THE COMPLETE FAMILY LAWYER

AN AUTHORITATIVE WORK ON ENGLISH LAW
APPLICABLE TO EVERYDAY MATTERS,
WHETHER CONNECTED WITH BUSINESS,
THE HOME, OR SOCIAL LIFE

Edited by

W. J. WESTON, M.A., B.Sc.,
BARRISTER-AT-LAW

The Contributors include:

T. H. COWPER
BARRISTER-AT-LAW

MAURICE SHARE
B.A., BARRISTER-AT-LAW

F. PORTER FAUSSET
M.A., BARRISTER-AT-LAW

C. T. SMITH
FELLOW OF THE INCORPORATED
SECRETARIES' ASSOCIATION

and

W. J. WESTON
M.A., B.Sc., BARRISTER-AT-LAW

ASSOCIATED NEWSPAPERS, LTD.
LONDON, E.C.4

THE COMPLETE FAMILY LAWYER

AN AUTHORITATIVE WORK ON ENGLISH LAW APPLICABLE TO EVERYDAY MATTERS, WHETHER CONNECTED WITH BUSINESS, THE HOME, OR SOCIAL LIFE

Edited by

W. J. WESTON, M.A., B.Sc.
BARRISTER-AT-LAW

The Contributors include:

F. H. COWPER
BARRISTER-AT-LAW

MAURICE SHARE
B.A., BARRISTER-AT-LAW

F. PORTER FAUSSET
M.A., BARRISTER-AT-LAW

C. T. SMITH
FELLOW OF THE INCORPORATED
SECRETARIES ASSOCIATION

and

W. J. WESTON
M.A., B.SC., BARRISTER-AT-LAW

ASSOCIATED NEWSPAPERS LTD.
LONDON, E.C.4

PRINTED IN GREAT BRITAIN BY
MORRISON AND GIBB LTD., LONDON AND EDINBURGH

FOREWORD

THE wish has often been expressed for a book that would give within small compass a complete statement, suitable for the layman, of the law of England.

Everyone understands that he is presumed to know the law, but what that law is in any particular case few have a ready means of discovering. The best advice, of course, is to consult a solicitor; for many reasons, however, this is impracticable, and the object of this book is to set before those who have not made an exhaustive study of English law the principles of law applicable to everyday matters, whether connected with business, the home and family, or with social engagements. It will not replace the solicitor, but it will tell when to consult a solicitor, which, from the point of view of the man in the street, is the next best thing.

It should be remembered that this is not a legal textbook, the traditional methods of textbook-writing have not been observed. The book is written from two points of view: first, that of the reader wishing for a readable exposition of the principles of law on some particular subject; and, secondly, that of the busy man with little time to spare who wishes to look up a special point rapidly. An exceptionally full index has been prepared which will immediately guide him to the page he wants. The book has, therefore, all the advantages of an alphabetical arrangement without its obvious disadvantages.

The lawyer expresses his opinion on a question of law, and that opinion is frequently based on inference from general principles. But it would be dangerous for the layman to attempt to draw inferences from previous cases, so here the authors have drawn the inferences for him. Whether he wishes to know his position when he is bitten by a dog, or when forming a company, or when his credit is pledged by his wife without authority, he will find the point referred to in the index, and quickly discover his true legal position.

CONTENTS

v

CONTENTS

INDEX

INSETS

vi   CONTENTS

CHURCH LAW
INCOME TAX
RATING

NOTE ON THE LAWS

"Our art," said a great lawyer, "like all arts and sciences, must have its proper terms, which can be understood only by training, and rightly used only with trained experience. But there is no reason why its broad principles and even much of its particular applications should not be set forth in language intelligible to the educated man."

We try to do that in this book. We do not seek to oust the practising lawyer. No book could. Some affairs of life—the conveyance of land, the arrangements between partners, the bequest of property—may still be quite complicated, even though the law has been so greatly simplified of late. To suggest that these affairs should be carried through without professional help would be misleading and dangerous. We do, however, seek to afford guidance upon legal rights and duties in the ordinary relations of business and social life.

WHAT ARE LAWS?

The laws are those rules of conduct to which the State requires adherence. If we do not adhere to them the possibility of penalty is present. The penalty may consist in the State's ignoring such acts as do not conform to its rules. A will is made; and the legal requirements of a valid will are not present. The State declares the attempted bequest a nullity. Payments are made, to be dependent upon the result of the Derby. The State will lend no aid to enforce payment, one way or the other, when the race has been lost and won. The State may, however, intervene and take an active part in suppressing conduct contrary to its rules. It intervenes either on its own initiative, or when invoked by one who is aggrieved by the unlawful act. Then the State either punishes the act or prevents its intended effect. This intervention of the State we call the *sanction of law*.

The State forbids, as every settled State must forbid, certain acts as being against the good of the State. These forbidden acts are then *crimes*. Moreover, certain acts inflicting damage upon our neighbours may give them a claim upon us. Such acts may be crimes; they are certainly *civil wrongs* or *torts*. A theft can be

1

prosecuted as a crime; it may also be sued upon as a conversion. Some unlawful acts that inflict damage are only civil wrongs. As regards these, the State leaves to the injured party the initiative for getting redress. Thus, it is not a crime to enter upon another's field. Trespassers cannot be prosecuted for crime. But they can be sued for the tort of trespass and be obliged to pay damages.

And when we make bargains, or *contracts*, the law constrains us to carry them out or to pay damages for not doing so. The laws relating to *crimes, torts, contracts*, all place obligations (duties) upon us. Failure to fulfil the obligations renders us liable to a prosecution for crime, or to an action for tort or breach of contract.

When a crime is the question before the Court, the Crown *prosecutes*. The case is *The King* v. *The Accused. Punishment* of a wrongdoer is sought by the Head of the State. This is sometimes expressed by saying that criminal cases are "pleas of the Crown." When "common pleas" (actions brought by one subject against another) are before the Court, then the person injured by a "civil wrong" or by a breach of contract *sues* for *compensation*.

SELF-HELP NO LONGER ALLOWED

In our days, the State itself makes its rules effective. We are not allowed to take the vindication of what we conceive to be our rights into our own hands. The State, not the individual claimant, enforces the laws. Where crimes are concerned, the State enforces them directly. It prosecutes; and, where guilt is proved, it fines or imprisons or in extreme cases kills. Where *civil wrongs* are concerned, the State enforces them indirectly. It gives its help if one who is wronged appeals to it. As a general rule the ancient right of self-help has been supplanted by the State's enforcing of the laws recognised. This we should welcome; for the extent to which the organised community, not the injured individual, maintains right is a measure of the degree of civilisation attained. We can hardly trust a man to be accuser, judge, and avenger in his own cause. Such slight remains of self-help as still exist—such as the landlord's right to distrain for rent due—are narrowly limited.

CODIFYING THE LAW

Rules of conduct must have been followed in the earliest period of our society. The rules had at first only the vague force of custom behind them. When, however, the old customs were enforced by the organised society, they became the "Common Law"; what was a matter of custom to the more enlightened people was made incumbent upon all. Immemorial custom when applied by the Courts becomes common law; and much of our life is still governed by custom, even though the books of statutes now make so imposing an array. It is, for instance, the custom that, when a woman marries, she takes her husband's name. No Act of Parliament enacts this. It is a custom so well recognised that we have never thought fit to follow the example of France, and make the rule a statutory one.

But these rules of conduct that we call laws are, to an ever-increasing extent, gathered together in Acts of Parliament, or Statutes. Legislation rather than custom is now the source of new law. In our criminal law, particularly, we have gone far towards codifying. In some aspects of contract law also, we have compiled several chapters of what will ultimately be a code of contract law. Thus, we have the legal rules, relating to the buying and selling of goods, skilfully drafted and logically arranged in the Sale of Goods Act, 1893. The law of tort, however, is still almost wholly to be found in judicial decisions—decisions that are understood to apply custom, "whereof the memory of man runneth not to the contrary," to the facts of our modern life.

SUPREMACY OF PARLIAMENT

When the law relevant to a particular topic is thus codified, Parliament wisely takes the opportunity of modifying the rules where it thinks fit. Decisions reached before the passing of the statute are then law so far as they are in harmony with the statute; they cease to be law if they are opposed to the statute.

For Parliament has supreme authority. Rules applicable to simpler conditions of life may be inapplicable to a complex society where we are all coagulated into groups. Parliament can change the rules. The judges cannot. Their duty is to interpret, not to make, the law; and they feel obliged to make their decisions consistent with statute or with former decisions. They may think the old custom irrelevant to modern life; but they have no power to change it.

Thus, Mr. Justice Rowlatt (*Orpen* v. *Haymarket Co.*, K.B., 1931) felt himself constrained to give effect to the long dormant Sunday Observance Act of 1781. Miss Millie Oppenheim changed her name to Miss Millie Orpen, " under which designation," said

the learned judge, "she could more colourably come forward
as the champion of the English Sunday." She laid her information: contrary to the Act certain places of entertainment had
charged for admission on Sunday. The information was accurate; these were the clear words of the statute: she was entitled
to the penalties claimed. "It is the duty of the Court to enforce
the Act of Parliament, and not to be perverse to find a way out
of it." Parliament, though, is unfettered. It can, and does,
constantly adapt the rules to the demands of the time.

THE PROCESS OF CODIFYING

In unostentatious manner, therefore, English law is being codified: we no longer have to consider a myriad of precedents when
trying to find the law relevant to a particular topic. For here
is the codifying statute.

The assumption is that, since the statute is expressed in
precise, well-considered terms, the ordinary educated layman can
understand the law and apply it to his own concerns. The
assumption is not invariably borne out in practice. Older
statutes, like the Statute of Frauds, 1677, have been the subject
of an enormous amount of litigation; and some of quite recent
date, like the Rent Restriction Acts, have given much work to
lawyers.

Yet, to have the rules expressed in a carefully compiled and
carefully considered statute means a vast improvement. It
lessens what one vigorous critic of "case-law" called "the in-
cognoscibility of the law and its extreme uncertainty." The
responsibility for the rather terrifying word is with Bentham,
who constantly gave voice to a demand for codifying the law.
He contrasts the law properly codified with the law as derivable
from former cases, statute law as against case law—

"On the question what the law is, so long as the rule of action
is kept in the state of common, *alias* unwritten, *alias* imaginary
law, authority is everything. The question is what on a given
occasion A (the judge) is likely to think. Wait till your fortune
has been spent in the inquiry, and you will know. But, forasmuch
as it is naturally a man's wish to be able to give a guess on what
the result will eventually be, before he has spent his fortune, he
applies, through the medium of B (an attorney) for an opinion
to C (a counsel), who, considering what D (a former judge) has
said or been supposed to say, deduces therefrom his guess as to
what, when the time comes, judge A, he thinks, will say."

DRAFTING AN ACT

Still, a *badly* worded statute may itself give rise to many contentions; and, where the subject-matter of the statute is wide, the draftsman may have failed to make provision for all cases. Thus, the various Rent Restriction Acts have cured a great deal of unemployment among lawyers; workmen's compensation cases are a fertile source of income; and we have continually before the Courts questions arising under the Finance Acts. The taxpayer pays his taxes with such resignation as he can muster. He is, however, reluctant to pay more than he need pay; and, when the command to pay can reasonably be construed to two ways, he adopts the interpretation the more favourable to his pocket. If people can dodge a tax, they will dodge it; and, despite all his ingenuity, the Parliamentary draftsman sometimes leaves loopholes. The case, *Payne* v. *Allcock*, decided in the Divisional Court in April, 1932, illustrates the point. The question answered in the case, a question of importance to all owners of motor-cars, was this: is a private motor-car subject to a higher rate of duty when it is used for carrying goods? The Cardiff Stipendiary Magistrate said "Yes." Appeal was made to the Divisional Court, where two of its members, including the Lord Chief Justice, agreed with the magistrate's finding, and one of its members disagreed.

DIFFERING INTERPRETATIONS

Mr. Allcock, the local taxation officer of the Cardiff City Council, laid an information before the magistrate. The information charged Mr. Payne, a greengrocer and florist, with an offence under the Finance Acts: he had taken out a licence for a motor-car, and had used the car for a purpose whereby a higher rate of duty was payable. The magistrate convicted, Mr. Payne was fined ten shillings, and he appealed to the Divisional Court. The two relevant Sections of the Finance Act, 1930, regarding the licence duty, are these: (5) *Vehicles constructed or adapted for use, and used for the conveyance of goods, whether in the course of trade or otherwise, if exceeding 1 ton but not exceeding 1½ tons in weight unladen, £20;* (6) *Any vehicle other than those charged with duty under the foregoing provision not exceeding six horse-power, £6; exceeding six horse-power, £1 for each unit or part of a unit of horse-power.* Now, Mr. Payne's car, rated at sixteen horse-power, was of the ordinary saloon type, neither constructed nor adapted for the conveyance of goods. Under Paragraph (5) the licence would have cost £20, under (6) it would have cost £16; and, not unnaturally, Mr. Payne chose the latter. The taxation officer demurred. For, on occasion, vegetables and other goods were carried in the back of the car. The magistrate considered that how the car was used determined the tax payable, not the mode of construction. This was the decision of the majority of the Divisional Court also. The court recognised the curious results that might follow from the decision: any private car owner who carried his own luggage or other "goods or burden" should, strictly speaking, pay at the higher rate; on the other hand, the owner of a high-powered private car could avoid the horse-power tax by fitting on a luggage carrier. Still, there were the plain words of the Act; and a judge's duty is to apply not to criticise the Act. Dislike it he may; but, since Parliament is sovereign in the State, none of its Acts can be *ultra vires*.

STATUTES THAT ARE DEAD LETTERS

Parliament may, indeed, have been induced to pass the Act owing to a transitory feeling. Such was the Act of 1745 against the "horrid, execrable, and impious vice" of profane swearing. It is still law and a constable, under a penalty of forty shillings, must arrest an offender who swears in his presence. Under the Act a "day-labourer" forfeits one shilling; every other person "under the degree of a gentleman" forfeits two shillings; every gentleman or "person above the degree of a gentleman" forfeits five shillings for each oath sworn. The Act is a "dead letter," a matter of interest to the social student but a matter having no bearing upon the lives of present men. Yet, to be sure, invocation of the law is possible and occurs.

In *R.* v. *Scott* (1863 B. & S.), an information was laid that the defendant "did profanely curse one profane curse, to wit . . . twenty several times repeated"; and he was fined the cumulative penalty. Scott was a "mealman," presumably therefore "under the degree of a gentleman," and so he had "to forfeit and pay the sum of 2l. being at the rate of two shillings for each curse." The report is reticent about the particular profane oath that proved so expensive a luxury. Normally, however, the minatory clauses of the Act sleep undisturbed.

It would probably astonish many to learn what a number of "statutory offences" they do commit. They have perhaps the uneasy thought that they are not doing quite the right thing, but certainly have no thought that they are incurring a penalty prescribed by Parliament, that in one sense they are criminals. Thus, among a couple of hundred of offences for which the Public Health Act, 1875, directs a fine of 40s. (or imprisonment for fourteen days) are the following : sings a profane song in the street, shakes a mat in the street (except a door-mat before 8 a.m.), permits any person in his service to stand upon the sill of an upper window, wantonly disturbs any inhabitant by ringing a door-bell or knocking at a door.

Every now and then a delver into the records of past ages unearths from long undisturbed Statute Books an Act that has long slept uninvoked ; it has become a dead letter and has no terror for those who break it. He sets the machinery of the law in motion to make the command an effective one ; and, very likely, Parliament is constrained to pass an Act hurriedly repealing the ancient law. So it was when a student of our constitutional law found that a succession of Presidents of the Board of Trade had rendered themselves liable to heavy monetary penalties through accepting office without vacating their seats in Parliament and presenting themselves for re-election. At once an Act of Indemnity, remitting all the penalties payable, was rushed through Parliament, and the particular rule was repealed. Necessary it might once have been when bribery by the Crown was a real possibility ; it is hardly necessary in these days.

DOCTRINE OF " COMMON EMPLOYMENT "

The Act of Parliament, too, is the one way by which the law can be brought into harmony with modern needs. The Courts must stand upon former decisions ; for in many respects certainty in the laws is a virtue as important as goodness. We ensure in our system something like certainty by the rule that a decision of the House of Lords is binding not only upon all inferior courts but upon the House of Lords itself. Any later and similar case coming before the Courts must be determined in accordance with the precedent. Parliament is in no way bound. It can change its opinion as often as it chooses ; its last enactment settles the law ; and unjust rules of the Common Law disappear before the statutory rules. Thus, a rule of the Common Law is that an employer is not liable when one of his servants is injured by the negligence of a fellow servant in the same employment. This rule, the doctrine of "common employment," caused great hardship to workmen and aroused bitter hostility among them. It was certainly a perverse doctrine : "If there be a common master, a servant who unskilfully packs dynamite in a factory, and another who unpacks it at a distant factory and is injured by the explosion, are clearly in common employment." The idea underlying the rule is that a servant, when he enters into a contract for employment, agrees by implication to take upon himself the risk that his fellow-servants may be negligent. It is this rule that the successive Employers' Liability Acts have almost eaten away. The rule still remains; statute law has for the most part removed its hardships.

RELATION BETWEEN STATUTE LAW AND COMMON LAW

Two cases, decided in the closing weeks of 1930, will illustrate the relation between the law as enacted by Parliament and published as a statute and the law as based upon old custom enunciated by the superior judges—between Statute Law, that is, and Common Law.

Where the two conflict, the first governs. When an Act has been passed, former decisions are good only in so far as they are consistent with the Act. The effect of the former decision remains. For it is only in very rare instances that an Act of Parliament is made retrospective. A future decision upon similar facts would be different.

An unfortunate sale of Indian cattle cake gave rise to one case. The sellers, knowing that harmful ingredients were as likely as not to be present, expressly declined to give a warranty; they accepted no responsibility for quality, telling their buyers to take samples and use their own judgment. They expressly sold this cake " *Tel quel*," such as it is, a phrase putting upon the buyer the care to ascertain whether the thing sold is really what he wants.

At Common Law such a disclaimer would have constituted a defence against a suit to recover damages caused by the cake. But now we have upon the Statute Book the Fertilisers and Feeding Stuffs Act, 1926; and this provides that when cattle food is sold " there shall be implied a warranty, notwithstanding any contract or notice to the contrary, that the article is suitable."

Parliament intended the vendor of cattle food to take the responsibility of its fitness for that purpose; and no private arrangement can enable him to avoid the responsibility (*Dobell and Co., Ltd.* v. *Barber and Garratt*, A.C., 1930). The sellers, therefore, in spite of their express refusal to give a warranty were obliged to pay damages. Parliament limits the freedom of bargaining; and no contracting out of the Act is allowed.

AN " ENTIRE CONTRACT '

The second case is an interesting illustration of the manner in which Parliament seeks to temper the rigour of the law, when its logical application offends against the sense of justice. It shows, too, how the more recent statute modifies by implication any former statute not consistent with it.

At Common Law, if a ship was lost on a voyage, a seaman could recover nothing for his services. He had undertaken to serve during a voyage; and, though through no fault of his, he had not performed his contract. No wages were due for the time before the vessel was lost. To be sure, nothing is earned by the shipowner as freight through the seaman's services. But, then, the shipowner can usually guard against the contingency that his vessel has plied without profit.

The seaman needs statutory protection; and he has obtained it by the Merchant Shipping Act of 1894. This gave wages up to the time of the wreck that ended the service. But then comes the Merchant Shipping (International Labour Conventions) Act of 1925; and this enacts that " where, by the loss of the ship on which he is employed, a seaman is unemployed he shall be entitled for a period of two months to receive wages."

Suppose, though, the voyage under more favourable auspices, would have ended within a day or two of the wreck? Is the seaman in that event entitled to two months' pay? Apparently he is. It might be urged that Parliament could not have intended the seaman to profit through the owner's loss; it certainly is a strange result that a few hours may make a difference of two months' wages.

The *Celtic*, the vessel in question, foundered off Queenstown on 10th December, 1928, the contemplated end of her voyage being Liverpool on 11th December. At the first glance it would seem absurd to contend that the seamen were entitled to two months' pay for the one day lost. Still, we cannot disregard the clear words of the statute. One of the members of the Supreme Court expressed the matter thus: "My Lords, Parliament can, of course, do anything; and I hope that judicially I shall never be other than obedient to its directions, whatever, when they are clearly expressed, these directions may be." And it may well have been in the mind of Parliament that the wreck of his ship disappoints the seaman of a prospect of re-engagement for her next voyage. Difficulty of finding another ship might be compensated in some degree by the arbitrary two months, irrespective of the date on which the contract would have expired (*Oceanic Steam Navigation Company* v. *Comerford, H.L.*, 1930).

RELATION BETWEEN LAW AND CONVENTION

The publication of the "Highway Code," summarising the conduct we expect from all decent users of the roads, brings out a distinction between the positive injunctions of law and the customary behaviour of sensible and thoughtful people. The code is issued, in obedience to the instruction given in Section 45 of the Road Traffic Act, 1930, by the Minister of Transport. The Act specifically states that failure to observe the provisions of the code shall not of itself render any person liable to criminal proceedings of any kind : no penalty is prescribed for breaking the rule that "Motor horns should never be used to show annoyance or impatience," or the rule that "Pedestrians should walk on the footpath where one is provided." Yet it is enacted that in all legal proceedings, whether civil or criminal, evidence of failure to observe the code will be a most important matter to be weighed. Adherence or non-adherence to the conventions will be strong evidence when there is a question of fixing liability. There is, again, the rule of the road—not law yet but gradually stiffening into law. There are some criminal provisions (Section 28 of the Town Police Clauses Act, 1847), making it an offence not to keep to the left for the purpose of being passed. But there is no general law that vehicles must keep to the left and pedestrians to the right : "though a carriage might be driving on the wrong side of the road, yet if there was sufficient room for other carriages and horses to pass on the other, a person was not justified in asserting what he termed the right of the road." Still, to break the rule may be evidence of negligence. Conventions though the rules are, we had better conform to them, just as one conformed to the convention not to smoke in the lower compartment of buses. No law constrained us ; but, considering the comfort of others, we went aloft to smoke.

"ORDERS IN COUNCIL"

A modern, and in some ways a startling, extension of Statute

Law is the growing practice of enunciating in the Act of Parliament certain broad principles and leaving the application of those principles to be worked out later. A Minister of the Crown is authorised to frame "Statutory Orders in Council"; and these, being issued, have all the force of Acts of Parliament. They may, indeed, be challenged as not being derivable from the Act; they are then asserted to be beyond the powers (*ultra vires*) of the Minister who framed them. If the judge before whom the case is argued does so decide, he simply ignores the order. In so far, however, as they are covered by the Act they are law; and the Courts must give effect to them. Thus, Parliament passes a Transport Act; and, in accordance with that Act, the Minister of Transport issues a multiplicity of orders. The part played by the Council—the Privy Council—is only formal. The King is in presence; there is a quorum of three Privy Councillors, the Minister responsible for the Order or Orders being among them; no discussion takes place. The Orders are formally passed when the Lord President of the Council has satisfied himself that a Cabinet Minister has authorised them. Clearly, the striking extension of the practice has introduced a new and in some ways a disquieting element into the working of the State. (See pages 296–297.)

EFFECT OF CODE

When a code is compiled the law is made reasonably certain and impartial. But the most voluminous code cannot make provision for all incidents of our complex social and domestic life. An elastic element must still persist. There is room, therefore, for the "judge-made law" based upon decisions. This, the "Common Law," is in effect a developing survey of justice, duty, care, and the upright fulfilment of obligations. A code tends to rigidity; and, where so much is so rapidly changing, a great amount of flexibility is needed. At all events, English law seems to prefer to evolve slowly by adding rule to rule, rather than by enunciating great leading principles and then deducing rules from these.

STATUTE AND LITIGATION

Besides, a code is not always easily applicable to the concrete facts that arise; and many contentions may arise over a statute passed with the fullest intentions to make matters clear as crystal. Parliament, in 1928, passed the Rating and Valuation Act. This was passed to grant relief to "industrial hereditaments" from part of the burden of local taxation. Such a relief would conduce to prosperity in depressed industry. Ultimately, the Act may do this. Meantime, it has given much work to lawyers. Lord Buckmaster, delivering judgment in the House of Lords (*Moon v. London County Council*, 1930), stated that: "Upwards of 18,000 appeals are said to be pending to Quarter Sessions and 800 from Quarter Sessions to the Divisional Court; and we have been asked to take this case without delay in order that the plague of litigation may be stayed." The actual case itself had already had vicissitudes. The London County Council claimed that a building, used solely for the printing of tickets, posters, and so on for the tramway service, was an industrial hereditament, entitled, therefore, to the relief granted by the Act; and the assessment committee allowed the claim. The revenue officer objected. For though the premises were a "letterpress printing works" and as such exempt, they were merely an auxiliary of the tramway business, and as such not exempt. Quarter Sessions dismissed the revenue officer's appeal. A Divisional Court allowed the revenue officer's appeal. The Appeal Court restored the order of the Quarter Sessions; and the House of Lords was called upon to settle the matter. Happily, the supreme arbiters were unanimous: when a building is used solely as a factory or a workshop it is an "industrial hereditament," and, therefore, entitled to the relief stipulated in the Act. What the destiny of its products may be, whether they are for sale or for service, is immaterial. The London County Council was right; the revenue officer was wrong. There is a little light cast, at appalling expense, upon a dark place.

The same Act may, however, serve as illustration that differences of interpretation are the exception, not the rule. The question was: what is intended in the Act by "contiguous?"

Ratepayers are allowed to include "properties contiguous to one another," as being one with the "industrial building." Are the offices of a sugar factory, though separate from the factory by a public road, to be regarded as "contiguous"? They were, to be sure, a necessary adjunct to the mills, but was this enough? No; was the answer of a Divisional Court presided over by the Lord Chief Justice. When a word appears in an Act of Parliament we are to assume that the draftsman of the Act knows the correct meaning of the word; if he puts "contiguous to" he does not mean "neighbouring." In the judgment he read, the Lord Chief Justice comments upon the language of our statutes: " Dr. Johnson, of whom it may probably be said that he employed the English language with a more anxious precision than any other man who ever lived, defines 'contiguous' thus: 'Meeting so as to touch; bordering upon each other; not separate.' The counsel who sought to establish 'neighbouring' as the intended meaning gave as their chief reason the derating object of the Act; and the wider and looser meaning of the word would bring more derating. Another argument was hinted at, though counsel had not the hardihood to advance it, that in the use of any language by the legislature one should expect the loose and inexact rather than the correct and exact. It is true that one who spends much time in this Court might be tempted in his haste to make some such assertion. But if he allowed cynicism to be tempered with sympathy for the harassed Parliamentary draftsman, he would reflect that it is only in regard to phrases of doubtful import that this Court is called upon to apply a toilsome scrutiny. The task is pathological; and too much immersion in it may well induce oblivion of the fact that these difficult passages are rare. It ought to be the rule, and we are glad to think that it is the rule, that words are used in an Act of Parliament correctly and exactly."

CRIME AND TORT

A crime is an offence against the State, against the public organised for the purposes of government. A tort is a wrong against an individual. To be sure, the same act may be both a crime and a tort, just as a man may be both a son and a father; it depends upon the point of view. I take another's property without pretext of right: I am thereby under danger of being punished by the State for the crime of stealing; I am also liable to pay damages in an action for the tort of trespass. In the first case, I am prosecuted by the King in his capacity of maintainer of order. Any crime is an affront to him, just as brawling in a man's house would be an insult. In the second case, I am sued by the wronged person, who seeks monetary compensation for his wrong; there is a plaintiff, who declares to the Court that his legal rights have been infringed, and I am the defendant summoned to answer the complaint—to justify my action if I can, to pay damages if I cannot.

The criminal remedy and the civil remedy are quite independent of one another. The one has, indeed, usually grown out of the other: whenever the law-making power has come to regard any class of private wrong with dread, it has made of it a public wrong; it has erected the tort into a crime because it considered the civil remedy to be inadequate.

When, however, the State does make a private wrong into a crime it does not take away the injured person's right to claim compensation. He who assaults another or does malicious injury to property may be punished criminally, by imprisonment or fine; he may also be compelled in a civil suit to make compensation or to restore property. There is one limitation, though, that should be noted. When the tort is also a felony—such a crime as is regarded by the State with peculiar loathing—the wrongdoer must be prosecuted for the felony before he is sued for the tort. This rule is designed to ensure the punishment of criminals; it compels those injured by criminal offences to fulfil their duty as citizens of prosecuting the offender, and not content themselves with seeking enforcement of private rights. In one case, where this rule was successfully pleaded as a bar to an action for tort, the judge said: "It is a well-established rule of law that a plaintiff against whom a felony has been committed by the defendant cannot make that felony the foundation of a cause of action unless the defendant has been prosecuted, or a reasonable excuse has been shown for his not having been prosecuted."

BREACH OF CONTRACT AND TORT

There is less difficulty in realising that the same action may be both a breach of contract and a tort. Both are civil wrongs. An undertaking has been given, and it has not been fulfilled; the aggrieved party is entitled to damages for breach of contract. Injury has resulted from negligence; the aggrieved party is entitled to damages for the tort of negligence. In a railway case, the Master of the Rolls declared, "The plaintiff might maintain an action either in contract or in tort. In the former case, he might allege a contract by the railway company to carry him with reasonable care and skill, and a breach of that contract. On the other hand, he might allege that he was being carried by the railway company to the knowledge of their servants, who were bound not to injure him by any negligence; and, if they were negligent, that was a matter on which an action of tort could be brought. A plaintiff may frame his claim in either way."

TORT BECOMES CRIME

We are to notice this also. When a merely civil wrong becomes a serious menace, Parliament makes it into a crime : the State, that is, does not choose to allow the law to remain at the mercy of the individual citizen who may have been wronged. Its own officials seek to enforce it. Thus, in 1857, Parliament made a fraudulent breach of trust, till then only a civil wrong for which the fraudulent trustee could be sued for damages, into a crime punishable by imprisonment up to a maximum of seven years.

A more recent instance affects all officials of joint stock companies. The 1929 Companies Act has many penal clauses. One of the features of that Act is the making more stringent of the obligation placed upon the officials of a company—upon the directors in their duty of safeguarding the interests of the shareholders, upon the auditor in his duty to see that the accounts give the true position of the company. The civil liability remains, indeed. But there is added a criminal liability also.

A breach of the duty imposed subjects the erring officials to a prosecution for crime. The harm done is, true, against individuals. But then the harm done is of such a nature that the public at large is affronted. There has been breach of faith in business matters ; and the smooth transaction of business depends largely upon this faith. In an indefinable but none the less real way, the community has been injured. In order, therefore, to deter from the harmful practice, a positive injunction goes against it. The State makes a crime of what before was merely a civil wrong.

DIRECTORS' CRIMINAL LIABILITY

The personal responsibility of directors is emphasised. A new section directs the prosecution of delinquent directors. If it appears to the Court in the course of a winding up that any past or present director has been guilty of any offence in relation to the company, for which he is criminally liable, the Court may direct the liquidator either himself to prosecute an offender or to refer the matter to the Director of Public Prosecutions. Misleading the shareholders has now the incident that it exposes the director to criminal prosecution as well as to an action for damages.

This method of constructing a body of law has its advantages : the law develops in response to our economic needs. Thus, our mercantile law has largely come into being by an adoption of the custom of merchants. Our judges gave the force of law to the usages that had fostered trade and had promoted rectitude in dealings; and, in the fullness of time, Parliament gave a statutory recognition to these usages.

LAW AND BUSINESS LIFE

For in this country the lawyer never belonged to a class apart, as he does in some countries. The Inns of Court and Chancery Lane are in no secluded spot, away from the stress and stir of market activities. They are where the City of London meets the City of Westminster. The barristers and solicitors gathered there are in touch with the merchant and the member of Parliament. In our own days we have had a merchant leaving the City and ultimately reaching the Woolsack; we have had a Lord Chancellor leaving the Woolsack for the greater material gains of the City.

The close connection has had something to do with the important fact that our legislators in their law-making have been intent upon making the economic machine run more smoothly, and that our judges in their law-interpreting have, in the main, sought to promote straight dealing in business transactions. "I have so great a veneration for the law," declared one of our great judges, "as to suppose that nothing can be law which is not founded in common sense and common honesty."

We must not imagine this attitude, this eagerness to enforce upright dealing, to have been from all time. To some judges of bygone days—to none in modern times—there seemed to be nothing reprehensible in sharp practice by which one trader tricked another. "Are we to indict one man for making a fool of another?" was the astonished question of a judge that delighted in a contest of wits. *Caveat emptor* once ruled: a man has only himself to blame if he is deceived. In our days, when we recognise good faith as being the foundation of business, the rule of *caveat emptor* has been well night eaten up by its exceptions.

DIRECTORS' LIABILITY ACT

The response of law to business needs has not often been so prompt as when the Directors' Liability Act of 1890 (now included in the Companies Act) made directors liable for any false statements: though they honestly believe the statements, yet, in the absence of a reasonable ground for belief, they must compensate shareholders misled to their loss by the statements. The year before the Act, the well-known case *Derry* v. *Peek* had been decided. There the liability of directors for a statement honestly believed, but in fact untrue, was negatived. That is, the general rule was applied; you cannot succeed in an action of fraud unless you prove that the defendant is fraudulent, that he made the statement knowing it was false, or, recklessly, careless of whether it was false or true.

The directors were exonerated. "Yet," said one of the judges of the Supreme Court, "I think those who put before the public a prospectus to induce them to embark their money in a commercial enterprise ought to be vigilant to see that it contains such representations only as are in strict accordance with fact. I think that this moral duty ought to be converted into a legal obligation." The legislature straightway acted upon the suggestion, which indeed was vigorously supported by commercial men, anxious that the confidence with which men invested in business enterprise should grow stronger.

PROPERTY ACTS

The adjustment of legal rules to economic requirements is too long deferred at times. Indeed, where the apparent interest of a ruling minority dictates the legal rules, these may persist long after they have ceased to promote any useful purpose. Such were the legal rules relating to the transfer of land. The intricate and shackling customs of far-off feudal times were not superseded by more sensible rules until the Property Acts of 1922–1925. Before these Acts the law relating to land was a maze of technical rules. The would-be buyer of land could hardly know that his title would be unassailable. Nor could the seller give him the assurance.

The influence of feudal ideas produced laws devised to keep land in large masses. When intestacy occurred the eldest son inherited. A testator, indeed, was not bound by this rule; but the practice of entailing estates made the so-called owner usually no more than a life tenant. The aspiration, "to make land as easily transferable as stock," has not yet been realised; but we have gone far towards achieving this desirable end. The system of registration now enables certainty of title to be given. Transfers are facilitated and the land goes, we may assume, into the hands of those who can make it perform the greatest economic service.

PRACTICE, NOT THEORY

English lawyers, including English judges, have applied their minds to concrete cases. They have sought to do justice to litigants seeking a decision in circumstances that had actually arisen. They concerned themselves little with abstract principles. By so doing they have kept touch with the realities of business life. "The Roman Law," said Lord Sankey, "dealt with abstract theories; the English Law is engaged on concrete cases. The politician invents slogans and shibboleths. The trouble is that when the lawyer has to translate the shibboleths into concrete practice he finds people differing as to the meaning of them. Vague political phrases have to be turned into clear and practical legal concepts." The reluctance of English judges to formulate general statements is well illustrated in a workman's compensation case that reached the House of Lords (*L.N.E. Ry.* v. *Brentnall*, H.L., 1933). The question was whether an injury sustained by an engine-driver, who slipped and fell at a hostel provided by the company for rest between turns of duty, was an accident "arising out of and in the course of his employment." The amount involved was small; but the company was anxious to get a definite ruling about the extent of their liability in like cases. The company got only slight guidance: "I am afraid it is impossible to give them any ruling extending beyond the special facts of this case. It is not a prudent course to attempt to lay down general principles in cases of this kind. It is wiser to confine each case to the particular circumstances in which it arises." The company's appeal was dismissed: since the driver was bound to go to the hostel and rest there, the accident arose out of and in the course of his employment.

MENTAL ATTITUDE

When breaches of contract are before the court the mental or moral condition of the defaulter has no effect upon the question of his liability or non-liability. In civil wrongs (or torts) the mental condition of the wrongdoer is rarely regarded. But in criminal law no action, however serious or even fatal its results, is punished unless the actor has a guilty mind—unless he intends the act.

Note, too, that a lawful act does not become unlawful simply because it is done out of spite or other blameworthy motive. A landowner put pressure upon a town corporation to buy his land: he intercepted the underground water that would have flowed into the corporation's reservoir. It was held that the plaintiffs had no legal remedy: "No use of property which would be legal if due to a proper motive can become illegal because it is prompted by a motive which is improper or even malicious. In such a case motives are immaterial. It is the act, not the motives for the act, that must be regarded " (*The Mayor of Bradford* v. *Pickles*, A.C., 1895). And in the same case : "If it was a lawful act, however ill the motive might be, he had a right to do it. If it was an unlawful act, however good his motive might be, he would have no right to do it. Motives and intentions in such a question as is now before your lordships seem to me to be absolutely irrelevant."

The law, that is, does not provide a remedy for all the ills of life. A lady, baulked of an advantageous marriage, sues the persons who had persuaded her fiancé to break off the engagement. By reason of the "acts of the defendants in causing the breach of the said contract of marriage, plaintiff had sustained the loss of an advantageous matrimonial connection; plaintiff's affections had been disregarded and blighted, and her spirit and feelings wounded, resulting in great mental distress and humiliation." The remarks of the judge in dismissing the plaintiff's appeal are : "The right of engaged parties to ask advice of their friends and the right of the friends to give advice has never been denied. To hold that a third party may be subject to answer in damages for advising or inducing an engaged person to break the engagement might result in a suit by every disappointed lover against his successful rival."

INJURY WITHOUT REMEDY

The notion, indeed, seems to prevail that, whenever one man suffers injury or loss through another's action, then he is entitled to compensation. If the law does not admit a claim for compensation, then the law is defective and a way of reformation is indicated. A new house rears its head in front of an old one. It deprives the old one of a pleasant prospect over a broad stretch of sea, of the health-giving ocean breezes, of a certain amount of sunlight. Is not our law a-wanting if it leaves the owner of the old house helpless in the matter? Is he confined to a remonstrance only too likely to be ineffective? Well, unless the law provides a remedy for the wrong complained of, he is so confined.

We must reconcile ourselves to the fact that, living as we do in close company with our fellows, we are like to suffer many crosses. Their very presence may at times be irksome. We, too, may annoy others and cause them loss; yet they have no legal remedy. Our gramophone grinds out tunes obnoxious to their cultivated tastes, our successful business enterprise turns their anticipated profit into actual loss, our exhibition of bigger and

better gooseberries prevents their gaining the prize at the flower
show. The law prescribes no remedy.

Nor does it prescribe one in this matter of blocking a favourite
view. Roman law did; but English law, reluctant to admit a
property in a prospect, does not. Nor can the sea breezes be
appropriated, so that we have a right against one who interferes
with our enjoyment of them. The right to light is recognised;
but the recognition is not by any means absolute. However
long I have enjoyed the light coming in at my windows the
diminution of the light by another erection does not of itself
entitle me to a remedy. To sustain an action there must be,
said one judgment, "a substantial privation of light, sufficient
to render the occupation of the house uncomfortable. It might
be difficult to draw the line; but the jury must distinguish between *a partial inconvenience* and *a real injury* to the plaintiff
in his enjoyment of the premises." If a man is to succeed
in an action for deprivation of light he must show (1) that
he has had twenty years' continuous enjoyment of the light so
that he has, we say, "a right of ancient light"; (2) that his
comfort or his profit has been substantially reduced by the
obstruction.

In regard to trade combinations the doctrine, that a man is
free to follow his interests, has lately been pushed far. Where
the combinations are made to promote the interests of those who
have entered into them, then, though they may inflict injury upon
outsiders, these outsiders have no remedy. *Sorrell* v. *Smith*, decided in the House of Lords in 1925, is a case in point. Sorrell was
a retail newsagent; Smith was the circulation manager of the
chief London dailies. The dailies had a "distance limit policy"
preventing newcomers from opening shops in areas where already
there were enough retailers. In pursuance of this policy, Smith
refused to supply Sorrell. Sorrell asked the Court to make Smith
deal with him. He asked, that is, for a mandatory injunction
addressed to Smith's. But the Court refused to interfere. The
rules laid down by the Court were—

1. In general a combination of two or more persons wilfully
to injure a man in his trade is unlawful and, if it results in
damage to him, is actionable.

2. But, if the real purpose of the combination is, not to injure
another, but to forward or defend the interests of those who enter
into it, then no wrong is committed and no action will lie, although
damage to another ensues.

Injury, that is, lies where it falls, unless the law recognises a reason for shifting it.

LEGAL RIGHTS ARE LIMITED

Legal rights are those rights that the law tries to enforce. They are less numerous than is sometimes supposed. The Courts would have a task far beyond their powers if they sought to make good all the rights that people think their due. I do many kindnesses to a person. I may think I have a right to kindness, too. So I have; but it is not a legal right. The Court might sympathise with me if I complained of ingratitude. It could not, however, afford me any remedy; for there is no legal right to gratitude.

Or a friend promises to give me a lift to Brighton; and, relying on his promise, I make arrangements to go. He gets nothing, beyond thanks, for his service; but yet I have a right to expect that what he has undertaken he will perform. Again, however, I have no legal right. If, unluckily, he forgets his promise I cannot obtain damages for breach of contract. Quite likely, I suffer inconvenience, quite likely incur expense through his breaking of his promise. But it is a gratuitous promise; it is not a business agreement for which, in return for his service, he gets something measurable in money. And, so far as the law is concerned, he can break such a gratuitous promise without coming under any legal liability.

It is often supposed, too, that because a person has inflicted injury upon me he can be made to pay me compensation in money. In a limited number of cases he can be so compelled. In the majority of cases, however, I invoke the law in vain; I must, if I can, guard myself against loss by devices of my own. My neighbour allows weeds to overrun his garden, and each gust of wind sends showers of seeds into mine. My efforts to eliminate weeds are frustrated through his neglect. Yet my only recourse is a friendly remonstrance, or maybe the effect of a good example.

Unless I am able to point to a legal rule whereby I can shift my injury on to another's shoulders, I must bear it myself. I am badly bruised by a motor car. Yet I can obtain the money I spend to get cured and the money I lose through my enforced absence from work only under certain conditions. I must show, first of all, that the motorist was careless in his driving; for he owes the duty of taking care to all users of the public highway. I must also show that my own conduct at the time was reasonable; I was taking care myself. His lack of care, therefore, where he owed a duty to exercise care was the sole cause of the accident.

The injury I suffer may actually have been intended. A rival has prevented success in my suit; he has married the lady I loved. Yet I have no legal redress any more than I have against the trader who, giving better value or making his shop more attractive, has taken my customers from me. The law is, indeed, very solicitous over the preservation of this right to compete freely—this right to make one's living as one thinks best. I may think the competition unfair; my competitor may deliberately cut his prices in order to drive me out of the trade. That gives me no legal right against him. As the judge put the matter in a well-known case: "All commercial men with capital are acquainted with the ordinary expedient of sowing one year a crop of apparently unfruitful prices, in order by driving competition away to reap a fuller harvest of profit in the future. And until the present argument at the Bar it may be doubtful whether shipowners or merchants were ever deemed by law to conform to some imaginary normal standard of freights or prices, or that law courts had a right to say to them in respect to their competitive tariffs: 'Thus far shalt thou go, and no further.'" The Mogul Steamship Company had complained about the "unfair" practices of a shipping "ring." The "ring" had offered big rebates upon freights to tea shippers who undertook to ship goods solely in the "ring's" vessels. Such an offer evidently militated against the chances of vessels outside the "ring." Yet "to say that a man is to trade freely but is to stop short at any act (designed to attract business to his own shop) which is calculated to harm other tradesmen, would be a strange and impossible counsel of perfection" (*Mogul Steamship Co.* v. *McGregor, etc.*). The harm done to the individual is more than balanced by the benefit to the public; in the interest of the greater good the law countenances even competition harmful to the single person.

Here and there, too, are those who resent to see their photographs reproduced in newspapers. They feel that an unwarranted intrusion has been made upon their privacy—their *right* of privacy, they say. This is no legal right, though. A dentist could get no legal protection against the "annoyance and indignity" to which his neighbours at Balham were subjecting him. They had erected in their garden an arrangement of mirrors enabling them to see all that happened in his operating room.

Harmful the acts of the inquisitive family might have been; they were not wrongful in the legal sense. The dentist could neither recover damages nor get an order restraining them from their irritating practice. Nor could the tenant of a flat obtain an injunction to forbid the tenant of the flat above, with the licence of the common landlord, from building an outside iron staircase to the upper flat. That the lower tenant's bedrooms were overlooked was a wrong without a remedy.

So with the photograph. "No one possesses a right of preventing another person from photographing him; any more than he has a right of preventing another from giving a description of him (provided that the description is not libellous or otherwise wrongful)." Miss Roberson sought damages against the Franklin Mills Flour Company because it had used her likeness for advertising purposes without her consent. Above the portrait was the note "Flour of the Family," below was the note "Franklin Mills Flour"—the advertiser wishing to suggest that just as the lady was the flower of the flock, the pick of the bunch, so the flour was the choicest on the market.

"Such publicity," said the judge, "which some find agreeable, is to the plaintiff very distasteful. Because of defendants' impertinence in using her picture without her consent for their own business purposes, she has been caused to suffer mental distress. Others would have appreciated the compliment to their beauty implied in the selection of the picture for such purposes; but, as it is distasteful to her, she seeks the aid of the Court." The Court could, however, render no aid. For the Court can intervene only where a legal right is infringed; and there is no legal right to privacy. This was an American case. But there is no doubt that a similar decision would have been reached by the English Courts. Parliament could, certainly, create a right such as was claimed. It could enact that no one should be allowed to use another's picture for advertising purposes without his consent. Till Parliament does speak, the right claimed is no legal right.

LEGAL REMEDY NOT ALWAYS ADEQUATE

A man is wronged. His right to reputation has been infringed by a libel, or his right to property by a trespass; and invocation of the law gives him a remedy for the wrong. We are bound to face the fact, though, that the remedy provided by the law is not invariably an adequate one. It may, indeed, fail lamentably to compensate for the injury suffered by the successful claimant.

Particularly is this so, when the wrongdoer is a man of straw. Judgment may be obtained against such a man; but the one effect of the judgment is to vindicate the plaintiff, at his own great expense. A prominent author is falsely accused of filching his plots and of employing ghosts to write his books; and a jury assesses his damages at a thousand pounds. The verdict is little to the purpose where the defendant has hardly a thousand pence. In this sense, indeed, there is one law for the poor and another— a harsher one—for the rich. The poor man does with impunity what the rich man does at the risk of heavy loss.

Often enough it is the sounder policy to bear one's wrongs without invoking the law. The tendency to do this is the stronger in matters of libel by reason of the fact that all statements made in court are absolutely privileged. Neither witness nor counsel is under restraint except in so far as the judge controls; either is free to vilify the other party. As one judgment declared: "This absolute privilege has been conceded on the grounds of public policy to ensure freedom of speech where it is essential that freedom of speech should exist, and with the knowledge that courts of justice are presided over by those who from their high character are not likely to abuse the privilege, and who have the power and ought to have the will to check any abuse of it by those who appear before them."

So with trespass. I may be subjected to continual annoyance by an intruder on my property. He offers me a shilling to cover the damage done by his technical trespass, and at Common Law I have no further remedy. That is one reason why the Chancery devised the injunction. In suitable cases the Chancellor's Court would forbid the conduct complained of; and where the Common Law remedy is inadequate there is a suitable case. Disobedience of the injunction is disobedience of the Court. The quarrel is shifted from the petitioner; the wrongdoer who persists in his wrongdoing is attached for contempt of court; and, till he purges his contempt by contrition and submission, he languishes in prison.

In business matters themselves a legal remedy may be lacking. Thus, the "honourable understanding," the "gentleman's agreement," that exists in business as out of it, does not fall within the cognisance of the Courts. If one party acts contrary to the understanding, that concerns his conscience and maybe his business reputation. The law cannot interfere when there is only a vague ill-defined understanding: "If there are any essential terms of a contract undertermined—and, therefore, to be determined by a subsequent contract, there is no enforceable contract." (So the Court of Appeal declared in *Hillas* v. *Arcos*.) An agreement to make an agreement is no contract.

Yet business relations arise that contemplate future arrangements. "A price to be agreed," "A salary to be fixed," are terms met with in agreements. The parties must, in these, trust to the honour of those with whom they deal. If it turns out that they have trusted those unworthy of trust, the difficulty consist in the imperfections inherent in human nature, not in the defects of the law.

This means a divergence between mercantile law and business practice. This is an unfortunate position; and dissatisfaction with it finds expression at times. "I regret," said Lord Justice Scrutton in *Hillas* v. *Arcos* (C.A. 1931), "that in many material matters the English law and the practice of commercial men are getting wider apart, with the result that commercial business is leaving the Courts and being decided by commercial arbitrators, with infrequent reference to the Courts. Commercial men carry on an enormous mass of business under the system of 'string contracts,' under which A, who has made a contract with B, goes to arbitration with Z, of whom he never before heard and with whom he has in the eyes of the law no contractual relations. The commercial man does not think there can be no contract to make a contract when every day he finds a policy, 'premium to be arranged,' treated as a contract." Custom has, in fact, brought it about that the Courts treat this last phrase, though it contemplates a future agreement, as in reality a present agreement to hold the risk covered at a reasonable premium.

In the actual case, Hillas & Co., timber merchants of Hull, had entered into a contract with Arcos, Ltd., for the purchase during 1930 of a large quantity of Russian timber. As an inducement to buy—at that time there was something like a boycott of Russian goods—Hillas obtained an option to buy further timber in 1931. The option clause did not specify the kinds of timber nor the ports of shipment. Doubtless, these matters could, assuming the will to settle, have been settled. Yet Arcos repudiated the agreement and the Court of Appeal could not help the plaintiff: "There is no enforceable contract. I have come to the conclusion with great regret. I have no doubt that the plaintiffs' thought they had secured a valuable option. I have also no doubt that the defendants' representatives in this country thought they had given a valuable option, and that both parties thought there was a concluded contract. I should have been glad to think that the Court could have enforced what both parties thought was a contractual obligation. The difficulty of doing so arises from the nature of a contract. If there remain essential terms that have not been agreed, the Court cannot award damages for a contract which had never come into existence."

The House of Lords was less diffident about its power to amend matters. That august court had temerity enough to affirm (H.L., 1932) that Hillas & Co. were entitled to the damages they sought, even though the agreement left so many things to be settled. For, where doubt existed, an independent arbitrator could resolve the doubt. The House of Lords thereby struck a mighty blow on behalf of business integrity. To shuffle out of the obligations even of a "gentleman's understanding" will in the future be fraught with the danger of damages. The decision has brought the law and the practice of the commercial community sensibly nearer.

DEAD LETTER LAWS

A *Law* ought to be a rule of conduct, followed in all but the rarest exception. And when those exceptions do occur, there ought to be a strong probability that the transgressor of the rule will be punished. Most of our laws are of this kind. This is well; for, when a law is constantly broken with impunity, there is engendered a contempt for laws in general. The breach of one law suggests the breach of another; and the community becomes less law-abiding. Very likely the inefficacy of the Prohibition Laws in the United States had much to do with the wave of lawlessness that swept over that country.

In our country, too, there are laws that are dead letters. Enacted by Parliament under the influence of a powerful though transitory feeling, or with the laudable motive of meeting exceptional conditions (as when the strange series of "Profiteering Acts" came during the War years) they persist as laws. But their effect upon the lives of people is negligible. The Sunday Observance Act, 1677, for example, still prohibits the exercise of "any worldly business or work on the Lord's Day," still prescribes penalties for any one who cries his wares on Sunday; but the Act permitted the milkman to emit his peculiar cry before eight in the morning; and the mackerel seller could get his customers "before the hours of divine service." Other invitations to buy were penalised. They are still. Yet, nowadays, noises long and loud and various assail us even on a somnolent Sunday afternoon. And none dreams of invoking the Statute.

A "KNOCK-OUT AUCTION"

There is no need, though, to go far back to find examples of laws that are quite or almost nugatory. Enacted through the best of motives they are like ineffective scarecrows on which the birds perch unafraid. In *Rawlings* v. *General Trading Co.*, the Court of Appeal decided in 1921 that a "knock-out" among dealers, a combination among the intending bidders at an auction not to bid against one another, was not illegal at Common Law. A man cannot be constrained to make an offer. An auction may, therefore, become a sham; the goods are knocked down to one member of the ring, and the ring afterwards divide the spoils. In the attempt to counter the manifest unfairness to the seller, Parliament passed the Auction (Bidding Agreements) Act, 1927. This Act penalises any dealer who gives or offers an inducement to abstain from bidding at an auction sale; it penalises also (by fine not exceeding £100, or six months' imprisonment, or both) the person who seeks such an inducement from a dealer. A dealer is defined as "one who in the normal course of his business attends sales by auction for the purpose of purchasing goods with a view to re-selling them." The consent of the Attorney-General, however, is a necessary preliminary to a prosecution; and it does not appear that any conviction under the Act has been secured. Nor, seeing that the parties to the agreement will not publish their bargain from the housetops, need we be surprised.

ILLICIT COMMISSIONERS

The Acts against the giving and receiving of secret commissions are of the same nature. The nature of the relation between the principal and his agent is vitiated when the agent has the third party's interests in mind. Nothing, therefore, can justify his making an undisclosed profit from the transactions entered upon on his principal's account. This is an unbending rule of Common Law. When an agent is promised something that might induce him to act disloyally to his employer, or even diminish his interest in his employer's business, the law will not help him to recover what has been promised. And, if he does obtain something, he is bound to account for it to his principal. The law does not allow him to have an interest conflicting with his duty. But

2

the very name, "secret commission," applied to these bribes suggests the difficulty of preventing them. Parliament accordingly thought to strengthen the civil remedy by making the giving or the taking of bribes a crime. The Prevention of Corruption Act, 1906, creates the misdemeanour of accepting or of giving bribes, and prescribes for the misdemeanour the punishment, upon indictment, of a fine of £500 or imprisonment for two years. Another Act, ten years later, imposed substantially greater penalties where the contract in which the illegal commission was paid concerned the Government. The Acts, are, it may be, some slight deterrent, just as threats unlikely to bear fruit in deeds may yet deter timid souls. Probably, however, we shall still need to depend for honourable dealings upon the probity of business men rather than upon the severity of penal laws. To break the law and evade the punishment must be particularly easy where both giver and taker of the bribe are anxious for secrecy.

JUVENILE SMOKING

What our ancestors irreverently called "grand-motherly legis-lation" has some striking illustrations in the Children and Young Persons Act, 1933. The Act expounds in great detail the duties of parents and others towards children, enjoining conditions con-ducing to the welfare of body, mind, and spirit. All the clauses of the Act are inoperative. Some clauses are, and from their nature they must be, merely pious aspirations with no effect in practice. Section 7, for instance, prohibits the sale of cigarettes and other smoking mixtures to any one who appears to be under the age of 16. This throws a good deal of discretion to the sellers of cigarettes and, in cases of doubt, these may well give them-selves the benefit of the doubt. The same section also empowers park-keepers and constables to seize any cigarettes found on any such child or young person in a street or public place. This seems a precarious power to exercise; for an injudicious exercise of it might give rise to an action for assault, and the Act gives no indemnity in advance.

INFANTS

DATE OF MAJORITY

AN infant is one that, in contemplation of law, has not yet reached maturity of judgment. The law, therefore, lightens the obligations upon the infant in dealings with others. There is a legal presumption that a child under eight cannot commit a crime. And the presumption is irrebuttable: any evidence that may be brought forward to show that in fact such a child did commit a crime must be rejected. Before the Children and Young Persons Act, 1933, seven was the age. The presumption continues to the age of 14; but evidence to the contrary may rebut the presumption. Where contracts are concerned the law's protection of the infant persists up to 21.

Since the law does not recognise fractions of a day, an infant becomes of full age on the day before his twenty-first birthday; he is then regarded as having completed his twenty-first year. The sovereign, however, becomes of full age when he (or she) attains the age of eighteen years.

PARENTS' DUTY TO MAINTAIN

The moral duty of a father (or, failing him, of a mother) to maintain his child has been made into a legal duty by the Poor Law Act, 1930. This re-enacts, in Section 41 (1), with modifications, the famous 43 Eliz.: "It shall be the duty of the father, grandfather, mother, grandmother, or child, of a poor, old, blind, lame, and impotent person or other poor person not able to work, if possessed of sufficient means, to relieve and maintain such person." The duty, that is, is a reciprocal one: the parent is obliged to maintain the child; the child is obliged to maintain the parent. Section 41 (3) adds the further obligation that a man is liable to maintain also the children, legitimate or illegitimate, of his wife born before his marriage.

The statutory duty ceases when the child reaches sixteen, if it can then maintain itself; it ceases, in any event, when the child reaches twenty-one.

The Children and Young Persons Act, 1933, makes parents liable to contribute, according to the scale prescribed by the Home Office, to the maintenance of children committed to the care of "fit persons" or sent to approved schools. (Sects. 86, 87.)

NO LIABILITY FOR CHILD'S DEBT

The duty to maintain does not include a duty to pay debts incurred by the child, even though those debts incurred by the child should be for necessaries supplied: "A man is to maintain his children as he himself shall think proper, and it requires a contract to enable another to do so and charge him for it in an action." However, it does not need very strong evidence to show that the parent has invested the child with authority as an agent. But, unless a trader can show that he had a right to assume such an authority to get goods on the parent's credit, the trader cannot recover from the parent the price of goods supplied to the infant.

RELIGIOUS EDUCATION OF A CHILD

The Common Law gave the father the right and imposed upon him the duty both to direct the secular education of his legitimate children and also to select the religion in which they were to be instructed. The only control possible was that of the Court of Chancery which—acting for the King as *parens patriae*—could interfere in the interests of the children.

In a case decided in 1933, the duty of the parents was put thus: "Infants are, or ought to be, instructed in religious matters by their parents, and as a general rule have no choice of their own in such matters. The parents' duty is to be discharged with a view to the moral and spiritual welfare of the children, and ought not to be influenced by mercenary considerations affecting their worldly welfare."

The children concerned were entitled to benefit under their grandfather's will, but a condition was imposed in the will: "If any grandchild of the said Sir Robert Hudson Borwick shall at any time before attaining a vested interest under the trusts here-inbefore declared, be, or become a Roman Catholic, such grandchild shall thereupon forfeit and lose one moiety of all the right in the capital or income of the said trust."

The question was whether or not this condition was valid. The Court decided not; for it would hamper and influence the parents in discharging their parental duty with regard to the religious instruction. They might be affected in their discretion by the knowledge that the instruction that was best for the children from the religious point of view might endanger the worldly welfare of the children. The condition was bad because it operated to restrain a man from doing his duty. (*In re Borwick's Settlement*, Ch., 1933.) It could, therefore, be ignored.

The Guardianship of Infants Act, 1925, only declared the Common Law. It makes the interests of the child the first consideration, the wishes of the father not indeed being ignored but not being the supreme question. In *Ward* v. *Laverty* (H.L. 1925), the law upon the matter is thus stated : "On the question of the religion in which a young child is to be brought up, the wishes of the father are to be considered ; and, if there is no other matter to be taken into account, the wishes of the father prevail. But it is the welfare of the children which forms the paramount consideration. It is still true that a sufficient case must be made for going contrary to the father's wishes. But, if such a case is made, the Court has no hesitation in deciding upon the whole facts of the case."

INSURANCE OF CHILDREN

It has been held (*Worthington* v. *Curtis*, Ch. 1875) that a father has no insurable interest in the life of his child. The Children Act, 1908 (Section 7), forbids a person who keeps a child for reward to insure the life of that child. The Industrial Assurance Act, 1923, restricts the amount of insurance that may be made upon a child to £6 (under three), £10 (under six), £15 (under ten).

PARENT'S DUTY TO EDUCATE

This is created by the Education Act, 1921, which places a duty upon the parent of providing an adequate *secular* education for the child. This must be continuous between the ages of five and fourteen.

CHILDREN AND YOUNG PERSONS ACT, 1933

This Act imposes a number of duties upon parents, and others in the place of parents, for the preservation of the health and safety of the child.

FATHER'S (AND TEACHER'S) POWER OF CONTROL

Legally, the father can control his child's actions (by force, if necessary), and he can delegate his power of moderate chastisement to a person, schoolmaster or other, having custody of the child : "It is clear law that a father has the right to inflict reasonable personal chastisement on his own children. It is equally the law that he may delegate this right to the schoolmaster. Such a right has always commended itself to the common sense of mankind. Nor is the authority delegated to the schoolmaster limited to the four walls of the school." (*Cleary* v. *Booth*, Q.B., 1893.)

The parent or teacher must use reasonable discretion. But "he is the judge; and, like all others clothed with discretion, he cannot be made responsible for error in judgment, when he has acted in good faith and without malice."

Apparently, however, when a child has reached an age of discretion and has left its father's control, the Court will not order return against the child's will. What this age of discretion is appears doubtful, perhaps fourteen for a boy, and sixteen for a girl.

PARENT'S POWERS MAY BE CONTROLLED

It is the duty, as well as the prerogative, of the King to protect all his subjects, including children, against wrong. He performs the duty through the courts. Lord Justice FitzGibbon explains the point, *In re O'Hara* (1900): "At Common Law, the parent has an absolute right to the custody of a child of tender years, unless he or she has forfeited it by certain sorts of misconduct. Chancery, when a separate tribunal, possessed a jurisdiction different from that of Queen's Bench, a jurisdiction essentially parental, in the exercise of which the main consideration was the welfare of the child, and the Court did what, on consideration of all the circumstances, it was judicially satisfied that a wise parent, acting for the true interests of the child, would or ought to do, even though the natural parent desired and had the Common Law right to do otherwise, and had not been guilty of misconduct. The Judicature Act has made it the duty of every Division of the High Court to exercise the Chancery jurisdiction. In exercising the jurisdiction to control or ignore the parental right, the court must act cautiously, not as if it were a private person acting with regard to his own child, but acting in opposition to the parent only when judicially satisfied that the welfare of the child requires that the parental right should be suspended or superseded."

AFFILIATION OF ILLEGITIMATE CHILDREN

This is regulated by the Bastardy Laws Amendment Act, 1872. A single woman (which includes a widow or a wife judicially separated from her husband) applies to a Justice for a summons to the alleged father. The application must be made within a year from the child's birth unless—

1. She declares upon oath that during the year the alleged father paid towards the child's maintenance.

2. The alleged father has left England, in which event she may apply within a year after his return.

A married woman cannot be heard to say that another than her husband is father of the child until independent testimony of "non-access" of the husband has been given. The law presumes that a child born in wedlock is legitimate, and "the evidence for the purpose of repelling the presumption must be strong, distinct, satisfactory, and conclusive."

"If the evidence of the mother be corroborated in some material particular by other evidence to the satisfaction of the Justices, they may adjudge the man to be the putative father of the said child, and may also make an order upon him not exceeding twenty shillings per week for the maintenance and education of the child with, in their discretion, the expenses of its birth." (Bastardy Act, 1923.)

An officer of the court (Affiliation Orders Act, 1916) now collects money due, and he may, on written request from the mother, sue for arrears.

The affiliation order ceases to have effect—

1. Upon the death of the child.

2. Upon its attaining the age of thirteen, an age which may, however, be extended in the Justices' order to sixteen.

The man against whom an affiliation order is made has the right to appeal to Quarter Sessions, and now (since the Criminal Justice Administration Act, 1914), a woman who has been refused an order has a similar right.

LEGITIMATING OF ILLEGITIMATE CHILDREN

The Legitimacy Act, 1926, enacts (Section 1) that "where the parents of an illegitimate person marry one another the marriage shall, if the father at the date of marriage is domiciled in England or Wales, render that person legitimate." But "nothing in this Act shall operate to legitimate a person whose father or mother was married to a third person when the illegitimate person was born." It appears, however, that the law of the domicile is recognized in this matter also. The child of a British subject domiciled in Germany was born in Germany at a time when its father was married to a woman not being the child's mother. The father was divorced in Germany, and married the child's mother. German law automatically legitimated the child, and it was held (*Collins* v. *A.-G.*, 1931) that the child was entitled to a declaration of legitimacy under the Act. In *Newbould* v. *A.-G.*

(Probate, 1931), the effect of a decree declaring a former marriage to have been null was considered. The petitioner (praying by his father) sought a declaration of legitimacy. The child was born in 1929 of parents married in the same year. The question was whether the proviso, "Nothing in this Act shall operate to legitimate a person whose father or mother was married to a third person when the illegitimate person was born," prevents a decree. For the father had in 1909 gone through a ceremony of marriage, and a decree for nullity was pronounced subsequently to the birth of the child. The President decided that the proviso was not applicable to this case. For "a decree of nullity for impotence has a retrospective operation; it amounts to a declaration that there was no marriage at all. The petitioner is entitled to the declaration his father now seeks on his behalf."

A petition for a declaration of legitimacy under the Act may be presented either to the County Court or to the Probate Division of the High Court.

The Act also removes a palpable injustice in regard to illegitimate children with reference to property. Section 9 enacts—

1. Where the mother of an illegitimate child dies intestate, and does not leave any legitimate issue, the illegitimate child shall be entitled to take interest in her real and personal property as if he had been born legitimate.

2. Where an illegitimate child dies intestate, the mother shall be entitled to take the interests to which she would have been entitled if the child had been born legitimate and she had been the only surviving parent.

ADOPTION OF CHILDREN

The Adoption of Children Act, 1926, enables a Juvenile Court to make an adoption order. The effect of the order is to extinguish all rights and liabilities of the parents or guardians of the child, and to transfer those rights and liabilities to the applicant or applicants. The adopter will then stand towards the child as though the child had been born to him or her in lawful wedlock, and the child, in respect of liability to maintain its parents, stands to the adopter as though born to him or her in lawful wedlock.

Before making the order the Court must be satisfied—

1. That every person whose consent is necessary understands the effect of the adoption order, in particular that a parent realises that he or she will be permanently deprived of his parental rights.

2. That the order will be for the welfare of the infant.

3. That the applicant is not adopting the child for purposes of gain.

An applicant for the order must, in general, not be under 25; he must be at least 21 years older than the infant; and, unless there are special circumstances, an order cannot be made where the sole applicant is a male and the infant a female.

ACTIONS FOR SEDUCTION

It seems that a parent, as such, cannot bring an action for damages against one who wrongs his or her child. Certainly he has a right to have the child in his keeping during its infancy, and if another deprives him of this right, he may recover possession by means of a writ of *Habeas Corpus* (see page 157).

As one entitled to and enjoying the services of his child, however, he may obtain damages against one who wrongfully prevents the rendering of those services. This is, absurdly enough, still the basis upon which actions for seduction are tried. The question is, "Was the claimant, by the wrongful act of the defendant, deprived of the services of the girl?" The absurdity is put strongly in the judicial statement that the law affords protection to the rich man, whose daughter occasionally makes his tea, but leaves without redress the poor man whose child is sent, unprotected, to earn her bread among strangers. If, however, this question is answered Yes, the damages awarded may have no relation to the value of the services rendered; they may be "exemplary damages" far in excess of the loss incurred. Moreover, the Courts accept even trivial acts as evidence of service in order to give a basis for what is really being tried—what damages ought to be awarded for the injury to the family's honour and feelings: "Even making tea has been regarded as an act of service."

It even seems to be enough if the plaintiff can show—

1. That the child was old enough to perform acts of service.

2. That the child resided with him, or was only temporarily absent.

In an action where a father succeeded in obtaining damages for an assault upon his son, the Chief Justice ruled that "it was sufficient to show that the son lived in, and was part of, his father's family; this would raise a service by implication."

The action available to a parent considers him as an employer of the girl seduced; and the action is similarly available for any other employer deprived by a wrongful act of the services of a servant. The converse of the rule is that a parent is responsible for the actions of his child only to the extent that the relation of master and servant may be looked upon as existing between them.

RIGHTS AND LIABILITIES OF AN INFANT (CONTRACT)

For contract law, an infant is one who has not yet completed his twentieth year. Full contractual capacity begins on the day preceding his or her twenty-first birthday.

The Infants' Relief Act, 1874, determines the infant's liability under contract.

1. All contracts whether by specialty (i.e. evidenced by a deed or sealed writing) or by simple contract henceforth entered into by infants for the repayment of money lent or to be lent, or for goods supplied or to be supplied (other than contracts for necessaries), and all accounts stated with infants, shall be absolutely void.

2. No action shall be brought whereby to charge any person upon any promise made after full age to pay any debt contracted during infancy, or upon any ratification made after full age of any promise or contract made during infancy, whether there shall or shall not be any new consideration for such promise or ratification after full age.

The protection afforded by the Act is far reaching. Not even a promise made after majority can render him legally liable for what took place in infancy. Nor does the fact that the infant has deceived the other party into an unfounded belief that the infant is of full age affect the matter.

In *Leslie* v. *Sheill* (K.B. 1914), where an infant by fraudulently representing himself of full age obtained £400 from a money lender, the plaintiff failed to recover: "the protection was a shield not a sword: therefore if an infant commit an assault or utter slander he is answerable for it in a Court of Justice. But, where an infant has made an improvident contract with a person, such person cannot resort to the court to enforce the contract. It is perhaps a pity that no exception was made, where, as here, the infant's wickedness was at least equal to that of the person that innocently contracted with him. But so it is. It was thought necessary to safeguard the weakness of infants at large, even though here and there a juvenile knave slipped through."

A contract with an infant, that is, cannot be enforced indirectly by means of an action for tort; "A tradesman dealing on credit with an infant does so at his peril, and must lose his money (that is, if the infant does not voluntarily pay him) unless he can prove that the goods supplied were necessaries for the infant according to his station in life." An infant is, indeed, liable for a civil wrong apart from contract. Two contrasted cases illustrate the distinction. In *Jennings* v. *Rundall* (1799, T.R.) the plaintiff failed: he had lent to an infant a mare for riding; the infant injured the mare through over-riding; the plaintiff sued for negligence. But it was held that to admit his claim against the infant would be another way of awarding damages for an infant's breach of contract. In *Burnard* v. *Haggis* (C.P., 1863), however, the plaintiff succeeded. An infant hired a horse for riding; the owner expressly refused to hire it for jumping; the infant lent it to a friend who jumped it at a hedge and so injured it that it was killed. The infant was held liable: "What was done by the defendant was not an abuse of the contract. It was a bare trespass, not within the object and purpose of the hiring. It was doing an act altogether forbidden by the owner."

NATURE OF PROTECTION AFFORDED

So, an infant trader cannot be made bankrupt. An infant was convicted for having defrauded his creditors (Debtors' Act, 1869). The conviction was quashed: the transactions were void under the Infants Relief Act; there were consequently no creditors to defraud. (*Reg.* v. *Wilson*, Q.B. 1879.)

The protection afforded does not, however, extend farther than the statute indicates. If an infant has paid money and taken benefit under a contract, he cannot recover his money. If he has acquired shares in his minority he may (in the absence of a disclaimer upon his reaching majority) be held liable as a contributory in the winding up.

And "necessaries" are construed widely. In *Roberts* v. *Gray* (K.B. 1913) it was applied to a contract whereby the infant Gray stipulated to tour in order to play with the veteran Roberts a series of exhibition games at billiards. He broke his agreement; and Roberts obtained damages: "The contract was one for necessaries within the meaning which that phrase had had attached to it. It is for board, lodging, employment found at the plaintiff's expense, and for the education which a billiard player of receptive capacity could not fail to obtain from playing with a great billiard player like John Roberts. Every item which goes to make up 'necessaries' in the sense of a labour and education contract—except the express term to give the education, which would be necessary if it were an apprenticeship deed—is in this particular contract as much as though, instead of finding the board and lodging on board ship and in various hotels, Roberts had found it in a house of his own where he gave exhibitions."

A loan of money too, supplied to be spent on immediate necessaries and actually so spent can be recovered. The lender is regarded as having supplied necessaries; he is entitled to stand in the place of the person paid by the borrowed money (be subrogated to him is the phrase).

OTHER PROTECTIONS OF INFANTS

(a) The Betting and Loans (Infants) Act, 1892, penalises any inciting of infants to betting or wagering or borrowing money. Section 5 enacts, moreover: "If any infant, who has contracted a loan which is void in law, agrees after he comes of age to pay any money which in whole or in part represents or is agreed to be paid in respect of any such loan, and is not a new advance, such agreement . . . shall be void absolutely as against all persons whomsoever." Even a negotiable instrument given in respect of such a loan is void.

(b) The Moneylenders Act, 1900, establishes the presumption that the moneylender knew that the person whom he incited to borrow was an infant. He can rebut this presumption only by proving that he had reasonable grounds for believing the infant to be of full age.

(c) Though an infant may be a member of a Building Society, he cannot execute a valid mortgage as a security for advances made to him by the society. In the absence of fraud or misrepresentation on the infant's part, the Court will order such a mortgage to be delivered up and cancelled.

HUSBAND AND WIFE

WOMEN

WE may well speak of a revolution in the legal position of women. Nineteenth century dependence has been displaced by twentieth century independence. Mill could write in 1848: "Women are as capable as men of appreciating and managing their own concerns, and the only hindrance to their doing so arises from the injustice of their present social position. When the law makes everything which the wife acquires the property of the husband, while by compelling her to live with him it forces her to submit to almost any amount of moral and even physical tyranny which he may choose to inflict, there is some ground for regarding every act done by her as done under coercion. But it is the great error of reformers and philanthropists in our time to nibble at the consequences of unjust power, instead of redressing the injustice itself. If women had as absolute control as men have over their own persons and their patrimony or acquisitions, there would be no plea for limiting the hours of labour for them in order that they might have time to labour for the husband in what is called, by the advocates of restriction, *his* home." All that Mill deplored in the matter has now been removed. The Sex Disqualification (Removal) Act of 1919 was simply a statutory recognition of the striking changes that had silently been in progress.

Till recent statutory changes, reflecting changes in the social system, marriage placed a wife into a position of subordination to her husband. Her promise to "obey" received a literal interpretation. Whatever property she had became her husband's; he could restrain her liberty at his pleasure; and, always subject to the rule of moderation, he could administer physical correction at his discretion. "The husband hath by law power and dominion over his wife" (Lord Bacon).

Outside the home her powers were narrowly restricted. Without the authority of her husband she could enter into no contract. If with his authority she made a contract, it was his contract alone; and he alone could sue or be sued on it. If she committed a wrong, the husband could be sued on the ground that he had permitted her to do it. If she committed a felony in the presence of her husband it was "marital coercion" that made her do it, and she was exempt from responsibility.* She could not vote. She could not enter a profession.

Matters are now almost wholly altered. Some slight limitations of freedom remain. The ecclesiastical profession is still closed to her. Property may still be left to her "with a restraint on anticipation" (a device invented for her protection), so that she can touch only the income from the property. The restrictions are now, however, almost negligible. The Sex Disqualification (Removal) Act of 1919, later completed by the extension of the suffrage to women of 21, removed inequalities.

MARRIED WOMEN'S LIABILITY UNDER CONTRACT

The Married Women's Property Act (1882) with its amendment of 1893 defines the contractual capacity of a married woman—

1. She has full capacity to acquire and to dispose of property and to contract.

2. As promisee she has the same rights as a man.

3. As promisor her liability is a peculiar one. She is not personally liable. Her separate contracts can be enforced against her separate estate only. And, if this is subject to a "restraint on anticipation," the accrued income alone is liable. If a judgment is given against her, the question of the property available for satisfaction of the judgment is thus decided: how much free property had she *at the time of making the contract*? If, at the time of entering into the contract or at any time thereafter, she has separate property which she is restrained from anticipating, such property cannot be made liable for her contracts.

The Married Women's Property Act, 1893, extends the 1882 Act a little. Every contract now made by a married woman, otherwise than as an agent, binds her separate estate and binds, too, property acquired *after* the contract was made. The exemption of property subject to a "restraint on anticipation" remains however. (See page 45.)

"Otherwise than as agent" has been interpreted to mean that, if the wife actually has authority from her husband to pledge his credit, her separate estate is not liable. The tradesman may not

---

* This presumption (or fiction) had been, indeed, invented for the woman's benefit. But the very circumstances of its origin emphasises the law's former unfairness towards women. A man charged with felony could "plead his clergy," he could as they said "hack out his neck verse" and, by so exhibiting a nodding acquaintance with learning, he escaped hanging. A woman, however, could not become a priest; she, therefore, however learned, could not plead clergy. The real culprit got off; the less guilty suffered death. So, at an early period the Judges invented the humane presumption.

know that she has her husband's authority; still, if she has it, he cannot make her liable.

In *Paquin* v. *Beauclerk* (A.C. 1906), where a dressmaker failed to recover, the matter was thus put—

"The law governing the case is the 1st Section of the Married Women's Property Act, 1893: 'Every contract hereafter entered into by a married woman, otherwise than as agent, shall be deemed to be a contract entered into by her with respect to, and to bind her separate property whether she is or is not, in fact, possessed of or entitled to any separate property at the time when she enters into such contract.' The separate property is not to answer when she enters into the contract as an agent. Did the defendant make this contract as agent for her husband; has she his authority, express or implied? The evidence, which was uncontradicted and not impugned by cross-examination, leaves it beyond reasonable doubt that she did act with his authority. That is sufficient to establish her case."

HUSBAND RESPONSIBLE FOR WIFE'S TORTS

In some ways the strangest liability of all is that of a husband for his wife's torts. This liability is, indeed, a survival from the times when a wife was looked upon as her husband's chattel, when she could neither own property nor make contracts. "By marriage, husband and wife are one person; and that person is the husband." Just as a man was answerable for damage his cattle did when trespassing, so he was held liable for the wrong of his wife. Nor, whether as regarded wife or cattle, did his greatest effort to prevent the wrong or the damage exempt him from liability. Desirable changes in the law are sometimes made without all the consequences of the changes being provided for. In the old days it was logical to hold the husband liable, as it still is logical to hold the owner liable for damage wrought by his straying cattle. It is not logical now that the married woman has full control of her property and pretty nearly full control of her life. Yet the rule persists. In one case, a woman eloped with her lover, using her husband's car for the purpose. Her perturbation of mind caused her to drive recklessly, and she damaged a municipal lamp-post. The husband was in law liable to the municipality; so that he lost wife and car, and was mulcted in damages into the bargain.

This Common Law doctrine is still the rule in regard to income tax. The wife's income is looked upon as part of the husband's;

and if the tax is not paid, even though the husband cannot get from his wife the means of paying, the husband is liable. The husband, too, is bound to provide "necessaries" for his wife, even if she has a separate income. In most other respects the Common Law rule has been whittled away. Even in regard to torts (wrong-doings) the rule is modified. The husband is now liable for his wife's torts committed before marriage only to the extent of the property he has acquired from her through the marriage. The injured party is, therefore, in no worse position. The wife is responsible so far as her separate estate is concerned for torts after her marriage. But the wronged party has another remedy, too. For the husband also is made liable. The husband's liability is ended by a divorce or by a judicial separation. This is so even if the tort were committed before the divorce or judicial separation, and even if proceedings in respect of the tort had been begun.

WIFE OBTAINING GOODS ON HUSBAND'S CREDIT

A husband must maintain his wife and family. If he leaves his wife without "necessaries"—i.e. things suitable to the station in life that the husband occupies, such things not being in excess of the wife's actual requirements at the time—she becomes his "agent of necessity," and may supply her wants upon his credit.

A tradesman may succeed in getting payment from the husband for goods supplied to the wife. He will, if he establishes one of two facts: he shows that the goods supplied were necessaries, and the husband had neither supplied them nor made an adequate allowance to his wife; or he shows that he was justified in assuming that the wife had her husband's authority to pledge his credit.

'NECESSARIES ' FOR A WIFE

The tradesman's task is an exacting one. First, he must satisfy the Court that the goods were suitable to the station in life chosen by the husband, not by the wife. Next, he must show that the goods were not in excess of the wife's actual requirements at the time: if she has plenty then, whether he knows or not, he fails: "A person who deals with a married woman on credit does so, so far as regards a remedy against the husband, at his own risk." So said the judge in *Martial and Armand* v. *Frankau* (K.B. 1931), where a dressmaker failed in her suit against the husband—failed because, though she was ignorant of the fact, the husband had made his wife a generous allowance.

But this does not complete the task. The husband may have

given his wife an adequate allowance for those particular goods. He is thereby exonerated. That she has diverted the allowance into other channels does not help the tradesman.

As regards imputed agency we are to ask, Did the husband by his conduct give the tradesman to understand that he would be answerable for the debts; had he paid former bills without demur, had he helped to select the goods? For marriage does not as a matter of course make the wife her husband's agent. If men become partners, that very fact makes them agents for one another in the business of the partnership. But marriage is not a partnership of this kind. That a man allows a woman to manage his house raises a presumption that he looks upon her as his agent. But it is a presumption only, and may be rebutted; and one way of rebutting the presumption is to show that an adequate allowance was made.

RESTRAINT OF WIFE BY HUSBAND

In the Matrimonial Causes Act, 1884, it was enacted that no decree for the restitution of conjugal rights could be enforced by attachment. That is, in spite of the decree, neither husband nor wife could force the other to return under penalty of imprisonment by the Court. *R.* v. *Jackson* (Q.B. 1891), supplies a commentary. The husband sought to justify the imprisonment of his wife, affirming that he was "using no more force or restraint than was necessary to prevent her from returning to her relations; and that he could lawfully use such restraint in order to have an opportunity of regaining the affection of his wife." The Court of Appeal rejected this contention with emphasis; and it is now clear that a married woman is free, if she wishes to do so, to leave her house and her husband.

Formerly the law gave a remedy to the husband or the wife whose spouse had been "enticed" away. In a case of 1932 (*Place* v. *Searle*, K.B.), Mr. Justice McCardie decided that the old action for "enticement" cannot be reconciled with the independence which the modern law has given to married women. He was overruled on the point by the Court of Appeal, which decided that a jury must determine whether or not the deserted husband should obtain damages. At the new trial the husband was in fact awarded damages. But the learned Judge's remarks illustrate the trend of events.

EVIDENCE OF HUSBAND OR WIFE

The old idea was "Husband and wife are considered as one and the same person in law, and to have the same affections and interests; from whence it has been established as a general rule that the husband cannot be a witness for or against the wife, nor the wife be a witness for or against the husband, by reason of the implacable dissension which might be caused by it, and the great danger of perjury from taking the oaths of persons under so great a bias, and the extreme hardship of the case."

Even before modern reforms this rule was relaxed where violence was used or threatened. The State must protect its subjects, and any supposed unity of person in husband and wife must not interfere with the duty. An injured spouse was always a competent witness against the injurer.

The present rule is stated in the Evidence Amendment Act, 1853.

1. In a civil suit the husbands and wives of the parties are both *competent* and *compellable* to give evidence;

2. In a criminal proceeding the husband is neither *competent* nor *compellable* to give evidence against his wife, nor the wife against her husband;

3. A husband shall not be compellable to disclose any communication made to him by his wife during the marriage, nor the wife to disclose any communication made to her by her husband during the marriage;

4. On the application of the person charged the wife or husband is a *competent* witness for the defence.

When marriage has been admitted or proved, neither husband nor wife will be heard to deny that sexual intercourse has taken place between them. (*Russell* v. *Russell*, H.L. 1924.)

CONTRACT TO MARRY (BREACH OF PROMISE)

In order that such a contract shall entitle a party to damages for breach it is not absolutely necessary that written evidence shall be forthcoming. But *some* corroborative evidence there must be; the claimant's evidence is not adequate. This is one of the few instances where statute (Evidence Act, 1869, Section 2) requires some added proof to the evidence of a single witness.

Where no time is expressed in the promise, the assumption is that the parties contemplated marriage within a reasonable time. It is then necessary, in an action for breach, for the plaintiff to make a request and to allege refusal. Clearly, however, if the defendant has made his promise impossible of performance through his marrying someone else, the request is not called for. It seems (*Hall* v. *Wright*, Q.B. 1858) that it is no answer to the plaintiff's plea for compensation that, since the promise, the defendant's bodily or mental or financial position has changed for the worse. The plaintiff is entitled to elect whether or not she will carry on with the contract, despite its being less favourable to her than she expected; and, as the Court informed the defendant upon his plea that he had a dangerous illness rendering him quite unfit for marriage, "Perhaps the lady might like to be his widow."

MARRIAGE

The marriage recognised by English law is " the voluntary union for life of one man with one woman to the exclusion of all others."

To be valid—

1. The parties shall be capable of contracting a marriage: there may be mental incapacity, when a party is not able to understand what is taking place in the marriage ceremony; there may be, since 1929, incapacity through not having reached the age of 16; there may be physical incapacity through inability to consummate the marriage.

2. The parties shall not be within the prohibited degrees of kindred.

3. Neither of the parties shall have a living spouse.

4. Certain forms shall be observed, and there shall be free consent. (See the case *Ogden* v. *Ogden* discussed below.)

The Courts regard marriage as a contract resulting in a *status ;* the Church tends to regard marriage as a contract resulting in a *relationship*. The status may, in suitable causes, be altered. The relationship once established cannot be altered.

DIVORCE AND MATRIMONIAL CAUSES ACT, 1857

Under this Act—

1. A woman divorced from her husband is restored to the position of a single woman (*feme sole*).

2. Judicial separation also causes the wife to be considered as a *feme sole* for any judicial proceedings.

WIFE'S SEPARATE ESTATE

"Husband and wife are one person; and the husband is that one." Such was the maxim of the Common Law; and Equity sought ways whereby, in spite of the maxim, property could be secured to the separate use of the wife. This explains what may still persist: a married woman holds property from which she derives an income at her free disposal, but which she cannot alienate nor charge with future debts. She holds it with a "restraint on anticipation"; for the legal owners are the trustees to whom she, or someone on her behalf, has conveyed the property "for her use."

MARRIAGE OF INFANTS

The Age of Marriage Act, 1929, makes void a marriage between persons either of whom is under 16. The consent of parents is necessary for the marriage of an infant between 16 and 21. But, where a parent or guardian refuses consent to the marriage of an infant, a court of summary jurisdiction may give consent; and suggestions are made that in proper cases magistrates shall be empowered to allow marriage, though the boy or girl is under 16.

PLACE DETERMINES VALIDITY

Whether or not a marriage is valid depends upon its being in accordance with the law of the *place* where it was made. When this place differs from the domicile, complications may arise.

Thus, a marriage between persons domiciled in the Province of Quebec was solemnised in France according to the rites of the Roman Catholic Church, but without a civil ceremony. The Judicial Committee considered that such a marriage, being a nullity under French law, is a nullity also in Quebec. The Court has no discretion to declare the marriage valid. Still, where as in the particular case the putative wife acts in good faith, she gets civil rights that include a right to alimony. (*Berthiaume* v. *Dastous*, J.C. 1929.)

LOCUS REGIT ACTUM (the place determines the nature of the Act)

If a marriage is good by the laws of the country where it is effected, English law holds it good all the world over. It is immaterial whether the proceeding or ceremony which constituted marriage according to the law of the place would or would not constitute marriage in the country of the domicile of one or other of the spouses. Conversely, if the so-called marriage is no marriage in the place where it is celebrated, it is no marriage anywhere. This is so although the ceremony or proceeding, if conducted in the place of the parties' domicile, would be considered a good marriage.

This rule has, in one case, been altered by statute law. Marriage in Scotland can be constituted by mere words of consent *de praesenti* (in the, presence of witnesses) ; and English couples used to cross the border to Gretna Green to be married by interchange of consent in the presence of the blacksmith and his assistant. The Marriage Act of 1856 declares a marriage constituted by " consent *de praesenti* " null where the parties had not previously resided in Scotland for at least three weeks.

MAINTENANCE ORDER AND SEPARATION AGREEMENT

A separation agreement, under which a wife undertakes not to take proceedings under the Summary Jurisdiction (Separation and Maintenance) Acts, 1895 to 1925, is not necessarily a bar to the jurisdiction of the Justices. The agreement is, indeed, evidence on the question as to what is reasonable maintenance and whether the husband has wilfully failed to provide it. The question for the Court is always, under the Acts, can the woman show that the man, being in a position to contribute to her maintenance, has wilfully neglected to do so and that she cannot under the agreement maintain herself ? So the President of the Divorce Divisional Court, on appeal from the order of a police magistrate, decided in *Matthews* v. *Matthews* (1932). The husband had agreed to set his wife up in business and to make certain payments. He carried out his undertaking and sought, unsuccessfully, when the wife's business failed, to have the validity of the clause acknowledged : "In consideration of the agreement of the husband herein, the wife agrees with the husband that so long as he observes and performs the agreement, the wife will not at any time hereafter make a claim or demand upon the husband for maintenance or institute any legal proceedings against him."

GENERAL RULES RELATING TO MARRIAGE

All persons are free to marry provided that they fulfil legal requirements (*a*) age, (*b*) mental and physical capacity, (*c*) relationship, (*d*) free consent of the parties. Failure in any of these respects renders the marriage of no effect.

Persons fulfilling these conditions are married by conforming with the various formalities required by law. Failure to conform may render the parties liable to penalties. At times, also, though rarely and only when both parties knew they were breaking a regulation laid down by statute, the marriage celebrated will be of no effect.

CAPACITY

Want of physical capacity makes a marriage voidable; the party prejudiced by the incapacity can seek a declaration from the Court that there has been no marriage. It should be noted, however, that it is not the physical or mental infirmity likely to be transmitted to children that will cause a Court to pronounce a marriage void; the incapacity is that of procreating or conceiving children.

CONDITION

The person marrying in England must have no spouse living recognised by the law. When a person has been married before, he may marry again if (a) the previous spouse is dead, (b) the previous marriage has been dissolved by a Court, the jurisdiction of which is recognised by the English Court, or (c) if the spouse has been continuously absent for seven years and is not known to be living. In the first two cases the marriage is perfect in all respects; in the third case the marriage is voided if the absent spouse should reappear. The person marrying under condition (c) is described as *widow* or *widower*. It may be noted that a second marriage may take place (without any liability in crime) even within seven years, if honest and reasonable belief exists that the other party to the first marriage is dead.

The first defence against a possible prosecution for bigamy, is a statutory one, the second is a Common Law defence. Thus in *R.* v. *Tolson* (1889) the Criminal Courts were obliged to consider the exact meaning of the words of the statute exempting a person from crime who married after seven years' absence without news of the former spouse.

It looked as though Parliament, when defining the crime of bigamy, had enacted that a defence of ignorance should not prevail until seven years had passed. At the Assizes, therefore, Mrs. Tolson who, reasonably thinking her husband drowned, had married within seven years, was found guilty of bigamy. The Court of Criminal Appeal, however, quashed the conviction; for there was no guilty intentions—which is almost invariably requisite to constitute a crime. "At Common Law," the judgment declared, "an honest and reasonable belief in the existence of circumstances, which, if true, would make the act for which the prisoner is indicated an innocent act, has always been held to be a good defence."

It should be noted, too, that the dissolution of a marriage does not take place when a *decree nisi* is pronounced in the Divorce Court. The dissolution takes place when the decree is made "absolute"; and during a period of six months it is the duty of a specially appointed office—the *King's Proctor*—to ascertain whether any reasons exist why the decree should not be made absolute. It is only after the decree absolute that re-marriage can take place.

PROHIBITED DEGREES

The Table conveniently bound up in the Book of Common Prayer is part of the law of England; for it was re-enacted by Parliament in 1835. It is, therefore, binding upon all domiciled here irrespective of whether or not they use the Church of England prayer book. The Table has been modified by the following enactments—

(*a*) 1907. By the Deceased Wife's Sister's Marriage Act a man may now lawfully marry the sister of his dead wife. And, contrary to the vast majority of Acts of Parliament, the Act was made retrospective. That is, it made lawful such marriages between a man and his dead wife's sister as had occurred before the passing of the Act. In this way children born of the marriages were made legitimate. The status of the wife's sister is preserved by the Act during the wife's lifetime. It expressly continues, for instance, the former rule that illicit connection with a living wife's sister is *incest*, even though ordinarily incest means connection with a person whom the accused could never marry.

It should be noted, too, that the Act expressly forbids marriage with the sister of a divorced wife during the divorced wife's lifetime. This express prohibition was necessary in view of the fact that divorced persons are, by statute, in the same position as if their marriage had been dissolved by death.

(*b*) 1921. By the Deceased Husband's Brother's Marriage Act the permission afforded to the man by the previously noted Act has been extended in analogous conditions to the woman. She may now marry the brother of her dead husband.

(*c*) 1931. By an Act passed in this year marriage to a nephew or a niece by marriage (i.e. to the dead wife's niece or aunt, or to the dead husband's nephew or uncle) is made lawful.

A summary of the "prohibited degree" is—

1. Ascendants and descendants may not intermarry.

2. Persons related within the third degree may not intermarry. A man, for instance, may not marry his niece: for from him to his

father is *one* degree, from father to brother or sister is a *second* degree, from brother or sister to niece is a *third*. Cousins, however, may marry: they are related in the *fourth* degree.

3. Kindred of husband are not of affinity with kindred of wife.

4. Relationship by the half blood is on the same footing as relationship of the whole blood.

INCAPACITY A PERSONAL ONE

Peal v. *Peal* (Probate Divorce, 1930) well illustrates the rule that the marriage law is a personal one. Residence elsewhere does not relax the rules regarding British subjects. Thus, an impediment to marriage arising from consanguinity is not removed by a customary law of local observance, nor by a dispensation from a religious community. The petitioner and the respondent at the time of marriage in India were British subjects of the Roman Catholic faith. They obtained from their proper ecclesiastical authority a special dispensation for their marriage. The dispensation was necessary because the petitioner was the daughter of the respondent's grandfather.

The petitioner sought restitution of conjugal rights; the respondent cross-petitioned for a decree of nullity. The respondent succeeded on both issues: "Are British subjects in India, as regards competency to marry, persons in a distinct and legally different class from their British fellow subjects? If they are, they could, by their own volition, and contrary to the general law, by marriage within the prohibited degrees create relationships and confer successional rights or interests in prejudice of the statutory rights and interests of their kinsfolk. As regards British subjects domiciled in India the personal law to which they are subject as regards capacity to marry is the law of England." The ceremony of marriage had between them in India was accordingly decreed to be null and void.

CONSENT

As to this it should be noted that, since a marriage is more than a contract (for it effects a change of status), no amount of fraud will make invalid an English marriage. When there has been a real (not merely an apparent) consent, the validity of the marriage will not be affected even though the consent has been obtained by fraud. A judgment expresses the notion thus: "Suppose a young man of sixteen, in the first bloom of youth, the representative of a noble family, and the inheritor of a splendid fortune. Suppose that he is induced by persons connected with a female in all respects unworthy of such an alliance to contract marriage with her after the publication of banns in a parish church to which both are strangers; the strongest case you could establish of the most deliberate plot would not enable this Court to release him from chains which, though forged by others, he has riveted on himself. If he is capable of consent, and has consented, the law does not ask how the consent has been induced." The Guardianship of Infants Act, 1925, has made this judgment largely inapplicable to persons under 21.

CONSENT OF PARENTS NECESSARY FOR MINORS TO MARRY

Before this Act, parents had little or no voice in the marriage of their children. The position is now greatly changed.

1. Who may "forbid the banns" or refuse their consent when application is made for a church licence, or for the licence of a superintendent registrar?

(*a*) *When the infant is legitimate*—

(i) Both parents, when they are living together.

(ii) The parent having custody of the child, when the parents are divorced or separated.

(iii) The guardian appointed by the Court, when both parents are dead or have been deprived of the custody of the child.

(iv) A surviving parent, if there is no other guardian.

(v) A surviving parent and the guardian appointed by the other parent. (Either parent may by deed or will appoint a guardian who then has equal powers with the other parent.)

(vi) The guardians appointed by the parents.

(*b*) *When the infant is illegitimate*—

(i) The mother.

(ii) The guardian appointed by the mother or the Court.

Provisions are made whereby, in the event of consent being unobtainable or being unreasonably withheld, the marriage contemplated may proceed.

For Section 9 provides—

(*a*) If the superintendent registrar is satisfied that the consent of any person whose consent is required cannot be obtained by reason of absence or inaccessibility or by reason of his being under any disability, the necessity for the consent of that person shall be dispensed with if there is any other person whose consent is also required, and the Registrar General may dispense with the necessity of obtaining any consent, or the Court may, on application being made, give its consent. Consent so given shall have the same effect as if it had been given by the person whose consent cannot be so obtained.

(*b*) If any person where consent is required refuses his consent, the Court may, on application being made, consent to the marriage; and the consent of the Court so given shall have the same effect as if it had been given by the person whose consent is so refused.

The infant to whom parents or guardians refuse consent may apply—

1. To the High Court, when the application will be heard in Chambers (i.e. not in public).

2. To the County Court, when the application will be heard by the Registrar (subject to appeal to the Judge).

3. To a Court of Summary Jurisdiction, when the application will be heard and determined otherwise than in open court.

Notice of the application must be given to the person who has refused consent so that he may, if he chooses, be present in order to justify his refusal to the Court.

The section carefully provides that: "Nothing in this section shall dispense with the necessity of obtaining the consent of the High Court to the marriage of a ward of Court." (Under the Adoption of Children Act, 1926, the rights of the parents as regards consent become vested in the adopter or adopters.)

MARRIAGE OF MINORS WITHOUT CONSENT OF PARENTS

The consent of the parents is regarded as part of the English marriage ceremony. The absence of consent is not a disability to marry. If, therefore, minors are married in a place where consent of parents is not an essential part of the ceremony, the marriage would be recognised in England.

BANNS OF MARRIAGE

These are public announcements, primarily intended to prevent clandestine marriages, of an intended marriage. The banns are published in the church of the parish "wherein the persons to be married shall dwell." If the parties live in different parishes the banns must be published in both. Dwelling means residence; if a person makes a parish his sleeping place for a few weeks he is dwelling there, and has a right to ask the clergyman of the parish to publish his banns. But the clergyman is entitled to ascertain whether the residence is acquired for a wrongful purpose; and for this he is entitled to *a notice of seven days at the least before the first publication*, in writing, of the true christian names and surnames, of the house inhabited in the parish, and of the length of habitation. Residence must continue throughout the period of publication.

The banns are published on three Sundays, normally at the morning service. The Sundays need not be consecutive. If the marriage contemplated does not take place within three months after the first completed publication, republication is necessary.

Where banns have been called in another parish the minister officiating at a marriage must not proceed with the ceremony unless he has a certificate from the minister in that other parish that the banns have been thrice called by him. The marriage takes place in one of the churches where the banns were published; the church (or chapel) must be authorised for the celebration of marriages; the ceremony must be performed by a clerk in Holy Orders in the presence of at least two witnesses; it must be performed within the canonical hours of 8 a.m. and 3 p.m. The clergyman cannot be a witness also. Nor has he power to celebrate his own marriage.

The Naval Marriage Act, 1908, enacts that, when a man is borne on the books of one of His Majesty's ships at sea, banns may be published by the chaplain or officer commanding.

The Marriage Act, 1823, declares a marriage void when the parties "knowingly and wilfully intermarry without due publication of banns." In *Small* v. *Small and Furber* this Act was applied. Smallwood in 1915 married, banns being read in the name of Small. Both parties knew this name to be assumed, Smallwood having adopted the alias to hide the fact that he had deserted one regiment and joined another. The woman later married another man; and, when she was convicted of bigamy, Small obtained a *decree nisi*. On the intervention of the King s Proctor, however the Court held that he had never been married. The woman was therefore, not guilty of bigamy, the first ceremony being no marriage.

SUPERINTENDENT REGISTRAR'S CERTIFICATE

The Civil Marriage Act, 1836, authorised a superintendent registrar to issue a certificate that should stand in place of the publication of banns. And every parson must solemnise marriage after such notice and certificate in like manner as after due publication of banns.

BISHOP'S LICENCE

A bishop (the "ordinary" whose injunctions the parson is obliged to obey) may issue a licence. Such a licence is a dispensation from the need for banns. The bishop's fee for granting it is £2 2s. 6d. and there is a 10s. Government stamp. As with banns, so with the bishop's licence, the marriage to be valid must follow within three months. One of the parties seeking the licence must swear that he, or she, knows no lawful impediment to the marriage, that one of the parties has lived for fifteen days in the parish where the marriage is to be celebrated, and that when necessary the consent of parent or guardian has been given.

The licence is not granted as of right. But being granted the clergyman of the parish is apparently bound to perform the marriage ceremony except where (as in the Matrimonial Causes Act, 1857) a clergyman is given an option. It was thus put by the Master of the Rolls in *Barmister and Wife* v. *Thompson*: "One of the duties of clergymen within this realm is to perform the ceremony of marriage, and parishioners have the right to have the ceremony performed in their parish church. By Section 57 of the Matrimonial Causes Act, 1857, liberty to re-marry was given to both parties if the decree of divorce had been made absolute. But the Act contained the following proviso, in view of the scruples of many clergymen regarding these newly legalised marriages. 'Provided always that no clergyman shall be compelled to solemnise the marriages of any person whose marriage may have been dissolved on the ground of his or her adultery.' The protection given is an exceedingly narrow one; it will not protect the clergyman in refusing to perform acts connected with the marriage, such as publication of banns."

If a clergyman elects not to perform the ceremony, the Act requires him to allow another clergyman of the Church of England, entitled to officiate in the diocese, to use the church for the ceremony. The rule is different in regard to marriage with a deceased wife's sister; the clergyman can refuse to perform the ceremony, and he can refuse the use of his church for the purpose.

SPECIAL LICENCE

There are dispensations that enable a marriage to be celebrated at any convenient time and place, even in a private dwelling house. They are granted by the Archbishop of Canterbury (his fee being £25 and £5 stamp duty), and only when the applicants "allege very strong and weighty reasons for such indulgence arising from the particular circumstances of their case, and prove the same to the satisfaction of the Archbishop."

The time of marriage, *apart from such licence*, is between 8 a.m. and 6 p.m. The object of the various rules is that those persons who know the parties to the marriage shall know of the marriage also.

THE MARRIAGE CEREMONY

1. The ceremony takes place with open doors. For, before the actual marriage, the minister must ask for the last time whether any person knows of a just cause or impediment against the marriage.

2. The persons present need include only the minister, the parties, and two witnesses.

3. The essential part of the ceremony is a declaration by each party of the words "I do solemnly declare that I know not of any lawful impediment why I, A. B., may not be joined in matrimony to C. D.," and a mutual undertaking, "I call upon these persons here present to witness that I, A. B. do take thee, C. D. to be my lawful wedded wife (or husband)." It is these essentials that must be performed before 6 p.m. Elaborations of the ceremony may go on as long as the parties choose.

4. The ring, though a pleasing token, is not material.

5. The parties sign the register *after* the ceremony.

MARRIAGE IN PLACES OF WORSHIP OTHER THAN CHURCHES OF THE CHURCH OF ENGLAND

The Marriage Act, 1836, enables marriages to be celebrated in places of worship of all denominations if their congregations wish. There must be present, however, a duly authorised person to represent the State. Since 1898 the duly authorised person may be the minister of the church or chapel. The building must be registered before marriages may take place in it.

CIVIL MARRIAGE

Persons may marry, by certificate showing that banns have been read or by licence, in the district registry office. The registrar and two witnesses must be present, the doors must be open ,the hours of 8 a.m.to 3 p.m. must be observed, and the solemn declaration must be made.

MARRIAGES WITH FOREIGNERS

Several cases indicate the risks run when an English girl marries a foreigner. Thus—

In 1898, a ceremony of marriage in English form was celebrated in England between a domiciled Englishwoman and P., a domiciled Frenchman. By a decree of the French Court in 1901, this marriage was annulled, the consent of the parent as required by French law when the party is below 25 not having been obtained. P. subsequently married in France, and in 1903 the Englishwoman sought for a dissolution of her marriage on the ground of P.'s adultery and desertion. The Court dismissed this petition, considering itself to have no jurisdiction, the domicile of the parties being in France. In 1904 the Englishwoman went through a ceremony of marriage in England with Ogden, a domiciled Englishman, describing herself as a widow. The Court held, at the suit of Ogden in 1908 that this later marriage was bigamous and must be annulled.

The Court considered, however, that, in view of the hardship upon the woman who was a wife in England but no wife in France, the Court in 1903 might have assumed jurisdiction and have treated the Englishwoman as having a domicile in her own country sufficient to support her divorce suit.

English law is certainly in this matter more in accord with reason and justice than French law. We hold that a marriage contract, valid in the place where it was celebrated, is binding though in the domicile of one of the parties it would be void or voidable. "How," asked a Judge, "are the inhabitants of any country to ascertain the condition of a stranger dwelling among them as fixed by the law of his domicile? Even courts of justice do not assume to know what the laws of a foreign country are; but require them to be proved. How, then, shall private persons be presumed to have better means of knowledge? Contracts ought to be governed by the law of the country where they are made, as to the competence of the parties to make them and as to their validity. Such a rule has certainty and simplicity in its application."

France has ventured upon the bold doctrine that the marriages of Frenchmen in foreign countries shall not be deemed valid if the parties are not by its own law competent to contract by reason of their being under the parental power. There can be little doubt that foreign countries where such marriages are celebrated will follow their own law, and disregard that of France.

On the other hand, a marriage not valid in the place where it was celebrated cannot be recognised as valid in this country, even though everything necessary for its validity here had been performed. An illustration is *Berthiaume* v. *Dastous* (J.C. 1929).

In 1913 the respondent a French Canadian of the Roman Catholic faith, being then a girl 17 years of age who had just graduated from a convent in a small town in Montreal, went on a trip to Europe with her father. She there met the appellant, a member of a Quebec family and also of the Roman Catholic faith, who had been living in Paris for several years. He proposed marriage to her, and she accepted. The appellant asked the respondent to make the necessary arrangements, and she called on the *curé* of the parish where her fiancé had been residing, and where she was temporarily residing. The *curé* informed her that there were certain civil formalities to be gone through, and that he would celebrate the marriage. She asked her fiancé to attend to the civil formalities, and he took her to the British Consulate where certain papers were signed and a certificate, which was given to the fiancé, was issued. After that the parties proceeded to the church. The certificate was handed to the *curé*, who then proceeded to celebrate the marriage according to the rites of the Roman Catholic Church. The parties lived together, until the respondent discovered that the appellant had been guilty of infidelity. The respondent applied to the Court in Paris for a divorce. The Court asked for the civil certificate of marriage. The respondent then discovered that the certificate procured at the British Consulate was only a notice of intended marriage, and that the officiating *curé* had carelessly omitted to notice that it was not a certificate of marriage. He had, indeed, exposed himself to heavy penalties by celebrating the religious ceremony without the production of a certificate. As no certificate of marriage could be produced, the Court declined to proceed with the case for divorce.

DOMICILE

1. This is a person's *home*, and is not necessarily determined by his nationality: it may be a "domicile of origin" or a "domicile of choice."

2. A person's domicile of origin is that received at birth; for a legitimate child it is that of the father, for a posthumous legitimate or an illegitimate child that of the mother.

3. The domicile of a married woman is that of her husband

while the marriage subsists. A widow, or a divorced wife, retains the husband's domicile till she changes it.

4. Any person can acquire a domicile *by the fact* of residence and *the intention* of permanent residence (*animus manendi*).

There is a presumption in favour of the domicile of origin. A change of domicile must be proved by strong evidence. (See page 289.)

5. Before the Court can grant a decree upon a petition for dissolution of marriage, it must be satisfied that the domicile of the parties was English when the suit was instituted.

DISSOLUTION OF MARRIAGE

Until the Matrimonial Causes Act, 1857, to obtain dissolution of the marriage tie was a tedious and most costly process. This Act made the lay Courts the competent tribunals for matters connected with divorce. The parties obtained the right to trial by jury of all disputed matters of fact; the Common Law rules of evidence were made applicable; and an appeal was made possible.

The husband could obtain a divorce for *adultery* ; the wife could obtain a divorce for *adultery coupled with cruelty or desertion for two or more years*, for *incestuous or bigamous adultery*, for *rape or unnatural offences.*

In a petition presented by the husband he must, unless excused by the Court, make the alleged adulterer a party (a *co-respondent*). It is not, however, essential that the wife should make the alleged adulteress a co-respondent.

The Matrimonial Causes Act, 1923, equalised the grounds of divorce for both sexes, so far as adultery is concerned.

BARS TO RELIEF

These are some absolute bars to relief. The Courts *must* dismiss a petition if satisfied that there has been (1) *connivance*, (2) *collusion*, (3) *condonation* (unless the former matrimonial offence is revived by a later one).

These are also discretionary bars to relief. The Courts *may* dismiss a petition because of (1) *Undue delay in presenting it.* (2) *Conduct by the petitioner conducing to the other party's adultery.* (3) *The petitioner's own adultery.*

THE STATE AN INTERESTED PARTY

The office of the King's Proctor and his possible intervention indicate the difference between the Divorce Court and the other divisions of the High Court. A petition for divorce is more than the private concern of the parties: the State requires, in its own interests, protection of marriage. Therefore it is that a divorce petition, even if undefended, will not be granted unless the petitioner shows fully that he or she is entitled to the relief sought.

So the "King's Proctor" has the duty of considering whether there has been *connivance** (the adultery of one spouse has been caused by or has been knowingly or recklessly permitted by the other).

CONDONATION

This means the forgiveness of a conjugal offence with a full knowledge of all the circumstances, the offending party being restored to the former position. Thus, "a husband who has sexual relations with his wife after knowledge of her adultery, must be conclusively presumed to have condoned her offence." (*Cramp* v. *Cramp*, 1920.) In such an event the Court is without power to grant a petition.

COLLUSION

This is a bargain between the parties for the procuring of a divorce, the true facts being hidden. Thus, one of the parties may obtain a money consideration from the other for not defending the petition, or adultery may be procured or pretended in order to secure dissolution. Thus in *Aylward* v. *Aylward* (1928) the Court made a stand against "hotel evidence." Since the 1923 Act the number of petitions, supported by evidence of a single instance of adultery at a hotel by the husband with a woman unknown, had greatly increased. The petition was dismissed; but a second petition, citing a named woman, succeeded.

In *Woolf* v. *Woolf* (Divorce Court, 1930), the President had refused to draw an obvious inference. The husband had shown an eagerness to be divorced, and had tendered to his wife "hotel evidence" that would support her petition. The President said: "The argument pointed to the view that where one party to the marriage tenders grounds for supposing he has been unfaithful and the other party is willing to accept them, the Court should

---

* But an agreement for a separation does not of itself amount to connivance. In *Prager* v. *Prager* (1926) a Jewish couple were divorced in accordance with the law of the rabbis. Both knew such a divorce to be of no validity in English law; yet the husband went through a Jewish form of marriage with another woman. To the wife's ensuing petition he pleaded connivance and conduct conducing. But the Court granted the wife's petition, holding that she had assented to a separation only.

3

shut its eyes to the true view of the facts and under its statutory powers should say, 'Very well; there shall be a decree.' At present that is not the law. A judge sitting here has not to make law or to amend it, or adapt it, or manoeuvre against its proper effects. He is sitting here to administer the law."

The Court of Appeal held, however, that—unless the King's Proctor could adduce cogent evidence to rebut the obvious conclusion—the inference should have been drawn; and the petitioner obtained the decree she sought.

DISCRETIONARY BARS

Whether or not the discretionary bars exist must also be considered. Thus—

1. *Unreasonable Delay.* The Court will be indisposed to relieve a party who "appears to have slumbered in sufficient comfort. It will be inclined to infer either an insincerity in the complaint, or an acquiescence in the injury whether real or supposed, or a condonation of it." But where sufficient explanation has been given the Court will not dismiss a petition on the ground of delay.

2. *Conduct Conducing, Cruelty, Desertion.* Any of these on the part of the petitioner may, in the discretion of the Court, constitute a bar; "It must not be supposed that a husband can neglect and throw aside his wife, and afterwards, if she is unfaithful to him, obtain a divorce on account of her infidelity." Thus, consider *Lander* v. *Lander* (1890): the husband would not see his wife, made her an allowance through a third party, and wrote that she must not inquire into his mode of life and he would not inquire into hers. His petition was dismissed on the ground of "conduct conducing"; and, though a second petition was successful, the Court refused to make it absolute until he had made provision for his wife's maintenance. Nor would the Court permit the inclusion in the agreement of a *dum sola et casta* (while she is unmarried and chaste) clause.

3. *Petitioner's Adultery.* As a sequel to the judgment in *Apted* v. *Apted and Bliss* (1930), the following Direction about Discretion Cases was issued: "It is directed by the President, in pursuance of his judgment in the above case, that when it is intended to ask, at the hearing of a matrimonial cause, that the discretion of the Court be exercised on behalf of either party, the petition (or answer) shall contain a prayer to this effect.

It must also be stated, in every application for the Registrar's certificate, whether or not the Court will be asked to exercise its discretion on behalf of either party. If the exercise of the discretion is sought, there must be lodged with the application for certificate a statement, signed by such party or his solicitor, setting forth all the facts which require the discretion to be exercised, and the grounds upon which such discretion is prayed."

"The discretion is not," said the President in *Wilson* v. *Wilson* (K.B. 1920) "to be exercised readily but with stringency. When the guilty petitioner is the husband and the Court is convinced of his *bona fides*, the following may be considered : (1) the position and interests of his children, (2) the interest of the woman with whom he has misconducted himself, (3) the fact that the withholding of a decree will not be likely to reconcile husband and wife, (4) the interest of the husband himself that he may remarry and lead a respectable life."

MISCONDUCT A BAR

It might appear illogical to refuse a decree because the plaintiff has been guilty of misconduct. It might be argued that if divorce is to be granted at all, the fact that both spouses had failed to keep the compact is an added cause (not a bar) for granting relief. But so it is. Unless the Judge, on cause shown, exercises his discretion in favour of a plaintiff who has been guilty of misconduct, the plaintiff cannot succeed in an English Court. The plaintiff would succeed in a Scottish Court.

JUDICIAL SEPARATION AND RESTITUTION OF CONJUGAL RIGHTS

The Divorce Court (under the Judicature Act, 1925, Section 185) has power to decree "judicial separation" or "restitution of conjugal rights" :

1. A petition for judicial separation may be presented to the Court either by the husband or the wife on the ground of adultery or cruelty, desertion without cause for not less than two years, failure to comply with a decree for restitution of conjugal rights, or on any ground on which a decree for divorce *a mensa et thoro* (from bed and board) might have been pronounced before 1857."

2. The Court may, on being satisfied that the allegations contained in the petition are true, and that there is no legal ground why the petition should not be granted, make a decree for judicial separation.

"Legal Desertion" is a withdrawal for two years and upwards from cohabitation, contrary to the wish of the petitioning party.

The disobedience of an order for "restitution of conjugal rights" is not now, as it was formerly, punished by attachment of the disobedient spouse. The practical effect is this. It enables a wife to obtain a decree of "judicial separation" before two years of desertion have passed; and she can in the decree obtain an order for payments.

JUDICIAL SEPARATION

Where a decree of separation is given by the Court the wife, so long as separation lasts, is in regard to property considered as a *feme sole*; if she should die intestate, her property devolves as if she had been a single woman. She may not, indeed, marry again during the life of her husband. A judicial separation is not quite the equivalent of a divorce. Nor does a judicial separation enable the wife to acquire a separate domicile from her husband; and it is the court of domicile (not of nationality) that settles questions of divorce or nullity (*Salveson* v. *Administrator of Austrian Property*, A.C., 1927).

But a suit for judicial separation—which means a divorce from bed and board (divorce *a mensa et thoro*) as distinct from a divorce from the bond of marriage (divorce *a vinculo matrimonii*)—can be granted by the English Courts whatever the domicile. For such a suit is instituted primarily, not for the purpose of dissolving the marriage, but for the protection of wife or husband. In other words, no change of *status* of either party is involved by the making of such a decree. The Courts, therefore, carrying out as they are bound to do, the Sovereign's duty to protect all who are living under allegiance, permanent or temporary, to him, assumes jurisdiction.

RIGHTS TO REMARRY

"As soon as any decree for divorce is made absolute, either of the parties may, if there is no right of appeal against the decree absolute, or if the time for appeal has passed, marry again as if the prior marriage had been dissolved by death." (Judicature Act, 1925, Section 184.) Six weeks are allowed for appeal against a decree absolute.

"Every decree for a divorce or for nullity of marriage shall, in the first instance, be a decree *nisi* not to be made absolute until the expiration of six months after decree." During this period *any* person (other than the parties) may show cause why the decree should not be made absolute. In practice it is the King's Proctor that intervenes. If the party against whom the decree is made should be dissatisfied, he applies for a new trial.

EXERCISE OF DISCRETION BY THE COURT

The limits within which the Court will exercise its discretion and allow a petitioner to succeed in spite of misconduct, are well shown in a case of 1926. In *Lowell* v. *Lowell*, a suit brought under the Poor Person's Rules, the King's Proctor intervened alleging that a decree *nisi* pronounced at Durham Assizes was obtained by the presentation of a false case. This the petitioner admitted; but she prayed the Court to exercise its discretion notwithstanding her failure to disclose all the material facts, on the ground that she did not appreciate the importance of so doing.

The President, in giving judgment, said that the facts which had been presented at the instance of the King's Proctor ought to have been before the Judge at the hearing. One difficulty in these cases was to avoid the possibility of an unwarrantable hardship by reason of the resentment which a Judge must inevitably feel at the course of perjury and concealment designed to deceive the Court.

Many people did not understand how material and very important it was in the common interests of a community like theirs that divorces should not be scattered at the instance of all sorts of profligate people just because they wished it. That would completely destroy the marriage tie; and it struck at the roots of society.

The easy course would be to rescind the decree and dismiss the suit; but he did not propose to do that. The intervention of the King's Proctor was necessary, and it would be allowed with costs. The decree *nisi* must not be made absolute till the King's Proctor was satisfied that an honest attempt was being made to provide for those costs. When that was done the decree *nisi* might be made absolute.

It seems a good method of making pretty certain that the King's Proctor costs will be forthcoming.

THE KING'S PROCTOR

"Procurator General" is his formal title. He has special duties of intervention where the circumstances warrant it. He is required to help the Court "to satisfy itself so far as it reasonably can both as to the facts alleged and also as to whether the petitioner has been accessory to or has connived at or condoned the adultery or not, and also to inquire into any counter-charge which is made against the petitioner."

ALIMONY

The Court orders payment by the husband to the wife—

1. *Pendente lite* (till the suit has been brought). The amount may be agreed upon. If not it is, as a rule, *one-fifth* of the *joint income* of husband and wife.

2. *Permanent Maintenance.* When a decree of judicial separation has been pronounced. It is, as a rule, *one-third* of the joint incomes; but, in addition, the husband may be ordered to support the young children of the marriage.

MAINTENANCE

An order for maintenance is not embodied in the decree of divorce, but is a matter for subsequent proceedings. This amount, too, is usually settled at one-third of the joint incomes.

CUSTODY OF CHILDREN

In making an order about custody of the children of a marriage the Court regards (1) the benefit of the children, (2) the interests of the innocent party, (3) the health of the mother.

RULES RELATING TO ALIMONY

1. The provision may be made by the Court for the maintenance of a wife, whether petitioner or respondent, during the pendency of a suit. This provision is alimony *pendente lite* (alimony pending suit). It is applied for by petition, *after* making the main petition, or *after* appearance in answer to the writ of summons. Application for maintenance of the children of the marriage may accompany the alimony petition.

2. Where any decree for judicial separation is made on the application of the wife, the Court may make such order for alimony as it thinks just. The wife petitions for permanent alimony.

RULES RELATING TO MAINTENANCE

1. When the Court decrees divorce or nullity of marriage it may order the husband (*a*) to secure, by a method approved of by an officer of the Court, either such a gross sum or an annual sum as shall appear to be reasonable, (*b*) to pay such a monthly or weekly sum for her maintenance and support as the Court may think reasonable.

2. Maintenance is petitioned for at any time after decree *nisi*, but (except by leave of the Judge) not later than one calendar month after decree absolute.

ASSESSMENT OF DAMAGES

Section 189, Judicature Act, 1925, enacts "A husband may, on a petition for divorce or for judicial separation or for damages only, claim damages from any person on the ground of adultery with the wife of the petitioner." The measure of damages is the loss sustained by the husband through being deprived of his wife and having indignity thrust upon him. Damages are for compensation not punishment. It is clear, however, that many other considerations usually enter into the assessment. An agreed amount may be mentioned to the jury; and, though they are not bound to do so, they usually assess damages at the agreed amount.

Apart from an agreed amount, the strict rule applies that the jury must not be told what amount the petitioner claims. In *Hinton* v. *Hinton and Spillett* (1930), the jury awarded £750 though the amount claimed was £250; the Judge allowed amendment of the petition and gave judgment for the larger amount. But the Court of Appeal held that this could not be done, the Master of the Rolls declaring it a primary rule of justice that no order should be made against anyone unless he was told what was being asked. The obvious deduction, therefore, is that a petitioner who seeks damages should assess them at an amount large enough to avoid likelihood of an over-award.

A jury is not bound to award damages, even though the petitionary husband succeeds.

Damages cannot be recovered from the estate of a co-respondent who dies before the order of the Court against him is executed.

That a co-respondent did not know of the marriage of the respondent may serve to mitigate damages; it is no reason for not awarding damages.

SUING FOR DAMAGES ONLY

It is possible, though seldom done, for a husband to sue for damages alone from a man he accuses of adultery with his wife. In *Bell* v. *Bell and Cooke* (Divorce Court, 1932) the petitioner, domiciled in Scotland, obtained there a divorce. He had claimed damages also; but Cooke, the co-respondent cited, had contended that his being domiciled in England prevented the Scottish Court from awarding damages. The Scottish Court agreed; and Bell petitioned in the English Divorce Court for damages only. He was empowered to do this under Section 189 of the Supreme Court of Judicature (Consolidation) Act, 1925—

1. A husband may on a petition for divorce or for judicial separation or for damages only, claim damages from any person on the ground of adultery with the wife of the petitioner.

2. A claim for damages shall be tried on the same principles and in the same manner as actions for criminal conversation were tried immediately before the Matrimonial Causes Act, 1857.

The jury awarded £750 damages.

COSTS IN DIVORCE SUITS

Costs are in the absolute discretion of the Court. They do not of necessity follow the event. For the wife, whether innocent or guilty, nearly always obtains costs "of and incidental to the trial." In a case, before the Married Women's Property Act gave woman economic independence, the rule was put thus: "When the wife has to take proceedings against her husband, or he against her—she ought to be provided at his expense with the means of bringing her case before the Court, or of properly defending the case brought against her." The rule is still followed except where a guilty wife has separate estate. The expenses of proceedings justifiably taken by the wife are Common Law necessaries; for these she is entitled to pledge her husband's credit.

But the proceedings must be reasonably undertaken.

A wife cannot pledge her husband's credit for her solicitor's costs where she herself has been guilty. In *Darnford* v. *Baker* (C.A. 1924), solicitors unsuccessfully sued the husband. They had acted for a petitionary wife, but had abandoned the suit when they became aware of the wife's guilt. "I do not think," said one judgment, "that it is sufficient—if the solicitor is to recover at Common Law—that he should believe the proceedings to be reasonably founded. Such a rule would enable a wife to devise a plot against her husband, convince a solicitor with a plausible tale, and thereby render her husband liable for her costs of presenting a fraudulent petition. Proceedings reasonably instituted must mean reasonably instituted in view of the knowledge possessed by the wife."

Upon a successful petition an order is usually made against a co-respondent for full costs, including the wife's costs.

MAGISTRATES' JURISDICTION IN MATRIMONIAL CAUSES

A Magistrates' Court (a Stipendiary Magistrate or two Justices at least, sitting in public as a petty sessions) has power to make summary orders as follows—

1. *To a wife for a separation or maintenance.* (*a*) Where a husband has been convicted summarily of an aggravated assault on her. (*b*) Where the husband has been sentenced on indictment either to over two months' imprisonment or to pay a fine of more than £5 for an assault on her. (*c*) For desertion. (*d*) For persistent cruelty to her or her children. (*e*) For wilful neglect to provide reasonable maintenance for her or her infant children. (*f*) Where the husband knowingly communicates venereal disease to her. (*g*) Where the husband coerces her into acting as a prostitute. (*h*) Where the husband is an habitual drunkard or drug-taker or is incapable of the management of his affairs (though not a lunatic).

2. *To an husband* for a separation. (*a*) Where the wife is an habitual drunkard. (*b*) Where the wife has been persistently cruel to him or to the children.

The Summary Jurisdiction Act, 1848, limits the time within which a complaint must be made to *six months from the cause of complaint.*

An Appeal lies to a *Divisional Court,* consisting of two Judges of the Court of Appeal.

VALIDITY OF MARRIAGES CONTRACTED ABROAD

The general rule is that English law recognises these if (*a*) they are valid according to the law of the place where contracted, (*b*) they are monogamous.

"Marriage in English law means a voluntary union of one man and one woman to the exclusion of all other. It is a status arising out of a contract to which each country is entitled to attach its own conditions, both as to its creation and duration." Thus, a marriage is regarded as valid even where, as in Soviet Russia, either spouse may divorce the other without showing any cause, and simply by registering the fact at the marriage registration office. So it was decided in *Nachimson* v. *Nachimson* (C.A. 1930). The means of dissolving a marriage is no test of its validity.

English law also recognises in general a divorce pronounced by a competent court in the country of the parties' domicile. But it will not recognise the right of one party to loosen the tie at his pleasure. Mir-Anwarrudin was a Mahommedan whose domicile was Madras. He married an Englishwoman in England, left her on his return to Madras, came back to England, and wished to marry another Englishwoman. He, therefore, by the Mahommedan *talak* dissolved his marriage. He petitioned the Court for a divorce; but the Court considered itself to have no jurisdiction. He then sought a marriage licence. On the Registrar's refusal he appealed, first to the King's Bench Divisional Court, then to the Appeal Court. Neither Court would grant a mandamus that should command the Hammersmith Registrar to issue a marriage licence. All the Courts held that the first marriage still subsisted. A decree of a Court of the domicile is, however, recognised by the English Courts, though granted upon grounds inadequate in England.

DIVORCE COURT CONTROLS PAYMENTS

In the Autumn of 1932, under the Debtors Act (Matrimonial Causes) Jurisdiction Order, 1932, the Divorce Court resumed its control over payments in matrimonial causes. The President took the occasion of saying that he thought it very proper that this class of proceedings should be dealt with by the Court which primarily dealt with matrimonial relations. In each of the applications which he had heard the husband had been in default in his obligations as a husband. It was one of the duties of the Court to see that the marital obligation, which involved a contribution to the maintenance of the wife by the husband, was properly enforced.

In this jurisdiction the object in view must be to see that, until the marital rights of the wife had been varied by the Court, they should be observed and completed by the husband to the extent of his ability to satisfy them.

The method of enforcing payment is that of attachment. In one of the summons heard, the debtor was the husband respondent in a wife's suit for restitution of conjugal rights. An order for alimony of £2 a week *pendente lite* had been ignored, and the President ordered that the respondent be committed to prison, but said that the order would be suspended if within the next seven days the arrears were paid.

MASTER AND SERVANT

APPRENTICESHIP

An apprenticeship agreement needs a sealed writing, in order to be binding. The consent of the apprentice to the agreement is needed.

The infant apprentice cannot cancel the agreement; but, upon reaching 21, he is entitled to do so upon giving reasonable notice. Death of the master terminates the agreement; and, since there is only a partial not a total failure of consideration, no premium can be recovered from the master's representatives. It seems, however, that when it is a case of serving under articles to a solicitor the Court may order return of a portion of the premium. For a solicitor is an officer of the Court; and the Court may direct its officers, or their representatives, to do what is equitable.

In the event of the apprentice's misbehaviour the master is not entitled to punish him or to deprive him of the wages or maintenance agreed upon. But the master can complain to a magistrate (Employers and Workmen Act, 1875). The magistrate can order the apprentice to carry out his duties. The apprentice is given a month's grace. If he is still unruly he can be imprisoned for not more than fourteen days. Moreover, in the following events the master can terminate the apprenticeship and need not return any premium that may have been paid—

1. If misbehaviour or laziness renders teaching impossible.

2. If the misbehaviour causes injury to the master.

3. If the apprentice is an habitual thief, the Queen's Bench decided in *Learoyd* v. *Brook*, 1891, that proof of this constituted a good defence to a silversmith sued for breach of his covenant to teach.

Under the National Insurance Act, 1924, an apprentice of 16 or over who receives a money payment from the master must be insured under the scheme. Moreover, the apprentice is "a workman," entitled to compensation for accident under the Workmen's Compensation Act, 1925.

See "Restraint of Trade," page 722, for information about agreements made by the apprentice to do or not to do things after the apprenticeship is over.

A specimen Deed of Apprenticeship follows—

This Deed made the *Fourteenth* day of *September, 19..*
BETWEEN JAMES BROWN AND SONS LIMITED of
the Eagle Works Barton in the County of Blankshire (herein-
STAMP   after called "the Employers") of the first part *Samuel
Smith* of *97 Victoria Road, Barton* (aged *14*
years) (hereinafter called "the Apprentice") of the second
part and   *James Smith* of   *97 Victoria Road, Barton*   the parent or
guardian of the apprentice (hereinafter called "the Guardian") of the third part
WITNESSETH that the Apprentice of his own free will and with the consent
of the Guardian HEREBY BINDS himself from this date for a term of   *Seven*
years computed from the   *14th*   day of   *September*   One thous-
and nine hundred and............ And the Apprentice and also the Guardian
as surety for the Apprentice HEREBY JOINTLY AND SEVERALLY COVE-
NANT with the Employers as follows—

1. That the Apprentice will during the said term faithfully honestly and diligently serve the Employers and diligently attend to the said trade or business at all times The Company's secrets keep and their or their representatives' lawful commands willingly obey And shall not absent himself from
   their service during the usual working hours without their consent Nor do
   or willingly suffer any damage to be done to the goods of the Company.
2. That the Apprentice will duly and punctually attend at the Eagle Works
   or the Employers' place of business between the hours of 8 a.m. and 1 p.m.
   and 2 p.m. and 6.30 p.m. of each week day and 8 a.m. and 1 p.m. on Saturdays or during the regular working hours for the time being.
3. That the Apprentice will attend and diligently work at the Barton Technical
   School or elsewhere in Barton between the hours of 10 a.m. and 10 p.m. but
   so that the total hours of work and instruction shall not exceed fifty-four
   per week The cost of such instruction to be paid by the Employers.
4. That if and whenever the Apprentice is absent from his work from any cause
   the wages for the time lost shall be deducted from his weekly wages and that
   if the Apprentice shall be guilty of gross misconduct by repeatedly disobeying the commands of the Employers or their representatives embezzle or
   make away with any of the goods or effects which may be entrusted to his
   care or in case of the breach or non-performance of any of the covenants or
   agreements herein contained on the part of the Apprentice the Employers
   may forthwith discharge the Apprentice and cancel this Indenture whereupon the weekly wages shall immediately cease and be no longer payable
   and this Indenture and every covenant clause and thing herein contained
   shall be void and absolutely determined.

And in consideration of such service the Employers HEREBY COVENANT
with the Apprentice and also with the Guardian as follows—

1. That the Employers by their manager or assistants will during the said term
   according to the best of their power skill and knowledge teach and instruct
   or cause to be taught or instructed the Apprentice.
2. That the Employers will pay the Apprentice during the said term during such
   time as he shall be able to and actually perform his service weekly and every
   week

   during the FIRST year of the term   *Ten*   shillings p.w.
   during the SECOND year of the term   *Eleven*   shillings p.w.
   during the THIRD year of the term   *Fifteen*   shillings p.w.
   during the FOURTH year of the term   *Nineteen*   shillings p.w.
   during the FIFTH year of the term   *Twenty-three*   shillings p.w.
   during the SIXTH year of the term   *Twenty-seven*   shillings p.w.
   during the SEVENTH year of the term   *Thirty*   shillings p.w.

IN WITNESS the Employers have hereunto set their Common Seal and the
Apprentice and Guardian have hereunto set their hands and seals respectively
the day and year first above written.

The Common Seal of James Brown and
Sons Limited was hereunto affixed in
the presence of

       James Brown   Seal.

       Governing Director.

SIGNED SEALED AND DELIVERED
by the Apprentice in the presence of   } *Samuel Smith*   O

Name   *Fred Johnson*

Address   *44 Harcourt Road*
               Barton.

SIGNED SEALED AND DELIVERED
by the Guardian in the presence of   } *James Smith*   O

Name   *Henry Green*

Address   *711 Warwick Lane,*
               Barton.

CONTRACT OF EMPLOYMENT

An agreement between an employer and an employee may, like
most other contracts, be made quite informally and by word of
mouth. From every point of view it is better, however, to have
the terms set out expressly in a written agreement. And such an
agreement should stipulate what amount of notice on either side
may determine the employment. Where an engagement for a
period exceeding a year has been made, the contract of service,
to be enforceable either by master or servant, *must* be evidenced
in writing in order to satisfy the Statute of Frauds (1677). This
is so even if the engagement is stated to be subject to determination by six months' notice. (*Hanau* v. *Erlich*, A.C. 1912.)

LENGTH OF NOTICE

Where this length of notice is not set out formally, "reasonable
notice" must be given. The length of this "reasonable notice" is
determined by—

1. The custom prevailing in the particular industry (the wage-
period may have some bearing on the custom). Thus (in *George*
v. *Davies*, K.B. 1911) it was held that a Judge is entitled to take
judicial notice of and to apply the custom in regard to *domestic
service* that either master or servant may end the service agreement at the end of the first month by giving notice *at or before
the end of the first fortnight.**

* To establish that a custom does exist the questions following need to be
answered in the affirmative: 1. Is this method of dealing adopted generally?
2. Is it well-established? 3. Is it sufficiently well-known to justify the assumption that people make their contracts understanding the incorporation of it in
those contracts?

2. The nature of the employment in the particular industry. (Thus a newspaper editor has been held entitled to a year's notice —*Grundy* v. *Sun Printing and Publishing Association*, 1916. A commercial traveller has been held entitled to three months' notice—*Grundow* v. *Master & Co.*, 1885.)

OTHER RULES ABOUT NOTICE

1. Apart from express stipulation or from established custom about notice, the hiring of the servant is presumed to be for a year. Moreover, a reasonable notice—at least a month,—to expire at the end of the year, is requisite.

2. Where wages are paid weekly, the presumption is a weekly hiring; and a week's notice given by either master or servant is enough.

3. A clerk seems to be entitled to three months' notice (apart from an express term in his agreement); a menial servant (which includes, among others, a head gardener, and a huntsman, though not living within the house) is entitled to a month.

The notice may be given by word of mouth, even though the agreement for employment is in writing.

DISMISSAL WITHOUT NOTICE

Dismissal without notice is possible for—

1. *Incompetence.* This includes incapacitating illness; but the employee is entitled to his wages during illness so long as the contract remains. The test to be applied in order to determine whether the illness justifies dismissal is this : does the illness defeat the object of the employment?

2. *Disobedience or Neglect.* The disobedience must be of an order that the employer was entitled to give. The degree of neglect justifying dismissal without notice depends upon circumstances. Dismissal was held to be justified when a farm servant refused to work during the harvest unless beer was provided (*Lilley* v. *Elwin*, Q.B. 1848). On the other hand, it was held not to be justified when a dyer refused to work during the hours of divine service. For the "command to do so was an unlawful command, and the obstinate refusal was to the servant's credit."

3. *Misconduct.* So, too, does the degree of misconduct justifying dismissal without notice depend upon circumstances. It seems that the test is, "does the misconduct interfere with the business of the employer or with the ability of the employee to perform his duties under the service contract." Thus, the manager of a

limited company who had accepted commission on the insurance of the company's premises was held liable to dismissal without notice. Even misconduct outside the business may be justification. (*Pearce* v. *Foster*, Q.B. 1886), illustrates the point. The plaintiff had been the confidential clerk of the defendants, general merchants and commission agents. They found that Pearce had been speculating wildly on the Stock Exchange, felt they could no longer trust him, and (though he was quite efficient) they dismissed him. In the circumstances the Court considered the dismissal justified.

Accepting secret commissions may very well justify dismissal without notice; for such acceptance may lead a servant to promote another's interests against his master's.

Apparently it is still the prerogative of the Crown (*Denning* v. *Secretary of State for India*, 1920) to dismiss its servants at pleasure, even when no misconduct is alleged and the agreement implies that the engagement can be ended only by the servant's misconduct.

CIVIL SERVANT'S POSITION

The civil servant's position is, however, peculiar in many ways. In theory he can be dismissed without cause shown and without notice; he can claim no pension, as he has no legal right to it; if he should be kept without salary, he can claim it only when the Crown grants his Petition of Right and allows him to claim. In practice he has a much greater security of tenure than he would have outside the Civil Service. For he remains through political changes. We have nothing in this country like the "spoils system" of the United States, where even minor officials depend for their office on the political fortunes of their party. His payments are assured. And he is under no political or legal responsibility for his errors (that responsibility belongs to the Minister of State under whom he serves). But the counterpart of this practical freedom from the ordinary risks of life comes with several (probably unimportant) disabilities: (1) though the civil servant has power to vote for a Member of Parliament, he must take no active part in politics; (2) he is ineligible for a seat in the House of Commons while he remains a civil servant, and if he decides to offer himself as a candidate he is required, by Treasury regulations, to resign his post; (3) under the Trade Disputes and Trade Union Act, 1927, though he can be a member of a trade union composed wholly of civil servants, he cannot be a member of a union that is affiliated to a union of persons not in the employment of the Crown.

PAYMENT UPON DISMISSAL

If an employee has rendered himself liable to dismissal without notice, and has been dismissed, he is entitled to no wages for the broken period since his wages last became due. Thus, a domestic servant who has been justifiably dismissed (or who gives up her post without notice) before she has worked a month is entitled to no wages.

Damages for a wrongful dismissal are usually measured by the amount of wages that would have been earned during that period of notice. This amount may be augmented by the estimated amount of commissions (which the employer's wrongful act has prevented the servant from earning) and of tips during the period. In one curious case (*Turner* v. *Goldsmith*, Q.B. 1891), a shirt-maker's traveller was unable to earn commission owing to the destruction by fire of his employer's factory. He sued, and the Court awarded him damages against his employer. But, if similar employment is at once available, only nominal damages are payable; and, in any event, no damages are awarded as a solace to the dismissed servant's feelings or as a compensation for added difficulty in obtaining another post.

If the employee leaves without notice, the employer is entitled to damages measured by the loss he can establish.

The bankruptcy of an employer or the winding-up of a company operates as a termination of an employment. In either event the following payments must be made to employees in priority to all other debts—

1. The wages or salary of a clerk or servant up to £50 in respect of work during the four months before the date of the receiving order.

2. The wages of a labourer or workman up to £25 in respect of work during the two months before the date of the receiving order. (Bankruptcy Act, 1914.)

INTERFERENCE WITH THE CONTRACT OF SERVICE

Any unjustified interference with rights under a contract is an actionable wrong. A persuasion either of master or servant to break a contract may be such an interference. Nor does it excuse the persuasion that the interferer had a laudable motive for his interference. Law admits few valid reasons. "The authorities," one judgment ran, "are numerous and uniform, that an action will lie by a master against a person who procures that a servant should unlawfully leave his service. The nature of the service contracted for is immaterial. He who maliciously procures a damage to another by violation of his rights ought to be made to indemnify; and that, whether he procures an actionable wrong or a breach of contract." (*Lumley* v. *Gye*, Q.B. 1853.) The "malice" spoken of is "legal malice," which exists when there is *knowledge of the contract interfered with* and also *absence of adequate justification for the interference.*

Seduction of a female servant may also constitute such an interference. The woman cannot bring the action; for she has been a consenting party, and *volenti non fit injuria* (she who is the author of her own wrong may not complain of it). The employer (or the parent, who by a fiction of law is supposed to enjoy the services of his daughter) can, however, bring an action; and it seems that juries are not restricted, in their assessment of damages, to the actual loss proved. They may award a sum as a measure of compensation for grief and outraged dignity.

" CHARACTER "

An employer is not compelled to give a testimonial to an employee who leaves him. If, however, he does so he is required to state what he believes to be true. The document enjoys a "qualified privilege." If it should be untrue, the employee can recover damages for libel only if he succeeds in showing that malice dictated the statements. It is the plaintiff that must prove the malice; for, if the defendant believes his defamatory statement to be true, the mere fact that his belief is against reason will not defeat his privilege. Absence of genuine belief in the statement is conclusive proof of genuine malice; for the defendant cannot have a proper motive in saying what he did not believe to be true. Moreover, an employer may not make use of his qualified privilege unless a proper occasion arises for its exercise; unless, for instance, he is asked by a prospective employer for a character of the servant. Whether an occasion is privileged is matter of law for the Judge. Whether "malice" (i.e. improper motive) has deprived the defendant of his privilege is matter of fact for the jury to decide.

There exists a social duty upon the employer (or former employer) to give with reasonable fullness his opinion of an employee. For it is clear that an employer is under a duty to be careful in selecting his servants. This is especially so where the servants are to be employed in circumstances offering great temptations to dishonesty. Thus the Lord Chief Justice allowed the claim of a lady for loss of jewellery, stolen, it was alleged, by the defendant's workman. The defendant had engaged the workman in reliance upon a testimonial that, it appeared afterwards, was fictitious. The workman was employed to visit various houses and care for the clocks; and it was on one such visit that the theft occurred. The defendant had been negligent in not testing the reference; a little inquiry would have shown it to be false. (*De Parrell* v. *Walker*, K.B. 1932.)

AMOUNT AND MANNER OF PAYING WAGES

Where there is something like equality in bargaining power between employer and employed these terms are settled by agreement. But in certain industries, employing low-grade labour that cannot organise itself, the State has intervened. Trade Boards have been set up to determine minimum rates of wage (Trade Board Act, 1909).

The Minister of Labour has power to make a Special Order applying the Act to trades where there is inadequate machinery for regulating wages.

TRADE BOARD

A Trade Board consists of—

1. Representatives of employers and employees in the trade in equal numbers.

2. Members, to a number less than half the total of the representatives, appointed by the Minister of Labour.

The chairman is appointed by the Minister from among the members; and the Minister also appoints a secretary.

The minimum rate fixed by the Board must be paid free of all deductions except such as are authorised by statute. The penalty attaching to non-payment of the rate is a fine not exceeding £20. The Board have power to exempt from the minimum rate workers who are incapable of earning the rate.

"TRUCK ACTS," 1831 to 1896

The results of the various "truck acts" are these—

1. A contract for the payment of any part of the wages otherwise than in current coin of the realm is illegal. ("Current coin" now includes Bank of England notes. And, if the employee

consents, payment by cheque drawn on a bank within fifteen miles is good.).

2. A contract stipulating the place or the manner in which the wages are to be spent is illegal.

In *Hewlett* v. *Allen* (Q.B. 1892) is the statement, "The clear intention of the Truck Acts was to ensure to workmen their wages in actual current coin of the realm, unfettered by any promise or obligation that it should be spent in any particular manner or at any particular shop. The legislature endeavoured to secure that the workman might have in his hand the actual coin representing his wages in order that he and his family might freely carry it home, or expend it without impediment in the open market."

Thus, in an action for wages, no set-off is allowable either for (1) goods supplied by the employer, or by any shop in which the employer has an interest, or for (2) goods supplied to the workman under any order of the employer. An employer must not deduct from wages any payment for goods previously supplied. Even a deduction for payment of shares agreed to be bought by the workman in the employer's company conflicts with the Truck Acts (*Redgrave* v. *Kelly*, 1899). It seems, however, that a set-off still exists for money paid for the person employed at his or her request.

3. An employee cannot be sued for payment for goods bought at a shop in which his employer has an interest.

The employees to whom the Act apply are all persons engaged in manual labour under a service contract, with the exception of domestic servants.

It may be noted that no subterfuge will be permitted to disguise the fact that wages are being paid otherwise than in money. Even when an employee voluntarily receives goods at a shop belonging to his employer it is against the Acts for the employer to deduct the price from the next week's wages. An employer may give a present, at Christmas or at another time, when he wishes to show special kindness. But if the present becomes habitual it may be looked on as illegal. It is, if the employee has come to regard it as a right. In a co-partnership bonus scheme the shares given must be quite apart from the agreed wages. Thus in *Glasgow* v. *Independent Printing Co.* (1901 I.R.), the agreement was for wages of 22s. to be paid as 20s. in cash and 2s. in shares. The agreement was declared void: the employee must not be able to claim a share as of right.

PERMITTED DEDUCTIONS

Deductions from the wages agreed upon may, however, be made—

(*a*) For *goods* to be used by the employee in his work. The "goods" include tools, space, light, heat. But the deductions are allowable only when—

    1. There is an express written agreement by the employee (or a clear notice is posted up).

    2. The employer charges no more than the cost of materials.

    3. The sum charged for space, light, heat, is "reasonable."

(*b*) For *bad or negligent* work, possible when—

    1. There is express written agreement or adequate notice.

    2. The deduction is no more than the actual loss.

    3. The loss is through the default of the person penalised.

    4. The deduction is fair and reasonable.

(*c*) For *fines*, where—

    1. There is an express written agreement about such fines.

    2. The act is likely to cause damage or hindrance to the employer's business.

    3. The fine is fair and reasonable.

(*d*) For *medicine, or food* to be eaten in the place of employment, or house, where—

    1. There is a written agreement about such deductions.

    2. The amount charged shall not exceed the real and true value of the thing supplied.

PRESSURE UPON THE EMPLOYEE

Apparently the selling device popularly, probably without justification, associated with Mr. Henry Ford—of "firing" an employee neglecting to buy a car—is an offence against the Truck Act. The Chester-le-street Co-operative Society (Oct., 1932) was fined heavily upon two charges, (1) that the contract of employment unlawfully stipulated that part of an employee's wages should be spent on the society's goods, (2) that the society imposed, as one condition of employment, dealing in the society's goods. The pressure was exerted by a letter containing the statement "You are under a strong moral obligation loyally to trade with the society . . . Unless a substantial improvement is made, the board intend to go further into the position." In fact, an employee was subsequently dismissed for not spending enough with the society. The Court was satisfied that the society's action constituted a contravention of the Truck Acts.

FACTORY AND WORKSHOP ACT

The Factory and Workshop Act, 1901, consolidated the regulations about conditions of work in factories and workshops. There have been many minor Acts since, as well as a vast number of Home Office Orders. These latter, in so far as they fall within the powers delegated by Parliament to the Secretary, have full legal force. The whole makes up a formidable volume.

The Acts and Orders, which are enforced by means of visits of Home Office Inspectors, make provisions in regard to: *Cleanliness* of the workplace, *Overcrowding*, *Temperature*, *Ventilation*, *Sanitary Conveniences*.

There are elaborate regulations to ensure safety, and first-aid appliances are prescribed for speedy use in the event of accident.

Length of working day is prescribed and conditions regarding meal-times are enacted.

CHILDREN AND YOUNG PERSONS, EMPLOYMENT OF

The Children and Young Persons Act, 1933, provides that no child under 12 can be employed. Children under 16 cannot, unless a special by-law authorises it, be employed before the close of school hours on any day on which they are to attend school; but by-laws may authorise employment before school hours for not more than one hour. Being under sixteen they cannot be employed before 6 a.m. nor after 8 p.m.; and they must not be employed for more than two hours on any school day. On Sunday they must not work for more than two hours. They must not be employed in any work likely to injure them. By-laws may restrict their employment still further.

Local authorities make by-laws as to the number of hours of work, time for meals and rest, and holidays or half-holidays of people between the ages of 16 and 18.

Nobody under 16 can be employed in street-trading, except that by-laws may make it legal for parents to employ their children.

EMPLOYERS' LIABILITY FOR ACCIDENTS

The Common Law liability of employers is still important, though most cases are covered by Act of Parliament. There are cases where although an Act of Parliament applies, the Common Law remedy is still available. The injured person may for his own reasons prefer to proceed by Common Law.

Consider the case *Kinnell Coal Co.* v. *Sneddon* (H.L. 1932), a case under the Workmen's Compensation Act, 1925. The Act gives a statutory remedy to a workman injured by the negligence of the employer. But it does not take away the Common Law remedy; and a workman, or his representatives, may choose the remedy. Now, the Act (Section 29) reads: "The workman may, at his option, either claim compensation under this Act, or take proceedings independently of this Act; but the employer shall not be liable both independently of and also under this Act." This would appear to guard an employer against two actions. But it does not. One dependant of a workman who had been killed, sued the employers under the Act: and the employers paid into Court the maximum compensation payable under the Act. Another dependant sued under the Common Law, thinking to get more than this maximum. For no limitations exist at Common Law to the damages that may be awarded. The claim of the employers that, having paid the maximum specified in the Act, they were exempt from further liability, was negatived. The section applies only in this sense, that one person cannot avail himself of both remedies. His choosing one does not, however, prevent another person, also damaged by the same accident, from choosing the other remedy. The Common Law remedy exists to its full extent. It is not cut down by the conditions and limitations of the statutory remedy.

COMMON LAW LIABILITY

The Common Law rule is this: If an employee is injured in consequence of a direct breach of contract by his employer the employer is liable. The employer is also liable when an accident to an employee occurs in consequence of his employer's negligence, unless the employee either accepted the risk or was himself guilty of contributory negligence. To prove acceptance of risk, it is necessary to prove not only that the employee knew of the risk but also that he acquiesced in it. Thus in *Smith* v. *Baker & Sons* (1891), where the House of Lords decided in favour of the injured employee who, though he knew of the risk he ran and had complained of it, remained in his employment, it was said: "Where a risk has been created or enhanced by the negligence of the employer, does the mere continuance in service, with knowledge of the risk, preclude the employed, if he suffer from such negligence, from recovering?" The Court could not assent to the proposition that the maxim, *Volenti non fit injuria*, applied to such a case, and that the employer could invoke its aid to protect him from liability for his wrong.

Even the employee's voluntary acceptance of the risk will not suffice if the employer's negligence is a breach of a statutory duty. For instance, it may be a breach of the Factory Acts. Neither the employee's willingness to accept the risks nor his contributory negligence will then avail as a defence. When the injury is caused not by the employer, but by a fellow employee, the employer is not liable. This is the doctrine of Common Employment. The assumption of the Common Law is that in accepting an employment the worker agrees to accept the risks of that employment, including the risks from the negligence of his fellow workers. The employment is common where both employees are working under the orders of the same employer, although not necessarily in the same trade. Thus an overseer in a mine is in one employment with a miner.

EMPLOYERS' LIABILITY UNDER THE ACT OF 1880

This Act excludes the defence of common employment, where injury arises from—

1. Any defect in the condition of the ways, works, machinery, or plant connected with or used in the business of the employer if arising from or if it has not been discovered or remedied, due to the negligence of the employer, or some person in the service of the employer whose sole duty was that of seeing that these things were in proper condition, or

2. The negligence of any person in the service of the employer who has any superintendence entrusted to him, whilst in the exercise of such superintendence and who is not ordinarily engaged in manual labour, or

3. The act or omission of any person in the service of the employer, done or made in obedience to the rule or order of the employer, or in obedience to particular instructions given by any person delegated with the authority of the employer in that behalf, or

4. The negligence of any person in the service of the employer who has the charge or control of any signal points, locomotive engine, or train upon the railway.

This Act applies to—

1. Railway employees.

2. Persons to whom the Employer's and Workmen's Act, 1875, applies.

The amount of compensation that may be recovered is limited to three years' earnings in the employment in question.

Written notice of injury must be given to the employer within

six weeks of its occurrence. But the Court has power to dispense
with this regulation in fatal cases. Every action must be commenced in the County Court and within six months of the occurrence. But in fatal cases the period is twelve months.

FATAL ACCIDENTS ACT, 1846

At Common Law no action may lie against a person for negligence if the injured person dies in consequence. But under this
Act a personal representative of the person dying under such
circumstances, is entitled to maintain an action for the benefit
of wife, husband, parent, grandparent, stepfather, stepmother,
child, stepchild, and grandchild of the deceased person. The
relation in question must prove a definite money loss. In computing the loss no account should be taken of any sum payable on
the death of the deceased under insurance contracts.

WORKMEN'S COMPENSATION ACT

The law regarding workmen's compensation was consolidated
in the Act of 1925.

The effect of it is to make the employer the insurer of the
worker during the course of the employment. Compensation is
to be paid for—

1. Injury through an accident, or
2. Injury to health from industrial disease.

The Act does not cover all employed persons. It covers—

1. All those who are engaged in manual labour.
2. Other employees whose wages do not exceed £350 a year.

It covers apprentices, but it does not cover out-workers who
are casual employees employed for another purpose than the
employer's trade or business. Thus if a man engages someone to
carry his bag, this carrier is not covered.

Where the injury results in the employee's death, the persons
who are entitled to compensation are those dependants of the
employee who are members of his family and who are alive when
the compensation agreement or award is made.

INDUSTRIAL DISEASE

In cases of industrial disease, the person liable to pay the compensation is the employer who, during the year previous to the
time when the employee was disabled, last employed him in
the kind of work from which the disease arose. If, however,
that employer proves that the disease was contracted in the

employment of another person, the latter is liable. The rule made when the employer becomes bankrupt or the employing company is wound-up is this: The employer's rights to call upon an insurance company to pay the employee's claim under an insurance policy are transferred from the employer to the employee. The injured workman can, therefore, claim direct from the insurance company. Naturally, the liability of the insurance company is limited under the employer's policy. Where a firm only partly covers its employees they have to prove for the balance in the bankruptcy or the winding-up.

No employer may contract out of his liability under the Workmen's Compensation Acts; an agreement with the employee to pay otherwise than as the Acts direct is void. The employer may, of course, and usually does, transfer his risk under the Acts to an insurance company. But, if this insurer whom the employer has selected fails to pay, the workman's claim reverts to the employer.

ACCIDENTS AND COMPENSATION

The accidents in which compensation is payable are those which arise out of, and in the course of, the employment. The employee in each case must be disabled for more than three days from earning full wages before he can claim.

The definition of accident is "an unlooked-for mishap or an untoward event which is not expected or designed." Even the contracting of a disease by infection may be such an "accident" as will give a right to compensation.

In order to prove that an accident arises out of and in the course of employment, it is necessary to prove that it arose because the employee was at the time doing something he was employed to do, or because his employment exposed him to the risk of that accident, which took place after the commencement and before the end of his employment.

THE "COURSE OF EMPLOYMENT" ILLUSTRATED

The effect of the Act was well illustrated in *Thomas* v. *Ocean Coal Co.* (H.L. 1932), where, in spite of the fact that the man had at the time of his death been breaking a rule laid down by Act of Parliament, the widow recovered compensation.

The dead man had been employed as a hitcher in the colliery in question and his duties included, *inter alia*, the controlling of and sending up full trams to the surface. The duties were performed by him on both sides of the pit bottom, and he could pass from one side to the other side of the pit bottom by a passageway-around the pit shaft, or by crossing the pit bottom in the shaft itself.

A regulation under the Coal Mines Act, 1911, prohibited crossing in the shaft: "No person shall attempt to go across the uncovered space of the shaft bottom, except for the purpose of working in the shaft bottom, and no person shall be allowed to work in such place unless the cages are stopped."

Did the sub-section cover even this disobedience? The House of Lords considered that it did. The accident arose out of the employment certainly. It was, besides, in the course of it, seeing that, apart from the prohibition, the action though hazardous was due to the man's desire to expedite the process he was engaged to control. The sub-section was applicable—

"For the purposes of this Act, an accident resulting in the death, or serious and permanent disablement, of a workman shall be deemed to arise out of and in the course of his employment, notwithstanding that the workman was, at the time when the accident happened, acting in contravention of any statutory or other regulation applicable to his employment. . . if such act was done by the workman for the purposes of and in connection with his employer's trade or business."

The respondent's husband, while employed with other workmen in sorting wool in the appellant's factory, became infected with anthrax and died of it. In an arbitration, after hearing medical evidence, the county court judge awarded compensation to the respondent, saying: "I find as a fact that the anthrax, which was the immediate cause of death, was caused by the accidental alighting of a bacillus from the infected wool on a part of the deceased's person, which afforded the harbour in which it could multiply and grow and so cause death. I can see no distinction in principle between the accidental entry of a spark of an anvil or the accidental squirting of scalding water or some poisonous liquid into the eye. The only difference is that in that case the foreign substance would be so large as to be visible. In this case the foreign substance is microscopic." The decision was affirmed in the House of Lords: "Probably it is true to say that in the strictest sense, and dealing with the region of physical nature, there is no such thing as an accident. The smallest particle of dust swept by the storm is where it is by the operation of physical causes, which if you knew beforehand you could predict with absolute certainty that it would alight where it did. But when the

Act now under consideration enacted that if, in any employment to which the Act applied, personal injury by accident arising out of and in the course of his employment is caused to a workman his employers shall pay compensation, I think it meant that apart from negligence of any sort—either employers' or employed—the industry itself should be taxed with an obligation to indemnify the sufferer for what ever the accident causing damage." (*Brinton's, Ltd.* v. *Turvey*, H.L. 1905.)

MEDICAL REFEREES

Medical referees are appointed by the Home Secretary for the purpose of settling disputes as to physical condition and fitness for work. The insured person has first to be medically examined. Within six days a copy of the report must be supplied to the company if the examination was made by the employer's doctor, or to the employer if the examination was made by the insured person's doctor. On the appeal of either party, the County Court may refer the matter to a medical referee. The medical referee's certificate is conclusive.

WHO IS A SERVANT?

Whether or not a person stands in the relation of servant to master may at times be difficult to answer. A taxi-cab driver, injured in the course of his occupation, claimed under the Workmen's Compensation Acts from the firm owning the taxi-cab. The hiring was on the basis of the firm's receiving 75 per cent of the registered takings. No control was exercised over the driver, who was required to sign this undertaking—

"I, the undersigned driver, hereby declare that I have taken the cab No. ... complete with number plate and police licence. I will be personally responsible for any violation of the police regulations."

Was the driver a servant of the firm? No, said the Court; the hiring of the cab was a bailment only. In the absence of control over him, he was not a servant of the firm.

ACCIDENT INSURANCE

Strictly speaking, the term "accident" in the sense of contingency covers the whole field of insurance.

But if we mark off, on the one hand, the larger risks of death, fire, and maritime loss, and on the other hand the minor casualties of life, there remain bodily accidents which incapacitate from work and involve medical expense. The business of insurance against these comprises—

1. Personal accidents.

2. Liability of employers for injuries to their workmen.

It is necessary to divide the insured workers into different classes to which different rates of premium are applicable.

This classification at first was as follows—

1. Professional men and others not liable to accident by reason of their occupation.

2. Master tradesmen who superintend their business only, and do not actually take part in it.

3. Mechanics and workmen generally, engaged in comparatively non-hazardous occupations.

4. Those engaged in hazardous work.

5. A class usually uninsurable.

Later, some companies adopted the principle of "specific compensation." This consists of setting against specific injuries fixed sums payable in proportion to the maximum amount payable in case of death.

The basis for a contract of this kind of insurance is the proposal form, which embodies statements as to occupation, physical condition, health, and as to other previously-existing similar insurances, the latter provison being made with a view of preventing over-insurance and securing that the contract, to that extent, shall be one of indemnity.

The company reserves the right to determine the policy at the end of any year.

WORKMEN'S COMPENSATION ACTS

In the Workmen's Compensation Act, 1906 (and subsequent amending Acts) the whole consolidated in the Workmen's Compensation Act, 1925, the following provisions are made—

Firstly. The word "employer" covers sole trader (man or woman), partnership, limited liability company, executor of a deceased employer, and (where an employer lends out or temporarily hires out a servant to a third person) this third person.

Secondly. The word "workman" means any person, male or female, who has entered into or works under a contract of service or apprenticeship with an employer, whether by way of manual labour, clerical work, or otherwise, or whether the contract is expressed or implied, is oral or is in writing.

The exceptions are—

1. Persons earning more than £350 a year, not in manual labour.
2. Persons casually employed outside the employer's trade or business.
3. Members of a police force.
4. Outworkers.
5. Members of the employer's family dwelling in his house.

Thirdly. The employer's liability in the case of death to a workman through accident extends to the workman's dependants; i.e. to those members of the family wholly or in part dependent upon the workman's earnings at the time of death; and illegitimacy, either of the workman or his dependants is no bar, provided that those members of the family were to any extent reliant upon the workman's support.

Fourthly. The workman may have contributed to the accident by his own carelessness; he may have disobeyed his employer's lawful orders. But he may still be entitled to compensation provided that the accident arose out of and in the course of his employment.

The only defence which can be raised is that the workman's accident was caused through his own serious wilful misconduct. If the accident results in serious disablement or fatal injury, even this defence is not available.

COMPENSATION PAYABLE

Compensation is payable as follows—

1. In the case of death.

If the dependants are wholly dependent, they may recover a sum equal to the earnings of the deceased for three years prior to the accident. In no case may compensation exceed £600.

If the workman leaves no dependants then the amount payable is that of reasonable medical expenses, and funeral expenses not exceeding £15.

2. In the case of total or partial incapacity.

A workman may be awarded a weekly sum during incapacity, not exceeding 50 per cent of his average weekly earnings during the previous twelve months; if he has not been so long employed during the period of his employment, with the same employer, such weekly payment is not to exceed 30s.

Compensation is payable if there is disablement for more than three days; but nothing is payable for the first three days, unless incapacity lasts for four weeks.

NOTE ON WORKMEN'S COMPENSATION

The various Compensation Acts have done much to substitute a milder code for the harsh individualism of the Common Law. Ever-growing mechanisation of industry had been, for some time before the 1897 Act, swinging the balance of social responsibility for industrial accidents against the employed classes. The Act sought to restore the balance by making the employer the insurer in his industry : the public as a whole bears the burden in the form of increased prices.

The purpose of the propounders of the original Act failed in one respect. It was thought that to make the employer liable for all accidents "arising out of and in the course of employment" would avoid law-suits. Whether or not the claimant was engaged in his employment when the accident happened or the disease was contracted would be obvious to all. In fact, much litigation has been necessary to interpret the phrase. And the tendency has been to favour social responsibility for individual misfortune. The interpretations of the judges have tended towards the greater protection of the worker; decided cases have supplemented the declared intention of Parliament. Injuries received from lightning on a high and unusually exposed scaffold, from the bite of a cat habitually kept in the place of employment, from an attack upon a cashier travelling with a large sum of money : these have all been held to have arisen in the course and out of the employment. A railway guard slipped and injured himself on the steps of a hostel where he was to sleep before his return journey. That, too, was in the course of his employment; for he was under instructions to rest at the place. In *Morgan* v. *Owners of Steamship Zenaida* (C.A., 1909) the applicant for compensation was an ordinary seaman. While the ship was lying off the Mexican coast he was told to go over the side to paint. The heat was great and he was seized with sunstroke, which permanently impaired his health. It was urged that the illness arose from a purely natural cause, the heat of the sun; it did not arise out of his employment. The County Court judge held, however, that the accident was covered by the Act; and the Court of Appeal upheld the award.

SHOPS

FREEDOM of bargaining is by no means unrestricted among us: in countless directions the State steps in and restrains one or both of the bargainers. The regulations relating to factories and workshops have been dealt with at page 79. Here we deal with the main regulations concerning shops and the sale of food and drugs.

SHOP HOLIDAYS

Every shop assistant must have at least one half holiday each week, such holiday beginning not later than 1 p.m. A notice exhibited in the shop must state on which day the weekly half holiday occurs; and no assistant must be deprived of the holiday by being sent to work in another shop.

In general all the shops in an area close not later than 1 p.m. on a specified day, usually fixed by the local authority, though at times by arrangement among the shopkeepers themselves. The local authority has power to fix different days for different classes of shops: thus the butchers may prefer Monday afternoon, the drapers Wednesday, and the authority is entitled to give effect to their wishes.

BANK HOLIDAY

In the week preceding a Bank Holiday the half holiday need not be given provided that, on some day in that week, employment ceases not later than 1.30 p.m.

SHOP HOURS

The Shops Act enacts that all assistants—not being members of the employer's family—shall have reasonable intervals for meals. Work must not be continuous for over six hours without at least 20 minutes' interval; between 11.30 a.m. and 2.30 p.m. there must be an interval of at least 45 minutes for dinner (an hour if the meal is taken off the shop premises); between 4 p.m. and 7 p.m., there must be an interval of not less than 30 minutes for tea.

SHOPS SELLING REFRESHMENTS

Modifications of these times are allowable in regard to assistants engaged in selling refreshments, including intoxicating liquors.

Their dinner interval may not end earlier than 11.30 a.m. or begin later than 2.30 p.m. And an Act of 1913 gives the sellers of refreshments, under specified conditions, an option to be exempted altogether from the operation of the main Act. Public notice must indicate that the option is being exercised.

The conditions are—

1. Hours of employment, exclusive of meal-times, must not exceed 65 in the week.

2. Assistants must have 52 whole holidays on week-days and 26 on Sundays during the year, two half holidays counting as one day.

3. There must not be continuous employment for more than 6 hours without a break of 30 minutes, and on half holidays there must be intervals for meals of at least 45 minutes, and intervals of 2 hours on other days.

SEATS FOR ASSISTANTS

The main Act of 1912 also prescribes that seats, not fewer than one for each three assistants, must be provided for female employees.

CLOSING HOURS

Till 1928 these were at the discretion of the local authorities. In 1928 an Act fixed the closing hours for all such shops as were not specifically excepted. On the first five days of the week 8 o'clock is the latest hour for closing. The shop may remain open till 9 on Saturdays, unless the local authority decides upon some other day as the late day.

For the shops where table waters, sweets, chocolates, or other sugar confectionery or ice-cream are sold, 9.30 p.m. is the prescribed hour on the five days and 10 p.m. on Saturdays.

There are several necessary modifications of these hours. At holiday resorts and places where sea fishing is carried on during the fishing season the local authority may suspend closing on half holidays or the general closing hours. The period of suspension must not, however, exceed four months in the year on the whole. And if a trader at a holiday resort proves to the local authority that he allows all his assistants a holiday on full pay during not less than two weeks in the year, he may be exempted from the obligation to give his assistants the weekly half holiday. He must also exhibit in his shop a notice that he does so.

The local authority is also given power to fix a general closing hour, not later than 10 p.m., for retail trades carried on at an exhibition or show in the area; and it may extend the general closing time for tobacconists' shops to 10 p.m. on a late day and 9.30 p.m. on other days.

EXCEPTIONS TO CLOSING HOURS

The following exceptions are possible to the closing order—

1. A person in the shop before closing hour may be served.

2. An article required in case of illness may be supplied after closing hours.

3. Meals or refreshments for consumption on the premises may be sold.

4. Newly-cooked provisions to be consumed off the premises may be sold.

5. Intoxicating liquors either for on or off consumption, or tobacco, table waters, or matches by a licensed victualler on licensed premises may be sold; but such sale is allowed only during the hours in which intoxicating liquors may be sold.

6. Tobacco, matches, table waters, sweets, chocolates, sugar confectionery or ice-cream may be sold during the performance to members of the audience at a theatre, cinema, music hall, or other place of entertainment.

7. Provided that the shop is kept open only long enough to serve the customer there may be sales of medicine or medical or surgical appliances.

8. At such railway-station bookstalls as may be approved by the Home Secretary, there may be sales of newspapers, periodicals, and books.

9. When required for urgent and immediate use it is permitted to sell aircraft, motor and cycle supplies or accessories.

10. Articles urgently required for the Forces or for ships may be sold after hours.

FOOD AND DRUGS

The community as a whole, too, through its representatives in Parliament, takes an increasing notice of the manner in which food and drugs are made and sold. When, as in former days, buyer and seller—consumer and producer—were in close contact with one another, the free play of bargaining might be tolerated. Now that the producer is far removed from the ultimate consumer, safeguards are necessary. So we have the various statutes affecting food and drugs.

4

(1) The Food and Drugs (Adulteration) Act, 1928, enacts, under penalties ranging from fines up to £50 to imprisonment for six months, that food and drugs must not be mixed or coloured with materials injurious to health. There is prohibition of (1) sales to the prejudice of the purchaser of any article of food or any drug not of the nature, substance, or quality demanded; (2) the abstraction of anything from food so as to affect injuriously its quality, substance, or nature, unless the abstraction is disclosed to the buyer; (3) the addition of preservatives to butter or cream (a list of articles that may contain specified preservatives is shown in the Public Health (Preservative) Regulations, obtainable at 4½d. from H.M. Stationery Office, Adastral House, Kingsway, London, W.C.2); (4) the exposure of unwholesome food for sale. The duty of seeing that the law relating to the exposure of unwholesome food is enforced falls upon the local authorities, whose medical officers and food inspectors have a right of entry and inspection wherever such food is deposited.

2. The Sale of Food (Weights and Measures) Act, 1926, prohibits the giving of short weight, measure, or number. The Act gives the Board of Trade power to make Regulations adding to the scope of the Act. Under it, for example, *bread* must be sold by weight; the buyer may demand that a loaf shall be weighed in his presence. (An exception is made of "fancy bread," made up as rolls or other shapes of less than a pound's weight.) The Act applies also to butcher's meat and to milk.

CHEMISTS AND DRUGGISTS

As is to be expected, seeing that they deal in drugs dangerous to human life when improperly used, chemists and druggists are subject to a number of minute regulations. It would obviously be impossible even to summarise them here; and the attempt might lull the practising chemist into a dangerous sense of security. The Pharmaceutical Society, which is the statutory governing body for chemists and druggists, will afford full information to applicants.

POISONS

Particular precautions are, naturally, prescribed in regard to poisons. The container must be distinctly labelled with the name of the article and the word "Poison "; and the name and address of the seller must appear plainly. For certain specified poisons more stringent regulations are laid down.

TRADE DISPUTES AND TRADE UNIONS

NO SPECIFIC RIGHT TO COMBINE

THERE is, in English law, no definite sanction of the right to enter into voluntary combination—in "club," or "union," or "society," or "institute." On the other hand, there is no definite prohibition of combination; and, in fact, people do combine for all manner of purposes. The combinations are lawful if they are for purposes not repellent to the law. It is with a combination for enduring purposes as with a meeting for a passing purpose. Just as an assembly gathered together with the avowed intention of holding a prohibited meeting is an "unlawful assembly," all who take part in it being guilty of a Common Law misdemeanour, so all who enter into association for purposes repellent to the law are guilty of the crime of "criminal conspiracy." Thus an association for military education, so that, in certain events, resistance might effectively be offered to the orders of the State, would clearly be a criminal conspiracy.

It must be remembered, however, that a combination even for lawful purposes is not exempt from the obligations of the common law. If the combination seeks to achieve its purposes by coercion, or intimidation, or threats, the law gives a remedy. Many may agree to use what are undoubtedly their legal rights in order to compel people to do harm to a plaintiff—not to deal with him or employ him or invite him to their homes. Then it is that a plaintiff has his legal remedy. "A number of acts and things not in themselves actionable or unlawful if done separately without conspiracy may, with conspiracy, become dangerous and alarming. So a grain of gunpowder is harmless but a pound may be highly destructive, or the administration of one grain of a particular drug may be most beneficial as a medicine but administered frequently and in larger quantities with a view to harm may be fatal as a poison." This was said in the well-known case *Quinn* v. *Leathem* (H.L. 1901) where the rights of many to act in unison were considered. The law was thus laid down: "Intentional damage, arising from the mere exercise of the rights of many, is not actionable. To hold the contrary would be unduly to restrict the liberty of one set of persons in order to uphold the liberty of another set. Competition with all its drawbacks, not only between individuals, but between associations, and between them and individuals, is permissible, *provided nobody's rights are infringed*. But coercion by threats, open or disguised, is a wrong; and, in considering whether coercion has been applied or not, numbers cannot be disregarded." See the case further discussed on page 103.

ILLEGAL ACTIONS BY COMBINATIONS

To persuade a man not to enter into a contract is lawful; to coerce a man not to enter into a contract is unlawful. And the action of combinations usually means coercion. What may begin as peaceable persuasion easily becomes, in trade disputes generally becomes, peremptory ordering, with threats open or covert of very unpleasant consequences to those who resist persuasion. A combination not to work is lawful. A combination to prevent others from working, by annoying them if they do, is unlawful.

DEFINITION OF TRADE UNION

The statutory definition of a trade union is: "The term 'trade union' means any combination whether temporary or permanent, for regulating the relations between workmen and masters, or between workmen and workmen, or between masters and masters, or for imposing restrictive conditions on the conduct of any trade or business." Trade union, therefore, includes even such an association as the Motor Trade Association, though that is an unregistered association of motor-dealers and manufacturers having little connection with labour questions and being essentially a union of traders for protecting their trade interests.

The questions arise: how far are such combinations recognised by our English Law? What are the legal powers possessed by a trade union? Under what legal obligations do they lie? The summary answers to these questions are: recognition is now complete; the powers are now surprisingly great; the obligations now surprisingly small.

THE POWER WITHIN THE STATE

The extent to which the right of combination should be allowed must obviously always present difficulties. For the combination becomes a Power within the State, an *Imperium in Imperio*. In almost every country some forms of association force upon public attention the practical difficulty of so regulating the right of association that its exercise may neither trench upon each citizen's individual freedom nor shake the supreme authority of the State. "How can the right of combined action be curtailed without depriving individual liberty of half its value; how can it be left unrestricted without destroying the liberty of individual citizens, or the power of the Government?"—Dicey, *Law and Opinion*.

COMMON LAW ATTITUDE TOWARDS COMBINATIONS

As regards combinations among workmen the old legislators and judges had no doubt whatever. Such combinations were conspiracies; and a conspiracy is an offence at Common Law, although the matter about which the offenders conspired might have been lawful for them. In one case where seven Liverpool tailors were sent to gaol for six months for agreeing to stand out for higher payment, Lord Mansfield said: "The illegal combination is the gist of the offence: persons in possession of any articles of trade may sell them at such prices as they may individually please, but if they confederate and agree not to sell them under certain prices, it is conspiracy; so every man may work at what price he pleases, but a combination not to work under certain prices is an indictable offence."

CIVIL DISABILITY OF THE UNION

The danger of indictment for the criminal offence of conspiracy was certainly a serious obstacle to trade union action. At least as serious, until 1871, was the fact that the associations were not recognised in law. For they had been formed for purposes that were "in restraint of trade"; they limited the liberty of a man to dispose of his time and his talents as he chose. Hornby was president of the Bradford Branch of the Boilermakers' Society; Close, a member, would not give up money belonging to the society. Hornby brought an action at law to recover the money. He failed, however, on the ground that the society was formed for illegal purposes. It was "in restraint of trade depriving, as it did, the workman of the free exercise of his will in the employment of his labour; tending to the encouraging and maintaining of strikes."

Of this decision, declaring in effect that property of a combination might be enjoyed by anyone clever enough to get it into his possession, a member of the Royal Commission then assembled, wrote: "the judgment lays down that trade unions, of whatever sort, are in their nature contrary to public policy, and that their object in itself will vitiate every association and every transaction into which it enters. Unionism becomes like betting and gambling, public nuisances and immoral considerations—things condemned and suppressed by law." The unions would have no help in recovering or preserving their property; they had no legal right even to recover their own money from their own bankers.

The Trade Union Act, 1871, gave protection to the funds of the unions by Section 12: "If any officer, having trade union money in his possession, wilfully withhold or fraudulently misapply the same, a Court of Summary Jurisdiction may order him to deliver up such money, or in default to be imprisoned." The interpretation of this section was considered in *Best* v. *Butler and Fitzgibbon* (K.B., 1932) where an information was preferred under the section against two trade union officials. The magistrate dismissed the summons on the intelligible but strange ground that "although there was a discrepancy in the accounts, a man cannot withhold what he has squandered." But the Divisional Court allowed the appeal, the Chief Justice remarking, "The term 'wilfully withhold' indicates a continuing offence; there is really no difference between wilful withholding and neglecting or refusing to deliver."

REMOVAL OF CRIMINAL AND CIVIL LIABILITY

The liability to an indictment for the crime of conspiracy was removed by the Conspiracy and Protection of Property Act, 1875. There still remained the civil liability, however: this, too, was removed by the Trade Disputes Act, 1906, Section 1 of which enacts—

"An act done in pursuance of an agreement or combination by two or more persons shall, if done in contemplation or furtherance of a trade dispute, not be actionable unless the act if done without any such agreement or combination would be actionable."

Section 3 of the Trade Disputes Act provides that "an act done in contemplation or furtherance of a trade dispute shall not be actionable on the ground only that it is an interference with the trade, business, or employment of some other person, or with the right of some other person to dispose of his capital or his labour as he wills."

Nor is the protection restricted to acts "done in contemplation or furtherance of a trade dispute": it extends, apparently, to all tortious acts. Vacher Sons are printers carrying on business in Westminster. Though no trade dispute was pending, they were libelled in a publication issued by the London Society of Compositors. Action was barred by Section 4 of the Act: "an action against a trade union or against any members or officials thereof, in respect of any tortious act alleged to have been committed by or on behalf of the trade union, shall not be entertained by any Court." The deduction is obvious, and involves a complete reversal of the Common Law attitude. According to the latter the combination to injure another was a wrong, even though the acts in contemplation were themselves innocent; according to the Trade Disputes Act the fact that a combination exists makes an otherwise wrongful act into an innocent one.

Here, for instance, is a letter sent out by a Trade Association to members who have broken its rules. An individual sending it out would be convicted of blackmail: it is an extortion of money through a threat. The Association sends it out with impunity.

"With reference to your appearance before the Stop List Committee at their meeting on — the —, we beg to inform you, that the Committee fully considered the evidence placed before them and came to the conclusion that the infringement of our recognised principles of price regulation, alleged as already stated to you, was proved to their satisfaction.

"The Committee under all circumstances are prepared to recommend to the Council that if you will pay a sum of £200 to our Indemnity Fund (which is applied towards expenses) to mark your regret; sign and pay for the insertion of the enclosed undertaking and also repurchase the article purchased from you, that this shall be regarded on this occasion as a satisfactory ending of the matter.

"Please let us hear from you by — the —, if you agree, and in that event let us have your cheque for £—, and sign the undertaking."

No individual could with safety sign such a letter; the Association sends it out as a matter of course.

It is well, perhaps, to point out that personal liability by an agent of the union is not removed by the Act. The injured employer, if he thinks it worth while, may sue the agent in his individual capacity. For instance, in *Bussey* v. *Amalgamated Society of Railway Servants*, 1908, a trade union official was made personally liable for tortious acts committed on behalf of the trade union.

PROTECTING TRADE UNION FUNDS

Protection of trade union funds was afforded by the Trades Union Act of 1871. Yet the Act did not enable the Courts to take cognisance of the internal workings of a trade union. Rigby, a member of a trade union, sought an injunction restraining the union from expelling him. He failed, however, the Master of the Rolls holding that the Court had no jurisdiction over the internal affairs of a union: "That Act, no doubt, was passed primarily with a view to preventing the officers of these societies from robbing them. That was the chief object. It was discovered that some of these men, abusing the confidence reposed in them, took advantage of the law which made these societies illegal, by appropriating their funds and property to their own use. The Act was passed to get at these men. Another object was this: the Act enabled these societies to sue in respect of their property and to hold property. But it was not intended that the contracts entered into by the members of the society should be made legal contracts *inter se*, so that Courts of Justice should interfere to enforce them."

SPENDING FOR POLITICAL OBJECTS

The manner of disposing of the union's funds is in some slight measure restricted. Before the decision in *Amalgamated Society of Railway Servants* v. *Osborne* (A.C. 1930) spending of the funds "to improve the conditions of work" received the widest possible interpretation: it was taken to include in its wide scope any object whatever sanctioned by majority vote. It therefore included among other things the spending upon political objects, the paying of candidates' expenses, and the supplementing of members' salaries, whether the candidates sought election to Parliament or to a Local Authority. The minority in a union might well, therefore, be contributing towards the funds of a hostile political party. The decision in the Osborne case declared such payments to be *ultra vires*. The payments were outside the scope of the Trade Union Acts: "It would be as unjust and oppressive as it is illegal to compel a member of a trade union either to contribute to the promotion of a political policy of which he might possibly disapprove, or be expelled from the union." The judgment in this case makes clear the legal status of a trade union: "They are quasi-corporations, resembling much more closely railway companies incorporated by statute than voluntary associations of individuals merely bound together by contract or agreement, express or implied. And it is plain that as soon as this character was given to them, and the rights and privileges they now enjoy were conferred upon them, it became a matter of necessity to define the purposes and objects to which they were at liberty to devote the funds raised from their members by enforced contributions. It is contended that it is only fair to imply that they have the power of securing parliamentary representation. For such a representation would afford the most effective means of accomplishing their objects.

"But trade unions are in this respect in precisely the same position as all corporations, municipal or commercial. These bodies, like the trade unions, may by legislation be helped or hindered in carrying out their objects. If, despite this, the intention never has been, and cannot be, imputed to the Legislature to confer on such corporations the power to devote their funds to the procurement of parliamentary representation, how can such an intention be imputed in the case of quasi-corporations such as registered trade unions?"

Agitation against the decision was successful. The Trade Union Act of 1913 provides that a trade union may apply its funds for political objects. Two conditions are, however, now required: first, a resolution in favour of such spending has been passed by secret ballot; second, no member must be charged the political levy unless he delivers to his trade union a notice to the following effect: "I hereby give notice that I am willing and agree to contribute to the Political Fund of the . . . Union, and I understand that I shall in consequence be liable to contribute to that Fund, and shall continue to be so liable unless I deliver . . . a written notice of withdrawal." (Trade Disputes Act, 1927.)

LEGALITY OF TRADE UNION ACTS

Group bargaining instead of individual bargaining, rules out the particular needs or the particular aptitudes of the individual worker. When the group that bargains consists of all in a certain trade, then the special circumstances of the individual employer as well as of the individual worker are eliminated. Group bargaining is now the typical method of bargaining. This is so much recognised, in the building trades for instance, that County Court Judges—called upon to determine questions under the Workmen's Compensation Acts—hold that the "working rules" of the district form part of the wage agreement, unless those rules are expressly excluded.

Since collective bargaining is the means upon which unions place reliance for obtaining a fair deal, it is necessary that the workers should be permitted not only to combine but to act in combination. In other words, the right to strike is inseparable from the right to bargain as a body.

Till the modern freedom of combination was achieved, a strike was a crime. One judgment ran: "The indictment, it is true, sets forth that the defendants refused to work under the wages which they demanded: yet it is not for the refusing to work, but for conspiracy, that they are indicted. And a conspiracy of any kind is illegal, although the matter about which they conspired might have been lawful for them to do if they had not conspired to do it."

The one limitation upon the right to strike is set forth in the Conspiracy and Protection of Property Act of 1875: "Persons employed in the public supply of gas or water, or to whose charge is specially committed the care of human life or of valuable property, who wilfully and maliciously break their contract of service, are liable to a penalty of £20 or of imprisonment, with or without hard labour, for three months." It will be noted that this exception is a peculiarly elastic one, and in some moods of the public mind would be construed as covering a very wide area; it would, for instance, easily cover the strike of "safety men," in a mine or signalmen on a railway.

INCIDENTS OF A STRIKE

The mode of conducting such a concerted refusal to work is noted in Section 7 of the Act. This penalises possible molestation and obstruction. If individual workers broke away from the group, group bargaining could hardly be achieved; and these—deserters in the eyes of the rest of the group—would perhaps be subject to the coercion of their fellow-workers. The penalties decreed are applicable against any one, who, with a view to dissuading another from doing what that other has a right to do—

1. Uses violence or intimidates.
2. Persistently follows that other.
3. Hides the tools or other property of that other.
4. Watches or besets the house or place of employment of that other.
5. With two or more fellows follows that other in a disorderly manner.

The liberty of what is called "peaceful picketing" is, however, provided for in the Act: "Attending in order merely to obtain or communicate information shall not be deemed a watch or a besetting." The Trade Disputes Act of 1906 extends this definition of peaceful picketing and adds "or of peacefully persuading any person to work or abstain from working."

INDUCING BREACH OF CONTRACT

The Conspiracy Act removed the liability to criminal proceedings for striking. But it left undisturbed possible civil remedy. If, without reasonable cause, I persuade another to break his contract, I am liable to an action by the aggrieved party. For I have infringed the rights he has acquired under the contract. Moreover, even without a breach of contract, if my persuasion or force prevents another from doing business with another, then —unless I have what the Courts will regard as reasonable cause— I am liable to action. The remedy against an individual workman, who probably would have been unable to pay damages awarded against him, would be of no great worth to an employer. The union, however, had property; if the union could be made civilly liable for disturbance of trade, the employer still had an adequate remedy for unjustifiable interference with his business.

The rule of law still holds good in regard to individuals who intentionally and without lawful justification induce any one to break a contract made by him with another. As it was put: "A violation of legal right committed knowingly is a cause of action. And it is a violation of legal right to interfere with contractual relations, if there is not sufficient justification for the interference."

Thus, Miss Wagner had signed a contract with Lumley, the proprietor of one theatre; but Gye, the proprietor of another, induced her not to fulfil the contract. It was held that Lumley could recover damages from Gye: "It is clear law, that a person who wrongfully and maliciously—or, which is the same thing, with notice—interrupts the relations subsisting between master and servant commits a wrongful act for which he is responsible at law. The rule applies wherever the wrongful interruption operates to prevent the service."

Whether "lawful justification" exists depends upon the facts. "No doubt, there are circumstances in which A is entitled to induce B to break a contract entered into by B with C. Thus, for instance, if the contract between B and C is one which B could not make consistently with his preceding contractual obligations towards A, A may not only induce him to break it, but may invoke the assistance of a court of justice to make him break it." A parent is presumably justified in inducing his child to break off an undesirable engagement; a doctor may well persuade his patient to break a contract of service. In *Brimelow* v. *Casson* (K.B. 1924), Casson was held justified in inducing theatre

managers to break their contracts with Brimelow on the ground
that Brimelow paid disgracefully low wages to artistes.

A TRADE UNION NOW EXEMPT FROM ACTION

It was the successful suit of the *Taff Vale Railway* v. *Amalgamated Society of Railway Servants* (1901) that made possible
the suing of a trade union as a person. In practice, a voluntary association does act as a unit. It would appear that the
liability ought also to be that of the unit. To the man in the
street who deals with the labour union or a club, there is no difference apparent between the conduct of that organisation unincorporated, and the conduct of a similar incorporated association.
"If the Legislature, has created a thing which can own property,
which can employ servants, and which can inflict injury, it must
be taken, I think, to have impliedly given power to make it suable
in a Court of Law for injuries purposely done by its authority and
procurement." And Lord Lindley said, "I repudiate the notion
that the effect of the Trade Union Act, 1871, is to legalise trade
unions and confer on them the right to acquire and hold property
and, at the same time, to protect the union from legal proceedings."
In accordance with this reasoning the trade union was mulcted
in damages.

The power to sue the union in such an event is now taken away.
For the Trade Disputes Act enacts in Section 3 that "An act done
by a person in contemplation or furtherance of a trade dispute
shall not be actionable upon the ground only that it induces some
other person to break a contract of employment." There is now
no necessity imposed upon a union of respecting the contractual
rights of employers.

PERSUASION AGAINST CONTRACTING

Interference with contractual rights is one thing; persuading
people not to enter into contracts is a different thing. The man
who induces another to break a contract induces him to do what
is in itself actionable; but no liability attaches to the refusal to
make a contract. How far may a person, or a combination, go in
inducing others not to make contracts?

Very far indeed, it would seem; to be actionable, the inducement must be of an unlawful kind, as, for example, acts of coercion
or intimidation. The famous trilogy of cases, *Allen* v. *Flood* (1897),
Mogul Steamship Co. v. *McGregor* (1892), and *Quinn* v. *Leathem*
(1901), makes clear the distinction between inducement that is
permissible and inducement that is actionable.

The Mogul case establishes the right of competition, even when the means employed are so unusual as to be unfair. It supports undercutting to the extent of actual loss; it supports intimidation of others, provided that the intimidation consists only in a threat to use one's legal rights. Nor does the malicious intention to injure the complaining party take away the right. The plaintiffs in the case showed that the defendants, wishing to retain a monopoly of the China tea trade, had wilfully injured them in their attempt to obtain part of the trade. McGregor and his associates had, by threatening to withdraw their custom from the Chinese merchants, obliged those merchants to give up the agency of the Mogul Co. The House of Lords held both the undercutting and the threatening to be justified.

LIMITS OF COMPETITION

As to the undercutting the judgment stated: "All commercial men with capital are acquainted with the ordinary expedient of sowing one year a crop of apparently unfruitful prices, in order by driving competition away to reap a fuller harvest of profits in the future. As to the threatening not to employ one's agents, this was merely a threat to exercise one's legal rights. All the acts done and all the means used were acts of competition."

The bias is in favour of freedom, whether in bargaining about commodities or about services. It is a doctrine for the strong not the weak. Mature men and women should, the law declares, be able to take care of their own interests. In contrast to the old adversity to agreements in restraint of trade, the courts now actually give their praise to combinations for regulating supply and so keeping up prices.

In *North Western Salt Co.* v. *Electrolytic Alkali Co.* (A.C. 1914), the Lord Chancellor [Haldane] said: "An ill-regulated supply and unremunerative prices may, in point of fact, be disadvantageous to the public. Such a state of things, if not controlled, may drive manufacturers out of business or lower wages, so causing unemployment or labour disturbances." And another Law Lord added: "Some combination limiting output and regulating competition so as to secure reasonable prices may have been necessary, not only in the interests of the salt producers themselves, but in the interest of the public generally. For it cannot be to the public advantage that the trade of a large area should be ruined by a cut-throat competition."

The appellants were a combination of salt manufacturers. They included practically all the salt manufacturers in north-west England. They made a contract with the respondents whereby they bought a stipulated amount of salt each year, their object being to control supply and so regulate prices. The respondents agreed not to sell salt otherwise than as agreed with the combination. In breach of their undertaking they sold to customers. The combination discovered the sales and claimed damages. The Appeal Court had held the contract illegal as being in restraint of trade, and as forming part of a scheme for securing a monopoly by restricting output and raising prices. The House of Lords, however, granted the appeal.

THE INTENT TO INJURE

Seemingly, too, the fact that a malicious intention is the motive for exercising a legal right makes no difference. "The existence of a bad motive in the case of an act which is not in itself illegal will not convert that act into a civil wrong." So it was declared in *Allen* v. *Flood*. Allen, a delegate of the boilermakers' society, had obtained the discharge of a non-member, Flood, by his employer, through what the House of Lords considered a warning that, unless Flood was discharged, the other men in the employer's service would be withdrawn. Flood could obtain no remedy for his loss of employment. For "To persuade a person to do or abstain from doing is lawful, and in some cases meritorious, although the result of the advice may be damage to another." The dividing line between an innocent warning and an illegal threat is, however, easily crossed.

LANDLORD AND TENANT

THE tenant has a different relation towards his landlord from that of the lodger. The lodger has licence to use what his landlord also uses; the tenant has for a period exclusive possession of land or buildings in which the landlord has an estate. In virtue of his lease the tenant has a smaller estate carved out of the larger estate of his landlord. The landlord retains some interest; otherwise the bargain would be a sale, not a letting (or leasing). The interest retained by the landlord is called the *reversion*.

LENGTH OF LEASE

1. An owner of a *fee-simple* (a freehold estate) may do with it what he pleases, may sell it or let it for a period, however long and on any conditions.

2. A *tenant-for-life* may grant (*a*) a building lease for not more than 999 years, (*b*) a mining lease for not more than 100 years, (*c*) any other lease for not more than 50 years.

3. A *mortgagor remaining in possession* of the mortgaged land may make an agricultural or occupation lease for 50 years and a building lease for 999 years. He may, however, have in the mortgage deed curtailed his powers.

4. A *tenant for years* may, unless his agreement expressly forbids him to do so, make an under-lease for any period less than his own term. So, too, may any other tenant.

Whether or not the power of sub-letting exists is usually made clear in the lease.

FORM OF LEASE

1. A *deed* (or *sealed writing*) is necessary in order to make enforceable (*a*) a lease for more than 3 years, (*b*) a lease, however short, that does not reserve as rent the best rent obtainable without payment of premium.

It should be noted, however, that the absence of a sealed writing is not material in practice. For, if there is a written agreement at all and the tenant enters into possession, the Court will construe the agreement as one for a lease upon the expressed conditions. And if there is only an agreement by word of mouth and the tenant enters into possession and pays rent, the tenant will be regarded as one from year to year.

2. A *written agreement* is necessary for any other letting. For such letting concerns an interest in land.

COVENANTS IN A LEASE

The covenants or undertakings entered into by landlord and tenant vary greatly. But the tenant usually covenants (*a*) to pay rent, rates, and taxes, (*b*) to repair, maintain, and insure the premises, (*c*) to use the premises in a stipulated manner only, (*d*) not to assign the lease or to underlet, (*e*) to yield up the premises at the end of the tenancy or upon the stipulated notice. And the landlord usually covenants that, so long as the tenant fulfils his obligations, neither the landlord nor any one claiming under him will disturb possession. The landlord often covenants also to do specified repairs.

STAMPING OF LEASES

The stamp duty payable is as follows—

1. 1d., paid by affixing an adhesive stamp, when there is a letting for a definite term, not exceeding a year, of a dwelling-house at a rent not exceeding £40 a year.

2. 5s., paid by affixing an adhesive stamp when there is an agreement to let for a definite term less than a year of a furnished dwelling-house or apartments at a rent less than £25.

3. *Ad valorem* duties on other leases in accordance with the table below.

Exceeding	Not exceeding	Not exceeding 35 years	Between 35 years and 100 years	Exceeding 100 years
£	£	£ s. d.	£ s. d.	£ s. d.
	5	1 –	6 –	12 –
5	10	2 –	12 –	1 4 –
10	15	3 –	18 –	1 16 –
15	20	4 –	1 4 –	2 8 –
20	25	5 –	1 10 –	3 – –
25	50	10 –	3 – –	6 – –
50	75	15 –	4 10 –	9 – –
75	100	1 – –	6 – –	12 – –
£100, for £50, or fractional part of £50		10 –	3 – –	6 – –

The stamp duty on a counterpart lease is 5s., unless the duty on the lease itself is less than 5s. In that event the duty on the counterpart is the same as on the original. Penalties are prescribed, unless an agreement not under seal is stamped within fourteen days from its execution, and an agreement under seal within thirty days.

TENANCIES

1. Apart from an express stipulation to the contrary, a tenancy is from year to year. Unless otherwise agreed, six months' notice, ending at the end of a year of the tenancy, terminates the tenancy. Thus, for a letting on the 1st July, the notice to terminate expires on the 30th June, and it must be given not later than noon on 1st January. Either landlord or tenant is entitled to give notice.

2. Where it is clear that the parties had no intention of creating a yearly tenancy the form of the agreement shows whether a *weekly* or *monthly* or *quarterly* tenancy was intended. Notice to quit will be of the same length as the tenancy.

3. A *tenancy at will* is one that may be ended at the option of either landlord or tenant.

4. A *tenancy on sufferance* is one in which the tenant continues in possession when notice has expired and without the consent of the landlord. The landlord may enter at any time or the tenant leave at any time.

TERMINATION OF TENANCY

Further notes on the ending of a tenancy are—

1. A weekly tenancy may be ended on the day of the week when it began, so long as notice is given on the corresponding day of the week before (*Newman* v. *Slade*, K.B. 1926).

2. Both the tenant and the landlord should know when the tenancy is to expire. In *Doe dem Finlayson* v. *Bayley* (C. & P. 1831), a landlord in a weekly tenancy was placed in an awkward position because he had forgotten (and the tenant did not choose to tell) whether the tenancy began on a Tuesday or a Wednesday. Notice to expire on a Tuesday would be insufficient for a Wednesday tenancy; notice on a Wednesday in a Tuesday tenancy would not expire on the right day. Two prevalent mistakes may be here noted. The first is that, where the landlord has bound himself to do the repairs, the tenant has a right to quit unless the repairs are done. There is no such right; the tenant's remedy is to sue for breach of contract. The second is that, on the failure of the landlord after notice, the tenant is entitled to effect the repairs and deduct the cost from his rent. The tenant is not so entitled. The rent must be paid in full, and again the tenant's remedy is to sue for the cost of the repairs.

PROTECTION OF THE TENANT

The Law of Property Act, 1925, protects, in certain events, a tenant from forfeiture of his lease. Where a tenant has broken a condition of the lease and where that breach is capable of being repaired, the tenant must be given a chance to repair it before being ejected from his holding.

NOTICE TO LICENSEE

The requirement of notice is not so exacting where a licence (not a tenancy) is concerned. If the grantor retains possession and gives the licensee a right to use, a "reasonable" notice will terminate the licence. The question arose in *Wilson* v. *Tavener* (Ch. 1901), whether an agreement to allow a bill-poster to erect a hoarding and to use a house wall, at a rental of £10 a year, was a licence or a tenancy. The agreement was held to be a licence merely, even though words applicable to a lease were used; and a three-months' notice was accordingly a reasonable and valid notice to end the licence.

FIXTURES

A question may arise whether or not at the end of a tenancy the tenant may remove "fixtures," things fastened to the premises so as to become part of it. In general he may not. When dispute arises, two questions must be answered: (1) was the article a fixture? (2) is there a rule of law allowing the tenant to remove it? As regards (1) there is no very ready way of determining. But (a) if the article cannot be removed without causing substantial damage or disfigurement to the land or building, it is a fixture, (b) if intended as a permanent improvement of land or building, it is a fixture. Thus doors, windows, locks, and keys, are fixtures. On the other hand the following, though in some way attached to land or building, have been held not to be fixtures : gas-brackets, tapestry, pictures, window-blinds, chairs screwed to the floor of a hall, ornamental chimney pieces, grates, stoves, and other articles of utility—always provided that they can be removed without doing substantial damage, and have not been substituted for landlord's fixtures.

As regards (2), the following are tenant's fixtures : What he has affixed to the premises for the purposes of his trade. Thus, a nurseryman may remove his greenhouses and small trees or shrubs that he has planted. One who is not carrying on gardening as his business may not.

If a fixture has been placed instead of a fixture in position at the beginning of the tenancy, the tenant must on removing his own fixture restore the old one or a similar one. Moreover, the tenant must remove his fixtures before his tenancy expires. For the law assumes that whatever is on the premises when the landlord resumes possession is his property.

FARMING FIXTURES

The right of the tenant farmer to remove fixtures is now a statutory one, defined by the Agricultural Holdings Act, 1923, Section 22. Any engine, machinery, fencing, or other fixture affixed to a holding by a tenant, and any building erected by him thereon for which he is not under the Act or otherwise entitled to compensation, and which is not affixed or erected in pursuance of some obligation or instead of some fixture belonging to the landlord, is the property of and is removable by the tenant before or within a reasonable time after the determination of the tenancy.

Provided that—

1. Before the removal of any fixture or building, the tenant shall pay all rent owing by him, and shall perform or satisfy all other of his obligations to the landlord in respect of the holding.

2. The tenant shall not do any avoidable damage.

3. Immediately after the removal of any fixture or building the tenant shall make good all damage occasioned to any other building by the removal.

4. The tenant shall not remove any fixture or building without giving one month's previous notice of his intention.

5. At any time before the expiration of the notice of removal, the landlord, by notice in writing given by him to the tenant, may elect to purchase any fixture or building comprised in the notice of removal, and this shall be left by the tenant and become the property of the landlord, who shall pay to the tenant the fair value thereof to an incoming tenant of the holding.

RENT

The payment made by the tenant to his landlord is nowadays almost always expressed as being so many pounds, shillings, and pence. Rarely, when it is desirable to give a tenancy instead of a licence, a nominal or "peppercorn" rent consisting of some small annual gift from the tenant is stipulated for.

Landlord and tenant make what bargain they choose; and the due date of the rent is usually, and wisely, clearly indicated. Where the bargain says nothing, the rent is due at the end of each period of letting; it is payable in advance only when the tenant has expressly agreed to this condition. Rent is not overdue and consequently the landlord has no right to levy distress, until midnight of the day when the rent should have been paid.

The tenant remains liable for rent so long as the tenancy lasts, even though fire or other cause has made the premises uninhabitable.

DOUBLE RENT

Where a tenant has power to end his tenancy and has given notice to end it, then, unless he gives up possession before the notice expires, he is liable for double rent for the period during which he holds over (Distress for Rent Act, 1737).

An earlier Act enacts that a tenant *for life* or *years* is liable for *double the yearly value of lands* in the circumstances following—

1. The tenant holds over after demand made and notice given by the landlord.

2. The tenant holds over well knowing that he has no right to retain possession.

THE LANDLORD'S REMEDIES WHEN RENT IS OVERDUE

1. The ordinary actions for the recovery of debts are available to the landlord when rent due is not paid. In addition, arising from the nature of the subject-matter, the landlord has other remedies—

2. A right, under certain conditions, to re-enter upon the premises.

3. Where a tenant has sublet, the superior landlord may require rent due to the tenant from the under-tenant to be paid direct to him.

4. A right to distrain, a curious and nowadays a very restricted survival of the ancient right of self-help.

DISTRESS (DISTRAINT) FOR RENT

This is the right of a landlord *when rent is overdue* (1) to enter upon the premises let, (2) to seize goods there, (3) and to sell them so as to cover his rent. The landlord may even, under the conditions below, follow goods that have been removed: (*a*) the tenant has, with the view of defeating the landlord's right to distrain, removed his own goods; (*b*) the tenant has not left goods enough to satisfy the landlord's claim; (*c*) the landlord takes the goods within thirty days of the removal; (*d*) the goods have not been sold to a buyer ignorant of the fraudulent removal.

Other points relating to the following of goods removed are—

(*a*) The landlord may, if he finds that the removed goods are locked away in a building, *with the help of a constable* and *by day*, break into the building and take the goods.

(*b*) If the building is a dwelling-house the landlord must, before breaking in, make oath before a J.P. that he has reason to believe the goods are there.

(*c*) After the tenancy is ended the landlord *cannot* follow goods. This is so even though the goods were removed *before* the tenancy ended.

(*d*) Where the goods removed do not exceed £50 in value, the landlord may obtain a Justices' order that the tenant shall pay double the value.

LIMITATIONS OF LANDLORD'S RIGHT TO DISTRAIN

1. Things upon which distress for rent may not be made include—

(*a*) *Things that cannot in any event be taken* (*things absolutely privileged*)—

(1) Fixtures; (2) things that cannot be restored in as good a state as when taken; (3) animals not domesticated (*ferae naturae*); (4) things delivered to a person (carrier, worker, repairer) in the way of his trade; (5) things in custody of the law (e.g. goods noted by the sheriff for sale to satisfy a judgment debt); (6) money.

These are exempt from seizure by Common Law. Various statutes add others: (1) Goods of an ambassador; (2) machines, materials, and tools for textile manufactures, and not belonging to the tenant; (3) gas, water, and electric fittings; (4) railway rolling stock; (5) the wearing apparel and bedding of the tenant and his family, and the tools and instruments of his trade to the value of £5 (in all) [Note that a cab, though over £5 in value, the only thing on the premises and the only means whereby its owner could ply his trade, came within the protection (*Lavell v. Richings*, K.B. 1906)]; (6) agricultural machinery hired; (7) goods of an under-tenant or lodger (subject to the condition that the under-tenant or lodger shall serve on the landlord a declaration of ownership).

(b) *Things that can be taken only when there is not enough property otherwise to distrain upon*—

(1) Tools and instruments of a man's trade or profession, and implements of husbandry though not in actual use; (2) beasts of the plough, and sheep; (3) live stock taken on an agricultural holding to be fed.

Bill of Sale gives Similar Power. An express agreement, as between, for instance, a borrower and a lender, may give to the lender a right to seize the borrower's goods in the event of default in payments. The written agreement conferring this right is a bill of sale, and is subject to the regulations of the Bills of Sale Act. Thus, unless it is registered in regard to the goods seized, it is of no effect against (a) a trustee in bankruptcy, (b) a creditor under an assignment, (c) an execution creditor.

2. The landlord must distrain personally or by an authorised bailiff. A list of such, holding a certificate from the County Court judge, is shown in the office of every County Court. There, too, may be seen the authorised charges.

3. A distrainor may *not* force or unfasten an *outer* door or gate or a window in order to effect entry. He may climb a wall or fence, but must not break it down. When entry has been effected, he may open inner doors or locks in order to reach the goods distrained upon. If, once having obtained lawful entry, the distrainor is driven out, or if after leaving for an unavoidable reason he is refused re-admission, he may *with the help of a constable* break into the premises. The tenant is under no obligation to supply with food or drink a man left in possession.

4. *Seizure* is effected (a) by taking hold of an article and declaring it a distress as representative of the goods seized, (b) by giving to the tenant, or by fixing in a conspicuous place, a list of the goods distrained upon. These goods should be enough to cover rent arrears; for a second distress cannot be made. But they must not be excessive; for then the tenant has an action for illegal distress.

5. Neither entry nor seizure may be made on Sunday, Christmas Day, or Good Friday. And it must be made between sunrise and sunset.

6. Five clear days (extended to fifteen when the tenant, or the owner of the goods, makes a written request) must elapse between seizure and sale. This interval is available (a) to give time for an application to the registrar of the County Court for redelivery, (b) to enable the tenant to redeem the goods.

7. Subsequent sale must be a real one, and every reasonable

effort must be made to obtain the best prices. It is to be noted that the buyer at such a sale of an article that ought not to have been seized obtains no good title. He does, however, obtain a good title where the illegality is excessive distraint only.

When no rent is really due, the landlord is liable for double the value of the goods distrained and sold.

LODGERS' GOODS PROTECTION ACT (1908)

The effect of this Act in removing risk from the lodger is well shown in *Thwaites* v. *Wilding* (Q.B. 1883). When a lodger's goods have been seized he recovers them if (*a*) he writes out a declaration and an inventory, (*b*) he delivers this to the landlord or to the bailiff employed by him, (*c*) he tenders to the landlord any rent due to the tenant distrained upon. A lodger must make a fresh declaration each time that a distress is levied upon his goods. For the statute is not for the benefit of the lodger alone. The superior landlord is to enjoy a correlative benefit : he is to receive, in part discharge of his claim, payment of any rent which may be due from the lodger to his immediate landlord.

Note that the making of a declaration or an inventory, knowing it to be untrue in a material point, is a misdemeanour punishable under the Perjury Act, 1911.

WHO DOES REPAIRS ?

For dwelling-houses, at a rent not exceeding £40 a year in London, not exceeding £26 elsewhere, the implication is that the landlord keeps it throughout the tenancy reasonably fit for human habitation. There is now also a statutory requirement in regard to houses intended for living in by the "working classes." Before rent is demanded there must be delivered in writing (in the rent book usually) to the tenant (*a*) the name and address of the medical officer of health for the district, (*b*) the name of the landlord or other person directly responsible for keeping the house fit for living in. Apart from these requirements, the matter is one of specific agreement. But the points following merit careful note.

WARRANTY OF FITNESS FOR HABITATION (NEW HOUSE)

Miller v. *Cannon Hill Estates, Ltd.* (K.B. 1931) decided that there is an implied warranty, when one enters into contract with a builder to buy a house to be built, that it shall be fit for human habitation.

IMPLIED UNDERTAKING OF FITNESS

If a furnished house is hired for a short period, the London season, for instance, the landlord impliedly undertakes that it shall be reasonably fit for immediate habitation. If it is not so fit the hirer may throw up his lease and sue for damages: "he is offered something substantially different from that which was contracted for."

And by the Housing Act, 1925, there is implied in the letting of a house (at £40 in London, or £26 elsewhere) a condition that the house is fit for human habitation, and that it will be kept fit during the tenancy by the landlord. Where the tenant obtains a lease of three years or longer, and in the lease undertakes to keep the house fit for habitation, the condition does not apply.

From the landlord's point of view, unluckily, there is no corresponding warranty that the intending tenant is a fit and proper person to occupy the house.

No undertaking applies to houses of a greater rental let for a term of years. In *Keates* v. *Lord Cadogan* (C.P. 1851), where the plaintiff sued for fraud in that the defendant did not disclose that the house, required for immediate occupation, was in a ruinous condition, the Chief Justice said: "It is not pretended that there was any warranty, express or implied, that the house was fit for immediate occupation. . . . The declaration does not allege that the defendant made any misrepresentation, or that he had reason to suppose that the plaintiff would not do, what any man in his senses would do—make proper investigation, and satisfy himself as to the condition of the house before he entered upon the occupation of it. There is nothing amounting to deceit."

RESPONSIBILITY OF OCCUPIER AND OWNER

Injury has befallen one who has entered house, shop, factory, or field. Is the occupier liable to compensate the injured person? He is if he owes a duty of carefulness towards *that person* and if the injured person can prove a failure of the duty. The hotel-keeper, who gains through the presence of his guest, is liable if one of them catches cold through being put into a damp bed; care for his comfort and safety is one of the things the guest pays for in his bill. The hostess is not liable when one of her weekend guests similarly contracts cold; her guests take the perils of the place along with the permission to abide in it. The landlord who has sent a plumber to repair pipes is responsible, if that plumber breaks his ankle on a faulty staircase. The landlord is not responsible when a visitor to a tenant so suffers injury.

Three degrees of care are, in fact, applicable to three different classes—to the *invitee*, to the *licensee*, to the *trespasser*. To the man who comes upon the premises in the interest of the owner or occupier, to the *invitee*, there is responsibility for any negligence in construction or management.

To the man who comes as a gratuitous guest, to the *licensee*, there is only responsibility for some known but concealed danger —for what is called a "trap." Thus : "a permission to use a way is in the character of a gift. The principle of law as to gifts is that the giver is not responsible for damage resulting from the insecurity of the thing, unless he knew its evil character at the time and omitted to caution the donee. There must be something like fraud on the part of the giver, before he can be made answerable. Otherwise, a man who allows strangers to roam over his property would be answerable for any damage which they might encounter whilst using the licence."

To the man who comes upon the property against the wish of the occupier, to the *trespasser*, there is only responsibility for the creation of a peril, like a spring-gun or a man-trap, that is serious and concealed. The occupier must do what is reasonably necessary to ensure the safety of the invitee ; he need do nothing except warn the licensee ; he need not even warn the trespasser. The notice to "Beware of the Dog" would not absolve him from liability for the dog's attack upon a paying guest ; it would, if the attack was upon a gratuitous guest ; it would not even be needed, if the attack was upon a burglar.

Thus in *Fairman* v. *Perpetual Investment Building Society* (A.C. 1923) it was decided that a landlord who lets out flats but keeps the common staircase under his control is responsible to his tenants for negligence in repair or lighting. They are his *invitees*. But he is not responsible in respect of visitors to his tenants. They are the invitees of his tenants ; so far as he is concerned they are *licensees* only. And he certainly is not responsible in regard to one who came to pillage, in regard to a trespasser.

LICENSEE OR TRESPASSER ?

Whether a person can recover damages for injury often depends, therefore, upon whether he was an invitee or a licensee or a trespasser. The Manchester Corporation was developing a building estate, and had levelled a rough road to the houses in construction. Till the houses were erected this road, not yet a public highway, gave a short cut to a favourite walk over the golf links; and one unlucky Sunday evening the plaintiff, who was engaged to a young lady in the neighbourhood, took this road with his affianced. He may have been watching his step with less attention than usual. At all events, he fell into a trench along which an electric main was to run. He was injured, and he claimed compensation from the corporation. The corporation having tacitly invited him to use the road ought to have rendered it secure, ought to have fenced the trench or placed warning lights along it. By leaving the way open the corporation had guaranteed its safety. (*Camerford* v. *Manchester Corporation*, K.B., 1931.)

The corporation contended, however, that if not a trespasser, the plaintiff was, in the most favourable supposition, a mere licensee. As such, he must take the land as he found it and himself run ordinary risks. And the corporation's contention prevailed. A jury had awarded him damages at the Assizes, but the Court of Appeal considered that the judge should not have submitted the question to the jury. The judgment concluded: "Having regard to the fact that the plaintiff entered the road in daylight and that it was obviously an unfinished, an unlighted road, I cannot see any evidence on which a jury could find a concealed danger. For these reasons I think Mr. Justice Acton should have withdrawn the case from the jury on the ground that the danger to which the plaintiff was exposed was obvious to a reasonable man. The plaintiff being at the best a bare licensee, the defendants owed no duty to him in respect of such a danger. The appeal should be allowed and judgment entered for the defendants, with costs here and below."

It would seem consonant with sound sense, as well as with justice, that a person who voluntarily runs a risk cannot be heard to complain when the risk he runs has become a reality. If I enter upon what many people call a game of Rugby, I must expect now and again to be, without ceremony, dashed to the ground; and, though damaged in the process, I cannot obtain compensation. For my own action, my own foolishness say some, has invited the happening. So, too, if I take advantage of an owner's permission to wander through his deer park, I must myself be responsible when one of the deer forgets its reputation for gentleness and forcibly repels my advances. Permission is a gift; and one must not look a gift-horse in the mouth.

The leading case is that of the *Mersey Docks and Harbour Board* v. *Proctor* (Appeal Court, 1923). In that case the position of a licensee is concisely and lucidly summed up: "A licensee takes premises, which he is merely permitted to enter, just as he finds them. The one exception to this is that the occupier must not lay a trap for him; the occupier must not expose him to a danger not obvious nor to be expected there under the circumstances. If the danger is obvious, the licensee must look out for himself; if it is one to be expected, he must expect it and take his own precautions. The licensor must act with reasonable diligence to prevent his premises from misleading or entrapping a licensee who on his side uses reasonable judgment. The licensee is to take reasonable care of himself and cannot call a thing a trap, the existence of which a reasonable man would have expected." To such a licensee, in short, the duty of the occupier is not to make his premises safe, but merely to give warning that they are not safe.

THE TENANT'S OBLIGATIONS

Even apart from specific promise, the tenant may be required to use the premises rented "in a tenant-like manner." This implies that he will not permit anything that will substantially lessen the value of the reversion to the landlord. He will, for instance, keep a building wind- and water-tight. His agreement usually extends his obligations.

1. *Damage Through Fire.* When a tenant has undertaken without reservation to repair, he is under legal obligation to restore buildings destroyed or damaged by accidental fire or lightning. And, whether he has undertaken or not to repair, he is liable for a fire caused by his negligence. Moreover, though he may not be bound to rebuild yet, unless he has protected himself in the agreement, he is liable for rent during the tenancy.

2. *Public Nuisance.* Through non-repair, buildings may become so unsafe as to be a menace to people passing. They are then a public nuisance and, in general, the tenant is liable for injury. But the landlord is liable (*a*) if he knew that the buildings were in a dangerous state when he let them, or (*b*) if, having undertaken to repair, he has knowingly neglected to repair.

3. *Use of Premises.* There may be restrictions in the tenancy agreement; and to these the tenant must conform. Apart from restrictions the tenant may use the premises in any lawful way. The common restriction to use the premises "only as a private

dwelling-house" implies that neither the public as a whole, nor any considerable section of it, shall be invited for business purposes : the stipulation would be broken by using the house as a school or a boarding house. "Trade" seems to be confined to buying and selling; "trade or business" seems to extend the prohibition to any use that habitually brings many people to the house. Thus, the maintenance of a hospital for the poor or a school for the ignorant, even though no payment is exacted, infringes the restriction.

4. *Subletting.* Unless he has agreed to the contrary, a tenant may assign his tenancy. Or he may sublet the whole or part of the premises leased. (But, if he sublets the whole of premises to which the Rent Restriction Acts apply, he gives the landlord a right to resume possession.)

It may be noted that a condition against "subletting the premises" does not prevent the tenant from letting part of them, or from taking lodgers.

FORFEITURE

The idea is current that failure of a tenant to pay rent or to observe other conditions of his lease gives to the landlord a right to eject him. This is not so unless the lease contains, as a well-drawn lease always will, a "proviso for re-entry." Even so, the Court will, where it can, relieve a tenant from the consequences of his failure. Thus, acceptance by the landlord of rent that has become due since the cause of forfeiture is readily taken as a waiver of the forfeiture. As in their dealing with the man obliged to mortgage his land as security, the Courts give the erring tenant "just one more chance." And the Law of Property Act, 1925, Section 146, greatly extends the powers of the Court to relieve. It enables the tenant to make good his default, and not suffer the possibly heavy and quite inordinate loss of forfeiture. "A right of re-entry or forfeiture under any proviso or stipulation in a lease for a breach of any covenant or condition in the lease, shall not be enforceable, by action or otherwise, unless and until the lessor serves on the lessee a notice specifying the particular breach complained of, and, if the breach is capable of remedy, requiring the lessee to remedy the breach, and, in any case, requiring the lessee to make compensation in money for the breach, and the lessee fails, within a reasonable time thereafter, to remedy the breach or to make reasonable compensation in money."

This relief is not available (1) where the tenant has broken a condition against assigning or underletting (2) where the tenant has become bankrupt, (3) where, having a mining lease, the tenant denies access to the books of the enterprise or to the mine workings, (4) where the forfeiture is for non-payment of rent.

NOTICES TO QUIT

(1) No special wording is needed. So long as it is clear that the tenancy is to end at a definite date, that is enough. But no condition must be attached. For a tenant to say or write "I hereby give you notice to quit, if I have found another house," or for a landlord to say "You must quit unless you repair" is no valid notice. It is a valid notice, however, when accompanied by an offer to create a new tenancy. Thus, the tenant may give notice and state also that he is willing to stay on upon modified terms.

(2) The right and liability to give and receive notice passes to the executor (or administrator) of a landlord or a tenant who dies.

(3) A notice to quit *part* only of the premises is not valid. The person, however, to whom it is given may accept it and act upon it; or he may treat it as a notice applying to the *whole* of the premises.

(4) Personal service is not needed. But it may be necessary to prove that the person entitled to notice did have notice, or should have had it. Thus, a notice given to a man's wife at the house or delivered by post may be valid.

(5) Notice once given cannot be withdrawn without the consent of the other party; and this consent to withdrawal may be implied from his doing some act (such as receiving rent for a period after the notice expired) showing that he waived notice.

Their Effect. The tenancy having been ended, it is the tenant's duty to give the landlord complete possession. This he usually does by handing over the keys of the house to the landlord or his agent. The landlord may, in the event of the tenant's failure to deliver possession, either (*a*) re-enter and take possession, *if he can do so without force*, or (*b*) bring an action for ejectment, or (*c*) where the rent does not exceed £20 a year, apply to a magistrate for a warrant directing the police to enter and give the landlord possession.

(Note that an order for ejectment cannot be enforced against a tenant insured under the National Health Insurance Act, 1924, when a doctor certifies that danger to the tenant's life would ensue.)

RENT RESTRICTION

War conditions made necessary various acts restraining landlords from excessive increases in the rents demanded; and,
though the housing shortage has been largely met, restrictions
still apply to the landlord's power. Indeed, until 24th June, 1938,
a County Court has power to refuse or to postpone an application
for possession or for ejectment when (1) it is harsh or oppressive,
or (2) it is likely to cause great hardship to the tenant. That is,
the tenant of a house to which the Acts apply—a *statutory tenant*
he is called—is protected against ejectment so long as he fulfils
the original terms of his tenancy agreement.

Rent restrictions apply, in general, to every dwelling-house
(or part of a house let as a separate dwelling) of which (1) the
standard rent does not exceed £105 a year in London, £90 in
Scotland, £78 elsewhere; (2) neither the *recoverable rent* nor the
rateable value exceeded £45 a year in London and Scotland, or
£35 elsewhere on 1st April, 1931.

The restrictions do not apply (1) to a house completed after
2nd April, 1919, (2) to premises let for business purposes, (3) to
a house let with land, where the value of the land is more than a
quarter of the rateable value of the house, (4) to a house of which
the landlord has come into actual possession since 31st July, 1923,
except houses of which the *recoverable rent* and rateable value
did not in London on 6th April, 1931, exceed £20; in Scotland
on 16th May, 1931, £26; and elsewhere on the 1st April, 1931,
£13, (5) to premises let for the sale of intoxicating liquor.

The *standard rent* is the rental on 3rd August, 1914, or if the
house was first let after 3rd August on the date on which it was
first let.

The *recoverable rent* means the maximum rent permitted.

PERMITTED INCREASES IN RENT

The Acts allow increases in rent in the following circumstances—

(*a*) 8 per cent of the expenditure incurred by the landlord on
improvement *in the structure* (not decoration or repairs). The
tenant can appeal to the County Court if he considers the expenditure unnecessary.

(*b*) Where the landlord pays rates, up to any addition since
3rd August, 1914.

(*c*) 15 per cent of the "net rent," i.e. the "standard rent" less
rates.

(*d*) 25 per cent where the landlord does repairs.

When the tenant sublets, he may charge 10 per cent in addition to the "net rent"; and of this increase the landlord may require half.

One who has paid more rent than the Acts allow may recover any excess paid during the previous six months.

It is illegal for the landlord of premises protected by the Acts to require a premium upon a change of tenancies.

Barrell v. *Fordree* (which in 1932 actually reached the House of Lords) illustrates the kind of contentions that may arise under the protecting Acts. A tenant rented a dwelling-house of six rooms and a scullery at 14s. 4d. a week. She sublet two rooms furnished at £1 a week, three partly furnished at £1 2s. a week, both her under-tenants having exclusive possession. The landlord claimed possession of the sublet rooms. The County Court judge rejected his claim, apparently on the ground that the 1920 Act, though it applied to a "house," did not apply to part of a house. All three of the higher Courts declared him to be wrong, and the landlord recovered possession.

OBTAINING POSSESSION

Where premises are controlled the landlord may obtain possession if the Court thinks it reasonable and is satisfied that suitable alternative accommodation is available for the tenant or if—

(*a*) Any rent lawfully due from the tenant has not been paid, or any other obligation of the tenancy (whether under the contract of tenancy or under the principal Acts), so far as the obligation is consistent with the provisions of the principal Acts, has been broken or not performed;

(*b*) The tenant or any person residing or lodging with him or being his sub-tenant has been guilty of conduct which is a nuisance or annoyance to adjoining occupiers, or has been convicted of using the premises or allowing the premises to be used for an immoral or illegal purpose, or the condition of the dwelling-house has, in the opinion of the Court, deteriorated owing to acts of waste by, or the neglect or default of, the tenant or any such person, and, where such person is a lodger or sub-tenant, the Court is satisfied that the tenant has not, before the making or giving of the order or judgment, taken such steps as he ought reasonably to have taken for the removal of the lodger or sub-tenant;

(*c*) The tenant has given notice to quit, and, in consequence of that notice, the landlord has contracted to sell or let the dwelling-houses or has taken any other steps as a result of which he would, in the opinion of the Court, be seriously prejudiced if he could not obtain possession;

(d) The tenant without the consent of the landlord has at any time after the thirty-first day of July, nineteen hundred and twenty-three, assigned or sublet the whole of the dwelling-house or sublet part of the dwelling-house, the remainder being already sublet;

(e) The dwelling-house consists of or includes premises licensed for the sale of intoxicating liquor not to be consumed on the premises, and the tenant has committed an offence as holder of the licence or has not conducted the business to the satisfaction of the licensing justices or the police authority, or has carried it on in a manner detrimental to the public interest, or the renewal of the licence has for any reason been refused;

(f) The dwelling-house is so overcrowded as to be dangerous or injurious to the health of the inmates, and the Court is satisfied that the overcrowding could have been abated by the removal of any lodger or sub-tenant (not being a parent or child of the tenant) whom it would, having regard to all the circumstances of the case, including the question whether other accommodation is available for him, have been reasonable to remove, and that the tenant has not taken such steps as he ought reasonably to have taken for his removal;

(g) The dwelling-house is reasonably required by the landlord for occupation as a residence for some person engaged in his whole-time employment or in the whole-time employment of some tenant from him or with whom, conditional on housing accommodation being provided, a contract for such employment has been entered into, and either—

(i) The tenant was in the employment of the landlord or a former landlord, and the dwelling-house was let to him in consequence of that employment and he has ceased to be in that employment; or

(ii) The Court is satisfied by a certificate of the county agricultural committee, or where there is no such committee, of the Minister of Agriculture and Fisheries, that the person for whose occupation the dwelling-house is required by the landlord is, or is to be, employed on work necessary for the proper working of an agricultural holding or as an estate workman on the maintenance and repair of the buildings, plant, or equipment, of agricultural holdings comprised in the estate;

(h) The dwelling-house is reasonably required by the landlord (not being a landlord who has become landlord by purchasing the dwelling-house or any interest therein after the eleventh day of July, nineteen hundred and thirty-one) for occupation as a residence for—

    (i) Himself; or

    (ii) Any son or daughter of his over eighteen years of age; or

    (iii) His father or mother;

UNDECONTROLLABLE HOUSES (CLASS C)

Reference has already been made to houses of low rent or rateable value. These are known as "Class C" houses and, under the Rent Restrictions Act of 1933, they are made undecontrollable.

Where, however, the landlord of a Class C house claimed that it was decontrolled before the passing of the 1933 Act he was given three months in which to apply to the local authority for registration of the premises as decontrolled. If he failed to have such premises registered they are undecontrollable.

PREMISES DECONTROLLED

The Rent and Mortgage Interest Restrictions (Amendment) Act, 1933, in addition to many other important changes in the law of rent restriction effected the decontrol of premises of which the recoverable rent or rateable value was more than £35 (in London and Scotland £45). Prior to the passing of this Act houses having a standard rent of £78 or less (£105 in London and £90 in Scotland) were controlled.

Tenants of houses now decontrolled are entitled to retain possession of them until the date specified in a notice served upon them by the landlords. Until this notice is given the old conditions apply. The notice, for the purpose of removing the restriction, must be in writing and should inform the tenant either that he is required to give up possession of the dwelling-house, or that he will be so required unless he makes a new agreement for tenancy with his landlord.

Contrary to the usual regulations in regard to the giving of notice, it is stipulated that the acceptance of rent by the landlord after the date specified in the notice is not to affect the validity of the notice.

Moreover, the notice may contain a statement that, if the

5

tenant retains possession of the dwelling-house after the date without having made an agreement with the landlord, he will be understood to remain on the landlord's terms, these terms being indicated in the notice.

PREVENTION OF EXCESSIVE CHARGES FOR SUBLETTING

There are provisions to prevent a tenant from charging excessively when he lets part of a dwelling-house. Where the Court considers it reasonable to do so, it may give an order for the recovery of a dwelling-house even though the Principal Acts apply to the affected tenant, if he should sublet part of the dwelling-house at more than the recoverable rent of that part.

If such an application for possession is made, and there has neither been an apportionment of standard rent between the dwelling-house and the sublet part, nor a determination of the recoverable rent of the sublet part; then the Court must make such apportionment or determination. This it must do whether or not it grants an order for recovery of possession or ejectment of the tenant.

DEATH OF STATUTORY TENANT

On the death of a statutory tenant the tenancy does not pass to the personal representatives of the tenant as in the case of an ordinary contractual tenancy, but in the event of the tenant dying intestate (i.e. without making a will disposing of the tenancy) his tenancy passes to his widow if she was residing with him at the time of his death or if the tenant leaves no widow, or is a woman the tenancy goes to such member of the tenant's family as has resided with him for six months before his death.

On the death of the person succeeding the statutory tenant in this way the statutory tenancy entirely ceases.

If the tenant attempts to assign his tenancy by will the tenancy does not pass to the person entitled but ceases altogether.

BUSINESS PREMISES

The Landlord and Tenant Act, 1927, encourages the improvement of leased premises by giving the tenant compensation for his improvements when these improvements have materially augmented the value of the holding to the landlord. And, if the tenant's conducting of business has created a goodwill, he either obtains payment for this or a right to obtain a new lease upon the ending of an old one.

The Act does not apply to dwelling-houses nor to agricultural holdings (which are dealt with on similar lines in the Agricultural Holdings Act, 1923). The Act applies to holdings for trade or business; and it provides compensation for improvements, (1) *other than such as the tenant was under contract to effect ;* (2) *effected not less than three years before the end of the tenancy.* It affects all properties, including the properties of the Crown and of the Duchies of Lancaster and Cornwall.

The County Court (or, with the consent of both parties, the High Court) determines questions under the Act when agreement cannot be reached.

Procedure under the Act is as follows— .

1. The tenant serves on his landlord notice of his intention to make an improvement which he adequately specifies.

2. The landlord has a right, within three months, to give notice of objection.

3. The tenant may then apply to the County Court judge, and he, being satisfied on the points below, will give his certificate that the proposed improvement is a proper one : (*a*) the improvement will add to the letting value of the holding; (*b*) it is reasonable and suitable to the character of the holding; (*c*) it will not detract from the value of any other property belonging to the landlord. The judge may modify the plan if he thinks fit, and he must not certify when the landlord shows that he offered to effect the improvement in return for a reasonable increase of rent.

4. When no objection has been lodged, or when the Court has given its certificate, the tenant may effect the improvement, even though it is against a stipulation in his lease. In effect, the Act has introduced into all leases an agreement that the landlord's consent to an improvement is not to be unreasonably withheld; but it is not unreasonable to require payment enough to cover loss that will be caused to other property owned by the landlord.

COMPENSATION FOR IMPROVEMENTS

It is in respect of improvements effected as above that the Act affords compensation. The amount payable will not exceed the value added to the property by the improvement. That is, not the loss to the tenant from being obliged to relinquish his holding, but the gain to the landlord when he seeks to relet, is the measure of the amount. Nor will compensation be payable if the landlord offers (within two months after the tenant has made a claim) a renewal of the lease upon reasonable terms. It is, in fact, the purpose of the Act to enable the tenant to carry on his trade under a new lease.

The claim, both as regards improvements and goodwill, is made in writing, (1) within a month after notice to end tenancy, (2) in tenancies not subject to notice, not more than 36 or less than 12 months before the tenancy ends.

Compensation for goodwill cannot be claimed by professional men, doctors or solicitors or the like; and, when the Court awards a business tenant such compensation, a condition may restrict his competing within a limited area. A goodwill created by the landlord, perhaps through his imposing restrictions upon other tenants, gives rise to no claim for compensation.

PAYMENT OF RATES, Etc.

1. *Landlord's Property Tax* (Income Tax under Schedule A), assessed upon the annual value of the property, is payable *by the owner*. It is, however, for convenience, collected from the occupier; but he may deduct what he pays as property tax from his next payment of rent. A landlord not allowing the deduction is liable to a £50 penalty.

2. *Land Tax*, payable upon freeholds and leaseholds over £1 a year value, is payable *by the tenant*. But, unless there is a specific agreement to the contrary, he may deduct the amount paid from the rent payable.

3. *Tithe Rent Charges* have mostly been redeemed. Where they still remain they are payable *by the landlord*; any contract, made since 26th March, 1891, for placing the burden upon the tenant, is void.

4. *Rates* are payable *by the occupier* (whether owner or tenant). In regard to these the points following merit notice—

(*a*) Rates are not payable on unoccupied premises; and, when there has been a change of occupiers during the period for which rates are levied, the payments are apportioned in accordance with the periods of occupation.

(*b*) The local authority may, if it chooses, require the landlord instead of the occupier to pay the *General Rate* in the cases following—

    (i) Where the rateable value of the premises does not exceed £10.

    (ii) Where the premises are let to weekly or monthly tenants.

    (iii) Where the premises are let in separate apartments.

(iv) Where the rents are payable at any shorter period than quarterly.

The landlord may pass on the charge. Where he does, the receipt for rent must state the amount charged for rates. An owner, paying as above, is entitled to an abatement of from 5 to 15 per cent in accordance with his choice (1) to pay rates whether or not the premises assessed are occupied (15 per cent), (2) to pay rates when premises are occupied ($7\frac{1}{2}$ per cent), (3) to collect rates from occupiers (5 per cent).

5. *Water Rate* is paid *by the tenant*, apart from specific agreement. Whether an agreement exists or not, the water company (or the local authority) may require payment from the occupier. For a house, however, the value of which does not exceed £10 a year, the rate is paid *by the owner*; and the water authority may not cut off the water supply for non-payment. The occupier may be required to pay. If he does, he may deduct the payment from the rent payable.

AN AGREEMENT BETWEEN LANDLORD AND TENANT

(*Note.* This agreement needs a penny stamp if the rent does not exceed £40 a year. In other cases it is stamped according to the rent.)

AGREEMENT FOR RENTING A COTTAGE FOR A YEAR OR LESS

AGREEMENT made the 19th day of April, 1933, between James Henry Montagu of Wandsworth Hall, Balham (hereinafter called the landlord), of the one part, and Thomas Johnson of 13 Willomatt Road, Tooting (hereinafter called the tenant), of the other part. Witnesseth as follows—

(1) The landlord hereby rents to the tenant all that cottage known as Seaview, Worthing, with outbuildings, garden, and premises thereunto belonging for the term of one year commencing from the 1st day of May, 1933, at a rent of fifteen shillings a week, payable in advance, the first payment being made this day the receipt whereof the landlord hereby acknowledges.

(2) The tenant hereby agrees to pay the rent, to keep the internal part of the cottage clean and in sanitary condition, and tenantable repair during the tenancy, accidental damage excepted. To leave the same in such repair and, according to the terms of the tenancy, to allow the landlord to inspect the premises, and not to sublet the cottage or any part thereof without the landlord's consent in writing.

(3) If the tenant shall not pay the said rent when and as it shall become due, or if the tenant without the consent of the landlord shall underlet the said premises or any part of them, or shall use the said cottage as a beer shop, workshop, or place of public sale or public worship, the tenancy shall in any of such events cease, and it shall be lawful for the landlord to re-enter and take full possession of the premises, and to remove the tenant and his family, also all other persons there being and also his and their effects.

(4) The landlord will pay all rates and taxes payable in respect of the premises and keep the external parts of the said cottage in tenantable repair.

(5) Either party may end the tenancy hereby created at any time of the year on giving to the other of them one week's notice in writing for that purpose. Leaving such notice at the said cottage with some adult person therein or if vacant by affixing it to the door thereof or sending it by post to the last known place of abode of the tenant shall be taken as sufficient service thereof.

JAMES HENRY MONTAGU
THOMAS JOHNSON

Signatures of both parties.

[AGREEMENT FOR TENANCY OF HOUSE]

MEMORANDUM OF AGREEMENT

made and entered into this twenty-fourth day of June, One thousand nine hundred and   BETWEEN Arthur Brown of 4 White Street in the City of Sheffield, Tailor, of the one part, and Charles Dawson of 5 Black Street in the same City, Grocer, of the other part.

THE said Arthur Brown hereby agrees to let and the said Charles Dawson hereby agrees to take ALL that messuage and dwelling-house situate and being No. 495 Burngreave Road in the City of Sheffield for the term of Three Years from the date hereof at and under the yearly rent of FORTY POUNDS payable without deduction except on account of the Landlord's property and income tax in equal quarterly payments of Ten pounds on the usual quarter-days the first quarterly payment to be made on the twenty-ninth day of September, One thousand nine hundred and   .

AND the said Charles Dawson doth hereby agree with the said Arthur Brown that he the said Charles Dawson his executors or administrators shall and will from time to time during the period that he or they shall continue to occupy the said premises under this Agreement keep repaired at his or their own expense all the windows doors locks bells and all other fixtures in and belonging to the said premises and all the internal parts thereof and so leave the same at the end of the said term (reasonable wear and tear and accidents by fire flood and tempest only excepted).

AND ALSO that he will not assign or underlet the said premises without the consent in writing of the said Arthur Brown (such consent not to be unreasonably withheld in the case of a respectable and responsible person) nor use the same other than and except as a private dwelling-house.

AND the said Arthur Brown agrees to keep all the external parts of the said premises in good repair.

PROVIDED ALWAYS that the said term hereby agreed to be granted shall cease and determine and the said Arthur Brown his executors administrators or assigns shall have an immediate right of re-entry in case the rent hereby reserved shall (whether it has been demanded or not) be in arrear more than twenty-one days next after any of the said quarter-days on which the said rent is payable or in case the said Charles Dawson his executors or administrators shall after notice refuse to observe and perform the agreements and conditions hereinbefore mentioned or shall assign or underlet the said premises without such licence in writing as aforesaid or in case the said Charles Dawson shall become bankrupt or shall permit any writ of execution to be levied upon his goods.

IN WITNESS whereof the said parties to this agreement hereinbefore mentioned have hereunto set their hands the day and the year above mentioned.

(Signed) ARTHUR BROWN
CHARLES DAWSON

WITNESS—
Joseph Davies,
75 Christ Church Road,
Pitsmoor, Sheffield. *Hosier.*

PERSONAL RIGHTS AND LIABILITIES

RIGHTS RECOGNISED IN LAW

THE law attributes to every man and woman a number of "rights." The number is limited. The tendency is to assume many more rights than are legally enforceable. Many are surprised to learn that the law does not recognise a right to privacy, a right to be protected from ruinous competition, a right to build on one's land as he pleases. Legally protected rights are, however, by no means negligible. Thus, a man has a right to the reputation he has gained by his life and his work. One who, without justification, detracts from this reputation can be sued for slander or libel. A man has a right to the property he has acquired whether by gift or fair bargain. One who transgresses that right can be sued for a trespass. A man has a right to go about his lawful business without being molested. One who interferes without cause can be sued for assault or for false imprisonment. An encroachment on any of the recognised rights is a *tort*, a wrong; and the Court will award the wronged person a sum of money to be paid by the wronger. This award is called "damages."

CONDITIONS FOR OBTAINING DAMAGES

In order to obtain damages a claimant must show that—

(*a*) He has suffered monetary loss through the defendant's act.

(*b*) The act constituted a neglect of the duty owed by the defendant towards the plaintiff.

(*c*) The claimant himself did not contribute towards the damage.

It is the second point that is usually the most difficult to establish. A man is knocked down in the street by a motor-car, and he sustains damage. Now, users of the roads owe a duty to take care towards all other users of the roads, towards pedestrians as well as towards riders. But the burden of proving a failure of duty is upon the claimant; and if there is no reasonable evidence of negligence, it is the duty of the judge to withdraw the case from the jury. The third point, too, introduces a complication: the defence of contributory negligence on the part of the claimant is a frequent one and is sometimes successful.

ABSOLUTE LIABILITY: VICARIOUS LIABILITY

In a very small number of events a man is liable to pay damages, though he has used all possible care. A man is liable for the harm his straying cattle have done, whatever precaution he took to prevent their straying. On the same principle he is liable for the damage done by the escape of anything (water, fire, wild animals) he has brought upon his land; he has brought them there for his own purposes, and he is required to protect his neighbours from the result of his action.

Moreover, one person may be considered answerable for an act, even unauthorised, of another. A master is answerable for the wrongdoings of his servant, when those wrongdoings are done in the course of the servant's employment. A principal is answerable for the wrongs done by his agent, in so far as these wrongs are done in the carrying out of the principal's business. And a husband is in general answerable for the wrongs his wife commits.

" REASONABLE " CONDUCT EXPECTED

It is no answer to a damaged claimant that no harm was intended by the defendant. A person injuring another by doing what the ordinary intelligent man would not do may have to pay damages, even though his intention was harmless. A good intention itself is not a justification of a wrongful act. A man is presumed to intend the natural consequences of his acts. In *Wilkinson* v. *Downton* (Q.B. 1897) the defendant was obliged to pay for the ill effects of a practical joke. He told the plaintiff, falsely, that her husband had broken both legs; she suffered a shock and sued him for the fraud that had caused it; and he pleaded high spirits as his excuse. He had no intention to injure.

But the judge said: "The question is, whether the defendant's act was so plainly calculated to produce some effect of the kind which was produced that an intention to produce it ought to be imputed to the defendant. I think it was." Terror wrongfully induced and inducing physical mischief gives a cause of action.

PUNISHING A PRACTICAL JOKE

Yet a person suffering through a practical joke is not justified in causing excessive harm upon the perpetrator. Violence in self-defence is a battery when it is out of all proportion to the injury suffered or apprehended. As Holt, C. J. said: "Neither ought a man, in case of a small assault, to give a violent or an unsuitable return. But, in such cases, plead what is necessary for a man's defence, and not who struck first. Hitting a man a little blow with a little stick on the shoulder, is not a reason for drawing a sword and cutting and hewing."

NEGLIGENCE

Negligence of the defendant has usually to be established before a plaintiff can recover damages. The term is difficult to define. The one test available is: "What would a prudent and reasonable man have done in the particular circumstances?" It is a question for a jury, the judge submitting it to them when he thinks there is enough evidence to justify the submission. And different juries may give inconsistent answers to the question.

CONTRIBUTORY NEGLIGENCE DEFEATS CLAIM

The difficulty is the greater in that the claimant may at some point leading to the damage have himself been negligent. If such negligence of the plaintiff's has *immediately* contributed to the accident, he cannot recover damages. The question always is: "Whose negligence was the immediate cause of the damage?"

In *Davies* v. *Mann*, the well-known tethered donkey case, the plaintiff recovered damages though he had himself been negligent. He had left his donkey with legs tied in the highway, and the highway is intended for passage only, not for grazing. The defendant carelessly drove his waggon against the donkey and was held liable for its injuries: "Although the ass may have been wrongfully there, still the defendant was bound to go along the road at such a pace as would be likely to prevent mischief. Were this not so, a man might justify the driving over a man lying asleep on a public highway, or the purposely running against a carriage going on the wrong side of the road."

In going about our business we are to *look and listen*: we are not entitled to suppose that everyone else is doing just what he should. We must ourselves be vigilant, and not trust to the vigilance of others. For he who has the *last clear chance* of avoiding an accident is the one liable. The claimant is not to lose his remedy merely because he has been negligent at some stage of the business. He is to lose his remedy if he has been negligent in the final stage and at the decisive point of the event, so that the mischief is immediately due to his own want of care and not the defendant's. If both parties are negligent, any damage suffered lies where it falls; the law declining to shift it from the sufferer to another.

When a defendant asserts "contributory negligence" as his defence, he is required to prove it, just as a plaintiff is required to prove the negligence of the defendant.

CONTRIBUTORY NEGLIGENCE IN THE ADMIRALTY COURT

The Maritime Conventions Act, 1911, Section 1, enacts a different rule when accidents at sea are caused by the negligence of both parties. The Act makes statutory what had long been the custom in the Admiralty Court. The greater the fault, the greater the liability. The Court tries to assess the degree to which each party contributed to the accident, and it apportions the liability in proportion: "Where, by the fault of two or more vessels damage or loss is caused . . . the liability to make good the damage or loss shall be in proportion to the degree in which each vessel was in fault: provided that if it is not possible to establish different degrees of fault, the liability shall be apportioned equally." Away from the Admiralty Court, however, the person damaged gets nothing at all when his opponent establishes contributory negligence.

DAMAGES IN MARITIME CASES

The manner in which damages are apportioned in maritime law was well illustrated in the case of the *Bremen* (1930). Among the "Regulations for Preventing Collisions at Sea" is one that requires a steam vessel, hearing the fog signals of a vessel apparently forward of the beam, to stop her engines and then navigate with care.

The *Bremen*, going down Channel in a dense fog at about four knots' speed, heard the fog whistle of the *British Grenadier*. It appeared to be abeam or a little abaft of it, and after it had been heard several times, the master of the *Bremen* starboarded and put his engines ahead to assist his helm. The *British Grenadier* then came into sight about 100 yards away on the starboard side crossing the bows of the *Bremen* from starboard to port, and the vessels collided.

"I conclude," ran the judgment, "that both vessels are to blame, the *British Grenadier* to the extent of 80 per cent, and the *Bremen* 20 per cent. The real and main cause of the collision was the excessive speed of the *British Grenadier* during the last ten minutes before the collision. Her general navigation could hardly have been worse. The navigation of the *Bremen*, on the other hand, was most careful. She was very unlucky to have met the *British Grenadier*. But I cannot excuse her entirely for her navigation after hearing the fog signals. That the signals keep the same bearing and get louder is clear indication of danger. Right navigation is to wait and see. Stop your engines as soon as you realise that the bearing is not changing. You are not bound to stop under the rules, because the fog signals are not forward of your beam. But prudence dictates stopping as the right manoeuvre."

CONSENT EXCLUDES CIVIL LIABILITY

A person injured by another's act cannot obtain damages when he has, expressly or by implication, assented to the act; a boxer or a football player has no cause of action against his opponent for accidents in the course of the contest. Such a consent does not, indeed, exclude criminal liability: a man may be prosecuted for harming another in a prize-fight, though he could not be sued for damages in a civil action. So far as civil liability is concerned, the maxim holds good, *volenti non fit injuria*, one who has assented to the act of the defendant cannot complain about its results.

Knowledge of a risk is not always to be interpreted as a consent to run the risk. The plaintiff may have no choice between bearing the risk and a greater evil—that of losing his means of living, for instance. In *Yarmouth* v. *France* (Q.B. 1887), the plaintiff was a carter employed by the defendant. The foreman had ordered the carter, in spite of his protests, to drive a horse known by both to be vicious. The plaintiff was injured and was held entitled to damages against the employer.

LAW REGARDS PROXIMATE, NOT REMOTE, CAUSES AND EFFECTS

The law declines, moreover, the attempt to estimate the remote consequences of a wrongful act, just as it declines to trace causes to their beginning. In *Sharp* v. *Powell* (Court of Common Pleas, 1872), the defendant had caused a van to be washed in the street, water had accumulated and had frozen, and plaintiff's horse fell upon the ice. Plaintiff sought unsuccessfully for damages: "The act of the defendant was not the proximate cause of the damage to the plaintiff's horse, or within the ordinary consequences which the defendant may be presumed to have contemplated, or for which he is responsible. There must be some limit to the liability of a man for the consequences of a wrongful act."

So, too, a railway company was held not to be liable to a passenger who, in a crowded compartment, was hustled and robbed by his fellow passengers. The company was perhaps negligent in allowing the carriage to be overcrowded: "It was the duty of the defendants not to allow their carriage to be overcrowded. But then it is necessary to show that the alleged damage was such as would naturally and ordinarily result from such breach of duty. It cannot be considered as the probable and ordinary result of allowing a compartment of a railway carriage to be overcrowded that a passenger should be robbed by his fellow-passengers. The damage alleged is too remote."

PRESUMPTION IS THAT DAMAGE LIES WHERE IT FALLS

In general, the law requires the claimant to show that his claim is justified. Just as our English law makes the generous assumption that a man is innocent until the prosecution proves him to be guilty, so a man is held to be exempt from an obligation to pay damages until a plaintiff makes good a case against him. A man does harm against his will. He is under no legal obligation to excuse himself by proving that the accident could not have been avoided by any care on his part. It is for the injured person to prove the negligence he asserts. I am injured by a motor driver's car. Yet this fact in itself gives me no title to a money compensation. Three questions must be answered affirmatively before such a title is established. Did he owe a duty of care towards me? Did he fail in that duty? Did I, by my failure to be careful, materially contribute to my misfortune? The first question is answered without ado in my favour; I need bring no evidence in regard to that. For one who uses the road owes a duty of care towards the other users, whether they ride or walk. The second question presents more difficulty. By my own evidence or by that of onlookers or by the admissions of the defendant, I must satisfy a jury that the effective cause of the accident was the negligence of the driver.

The burden of proof is upon me. But now comes another and a difficult question, too: was there contributory negligence on my part? My own evidence may already have shown that there was, or the defendant may have witnesses to establish the fact. If he can do so, then, though he was negligent, he escapes liability —legal liability, at any rate.

BURDEN OF PROOF ON CLAIMANT

That a pedestrian has been run down by a motor driver, even

by a careless driver, does not of itself constitute a valid claim for damages. Clearly, the question whether or not there has been contributory negligence serious enough to defeat a claim, bristles with difficulties. How careful must I be when crossing a road in these days of swift-moving traffic? What constitutes the standard of *reasonable care* that every user of the road must observe towards other users? The judge must often feel relieved when he can say to the jury: "Well, members of the jury, it is for you, not me, to say whether the plaintiff, by his failure to take ordinary precautions, helped to bring about this accident. If I should cross Piccadilly Circus with my eyes poring upon a legal treatise I am asking for trouble. The plaintiff must show carelessness on the part of the defendant, and this burden he has, you will agree with me, successfully discharged. But on the evidence brought forward, can you acquit the plaintiff of negligence?"

To be sure, when an accident happens, the plaintiff must have contributed to it in one sense.

If he had not been in the road at that particular time, if he had looked a little longer into a shop window, if he had not accepted his friend's invitation to lunch—a thousand and one possible things present themselves. But in this sense, of course, nothing is an *accident*; provided that we know all that preceded it, we see that the happening was inevitable. The *immediate* cause, or causes, we can, however, usually assign with some degree of sureness, and this is all we want to do when determining who is responsible. Negligence at some stage in the events leading to the accident is not in itself a bar to a claim. So it was held by the House of Lords in an interesting running-down case. The plaintiff might well have shown more care than, in fact, she appeared to have done; but the *proximate* cause of the accident was the negligence of the driver.

QUESTION OF CONTRIBUTORY NEGLIGENCE

The claimant was a shop girl who, on alighting from an east-going tramcar in Glasgow and crossing to the south side of the road, was knocked down and injured by a west-going motor-car. There was no doubt about the excessive speed and the failure to keep an adequate look-out of the motorist; but should not the claimant have looked and waited until the danger was past? The House of Lords decided not; a pedestrian, taking reasonable care, may run some risks without barring a claim. "Did the claimant materially contribute to the accident? No doubt in a sense she did, because if she had not come out into what might be called the danger zone, and had not proceeded to cross the street, she would not have been struck down by the car. She may have been negligent in so doing. But that does not bar her claim if the defendant, by the exercise of reasonable care and skill (which does not mean anything superhuman or exceptional, with all allowance for what is called the agony of the moment) could have avoided her. This is so, even if her negligence continued right up to the moment of impact." (*M'Lean* v. *Bell*, H.L. 1932.)

"THE LAST CLEAR CHANCE"

Who had the best chance of avoiding the accident? Or rather who ought to have had the last chance if he had fulfilled his legal duties? The answer to that question settles responsibility. A man was killed while driving his buggy over a level crossing. He had not looked to see whether an electric car was coming. The driver of the car saw the horses when he was about 400 ft. away from the crossing, and he at once applied his brake. If the brake had been in good order, the car would have stopped before the crossing was reached. The brake was, in fact, defective, and upon this ground the railway company was held liable (*British Columbia Electric Railway Company* v. *Loach*, A.C. 1916).

Perhaps the best statement of the law in these collision cases was made in *Swadling* v. *Cooper* (H.L. 1931). A motor-car and a motor-cycle collided at cross roads, where neither rider could have seen the other in time to avoid the collision. The plaintiff failed to recover damages. For, when the parties became aware of their respective positions, there could have been no time for the defendant to avoid the impact and, the plaintiff being also in fault, the negligence of each party contributed to the collision. The statement is in Lord Hailsham's judgment: "In order to succeed, the plaintiff must establish that the defendant was negligent and that that negligence caused the collision of which he complains. If it is established from his own evidence adduced on behalf of the defendant, that the plaintiff could have avoided the accident by the exercise of reasonable care, then the plaintiff fails, because the injury is due to his own negligence in failing to take reasonable care. If, although the plaintiff was negligent, the defendant could have avoided the collision by the exercise of reasonable care, then it is the defendant's failure to take that reasonable care to which the resulting damage is due, and the plaintiff is entitled to recover."

THE DOCTRINE OF IDENTIFICATION

The contributory negligence that could bar a claim once had a strange extension. An injured person, though not careless himself, might be so identified with another who was careless, that he failed to recover. This doctrine of identification was at the basis of the judgment in *Thorogood* v. *Bryan* (C.B. 1849). In that case a passenger in an omnibus, who had been injured partly by the negligence of the driver of his own omnibus and partly by the negligence of another driver, failed to recover from the owner of the other vehicle. It was said that he was identified with the driver of the omnibus in which he had been travelling. In a later case (*Mills* v. *Armstrong*, H.L. 1888), the House of Lords overruled the unreasonable imputation to the passenger of contributory negligence. "The theory of the identification of the passengers with the driver is a fallacy and a fiction, contrary to sound law and opposed to every principle of justice. The driver is the servant of the owner, not of the passengers. He does not look to them for orders, and they have no right to interfere with his conduct of the vehicle, except perhaps the right of remonstrance when he is doing (or threatens to do) something that is wrong and inconsistent with their safety."

Yet curious results may follow. In *Somerset* v. *London C.C.* (K.B. 1923), the Council had to pay £500 to the wife of a costermonger in these circumstances. The costermonger and his wife had finished their "round" and the husband was urging his horse home so that he might attend a football match. At a crossing there was a collision with an L.C.C. tramcar going to the depot and, it appeared, at more than the ordinary speed. The wife was thrown out; her counsel vividly described her consequent sufferings; an emotional jury, struck by the discrepancy between the litigants—the mighty Corporation against the poor trader—awarded substantial damage. The husband himself could not recover; he was, indeed, mainly to blame. Yet the wife who sat beside him could.

In *Oliver* v. *Birmingham & Midland Omnibus Company* (K.B. 1932), an attempt was made to revive the doctrine, though in a slightly modified form. The infant plaintiff, who was four years old, and his grandfather were crossing a road to board an omnibus. They were walking hand-in-hand when the grandfather suddenly became aware of the approach of the defendant's omnibus and let go the hand of the infant plaintiff. He himself was able to jump back to a place of safety, but the infant plaintiff was struck by the defendant's omnibus and sustained severe injuries. At the trial the judge left two questions to the jury—

1. Was the defendant's driver guilty of negligence?

2. Was the infant plaintiff's grandfather guilty of contributory negligence?

The jury answered both questions in the affirmative, and the judge awarded damages. It was submitted to the judge that the infant plaintiff was so identified with his grandfather, in whose charge he was, as to disentitle him to recover from a person whose negligence had contributed to the accident. The judge, however, expressed the view that the doctrine of identification was no longer part of the law of England. And on appeal this judgment was upheld. "An infant a day old has legal rights, and no one has any right to injure it by his negligence. The County Court judge was, therefore, right in holding that the doctrine laid down in *Thorogood* v. *Bryan* is no longer the law of the country, and in entering judgment for the infant plaintiff. The appeal would be dismissed."

SHIFTING THE BURDEN OF PROOF

Many people consider that in running-down cases, where a pedestrian has been injured by a motor-car, the burden of proof should be shifted. Instead of requiring the plaintiff to prove negligence, the law should require the defendant to prove care. That was the gist of a bill introduced and read in the House of Lords in 1932; the defendant is presumed to be liable until he establishes that he acted as a prudent and sensible man would have acted in the circumstances. The bill did not, however, become an act. The law, therefore, remains, that the injured claimant must prove negligence.

This presumption of liability suggested in the bill is not quite a new thing in our law. Even in criminal law, statute sometimes requires a person charged to assume the burden of proof; he is assumed to be guilty of an offence till he establishes his innocence. One found at night with a burglar's outfit must submit a reasonable explanation of his possession, if he is to escape punishment. So with an accident. The true cause may lie solely within the knowledge of the person who caused it. Indeed, where a person has been killed by a motor-car, the most important witness against the driver has been effectively removed, and, even when death has not ensued, the injured person was probably so bewildered as not to realise what was happening. In such cases, we may say that the accident speaks for itself (*res ipsa loquitur*). Thus, in one case, it was said, "Where the thing is shown to be under the management of the defendant or his servants, and the accident is such as in the ordinary course of things does not happen if those who have the management use proper care, it affords reasonable evidence, in the absence of explanation by the defendant, that the accident arose from want of care." The extension of the idea to motor traffic would mean this. A man takes a car on to the highway under much the same obligations as he takes a dog known to be savage. If harm does occur through the presence of car or dog, he is answerable for the harm unless he can do one of two things. Either he shows that he was exercising all possible care. Or he shows that the injured person had himself conduced materially to the accident; he had teased the dog, or had crossed the road in front of the car despite a policeman's warning.

DUTY TO TAKE CARE

The breach of the defendant's contract with A to use care and skill in the making or repair of an article does not of itself give any case of action to B, when he is injured by reason of the article's proving defective. The exceptions to this general rule are these—

(i) Where an article is dangerous in itself.

(ii) Where an article not in itself dangerous is, in fact, dangerous through some defect known to the maker.

(iii) Where a manufacturer sells his products in such a form as shows that he intends them to reach the ultimate customer in that form. There is no reasonable possibility of intermediate examination, and there is knowledge that the absence of care in the preparation or putting up of the products is likely to result in injury to the consumer's life or property.

In all these cases a duty to take care is owed to the user, even though no contractual relations exist between him and the maker. As regards (i) the maxim, that we are required to use our own so as not to injure another, applies. As regards (ii), knowledge of the danger creates the obligation to warn: to conceal the danger partakes of the nature of fraud. The obligation is similar to the obligation imposed upon the occupiers of land or buildings, that he must have no "concealed traps" whereby one whom he invites or permits on his premises may be injured. As regards (iii) it seems that there should be no diminution of the duty of care merely because the article that did the damage has passed through the hands of a middleman or middlemen. Provided it reaches the consumer in the form it left the maker, the maker's obligation persists. For the ultimate consumer to sue the maker merely short-circuits the series of actions possible based upon contract. The injured consumer could maintain an action against his immediate supplier; that supplier could have sued his, and, so, by a snowball accretion of costs, damages out of all proportion to the actual loss be sought from the maker. To give the person damaged by the negligence right of action against the original supplier would seem to be a much more expeditious and less costly method.

WHAT CONSTITUTES LEGAL "NEGLIGENCE"?

In the now well-known case (*Donoghue* v. *Stevenson*, H.L. 1932), the snail in the ginger-beer bottle case, the question was discussed at length. The law takes cognisance of carelessness only where there is a duty to take care and where failure in that duty has caused damage. In such circumstances, carelessness assumes the legal quality of negligence, and entails the consequences in law of negligence. What, then, are the circumstances which give rise to this duty to take care? In the daily contacts of social and business life human beings are thrown into or place themselves in an infinite variety of relationships with their fellows, and the law can refer only to the standards of the reasonable man in order to determine whether any particular relationship gives rise to a duty to take care as between those who stand in that relationship to each other. The grounds of action may be as various and manifold as human errancy. The conception of legal responsibility may develop in adaptation to altering social conditions and standards. In our own system of law, which has always been averse from fixing itself into rigid codes, the criterion of judgment must adjust and adapt itself to the changing circumstances of life. The categories of negligence are never closed. The cardinal principle of liability is that the party complained of should owe to the party complaining a duty to take care, and that the party complaining should be able to prove that he has suffered damage in consequence of a breach of that duty.

THE MANUFACTURER'S OBLIGATION

Thus, a person who for gain engages in the making of articles of food or drink, intended for consumption by members of the public in the form in which he issues them, is under a duty to take care in the making. He owes that duty to those whom he intends to consume his products. He places himself in a relationship with the potential consumers of his commodities. That relationship, which he assumes and desires for his own ends, imposes upon him a duty to take care to avoid injuring them. A citizen's duty is to carry on his business with as little injury as may be to his fellows; if he turns dangerous or noxious things loose on the world without giving adequate warning, he is responsible for the damage they do.

PERFORMING SERVICES UNASKED

I realise that my action would be of great benefit to my neighbour; I believe that, if he were present, he, too, would realise the benefit and ask me to perform the service. My social duty it is, perhaps, to perform the service, but not my legal duty. If I do perform the service, incurring trouble and possibly expense by doing so, have I a claim for compensation? In all but the rarest cases, no. As so often in this imperfect world of ours, I must be content with the approbation of my own conscience. Virtue must be its own reward. For the view of the law is that, if I choose to give services rather than sell them, I cannot afterwards modify my choice. I cannot impose upon another a duty of payment for services rendered. That other, indeed, may resent my interference with his affairs as being an uncalled for impertinence. A stranger to me is driving away in my neighbour's car. Ought I to prevent what I have reason to believe a theft? How if it should turn out that this driver is not at all a stranger to my neighbour, and sanction of the use of the car has been given? How if my neighbour would have borne with equanimity the theft of the car, and felt a little irritation because my zeal prevented his recourse to the insurers? They would pay; and pay handsomely. At any rate, the rule as regards land services is firmly established, that unless there is an actual request or unless a request can be implied for them, services rendered give no claim for reward. The common, and peculiarly Anglo-Saxon, phrase, "Mind your own business" expresses the independent attitude of our people; and our legal system supports the phrase. I mustn't do harm. But I needn't go out of my way to prevent harm: "Thou shalt not kill, but need'st not strive, officiously to keep alive."

ALTRUISM NOT A LEGAL DUTY

To this rule—that unless an express or implied promise has

been made by the recipient of my benefit, I cannot enforce payment for services rendered—a counterpart exists. The counterpart is this: unless I am promised something for my pains, I am under no legal obligation to render services. I see a dog trampling over the flowers my neighbour prizes so highly. A little trouble on my part would avoid further damage. A social duty rests upon me to take the trouble; but legal duty there is none. Among less self-centred people there would be such a duty, and our position has had—still has—its vigorous critics. One of these was Bentham: "A woman's head-dress catches fire: water is at hand: a man, instead of assisting to quench the fire, looks on, and laughs at it. A drunken man, falling with his face downwards into a puddle, is in danger of suffocation: lifting his head a little on one side would save him: another man sees this and lets him lie. A quantity of gunpowder lies scattered about a room: a man is going into it with a lighted candle: another, knowing this, lets him go in without warning. Who is there that in any of these cases would think punishment misapplied?" Yet the only punishment is the contempt of others. Indeed, it is difficult to see how definite rules could be laid down in the matter; no law could constrain a weak swimmer to venture into a raging sea to save one drowning, though he might well be put under obligation to lift the drunkard out of the puddle. But where draw the line?

RATIFICATION

True, a man having the option of rejecting the services proffered may yet accept them. His promise to pay a reasonable reward may then be implied without great difficulty. In one case it was said: "Money has been expended for the benefit of another person under such circumstances that an option is allowed to him to adopt or decline the benefit. In this case, if he exercises his option to adopt the benefit, he will be liable to repay the money expended. But if he declines the benefit he will not be liable." One cannot force benefits upon another, and then charge him for them. It is true, also, that the person for whose sake the good deed has been performed may, when he learns of it, approve, and thank his benefactor. He ratifies the act. So doing, he becomes liable as principal to indemnify his agent; the convenient fiction is that he had, even before the act, given authority for it. Still, the would-be agent runs the risk that ratification may not follow. Walter accepted (as agent) a bill drawn upon his former partner, thinking to save him expense. For the presenter of the bill informed Walter that it would be protested if not accepted. Walter thereupon accepted the bill as by procuration of the drawee. The drawee on being told expressed regret, refused to pay the bill, and Polhill, into whose hands it had come during the course of business, enforced payment from Walter (*Polhill* v. *Walter*, K.B. 1832). "A stranger," it was said, "who accepts a bill as agent for the drawee on the chance of his ratifying the acceptance acts at his peril."

SALVAGE AT SEA

Unsought services on land give rise to no claim for reward: "An action cannot be maintained for remuneration merely because it may appear to be reasonable." Services rendered at sea, though unsought by him whom they benefit, do often give rise to a claim for reward. The dream of the tramp captain is that he shall come across a rudderless Cunarder in mid-Atlantic and tow her into safety. He would retire from the sea and live upon the salvage earned. He would, it is true, get nothing, except maybe the Royal Society's medal, for saving life at sea; he would get a very substantial reward for saving valuable property at sea. From the earliest days of sea-traffic the law of merchants stimulated the efforts of rescuers by allowing a share in the thing rescued. Why the rescuer on land is not rewarded is not apparent. In one case where a claim was made, it failed; for "there is no case in any English court in which the question of salvage reward has even been entertained unless the subject of the salvage service was a ship, her apparel, or cargo." "At sea," said Lord Justice Bowden, "the maritime law—for the purposes of public policy and for the advantage of trade—imposes in these cases a liability upon the thing saved, a liability which is a special consequence arising out of the character of mercantile enterprises, the nature of sea perils, and the fact that the thing saved was saved under great stress and exceptional circumstances." (*Falcke* v. *Scottish Imperial Insurance Co.*, 1886, Ch.)

REMEDYING LEGAL WRONGS

Legal wrongs (*or torts*) may be redressed in two ways—

1. *By invoking the aid of the Court.* In modern times this is the almost universal remedy.

The Court will (*a*) award damages for a wrong; (*b*) issue an injunction forbidding its continuance; (*c*) order that property wrongfully taken be restored to its rightful possessor.

2. *By self-help.* This is now narrowly restricted.

The modes of self-help still authorised by law are—

(*a*) *Defence of the person against unlawful violence.* But the force used against the offered violence must be no greater than is requisite for the purpose, nor must it be out of proportion to the evil feared. A man is not obliged to adopt an attitude of passive defence against violence; but he is not entitled to kill or do grievous bodily harm to defend himself against a trivial assault.

(*b*) *Prevention of trespass.* The occupier—of land or of building— or another for the occupier, is entitled to use force to prevent a trespasser from entering, or to eject him after he has entered. But the force must be no more than is requisite for the purpose. Nor may force be used until a request has been made to the trespasser to leave, and he has had reasonable time to leave.

(*c*) *Defence and re-taking of personal property.* A man is entitled to defend his personal property, using a reasonable amount of force. He is also entitled to retake it, by force if necessary. In this respect personal property differs from land. The dispossessed owner is forbidden by Act of Parliament—an old Act of Richard II—from using force to take his land; he must have recourse to the Courts.

(*d*) *Abatement of nuisances.* An occupier of land (or one invested with his authority) is entitled to remove things doing injury to his land. He may cut off the branches of a neighbour's tree if they overhang his land. In cases of emergency he may even enter upon his neighbour's land to abate the nuisance. And any person is entitled to remove an obstruction whereby his right of way is impeded.

(*e*) *"Distress damage feasant"* (i.e. a seizing while doing damage). An occupier of land is entitled to impound cattle doing damage to his land, and he may keep them till he has received compensation for the damage done.

(*f*) *"Distress" for non-payment of rent.* (See "Landlord and Tenant".)

TRESPASS

"Trespass" is a term having a very wide sense in law.

There is a trespass when—

1. A defendant *enters*, without actual or implied invitation, upon land or buildings occupied by the plaintiff.

2. A defendant, having licence to enter upon land, *abuses* his privilege. Thus, a public highway is dedicated to the public "for

passing and repassing." If one uses the highway for pasturing cattle, or for interfering with the adjoining land—spying on horses exercising, or frightening game, for instance—he is a trespasser even on the highway.

3. A defendant *remains* on land after his licence to remain has ended. This does not apply to one who holds over after his lease of land or buildings is finished. For trespass can be committed only against the present occupier.

4. A defendant has, without licence, *placed* things—stones, rubbish, cattle, nails—upon land or buildings.

Trespass is possible below the surface, as when the defendant abstracts coal from underneath the plaintiff's land.

So, too, trespass above the soil is possible. It seems that an occupier can cut and remove a telegraph wire, however high it may be, and however little damage he suffers from it. (*Wandsworth Board of Works* v. *United Telephone Co.*, Q.B. 1884.)

Technically, indeed, flying a kite or an aeroplane over land is a trespass ; though there the maxim *de minimis non curat lex* (the law can't concern itself about utter trifles) would bar legal remedy ; and self-help, by removal of the offending thing, is impracticable. (See "Who Owns the Air," page 477.)

NUISANCE

A wrong to property that is not a trespass is a "private nuisance." A private nuisance may be one of two kinds—

1. The defendant has *interfered with the plaintiff's rights over land*. Thus, by an obstruction he has substantially diminished the light falling upon the plaintiff's windows, the plaintiff having had twenty years' continuous enjoyment of the light.

2. The defendant has either *caused* or *allowed harmful things*— smoke, smells, noise, water—to *escape on to another's land. Hoare* v. *McAlphine*, where a brewer obtained damages from a builder, decided that even the escape of vibration (due to the driving in of piles) gives a right of action when the vibration can be shown to cause damage.

To obtain damages for a nuisance, the plaintiff must show that the injury he has suffered is considerable. The "inconvenience is more than fanciful, more than one of mere delicacy or fastidiousness. It is an inconvenience materially interfering with the ordinary physical comfort of human existence; not merely according to elegant or dainty modes and habits of living, but according to plain and sober and simple notions among the

English people." The character of the locality, too, must be considered: "what would be a nuisance in Belgrave Square would not necessarily be so in Bermondsey, and where a locality is devoted to a particular trade or manufacture, judges and juries would be justified in finding that a trade or manufacture, carried on in a recognised manner in that locality, is not a private wrong."

ESCAPE OF HARMFUL THINGS

Am I answerable for damages done when, against my wish, harmful things escape from my land? Yes; if I have myself caused those harmful things to be upon my land. Then I must keep them in at my peril. The liability is a high one; for it exists though I am ignorant of the escape, and though I have taken every reasonable precaution to prevent it. In the leading case (*Rylands* v. *Fletcher*, A.C. 1868) the rule was put thus: "The person whose grass or corn is eaten down by the escaping cattle of his neighbour, or whose mine is flooded by the water from his neighbour's reservoir, or whose habitation is made unhealthy by the fumes and noisome vapours of his neighbour's alkali works, is damnified without any fault of his own. And it seems but reasonable and just that the neighbour who has brought on his own property something that was not naturally there—harmless to others so long as it is confined to his own property, but mischievous if it gets on his neighbour's—should be obliged to make good the damage which ensues if he does not succeed in confining it to his own property."

The law is, however, reasonable. If the plaintiff has caused the escape, he cannot recover damages. If the escape has been caused by a quite unforeseen occurrence, against which no precautions reasonably to be expected would have availed,—by what is called *vis major*, or "Act of God"—the defendant is excused. Moreover, when animals are being driven along the highway, the owner is only answerable for damage arising through his negligence. In *Tillet* v. *Ward* (Q.B. 1882), the plaintiff sued for damages done by the defendant's ox which swerved from the roadway into Tillet's ironmonger's shop. He failed, however: "When a man has placed his catt'e in a field it is his duty to keep them from trespassing; but while he is driving them upon a highway he is not responsible, without proof of negligence, for any injury they may do upon the highway. Moreover, he is not responsible when the injury is done to property adjoining the highway— an exception which is absolutely necessary for the conduct of

the common affairs of life. I see no distinction between an animal
straying on to an unfenced field or into an open shop in a town."

That is, property adjoining a spot on which the public have
a right to carry on traffic must run some risk; it is liable to be
injured by that traffic. The owner of the injured property must
bear his own loss, unless he can establish that some other person
is in fault and liable to make it good. He does not establish this
against a person merely by showing that that person is the owner
of the carriage or ship or animal that did the mischief. There
must also be evidence of negligence. Thus (*Gaylor & Pope* v.
Davies & Son, K.B. 1924), the bolting of a pony, left unattended
in the street, was accepted as evidence of negligence; and, in
the absence of rebutting evidence, the owner of the property was
held entitled to damages.

For the escape of things *naturally* on his land, the owner is
under no liability. Giles sued Walker because thistle seeds in
great quantity invaded the plaintiff's land from the adjoining
and untended land of the defendant. He failed to recover:
"There can be no duty as between adjoining occupiers to cut the
thistles, which are the natural growth of the soil." (*Giles* v.
Walker, Q.B. 1880). True, if the occupier has by his action increased the accumulation—if he has for purposes of sport collected
rabbits or game upon his land—he is liable for damage done to
neighbours' property. And he will be liable if he *causes* the escape
of harmful things: "If any one by an artificial erection on his
own land causes water, even though arising from natural rainfall
only, to pass into his neighbour's land and thus substantially
to interfere with its enjoyment, he will be liable to an action at
the suit of him who is so injured."

RESPONSIBILITY FOR ANOTHER

The actual wrongdoer may not be worth suing. Then the question arises, "Could not a more substantial person be fixed with
liability?" In an increasing number of instances he can. The
most striking extension of this liability for others was effected
by the compulsory insurance clauses of the Road Transport Act.
Before that Act, a pedestrian, injured through the negligent
driving of a motorist, too often found himself without effective
remedy. The law, doubtless, would award damages against the
motorist. But he had no money worth speaking of; and he was
not insured against third party risks. That an insurance company
is now behind every motorist is an immense improvement.

Perhaps the greater readiness to hold an employer answerable for the wrongdoing of his servant must also be looked upon with approval. For it renders the legal remedy worth pursuing in practice. A carter sees a boy touching one of the bags on the cart; he thinks the boy about to steal, and strikes him; injury follows, and the employer is held liable. True, the employer had not authorised the particular act that caused the injury, but he had employed the carter to carry the bags safely, and he was answerable for the manner in which the carter did the work. It would appear that, provided a reasonable person would suppose the act incidental to the employment, the employer has, by implication, sanctioned the act, and is, therefore, answerable for the consequences of it.

RESPONDEAT SUPERIOR (LET THE MASTER ANSWER)

The porter to whom I have entrusted my luggage abstracts one of the suit cases. Is the railway company liable? Must it pay me damages enough to cover my loss? Consider the injustice to the passenger if the company should be able to disclaim liability on the ground that the porter was employed to take care of the passenger's luggage, not to pillage the passenger. To be sure, the erring porter can be sued for conversion. But then, before this can be done, it will be necessary to prosecute him for the crime of stealing. For the act of the porter is both a felony and a tort; it is an offence against the public; it is also a wrong against an individual. And we have this rule in our English law : that, when a wrong is also a felony, then, till the defendant has been prosecuted for the felony, he cannot be summoned for the wrong. The public duty must first be fulfilled of preserving law and order in the State; the injured man must not content himself with the enforcement of his private right. "It is," declared a great judge, "a well-established rule of law that a plaintiff against whom a felony has been committed by the defendant cannot make that felony the foundation of an action unless the defendant has been prosecuted." Even if the passenger could bring his action against the porter, he would most likely gain nothing by it; for a porter is not often found to have a substantial banking account. The law, therefore, makes the company liable. The law does this on the quite sound reasoning that the company, by its choice, assures the passenger that the porter is competent and honest. "The master is responsible for the acts of his servant, and that person is undoubtedly liable who stood in the relation of master to the wrongdoer, he who selected the servant from a knowledge of or belief in his skill and care, who could remove him for misconduct, and whose orders he was bound to receive and obey." *Respondeat superior*, let the master answer.

SCOPE OF EMPLOYMENT

We must not, indeed, press the principle beyond reason. The man who seeks to make me answerable must establish two things; the wrongdoer was my servant at the time of the wrongdoing; the act was done in the course of his employment. I take a taxi to the station, and I may, in fact, give the driver some general directions—that he should lose no time; that he should avoid the main stream of traffic. Yet he is not my servant. He is one with whom I have made a contract. If, in performing that contract, he, by his negligence or want of skill, injures another, I am not answerable. I should, though, be answerable for my chauffeur's negligent driving; I should be answerable even if the negligence occurred when I could not restrain his propensity towards reckless driving, when perhaps he was on his way to meet me at the station. More than that, I should be answerable, though I had forbidden his driving beyond a certain speed. For, undoubtedly, he is my servant, and undoubtedly, too, he was doing what I had engaged him to do. As was decided in a well-known case: "Those instructions, not to perform his duty in a dangerous manner, are immaterial. If disobeyed, the law still casts upon the master a liability for the act of his servant in the course of his employment. The law is not so futile as to allow a master, by giving secret instructions to his servant, to discharge himself from liability." (*Limpus* v. *L.G.O.C.*, Ex., 1862.)

CASES ON THE MARGIN

Whether the wrongdoer was in the course of his employment, is often more difficult to determine. The bus company is certainly liable for whatever damage the negligence of the driver causes while he is actually driving; it is certainly not liable, if the driver, seeing his enemy, alights from his seat and administers a thrashing. Between these two certainties there are degrees of doubt. Thus, in one of two cases where a London bus did damage, the bus company was held liable; in the other, it was held exempt from liability. In *Ricketts* v. *Thomas Tilling*, *Ltd.* (K.B. 1915), the driver allowed the conductor to drive. The conductor's unskilful driving caused damage, and, though the company's rules forbade the driver to delegate his duty, the company was held liable. For the employer has not fulfilled his duty by the issue of sensible instructions; he must also see that those instructions are obeyed. In the other case, also, the conductor negligently drove the bus. The journey had ended; the driver was away; the too officious conductor tried to turn the bus for the return journey. Clearly, the act was not at all incidental to the conductor's work. He had gone outside the scope of his employment, and the company could not be held answerable for an act quite remote from the conductor's duties (*Beard* v. *London General Omnibus Company*). On the other hand, the company would be liable if the conductor had deliberately given me short change, or had carelessly started while I was alighting and caused me to fall. For he is employed to do this particular kind of acts, and the employer is answerable for negligence, fraud, or mistake, in doing them.

LIABILITY FOR ANIMALS

The owner of an animal is, in general, liable for the mischief done by it in either of these two events—

1. The mischief is such as people might expect an animal of that kind to do.

2. The owner knew that the particular animal (though of a species usually harmless) might do such mischief.

Nor does the plaintiff require to prove negligence on the part of the defendant: "A person keeping a mischievous animal with knowledge of its propensities is bound to keep it secure at his peril, and if it does mischief, negligence is presumed." This was said in a case where the plaintiff was bitten by a monkey, and where the defendant unsuccessfully pleaded that he was liable only for lack of taking precautions.

There is nothing wrong in keeping an animal even if naturally wild (*ferae naturae*). "But as soon as the animal has done an injury to any person, then the act of keeping it becomes, as regards that person, an act for which the owner is responsible."

When an animal is domesticated (*mansuetae naturae*), proof must be given that the owner knew of its mischievous tendency before the owner can be made liable. Thus, "the law takes notice that a dog is not of a fierce nature, but rather the contrary." When, therefore, a dog bites a person, damages can be obtained only by showing that the owner knew of the tendency to bite.

Moreover, the harbourer of a savage dog can be sued for damage done by it: "the harbouring of a dog about one's premises, or allowing him to resort there, is a sufficient keeping of the dog to support this form of action. It was the defendant's duty either to have destroyed the dog or to have him sent away, as soon as he found that he was mischievous."

DOMESTIC ANIMALS

The Court of Appeal has decided that the same rule is applicable to a cat. An unsuccessful action was brought by a pigeon owner in the County Court. Now, an appeal from the County Court is possible upon a point of law, not upon a point of fact. The necessary permission to appeal may be conditional upon the appellant's finding security for possible costs he may be required to pay to the respondent. This course was taken in *Buckle* v. *Holmes* (C.A. 1926). The pigeon fancier sought answer to the question whether the owner of a cat is in law answerable for the damage it does when straying. The Court of Appeal said no. The owner of the cat, like the owner of a dog, is not bound to keep the animal from straying. And if, following its ordinary instincts, it does damage while straying, still the owner is not answerable.

The law was thus explained in the Court of Appeal—

"The responsibility of the owners of animals for damage done by them has developed along two main lines, one a branch of the law of trespass, and the other a branch of the law which imposes upon the owner of a dangerous animal or thing a duty to take measures to prevent it from doing damage. With respect to this second branch there are two classes of animals. The first includes animals *ferae naturae*, for example, a tiger or a gorilla. A person who keeps an animal of this class keeps it at his peril. If he loses control of it and it does damage he is responsible. The second class includes dogs, cows, and horses, which are not naturally dangerous to mankind. Of this class individuals may develop dangerous propensities, but unless and until they do so they are not treated as animals which the owner keeps at his peril, and the owner is not responsible for damages which these animals may do when not trespassing. An individual of this class may, however, cease to be one for whose damage its owner is not responsible. If it has given him indications of a vicious or dangerous disposition he keeps it at his peril.

"Generally speaking, the owner of an animal is responsible if it trespasses, but the Common Law in its common sense admits exceptions to this general rule, and among the exceptions to this is the dog. I can see no possible distinction between a dog and a cat."

The Dogs Act, 1906, introduces a modification where cattle are concerned. "Cattle" here include not only cows but horses, sheep, goats, swine. By Section 7 of the Act: "The owner of a dog shall be liable in damages for any injury done to any cattle by that dog, and it shall not be necessary for the person seeking such damages to show a previous mischievous propensity in that dog, or the owner's knowledge of such mischievous propensity, or to show that the injury was attributable to neglect on the part of the owner." The Dogs (Amendment) Act, 1928, extends the liability; the owner is answerable for injuries to poultry (fowls, turkeys, geese, ducks, pigeons). The curious result emerges that human beings are, in respect of attacks by dogs, less protected than "cattle" are.

Possible defences against claims for damages done by animals are—

(a) Contributory negligence on plaintiff's part: he has irritated the animal or loosened it from custody.

(b) The plaintiff was injured (by a bull or a dog, for instance) while trespassing.

(c) The actual injury was of a kind not to be anticipated (e.g. a plaintiff failed in an action where the defendant's dog jumped over a low wall into a garden upon the plaintiff who was digging a well). And in *Heath's Garage, Ltd.* v. *Hodges* (K.B. 1916), where a motor car was upset in daylight by sheep straying on the highway, the damage to the car was held not to be a natural consequence of the straying.

MINISTRY REGULATIONS RELATING TO DOGS

The Ministry of Agriculture and Fisheries issues orders relating to dogs.

An annual licence, costing 7s. 6d. for each dog above the age of six months, is needed to keep dogs, unless kept—

(a) By a blind person for guidance.

(b) For tending sheep and cattle (in this event a certificate of exemption must be obtained from a court of petty sessions).

The penalty for keeping a dog without a licence is £5.

STRAY DOGS

A person taking possession of a stray dog is required (Act of 1928) to return the dog to its owner, or take the dog to the nearest police station. The police officer shall, if the finder wishes to keep the dog, give a certificate containing—

1. A description of the dog.
2. Where it was found.
3. Name and address of finder.

The finder can then take it away. But he must keep it, against possible claims, for at least a month. If the finder does not want it, and the owner does not claim it within seven days, it is sold or destroyed. This happens also when stray dogs are seized by the police.

WRONGS AGAINST PERSONAL SECURITY

At Common Law no damages were awarded in respect of death, though resulting from the wrongdoing of the defendant. For the rule of Common Law is "A personal action dies with the person" (*Actio personalis moritur cum persona*). Unlike a claim arising out of contract, a claim arising out of a wrong could not be pursued if either the wronger or the wronged died. And relatives, who might have suffered loss through the death, were too remote to maintain an action.

DAMAGES FOR CAUSING DEATH

This Common Law rule has been greatly modified.

1. *Judicial decision* has modified it where the wrong is also a breach of contract. Thus, in *Jackson* v. *Watson and Sons* (K.B. 1909), the plaintiff recovered substantial damages for the death of his wife, who had died through eating salmon bought by the plaintiff from the defendant. There was an implied warranty that the salmon was fit for food; the warranty was broken; and the plaintiff had lost through the breach.

2. *Statute* has modified the rule by the Fatal Accidents Act, 1846. This gives to the near relatives of one killed the right to damages when (*a*) the person killed would have been able to claim damages if he had been only injured, (*b*) the relatives can show that the death has meant monetary loss to them.

Further, by the Law Reform (Miscellaneous Provisions) Act, 1934, the common law rule is almost entirely swept away. This Act provides that on the death of any person all causes of action subsisting against or vested in him shall survive against or for the benefit of his estate. The Act does not, however, apply to causes of action for defamation or seduction or for inducing one spouse to leave or remain apart from the other or to certain claims for damages on the ground of adultery.

ASSAULT AND BATTERY AS CIVIL WRONG

A man or woman has a right to go about his or her business without being interfered with. An interference which the law will restrain and, if necessary, penalise, may take the form of *assault* or *battery* or *false* imprisonment. *Assault* includes (1) actions calculated to make a person fear violence to his person: thus, shaking one's fist in anger at a man is an assault; (2) actual striking, sometimes called *battery*.

Both kinds are crimes as well as civil wrongs and, till 1862, a criminal prosecution did not bar a civil action. Now, however, it does when the magistrate, who tries the case and disposes of it summarily, gives a certificate. This is in virtue of Section 45 of Offences Against the Person Act, 1861: the offender is released from all further or other proceedings for the same cause. But this release does not operate to protect the employer of the offender from a civil action. In *Dyer* v. *Munday* (Q.B. 1895) the manager of a hire-purchase business was fined for assaulting a customer, and the Court gave the certificate of exemption. It was held that the employer of the manager was still liable to a civil action for damages.

DAMAGES FOR ASSAULT

A jury in awarding damages for assault may take all manner of circumstances into account whether to mitigate or to aggravate the amount. "I remember," said Mr. Justice Heath in *Merest* v. *Harvey* (1814), "a case where a jury gave £500 damages for merely knocking a man's hat off, and the Court refused a new trial. There was not one country gentleman in a hundred that would have behaved with the laudable and dignified coolness of this plaintiff. It goes to prevent the practice of duelling, if juries are permitted to punish insult by exemplary damages."

PERIOD WITHIN WHICH ACTIONS MUST BE BROUGHT

Actions for assault, false imprisonment, and trespasses to the person, actions for *any* form of injury to the person, must be brought within four years of the cause of action. (Statute of Limitations, 1624.)

WHAT CONSTITUTES ASSAULT OR BATTERY

Accidental touching of another person does not constitute an

6

assault; intention and hostility are present in an assault. More-over, there is no assault when a man uses reasonable force in protection of his person (or that of near relatives) or in expelling a trespasser on his property. Nor, it seems, is a man, threatened with violence, bound to remain passive in defence. He may repel force by aggression, always provided that he does not go beyond what is reasonable: "hitting a man a blow on the shoulder with a little stick is not a reason for him to drive a sword and cut and hew the other." It seems that even a *legal right of precedence* may be thus protected. Such a defence, however, failed in one curious case: in a funeral procession at Plymouth, the wife of a J.P. gently pushed aside the wife of a D.D. The Court declined to settle the delicate point of whether a legal right of precedence had been involved, so that there was technically a "battery."

Further, there is no assault when there is consent; a man en-gaged in a boxing match cannot maintain an action against his opponent. The maxim is *Volenti non fit injuria* (wrong is not done to one who invites it). And the consent may be implied as well as express: to place a boy in a schoolmaster's care is an authorising of reasonable correction. The reasoning is similar to that followed when the question of contributory negligence is considered. Did the injured person by his own action, his own want of care, his own willingness to incur risks, help to bring about the injury of which he complains? "If one goes across a public cricket-ground whilst they are playing there, and the ball being struck chances to hurt him, the person to blame is not the innocent striker of the ball, but he who imprudently sought out the danger." And if one enters into what people call "a battle of flowers," or takes part in a "gala dance," where balloons and similar accessories are much in use, he must be taken to have invited the assaults of his neighbours.

MENTAL SHOCK MAY BE ACTIONABLE

Mental shock, if it causes physical harm, gives a cause of action. To bring about mere mental distress is not, however, actionable: "Mental pain or anxiety the law cannot value and does not pre-tend to redress." *Dulieu* v. *White and Sons* (K.B. 1901) illus-trates this. There damages were received for a shock leading to physical ill: "terror wrongfully induced and inducing physical mischief gives a cause of action. Thus, there are cases where fear of impending danger has induced a passenger to take means of escape which have in the result proved injurious to him. There the carrier has been held liable." *Hambrook* v. *Stokes* (A.C. 1924) carries the principle still further. It decides that fear even for another may produce the shock, and give rise to an action against the person causing the fear.

FALSE IMPRISONMENT

This wrong is committed when one prevents another, without lawful justification, from leaving a place. "False" here means "wrongful." To constitute the wrong the plaintiff must either have been under actual constraint or have been aware that constraint would be used against him if he moved away: "There is an imprisonment in every case where a man is detained forcibly and against his will; whether he be imprisoned in a house or in the open street or elsewhere." No violence is necessary; I may be sued for false imprisonment even if I turn a key in a lock and so confine a person, or if on an unfounded charge I give a person into custody.

"Lawful justification" for an imprisonment has a wider meaning for a constable than for a private person. A constable sued for false imprisonment has a defence, if he can show that there was reasonable suspicion, that the person arrested had committed a felony. He need not show that a felony had actually been committed. To have a valid defence, a private person must show this also.

Action for false imprisonment has been brought against a teacher. But the "keeping-in" of pupils for a short time after a school has closed, as a penalty for some shortcoming, is one of the recognised methods of enforcing discipline in schools. It is a mild method, and inflicts no disgrace on the pupil. However mistaken a teacher may be as to the justice of imposing such a penalty in any particular case, it is not a false imprisonment, unless imposed from malicious motives.

VINDICATING PERSONAL FREEDOM

We should note, however, that the Courts are diligent in upholding personal freedom and, at any rate in time of peace, will severely penalise arbitrary imprisonment, whether by government officials or by private individuals. Moreover, by the writ of *habeas corpus*, there is an effective machinery for securing that anyone detained shall be brought before the Court so that it may be ascertained whether his detention is legal or not.

In 1923, for instance, the Court of Appeal by a unanimous

decision, obtained release of a number of persons interned in the Irish Free State. They had been arrested in England and deported under a regulation believed by the law officers to be still in force, though, in fact, it had been abrogated by the establishment of the Irish Free State. Parliament, indeed, passed an Act giving indemnity to the Home Secretary who had ordered the arrest. At the same time, however, Parliament set up a tribunal to assess damages for the false imprisonment. (*Ex parte* Art O'Brien.)

MALICIOUS PROSECUTION

"Malicious prosecution" is akin to "false imprisonment." The distinction lies in this; the restraint in the first is the *indirect* result of the defendant's action; the restraint in the second is the *direct* result. "The distinction between false imprisonment and malicious prosecution is well illustrated by the case where parties, being before a magistrate, one makes a charge against another, whereupon the magistrate orders the person charged to be taken into custody and detained until the matter can be investigated. The party making the charge is not liable to an action for false imprisonment, because he does not set 'a ministerial' but a 'judicial' officer in motion. The opinion and judgment of a judicial officer are interposed between the charge and the imprisonment."

To recover damages for malicious prosecution, a plaintiff must show: (1) that the defendant charged him with a crime; (2) that the defendant acted maliciously (i.e. under a motive that the law regards as an improper one); (3) that the defendant had no reasonable cause for prosecution; (4) that the proceedings had ended in the plaintiff's acquittal.

We should note, however, that it is to the interest of the community that crime should be prosecuted and punished. The law, therefore, will not lightly find that the wrong of malicious prosecution has been committed.

Thus, the House of Lords decided that, in the absence of proof of wrong motive, the plaintiff could not recover in an action for malicious prosecution (*Abrath* v. *N.E.Rly. Co.*, H.L. 1883). The plaintiff, a doctor, had attended one for injuries sustained, it was alleged, in a collision. The company paid a large sum in compensation, but afterwards, upon information received, prosecuted Dr. Abrath for a conspiracy to defraud. Dr. Abrath was tried and acquitted. He then brought his action, but failed to discharge the heavy burden of proof required from a plaintiff in such an action: "In an action for malicious prosecution, the plaintiff has the burden throughout of establishing that the circumstances of the prosecution were such that a judge can see no reasonable or probable cause for instituting it. It is not true that mere innocence is proof of want of reasonable and probable cause."

An evil motive is an essential ingredient of the wrong. The law might have given redress whenever proceedings against an innocent person are initiated without reasonable and probable cause. For the person proceeded against suffers injury. The law gives no remedy, however, unless malice prompts the prosecution. It does this on the very sound ground that—unless the man acting in good faith is exempt from liability—people would be too much deterred from enforcing the law. This would be to the disadvantage of the public. The prosecutor who really believes in the justice of his action is protected though he causes injury. But, if he abuses his privilege in order to indulge personal spite, he loses the protection: he is liable in damages, not for the malice prompting his act, but for the wrong done in subjecting another to the annoyance, expense, and possible loss of reputation by a causeless prosecution.

PROTECTION OF FREEDOM

The liberty of the subject is implied in these two rules: (*a*) That the subject may say or do what he pleases provided he does not break the law or infringe the legal rights of others; (*b*) That the public authorities (including the Crown) can do nothing except what a rule of a Common Law authorises them to do. The subject, indeed, possesses no guaranteed rights. For Parliament is supreme and may pass what law it chooses. Still, we may say that the liberty of the British subject is protected by—

1. A very great development of the action for trespass. For this see *Huckle* v. *Money*, noted below.

2. By the writ of *habeas corpus*.

3. By the right to have actions affecting Common Law rights and also accusations of serious crime tried by non-professional representatives of public opinion, by a jury that is.

4. By the fact that all persons are equally liable to the jurisdiction of the Courts, and may be made liable for infringement of rights. Some limitations there are on this rule: the king and the judges are totally exempt from process, and public authorities enjoy some amount of protection.

5. By the rule of construction of statutes in favour of non-interference with the rights of the subject.

HUCKLE v. MONEY

How carefully the law defends the liberty of the subject is well illustrated in the famous case of *Huckle* v. *Money* (Court of Common Pleas, 1763), where the illegality of a "general warrant" (one mentioning no name) was established. A person may be arrested; but it must be by a special warrant, duly signed by a justice of the peace, upon complaint against that person himself who is named in the warrant. A general authority to arrest is no authority. As so often the judges, by firmly asserting the principles of the Common Law, protected the ordinary man against the arbitrary acts of the executive. At the trial before the Lord Chief Justice it was proved that the plaintiff was a journeyman printer taken into custody by the defendant (a King's Messenger) upon suspicion of having printed the *North Briton*. The defendant kept him in custody about six hours, but used him civilly by treating him with beef steaks and beer, so that he suffered little or no damages. The defendant attempted to justify under a general warrant of a Secretary of State to apprehend the printers and publishers of the *North Briton*. The jury gave £300 damages.

It was then moved that the verdict might be set aside and a new trial had, as £300 were most outrageous damages. The Court, however, refused a new trial.

The Lord Chief Justice said—

"I shall now state the nature of this case as it appeared upon the evidence at the trial. A warrant was granted by Lord Halifax, Secretary of State, directed to four messengers, to apprehend and seize the printers and publishers of a paper called the *North Briton*, without information or charge laid before Secretary of State previous to the granting thereof, and without naming any persons whatsoever in the warrant. Carrington, the first of the messengers, to whom the warrant was directed, from some private intelligence he had got that Leech was the printer of the *North Briton*, No. 45, directed the defendant to execute the warrant upon the plaintiff (one of Leech's journeymen) and took him into custody about six hours, and during that time treated him well. The personal injury done to him was very small, so that if the jury had been confined by their oath to consider the mere personal injury only, perhaps £20 damages would have been thought damages sufficient. But the small injury done to the plaintiff, or the inconsiderableness of his station and rank in life, did not appear to the jury in that striking light, in which the great point of law touching the liberty of the subject appeared to them at the trial. They saw the magistrate over all the king's subjects, exercising arbitrary power, violating Magna Charta, and attempting to destroy the liberty of the kingdom by insisting upon the legality of this general warrant before them; they heard the king's counsel, and saw the solicitor of the treasury, endeavouring to support and maintain the legality of the warrant in a tyrannical and severe manner. These are the ideas which struck the jury on the trial, and I think they have done right in giving exemplary damages. To enter a man's house by virtue of a nameless warrant in order to procure evidence, is worse than the Spanish Inquisition; a law under which no Englishman would wish to live an hour; it was a most daring public attack made upon the liberty of the subject. I thought that the twenty-ninth chapter of Magna Charta, *Nullus liber homo capiatur vel imprisonetur*, etc., *nisi per legale judicium parum suorum vel per legem terrae*, etc., [let no free man be taken or imprisoned unless by the lawful judgment of his peers or by the law of the land], which is pointed against arbitrary power, was violated, I cannot say what damages I should have given if I had been upon the jury, but I directed and told them they were not bound to any certain damages, against the Solicitor-General's argument. Upon the whole, I am of opinion the damages are not excessive, and that it is very dangerous for the judges to intermeddle in damages for torts. It must be a glaring case indeed of outrageous damages in a tort, and which all mankind at first blush must think so, to induce a court to grant a new trial for excessive damages."

ENTICK v. CARRINGTON

The judges were likewise stalwart defenders of the liberty of the subject when they gave verdict against the executive on the question of search warrants. In *Entick* v. *Carrington* (Court of Common Pleas, 1765), the Lord Chief Justice gave judgment for the plaintiff who had brought an action of trespass against messengers acting under a warrant from a Secretary of State. Under the warrant the messengers had broken into the plaintiff's house, searched his boxes, and carried away papers.

The Lord Chief Justice said—

"The defendants are under a necessity to maintain the legality of the warrant under which they have acted, and to show that the Secretary of State, in the instance now before us, had jurisdiction to seize the plaintiff's papers. If he had no such jurisdiction the law is clear: that the officers are as much responsible for the trespass as their superior. If this point should be determined in favour of the jurisdiction, the secret cabinets and bureaux of every subject in this kingdom will be thrown open to the search and inspection of a messenger, whenever the Secretary of State shall think fit to charge, or even to suspect, a person to be the author, printer, or publisher of a seditious libel.

GENERAL SEARCH WARRANT

"The messenger, under this warrant, is commanded to seize the person described, and to bring him with his papers to be examined before the Secretary of State. In consequence of this, the house must be searched; the locks and doors of every room, box, or trunk must be broken open: all the papers and books without exception, if the warrant be executed according to its tenor, must be seized and carried away; for it is observable that nothing is left either to the discretion or to the humanity of the officer.

"This power so assumed by the Secretary of State is an execution upon all the party's papers, in the first instance. His house is rifled; his most valuable secrets are taken out of his possession, before the paper for which he is charged is found to be criminal by any competent jurisdiction, and before he is convicted either of writing, publishing, or being concerned in it.

"This power, so claimed by the Secretary of State is not supported by one single citation from any law book extant. It is claimed by no other magistrate in the kingdom but himself: the great executive hand of criminal justice, the Lord Chief Justice of the Court of King's Bench, never having assumed this authority.

"The arguments, which the defendants' counsel have thought fit to urge in support of this practice, are of this kind. That such warrants have been issued frequently since the Revolution. They say, too, that they have been executed without resistance upon many printers, booksellers, and authors, who have quietly submitted to the authority. And it is further insisted that this power is essential to government, and the only means of quieting clamours and sedition. These arguments, if they can be called arguments, shall be all taken notice of, because upon this question I am desirous of removing every colour of plausibility.

ARGUMENTS FOR GENERAL WARRANTS EXAMINED

"The great end, for which men entered into society, was to secure their property. That right is preserved sacred and incommunicable in all instances where it has not been taken away or abridged by some public law for the good of the whole. The cases where this right of property is set aside by positive law are various. Distresses, executions, forfeitures, taxes, etc., are all of this description; wherein every man by common consent gives up that right for the sake of justice and the general good. By the laws of England, every invasion of private property, be it ever so minute, is a trespass. No man can set his foot upon my ground without my licence but he is liable to an action, though the damage be nothing.

"The warrant bears a resemblance, as was urged, to the known case of search and seizure for stolen goods.

"I answer, that the difference is apparent. In the one, I am permitted to seize my own goods, which are placed in the hands of a public officer till the felon's conviction shall entitle me to restitution. In the other, the party's own property is seized before and without conviction, and he has no power to reclaim his goods, even after his innocence is cleared by acquittal.

"The case of searching for stolen goods crept into the law by imperceptible practice. It is the only case of the kind that is to be met with. No less a person than my Lord Coke denied its legality, and, therefore, if the two cases resembled each other more than they do, we have no right, without an Act of Parliament, to adopt a new practice in the criminal law, which was never yet allowed from all antiquity.

"Observe, too, the caution with which the law proceeds in this singular case. There must be a full charge upon oath of a theft committed. The owner must swear that the goods are lodged in such a place. He must attend at the execution of the warrant to show them to the officer, who must see that they answer the description. And, lastly, the owner must abide the event at his peril: for if the goods are not found, he is a trespasser; and the officer, being an innocent person, will be always a ready and convenient witness against him.

"What would the Parliament say if the judges should take upon themselves to mould an unlawful power into a convenient authority by new restrictions? That would be not judgment but legislation.

"With respect to the practice itself, if it goes no higher, every lawyer will tell you it is much too modern to be evidence of the Common Law. And if it should be added that these warrants ough⁺ to acquire some strength by the silence of those courts, which have heard them read so often upon returns without censure or animadversion, I am able to borrow my answer to that pretence from the Court of King's Bench, which lately declared with great unanimity in the Case of General Warrants, that as no objection was taken to them upon the returns, and the matter passed *sub silentio*, the precedents were of no weight. I most heartily concur in that opinion, and the reason is more pertinent here, because the Court had no authority in the present case to determine against the seizure of papers which was not before them, whereas in the other they might, if they had thought fit, have declared the warrant void, and discharged the prisoner *ex officio*.

"To search, seize, and carry away all the papers of the subject upon the first warrant: that such a right should have existed from the time whereof the memory of man runneth not to the contrary, and never yet have found a place in any book of law, is incredible. But if so strange a thing could be supposed, I do not see how we could declare the law upon such evidence. But still it is insisted that there has been a general submission and no action brought to try the right.

"I answer, there has been a submission of guilt and poverty to power and the terror of punishment."

PRECAUTIONS OF LAW AGAINST WRONGFUL ARREST

Even when a statutory power to arrest on suspicion has been given (as by Section 66 of Offences Against the Person Act, 1861), this power is carefully guarded. The constable effecting the arrest must have good cause of suspicion, and there must be speedy investigation: "Any constable or peace officer may take into custody, without a warrant, any person whom he shall find lying or loitering in any highway, yard, or other place during the night, and whom he shall have good cause to suspect of having committed or being about to commit any felony, and shall take such person as soon as reasonably may be before a justice, to be dealt with according to law."

It is sufficiently remarkable to note that in our constitution, as distinct from most other constitutions, the freedom of the subject from arbitrary action on the part of the executive is derived from the ordinary law of the land. It does not depend upon formal sanctions.

FRAUDULENT ASSUMPTION OF NAME

Where in making a bargain the personality of one party may be a matter of concern to the other, there the assumption of a false name is a species of fraud. The contract entered upon may, therefore, be avoided by the party deceived. Thus, in *Gordon* v. *Street* (Q.B. 1899) the defendant was induced to borrow money from the plaintiff, who was notorious for the harshness of his dealings with his clients. He had on this occasion assumed the name of Addison. Street was held to be entitled to repudiate the contract.

THE WRONG OF DECEIT

A plaintiff can recover damages for the wrong of deceit (or fraud) when (*a*) the defendant has made a statement either false to his knowledge or recklessly, careless of whether it is false or true, (*b*) the defendant intended the plaintiff to act upon it, (*c*) the plaintiff has acted upon it and has suffered loss in consequence of doing so.

GOOD INTENTION NO EXCUSE

A person is liable for fraudulent misrepresentation, even if his motive is good. A bill had been drawn upon Walter's former partner. The bill was left for acceptance, and when the payee called for it Walter said that the drawee was out of town, and that the bill had better be presented again. The payee refused, and said that he would protest the bill. Thereupon, Walter, wishing to save trouble and expense, accepted the bill *per procuration* of the drawee. He believed, of course, that his action would be adopted by the drawee, would be sanctioned (or ratified). In fact it was not. For the drawee on being told, expressed regret at Walter's action and refused to pay the bill. It seems that he was under no duty to pay.

"If the defendant, when he wrote the acceptance (thereby representing that he had authority from the drawee), knew he had no authority, the representation was untrue to his knowledge, and an action will lie against him by the plaintiff for the damage sustained in consequence. The defendant no doubt believed that the acceptance would be ratified, and the bill paid when due. If he had done no more than make a statement of that belief, he would have been blameless. But, then, the bill would never have circulated as an *accepted* bill." (*Polhill* v. *Walter*, A.C. 1832.)

EFFECT OF "INNOCENT" MISREPRESENTATION

Mere negligence in the making of statements, even though they should prove to be false and cause loss to the plaintiff, is not, however, actionable. Such "innocent misrepresentation" will, it is true, enable the deceived party to cancel a contract made with the misleader, provided that he can restore things to their former state. But it gives rise to no action for deceit. This was laid down by the House of Lords in *Derry* v. *Peek* (1889): "Making a false statement through want of care falls far short of, and is a very different thing from, fraud. Nothing less than fraud will render directors or any other persons liable to an action for deceit." To sustain an action for fraud the false statement must be shown to be made with an actual disregard of truth. Negligence is not enough. A company obtained a special Act authorising it to make and work tramways; with the consent of the Board of Trade the power might be steam power. Consent was expected as a matter of course, and the directors in their prospectus said: "The company has the right to use steam or mechanical motive power instead of horses, and it is fully expected that this will result in a considerable saving in the working expenses." The Board of Trade did not, in fact, give its consent; and ultimately the company was wound up.

Peek, relying as he said upon the statements in the prospectus, invested money in the company and lost it. He sued the directors for deceit; but, though judgment went in his favour at first, the House of Lords decided against him. "An action of deceit differs essentially from one brought to obtain rescission of a contract on the ground of misrepresentation of a material fact. Where rescission is claimed, it is only necessary to prove misrepresentation. Then, however honestly the misrepresentation was made, the contract cannot stand. In an action of deceit, something more must be proved to cast liability on the defendant. There must be proof of fraud. And fraud is proved when it is shown that a false representation has been made (1) knowingly, or (2) without belief in the truth, or (3) recklessly, careless whether it is true or false. Making a false statement through want of care falls far short of, and is a very different thing from, fraud, and the same may be said of a false representation honestly believed, though on insufficient grounds."

(Note that it was this decision that caused Parliament to pass legislation, making more stringent the liability of directors for statements in prospectuses.)

DAMAGE THROUGH MISREPRESENTATION

Where there is no contract, apparently no remedy exists for loss through an innocent misrepresentation.

In *Le Lievre* v. *Gould* (Q.B. 1893), the defendant, a surveyor, had given certificates relating to work done. The certificates were not accurate, the surveyor having been tricked by the builder to whom he gave them. On the faith of these certificates the plaintiffs made advances on mortgage to the builders. The plaintiffs lost money and they sued the surveyor; since it was upon his statements that they had lent. The Court considered, however, that, in the absence of a duty owed by the surveyor to the mortgagees, they could not recover. "No doubt," said the Master of the Rolls, "the defendant did give untrue certificates. It was negligent on his part to do so. But can the plaintiffs rely upon negligence in the absence of fraud? The question of liability for negligence cannot arise at all until it is established that the man who has been negligent owes some duty to the person who seeks to make him liable. What duty is there when there is no relation between the parties by contract? A man is entitled to be as negligent as he pleases towards the whole world if he owes no duty to them." Therefore it was that the injured plaintiffs failed to recover damages in the curious case *Dickson* v. *Reuter's Telegram Co.* (C.A. 1877). The company had, indeed, broken its contract to deliver a telegram correctly; but, since the contract was not made with the plaintiffs, he could not maintain his action.

The plaintiffs were merchants at Valparaiso; the defendants were a telegraph company; the plaintiffs received at Valparaiso a telegraphic message, which they understood, and reasonably understood, to be a direction to ship barley to England. But the message was not, in fact, intended for the plaintiffs. The misdelivery was caused by the negligence of the defendants or their agents. On receiving the telegram, the plaintiffs proceeded to execute the supposed order, and shipped large quantities of barley to England. Owing to a fall in the market for barley, the plaintiffs, by reason of the shipments, sustained a serious loss, and they claimed that the defendants' company should reimburse them for that loss.

INNOCENT MISREPRESENTATION SOMETIMES ACTIONABLE

This rule, that false statements, with an honest belief in

their truth, do not render their makers liable for damage caused, is subject to exceptions—

(*a*) Where there is a contract implying a duty of taking care in making statements.

Thus, in *De la Bere* v. *Pearson* (K.B. 1908), the plaintiff suffered loss through following the advice given to him in a newspaper. It was not disputed that the offer was made and was accepted; but it was contended that the defendant gave no consideration for the service he received. The Court thought, however, that there was consideration for the promise and that, therefore, the plaintiff had a right to compensation for acting on the misleading advice. "The defendants advertised, offering to give advice with reference to investments. The plaintiff asked for the name of a good stockbroker. The questions and answers were, if the defendants chose, to be inserted in their paper as published. Such publication might obviously have a tendency to increase the sale of the defendants' paper. I think that this offer, when accepted, resulted in a contract for good consideration."

(*b*) One who acts as an agent is understood to imply that he has authority from his supposed principal. If he is, in fact, acting without authority he can be sued for a "breach of warranty of authority," and this even if he supposed himself to have the authority.

Wright, land-agent for Gardner, let a farm to Collen on a long lease. Collen entered upon the farm in pursuance of the lease. Gardner, however, refused to execute the lease; and, in fact, Wright, in negotiating it, had exceeded his authority. Collen brought an action for specific performance against Gardner, but, of course, failed when Gardner showed the limitation of his agent's authority. Wright's executors were held liable to recoup Collen for the loss he had sustained in entering on the farm and in bringing his action. "Persons who induce others to act on the supposition that they have authority to enter into a binding contract on behalf of third parties, on it turning out that they have no such authority, may be sued for damages for the breach of an implied warranty of authority " (*Collen* v. *Wright*, Q.B. 1857).

(*c*) The Companies Act, 1929, makes the promoters or directors of a company liable for negligent, misleading statements in a prospectus; this Act incorporates the provisions of the Directors' Liability Act, 1890.

ADOPTION OF NAME

English law is singularly tolerant in regard to the use of names.

A man may call himself by whatever name he pleases. He can even call himself by different names for different purposes. So a woman, without infringing any law, may call herself Miss, though married, or Mrs., though single. It has even been held (by the Court of Appeal, 1908, in *Cowley* v. *Cowley*) that the divorced wife of a peer may retain the title acquired by her through the first marriage. The one limitation on the adoption of a name is that it must not be an instrument of deceit; to assume another's name for the purpose of signing a cheque makes one guilty of forgery; to assume another's name for the purpose of deceiving the public is a species of fraud. The former is punished as a crime. The latter can be prevented by injunction; it may also, in some circumstances, be a crime. There are also now certain statutory requirements regarding the registration of business names.

Thus, the Medical Council brought an information against a bonesetter not registered under the Medical Act, 1858, but who had a name plate, "Prof. A. S. Shakesby, D.O. (Lond.), Bonesetter, Osteopathic Physician and Surgeon." The magistrate dismissed the information, holding that the titles assumed was a mere amplification of the description "bonesetter." The Divisional Court, however, sent the case back to the magistrate with an order to convict, holding that the names assumed suggested qualifications not, in fact, possessed (*Whitwell* v. *Shakesby*, 1932).

CHANGE OF NAME

Difficulties of identification make it highly desirable to ensure publicity when a change of name is contemplated. Often, indeed, the publicity is essential. When a matriculant wishes to proceed to a degree in a name that differs from that upon his birth certificate, the registrar of the university would probably require formal evidence of identification. Advertisement of the intention to change a name may at times suffice: we frequently see such advertisements in *The Times*, particularly when the change of name is accompanied by the announcement that the Home Secretary is being petitioned for letters of naturalisation as British subjects.

CHANGE BY DEED

The usual method of perpetuating the evidence of change, and probably the cheapest in the long run, is this: The person desirous of changing his name declares his intention in a formal document, signed, sealed, and witnessed (a "deed poll" it used to be called, since it had a straight or "polled" edge). He advertises his intention. Then he obtains registration of the deed in the Central Office of the Law Courts. The cost, including the advertisement, the registration charges, and the deed stamp of 10s. would be covered by £5.

To obtain a Royal licence to use a new name is a possible method. The Home Secretary grants the licence upon payment of a stamp duty of £10. If, however, the change is necessitated in order to obtain the benefit of a claim in a will, the testator making the adoption of a new name the condition under which the benefit can be taken, the stamp duty is £50.

The law relating to names was stated very clearly in an action by Jay's, Ltd., where they sought unsuccessfully to restrain two ladies from carrying on a business as "Jays." The first defendant had for many years been manageress of a ladies' outfitters' business, and, though her real name was Mrs. Jacobi, had been known to the staff and the customers as Miss Jay. Her engagement was ended by the liquidation of the company; she opened a new business in partnership, and, after some considerable time, the plaintiffs brought their action.

"Whether they are entitled to any relief at all depends on the answer to the question whether the defendants have done anything calculated to produce the belief in the mind of a reasonable person, that their business is that of, or connected with that of, the plaintiffs.

" In my opinion Mrs. Jacobi has acquired the surname of Jay by reputation, and is entitled to carry on a business under that name if she thinks fit.

"As the owner by reputation of the name of Jay, she has the right to trade under that name, and, so long as she acts honestly, cannot be restrained from so doing, even though the similarity of the name to that of the plaintiffs might occasionally lead to confusion. There is not a line of evidence to show that the defendants have used the name 'Jays' in such a way as to suggest that their goods are the plaintiffs' goods or that their business is one connected with the plaintiffs. The defendants had complied in all respects with the Registration of Business Names Act, 1916, and in the stationery and invoices their names are disclosed under the shortened letters 'AY' in the middle of 'Jays.' The action will be dismissed with costs " (*Jay's, Ltd.* v. *Jacobi*, Ch., 1933).

LIBEL AND SLANDER

DEFAMATION

I HAVE a right to the reputation I have gained by my conduct in life. A false statement against my personal reputation is the wrong of *Defamation*, which may be—

1. *Libel*, when the defamatory statement is in a visible and enduring form—in writing or print or picture.

2. *Slander*, when the defamation is in a passing form—in spoken words, even in gestures or inarticulate sounds when these gestures or sound convey a meaning. "There is a marked distinction between oral and written slander. The latter is premeditated, and shows design; it is more permanent, and calculated to do a much greater injury than slander merely spoken."

LIBEL MAY BE A CRIME

Libel is a wrong: it is also a crime; for it may incite to a breach of the peace. To prosecute a libeller for crime is, indeed, sometimes a more eligible remedy than to sue him for wrong (tort). He may have no money, nor much else. In that event the plaintiff's judgment is worthless; to the wrong of the libel has been added the expense involved in vindicating himself. Or the person wronged may disdain damages or consider them no effective deterrent. Besides, a prosecution for criminal libel is the only way of punishing one who publishes what is truth, but publishes it quite unnecessarily and with the malicious desire to vilify the prosecutor. For to show the truth of the statement is a good defence against a civil claim. To a charge of criminal libel it is no defence to establish the truth of the statement of which complaint is made. He who seeks to justify must also show that the public has an interest in knowing that truth. If spite alone prompts the publication, then "the greater the truth, the greater the libel."

SLANDER A CIVIL WRONG ONLY

Slander is a wrong merely: "hard words break no bones," and do not provoke retaliation, or ought not to. Moreover, the plaintiff need not prove damage in libel; damage is assumed from the nature of the wrong. But, if he is to recover for slander, the plaintiff must show actual ("special") damage, unless the slander imputes that the plaintiff—

1. Has committed a crime punishable by imprisonment.

171

2. Suffers from a contagious disease.

3. Being a woman, is unchaste.

4. Conducts his business or fulfils his office badly.

As regards this it would appear that, to sustain an action, the slander must be clearly in respect of the calling. Some of the cases are rather surprising: a clergyman has failed to obtain redress for the imputation of adultery, and a schoolmistress has been declared incompetent to maintain an action for a charge of prostitution. Yet these imputations were undeniably calculated to injure the success of the plaintiffs in their professions. But not being applicable to their conduct in their professions, no action lay. In *Doyley* v. *Roberts* (Court of Common Pleas, 1837) the plaintiff was an attorney (who studied racing more than law) of whom the defendant said he had been "horsewhipped off the course at Doncaster" for "defrauding his creditors." The jury considered that the words were not spoken of him in his business of an attorney, and, though the words had a tendency to injure him morally and professionally, he failed to recover damages: "The words are abusive but, spoken of an attorney, they do not touch him in his profession, any more than they would touch a person in any other trade or profession." If the phrase used had been "defrauding his clients," that would have been a different matter.

In these four species of slander the damage suffered by the plaintiff is presumed without proof. The "special damage" that the plaintiff must prove is more than mere loss of reputation. It must be the loss of some material advantage; if the plaintiff can show the loss of the voluntary hospitality of friends, that suffices. The damage, moreover, must not be too remote. It is too remote, for instance, when due, not to the original slander, but to the repetition of it by others.

An insult—words and conduct that offend a man's dignity— is no defamation, unless there is also a false statement. Insults are not in themselves likely to diminish the good opinion people have of the plaintiff, as suggestions of crime, dishonesty, cruelty are likely. On the other hand, to impute insanity to a sane man is defamation, even though insanity is a misfortune rather than a fault; to impute insolvency to a solvent trader is defamation, even though the imputation carries no moral censure. For either statement is likely to do material harm to the person defamed.

WHO DECIDES THAT STATEMENTS ARE DEFAMATORY?

A man can, in this country, publish what he pleases; he needs no preliminary licence. That only is what we mean by "freedom of speech." But a man is answerable for what he publishes, and if he should reflect discredit on another—even in ignorance and without intention—he may be made to pay damages. The question whether or not his statement is defamatory is answered by a jury: would the members, as ordinary intelligent citizens, consider the statement—

1. As being applicable to the plaintiff.

2. As being derogatory to his reputation, as tending to bring him into hatred or ridicule or contempt, or as tending to injure him in his office, profession, or trade?

Even statements in fiction writing are defamatory if they satisfy these two requirements: a writer may libel one of whose existence he was unaware. And it seems that the guarding statement made at times—"all the characters in this novel are entirely fictitious and have no reference to any living person" —does not alter the matter. If the jury thinks that readers might reasonably apply defamatory statements to persons living, the writer and the publisher are answerable. So it was decided in the well-known case *Jones* v. *Hulton* (H.L. 1910). By a curious coincidence the writer of a sprightly newspaper article depicting "Gay Life in Ostend" selected a name, *Artemus Jones*, borne by a respectable barrister. Possibly he thought that no one called *Jones* could also be called *Artemus*. The House of Lords decided, however, that if reasonable people, knowing the plaintiff, might think the article applied to him, he was entitled to damages.

The judge, however, must, before he submits the questions to the jury, first decide two questions—

1. Is the statement reasonably capable of bearing the meaning of which the plaintiff complains?

2. Is such a meaning defamatory in law?

For, if I assert that a parson knows no more law than a donkey, I do not defame him: he can be a very good parson, and yet be profoundly ignorant of law. If, however, I assert that a solicitor knows no law, I defame him: he cannot be a good solicitor without considerable knowledge of law. The judge decides the questions of law, before the jury is called upon to decide the questions of fact.

DEFAMATION IS INDEPENDENT OF INTENTION

A racehorse owner was photographed with a lady, and a newspaper, with his sanction, possibly given in jest, published the photograph with an inscription to the effect that the lady was she whom he would shortly marry. He was, in fact, married at the time; and his wife, not unnaturally, objected to the publication. It suggested that, though living with him, she was not his wife. Though the newspaper had throughout acted in good faith, she obtained substantial damages. One of the Law Lords explained the principle—

"Liability for libel does not depend on the intention of the defamer, but on the fact of defamation. If you once reach the conclusion that the published matter amounts to or involves a statement that Mr. C. is an unmarried man, then those persons who knew the circumstances might reasonably consider the statement defamatory of the plaintiff. The statement being capable of a meaning defamatory to the plaintiff, it was for the jury upon the evidence adduced to decide whether the plaintiff had been libelled or not.

"It was said that it would be a great hardship on the defendants if they were made liable in consequence of a statement innocent on its face and published by them in good faith. The answer to this appeal for sympathy seems to be to point out that, in stating to the world that Mr. C. was an unmarried man they, in fact, stated what was false. From a business point of view, no doubt, it may pay them not to spend time or money in making inquiries, or verifying statements before publication, but if they had not made a false statement, they would not now be suffering in damages. They are paying a price for their methods of business."

PUBLICATION OF A LIBEL

There is no wrong for which a plaintiff can take action, until the libel or slander has been made known by the defendant to another person than the plaintiff. (To publish to the prosecutor alone is enough to make a criminal libel, the essence of which is that it tends to a breach of the peace.) Saying or writing the defamatory statement to the plaintiff is not enough; for this will not cause others to think less well of him.

There is no publication when the maker of the defamatory statement communicates it to his wife (or to her husband). The unity of husband and wife is here assumed. There is, however, a publication when the defendant makes known the statement to the wife (or husband) of the plaintiff. To assume the unity of husband and wife for this purpose would afford a most dangerous protection to the makers of defamatory statements.

UNWITTING PUBLICATION MAY BE EXCUSED

Where there is no negligence, the unintentional disseminator of defamatory statements is not answerable. Thus, in *Bottomley* v. *Woolworth & Co.* (K.B. 1932) the defendants successfully pleaded that they had no reason to suspect the presence, in a magazine sold by them, of a libel on the plaintiff. In an earlier case (*Emmens* v. *Pottle*, Q.B. 1865) the point was put thus: "The defendants were innocent carriers of that which they did not know contained libellous matter, and which they had no reason to suppose was likely to contain libellous matter. A newspaper is not like a fire; a man may carry it about without being bound to suppose that it is likely to do an injury. . . . But I by no means intend to say that the vendor of a newspaper will not be responsible for a libel contained in it if he knows, or *ought to know*, that the paper is one which is likely to contain a libel." It may be that a duty lies upon distributing agents to examine some books carefully, because of their titles or their authors. It would be asking too much to go beyond that.

THE PLEA OF JUSTIFICATION

The defendant can escape liability in an action for damages if he proves that his statement is substantially true. A failure in such an attempt may, however, be looked upon as an additional injury for which the plaintiff must be compensated.

Truth is now also a defence in criminal proceedings, if the jury thinks the publication to have been for the public benefit— but not unless.

PRIVILEGE

A defendant may be able to plead *privilege* in regard to a defamatory statement published by him. Though the statement is admittedly defamatory, its maker is for one reason or another protected in making it. In some circumstances it is in the public interest to allow the utmost freedom. There is then an *absolute privilege*. Thus, however false or malicious the statements may be, no action lies when the statements are made—

1. In the course of judicial proceedings (by judge, member of the jury, either party, witness, or advocate). Thus, in the notorious "Baccarat Scandal" case, where the Prince of Wales was called as a witness, we have this from Lord Coleridge, Chief Justice. The plaintiff in the case had brought an action for defamation against defendants who had accused him of cheating at cards—

now, since the Gaming Act of 1845, an indictable misdemeanour. A witness for the defence complained of an unjustifiable attack by the counsel for the plaintiff. The presiding judge, while expressing his sympathy, said: "Counsel must always speak under the sanction and control of their professional duty: there is absolutely no restraint on the language of counsel when it is relevant, and, indeed, it is very doubtful whether there is restraint when the language is not relevant." This absolute privilege has been conceded on the grounds of public policy to ensure freedom of speech where it is essential that freedom of speech should exist, and with the knowledge that the Courts of Justice are presided over by those who from their high character are not likely to abuse the privilege, and who have the power and ought to have the will to check any abuse of it by those who appear before them.

2. In Parliament by a member of either House. (That is why we have the entertaining spectacle of one member, being attacked by another in the House, inviting another "to repeat his remarks outside"—where there is no privilege and when, therefore, an action for defamation might succeed.)

3. By one officer of State to another in the course of his duty.

4. In fair and accurate reports, at the time, of public judicial proceedings (The Law of Libel Amendment Act, 1888, enacts in Section 3: "A fair and accurate report in any newspaper of proceedings publicly heard before any court exercising judicial authority shall, if published contemporaneously with such proceedings, be privileged; provided that nothing in this section shall authorise the publication of any blasphemous or indecent matter").

5. In Parliamentary papers, published by the authority of either House (Parliamentary Papers Act, 1840).

(The first three are Common Law exemptions from liability; the last two are Statutory exemptions.)

QUALIFIED PRIVILEGE

In other circumstances, social interests require that statements *made in good faith* shall not expose their authors to action. There is then a *qualified privilege*, which is lost if the plaintiff can show that the statement is not only false but has been made out of malice. Thus, the "characters" or "testimonials," given by employers enjoy a qualified privilege: if the writer really believes what he states, no action lies against him.

"PUBLICATION" AS APPLIED TO "PRIVILEGED" COMMUNICATIONS

He who makes a privileged statement is not entitled to make it to those having no interest in receiving it: he may not publish a defamatory statement, though privileged, to the world at large. Yet the privilege covers all incidents of the transmission and treatment of that communication which are in accordance with the usual course of business. If third parties—clerks or others— are thereby enabled to obtain knowledge of the defamatory statement, the privilege still remains. In *Lawless* v. *Anglo-Egyptian Cotton Co.* (L.R. 4 Q.B.), the company directors had authorised the printing of a report, containing matter defamatory of the plaintiff, for circulation among the shareholders. Publication to the shareholders was privileged, but did the privilege cover publication to the printer? The Court said it did. For printing of the report was the ordinary and reasonable mode of doing what the occasion entitled the company to do—communicate the report to the shareholders.

In *Minter* v. *Priest* (H.L. 1930) the question of privilege in regard to communications between a solicitor and a prospective client was considered. Such communications are privileged, even if the solicitor does not accept the client. They are protected from disclosure; for they are made for the purpose of giving or receiving professional advice. But they must be, in order to obtain privilege, reasonably relevant to the subject upon which the client seeks advice. A solicitor is not entitled, simply because he is a solicitor and is talking to a client, to defame a third party.

Whether or not the statement enjoys a qualified privilege is a question of law for the judge. Whether there has been malice, so as to destroy the privilege, is a question of fact for the jury. And it seems (*Minter* v. *Priest*, H.L. 1930) that the judge must decide the question of law before he asks the jury to determine the question of fact.

A qualified privilege is enjoyed by—

1. Statements made in fulfilling a social duty (e.g. answering questions about former servants).

2. Statements made to protect an interest (e.g. partners may warn one another against business associates).

3. Fair comment upon matters of public interest (e.g. the writer of a novel or the producer of a play invites criticism).

4. Reports of public proceedings.

" DOMESTIC INQUIRIES "

By these we mean such as are instituted by those in executive control of clubs, trade unions, and other associations. The attitude of the Courts in regard to domestic inquiries is this. The inquiry is conducted by a regularly constituted governing body. This governing body may have an *absolute* power. Such a power may be conferred by Act of Parliament, or it may result from contract, from the terms upon which appointment is offered and accepted. The Courts will interfere with the discretion exercised in such case only when there has been fraud. Probably the Benchers of an Inn of Court have this absolute power over their members.

Usually, however, it is a *judicial* power that is being exercised. Then it is that the Courts will interfere to ensure that the rules of justice are observed. A person is alleged to have transgressed the rules of his association; the question is whether or not he shall be deprived of an office or of an interest in the property administered by the association for the benefit of its members. The Court will not judge the merits of the question as if it were a Court of Appeal. But it will see that the alleged offender has notice of the charge against him, that he has every chance of being heard in his defence, that any rules relating to the proceedings are observed, and that the decision is reached in good faith and with the desire to promote the common good. Nor, if the decisions have been reached in good faith—even though trained judges might have reached a different decision upon the facts—will an action for defamation lie when the decisions are made public. To uphold such an action, would be to bring about an indirect review of the domestic tribunal's inquiries. Publication of the decisions, in the authorized medium of publication, is held to be privileged.

" PRIVILEGED PUBLICATIONS "

The extent to which a qualified privilege protects against an action for libel was considered in the much discussed case of *Chapman* v. *Lord Ellesmere and Others* (C.A. 1932).

The plaintiff was a trainer of horses, the defendants were Stewards of the Jockey Club. *The Times* newspaper was added as a defendant. One of the rules of the Jockey Club is: "The Stewards of the Jockey Club have power at their discretion to grant and withdraw licences to officials, trainers, jockeys, and racecourses; to refuse to allow any person to act or continue to act as an authorized agent; to fix the dates on which all meetings are held; to make inquiries into and deal with any matter relating to racing, and to warn any person off Newmarket Heath; and to advise the public in the Racing Calendar of their decisions respecting any of the above matters."

The Jockey Club, that is, was the properly constituted domestic tribunal to which all the racing fraternity had voluntarily submitted themselves.

A horse named *Don Pat* trained by the plaintiff aroused the suspicions of the Stewards. The horse was examined, the surgeon's report—that the horse must have had a fairly big dose of the stimulant caffein—was carefully considered, the trainer was questioned, and was given every chance of stating his case.

In the event the Stewards issued the following report: "The Stewards satisfied themselves that a drug had been administered to the horse for the purpose of the race in question. They disqualified the horse for the race under the rules and warned C. C. Chapman, the trainer of the horse, off Newmarket Heath." The plaintiff claimed damages alleging that the publication of the statement was defamatory, since, although it was established that he himself was innocent of the doping of the horse, the general public would infer that he was guilty. The defendants pleaded (1) that the words were true in their natural and ordinary meaning; (2) they contended, too, that the natural and ordinary meaning of the words was that the trainer had been warned off for failing in his duty to protect the horse from being doped.

In the lower court the jury awarded heavy damages against the Stewards and against *The Times* on the ground that, from the wording of the announcement, the ordinary reader would assume that the plaintiff had been an actual party to the doping.

" DOMESTIC " TRIBUNAL

But the Court of Appeal decided that the jury's verdict must be set aside. The Appeal Court grounded their decision chiefly upon the reason that the publication of the decision of a domestic tribunal, in the terms in which the tribunal *bona fide* embodied it, in the publication chosen as means of communication between the tribunal and the public interested, is privileged; and since there was no malice established, the privilege had not been destroyed. Nor does it give rise to an action for damages that the outside public may think other than what was intended to be thought: "The domestic tribunal uses terms which are intended to convey the proper meaning to those who understand the terms and have knowledge of the jurisdiction exercised. It does not establish a good cause of action to prove that by some others, outside and beyond, one or other different meanings are placed upon the words for which a responsibility is sought to be charged upon the members of the domestic tribunal." The Stewards of the Jockey Club were, therefore, exempt from liability.

The publication in *The Times* was not, however, privileged. For the statement was made as a fresh item of news; it was not in answer to a widely circulated charge. Since, however, the amounts awarded were excessive, since they showed that the jury must have contemplated that the plaintiff had been deprived of his livelihood—a deprivation due not to the publication of the report but to the withdrawal of the licence—there must be a new trial of the whole of this part of the case.

When an occasion is privileged, whether a person has reasonable grounds for believing the statements he made does not matter. If he does believe, then his privilege is not destroyed. So the Criminal Appeal Court felt obliged to quash a conviction for criminal libel because the Recorder had given a wrong direction to the jury. He had said: "A privileged occasion means an occasion when you are entitled to say what you honestly believe to be true on reasonable grounds, even though it is not true, because you have a social or moral duty to make the communication."

The accused had stated of Mr. X that he had been convicted as a spy and had been sentenced to penal servitude. In fact, it was incumbent upon the prosecution to satisfy the jury not only that the statement was false, but that the accused knew it to be false. If he believed it, whether reasonable or not, that was enough, and apparently he did believe it (*R.* v. *Black*, C.C.A. 1932).

REASON FOR QUALIFIED PRIVILEGE

This qualified privilege has been established so that a desirable social duty may be fearlessly performed; and it needs strong proof of "malice" to defeat the privilege. So, where the point was raised that express malice was shown in that the language of the defamation was excessive the Court of Appeal gave its opinion that: "In order to justify leaving to the jury a case of excessive language as evidence of malice, the language used must be utterly beyond and disproportionate to the facts. The language must not be submitted to too strict a scrutinizing, otherwise the whole value of the law in reference to privilege would be taken away" (*Bentley* v. *Central, Etc.*, C.A. 1920).

Still, moderation is necessary. A privilege does not justify publication in excess of the purpose giving rise to it. A man may in good faith complain of the conduct of a servant to the master of the servant, even though the complaint amounts to defamation; but he is not protected if he published the complaint in a newspaper.

A communication that would be privileged if sent by letter becomes unprivileged if sent through the telegraph office. For it is communicated to all the clerks through whose hands it passes.

"MALICE" MEANS A WRONGFUL MOTIVE

The "malice" that destroys a qualified privilege is simply a motive other than the one recognised by law as a sufficient and proper one for the act in question; it has a sense, therefore, far wider than the ordinary sense of malice. The ordinary sense of malice is ill-will against a person, a spiteful wish to injure him; the legal sense is a wrongful act, done intentionally, without just cause or excuse.

Thus, in *Whistler* v. *Ruskin* (Q.B. 1878), the judge instructed the jury that it is not "Fair Comment" when a critic runs into "reckless attack merely from the love of exercising his power of denunciation;" and the painter was awarded damages (though only a farthing) because the critic described him as "a coxcomb who asks two hundred guineas for flinging a pot of paint in the public's face," the particular picture being an "ill-educated conceit nearly approaching the aspect of wilful imposture."

Even the wish to talk in an interesting way may be "malice." It is when the talk consists of repetition of news that is false, and that does material damage. The statement complained of in *Bromage* v. *Prosser* (K.B. 1825) was, "I've been told that Bromage's bank has stopped payment." The defendant had, in fact, been told that there had been a run on the bank (which was true). He had amplified the report into what was not true, and was held liable to pay damages.

"FAIR COMMENT" IS A GOOD DEFENCE

Where comment is made upon a person, and the commentator can show that the public has an interest to know the comment, and that he has made it with no other motive than to give desirable criticism or to provide entertaining reading, no action lies. The commentator must not state *facts* that are untrue; he must confine himself to opinions which he *bona fide* holds. That others disagree with the opinions is no reason for not publishing them so long as they are honestly held.

Where, as is often the case, statement of fact and opinion are closely combined, a defence will be that: "In so far as the statements complained of are statements of fact, they are true in substance and in fact, and, in so far as they consist of comment, they are fair comment upon a matter of public interest." In *Campbell* v. *Spottiswoode* (Q.B. 1863), where the plaintiff obtained damages against the printer of *The Saturday Review*, the L.C. Justice told the jury that they should find for the defendant if they thought the article complained of fairly criticized, though in a hostile spirit, the scheme publicly put forward by the plaintiff. But they should find for the plaintiff if they thought the article went beyond that, and imputed to the plaintiff base and sordid motives. Further, it was no defence that the writer honestly believed the imputation made to be well founded.

DOES THE ANSWER TO A TRADE INQUIRY ENJOY A QUALIFIED PRIVILEGE?

If a person who is thinking of dealing with another in any matter of business asks a question about his character from some one who has the means of knowledge, it is for the interests of society that the question should be answered, and if answered *bona fide* and without malice, the answer is a privileged communication. A privileged communication is one made in discharge of a duty, legal, moral, or social—either a legal duty or a duty of imperfect obligation. A duty of imperfect obligation attaches on every one to do what is for the good of society. In that sense, it is the duty of those who have knowledge as to persons seeking charitable relief to communicate it, when asked by persons who wish to know whether the applicants are deserving objects.

Thus, the House of Lords (in an appeal by the *London Association for Protection of Trade* against *Greenlands, Ltd.*, 1916) held that the secretary in making inquiries on behalf of a member of the association, and in reporting the result of his inquiries was acting as the confidential agent of the inquiring member. The publication was, therefore, a privileged one. But one judgment contained the warning: "It is right that proper facilities should be given for ascertaining the financial position of traders. But we must remember that private reputations are at stake, and I cannot think that privilege should be allowed unless there is not merely good faith but also real care to make inquiry only in reliable quarters, and to verify it where practicable." That is to say, an answer to a trade inquiry enjoys a privilege. It gives no ground for an action unless the person defamed can show (1) that the answer was misleading, (2) that it was made with a knowledge of its falsity, or so carelessly that such a knowledge must be assumed.

FALSE STATEMENTS, KNOWINGLY MADE, MAY BE ACTIONABLE

Akin to slander and libel is the wrong of false statement which though not defamatory, yet causes loss. If its author knows it to be untrue, and if it produces damage of a kind it is likely to produce, the person harmed by it can recover. In *Ratcliffe* v. *Evans* (C.A. 1892) the defendant published that plaintiff had retired from business. The statement was not true, nor was it published *bona fide*. The plaintiff recovered damages for the decline in his business: "In an action for falsehood producing damage to a man's trade, evidence of a general loss of business is admissible. In this case a falsehood is openly disseminated through the Press—probably read, and possibly acted on, by persons of whom the plaintiff never heard. To refuse to admit such evidence would involve a denial of justice and of redress for the very mischief that was intended."

TRUSTS AND TRUSTEES

THE NATURE OF A TRUST

THE idea of a "trust" seems peculiar to this country. There is, at all events, no corresponding system in Continental countries. Smith owns certain property. He has such confidence in Brown that he gives him control of it, with an obligation, which the Courts of Equity will enforce, that he shall hold it or exercise a power over it for the benefit of another person or persons (of whom Smith may be one), any one of whom may enforce the obligation. This is scarcely a definition. But it is hard to give a clear definition; and it is sufficient to bear in mind this general illustration, remembering that Brown is the trustee and that the person or persons who benefit by the trust are described in law as the beneficiaries or *cestuis que trust*. The property in question is known as the trust property or trust estate, and it is usually in the legal ownership of the trustee, while the *cestui que trust* is only the equitable owner. But the trustee is sometimes (and perhaps better) described as the nominal owner, the *cestui que trust* being the beneficial owner.

Formerly a trust, of real or of personal property, might have been created by word of mouth; but the Law of Property Act, 1925, Section 53, declares that a declaration of trust affecting land must be proved by writing signed by the party who is able to declare the trust, or by his will. It appears, however, that a trust of chattels (i.e. personalty) can still be created by word of mouth, provided that it is not meant to take the place of a will. An assignment of a trust must also be in writing; for by Section 53, sub-sec. 1 (c) "a disposition of an equitable interest or trust must be in writing signed by the person disposing of the same, or by his agent lawfully authorised." A trust which is to take effect on death must, however, be created by will, whatever its nature may be, and the provisions of the Wills Act, 1837, as to execution, signature, and witnesses apply to such a trust.

Three certainties are required for the creation of a trust: The words used must be imperative; the subject-matter of the trust must be certain; the persons intended to benefit must be certain.

DIFFERENT KINDS OF TRUSTS

Trusts may be either (*a*) Express, (*b*) Implied, or (*c*) Constructive.

(*a*) In an express trust there is an express declaration of trust in the instrument creating it, e.g. Smith declares that he holds the trust estate in trust for B, or Smith conveys it to Brown with an express provision that Brown is to hold it on trust for C.

(*b*) A trust may be implied. Thus, in the case just mentioned, C may die, and the trust come to an end. In that case there is an implied trust, which will be enforced in equity, that Brown shall hold the property not for his own benefit but for the benefit of Smith who created the trust, or for his next of kin, in case the *cestui que trust* is dead. If there is no next of kin, the property will go to the Crown as *bona vacantia*, subject to payment of debts. Formerly, the executor of a testator who died without expressly disposing of all his residue was entitled to claim the property not disposed of by the will. But a Statute of 1830 provided that the executor should hold it for the next of kin, and in the absence of any next of kin it goes to the Crown.

(*c*) There are also trusts known to equity as constructive trusts, so called because they arise from construction of equity and not from any trust instrument. The most common instance arises upon a contract for the sale of land or houses. Here the vendor has a lien on the property in equity until the price is paid. Even if he has conveyed the property to the purchaser the purchaser is a constructive trustee to the vendor.

Trusts are sometimes divided into *public* and *private* trusts, the former being charitable trusts and the latter the ordinary trusts which arise in private family life.

Public or charitable trusts, i.e. trusts for public charitable objects, are outside the scope of this book. It is sufficient to say that a charitable trust never fails; for if the particular charitable object fails it will be applied by the court *cy-près*, i.e. "as nearly as possible" to benefit a charitable object resembling nearly the original object. Charities, too, are exempt from the rule against perpetuities. The property can be devoted to a charity *for ever*, unlike private trusts in which the property must vest in some person absolutely within a life or lives in being and twenty-one years after the end of such life or lives. If not, a private trust is said to offend against the rule forbidding a perpetuity.

Another classification of trusts divides them into *executed* trusts, which are so called when the trust instrument itself states clearly the term of the trust, and *executory* trusts, when another instrument has to be executed at some future time defining the terms of the trust with greater precision. Sometimes the term "Precatory" trust is used in legal documents, and such a trust arises when the person creating the trust uses words of request or desire that property shall be applied for the benefit of a third person. These precatory words will not always be enforced in the Courts, being nothing more than an expression of hope. But when they are strong enough to be enforced they constitute a precatory trust, which is enforceable like any other trust.

Trusts are described in law as equitable obligations. That is to say they can be enforced in a Court of Equity acting as a Court of Conscience. The Common Law Courts refused to recognise trusts, and so they became the special province of the Court of Chancery. In 1875, however, the Judicature Act, which then became law, had the effect of fusing Common Law and Equity; and, although trusts are still administered in the Chancery Division of the High Court and not in the King's Bench (or Common Law) Division, equitable relief and with it the enforcement of a trust can now be obtained in any Court, whether King's Bench or Chancery. The same applies in the County Court. But the common lawyer will always admit that his knowledge of trusts is not equal to that of an equity lawyer, and actions connected with trusts are brought on the Chancery side of the High Court.

THE TRUSTEE ACT, 1925

The Act which at present governs the law relating to trusts is the Trustee Act, 1925. This consolidates the previous law on the subject and repeals the Trustee Act, 1893, which was the chief statute then in force. The Act of 1925 deals (Part I) with the investments which are open to trustees and defines them: (Part II) with the general powers of trustees and personal representatives: (Part III) with the appointment and discharge of trustees. Finally (Part IV) deals with the powers of the Court over trustees; for, in several matters, as, for instance, in the appointment of new trustees where there are no powers in the trust instrument in the right of trustees to pay money into Court, and so free themselves from liability for trust moneys, etc., the Court exercises a fatherly control over trusts and trustees. A large part of the work of the trustees in Chancery and indeed of the judges consists in superintending trusts and deciding questions relating to them.

APPOINTMENT OF TRUSTEES

Any one of full age is capable of acting as trustee, including a married woman or a corporation. Indeed, the appointment of a trust corporation is encouraged by the Trustee Act, 1925, which defines such a corporation as including the Public Trustee or a corporation appointed by the Court to be trustee in a particular case, or entitled by the rules of the Trustee Act, 1906, to act as custodian trustee.

Difficulties arise in some cases where a corporation is not entitled to hold land, and, where the trust property consists of land; but the Companies Act, 1929, Section 14, now enables a company registered under that Act to hold lands without licence. The Public Trustee Act, 1906, provides for the appointment of the Public Trustee as "custodian trustee" with another, and this is often a convenient way for insuring the continuity of the trust and the safety and stability of the trust investments. An infant cannot now act as trustee, and such an appointment would be void, with the result that a new trustee would have to be appointed to fill the vacancy: Law of Property Act, 1925, Section 20.

If the legal estate is conveyed to an infant jointly with other persons of full age upon trust, the conveyance operates to vest the legal estate in the other person only. A conveyance to an infant alone upon trust does not convey the legal estate at all and is void.

If a trustee becomes a lunatic, the committee or receiver of his estate can convey the property in his name or on his behalf. If land is held on trust for sale and one of the trustees is a lunatic, a new trustee should be appointed and the lunatic trustee will be thereby discharged.

The usual course in making the appointment is for the person who creates the trust and settles the property whether real or personal to appoint the trustees. If he fails to do so, the beneficiaries if they are all *sui juris* (having full legal rights) may appoint, or the appointment may be made by the Court on application by one of the parties interested.

But Section 36 of the Trustee Act, 1925, contains elaborate provisions for the appointment of new or additional trustees in certain cases.

These are as follows—

1. Where a trustee is dead.

2. Where he remains out of the Kingdom for more than 12 months.

7

3. Where he desires to be discharged from the trusts.

4. Where he refuses or is unfit to act, or is incapable of acting.

5. Where he is an infant.

In the above cases, the persons nominated for the purpose in the instrument creating the trust can appoint; or, if there is no such person, then the surviving trustees or trustee for the time being or the personal representatives of the remaining trustee, may by writing appoint a trustee to act in place of the dead or retiring trustee.

Where a trustee has been removed under power in the instrument, a new trustee may be appointed in his place, as if he were dead, or in the case of a corporation, as if he were discharged. Where a sole trustee (not a corporation) is appointed and there are not more than three trustees, the persons nominated in the instrument or, if there are no such persons, then the trustees for the time being may by writing appoint additional trustees. But this is not obligatory unless the instrument itself so provides, and the number of trustees is not to be increased beyond four.

A few points laid down in the Trustee Act, 1925, as to new trustees are worthy of mention in addition to the above—

1. Subject to the restrictions laid down by the Act, the number of trustees may always be increased: Section 37, subsection 1 (*b*).

2. Where there are distinct trusts in the same settlement, separate trustees may be appointed to manage any particular trust, without the other trusts in the settlement being affected: Section 37, subsection 1 (*c*).

3. Where only one trustee was originally appointed, it is not necessary to appoint more than one. If there were more than two trustees originally, the original number need not be filled up, but, except in those cases where only one trustee was originally appointed, who is able to give receipts for capital moneys, a trustee will not be discharged from his trust unless there remain either a trust corporation or at least two individuals to act as trustees and perform the trust: Section 37, subsection 3.

4. Where a new trustee is appointed to take the place of an existing trustee who retires, the deed by which he is appointed should state the reason for the retirement and that statement will be conclusive. The deed should also vest the property in the new trustee: Section 40.

5. When a trustee desires to be discharged, and a trust corporation or at least two individuals are left to perform the trust, it is not necessary to appoint a new trustee. The retiring trustee

should execute a deed expressing his wish to retire, and the co-trustees, together with the person empowered to appoint new trustees, should express their consent to his discharge, and to the vesting of the trust property in the remaining trustees: Section 39.

6. After the passing of the Trustee Act, 1925, a deed which does not contain a declaration vesting the property, will have the same effect as if it contained such a declaration: Section 40, subsection 3.

The above provisions, however, do not extend to—

(a) A mortgage of land for securing money subject to the trust, except debentures or debenture stock.

(b) Land held on lease with a covenant against assignment without consent, unless the necessary consent has been obtained.

(c) Stock, etc., transferable only in books kept by a Company or in manner directed by Act of Parliament; Section 40, subsection 4.

NUMBER OF TRUSTEES

In the case of settlements of *land*, the number of trustees is not to be more than four. Where the trust deed provides for more than four, the four first named, alone, are trustees. The others do not become so unless appointed on the occurrence of a vacancy: Section 34. This section does not apply to settlements of land for charitable, ecclesiastical, or public purposes, or where land is to be sold for like purposes.

THE PUBLIC TRUSTEE

The Public Trustee Act, 1906, enables the Court on application by the trustee or beneficiary in a will or settlement to appoint the Public Trustee to be a new or additional trustee even though the trust instrument contains a direction to the contrary. But, apart from this, any one can appoint the Public Trustee to act either alone or in conjunction with others, either as a new or additional trustee. The advantages of appointing him as trustee are that, being a "corporation," he never dies, and that it is not necessary to appoint new trustees from time to time. Also, the State is responsible for any loss to the trust estate arising from a breach of trust on his part. He may be called upon to act either as an ordinary trustee or as "custodian trustee." In this latter capacity, the trust property will be transferred to him as if he were sole trustee and all the securities and documents of title connected with the trust remain in his sole custody. All sums payable out of income are paid to or by him, except that he may allow dividends, etc., to be paid to the other trustees ("managing trustees"). The management of the trust is thus vested in the "managing trustees," but the concurrence of the Public Trustee is necessary to give them access to securities and documents.

Insurance companies, guarantee companies, and banks also act as custodian trustees. As regards the expenses of the trust, it should be realised that the ordinary trustee, in the absence of express power in the trust deed, cannot charge for his services. But he can employ a solicitor who will charge the usual professional fees for conducting correspondence, altering trust investments, or appointing new trustees. The Public Trustee and also banks and other trustee companies, have a regular scale of charges, consisting of an annual percentage upon income, and a lump sum based on capital for change in trust investments. Whatever plan is adopted, the creation and execution of a trust is not without expense, and this should be considered carefully in the first instance.

DUTIES OF TRUSTEE

The trustee, upon taking up his office, should find out exactly what are the terms of the trust which he is undertaking and of what the trust property consists. For this purpose he should look at the deeds and other documents relating to the trust property. He should see that any trust property which is outstanding is got in, and should recover all debts and funds due to the estate. If necessary, he may have to institute legal proceedings or defend actions in respect of the trust property. But where action would be useless, owing to the insolvency of the proposed defendant, he is not required to take proceedings.

He must carry out the terms of the trust, and, if it is necessary for him to deviate in any way, he should obtain the consent of all the beneficiaries if they are *sui juris*. If there are infant beneficiaries or if infant beneficiaries are likely to come into being in the future who will be prejudiced by his act, it may be necessary for him to obtain the leave of the Court, which he does by a summons in the Chancery Division.

The standard of care which is required of a trustee is that of the ordinary prudent man of business. It is the standard which such a man would adopt in the conduct of his own affairs. In cases of doubt he may take legal advice and if it is reasonable advice he may act on it with the knowledge that it will relieve him from responsibility. But, where the amount involved is considerable and the doubt is serious, he should obtain the opinion of the Court. It is always possible to obtain the opinion of the Court upon the construction of a clause in a trust deed or in a will, by an originating summons in Chancery, upon which the matter will be decided in Court, and the decision will relieve the trustee from any liability for his action.

It is an old maxim that a trustee is not entitled to make any profit or advantage out of the trust; and this rule is rigorously enforced. Indeed, the trustee may not enter into any personal engagements in which his own interest would conflict with the interests of the beneficiaries under the trust.

A trustee, although he can take legal advice, cannot escape responsibility by leaving it to another person entirely to carry out the trust. He must make up his own mind and act accordingly. He cannot be heard to say that he left matters to his co-trustee except so far as is allowed by the Trustee Act. The power to employ agents, however, is given by Section 23 of the Act. This section provides that instead of acting personally, the trustee may employ and pay an agent, whether a solicitor, banker, stockbroker, or other persons to transact any business or do any act required in the execution of the trust, including the receipt and payment of money. He is entitled to be allowed and paid all charges and expenses so incurred, and is not responsible for the default of the agent if he employs him in good faith. Trustees may (by the same section) appoint a person to act as agent or attorney in selling, collecting property, or in executing insurances, or otherwise administering the property or exercising their powers, and they may appoint substitutes and are not by reason only of their appointment liable for any loss arising thereby.

A trustee may also appoint a solicitor to receive and give a discharge for money or property receivable under the trust, by permitting him to have custody of and to produce a deed having upon it a receipt for such money or property, the deed being executed, or the endorsed receipt being signed by the person entitled to give a receipt for that consideration. A trustee is not chargeable with breach of trust by reason only of having made or concurred in making such appointment, and the production of the deed by the solicitor has the same statutory validity as if the person appointing him had not been a trustee. The section also enables the trustee to appoint a banker or solicitor to be his agent to receive and give a discharge for money payable to the trustee under a policy of insurance. He may permit the banker or solicitor to have custody of and produce the insurance policy with a receipt signed by the trustee, and the trustee is not liable for breach of trust by reason only of having made the appointment. But the trustee must not allow the money or property to remain in the agent's possession longer than is reasonably necessary to enable him to pay it over to the trustee.

MAINTENANCE AND ADVANCEMENT OF INFANTS

Difficulties often arise in connection with trusts where some of the beneficiaries are infants, and have to be maintained or educated. In these cases the Act (Section 31) provides that trustees may pay out to the parent or guardian the income of the property forming the subject of the trust to which the infant would be entitled, if of age. This may be done whether there is any other fund available or not, and whether there is any obligation to provide for maintenance or education or not. After the infant reaches the age of 21 years, if he is still not entitled to the capital, the trustees may continue the payments until the infant attains a vested interest or dies, or until failure of the interest. Regard must be had to the age of the infant and his requirements generally, and to what other income is available. During infancy the residue of the income must be invested, and the proceeds accumulated with compound interest until the infant reaches 21 years or marries.

These accumulations are to be held for such person absolutely, without prejudice to any marriage settlement entered into by him. In any other case, the accumulations are to be held as an accretion to capital. The trustees may apply the accumulations during infancy at any time as if they were interest for the current year. These provisions apply to interest arising after 1st January, 1926. The Act (Section 32) also enables trustees to apply capital moneys for the advancement and benefit of any person entitled to the capital absolutely or contingently on his attaining a specified age. This power extends to one-half the person's interest in the trust property. Upon his becoming indefeasibly entitled, the money so advanced must be brought into account. Such payments must not be allowed to prejudice persons entitled to a prior life interest or other interest whether vested or contingent. This provision only applies to trusts created after 1st January, 1926, and does not apply to capital money for the purpose of the Settled Land Act, 1925.

LIABILITY FOR BREACH OF TRUST

The office of trustee is a somewhat thankless one—the trustee is often asked to do what he is not legally entitled to do, in the interest or supposed interest of some of the beneficiaries. His best course is then to get a legal opinion on the question from some barrister or solicitor and send a copy of it to the unfortunate beneficiary, at the same time expressing the trustee's regrets that he is unable, owing to the legal aspect of the case, to carry out the proposal. There is no greater mistake than to yield in the hope of preserving friendly relations with the beneficiary. Time passes quickly, and in the course of years another beneficiary will fasten on to his conduct, if he gives way, as a breach of trust, which may have expensive and unfortunate consequences for the trustee. At the same time, the trustee is now protected by statute from the consequences of a breach of trust, as to which he can plead that he was not guilty of any personal neglect or default. Under the Trustee Act, 1925, Section 30, a trustee is only liable for money and securities actually received by him. Even if he has signed a receipt for the sake of conformity, provided that he has not committed any act or default, he is not answerable for the acts or defaults of a co-trustee or of a banker, broker, or other person with whom trust money or securities have been deposited. If there is an insufficiency or deficiency of securities or any other loss, he is still only responsible for loss occurring through his own wilful default. This is not a new principle established by the Act of 1925; it has always been the rule in equity, but it is now also a provision of statute. The trustee must not, however, improperly allow his co-trustee to receive the trust property or to have sole control over it, as this will constitute a neglect of duty for which he may very likely be held liable. He must not appoint agents otherwise than is allowed by the Act (see "Duties of Trustee," p. 190) or leave the trust property in their control, nor above all must he invest in improper securities (see "Trust Investments," p. 194). In such cases, if he is at fault, his only hope is that there may be a clause in the trust deed which will exempt him from liability for the breach of trust. Some inconsistency may appear to exist between the effect of Section 30 (above) and the rule that the trustee must not leave the property in the hands of his co-trustee. The answer is that it is a question of time. The trustee may join in a receipt for money which is paid to his co-trustee, but he must not allow the money *to remain* in the hands of his co-trustee for longer than is absolutely necessary. The money must be paid into an account at the bank in their joint names or otherwise applied to the purpose for which it was intended.

An executor trustee is in a somewhat better position as regards his co-executor. Each executor has legally complete control over the testator's property so there is no need for a co-executor to join in a receipt in order to give a discharge to the debtor. If, therefore, a co-executor is asked to join in a receipt there is no need for him to do so and when the money is paid over to the joint control he can refuse. On the other hand, the joining in a receipt by a co-executor is strong evidence that he has actually received the money in addition to his co-executor. It is not ordinarily so in the case of a trustee who signs merely for conformity with his co-trustee.

Where two or more trustees have committed a breach of trust, each of them is liable for the whole amount of the loss, and judgment may be executed against any one of them for the whole amount. But, as between themselves, there is a right of contribution. That is to say, if A and B are trustees and A pays more than his share of the liability he can claim contribution from B, so that as between themselves each pays the same amount. There are three cases in which one trustee must indemnify the others, namely—

1. If one trustee has received the trust money and misappropriated it or is otherwise alone morally guilty.

2. If one of the trustees has acted as solicitor to the trust and the breach of trust was committed on advice.

3. Where one of the trustees is a beneficiary the breach of trust will be made good out of his beneficial interest, and to that extent he must indemnify his co-trustee.

The measure of liability for a breach of trust is the actual loss to the trust estate. But where the trustee has improperly advanced too large a sum upon mortgage so that the margin of security is too small, the security is deemed to be an authorised investment up to the statutory limit and the trustee is only liable to make good the sum advanced in excess of his limit, with interest. Trustee Act, 1925, Section 9.

TRUST INVESTMENTS

Trustees should not allow the trust funds to remain idle, but should invest them as soon as possible in one or other of the authorised investments. The investments open to the trustee are declared in the trust instrument. For this purpose the person creating the trust usually confines himself to directing "the usual trust investments" or the "investments allowed by the Trustee Act, 1925." But he may not be satisfied with these or may desire to give a wider range, so as to include (for instance) "the preference stock or shares of any company in the United Kingdom." Or he may give power to the trustees to retain existing investments, which means that the trustee may at his discretion so retain them, but, if he sells out, he must invest the proceeds in the recognised trust securities. These are defined by the Trustee Act, 1925, Section 1, as follows—

(*a*) Parliamentary stocks or public funds or Government securities of the United Kingdom.

(*b*) Real securities in the United Kingdom.

(*c*) Stock of the Bank of England or the Bank of Ireland.

(*d*) India Stocks.

(*e*) Securities, the interest of which is guaranteed by Parliament.

(*f*) Metropolitan Board of Works Stock, London County Council Stock, or Metropolitan Water Stock.

(*g*) Debenture, rent charge, guaranteed or preference stock of any railway company in the United Kingdom, which has paid not less than 3 per cent on its ordinary stock for the past ten years.

(*h*) Railway or canal stock where the undertaking is leased for 200 years at a fixed rental to railways as in (*g*).

(*i*) Debenture stock of Indian Railway Companies whose interest is paid or guaranteed by the Secretary of State in Council of India.

(*j*) Certain Indian railway annuities.

(*k*) Certain other Indian railway stock.

(*l*) Debenture or guaranteed or preference stock of water companies in the United Kingdom, which have paid a dividend of not less than 5 per cent on their ordinary stock for the past ten years.

(*m*) Municipal corporation stock where the population of the municipality exceeds 50,000.

(*n*) Stock issued by authority of Parliament for water supply where the population exceeds 50,000, and the water rates are not more than 80 per cent of the amount authorised.

(*o*) Stocks authorised under the Colonial Stocks Act, 1900.

(*p*) Local Housing bonds.

(*q*) Stock issued by the Government of Northern Ireland.

(*r*) Stocks, funds or securities for the time being authorised for investment of cash under control of the Court.

The trustees have also power to vary such investments and may continue to hold any of the above investments even if they have ceased to be authorised investments: Trustee Act, 1925, Section 4.

It is to be observed that the section allows two kinds of investments (1) the stocks authorised in (a) to (q) of the above list and (2) the stocks and securities as in (r) authorised by the Court for funds under the control of the Court. These latter are called "Chancery" stocks. This creates at least one strange inconsistency. Thus, in the case of railway stocks, investment is allowed in (g) where the company has paid at least 3 per cent on its ordinary stock in the past ten years.

In the case of "Chancery" stocks, however, investment is allowed in the debenture, preference, guaranteed, or rent charge stock, of railway companies in Great Britain or Northern Ireland, having paid any dividend on the ordinary stock for the past ten years. This will explain why railway companies, which have been doing badly of late, have paid so small a dividend as 2s. 6d. per cent on their ordinary stock, because this payment is enough to preserve their stocks as "Chancery" trustee stocks at any rate, and so to keep them available for trust investment. Notice should be taken, too, of the fact that it is the condition of the stock *at the time of investment* which decides whether the stock is trustee stock or not. If a stock ceases to be an authorised stock, the trustee is not obliged to sell out, although he may, of course, think it wise to do so.

Trustees may purchase any of the stocks above-mentioned, notwithstanding that they are redeemable and that the price exceeds the redemption value. But the securities must not be purchased at a price exceeding the redemption figure if they are liable to be redeemed within 15 years, or even if redeemable after that time at a price exceeding the redemption value. A trustee may retain until redemption any redeemable stock properly purchased.

REAL SECURITIES

Trustees are entitled to lend on first mortgage of freehold land, but not on second mortgage, unless expressly authorised. They can only lend on mortgage of *leasehold* property, if the lease is held for an unexpired term of not less than 200 years, and is not subject to a ground rent greater than a shilling a year, or to any right of redemption or to any condition for re-entry, except for non-payment of rent. This includes a charge or mortgage of any charge made under the Improvement of Land Act, 1864. The security may be in the form of a charge by way of legal mortgage, or an existing mortgage may be turned into a charge by way of legal mortgage. A trustee is not allowed to join in a contributory mortgage, because by doing so he parts with his sole control over the trust property. While Section 1, subsection 1 (*b*) of the Act allows a trustee to invest in real securities, it does not thereby allow him to *purchase* land; for this would involve a change in the trust funds from money into land, and in the absence of express power in the trust instrument, this is not permitted. If a purchaser of land is so authorised, he is entitled to sell it at any time at his discretion, because the Law of Property Act, 1925, Section 32, enacts that land bought by trustees under express power in the trust instrument is to be held on trust for sale unless the settlement otherwise provides. This power of sale also arises under the general power in trustees to vary trust investments.

The margin of security allowed to trustees who lend trust money on mortgage is laid down by the Trustee Act, 1925, Section 8. This section protects trustees in cases where the land or houses constituting the security have depreciated in value so as to cause loss, if the following conditions are observed—

(*a*) If the trustee takes the opinion of an independent able and practical surveyor or valuer.

(*b*) If the loan does not exceed two-thirds of the value of the property as stated in the report.

(*c*) If the loan was made under the advice of the surveyor or valuer expressed in the report.

A trustee lending money on leasehold security is not chargeable with breach of trust merely because in making the loan he dispensed with production or investigation of the lessor's title. A trustee is not liable for breach of trust in the purchase of property or in lending money on mortgage generally, merely because he accepted a shorter title than he might have required, provided that he acted with ordinary prudence and caution.

Trustees lending money on mortgage can contract that the money shall not be called in for a period of seven years from the time when the loan was made, provided that the interest is paid regularly every half year, and the mortgagor commits no breach of covenant in the mortgage deed : Section 10.

On a sale of freehold land for a term of 500 years still to run, trustees may allow part of the purchase money not exceeding two-thirds to remain on mortgage, but the mortgagor must covenant to keep the premises insured against fire to their full value. No report as to the value of the land is required in this case and the trustee will not be liable by reason only of the security being insufficient. When a company's securities are subject to a trust, the trustees may concur in a scheme of arrangement for reconstruction, sale, amalgamation, or variation of rights, in the same way as an individual shareholder, and may take up new shares without being responsible for any loss which may be incurred thereby, provided that they act in good faith. If any conditional or preferential right to subscribe for securities in a company is offered to trustees in respect of a holding in the company, the trustee may either accept, renounce, or assign for value the shares or stock offered and will not be liable for loss, provided that he acts in good faith. The consideration for the sale in case of assignment is to be held as capital money of the trust. The powers conferred by Section 10 (*supra*) are to be exercised subject to the consent of any person whose consent is required, under the terms of the trust deed, to a change of investment. Pending the preparation of a mortgage, or choice of investment, trust money may be kept on deposit at the bank and the interest applied as income. Capital money may also be applied in payment of calls due on any shares subject to the same trust.

UNAUTHORISED INVESTMENTS

Trustees should always confine themselves to the investments allowed by the powers contained in the trust deed. There is, however, a provision in the Trustee Act, 1925, which may assist them where some unauthorised investment is desired or if a mistake has been made. By Section 57, where an investment is expedient in the opinion of the Court, but cannot be effected owing to absence of powers in the trust instrument or by law, the Court may give the trustees the necessary power to invest. The same discretion is given to the Court where the trustees wish to effect a "sale, lease, mortgage, surrender, release, purchase, acquisition, expenditure, or other transaction."

TRUSTS UNDER WILLS

It is the duty of the trustees to hold the scales evenly between tenants for life and persons entitled in remainder. That is to say, the tenants for life must not enjoy a good income in a depreciating security, at the expense of the persons entitled in remainder. This is particularly the case where the trust is declared *by Will.* It is known as the rule in *Howe* v. *Lord Dartmouth* (1862).

The rule laid down in that case seventy years ago, is still good law, that in the case of trusts arising under wills, wasting and hazardous securities such as leaseholds, coalmines, etc., are to be sold, and the proceeds to be invested in some permanent security. This is in the interests of persons entitled in remainder after the death of the tenant for life. But the reverse is true where the trust property consists of an interest which does not yield an income, e.g. a life insurance policy or other property expectant on death. The duty to convert, however, does not ordinarily arise where the trust property is settled by deed, but only in trusts arising under a will, where the testator has given interests in residue to several persons in succession, e.g. a testator gives the residue of his personal estate upon trust to pay the income to A for life and on C's death to D absolutely. As in most matters arising under wills, this duty to convert wasting assets must be exercised within one year after the death of the testator.

Exceptions to the rule as to conversion exist where there is a clear direction to the contrary in the will, or where there is an indication in the will that the testator intended to exclude it.

For instance, the testator gives his trustees powers to sell when and as they may deem expedient, or he directs that the income of the residue of his property is to be enjoyed *in specie* : in neither of these cases does the duty to convert arise.

As between tenant for life and remainderman, the tenant for life is usually entitled to the income as from the date of the death. In this the difference between beneficiary under a trust and legatee is to be noticed, the latter being only entitled to claim his legacy (without interest) twelve months after the date of the death, unless the estate is wound up before that date.

In the case of wasting securities which the trustee has to convert the tenant for life cannot claim the full income from the testator's death, but only interest at 4 per cent, the balance being capitalised and the income thereon being payable also to the tenant for life.

In the case of non-paying securities, a similar rule applies when the interest is sold or otherwise falls in. The sum is apportioned and 4 per cent is payable to the tenant for life on the actual capital, unless the will shows that the tenant for life is to enjoy the "actual income," when he takes all or none as the case may be.

TRUST ACCOUNTS

It is the duty of a trustee to keep accounts, to produce these to the beneficiaries when required, and to give them information as to the administration of the trusts, and the trust investments. If this is not done, the trustees may be brought to book upon application to the Court by the beneficiaries. Trustees may from time to time have the trust property valued by duly qualified valuers.

Once every three years they may cause the accounts to be examined or audited by an independent accountant. They will then produce vouchers and give the accountant such information as he may require. The costs of such examination or audit, including the auditor's fee, is to be paid out of the capital or income of the trust property, or divided between them, as the trustees in their discretion think fit. In default of any direction to the trustees to the contrary, the costs attributable to capital are paid out of income, and those attributable to income out of income: Section 22 (4). Under the Public Trustee Act, 1906, Section 13, either the unofficial trustee or a beneficiary may apply to the Public Trustee for an audit and investigation of trust accounts. But this cannot take place more than once a year. The Public Trustee has power to order the applicant to pay the costs of the investigation, and the right to apply is not to be exercised except in a really urgent case, as the expense is considerable.

VOLUNTARY SETTLEMENTS

Voluntary settlements (for which there is no consideration) are liable to be upset in the interests of creditors, both where there is an intention to defraud and where, although there is no fraud, the effect is to deprive creditors of their rights. The Law of Property Act, 1925, Section 172, states clearly that conveyances made with intent to defeat creditors are voidable at the instance of persons prejudiced. But this does not extend to settlements made in good faith and for valuable consideration, or upon good consideration and in good faith to any person not having, at the time of the conveyance, notice of the intent to defraud creditors. "Valuable" consideration may be either some adequate money value given, or else marriage, which is the consideration for the ordinary marriage settlement. So an ordinary ante-nuptial settlement cannot afterwards be set aside, unless it be shown that there was a fraudulent intent and the wife was aware of it.

Putting these settlements for value on one side there are still those voluntary settlements to be considered which are open to attack by a trustee in bankruptcy. Even where bankruptcy does not supervene, and the settlor is found to be insolvent only, it is possible for creditors to apply to the Court to avoid the settlement and attach the property settled. But that is by an old Statute of Elizabeth (1 Eliz. ch. 5), and it is of more practical value to consider the provisions of the Bankruptcy Act, 1914, in this connection; which are designed to protect creditors in bankruptcy against being thwarted by the trusts of *ordinary* settlements.

Such a settlement is one "not made before or in consideration of marriage or in favour of a purchaser or incumbrancer in good faith and for valuable consideration, nor on the settlor's wife or children, of property which has accrued to the settlor after marriage in right of his wife."

A voluntary settlement in this sense is void against the trustee in bankruptcy if the settlor becomes bankrupt within two years, or if he becomes bankrupt within ten years, unless persons claiming under the settlement can prove (1) that the settlor was, at the time of making the settlement, able to pay all his debts without the aid of the property comprised in the settlement, and (2) that his interest in the property passed to the trustees of the settlement on the execution thereof; Bankruptcy Act, 1914, Section 42.

TRUSTEES OF SETTLED LAND

The usual form of settlement of land is that the land is settled on A for life with remainder to his eldest son in tail, and on failure of issue there is an ultimate reversion to the settlor. The result used to be that A, being only tenant for life, could not sell the property, nor could his son, being still an infant. The only opportunity arose when the son reached 21 years. They could then join together in "barring the entail." But the usual course was then to resettle the land on the son and proceed as before. The land often depreciated in value in a generation and families were found to be living in comparative poverty upon a large landed estate. By the Settled Land Act, 1882, this was altered in that the Act enabled A, the tenant for life, to sell the whole fee simple. The proceeds of the estate were tied up in the same way as the land, and except that the land was turned into money, the parties were in the same position as before. Other Settled Land Acts followed, but the whole are now collected together in the Settled Land Act, 1925. The process is carried out in the following way.

There is a "vesting deed" by which the fee simple is declared to be vested in A the tenant for life.

A then sells the estate free from all charges and interests except (1) legal mortgages, (2) leases and easements created under the settlement, provided they are duly registered. The sale is free from annuities, limited owner's charges, and general equitable charges, even if they are registered. The tenant for life is not the trustee of the settlement. He must give one month's notice of the sale to the trustees of the settlement, of whom there must be at least two. If the latter think that he is acting unfairly, they can appeal to the Court, but apart from this the sale is not dependent on their consent. The sale must be at the best price which can reasonably be obtained, and the purchase money must be paid to the trustees and invested by them, the investments being held on the same trusts as the land. The tenant for life can also grant leases for a term beyond his own life, but he must give notice to the trustees. The rent must be the best that can be obtained and the lease must take effect in possession within twelve months.

Leases for more than three years' duration must be by deed. The effect of the Settled Land Acts cannot be over-estimated. They have assisted both the tenant for life, who is able to enjoy the income from the investments instead of a precarious income, or perhaps no income at all, from the land itself, while persons entitled in remainder can look forward to succeeding in the future to a certain sum of money instead of to a house or other landed property, which may by that time have ceased to be remunerative, and which would involve them in expenditure which they are no longer able to keep up.

THE EXECUTOR TRUSTEE

No section on the subject of trusts would be complete at the present time without a note dealing with trustees who are also executors or administrators. Upon the death of a person intestate, letters of administration are granted to his personal representatives who take all his real and personal estate. They hold it upon trust for sale, except as to actual cash, with power to postpone the sale if they think fit. Their first duty is to pay funeral expenses and debts of the deceased together with expenses connected with the administration. The residue is then distributed among the family as follows—

If the deceased left a husband or wife, the husband or wife takes—

1. Furniture, plate, pictures, etc., absolutely.

2. £1,000 free of death duties with interest at 5 per cent from the death.

3. The income of the residue for life, if there is no issue of the marriage.

4. The income of half the residue for life, if there is issue.

Subject to these rights of the husband or wife, the personal representatives hold the residue upon the following *statutory trusts* for the children of the intestate—

1. For children living at the death of the intestate, who reach 21 years of age and marry, in equal shares.

(If any child dies before the intestate, his issue who survive and reach 21 or marry take the share of their parent.)

2. If the intestate leaves no issue, the residue belongs to his father and mother in equal shares, or if one only survives, then to him or her absolutely.

3. If the intestate leaves no issue and no parent, the residue is held by the personal representatives in trust for the following persons in the order given—

(a) Brothers and sisters of the whole blood on the statutory trusts (see above).

(b) Grand-parents in equal shares.

(c) Uncles and aunts of the whole blood on the statutory trusts.

(d) Uncles and aunts of the half blood on the statutory trusts (see above).

(e) Husband and wife absolutely.

As previously explained, if none of these next of kin survive the intestate, the whole of the residue belongs to the Crown as *bona vacantia*.

The above rules are laid down for personal representatives of a person dying intestate after 1st January, 1926, by the Administration of Estates Act, 1925.

TRUSTEE'S PROTECTION

A trustee is liable for negligence or breach of trust if loss is caused thereby to the beneficiaries, but he may in a proper case claim the protection of the Trustee Act, Section 61. This section gives the Court power to relieve him, provided that the trustee has " acted honestly and reasonably and ought fairly to be excused for the breach of trust and for omitting to obtain the directions of the Court in the matter." The same relief is given to trustee executors and administrators of the estate of a deceased person.

The question arises how far the Statute of Limitations runs in favour of trustees so as to bar actions by beneficiaries for breaches of trust unless they are brought within six years. Limitation Act, 1623.

The law now is that a trustee is entitled to plead the Statute of Limitations in answer to any claim that is brought against him, whether the trust is express or implied. The Act, however, does not enable a trustee to plead lapse of time where the claim against him is founded on fraud or fraudulent breach of trust to which the trustee was a party, or where it is sought to recover trust property or the proceeds which are still in the hands of the trustee. In other cases, however, the trustee, where he is innocent, enjoys the same rights under the Statute of Limitations as other persons, which are that claims against a trustee must be confined to those which arise within six years before the commencement of the action. In other words, claims against him are barred in six years.

It is to be observed that time begins to run for this purpose as soon as the breach of trust is committed, and it is no answer to say that the beneficiary was not aware of it, unless the beneficiary was under a disability or where his interest is reversionary, in which case time only begins to run when it falls into possession. In such cases, the Court will order the trustee to restore the money for the benefit of the person entitled in reversion, and to take the interest on the money until the death of the tenant for life. The Bankruptcy Act, 1914, provides that except in cases of fraud a discharge in bankruptcy will release a trustee from the consequences of a breach of trust.

A claim against a trustee for breach of trust will also be barred, if the trustee can show that the beneficiary who is making the claim acquiesced in or allowed it with full knowledge of the facts, provided he was not an infant but was *sui juris* at the time. The Trustee Act, 1925, Section 62, provides for this in that the Court has power, even in the case of a married woman who is restrained from anticipation, to order that the interest of the beneficiary in question in the trust may be impounded by way of indemnity to the trustee or persons claiming through him. This section applies to breaches of trust committed before or after the date of the Act.

In conclusion, an executor may demand a formal release on handing over the residue to the residuary legatee, but whether a trustee can strictly do so is doubtful. He is certainly entitled to have his accounts examined and approved by the beneficiaries, and this in itself should constitute a release. A study of the foregoing pages will confirm the view that the trustee is entitled not only to a formal release, but to the thanks of the beneficiaries for his onerous services.

RETIRING FROM A TRUST

A trustee, whether appointed by deed or will, is not bound to act. He may disclaim the trust at any time before doing any act which shows that he has accepted it. For this purpose a written disclaimer is sufficient, although a deed is advisable. Even after the trustee has accepted the trust he can at any time retire by executing a deed to that effect, provided that either a corporation or two individuals, apart from a custodian trustee, are left to act as trustees. The consent of the continuing trustees and of the person entitled to appoint new trustees is necessary to the discharge, and this should be expressed in the deed. The deed should also contain a declaration vesting the trust property in the trustees who are left to carry on the trust. In this way the retiring trustee obtains his discharge: Trustee Act, 1925, Sections 39 and 40. By the Public Trustee Act, 1906, Section 5, a trustee may retire on the appointment of the Public Trustee as an ordinary trustee, although there are not more than two trustees, and without the consents required by Section 39 of the Trustee Act, 1925.

CRIMINAL LAW

Criminal Justice is administered by—

1. *Justices of the Peace*, unpaid magistrates who have the King's commission to preserve peace and order in his realm. The justices preside over: (*a*) a Single Magistrate's Court; (*b*) Petty Sessions; (*c*) Quarter Sessions.

2. *Recorders*, who are part-time judges appointed from barristers of not less than seven years' standing. They conduct trials in the more important boroughs.

3. *Stipendiary Magistrates.* These are paid Justices of the Peace appointed for the most important boroughs, and each is invested with the powers of two unpaid justices in Petty Sessions.

4. *The King's Bench Judges.* These take the more serious cases at the Central Criminal Court (Old Bailey), and travel to the various County Assizes.

5. The *Recorder*, the *Common Sergeant*, and the *Judges* of the *Mayor's and City of London Court.* These do most of the work of the Central Criminal Court.

The head of the criminal judiciary is the *Lord Chief Justice.* In order that the criminal law shall be effectively and systematically applied, there is a *Director of Public Prosecutions.* His office is 1 Richmond Terrace, Whitehall, London, S.W.1.

GROWING WORK OF JUSTICES

The striking change that is coming over our criminal administration is the gradual disappearance of trial by jury on indictment, and the corresponding increase in the trials by justices with power to sentence summarily.

JUSTICES OF THE PEACE

The justices, now drawn from all classes and including women as well as men, have many of the characteristics of a jury. Apart from the recorders and stipendiary magistrates, who are judicial officers of the Crown and have many of the characteristics of the judges, the Justices of the Peace are as remarkable a body of unpaid servants of the community as ever existed. They are lay people, not of necessity possessed of a legal qualification, and are guided, but not controlled, in their duty of administering the law by a trained clerk. They decide, however, by majority, not by unanimity, as a jury normally does. Where there is equality in voting the chairman has no casting vote; and if, after a rehearing before a reconstituted court, the voting is still equal, the accused should be discharged.

Such a discharge will be an answer to a second charge for the same crime, the plea of the accused being *Autrefois Acquit.*

SUMMARY TRIAL AND TRIAL UPON INDICTMENT

One might suppose a haphazard court of lay members to be a most unsatisfactory one. Yet most prisoners, faced with the choice of being tried either by the justices in petty sessions or upon indictment at quarter sessions or at the assizes, choose the former. And their confidence, that they will get a fair and sympathetic trial, is almost invariably well grounded. The fact that the penalties that can be inflicted at quarter sessions or at the assizes are much more severe than those possible on summary trial has, no doubt, something to do with the choice. The chief reason, however, is the speedier trial expected.

ADMINISTRATIVE WORK OF JUSTICES

The Government, too, by constantly committing to the jurisdiction of magistrates more and ever more judicial and administrative duties, evinces its confidence in the ability of the layman to administer justice. The duties under the Road Traffic Act of 1930 are a striking illustration. In petty sessions, where two magistrates sit, they sit without a jury and deal with offences, not all minor, in a summary manner though not, of course, without careful investigation. In quarter sessions the whole body of justices is called to act under their chairman; there are elaborate preliminaries, including the indictment; and a jury is empanelled to answer questions of fact. The chairman consults his colleagues upon important points. But, in effect, he is an unpaid judge; and an accused may feel that at quarter sessions he will be tried by a benevolent gentleman who requires a most serious offence before he sends a man to gaol, but at the assizes by a stern judge keenly anxious that law shall be vindicated.

It is also the justice who as a rule signs the summons or warrant that operates to bring an accused before a court for examination.

SUMMONS TO APPEAR

When a complaint is made against a person, the justice may

summon that person to appear before him. The information upon which the summons is issued need not be written and need not be supported by oath. The summons is served upon the accused personally by a constable, or is delivered to an adult person for him at his usual place of abode. The object of this summons is to inform the accused, in clear simple language, with what he is charged—

"To Thomas Atkins of ...., farm-worker. Whereas you have this day been charged before the undersigned, one of His Majesty's justices of the peace in and for the county of .... for that you on .... at ....did............... These are therefore to command you in His Majesty's name, to be and appear before me on Wednesday, the 25th day of January, at eleven o'clock in the forenoon at ...., or before such other justice or justices of the peace for the said county as may then be there, to answer to the said charge, and to be further dealt with according to law. Herein fail not.

Given under my hand and seal, this 23rd day of January, in the year of our Lord 19.., at ...., in the county aforesaid.

A. B.

WARRANT TO ARREST

A warrant to arrest can be issued only upon an information and complaint in writing, sworn to or affirmed by the informant. It is directed to a particular constable or to the constables in the jurisdiction of the justice signing it. As the summons does, the warrant describes the offence: "The statement shall describe the offence shortly in ordinary language, avoiding as far as possible the use of technical terms; and, if the offence is created by statute, shall contain a reference to the section of the statute creating it." Such a warrant is—

To the constable of .... and to all other peace officers in the said county of .... Whereas Thomas Atkins of ...., farm-worker, hath this day been charged upon oath before the undersigned, one of His Majesty's justices of the peace, in and for the said county of ...., for that he on .... at .... did .... These are therefore to command you, in His Majesty's name, forthwith to apprehend the said Thomas Atkins and to bring him before me ....

A. B.

PRECAUTIONARY REQUIREMENTS

In fulfilment of their duty to preserve the King's peace the justices may, and must when the need is evident, take precautionary measures. They can require a person to find sureties to be of good behaviour and, in the event of refusal or failure to find them, can commit to prison. The magistrate's warrant of committal in such case would be an adequate answer to a writ of *Habeas Corpus*.

This power of the justices is a Common Law power, made statutory by an Act of Edward III, and is obviously a power called for in the interests of the community. And we have ample safeguards against its arbitrary exercise.

Following one much debated instance in 1933 of committal to prison though no actual offence had been committed, the Home Secretary explained the matter. There had been disturbances in connection with demonstrations of the unemployed; and the police authorities had reason to anticipate a recurrence. The Director of Public Prosecutions, therefore, with the approval of the Home Secretary and of the Attorney-General, applied to a Chief Magistrate that he should order two officials, of the association that had, apparently, helped in creating the former disturbances, to keep the peace.

"The Magistrate" (the Home Secretary pointed out in a letter to the Leader of the Opposition), "was satisfied that the evidence was such as to justify a reasonable apprehension that a breach of the peace was likely to ensue; and he accordingly required Mr. Mann and Mr. Llewellyn, as the two responsible officials of the body organising these activities, to enter into a recognisance with sureties to be of good behaviour and to keep the peace for 12 months, or in default to go to prison for two months. There was nothing to prevent both or either of them from entering into recognisances and finding sureties to secure their good behaviour. Had they chosen to do so, no question of imprisonment would have arisen. They were asked solely to refrain from promoting a repetition of the recent disorders; they were not asked to refrain from the expression of opinion or from helping in an orderly way to convey a petition to the House of Commons.

With reference to the criticism of the use in these proceedings of the Statute of Edward III, proceedings with a view to an order of the Court requiring a person or persons to keep the peace and to give sureties for their good behaviour are of very frequent occurrence. The provisions of this Act merely give statutory recognition of the Common Law power of Justices of the Peace. This jurisdiction has been judicially described as a branch of preventive justice in the exercise of which magistrates are invested with large discretionary powers for the maintenance of order and the preservation of the public peace, and is, and always has been, of the very essence of the justices' function.

The proceedings taken in these cases in no way infringe the right of freedom of speech or the right of lawful public meetings. In fact, they lie at the very foundation of the security for civil liberty peacefully enjoyed by the community as a whole. The executive Government would be guilty of the gravest dereliction of their primary duty to the public if they failed at any time to take all proper steps for the maintenance of law and public order threatened by the action contemplated by the N.U.W.M. (National Unemployed Workers' Movement), and no Government worthy of the name could shirk its responsibility in this matter."

JUSTICES AND MAINTENANCE ORDERS

The justices have what may well be an even more delicate task than the trial of crimes. They have jurisdiction over maintenance to be paid by husband to wife. But an appeal lies to a divisional court consisting of two judges of the Probate, Divorce, and Admiralty Division. Such an appeal was made (*Millichamp* v. *Millichamp*) in 1931. The complainant took out a summons under the Separation and Maintenance Acts, 1895–1925, alleging that her husband had wilfully failed to provide her with reasonable maintenance. The parties had before marriage agreed that the wife should live with the husband's mother; but dissensions soon arose between wife and mother-in-law. The justices (Frodsham, Cheshire), holding that a man's first duty was towards his wife, made an order that he should pay £1 a week for wife and child, the wife to live separate. The husband appealed; but, except in so far as the amount was reduced a little, failed in his appeal. The President said: "One cannot distribute the blame between these people, who were placed in a very tight fix. It is natural enough and creditable that this man feels his filial obligations to his mother. It is natural enough that the wife says she cannot really live under those conditions. Thus this *impasse*. The justices had to deal with the matter according to law, and to find whether or not the husband had in breach of his duty wilfully neglected to provide maintenance for his wife. They came to the conclusion that he had so neglected his duty. With every sympathy for the parties I have come to the conclusion that the decision was right. The husband's first duty was to his wife."

JURISDICTION OF QUARTER SESSIONS

Most misdemeanours, *with the consent of the accused*, can be dealt with in petty sessions without a jury. The justices assembled in quarter sessions have jurisdiction limited only in regard to the most serious or most difficult charges. Such, reserved for the assizes, are—

1. Treason or misprision of treason.
2. Murder.
3. Any capital felonies or such as are punishable by penal servitude for life.
4. Blasphemy and offences against religion.
5. Bigamy and other offences against the marriage laws.
6. Abduction of women and girls.
7. Incest.
8. Perjury.
9. Offences under the Officials Secrets Act, 1911.
10. Child destruction.

ASSIZES

The King's Bench judges, sent to the assizes held in the county towns, have a jurisdiction over crime that is unlimited. Thrice a year they visit the counties with the King's authority and his commission to hear and decide upon the charges presented by the Grand Jury.

It appears that the Central Criminal Court, also, has a concurrent and equal jurisdiction with the King's Bench.

The *Central Criminal Court* ("Old Bailey") has as its permanent judges the *Recorder* of the City of London, the *Common Sergeant*, and the *Judge of the Mayor's Court*. These are invariably trained lawyers and deal with most of the serious criminal matters that arise in the metropolitan area. The most serious crimes of all are dealt with by a King's Bench judge.

The Home Office, which is responsible for peace and order in this country, issues figures showing the extent to which crime is prevalent. In a typical year, in England and Wales, by far the greatest number of offences were those against property. The numbers were: (1) against the person 5,669; (2) against property, (a) with violence 26,248, (b) without violence 110,159; (3) malicious injury to property 351 (including 107 cases of arson); (4) forgery and currency offences 1,072; (5) other offences 3,532.

The crimes of violence against the person were thus classified: (1) murder 122; (2) attempts and threats to murder 91; (3)

manslaughter 162; (4) infanticide 16; (5) concealment of birth 95; (6) wounding (felonies 192, misdemeanours 1,251); (7) endangering railway passengers 22; (8) assault 27; (9) intimidation 6; (10) cruelty to children 23; (11) child stealing 4; (12) procuring abortion 98.

Sexual crimes were: (1) rape 89; (2) defilement (girls under thirteen 58, girls between thirteen and sixteen 402); (3) indecent assaults 1,871; (4) incest 76; (5) procuration 15; (6) abduction 13; (7) bigamy 374; (8) unnatural offences 648.

The crimes of violence against property were: (1) sacrilege 163; (2) burglary 1,449; (3) housebreaking 9,720; (4) shopbreaking 11,846; (5) attempts to break in 1,259; (6) entering with intent 1,233; (7) possessing housebreaking tools 267; (8) robbery 217; (9) extortion by threats 94.

Crimes against property, without violence were: (1) larceny (*Simple* 84,697, *aggravated* by reason of the matter of the theft, or its place, or its perpetrator (*a*) horses and cattle 130, (*b*) from person 1,984, (*c*) in house 1,697, (*d*) by servant 3,575, (*e*) of post letters 347, (*f*) embezzlement 2,150, (*g*) other aggravated larcenies 144); (2) obtaining by false pretences 11,296; (3) frauds by agents 676; (4) falsifying accounts 267; (5) other frauds 998; (6) receiving stolen goods 2,102; (7) bankruptcy offences 104.

Motoring offences account for the great bulk of the work of summary courts. Drunkenness is a steadily diminishing crime.

We are, it will be seen from these figures, as a nation singularly law-abiding: our criminal laws are really rules of conduct, obeyed in all but rare cases. See, however, note on page 272.

ASSUMPTION OF INNOCENCE

The English idea—in marked contrast to the idea of many continental systems of law—is that it is not the business of a court of justice to be an inquisitor. The accused must be treated as innocent, until evidence adduced in court has shown him to be guilty; he must not be questioned as though it were incumbent on him to show his innocence. The voluntary admissions of an accused are themselves accepted only under strict conditions; if they are induced by promises or threats, they are rejected.

How far the Courts go in their insistence that an accused is not to be called upon to incriminate himself surprises at times. Thus, the Court of Criminal Appeal in 1932 rejected a statement obtained by the police because it had been elicited by a suggestion: "To say to a person in custody 'It is alleged so-and-so

. . .' is only a subtle form of cross-examination by the police, and a statement in response is not admissible." And, in spite of a plea of guilty, the Court will review a conviction when there is a good defence in law. A defendant pleaded guilty to an indictment for bigamy, though he had a statutory defence to the charge—the wife had been continuously absent from the husband for the space of seven years before the second marriage, and there was no evidence that the appellant knew that she was alive within that time. For the burden of showing this lies upon the prosecutor. The conviction for bigamy was quashed (C.C.A. 1932, *R.* v. *Griffiths*). The business of the Courts is judicial, to decide between two contending litigants upon the evidence brought before it; even in a criminal cause it is the King, represented by the prosecution, who declares that an accused, having broken one of his laws, has made himself liable to pay a penalty. The King must prove his charge "beyond reasonable doubt." If the accused is found not to be the guilty person, it is not for the Court to make a roving inquiry, and hazard conjectures about who should have been arraigned.

CORONER AND HIS DUTY

The duty of inquiring is that of the coroner helped by the police. All the judges of the High Court, are, indeed, coroners *ex officio*; and the Lord Chief Justice is the supreme coroner for England. But on the judicial bench they judge, not inquire. Of course, a judge may, and does, ask questions from the witnesses when he pleases; but the questions are confined to the elucidation of the question: "Is the accused guilty of the particular charge laid against him."

The *coroner* has the duty of inquiring—

1. When treasure has been found (treasure-trove).

2. When a person has been killed or has died in circumstances that call for inquiry, or in prison, or in a mental hospital.

The coroner himself must view the body. The rule that an inquest must be held *super visum corporis* is not affected by the Coroners Act, 1887. Where the coroner inadvertently omits to view the body, the inquest is a nullity and a fresh inquest must be made (*R.* v. *Haslewood*, 1926).

His court is a "court of record": what actually took place in his court is conclusively proved by production of its records. He has power to examine on oath; and one giving false evidence before him is guilty of perjury. He is by Common Law a

conservator of the King's peace, and therefore can give a warrant
to arrest offenders. He can summons a jury, of from seven to
eleven persons, to help him in his inquiry into sudden or suspicious
deaths; and, if the minority should be not more than two, he
may accept the verdict of the majority. At his discretion he may
direct that a *post-mortem* examination shall be held.

The coroner has not an absolute right to hold inquests in
every case in which he chooses to do so. It would be intolerable
if he had power to intrude without adequate cause upon the
privacy of a family in distress and to interfere with their arrangements for a funeral. But (as *R.* v. *Price*, Q.B. 1884, shows) it is
a misdemeanour to prevent the holding of an inquest, which
ought to be held, by disposing of the body.

When a sentence of death has been executed by the prison
authorities, it is his duty—

1. Within twenty-four hours to conduct an inquest with the
help of a jury.

2. To have the body identified.

3. To report that the judgment was duly executed.

The Coroners (Amendment) Act, 1926, authorises him—

1. When criminal proceedings for murder or manslaughter are
pending, to adjourn his inquiry until such proceedings end.

2. To dispense with juries in minor cases.

3. To have a body viewed by the jury only when he thinks it
necessary.

CORONER'S APPOINTMENT

The coroner is appointed by a county council or by a borough
council with a quarter sessions of its own. The Lord Chancellor
has power to remove him on good cause shown. When a vacancy
occurs the council concerned gives notice to the Home Secretary
of State, and within three months proceeds to appoint a duly
qualified person. To be qualified for appointment a person must—

1. Be a barrister, or a solicitor, or a legally qualified medical
practitioner of not less than five years' standing in his profession.

2. Reside in the district of his inquisition, or within two miles
of its boundary.

A mayor, or alderman, or councillor of the appointing authority
is disqualified; and the disqualification lasts for six months after
the relinquishing of the office held.

NATURE OF CRIME

A crime is the disobeying of a command issued and enforced

by the sovereign power of the State. It is a wrong not so much against an individual as against the community in general.

Most crimes are now carefully defined by Act of Parliament and the maximum punishments set out; and it may be that we shall soon have a complete code of criminal law. Meantime, as *Rex* v. *Manley* noted below shows, it is perhaps well that the Common Law still has power of adapting itself to new conditions.

KINDS OF CRIME

Crime is any form of conduct which is forbidden under pain of some punishment. Some acts are so obviously evil that one instinctively recognises them as wrong. They are *mala in se*, evils in themselves. Such is the murdering of a man in order to take his property; such is the malicious burning of a stack that its owner has laboriously garnered for the winter. None would hesitate to call these acts "crimes"; few would deny that the actors should be punished. Such acts have always been common law crimes, though now they are covered by statute. They constituted conduct that was anti-social, conduct that is spontaneously regarded as being against the welfare of the community. It is true that in the beginning of our organised community, the exaction of vengeance even for these departures from social co-operation was left to the individuals who were wronged by them. But that was because the State did not then possess an efficient police system that would enable it to supersede self-help. There is no hesitation now to consider them as matters *primarily* for the State, and only *secondarily* for the individuals aggrieved. It is only these more serious offences against the community that gives a stigma to the offender. If every breach of law made one a criminal, the whole community, with rare exceptions, would be included in the criminal class.

Other acts there are, however—and with every session of Parliament the number increases, that are made crimes simply because Parliament, giving effect to the will of the electorate, prohibits them. In other, perhaps simpler times, the acts were innocent, even laudable. They are not evils in themselves, they are crimes because, for some reason or other, Parliament has thought fit to make them so. They are *mala prohibita*, evils because prohibited. Such is the keeping of a tobacco shop open after eight o'clock; such is the neglect to provide fire-guards in a room where young children are left.

The reasons prompting Parliament are various. The ill-result of an act, or of a neglect to act, may become so obvious that the conscience of the community is awakened, as when the Education Act made it a crime not to provide education for children. Or the civil remedy may so seldom be invoked, or may prove so inadequate to repel the wrong course of conduct, that Parliament turns the civil wrong into a crime. Thus, till 1857, for a breach of trust, however fraudulent it might have been, there was no criminal punishment. Yet, in our increasingly complex social system, a man might be a trustee for all kinds of property. He was the legal owner; but he was under an equitable obligation to let another have all the benefits of the property. Parliament, therefore, came to the conclusion that it needed a stronger deterrent to a breach of trust than was afforded by the possibility of an action in a civil court. Fraudulent breach of trust was made a crime.

We should note, too, that with changing conditions of life, and with consequent changes in ideas, certain actions cease to be either crimes or civil wrongs. For they cause neither resentment nor fear. No employer would be a criminal, as he would once have been, for paying more than the ordinary wage to his employee; no charge would lie against "John delylls wyffe" for "waring a peticot adorned with vellat."

The position in regard to "maintenance" and "champerty" (noted on page 260) affords a curious contrast to this tendency to erect civil wrongs into crimes against the public. These two illegalities, once common law crimes, are now looked upon merely as civil wrongs.

THE MISDEMEANOUR OF PRODUCING A PUBLIC MISCHIEF

That the Common Law still has abundant vitality we need not doubt. The King's judges resort to the Law of Nature, which is the ground of all laws. Or perhaps it is more accurate to say they expect a man to act with reason. The law expects a man to act with not less judgment than a man of ordinary sense and prudence may be expected to show : a man foolishly and wilfully harming the community in its working is liable to punishment. Codes come—codes go sometimes—but the Common Law goes on for ever developing and expanding.

"Justice, moral fitness, and public convenience, when applied to a new subject, make Common Law without a precedent." This was said when the Court decided that it was a punishable misdemeanour to incite a servant to rob his master. And now we have a new species of crime, the Common Law misdemeanour of creating a public mischief by making false complaints to the police. The objection that was once valid, is no longer valid. "Formerly," said Lord Chief Justice Wilmot, in a well-known case, "there was too confined a way of thinking in the justices of the Common Law; and the Courts of Equity have risen by the judges not properly applying the principles of the Common Law, being too narrowly governed by old cases and maxims. The jurisdiction of the Courts of Equity would never have swelled to that enormous bulk we now see, if the judges of the Courts of Common Law had been anciently as liberal as they have been in later times."

The pestilent desire for cheap notoriety will be controlled, at any rate a little, by the decision of the Criminal Appeal Court. In *Rex* v. *Manley* (1932), the accused had made a statement that she had been attacked and robbed by a man of whom she gave a description to the police. The police spent a considerable time in investigating the matter before they found that the statement was false. At the Central Criminal Court the Recorder determined that the offence committed was the Common Law misdemeanour of doing an act tending to produce a public mischief. On appeal the Court confirmed the conviction. It was urged that no such offence was known to the law. But the Court accepted the argument that the class of offence was a fraud affecting the Crown. Public servants had been diverted from their duties, and any one who might have corresponded with the description given was put in jeopardy. The Lord Chief Justice said: "All offences of a public nature, all such acts or attempts as tend to the prejudice of the community are indictable. The conviction must stand and the appeal be dismissed."

FELONIES AND MISDEMEANOURS

The chief acts dealing with crimes are the Offences Against the Person Act, 1861, and the Larceny Act, 1916, dealing with offences against property.

In general the more serious crimes are *Felonies*, the less serious *Misdemeanours*. In a narrower sense Misdemeanours are indictable crimes that cannot, unless under the authority of an Act of Parliament, be tried in summary fashion in a Court of petty sessions. *Treasons*, crimes against the Crown, are in a class apart.

Conviction for treason and felony does not now involve forfeiture of lands and goods (Forfeiture Act, 1870). But any person convicted of treason or felony, for which he shall be sentenced to *death or penal servitude*, or for *any term of imprisonment with hard labour*, or *exceeding twelve months*—

1. Will forfeit any military or naval or civil office under the Crown.

2. Will forfeit any pension or superannuation allowance payable out of public funds (unless a free pardon is granted within two months after conviction).

3. Will during imprisonment be disqualified from holding any public office, and from voting either for Parliament or for a local authority.

The War Pensions Act, 1920, gives, however, to the Minister of Pensions power to restore forfeited pensions, and power also, while the pensioner is imprisoned, to apply his pension for the benefit of his dependants.

COMPENSATION IN CRIMINAL CASES

The Forfeiture Act made another innovation in criminal law. The ancient idea was that the prosecutor of a crime sought no benefit for himself; his thought was for the welfare of the State, wronged by the accused's offence. He sought punishment of the prisoner, not compensation for himself. The Act now allows the Court to award, *immediately after conviction and as an addition to the punishment of the crime, and on the application of a person aggrieved*, a sum not exceeding £100 for loss of property through the felony. Another change modifies the old rule that the Crown never pays nor asks for costs : one convicted of a crime may be ordered to contribute towards the costs of the prosecution. Thus, Mr. Compton Mackenzie, charged and convicted (under the Official Secrets Act, 1911) for divulging confidential documents, was fined £100 and also ordered to pay a sum not exceeding £100 towards the costs of the prosecution (Central Criminal Court, 1933).

PROCEDURE IN FELONY AND MISDEMEANOUR

Certain distinction of procedure may also be noted—

1. A private person may without warrant (he is, indeed, under legal obligation to do so) arrest a felon.

2. The examining magistrate may refuse bail to one charged with felony.

3. One accused of felony can, without explanation, object to jurors ("has the power of peremptory challenge" is the phrase).

4. Peers accused of felony are entitled to be tried by their fellow-peers.

DEGREES OF GUILT

In a felony there may be a *"principal in the second degree,"* one who is present at the crime and actively aiding the principal offender; there may also be an *"accessory before the fact,"* one knowing of the project to commit the crime and either aiding in its preparation or remaining passive where he should give information; there may also be an *"accessory after the fact,"* one who knowing of the crime harbours and comforts the criminal. Wife (or husband) of a criminal cannot, however, be an *accessory after the fact*: the law is not foolish and will not impose too heavy a burden upon people.

Both the *principal in the second degree* and the *accessory before the fact* are punishable in the same manner as the *principal in the first degree*. In all felonies, except murder, the *accessory after the fact* is liable to be imprisoned for any term not exceeding two years, with or without hard labour; in murder such an accessory is liable to penal servitude for life.

In misdemeanours all who take part are liable as principals: "Whosoever shall counsel, aid, or abet the commission of an indictable misdemeanour shall be liable to be proceeded against, indicted, and punished as a principal offender." So, too, from the assumed greater seriousness of the crime, all concerned in a treason are principals.

DISTINCTION OF NO GREAT VALUE

There seems to be little point in maintaining a distinction between felonies and misdemeanours; and the distinction at times leads to absurdity. Thus, apart from statutory authority, a prisoner indicted for felony cannot be convicted of a misdemeanour. In *R.* v. *Thomas* (C.C.R. 1875), the accused was indicted for the felony of uttering counterfeit coin after a previous conviction for uttering. To utter counterfeit coin is a misdemeanour; to utter after previous conviction is a felony. At a trial the subsequent misdemeanour is first dealt with; if the accused is found guilty, the previous conviction is gone into. In this case, the jury found the uttering, but not the previous conviction. The charge of felony therefore failed. The charge of misdemeanour failed, too; for the Act gave no authority for conviction as for a misdemeanour.

8

PRINCIPAL IN CRIME AND IN CONTRACT

It is perhaps worth noting that in criminal law "Principal" has a different sense from the sense it has in civil law. When we speak of "Principal and Agent" in contract, the principal is the one for whom the agent strikes the bargain. The principal is in the background; the agent is the active party. The principal in criminal law is the actual doer of the prohibited act. If there is an instigator behind him, the instigator will be an "accessory before the fact" in a felony, a "principal" in a misdemeanour.

Even if a felony or misdemeanour is not actually committed, one who persuades another to commit it is guilty of the misdemeanour of "Incitement to Commit a Crime": in *R.* v. *de Kromme* (1892, C.R.), the accused was convicted of "inciting to conspire to cheat and defraud," because he had offered to a servant a bribe as an inducement to sell the master's goods below their value. This was a case stated by the London Recorder.

ATTEMPTS TO COMMIT CRIME

An attempt to commit a crime is itself a crime. Statute law has, indeed, as in the case of murder, sometimes made the attempt a felony. The mere intention or empty threat, however, without an act immediately aimed at the commission of the crime, is not such an attempt as is contemplated in criminal law. Where the act is only preparation for a crime—as buying a revolver in order to commit murder, or procuring fuel in order to commit arson—there is no attempt. Such an act is too remote; for it might be possible of an innocent explanation.

STATUTORY CRIMES

One further distinction among crimes may be repeated. Some crimes are such as would from their very nature be condemned by right-thinking people. They are evils in themselves, *mala in se.* Such are most of the Common Law crimes, murder, theft, arson, and the rest. Other crimes would have been quite innocent actions, if Parliament had not passed an Act aiming at their prohibition. They are evils because forbidden by the sovereign authority of the State, *mala prohibita.* Such is the law against selling cigarettes after eight o'clock. (See page 215.)

GUILTY INTENTION NECESSARY TO CONSTITUTE CRIME

Only in exceptional circumstances can one commit a crime without the intention to do the particular act, or, at all events, an act likely to result in the crime—an intention called "malice." Such an exceptional circumstance is created, for instance, by the Licensing Act, 1872, which enacts : "If any licensed person sells intoxicating liquor to any drunken person, he shall be liable to a penalty." The words amount to an absolute prohibition; and it is no answer to the charge that there was a reasonable doubt about the condition of the person served. Where there is not, as usually there is not, such an absolute prohibition, a guilty mind is necessary to constitute a crime : there must be *mens rea* as well as *actus reum*. An act done without the will, perhaps while sleep-walking, cannot be a crime ; we cannot impute a blameworthy condition of mind when the act is involuntary.

INSANITY AS A DEFENCE

A man is presumed to be sane ; the burden of proving insanity is therefore upon the defence. What is needed to establish the defence was laid down by the judges in a series of answers to questions set by the House of Lords.

1. To establish a defence on the ground of insanity, it must be clearly proved that, at the time of the committing of the act, the party accused was labouring under such a defect of reason, from disease of the mind, as not to know the nature and quality of the act he was doing, or, if he did know it, that he did not know he was doing what was wrong.

2. Where insanity exists on some matters only, the person must be considered in the same situation as to responsibility as if the facts with respect to which the delusion exists were real. If, for example, he is under the delusion that any other man is in the act of attempting to take away his life, and he kills that man as he supposes in self-defence, he would be exempt from punishment. If his delusion was that the deceased has inflicted a serious injury to his character and fortune, and he killed him in revenge for such supposed injury, he would be liable to punishment.

3. Notwithstanding that the person accused did the act with a view, under the influence of insane delusion, of redressing or revenging some supposed grievance or injury, or of producing some public benefit, he is nevertheless punishable if he knew at the time of committing such crime that he was acting contrary to the law of the land.

BAIL IN FELONY AND CERTAIN MISDEMEANOURS

Where, as in some misdemeanours, it is a matter of discretion whether or not to allow bail, the magistrate who decides not to allow it must inform the accused of his right to appeal to a High Court judge for bail. In the cases below the magistrate has discretion. The rule about bail is given in Section 23 of the Indictable Offences Act, 1848: "Where any person shall be brought before a justice of the peace charged with any felony, or with assault with intent to commit a felony, or with attempt to commit a felony, or with obtaining or attempting to obtain property by false pretences, or with a misdemeanour in receiving property stolen or obtained by false pretences, or with perjury or subornation of perjury, or with concealing the birth of a child by secret burying or otherwise, or with wilful or indecent exposure of the person, or with riot, or with assault in pursuance of a conspiracy to raise wages, or assault upon a peace officer in the execution of his duty or, upon any one coming to his aid, such justice of the peace may, in his discretion, admit such person to bail."

INDICTABLE OFFENCES

These are offences upon which an indictment (or formal charge) is laid by the grand jury before a Court of *Oyer and Terminer* ("to hear and to decide") or of "General Gaol Delivery," or before Quarter Sessions. The indictment is a written accusation charging one or more persons with the commission of one or more crimes. The grand jury, that is, accuses, not judges; when it finds a "true bill" against a person there need not be unanimity, though at least twelve jurors must concur in the charge. When the grand jury, deliberating in private, has decided that the person charged must answer the charge, the trial takes place in public before the petty jury.

The indictment states the place of commission of the crime (and normally of trial) and the nature of the crime. The Indictments Act, 1915, has simplified the form of indictment and has given the Court wide powers to amend. Still, the Criminal Appeal Court is insistent that the indictment shall give ample information to an accused. In one case (*R.* v. *Kitching*, 1929) the Court quashed a conviction in the following curious circumstances. An indictment for rape had been put before the grand jury. They endorsed on the charge: "No true bill for rape. A true bill for indecent assault (aggravated)." There was, however, no indictment for indecent assault before the grand jury.

The trial proceeded as if a true bill had been found, though the charge was indecent assault. The grand jury might have ignored the indictment for rape; it might have presented the appellant upon the other charge; it contented itself with the suggestion of an alternative indictment.

(The appellant here was not, however, so lucky as some whose convictions have been quashed on a technical point. For the quashing of his conviction on the first indictment did not operate as a bar to his trial on a second indictment for indecent assault. He could not raise the defence that he had formerly been convicted (*autrefois convict*); for he had never been tried on the charge. He was, in fact, indicted on the less serious charge and duly convicted and imprisoned.)

The act requires that an indictment shall contain "a statement of the specific offence or offences with which an accused person is charged, together with such particulars as may be necessary for giving reasonable information as to the nature of the charge." The indictment states—

1. The case and the Court of trial.
2. The offence.
3. Particulars of offence.

Thus—

The King v. A.B.

Court of Trial (e.g. *Central Criminal Court or Durham County Assizes, held at Durham, or Hants Quarter Sessions, held at Winchester*).

PRESENTMENT OF THE GRAND JURY

Statement of offence

A.B. is charged with the following offences :

Arson, contrary to Section 2 of the Malicious Damage Act, 1861

Particulars of offence

A.B., on the .... day of ...., in the County of .... *maliciously set fire to a dwelling-house, one F.G. being therein.*

Here there is one "count" only; but, of course, there may be more than one.

The grand jury does not try a case; its proceedings are secret; and the accused is not present at its deliberations. The ancient form of oath still administered clearly indicates the function of the grand jury: "You, as Foreman of this Grand Inquest for our Sovereign Lord the King and the body of this County, shall diligently inquire and true presentment make of all such things as shall be given to you in charge or otherwise come to your notice touching this present service."

"The King's counsel, your fellows', and your own, you shall observe and keep secret. You shall present no man for envy, hatred, or malice, neither shall you leave any one unpresented for fear, favour, affection, gain, or reward."

CRIMINAL INFORMATION

A prosecution may also be initiated by a *criminal information*, a formal alleging of an offence, filed by the Attorney-General in the King's Bench. A criminal information can be filed for a *misdemeanour* only: in *treason* and *felony* a grand jury should present an accused upon their oaths.

CORONER'S INQUISITION

The verdict found at a coroner's inquisition may also serve to charge an accused before the petty jury. But, where a person is charged with murder, manslaughter, or infanticide, the offence is also always the subject of inquiry before justices. The person charged may, therefore, also be indicted before the grand jury. Yet, if the grand jury find "no true bill," the accused may still be arraigned upon the coroner's inquisition (*R.* v. *Coleman*, 1911, *Justice of the Peace*, 75). In such a case, however, the Crown will usually offer no evidence upon the inquisition.

PROSECUTOR OF A CRIME

Different in this respect from Scots law, English law permits any one to set the criminal law in motion. There are two checks upon this power—

1. If a man makes a bad use of this permission he may himself be accused of "malicious prosecution."

2. In many crimes the consent of the Attorney-General or of the Solicitor-General has been made necessary before a prosecution can be begun.

This is so, for instance, under the Prevention of Corruption Act, 1906, for frauds by trustees, for various highway offences, and for offences under the Punishment of Incest Act, 1908. Doubtless, too, the power that the justices have in a summary trial of awarding costs to the prisoner who has been prosecuted without good cause has a limiting effect.

Where the Act creating or defining the offence says nothing to the contrary, any one may prosecute. Thus, it was not at Common Law a crime to kill a pigeon. It was made a crime by the Larceny Act, 1861, Section 23. In *Smith* v. *Dear* (K.B. 1903), the killer of a pigeon made compensation to the owner, but was prosecuted by the secretary of the local association for prevention of cruelty to animals (R.S.P.C.A.). The magistrate held that a third party, who had no rights in the pigeon, could not prosecute the killer of it. But on appeal the Lord Chief Justice said: "As there is nothing in the Act to limit to the owner of the bird the right to prosecute, any person can prosecute."

In certain events, indeed, the law gives the prosecutor a reward more substantial than the thought that he has fulfilled his duty as a good citizen in helping to repress crime. It allots him all or part of the fine inflicted on the delinquent. Thus, under the Regulations of Railways Act, 1868, Section 21, a company knowingly providing a special train for conveying parties to a prize fight is liable to a penalty not less than £200 or more than £500. The penalty is recoverable summarily, and half is to be paid to the person at whose suit the summons was issued.

PENALTIES FOR CRIME

No judge, now, in passing sentence, may inflict punishment other than those prescribed by statute or resulting from long custom. He cannot, whether in order to make "the punishment fit the crime" or any other reason, impose any arbitrary penalty. Usually, however—when, as is now the case with most crimes, a statute deals with it—a maximum penalty is prescribed, and the judge exercises his discretion up to this maximum. In rare instances, as in a sentence for murder, or for burning arsenals or ships of war, he has no discretion: one penalty in these cases, that of death, alone is possible.

The tendency nowadays is to regard punishment rather as directed to reformation than to the exacting of a savage punishment or to the repellent effect upon others. Recently, therefore, other devices, aiming at preventing rather than punishing crime, impose prescribed restraints upon criminals or possible criminals.

DEATH PENALTY

This is now confined to—
1. High treason.
2. Murder.
3. Piracy with violence.
4. Arson of dockyards, ship of war, naval stores.

Hanging is the mode of execution, and the hanging (since 1868) is within the prison walls, where, after a coroner's inquest, the body is buried. The orderly execution of the sentence is assured by—

1. The verdict of the coroner's jury.
2. The sheriff's declaration.
3. The posting outside the prison walls of the surgeon's certificate of death.

PENAL SERVITUDE

This can be given only for such crimes as are tried before a petty jury, on indictment by a grand jury. Three years is the minimum period. The punishment consists in compulsory work out of doors in convict settlements.

Through good behaviour, convicts may obtain a licence or "ticket of leave" whereby, on condition that they do certain things (including periodic reporting to the police), they are at liberty during the last portion of their sentence.

When a long sentence has been passed, the rule of the Home Office is to bring the sentence under review at intervals of ten, fifteen, twenty years. Penal servitude for life means, assuming satisfactory conduct, the serving of about 26 years, 8 months.

IMPRISONMENT

This, especially when accompanied by hard labour, is almost invariably limited to two years.

" DIVISIONS " OF PRISON

1. "Hard labour," in the sense of severe physical exertion imposed upon prisoners, does not now exist. Apparently, the only added hardship nowadays upon one sentenced to imprisonment with hard labour is that, for the first fourteen days of his sentence, he sleeps upon a plank bed without a mattress.

2. In the "First" and "Second Division" prisoners have more privileges, chiefly in regard to the sending and receiving of letters and the number of visitors allowed, than ordinary prisoners. And, unless their own clothes are unfit to wear, they are not obliged to wear prison garb.

WHIPPING

This penalty, strictly defined and limited by Act of Parliament, still exists for male offenders. The Court, in ordering whipping of one convicted under the Offences Against the Person Act, 1861, or the Larceny Act, 1916, must prescribe the instrument to be used and the number of strokes to be inflicted—

1. The maximum number for boys under sixteen is twenty-five, a birch rod being the instrument.

2. The maximum number for those older is fifty.

3. Magistrates must not order more than twelve strokes upon a boy under fourteen.

No person must be whipped more than once for the same offence.

FINES

These, like the terms of imprisonment, are now almost without exception limited by statute. They are meant to be a lighter punishment than imprisonment; and for that reason the Criminal Justice Administration Act, 1914, sought, in effect, to make imprisonment for non-payment necessary only for refusal, not for inability, to pay. In fixing the fine the Court is to take into account the apparent means of the prisoner, is in most cases to allow time for payment, is to reduce the period of imprisonment upon part payment. There is, too, an obligation to allow time for payment of fines: "A warrant committing a person to prison in respect of non-payment of a fine shall not be issued forthwith unless the court which passed the sentence is satisfied that he is possessed of sufficient means to enable him to pay the sum forthwith, or unless upon being asked whether he wants time to be allowed for payment he expresses no such desire."

POLICE SUPERVISION

When, in a trial for an indictable offence, the accused is shown to have been previously convicted of crime, he may be sentenced to a period under police supervision, in addition to a sentence of imprisonment or penal servitude. While under police supervision he must report himself to the chief police officer of his district, and keep him informed of any change of address.

PREVENTIVE DETENTION, AND THE BORSTAL SYSTEM

The Prevention of Crime Act, 1908, enacts—

1. That when *youthful offenders* (i.e. between 16 and 21) have been convicted of an offence entailing penal servitude or imprisonment they may be sentenced instead to detention in a "Borstal Institution" for not less than one or more than three years. ("Borstal" is the name adopted for the new treatment from the

name of the place where the first of such reformatories was established.)

The object of such detention, whether as an offender in a Borstal institution or as an "habitual criminal," is "to give such industrial and other instruction and to apply such disciplining and moral influences as will conduce to the reformation of the inmates and the prevention of crime."

2. That an "habitual criminal" may be sentenced to be detained for a minimum of five and a maximum of ten years. The "habitual criminal" is one who—

(a) Has been sentenced to penal servitude for a felony or a serious misdemeanour.

(b) Has at least three times previously been convicted of a similar crime, and is leading a dishonest or criminal life.

The object is to prepare him, if he will, to earn an honest living on being discharged.

Both the "Borstal inmate" and the "habitual criminal" may be allowed out on probation. The Home Secretary must at the end of each three years consider whether or not an habitual criminal may be so released.

PROBATION OF OFFENDERS ACT, 1907

This Act has given the Court a wide power of affording even a guilty prisoner one more chance. The Act permits the Court, in its discretion, either to dismiss the information or charge or to release the prisoner on probation when it would be a benefit to society to do so: "Where any person is charged before a court of summary jurisdiction and the Court thinks that the charge is proved but is of opinion that, having regard to the character, antecedents, age, health, or mental condition of the person charged, or to the trivial nature of the offence, or to the extenuating circumstances under which the offence was committed, it is inexpedient to inflict any punishment or any other than a nominal punishment, or that it is expedient to release the offender on probation, the Court may, without proceeding to sentence, make an order either—

1. Dismissing the information or charge, or

2. Discharging the offender conditionally on his entering into a recognisance, with or without sureties, to be of good behaviour and to appear for conviction and sentence when called on at any time during such period, not exceeding three years, as may be specified in the order."

CONDITIONS OF RELEASE ON PROBATION

The released prisoner enters into a recognisance—

1. To be of good behaviour.

2. To appear if called on for sentence within a period limited to three years.

3. To make good the damage he has done.

There may also be a condition that he shall place himself under the supervision of an officer of the Court—the *probation officer*, whose duty is to advise and befriend the person released, to find him employment, to report to the Court upon his conduct; and there may be additional conditions of residence (in an institution or elsewhere) and of abstention from intoxicants.

CONDITIONS OF COMMITTAL FOR PREVENTIVE DETENTION

The power is given by the Criminal Justice Administration Act, 1914 (supplemented by the Criminal Justice Act, 1925).

The justices must be satisfied that the offender is—

1. Not less than sixteen nor more than twenty-one years of age.

2. That he has been previously convicted or, having been discharged on probation, he broke his recognisance.

3. That, by reason of his criminal habits or tendencies, or association with persons of bad character, it is expedient that he should be subject to detention for such term and under such instruction and discipline as appear most conducive to his reformation and the repression of crime.

Then, instead of passing sentence, they may commit the offender to prison till the next assizes or quarter sessions. The question of detention is decided there.

AGE DETERMINED AT TIME OF COMMITTAL

It seems that a sentence of detention in a Borstal institution cannot be passed upon an offender who is over twenty-one at the date of the commencement of the assizes or quarter sessions to which he has been committed for sentence, even though he was under twenty-one at the date of his conviction at petty sessions.

In *R. v. Scoffin* (C.C.A. 1930) sentence of three years' detention in a Borstal institution was passed on an offender who, under twenty-one when he appeared before the justices, had reached twenty-one when he appeared at the assizes. On appeal the sentence was varied. Counsel for the Crown suggested that "not more than twenty-one" might be interpreted as anything up to twenty-two, or that the relevant age should be that of conviction, not of sentence. Both suggestions failed to convince the Court. The Lord Chief Justice said: "The appellant, according to his birth certificate, was born on the 17th day of February, 1909, and he, therefore, completed twenty-one years on the 16th day of February, 1930. His conviction at petty sessions was on the 22nd day of January, 1930, but the commission day for Manchester Assizes was on the 17th day of February, 1930, and, in fact, sentence was passed on the 18th day of February, 1930.

It is perfectly obvious, therefore, that on the commission day of the assizes he was more than twenty-one years of age. Counsel for the Crown has put forward an ingenious argument; but two serious difficulties stand in his way. The first is to convince us that 'not more than twenty-one years of age' means 'not so much more than twenty-one,' and the second is to convince us that, in a proper case, 'is' means 'was.' If those difficulties could have been surmounted, our decision might have been different. There is much to be said for the view that the statute might well have been framed somewhat differently. But that is a matter for separate inquiry. We have no doubt that the appellant was above the age prescribed by the statute, and he must therefore be denied the benefits of Borstal, and must, instead, go to prison for six months in the second division."

IMPRISONMENT IN LIEU OF PAYING FINES

Imprisonment for not paying is limited, by the Summary Jurisdiction Acts, in accordance with the money due: 10s., not exceeding seven days; £1, fourteen days; £5, one month; £20, two months; over £20, three months.

PREROGATIVE OF MERCY

This power of the Sovereign to pardon convicted persons is indispensable if the two desirable things—the vindication of law, the prevention of wrong through a too rigid adherence to law— are to be achieved together. The power is quite apart and quite different from the reviewing of a decision by a Court: the decision is not questioned in the slightest; the only point considered by the Sovereign—in effect by the executive—is whether or not it is expedient to remit part or all of the sentence period. When the Home Secretary decides, in reliance on the opinion of the judge who tried the case, or after sympathetic consideration of the jury's recommendation to mercy, that the case is one where the prerogative might well be exercised he advises the Sovereign; and the Sovereign acts on the Home Secretary's advice.

There is one Common Law restriction on the Sovereign's power to pardon and one statutory restriction—

1. Where private interests are principally concerned. Thus, the crime of a public nuisance cannot be pardoned while the nuisance continues.

2. Under the Habeas Corpus Act a pardon cannot be pleaded when the offender is guilty of the offence of committing a man to prison out of this realm.

A pardon may be conditional. It often is when a murderer, upon whom no sentence but that of death can be passed, is pardoned: the condition is that he shall serve a sentence of imprisonment or of penal servitude.

REPRIEVE

Akin to the power to pardon is that of a *reprieve*, so that for an interval execution of a criminal is postponed. Reprieve may be granted by the Sovereign or by the Court that awards execution. In two events the Court is obliged to reprieve—

1. When it is stated (and found to be so by a jury of twelve matrons) that a woman sentenced to death is pregnant.

2. When a prisoner has become insane after judgment passed.

CRIMES ARE CLASSIFIED AS FOLLOWS—

1. Offences against persons.
2. Offences against property.
3. Offences against public rights.

The first class of crimes, against persons, includes—

Homicides that are not justified. The taking of life is justifiable in these cases only—

1. When it is necessary to carry out public justice (the hangman, carrying out the sentence of the Court, incurs no liability).

2. When it is needed to advance public justice, or to maintain peace, as to arrest a felon or suppress a riot.

3. When it is needed in self-defence. But the necessity must be evident, and the burden is upon the killer to show that he could not have defended himself in any other way.

In other cases the taking of life is an offence whether it is one or another of the following—

1. *Felonia de se* (that is, suicide). An attempt to commit suicide is a misdemeanour. And, if two agree to commit suicide and only one succeeds, the survivor is guilty of murder; he has

successfully instigated the other to kill himself, and, so far as regards the person dead, he has been a "principal in the second degree."

2. *Manslaughter* is the killing unlawfully, but without the "malice aforethought" necessary to constitute murder.

3. *Murder* is unlawful homicide "with malice aforethought," the death occurring within a year and a day from the injury. "Malice aforethought" is here no more than a deliberate intention to do the act that caused the death. Moreover, it is murder when, through the perpetration of a felonious act (robbery with violence, for instance), a person brings about the death of a fellow creature —unless, indeed, when the chance of death resulting from the committing of the felonious act was so remote that no reasonable man would have anticipated it.

MURDER AND MANSLAUGHTER

The killing of a person is not readily reduced to manslaughter, still less to justifiable homicide. Before a man can avail himself of the defence that, in taking another's life, he was acting in self-defence he must show—

1. The act was necessary to protect his life.
2. He did all he could to avoid it.
3. He had reasonable fear that his life was in danger.

Before he can avail himself of the defence that he was protecting his property he must show that he was preventing a serious felony, intended to be carried out by force   Obviously, the defence is less likely to prevail when it is property, not personal security, that is menaced.

In *R.* v. *Symondson* (Central Criminal Court, 1896), Kennedy, J., explained the matter clearly. The prisoner had killed by shooting a man who, among others, threatened to break into his home and take away property: "There are cases in which the life of another may be taken not unlawfully, but such cases, where persons take the law into their own hands, must be watched very carefully. It is not any assault that will justify the use of a pistol; the danger measures the right. The infliction of death must be to prevent no ordinary crime. You must not shoot a trespasser merely because he is a trespasser. If he shows an intention to accomplish a felonious purpose by force, extreme measures may be used."

"MALICE AFORETHOUGHT" AN ESSENTIAL OF MURDER

Premeditation ("malice aforethought") is the element usually invoked to establish that an unlawful killing is the crime of murder, not of manslaughter; and the premeditation is shown by such facts as the preparing of a plan, the procuring of poison or a deadly weapon, or the utterance of threats. In some way or other the prosecution must prove that the accused intended the act resulting in the death.

Manslaughter is unlawful homicide committed without premeditation. No provocation will excuse manslaughter; but, if the accused was smarting under a provocation so recent and so strong as not to be master of his understanding, his killing is reduced from murder to manslaughter. Thus, the crime of killing has been considered manslaughter where a man suddenly hears from his wife that she had committed adultery. The following have entailed conviction for manslaughter: where a man not qualified in surgery has performed an operation that killed the patient; where "Peculiar People," conscientiously objecting to call in medical assistance and believing it wrong to do so, have in the opinion of the jury by that neglect accelerated a death. Thus, an infant nine months old died of pneumonia; evidence showed that life would have been saved if medical help had been obtained; the jury found manslaughter, but added that the accused had done all that was possible for the child except in not calling in a doctor. The conviction was upheld upon appeal, the Lord Chief Justice saying that there had been "wilful neglect," *wilful* being applied to what was done deliberately, and *neglect* being a failure to do what an ordinary careful parent would do.

Murder, manslaughter, and *attempt to murder* all belong to the class of crimes called *felonies*, a class that, before 1870, entailed forfeiture to the King of all the felon's goods.

ASSAULT

This is an attempt to do bodily injury to another without his consent. If the attempt succeeds, the assault is also a *battery*. It has been held that it is an assault by a constable when, in order to obtain the name and address of a cyclist riding at night without light, he caught hold of the bicycle and caused the rider to fall (*Hatton* v. *Treeby*, Q.B. 1897). On the other hand it is no assault when a teacher administers reasonable corporal punishment to a pupil; for a parent is assumed to delegate to the teacher the power he himself has of punishing without causing serious injury (*Mansell* v. *Griffin*, K.B. 1908). Assaults are classed as—

1. Common assaults.

2. Aggravated assault on women and children (upon a male child under fourteen or upon a female).

3. Indecent assault.

The first two classes can be dealt with summarily by the justices, the third is an indictable offence, triable at quarter sessions or at the assizes unless the accused consents to be tried summarily. As to this possible choice the Criminal Justice Act, 1925, Section 24, gives directions—

1. Where a person who is an adult (in this connection one aged 16 or upwards) is charged before a court of summary jurisdiction with an indictable offence (beng one of the offences scheduled in this Act) the Court, if it thinks it expedient to do so, having *regard to any representation made in presence of the accused by the prosecutor, the character and antecedents of the accused, the nature of the offence, the absence of circumstances which would render the offence one of grave or serious character, and the adequacy of the punishment which a court of summary jurisdiction has power to inflict,* and if the accused, when informed by the Court of his right to be tried by a jury, consents to be dealt with summarily, may deal summarily with the offence. If the accused is found guilty the Court may sentence him to be imprisoned for a term not exceeding six months, or to a fine not exceeding £100, or to both. Where, however, the offence affects the property of the Crown or of a public body, or where the Director of Public Prosecutions is conducting the case, the consent of the prosecutor is needed for the summary trial.

2. If the Court is satisfied that it would be expedient to try the case summarily, the charge is put into writing and read to the accused. He is then asked: "Do you desire to be tried by a jury, or do you consent to the case being dealt with summarily?" If necessary, explanations must be given of what is implied in the question.

An assault, it will be noted, is both a *crime* and a civil *wrong*; and, since it is a misdemeanour and not a felony, the person injured by the assault can sue for damages even though he does not prosecute for crime.

SUICIDE, SUICIDE ATTEMPTS, AND SUICIDE PACTS

He who, being of sound mind, kills himself is *felo de se*: he has committed a felony against himself. His attempt at suicide is, therefore, an attempt at a felony, and—different in this respect from Scots and most other systems of law—English law considers the attempt as an *indictable misdemeanour*. Moreover, he who enters into a "suicide pact" with another is guilty of murder when he fails to kill himself and the other succeeds. For he has been a "principal in the second degree" in the killing.

The savage rules against suicides are now abrogated. There is no longer forfeiture of goods nor opprobrious burial. The former was abolished by the Forfeiture Act, 1870, the latter by the Interments (Felo de se) Act, 1882, which authorises burial "either without any religious service or with such Christian and orderly religious service at the grave as the person having charge of the burial thinks fit."

It may seem strange to punish attempts at suicide. Perhaps, in its logic, law seeks to prevent a person from exacting vengeance even on himself. Law was in the beginning a substitute for self-help or unrestrained private vengeance. "Revenge is a kind of wild justice," wrote Bacon, "which the more man's nature runs to, the more ought law to weed it out." Blackstone, the great apologist for English law, intent on showing that English law is "wisely and religiously considered," advances two reasons for maintaining a punishment for attempts at suicide. It penalises ill manners in that the would-be suicide is "invading the prerogative of the Almighty, and rushing into his immediate presence uncalled for." One may attach more importance to the second, to the temporal than to the spiritual reason : the attempt is "against the King, who hath an interest in the preservation of all his subjects." So the King's lawyers made suicide a felony, that the King might have advantage from the goods, if not from the life, of the suicide.

To make the attempt to kill oneself a crime it is, apparently, necessary that the person charged shall be of sound mind and of full age : one under 21 cannot commit the crime.

BIGAMY

This crime is defined in the Judicature Consolidation Act, 1925 : "It is bigamy when there is a marriage of any person, being married, to any other person during the life of the former husband or wife, whether the second marriage shall have taken place within the dominions of His Majesty or elsewhere." There are, however, three limiting provisions in the Act. There is an answer to the charge when—

1. The second marriage has been contracted, by any other than a subject of his Majesty, elsewhere than in England and

Ireland (but it is bigamy when the second marriage is contracted in England even though the person contracting it belongs to a country where polygamy is recognised).

2. The person contracting the second marriage is one whose husband or wife has been continuously absent for seven years, and is not known by the person charged to have been living within that time. (This does not mean that the second marriage is recognised as valid. It means only that the person charged with bigamy has a valid defence to the charge.)

3. The first marriage has been dissolved by divorce or has been declared void by a court of competent jurisdiction.

When a charge of bigamy is made, production of the registrar's certificate of the first marriage is necessary; it seems that the prisoner's admission is not enough. This is no more than an application of the general rule that a charge must be fully made out by the prosecution. The Criminal Justice Administration Act, 1914, makes the wife or husband of a person charged with bigamy a competent witness, either for the prosecution or the defence and without the accused's consent. Yet he or she is not compellable, and may when called elect not to give evidence.

It should be noted that a reasonable belief in the death of a spouse is an answer to a charge, even though the statutory space of seven years had not elapsed when the second marriage took place. For such a belief excludes one essential of a crime; there can be then no *mens rea*, no guilty intention. In *Reg.* v. *Tolson* (Q.B. 1889) nine judges to five held that a wife (whose husband had been absent for about six years, and whom she thought drowned on a voyage to Australia) could not be convicted for bigamy upon re-marrying, when on reasonable grounds she supposed her first husband dead. The statutory defence given by Parliament does not exclude such a Common Law defence as was available before the statute.

PRESUMPTION OF CONTINUANCE OF LIFE

The strictness of English criminal law, in requiring that the prosecution must fully establish the crime, enabled the accused to escape punishment in the strange case, *R.* v. *Willshire* (Q.B. 1880). On appeal a conviction for bigamy was quashed. Willshire had married in 1864, and had been convicted for re-marrying in 1868, his wife being alive. In 1879 he married again, in 1880 yet again, the woman with whom he went through the ceremony in 1879 being alive. Evidence for the defence consisted of the former conviction: this showed that the wife of 1864 had been alive in 1868, and presumably also in 1879. The 1880 marriage *might* have been non-bigamous: it would if the first wife had died in the interval between the last two ceremonies; and in any event there was the statutory defence of seven years' absence. The conviction was quashed because this question had not been left to the jury. Willshire was peculiarly lucky in the matter. For—

1. A new trial with a proper direction to the jury was barred by the rule that no man can be tried twice for the same offence.

2. An acquittal by the jury, under the proper direction, would have implied that they thought him guilty of bigamy in 1879, a crime for which he had escaped indictment.

PRESUMPTION OF INNOCENCE

R. v. *The Inhabitants of Twyning* is also an instructive case. The question was whether the children of a female pauper, born of a second marriage, were legitimate or not. The woman had married Winter and had lived with him for a few months. He enlisted, went abroad on service, and was not afterwards heard of. Twelve months after his leaving she married Burns. The Court held that the children of the second marriage were legitimate: "This is a case of conflicting presumptions. Which is to prevail? The law presumes the continuation of life; but it also presumes against the commission of crimes. There is a marriage of the pauper with Francis Burns, which is *prima facie* valid; but the year before that took place, she was the wife of Richard Winter, and if he was alive at the time of the second marriage, it was illegal, and she was guilty of bigamy. But are we to presume that Winter was then alive? If the pauper had been indicted for bigamy, it would clearly not be sufficient. In that case Winter must have been proved to have been alive at the time of the second marriage. It is contended that his death ought to have been proved; but the presumption of law is that he was not alive when the consequence of his being so is that another person has committed a criminal act. The sessions decided right in holding the second marriage to have been valid, unless proof had been given that the first husband was alive at the time."

But in *R.* v. *Thomson* (1906), at the Central Criminal Court, the Common Sergeant, when a prisoner charged with bigamy alleged that his first marriage was invalid (his first wife having a husband living), and when the prosecution had proved the two marriages, held that the prisoner must prove what he alleged.

BIGAMY A FELONY

Bigamy is a felony, and may be punished by seven years' penal servitude. If the other party to the bigamous marriage knows its nature, he or she is a "principal in the second degree," liable, therefore, to the same penalty.

What is the position of a man who goes through a marriage ceremony with a woman whose husband—he knows, though she does not—is alive and undivorced? It seems that he is still a "principal in the second degree," still liable to seven years' penal servitude. For the marriage is a bigamous one though the woman may have a statutory or a Common Law defence. There exists, therefore, a "principal in the second degree" without there being a "principal in the first degree"; the man can be punished though the woman cannot.

DEFAMATION (CRIMINAL LIBEL)

This is made a crime not because private reputation may be injured, but because public safety may be disturbed. Whether, for the purpose of criminal law, the defamation is true or false does not matter. Indeed it is said: "The greater the truth, the greater the libel," as being the more likely to provoke retaliation. Truth is an answer to a civil action. In a criminal cause the accused must not only show the truth; he must also show that the public benefits from his disclosure, and that he was not actuated by malice. Nor does it matter that there has been no such publication as would justify a civil action; it is enough that a person has, by it, been induced to break the peace. That is, the sending of the libel to the prosecutor is a "publication" for a criminal charge.

But this likelihood of provoking retaliation that would break the peace is necessary to constitute the crime. There must be a public interest concerned, something affecting the guardians of the public peace, to justify the recourse by a private person to a criminal remedy. A personal squabble between two individuals should not be the subject of a criminal indictment. Unless the libel is particularly obnoxious, or unless it is persistently repeated, the aggrieved party is left to his civil remedy.

The criminal libel consists of slanders, put into printing or other durable form, tending to blacken the memory of one dead, or to damage the reputation of one alive and expose him to disgrace, ridicule, or contempt. It seems that to libel a dead person will be a crime only when there is a purpose of injuring his posterity.

It is an indictable misdemeanour—

1. To publish, or threaten to publish, a libel upon a person living or dead—or to offer to prevent the publication—for the purpose of extortion (Larceny Act, 1916, Section 31). An offer to withdraw a notice of objection to a justices' licence has been punished under this section.

2. Maliciously to publish any defamatory libel knowing it to be false (Libel Act, 1843, Section 4).

3. Maliciously to publish any defamatory libel (Libel Act, 1843, Section 5).

LIBELS IN NEWSPAPERS

The Law of Libel Amendment Act, 1888, modifies the law in relation to newspapers.

1. No criminal prosecution can be begun against any one connected with the publication of a libel in a newspaper without an order of a judge in chambers. The person accused must have notice and may oppose the application.

2. Fair and accurate reports of public proceedings before any court exercising judicial authority are privileged when published contemporaneously with the proceedings (Section 3). But the section does not authorise publication of blasphemous or indecent matter. Nor does it limit the power of the King's Bench to make a person answerable for contempt of court in publishing what might prejudice a fair trial. Thus, to publish a photograph of one accused, an identification parade being thereby spoiled, is such a contempt.

3. Fair and accurate newspaper reports are privileged of (a) a public meeting, a public meeting being one for the furtherance or discussion of any matter of public concern; (b) meetings of local authorities—vestries, town councils, and so on—or of any committees of these bodies (unless the public and newspaper reporters are excluded from such meetings); (c) royal and other Government commissions; (d) notices and reports issued by a Government department or by a police authority.

In all cases the privilege is destroyed when it is shown that malice dictated the publication. Nor is the defence available when the person defamed has asked the newspaper to publish a reasonable letter contradicting or explaining the report, and his request has been refused.

"Criminal libel" is the term applied also to publications that, being *blasphemous, seditious,* or *obscene,* tend to a breach of the peace.

The Judicial Proceedings (Regulations of Reports) Act, 1926, should also be noted (see page 899).

PROPERTY RIGHTS

How tenderly the law regards the rights of property, how severely it penalises the meddling with another's property, is admirably illustrated in *Betts* v. *Receiver for the Metropolitan Police, and Carter Paterson & Co.* (King's Bench, 1932). The plaintiff, a general dealer, had in 1925 been convicted for receiving a quantity of jewellery, knowing it to have been stolen. He was sentenced to five years' penal servitude. The police at the time took possession of some rolls of cloth, and these were the subject-matter of a second charge. The second charge was not, however, proceeded with. That being so, the cloth was still, so far as the law is concerned, the property of the person in whose possession it was; and the duty of the police was to hold it for him and to restore it in due course. Carter Paterson, however, claimed the cloth as being stolen from their warehouse; and the police, satisfied of the validity of the claim, handed over the cloth. By doing so, both the police and Carter Paterson were converting the plaintiff's goods, the police by handing them over, Carter Paterson by taking them. For no process of law had shown them to be other than the plaintiff's property. "There was no doubt," said the presiding judge, "that the police acted in good faith and there was a high probability that it did not belong to Betts." But probability is not certainty, in law or anything else. The police receiver was protected by the Public Authorities' Protection Act, 1893. This enacts that an action not begun within six months from the cause of action, is barred against public authorities. Carter Paterson's were not protected; and they were constrained to pay £150.

GENERAL RULE REGARDING PROPERTY

Only the owner, or one invested with his authority, can divest himself of his property rights. Parliament, no doubt, which in matters of law is omnipotent, can, for public purposes, modify this rule. It does, in fact, modify the rule when it grants permission for such an enterprise as the construction of a railway. For then it enacts that a landowner, however reluctant he may be to do so, must sell what land the railway company requires for its enterprise. And Parliament has made regulations concerning property coming into the possession of the police. The Police Property Act, 1897, prescribes what is to be done when, for example, the police have raided a receiver's premises, have taken a deal of property, and no one makes a plausible claim to it. The police apply to a magistrate for an order under the Act. Having the order they can sell the goods, placing the proceeds to the Prisoner's Property Fund—that is, in effect, to the country. After twelve months the police can sell without the magistrate's order.

Apart from these statutory powers the police are like any one else into whose possession another person's property comes. They become bailees of the property, are bound to exercise reasonable care in safeguarding it, and must hand it over when a claim to it has been substantiated. If more than one claimant appears, the claimants are told to apply to Bow Street for a magistrate's order. There the validity of the claims is tested.

WRONGFUL INTENTION NOT NECESSARY

An innocent agent himself may be liable for a conversion. He is when, though in perfect good faith, he has dealt with the goods of another without that other's authority. A bankrupt, acting in fraud of his creditors, sold goods belonging to his trustees in bankruptcy. Elwall bought in good faith for a foreign principal, paid for the goods, and forwarded them. He was held liable to the trustees for a conversion. The hardship is undeniable; but the Court is bound to administer the law, and must not be swayed by the hardship of any particular case (*Stephens* v. *Elwall*, K.B. 1815). Comment in a later judgment on a similar decision involving an innocent agent was: "It is a matter of everyday experience that one cannot always be perfectly secure from loss in his dealings with others. And the defendant here is in the position of a person who has trusted to the honesty of another, and has been deceived. He undertook to act as agent for one who (it now appears) was a thief; and, relying on his representations, he aided this principal to convert the plaintiff's property into money. It is no greater hardship to require him to pay to the plaintiff the value of this property than it would be to take it away from any innocent vendee who purchased and paid for it. And it is universally held that the purchaser of stolen property, no matter how innocent or free from negligence in the matter, acquires no title to such property as against the owner." Hardship it may be; but it does conduce to the security of property. For it obliges dealers in property to have a care.

WHAT IS NOT CONVERSION

The wrong of conversion implies action in relation to the goods. It is no conversion where a broker, auctioneer, or other, simply negotiates the sale from a non-owner to the buyer. If the broker never has had possession of the goods he cannot be liable in conversion. Nor is a carrier liable for conversion simply by performing the act of carriage: "If a thief had given his stolen goods to a carrier to be carried, and the latter (at the end of the journey) had returned the goods to the thief, upon the thief's discharging the lien for the carriage, no action would lie against the carrier at the suit of the true owner. It would be different if, before the thief repossessed himself of the goods, the true owner were to demand possession. For, if he did so, and possession were refused, the carrier would be guilty of conversion" (*Union Credit Bank* v. *Mersey Docks*, Q.B. 1899). Where there is doubt regarding which of rival claimants is entitled to the goods the carrier can protect himself either by an application to the Court in an interpleader action, or by taking an indemnity from the claimant to whom he delivers.

DEFINITION OF " STEALING "

Stealing is carefully defined in the Larceny Act, 1916. A person steals when he—

1. Without the consent of the owner;
2. Fraudulently and without a claim of right made in good faith;
3. Takes and carries away anything capable of being stolen;
4. With intent, at the time of such taking, permanently to deprive the owner thereof. Even if a person has lawful possession of a thing—as when he is a bailee or a part owner of it—he is guilty of stealing when he fraudulently converts the thing to his own use or to any one else's use except the owner's (see *Betts* v. *Police Receiver*, above). A "bailee" here means one who is bound to return the specific thing entrusted to him; it does not include, for instance, the treasurer of a club, who is under no obligation to keep the identical money given to him.

All four characteristics must be shown to have been present before the person charged can be convicted of larceny.

(3) is the *asportation* (i.e. the carrying away); (4) is the *felonious intent*; and both are essential to constitute this crime.

1. The owner's consent is not obtained when possession is obtained—

(a) By a trick.

(b) By intimidation.

(c) Under a mistake of the owner, the taker knowing that a mistake had been made (thus if I give a beggar a gold coin in mistake for a shilling, he is a thief when, knowing that I have not intended such a gift, he retains it).

(d) By finding, when the finder believes that the owner can be discovered by taking reasonable steps (the finder is, however, having taken these reasonable steps, entitled to retain the property against all the world except the true owner). It is the duty of the finder to take reasonable steps to find the owner; and, if unsuccessful in his search, to keep with reasonable care the thing found. (When he finds a thing and takes it up, he becomes a "voluntary bailee" of it; and is accordingly obliged to take such care of it as a prudent man would take of his own goods.)

2. "Carries away" has an elastic meaning. It includes the removal of anything from the place it occupies: thus, it was held to be a "carrying away" when, in an attempt at theft, an ear-ring was detached from the ear but was caught in the wearer's hair.

3. The difficulty of establishing that the taker intended "permanently to deprive the owner thereof" led, in the case of motor-cars, to the Act whereby stealing a ride is a crime punished by a summary process.

WHO IS THE "OWNER"

The "owner" includes any person, like a carrier or a pawnbroker, who rightly has possession of another's property. The "owner" may even be one who was unaware that he possessed the articles taken. Thus *The South Staffordshire Water Company* in 1896 recovered two gold rings from *Sharman* (Q.B.), a workman who had found them while cleaning out a pool of which the plaintiffs were owners. For where a person has possession of house or land, with a manifest intention to exercise control over it, then, if something is found on that land, whether by an employee of the owner or by a stranger, the presumption is that the possession of that thing is in the owner of the house or land. And, till a claimant appears who can establish a stronger claim, the constructive possessor can retain the goods found.

A KNOCK-OUT AUCTION

After some difference of judicial opinion it was settled that a combination between intending bidders to refrain from bidding against one another is not illegal. The seller at an auction can protect himself by fixing reserve prices (*Rawlings* v. *General Trading Co.*, C.A. 1921).

The Auctions (Bidding Agreements) Act of 1927 was an attempt, not very successful it seems, to neutralise this decision. It imposes penalties (fines not exceeding £100 and imprisonment not exceeding six months) upon any dealer who rewards a person for abstaining from bidding at an auction, and upon the person who takes the reward.

But a prosecution under the Act can be instituted only with the consent of the Attorney-General or the Solicitor-General; and it is difficult to see how a conviction can be secured. (See page 27.)

WHAT MAY BE STOLEN

Anything that is valuable property may be subject to theft. But things attached to land (like growing trees) can be stolen only after they have been severed and possession has been abandoned after severance. And the carcasses of wild animals, not reduced into possession while living, can only be stolen by the person who has killed them when he has abandoned possession: he has left them temporarily and has returned for them.

SIMPLE LARCENY

Stealing that is not made more serious by an accompaniment— as stealing with violence, stealing by breaking into a house, stealing by persons in position of trust, and so on—is "simple larceny." This is a felony punishable with penal servitude up to five years. The offender, being a male under sixteen, is also liable to be once privately whipped. Other larcenies are *compound larcenies*.

" FALSE PRETENCES "

This misdemeanour (which may be punished by penal servitude for not exceeding five years) is defined in the Summary Jurisdiction Act of 1899. A false pretence means a false representation, by words, writing, or conduct, that some fact exists or existed. It is a lie about the past or present. Thus if a man obtains a meal at a restaurant and has no means of payment, he is guilty of the crime of obtaining credit by false pretences. For his seating himself and ordering the meal affirms that he has money to pay. A promise as to future conduct, even though not intended to be kept, is not in itself a false pretence.

ROBBERY

Robbery is theft aggravated in that it is taking another's property, from his person or in his presence, by violence or by putting him in fear. The Larceny Act, 1916, makes it a felony (punishable by penal servitude for life, whipping being possible for a male offender) when—

1. A person being armed with any offensive instrument, or being together with one other person or more, robs or assaults with intent to rob any person; or

2. A person robs another, and immediately before or immediately after such robbery, uses any personal violence.

" ROBBERY DISTINCT FROM LARCENY "

The distinction between simple larceny and robbery is a very old one. In the King's Bench of 1584 it was thus explained: "A man cutteth my girdle privily, my purse hanging thereat, and the purse and the girdle fall to the ground; but he did not take them up (for that he was espied). This is no felony; for that the thief never had an actual possession thereof, severed from my person. But if he had holden the purse in his hand and then cut the girdle (although it had fallen to the ground, and that he took it up no more), then had it been felony. For then he had it once in his possession. But these secret and privy takings from my person are no robbery; for he neither assaulted me, nor put me in any fear."

PARTICULAR OFFENCES UNDER THE LARCENY ACT, 1916

1. *Night offences* ("night" here meaning between 9 o'clock in the evening and 6 o'clock in the morning, 10 and 7 summer time): a person is guilty of a misdemeanour if found by night—

(*a*) Armed with any dangerous or offensive weapon, with intent to break into a building and commit a felony.

(*b*) Having in his possession without lawful excuse— the burden of showing which is upon the accused—any housebreaking implements, like keys, picklocks, jacks. (This constitutes one of the few instances where guilt is presumed, and innocence must be established.)

(c) Having his face blackened or disguised with intent to commit a felony.

2. *Animals.* It is a felony to steal horse, cattle, sheep, pig; or to kill an animal in order to steal carcass or skin.

3. *Dogs.* It is a misdemeanour (punishable by imprisonment up to eighteen months, with or without hard labour)—

(a) To steal a dog, after a previous summary conviction.

(b) To have in his possession a stolen dog, after a previous summary conviction.

(c) Corruptly to take reward under pretence of recovering a a stolen dog.

4. *Larceny by Servants, and Embezzlement.* A clerk or servant embezzles when he appropriates to his own use money or other property taken into possession for his employer or for his office. A clerk or servant steals when he takes *out of his employer's possession* personal property for his own use. The distinction may be illustrated thus. If a shopman puts money given by a customer into his pocket instead of into the till, that is embezzlement. If he takes money out of the till, that is stealing. The distinction is not now very material. For a jury has power to find one charged with embezzlement to be guilty of stealing, or *vice versa.* (Such power constitutes an exception to the merciful rule that a man charged with one crime cannot be found guilty of another. Here, however, no hardship can result from the breaking of the rule; for the accused has in either event full information of the crime with which he is charged.)

5. *Burglary.* Two essentials of this crime are—

(a) It can be committed only in a dwelling-house.

(b) It can be committed only at night (between 9 p.m. and 6 a.m., which means during "summer time" between 10 p.m. and 7 a.m.).

The definition in the Act is: "in the night—

(a) Breaking and entering the dwelling-house of another with intent to commit a felony; or

(b) Breaking out of the dwelling-house of another with intent to commit a felony, or having committed a felony."

(That is, even if the breaking-in is by day or even if the entrance has been made without a breaking-in, the offence is burglary when the breaking-out is by night.)

The Act explains that "dwelling-house" does not include a building, a garage, for instance, though within the same curtilage (i.e. the area attached to the dwelling-house), unless there is a covered and enclosed passage leading from it to the dwelling-house.

"Breaking-in" may consist of unlocking a door, raising a trap-door held down by its own weight, opening a window by pulling up the sash. But entering by an open door or window will not be a breaking-in.

Burglary is a felony punishable by penal servitude for life.

6. *Housebreaking.* This is a less serious offence than burglary and is punishable by a maximum of fourteen years' penal servitude. The crime consists in breaking into *any* building (not merely a dwelling-house) and at any time for the purpose of committing a felony. It should be noted that the intent must be to commit a felony. One who breaks into a building in order to sleep there cannot be convicted of housebreaking: his intention was to trespass merely, a civil wrong, or to commit a public nuisance, a misdemeanour.

7. *Sacrilege.* This is a felony and consists in breaking in and entering any place of divine worship and committing felony within.

8. *Being a director, manager, or public officer of any body corporate or public company makes or helps to make a written statement of accounts which he knows to be false in any material particular, with intent to deceive or defraud any member, shareholder, or creditor, or with intent to induce anybody to become a shareholder or to advance money to the company.*

In *R.* v. *Kylsant* (C.C.A. 1932), the accused was held to have been rightly convicted under this head. A prospectus invited subscriptions to a debenture issue. There were no figures or statements inaccurate in themselves. But the whole was calculated to make people suppose what was not the fact—that, though times had been bad, dividends continued to be paid out of profits. The dividends had in fact been paid out of secret reserves.

FALSE PRETENCES

There may be difficulty at times in distinguishing between the *felony of larceny* and the misdemeanour of *obtaining by false pretences*. The latter is defined (Section 52 of the Larceny Act, 1916) as—

1. "By any false pretence, with intent to defraud, obtaining from any other person any chattel, money, or valuable security,

or causes or procures any money to be paid, or any chattel or
valuable security to be delivered to himself or to any other
person."

2. "With intent to defraud or injure any other person, fraudulently causes or induces any other person to execute, make, accept,
or destroy the whole or any part of a valuable security."

Fraudulently obtaining credit should also be added: incurring
any debt or liability by obtaining credit under false pretences
or by means of any other fraud is a misdemeanour punishable
by imprisonment not exceeding one year under the Debtors
Act, 1869, Section 13.

Thus, it is false pretence to cry false news in a street and
thereby obtain money for a paper falsely said to contain the
news; to assume without right the cap and gown of a commoner
at Oxford and thereby obtain credit; to sell furniture without
telling the buyer that a bill of sale covered it. But the latitude
allowed to traders of exaggerating the merits and minimising the
defects of their goods still imposes upon a customer the duty of
taking precaution if he is not to be tricked. That is, *caveat
emptor* is not yet a needless warning.

"LARCENY" AND "FALSE PRETENCES"

The distinction between *obtaining by false pretences* and *larceny*
is usually put thus: if, as the result of the trick, the person
defrauded intends to part with both the possession and the
property in the goods it is false pretences; but if he is induced
merely to part with the possession of the goods, and does not
intend to part with the property, the offence is larceny by trick.
When John Roe pretends to be Sir Richard Doe and obtains from
a jeweller a ring on credit, not intending to pay, that is *obtaining
by false pretences*: the property in the ring has passed to him for
a time, and he may give a good title to the ring to one (a pawnbroker, for instance) who takes it from him in good faith (*Phillips
v. Brooks*, K.B. 1919). When Blenkarn orders goods in the name
of "Blenkiron and Co.," and the manufacturer supplies them to
Blenkarn, that is *larceny by a trick* on Blenkarn's part: no
property has passed and even a buyer in good faith from the
trickster acquires no right (*Cundy v. Lindsay*, A.C. 1878). In
the first case a contract, though a voidable one, has been made;
and till the contract had been avoided (rescinded) the property
had passed. In the second case, no contract had been made;
no property, therefore, had passed.

EFFECTS OF DISTINCTION

1. From the point of view of the accused it matters little what name is given to his offence : the penalty on conviction will be much the same; and he will not escape upon a technical error in the indictment. The Larceny Act, Section 44, provides : "If on the trial of any indictment for stealing it is proved that the offence amounts in law to obtaining by false pretences with intent to defraud, the jury may acquit the defendant of stealing and find him guilty of obtaining by false pretences," and "If, being tried for false pretences, it is proved that he stole the property, he shall not by reason thereof be entitled to be acquitted of obtaining by false pretences." This provision is designed to overcome the strict rule of criminal law that an indictment cannot be framed in the alternative, that being charged with one offence an accused cannot be found guilty of another. (See the note on "Embezzlement" above.)

With the accused's consent the charge of false pretences may be dealt with summarily, the Court being required to explain to the accused that, "A false pretence means a false representation by words, writing, or conduct that some fact exists or existed, and that a promise as to future conduct not intended to be kept is not by itself a false pretence."

2. The great distinction is in regard to other (collateral) transactions. The false pretender can give a good title; the thief cannot. In the *Cundy* v. *Lindsay* case it was thus explained : "If the chattel has come into the hands of the person who professed to sell it by a *de facto* contract, that is to say, a contract which has purported to pass the property to him from the owner of the property, then the purchaser will obtain a good title, even although afterwards it should appear that there were circumstances connected with that contract which would enable the original owner of the goods to reduce it, and set it aside." The transaction, that is, can be set aside. But, till it is, the trickster can deal with the property as its owner. Not so the thief. That a contract is induced by fraud does not make the contract void. Nor does it prevent property from passing. It merely gives a party defrauded the right, on discovering the fraud, to elect whether he will continue to treat the contract as binding, or will disaffirm the contract and resume his property. The contract is valid till he avoids it. But if, while he is deliberating or before he learns of the fraud, an innocent third party acquires an interest in the property, the right to resume the property is gone.

DAMAGE TO PROPERTY

The Larceny Act, 1916, amply guards the owner of property against wrongful appropriation. The Malicious Damage Act, 1861, guards him against most other infringements of his property rights. "Malicious" here has the wide sense of "wilful" as distinct from "accidental." The ordinary sense of "malice," a desire and an intention to injure a person, need not be present. In *R*. v. *Ward* (C.C.R. 1872), the accused fired at a boat with the intention of deterring the occupants from shooting wild fowl; he unintentionally hit a man in the boat. It was held that the wounding was malicious: "No person can shelter himself from punishment on the ground that the mischief he committed was wider in its consequences than he originally intended." So in *Roper* v. *Knott* (Q.B. 1898), a divisional court held that a milkman, who had watered his master's milk in order that he himself might profit, ought to have been convicted of malicious damage.

The extent to which an owner is entitled to protect property is great; some of the cases may well occasion surprise. Thus, the owner was exempt from liability for the death of a dog killed by contact with an electric fence erected to repel straying cats; a conviction under Section 41 of the Act, the accused having set a rat-trap in his garden to catch trespassing cats or dogs,* was quashed on appeal; in *Daniel* v. *Jones* (C.P. 1877), the Court decided that placing poison in a garden to kill a dog in the habit of trespassing was not acting maliciously.

UNLAWFUL AND MALICIOUS DAMAGE IN GENERAL

So as to cover damage not mentioned specially, the Act makes it a misdemeanour (Section 51) "unlawfully and maliciously to commit any damage, injury, or spoil to or upon any real or personal property whatsoever, either of a public or private nature, for which no punishment is by this Act hereinbefore provided." An act done by night is liable to a much heavier penalty than one done by day. Night acts have always been peculiarly repugnant to the law; a right by day may, indeed, be a wrong by night: "If Adam places a fence where his neighbour B hath a right of driftway to his common of pasture, then B commits no tort if, freshly on the placing thereof, he do abate it in the daytime. But

---

*"Unlawfully and maliciously kill, maim, or wound any dog, bird, beast, or any animal not being cattle but being either the subject of larceny at Common Law, or being ordinarily kept in a state of confinement, or for any domestic purpose."

there will be a tort if he abate it by night, albeit it was placed unlawfully" (*Year Books* of Edward I).

This provision in Section 51 appears wide enough; but some limits of its application should be noted.

1. A mere trespass, where the damage is not substantial, cannot be made into a crime under this section.

The justices convicted footballers, who, after being asked to leave, continued playing in an enclosed field, of "unlawfully and maliciously doing damage with intent to destroy grass, the food of beasts." On appeal it was held that the conviction was wrong: there was no intent to damage (*Eley* v. *Lylle*, 1885). So it seems to be no crime to take mushrooms, blackberries, primroses, or wild plants of any kind, nor to trespass in search of them. Even yet, "Trespassers cannot be prosecuted"; they can only be sued in civil court.

2. The section does not apply when the accused acted under a fair and reasonable supposition that he had a right to do the act complained of.

The claim of right must not be a mere assertion; if there *may* be something in it, however, the prosecutor must have recourse to his civil remedy. In *Usher* v. *Luxmore* (Q.B. 1889), the Queen's Bench Division quashed a conviction by the justices: the appellants had acted under a fair and reasonable supposition that they were acting within their rights. The owner of land over which a public footpath crossed erected two posts in the middle of the path so that his cattle might not stray. The appellants were among those who pulled up one of the posts, and threw it over the hedge. (So, too, in *Heard* v. *Coles*) the justices convicted Heard on the facts following—

The complainant and the appellant had gardens adjoining and separated by a wire fence.

The complainant's clothes line overlapped the appellant's garden, and soapy water dropped upon broccoli.

The appellant cut the line, the clothes fell into the garden and were damaged.

The justices considered that Heard should have made request before cutting; but the Divisional Court held that since Heard was exercising his right in cutting the line, the justices were wrong (see *Lemmon* v. *Webb*, page 536, for this right to abate a nuisance).

WILFUL DAMAGE BY FIRE

The ancient terror of fire is illustrated by the severity with

9

which the law dealt, and still deals, with it. The *civil remedy* is wide: before a statute of Queen Anne's reign a man who kindled a fire was answerable for any damage it did, even though he was innocent of negligence, and, of course, even though he had no wish to cause damage. The statute makes "accidental" fire no longer a liability; but "accidental" does not exclude negligence. In *Filliter* v. *Shippard* (Q.B. 1847), the Court decided on appeal that the defendant was rightly made liable, the plaintiff having shown that his trees and hedges were burnt by a fire which the negligence of the defendant had allowed to escape: "The ancient custom of England was that a person in whose house a fire originated, which afterwards spread to his neighbour's property and destroyed it, must make good the loss. Does the exemption of 'accidental' fires protect the defendant? It is true that, in strictness, the word *accidental* may be employed in contradistinction to *wilful*; and so the same fire might both begin accidentally and be the result of negligence. But it may equally mean a fire produced by mere chance, or incapable of being traced to any cause; and so would stand opposed to the negligence of either servants or masters. And when we find it used in statutes which do not speak of wilful fires but make an important provision with respect to such as are accidental—and consider how great a change in the law would be effected, and how great encouragement would be given to that carelessness of which masters may be guilty as well as servants—we think the plaintiff's construction much the more reasonable of the two."

Wilful firing is severely punished as a crime. In the following circumstances it is a felony—

1. *Burning a Dwelling-house, any Person Being Therein.* This is the ancient crime of *arson.* In spite of the practice of fire insurance—or, maybe, because of the practice—it still retains its serious character and is punishable by penal servitude for life.

2. *Burning a Church or Chapel.* By the Act this has been made a crime equal in heinousness to the crime of arson and is similarly punishable.

3. *Burning a House, Trade, or Farm Building; A Railway Station; a Public Building.* All these are punishable by penal servitude for life.

4. *Burning other Buildings, Goods in Buildings.* Felony punishable by fourteen years' penal servitude.

5. *Attempting to Set Fire to any of the Above is Itself a Felony.*

6. *Burning Stacks* (*of Hay or Corn or Other Crops*) is a felony punishable by penal servitude for life; *burning crops*, whether standing or cut down, or *burning woods* or plantations or heaths, is a felony punishable by fourteen years' penal servitude.

PUBLIC (COMMON) NUISANCE

A *public* (*or common*) *nuisance* is "an act not warranted by law, or an omission to discharge a legal duty, which act or omission obstructs or causes inconvenience or damage to the public in the exercise of rights common to all His Majesty's subjects." It is an annoyance to the community at large, not of a few individuals only, and is indictable as a misdemeanour. Thus, the keeping of a common gaming house is a public nuisance; the obstruction of a highway, or the making it dangerous, is a public nuisance. "If an unreasonable time is occupied in the operations of delivering beer from a brewer's dray into the cellar of a publican, this certainly is a nuisance. A cart or wagon may be unloaded at a gateway; but this must be done with promptitude. No man can make a stable-yard out of the King's highway. . . . I cannot doubt the guilt of the present defendant. He is not to eke out the inconvenience of his own premises by taking in the public highway into his timber-yard; and if the street be narrow, he must remove to a more commodious situation for carrying on his business" (*R.* v. *Jones, Nisi Prius,* 1812).

So it was ruled that to hold a meeting in Trafalgar Square or any other public place, preventing as it does the right of passage, is a public nuisance (*R.* v. *Graham and Burns,* 1888). The following have been held to constitute a nuisance: drawing a crowd of disorderly persons by music and fireworks, obstructing the access to a plaintiff's premises by a theatre queue, placing a gipsy encampment, causing excessive noise by a "merry-go-round," keeping ferocious animals without proper control.

NUISANCE ON A HIGHWAY

To tether cattle on the highway, to ride a horse or a bicycle upon the footpath by the side of the road, to play cards or football on the highway, to fire guns or let off fireworks within 50 feet of the centre of a highway, to deposit rubbish upon the highway—all these, prejudicing the public right of free passage, are public nuisances. The test seems to be: Did the accused's act either (1) *injure the highway*; or (2) *injure, interrupt, or put into personal danger a person travelling thereon*? Thus, on appeal, it was held that the appellant, who had rolled a lighted tar barrel along the highway on the Fifth of November, had been wrongly convicted. For there was no injury to the highway, nor, it seemed in the circumstances, any danger to the public (*Hill* v. *Somerset*).

The various Public Health Acts have created a great number of statutory nuisances.

PUBLIC NUISANCE MAY ALSO BE A CIVIL WRONG

When an individual suffers a special damage from a nuisance he can bring a civil action against the offender. He need not invoke the method of indictment, nor move the Attorney-General to take action; he can begin proceedings simply by issuing a writ. And he can seek, not punishment of the wrongdoer, but compensation for himself and an injunction against the continuance of the nuisance. To sustain the civil action, however, he must show a particular and substantial injury to himself beyond what is suffered by the rest of the public. Thus, if the alleged nuisance is obstruction of a highway the civil claimant must show such things as that free passage of light and air to his own premises was hindered.

UNLAWFUL ASSEMBLY, ROUT, RIOT, STATUTORY RIOT

These are crimes of increasing seriousness connected with meetings.

1. An *unlawful assembly* is a meeting that attempts to carry out any common purpose, lawful or unlawful, in such a manner as to give other people reason to fear a breach of the peace.

2. The unlawful assembly becomes a *rout*, a graver crime, when the meeting proceeds to carry out an unlawful purpose but does not execute it.

3. A *riot* is a tumultuous disturbance of the peace by three or more persons, assembled with an intention to help one another, even by violence if necessary, in carrying out an enterprise of a private nature: "A riot is a tumultuous meeting of persons who are guilty of actual violence; a rout where they endeavour to commit an act which would make them riotous; and an unlawful assembly when they meet with an intention to make a riot, but neither carry their purpose into effect nor make any endeavours towards .t."

4. A riot becomes a *statutory riot* when the public authorities are flouted.

READING THE RIOT ACT

The Riot Act, 1714, makes it a felony of anyone who—

1. Being one of at least twelve, unlawfully, riotously, and tumultuously assembled, to the disturbance of the public peace.

2. Being required by a justice, sheriff, mayor, or other person in authority, by proclamation in the King's name in the form given in the Act, to disperse themselves and peaceably depart.

3. Remain, to the number of twelve or more, and unlawfully, riotously, and tumultuously continue together for one hour after the proclamation (Section 1).

The form of proclamation is: "Our Sovereign Lord the King chargeth and commandeth all persons, being assembled, immediately to disperse themselves, and peaceably to depart to their habitations, or to their lawful business, upon the pains contained in the Act made in the first year of King George the First for preventing tumults and riotous assemblies. God save the King." Making the proclamation is sometimes spoken of as "reading the Riot Act."

CIVIL AUTHORITIES, NOT MILITARY, ARE RESPONSIBLE

The effect of reading the proclamation is to turn a misdemeanour into a felony, more heavily punished; and if stern measures are taken to repress disorders, it will be strong evidence that such measures were needed. But it does not modify the duty of the public authorities to preserve peace, if necessary, by forcible measures. Where it is necessary, the magistrate may seek the aid of the military power to repress disorder; but responsibility still remains with the magistrate in his primary duty as preserver of the peace. It is, indeed, incumbent upon the military officer—as it is in fact upon all citizens—to do what is necessary to repel riot. It is not incumbent upon him to await the magistrate's order to use the force at his disposal: if he does wait beyond what is reasonable, he himself fails in his duty. A commission reported to the House of Commons: "An order to fire from the magistrate who is present is required by military regulations; and wisdom and discretion are entirely in favour of the observance of such a practice. But the order of the magistrate has at law no legal effect. Its presence does not justify the firing if the magistrate is wrong. Its absence does not. excuse the officer for declining to fire when the necessity exists." Yet the King's Regulations, to which an officer is required to adhere, makes a magistrate's order a condition for a command to fire.

In some circumstances, happily in these days unlikely, the officer may be in a very difficult position.

The relevant regulations are—

1. "No officer is to take out troops for the purpose of aiding in the suppression of riot, the maintenance of the public peace, or the execution of the law, except upon the requisition in writing of a magistrate, or in cases of great and sudden emergency. Nor are troops to be sent to assist the civil force in case of expected riot except upon the written requisition of the lord-lieutenant, sheriff, or a magistrate or magistrates having jurisdiction in the place where a riot is expected, or in case of emergency on the receipt of a telegram from such authorities.

2. "The magistrate is to accompany the troops, and the officer is to remain near him.

3. "The troops are not on any account to fire except by word of command of their officer, who is to exercise a humane discretion respecting the extent of the line of fire, and is not to give the word of command to fire unless distinctly required to do so by the magistrate."

The magistrate's duty of reading the proclamation prescribed in the Riot Act is one remainder of the former extensive executive duties he had, duties of so extensive a nature that the justice was the maid-of-all-work to the Tudor Government.

DAMAGE BY RIOT

The local authorities—in counties, the county council; in boroughs, the town council—are bound to compensate for injuries done to house, shop, or building, or the property therein, by a riot (Riot Damage Act, 1886).

1. Claims are to be made within 14 days.

2. The police authority is entitled to ask for statutory declarations regarding the extent of damage.

3. Where an insurance policy covers part or whole of the loss the compensation payable is reduced by the amount recovered under the policy.

The "riot" intended in the Act is the Common Law riot, and the five essentials of such a riot must be proved—

1. Three persons at least.

2. A common purpose.

3. The execution of the common purpose.

4. An intent to help one another.

5. Such force or violence as would alarm a person of reasonable firmness and courage.

FORGERY

A forged document is one that tells a lie about itself. A misdemeanour at Common Law—"the fraudulent making or alteration of a writing to the prejudice of another man's right" —it has, by the Forgery Act, 1913, been made a felony. "Forgery is the making of a false document in order that it may be used as genuine, and the counterfeiting of specific seals and dies with an intent to defraud or deceive."

A document is false if the whole or any material part pretends to be made by or with the authority of one who did not make it nor authorise its making. In particular a document is false—

1. When an unauthorised alteration in a material point has been made in it.

2. When a document pretends to be made by a fictitious or deceased person.

The mention in the Act of ways in which a document may be false does not preclude other ways: the Criminal Justice Act, 1925, enacts: "For the purpose of removing doubts it is hereby declared that a document may be a false document for the Forgery Act, 1913, notwithstanding that it is not false in any such manner as is described in the Act." Forgery, therefore, is by no means limited to the popular sense of signing another's name: the falsity may be in any material point.

Intent to defraud is an essential to the crime of forgery. Where this is present, and where the false documents operate to transfer property, the crime is a felony punishable by penal servitude for life. Such documents are—

1. A will, codicil, or other testamentary document, either of a dead or a living person.

2. A deed or bond.

3. A bank-note.

4. A valuable security, including cheques and bills of exchange.

5. Documents of title to land or goods.

6. Charter-parties or assignments of them.

The crime is felony also when it strikes against the confidence felt in public documents, when it relates to such documents as—

1. Registers of births, deaths, marriages.

2. Official documents of any court of justice.

3. Any certificate needed for the celebration of marriage.

4. Any customs or excise permit.

Demanding property on forged documents, with intent to defraud, is also a felony. Under this head a telegram, sent by a telegraph clerk in another person's name to make a bet on a race that had already been run, was held to be a forged instrument.

It is a misdemeanour to forge, with intent to defraud, any document the forgery of which is not made a felony.

The "uttering" of a forged document—the utilising of it, knowing it to be forged for the fraudulent purpose—is punishable as a felony or a misdemeanour in like manner as the forgery itself.

PERJURY

Perjury, the most serious of the attempts to obstruct or to pervert justice, is now defined by the Perjury Act, 1911. It is still a misdemeanour only; but it is one punishable by seven years' penal servitude. The essentials of the crime are—

1. The person making the statement has been sworn as a witness or as an interpreter in a judicial proceeding.

2. The statement is a material one: its truth or falsehood has a direct bearing upon the decision that will be reached.

3. The person knows the statement to be false, or does not believe it to be true.

The forms and ceremonies used in administering the oath are immaterial, so long as the person taking the oath has accepted them without objection. And those allowed to "affirm" or "declare" instead of swearing are under the same obligation to tell the truth.

"Judicial proceeding" means a proceeding before a tribunal that has power to receive evidence on oath. Thus, on appeal to the Queen's Bench (*R.* v. *Lloyd*, Q.B. 1887), a conviction for perjury was quashed on the ground that the false statement was not made before a court of competent jurisdiction. Lloyd had been summoned before a registrar in bankruptcy, was sworn before him, but—for convenience, as it appeared—was examined in the presence of his own solicitor by the solicitor for the official receiver in a room adjoining that of the registrar.

We may perhaps assert that English law seeks rather to prevent perjury than to punish it; for it is anxious that witnesses shall speak freely of what they know, without the constant fear that one whom their evidence condemns may aver perjury. The strictest proof is needed both as to what the accused actually swore, and as to the materiality of his statement. Moreover, corroboration is needed before a conviction can be recorded:

"A person shall not be liable to be convicted of any offence against this Act solely upon the evidence of one witness" (Section 13). The evidence of that witness must be supported by other material evidence.

False statements other than perjury may be punishable misdemeanours. Such are—

1. *False Statements on Oath not in Judicial Proceeding.* This includes a false affidavit for the purposes of bills of sale.

2. *False Statements in Relation to Marriage.* This includes false declarations to secure a certificate or licence for marriage, or false declarations about any particular required to be registered. It also covers a false representation of a person that his consent to the marriage is required by law, and who forbids the issue of a certificate or licence for marriage.

3. *False Statements to the Registrar of Births or Deaths.*

4. *False Statutory Declarations.* The form of declarations which may be required when a birth or other certificate is unobtainable, or when statements of income are needed in order to assess scholarship grants, is "I, A. B., do solemnly and sincerely declare, that . . . and I make this solemn declaration conscientiously believing the same to be true, and by virtue of the provisions of the 'Statutory Declarations Act, 1835'." One who knowingly makes a false and material statement is liable to imprisonment for two years and fine.

5. *False Declarations in Order to Obtain Registry* as being qualified to practise any vocation or calling.

MISCELLANEOUS CRIMES AND ILLEGALITIES

1. "*Subornation of Perjury.*" This is an attempt to induce a person to commit any of the offences punishable under the Perjury Act, 1911. The offence is a misdemeanour: "Every person who incites or attempts to procure or suborn another to commit an offence against this Act shall be guilty of a misdemeanour." He "suborns" who induces, by bribery or otherwise. He is tried and punished as if he were a principal offender.

2. "*Misprision of Treason or of Felony.*" It is the duty of a good citizen to prevent the commission of a crime or to help in its punishment. To conceal a felony is, therefore, an indictable misdemeanour: where a person, not being concerned in the crime, conceals his knowledge, he is guilty of "misprision of felony (or of treason)." Apparently, there is no similar obligation to disclose misdemeanours.

3. "*Embracery.*" This Common Law misdemeanour consists in the attempt to pervert justice by corrupting juries or court officials. It is an effort to influence, by bribes or by any means other than evidence and argument in open court, a judicial decision.

4. "*Maintenance.*" It is recognised that litigation should not arise without good cause. If, therefore, a man by money or other help stirs another to prosecute a suit, in which he himself has no concern and simply for the satisfaction of seeing a quarrel, he is liable to an action for the tort of "maintenance." It is not, of course, wrong, out of disinterested charity, to enable a poor man to maintain his suit. But "it is unlawful for a stranger to render officious assistance, by money or otherwise, to another person in a suit in which that third person has himself no legal interest" (*Neville* v. *London Express*, A.C. 1919).

Maintenance does not apply to criminal cases. There must be no impediment for crime hindering a prosecution. If a person puts the criminal law in motion from an irregular motive, the aggrieved person has his remedy in an action for malicious prosecution.

5. "*Champerty*" is the supporting of a quarrel for a share in the proceeds, when "he who maintains another is to have by agreement part of the land, or debt, in suit." Both maintenance and champerty, though at Common Law misdemeanours as tending to the stirring up of strife, have now ceased to be crimes, the remedy in tort being possibly adequate for their suppression.

6. "*Compounding a felony*" (or other offence) is the making a bargain to conceal a felony (or other offence). A person, knowing that a felony has been committed, who agrees to abstain from prosecuting is guilty of the offence. To advertise a reward for stolen goods, with an intimation that "no questions will be asked," is such an offence. The bargain is not only a misdemeanour; it is void in law, and the Court may cancel its effects. The secretary of a friendly society embezzled the society's money; the directors threatened prosecution; relatives of the secretary gave promissory notes to the society. The directors made no express promise not to prosecute. But they were aware that the stifling of a prosecution was the motive of the relatives; and the Court of Appeal held—after the secretary's death—that there was an implied agreement on the part of the directors not to prosecute, and ordered the notes to be cancelled (*Jones* v. *Merionethshire Building Society*, Ch. 1892).

7. *Prize-fighting.* An exhibition of sparring is lawful. A

prize-fight, where the combatants intend to fight till one gives in from exhaustion or injury, is an indictable misdemeanour, whether or not gloves are worn. Each combatant is guilty of assault upon the other; for, though the consent to battery will bar a civil action by either, no one by consent can change a crime into an innocent act. So, too, if a man is killed in a duel, it is murder on the part of all directly concerned.

8. *Forcible Entry.* English law does, in general, allow a man to take his property from one wrongfully possessed of it. But, when there might be grave danger of a breach of the peace, statute law has taken this right away. It has done this in the case of land: the rightful owner must recover that by due process of law. For forcibly to enter and take possession of lands and tenements, with menaces, force, and arms, is an indictable misdemeanour. But (*Hemmings and Wife* v. *Stoke Poges Golf Club,* K.B. 1920) settles that, when one is in possession of premises as a trespasser, he can recover no damages unless more force than necessary is used for his removal.

9. *Blasphemy.* This crime consists in reviling Christianity. Mere denial of what Christianity teaches is not blasphemy, nor is serious argument against it. If the decencies of controversy are observed, even the fundamentals of religion may be attacked. Where insulting words are calculated to bring Christianity into ridicule and contempt so that believers are incited to a breach of the peace, blasphemy is committed. The essence of the crime is the likelihood that violent reprisals may result.

10. *Rescue.* This is the forcible liberation of another from lawful custody. To constitute this crime the rescuer must be aware of the lawful custody: if the custody is by a constable, the knowledge is presumed; if by a private individual, the knowledge must be proved.

11. *Supporting Foreign Quarrels.* It would undoubtedly seriously affect friendly relations if British subjects were to intervene in quarrels with which this country has no concern. There is, therefore, a duty to abstain from foreign quarrels.

The Foreign Enlistment Act, 1870, makes it a criminal offence for a British subject wherever he lives—

1. To enlist in the service of a state at war with a state with which we are at peace.

2. To persuade or help others so to enlist.

3. To help to furnish vessels of war, having reason to believe that they will be used in the service of the warring state.

4. To fit out any naval or military expedition against a friendly state, unless with the licence of the Crown.

Moreover, any agreement that contemplates action hostile to a friendly state is unlawful and cannot be enforced.

12. *Child Destruction.* This is a statutory crime, created by the Infant Life (Preservation) Act, 1929. A person who, with intent to destroy the life of a child capable of being alive, by any wilful act causes a child to die before it has an existence independent of its mother, is guilty of the felony of "Child Destruction." Penal servitude for life may be awarded to one convicted. An act done in good faith, for the purpose of preserving the life of its mother, does not of course make a person guilty of the crime.

13. *Infanticide.* The Infanticide Act (1922) makes the killing of a newly born child by the mother, "when the effect of giving birth to the child has disturbed the balance of her mind," into the crime of *infanticide*, which must be regarded as manslaughter, not as murder.

The Court has power, in the event of acquittal and if evidence establishes the fact, to find the accused guilty of "Concealment of Birth." This misdemeanour consists in the secret disposition of the dead body in the effort to conceal the birth.

So, too, there is power to return a verdict of "manslaughter" or of "guilty but insane."

14. *Sedition (Treason-Felony), or Incitement to Sedition.* This, the vaguest of crimes, consists in the attempt, either by writing or speech—

1. To vilify or degrade the King in the esteem of his subjects.

2. To create discontent or disaffection.

3. To incite to tumult, violence, or disorder.

4. To bring the Government or Constitution into hatred or contempt.

5. To recommend force for the effecting of a change in the law.

Clearly, a wide interpretation would preclude any criticism, however fair and however decently expressed, of the Government. All opposition could be effectively prevented. Freedom of speech upon political matters would be annihilated. In ordinary times, however, nothing but language passing all bounds of sober and decent argument is prosecuted. The bounds are usually far-stretching. Persons convicted of sedition, or of seditious libel, are to be imprisoned in the First Division. If, however, an alien *incites to sedition*, he is liable to penal servitude on conviction on indictment for ten years, and to imprisonment on summary conviction for three months: "If any alien attempts or does any act calculated or likely to cause sedition or disaffection amongst any of His Majesty's Forces, or amongst the civilian population, he shall be liable on conviction on indictment to penal servitude for a term not exceeding ten years, or on summary conviction to imprisonment for a term not exceeding three months" (Aliens Restriction Act, 1919).

15. *Blackmail.* The Larceny Act, 1916, makes it an offence—punishable by penal servitude for life—to threaten to accuse a person of a crime "with intent to extort or gain any property or valuable thing." That the offence may conceivably be committed even when one is seeking what one believes his due was shown in *R.* v. *Kerr* (Central Criminal Court, 1931). The prosecutor admitted that he owed the accused money; but the Recorder said: "I shall tell the jury that they may hold a man guilty of intent to extort if—although he honestly believes a debt is due—he threatens to employ discreditable means whereby to injure his debtor, either physically or morally. I believe that to be the law because it is only common sense and common justice."

It is legal to demand money due; it is illegal to enforce payment by threatening to expose misconduct.

A similar decision had been reached in *R.* v. *Denyer*, 1926, where the Criminal Appeal Court decided that the offence had been committed of "uttering, knowing the contents, a letter demanding with menaces and without any reasonable or probable cause any property." Denyer's proposal—he was the agent of a trade association—to the prosecutor was to pay in order that the prosecutor's name should not appear on a "stop list." The prosecutor had acted in contravention of the rules of his association; inclusion in the "stop list" would have meant ruin; and the defence was that the proposal was lawful and reasonable in that it lessened the penalty. But the Court declared: "It is an excuse that might be offered by blackmailers to an indefinite extent. There is not the remotest nexus or relationship between a right to put the name upon the stop list and a right to demand £257 as the price of abstaining from that course."

It is not necessary that the letter demanding money or other property shall contain a direct threat; if a threat can be fairly implied that is enough to establish the crime. Nor does **the truth** or falsehood of the accusation matter; the one question is: Did the accused intend to extort by threatening to make the accusation?

16. "*Welshing*" at Races. This is a species of the big genus, obtaining money by false pretences. It is a theft accomplished through a pretence to contract. The bookmaker who absconds with a backer's money is guilty of larceny by a trick (*R.* v. *Buckmaster*, Q.B. 1888). For he had intended not to contract but to steal. It should be noted, though, that the winner of the bet cannot sue the bookmaker for the winnings, nor can he sue even for the stake back. The "welsher" can be prosecuted for a crime; he cannot be made liable in a civil court.*

One famous chief justice became rhetorical in dismissing an application for money due under an illegal contract.

"No polluted hand shall touch the pure fountains of justice. Whoever is a party to an unlawful contract, if he hath once paid the money stipulated to be paid in pursuance thereof, he shall not have the help of a Court to fetch it back again. You shall not have a right of action when you come into a court of justice in this unclean manner to recover it back. '*Procul O! procul este profani*'."

---

* FRAUD NOT NECESSARILY A CRIME. One must admit that at times the line marking off frauds that give rise only to an action for damages, and the crime of obtaining money by false pretences, for which a prosecution may be instituted, is difficult to draw. And it would be drawn differently in different periods. The present Criminal Courts take note of many predatory activities that the Courts two hundred years ago would have thought outside their province.

In *Regina* v. *Nehuff* (Q.B. 1706), there was a motion for a certiorari to remove an indictment found at the Old Bailey for a cheat. The defendant had borrowed £600 from a *femme covert*, and promised to send her some fine cloth and gold dust as a pledge. He sent no gold dust, but some coarse cloth worth little or nothing.

The Court granted a certiorari, because the fact was not a matter criminal (for it was the prosecutor's fault to repose such a confidence in the defendant). And it was an absurd prosecution. That is to say the defrauded wife—*femme covert*—was left to her civil remedy.

So, too, in *R.* v. *Wheatley*, the King's Bench, in 1760, refused to consider a breach of contract as a crime. The prosecutor had paid the accused for a quantity of beer; the beer was not delivered; instead of bringing an action for breach of contract, the aggrieved party prosecuted for crime. A crime, however, concerns the public, and, the Court said: "What is it to the public whether R. W. has or has not his eighteen gallons of amber beer?"

All this is in the spirit of the old idea that, as against the majesty of the law and the upholding of its principles, the individual is nothing.

An advocate pleaded that if his client should be held responsible for a number of fires caused by the escape of fire from his own premises he would be ruined. The contention received slight consideration from the Court. "This defendant will be undone and impoverished for ever, if this action be allowed against him; for then twenty other such actions will be brought against him for like matter." "What is that to us?" asked the Court. "It is better that he should be utterly undone than that, for him, the law should be changed" (*Year Book*, 1401, *Beaulieu* v. *Finglam*).

17. *Dangerous Driving of Motor Vehicle.* One charged with an offence should have every facility to defend himself. How anxious the Court is to ensure this was well illustrated in *R.* v. *Bolkis* (C.C.A. 1932). There the Court quashed the conviction of Bolkis, who had been convicted at Gloucester Assizes for dangerous driving. The point upon which the appeal succeeded was that notice of the intended prosecution had not been given in good time to the owner of the car involved. " Good time " is now defined by statute, by the Road Traffic Act, 1930, which—while in Section 11 it creates the crime of " dangerous driving "—in Section 21 makes provision for fair trial of the accused.

Section 21 provides as follows—

Where a person is prosecuted for an offence under any of the provisions of this part of this Act relating respectively to the maximum speed at which motor vehicles may be driven, he shall not be convicted unless either—

(*a*) He was warned at the time the offence was committed that the question of prosecuting him for an offence under some one or other of the provisions aforesaid would be taken into consideration ; *or*

(*b*) Within 14 days of the commission of the offence a summons for the offence was served on him ; *or*

(*c*) Within the said 14 days a notice of the intended prosecution specifying the nature of the alleged offence and the time and place where it is alleged to have been committed was served on or sent by registered post to him or the person registered as the owner of the vehicle at the time of the commission of the offence.

Provided that—

(i) Failure to comply with this requirement shall not be a bar to the conviction of the accused in any case where the Court is satisfied that—

(1) Neither the name and address of the accused nor the name and address of the registered owner of the vehicle, could with reasonable diligence have been ascertained in time for a summons to be served or for notice to be served or sent as aforesaid.

(2) The accused by his own conduct contributed to the failure ; and

(ii) The requirement of this section shall in every case be deemed to have been complied with unless and until the contrary is proved.

The judgment of the Court ran—

"Although the name and address of the accused could not, with reasonable diligence, have been ascertained in time, there was no such difficulty about the name and address of the registered owner of the vehicle, which were in fact known to the Gloucestershire police seven days only after the commission of the offence, namely, on 18th August; and that there was therefore ample time for doing that which by Section 21 (a) is enough to justify a conviction under Section 11, that is, serve on, or send by registered post to the registered owner of the vehicle a notice of the intended prosecution.

"We think that this is fatal to the conviction.

"One of three conditions must be performed if a conviction is to be good for an offence to which the section relates; but if none of them could be performed, because the relevant names and addresses could not be, with reasonable diligence, obtained in time, the failure to perform them is excused. Here the prosecution have only shown that two of the conditions could not be performed for the reason stated, and they have therefore not excused their failure to perform any of the three."

OFFENCES IN REGARD TO CHILDREN

A number of these, some serious enough to be punished by imprisonment, some quite trivial, are to be found in the Children and Young Persons Act, 1933. Such are—

1. Causing or allowing a person under 16 to be in a street for the purpose of begging (penalty, three months' hard labour or £25 fine).

2. Allowing a child under 7 to be in a room with an open fire grate not sufficiently protected.

3. Allowing a child between 4 and 16 to reside in or to frequent a brothel.

4. Parents causing or encouraging the seduction or prostitution or unlawful carnal knowledge of girl under 16.

5. Persons failing to give notice in writing to the local authority that they have undertaken the nursing and maintenance of an infant under 7 (see the note below) apart from its parents.

6. Selling tobacco to children under 16.

7. Buying old metal from children under 16.

8. Taking articles in pawn from children under 14.

9. Giving a child under 5, except upon the order of a qualified doctor, intoxicating liquor.

10. Allowing a child in the bars of licensed premises during opening hours.

11. Failing to take adequate precautions for the safety of children at entertainments.

(Where "child" and "young person" are contrasted, "child" refers to one under 14, "young person" to one under 17.)

CARE AND PROTECTION OF JUVENILES

The 1933 Children and Young Persons Act penalises general neglect of young persons or children. Sections 61 and 62 enable any constable or "authorised person"—including the officer of a society authorised by the Home Secretary—to bring a child or young person before a Juvenile Court and to remove that child or young person to a place of safety pending the hearing. The power can be exercised when there is no parent or guardian, or the parent or guardian is bad or useless, or when the child is in company of vagrants who are preventing him from receiving education.

It is, moreover, a penal offence: (1) for a person under 16 to trade in the streets; (2) to permit a child under the age of 14 to take part in any entertainment for which a charge is made without a licence from the local education authority; (3) to permit a boy or girl under 16 to take part in any performance in which life or limb is endangered; (4) to allow a juvenile under 18 to go abroad to perform for profit without a special licence from a police magistrate, who may at his discretion impose restrictions.

FIREARMS (GUN LICENCE)

"To ride or go armed" without authority has long been in this country an indictable offence. The Firearms Act, 1920, now regulates the matter. No one may buy or have any firearm or ammunition until he holds a "firearm certificate." This is obtained upon application to the chief officer of police of the district. The officer grants it when satisfied that the applicant has a good reason for wanting the certificate, and that danger to the public safety or to peace will not be increased by granting the request. An appeal from a refusal lies to a court of summary jurisdiction. (The maximum penalty prescribed is £50 fine, or three months' hard labour, or both.) No person under 14 may have firearm or ammunition. Dealers in firearms must be registered, must keep a record of transactions, and must before selling arms or ammunition require the firearm certificate to be produced.

The Gun Licences Act, 1870, makes it an offence (penalty £10) to carry outside the bounds of his house firearm or any kind of gun from which a missile can be discharged without having a licence. A *licence to kill game* renders unnecessary a gun licence. Other exemptions arise from the nature of the matter : common carriers in the pursuance of their business, soldiers, etc., on duty, persons scaring birds or killing vermin (including rabbits) on their own land, need have no licence. By the Game Licence Act, 1860, an excise penalty of £20 is prescribed for the offence of "pursuing game without a licence" (see also below Ground Game Act).

GAME

Offences in regard to "game" are statutory offences. For at Common Law wild animals when alive are no one's property. The only remedy, therefore, apart from statute, a landowner would have against a "poacher" was to sue him for trespass. A number of Acts now give him far-reaching remedies.

"Game" consists of "hares, pheasants, partridges, grouse, heath or moor game, black game, and bustards" (Game Act, 1831).

"*Close Times*" for game during which it is a penalty to kill are—

1. *Partridge* between 1st February and 1st September.
2. *Black Game*, 10th December and 20th August.
3. *Bustard*, 1st March and 1st September.
4. *Pheasant*, 1st February and 1st October.
5. *Grouse*, 10th December and 12th August.
6. *Hares*, 1st March and 31st July.

A penalty of £1 per head of game killed during the close season is prescribed ; and there is a special penalty of £5 for hunting on Sunday or Christmas Day (Game Act, 1831).

Under the Act a tenant of land has the right to kill game, unless the landlord has expressly reserved the right. As a rule no one may trap or kill game without a game licence, every occupier of land, however, has " as incident to and inseparable from his occupation of the land, the right to kill and take ground game thereon, concurrently with any other person who may have the right." Any agreement whereby the occupier is deprived of this right is of no effect. The occupier need not take out a licence to kill ground game, nor need those—members of his household or persons in his service—whom he authorises to kill. He must not use firearms at night-time, nor employ spring traps (except in rabbit-holes), nor use poison.

POACHING

This statutory offence consists in trespassing in pursuit of "game" which, since the Poaching Prevention Act, 1862, includes, in addition to the items noted above, rabbits and the eggs of game birds. Penalties of increasing severity are prescribed in accordance with the assumed greater seriousness of the offence—

1. *Poaching in the day-time, penalty £2.*

2. *Five or more poaching together, £5 each person.*

3. *Any of these five being armed or offering violence to game-keepers or others entitled to prevent trespass, £5 in addition to any other penalty.*

4. *Poaching by night. First offence, imprisonment with hard labour for three months and afterwards to find sureties, fine £25. Penalties are doubled for a second offence, the accused having, however, the option of trial by jury.*

5. *Poaching by night and offering violence to owner or occupier. Penal servitude for seven years upon indictment.*

6. *Three or more together, any being armed. Penal servitude for fourteen years upon indictment.*

RIGHTS OF SEARCH

Peculiar and very exceptional rights of search and of arrest are given by the various Acts in regard to the offence of poaching—

1. If a trespasser in pursuit of game does not give his real name and address when required to do so by a gamekeeper, or if he does not quit the land when asked, the gamekeeper may arrest him and take him within twelve hours before a magistrate. There must be no longer detention; if he cannot be taken before a magistrate the ordinary proceeding by summons or warrant must be followed. It would seem that the person arrested, if he could show that though a trespasser he was not "in pursuit of game," would have a valid claim for damages for false imprisonment.

2. When any person is found on land in pursuit of game with any game in his possession that appears to have been recently killed, the occupier or gamekeeper may demand the game and upon refusal take it by force. Here, again, it would seem that

the occupier might very well be incurring the penalties prescribed for the felony of "robbery." For, if the trespasser successfully establishes his title to the particular game, then the occupier has "taken property from his person by violence or threat of violence."

3. A police officer may search any person whom he may reasonably suspect of coming from land where he has unlawfully been in pursuit of game. He may take guns or other poaching apparatus or any game being carried, and summon before two magistrates (Poaching Prevention Act, 1862). He may also stop and search a cart or other conveyance. Unless, however, his reasons commend themselves to the Court he may, if nothing illicit is found, himself become a trespasser. For the law leans against any invasion of person or property, and requires a strong justification of it.

SEARCH WARRANTS

This is illustrated by the precautions taken in regard to a search warrant. This is an authority *to a special officer, to enter a specific house, to search for and seize specified property*. The Larceny Act, 1861, Section 103, enacts that a justice of the peace may grant a warrant, even on oath that there is reasonable cause to suspect stolen goods to be in a certain place.

In the search warrant for stolen goods—

1. There must be a full charge upon oath of a theft.

2. The owner must attend at the examination of the warrant to show the goods to the officer, who must see that they answer the description.

3. The owner abides the event at his peril; if the goods are not found he is a trespasser, and the officer, being an innocent person, is a convenient witness against him.

FOX-HUNTING

No question of poaching arises here, since a fox is not game. Still, a fox-hunter may be a trespasser. For, though public necessity may justify what otherwise would be a trespass, there is no such necessity in fox-hunting. The Court of Queen's Bench (*Paul, etc.* v. *Summerhayes*, 1878), considered the matter upon a case, stated by the justice. The justices had awarded the respondent damages against fox-hunters, who had resented and resisted his opposition to entry of the chase on his father's land, and the Chief Justice upheld the award: "Was the respondent justified in resisting the entry of the appellants on his father's land? I think he was. Fox-hunting must be carried on in subordination to the ordinary rights of property."

INDICTMENT OF A JOINT STOCK COMPANY

A corporation is a legal person and may, in certain events, be made liable even for crime. But there are obvious limitations upon such liability.

During a mining strike, when disturbances were feared, the managers of Cory Brothers & Co. defended their premises against possible trespassers by a live electric fence. They gave adequate notice that they had done so. An attack on the premises was, in fact, made by the strikers, and one of these, coming into contact with the fence, was killed. The company along with three individuals was indicted at Glamorgan County Assizes. The first count in the indictment was *manslaughter*. The second count was *setting up an engine calculated to destroy human life or inflict grievous bodily harm with intent against trespassers or other persons*. This second offence is forbidden by Section 31 of the Offences Against the Person Act, 1861.

It was held, however, that the indictment of the company must be quashed. The technical reason is, perhaps, that on an indictment the body of the criminal must be before the Court. The corporation clearly cannot be indicted for a felony or for a misdemeanour involving personal violence (*R.* v. *Cory*, K.B. 1927).

RESERVING A DEFENCE

The Court of Criminal Appeal anxiously and scrupulously guards the rights of an accused. He must, when charged with an offence, be brought to speedy trial: the police have only a restricted time within which to prepare the case against him. Nor need he answer a charge.

The Recorder, in his summing up to the jury, commented adversely on the fact that the prisoner had failed to disclose his defence at the preliminary hearing before the magistrate. The Court of Criminal Appeal quashed the conviction on the ground that such comments were improper. A man has a right to reserve his defence. Perhaps the police are put under a handicap through this. For they are unaware of what defences they will meet. But it is for the prosecution to make out its case; then only need the accused bring forward his defence: Court of Criminal Appeal (*R.* v. *Naylor*, 1932).

DEFENCE OF " AUTREFOIS ACQUIT "

It is a rule of Criminal Law that to be acquitted or to be convicted upon a charge is a bar to a subsequent trial upon the
same charge. The existence of this rule is, however, sometimes
not quite understood. The test whether *autrefois convict* or
autrefois acquit has been established is not whether the facts
relied upon by the Crown are the same in both cases. The test
is whether the offence charged is the same, whether the accused
has been in jeopardy twice on the same charge. An accused was
convicted of arson, though the jury on the same facts acquitted
him of murder. He had, in order to obtain insurance money,
burnt down his house and had—inadvertently and, indeed, to
his evident great distress—by the felony caused the death of his
son. Technically, this was murder; but a compassionate jury
acquitted him. He was, however, subsequently convicted of arson.
Similarly, one acquitted of manslaughter may be convicted upon
the same facts of dangerous driving. The Lord Chief Justice
in *R.* v. *Stringer* (C.C.A. 1933), explains the position: "With
regard to the two counts of the indictment it is to be remembered
that each count is a separate indictment. It is to be observed
that on the first count for manslaughter the appellant could not
have been convicted of dangerous driving. In other words, on
the charge of manslaughter, the appellant was never in jeopardy
on the charge under the Road Traffic Act, 1930. If there had
been two separate indictments at separate times he could not
successfully have put forward a plea of *autrefois acquit*. But in
the opinion of the Court it is not desirable that a charge under
Section 11 of the Road Traffic Act, 1930, should be made a
count in an indictment charging manslaughter. If the two charges
are to be made they should be made in two separate indictments.
Any confusion would then be avoided."

The test is whether the accused is charged with an offence which
is the same, or practically the same. Thus, the offence of threatening to publish with intent to extort (Section 31, Larceny Act,
1916), and of uttering a letter demanding money with menaces
(Section 29, Larceny Act, 1916), are quite distinct charges.

INTOXICATING LIQUOR

THE law governing the sale and consumption of alcoholic liquor in England and Wales is contained chiefly in the Licensing (Consolidation) Act, 1910, and the Licensing Act, 1921. The 1910 Act is an Act consolidating in one head the legislation up to that date that had not been repealed, and the 1921 Act modified, to some extent, restrictions imposed during the war. In addition, legislation concerning the licensed trade is to be found in the various Finance Acts passed yearly, embodying budget provisions.

SPHERE OF LEGISLATION

While it is possible to indicate only main points herein, the licensing legislation now in force covers the vast fields of manufacture, sale and consumption, quality and purity of the liquor, hours of and premises for sale thereof, fitness of persons to sell and consume, sale to young people, regulations for clubs, insobriety, etc.

Administration of the law is in the hands of the police acting for the Licensing Justices of the various licensing divisions, and due regard is paid to complaints about a licensed house or licensee at each general annual licensing meeting (February) and the other (transfer) sessions during the year. Ignorance of law is no plea in court.

WHAT IS INTOXICATING LIQUOR?

For the purpose of licensing law, "intoxicating liquor" is defined (Section 110, Act of 1910) as "spirits, wine, beer, porter, cider, perry, and sweets, and any fermented, distilled, or spirituous liquor which cannot, according to any law for the time being in force, be legally sold without an excise license."

LICENCES

Licences are required for the manufacture of, and dealing in, intoxicating liquor, wholesale or retail, subject to certain exemptions granted in the case of small quantities brewed by a private individual for domestic consumption only. Thus brewers, distillers, wine and spirit merchants, keepers of hotels, inns, and all licensed houses require a licence to sell. A manufacturer's licence usually covers wholesale dealing; licences required for the retailing of intoxicating liquor are, as a rule, of two kinds—

(*a*) *Justices' Licence* of fitness to apply for and to hold an excise licence. This may be for one year or for a term of years not exceeding seven. It is granted at the general annual licensing meeting of the county, borough, or division, and expires on 5th April where annual.

(*b*) *Excise Retailer's Licence*, certifying that requisite excise duty has been duly paid.

Exceptions to this requirement are of a minor nature and are enumerated in the Licensing Act, 1910, Sections 64, 88, 111, and Section E of Schedule I of the Finance Act, 1909–10.

Opposition to the grant of a licence may be offered, on reasonable grounds, provided previous written objection is made. In practice, no excise licence is needed by doctors and chemists for the sale of medicines containing spirits (Section 111).

Retailers' Excise Licences may be ON or OFF and expire, as a rule, on 30th September. The ON-licence authorises sale for consumption either on or off the premises; the OFF-licence permits of sale only for consumption *off* the premises. Both ON- and OFF-licences are subject to payment of the excise duty set out in Schedule I, Finance Act, 1909–10.

Passenger vessels, hotels, public buildings, theatres, music-halls, railway refreshment rooms and restaurant cars all require excise licences (Finance Act, 1909–10, Schedule I) but no justices' licence. In general, the law as to hours of sale must be complied with. For "Clubs," see p. 277.

Early-closing and Six-day Licences are not so common. The former requires a house to close one hour earlier than ordinary houses, but there is nothing to prevent the sale of soft drinks after the restricted hour.

The six-day licence may not open on Sundays, although liquor may be supplied to persons lodging in the house. Both these licences carry with them a remission of excise duty amounting to one-seventh the ordinary rate.

Occasional Licences. The term given to special permits granted for the sale of liquor at a place other than a licensed house at a special time, e.g. balls, dances, shows, dinners, sports meetings, etc. Application has to be made to the local police for this kind of licence.

The police also have power to grant to licence-holders special **extensions of** time beyond customary opening-hours for specific purposes. Such extensions are not to be of such regularity as to effect a permanent extension of hours.

KINDS OF RETAIL EXCISE LICENCES

Authorises Sale of

1. *Publican's full licence* . Spirits, beer, cider, wine, sweets ON or OFF the premises.
2. *Beer ON-licence* . Beer and cider ON or OFF.
3. *Cider ON-licence* . Cider only, ON or OFF.
4. *Wine ON-licence* . Wine and sweets ON or OFF.
5. *Sweets ON-licence* . Sweets, ON or OFF.
6. *Spirits OFF-licence* . Spirits OFF only, but not in open vessels or less than one reputed quart.
7. *Beer OFF-licence* . Beer and cider off.
8. *Cider OFF-licence* . Cider off.
9. *Wine OFF-licence* . Wine and sweets off, not in open vessels and not less than one reputed pint.
10. *Sweets off* . . . Sweets off.

Sweets is defined (Finance Act, 1909–10, Section 52) as any liquor made from fruit and sugar, or fruit or sugar mixed with any other material, which has undergone fermentation in the manufacture, and includes British wines, made wines, mead, and metheglin.

In general, justices' licences are required for the above as well. All these excise licences expire on 30th September each year, and licensee's name and class of licence must be displayed clearly over the door of the premises, and kept legible.

RENEWAL OF LICENCES

Renewal of an ordinary ON-licence can be refused only by the justices without compensation being paid (1910 Act, Sections 17–18) for—

1. Misconduct of the premises.
2. Unsuitability of premises, or for a structural defect.
3. The unsatisfactory character of the applicant.
4. A legal reason which renders void a renewal.

For pre-1869 beerhouses and pre-1903 OFF-licences, there are certain qualifications of the above grounds for refusal. Licences granted after 15th August, 1904, are governed by Sections 14 and 29 of the Act.

TRANSFER OF LICENCES

During each year the licensing justices hold "transfer sessions" for the purpose of approving the transfer of the licence of a premises from one person to another. No transfer can take place without the consent of the justices.

In every case the transferee must show that he is a fit and proper person to hold a licence.

COMPENSATION

When an ON-licence is not renewed on the grounds that it is a redundant licence and not required, compensation becomes payable to the licensee, and his landlords (if any), for the removal of the licence. The compensation money is paid out of a central fund maintained largely by levy on all ON-licence holders. The scale of levy is set out in Schedule 3 of the Licensing Act, 1910. A yearly tenant may claim refund of his compensation levy from his landlord, and the amount that a lessee may claim from his landlord varies according to the unexpired term of his lease (Schedule 3, Part 2). In no case shall the amount repaid by the landlord exceed one-half of the amount of yearly rent.

REMOVALS

1. A brewer-owner or licensee may apply to the justices for the removal of the licence to more conveniently situated premises in the same district; *or*

2. For removal to fresh premises following demolition of the old for a public purpose or by reason of destruction by fire, etc.

There is no appeal permissible against the refusal of an application made under (1) above. Instances of such applications for "removal" occur, for example, where a slum-clearance scheme is undertaken.

PERMITTED HOURS

The actual opening and closing hours of licensed premises are fixed by the justices of the various licensing divisions. The 1921 Act provides that the maximum number of "open" hours daily shall be—

Metropolis, 9, weekdays and 5, Sundays.

Outside metropolis, 8, weekdays and 5, Sundays,

and, subject to special circumstances, these shall not be before 11 a.m. or after 11 p.m. (after 10 p.m. outside the metropolis). Also, there must be a break in the afternoon of at least 2 hours. "Sundays" here includes Christmas Day and Good Friday.

There is no Sunday opening in Wales and Monmouth. The penalty for contravening the permitted hours is a fine not exceeding £30. Special permission is necessary for the keeping open of licensed houses beyond the stipulated closing hour. The hours for clubs are dealt with below.

Consumption of alcoholic liquor may take place with a *bona fide* meal to within half-an-hour after the normal closing hour, but the liquor must have been ordered and supplied before that closing hour. Also, under Section 3, Licensing Act, 1921, the ordinary closing hour may be extended by one hour for the supply of food and of "drink ancillary to food" if the justices consider the premises structurally suitable for this facility. The words "food" and "meal" in this connection require definition. Presumably a sandwich is *not* a meal! The greatest care must obviously be exercised by a licensee who obtains such an extension of hours.

CLUBS

A club is a society of people associated for the furtherance of a common object other than the acquisition of gain : there is no satisfactory definition, unfortunately. It does not matter much *what* the club is for, but if intoxicating liquor is to be sold on its premises, the club must be registered with the police, and certain particulars filed annually (Sections 91, 110, Licensing Act, 1910). The club may be struck off the register and closed if the liquor supplied is not under the control of a committee of members. Duty must be paid annually on all purchases of liquor during the previous year. A record of members must be kept on the premises and be open to inspection by the public at reasonable times on payment of a fee of 1s.

Section 95 (i) Licensing Act, 1910, sets out the numerous obligations of a club. If struck off the register, the *same* club need not be re-registered and *cannot* be for at least a year from the date of closing. The law relating to sale of liquor is similar to that for a public house, but consumption on the premises may only be to *bona fide* members or their guests, and sales for off consumption may be made only to members.

A de-licensed public house may be refused registration as club premises, and will be until after expiration of twelve months from its closing as such.

Under Section 96 of the 1910 Act, any justice of the peace may issue to a constable a search warrant to enter and inspect the premises of the club and to seize any books or papers relating to its business.

Club Hours. By the Licensing Act, 1921, these are—

In Metropolis. Nine week-days.

Five Sundays, Christmas Day, and Good Friday.

Outside Metropolis. Eight and five hours respectively.

The members of a club may fix any open hours they wish subject to the above maxima being observed and the opening and closing hours respectively being not earlier than 11 a.m. or later than 11 p.m. with at least a two-hour break after 12 noon. Outside the metropolis the latest hour is 10 p.m. For Sundays, etc., the 5-hour period must not comprise more than two between 12 and 3, or three between 6 to 10 p.m.

Although a member may not be supplied with liquor after the permitted hours, he may *consume* it with a *meal*, any time within half-an-hour after permitted hours, provided the liquor was served at the same time as the consumption of the meal.

Residents in a club may be supplied with and consume liquor in the club at any time. Subject to certain conditions as to structure being complied with, the permitted hours in the evening may be extended by one hour where the premises are habitually used at that time for substantial refreshment to which drink is quite ancillary, and not the purpose for which people come in at that time (Section 3, 1921 Act). Liquor supplied so must be consumed at and with the meal. All other bars in the club must be closed in that hour. In addition, the half-hour's grace is allowed for consumption with the meal where this additional hour is granted and this facility applies in and outside the metropolis alike.

Generally, as to clubs, it is an offence—

1. To serve, or permit to be served, liquor after hours.

2. To consume in, or take from any club, liquor, save in the hours permitted under the club's certificate.

3. To give over-measure (long pull).

4. To give credit for intoxicating liquor supplied, but liquor supplied with a meal may be paid for on completion of the meal.

5. Unlawful games, or games which, if played, turn the club premises into a gaming house, are not permitted. "Tote" clubs are now held to be illegal and can be proceeded against.

Unless rules of a club definitely say so, a member is not liable for the debts of a club.

Subject to specific provision, club property, on a club being wound up, is equally divisible among its members, after discharge of liabilities.

The test with all clubs is : Is it a *bona fide* association of people with a common object not for gain, or is it a club opened by one or more for private profit intended to evade the law as to licensed premises ? If the latter, it is a bogus club, should not be on the register, and the conduct of it lays the officials open to heavy penalties. Clubs are in many ways privileged over licensed houses, and the law requires that these privileges should be honoured strictly.

LICENSED PREMISES

Not any form of premises can be used as a licensed house. Most existing houses date back many years, and new sites, when permitted, are subjected to close scrutiny "in the plan" before a licence is granted. All licensed premises are required by law to be structurally adapted to the class of licence and to provide adequate accommodation for the public.

ALTERATIONS

Alterations to premises require the previous consent of the justices.

CLOSING OF HOUSES

Power is given the justices to order the closing of any house if, in their opinion, that house is not fulfilling the purpose for which it was licensed. Appeal to quarter sessions is permitted. Compensation is paid, but not for OFF-licences.

INSPECTION

A licensed house is open to inspection by police at any time without a warrant. This is important. Officers of customs and excise are empowered to enter and take away samples for analysis.

OFFENCES

Offences against the law relating to licensed houses are too many to permit of full reference here.

It is important to note that intoxicating liquor may not be sold without the requisite licences or on unlicensed or unregistered premises. Such premises, once passed by the authorities, may not be structurally altered without consent, and must, at all times, be kept in a fit and proper state, and maintained in an orderly way. For music and dancing, permission has to be obtained. It is unwise to allow anything tending towards rowdiness on licensed premises, as objection can be lodged that the premises are an improperly conducted house. It follows that drunkenness is barred, sale to drunken people, or permitting drunkenness or drinking outside a house on the public highway.

It is an offence to allow children in any bar or to allow sale of liquor to young people under the age of 18, save that, for off-consumption only, liquor may be sold to a child over 14 if it is contained in a properly corked and sealed bottle.

In no case may intoxicating liquor be sold except in permitted hours, and, to stop canvassing, it is not permitted to take out on a barrow or van and deliver liquor that has not been previously ordered from the licensee and the order duly entered in a proper order book.

Consumption of intoxicants in premises licensed for OFF-consumption only is forbidden, as also are the giving of excessive measure (the "long pull") and allowing sales on credit. Spirits must not be sold if deficient in strength. The adulteration of any liquor is expressly forbidden.

Betting and gambling are not allowed on licensed premises. The games played have to be chosen by the proprietor with care.

While prostitutes and thieves are not barred from taking alcoholic refreshment, it is a serious offence to allow them to use licensed premises for their own purposes.

Under the Truck Acts, wages may not be paid in any public house.

The police are empowered to inspect licensed houses, but it is an offence to harbour the police, bribe them, or supply liquor to them when they are on duty. It is, of course, a serious offence to hinder the police in the performance of their duty.

A licensee has rights in his house. It is a punishable offence to render him liable to any penalty concerning the conduct of his house, or to refuse to leave the premises when asked.

CENTRAL AND LOCAL GOVERNMENT

THE KING

Succession to the throne is dependent upon the Act of Settlement (1710). The right of the King to reign is, therefore, a right conferred by Parliament. The descent is governed by feudal laws of inheritance with one exception: the rule of primogeniture gives the title to the eldest son, but where there is no son the eldest daughter inherits. There is not, as in the feudal laws, equality among the daughters.

Under the Act no Roman Catholic or person married to a Roman Catholic may reign.

Under the Accession Declaration Act, 1910, the King must take oath to uphold the enactments securing a Protestant succession, and he declares himself to be a Protestant.

The title of the King is (by the Royal and Parliamentary Titles Act, 1927), "George V by the Grace of God, of Great Britain, Ireland, and of the British Dominions beyond the Seas, King Defender of the Faith, Emperor of India."

The King's Privy Purse is distinct from the public revenue: under the 1910 Act it was fixed at £470,000 per annum.

The King's consent is necessary to make the marriage valid of a descendant of George II—except as regards the children of princesses married into foreign families—under twenty-five years of age. After that age they may marry without the consent, giving a year's notice, unless both Houses of Parliament disapprove of the contemplated marriage.

The Royal Victorian Order is personal to the King. Apart from this the responsibility of the King's ministers extends even to the distribution of honours. The granting of honours to residents in the Dominions is with the assent of the Dominion Governments. At present South Africa, Canada, and the Irish Free State refuse assent.

The Emergency Powers Act, 1920, empowers the King, when the community is threatened with the deprivation of the essentials of life, to proclaim a "state of emergency." Then Orders in Council (the Privy Council) may be made (as was done in the General Strike of 1926) for the preservation of public safety.

281

THE " CROWN "

It is customary, when regarding the King as the representative of his people, to speak of the " Crown." In a Revenue case, for instance, where the contention is whether or not a payment is due, the Crown stands for the rights of the public—the rights of all citizens other than those who are at the moment contesting with the Crown.

THE PRIVY COUNCIL

The Privy Council was originally an assembly of the King's chief advisers. The present number (about 300) of members who are Right Honourable Privy Councillors precludes it from being this. It meets as a whole only to proclaim a new sovereign. Its committees are, however, of the utmost importance. Its members include the Cabinet, the Archbishops, the Bishop of London, the chief Judges, and Ambassadors. Each Privy Councillor becomes a Justice of the Peace for every county. Each has the right to be present at debates in the House of Lords, a right reminding us that Parliament once consisted of a meeting of the King's council with barons, clergy, and commons.

Among its various committees is the Judicial Committee, the supreme court for appeals from the Empire and from ecclesiastical courts.

The Lord President of the Council is always in the Cabinet.

Orders in Council are issued to put into effect Acts of Parliament. A quorum of three Councillors assemble in the King's presence to issue the orders.

COUNCIL OF STATE

In 1928 George V had a lengthy illness, and it was deemed desirable to set up a Council of State to perform his office. He signed letters patent which authorised its creation under the Great Seal. The Council consisted of the Queen, the Prince of Wales, the Duke of York, the Archbishop of Canterbury, and the Prime Minister.

LOCAL ALLEGIANCE

All British subjects living in the country owe allegiance to the King, and, whether they approve of them or not, must conform to his laws. But, also, while living here all persons (other than invaders in time of war) owe a local allegiance. That a temporary dweller here lives normally under a different law is not accepted as an excuse for his breach of a British law.

OATH OF ALLEGIANCE

A British subject owes allegiance to the King reigning—to the King *de facto* is the term. Whether or not that King is King by right, *de jure*, does not matter. So the Treason Act enacts (1495). Or perhaps we may put it that a subject has no power, nor is any machinery available, to dispute the King's right to allegiance.

The duty of allegiance is not easily defined; but it certainly includes obedience to the King's laws. In this sense a temporary allegiance is owed even by aliens resident upon British territory. If, for instance, a non-British subject living in England helped his own countrymen in war against Britain, he would be guilty of treason; and while living here he is subject to English laws whether he knows them or not.

It may be that allegiance to a personal King supplies a very desirable link for the various peoples of the Empire.

An oath of allegiance could formerly be exacted from all who lived under the protection of the Crown. The Promissory Oaths Act, 1868, enacted that the oath should be required only:

1. From the officials of the Crown.
2. From clergymen of the Church of England upon their ordination.
3. From Members of Parliament on taking their seats.
4. From members of the armed forces.
5. From those upon whom dignities are conferred.

The Naturalisation Acts require the oath from aliens also, upon their becoming naturalised British subjects.

TREASON

A person obnoxious to the Government might, in former days, have been charged with treason against the Crown for all manner of things disliked by the rulers. The crime was a very elastic one; and anxiety to protect the subject against the executive made it one of the first to be defined by statute. Nowadays, the crime of high treason is strictly limited by statutes, beginning with the Statute of Treasons, 1351. All the acts constituting treason are such as threaten the King's safety or dignity. Four were defined by the early Act—

1. *Compassing or imagining the death of the King, Queen, or Prince of Wales.* ("Imagining" here means, of course, something

10

more than thinking about the matter; planning with others against the King would certainly be such imagining.)

2. *Levying war against the King or adhering to his enemies in his realm, giving his enemies aid or comfort, in his realm or elsewhere.*

3. *Violating the chastity of the Queen, the wife of the Prince of Wales, or the King's eldest daughter being unmarried.*

4. *Slaying the Chancellor, the Treasurer, or the Justices of the Benches, or Assize, or Oyer and Terminer, being in their places doing their offices.*

A fifth, once maybe of importance, now only a point of historic interest, was added when Parliament provided for the succession of George I:

5. *Questioning the title to the throne of Great Britain under the Act of Settlement, 1701.*

Prosecution for treason must in general take place within three years. But this limitation does not apply if the offence was committed outside the kingdom, or if the treason consisted in a plan to assassinate the sovereign. In such events the ordinary rule applies that a crime may be prosecuted no matter how long an interval has elapsed since its commission. *Nullum tempus occurrit regi :* Time does not run against the King. All persons concerned in treason are equally liable to death; there are no degrees of guilt, as there are in felonies.

BRITISH NATIONALITY

This is now determined by the British Nationality and Status of Aliens Acts (1914, 1922). A *Natural-born British subject* is—

1. Any person born on British territory (except children of invaders).

2. Any person born on a British ship, even in foreign waters (but not birth on a foreign ship in British waters).

3. A person born out of a British territory if

(a) the father was born on British territory; or

(b) the father has been naturalised; or

(c) the father is in the service of the Crown abroad.

4. A person born of a British father out of British territory if

(a) the child's birth is registered at a British consulate;

(b) Within a year of reaching twenty-one the child makes a formal declaration of British nationality.

This last provision enables retention of British nationality among British denizens in places, like the South American republics, containing a strong British colony.

NATURALISATION

This is given by a grant from the Home Secretary. The grant, which is discretionary, is only given when the applicant—

1. Has lived, during the year preceding his application, in the United Kingdom.

2. Has lived, for four years out of the last eight preceding his application, on British territory.

3. Knows English, is of good character, and intends to live on British territory.

(Service of the Crown abroad is equivalent to residence in the United Kingdom.) The grant does not become effective until the applicant has taken the oath of allegiance to the King; and it may be revoked for good causes.

A British subject automatically divests himself of his nationality by becoming naturalised in a foreign country.

NATIONALITY OF MARRIED WOMEN

Ordinarily a married woman takes the nationality of her husband. If, however, her husband renounces his British nationality, she can at her choice retain it. Moreover, if she has married an alien and his country declares war against Britain, she may be given a certificate of naturalisation.

VOTING QUALIFICATION

A person, to be entitled to the Parliamentary Franchise in any borough or county constituency, must be—

(a) twenty-one years of age on the last day of the qualifying period (a person reaches majority on the last day of his twentieth year).

(b) and have either a "residence qualification" or a "business qualification."

To obtain a "residence qualification" a person must have resided in premises in the same constituency for the previous three months, or if during that period he or she has removed from one residence to another, such removal must have been within the same parliamentary borough or parliamentary county, or from a borough or county contiguous thereto. Residence is held to be where a person usually lives and sleeps.

To obtain a "business premises qualification" a person must be or have been in occupation, in a constituency other than that in which he or she resides, for the purposes of business, profession, or trade, of land or other premises of a yearly value (defined as the gross estimated rental) of £10 or more. The occupation must have extended over the whole qualifying period, or successive occupation can be claimed from one set of premises to another within the same county or borough or contiguous counties or boroughs, as in the case of the "residential qualification."

The wife or husband of a person who has a business premises qualification is also entitled to be registered in respect of the business premises qualification.

Partners carrying on their profession, trade, or business on any land or premises may be registered as joint occupiers provided the yearly value is sufficient to allow £10 for each partner.

In any other case of joint occupation, only two persons can be registered in respect of the same land or premises.

The following are not allowed to vote—

DISQUALIFICATIONS

Idiots and lunatics, peers, convicts under sentence for treason or felony or for corrupt practices, and returning officers.

The following may not sit as members of Parliament—

Infants, lunatics, those convicted of treason or felony where the sentence exceeds a year's imprisonment, bankrupts, those convicted of corrupt practices as a parliamentary candidate, clergymen of the Church of England, or of the Church of Scotland, or of the Roman Catholic Church, members of the House of Lords, those holding a government contract, most civil servants.

LOCAL GOVERNMENT VOTERS

Men and Women. A person to be entitled to be a local government elector for a local government area, must be—

(a) twenty-one years of age and not subject to any legal incapacity.

(b) have occupied on the last day of a qualifying period, and for three months previously, or in immediate succession in the same administrative county or borough, land or premises, of any value.

(c) or be the husband or wife of a person entitled to be so registered in respect of premises in which both the person so entitled and the husband or wife, as the case may be, reside.

For the purpose of qualification a naval or military voter is deemed to be living at home, so as to qualify his wife.

The local government qualification applies to any person who occupies a "dwelling-house" by virtue of any office, service, or employment, if the dwelling-house is not inhabited by the employer, and also applies to a lodger occupying a room or rooms which have been let in an unfurnished state. A woman occupying unfurnished lodgings, or the husband of a woman or the wife of a man occupying unfurnished lodgings, can, under certain conditions, obtain a local government vote.

In the case of removals, the local government franchise can be retained only if the successive premises occupied for the qualifying period were within the same electoral area. It is not, therefore, possible to claim successive occupation from a county or borough or *vice versa*.

The provisions with regard to the "Absent Voters List" and "Voting by Proxy" do not apply to local government elections.

VOTING BY PROXY

Any person whose name is entered on the Absent Voters List, and who makes a statement in the prescribed form that there is a probability that he or she will, at the time of a parliamentary election, be at sea or out of the United Kingdom, and satisfies the registration officer as to the *bona fides* of such statement shall be entitled to appoint a proxy, and having appointed a proxy to vote by proxy.

It is necessary for an absent voter to claim to appoint a proxy to vote on his or her behalf.

The wife, husband, parent, brother, or sister (if of full age) of the elector, or any person who is a voter in the same constituency, may be appointed as proxy. A person shall not vote by proxy on behalf of more than two absent voters at an election in any constituency, unless that person is voting as the husband, or wife, or the parent, brother, or sister, of the absent voter.

The appointment of a proxy must be served on the Returning Officer one clear day prior to the day of nomination.

The appointment of a proxy may be cancelled by the voter any time up to the day of nomination at a parliamentary election.

UNIVERSITY CONSTITUENCIES

In University constituences the age qualification is twenty-one.

A person must have obtained a degree in the University for which he or she wishes to be registered.

TWO VOTES

At a General Parliamentary Election a person can vote once in respect of a residence qualification, and once more (if in another constituency) for any other qualification, either for business premises or for a University qualification. At a by-election a person may vote in any constituency where he or she is registered as a voter.

UNPAID SERVICES OF THE CITIZEN

The British subject is in many ways under legal obligation to help in the orderly governing of the country, either without pay or with an amount merely nominal—

1. In 1887 the Sheriffs Act reiterated the duty, recognised from the earliest times, of *helping to maintain order*: "every person in a county shall be ready and apparelled at the command of the sheriff and the cry of the county to arrest a felon." Refusal to help a constable when called upon is punishable by fine.

2. *Unpaid Offices.* Few of these now remain; but jurors are required to serve when called upon and receive no adequate money reward, and witnesses may be summoned under penalty (*sub poena*) to give evidence.

DISABILITIES OF THOSE WHO ARE NOT BRITISH SUBJECTS

1. Aliens are incapable of being (*a*) members of the Privy Council or of either House of Parliament; (*b*) appointed to any office of trust, either civil or military, or of being a member of the Civil Service; (*c*) recipient of any grants from the Crown.

2. They may not be registered as electors either in regard to the central government or to the local government.

3. They may not hold a pilotage certificate for a district in the United Kingdom.

4. They may not act as master, chief officer, or chief engineer of a British ship. Nor may they be employed in any capacity in a British ship unless they produce satisfactory proof of nationality (Aliens Restriction (Amendment) Act, 1919).

5. They are under restrictions in regard to possible concealment of real names.

6. They may not (even when enlisted in His Majesty's regular forces, with the consent of the Crown signified through the Secretary of State) hold any rank higher than that of warrant officer or non-commissioned officer.

ALIENS

An alien friend cannot own a British ship or part of one. Apart from this restriction his power to hold property or to contract is the same as that of a natural-born British subject. And he has the same rights of access to the British Courts. He has no political rights. The Home Secretary, in fulfilling his duty to preserve the peace of the King, may make an order for the deportation of an undesirable alien. Nor, it seems (*ex parte Venicoff*, K.B. 1920), would the Courts issue a writ of *certiorari* (transferring the proceedings from the Minister to a superior Court) against the Home Secretary. For his action would be an executive one in his capacity as representative of the Crown, not a judicial one.

AN ALIEN ENEMY

1. Cannot enter into contract with a British subject during war.
2. He cannot sue in the King's courts.
3. He may, however, if he can be served with a writ, be summoned and appear as defendant; and he is not debarred from an appeal. That would be to deny him justice; and, in war time as in peace time, the Courts consider it their primary duty to further justice.
4. Contracts made before the war, like partnerships involving intercourse with the enemy, are dissolved by the outbreak of war.

The status of an *alien enemy* is determined by the *place where the person in question lives* : an enemy subject living in a neutral country, or (under licence from the Crown) in Great Britain, is, so far as regards contract, in the position of an alien friend.

NATIONALITY AND DOMICILE

It may be well to note that *nationality* and *domicile* are not the same. The first is independent of place of residence, the second depends upon (*a*) actual residence; (*b*) intention of making the residence a permanent one. Moreover, within the same nationality there may be several possible domiciles. There is a British nationality (not an English or a Scottish nationality). On the other hand, there is an *English domicile* or a *Scottish domicile* (never a British domicile). Nor, though to be sure it is a strong fact, does a change of nationality of itself involve a change of domicile.

DETERMINATION OF DOMICILE

In *Wahl* v. *A. G.* (H.L. 1932) the points that may arise regarding domicile were discussed at length. The Attorney-General sought death duties on the estate of one who lived in Germany as well as in England. The Court of Appeal decided in favour of the Crown, decided that is that the death duties were payable. The executor appealed. After considerable difference of judicial opinion the House of Lords by a majority decided that the deceased, born a German though he became a naturalised Englishman, had reverted to his domicile of origin. Some of the Law Lords, indeed, doubted whether, in spite of his being naturalised and in spite of his residence and marriage in this country, he had ever made this country his domicile of choice.

Lord Atkin said: "The deceased died in England in 1915. His domicile of origin was German. Did he abandon his German domicile and acquire an English domicile of choice? If so, did he subsequently abandon his English domicile and reacquire a German domicile? The onus of proving the first is on the respondent: if he succeeds, the onus of proving the second is on the appellant. I am of opinion that the Attorney-General has not discharged the onus of proof that the deceased ever acquired an English domicile. The evidence falls far short of what is necessary to prove such a serious change in a man's status. His father had a sugar manufacturing business in Germany; and the deceased came to England to manage the export business here. He does not appear to have severed a single tie with Germany. I see no proof that he either had the intention, or that he carried out an intention, to make his principal or only home in this country. The evidence negatives both the *animus* and the *factum*, the mind and the deed. It seems to have been thought that the declaration made for naturalisation —that the applicant intended to reside permanently within the United Kingdom—is conclusive proof of the acquisition of a new domicile. This is not so. It is worth noting that the words occur in print, and in a form that goes beyond the requirements of the statute. I am far from saying that because they appear in print the declarant is absolved from an obligation to make the full declaration truthfully. But I think they might be understood by him and his advisers as not intended to go beyond the statutory requirements. Naturalisation is one thing, change of domicile is another: it is not the law, either, that a change of domicile is a condition of naturalisation, or that naturalisation involves necessarily a change of domicile. Indeed, when we note that the 1914 Act makes the five years' previous residence (necessary for naturalisation) to include possibly four in the British Dominions, the distinction is clear."

DIPLOMATIC IMMUNITY

The fiction is that a duly accredited representative of a foreign power lives, though in London, in his own country. He is, therefore, outside the jurisdiction of our Courts. This immunity is a rule of international law and has always been recognized in our Common Law. It extends not only to ambassadors but to all members of an embassy. An Act in 1708 made the immunity into a statutory one. The Act was passed to assuage the wrath of the Czar of Russia, indignant that his representative had been arrested for debt. It did no more than declare existing law. Yet it seemed to have served in lieu of the punishment that the Czar requested, the execution of the wrongdoers.

The privilege of diplomatic immunity cannot be waived unless the sovereign consents. Where the consent is obtained, the representative submits to the jurisdiction of the Court; and the trial proceeds as against ordinary persons.

RIGHT OF SUBROGATION AND DIPLOMATIC IMMUNITY

Dickinson v. *Del Solar* (K.B. 1930) supplies an effective illustration. This was an insurance case, where the insurance company urged its *right of subrogation* : when an insurer undertakes to indemnify against a specified loss, he is entitled to take to himself all the means that the insured has of mitigating the loss. If the insured renounces rights that he could have exercised, he may be compelled to make good to the insurer the full value of these rights.

Del Solar, driving a car in Hyde Park, injured a pedestrian. Negligence was not contested, and the claim for damages would ordinarily have been paid by the insurance company without demur. Here, though, the wrongdoer was a member of a diplomatic corps. As such he had diplomatic immunity and could successfully plead it in an action for damages. He waived the privilege, thereby depriving the insurance company of a means of resisting payment. The Court, being invoked, declined to help the company in the matter. Nor could the Court have constrained the diplomat to plead his privilege.

DETERMINING DIPLOMATIC IMMUNITY

For it appears (*Engelke* v. *Musmann*, H.L. 1928) that the Courts are under a duty to accept without question the decision of the Foreign Secretary that the particular defendant is entitled to diplomatic immunity. A writ was taken out against a member of the staff of the German Embassy for arrears of rent. The member took out a summons to set aside the writ, claiming diplomatic immunity and making an affidavit to that effect. The landlord sought leave to cross-examine on the affidavit; but the House of Lords decided that no such cross-examination could take place: "The sole question is the method by which the status of any person claiming the privilege is to be determined. For the appellant it is contended that the statement of the Attorney-General on the instruction of the Foreign Office is for this purpose conclusive, while the respondent asserts that any such dispute should be ascertained in the ordinary way, according to the usual rules of evidence.

"The proper course is that the Court should apply to His Majesty's Government, and that in any such matter it is bound to act on the information given them through the proper department. Such information is not in the nature of evidence. It is a statement by the Sovereign of the country through one of his ministers upon a matter which is peculiarly within his cognisance."

FUNCTIONS OF GOVERNMENT

The work of government consists of law-making, law-enforcing, and law-interpreting.

The first is the work of the legislative, of the *King in Parliament*; and there, in this country, resides the sovereign power. The second is the work of the executive, of the *Ministers* who have the support of a majority in the House of Commons, and of the permanent Civil Service, over which the Ministers of the Crown become more or less temporary heads. The wise and effective administration of the law is, undoubtedly, the most important duty of government. But administration makes less appeal to the electorate than legislation does; and no political party is content to rely for continuance of support upon its success in administration. Each party seeks to influence votes by its law-making proposals. The *third* function is the work of the judicature, of the High Court judges and the judges of the various inferior Courts. (See Lord Haldane's remarks in the Vacher case, page 93.)

THE HOUSE OF LORDS

The House of Lords debates important questions with ability and effectiveness. Occasionally, when the Government commands a majority in that House, less important measures pass through their first stages in the House. And it constitutes a dignified and impressive assembly upon great State occasions.

But modern developments—culminating in the Parliament Act, 1911—have shorn it of its former great, indeed predominant,

powers. Even a Bill other than a Money Bill may become law
without the assent of the Lords. The House of Lords can exercise
only a suspensive veto: "If any Public Bill is passed by the
House of Commons in three successive sessions, and is rejected
by the House of Lords in each of the sessions, the Bill shall on
its rejection a third time by the House of Lords be presented to
the King and become an Act of Parliament on the Royal Assent
being signified thereto." (Section 2 of Parliament Act, 1911.)

Possibly this provision is more palatable to the House of Lords
than what had come to be regarded as the effective way to coerce
the House of Lords to conform to the will of a House of Commons
obviously having the wishes of the people behind it. This way
was the change, or threatened change, in the composition of the
House, by the creation of a sufficient number of new peers favourable to the Government's proposal. Such a threat resulted in the
passing of the First Reform Bill and of the Parliament Act, 1911,
the majority of the House being strongly opposed to both measures.

The great majority of the House of Lords consists of hereditary
peers. But there are also the Lords Spiritual—the Archbishops
of Canterbury and of York, the Bishops of London, Winchester
and Durham, and twenty-one other Bishops in order of seniority
of creation: there are Scottish and Irish peers, the former elected
for each Parliament, the latter for life: and there are the seven
Lords of Appeal in Ordinary, appointed for the effective performance of the House of Lord's function as Supreme Court of Justice.
No woman sits in the House. It was decided (Lady Rhondda's
Case, H.L. 1922), that the Sex Disqualification (Removal) Act,
1919, had not effected such a change as to allow peeresses in their
own right to claim a right of summons.

THE HOUSE OF COMMONS

The 615 elected members of the House of Commons include
seventy-four from Scottish constituencies, and thirteen from
Northern Ireland. The City of London and twelve boroughs have
two members each, the other constituencies one each. A majority
vote decides, except in the University constituencies, where the
principle of proportional representation applies. Since 1872 voting
for members of the House has been by secret ballot.

HOUSE OF COMMONS CONTROLS MONEY MATTERS

The Representative House has gradually drawn to itself control
over both the raising and the spending of revenue, its last notable

step in the matter being the Parliament Act, 1911. This, among the innovations, took away from the House of Lords power to prevent the passage of "money bills." Section 1 enacts: "If a Money Bill is sent up to the House of Lords at least one month before the end of the session and is not passed by the House of Lords without amendment within one month after it is sent up, the Bill shall, unless the House of Commons directs the contrary, be presented to the King and become an Act of Parliament on the Royal Assent being signified, notwithstanding that the House of Lords have not consented to the Bill."

PARLIAMENT IS SUPREME

The House of Commons, that is, can do what it chooses both in regard to money matters and other problems of government. Nor will the Courts countenance any indirect attempt to deprive the Representative House of such absolute control. The acts of the executive are subject to judicial consideration; and, if those acts are beyond the powers granted by Parliament, they are declared to be of no effect.

This attitude, which is constantly shown whenever executive acts are challenged, is traditional. It was well exemplified when, in 1688, James II issued a command to all clergy to read his Declaration of Indulgence, giving a general suspension of all penal laws against those who were not members of the Church of England. The Archbishop of Canterbury and six bishops petitioned to be excused from reading the Declaration; the petition became the subject-matter of a charge of seditious libel; the defence was that the Declaration, not being sanctioned by Parliament, was illegal and that therefore their petition was a proper one. The King's Bench judge directed the jury that, if the executive assumed such power as the Declaration evidenced, "it would be an abrogation and utter repeal of all the laws. There will need no Parliament. All the legislature will be in the King, which is a thing worth considering, and I leave the issue to God and your consciences." The jury—greatly daring, for Judge Jeffreys was to be feared, and *Bushell's* case affirming the immunity of juries was still recent—found the accused innocent of the charge.

HOUSE OF COMMONS CONTROLS POLICY

The Representative House controls policy also. For the Ministers responsible for policy depend upon the retention of a majority in the House of Commons favourable to their policy. It is a custom—a convention of the constitution—that when the Prime Minister finds his policy unacceptable to the House of Commons he either (1) resigns office, or (2) advises the King to dissolve Parliament. If he chooses the first course he has the duty of indicating to the King the particular statesman who might be invited to form a new ministry. If he chooses the second course he, in effect, appeals to the electorate from the opinion of the House that is unfavourable to him. He asks the electorate to choose a new House of Commons that will approve of his policy.

This power of dissolution—for it is most unlikely that the King would reject the advice to dissolve Parliament—is a potent weapon in the hands of the Prime Minister. He can so use it as almost to compel his followers to conform to his wishes. It enables him to submit them to the hazards and expense of an election before the normal five years of the life of a House of Commons has expired. Moreover if, as is natural, these followers believe that the well-being of the country depends largely upon the continuance of their party in office as administrators, serious defections need not be feared.

THE CABINET

In theory a kind of committee of the Privy Council, the Cabinet is, in fact, the most important body in the State. Yet they have no collective official title. Their summons to meeting is: "A meeting of His Majesty's Servants will be held at 10 Downing Street at . . . o'clock on . . . the . . . which . . . . . is desired to attend."

The Prime Minister is the "keystone of the Cabinet arch." Members are heads of various administrative departments of State and are responsible for these departments to the House of Parliament. They are also the political chiefs commanding a majority in the House of Commons. The making of laws and their execution may, therefore, be expected to be in harmony.

The Lord Chancellor, the head of the judiciary, is also in the Cabinet; but he is a member of the Cabinet rather as a political chief and the Speaker of the House of Lords, than as a judge. For the executive and the judiciary must be kept separate in order to provide that the judges should act as checks upon the executive, and prevent the assumption of powers unauthorised by Parliament.

Through the Prime Minister, who invites the ministers to serve in the Cabinet, there is a collective responsibility. If the policy of the Government meets disapproval, the whole Cabinet resigns.

What takes place at its meetings remains normally undisclosed, Cabinet decisions being announced as those of a unit. Secrecy follows, or ought to follow, from the oath of a Privy Councillor; and a prosecution under the Official Secrets Act is possible for an unauthorised divulgence.

DELEGATION OF PARLIAMENT'S POWERS

Parliament is supreme; no authority may dispute its decisions. If the law is clearly expressed it must be followed, however unsatisfactory it may appear to the Courts. Parliament can also delegate powers; and to an increasing extent does do so. It endows an official with law-making powers; and, though vigorous protests both here and in the United States have been made against "government by bureaucracy," the increasing duties of the Government probably makes such delegation inevitable. The extent to which Parliament does delegate is well shown in *Arlidge* v. *Local Government Board*, (H.L. 1915). The Housing Act, 1909, gives a local authority upon the representation of its medical officer, power to issue a "closing order" prohibiting the use of dwelling-houses as being unfit for human habitation. An appeal lies to the Ministry of Health, which must hold a public local inquiry and which, upon a question of law, may be required to state a special case for the High Court's opinion. The procedure to be followed "shall be such as the Board may determine." And "the Board may make such order in the matter as they think equitable, and any order so made shall be binding and conclusive on all parties."

The Board held an inquiry under the Act at which Arlidge, the owner of the condemned house, was represented. The Board dismissed his appeal against a demolition order. He did not exercise his right to require the Board to state a special case. But he appealed to the Courts to quash the order; his reasons were that the order did not disclose what officer of the Board had decided the appeal, and that the report of the Inspector who conducted the inquiry was not made public. The House of Lords held that since the Board could, by the Act, determine its own procedure, no court of law could interfere with an order that was made by Parliament "binding and conclusive."

PARLIAMENT UNRESTRICTED

Parliament can make what laws it chooses, and it can change existing law in order to bring it into harmony with present conditions. A rigid observance of Sunday becomes irksome; and Parliament passes The Sunday Entertainments Act, 1932. This makes provision for cinematograph exhibitions and other entertainments and appoints a poll to decide whether such entertainments are wanted by the inhabitants of an area. Even before, however, authorities, relying on the decision in *Williams* v. *Wright* (1887), had granted licences for entertainments. It was held in that case that, where admission is free to some, it is legal to make a charge for a reserved seat. If this is done no offence is committed against the Sunday Observance Act, 1780. The new Act does not modify this decision.

The licensing authority have power to attach special conditions when allowing Sunday entertainments. No person shall be guilty of an offence, or be subject to any penalty under the Sunday Observance Acts, 1625 to 1780, by reason of his having taken part or attended a cinematograph entertainment at any place licensed in accordance with the Act, or any musical entertainment, or any lecture or debate.

Parliament can make general laws for a great community; it can deal with individuals, as when, in Henry VIII's reign, it provided for "boiling the Bishop of Rochester's cook to death without having any advantage of his clergy."

DELEGATING LAW MAKING POWER

Parliament can also delegate its power to make laws. It gives authority to a Minister or other State official to make rules relating to a particular topic: and, to the extent that these rules fall within the scope of the authority conferred, they are laws. Thus, the Registrar of Joint-Stock Companies is entrusted with Parliament's power of creating these artificial legal persons. He incorporates joint-stock companies through the power given by the Companies Act of 1929. The Minister of Transport is another law-maker. He emits a continuous stream of statutory orders by virtue of the power given by the Road Traffic Act of 1930; and these orders become laws that must be obeyed under risk of penalty.

During the War years, in the general upheaval of social and industrial life, rules in profusion were issued under the Defence of the Realm Acts—under "Dora," as people said. Delegation was certainly necessary then. For, in view of the enormous amount of work that modern conditions impose upon Parliament, it would have been impossible to discuss every matter needing attention.

Delegation is probably necessary still. Ignorance of the law cannot be admitted as an excuse for breaking the law; but how unfair this maxim becomes when a new regulation, issued without adequate warning, subjects people to new duties and restrictions. One attack on the delegation of Parliament's law-making power was launched by the Lord Chief Justice himself.

The attack led to the appointment by the Lord Chancellor of a Committee on Minister's Powers. Its report duly appeared. Delegation is desirable; it is quite often inevitable; and, with proper safeguards, no hardship need result. So long as Parliament keeps effective control over Ministers, and so long as the Courts are available to test whether or not authority is exceeded, the rules must be in accordance with public opinion. But, the Committee points out, "We doubt whether Parliament itself has fully realised how extensive the practice of delegation has become, or the extent to which it has surrendered its own function in the process, or how easily the practice might be abused."

CONTROL OF MINISTER'S POWERS

True, where Parliament can determine, it should determine. When the Minister in charge of a Bill wants a "Henry VIII clause," whereby he can make statutory orders, he must show that it would be impossible to work the Act without such a clause. The power granted should be carefully defined. Even so, the jurisdiction of the Courts of Law must be carefully preserved in determining whether or not, in making his order, the Minister has acted within the scope of his authority. There should, indeed, be a simpler procedure than the present cumbrous and expensive one.

At present, this is by seeking a *writ of prohibition*. Thus, in 1932, Sir Walter Berry, a large producer of English hops, sought and obtained from the Divisional Court a rule *nisi* for a writ to prohibit the Minister of Agriculture from proceeding with his scheme for the marketing of English hops. The scheme had been made under the Agricultural Marketing Act, 1931, and the contention was that it exceeded the powers given by the Act. The rule *nisi* was obtained. It was debated at length in successive Courts, the conclusion ultimately reached being that the Minister had not exceeded his powers. That is, four successive discussions took place. A speedier procedure is easily conceivable.

A duty is incumbent upon Parliament to supervise its delegates in their law-making. The present method does not seem very effective. The orders made are "placed on the table"; but Members seldom look at them.

Indeed, in a recent road transport case a prominent King's Counsel, who had long been a Member of Parliament, confessed that he had never found out which table was meant. The Committee, therefore, made the suggestion—

(1) That every Bill containing proposals to confer law-making powers on Ministers should be accompanied by a memorandum explaining what the powers are, why they are needed, how they would be used, and what safeguards there would be.

(2) A standing committee should scrutinise every rule made under the powers, and should report to the House upon it.

SUPREMACY OF THE LAW

The supremacy of the law must be maintained. This implies that no Minister shall be given arbitrary power, and that when a question arises between the Minister and the subject, there shall be equality before the law. In the many instances where a Minister or one of his officials is required to make a decision involving the rights of contending parties, the principles of natural justice must be followed, principles that our law courts scrupulously observe.

The first great principle is this: *no man should be a judge in his own cause.* Obviously, pecuniary interest in the matter disqualifies one from being a judge. But then also there may be a strong and sincere conviction of what public policy requires; and this will militate against impartiality even more effectively than pecuniary interest does.

The second great principle of natural justice is this: *no man ought to be condemned unheard, and he must know in good time the case he has to meet.*

The committee disliked the idea of allowing the Minister to perform the office of a judge. He must, of course, come to decisions about administrative matters. Only very exceptionally should he make judicial decisions; and an aggrieved party must continue to have a right to appeal to the High Court of Justice on any point of law. When it is necessary to clothe the Minister, or a tribunal appointed by him, with power to determine disputes between parties, the four requisites of a true judicial decision must be kept in view.

1. *The parties must, orally or in writing, present their case.*
2. *Disputed facts must be ascertained by means of evidence.*

3. *Any question of law must be settled by argument.*

4. *Decision must dispose of the whole matter ; it must declare the truth about disputed facts, and it must apply the law of the land to the facts.*

TESTING THE POWERS

Whether or not the delegate of Parliament is acting within the powers conferred upon him is at times difficult to determine. One wishing to test it applies to the Court for a "writ of prohibition," an order from the Court to the delegate not to exceed his powers in the particular matter.

If, as may happen, the writ is issued, we have the curious position of one representative of the Crown nominally (though, of course, in reality on behalf of some subject who feels himself aggrieved by the order) in litigation with another representative of the Crown. It becomes a case of *Rex* v. *Minister of Labour* and the like.

Thus under the Trade Boards Act, 1918, the Minister of Labour has power to set up a Board that will prevent "sweating" in an industry. He can do this "where no adequate machinery exists for the effective regulation of wages."

The Minister notified his intention to use his power in respect of "the catering trade." A Divisional Court made a rule prohibiting the Minister from making a special order. On appeal the rule was discharged. That is, the Court of Appeal held that the Minister of Labour was competent to make the order. (*R.* v. *Minister of Labour, ex parte National Trade Association*, C.A. 1932.)

So, too, Parliament may endow an executive Minister with judicial discretion. Then it is that his decision may come before the Court, but only on a point of law. That is, the Court will interfere with the Minister's decision only when it is clear that the Minister has made a mistake in the law. Thus, the Minister of Health decided under the National Health Insurance Act, 1924, that a music-hall artist, doing an acrobatic turn, was employed in "manual labour," and was, therefore, an insured person irrespective of his remuneration. But Roche, J. said: "I can find no evidence to support the decision of the Minister of Health. Mr. McManus is both an acrobat and a clown. What he did in his performance involved not only physical exertion but dexterity. The appeal must be allowed." (*In re McManus*, 1933.)

JUDICIARY AND THE EXECUTIVE

The Courts have, indeed—at any rate since the seventeenth century—been ready to intervene to check the arbitrary acts of the executive.

So, it was in 1913 (*Bowles* v. *Bank of England*) that the Chancery Court held that to deduct income tax, before an Act of Parliament authorises the deduction, is illegal. This forced the Government to take action. To avoid the loss of revenue that would result unless a tax can be collected as soon as the intention to impose it is disclosed, the Government induced Parliament to pass the Provisional Collection of Taxes Act, 1913. This Act gives the requisite authority for collecting income tax, or customs duties, if within four months an Act imposing the tax has been passed.

A more recent example arose out of an order of the war-time Food Controller. Under powers given by the Defence of the Realm Acts, the executive forbade the removal of milk from one area to another except under licence. Where licences were granted the Food Controller charged 2d. a gallon on the milk moved. This charge the Wilts United Dairies challenged as being taxation without Parliamentary authority; and the Court upheld the challenge (*A. G.* v. *Wilts United Dairies*, 1921). As a result the Government was obliged to procure the passing of the War Charges (Validity) Act, 1925.

In the case that led to the passing of this Act Lord Atkin put the matter clearly and forcibly:

"We know how strictly Parliament has maintained this right of imposing taxes, in particular how jealous the House of Commons has asserted its predominance in the power of raising money. An elaborate custom of Parliament has prevailed by which money for the service of the Crown is only granted at the request of the Crown made by a responsible Minister, and assented to by the House in Committee. By constitutional usage no money proposal can be altered by the Second Chamber, whose powers are confined to acceptance or rejection.

If an officer of the executive seeks to justify a charge upon the subject made for the use of the Crown (which includes all the purposes of the public revenue), he must show in clear terms that Parliament has authorised the particular charge. The intention of the Legislature is to be inferred from the language used; and the grant of powers, though not expressed, may have to be implied, as necessarily arising from the words of a statute. But (in view of the historic struggle of the Legislature to secure for itself the sole power to levy money upon the subject, its complete success in that struggle, the elaborate means adopted by the Representative House to control the amount, the condition, and the purposes of the levy) the circumstances would be remarkable indeed which would induce the Court to believe that the Legislature had sacrificed all the well-known checks and precautions and, not in express words but merely by implication, had entrusted a Minister of the Crown with undefined and unlimited powers of imposing charges upon the subject for purposes connected with his department.

I am clearly of opinion that no such powers, and indeed no powers at all, of imposing any such charge are given to the Minister of Food. The Solicitor-General urged that while it was true that a licensing authority may not require a money payment for public uses in excess of amounts fixed in accordance with statute, as a condition of its licence, yet here the subject has no right to a licence, and therefore that the Food Controller might make his own conditions. The answer is that he may not, if one of those conditions amounts to levying money for or to the use of the Crown.

It makes no difference that the obligation to pay the money is expressed in the form of an agreement. It was illegal for the Food Controller to require such an agreement as a condition of any licence. It was illegal for him to enter into such an agreement. The agreement itself is not enforceable against the other contracting party; and if he has paid under protest, he may recover it back as money had and received to his use. I say nothing as to the alleged purposes to which the money so raised was destined, except to point out that the vagueness of the intention to apply it later for the benefit of the public by a reduction of prices of milk or milk products, or in some similar way, illustrates the wisdom of Parliament in retaining in its own hands the control of the expenditure of public money.

I have no doubt whatever as to the good faith of the Food Controller. His intention in making the charge may have been excellent; but he adopted methods which are unconstitutional and contrary to law, and his agreements cannot be enforced."

ESTATE DUTIES

The power of Parliament to raise revenue is subject to practical difficulties. It may decide upon a tax, and the tax may meet with active or passive resistance that will make Parliament's decree of little effect. For unless the approval of a man's conscience goes with a restraint put upon him he resents the restraint; and, when he can, he evades it. This is particularly evident in relation to taxes. These in effect limit our power of individual spending in order that there shall be more collective spending. The limitation imposed is greater, or appears to be greater, upon some than upon others. The tendency is, therefore, to devise schemes whereby an unfairly stringent limitation may be escaped. We have a continuous contest. The individual eagerly seeks, in ways not definitely prohibited, to evade the obligations that Parliament intended him to assume. Parliament, slow-footed and ill-equipped to cope with all the ingenious dodges of those who do not care to pay more taxes than their neighbours do, seeks to close up the meshes through which the individual escapes from the tax-gatherer's net.

So it has been with Estate Duties. These are, in fact, bound to be inequitable; for they depend upon the chance of death. It is true that the Finance Act makes some provision for removing gross injustices. When property passes in quick succession, the burden of the tax is lightened: "Where property consists of land or a business not carried on by a company, and estate duty has been paid in respect thereof within five years of another estate duty becoming payable in respect thereof, the amount payable on the last occasion shall be reduced, if the second death occurs within one year of the first death, by 50 per cent; two years by 40 per cent; three years, by 30 per cent; four years, by 20 per cent; and five years, by 10 per cent."

INEQUITY ENCOURAGES EVASION

The alleviation is something to the good. None the less the second payment, coming so closely after the first, is felt as a grievance. Besides, many are inclined to think the estate duties inequitable for a reason other than the varying intervals of payment. They are, say the objectors, voted by those who have no property subject to them; they are paid by the minority that has such property. At all events, efforts are made to evade them. It was against a particularly successful effort that Part III of the Finance Act, 1930, was directed. The method of evasion was, in effect, this: the owner of a large estate, dreading lest the estate should be cut up in order to pay estate duties, turned himself and his heir into a limited liability company. His tenants and others would then deal not with the Duke of Westminster but with Mayfair Estates, Ltd., or some such incorporation. He and his prospective heir would be registered as the joint holders of the shares; and, when one joint holder dies, the other is entitled to the shares. They pass without any proving of wills or being subject to the tax collector's scrutiny. For, of course, the artificial person that we call a corporation does not die, of old age or of anything else; "a corporation aggregate of many is invisible, immortal, and rests only in intendment and consideration of law. It has no soul, neither is it subject to the imbecilities of the body." The company may, indeed, be wound up and pass out of existence in that way. But it need not be; it is devised for immortality.

MAKING A SETTLEMENT

We are to remember that most "landowners" are in reality no more than tenants for life; they have possession rather than property of the land. They have a right to what income is derivable from it. But they are not free to sell it. The land is "entailed" land, the entail being brought about by some such settlement as this. One who has the freehold of land wishes to keep the land in his family as long as possible. The family looms larger than the individual; and, in the interest of family, he curtails his own rights. Upon his marriage he makes a settlement. He conveys the estate to himself for life, the remainder to go to his unborn sons in the order of their seniority. He cannot tie up the estate for a longer period. For the "rule against perpetuities" makes void any settlement which is not certain to take effect within the lives in being and twenty-one years afterwards. The eldest son has the remainder; the settlor—who is called the "Protector of the Settlement"—has divested himself the power of determining how the property shall pass at his death. When, however, the eldest son reaches twenty-one he and his father together can "break the entail." They can, if they choose, tie up the land for another generation. A settlement gives the son a life-estate, after the father's life estate, with remainder to the unborn sons of the son. They can also, if they choose, convey the land to a limited company. It is this latter that Section 35 of Part III of the Finance Act, 1930, contemplates.

FINANCE ACT, 1930

The section runs: "When at any time before the death of a person dying after the commencement of this Act any property in which the deceased had an estate or interest limited to cease at his death, was transferred by the deceased and the person interested in the remainder or reversion, whether directly or indirectly, and whether by one or more transactions to or for the benefit of a company, then the property shall be deemed for the purpose of estate duty to pass on the death in like manner as if the estate or interest of the deceased therein had continued until the death." There seems to be slight prospect of escaping this wide-sweeping proviso; but one never knows. The Act places upon the company responsibility for the payments due. Section 36 enacts: 1. The estate duty payable in respect of any property deemed to pass on the death of any person shall be a debt due from the company concerned to His Majesty. 2. The company concerned shall be accountable for any such duty. 3. Where a claim for duty arises, the company concerned shall notify the Commissioners of Inland Revenue of the death of the person; the penalty for failure to do so is £500. 4. The Commissioners of Inland Revenue may require balance sheets, etc. There are exceptions, which arise from the nature of the matter, provided for in Section 35. Thus, if the deceased had only an interest in expectation and the interest had never come into possession, no property would pass on his death, and no estate duty is chargeable.

If there has been a transfer for consideration other than an allotment of shares—if there has been an out-and-out sale—the statute does not apply. Nor does it apply where the deceased had, at least three years before his death, relinquished all interest in the property. The Act, that is, concerns itself with fictitious not with genuine transactions.

ESTATE DUTY

The rules relating to estate duty are complicated and many. They are set forth at length in Form A—2, which can be obtained upon application at the Estate Duty Office, Somerset House, London, W.C.2. The main points are the following—

1. Estate duty is leviable upon the principal value of both real and personal property passing upon death, including

(i) Whatever property the deceased could have disposed of, whether he did dispose of it by will or not;

(ii) Gifts made in anticipation of death (donations *mortis causa*). These are gifts that are assumed to be conditional upon the giver's death. They are of no effect, therefore, if the giver recovers. Such gifts unlike gifts *inter vivos*, are not only revocable and liable to estate duty but are also available for payment of the deceased's debts, if his other property is not enough;

(iii) Gifts made within three years of death, except so far as these are:

(*a*) Gifts made more than twelve months before death, and for public or charitable purposes;

(*b*) Gifts made in consideration of marriage;

(*c*) Gifts that are shown to be part of the deceased's normal expenditure;

(*d*) Gifts not exceeding £100 to any one person;

(iv) Gifts made with reservation of a power to resume the property;

(v) Property which the deceased had transferred to another person jointly with himself;

(vi) Deceased's share of any joint property;

(vii) Life interests of the deceased;

(viii) Life insurance policy payments.

2. Real property situated out of Great Britain is not chargeable; but movable property is chargeable when

(*a*) The deceased was the owner.

(*b*) The deceased was domiciled in Britain.

3. Exemptions from estate duty—

(i) The property of seamen, marines, soldiers, or airmen slain or dying in His Majesty's Service is not chargeable;

(ii) Where the deceased died on active service, or within three years from a cause incurred on active service, and was a member of His Majesty's forces, the Treasury may afford total exemption from all death duties in respect to the first £5,000 passing to widow and lineal relations or to brothers and sisters, and on the excess over £5,000 the duty is to be discounted for a period equal to the normal expectation of life of the deceased;

(iii) When property reverts to a settlor on the death of one to whom he had granted a limited estate;

(iv) Property destined by its owner for transfer to the National Debt Commissioners for the reduction of the National Debt;

(v) Things of national, scientific, or historic interest given for national purposes, or to any University, or to any County Council or Municipal Corporation;

(vi) Estates in land given to the National Trust inalienably for the public benefit, or to the Commissioners of Works or a local authority.

4. Fixing the rate of estate duty: to find this all property on

which estate duty is leviable passing at the death is aggregated so as to form an estate; the rate is then found from the table below.

5. Executor is accountable for duty; but the executor is not liable for any estate duty in excess of the assets which he has received as executor, or might, but for his own neglect or default, have received.

6. (i) A *bona fide* purchaser for valuable consideration without notice is not liable to or accountable for duty;

(ii) A purchaser acquiring a legal estate in land (other than registered land) takes it free from any charge for death duties, except when such a charge has been registered as a land charge.

7. Time of payment: the account upon which the estate duty is charged must be delivered to the Commissioners of Inland Revenue within six months of the death by the person accountable. The duty, to be collected upon an Inland Revenue Affidavit or Account, is due on delivery of this Account or at the expiration of six months from the death, whichever first happens.

FIXING THE VALUE

The Commissioners, in estimating the principal value of any property, are to fix the price according to the market price at the time of the death, without allowing any reduction on the ground that the whole property is to be placed on the market at one and the same time, unless it is proved to the Commissioners that the value of the property has been depreciated by reason of the death of the deceased, in which case such depreciation is to be taken into account. In estimating the principal value of any agricultural property which comprises cottages occupied by persons employed solely for agricultural purposes in connection with the property, no account is to be taken of any value attributable to the fact that the cottages are suitable for the residential purposes of any persons other than agricultural labourers or workmen on the estate.

In the case of shares in a company (not being preference shares) passing on a death on or after the 1st August, 1930, where either (a) a sum of money computed by reference to the value of the total assets of the company is deemed to pass in connection with the death of the deceased by virtue of Section 34 of the Finance Act, 1930, or (b) the deceased, immediately before death, held a controlling interest in the company, then, unless such shares have, within the period of twelve months preceding the death, been subject to dealings on a recognised stock exchange in the United Kingdom or been quoted in the official list of such exchange, the principal value of those shares for the purposes of estate duty is by reference to the value of the total assets of the company.

INTEREST ON DUTY

Simple interest at 4 per cent per annum, without deduction for income tax, is payable upon all estate duty from the date of the deceased's death.

INSTALMENTS ON REAL PROPERTY

The estate duty due upon an account of real property may, at the option of the person delivering the account, be paid by eight

RATE OF DUTY

Principal Value of the Estate				Rate per cent	Values below which Section 13 (1) of the Finance Act, 1914, comes into operation
£			£	£	£ s. d.
	Does not exceed		100	0	
Exceeds	100	and does not exceed	500	1	101 – 3
,,	500	,,	,,	1,000	2	505 2 1
,,	1,000	,,	,,	5,000	3	1,010 6 3
,,	5,000	,,	,,	10,000	4	5,052 1 8
,,	10,000	,,	,,	12,500	5	10,105 5 4
,,	12,500	,,	,,	15,000	6	12,632 19 7
,,	15,000	,,	,,	18,000	7	15,161 5 10
,,	18,000	,,	,,	21,000	8	18,195 13 1
,,	21,000	,,	,,	25,000	9	21,230 15 7
,,	25,000	,,	,,	30,000	10	25,277 15 7
,,	30,000	,,	,,	35,000	11	30,337 1 7
,,	35,000	,,	,,	40,000	12	35,397 14 7
,,	40,000	,,	,,	45,000	13	40,459 15 5
,,	45,000	,,	,,	50,000	14	45,523 5 2
,,	50,000	,,	,,	55,000	15	50,588 4 9
,,	55,000	,,	,,	65,000	16	55,654 15 3
,,	65,000	,,	,,	75,000	17	65,783 2 8
,,	75,000	,,	,,	85,000	18	75,914 12 9
,,	85,000	,,	,,	100,000	19	86,049 7 8
,,	100,000	,,	,,	120,000	20	101,250 – –
,,	120,000	,,	,,	150,000	22	123,076 18 6
,,	150,000	,,	,,	200,000	24	153,947 7 5
,,	200,000	,,	,,	250,000	26	205,405 8 2
,,	250,000	,,	,,	300,000	28	256,944 8 11
,,	300,000	,,	,,	400,000	30	308,571 8 7
,,	400,000	,,	,,	500,000	32	411,764 14 2
,,	500,000	,,	,,	600,000	34	515,151 10 4
,,	600,000	,,	,,	800,000	36	618,750 – –
,,	800,000	,,	,,	1,000,000	38	825,806 9 1
,,	1,000,000	,,	,,	1,250,000	40	1,033,333 6 8
,,	1,250,000	,,	,,	1,500,000	42	1,293,103 9 –
,,	1,500,000	,,	,,	2,000,000	45	1,581,818 3 8
,,	2,000,000				50	2,200,000 – –

equal yearly instalments or sixteen half-yearly instalments, with interest from the date at which the first instalment is due. The first instalment is to be due at the expiration of twelve months from the death, and the interest on the unpaid portion of the duty is to be added to each instalment and paid accordingly. But the duty for the time being unpaid, with such interest to the date of payment, may be paid at any time. And, in case the property is sold, the duty is to be paid on completion of the sale, and if not so paid, is to be duty in arrear.

POWER TO TRANSFER LAND IN SATISFACTION OF DUTY

The Commissioners may, if they think fit, on the application of any person liable to pay estate duty or settlement estate duty in respect of any real (including leasehold) property, accept in satisfaction of the whole or any part of such duties, such part of the property as may be agreed upon between the Commissioners and that person.

TAX REVENUE COLLECTED BY MEANS OF STAMPS AND DUTIES

These are mainly regulated by the Stamps Act, 1891, and the various Finance Acts. The present duties payable are—

	£	s.	d.
Admission to the degree of a barrister	50	—	—
As solicitor or proctor, or W.S. (Writer of the Signet)	25	—	—
As students to any Inn of Court	25	—	—
As Fellows of College of Physicians	25	—	—
As Burgess, by birth, apprenticeship, or marriage, England or Ireland	1	—	—
On any other ground	3	—	—
Faculty as a Notary Public, England	30	—	—
Affidavit, or statutory declaration		2	6
Agreement, or memorandum of agreement, under hand only, not otherwise charged			6
Agreement for Lease, for less than a year of a furnished house, the rent exceeding £25		5	—
Alkali Works, Cert. of Registration	10	—	—
Appointment of a new trustee and in execution of a power of property, not being by a Will		10	—
Appraisement or Valuation of any property, or of dilapidations, or of repairs wanted, or of materials and labour, where the amount of the appraisement shall not exceed £5			3
Not exceeding £10			6
,, ,, 20		1	—
,, ,, 30		1	6
,, ,, 40		2	—
,, ,, 50		2	6

	£	s.	d.
Not exceeding £100		5	–
,, ,, 200		10	–
,, ,, 500		15	–
Exceeding £500	1	–	–
Apprenticeship Indentures		2	6
Arms, grant of, stamp duty on	10	–	–
Articles of Clerkship to solicitor	80	–	–
Award		10	–
Banker's Annual Licence, U.K.	30	–	–
Bankers' Cheques			2
Bills of Exchange, *Inland* or *Foreign*, payable on demand, or within 3 days after date or sight, for any amount			2
Bill of Exchange, *Inland*, not payable on demand or within 3 days; also Promissory Notes—			
Not exceeding £10			2
Exceeding £10 and not exceeding £25			3
,, 25 ,, ,, ,, 50			6
,, 50 ,, ,, ,, 75			9
,, 75 ,, ,, 100		1	–
Every £100 and also for any fractional part of £100, of such amount		1	–
Bills of Exchange, *Foreign* (i.e. drawn, and expressed to be payable, out of U.K.), not payable on demand or within 3 days. When paid, or endorsed, or negotiated in U.K. : not exceeding £10			2
Exceeding £10 and not exceeding £25			3
,, 25 ,, ,, ,, 100			6
Every £100 or fractional part			6
Bill of Lading			6
Capital Duty (Share). Companies and Corporations with limited liability, on every £100 of the nominal capital		10	–
Statement of amount of any increase of registered capital shall be delivered duly stamped within fifteen days after the passing of the resolution.			
Capital Duty (Loan). On issues by Local Authorities, Companies, and Corporations, etc., on every £100 of amount secured		2	6
2s. in the £ is repayable if the Capital is applied in conversion of an existing loan.			
Certificate—to be taken out yearly by every solicitor, law agent, or writer to the signet, notary public, conveyancer, special pleader, and draftsman in equity, practising within 10 miles of the General Post Office, London; or in the city or shire of Edinburgh, or within 3 mile thereof	9	–	–
If practising elsewhere	6	–	–
(During first three years one half only.)			
Certificate of birth, baptism, marriage, death, or burial			1
Charter-party			6
Cheques, or drafts, payable on demand or to order			2
Collateral security, for every £100			6
Maximum duty		10	–
Commission of Lunacy		5	–
Contract Note for the sale or purchase of any stock or marketable security: where the value of the stock or marketable security—			
Is £5 and does not exceed £100			6
Exceeds 100 ,, ,, 500		1	–
,, 500 ,, ,, 1,000		2	–
,, 1,000 ,, ,, 1,500		3	–
,, 1,500 ,, ,, 2,500		4	–

						£	s.	d.
Exceeds £2,500 and does not exceed £5,000 .				. . . .			6	–
,,	5,000	,,	,,	7,500 .	. . . .		8	–
,,	7,500	,,	,,	10,000 .	. . . .		10	–
,,	10,000	,,	,,	12,500 .	. . . .		12	–
,,	12,500	,,	,,	15,000 .	. . . .		14	–
,,	15,000	,,	,,	17,500 .	. . . .		16	–
,,	17,500	,,	,,	20,000 .	. . . .		18	–
,,	20,000	. . .	. .	. . .	. . .	1	–	–

(Special adhesive stamps.)

Continuation Notes are chargeable on one only of the two transactions embraced.

Option Contract Notes are chargeable with half the above rates only, unless the option is a double one.

Contract Note following a duly stamped option contract note chargeable with half the above rates only.

	£	s.	d.
Contract or Grant for payment of a superannuation Annuity: for every £5 or fractional part of £5		6	
Conveyance or Transfer: of Bank of England stock . . .	15	6	
Of any Colonial Stock forming part of public debt of Colony, if register is kept in U.K. and the Stock is declared under the Colonial Stock Act, 1877: for every £100, or fractional part of £100, of nominal amount transferred		5	–
Conveyance or transfer on sale of any stock (except as aforesaid), shares, or marketable security: where the purchase money shall not exceed £5		1	–
Exceeding £5 and not exceeding £10		2	–
,, 10 ,, ,, 15		3	–
,, 15 ,, ,, 20		4	–
,, 20 ,, ,, 25		5	–
For every additional £25 up to £300		5	–
If exceeding £300, then for every £50		10	–
Conveyance or transfer on sale of any property (except as above); where the purchase money shall not exceed £5		1	–
Exceeding £5 and not exceeding £10		2	–
,, 10 ,, ,, 15		3	–
,, 15 ,, ,, 20		4	–
,, 20 ,, ,, 25		5	–
For every additional £25 up to £300		5	–
If exceeding £300, then for every £50		10	–
Of any kind not otherwise charged		10	–

Conveyance by way of gift " inter vivos " are charged as conveyances on sale. Exceptions for marriage settlements, and certain gifts of property for preservation of open spaces, and for conveyances to appoint new trustees.

	£	s.	d.
Copy or Extract (attested or authenticated), the same duty as original, but not to exceed			1
Declaration of Trust, not being a Will or Settlement		10	–
Deed of any kind not charged under some special head . . .		10	–
Deputation or appointment of a Gamekeeper		10	–
Ecclesiastical Licences—			
To hold the office of lecturer		10	–
For licensing a building for divine service, and any chapel for solemnising marriages		10	–
Licence not otherwise charged	2	–	–
Equitable Mortgages under hand only. For every £100 or part thereof		1	–
Faculty or Dispensation—			
In England, in all cases	30	–	–

£　s.　d.

Hire-purchase agreements—
　Under hand　.　.　.　.　.　.　.　.　.　.　　　6
　Under seal　.　.　.　.　.　.　.　.　.　　10　–
Inebriates' Retreats Licences　.　.　.　.　.　.　5　–　–
　(10s. additional is payable for every patient over 10 in number.)
Insurance Polices : Life—
　For any sum not exceeding £10　.　.　.　.　.　.　　　　1
　Exceeding £10 and not exceeding £25　.　.　.　.　　　　3
　Exceeding £25 and not exceeding £500, for every £50 or fractional
　　part of £50　.　.　.　.　.　.　.　.　.　　　　6
　Exceeding £500 and not exceeding £1,000, for every £100 or frac-
　　tional part of £100　.　.　.　.　.　.　.　　1　–
　Exceeding £1,000, for every £1,000 or any fractional part of £1,000　　10　–
Policies of Indemnity against loss under the Employers' Liability Act,
　1880, and the Workmen's Compensation Acts
　　Under hand .　.　.　.　.　.　.　.　.　.　　　　6
　　Under seal　.　.　.　.　.　.　.　.　.　　10　–
Accidental Death, or Personal Injury, or on periodical payments dur-
　ing sickness, or loss or damage upon Property　.　.　.　.　　　　6
Insurance Polices : Sea—
　Where the premium does not exceed 2s. 6d. per cent　.　.　.　　　　1
Where the premium exceeds 2s. 6d. per cent—
　For any voyage—
　　Where the sum insured does not exceed £250　.　.　.　　　　3
　　Exceeds £250 but does not exceed £500　.　.　.　.　　　　6
　　　,,　　500　,,　,,　　,,　　,,　　750　.　.　.　.　.　　　　9
　　　,,　　750　,,　,,　　,,　　,,　1,000　.　.　.　.　.　　1　.,
　　　,,　1,000 for every £500 or fractional part of £500　.　.　　　　6
For Time—
　Where the insurance is made for any time—
　(1) Not exceeding 6 months, three times the amount which would
　　　be payable if the insurance were made upon a voyage;
　(2) Exceeding 6 months and not exceeding 12 months, six times
　　　the amount which would be payable if the insurance were
　　　made upon a voyage.
Penalty for fraud, or evasion of Sea Policy duty　.　.　.　.　100　–　–
Legacy and Succession Duties.
No succession duty is payable where the principal value of all the
　successions on the same death does not amount to £100.
To Husband, or Wife or Children of the deceased, or their Descendants,
　or to the Father or Mother or other Lineal Ancestor of the deceased
　　　　　　　　　　　　　　　　　　　　£1 per cent.

Exceptions. Estates not exceeding £15,000—
　Legacies and successions of less than £1,000 (£2,000 in the case of
　　widow or child under the age of 21 of deceased), whatever may be
　　value of whole estate.
　To Brothers and Sisters of the Deceased or their Descendants, or
　　their Wives or Husbands　　　　　　　　£5 per cent
　To Brothers and Sisters of the Father or Mother of the⎫
　　Deceased, or their Descendants　.　.　.　.　｜　£10
　To Brothers and Sisters of the Grandfather or Grandmother⎬　per
　　of the Deceased, or their Descendants　.　.　.　｜　cent.
　To any Person in any other degree of collateral Consanguinity｜
　　or to a Stranger in Blood to the Deceased .　.　.　⎭
　The Husband or Wife is chargeable with Estate Duty and Legacy
　　and Succession Duty; and the Husband or Wife of a relation is
　　chargeable at the rate at which the relation would be charged.
Letters of Allotment and of Renunciation.
　Less than £5, 1d. ; £5 and upwards, 6d.

	£	s.	d
Letters of Marque and Reprisal	5	–	–
Letters Patent, Grant of, to any honour or dignity, Duke, £350; Marquis, £300; Earl, £250; Viscount, £200; Baron, £150; Precedence, £100; Baronet, £100; *Congé d'élire* to elect an Archbishop or Bishop, £30; any other honour, dignity, or franchise, £30. Change of surname or arms, in accordance with will, £50; upon voluntary application, £10.			
Lunacy Act, Licence for House		10	–
Lunatic: Grant of custody of person or estate	2	–	–
Marriage Licence, special, England and Ireland	5	–	–
Not special		10	–
Money Lenders' Registration Fees	1	–	–
Mortgage Bond, not exceeding £10			3
„ „ 25			8
„ „ 50		1	3
„ „ 100		2	6
„ „ 150		3	9
„ „ 200		5	–
„ „ 250		6	3
„ „ 300		7	6
Exceeding £300, for every £100 and fractional part of £100 .		2	6
Transfer of Mortgage (except marketable securities), for every £100			6
Reconveyance, Release, for every £100			6
Passport (The passport itself costs 15s. and its renewal 10s.) . .			6
Patent (Letters) for inventions—			
On application for provisional protection	1	–	–
On filing complete specification	3	–	–
On notice of desire to have patent sealed	1	–	–
Application for certificate of payment of renewal—			
Before the expiration of the 4th year from the date of the patent, and in respect of the 5th year	5	–	–
6th „	6	–	–
7th „	7	–	–
8th „	8	–	–
9th „	9	–	–
10th „	10	–	–
11th „	11	–	–
12th „	12	–	–
13th „	13	–	–
14th „	14	–	–
15th „	15	–	–
16th „	16	–	–
Power of Attorney, receiving prize-money or wages		1	–
For the receipt of any money, or bill, or note, not exceeding £20, or of any periodical payments not exceeding £10 annually . .		5	–
For the receipt of dividends or interest of any stock, if for one payment only		1	–
In any other case		5	–
Proxy to vote at a meeting			1
Power of Attorney of any other kind		10	–
Protest of any Bill of Exchange—			
Where the duty on the Bill or Note does not exceed 1s., the same duty as the Bill or Note.			
In any other case		1	–
Receipts, £2 or upwards			2
Penalty for not stamping	10	–	–

	£	s.	d.
Revocation of any Trust or Property, not being a Will		10	–
Warrant for Goods			3

Note. The instruments for which the use of Postage adhesive stamps is permitted under the Stamp Act, 1891 are—
Agreements liable to the duty of 6d. Bills of Exchange (including cheques) for payment of money on demand. Certified copies of or extracts from registers of births, etc. Charter-parties. Lease: (i) of a dwelling-house, or part of it, for a definite term not exceeding a year, at a rent not exceeding the rate of £10 per annum; (ii) of any furnished dwelling-house or apartments for any definite term less than a year, where the rent for such term does not exceed £10. Letter of renunciation. Notarial Acts. Policies of Insurance (not life or marine). Protests of bills of exchange and promissory notes. Proxies liable to the duty of 1d. Receipts. Transfers of shares in Cost-book mines. Voting papers. Warrants for goods.

ENTERTAINMENTS TAX

In its anxious search for further sources of income, Parliament (in the Finance Act, 1916) instituted the Entertainments Tax. The tax is now (1933) established at the rate following—

Where payment is below	$2\frac{1}{2}$d.,	tax at	$\frac{1}{2}$d.
,, ,, ,, ,,	6d.,	,, ,,	1d.
,, ,, ,, ,,	$7\frac{1}{2}$d.,	,, ,,	$1\frac{1}{2}$d.
,, ,, ,, ,,	10d.,	,, ,,	2d.
,, ,, ,, ,,	1s. $0\frac{1}{2}$d.,	,, ,,	$2\frac{1}{2}$d.
,, ,, ,, ,,	1s. 3d.	,, ,,	3d.

Then 1d. additional for every 5d. or part of 5d. over 1s. 3d. That is, the tax is fixed as nearly as may be at 20 per cent of the admission price.

The duty is charged: (*a*) by means of a ticket stamped with a stamp denoting that the proper entertainments duty has been paid; or (*b*) with the approval of the Tax Commissioners by means of a barrier where, by an automatic register, the number of persons admitted is recorded.

The proprietor of the entertainment may also make other arrangements with the Commissioners for furnishing return payments.

The duty is not charged where the Commissioners are satisfied: (*a*) that the whole of the takings are devoted to philanthropic or charitable purposes, without any charge for expenses; (*b*) that the entertainment is of a wholly educational character; (*c*) that the entertainment is intended only for the amusement of children, and that the charge is not more than two-pence per person; (*d*) that the entertainment is provided for partly educational or partly scientific purposes by a society, institution, or committee not established for profit, or is provided by any such society or institution that has been founded with the object of reviving national pastimes, in furtherance of that object.

The definition of "payment for admission" adopted in the decided cases is far reaching. It has been held that the 2d. paid for a chair inside a band hall or a pier is subject to duty (*Cordiner* v. *Stockham*, K.B. 1920); that, where members of a cricket club pay an annual sum for a ticket entitling them to free admission to matches, an arrangement about the amount of entertainment duty payable must be made with the Commissioners (*Att.-Gen.* v. *Swan*, K.B. 1922); and that payment for the use of a window from which to view a street procession is chargeable (*Gibson* v. *Reach*, 1923).

It may be noted that where music was provided in a restaurant during meals, but no charge was made except for articles consumed, no entertainment duty is payable. (*J. Lyons & Co., Ltd.* v. *Fox*, K.B. 1919.)

MEETINGS

Public Meetings. No specific law recognises a right of public meeting. But individuals, in the exercise of their freedom, can meet together if they choose: there is nothing to prevent them. If meeting together they break the law, they are prosecuted not for meeting but for the particular breach of law. The right to hold a public meeting is merely a deduction from the right of each individual to go where he pleases, so long as he does not trespass; the right of free speech is a deduction from the right to say what he chooses, so long as he does not libel or blaspheme or talk sedition.

Public Highway. Thus, people have no right to meet in a public highway in such a manner as to prevent its being used for the purpose for which it was dedicated, free passage: "There is no such thing," said Lord Dunedin (*McAra* v. *Edinburgh City Corporation*, 1913), "as a right in the public to hold meetings as such in the streets. . . . That does not necessarily mean that anyone is doing an illegal act if he is not at the moment passing along. Citizens may meet and may stop and speak to each other. It is a question of degree."

In *Burden* v. *Rigler* (K.B. 1911) it was held that the magistrates were wrong in assuming that, because a meeting was held on the public highway, it was, of course, illegal, and that therefore the disturbance of such a meeting could not be an offence under the Public Meetings Act, 1908.

Legal Position of Audience. (1) When no charge is made for admission to a meeting, those who attend are licensees of the conveners of the meeting. Disorderly conduct on their part will, therefore, make them into trespassers; the unruly behaviour, being alien from the purpose for which the licence was granted, has turned the lawful entry into an unlawful intrusion. The conveners may ask them to withdraw: and, after a reasonable time for compliance, may use the force necessary to eject them.

(2) When a charge is made, the licence to attend cannot be withdrawn. The only remedy against one who oversteps the limits of fair criticism and comment is to take proceedings under the Public Meeting Act. (See p. 318.)

Dispersing or Forbidding a Meeting. Where magistrates have reason to fear a breach of the peace as the result of a meeting, they have ordered the police to disperse it or have forbidden it. The magistrates have done this in fulfilling their duty as "conservators of the King's peace." If no other means of preserving the peace is available, their action is justified: "Where a public meeting, though the object of the meeting and the conduct of the members thereof are strictly lawful, provokes a breach of the peace, and it is impossible to preserve or restore the peace by any other means than by dispersing the meeting, the magistrates, constables, and other persons in authority, may call upon the meeting to disperse, and if the meeting does not disperse it becomes an unlawful assembly."

But the necessity must be clear: "If danger arises of a breach of the peace from the exercise of lawful rights, the remedy is the presence of sufficient force to prevent that result, not the legal condemnation of those who exercise those rights."

Unlawful Assembly. Even a lawful meeting becomes unlawful when it is so conducted that people of ordinary courage in the neighbourhood fear a breach of the peace as a result of it. To take part in such a meeting is a misdemeanour punishable by fine and imprisonment without hard labour.

Common Law Riot. The unlawful assembly may develop into a riot. It does when the assembly proceeds to carry out its unlawful purpose, by force if necessary. Those taking part are then committing a misdemeanour.

"Statutory Riot." The Riot Act (1714) enacts that if *twelve* or more persons are assembled together to the disturbance of the public peace, it is the duty of magistrates to go to the assembly and read a proclamation prescribed in the Act ("reading the Riot Act" is the popular phrase). The proclamation calls for dispersion. Those who do not disperse within an hour are declared to be

guilty of felony. That is, the proclamation being read, a misdemeanour becomes a felony.

The magistrates may take other desirable measures for preserving the King's peace, including the closing of public houses in the neighbourhood.

The County Council is liable for damages caused by a riot. Claims must be made in a prescribed form within fourteen days of the riot.

Freedom of Speech. Every person can say what he or she pleases. But a breach of the law against slander, blasphemy, treason, will be punished. Similarly, a writer or a printer need obtain no preliminary licence to write or print. But, again, an unlawful use of the freedom is penalised.

A paper can publish a writing or a picture without obtaining previous sanction. But it acts at its peril. How much so was vividly illustrated when the *Daily Mirror* was constrained to pay Mrs. Cassidy heavy damages, though there was no knowledge of the lady and certainly no wish to defame her. Mr. Cassidy allowed a *Daily Mirror* representative to take a photograph of him on a racecourse, along with a lady to whom, he said jestingly, he was engaged. The photograph was published with the announcement. Mrs. Cassidy resented this, as it suggested that, though she posed as Mr. Cassidy's wife, she was not really married to him ; and the jury agreed that she was wronged and that the defendants were liable. Nor did the Court of Appeal disturb the verdict. (C.A. 1932.) The one exception to this freedom from preliminary licences seems to be in regard to *Dramatic Performances.* Before a theatres proprietor exhibits plays and charges for admission, he must procure from the Lord Chamberlain or the magistrates a licence. Nor may he exhibit a play that has not been submitted to the Lord Chamberlain and received his approval. Even this restriction does not apply when no charge is made for admission.

Blasphemy. This is a criminal offence. For it is likely to lead to a breach of the peace. It consists in the use of such language attacking religion as is likely to shock and insult believers. But "The Common Law of England, which is only common reason or usage, knows of no prosecution for mere opinions. If the decencies of controversy are observed even the fundamentals of religion may be attacked without a person being guilty of blasphemous libel."

"Brawling in Church." The Places of Religious Worship Act, 1812 (extended to all assemblies for religious worship by the Religious Disabilities Act, 1846), enacts that "If any person shall

maliciously disquiet a congregation he shall suffer the pain and penalty of forty pounds."

Disturbance of Public Meetings. The Public Meeting Act, 1898, protects lawful public meetings against disturbance calculated to prevent the transaction of business. One who designedly upsets a *political meeting* in a constituency, between the issue of a writ for the return of a member and the election, is guilty of an *illegal practice* (Corrupt and Illegal Practices Prevention Act, 1883). One who designedly upsets any other lawful public meeting may be summarily sentenced to a fine of £5 or to imprisonment not exceeding one month.

Chairman's Election. Where, in the absence of someone with a right to preside, it is necessary to appoint a chairman, a member of the meeting proposes "I move that Mr. X take the chair," another member says, "I second that motion." No other being nominated, the proposer puts the motion to the meeting; and Mr. X presides with a view to the effective dispatch of the business to be transacted.

Majority Rule. Where no special requirement exists—as it does for instance in regard to a "special resolution" under the Companies Act, 1929—the rule is that a majority *of those who vote* (ignoring those who do not vote) determines the will of the meeting. Those present may be reckoned in the *quorum* necessary, even though they do not vote.

Chairman's Duties.

1. To see whether the meeting has been properly convened.

2. To see that the requisite quorum is present.

3. To have the correspondence read (or to read it).

4. To have the minutes of the previous meeting confirmed and to sign them.

5. To conduct the business as far as practicable in accordance with the prepared agenda.

Agenda. The agenda must include nothing of any importance except that of which due notice has been given to those entitled to vote. Otherwise a resolution upon it may be challenged: "The notice convening the meeting should contain sufficient description of the important business which the meeting is to transact. The meeting cannot in ordinary circumstances go outside the business mentioned in that notice."

Resolutions of a Meeting. A proposal is moved. Unless someone approves of it sufficiently to second it the motion drops. Its discussion after seconding may be interrupted by—

1. The moving and seconding of an amendment.
2. The moving and seconding of "the previous question."
(This is, in effect, a proposal to postpone discussion. It takes the form usually of a motion, "That this motion be now put." That is the previous question which must be settled before the main question. A motion "to proceed to the next business" also aims at a postponement.)
3. The moving and seconding of the closure.
4. The adjournment of the discussion or of the meeting.

It would seem that the seconding of a motion or even of its formal proposal is not essential to its validity. If a resolution can be shown to express the sense of a meeting, it is valid. So the Chancery Court held in *re Horbury Bridge Coal Company* (1879): "Is there any law of the land that at a meeting of shareholders a motion cannot be put unless it is seconded? I am not aware of any. No doubt it is the practice of the House of Commons. And that practice is commonly followed at meetings. But, in my opinion, if the chairman put the question without its having been proposed or seconded by anybody, that would be perfectly good."

Closure of Debate. A determined minority might prevent the will of a meeting from being expressed in a resolution. The power of the chairman to accept and to put to the meeting a motion for closure is, therefore, inherent in his office. Adequate discussion he must allow; excessive, he need not. The Court of Appeal (*Wall* v. *The London and Northern Assets Corporation*, 1898) put the point thus: "As to the closure, if we laid down that the chairman, supported by a majority, could not put a termination to the speeches of those who were desirous of addressing the meeting, we should allow a small minority, or even a member or two, to tyrannise over the majority. We should put a weapon of terrorism into the hands of the minority, which might involve the company in all-night sittings. That is an extravagant proposition. And in this particular case there seems to have been nothing arbitrary or vexatious on the part of the chairman or of the majority."

Trespassers may be Removed. One who gives another a licence (by invitation or permission) to enter upon his premises may revoke the licence. The licensee then becomes a trespasser and, being asked to withdraw, he must do so within a reasonable time. Failing withdrawal he may be ejected by force and his resistance is an unlawful act. Thus where a guest, ejected from a public house where he was behaving in a disorderly manner, sued the landlord for assault, the judge explained the law to the jury:

"If a man goes into a public house and conducts himself in a disorderly manner, and the landlord requests him to go out and he will not, the landlord may turn him out. There is no doubt that a landlord may turn out a person who is making a disturbance in a public house, though such disturbance does not amount to a breach of the peace. But if the person resists and lays hands on the landlord, that is an unjustifiable assault on the landlord." (*Howell* v. *Jackson*.)

Disorder, not amounting to a breach of the peace, does not, however, justify giving the disturber into custody. In a case where the plaintiff in an action for false imprisonment obtained damages, the judge told the jury that annoyance and disturbance—the iteration of "hear, hear," the incessant flow of questions, the comments on a speaker's statements—were not enough justification; the jury must find for the plaintiff unless they were satisfied that what he did amounted to a breach of the peace.

Admission of the Press to Meetings of Local Authorities. The right of representatives of the Press to attend meetings of local authorities depends upon the Local Authorities (Admission of the Press to Meetings) Act, 1908.

The Act gives no right to attend committees; and it is subject to the limitation that: "A local authority may temporarily exclude such representatives from a meeting as often as may be desirable when, in the opinion expressed by resolution of a majority of the members of a local authority present, in view of the special nature of the business then being dealt with or about to be dealt with, such exclusion is desirable in the public interest."

IMPORTANCE OF LOCAL GOVERNMENT

There is no essential difference between the rates we pay to the local authorities and the taxes we pay to the central authorities. Both are compulsory payments for public services; both constitute a curtailing of individual spending so that there shall be more collective spending. And with the continued extension of the government, central and local, into spheres once thought fitting for private enterprise only, both are bound to increase.

The importance of local government will be realised from the fact that about one-ninth of the national income, possibly more, is annexed in the form of local rates and is spent collectively. In some boroughs one in ten of the working population is employed as a servant of the local administration. The services performed by the hundreds of authorities are many and varied: education, the maintenance of the highways, policing, housing, the provision of parks and recreation grounds, street lighting, and a host of other necessary works are functions of the local authorities.

The existence of towns would be impossible without some such method of pooling a part of the individual's resources in order that certain problems may be solved by collective spending, by the compulsory co-operation, that is, of all the citizens.

CENTRAL AUTHORITY EXERCISES CONTROL

In view of the enormous and increasing responsibilities incumbent upon local authorities, it is clear that there should be some uniformity in methods and policies, so that work may proceed with as little friction as possible. Yet the first thing that strikes one about the division of this country into self-governing localities is the utter lack of any uniformity or system. The boundaries are often artificial, bearing no relation to the natural or economic divisions of the territory. The classification of the local authorities as Borough or District Councils is in many cases illogical and unjust. In rateable value, population, territorial extent, and status and powers of the respective authorities, there are great variations between different localities.

The original determination of the extent of the units of local administration was entirely haphazard; and the passage of time has introduced fresh anomalies. The counties have been in existence since pre-feudal times, and in most cases still keep their old boundaries. The parishes, which have been units of local government since the Middle Ages, were small enough to permit the clergy to complete their day's round on foot. Modern conditions, and gradual changes in the relative importance of different localities, have called for a revision of the boundaries of many of the local authorities.

LOCAL GOVERNMENT ACT, 1929

The County Councils are empowered by the Local Government Act of 1929 to review periodically the boundaries of their parishes. Any parish that considers itself aggrieved may, however, petition the Ministry of Health and demand that a local inquiry should be held. This is a slow and expensive process, and it seems that the parish boundaries, even though they be absurd anachronisms, must remain with little alterations for many years to come.

It is patently impossible for bodies which vary to so large an extent in size, wealth, and population to perform with an equal

degree of efficiency the many duties imposed upon them. In the
business world, the tendency has been towards the combination
of individually impotent units in order to form one powerful
whole. The same advantages which accrue to a manufacturer who
can produce on a large scale, some of them at least, should hold
good for a local authority which is able to increase the area over
which it has authority. This becomes more evident when it is
realised that the duties of the local authorities may include such
functions as the supply of electricity, in which a considerable
reduction might be made in the cost of production of the electric
power if a larger scale of activities were possible.

In such matters as land drainage, and water supply, a large unit
of administration is desirable. Failing this, co-operation by the
smaller units is essential to efficiency. Yet, until quite recently,
we had no larger authority than the county for drainage, and within
this there were independent County Boroughs. Effective drainage
could not be performed by a number of small and quite artificially
formed units, especially when there was no power to compel
co-operation. The natural unit of drainage is, of course, the river
basin; and water partings should form the boundaries of areas
under single authorities. When this natural area is divided into
several independent authorities, efficient drainage becomes impossible. This is very evident when it is seen that, if one of these
authorities neglects its duties, it will affect the work of all authorities within the drainage area.

CO-OPERATION AMONG LOCAL AUTHORITIES

Fortunately, the need for larger authorities has been realised
by Parliament so far as drainage is concerned; and this may
possibly be regarded as a step in the right direction which will
be followed by further unification in the other functions of the
local authorities. Lord Noel Buxton's Drainage Bill, has remedied
many of the faults of the old system of drainage. The Report of
the Royal Commission on Land Drainage, which preceded Lord
Buxton's Bill, called attention to the unnatural composition of the
units of drainage authority. It recommended that the drainage
unit should take the form of the Catchment Area, or the whole of
the land which directs the drainage towards one river, ending in
the sea.

The Commission suggested that there should be set up for each
Catchment Area one authority only, which was to attend to all
the drainage problems within that area. The authority was to be

composed of representatives from the councils of the counties included within the area, from the County Boroughs and from certain other interests. Urban District Councils and Non-County Boroughs were not to be permitted to appoint representatives. The counties were to submit, within a specified time, a proposed scheme of amalgamation. In the event of default, the Ministry of Agriculture was empowered to enforce the unification for drainage purposes of counties within a drainage area. It was stressed that co-operation should be obligatory and not merely permissive ; because no scheme of drainage can be successful if one area refuses to perform its part or is negligent in the acquittal of its duties.

DELEGATING POWERS

Parliament legislates in general terms, and defines the powers and duties of local authorities. The government of each locality is supposed to attend to the enforcement of the general rules laid down by the central authority and to make any necessary by-laws. In addition, each locality must perform as efficiently as possible the many duties imposed upon it by Parliament. By this delegation of authority, the Central Government is relieved of an enormous mass of intricate detail, to deal adequately with which would be beyond the powers of one body. It was hoped that the system of local government would prove "flexible and responsive to particular needs," and that many small and scattered authorities, each cognisant of and sympathetic with local circumstances, would administer regulations far more effectively than one central body could. Events have proved this hope to have been too sanguine. In many branches, the work of local authorities has been performed in a none too efficient manner.

As long ago as 1869, a Sanitary Commission enumerated the following as the normal requirements of a community which should be satisfied by the local authority—

1. An adequate supply of clean, healthy water.
2. The regulation of building and town planning.
3. The maintenance of the streets in good repair.
4. The prevention of pollution of rivers and other waterways.
5. The provision of means for the disposal of sewage.
6. Inspection of food.
7. Abatement of smoke.
8. Prevention of the spreading of epidemics, and the care of the public health at all times.

In the last sixty-five years we should certainly have made some progress, and our standards should not be lower than those suggested by the Commission of 1869. Yet there are many localities to-day which fail abjectly to provide the minimum amenities regarded as essential by the mid-Victorians.

It appears that much of the inefficiency of the local authorities may be attributed to the small scale of their operations, and to the paucity of their resources. There are at present over 430 districts which could not raise £100 by the imposition of a penny rate. Clearly it is impossible for these localities to effect any considerable improvements in their conditions, even though they were prepared to raise their rates to an exorbitant figure. Little justification can be found for the small size of our units of local government. The sizes were determined when a more centralised system was impracticable. Since then, improved means of communication and a growing sense of discipline have made possible some unification of the system. It is sometimes urged that any alteration is undesirable as it would destroy local patriotism. This defence of our system is untenable; local patriotism, where it exists, usually runs to resentment to other localities, and is more a bar than an incentive to progress. Our units of local authority must not be kept small and impotent merely to foster a perverted sense of patriotism; for patriotism of a finer kind is induced by centralisation. Even a unit as large as the British Empire may have its spirit of patriotism.

THE UNITS OF LOCAL GOVERNMENT: THE PARISH

The Parish has long been a unit of ecclesiastical administration; but its position in our local government system was fixed by the Local Government Act of 1894. The Parish may be either a rural or an urban locality, and for purposes of local government is defined as "a place for which, prior to the Rating and Valuation Act, 1925, a separate poor rate was or could have been made, or for which a separate overseer was or could have been appointed."

There are two types of governing body which may exist in a parish, namely, the Parish Meeting and the Parish Council. The Parish Meeting is an assembly of all the local government electors resident within a parish. The possession of such a meeting is compulsory for rural parishes, but optional for urban parishes. In parishes with a population of under one hundred, or between one and three hundred in cases where special application has not been made to the County Council, the Parish Meeting is the only representative authority. However, it is open to the County

Councils to permit, at their discretion, parishes with a population of under a hundred to hold a Parish Council in addition to the Meeting. In the absence of a Parish Council, the Chairman of the Meeting, who is elected annually, and the Rural District Councillors are a corporate body with perpetual succession.

POWERS AND DUTIES OF THE PARISH MEETING

The Parish Meeting may, in parishes which do not possess a council, appoint two representatives on the Rating Committee.

The disposal and administration of parish property is a function of the Meeting.

The Parish Meeting is not empowered to levy a rate. If and when it incurs any expenses, which must be limited by the proceeds of an eightpenny rate, it may make payment by means of orders on the Rating Authority. Accounts must be made up annually to the 31st March, and are audited by the District Auditor of the Ministry of Health.

The Parish Meeting has the right to veto in the following cases—

(*a*) Any expenses which will necessitate a rate of over 4d.

(*b*) The borrowing of any money.

(*c*) The adoption of the Adoptive Acts by the Parish Council.

(*d*) The proposed stopping or diversion of a highway.

MEETINGS

There must be at least two meetings of the electors every year, one of which must be held between 1st March and 1st April. Further meetings may be called, on due notice, by any six electors or by the Chairman. Such meetings must always be held in the evenings, after 6 p.m., presumably to ensure a representative attendance.

Each elector has one vote, and all matters are decided in the first place by the majority of those present at the meetings. A minority of at least one-third of the voters, provided that it is not less than five persons, may, however, demand that a poll shall be taken of all the electors within the parish. Polls, in such cases, must be taken by ballot.

THE PARISH COUNCIL

There is a second representative unit in larger parishes, namely, the Parish Council. In rural parishes with a population exceeding three hundred, the election of a Council is obligatory. In parishes with between one and three hundred inhabitants, the Parish Meeting may elect a Council, provided that it notifies the County authorities. If a parish has less than a hundred inhabitants, it may elect a Council only with the special permission of the County Council. The election of the Council is in all cases held at the annual Parish Meeting.

The Parish Council may consist of any number of members from five to fifteen, who are elected to serve for three years. It is usual for one-third of the councillors to retire at the end of each year. This tends to continuity in the policy of the Council, and permits of changes to be made only gradually. The necessary qualifications which candidates for seats on the Council must possess are—

(a) Residence in the parish, or

(b) Ownership of property within the parish, or

(c) The possession of a vote in the local government.

The Parish Council, like the Parish Meeting, is a unit of representation rather than administration. Its scope of authority is very limited, and perhaps its chief function is to call attention to the omissions of the more potent units of authority. For instance, the Council may petition the Ministry of Health if the parish water supply is unsatisfactory; it may request that an order by the County Council to alter its boundaries should be annulled; it may call to the attention of the proper authorities the existence of dangerous corners, or the dilapidated state of the highways.

The parish authorities have very little power of their own, especially since the abolition of the Boards of Guardians by the Local Government Act of 1929. The infinitesimal scale of their activities may be judged from the fact that their average expenditure in a typical financial year was only £31, and that their income from rates, levied through the County authorities, did not exceed £21. The value of the Parish Council seems to lie not in the work that it does, but in the calling of attention to the need for work to be done, and the semblance which it maintains of local self-government. It is frequently stated that it is a good influence if the parishioners know that they have a representative body, however limited the scope of its authority, and if they can closely follow its various activities. This argument is, perhaps, rendered void by the deplorable lack of interest in local government. It is quite common for councillors to be returned unopposed at the elections; and there are many cases on record where the council could not sit in full force for want of candidates at the elections. Local government elections arouse very little enthusiasm, and a poll of 10 per cent of the electorate is unusually large.

POWERS AND DUTIES OF THE PARISH COUNCIL

The Parish Council may appoint two representatives on the County Rating Committee, and may appeal to the Quarter Sessions or to the Assessment Committee on questions concerning rating and valuation.

The Council may provide and maintain a Parish Hall or Rooms, and has custody of the books and records.

It has the right of veto on proposals relating to the stopping or diversion of highways. The Council does not build or maintain highways, although it may supervise footpaths, and preserve rights of way.

It may provide land for certain authorised purposes including recreation grounds, markets, and allotments.

With the sanction of the Parish Meeting it may administer the Adoptive Acts.

The Parish Council is not entitled to levy a rate. As with the Parish Meeting, expenditure is met by precepts on the County Rating Authority. This expenditure is limited to the proceeds of a 4d. rate, or, with the approval of the Meeting, an 8d. rate, plus any other amounts that may be required for the execution of the Adoptive Acts. But even in this latter indefinite amount the Meeting exercises some control, since it may forbid the Council to adopt the Adoptive Acts.

With the sanction of the County Council and the Parish Meeting the Parish Council may raise loans for authorised purposes.

Accounts are made up annually to 31st March and are audited by the District Auditor of the Ministry of Health.

MEETINGS

At least four meetings of the Parish Council must be held every year, one of which must be between 8th April and 22nd April. Further meetings may be called, on due notice by the chairman or by any two councillors.

THE DISTRICT

The District is the unit of local government for sanitary purposes, and consists of a number of parishes. This number is not regulated, but may vary within wide limits.

A district may be governed by a Rural or an Urban District Council; the former, of course, is intended to serve as the local government authority in country areas, and the latter in town areas. This distinction, however, is not as fine as it might be, and there are many cases of urban communities which are governed by Rural District Councils, or even by Parish Councils. Machinery exists to remedy these anomalies. By the provisions of the Local Government Acts of 1888 and 1894, the County Councils may cause local inquiries to be made if they consider that an Urban District is called for, or if they receive memorials from the Parish Councils concerned. The Local Government Act of 1929 makes it obligatory for the County Councils periodically to review their boundaries, with the object of preventing the continuance of anachronism. The interval between successive reviews must not be less than ten years.

CONSTITUTION OF THE COUNCILS

Those who may serve on the District Councils are—
1. Local government electors;
2. Residents in the district;
3. Owners of property;
provided that they are not disqualified on account of infancy, lunacy, etc. The number of members on the Council is not fixed, but there is a minimum of at least one councillor for each parish with a population of three hundred or more.

The election of Councillors takes place in April. Voting is by ballot, and each local government elector has one vote for each seat to be filled. The councillors are elected for a period of three years, and it is customary for one-third of them to retire annually, to prevent sudden changes of policy. But with the consent of two-thirds of the District Councillors and a majority of the County Council, the entire District Council may give up office at the end of every third year.

MEETINGS

The District Council must meet at least once a month. Additional meetings may be summoned by the chairman and any two councillors. A quorum consists of one-third of the number of councillors, but must not be less than seven.

ACCOUNTS

Accounts are made up annually to 31st March, and are audited by the District Auditors of the Ministry of Health.

RATES

All District Councils are entitled to levy rates to meet any expenses which are not by law or custom paid from particular funds. Rateable property within the district is valued by the Rating Authority, and the lists are revised periodically by the Assessment Committee. A General Rate may be levied on the basis of the Valuation Lists, and a salaried official is responsible to the District Council for its collection.

Certain properties, such as agricultural land and woodlands and church halls, are exempted from the liability of bearing a rate. Others, such as factories and railway property in urban districts are rated at a quarter of their annual value.

A Private Improvement Rate may be levied in respect of premises for the specific improvement or benefit of which expenses have been incurred by the Council, e.g. Road Charges. No portion of these expenses may remain outstanding after thirty years have elapsed from the date of their being incurred.

BORROWING CAPITAL

Capital expenditure on sanitary works or housing schemes may be met by the borrowing of money. There is no limit to the total amount which may be outstanding at any particular time; but loans must be repaid within sixty years if made for sanitary purposes, or within eighty years if for housing schemes or the acquisition of land.

MUNICIPAL TRADING

The Urban District Council may carry on certain permitted "trading enterprises," such as the provision of electricity or the running of tramways.

It has power of raising loans by the issue of stock, as provided for by the Public Health Amendment Act, Part V.

The Councils of Urban Districts with over 20,000 inhabitants are the authorities under the Shop Acts, The Old Age Pensions Acts, and the National Health Insurance Acts. Regardless of population, the Urban District Council is the authority under the War Charities Act.

TRANSITION FROM URBAN DISTRICT TO BOROUGH STATUS

By the terms of the Municipal Incorporation Act of 1882, the inhabitants of an Urban District may petition the Ministry of Health for a Charter of Incorporation, which, if granted, will give them County Borough status. The expenses incurred in the attempt to obtain this Charter must not constitute a charge on the rates of the Urban District; but if the Charter is granted, they may be paid from the fund of the newly constituted borough.

POWERS AND DUTIES PECULIAR TO RURAL DISTRICT COUNCILS

The Rural District Council is allowed to delegate some of its sanitary functions to the Council of the parishes within its area. If the boundaries of the Rural District are identical to or include those of a parish, the Rural District Council is entrusted with all the functions of a Parish Council.

Rural District Councils have special duties to perform under the Public Health (Water) Act, 1878, which requires them to provide, or to enforce the provision of, an adequate supply of water at a reasonable proximity to any occupied house within its area.

The Ministry of Health may grant the Rural District any of the powers of an Urban District which it thinks fit, or may make it into an Urban District.

POWERS AND DUTIES OF DISTRICT COUNCILS

The functions of an Urban District Council differ considerably from those of a Rural District Council. As a general rule, it may be stated that the Urban District Council is entrusted with those special duties which are made necessary by the nature of life in towns, while the Rural District Councils are given the functions peculiar to country life. The duties of the Urban District Council are rather more onerous, and its powers greater, than those of a Rural District Council. Some duties, however, are common to all District Councils, no matter whether they have jurisdiction over urban or rural areas.

They are as follows—

PUBLIC HEALTH

There is a similarity in the power of appointing officials; for all District Councils must have a Sanitary Inspector and a Medical Officer. The similarity is limited; for the Urban Districts must maintain more public health services than the Rural Districts.

The Public Health functions which are common to both Urban and Rural District Councils are as follows—

Abatement of nuisances.

Drainage and sewerage.

Disposal of water refuse.

Provision of water supply.

Inspection of food.

Inspection of regulations of dairies, workshops, laundries, lodging houses, etc.

Provision of hospitals and cemeteries.

Prevention of spread of infectious diseases.

Regulation of building and town planning.

Housing.

In addition, all District Councils have power to make such by-laws on the subject of public health as will be conducive to good government, provided that they meet with the approval of the Ministry of Health.

Highways. Since the passing of the 1930 Act the duties common to all District Councils on the subject of Highways are limited to the protection of rights of way. The Urban District Council still have control of all streets within their area.

Allotments. The provision and administration of allotments is performed by the Councils of both Urban and Rural Districts.

Other functions common to all District Councils include the powers and duties of Justices out of Session, the protection of rights to common, and the granting of licences to pawnbrokers, game dealers, gang masters, etc.

POWERS AND DUTIES PECULIAR TO URBAN DISTRICT COUNCILS

Public Health. The Urban District Council is entrusted with certain special functions under this heading, namely—

The provision of bath, wash houses, and conveniences.

Street cleaning, lighting, and watering.

Inspection and regulation of slaughter houses.

Education. The powers of the Urban District Council in this direction are dependent to a certain extent on the population of the area over which it has jurisdiction. However, all Urban District Councils, no matter what the population may be, are allowed to provide secondary or higher education to the extent of the proceeds of a penny rate.

If the population is 20,000 or more, the Urban District Council is the local education authority. For smaller districts the authority is the County Council.

THE COUNTY

The administrative county, which shares with the County Borough a place of pre-eminence in local government, is distinct from the geographical county. In the majority of cases, the boundaries of the geographical and administrative counties coincide. But there are some instances of a geographical county being split into several independent units of local authority. For example, both Yorkshire and Lincolnshire are divided into three separate administrative counties. Suffolk and Sussex are each divided into two counties for local government purposes. Further instances of variation in the extent of geographical and administrative counties are provided by the Soke of Peterborough, the Isle of Wight, and the Isle of Ely. Each of these localities is governed by an independent County Council, although it constitutes but a small section of a geographical county. In all, there are sixty-two administrative counties, as against the fifty-two geographical divisions.

The local authority in a County, the County Council, is a corporate body having the right to a common seal and perpetual succession. The personnel of the Council consists of a chairman, aldermen, and councillors. The Council is elected by ballot, at which all the local government electors are entitled to vote.

ELECTION OF THE COUNCIL

County Councillors are elected for a period of three years, and the whole Council retires triennially. For the purpose of electing the Council, the County is split into a number of divisions, each of which choses one representative on the Council. No local government elector may vote in more than one division, even though he has property in several divisions which would normally entitle the owner to a vote.

The election of the County Council usually takes place on 8th March; but by resolution of the retiring Council, it may be held on any day in the preceding week.

QUALIFICATION OF COUNCILLORS

The qualifications required of County Councillors are similar to those of County Borough Councillors, except that the residential qualification is extended to twelve months. In cases where qualification is by virtue of the possession of property in the County the conditions are as follow—

1. In counties of less than four divisions, the owner of property valued at £500, or at £15 a year for rating purposes, is eligible for seat on the councils.

2. In counties containing four or more divisions, property to

the value of £1,000, or property rated at £30 qualifies for membership of the council.

ALDERMEN

County Aldermen are elected by the County Councillors from among their number, or from those qualified to be councillors. One alderman is elected for every three councillors. Aldermen serve for a period of six years, and half of them retire triennially.

CHAIRMAN

The chairman of the County Council is elected by the councillors and the senior aldermen from their number. He officiates at all meetings of the full Council.

MEETINGS

The full Council usually meets four times in the year. The first statutory meeting of the newly elected Council must be held on 16th March, or on the succeeding day if the 16th falls on a Sunday. In the second year of its term of office, the Council may hold its statutory annual meeting in either March, April, or May. Three other meetings of the Council must be held every year in addition to the statutory meeting. The various committees of the Council meet as frequently as their work necessitates.

POWERS AND DUTIES OF THE COUNTY COUNCIL

A County includes a large number of authorities invested with varying degrees of responsibility. One of the main functions of the County Council, therefore, is the control and supervision which it exercises over the less powerful local authorities which constitute its area. The extent of this control varies in inverse ratio with the powers of the respective authorities. Thus, the Parish Meeting, a relatively impotent body, may do little without the sanction of the County Council, while the County Borough acts independently of the County Council.

The County Council may intervene if the sanitary functions of its component localities are inefficiently carried on. In the matters of housing, the building of hospitals and schools, and the maintenance in good repair of the highways, the County Council exercises a control. The Council may alter the boundaries of its constituent localities, subject, in the event of appeal, to the approval of the Minister of Health.

COMMITTEES

The work of the County Council is for the most part delegated to committees. No committee, however, may have conferred upon it the power to raise money, whether by means of a rate or loan.

Committees formed by the County Council may be divided into two main classes, viz. the statutory or compulsory committees, and the optional ones, appointed according to the Standing Orders of the Council. Each class may be subdivided into ordinary and joint committees, the distinction arising from the fact that representatives of the smaller units of local authority contained in the County may serve on the latter.

Statutory Committees, which must be appointed by all County Councils, include those formed for the following functions—

Finance.

Valuation.

Housing.

Education.

Pensions.

Public Assistance.

The Administration of the Shops Acts.

The Standing Joint Committee, which deals with the property of the Council and appoints certain of its officials.

Great innovations of the Local Government Act were—

1. "Public Assistance" now takes the place of the old "Poor relief"; and the poor law functions of the old Boards of Guardians are now performed by the Councils of Counties or of County Boroughs.

2. Roads are controlled by the County Councils; and in both *Rural Districts* and *Non-County Boroughs* and *Urban Districts* the expenses of the maintenance, repair, and improvement of the roads are General County expenses.

3. Powers are given to County Councils to initiate, if thought desirable, with local authorities *town-planning* schemes.

THE BOROUGH

The Borough is the most dignified form of self-governing urban locality. Boroughs may be divided into two categories, according to their status in relation to the County. Firstly, there are the County Boroughs, units of local authority possessing, to all intents and purposes, the powers and duties of the counties. They are, in fact, independent counties within counties. The second type is the Non-County Borough, which does not enjoy such a large degree of independence as the County Borough. It is subordinated in some respects to the County, and is forced to contribute to its funds.

From the point of view of the ratepayer, some disadvantages may be said to accrue from government by a Borough. It is possible that the rates levied will be such a large sum as is compatible with the dignity and standing of the municipality. Another factor which may lead to higher expenditure is the limitation of the power of the Borough auditors. Except for accounts concerning functions for which State assistance is provided, the Boroughs are exempted from the audit of the Ministry of Health. For the most part the Boroughs are allowed to appoint their own auditors, and these are not empowered to surcharge any expenses.

CONSTITUTION OF THE GOVERNING BODY

The body which governs a Borough is a Municipal corporation, which enjoys the right of perpetual succession, and has a common seal. The personnel of the corporation consists of the Mayor, the aldermen, and the burgesses. All the powers and duties of the corporation may, however, be delegated to the Borough Council, a body which is elected by the burgesses.

Burgess. The term "burgess" is almost synonymous with "local government elector." Any person who, being duly qualified, has his name on the burgess rolls of the borough, is a burgess. The "due qualification" is the only distinction between a burgess and a local government elector. A person may have got his name included in the burgess rolls by misrepresentation, although he is not qualified. In such a case, it may be impossible to prevent him from voting; but he is not a burgess.

To be eligible as a burgess, a person must satisfy one of the two following conditions—

1. He must occupy premises within the borough, and must have done so during the six months preceding the compiling of the register.

2. He, or she, must be the spouse of a person qualified under (1)

In both cases eligibility is dependent on freedom from legal disqualification on account of minority, unsound mind, felony, etc.

The direct control of the burgesses in the affairs of the borough is negligible; by means of his vote he delegates his authority to the Council. However, he is allowed to inspect the minutes of the Council on payment of a fee not in excess of one shilling; he may criticise the policy of the Council, and may insist on its fulfilling its statutory obligations, and restrain it from performing actions outside the scope of its authority.

Councillors. The number of Councillors in a borough is fixed by its Charter of Incorporation, and may be revised by Act of Parliament or by Orders in Council. The borough is divided into wards, and for each ward there must be appointed three councillors, or some multiple of three. The councillors are elected by the burgesses at the local government elections held on 1st November. Councillors are elected for a period of three years, and it is customary for one-third of their number to retire annually, to ensure continuity of policy. In some places, and throughout London in particular, the entire Council retires at the end of every third year.

The polling is by ballot, and each local government elector is allowed one vote for every seat to be filled. But no person may give more than one vote to any one candidate.

Those qualified to act as councillors are burgesses and owners of property within the borough of a capital value of £1,000, or a rateable value of £30. (In boroughs with less than three wards, the capital value need be only £500, or the rateable value £15.) However, no person may be a councillor if—

1. He holds any remunerative office in the gift of the Council (other than mayor or sheriff).

2. He is an undischarged bankrupt, or a felon.

3. He has been found guilty of corrupt practices at elections.

4. He has resided for six successive months in the last year outside the borough (unless qualified by ownership of property).

5. He is interested in any contract made with the Council.

In addition the usual disqualifications exists in regard to infants, aliens, officers of the regular forces on the active list (Army Act). Such officers are, it should be noted, eligible for election to the County Councils. Since 1925 (Removal of Disqualifications Act), ministers of religion are eligible.

Aldermen. Aldermen are elected by the councillors from any of their number, or from among those qualified to be councillors. The period of office is six years, and half of the aldermen retire at the end of every third year. One alderman is elected for every three councillors. The election of aldermen is held on 9th November, and is conducted by an open poll. Each councillor has one vote for each seat to be filled, but may not give more than one vote to any candidate.

Aldermen are members of the Council, and have no greater

powers or duties than the other councillors. Their only special function is to act as returning officers at the local government elections. Their social status is higher than that of the common councillor.

Mayor. The mayor is chosen annually on 9th November by the council to act as its president and chairman, and is nominally the head man in the borough. He must be elected from among the councillors, or from those qualified to be councillors. An additional qualification is necessary for the office of mayor in that not more than two months' residence outside the borough is permitted, as against the six months permitted in the case of councillors. The outgoing mayor may present himself for re-election.

The office may be, but is not of necessity, a salaried one, and carries with it, in certain districts the right to the title "Right Honourable."

The mayor is, *ex officio*, a Justice of the Peace for the Borough, and also for the County, unless his is a County Borough. His office as a Justice of the Peace continues for one year after he ceases to be mayor, unless in that period be becomes disqualified to act as mayor. He is also, *ex officio*, a member of the Watch Committee, and Head Magistrate during his term of office.

The mayor may appoint in writing a deputy to act on his behalf at any meeting of the Council.

FINANCE AND ACCOUNTS

The borough meets its expenses by means of the rates which it levies, State grants, loans, surpluses from "trading ventures," fines and tolls, and rents from borough property.

Rates. The borough may levy a General Rate to make good any deficiency on the year's accounts. In addition, special rates may be levied in respect of particular functions, such as a Watch Rate in boroughs which maintain their own police force. Rates are collected by a salaried official.

Loans. Loans may be raised for sanitary or building purposes, though usually it is necessary to obtain the permission of the Ministry of Health. Loans for sanitary work must be repaid within sixty years, and loans made for the acquisition of land or for building, must be repaid within 80 years. There is no statutory limit to the total amount which may be outstanding at any one time.

Accounts are made up annually to any date that the borough decides, provided that it meets the approval of the Ministry of

Health. It is usual for them to be made up to 31st March, the end of the fiscal year. They are audited for the most part by the borough auditors, two of whom are elected by the Council, while the third is nominated by the mayor. The borough auditors must have the same qualifications as are required for membership of the Council, but they must not be councillors. They have no power to surcharge.

Accounts relating to housing, education, and public assistance, functions in respect of which State grants are received, are audited by the District Auditor of the Ministry of Health, who may surcharge expenses contrary to law.

POWERS AND DUTIES OF THE BOROUGH COUNCIL

The scope of the authority of a Borough Council depends on whether the borough in question is a County or a Non-County Borough. The powers of the Council also vary with the population of the borough.

FUNCTIONS DEPENDENT ON POPULATION

The Councils of boroughs with a population of 10,000 or more are the authorities under the following Acts—

Weights and Measures Act.

Diseases of Animals Act.

Food and Drugs Act.

Education Act, 1921, for elementary education.

The Councils of boroughs with a population of 20,000 or more are the local authorities under the Old Age Pensions Act.

They may apply to the Home Office for permission to maintain a separate police force. In the event of the permission being granted, the police force is controlled by a Watch Committee. (Separate police forces may also be maintained by boroughs which had a population of between 10,000 and 20,000 at the 1881 census, provided that a force has been in uninterrupted existence since 1881.)

RECEIPT OF PUBLIC ASSISTANCE (POOR RELIEF)

This disqualifies for the office of Borough or County Councillor. But the disqualification does not apply if only—

1. He or a member of his family has received medical or surgical treatment.

2. He has received relief under the Blind Persons Act, 1920.

3. He has received relief as a rate-aided patient.

4. He received relief before 27th March, 1929.

HOUSING

Great progress has been made since the War in the work of remedying over-crowded dwellings. During the last ten years, more than 1,400,000 new houses have been built; it is estimated that they provide accommodation for some 7,000,000 of people. The majority of these new houses, however, are being occupied by the middle classes. They are let at rents which the unskilled artisan cannot pay, or have been bought on money advanced by Building Societies at repayment rates beyond the income of the common labourer.

As a result, in spite of this post-war building activity, there were, in 1930, great numbers of slum dwellers. Although these people paid low rents, they tolerated such a low degree of comfort that their accommodation was relatively expensive. For some time previously, the local authorities had been making sporadic attempts at providing better houses at low rents for the working classes; but the number of persons who could live in the Council houses and flats was insignificant when compared with the enormous army of slum dwellers. It often happened that Council flats were let at rents which excluded the ordinary wage earner. In such cases it was not uncommon for middle class families, who could have afforded a higher rental, to be living in dwellings subsidised by the State and the Municipality. An increase in the extent of slums was then to be expected; for the houses vacated by these middle class families would often be divided into tenements. Such tenements, let at low rents and overcrowded, would develop into slums.

The system on which the State grants were paid to assist the provision of cheap housing facilities was, before the 1930 Act came into force, illogical and unsatisfactory. The State used to pay the Municipalities a yearly sum not exceeding 50 per cent of the amount that they had expended on the provision of houses during the year. Grants in aid were allocated in proportion to the ability to spend, rather than on the need for service. This, coupled with the fact that the charge on the State was indefinite, and its precise magnitude dependent on the profligacy of the local councillors, called for an entire revision of the system.

The 1930 Housing Act (Part 2) was introduced by the Minister of Health in order to remedy the defects in the old system of Municipal Housing. It abolished the percentage basis of grants and introduced a unit system. A grant is now made by the Central Government to the local authorities towards the cost

of buildings at so much per annum for every person displaced
from the slums who is accommodated in the council dwellings.
The normal rate is 45s. per head per annum in England and Wales,
and is payable for a period of forty years from the date of its
inception. In the case of rural parishes, and in towns where high
buildings are made necessary by the cost of land, the grant may
be increased as under—

1. Rural parishes, which are defined as parishes in which at
least a quarter of the assessable value arises from agricultural
land and buildings, and in which the population does not exceed
320 persons per square mile. In such parishes, the grant is 50s.
per annum for every displaced person. In addition to this State
subsidy, further facilities are provided to ensure better rural
houses. The County Councils are obliged to contribute towards
the cost of building or improving rural dwellings an amount of
£1 per annum for every person for whom house accommodation
is provided. This subsidy must continue for forty years. It has
the effect of decreasing the burden on the parish by spreading its
incidence over the entire county.

2. High building in towns. It is often necessary for urban workers to live close to their places of employment. When hours are
long, or when work starts exceptionally early, it is particularly
desirable that travelling time and expense should be reduced to
a minimum. In large towns, therefore, the council dwellings may
have to be built on expensive land, near the heart of the city.
When this is so, it will be more economical to build high on small
sites. But high buildings are relatively more costly than low
buildings. In recognition of this, the 1930 Act provides that in
cases where houses of at least three storeys are erected on land
which cost more than £3,000 an acre, the annual per capita grant
shall be increased to 70s.

The local authorities must undertake to let the subsidised
dwellings at a rental not in excess of the difference between the
average annual cost of building and maintenance and the State
grant received. It is intended that the accommodation shall be
let to poor persons deserving the subsidy, that is, in the main, to
the displaced slum dwellers. The tenants are not intended to pay
an economic rent; every family housed by the municipalities
will constitute a charge on the national and municipal revenues
for a period of forty years. To provide a certain amount of elasticity in the actual amount of this charge, the Act includes a clause
which permits a periodical revision of the amount of the State grant.

There are no statutory regulations as to the precise amount of rent which shall be charged. The local authorities are allowed to differentiate, and may enforce higher payment from one family than from another for identical accommodation. It is intended, as far as possible, that the rent shall be determined by the ability of the tenant to pay. The success of the Act depends, in a large measure, on the willingness of the local authority to grant housing accommodation to poor people at rock bottom rents, even though the result is a considerable charge on the rates.

Several methods have been suggested for the determination of the rent to be charged for particular families. Of these, the more important are—

1. A fixed proportion of the family income.

2. A standard rate, with deductions in respect of dependent children, and increased payments when the children are at work. Thus, the married couple with no children, living in a state of comparative opulence, would pay the full standard rent. With the arrival of each child, as the family expenses rose, the rent would be reduced by a small amount. In the second period of affluence, when the children were earning, the rent would be raised.

Opponents of this scheme maintain that it would encourage improvident marriages and unduly large families. Can it be seriously suggested that the promise of a reduction of, say, a shilling a week in the rent will induce a couple to bring an unwanted child into the world?

DEMOLITION

Before much progress can be made in the work of providing subsidised dwellings, the actual clearance of slums must be attended to. Clearance work is divided by the Act into three categories, each of which must receive a different type of treatment. They are—

1. *Clearance Areas.* These are areas which are unhabitable throughout. Such slums should be entirely demolished, and new and better houses built in their place.

2. *Improvement Areas.* These are areas in which the dilapidation is only partial, and which may be made habitable by "patching up." In slums of this type, it is intended that the necessary alterations and improvements will be made, at a cost substantially lower than that of rebuilding.

3. *Individual Houses.* Detached and unhabitable dwellings, situated among houses in a reasonable condition, are to be demolished.

COST OF THE ACT TO THE STATE

Reckoning five persons to a dwelling, the capital value of the State subsidy, at the normal rate of 45s. per head is calculated at about £200 for every dwelling erected under the Act. In towns, where the higher rate of grant is paid, the capital value of the State contribution will be about £310 per dwelling. This represents the most generous subsidy to housing which has ever been made. The capital value of the State subsidy under the former plan was £130; the value of the earlier subsidy was £75.

The total amount which the State will have to expend under the Act depends, of course, on the extent of the slum clearance work of the local authorities. There is no coercion by the Central Government; the initiative must be taken locally, and the cost to the State will be dependent on the willingness of localities to do the work. However, it is safe to prophesy that something like £250,000,000 will have to be found by the taxpayer during the currency of the scheme.

INITIATIVE TAKEN BY AN OUTSIDE AUTHORITY

The erection of subsidised housing accommodation in a particular area, as distinct from the enforced demolition of insanitary buildings, is not invariably left to the local authority concerned. There is nothing to prevent the Council of a borough from acquiring land in the surrounding districts for the purpose of building. An example of such a procedure is provided by the estate of Becontree, in the County of Essex, which is being developed by the London County Council.

The motive which induces a locality to "colonise" places outside the area over which it has jurisdiction, is usually the scarcity and costliness of suitable sites within the locality. The building which is being carried on at Becontree is intended to benefit people who move out of London; it is in no sense designed to relieve any congestion which might formerly have existed in Essex. The London County Council have been forced to build outside their administrative area because London was overcrowded, and because building sites in the Metropolis are prohibitively expensive. They did not do so as an act of charity towards the poor of Becontree. Indeed, a locality may feel injured when another authority plants extensive housing estates within its area. The authorities of the localities which are being "colonised" have certain duties to perform towards their inhabitants. For instance, they may have to provide schools for the children resident within their area; they have to maintain roads, to provide an adequate water supply, and to carry out many other functions, the cost of which is dependent largely on population. Local authorities may resent colonisation from other areas; for the influx of population adds considerably to the cost of government. The existing amenities are insufficient for an increased population, and the local authority is forced to extend its activities. Considerable capital outlay may be necessary, unduly taxing the resources and the borrowing powers of the locality.

In answer to this objection, the Council which is responsible for the erection of the houses may state that it has used the money of its own ratepayers to create rateable value in another locality. The population of the colonised area, and consequently the expense of governing it, have admittedly increased; but it is held that its income from rates will increase proportionately. Authorities which are forced to build outside their administrative area often advance this state of affairs as an argument in favour of an extension of their boundaries, to include the newly developed area.

The subsidy paid by the State must be so used as to provide houses at a lower price than would be possible without it. Thus the Burnham-on-Sea Urban District Council recovered subsidies paid to builders in the following circumstances—

The builders applied, under the Housing Acts, for assistance in the erection of cottages. The application stated that the selling price, including the subsidy, was to be £625. The cottages were, however, sold for sums considerably over this amount, the additional amounts being for extras supplied by the builders. The Ministry of Health, upon its attention being drawn to the matter, advised the Council to bring action for the recovery of the subsidies. The Council did recover.

"I think that the condition is good imposed by the Council that the house must not be sold for more than a definite sum. If the words 'selling price' in the conditions meant no more than the value of the house, and did not mean the maximum price at which the builder may sell, the whole provision is nugatory; and the Housing Acts are reduced almost to farce. It is well-known that the reason for granting these forms of assistance is to remedy the great lack of houses at a low price. If a builder could build a house at the price stipulated in the condition, and then sell it for more, the Act becomes of no effect; for the builder would pocket the subsidy and the working class get no benefit at all. The plaintiffs

are entitled to recover the sum paid, and the defendants must pay
the costs of the action." (*Burnham-on-Sea Urban District Council
v. Channing and Osmond*, Ch. 1932.)

OFFICIALS AND EMPLOYEES

The local authorities are allowed some amount of latitude in
the appointment of officials. There are some officials which certain types of authorities are bound by law to appoint; but there
are no statutory regulations concerning wages, superannuation, or
conditions of tenure of office. Broadly speaking, a local authority
is at liberty to appoint what officials it considers fit, over and
above the minimum which the law requires. With certain exceptions it may draw its recruits from wherever it pleases; it may
itself decide what wages and pensions shall be paid, subject always
to the risk of their being surcharged by the auditor if he considers
them excessively high.

WAGES

It is in this matter of wages that the greatest supervision is
exercised over the appointment of officials by the local authorities.
The view is often expressed that the State and the Municipalities
should be the ideal employers, and should serve as an example
to the capitalist employer. On the question of remuneration of its
servants, however, our local authorities are unable to act in an
exemplary manner. They cannot hold out a standard of wages
which other employers should strive to attain; for the wages they
pay must be based on the market price of labour.

Local authorities are not allowed to pay wages which are unreasonably large, and it is held that the current rate in the district
is *prima facie* reasonable. They may pay this rate with the addition of a small discretionary allowance, which since the Poplar
Wage Case has been fixed by the auditors at 10 per cent. So
much for the social reformer. He is confronted with the dogma:
"What is, is; and is therefore reasonable." Perhaps this decision
was unfortunate in one sense. For many local authorities under-
pay their employees, and the fixing of a maximum instead of
a minimum wage may tend to encourage the practice. It is
possible to be too economical even with ratepayers' money.

FUNCTIONS " ULTRA VIRES "

The directions in which a local authority may spend public
money are very limited, and are strictly defined by law. The scope

of its activities must not exceed that laid down as a general principle by the Central Government, except in the relatively few cases in which an ancient charter especially sanctions the performance of things not recognised by Parliament. If a local authority performs any act which is not within its powers, as determined by Parliament or by a special charter, or if it spends money in unauthorised directions, it purports to do what it cannot do. In contemplation of law it has not done the act. The authority acquires no legal rights as a result; it incurs no legal liabilities. The State may not interfere directly with a local authority, even though it be engaged in practices which are contrary to the law. It may not intervene to restrain or punish; but must confine its course of action to suing the defaulting Council in the Courts. The law then decides what penalties shall be exacted from those responsible for the acts, just as though it were an ordinary action between two persons.

These *ultra vires* actions fail of legal effect not on account of their nature, but merely because they do not fall within the scope of the authority of the performer. Our units of local government are supposed to do what they are told and nothing more. It is, apparently, a greater sin for them to perform worthy acts which have not been specifically sanctioned, than to neglect the administration of essential services. There is much to be said for this doctrine of *ultra vires*. It is, without doubt, an effective check on the wasting and misappropriation of public funds. It prevents the local authorities from embarking upon foolhardy and unnecessary ventures. On the other hand, it may constitute a definite bar to progress. It prevents a far-sighted local authority from instituting beneficial new services, even with the consent of the ratepayers, until the innovations have been sanctioned generally by Parliament. Our Central Government is notoriously conservative in its policy; and its reluctance to give the local authorities new powers may operate as a brake to progress. The use of the method of trial and error, which, though harsh in particular cases, is nevertheless valuable, is rendered impossible. Parliament refuses to permit individual localities to try, for fear that the experiment should result in error.

Items of expenditure may be *ultra vires* in extent as well as in nature; and here a great deal is left to the discretion of the District auditor. If the auditor considers that any payment, although made for a legitimate purpose, is unnecessarily or unreasonably large, he may cause it to be surcharged upon the councillors

responsible for it. It is true that the councillors have the right of
appeal to the High Courts or to the Ministry of Health; but this
still leaves the auditor as the sole arbiter of what is reasonable
and therefore legal, though his decisions may be subject to review
by the higher authority.

If a disbursement is surcharged on account of its unreasonable
magnitude, or because it was made for objects not sanctioned, the
councillors who authorised it are held personally liable. The
burden of expenses which are *ultra vires* is not allowed to fall on
the public funds, even though the expenses were incurred for the
furtherance of the public welfare. It makes no difference if the
amount of the expenditure was such as would have been sanctioned
by the majority of the electorate. If, in the opinion of the auditor,
subject in the event of appeal to revision by a higher authority,
the disbursement is excessively large, the amount may still be
surcharged.

Clearly, there is considerable scope for abuse in this arrangement, since so much is left to the good judgment and fairness of
the District Auditor. Experience has shown, however, that the
auditors are, on the whole, a body of men worthy of the trust
which is placed in them. The supervision which they exercise
leads to a better and more honourable administration of public
funds. It must be remembered, however, that the District
Auditors of the Ministry of Health are not concerned with the
accounts of Boroughs or Counties, except in so far as they relate
to Housing, Education, Highways, or Public Assistance.

The Poplar Wage Case (*Roberts* v. *Hopwood*, A.C. 1925) is
an illustration. In 1920, the Poplar Borough Council had been
paying a minimum wage of four pounds a week to its adult male
employees. This rate of remuneration was based on the cost of
living, and was in harmony with the general level of wages at the
time. During the following years, outside wages and the cost of
living both fell considerably; but the Poplar Borough Council
continued to pay the same wages as in 1920.

At the 1923 audit, the Ministry of Health auditor refused to
allow these minimum wages of four pounds a week as a charge
against the rates, because they were far higher than the current
rate of payment for work of a similar kind in the district. The
auditors held that the wages paid by the Municipality were unreasonably, and hence illegally, large, and caused an amount of
£5,000 to be surcharged on the councillors.

The Court upheld the decision of the auditors. The Poplar

councillors appealed against this finding. Lords Justice Scrutton and Atkins (Banks, L.J. dissenting), before whom the appeal was heard, reversed the decision of the King's Bench Division, and found in favour of the councillors. The councillors had contended that the municipalities should be the ideal employers, and that it was against public policy to pay wages lower than four pounds a week. The Lords Justices, while not in complete agreement with this statement, did not consider that the rate of wages in question was so far beyond the bounds of reason as to be surchargeable. Lord Justice Atkins suggested that the authority of the auditor was more limited than was generally supposed. He inferred that, since the auditor could exercise no definite control over the number of servants employed by a local authority, he had no right to object to the payment of wages at a rate rather higher than the capitalist standard. If the auditor could not force the municipality to reduce its staff of dustmen from forty to thirty, could it insist on a reduction in their wages from four to three pounds?

The House of Lords unanimously rejected the decision of the Court of Appeal, and upheld the previous finding of the King's Bench Division in favour of the auditors. Lord Atkinson held that, under the terms of Section 247 (7) of the Public Health Act, the auditor had power to inquire into the legality of every payment. If in his opinion any payment was contrary to law, he could cause it to be surcharged on the persons responsible for it. If payments were unreasonably large, the auditor could surcharge that portion of them which was excessive.

Lord Sumner maintained that the criterion of reason could not be simply the councillors' opinion. The ratepayers had to be protected against the misguided and costly idealism of the elected councillors. It was not necessary to prove bad faith before a sum could rightly be surcharged; it had only to be shown that the sum was unreasonably large. Clearly, the decision of this point must be made by a disinterested body, not by the councillors who authorised payment. "Any auditor . . . shall disallow every item of expenditure contrary to law, and surcharge the same on the person making or authorising the making of the illegal payment and shall charge against any person accounting the amount of any deficiency or loss incurred by the negligence or misconduct of that person, or if any sum which ought to have been but is not brought into account by that person, and shall in every case certify the amount due from such person."

12

AGENCY

RESPONSIBILITY FOR ANOTHER'S CONTRACT

THE question, how far one is answerable for the actions for another, is often difficult to answer. I entrust to another the making of a bargain for me; I tell him what I want and leave him some discretion in the matter.

There is then no doubt about his being my agent, and I his principal. He makes a foolish and losing bargain for me. Yet I must put up with it. I chose him as my agent; and it was an unlucky choice.

An agent is one employed in order to make contracts for his principal. As a rule, once the contract has been made, the agent drops out of the matter. The principal alone is liable on the contract and alone can sue on it. (Trade usage may, however, make an agent liable on the contract: it seems to do so when an agent buys goods for a principal abroad.) Where the agent does not disclose to the other party the existing agency, that other party has the option of holding either agent or principal liable on the contract.

AN INFANT AGENT

It is quite possible, indeed, that the law may consider the agent to lack capacity to contract. The law does in fact look upon the infant, he or she who has not yet reached the age of twenty-one, as being unripe in judgment, as being, therefore, incapable of striking a good bargain for itself. Still, though the infant cannot contract for himself, he can contract for me. I have chosen, and I must put up with the results of my choice.

But I may be answerable for the agent's act, though I had given him no definite instructions. For it is quite possible that I have behaved in such a manner as to induce the belief in other people that I look upon him as my agent.

He may have no actual authority from me; he may have, however, apparent authority. He, or usually she, has run up bills in the past; and I have paid them, so far as the trader knows, without demur. Until I tell him otherwise, he assumes (and, of course, he is entitled to assume) that I shall continue to pay. I cannot by private talk with my agent, limit the authority which I have allowed the outside world to suppose still continuing as wide as ever. If, as the saying is, I have "held out" one to be my agent, I am prevented from denying that he is so: "The rule is that the husband, as well as every principal, is concluded from denying that the agent had such authority as he was held out by his principal to have."

IMPLIED AUTHORITY OF AGENT

The law puts the matter in this way: "There are two cases in which a principal becomes liable for the acts of his agent: one when the agent acts within the limits of his authority, the other where he transgresses the actual limits but acts within the apparent limits, where those apparent limits have been sanctioned by the principal." Sheward employed his brother to sell a horse to Howard. He gave his brother instructions not to warrant the horse. The brother did, however, warrant it; and Howard, finding the horse to be unsound, sued Sheward for breach of warranty. Howard obtained damages. For the buyer was justified in supposing that the agent had instructions to warrant the horse: "The ostensible authority could not be negatived by showing a secret understanding between the horse-dealer and his agent." (*Howard* v. *Sheward*, C.P. 1866.)

WHEN HUSBAND ANSWERABLE FOR WIFE'S CONTRACTS

A husband, much against his will, may be held liable for debts incurred by his wife. In one way or another he has created an impression that he regards her as his agent; he has given her authority to pledge his credit. He is, whether he has given authority or not, liable for the supply of necessaries; and, if such are in question, the presumption is that he has asked his wife to buy them upon his undertaking to pay.

This presumption arises when wife and husband are living together; it arises, indeed, in relation to any woman with whom a man lives in the relation of husband to wife. But the presumption may be rebutted by the man's showing—

(i) That at the material time the wife was already provided with necessaries, or with the money to get them.

(ii) That he forbade her to pledge his credit.

(iii) That the credit was given to the woman herself.

OSTENSIBLE AUTHORITY MAY IMPOSE LIABILITY

In regard to other things than necessaries also he must pay, if the Court finds that he has behaved as a principal appointing his wife as his agent. The trader, that is, may reasonably suppose from the husband's conduct that the husband had said words to this effect, "Get the goods; let me have the bill."

No doubt, the trader is often put into a position calling for the exercise of exquisite tact in this matter. He needs to be an accomplished diplomat when it is the wife who gives the order, and it is the husband who may, or may not, be legally bound to pay the bill. The customer may resent, or simulate to resent, a question however carefully couched as to whether she really has her husband's authority to pledge his credit. Yet it appears that the trader desiring to hold the husband liable must obtain some evidence of authority other than the fact that the customer is the wife. For marriage does not, as partnership does, of itself constitute each party the agent of the other.

Goods were supplied to Mrs. Benedict; and, though the goods were like those of the jovial pedlar "Lawn as white as driven snow; Cyprus black as e'er was crow; Gloves as sweet as damask roses; Masks for faces and for noses," they satisfied one requisite of what the law calls "necessaries." For the law has a very elastic meaning of "necessaries"; and these were reasonably suitable for the station in life of the buyer. But they did not satisfy the other requisite. They were in excess of her actual requirements at the time; for Mr. Benedict had always been generous in his dress allowance. The goods were not "necessaries"; and Mr. Benedict had done nothing to give the trader cause to think that the buying was with his approval. The confiding trader was, therefore, unable to obtain payment, the Lord Chief Justice's comment being: "It may be hard on a fashionable milliner that she is precluded from supplying a lady without previous inquiry into her authority. The Court, however, cannot enter into these little delicacies, but must lay down a law that shall protect the husband from the extravagance of his wife" (*Seaton* v. *Benedict*, 1828).

MAKING THE HUSBAND LIABLE

The law, briefly, is this. There is a presumption that the wife has her husband's authority to make contracts as his agent in all domestic matters usually entrusted to a wife. That is the presumption. But, then, the presumption may be rebutted in several ways: that the husband had already obtained an ample supply of necessaries, or had given the money to get them, or that the credit had been given to the wife herself. The trader, therefore, who seeks to make a husband liable for his wife's debts must establish one of two facts. Either the goods supplied were necessaries, and the husband had not done his duty in providing them. Or, in one way or another, the trader was entitled to pledge his credit. The difficulty of establishing either fact is illustrated in *Mayfair Hotel Co.* v. *Lord Falkland* (K.B. 1929).

The Mayfair Hotel had provided upon Lady Falkland's request a "coming-out ball"; and Lord Falkland was sued for the price. Whether a ball that effectively ushers a lady into society is a necessary was left unsettled. There remained then the question of agency. The plaintiffs could not assert an actual giving of authority; for in fact the defendant had expressly forbidden his wife to pledge his credit. But there may be an ostensible giving of authority; the plaintiffs may have been misled by the defendant's conduct that he had given authority. Can a husband's quiet acquiescence in what is going on, be regarded as active approval? Is whatever is done in the household with his knowledge, and without his protest, to be taken as done with his authority?

The Lord Chief Justice decided not. "To make Lord Falkland liable it must appear that his wife had actual authority to make the contract for the ball, or that his conduct had been such that he was estopped from denying that she had authority. Actual authority had been negatived by the jury. The question of estoppel remained: had Lord Falkland by words or by conduct induced the plaintiffs reasonably to believe that his wife was authorised to make the contract on his behalf, and were the plaintiffs thereby induced to enter into the contract? It was urged that Lord Falkland knew that arrangements were being made for a ball and nevertheless did not inform the plaintiffs that he would not be responsible for the costs. Must that mere silence of the defendant be regarded as sufficient to raise an estoppel against him. I think not. And the attendance of Lord Falkland at the ball could not reasonably lead to the belief that he had authorised the pledging of his credit for the expenses."

So, too, in the leading case *Debenham* v. *Mellon* (A.C. 1880). Mr. Mellon had made his wife an adequate allowance for clothes; and though Messrs. Debenham (who supplied a great amount of clothing) were unaware of this, M was held exempt from liability. "It is urged," ran the judgment, "that it is hard to throw upon a tradesman the burden of inquiring into the fact of a wife's authority to buy necessaries upon her husband's credit. I assent to the answer that while the tradesman has at least the power to inquire or to forbear from giving credit, it is still harder to cast upon a husband the burden of debts which he has no power to control at all except by a public advertisement that his wife is not to be trusted, and in respect to which even after such advertisement he may be made liable to a tradesman who is able to swear that he never saw it." The rules laid down in that case are: (1) Except as regards necessaries, marriage of itself creates by implication no authority from the husband to his wife to pledge his credit. (2) Where the husband has habitually ratified (by paying the bills without apparent demur) the acts of his wife in pledging his credit, he cannot, as regards those whom he has thus induced to look to him for payment, revoke her authority without notice. (3) In the absence of such authority, arising from the husband's authority, the husband is entitled to revoke any express or implied authority which he may have given her.

DEFINITION OF AGENT

A man employed is not necessarily his employer's agent: the messenger that conveys an offer couched in specific terms is not an agent. The agent is, indeed, employed by his principal, but for a definite purpose. He is employed in order to make bargains with others. The agent is an extension of the principal's personality; he is the means whereby that principal can enter into contractual relations to a greater extent than through his own bargaining. In establishing those relations, the agent has some amount of discretion. He can relax terms, make concessions, assume obligations, and, so far as he appears to be acting within the limits of the authority conferred on him, his principal is bound by his bargains. He acts by virtue of this authority or mandate. The authority being withdrawn, or being automatically ended through *the death*, or *insanity* or *bankruptcy* of the principal, he ceases to be an agent.

RATIFYING A CONTRACT

A man may, indeed, strike a bargain for another, though he has no authority to do so; and the other, learning of the bargain, may express his contentment at it. He *ratifies* it; he wishes to adopt the agent's act as though, before the act, he had given authority. And the law allows him to do so.

It is a curious position. For the adoption of the pretended agent's act has a retrospective operation. But this permission to ratify is narrowly circumscribed. It can take place only when the *agent professed* to *contract for the principal who does ultimately ratify ; the person ratifying must have full knowledge of the facts ;* and *he must ratify in such manner as to admit of no doubt about his intention to do so.* The principal, too, must be in existence at the time of making the contract; a company cannot ratify contracts made in its name before incorporation.

There is no need for any formality in order to confer authority upon an agent. The conduct as well as the words of the principal may do so. In one event only is a formal deed needed to give authority: this is when the agent is to make a contract under seal. Such a formal authorising is a *power of attorney.* Below is a specimen of such a power of attorney, a deed giving authority to enter into dealings as agent of a property owner.

THIS POWER OF ATTORNEY is made the   *twentieth*   day of   *December,* 19— by me   *Henry Fitzsimmons, Baronet*   of   *Oxby Manor, Surrey.*

1. I hereby appoint   *Thomas Seecombe, Solicitor,* of   57 *Cheam Road, Croydon, in the County of Surrey*   to be my lawful Attorney for me and in my name to do and on my behalf to execute all or any of the following acts deeds and things that is to say—

(*a*) To act for me in all matters with regard to my property in England and to enter into any contracts or agreements on my behalf with regard thereto and to demand sue for recover and give receipts for all sums of money due or owing to me in respect thereof and for all claims by me against any other person in or arising thereout and to take or defend any legal proceedings relating to same and to settle and compromise the same as my Attorney may think fit.

(*b*) To purchase or sell any stocks shares or securities and to execute any transfers relating thereto and to vote in respect of any shares or debentures held by me at any meeting of share or debenture holders.

(*c*) To endorse all cheques bills of exchange or other securities payable to me and to draw upon any banking account standing in my name and sign any cheques thereon and to accept any bill of exchange or negotiable instrument.

(*d*) To engage or discharge any servants or employees in connection with my property and to appoint any substitute or agent for my Attorney to act under him in respect of all or any matters on such terms as my Attorney shall think fit.

(*e*) To sell let on lease or agreement or otherwise deal with any real or leasehold property belonging to me or over which I have any power of disposal.

(*f*) Generally to act on my behalf and to do all such acts deeds matters and things whatsoever in or about my property and affairs as fully and effectually to all intents and purposes as I could do in my own proper person if personally present.

And whatsoever my said Attorney shall lawfully do or cause to be done in or about the premises I hereby agree to ratify and confirm.

And I hereby declare that this power of attorney shall be irrevocable by me for the period of (not exceeding one year) from the date hereof.

IN WITNESS whereof I have hereunto set my hand and seal the day and year first above written.

SIGNED SEALED AND DELIVERED⎫
   by the said   ⎬*Henry Fitzsimmons,*
   in the presence of—   ⎭   *Bart.*

        M. C. Jennings,
          Solicitor's Clerk,
            6 Bunting Street,
               Croydon.

RESPONSIBILITY OF PRINCIPAL

When a man does enlarge his contractual capacity by appointing an agent, he also adds to his responsibility. How far is he answerable for what his agent does? The agent may be incompetent or dishonest or reckless; is it fair that the principal should be liable for the incompetency or dishonesty or recklessness? Well, the principal has freedom of choice. If he has chosen badly, that is his concern. At an early period in our legal history it was established that, where the agent is apparently acting under the authority of the principal, the principal is liable.

A buyer sues a seller for deceit. At the trial it appeared that there was no deceit in the seller; but that it was in his factor beyond sea. "And the doubt was, if this deceit could charge the merchant." Chief Justice Holt was of opinion "That the merchant was answerable for the deceit of his factor, though not *criminaliter*, yet *civiliter*." He could, that is, be made to pay damages for wrong though he could not be prosecuted for a crime. "For, seeing somebody must be a loser by his deceit, it is more reasonable that he who employs (and puts a trust and confidence in) the deceiver should be a loser, than a stranger."

As was decided in a later case, where a principal was made answerable for the unauthorised act of his agent: "The principal is answerable for every such wrong of his agent as is committed in the course of the service, though no express command be proved. Owners of ships are held liable for the acts of masters abroad; railway companies are held liable in cases where officers, entrusted with the execution of by-laws relating to imprisonment, and intending to act in the course of their duty, improperly imprison persons. It is true that the principal has not authorised the particular act. But he has put the agent in his place to do that class of acts."

We may, indeed, put the position more strongly still. A principal is responsible for his agent's acts though he has forbidden them, if such acts appear to others affected as being authorised by the principal. The liability is similar to the liability of a master for the acts of his servant "in the course of his employment." And the liability is based upon the same grounds. The master may not excuse damage to third parties by saying that his servant was disobedient; the principal may not excuse himself by saying that his agent was unauthorised. The question always is, "Was what the servant or the agent was doing apparently what the master or the principal had engaged him to do?"

In *Limpus* v. *L.G.O.C.* (Exchequer, 1862), where the company was held liable for the act of one of its drivers who, racing a rival's bus, had overturned it, the company brought forward evidence showing a prohibition of such racing. But the Court evidently thought that such a prohibition, which the company could hardly have wanted to see obeyed, was similar to an injunction, "Don't throw him into the horse-pond."

"In my opinion," ran the judgment, "those instructions are immaterial. If disobeyed, the law casts upon the master a liability for the act of his servant in the course of his employment and the law is not so futile as to allow a master, by giving such instructions to his servant, to discharge himself from liability." So, when an agent exceeds his authority, the principal will be bound if reasonable people would suppose him to have the authority.

AGENT PAYING PRINCIPAL'S DEBT

The business man would do well to garner and treasure the advice occasionally tendered by our judges in the course of their decisions. For, by their training—not in some secluded academy, but in the busy haunts of men—they can hardly help becoming sound men of affairs. Consider, the appeal case where brokers, who had already paid their foreign principal, failed to recover from the buyer the purchase price of timber sold. In the course of the transaction the buyer had discovered that his seller was one against whom he himself had a claim. He therefore, not unnaturally, set off the price of the timber against the former debt. In effect the decision was this: An agent made a contract between an undisclosed foreign seller and an English buyer. He claimed the price due under the contract from the buyer. The buyer said, "I have no contract with you; and I do not pay your seller because I have a set-off against him of a larger amount."

The case is another illustration of the rule that, once the contract is completed by the agent, he falls out of the matter; *the rights and liabilities under the contract are those of the principals only.*

The appellants had signed the contract in their capacity as brokers and they had, therefore, neither rights nor liabilities under the contract. But, Lord Justice Romer pointed out, when paying their foreign principal they could have safeguarded themselves.

They could have had an assignment of the debt made to them by their foreign principal. "I have," said the Lord Justice, "arrived at my conclusion with some regret, because I cannot help thinking that the plaintiffs, when they financed the sellers, did so in the belief that they were being secured by being entitled to receive the purchase money direct from the buyer. Feeling that regret, I will only add this: That brokers may in the future think it wise to have recourse to some equitable principle. If, when they finance their sellers, they get an equitable assignment of the purchase price from the sellers, and give notice of that equitable assignment to the buyer, they would find themselves in a much happier position than they are left in after this decision." (*Flatau, Dick & Co.* v. *Keeping,* C.A. 1931.)

POWER TO DELEGATE IS LIMITED

It is well to note that there are limitations upon our ability to conduct business by another's agency. From the very nature of the thing, we cannot, where personal qualifications are requisite, get another to act for us. A doctor could not appoint an unqualified man to sign certificates for him. The qualification, whether a doctor's, or a lawyer's, or an accountant's, or a secretary's, is in some measure an assurance to the public that they are dealing with a person judged competent by those entitled to express an opinion. To allow delegation would be, in effect, to allow any person having the requisite qualification to grant diplomas to unqualified persons.

Thus, on the motion of the Incorporated Law Society, an unqualified clerk acting as a solicitor was committed to prison for two months (*In re J. H. Thorpe,* Ch. 1932). It appeared that the clerk's employer, who was himself a solicitor with a large practice, had when leaving for a long absence abroad, given the respondent a power-of-attorney. The first clause purported to authorise the respondent "to manage, conduct, and act in my business of a solicitor." Relying on this, the respondent conducted litigation, though the Solicitors' Act, 1860, forbids an unqualified person to do so. Moreover, a solicitor is an officer of the Court, and is entered upon the rolls because there is abundant evidence that he or she is competent to help the Court in administering justice. The judge held that the enabling clause, "To act as a solicitor," was inoperative. "There had been a clear breach of the statute; the individual concerned was guilty of a misdemeanour; and he would go to prison for two months."

DUTY OF AGENT

The agent is employed in order that the principal, to the benefit of his business, may make more contracts. The duty of the agent is, therefore, clear: it is to make the best bargain possible for his principal. He must not let other considerations intervene; and if his interest and that of his principal conflict, still his principal's interest must prevail. He must not put himself into such a position as would make his own interest conflict with the interest of his principal. The principal must get all the benefit of the bargain entered into by the agent; the agent's benefit is confined to what has been agreed upon as his requital; he must make no profit unknown to the principal.

It was put thus in *Johnson* v. *Kearley* (1908, K.B.) where the broker, instructed to buy goods for his principal, had simply transferred some of his own goods to the order: "To add on to the price of the article bought an arbitrary sum is a taking of profit and not a commission, and is compatible only with a sale and resale. It is absolutely inconsistent with the duty of an agent for purchase, inasmuch as it is the essential idea of a purchase through a broker, or any other agent of the kind, that the whole benefit of the purchase should go to the principal; and that the sole interest of the agent should be in the commission allowed him by his principal. The office of a broker is to make privity of contract between two principals; and this is utterly incompatible with making a contract at one price with the one party, and a corresponding contract at another price with the other." (See, too, *Alexander* v. *Webber* (K.B. 1922), where the taking of a bribe by a chauffeur was held to justify his employer in rescinding a contract for the buying of a motor-car.)

DEL CREDERE AGENT

An agent may—usually in return for a commission additional —assume further obligations towards his principal. He may warrant that the third party, with whom he will bring his principal into contractual relations, will continue able to pay his debts. The agent then becomes a *"del credere* agent"*: he warrants that the principal's debtor will remain solvent.

In *Montagu Stanly & Co.* v. *Solomon, Ltd.* (K.B., 1932) the matter of contention was whether an agreement between the parties was a letter of indemnity or an undertaking to be a *del credere* agent. The plaintiffs, stockbrokers on the Stock Exchange, had agreed with the defendants to share commissions on business introduced. The letter expressing the agreement was—

Dear Sirs,

In consideration of your paying to J. C. Solomon. Limited. 50 per cent of any commission received on business introduced by them as agents, it is hereby agreed that the company shall be liable to you for 50 per cent of any loss sustained by you in connection with such business.

J. BARNES, *Secretary.*

J. C. SOLOMON, *Director.*

A customer introduced by the defendants executed a deed of assignment. Without waiting to see what proportion of their debt they would ultimately get from their customer, the plaintiffs claimed against the defendants for an immediate loss. The Court held, however, that the letter constituted a contract of indemnity, not a *del credere* agreement—in spite of the phrase "as agents." Till the amount of loss had actually been ascertained, the defendants were under no obligation.

PREVENTION OF CORRUPTION

Note that Parliament, in a laudable, but not very successful, effort to put obstacles in the way of secret commissions, enacted the Prevention of Corruption Act, 1906. The Common Law rights of the principal against the agent who has betrayed his trust and against the third party who has joined in the betrayal are now, therefore, supplemented by statutory rights. Both the receiving and the giving of a bribe have been made crimes—punishable by fine or by imprisonment with or without hard labour. When summary proceedings are taken the punishments possible are a fine of £50 or four months' imprisonment with hard labour, or both. When trial upon indictment at the Assizes takes place the possible punishments are a fine of £500 or two years' hard labour, or both. At Bow Street (1933) the magistrate imposed heavy fines on a managing director who had given bribes and an employee who had taken them. Both pleaded guilty. Bakelite, Ltd., were makers of a moulding powder used in manufacturing such things as telephone receivers. Till 1928 they had a monoply of the powder, which was made by a secret process. Then a rival firm placed on the market a similar powder. Subsequent inquiries showed that the director of the rival firm had bought the secret formula from a research chemist who was under agreement with Bakelite, Ltd., not to disclose it.

The later Prevention of Corruption Act, 1916, enacts that where the transaction, in which the secret commission is taken, is a contract with the Crown or a Government Department or any public body, the maximum punishment shall be increased to seven years' penal servitude. Both Acts, well-intentioned in their objects, are, unluckily, very largely, dead letters.

Nor, indeed, when both giver and taker are keenly concerned to keep the bribe secret, can we wonder at this.

A conviction is, however, secured at times. It was at the Eastbourne Police Court (1933), when an alderman and officials were charged under the Act of accepting bribes from the Pirelli General Cable Works as inducements to show favour. All the defendants were convicted. The prosecution was undertaken by the Director of Public Prosecutions.

NO UNDISCLOSED PROFIT

The rule that in making a contract for his principal the agent must keep his principal's interest ever before him, is clear. Its application is difficult at times. For rules of law need modification with changing conditions. In less complicated conditions it was possible to lay down as an *inflexible rule*, that an agent, in his principal's business, must make no undisclosed profit. So it was expressed in the well-known case, *Parker* v. *McKenna:* " It appears to me very important that we should concur in laying down again and again that in this Court no agent, in the course of his agency, can be allowed to make any profit without the knowledge and consent of his principal; that that rule is an inflexible rule and must be applied inexorably."

Yet, in *Harrod's* v. *Lemon* (C.A. 1931) it was not applied. For, in these days of great business enterprises, carrying on many functions and having a great many customers, it is possible for two principals to employ the one agent; and the agent may be quite unconscious that he is acting for both parties to the bargain. The estate agency department found a buyer for Mrs. Lemon; the building department, approached by the buyer, made an adverse report upon the drains and caused a diminution of the agreed price. In these circumstances the seller disclaimed her obligation to pay agent's commission. She was, however, adjudged liable. "It was abundantly clear," said the Master of the Rolls, "that no charge of fraud or conscious double dealing was made against the plaintiffs. The trouble arose through the ignorance of one department of what was being done by the other; and when Messrs. Harrod's attention was called to what had happened, they offered to stand down in the matter."

Mrs. Lemon was, if she chose, entitled to take the business from Harrod's; or she could conclude the bargain after an independent survey. She was not, however, entitled to accept Harrod's purchaser, and then to repudiate the liability to pay agent's commission.

SOLE AGENT

When an agent is authorised by his principal to sell property, and when the principal makes him "sole agent," has the principal thereby deprived himself of the power to sell his property? If the principal does find a buyer, without the intervention of the agent, is the agent entitled to commission? Where the agent has done much and spent much in the attempt to find a purchase, and has failed, is he entitled to payment of his out-of-pocket expenses? All these questions were answered in the negative, in *Bentall* v. *Vickary* (K.B. 1930). The authority of the agent to sell is conferred by the principal. By word of mouth, or by act, the principal can withdraw the authority; and the principal's sale of the property in question is a very effective withdrawal of authority. The undertaking to perform the task for a stipulated reward is not fulfilled by preliminaries to the performance: apart from special agreement, no payment is due for these preliminaries. This case is, in fact, another application of the rule in *Cutter* v. *Powell*: where an "entire contract" has been entered upon then, apart from an expressed or implied promise to pay on a *quantum meruit*, no payment is due for partial performance.

True, the parties may make what contracts they please. The principal can agree to pay commission, even if he does himself sell.

He can agree, often indeed does agree, to remunerate even unsuccessful efforts. If he does so agree, there is no reason why he should not be bound by the agreement.

It is important, though, to note that in certain trades, the word "agent" is often used loosely and without any reference to the law of principal and agent. The motor trade is an example. In that trade persons are described as agents who are not agents in regard to any principal, but are merchants who buy from manufacturers and sell independently of them. Such loose use may give rise to difficulties. It did in *Lamb* v. *Goring Brick Co.* (C.A., 1931). The plaintiffs had been appointed "sole selling agents." Did this, as the plaintiffs contended, prevent the manufacturers from selling? Or did it, as the defendants contended, mean merely that the defendants would sell through no other agents than the plaintiffs? The Court decided that the first interpretation was the correct one. "The fair construction of this agreement is that the parties intended that, the manufacturing part of the business being in the hands of the defendants, the selling part of it should be entrusted to the plaintiffs. The plaintiffs had the necessary selling organization, the necessary connection with possible buyers, and the hope of making bargains in the best way." It was the promise of the plaintiffs to put their organization and their service at the disposal of the defendants that formed the consideration for the defendant's promise to entrust to the plaintiffs the "selling part of the business." The plaintiffs should have been described as "merchants" making an independent bargain rather than as "agents." In one part of the agreement the plaintiffs were in fact described as "merchants," in another part "sole selling agents." The first was the correct description.

COMMISSION UNEARNED APART FROM SALE

In the case there was no such agreement (*Bentall, etc.*, v. *Vickary* K.B. Dec., 1930). The defendant had long wished to sell a rather large and secluded house in Hampshire. He had instructed several agents without satisfactory result; and the plaintiffs, a well-known firm of estate agents, suggested that they should be appointed "sole agents" on such terms as would enable them to use more effective means of finding a buyer. The material part of the agreement into which the defendant entered is embodied in the plaintiffs' letter—

"We now write as follows to outline the arrangement made and your instructions. We are to be appointed sole agents for the sale of the property. If we introduce a purchaser we are to receive a special commission of 5 per cent on the price realised. You authorise us to expend on your behalf up to the sum of £100 in advertising the property, and if we do not sell we are to bear 50 per cent of this cost."

In their energetic efforts to find a buyer the plaintiffs spent £35 10s. on advertising, and incurred other expenses of about £25. While they were so acting a lady who did not know of the plaintiffs and who had learnt from another source that the house was for sale, negotiated with the defendant and bought the whole property for £5,000. Were the plaintiffs entitled to £250 commission—5 per cent, that is, of the £5,000? No, said the Court; they had not introduced the buyer, and the one condition upon which they could obtain commission was "if we introduce a purchaser." But then, had not the defendant when he himself sold, broken his contract that he would make them sole agents?

No, was the decision: "The plaintiffs argued that it was an implied term of the contract that the defendant should not himself sell the property and so deprive the plaintiffs of the commission which they might perhaps be able to earn. But it was the plaintiffs and not the defendant who drafted the contract. Hence the words of the contract must be taken as strongly as possible against the plaintiffs. Nor should the Court introduce an implied term into the contract unless such implication was needed for the business efficacy of the transaction, unless the implied term must have been intended at all events by both parties.

The Court has no right to imply in a written contract any stipulation unless, on considering the terms of the contract in a reasonable and business manner, an implication necessarily arises that the parties must have intended that the suggested stipulation should exist. It is not enough to say that it would be a reasonable thing to make such an implication. It is to be noted that the contract contains no express words at all indicating a prohibition against a sale by the defendant himself. If the parties intended such a prohibition, nothing would have been easier than to insert the appropriate words. It is also to be noted that the defendant does not say by the contract 'I give you the sole right to sell,' only, 'I appoint you sole agents for the sale,' which is quite a different thing."

A " QUANTUM MERUIT "

But, then, were not the plaintiffs entitled to a *quantum meruit*, to what they had earned by their efforts, at all events to the money that they themselves had disbursed? No; "undoubtedly the plaintiffs had worked and incurred expenses. But that was quite a usual feature of an estate agent's vocation when he worked under a commission note which only gave him a right to recover commission when he fulfilled the terms of the note. He ran the risk of losing his labour and expenses unless he could comply with the conditions."

A man is bound by the bargain he makes. When he has used precise words, his rights under the bargain are circumscribed by those words. He cannot, when he has found that the agreement has ended badly for himself, introduce additional terms, or have the agreement construed in a manner more favourable to him than was intended at first. So with the earning of commission by agents. Thus, a shipbroker is not entitled to commission on "all hire earned" when, though he has done much to obtain cargo, the ship has not reached port. The broker can, however, guard his interests. If he expresses in the note that commission is payable "on the signing of the charter upon the gross estimated freights," then his commission becomes due even before the freight is fully earned.

AN AGENT'S REMUNERATION

Is an agent entitled to keep a deposit paid, though the contemplated sale has not been completed? It depends upon the wording of the agreement he made with his principal. For one risk that the agent runs is the possibility that he may do much, may even spend much, without achieving the result he and his principal desire. If he bargains for a commission "when a sale has been effected," he is entitled to nothing till the condition has been fulfilled. But, the question may arise, has a sale been effected when the agent has found an intending buyer who has paid a deposit? Has the agent done the work he undertook to do, and is he therefore entitled to his commission? Can he not, at all events, keep the deposit paid as being on account of commission? Apparently not, unless the buyer is able and willing to complete. If the sale drops, the agent must hand the deposit paid to his principal. So it was decided in *Martin* v. *Perry and Law* (K.B. 1931). The burden of showing that the third party was "able and willing to complete" should have been shouldered by the defendants; the payment of a deposit was not in itself sufficient to show this. The agent can protect himself and stipulate that, even though a sale has not been effected, he shall receive some compensation for his work.

NEGLIGENCE OF A BANKER

From one point of view the relation between a banker and his customer is that of debtor to creditor; the banker owes money to his customer and has undertaken to pay it back upon demand or at short notice. From another point of view the banker is his customer's agent, undertaking to carry out that customer's instructions upon certain specified points. What degree of care is expected of a banker? Both in regard to his customers' money or valuables and in regard to his agency this degree is great indeed. To many it would seem to be even more stringent than actual business requires. In *Lloyds Bank, Ltd.* v. *E. B. Savory & Co.* (House of Lords, 1932), the bank was held liable to pay to the respondents (plaintiffs in the orginal action), a firm of stockbrokers, some £5,000 obtained by means of stolen cheques. The bank pleaded that it was protected by Section 82 of the Bills of Exchange Act, 1882. The House of Lords decided, however, by a majority, that in the circumstances the bank was put upon inquiry. For the cheques were paid in by employees of the firm and were payable to another person than the employees.

Failure to make inquiry must, therefore, be construed as negligence. And when negligence is shown, the protection afforded by Section 82 is lost. A few sentences from the judgment are explanatory: "The respondents claim repayment of the amount of these cheques from the bank, who rely in answer on Section 82 of the Act. This section is: 'Where a banker in good faith and without negligence receives payment for a customer of a cheque crossed generally or specially to himself, and the customer has no title or a defective title thereto, the banker shall not incur any liability to the true owner of the cheque by reason only of having received such payment.' The risk of banking accounts being used for dishonest purposes is well known and realised by the banks. The appellants have, in fact, a book of rules designed to afford protection against misuse of their facilities. There is also a rule, not reduced into writing but said to be a well-known banking understanding, familiar to cashiers, as follows: banks do not take payments in, without inquiry, on cheques drawn by a firm in favour of a third party, and paid in by a person other than the payee. These rules and statements are not a legal measure of the liability of a bank. They may fall short, or they may exceed what the Courts may regard as their duty in a particular case. But they afford a very valuable criterion of obvious risks against which the banks think it is their duty to take precautions.

"It follows that the system of receiving payments in by an unknown hand at another branch completely defeats the protection which the unwritten rule is designed to afford. The bank that ultimately receives the proceeds is only informed from the branch which collects the cheque by a slip that gives no information whatever as to the drawer's name or that of the payee of the cheque. In other words, if the unwritten rule represents a measure of the prudent course of conducting business, then that prudence is completely neglected and ignored where the branch, to which the customer is entirely strange, is used as the means of collecting a cheque."

CHEQUES SIGNED "PER PRO."

So with cheques drawn on behalf of a principal by his agent. The duty of care in regard to the destination of payments made under these cheques is imposed upon the banker. Failing in the duty the Midland Bank was held liable in *Midland Bank* v. *Reckett* (House of Lords, 1932). R had created X his attorney for the conduct of R's business during his absence abroad. The attorney, who was a customer of the bank, paid cheques signed *per pro* R, into his own private account. The bank neglected to ask by what authority he did so. On appeal to the House of Lords the bank was obliged to credit R's account with the amount withdrawn on the intelligible ground that "a bank collecting cheques signed *per pro* by their customer under a power of attorney is by the form of signature given notice that the money is not their customer's." *Per pro* is a notice of limited authority on the face of the cheque. The bank is put upon inquiry and, if it neglects inquiry, it loses the protection afforded by Section 82 of the Bills of Exchange Act, 1882.

Another good illustration of the degree of care expected of the banker was afforded by the *Bank of Montreal* v. *Dominion*, etc. (A.C. 1930). The Bank of Montreal were the appellants to the Judicial Committee against the Dominion Gresham Guarantee and Casualty Co The respondents had insured the fidelity of the chief accountant of one of the Bank's customers. The accountant made defalcations; the insurers paid under their fidelity policy; and, being thereby subrogated to any rights their customers had of mitigating the loss, sued the bank. The contention was that the loss would not have occurred if the bank had exercised reasonable care. This contention the final Court accepted. The cheques had been drawn by the accountant and the director of a customer, and they had been made payable to the accountant's order. The fact that it was so payable put the bank upon inquiry, and inquiry had liable not been made.

BANKER'S LIABILITY AS AGENT

The banker's liability as agent is a heavy one, too. In *Wilson and Another* v. *United Counties Bank* (H.L. 1919), the bank was held liable for negligence and was mulcted in large amounts.

A trading customer of the bank had become bankrupt. The jury found that the bank had agreed with the customer to supervise the financial side of his business during his absence on military service, and to take all reasonable steps to maintain his credit and reputation; and that the negligence of the bank was the cause of the bankruptcy that ensued. The jury awarded £45,000 odd for the loss caused to the bankrupt's estate, and £7,500 damages for the injury caused by the bank's negligence to the bankrupt's credit and reputation.

The first amount went to the trustee in bankruptcy. The second amount, being damages in respect of injuries solely to the person and feelings of the bankrupt, did not pass to the trustee for the benefit of the creditors: "The right of action does not pass where the damages are to be estimated by immediate reference to pain felt by the bankrupt in respect of his body, mind, or character, and without immediate reference to his rights of property. Thus it has been laid down that the assignee cannot sue for breach of promise of marriage, for seduction, defamation, battery, injury to the person by negligence."

While all causes of action for damage to the property vest in the trustee, any cause of action for damage to the person or reputation to the bankrupt would remain vested in him in spite of his bankruptcy.

BANKER'S LIABILITY FOR CONVERSION

In 1896 Mrs. Langtry lost her jewels. Apparently—though the case was settled without the Court's decision on the point—the bankers with whom she had deposited them for safety was liable for conversion. Mrs. Langtry accepted a sum of £10,000 by way of compromise rather than, as her counsel said, "undertake the risks of protracted litigation, even though she had to forgo the pleasure of fixing a portion of the law of the land." The case, however, occasioned a careful survey by the bankers of their position as *gratuitous bailees*. As such they are bound to take the same care of the property entrusted to them as a reasonably prudent and careful man may be expected to take of his own property of the like description. The obligation is less than that of the *paid bailee* in this: the paid bailee is bound to adopt all precautions and means of ensuring safety; the gratuitous bailee is only bound to use what means he has got. Since, however, the banker in his business is provided with all the means that science has made available for ensuring safe custody, the distinction in his case is of no importance. "It is necessary to distinguish between cases in which valuables are by mistake delivered to the wrong person (as in Mrs. Langtry's case), and cases in which they are destroyed, lost, stolen or fraudulently abstracted, whether by an officer of the bank or by some other person." In the former case the question of the negligence of a bailee does not arise; the case is one of wrongful conversion apart from any question of negligence. The liability of the banker in the latter case, when the goods have been destroyed by fire, or lost, or stolen, whether by an officer of the bank or by a stranger, depends upon the question of the negligence of a bailee. The banker is a gratuitous bailee and would not be liable in any of these cases, if he has used the care which an ordinary prudent man would take of his own valuables. The question whether this amount of care has been used would necessarily be a question for the jury in each case."

PARTNERSHIP

HOW A PARTNERSHIP ARISES

PARTNERSHIP arises from an agreement of the parties concerned; and it can arise without any formalities. Moreover, it can be modified by a similar agreement as the partnership proceeds: "To constitute a partnership the parties must have agreed to carry on business and to share the profits in some way." And it can be dissolved without formality: "Voluntary societies derive their existence wholly from the consent of private individuals; and it is upon the continuance of that consent that the continuance of their existence depends." The foundation of the partnership is the members' confidence in the competency and integrity of one another. For the act of making a partnership in itself constitutes all the partners agents for one another in the business of the partnership. This aspect seems to be emphasised by the enactment that a partnership cannot be formed of more than *ten persons for banking*, or *twenty for any other business*. "Every partner is in contemplation of law, the general and accredited agent of the partnership, and may consequently bind all the other partners by his acts in all matters within the scope and objects of the partnership." The exception is where the other party knows of some limitation of the partner's authority to bind his fellows. For "partners may stipulate among themselves that some one of them only shall enter into particular contracts; but with such private arrangements third persons dealing with the firm without notice have no concern."

LIABILITY OF PARTNER

The liability of a partner for the firm's debts is a peculiar one. During his life he is jointly liable with the other partners; after his death, his estate is severally liable also. If a creditor proceeds against one partner and obtains judgment he cannot maintain an action against another living partner. But his action can be maintained against the estate of a dead partner.

The firm is answerable for each partner's acts in the business of the firm because, even though the other partners were unaware of the acts, they held the partner "out to the world as a person for whom they were responsible." Of course, though, if the debt contracted or the wrong done is clearly outside the partnership business, the other partners are no more liable than a principal would be for the unauthorised acts of his agent.

MEANING OF " NOVATION "

To become a partner in a firm does not entail liability for debts contracted before admission. Nor, on the other hand, does retirement of itself mean a cessation of liability for the debts and obligations incurred before the retirement. Usually, however, there is an agreement with the creditors that they shall accept the liability of the new firm in lieu of the old. When this tripartite agreement (between the creditor, the partner joining or leaving, and the other members of the firm) takes place, the retiring partner is discharged. Such a substitution of liability is called a *novation*.

INFANT AS PARTNER

The House of Lords decided (*Lovell & Christmas* v. *Beauchamp*, 1894) that an infant can be a partner and can enjoy the benefits of the partnership only by bearing its burdens : "There is nothing to prevent an infant trading, or becoming partner with a trader. Till he disaffirms the contract of partnership he is a member of the trading firm. But he cannot contract debts by such trading : although goods may be ordered for the firm he does not become a debtor in respect of them. The adult partner is, however, entitled to insist that the partnership assets shall be applied in payment of the liabilities of the partnership ; and that, until these are provided for, no part of them shall be received by the infant partner. This right of the adult partner can be made available for the benefit of the creditors."

Unless, within a reasonable time of his reaching the age of twenty-one, the infant repudiates the partnership agreement, he becomes fully liable as a partner. For he has allowed the world at large to assume that he is a partner.

PARTNERSHIP PROPERTY PROTECTED

Since the Partnership Act, 1890, the partnership property cannot be taken to satisfy a judgment debt against a partner for a debt on his own account. Formerly it was the sheriff's duty to sell the partner's interest in the goods seized, even though it was impossible to measure that interest unless by taking partnership accounts. Now it is enacted that "a writ of execution shall not issue against the firm." But a judgment creditor of a partner can get an "order charging that partner's interest in the partnership property and profits with payment of the judgment debt and interest thereon."

PARTNERSHIP RULES

The partners may agree among themselves to vary the following rules. Apart from such agreement, which may be deduced as a fact as well as be expressed, the rules are in Section 24—

1. All the partners are entitled to share equally in the capital and profits of the business, and must contribute equally towards the losses whether of capital or otherwise sustained by the firm. Thus if A and B become partners it may be that A provides the capital (say £10,000), and that B brings in only his technical skill and business ability. Nevertheless, apart from special agreement, B stands on an equality in regard to the sharing of profits; and if, at the conclusion of the joint enterprise, the capital assets are worth say £12,000, B is entitled to £1,000, i.e. half of the increment. For it is to be assumed that A's property and B's person have contributed equally to the accession. On the other hand, if the enterprise is a failure, if after paying partnership debts to outsiders only £4,000 is left for A, then B must bring in £3,000 as his share of loss of capital.

2. The firm must indemnify every partner in respect of payments made and personal liabilities incurred by him—

(a) In the ordinary and proper conduct of the business of the firm; or

(b) In or about anything necessarily done for the preservation of the business or property of the firm. This liability to contribute is akin to the liability of a principal for the necessary expenses of his agent; but it extends further. For it may cover what has neither expressly nor by implication been authorised by the other partners.

3. A partner making, for the purpose of the partnership, any actual payment or advance beyond the amount of capital which he has agreed to subscribe, is entitled to interest at the rate of 5 per cent per annum from the date of the payment or advance.

4. A partner is not entitled, before the ascertainment of profits, to interest on capital subscribed by him.

5. Every partner may take part in the management of the partnership business.

6. No partner shall be entitled to remuneration for acting in the partnership business.

7. No person may be introduced as a partner without the consent of all existing partners.

8. Any difference arising as to ordinary matters connected with the partnership business may be decided by a majority of

the partners, but no change may be made in the nature of the partnership business without the consent of all existing partners.

9. The partnership books are to be kept at the place of business of the partnership (or the principal place, if there is more than one), and every partner may, when he thinks fit, have access to and inspect and copy any of them.

It is to be noted that the first rule, of equality, exists though the amounts of capital ventured in the business may vary. For, clearly, a man's value to the partnership may be quite out of proportion to the capital he has put into it.

In practice it is common to modify Rule 5. The partners may agree that the management of the partnership affairs shall be confided to one or more of their number exclusively of the others, or that there shall be a division of the labour of management. Such an agreement is quite valid.

As regards Rule 7 the following points should be noted—

(*a*) The attempt of one partner to admit another without consent of his fellows would give the newcomer no rights at all against the firm. At best it would be a sub-partnership; the partner attempting to introduce the newcomer would share with him the profits of the firm.

(*b*) But it is common for a senior partner to reserve the power of admitting a new partner. A person so introduced, possibly a son, acquires a partner's rights.

(*c*) Just as a new partner cannot be introduced without the consent of all the others so no majority of the partners can expel any partner—again, of course, apart from special agreements among the partners.

DURATION OF PARTNERSHIP

A partnership is usually agreed upon to last for a fixed term or till dissolved "by mutual arrangement." Where it is not, any partner may dissolve the partnership at any time on giving notice of his intention so to do to all the other partners. Notice in writing is enough for this, though the partnership agreement may have been made by deed.

PROFITS IN PARTNERSHIPS

Just as an agent must make no undisclosed profit in his principal's business, so every partner must account to the firm for any benefit derived by him from the business of the partnership, or from use of the partnership name or business connection. To put in the partnership articles such a clause as, "The partners agree not to engage in any trade or business except upon the account and for the benefit of the partnership," adds nothing to the duty imposed by law.

ASSIGNING A SHARE

A partner may assign his share of the partnership. But this means only that the assignee is entitled to receive the assignor's share in the profits while the partnership is a going concern, and to receive the assignor's share in the partnership assets upon a dissolution. It does not entitle the assignee to interfere in the management or to inspect the partnership books.

DISSOLUTION OF PARTNERSHIP

Dissolution of a partnership takes place—

1. On the expiration of the agreed term.

2. On the notice of his intention to dissolve, given to his fellows by one of the partners when the partnership has been entered into for an undefined time.

3. On the death or bankruptcy of any partner.

4. On the happening of any event which makes it unlawful for the business of the firm to be carried on.

5. On a decree by the Court in certain prescribed events.

Moreover, if the other partner or partners so wish, the partnership is dissolved if a partner charges his share of the partnership property for his separate debt.

As regards No. 5, the circumstances must be such as, in the opinion of the Court, "render it just and equitable that the partnership be dissolved." It is, therefore, an application of the discretionary power of the Chancellor to modify the rigidity of the Common Law. Certain of the circumstances noted in the Act are—

(a) Lunacy of a partner.

(b) Incapacity of a partner from performing his part in the contract.

(c) Conduct of a partner, other than the partner who seeks the Court's help, that is to the prejudice of the business.

(d) Continued loss in the business.

SUBSTITUTED LIABILITY

When a change in the composition of a partnership occurs, the rules relating to substituted contracts apply. The creditors of the firm have the option of holding the retiring partner liable, or of accepting the liability of the firm as newly constituted. If the creditors agree to the substitution there is a *novation,* a tripartite arrangement (creditor, outgoing-partner, incoming-partner).

APPLICATION OF PARTNERSHIP PROPERTY

Upon a dissolution the property of the partnership is applied in the following order—

1. To pay the debts and other liabilities of the firm.
2. To pay *loans* made by the partners to the firm.
3. To pay *capital* placed in the firm by the partners.

Any residue is divided among the partners in the proportion in which they are entitled to profits. Similarly if losses are made, they are borne by the partners in the proportion to which they are entitled to share profits.

GOODWILL

If, as part of the partnership assets, the "goodwill" of the business is sold then—

1. The buyer alone may represent himself as carrying on the business.
2. The seller may carry on a competing business, but not under the old name, nor so as to suggest that he is carrying on the same business.
3. The seller may advertise his business; but he may not canvass customers of the old business, even if these customers have continued to deal with him.
4. The buyer has a right to the exclusive use of the old name of the business.

ADMINISTRATION OF PARTNERSHIP PROPERTY

If the High Court is called upon to administer the estates of deceased partners, and of bankrupt and insolvent partners, it observes these rules—

(*a*) Partnership property is applied as *joint estate* in payment of the debts of the firm to persons other than partners. The separate property of each partner is applied as *separate estate* in payment of his separate debts.

(*b*) After such payments the surplus, if any, of the joint estate is applied in payment of the separate debts of the partners. The surplus, if any, of the separate estate is applied in payment of the debts of the firm.

PARTNERSHIP AND JOINT-STOCK COMPANY

The difference between a partnership and a joint-stock com pany (a corporation) may be thus summed up.

A partnership may be a quite informal affair; it may be arranged in as casual a manner as many marriage partnerships are; it may be dissolved as readily as it can be formed. The law looks on the partnership merely as a collection of individuals who have agreed to act together for some specific business purpose. Individual responsibility still persists.

The corporation, however, the joint-stock company with or without limited liability of its members, is a very different thing. Its formation is attended by a ceremonial; the Registrar, to whom Parliament has delegated its power of creating new legal persons, ushers it into being only when a prescribed procedure has been followed. The conditions upon which its existence depends are determined; and these conditions cannot be modified without a procedure almost as elaborate as that attendant upon the birth of the corporation. The individuals that from time to time comprise the corporation have no individual responsibility for its affairs. The corporation is a person quite distinct from its constituent numbers; it persists as a separate legal person, endowed with its own powers, subject to its own liabilities, throughout all the alterations in the number of those entitled to a share in the profits earned by it. The members of the company are not responsible for one another's liabilities in regard to the company; the partners are responsible for one another in the business of the partnership. The members of a company most commonly know nothing of one another, and the majority of them have no part in the ordinary conduct of the company's business; the partners form the firm because they have confidence in one another, and each has, apart from agreement to the contrary, the same right in the conduct of the partnership business.

A PARTNERSHIP AGREEMENT

A partnership agreement form will vary with the nature and conditions of the partnership. A precedent will, however, be of service.

This Deed made the *thirteenth day* of *September* 19.. BETWEEN *James Smith* of 395 *Slope Street Ipswich in the county of Suffolk* of the one part and *Thomas Jones* of 521 *Right Place Colchester in the county of Essex* of the other part

WHEREAS the said *James Smith* and *Thomas Jones* have agreed to become partners in the trade or business of coal merchants as hereinafter mentioned for the term and subject to the conditions hereinafter contained

NOW THIS DEED WITNESSETH that in pursuance of the said agreement each of the said parties doth hereby covenant with the other as follows—

1. THE said *James Smith* and *Thomas Jones* shall become and remain partners in the trade or business of *Coal Merchants* for the term of *seven* years from the date hereof if both of them shall so long live.

2. THE business of the partnership shall be carried on under the style or firm of *Smith and Jones* at 395 *Slope Street Ipswich aforesaid* or at such other place or places as the partners shall from time to time determine.

3. THE capital of the partnership shall consist of the sum of £ 5,000 to be brought in by the partners in the following proportions, namely the sum of £ 3,000 by the said *James Smith* and the sum of £ 2,000 by the said *Thomas Jones* and the partners shall be entitled to the capital of the partnership in the same proportions and each partner shall be entitled to receive interest at the rate of £5 per cent per annum payable half-yearly from the commencement of the partnership on the amount of capital so brought in by him as aforesaid and shall be entitled to receive interest at the same rate payable half-yearly and to commence from the date of the advance on all sums of money which he may hereafter advance to the capital of the partnership. The said capital and the profits arising therefrom (including the premiums to be paid for any apprentice or apprentices to be taken by either of the partners) shall (subject as hereinafter mentioned) be employed in the said business.

4. THE bankers of the partnership shall be *the Eastern Counties Bank Limited* or such other bankers as the partners shall agree to appoint and all moneys of the partnership not required for current expenses shall be paid into the bank to the credit and on account of the firm.

5. THE rent of the partnership premises and all rates taxes payments for insurance cost of repairs and alterations and other outgoings whatsoever in respect of the same and the wages and remuneration of all persons employed in the business and the travelling expenses incurred by the partners in connection with the business and all other outgoings expenses debts liabilities and losses (including any loss of capital) incurred in the course of the business and all interest payable to either partner on any capital now brought in or hereafter to be advanced by him shall be paid and discharged out of the gross receipts and out of the capital of the partnership or in case the same shall be insufficient for the purpose by the partners in the proportions in which they are entitled to share in the net profits of the partnership.

6. EACH partner shall during the partnership employ himself diligently in the business of the partnership and shall carry on the same to the greatest advantage of the firm.

7. EACH partner shall be entitled to have *four* weeks' holiday in each year. In the first year of the partnership the said *James Smith* shall have the first choice of the time or times at which he will take his holiday and in the second year of the partnership the said *Thomas Jones* shall have the like choice and so on alternately during the continuance of the partnership.

8. NEITHER partner shall during the continuance of the partnership engage either directly or indirectly in any business other than the business of the partnership except with the previous consent in writing of the other partner.

9. No clerk traveller shopman apprentice or servant shall be engaged or be employed in the business or be dismissed from the business by either partner without the consent of the other partner.

10. NEITHER partner shall on account of the firm purchase goods or make contracts whereof or whereunder respectively the price or the liability incurred shall exceed the sum of £ 20 without the consent of the other partner and if either partner shall do so the other partner shall have the option of adopting or of repudiating the purchase or the contract on behalf of the firm and if he shall repudiate the same the purchasing or contracting partner shall solely bear and discharge and indemnify the firm the partnership property and the other partner against all liability thereunder but subject thereto may take the benefit thereof as his separate property.

11. NEITHER partner shall lend any of the moneys or deliver upon credit any of the goods of the partnership to any person or persons after he shall have been requested in writing by the other partner not to do so or without the consent of the other partner and except when in the ordinary course of business the contrary shall be unavoidable compound release or discharge any debt or security which shall be owing or belonging to the partnership or draw or accept any bill of exchange or promissory note on account of the firm and if either partner shall do so he shall (as the case may be) forthwith pay to the firm the full amount or value of the money so lent or the goods so delivered or the debt or security so released or discharged or the loss incurred by the firm by reason of such composition or solely bear and discharge and indemnify the firm the partnership property and the other partner against all liability under such bill or note.

12. NEITHER partner shall without the consent in writing of the other enter into any bond or become bail surety or security for any person or persons or corporation or subscribe any policy of insurance.

13. ALL contracts and engagements entered into by the partners on account of the partnership and all cheques drafts upon bankers bills of exchange promissory notes and other securities receipts and other evidence relating thereto shall be made given and taken respectively in the name of the firm.

14. THE partners shall keep or cause to be kept proper books of account and proper entries shall be made therein of all moneys received and paid and of all the sales purchases contracts engagements transactions and property of the partnership and of all other matters of which accounts or entries ought to be kept or made according to the usual

and regular course of the business and the said books of account and all deeds securities bills and papers belonging to the partnership shall be kept at the counting house at 395 *Slope Street* or at such other place of business of the partnership as the partners shall agree upon and each partner shall have free access at all times to examine and to take copies of the same.

15. ON the   31*st*   day of   *March*   in the year 19.. and on the   31*st* day of   *March*   in every succeeding year a general account shall be taken by the partners of all the receipts payments sales purchases transactions and engagements of the partnership during the then preceding year and of all the capital stock-in-trade property engagements and liabilities for the time being of the partnership and in taking such account a just valuation shall be made of all particulars requiring and capable of valuation and the said general account shall immediately after the same shall have been taken be written into two books and be signed in each such book by each of the partners and after such signature each partner shall keep one of the said books and shall be bound by every such account except that if any manifest error to the amount of £ 50   or upwards shall be found therein by either partner and signified to the other partner within six calendar months next after the signing thereof by both of them such error shall be rectified.

16. THE partners shall be entitled to the net profits of the said business (after paying all expenses and interest on capital as set out in clauses 3 and 5 hereof) in the following proportions the said   *James Smith* to   *three fifth*   parts thereof and the said   *Thomas Jones*   to the remaining   *two fifth*   parts thereof and the same shall be carried to their credit respectively in the books of the partnership immediately after every such annual account as aforesaid shall have been taken and signed and may be drawn out at pleasure.

17. THE said   *James Smith*   shall be at liberty to draw out of the profit of the business for his own use (in anticipation of his share in the net profits) any sum not exceeding the sum of £ 3   per   *week*   and the said   *Thomas Jones*   shall be at liberty so to draw out of the said profits for his own use any sum not exceeding the sum of £ 2   per *week*   but if at the end of any year of the partnership it shall appear upon taking the general account that the amount which either partner is entitled to receive for interest on capital brought in or advanced by him and his share for that year of the net profits of the business is less than the total amount which he shall have drawn out in pursuance of this clause during that year he shall forthwith repay to the partnership the difference between the amount so drawn out by him and the amount which he is entitled to receive as aforesaid.

18. WITHIN six calendar months after the expiration of the partnership otherwise than by the death of either partner a general account shall be taken by the partners of all the capital property engagements and liabilities of the partnership and immediately after such last mentioned account shall have been so taken and settled the partners shall forthwith make due provision for the payment of the debts and meeting all other liabilities of the partnership and subject thereto the capital

of the partnership shall be divided between the partners in the proportions in which they shall be entitled to the same and the residue of the property of the partnership shall be divided between the partners in the proportions in which they are entitled to the net profits of the partnership and all such deeds or instruments in writing shall be executed by the partners respectively for facilitating the getting in of the debts due to the partnership and for vesting the various parts or particulars of the partnership property in the partners to whom the same respectively shall upon such division belong and for releasing to each other all claims on account of the partnership and otherwise as are usual in similar cases.

19. If either partner shall die during the partnership his executors or administrators shall be entitled to—

(1) The amount of the sum brought in and any further advances made by him to the capital of the partnership

(2) The amount of what shall be due to him for interest unpaid thereon up to the day of his death

(3) The amount if any ascertained or to be ascertained by the annual account which was or should have been or should be taken on the annual account day next before his death or if he shall die on some annual account day on the day of his death to be due to him for his share in the net profits of the business and remaining at the time of his death unpaid to or not drawn upon by him

(4) If he shall die on any other day than an annual account day an allowance in lieu of net profits equal to interest at the rate of £ 5 per cent per annum on the amount of his aforesaid share in the capital of the partnership to be calculated if he shall die before the first annual account day from the commencement of the partnership and if he shall die after that day then from the annual account day next before his death And the said executors or administrators shall give credit for all sums drawn out by him since the commencement of the partnership or the last annual account day as the case may be.

The amounts to which the said executors or administrators shall be so entitled for interest on capital and share of and allowance in lieu of net profits shall be paid to them by the surviving partner on demand but the amount to which they shall be entitled for the deceased partner's said share in the capital of the partnership shall be paid to them by the surviving partner by three equal instalments to be payable together with interest thereon at the rate of £5 per cent per annum from the date of the death in the manner following (that is to say) the first of such instalments with the interest then due thereon and on the principal amount then remaining unpaid at the expiration of   *six* calendar months after the death the second of such instalments with the interest then due thereon and on the principal amount then remaining unpaid at the expiration of   *twelve*   calendar months after the death and the third of such instalments with the interest then due thereon at the expiration of   *eighteen*   calendar months after the death And the payment of the said instalments and interest shall be secured by the bond of the surviving partner in a sum of double the amount of the principal money to be paid conditioned to be void on payment of the said instalments and interest in manner aforesaid   And subject to the rights by this 19th clause of these presents secured to the said executors or administrators the whole of the property (including the goodwill) of the partnership shall as from the day of such death belong to the surviving partner and all the liabilities of the partnership shall as from that day be discharged by the surviving partner And all such assurances releases and instruments shall be executed by the said executors or administrators and the surviving partner respectively as shall be necessary or expedient to vest all the property of the partnership in the surviving partner alone and otherwise to give effect to the provisions of this clause and amongst other instruments a bond in a sufficient and reasonable penalty shall be executed to the said executors or administrators by the surviving partner his executors or administrators for indemnifying the heirs executors or administrators estate and effects of the deceased partner against all the liabilities of the partnership at or after such death and all actions proceedings expenses claims and demands on account of the same.

20. WHENEVER any difference or dispute shall arise between the parties hereto or their respective executors or administrators touching these presents or anything herein contained or provided for or the operation hereof or any of their respective rights duties or liabilities hereunder or under the partnership hereby constituted or otherwise in connection with the premises the matter in difference or dispute shall be referred to two arbitrators or their umpire one of such arbitrators to be appointed each by party pursuant to and so as with regard to the mode and consequences of the reference and in all other respects to conform to the provisions in that behalf of the Arbitration Act 1889 or any subsisting statutory modification thereof.

IN WITNESS whereof the said parties to these presents have hereunto set their hands and seals the day and year first above written.

SIGNED Sealed and Delivered by the above-named *in the presence of* *Alfred Robinson* 294 *Legal Square* *Ipswich* *Solicitor.*	*John Smith* *Thomas Jones*	L.S. L.S.

LIMITED PARTNERSHIPS

A more recent Act, the Limited Partnerships Act of 1907, has made it possible for a man to advance capital to a firm without incurring liability beyond the capital he has advanced. He is a sleeping (dormant) partner and must take no part in the management of the firm. Otherwise, he incurs the full liability of a partner. The "general partners," actively conducting the business, are liable for all debts and obligations of the firm. Though a "limited partner" may take no part in the management of the

13

partnership business and has no power to bind the firm, yet he is not debarred from tendering his advice to the managing partners. And he or his agent can examine the partnership books.

To obtain the privileges of this Act there must be registration in a prescribed form giving the essential particulars relative to the business. The Registrar of Joint-Stock Companies is appointed also Registrar of limited partnerships.

The prescribed forms are these—

No. of Certificate.　　　　　　　　　　　　　　　　　　Form No. L.P. 1.

LIMITED PARTNERSHIPS ACT, 1907

Application for registration
of a limited partnership.

A £2 fee stamp must be
impressed here.

We, the undersigned being the partners of the firm, hereby apply for registration as a limited partnership, and for that purpose supply the following particulars, pursuant to Section 8 of the Limited Partnerships Act, 1907—

The firm } name.

The general nature } of the business.

The principal place } of business.

The term, if any, for which the partnership is entered into, and the date of its commencement.

Term (if any) years.

If no definite term, the conditions of existence of the partnership.

Date of commencement.

The partnership is limited.

Presented or forwarded for filing by

Full name and address of
each of the partners.

General partners.

Limited partners.

*Amount contributed by each limited partner, and whether paid in cash, or how otherwise.

*A separate statement (Form L.P. 3) of the amounts contributed must accompany this application, for the purposes of payment of capital duty, pursuant to Section 11 of the Act.

Signature of all the } partners.

Date

No. of Certificate.   Form No. L.P. 3.

LIMITED PARTNERSHIPS ACT, 1907

*........................

Statement of the Capital contributed by Limited Partners made pursuant to Section 11 of the Limited Partnerships Act, 1907.

The amounts contributed in cash or otherwise by the limited partners of the firm*   are as follows—

Name and Addresses of Limited Partners	Amounts contributed in Cash or otherwise (If otherwise than in Cash, that fact, with particulars, must be stated)

Signature of a general partner

Date

Note.—The stamp duty on the nominal capital is five shillings for every £100, or fraction of £100, contributed by each limited partner.

This statement must accompany the application Form L.P. 1 for registration of a limited partnership.

Presented or forwarded for registration by

* Here insert name of firm or limited partnership.

COMPANIES

AN ARTIFICIAL PERSON

A PERSON, in the eyes of the law, is an individual possessed of rights and under obligation to perform duties. The person may be a human being. The person may also be a collection of property defined in some way or other. The Crown, as distinct from the King, is an instance of the latter. Each person is in general equally subject to the law, has the same rights and duties. "The law is no respecter of persons," we sometimes say: cook's son and duke's son get the same treatment. Still, from the very nature of the person with whom the law deals, there must be some modification of this rule. A child, immature in judgment, cannot be subjected to the same legal responsibilities as the adult mature in judgment shoulders; a married woman should perhaps be subject to fewer liabilities under the criminal law and under the law of torts than her unmarried sister is.

The chief variation from the general equality is in regard to what are sometimes called "artificial persons," persons created by law itself. The limited liability company is nowadays the chief example of such.

KINDS OF ARTIFICIAL PERSONS

Of these artificial persons there are—

1. *Corporations Sole.* Where a mass of property is owned by one person in virtue of his office. (Thus, the Postmaster-General is a corporation sole; he has rights and duties from his office quite apart from his rights and duties as a citizen.)

2. *Corporations Aggregate.* Where a number of people, maybe constantly changing, are regarded by law as a single body endowed with its own rights and obligations.

Of the *corporations aggregate* there are two kinds:

(a) those that have existed so long that their origin can only be surmised;

(b) those created by Act of Parliament (either directly, or by Parliament's delegate, the Registrar of Joint-Stock Companies).

As regards the powers of the corporations, there is an important distinction between the first and the second kind. The former (sometimes called "Common Law Corporations") can exercise whatever powers the managers think fit, provided that these powers are not expressly withheld. The latter are confined in their acts to what their constitution permits, either expressly or by reasonable implication: a joint-stock company may do nothing outside the powers taken in its Memorandum of Association; a railway company may do nothing outside the powers given in its Railway Act.

LIMITED LIABILITY COMPANY AN "ARTIFICIAL PERSON"

An incorporation or corporation is an "artificial person," artificial meaning in this connection in accordance with the rules of the (lawyer's) art. An incorporation is in other words a person in contemplation of law. "A corporation aggregate of many is invisible, immortal, and rests only in intendment and consideration of the law." Just so we might say that one will, being skilfully composed, is artificially drawn: another, drawn by one unacquainted with or using badly the lawyer's terms of art, is inartificial. The word does not, of course, mean fictitious; a limited liability company is real enough. A corporation is a legal person as an individual is. If a man trusts a corporation he trusts that legal person and can look only to its assets for payment. He can call upon individual members to contribute only in so far as the Act of Parliament or the charter creating the corporation has provided for it.

ULTRA VIRES ACTS

When an agent of a company enters into contracts in its name, he cannot be made personally responsible for the contracts. For, even if the contracts are in relation to objects for which the company has no powers, the other party to the contract is assumed to know the limitations placed upon the company. Its memorandum, and, when it has them, its articles of association, are public documents.

That one who has dealings with a limited liability company should make himself acquainted with its powers is effectively taught in the case of *Ashbury Railway Carriage Co.* v. *Riche* (H.L. 1875).

A corporation, like a limited liability company, being an artificial person created by law, is restricted in its powers. Its powers are restricted to what are given to it at its creation, or what may be reasonably deduced from these. Acts beyond those powers are beyond its capacity (*ultra vires*). So far as the corporation is concerned these acts give no rights and involve no liabilities.

A company was formed to make carriages, including locomotives. It entered into a contract with Riche that he should do work in connection with the construction of a railway line. Riche performed his part of the contract. The company did not pay. He sued; but he failed. For the construction of a railway is not incidental to the building of carriages: the *memorandum of association* took power to do the second; it took no power to do the first. And its power to alter its memorandum in order to enter into a new kind of contract is very restricted. The alteration must have the sanction of the Court; and it can be effected only to achieve an extension of its business by the addition of business of the same nature, or possibly to abandon some of its original objects (*Ashbury Railway Carriage Co.* v. *Riche*, H.L. 1875).

A company can alter the articles of association at its discretion. That is a purely domestic matter between directors and shareholders; and the Court will interfere only when some class of shareholders is patently treated with great unfairness. The memorandum is a different thing. For outsiders may have relied upon this when entering into contracts with the company.

A JOINT-STOCK COMPANY: COMPANIES ACT, 1929

The regulations relating to a joint-stock company are gathered together and arranged in orderly fashion in the Companies Act, 1929. A joint-stock company—like other corporations—is an artificial person created by law. Parliament can create a "person" endowed with certain rights and liable to certain duties, and Parliament can delegate its power of creation to an official. It does so in regard to joint-stock companies. And having come into existence, they need never die. Unlike a partnership where there are troublesome legal formalities on the death of a partner, a company enjoys perpetual succession. "A corporation aggregate is invisible, immortal. It has no soul, neither is it subject to the imbecilities of this body." Or, in more ordinary language: "It has neither soul to be saved nor body to be kicked." The members do not constitute the corporation. They are only the members for the time being.

FORMATION

A company can be formed for any lawful purpose by conforming to a few simple instructions. A *private company* can be formed by two persons; a *public company* by seven. These persons sign a *memorandum of association*, and obtain its registration at Somerset House. The registrators may, if they choose, subject themselves to unlimited liability in regard to the affairs of the company. Usually, and wisely, they take the privilege offered by the Act. They assume only a liability limited to the amount of capital they subscribe or guarantee.

The Act contains specimen memorandums. These show—

1. *The Proposed Name of the Company.* (Any name, with a few exceptions noted below, can be adopted provided it does not cause confusion in the public mind with another undertaking.)

2. *The Place of the Registered Office.*

3. *The Objects for which the Company is established.* (Whatever business the company enters upon must be covered by these objects; if it is not, the business is *ultra vires*, and, in the eyes of the law, is of no binding effect upon the company.)

4. *Whether or not the Liability of the Members is Limited by Shares or Guarantee.*

5. *The Share Capital and the Method of its Division.*

Under 2 note that a company incorporated in England and having its registered office in England is an English company, though its members may be other than British and though its business is carried on and controlled abroad. It is also a means whereby any restrictions in regard to foreigners may be evaded. Thus, none but a British subject may own a British ship, or part of a ship; but a company composed of members of any nationality may still be a British subject and able to own British ships. It seems, too, that the advantage may be had without the drawbacks incident to payment of income tax.

In the *Egyptian Delta Land and Investment Co.* v. *Todd* (H.L. 1929) it was held that for income-tax purposes the residence of an English Limited Liability Company depends not on its English registration and statutory obligations, but on the facts as to the mode and place in which it controls and directs its affairs. We can, that is, actually have—as in the case decided—a non-resident English company.

INCORPORATIONS OTHER THAN UNDER THE COMPANIES ACT

A royal charter may incorporate some legal persons. The Bank of England is one example.

A special Act of Parliament may be needed where it is desired to obtain land by compulsory purchase. Thus a railway company must obtain a private Act.

Old custom or public Act of Parliament creates other incorporations. Thus the modern municipal corporations are the delegates of Parliament, and make laws within the limited sphere allotted by Parliament.

PRIVILEGE OF LIMITED LIABILITY

Under the Companies Act the members may shoulder as much or as little of the risks of an undertaking as they choose. In a partnership there is individual responsibility for all the debts of the partnership : in the limited company there is responsibility only for an agreed amount of capital. The company may, indeed, be looked upon rather as an association of capitals than as an association of persons.

COMPANY, A DISTINCT LEGAL PERSON

The incorporated company is distinct, in the eyes of the law, from its constituent members. In a partnership a partner cannot enter into contract with his firm. For in effect he is contracting with himself; and a contract is a meeting of at least two minds at the one point. In a company a member can, and frequently does, contract with the company. For there are two legal persons—the company acting through its authorised agents, the member acting for himself. As the well-known case, *Salomon* v. *Salomon & Co., Ltd.* (H.L. 1897) shows, English law carries to its logical conclusion the idea of the separate entity of an incorporation.

THE REGISTRAR'S CERTIFICATE

Till the Registrar's certificate has been given, the company has no existence. Any contracts entered into on behalf of the proposed company are neither enforceable by the company nor enforceable against the company. The so-called agents of the company are personally liable on such contracts.

Thus, in *Kelner* v. *Baxter* (1866) the promoters of a company in contemplation made a contract on its behalf. The company when formed ratified the contract. The company was wound up before it had fulfilled its part of the contract, and the promoters were held personally liable. They argued that, by ratification, the liability had passed to the company. This could not be, however : "Ratification can only be by a person ascertained at the time of the act done—by a person in existence." Promoters can always protect themselves by introducing a condition in the contract excluding personal liability. They can make the contract conditional upon its being afterwards adopted by the company.

When the certificate has been given "the subscribers of the memorandum, together with such other persons as may from time to time become members of the company, shall be a body corporate by the name contained in the memorandum, capable forthwith of exercising all the functions of an incorporated company, and having perpetual succession and a common seal."

If it is a private company, it can get to business at once. If it is a public company, it can proceed to collect the necessary capital.

" PERPETUAL SUCCESSION "

This implies the continued existence of the company though its members are subject to change. Here is Blackstone's comment—

"As all personal rights die with the person, and as the necessary forms of investing a series of individuals, one after another, with the same identical rights, would be very inconvenient if not impracticable, it has been found necessary, when it is for the advantage of the public to have any particular rights kept on foot and continued, to constitute artificial persons, who may maintain a perpetual succession, and enjoy a kind of legal immortality."

PUBLICITY IN REGARD TO COMPANIES

Those who deal with a limited company have warning that it is to the subscribed capital alone that they can look for satisfaction of their claims. They cannot look to the individual responsibility of the members. This warning is given by the statutory obligation upon the company to use the word "Limited" (or its recognised abbreviations) as the last word of the company's name.

Moreover, all the documents relating to the company's capital are filed in Somerset House and are open to inspection. The public company is required, indeed, to file also a copy of its annual balance sheet.

SHARES AT A DISCOUNT

The creditors of the company are, however, entitled to look to the capital as declared in these public documents. There must be no issuing of shares at a discount, whereby the shareholder's contribution is less than it appears. It is beyond the power of a limited company to issue shares at a discount, by way of bonus or otherwise.

There is, however, an important exception to this, namely, where shares of a particular class have already been issued and it is desired to issue further shares of that class. In such a case the issue may be made at a discount provided certain formalities are complied with and that the sanction of the Court is obtained.

Where shares are issued at a discount under this exception to the general rule, every prospectus relating to the issue of the shares and every balance sheet issued subsequently to the issue of the shares must contain particulars of the discount.

The terms of the issue must be sanctioned by the Court, which has an unfettered discretion in the matter, and moreover the company must have been carrying on business for a year or more and the issue of the shares at a discount must have been approved by a general meeting.

" ONE MAN " COMPANY

English law recognises in the fullest measure the separate existence of the company. Even when one member provides the capital and conducts the business—the other member or members being his nominees—the company is a separate person. To this artificial person the member can "lend" the bulk of the capital on debenture. He thereby, in effect, obtains a charge upon his own property; so that, if winding up comes, he takes precedence of his own trade creditors. He becomes his own secured creditor.

Such a "no-liability company" was in the Court of Appeal treated as fraudulent; but the House of Lords reversed this judgment (*Salomon* v. *Salomon & Co.*, H.L. 1897). Once a company is incorporated it is a person able to contract with a member. However large the proportion of shares or debentures owned by him, and though he, as governing director, has control of the company's affairs, its acts are not his acts, nor its liabilities his liabilities.

SALOMON v. SALOMON & CO., LIMITED

The appellant, Aron Salomon, for many years carried on business on his own account as a leather merchant and wholesale boot manufacturer.

With the design of transferring his business to a joint-stock company to consist of himself and his family, he entered into an agreement on 20th July, 1892, with a trustee for the future company settling the terms of the transfer, one of the conditions being that in part payment he was to receive £10,000 in debentures of the company.

The intention throughout was to retain the business in the family and not to admit strangers. At the time of its transfer to the company the business was perfectly solvent.

The company lost heavily; a liquidator was appointed for the unsecured creditors. A balance of about £1,055 remained, and Salomon claimed this as debenture holder. In the two lower courts judgment was in favour of the liquidator against Salomon, the Court of Appeal considering that "the formation of the company and the issue of the debentures to Salomon were a mere scheme to enable him to carry on business in the name of the company with limited liability, contrary to the true intent and meaning of the Companies Act, 1862, and further to enable him to obtain a preference over other creditors of the company by procuring a first charge on the assets by means of such debentures." But the House of Lords reversed the decision: "It was essential to the artificial creation constituting a company that the law should recognise only that artificial existence, quite apart from the motives of the corporators. Once formed, the company must be treated like any other independent person; but assuming for the sake of argument that the formation of the company was a mere scheme to enable Salomon to carry on business in the name of the company, it did not follow that this was contrary to the intention of the Companies Act, which apparently gives a company a legal existence with its own rights and liabilities independently of the ideas of those who formed it. The Lords Justices had considered the inexpedience of permitting one man to be practically the whole of the company; and assuming that such a thing could not have been intended by the legislature they had sought to read into the Act some prohibition of such a result; but the question of policy was immaterial if the company had been duly constituted by law; and there was nothing in the evidence to show that Salomon intended to do anything dishonest. The judgment of the Court of Appeal should be reversed."

LIABILITY RESTRICTED

The Companies Act, 1929, has not modified the law in this respect. Under it the device of forming a joint-stock company with limited liability is open to any trader, being at the time solvent, who seeks to restrict his liability in his business. Now, indeed, when the "Private Company" is recognised, the man anxious to lessen his risks need obtain only another member. And that other may be his wife.

LIABILITY OF COMPANY FOR WRONGS

It was once thought that, since the joint-stock company is the creature of law, it could authorise no illegality: that clearly would be beyond the powers granted by it. Then, too, since a guilty mind is essential to a crime, the company, having no mind, could not be criminal. It is now settled, however, that a company can be made liable for the illegal acts of its agents just as can an individual principal. Whatever penalty is exacted must necessarily, however, be against the property held by the company.

A company's capital is liable for debts contracted on its behalf. Is it also liable for civil wrongs committed by its agents? It is now well settled that it is. This is so even when it is incorporated for public duties from which it derives no profit. ("A private corporation is but an association of individuals united for some common purpose, and permitted by the law to use a common name and to change its members without a dissolution of the association. The doctrine which formerly was sometimes asserted, that an action of tort will not lie against a corporation is exploded. The same rule now applies to corporations as to individuals. They are equally responsible for injuries done, in the course of their business, by their servants.")

Now that the limited liability company is the normal form of business enterprise, this is only fair. In the *Mersey Docks and Harbour Board* v. *Gibbs* (H.L. 1866), the judgment declared: "the legislation intends that the body, the creature of the statute, shall have the same duties, and that its funds shall be rendered subject to the same liabilities as the general law would impose on a private person." A company has in fact been held liable even for a wrong like libel.

An interesting case in 1931 emphasises the point.

JOINT-STOCK COMPANY AS A "DISORDERLY PERSON"

A common informer was awarded penalties against a joint-stock company acting, she showed, as a "disorderly person." Here was an interesting application of the idea that a company is a separate entity; it is a person with rights and liabilities distinct from those of its constituent members. Long before the first Companies Act, long before the joint-stock company had started on its course to become the typical business organisation, Parliament enacted the Sunday Observance Act, 1781. The Act penalises, to the extent of £200, any person who on Sunday opens a place of entertainment to which the public is admitted upon payment. And "in order to encourage prosecutions" the Act provided that two inhabitants of any parish might cause a constable to go with them to a justice; and that he, on their undertaking to prosecute, must issue a warrant to bring the offender before him. And if penalties were exacted the "common informers" were to have them. Parliament, anxious that a statute passed should not become a dead letter, "enlisted the motive of private greed to ensure that the offender should be made to answer for his offence." Obviously, the procedure contemplated is not practical against a company. An ingenious argument, therefore, suggested that—as one result of the laying down of this procedure—the Act had no application to a company. A company was certainly not in contemplation when the Act was passed. But then, the judge pointed out, the prescribing of a particular mode of procedure, devised to promote the application of the law, does not prevent a prosecution in other ways. You cannot arrest a company. You can, however, prosecute it for offences committed by its agents. You cannot seek its corporal punishment, you can proceed against its property; you can penalise its soul—which is its money, though you cannot pain its body. In short, "person" must be taken to include company even in an Act passed before the modern joint-stock company was contemplated. There are obvious limitations. You cannot sue a company for breach of promise nor prosecute it for murder. Thus an attempt to indict a joint-stock company for manslaughter failed in *R.* v. *Cory Bros., Ltd* (K.B. 1930), the technical reason given being that in the absence of the accused no trial for felony can proceed in any English court. Apart from these limitations a company is liable for the faults of the agents conducting its business.

PROMOTERS OF A COMPANY

The law, whether statutory or judicial, gives no rigid definition of this term: "The term promoter is not of law but of business, usefully summing up in a single word a number of business operations familiar to the commercial world by which a company is generally brought into existence." The promoter is considered to stand in the position of trustee towards the company; and a strict definition might exclude some whom it might be desirable to regard as promoters. "A very little will make people promoters of a company if it can be seen that they were really doing something in the way of speculation for their own interest, and not acting merely as agents for others."

The promoter, being in a position of trust towards the company, must make no undisclosed profits at the expense of the company. And, if he sells to the company, he must disclose to an independent board all the material facts. One Lord Chancellor declared: "I do not say that the owner of property may not promote and form a joint-stock company, and then sell his property to it. But I do say that, if he does, he is bound to take care that he sells it to the company through the medium of a board of directors who can and do exercise an independent and intelligent judgment of the transaction, and who are not left under the belief that the property belongs, not to the promoter, but to some other person."

MEMORANDUM OF ASSOCIATION

It is this document that determines the activities of a company. Investors, by looking at the "objects clause," can see how their capital is to be employed: they need take no blind risks. Those conducting business with the company can in like manner see whether or not they are able to hold the company liable for the dealings.

The memorandum is the fundamental law of the company; and it can be altered only with the consent of the Court, and then only in a restricted measure. Its registration gives birth to a *private company* or to a *public company*.

PRIVATE COMPANY

The articles of association (the rules under which the business of the company is to be transacted) of a private company—

1. Restrict the freedom to transfer shares.

2. Limit the number of members to fifty.

3. Prohibit invitation to the public to subscribe for shares or debentures.

Such a company—

1. Need not file a prospectus or statement.

2. Need not file an annual balance sheet.

3. Need not send to members copies of the balance sheet or the auditor's report.

It must, however, send two certificates each year to the Registrar—

1. That since the last annual return no invitation to the public had been issued.

2. That any excess over fifty members consists of employees or past employees of the company.

NAME OF COMPANY

As regards freedom of choice, the Board of Trade limits this in a few directions; its sanction must be obtained if the name is to contain—

1. The words "Chamber of Commerce"—which would suggest formation for public welfare rather than for private profit.

2. Words like "Royal," "Imperial," "Municipal," "Chartered," "Building Society," "Co-operative," which would suggest connection with the Royal Family or with the State or with organised societies.

A change of name is permitted when—

1. A special resolution approving of the change has been adopted.

2. The approval of the Board of Trade has been received.

ALTERATION OF THE MEMORANDUM

No alteration is possible without the sanction of the Court; and the Court is charged with the duty of seeing that no debenture holder or other creditor of the company is prejudiced by the alteration. Before petitioning to the Court for approval, the suggested alteration must be passed by special resolution. The alterations permitted include—

1. The adoption of means for carrying on the business more profitably.

2. Selling of the whole or part of the enterprise.

3. Amalgamation with any other company.

RIGHT OF INSPECTION

There is a general right of inspection of the documents kept by the Registrar of Companies. Copies may be procured on payment of a specified fee. Section 314 of the Act enacts: "Any person may inspect the documents kept by the Registrar of Companies on payment of such fees as may be appointed by the Board of Trade, not exceeding one shilling for each inspection, and any person may require a certificate of the incorporation of any company, or a copy or extract of any other document, or any part of any other document, to be certified by the registrar on payment for the certificate, certified copy, or extract, of such fees as the Board of Trade may appoint, not exceeding five shillings for a certificate of incorporation and not exceeding sixpence for each folio of a certified copy or extract."

A "folio" consists of seventy-two words.

ARTICLES OF ASSOCIATION

The Companies Act gives *general powers*. The memorandum takes *powers within those general powers*. The articles make regulations *within the powers taken*. "The articles of association play a part subsidiary to the memorandum of association. They accept the memorandum of association as the charter of incorporation of the company, and proceed to define the duties, the rights, and the powers of the governing body; and the mode in which the business of the company is to be carried on; and the mode in which changes in the internal regulations of the company may from time to time be made" (*Riche* v. *Ashbury Railway Carriage Co.*, H.L. 1875).

Both the memorandum and the articles are public documents. Those dealing with a company cannot, therefore, plead ignorance of them. On the other hand knowledge of the actual business transacted by the company is not to be assumed.

British Thomson-Houston Co. v. *Federated European Bank, Ltd.* (C.A. 1932) illustrates effectively the distinction between the articles of association, knowledge of which is assumed for certain purposes, and the internal management of the company. The plaintiffs sued and recovered on a guarantee in this form—

The Federated European Bank, Limited, 21 Soho Square, London, W.1. 11 June, 1931. To the British Thomson-Houston Co., Ltd., Rugby.

In consideration of your supplying or continuing to supply goods to Harris Williams (Servis), Limited, of 180 Albion Road, Stoke Newington, London, N.16. We hereby guarantee the payment of your account with them up to the sum of £200 (two hundred pounds) for three months from the date hereof, and you are at liberty to give any time or indulgence to the said Harris Williams (Servis), Ltd., for the whole or any part of your account without discharging us.

The Federated European Bank, Ltd.

(signed) N. Pal.

The writ was specially endorsed, and the plaintiffs issued a summons for leave to sign final judgment under Order XIV. In answer to the summons the manager of the defendant company stated in an affidavit that the company had not executed the guarantee, as any guarantee by them had to be executed by two directors. The Master gave leave to defend; it was admitted at the trial that N. Pal was chairman of the board of directors; and the judge gave decision for the plaintiff. It was against this decision that the bank appealed.

It appeared from the articles of association that the board had power to delegate to any manager or other officers the powers conferred on the directors, other than the powers to borrow and make calls. Delegation of the power to give guarantees had not in fact occurred. But the plaintiffs urged that they had no concern with the way in which the bank managed their affairs within the powers conferred by the articles. "If you are dealing with a director in a matter in which normally a director would have power to act for the company you are not obliged to inquire whether or not the formalities required by the articles have been complied with, before he exercises that power." And this contention was accepted by the Court of Appeal. "Those who have dealings with a company are affected with notice of all that is contained in its memorandum and articles of association. These confer upon the directors two powers: (1) to delegate to one or more of their number any of the powers of the board of directors; (2) to decide who shall sign contracts and other documents on the company's behalf. *Royal British Bank* v. *Turquand* decided that, if persons dealing with a company find an officer of the company openly exercising an authority which the directors have power to confer upon him, they are released from the duty of further inquiry, and are entitled to assume that the power has been regularly and duly conferred."

PROSPECTUS

This invitation to the public to invest money in a company or to buy its debentures must give sufficient accurate information to guide the prospective investor or creditor, including—

1. Contents of memorandum.
2. Names of directors.
3. Property to be bought by the capital to be raised.
4. Amount paid for goodwill.
5. Preliminary expenses.
6. Auditors' report.

LIABILITY FOR PROSPECTUS

Those responsible for issuing the prospectus are responsible for its accuracy and its fullness. The fact that a misrepresentation is innocent does not now protect them, if the Court decides that they should have had the knowledge they lacked. Whenever a misleading statement appears in a prospectus the directors responsible may be able to show that they should be excused, that though they had taken reasonable precautions they themselves had been misled. If they cannot, they "shall be liable to pay compensation to all persons who subscribe for any shares or debentures on the faith of the prospectus for the loss or damage they may have sustained by reason of any untrue statement therein" (Section 37). Where the misrepresentation is wilful, there has been added in the latest Company Act a criminal liability also upon the directors. Nor need the misrepresentation be in any specific point. It is enough if the whole tendency of the prospectus is to mislead. So it was put in *Aarons Reef* v. *Twiss* (A.C. 1896)—

"If the tendency of the prospectus as a whole is to deceive, there is no need, in order to claim rescission of a contract, to take shares, to show that certain specific statements are untrue.

" I protest against being called on only to look at some specific allegation in it; I think one is entitled to look at the whole document and see what it means taken together. Looking at the whole document, nobody can doubt that this was a fraudulent conspiracy. One or two of the learned judges below remarked upon the fact that Mr. Gilbert, who seems to have been the head and front of it, was not subjected to an inquiry in a criminal court. It is said there is no specific allegation of fact which is proved to be false. That is not the true test. Taking the whole thing together, was there false representation? I do not care by what means it is conveyed, by what trick or device or ambiguous language; all those are expedients by which fraudulent people seem to think they can escape from the real substance of the transaction. If by a number of statements you intentionally give a false impression and induce a person to act upon it, it is not the less false although if one takes each statement by itself there may be a difficulty in showing that any specific statement is untrue."

THE MISLED INVESTOR'S RIGHTS

Not only has the investor who has been misled in this way a right to damages. He has also a right to rescind his contract to take shares or debentures. But he must act promptly if he chooses to rescind: "The delay of a fortnight in repudiating the shares makes it, to my mind, doubtful whether the repudiation in the case of a going concern would have been in time. No doubt, where investigation is necessary, some time must be allowed. But where the shareholder is at once fully informed of the circumstances, he ought to lose no time in repudiating."

SHARES

A share is personal property and can be transferred in the manner described in the company's articles. It is issued under the seal of the company. The share is, therefore, a "specialty contract" between the holder and the company.

It should be noted that the share may contain other obligations than to pay money at stipulated times. Thus, in *Borland's Trustee* v. *Steel Bros. & Co., Ltd.* (Ch. 1901), it was held that a clause in the share certificate, giving directors a right to buy at par the shares of a bankrupt member, was valid: "A share is the interest of a shareholder in the company, measured by a sum of money, for the purpose of liability in the first place and of interest in the second, but also consisting of a series of mutual covenants entered into by all the shareholders."

Varying rights, too, may be given in different shares. Thus, one class of shares may confer a right to payment of a fixed dividend from profits before other shareholders participate.

The *share certificate* is not a negotiable instrument: the property in it is not transferable by mere delivery to one who buys it in good faith.

A *share warrant*, however, is a negotiable instrument. It is issued only in respect of shares fully paid up. The buyer in good faith becomes the owner of the shares specified in the warrant, even though the title of the previous holder was defective.

Under the 1929 Act, shares can now be issued at a discount provided the Court approves, provided also that all future balance sheets shall show the amount of discount. (See page 387.)

The prospectus is an invitation to the public to buy shares. The letter of application is the investor's *offer*; and, like other offers, it can be withdrawn before acceptance. Upon acceptance the offer is irrevocable: and acceptance means the posting of a *letter of allotment*. Such posting concludes the contract. This is so even if a revocation of the investor's offer is on its way, but has not yet been received.

STOCK

When shares are fully paid up so that, in the event of a winding-up, the shareholder would be under no further obligation, the company may consolidate its shares into stock. After the conversion a part-owner of the company holds so many pounds of the total stock : before he held so many shares of a specified amount.

A bequest of "shares" includes "stock." "The use of the term 'stock' merely denotes that the company has recognised the fact of the complete payment of the shares, and that the time has come when those shares may be assigned in fragments."

DEBENTURES (OR BONDS)

These are documents acknowledging that the holders are, to a specified amount, creditors of a company. Payment of interest on the debentures is part of the costs of the company, and is payable whether or not the company is making a profit. The debenture-holder can claim his interest just as the workman can claim his wages. On the other hand he has no voice in the management of the company. The debenture-holder may be a secured creditor through having either a *fixed* or a *floating* charge upon the company's property. The "floating" charge entitles him, if things go wrong, to fix upon assets that are continuously changing and sell them in satisfaction of his debt. The "fixed" charge is upon specific assets.

The debenture-holder who takes as his security a fixed charge—a mortgage on some specified property—runs the risk that the property may be worth little when he determines to close on it. He who takes a floating charge runs the risk, that, when he wishes to fix his charge, there is little to fix it on. For the floating security is an *equitable charge* upon the assets ; and a *legal charge* (which has priority) may have already been created on the assets.

Moreover, a floating charge created within *six months* of the beginning of a winding-up is valid only in regard to cash paid to the company at the time of creation of the charge, or subsequently. This rule does not apply if it can be shown that, at the time of creation of the floating charge, the company was solvent.

Debentures may be *perpetual*, no provision being made for their redemption, the loan being repaid only upon the winding up of the company, if at all. Or they may be *redeemable* at the end of a stated period, or at the option of the company. And they may be re-issued after redemption, unless the articles forbid the re-issue.

The Court may, if it thinks fit, enforce by a decree for specific performance a contract to take up debentures.

PREFERRED DEBTS

In a winding-up the following debts are payable before the debenture holder comes in—

1. *Rates and taxes*: due and payable within the twelve months before the winding-up.

2. *Wages or salary* of any clerk or servant: for services rendered during four months preceding the winding-up, and not exceeding fifty pounds.

3. *Wages of workman or labourer*; for services rendered within two months and not exceeding twenty-five pounds.

4. Payments under the Workmen's Compensation Act, 1925.

5. Payments under the Health and Unemployment Acts.

These preferred debts rank equally among themselves; and, if the assets are not enough to pay them in full, they all lose the same proportion.

RESTRICTING FREEDOM OF TRANSFER

The articles of a company may restrict freedom of transfer of shares. A private company is required to restrict the freedom. A public company usually takes powers to refuse to transfer shares not fully paid to one thought undesirable—one without means and therefore unable to answer calls, or an infant against whom calls cannot be enforced. Nor need the directors give a reason for refusing the transfer.

DEBENTURE CHARGES TO BE REGISTERED

Publicity in regard to the real position of a company is ensured by the enactment that charges are to be registered. The officials of a company incur penalties for failure to register. The lender, too, can register the charge; and he has a strong incentive to see to the registration. For, "the charges shall, so far as any security on the company's property is conferred, be void against the liquidator unless the prescribed particulars are delivered for registration within twenty-one days after the date of creation."

MEMBERS OF A COMPANY

The members are those who have subscribed the memorandum, or who have agreed to become members.

An infant may be a member. But, either during minority or

within a reasonable time after majority, he is entitled to repudiate his shares. If his shares, however, once had value in the market, he cannot recover money paid for them (*Steinberg* v. *Scala, Leeds*, 1922, Ch.).

One company (the "holding" company) may be a member and hold shares in another company (the "subsidiary" company).

A company cannot, however, by buying its own shares, become a member of itself. "It is inconsistent with the essential nature of a company that it should become a member of itself. It cannot be registered as a shareholder to the effect of becoming on the list of contributors in its own liquidation."

But it has been held that fully paid shares can be surrendered without leave of the Court provided the surrender does not involve a reduction of capital (*Rowell* v. *J. Rowell & Sons, Ltd.*, 1912).

A surrender will be void if it amounts to a purchase of the shares by the company, or if it is accepted for the purpose of relieving a member from his liabilities. A shareholder may transfer his shares to trustees in trust for the company by way of gift. This is not a surrender (*Cree* v. *Somervail*, 1879, A.C.).

Shares in a company can be held by an individual as trustee for the company, provided no funds of the company are used in acquiring them (*Kirby* v. *Williams*, 1929, Ch.). The trustee would have to be registered in his own right, but would be required to exercise his voting right in accordance with the directions of the company.

MODE OF CONDUCTING BUSINESS

Such control as the shareholders have over the company is exercised in *meetings*. "For the purpose of binding the company in its corporate capacity, individual assents given separately are not equivalent to the assent of the meeting."

The company is entitled to the protection afforded by a meeting, and by a resolution properly considered and carried, and duly recorded.

In general, the will of the majority prevails. But, for resolutions other than routine ones, a minority may prevent action. "A resolution shall be an extraordinary resolution when it has been passed by a majority of not less than three-fourths of such members as, being entitled so to do, vote in person or, where proxies are allowed, by proxy, at a general meeting of which notice specifying the intention to propose the resolution as an extraordinary resolution has been duly given." (Note that the members present and not voting are ignored for the purpose of determining whether or not the resolution is carried; if ten attend and three vote for and one votes against, the resolution is carried.) The same majority is needed for a *special* resolution.

VOTING

The chairman usually has a "casting" vote, a right when votes for and against are equal to determine one way or the other in regard to a question submitted to the meeting. He need not exercise the vote: if he does not, the motion is lost. It is the chairman's duty to decide how the voting has gone. Any one dissatisfied with the decision must take the appropriate steps to challenge it at once. If the voting is by show of hands, the dissatisfied party can demand a poll.

MEETINGS OF PUBLIC COMPANY

1. *A statutory* meeting, held within three months after the receipt of the Registrar's certificate enabling it to begin business. This meeting is, in effect, to discuss whether the flotation of the company has been a success.

2. *Extraordinary general* meeting, convened to consider and possibly pass an "extraordinary resolution."

3. *Annual general* meeting, to hear and approve of or criticise the directors' report, to consider accounts and a balance sheet, to declare dividends, and to elect directors and auditors. Such meeting must not be deferred more than fifteen months after the last general meeting.

NOTICE

The *usual* notice is seven days; and the seven days include the day of meeting but not the day on which notice is given.

For a *special resolution* there must be a notice in writing of at least twenty-one days. The notice must be "a fair, candid, and reasonable explanation of the business to be transacted. Otherwise the shareholder cannot decide whether or not it is worth while to be present." (Where, however, there is unanimity and no absentees any resolution is valid, even in the absence of notice.)

ADJOURNMENT OF MEETING

A meeting is adjourned: (1) when the requisite quorum fails to attend; (2) when the requisite quorum is no longer present ("a count out"); (3) when a resolution to adjourn has been carried.

When a meeting has been convened for some private purpose the convenors, or the chairman appointed by them, can adjourn the meeting even against the wishes of most present. The chairman of public meetings cannot, however, adjourn unless authorised to do so by the majority. If he should try to do so, those present can elect another chairman and continue the business. In *National Dwellings Society* v. *Sykes* (Ch. 1894), the judgment put the point thus: "The power which has been contended for is not within the scope of the authority of the chairman, namely, to stop the meeting at his own will and pleasure. He cannot say, after some particular business has been opened: 'I will have no more to do with it; I will not let this meeting proceed; I declare the meeting dissolved and I leave the chair.' The meeting by itself can resolve to go on with the business which the first chairman, forgetful of his duty or violating his duty, has tried to stop because the proceedings have taken a turn which he himself does not like."

SPECIAL RESOLUTION

This is needed—

1. To alter the memorandum with regard to the objects of the company.

2. To alter the articles.

3. To change the name of the company.

4. To create a reserve liability.

5. To reduce the share capital.

6. To make the liability of a director or manager an unlimited one.

7. To appoint inspectors to examine into the affairs of the company.

8. To wind up the company by the Court.

9. To wind up the company voluntarily.

10. To give the liquidators power to accept shares in another company as payment for the property of the company.

EXTRAORDINARY RESOLUTION

This is needed—

1. When it is desirable, the company being insolvent, to wind up voluntarily.

2. To give the liquidator power to pay any classes of creditors in full, to compromise with creditors and debtors of the company.

3. To dispose of the company's books and papers.

Copies of the resolutions are sent to the Registrar, whose duty it is to register them. Those having dealings with the company are thereby enabled to know the material facts about the financial position of the company.

If a resolution is passed at an *adjourned meeting*, the date of the resolution is that of the adjourned meeting, not of the original meeting.

PROXIES

Whether or not proxies are allowable depends upon the articles of the company. There is no Common Law right of voting by proxy. The articles may also determine that the proxy shall be a member.

A proxy can join in the demand for a poll, but he cannot (unless acting for a member of unsound mind and authorised by the committee in lunacy) vote on a show of hands. The proxy counts for *one* vote on a show of hands; on a poll he can vote himself, if entitled to do so, and also for those who have authorised him to do so.

MINUTES

Written records of the proceedings at a meeting are to be preserved in books specially provided. When signed by the chairman of the meeting, or of a succeeding meeting, the minutes are evidence of what took place.

A shareholder is entitled, if he chooses, to inspect the minute books at the registered office of the company, during at least two hours of the business hours.

BOOKS OF ACCOUNTS

Since the 1929 Act every company is under the statutory obligation (enforced by heavy fines upon the officials in default) to keep proper books of account.

There must also be prepared each year, for every public company, a profit and loss account and a balance sheet.

THE AUDITOR OF THE COMPANY

The 1929 Act makes abundantly clear that the auditor is the agent of the shareholders rather than of the directors. It is the

right of general meetings to appoint or remove auditors, and to
fix their remuneration. Section 134 explains the duty of the
auditor in relation to the balance sheet: "The auditors shall
make a report to the members on the accounts examined by them,
and on every balance sheet laid before the company in general
meeting during their tenure of office; and the report shall state
(a) whether or not they have obtained all the information and
explanations they have required; and (b) whether in their opinion,
the balance sheet referred to in the report is properly drawn up
so as to exhibit a true and correct view of the state of the
company's affairs." A positive injunction is given and an appropriate penalty prescribed if that injunction is not obeyed.

If, therefore, the auditor signs the report and he fails in his
duty, he is liable not to a civil action only but to a criminal
prosecution. It is true that the auditor is not expected to do
the impossible; he is not expected to penetrate into possible
fraud or wilful misleading by directors. It was judicially stated,
relating to the duties of an auditor: "The auditor is not appointed
to be a detective, or, as was stated, to approach his work with
suspicion or with the firm conclusion that there is something
wrong. He is a watchdog, not a bloodhound. If there is anything calculated to excite suspicion he should probe it to the
bottom; but in the absence of anything of that kind he is only
bound to be reasonably anxious and careful."

Or, again, in an action where an auditor was held liable to
repay to the company dividends that had been paid out of capital
the judgment stated: "It is not part of the auditor's duty to
give advice either to directors or shareholders. The auditor has
nothing to do with the prudence or imprudence of making loans
with or without security. His business is to ascertain what is the
true financial position of the company at the time of the audit,
and his duty is confined to that. But there comes the question:
How is he to ascertain such position? The answer is: By examining the books of the company. But he does not discharge this
duty by doing this casually and without taking any trouble to
see that the books of the company themselves show the company's true position. He must take reasonable care to ascertain
that they do. Unless he does this his duty will be worse than a
farce." These were cases where the civil remedy of damages was
sought. This remedy is still available; but there exists, in
addition, the criminal liability of the careless or dishonest
auditor.

WHO MAY NOT BE AN AUDITOR

The auditor is a check upon the directors, and the shareholders appoint him as a *person* whom they trust. Therefore none of these can be an auditor: (*a*) a director or officer of the company; (*b*) a partner or an employee of an officer of the company (unless the company is a private company); (*c*) a body corporate. This prohibition, introduced for the first time by the 1929 Act, emphasises the individual responsibility of the auditor. The prohibition extends to the offices of *liquidator* and *receiver*.

SECRET RESERVES

Apparently there is no legal objection to the practice of keeping undisclosed assets from which unexpected payments may be made. What was objected to and penalised in the Kylsant Case (1932) was the drawing from hidden reserves in order to give a misleading aspect of prosperity to the company.

BOARD OF DIRECTORS

The powers of the directors are given by the articles. The discretion necessarily conferred by the shareholders upon the board must be used in the interests of the company. For directors are in a fiduciary relationship towards the company.

It is the chairman's duty to conduct a meeting, and in a reasonably speedy fashion. He must see that no irregularity takes place and that the sense of the meeting is really obtained. On a vote he votes as a member.

CASTING VOTE

In order to obtain decisions it is usual for the articles to give the chairman, when votes for and against are equal, a second or "casting" vote. This vote is not a Common Law right of the chairman of a meeting; and, when the articles are silent, he has one vote only.

The chairman cannot stop a meeting unless authorised to do so by the majority of those present. If he should try to do so, the meeting—provided a quorum is present—may elect another chairman and conclude the business.

BUSINESS NAMES

A register open to inspection must be kept of the directors and managers of the company showing: (1) the present Christian name and the surname; (2) any former Christian name or surname;

(3) nationality; (4) nationality of origin (if other than the present nationality); (5) address; (6) other business if any. Companies registered after 1916 are subject to another restriction. The business documents of the company must also bear the directors names with the first four particulars. This rule applies also to all companies licensed under the Moneylenders Act, 1927.

CESSATION OF A COMPANY'S EXISTENCE

A company, though it may continue indefinitely, may end by: (1) being removed from the register, the Registrar being satisfied that no business is being done by the company; (2) amalgamation with another company; (3) winding-up.

The rules relating to winding-up are made by the Lord Chancellor with the concurrence of the President of the Board of Trade. The Board of Trade exercises control over the liquidator in winding-up.

Where the assets of the company are not enough to cover the costs of winding-up and to pay creditors, the liquidator is entitled to call upon shareholders to the extent of the liability they have assumed. The *shareholder* becomes a *contributory* and he may be asked to pay whatever part of his subscription is still unpaid.

One who has ceased to be a member for over a year is exempt from contributing. One who has been a member within a year before winding-up is called upon if the present members are unable to make the shares fully paid-up. But one who has transferred his shares is only liable for what his own transferee cannot pay, and only in respect of debts contracted before he ceased to be a member.

RULE OF EQUALITY PREVAILS

In a winding-up it seems that all shareholders, preference as well as ordinary, are—in the absence of express stipulations—entitled to participate in any surplus assets (*In re William Metcalfe and Sons, Limited*, C.A. 1932). After payment of debentures and all other debts, and the repayment of the paid-up capital, there remained a substantial sum. The preference shares had a right to fixed cumulative preference dividend, and also ranked as regards repayment of capital in priority to the ordinary shares. Were these preference shares in addition to come in upon a distribution of a surplus largely consisting of accumulated profits? The Court said, Yes; in spite of the fact that these profits might, at the director's option, have previously been paid on the ordinary shares. "There was nothing in memorandum or articles to displace the rule of parity. When the whole of the capital has been returned, both classes of shareholders are on the same footing, equally members and holding equal shares in the company, and they ought to be treated as equally entitled to its property."

BUILDING SOCIETIES

A striking development of late years is the borrowing for consumption as distinct from production. In housing it has developed far. The building society is in touch with the million; thousands are able to enjoy a comfortable house while paying for it; and a substantial body of law relating to building societies has come into being.

Like a joint-stock company, a building society is, in itself, a legal person, having rights and liabilities distinct from those of its members. These, indeed, may be constantly changing; the society itself has perpetual succession, and may endure indefinitely. Unlike the joint-stock company, however, building societies cannot specify for themselves their purposes. The scope of such societies is limited, by the Building Societies Act, 1874, to the one purpose "to raise by the subscription of members a stock or fund for making advances to members out of the funds of the society upon the security of freehold or leasehold estate by way of mortgage." A society that has obtained the Registrar's certificate obtains thereby the powers specified in the Act to enable it to fulfil its object. In effect, Parliament has delegated to the Registrar of Friendly Societies the power to create these artificial legal entities taking the powers conferred by the Act.

BORROWING POWERS

One such power, that of borrowing from other persons than its own members, is carefully guarded. A "terminating building society," designed to end when all its members have received advances enabling them to buy their homes, must not borrow more than two-thirds of the amount secured by mortgages from its members, or not exceeding twelve months' subscriptions on the shares in force at the time. That is, no more borrowing must be effected than what is amply covered by actual property in the hands of the society.

A "permanent society," into which new investing or borrowing members are constantly being enrolled, may borrow two-thirds

of the amount for the time being secured to the society by
members' mortgages. The design is, of course, to make certain
that no building society shall ever be other than perfectly solvent.

" ULTRA VIRES " ACTS

The doctrine of *ultra vires* obtains an excellent illustration
when applied to building societies. Briefly, the doctrine may be
expressed thus: an act done outside the powers conferred by
statute upon the society is, as regards the society, of no effect.
It is void, not because the act is illegal, but because the society
cannot do it. As a result, those who do the act, who borrow more
than the limited amount, who lend on other than the stipulated
security, are themselves responsible. They are responsible either
on the ground that, while purporting to act for the society, they
have really acted for themselves, or on the ground that they have
warranted an authority that they do not own.

In the famous *Amalgamated Society of Railway Servants* v.
Osborne, where it was decided that a trade union could not
spend its funds upon political objects, the position was clearly
put: "Companies incorporated by statute for special purposes,
and societies which owe their constitution and their status to
an Act of Parliament, having their objects and powers defined
thereby, cannot apply their funds for any purpose foreign to the
purpose for which they were established, or embark on any
undertaking in which they were not intended by Parliament to
be concerned."

This throws a quite heavy responsibility upon the directors of
a society. The society itself is not liable on any contract *ultra
vires*. Nor need it repay any money received as the result of
such a contract. But the officers are personally liable to third
parties, and are also responsible to the society itself for any loss
incurred. Equity gives, indeed, some degree of help to outsiders,
who have in good faith advanced to the society money that the
directors had no power to borrow. If any of the money so
borrowed has been expended in paying proper debts of the
society, then—although those who received the money had no
authority to bind the society—the lenders may in equity recover
from the company so much of that money as was expended in
paying debts of the company.

This right, an instance of the right of subrogation, whereby the
lender stands in the shoes of the creditor, was established in
The Blackburn Building Society v. *Cunliffe & Co.*, and is, of course,

only fair. It is what a court of conscience would impose as a duty upon one coming before the Court and petitioning for relief from a burden cast upon him by the Common Law.

CLUBS

An association like a social club partakes of the nature both of company and partnership. In one sense the committee acts as agent for the members. Yet it is clear that a member does not, simply by the act of joining a club, give the committee authority to pledge his credit for goods supplied to the club.

In one unsuccessful effort to make individual members responsible for debts incurred, it was said: "Clubs are associations of a peculiar nature. They are societies the members of which are perpetually changing. They are not partnerships; they are not associations for gain; and the factor that distinguishes them from other societies is that no member as such becomes liable to pay to the funds of the society, or to any one else, any money beyond the subscription required by the rules of the club to be paid so long as he remains a member. It is upon this fundamental condition, not usually expressed but understood by every one, that clubs are formed." (*Wise* v. *Perpetual Trustee Co.*, A.C., 1903.)

PROPRIETARY CLUBS

A club may, it is true, belong to an individual or a joint-stock company. Such a proprietor may act through officers of the club or through a committee. He, or it, remains the principal, responsible for the contracts of the agents. The members are under no personal liability for goods supplied, nor do they own property of the club.

MEMBERS' CLUB

This has no legal existence apart from the members. If it is to sue it can only do so by a member, suing on behalf of himself and all the other members. Similarly, one suing the club can do so by suing a member on behalf of the club. The funds of the club and its property belong to the members jointly. When a member obtains refreshments he consumes his own property, the other members releasing their interest on it upon terms fixed by the committee of management. It is not a sale for the purposes of the Licensing Acts. Joining the club is an implied undertaking to conform to the rules adopted for the orderly conduct of the club. One expelled by the committee acting in good faith and without malice has no legal redress provided he has had a fair hearing. For the Courts will not interfere in what is a domestic matter.

INTOXICANTS

When these are supplied to members or their guests, the club, whether a members' club or a proprietary club, must be registered. The secretary, or proprietor, gives each year a return of the club to the justices of petty sessions. The return states—

1. Name, objects, address of club.
2. Number of members.
3. Rules relating to—

(a) Election of members and terms of admission of temporary or honorary members.

(b) Terms of subscription.

(c) Hours of opening and closing.

(d) Cessation of membership.

(e) Mode of altering rules.

There must be kept upon the club premises a register of members and of the latest payment of subscriptions.

THE LICENSING ACT, 1910

This Act prescribes heavy penalties for default.

Upon complaint by any person that the club has been badly conducted, or that there have been illegal sales, or that the membership is below twenty-five, or other grounds specified in the Act, a justice of the peace has power to strike the club off the register.

A *members' club* has no need to take out an excise licence. For the dispensing of exciseable articles, upon conditions as to price and so on, to members is not a sale but merely a distribution to them of their own property. Nor does it matter whether the price charged to members is more or less than the cost price. The Board of Inland Revenue apparently considers the questions—

1. Is the body really a club, the members having gone through a proper form of election and paying a regular subscription?

2. Are the articles sold to members only? (In *Stevens* v. *Wood* a member of a working man's club was held liable for selling

without a licence in taking from a stranger, whose name he had written in the visitor's book, payment for the ale bought.)

3. Does any profit go to the club or to an individual?

In a members' club no guest must be permitted to pay for exciseable articles supplied to him; and where the club's rules permit of temporary or honorary membership, the rules giving the permission must be clearly expressed.

INSURANCE

Insurance is a contract whereby one who runs a risk procures, for a consideration called the premium, another who will run the risk for him. The person effecting the insurance must have what is called an "insurable interest." That is, he stands to lose money if the risk is realised. If he has not this insurable interest the contract is void. Indeed, it is now in marine insurance a criminal offence to enter into an insurance contract without a *bona fide* interest, or expectation of an interest, in the subject-matter of the insurance. In practice the terms "insurance" and "assurance" are interchangeable; but perhaps " assurance " is more correctly applied where life policies are concerned. For the event on which the policy depends is a certainty. In most insurances the uncertainty is as to *whether* the risk insured against will arise; in life insurance the uncertainty is as to *when* the event insured against will occur.

Insurance generally is dealt with in the Insurance Act of 1774. This Act forbids insurances on the lives of any persons unless the insurer has an insurable interest in those lives.

DEPOSITS REQUIRED FROM INSURANCE COMPANIES

The whole community is keenly interested that no claim under an insurance policy shall fail for want of funds. Every company is required, therefore, to keep deposited with the Paymaster-General £20,000 for each class of business carried on. The money is invested in securities approved by the Court and the dividends on the securities go to the insurance company.

Underwriters who are members of Lloyd's need deposit only £2,000. The underwriter's deposit with Lloyd's is, however, substantial; and insolvency is very unlikely.

The fund created for any class of business is to be "as absolutely the security of the policy holders of that class as though it belonged to a company carrying on no other business than assurance business of that class." It must not be applied, directly or indirectly, to any other contracts of the company.

Under Section 42 of the Road Traffic Act, 1930, a deposit of £15,000 is required from any company conducting insurances connected with the use of motor vehicles (including third-party risks).

INSURANCE CONTRACT

This is usually in a written "policy of insurance." The consideration is the "premium": the bargain struck is one whereby a risk is shifted from insured to insurer. The contract is distinct from a wager in this, that the interests of insured and insurer coincide : neither insurer nor insured wishes the risk to be realised. By means of the insurance the risk of an individual is merged into the risk of many : "Those whose fortune it shall be to have more than average success resign the overplus in favour of those who have less."

INDEMNITY

Apart from life and accident insurance all insurance contracts are contracts of indemnity. Life and accident insurance are for specified sums (irrespective of actual loss), and in neither are the rights of the insured transferred (subrogated) to the insurer. For, when an individual's life ceases or when his earning capacity diminishes through accident, no accurate measure of the loss is available. The insurance contract, therefore, stipulates for a fixed sum payable when the event insured against occurs. This fixed sum may be much more—as, indeed, it may be much less—than the actual loss sustained.

FULL DISCLOSURE OF MATERIAL FACTS

In an ordinary contract misrepresentation renders a contract voidable by the party deceived; in an insurance contract misrepresentation (or non-disclosure) renders a contract void. The proposal form is usually "the basis of the contract." In that event an inaccurate statement will make void the contract even though the statement is not material. And the insured must disclose to the insurer all "material facts," such facts as an underwriter is accustomed to take into consideration when determining (1) whether or not to accept the risk, (2) what premium to charge.

"The law as to a contract of insurance differs from that as to other contracts : concealment of a material fact, though made without any fraudulent intention, vitiates the policy." (*Ionides* v. *Pender*, Q.B. 1874.)

INSURABLE INTEREST

A person effecting an insurance must have a pecuniary interest in the person or thing insured. He must have benefit from the existence : prejudice from the destruction. Thus, a creditor may insure his debtor's life for the amount of the debt; and, provided he keeps up the premiums, he has a right to the amount upon the death even though the debt has been cancelled by payment.

INSURANCE POLICY AS SECURITY

A banker might insure the life of his debtor. For he has an insurable interest. In practice, however, it is the debtor that insures himself and uses his policy as a security for a loan. He may merely deposit the policy with his banker. The banker then has the rights of an equitable mortgagee; he can retain the policy until his debt is paid. Thus, where a depositor became bankrupt, it was held that the trustee in bankruptcy could not obtain the policy before satisfying the banker's claim (*Re Wallis*, K.B. 1902). Or the debtor may assign the policy in accordance with the 1867 Act, undertaking to keep the policy alive by payment of premiums and giving the banker a right to surrender the policy at its surrender value in case of need. The banker is then fully protected. The defect of the mere deposit, from the banker's point of view, is that in the absence of notice, payment by the company to the debtor would defeat the banker's claim.

DAYS OF GRACE

Assurance companies usually allow grace for the payment of renewal premiums. The insured is not entitled to rely upon this unless a clear statement, that such days are allowed, appears in the policy. For outside evidence to vary the terms of a written policy is not admissible. The contract expires when premiums are unpaid at the expiration of the days of grace (if any). But companies usually allow lapsed policies to be revived (on payment of premiums with interest). Again, however, the insured is not entitled to rely on this; for the company may, where the risk insured against has altered, decline the risk or accept it at an increased premium. "Days of Grace" as applied to the insurance premium are not the same as "Days of Grace" as applied to a bill of exchange: in the latter the extended time is a matter of statutory right; in the insurance premium it is, what the name suggests, a matter of favour.

ASSIGNMENT

The Policies of Insurance Act, 1867, allows a life policy to be assigned so that the assignee can claim upon it in his own name.

The assignment is made either by an indorsement on the policy, or by a separate document; written notice of the assignment must be given to the insurer, and he must give his certificate acknowledging the receipt of the notice. The assignee gets the rights of the assignor under the policy—no more; but also, of course, no less. Such an assignment may often serve as security for a loan.

AN INSURANCE CONTRACT IS ONE UBERRIMAE FIDEI

We have come to expect good faith in business dealings; and in the vast majority of transactions we are not disappointed. *Caveat emptor* is the general rule, it is true; but we are not thereby to be constantly and greatly suspicious. We can rely upon the performance of what has been promised to us, and are not forced to be for ever on guard against possible sharp practice. Without good faith, shown towards others and received from them, business would be a poor, cramped thing; and the Courts insist upon straightforwardness in contracts.

In no class of cases is the insistence more serviceable than in insurance cases. The amount of foreign insurance effected in London is enormous; and the main reason for this is the well-justified confidence that the insurers will do all, perhaps even a little more than, they have promised. The insurers are entitled to fairness in return.

In the absence of the utmost good faith an insurance contract may be held void. An illustration is provided by *Holt's Motors* v. *South-East Lancashire Insurance Co.* (Court of Appeal, 1930). The appeal of the claimants under an insurance policy was unanimously dismissed by the Court of Appeal. The claimants had, through their broker, proposed an insurance to the Bell Co., but this company declined the proposal "owing to information received." The brokers, in misguided but well-intentioned politeness, paraphrased this into a statement that the Bell Co. did not cover commercial cars. The brokers, however, placed the insurance with the Lion Co. But the Lion Co., at the end of the year, wrote that they could not invite renewal. This, it would seem, is the insurance way of saying: "You cannot go on with us; we shall not renew your insurance." That is was so understood is clear; because their brokers sent the notice to Holt's, adding "from which you will see that, owing to claims' experience, they cannot invite renewal." This certainly was a fact that possible insurers would like to know.

Such was the position when insurance was accepted by the company sued, the proposal form containing a number of questions, the answers to which were to be "the basis of the contract for the insurance hereby intended to be made." One question was: "Has any company or underwriter declined to insure you?" and the answer appended was "No." The proposer declares, at the end of the proposal form: "I warrant the truth of the foregoing" a declaration that effectively disposes of the possible excuse of ignorance.

EFFECT OF WARRANTY

That a lie is told in ignorance makes an alteration in its moral aspect; ignorance does not, however, excuse a breach of warranty. For the warranty implies that the statements governed by it are true in fact. It is not enough that there is absence of fraud. In other words, an innocent misrepresentation avoids the policy as effectively as a fraudulent one.

Was the answer of the proposer true in accordance with the warranty? The Court thought not. The fact that the proposers were given a fictitious reason for the Bell Co.'s declining did not make their answer true. The Lion Co., certainly, had not declined in set terms; you can hardly decline before you are asked. But then, in the insurance world a statement that "owing to claims' experience they will not invite renewal" would be regarded by everybody as declining. The claimant, therefore, failed.

A striking illustration is afforded by *Newsholme Bros.* v. *Road Transport and General Insurance Co.* (K.B. 1929). It does not introduce any new principle of law. It does, however, reiterate the rule that the agent is employed to further the interest of his principal, and that the agent's seeking to further his own ends is not to prejudice his principal. An agent for the defendant insurance company received from the plaintiffs true answers to questions in a proposal form. The agent, however, possibly in order that the insurance should go through and he thereby be enabled to earn his commission, mis-stated the answers in filling up the form. Now, he had no authority to fill up the form nor did the defendant company know that he had filled it. The plaintiffs signed the form, a premium was accepted, a policy was duly issued, and an accident happened to the motor-bus insured. The plaintiffs claimed under their policy. The defendants repudiated the claim on the ground that the written answers were untrue; and when the case came to the Court of Appeal, it was held that they were entitled to do this.

In Biggar's case (*Biggar* v. *Rock Life Assurance Co.*, K.B. 1902) the insurance agent was held to be, in his filling of the form, the agent of the insured not of the insurer. Where the party signs and acquiesces in a form, without choosing to read it, he must be considered as adopting the proposals. It was in the power of the assured by reasonable diligence to defeat the fraudulent intent. A signing of the application without reading it or hearing it read is inexcusable negligence; for a party is bound to know what he signs. It is well to have a comprehensive rule if at all possible; and there is no hardship in holding a man answerable for the statements to which he affixes his signature.

CARE IN INTERPRETING TERMS

The wording of a policy may introduce another difficulty: there may very well, without bad faith on either side, be a difference of opinion between insurer and insured about the extent of risk carried by the insurer.

It may, indeed, be that—tax our ingenuity as we may in order to frame the appropriate documents—we fail to anticipate all eventualities. An occurrence not contemplated has led the two parties to take differing views of the agreement entered upon. So with this insurance case, *Rogerson* v. *Scottish Automobile and General Insurance Co.* (C.A. 1930). The plaintiff was insured in respect of a car, and also in respect of "any car at the time of the accident being used instead of the insured car": if the insured's Baby Austin were laid up through a collision he could borrow his friends Rolls-Royce, a more dangerous implement. Now, the plaintiff sold the insured car, bought another, had an accident with the new car, and claimed under his policy. The insurers disputed the claim upon the ground that the policy did not include the insurance of a car bought to replace the insured car; such new car could not be regarded as being used "instead of the insured car." And the Appeal Court supported this contention.

DEFINITION OF MARINE INSURANCE

"Marine insurance is a contract by which one party, in consideration of a premium, engages to indemnify another against a contingent loss by making him a payment in compensation if, or when, the event shall happen by which the loss is to accrue."

The insurer, whether company or individual underwriter, is engaged not so much in assuming another's business risk, as in cancelling that risk by combining it with many others. Through his agency the few failures are set off against the many successes, the few wrecks against the many safe arrivals to port. The individual is uncertain; the average, where large numbers are concerned, is comparatively certain. The large number contributes to a common fund. They voluntarily suffer a small loss in order that a great loss, if it should fall upon one among them, shall be made good.

"EXCEPTED RISKS"

The shipper of goods desires safe carriage. The shipowner offers it, but with certain "excepted risks"—risks that the modern contract of affreightment has enormously extended. For apart from express stipulations, the Common Law obligations of the shipowner are onerous: he can excuse himself from delivery of merchandise entrusted to him in the same condition as when he received it, only by showing that his failure was due to *act of God* or of *the King's enemies* or to the *fault of the consignor himself*. Now, a loss occurs through "act of God" when it is due to natural causes, directly and exclusively, without human intervention: and the carrier must show that he could not have prevented it by any amount of foresight and care reasonably to be expected of him. He will have difficulty in showing this; and another Common Law excuse—of restraint by the King's enemies—is rarely available. The Carriage of Goods by Sea Act, 1924, however, has added a great many statutory immunities to the meagre ones of Common Law: *fire, perils of the sea, quarantine restrictions, riots*, and *civil commotions*, and so on. A multitude of pleas is thus available for the shipowner. The goods being lost through the realisation of one of these excepted risks, the shipowner has negatived liability. It is against such risks that the shipper seeks protection by way of insurance.

The earning of freight similarly depends upon the successful end of the adventure. The owner may have incurred much outlay and have had his ship long embarked upon the venture; and the venture may be frustrated in the end. The owner has a prospect of large gains. Wishing in no event to be a loser, he guards against the contingency by paying an underwriter part of the anticipated gains.

RIGHT OF SUBROGATION

If, therefore, the assured obtains an indemnity from the insurer, any rights of recovery that the assured may have against a third party pass to the insurer. This transfer of rights is "*subrogation*"; and it is to be noted that not merely is the insurer entitled to be put in the place of the assured for the purpose of enforcing rights of action, but he is to have all other rights that the assured might have had to diminish the loss. And if the assured has given up rights that, being exercised, would have lessened the loss, then he may be compelled to make good to the insurer the full value of those rights, unless he had made full disclosure of this fact.

IMPLIED TERMS

There are, too, mutual understandings that have all the force of expressed terms in the insurance contract. The assured, by the very fact of proposing a vessel for insurance, warrants by implication that he will take reasonable diligence to ensure seaworthiness so that the vessel insured is reasonably fit "as to repairs, equipment, and crew, and, in all other respects, to encounter the ordinary perils of the voyage insured at the time of sailing upon it." One need not inquire whether the assured did exercise such diligence. Unless he did, the underwriter is absolved from liability. Every ship insured on a *voyage* policy sails under this implied warranty.

Where special circumstances modify the meaning of this term, such special circumstances must be stated. If the underwriters then undertake the risk they are liable.

Another implied warranty, become prominent in recent years, is that the adventure is a lawful one and that, so far as the insured can control, it will be carried out in a lawful manner.

PURPOSE OF ANSWERS TO INSURER'S QUESTIONS

But the principle, that the answers of the insured must be scrupulously accurate in order that the insurer may know what risk he is running, must be taken reasonably. An insurer is not to escape his liability through a quibble. In *Morgan* v. *Provincial Insurance Co., Ltd.* (K.B. 1932), the arbitrator, the King's Bench Judge, and the three members of the Court of Appeal were at one in declaring that the insured was entitled to recover, even though his answers were not minutely correct. The proposal form, which was in regard to a motor lorry, contained the question: "State (*a*) the purposes (in full) for which the vehicle will be used; and (*b*) the nature of the goods to be carried." The answer was: (*a*) Delivery of Coal; (*b*) Coal." The policy issued had the usual clause *that its conditions must be observed*, and that it was a condition precedent *that the statements in the proposal were true, correct, and complete*. The plaintiff, after the issue of the policy, made a contract for hauling timber and used the lorry for timber as well as coal. The collision, in respect of which the claim arose, occurred at the end of a day's work during which both timber and coal had been carried. Only a small load of coal was, however, on the lorry at the time. The Court of Appeal held that the statements were not warranties: if they had been, any deviation, however innocent, would have been fatal to the claim. They were merely statements of the kind of work the insured intended it to do. The House of Lords concurred.

CERTIFICATE OF INSURANCE

A certificate of insurance is not to be regarded as equivalent, for the purposes of a c.i.f. contract, to the insurance policy. In *Diamond Alkali Export Corporation* v. *Bourgeois* (1921), 3 K.B. 443, the sellers under such a contract had tendered to the buyer a document in the terms: "This is to certify that on the 8th of November, 1920, this company insured under policy No. 2319 for D.A. Horan 5790 in 280 bags 58 per cent dense soda ash . . . This certificate represents and takes the place of the policy and conveys all the rights of the original policy-holder." The buyers were held entitled to reject this, the judgment declaring, "a document of insurance is not a good tender in England under an ordinary c.i.f. contract unless it be an actual policy and unless it falls within the provisions of the Marine Insurance Act, 1906."

The fact that it is customary to accept such a certificate or to accept a broker's cover note (a printed form issued pending the preparation of a policy) to the same effect does not alter the matter.

THE INSURANCE BROKER

The insurance contract is usually effected through a broker, and custom, now embodied in statute law (Marine Insurance

Act, Section 53), has made the insurance broker different from other agents in respect of legal liability. Ordinarily, when an agent has made a contract for his principal he drops out of the matter; he cannot sue, nor can he be sued. But the position in marine insurance is peculiar; the broker is the person to whom alone the underwriter can look for payment of premiums, though the insured may, in the event of loss, sue the underwriter. Against his liability the broker has a lien upon the policy issued in respect of the amount due to him from his principal.

GAMBLING POLICIES

Marine Insurance (Gambling Policies) Act, 1909, makes it a criminal offence to enter into a contract of marine insurance without a *bona fide* interest, or possibility of interest, in the subject-matter insured. No man is to put himself into a position where he would be better pleased with the failure than with the success of a maritime adventure.

EFFECT OF " SLIP "

The "slip," on which the insurance broker writes in short form the risk insured, is considered binding by insurers. But, in face of the words of the Act, it is not the policy. It is merely evidence that a contract has been made. Section 21 (Marine Insurance Act, 1906) enacts: "A contract of marine insurance is deemed to be concluded when the proposal was accepted by the insurer, whether the policy be then issued or not; and for the purpose of showing when the proposal was accepted, reference may be made to the slip or covering note or other customary memorandum of the contract, although it be unstamped." (See page 880.)

THE INSURANCE POLICY

1. Contrary to the usual rule, that when the subject matter of a contract has perished a contract in relation to it is void, the Marine Insurance Act enacts: "Where the loss has occurred before the contract is concluded, the risk attaches, unless at such time the assured was aware of the loss and the insurer was not." This is implied in the words of the policy "lost or not lost."

2. Recently a F.C.S. clause ("free of capture and seizure") has appeared in policies, over-riding the assumption of a risk of what "Men-of-War and enemies do." The inserted clause usually

runs: "Warranted nevertheless free of capture, seizure, and detention, and the consequences thereof, or of any attempt thereat, piracy excepted, and also from all consequences of hostilities or warlike operations, whether before or after declaration of war."

3. The words "all other perils, losses, and misfortunes" must be read as applicable only to those of the same class (*Ejusdem Generis*) as the ones specified in the paragraph. (See page 892.)

4. The "sue and labour" clause gives to the assured a permission to incur expenses in the effort to minimise a loss that has occurred. Such effort should, we may assume, result also in a lessening of the underwriter's loss.

5. The "waiver" clause is necessary. Otherwise an effort of the insured to save the vessel after he had given notice of abandonment might be construed as a waiving of his notice; or an attempt of the underwriters to save might be construed as an acceptance of abandonment.

6. The memorandum (the addition following N.B.) is a late importation into the policy. Goods liable to damage from other causes than the chances of the sea voyage are placed outside the underwriter's risk.

ASSIGNABILITY OF POLICY

A marine insurance policy is *assignable*. The assignee may sue upon the policy in his own name; nor—different in this respect from policies of life insurance—is there need to give to the underwriter formal notice of the assignment. It is to be noticed, however, that the assignee assumes only rights under the policy that could have been exercised by the assignor. Whatever defence would have been valid against the assignor is also valid against the assignee.

The underwriter's disclaimer of liability for damages sustained by collision with things other than vessels prompts the shipowner to have recourse to a "protection and indemnity association"; and occasionally the fixing of liability raises an interesting point.

THE F.P.A. CLAUSE

A usual clause limiting the cargo underwriter's liability is the "Free from Particular Average (F.P.A.) Clause." This clause extends the exemption—apart from the exceptions noted in the N.B (the memorandum)—to all partial losses other than general average, unless the vessel meets with a casualty. The warranty does not exempt the underwriter from charges, under the "Sue and Labour Clause," incurred in saving the subject-matter from loss for which he holds himself liable.

STATUTORY LIMITATION OF EXCEPTED RISKS

Since the Carriage of Goods by Sea Act, 1924, the number of excepted risks is limited. Even if the Charter Party or the Bill of Lading contain them, they are of no effect. Article III, Rule 8, enacts: "Any clause, covenant, or agreement in a contract of carriage relieving the carrier or the ship from liability for loss or damage to or in connection with goods arising from negligence, fault, or failure in the duties and obligations provided in this article or lessening such liability otherwise than as provided in these rules shall be null and void and of no effect." The number of excepted perils is still great, however, and makes it well nigh imperative on the shipper to insure.

FIRE INSURANCE

This is the typical contract of indemnity: the insured person, who has suffered loss from fire recovers from the insurer no more than the amount that will cover the loss. The maximum amount claimable is fixed in the policy; and, if this maximum amount should be less than the real value of the thing insured, the owner (or occupier) is understood to insure the balance himself. Thus if a building worth £10,000 is insured for £5,000 the insurer would be called upon to pay £5,000 in the event of a total loss, and for partial loss in proportion. (That is, he would in this case pay only half the amount.) Conversely, if a thing is insured for more than its value (if, for instance, two policies were effected by parties having an interest in the property insured) only the actual loss could be recovered. The loss being covered by one insurance company there would be a claim for contribution from the other company. That is, each company would bear half the loss incurred.

Since the contract is one of indemnity merely, the person insured—on being compensated by the insurer—relinquishes to the insurer any means available for mitigating the loss. Thus, any salvage, where insurance payment has been made as for a total loss, belongs to the insurer; any rights that the insured has against the person causing the loss become the rights of the insurer. The insurer stands in the shoes (is *subrogated* to) the insured.

This does not, however, apply to a life policy. Provided that an insurable interest exists at the time of effecting the insurance, it does not matter that the insurable interest ceases during the currency of the policy. Provided the premiums are kept up, the full amount insured for can be recovered upon the death. That is, no question of the amount of loss sustained by the death arises. Thus, a man may insure his debtor's life for a sum equal to the amount of debt, and may keep up the insurance though the debt has been paid. The contingency upon which a payment on a life assurance is made is also different from the contingency upon which a payment on an indemnity contract is made. In the first the event upon which payment depends is bound to happen; the doubtful point is *when*. In the second the event upon which payment depends may not happen; the doubtful point is *whether*.

In *Darrell* v. *Tibbits* (Q.B. 1880) the defendant was a landlord who had insured his houses against fire (including gas explosions) with the plaintiff. A steam-roller broke the gaspipes in a street, thus causing an explosion in one of the houses. The tenant, on a repairing lease, expended the money obtained as compensation from the Brighton Corporation on the necessary repairs. The landlord, therefore, lost nothing; and the insurers sought the return of the money paid under the policy. They succeeded: "If the landlord had been allowed to keep the money he would be not merely indemnified but paid twice over."

WHO HAS AN INSURABLE INTEREST?

One who would suffer a monetary loss if the event insured against happened has an insurable interest. Thus a trustee has, for the purpose of insurance, an insurable interest in the property held in trust; a carrier has an insurable interest in the goods carried by him; a pawnbroker has an insurable interest in his pledges. For all would be required to make good a loss that occurred. So, too, when an insurance company has insured property, it may reinsure with another company. It seems, however (*Maccura* v. *Northern Assurance Co.*, A.C. 1925), that a shareholder has no insurable interest in any particular asset of the company.

The question of insurable interest arose in *Piper* v. *Royal Exchange Assurance Co.* (K.B. 1932). The plaintiff had bought in Oslo a yacht at a "bargain price" of £1,000. The terms of sale included delivery here in the condition in which she was bought, the sellers insuring it for the voyage. For some reason the plaintiff also insured the yacht; it suffered damage; and the company paid the claim made. The yacht was valued in the policy at £2,500. Later, during repairs, two fires broke out and claims were made. The company resisted payments of these claims, on the ground that the excessive over-insurance amounted to concealment of a material fact and so avoided the policy. The company further counter-claimed for the money formerly paid, on the ground that at the time of the loss the plaintiff had no insurable interest in the thing insured. Any loss would have fallen on the sellers.

The company succeeded both on the claim and the counter-claim: "At the material time the plaintiff had no insurable interest in the yacht. On the ground of payment by mistake the defendants were entitled to recover the sum paid; and I give judgment for them on the counter-claim.

" As regards the claim for fire, although I have great suspicion, the onus of showing that the fires were not accidental was on the defendants. I do not think they have discharged it. The defence has not established that the fire was caused on purpose. But I am satisfied that the fire claim must be defeated on the ground of gross over-valuation and non-disclosure of the fact when the policy was taken out, by which time the plaintiff knew that the yacht was really unsaleable."

ALTERING A RISK AND ITS EFFECT

It is usually an express condition of the contract that, during the currency of the policy, the risk assured against shall not be increased (or modified) by—

1. Doing anything to the goods, or to the building housing them that would augment the risk of fire.

2. Removing the goods into another building.

3. Assigning the goods (unless by will).

RULES RELATING TO FIRE INSURANCE

Rules relating to fire insurance are—

1. Where an insured pays a premium to insure a greater value than the property insured, he can recover nothing more (upon a total loss) than the actual value. If, for instance, by an oversight, insurance is made in two offices, the offices share the loss.

2. Where an insured pays a premium covering only part of the actual value, the assumption is that he has decided to bear the uncovered risk himself. If, therefore, a loss occurs he has a

valid clause against the insurance for a proportionate amount only. Thus where goods are valued at £30,000, but insurance is effected for £20,000 and a loss of £3,000 occurs, the amount due from the underwriters is £2,000.

3. Though a *life insurance policy* may be assigned by a deed of assignment notice of which is given to the insurer, and a *marine insurance policy* may be assigned simply by endorsing the policy, no notice being necessary to the insurer, a *fire insurance policy* cannot be assigned without the previous assent of the insurer. It is, however, enacted (by Section 47 of the *Law of Property Act,* 1925), that where money becomes payable to a vendor of property (who has made a contract for sale but has not yet completed the transfer by a formal conveyance) he shall receive the money on behalf of the purchaser. When the sale is completed this money must be paid to the purchaser. This enactment would have made the £330 (in dispute in the Castellain case above) payable by the insurer, but to the buyer—not to the seller who had insured the property.

4. As in the other contracts of indemnity, an insurer who pays upon a loss is entitled to every right of the insured arising upon the occurrence. This is the right of *subrogation* : "A legal process arising out of the right of one party on payment of compensation to another to avail himself of any rights and remedies possessed by the other, against a third party in connection with the event which gave rise to the compensation." Thus X warehouses his goods and insures them against fire ; they are destroyed by fire through the negligence of the warehouseman ; the insurer pays the value, but has a corresponding claim against the warehouseman.

A curious illustration of the working of this right was afforded by *Midland Insurance Co.* v. *Smith* (Q.B. 1881). The house insured was purposely burnt by the wife of the insured—without his privity, however. Against any one except his wife the insured would have had a valid claim for damages. He could not, however, sue his wife ; and therefore the insurance company could not. The insurance company had to pay the full amount claimed, and had no means of mitigating their loss.

5. If a building is burnt in the Metropolis any person interested (insurer or other) may demand that the insurance money be spent in repairing or in rebuilding the structure. This is "in order to deter and hinder ill-minded persons from wilfully setting their houses or other buildings on fire, with a view of gaining to

themselves the insurance money" (Fire Prevention (Metropolis) Act, 1774).

6. Damages done by the Metropolitan Fire Brigade "in the due execution of their duties, shall be deemed to be damage by fire within the meaning of any policy of insurance against fire" (Metropolitan Fire Brigade Act, 1865).

7. As in other insurance contracts the party proposing the insurance, who is assumed to know more of the risk assured against than the insurer, is under the obligation to make the fullest disclosure. Otherwise, the contract is void, and his premiums liable to retention. Moreover, where the answers on the proposal form are stated to form the *basis* of the contract, it seems that an erroneous answer will avoid the contract even though the truth or untruth of the answer is really immaterial. So the House of Lords decided in *Dawson* v. *Bonmin* (1922). The appellants had insured their motor-lorry against fire, the proposal form having been filled up by an insurance agent and handed to the appellants' secretary for signature. The form asked for particulars including (2) *proposer's address*; (4) *full address at which the vehicle will usually be garaged.* The one address was given for both particulars though, in fact, the garage was elsewhere than at the proposer's address. The secretary did not notice the inaccuracy. The Lord Chancellor said: "The meaning and effect of the 'basis clause' is that any untrue statement in the proposal shall void the policy; and, if that be established, the question of materiality has not to be considered."

8. The fact that the withholding of a material fact is unintentional is no excuse for non-disclosure: "it is well established that the law as to a contract of insurance differs from that as to other contracts, and that a concealment of a material fact, though made without any fraudulent intention, vitiates the policy."

REPLACEMENT CLAUSE

For their own protection the insurers against loss from fire usually stipulate that, as an alternative to paying the amount claimed in money, they may reinstate the property insured.

HUSBAND'S INSURANCE POLICY IN FAVOUR OF WIFE

Section 11 of the Married Women's Property Act, 1882, deals with money payable under an insurance policy, on the husband's life, but expressed to be for the wife's benefit. Such money does not form part of the husband's estate, nor is it chargeable with his debts. Moreover, even if the wife dies before the husband, the money payable does not revert to the husband; it remains as part of the wife's estate. This was decided in *Cousins* v. *Sun Life Assurance Society* (C.A. 1932), where the effect of Section 11 was considered. "A policy of insurance effected by any man on his own life, and expressed to be for the benefit of his wife . . . shall create a trust, and the moneys payable under any such policy shall not, so long as any object of the trust remains unperformed, form part of the estate of the insured or be subject to his debts."

It was at first thought that the wife's interest was dependent upon her surviving her husband. But the Court of Appeal decided that no such dependence existed: "The trust is created in favour of the wife; she takes a vested interest as soon as the trust is created; and there is nothing to imperil that interest. No money, surrender value or any other, could revert to the husband; such money was payable to the wife's executors."

THIRD-PARTY RISKS

Third-party risks have been much discussed as a result of the compulsory insurance enjoined by the Road Traffic Act of 1930. Its initiation was a long overdue reform; the person injured by a reckless or incompetent motor driver is not now balked of his remedy merely because the culpable person is not worth suing. Fear was that this part of the Act would be difficult to carry out. But, through the energetic co-operation of the insurance companies—themselves keenly interested in the matter—the difficulties were quickly overcome. "Certificates of Security" are now in the hands of all insured motorists. One contingency still remains that would deprive the wronged party of remedy. This is the fact that, if the driver at fault dies before a legal settlement is made, the injured person is left without legal remedy. This contingency results from the Common Law rule that a personal action dies with either of the parties to the cause of the action (*actio personalis moritur cum persona*). An action for a wrong must be begun while both the wronged and the wrongdoer are alive; and, if either party dies before a verdict has been entered, the action abates. This Common Law rule—which the utmost ingenuity could not justify—has already been greatly modified in many directions. There is certainly no reason why it should not be modified in regard to third-party risks. All that is needed is a short supplementary Act to the effect that the death of a person responsible for the accident should not relieve an insurance company of liability. At present, the anomalous situation exists that the power of the injured to get compensation depends upon whether or not the injurer himself dies : where personal injuries are sustained by a third party owing to the negligent driving of the owner, and that owner dies before a verdict has been entered, the injured party's right against the motorist is lost and the insurance company is freed from liability.

DAMAGES IN THIRD-PARTY RISKS

One unexpected, but not unnatural, result of the compulsory insurance requirement in the Road Traffic Act of 1930 is this. Juries are likely to award heavy damages to those injured by careless motorists. For they know that an insurance company, presumably well supplied with funds, will pay. When juries were not allowed—as is the case still in ordinary actions—to know whether or not a defendant was insured, they were more inclined to hold the balance even between the claimant and the one liable. Appeals as to excessive damages will, therefore, increase ; and it seems that the Court of Appeal regards itself (since *Johnson* v. *G.W.R.*, K.B. 1904) as having a considerable power of review and reduction of a jury's verdict. It was once necessary to establish, in order to obtain reduction, that reasonable men could not have awarded the amount challenged. It is now enough to show that the jury must have taken into account, in assessing the damage, matters irrelevant. That the defendant was insured and that, consequently, he will not be required to pay, is clearly a matter irrelevant ; and it would be unfair to the insurance company, which technically is not a party and cannot plead hardship, not to admit an unbiased review.

ACCIDENT INSURANCE

The risk of *injury resulting from accident*—from a fortuitous and unexpected happening—can be insured against. For here, too, averages can be struck. And the "accident" insured against may be of a limited, specified class—to a passenger by rail, for instance —or may be generic, extending to all except "natural causes." The policy may also provide that, in the event of death, the accident has been the direct and sole cause of the death.

In any event the advice "Read your policy" is sound. For both insured and insurer have their legal rights and obligations limited by the express words of the policy, of the written contract of insurance.

"Accident," too, is a term not easily definable; and the Courts have often enough been asked to say whether or not death or injury resulted from such an accident as the policy contemplated. Thus, the Court held that an injury, brought about by a bicycle ride—there being no fall or collision, nothing that was not intended by the rider—was not accidental. Nor was it an "accident" when a man, having a weak heart, injured it by running for a train. On the other hand, if something happens not intended by the insured, there has been an "accident": a man used a pole to close a window; the pole slipped, and he was thrown against a table, injuring his kidneys; this was an accident (*Scott* v. *General Accident Assurance Co.*, K.B. 1905. (It may be worth noting, too, that the "accident" is connected with the person insured.) It does not necessitate an untoward happening to the railway or the locomotive to constitute an accident to a railway passenger. If, for instance, he slips when alighting from the compartment, that is enough to constitute the accident insured against.

PLATE-GLASS INSURANCE

This, a quite usual form of insurance, may contain exceptions leading to great contention. A common one is that the company will not be liable when the damage has been "caused directly by or arising from civil commotion or rioting." Another exception may be fire. For the insurance is essentially one against breakage. In *Marsden* v. *City and County Assurance Co.* (C.P. 1865), the plaintiff's shop-front was insured against "loss or damage originating from any cause whatsoever, except fire . . ." A fire broke out on adjoining premises; the fire slightly damaged the rear of the plaintiff's shop, but did not approach the front; a mob, attracted by the fire, tore down the shop-shutters for the purpose of looting and broke the glass. It was held that the plaintiff was entitled to compensation, since the fire was not the proximate cause of his loss: "The assembling of the crowd was caused by the fire; and but for the fire probably the plaintiff's windows would not have been broken. But the breakage was not caused by the fire; it was the result of the plaintiff's attempt to save his stock and furniture, coupled with the desire of the mob to seize what they could lay their hands on."

A policy specifies the nature and extent of the glass insured and the premiums are fixed in accordance. As would be anticipated glass that is stained or is otherwise (by lettering or painting) more valuable than the ordinary plate glass bears a higher premium.

BURGLARY INSURANCE

The burglary policies issued in relation to *private dwellings* usually cover also the risks of house-breaking (a day crime) and larceny without house-breaking. Where a plural tenancy exists or where a flat is not self-contained, larceny is probably excluded. The premiums are based on the value of the total contents. Where valuables—such as gold or silver articles or jewellery—make up more than a third of the value, an added premium is charged. The risk insured against includes also the risk of damage done by burglars in breaking into the house.

For *business premises* the risks undertaken by the insurer are usually more restricted; and the premiums vary widely with the nature of the stock. "Actual violent and forcible entry to the premises" may be one condition of payment of compensation.

PROFITS INSURANCE (CONSEQUENTIAL INSURANCE)

Loss of profits from a specified cause, fire, for example, is insured against by some companies. One may say, indeed, that when practically any risk calculable in some degree exists, then either the companies or more or less adventurous underwriters of Lloyd's are prepared to insure against it. One particular type is that of *Use and Occupancy Insurance*.

USE AND OCCUPANCY INSURANCE

When business is interrupted by fire or other unforeseen event a goodwill laboriously built up may be greatly impaired; and, of course, anticipated profits are not realised. The risk is guarded against by a *business interruption indemnity insurance*. Such an insurance is peculiarly acceptable to the makers of proprietary goods (especially when these are being extensively advertised under continuing contracts) to hotel proprietors, laundry keepers, to theatres, and to various public utilities. Full indemnity usually provides for payment for a year's estimate of profits together with expenses that continue despite the interruption of business.

FIDELITY INSURANCE

The Courts are reluctant to allow a man himself to be indemnified against the results of his own wrongful acts; but they raise no objection to his arranging that others shall be indemnified. Employers may have persons in positions of confidence ; they can insure against fraud or embezzlement by such persons. They may also require the employee to insure : in the latter event the employee makes the bargain with the insurance company, paying the premiums and acceding to the conditions required—including, usually, the giving of satisfactory references ; the benefit of the policy is for the employer. The employer's statement to the insurers is the basis of the contract. This statement normally includes the system of checking used ; and the consent of the insurers is needed for any alteration of such system.

Instead of an individual insurance, the insuring company may give a collective guarantee for the whole staff.

PROPERTY OWNERS' INDEMNITY

Another insurance countenanced against a person's wrongful acts is that against the risk borne by property holders of having to pay compensation for damage done by their property. Slates or copings may fall and cause injury to persons or damage to another's property ; there may be defective staircases or defective drains involving the owner of the property in liability to compensate. The policy covers the risks, the premiums being based upon the nature of the property and the risks insured against.

COUPON INSURANCE

This, offered often by newspapers to their subscribers, or by the sellers of "proprietary articles," is valid and gives an enforceable right to the person accepting the offer. The acceptance may consist of filling up a form and the sending of the form to a specified address—the insurances offered by the makers of diaries are usually of this type. Or it may simply consist in buying the paper or the article (see the case of *Carlill* v. *Carbolic Smoke Ball Co.*, p. 693). The risks insured against vary indefinitely, and no useful purpose can be served by an attempt to enumerate them. It is enough to say that the Courts will enforce the promises made when the insured person fulfils the conditions prescribed ; and that, as always when one party expresses the terms of the contract and the other party merely signifies his acceptance, where there is an ambiguity the interpretation is in favour of the party who accepts. Words are interpreted more strongly against the party whose words they are.

HOUSE PURCHASE AND INSURANCE

An interesting innovation in insurance business is the method whereby an occupier, who is buying his dwelling by means of a series of instalment payments, obtains the advance on mortgage from his building society and couples with it an insurance policy of a special type. One clause of the policy stipulates that, in the event of the insured's death, payments for the house shall cease. The burden of debt is thereby lifted from the shoulders of his dependants.

GROUP INSURANCE

This is an interesting extension of life insurance to groups of industrial workers. In the United States it has a great vogue; and it exists to some extent in this country. By means of a single premium covering his whole staff an employer effects an insurance on the life of each person in his employment. There may, too, be additional benefits, covering, for instance, sickness or accident; and there may be a method of obtaining contributions from employees. Such "group insurance," in other words, supplies a substitute for the National Insurance that has already developed far among us.

CASUALTY INSURANCE

This has developed rapidly along with the compiling of reliable figures upon which the calculation of risks can be based. It now includes the most diverse risks, obvious losses like those arising from fire, theft, storms, and floods, less obvious ones like those arising from damage to property through aeroplane accidents, loss of trade or forced stoppage of work through electric current interruption, even such loss as might occur through sprinkler leakage or engine breakdown. We may, indeed, generalise and say that wherever an objective risk is calculable there insurance is possible. Since the average can be struck of the days during the cricket season when "rain stops play," a professional cricketer can insure against the risk of his benefit match being spoiled by the weather; since statistics are available of twin births an insurance against such a contingency is possible.

NATIONAL INSURANCE

THE insurance of the whole—or the bulk—of society against the risks of illness and the loss of profitable work is a social service that modern conditions has made inevitable.

National Insurance concerns itself, as is natural and desirable, with *Personal* rather than *Property Insurance*. It seeks to counter-balance, in its entirety or partially, the loss of income or the added expenditure due to (1) *Death* (see the note on *Widows' and Orphans' Pensions* below); (2) *Survival* (our *Old Age Pensions* in some measure insure against this. See below); (3) *Impairment of Health* (the *National Health Insurance* scheme with its medical service afforded to "panel patients" was designed to counter this); (4) *Inability to sell Labour Power* (our *Unemployment Insurance*—the "dole" as it is sometimes, though erroneously, called—was intended to cope with this).

HEALTH AND PENSIONS INSURANCE

The National Insurance Act of 1911 established compulsory health insurance. After various amending Acts the Act of 1924 consolidated the provisions. Extensions were embodied in the Widows', Orphans', and Old Age Contributory Pensions Act, 1924, and the National Health Insurance Act, 1928.

Employed contributors, under these Acts, are all persons who, being between 16 and 65 years of age, are engaged under a contract of service (*a*) in manual labour, irrespective of the amount earned; (*b*) as paid apprentices; (*c*) in non-manual labour at not more than £250 a year; and (*d*), unless excluded by a special order, in manual labour in a fishing or other vessel. These must contribute, but there are also voluntary contributors.

VOLUNTARY CONTRIBUTIONS

These are, in general, such as have been compulsory contributors who wish to retain, if possible, the benefits of the scheme. Thus, serving in non-manual labour, their salary may have exceeded the £250-a-year limit. To belong to the insurance scheme is a privilege worth having, and it may be of interest to note who are entitled to become voluntary contributors. They include—

1. A person, other than a married woman, who has been insured for at least 104 weeks since the last entry into insurance, and who has ceased to be in insurable employment.

2. An uninsured man who marries an insured woman in respect of whom 104 contributions have been paid.

3. An employed person who shows that he or she has either a pension or salary of £26 not dependent on personal exertions can obtain a certificate exempting him or her (but not the employer) from payment of contribution. Such an "exempted person," in respect of whom 104 contributions have been paid, may continue paying when he or she ceases to be in such employment.

4. There are "excepted employments" in which employees are assured of sickness and disablement benefits equivalent to those under the National Health Insurance scheme. Such an employment under the Crown or a public authority; employment as a clerk or salaried official of a statutory company that gives rights in a statutory superannuative fund; and, under certain conditions, employment in statutory public utility undertakings, like gas and water companies. A person, other than a married woman, who ceases to be employed in these "excepted employments" may become a voluntary contributor.

The voluntary contributor pays the full contribution, except that the total amount is reduced by 3d. a week when the income exceeds £250 a year—such voluntary contributor not being entitled to medical attendance.

CONTRIBUTIONS

For the combined Health Insurance and Pensions the contributions are—

Male : employer, 9d.; employee, 9d.

Female : employer, 7d.; employee, 6d.

The employer pays both contributions, deducting that of the employee from wages payable. No contribution is payable for any week during which no wages are earned. When an insured person is employed by more than one employer in any week, the employer's obligations must be fulfilled by the employer who first employs him or her in that week.

The above are the general rates of contribution; but there are modifications in regard to earners of very low wages and in regard to workers over 65. The male employee earning 3s. a day or less (board and lodging not being provided by the employer) pays 4½d. only; the female employee 2d. The employer then pays 1s. 1½d. in respect of the male employee, 11d. in respect of the female employee.

The employer's contribution alone is payable in regard to persons over 65.

BENEFITS ASSURED UNDER THE NATIONAL HEALTH INSURANCE SCHEME

1. Immediately upon their entering into the scheme insured persons are entitled to *free medical attendance and medicine*.

2. After 104 weeks from entry into insurance and the payment of 104 weekly contributions *sickness benefit* is payable at the rate of 15s. a week for men, and 12s. a week for women. After 26 weeks from entry into insurance and the payment of 26 contributions the rates are 9s. for men and 7s. 6d. for women. The benefit begins on the fourth day of incapacity, and is given for a period not exceeding 26 weeks. It ceases to be payable when the age of 65 is reached, old age pension then being claimable by insured persons.

3. Further *disablement benefit*, after 26 weeks' sickness benefit, at the rate of 7s. 6d. a week. This, too, ceases when the age of 65 is reached.

4. 40s. *maternity benefit* payable to the wife of an insured man on her confinement or to an insured woman. If a married woman, whose husband is not insured, is an employed contributor the maternity benefit is £4. The title to maternity benefit arises after 42 weeks from entry into insurance.

Some regulations relating to benefits—

1. No benefit can be assigned to another.

2. An insured person is still entitled to medical attendance and medicine even though, on the ground that his sickness or disablement has been caused by his own misconduct, his society has suspended his sickness or disablement benefit.

3. Where both husband and wife are insured, a second maternity benefit is payable to the wife.

4. A person may be entitled to compensation for an injury or a disease. In such an event no sickness or disablement benefit is payable, unless the compensation is less than the benefit that would have been received: then the difference between the amounts is payable.

5. An insured person may become an inmate of a hospital, asylum, workhouse, or other public or charitable institution. Such person may not receive sickness or disablement benefit; nor may a woman, being an inmate of a public institution at the time of her confinement, obtain maternity benefit. The insurance

committee or the approved society may, after consulting the insured person, pay the amount to the dependents or to the institution. Any amount not so applied must be paid to the insured when he leaves the institution, or to his estate if he dies.

WHO ADMINISTERS HEALTH BENEFITS?

Contributors to the Health Insurance scheme are divided into (1) a large division belonging to *"approved societies"* which control payments; (2) a small division of *"deposit contributors,"* who have not joined an approved society and whose interests are guarded by *insurance committees* set up in each county and county borough. Probably one is well-advised to join an approved society.

APPROVED SOCIETIES

Before the Ministry of Health approves a society for the purposes of health insurance it must be satisfied (1) that the society is not carried on for profit; (2) that its members are able to control its proceedings; (3) that honorary members do not vote upon questions of health insurance; (4) that no applicant is refused admission to the society solely on the ground of age.

RULES OF APPROVED SOCIETIES

The rules of an approved society are subject to the consent of the Ministry of Health; and there are the restrictions that follow—

1. No rule shall impose a fine exceeding 10s., or, where there are repeated breaches of a rule, 20s.

2. Any rule concerning the visiting of insured persons by visitors of the society shall provide that women shall be visited by women only.

3. No rule shall subject an insured person to penalty—by way of suspension of benefits or otherwise—on account of refusal to submit to a surgical operation or to be vaccinated or inoculated. If, however, the refusal is one to undergo a minor surgical operation, and the society, or the Minister on appeal to him, considers the refusal unreasonable, the rule does not apply.

4. No rule shall inflict suspension of maternity benefit, upon the the confinement of the wife of an insured person, for breach of rules or for imposition unless the breach of rules or the imposition is that of the wife herself.

ADDITIONAL BENEFITS

An approved society having a surplus may, with the sanction of the Minister of Health, arrange for additional benefits including (a) an increase in amounts of benefit; (b) payment of benefit from the first day of incapacity; (c) allowance during convalescence; (d) payments to members compulsorily absent from work on account of infection; (e) payment for additional medical advice or surgical treatment; (f) expenses of travelling to hospitals; (g) payment of part or of the whole cost of dental treatment; (h) payment for ophthalmic treatment and of the cost of optical appliances; (i) payment of the cost of nurses for members.

EMPLOYEES' APPROVED SOCIETY

A work's benevolent fund may be an approved society under these conditions—

1. The representatives of the employees on the committee must be elected by ballot. Where the employer is answerable for the solvency of the fund, he may appoint up to one-fourth of the committee.

2. A member must be entitled at his option to transfer with his paid-up contributions to another approved society; and a member leaving the employment and being unable to obtain admission to another society must have the option of remaining in the fund.

3. Membership of the fund must not be a condition of employment.

4. The adoption of the scheme to administer the National Health Insurance must be dependent upon a ballot of the members of the benevolent fund.

Two other rules relating to such an "approved society" are—

1. If the fund consists of fewer than 5,000 members then, unless the employer makes himself answerable for the solvency of the fund and the payment of benefits, it must be grouped with other societies.

2. The employer may deduct, from his periodical payments to the fund, the amounts payable under the National Health Insurance Act, 1924, by him as employer.

INSURANCE COMMITTEE

An insurance committee is created by the National Health Insurance Acts (1924 and 1928) to administer the benefits to "deposit contributors," those, that is, who do not belong to an approved society. The committee is so framed that the insured population, the local authority, and the medical profession are all represented.

PENALTIES UNDER THE NATIONAL HEALTH INSURANCE ACTS

1. For making false statements, knowing them to be false, in order to obtain a benefit or to avoid a payment: three month's imprisonment.

2. For a failure on the employer's part to pay a contribution, for his attempt to deduct part of the contribution from the employee's wages, or for any other contravention of the Act in regard to payment: £10 fine for each offence. If the employer in fault should be a joint-stock company, each director in his individual capacity may be held liable.

3. For dealing in insurance cards, books, or stamps—selling or pawning them, buying or taking them in pledge: £20 fine.

Moreover, when an employee has suffered loss through an employer's failure to pay contributions, he may take summary proceedings to recover the amount lost from the employer.

Proceedings under the Act must be taken within a year, or within three months from the time when evidence is available, whichever period is the longer.

UNEMPLOYMENT INSURANCE

Workers who are to be insured for Health and Pensions benefit are, with the exceptions noted below, also to be insured against unemployment. Because the difficulties in administering appear well-nigh insuperable or for other reason, the following are not within the Unemployment Insurance scheme, though they are within the Health and Pensions scheme—

1. Those engaged in agriculture, including gardening.

2. Those engaged in domestic service, except where the employed person is employed in any trade or business carried on for the purposes of gain.

3. Those engaged as female professional nurses or as probationers training to become nurses.

As might be expected, "border-line cases" arise—and some of the decisions hardly appear consistent with one another. Persons employed during 48 hours in the week in a departmental store for cleaning were held to be insurable as being in domestic service in a business, whereas a charwoman employed to clean offices before and after business hours was held not to be insurable.

The King's Bench held (*in re Junior Carlton Club*, 1922) that the servants of the club were exempt from insurance, their duties not being connected with a profit-making concern : they came within the derivation of domestic servants as being servants whose main practice is to be about their employers' persons or their establishments for the purpose of ministering to their needs or the needs of members of their establishments, or of those resorting thereto, including guests. So a groundsman employed by a club is not insurable; for he is "engaged in agriculture." A golf caddie, however, is insurable; for he is engaged in casual employment for the purposes of a game.

RATES OF BENEFIT

The contributions under the Unemployment scheme were calculated in the hope and expectation that the scheme would be self-supporting. It was not anticipated that a long continued and most distressing period of widespread unemployment would render the fund insolvent. The rates may therefore change in the interval between writing and reading; and the reader should ascertain whether such change has taken place before he uses the figures in serious argument. The ordinary rates per week and the ordinary benefits under the Act are—

	Employer	Employee	Benefits
Man	8d.	7d.	17s.
Woman . . .	7d.	6d.	15s.
Young man (18–20) .	7d.	6d.	14s.
Young woman (18–20)	6d.	5d.	12s.
Boy (16–18) . .	4d.	3½d.	9s. (17–18) 6s. (16–17)
Girl (16–18) . .	3½d.	3d.	7s. 6d. (17–18) 5s. (16–17)

DEPENDANTS' BENEFIT

Where a man or a woman obtains "Dependants' Benefit" he or she also receives the 17s. or the 15s. "Ordinary Benefit." Such Dependant's Benefit is each week—

1. To husband in respect of his wife or of a "resident" or "non-resident housekeeper": 9s.

2. To a wife in respect of her infirm husband: 9s.

3. To man or woman in respect of dependant's father or mother (including stepmother or stepfather): 9s.

4. To man or woman in respect of dependent children or younger brothers and sisters : 2s. for each dependent child.

CONDITIONS FOR RECEIPT OF BENEFIT

The conditions, too, are in a state of flux. As contemplated by the Act they were—

1. That, during the two years preceding the application for benefit, no fewer than thirty contributions have been paid. (The protracted period of industrial depression necessitated an alternative to this condition: the claimant must show (a) that not fewer than eight contributions were paid in the two years, or that not fewer than thirty contributions have at any time been paid; (b) that he is normally employed in insurable employment, and that he will normally seek to obtain his livelihood by means of insurable employment.)

2. That the claimant has made application for benefit in the prescribed form and that he has been continuously unemployed since the date of application.

3. That the claimant is capable of and is available for work.

4. That, being so required, he has attended an instruction course.

DISQUALIFICATIONS FROM BENEFIT

A person may be deprived of benefit *for a maximum of six weeks* if (1) without good cause he has failed to apply for, or has refused to accept, a suitable situation; (2) without good cause he has failed to carry out any written directions given to him by an officer of an employment exchange with a view to assisting him to find suitable employment; (3) he has lost his employment through misconduct or has left it without just cause.

A person is disqualified to receive benefit *during the whole time* when (1) he is in prison or workhouse or other institution supported out of public funds; (2) he resides outside the United Kingdom; (3) he is receiving benefit under the National Health Insurance Act, 1924, or under the Blind Persons Act, 1920; (4) he has lost employment through a trade dispute at his place of employment.

NON-CONTRIBUTORY PENSIONS

Even when a person has not contributed to a pension's fund, the State grants a pension under the following conditions: (a) He or she has reached the age of 70 (where a birth certificate is not available the Pensions Officer will help the claimant to prove his age without the need to incur expense); (b) he or she has been a British subject for at least the past ten years; (c) he or she, being a natural-born British subject, has been resident in the United Kingdom for twelve years at least since attaining the age of fifty; or, being a naturalised British subject, has been resident at least twenty years in all. If the claimant has, though residing abroad, maintained dependants in the United Kingdom, such period may be reckoned as residence in the United Kingdom.

RATE OF PENSION

This depends on what other income the claimant has. A single person is allowed £39 per annum of income and a married person £78, apart from earnings without the right to the pension being effected. Thereafter the yearly income is taken into account in accordance with the following table—

YEARLY MEANS		Weekly Rate of Pension
Exceeding £ *s.* *d.*	*Not Exceeding* £ *s.* *d.*	*s.* *d.*
—	26 5 –	10 –
26 5 –	31 10 –	8 –
31 10 –	36 15 –	6 –
36 15 –	42 – –	4 –
42 – –	47 5 –	2 –
47 5 –	49 17 6	1 –
49 17 6	—	Nil

Whether or not a claimant is entitled to pension is decided by the local Pension Committee, to which the Pension Officer after investigation submits the claim. An appeal is possible within seven days from the Committee's decision: either the claimant or the Pension Officer may ask for the decision of the Ministry of Health.

BANKRUPTCY AND DEEDS OF ARRANGEMENT

CENTURIES have gone by since the broken bench of the Venetian financier indicated that its owner was insolvent and unable to carry on his business. But the word "bankruptcy" survives and to-day describes the method by which the property of an insolvent person is taken over by the State and distributed among his creditors. When this process is completed he himself, if he has acted honestly, obtains a release from his creditors and is able to start life once again with a clean sheet. At one time a bankrupt was looked upon as a criminal, and bankruptcy was regarded as a punishment. The law of bankruptcy was then applicable only to traders, but since 1861 it has been extended to all persons, whether traders or not.

The present Act dealing with bankruptcy is the Bankruptcy Act, 1914 (4 & 5 Geo. 5 Ch. 59), which consolidated the law on the subject. The administration of bankruptcy law is under the control of the Board of Trade which is responsible, under the guidance of the Lord Chancellor, for a series of rules dealing with the administration of the Act, known as the Bankruptcy Rules, 1915.

Any references made in this article relate to sections of the Act of 1914 or the Rules of 1915.

Bankruptcy proceedings are always begun by a *petition*, which must be founded on some definite *act of bankruptcy*, a term which we shall consider later. But before proceeding further the first question to be decided by the person presenting the petition is in what Court it is to be taken out. If the debtor has resided or carried on business in London for the previous six months, or is not resident in England, the petition must be presented to the High Court in London. In other cases the petition must be presented to the county court for the district in which the debtor has resided, or carried on business, for the previous six months. If the debtor has carried on business in one district and resided in another the petition is to be filed in the court of the district where he has carried on business. The judges of the various courts are assisted by Registrars who have full powers and who, in practice, determine most of the questions which arise in connection with the estate. The Board of Trade has the appointment of official receivers in bankruptcy who are attached to the various districts throughout the country. The duties of these officials are (1) to investigate the debtor's conduct and report thereon to the Board of Trade; and (2) to act as trustee and receiver of the assets until the appointment of a trustee by the creditors. Indeed, in many cases the Official Receiver acts as trustee and administers the estate throughout.

Before describing the various steps in the bankruptcy proceedings a few words are necessary as to the object and effect of bankruptcy from the creditors point of view, and the effect of the order upon the debtor. The chief penalty under which an undischarged bankrupt suffers is that he cannot obtain credit for more than £10 without informing his creditor that he is an undischarged bankrupt. This is a valuable check to the activities of insolvent persons, particularly if they are unscrupulous, and from this point of view bankruptcy is a useful weapon against fraud to traders and others who supply goods on credit. The Act also renders the bankrupt liable to punishment if he engages in trade under another name. But the individual creditor is chiefly concerned with the recovery of the debt due to him, and as to this the returns are not encouraging. Between four and five thousand receiving orders are made annually. The debtors' liabilities were estimated at nine and a half million pounds, while the debtors' estimated assets were under two million pounds. From these assets the costs of the proceedings and administration have to be deducted, and the fact is that bankruptcy proceedings are a last resort for an unpaid creditor, and that administration in bankruptcy is an expensive business. But a petition often leads to a scheme of arrangement by which the debtor's estate is handed over to a private trustee, who distributes the proceeds economically and equitably between the creditors. The great point about proceedings in bankruptcy is that all creditors are treated alike and receive the same dividend in the pound upon the amount of their debts. It is a frequent cause of complaint that there is a large number of undischarged bankrupts carrying on business in this country, the reason being that they are dishonest persons who dare not apply for a discharge as their conduct would then be investigated. It has often been suggested that every bankrupt should be compelled at a certain stage in the bankruptcy to apply for his discharge, but the legislature have not yet taken this view, on the ground that it is a favour to be sought by the bankrupt at the hands of the Court. It is certainly a luxury which the bankrupt has to pay for out of his own pocket and, in some cases, this may be the reason why a bankrupt does not take the trouble to make the application. It can at all events be said that recent legislation has made the path of the dishonest bankrupt more thorny than it was before 1914, and that the difficulty of obtaining credit, and the penalties attaching to dishonest conduct, render frauds by insolvent persons increasingly difficult to carry out.

THE PETITION

Before launching a petition against the debtor the creditor should consider whether he comes within the law of bankruptcy in this country. There is now no distinction between traders and non-traders, but the following exceptions to the general rule still exist—

A *foreigner* can only be made bankrupt if at the time when the act of bankruptcy was committed by him: (*a*) he was personally present in England; or (*b*) he ordinarily resides here; or (*c*) he was carrying on business in England personally or through an agent; or (*d*) he was a member of a firm carrying on business here.

An *infant* cannot be made bankrupt, except possibly upon a contract for necessaries. If an act of bankruptcy is committed by a firm and one of the partners is an infant, the receiving order can only be made against the partners "other than the infant partner."

A *married woman* can only be made bankrupt if she carries on a trade or business: she is then subject to bankruptcy law as if she were a single woman.

A *lunatic* can only be made bankrupt with the consent of the Court of Lunacy, which will appoint some person to represent him.

A *firm* is not supposed to exist in this country apart from the individual partners, but a petition may be presented against a firm and a receiving order will be made against the firm and will operate against each individual partner.

Companies do not come under the Bankruptcy Act but are wound up under the Companies Act, 1929.

The bankruptcy *petition* which must be signed by the petitioning creditor sets out the debtor's name, description, and address and the particular Act of bankruptcy on which the creditor relies. The creditor on filing the petition must deposit

£5 with the O.R.,[1] but this sum is afterwards repaid him out of the estate. The petition also requires a £5 stamp which has to be paid by the creditor. The petition is served personally by delivering a sealed copy to the debtor. Service of the petition is proved by affidavit, with a sealed copy of the petition attached, which is filed in court. If it is impossible to serve the petition personally the court may allow the petition to be delivered at the debtor's residence or place of business, or by registered letter, or advertisement. This is known as "substituted service." The various acts of bankruptcy on which a petition may be founded are to be found in Section 1 of the Act.

ACTS OF BANKRUPTCY

The eight specific acts of bankruptcy are defined in Section 1 as follows—

1. *If in England or elsewhere he makes a conveyance or assignment of his property to a trustee for the benefit of his creditors generally.*

This is an "act of bankruptcy," unless the assignment is duly registered under the Deeds of Arrangement Act, 1914. The clause only applies to an assignment by the debtor of *all* his property for the benefit of his creditors generally. Thus an assignment for the benefit of one class of creditors is not within its scope. Under the Deeds of Arrangement Act, 1914, the trustee of such a deed must give notice to creditors of the execution of the deed and of the necessary assent being obtained. Dissenting creditors have then one month within which they can serve a petition founded on the execution of the deed as an act of bankruptcy. If they do not exercise their right within that time they are debarred from doing so.

2. *If in England or elsewhere he makes a fraudulent conveyance gift, delivery, or transfer of his property, or any part thereof.*

This differs from the previous act of bankruptcy in that it relates to a fraudulent transfer only: the fraud consists in the debtor putting his property out of reach of his creditors. The fraudulent intention is a matter for the Court to decide, having regard to the circumstances of the case. If it appears that the debtor was insolvent when he made the assignment and that he intended to defraud creditors the assignment will be invalid. A typical case was that of an insolvent trader who turned his business into a one man company. He himself was the company and the consideration consisted of shares and an undertaking

---

[1] O.R. throughout this section means the "Official Receiver."

by the company to pay his debts. This was held to be a fraudulent transfer and an act of bankruptcy which the trustee in bankruptcy could set aside in the interest of creditors.

An assignment by a debtor of his property to a creditor in consideration of a past debt is another instance of an act of bankruptcy under this heading.

3. *If in England or elsewhere he makes any conveyance or transfer of his property or any part thereof or creates any charge thereon which would under this or any other Act be void as a fraudulent preference if he were adjudged bankrupt.*

Fraudulent preference is not often relied on in the petition as an act of bankruptcy. The fraud does not, as a rule, appear until after the receiving order, when the estate is being administered it can then be set aside under Section 44 of the Act.

4. *If with intent to defeat or delay his creditors he does any of the following things, namely, departs out of England, or being out of England remains out of England, or departs from his dwelling-house, or otherwise absents himself, or begins to keep house.*

Here again an intent to defeat creditors is a matter to be inferred from the debtor's conduct. If he leaves England without making provision for bills or debts becoming due, it may be assumed that he intended to defeat creditors. The phrase "keeping house" means that when creditors call he gives instructions to tell them that he is "not at home."

5. *If execution against him has been levied by seizure of his goods under process in an action in any Court, or in any civil proceeding in the High Court, and the goods have been either sold or held by the sheriff for twenty-one days.*

The sheriff is obliged to hold the goods of a debtor which he has seized in execution for twenty-one days before selling them in case some third person has a claim upon them. In the event of such a claim the sheriff serves a summons on the claimant and execution creditor to appear and have their rights decided. This is called an interpleader summons and the time elapsing between the date of the summons and the decision is not to be taken into account in calculating the period of twenty-one days. If the seizure and sale of the debtor's goods have taken place or the goods have been held by the sheriff for twenty-one days, that is an act of bankruptcy; but if the creditor has no notice of a bankruptcy petition or of the commission of an available act of bankruptcy by the debtor he can retain the benefit of the execution up to the date of the receiving order. After the receiving order is made no creditor can obtain any preference but must take his chance with the rest.

6. *If he files in the court a declaration of his inability to pay his debts or presents a bankruptcy petition against himself.*

Where a petition is filed by a debtor the Court will make a receiving order forthwith, whereas a creditor's petition is not heard until eight days have elapsed after service. As may be imagined, instances of debtor's petitions are rare.

7. *If a creditor has obtained a final judgment or order against the debtor for any amount, and, execution thereon not having been stayed, has served upon him a bankruptcy notice, and he does not within seven days either comply with the notice, or satisfy the Court that he has a counter-claim which equals or exceeds the amount of the judgment debt.*

This is the act of bankruptcy most commonly relied on in the petition. In a recent year "non-compliance with a bankruptcy notice" was the act complained of in 74 per cent of the cases in which receiving orders were made. A *bankruptcy notice* is a notice signed by the creditor or his solicitor requiring the debtor to pay the judgment debt or to secure or compound for it to the satisfaction of the creditor or the Court. In order to issue the notice a creditor must apply to the Registrar and produce an office copy of the judgment on which the notice is founded. Two or more judgment debts cannot be included in one notice, but interest may be claimed. If the debtor gives security for the debt, the creditor cannot issue another bankruptcy notice so long as the security is in force. If the debtor has a counter-claim of the amount referred to in the notice he should file an affidavit to that effect. The Registrar then fixes a day for the hearing, and if the counter-claim is made out the bankruptcy notice will be set aside. If it is not made out and the debtor does not comply with the notice by payment or otherwise within the time allowed, the act of bankruptcy is complete. The notice is not invalid if the amount of the debt is not exactly stated in it. If the sum stated exceeds the actual debt it is sufficient compliance if the debtor pays or gives satisfaction for the actual amount due.

8. *If the debtor gives notice to any of his creditors that he has suspended, or is about to suspend payment of his debts.*

The notice referred to in this clause need not be in writing, but it must be formal and deliberate. The test as to whether the notice amounts to an act of bankruptcy is the intention of the debtor and the effect of the notice on the minds of the creditors. If a debtor writes "being unable to meet my engagements I invite your attendance at No. 1, Green Street, when I will submit a statement of my position for your consideration and decision," this has been held to be a notice that the debtor is about to suspend payment.

These are the eight acts of bankruptcy specified in the Act. Not every such act will be available for a bankruptcy petition. It is a condition that the act of bankruptcy on which the petition is grounded must have occurred within three months before the presentation of the petition. Such an act is called in the Act an "available act of bankruptcy." Further, the debt owing to the petitioning creditor or creditors must amount to £50 and it must be a sum clearly payable either immediately or at some certain future time. It has already been pointed out that the debtor must be domiciled in England or have resided here or carried on business here within a year before the petition; or if a foreigner he must have carried on business here personally or by an agent or as a member of a firm carrying on business here. If these conditions are satisfied the creditor can proceed to issue his petition.

PROCEDURE ON PETITION

Having drawn up his petition the creditor must swear to the facts by an affidavit made before a commissioner of oaths. If he cannot verify all the facts himself, he must ask some person who can do so to swear an affidavit for him. These affidavits he files with the petition. The creditor or his solicitor must now serve a sealed copy of the petition by delivery to the debtor. After the presentation of the petition the court may appoint the O.R. as "receiver" of the property of the debtor to protect his estate in the interest of creditors. It may also stay any action against the debtor. If the debtor is carrying on a business the creditors may apply for the appointment of a special manager who will carry on the business on such terms as the creditors or the Board of Trade may direct, until a trustee is appointed.

At the hearing of the petition the petitioning creditor must prove his debt, service of the petition, and the act of bankruptcy. The hearing takes place eight days after the service of the petition, but may be adjourned for periods up to a month from the first hearing. The registrar may dismiss the petition or make a receiving order against the debtor, upon which the costs of the proceedings, including those of the petitioning creditor, become payable out of the estate.

THE RECEIVING ORDER

The receiving order is prepared by the Registrar. It contains a statement of the nature and date of the act of bankruptcy relied upon, and requires the debtor to attend before the O.R. on a certain date. The O.R. serves a copy of the order on the debtor. Upon the making of this order the O.R. is constituted receiver of the property of the debtor, and after that no creditor can commence legal proceedings against the debtor except by leave of the court. Secured creditors, however, can still deal with their securities and realise them for the discharge of their debts as before. It must be understood that the receiving order does not make the debtor a bankrupt. After the order the debtor hands over his property to the O.R. for the benefit of creditors: but he himself still has control over it and is the proper person to sue for its recovery if any action is necessary. The O.R. has to protect and preserve the property, and the only person who can interfere with it is the landlord, who can distrain for six months rent, accruing due before the order of adjudication.

Notice of the order with particulars and the date of the order and petition are now gazetted and advertised. As soon as possible a first meeting of creditors is held to consider whether a scheme of arrangement shall be accepted or whether the debtor shall be adjudged bankrupt.

Within seven days from the date of the order the debtor must submit to the O.R. a statement of affairs showing his assets, debts, and liabilities, the names of his creditors together with securities held by them. This statement is open to inspection by creditors or their agents.

A day is next fixed for the public examination of the debtor, and the Court holds this in public, and the debtor must attend for examination as to his conduct, dealings, and property. The examination is held as soon as possible after the statement of affairs. It is conducted mainly by the O.R., but creditors may question the debtor. Notes on the examination are taken down, read over to the debtor, and signed by him. They can be inspected by the creditors if desired. The examination may be adjourned by the Court, and when the debtor's affairs have been sufficiently investigated the Court declares the examination concluded, but not until after the day appointed for the first meeting of creditors.

No. 34

N.B.—you are required to fill up carefully, and accurately, this sheet, and such of the several sheets A, B, C, D, E, F, G, H, I, J and K (1) as are applicable showing the state of your affairs on the day on which the Receiving Order was made against you, viz.: the *10th* day of *October, 1932.*

Such sheets, when filled up will constitute your Statement of Affairs, and must be verified by oath or declaration.

(1) Sheet L should be substituted for any one or more of such of the sheets named as will have to be returned blank.

Statement of Affairs.

In the High Court of Justice

IN BANKRUPTCY.

No. 1436 of 193..

Re *John Stiggins.*

STATEMENT OF AFFAIRS

At *4th* day of *October,* 193., date of Receiving Order.

Verified Statement filed in Court this ___ *day of* ___ 19

Filed in the Office of the ___ *day of* ___ 19

Official Receiver, this

(2) Strike out words not applicable.

Gross Liabilities £ s. d.	Liabilities (as stated and estimated by Debtor)	Expected to Rank £ s. d.	Assets (as stated and estimated by Debtor)	Estimated to produce £ s. d.
	Unsecured Creditors as per list (A.)— £ s. d.		Property as per list (H.), viz.—	
			(a) Cash at banker's . . .	450
	Creditors fully secured as per list (B.) . . 1,500		(b) Cash in hand	
	Estimated value of securities. . . 2,000		(c) Cash deposited with Solicitor for Costs of Petition . .	50
			(d) Stock in Trade (cost £) .	
	Surplus 500			
	Less amount thereof carried to sheet (C.)		(e) Machinery . . .	
			(f) Trade Fixtures, Fittings, Utensils, &c. . .	1,000
	Balance thereof to *contra* . . £			
			(g) Farming stock . . .	
			(h) Growing Crops and Tenant Right	
	Creditors partly secured as per list (C.) . . 1,000		(i) Furniture	
	Less estimated value of securities. . . 500	500	(j) Life Policies . . .	
			(k) Stocks and Shares . .	
	Liabilities on Bills discounted other than Debtor's own acceptances for value as per list (D.), viz.—		(l) Reversionary or other interests under Wills . .	
			(m) Other property, viz.—	
	On accommodation Bills as Drawer, Acceptor, or Indorser . *nil*		Total as per list (H.) .	1,500
	On other bills as Drawer or Indorser . £ 800		Book debts, as per list (I.), viz.— Good . . . . . £ s. d.	3,000
			Doubtful . . 1,000	
	Of which it is expected will rank against the estate for dividend . . .	700	Bad . . . 500	
	Contingent or other Liabilities as per list (E.) . . . £ 400			1,500
	Of which it is expected will rank against the estate for dividend . .	200	Estimated to produce 700 . .	700
	Creditors for rent, &c., recoverable by distress as per list (F.) . . 100		Bills of Exchange or other similar securities on hand, as per list (J.) . . £	
			Estimated to produce . .	*nil*
	Creditors for rates, taxes, wages,&c., payable in full as per list (G.) . . 300		Surplus from securities in the hands of Creditors fully secured (*per contra*) .	
	Sheriff's charges payable under Sec. 41 of the Act, estimated at 25			£ 3,700
	£ 425		*Deduct creditors for distrainable rent and for preferential rates, taxes, wages, Sheriff's Charges, &c. (per contra)* .	500
	Deducted *contra* . £ 50	375		£ 3,200
	(2) Surplus explained in Statement (K)		(2) Deficiency explained in Statement (K)	*nil*
£		£ 1,775	£	

I. ___ in the County of ___ of ___ make oath and say that the above statement and the several lists hereunto annexed, marked A, B, C, D, E, F, G, H, I, J, K, and L, are, to the best of my knowledge and belief, a full, true and complete statement of my affairs on the date of the above-mentioned Receiving Order made against me.

Sworn at *Stoneyhurst,*
in the County of ___
this *1st* day of *December,* 193
Before me

)
) Signature *John Stiggins.*

(2207)

FORM I

Receiving Order on Creditor's Petition

In the High Court of Justice

IN BANKRUPTCY. No. *1436* of 193..

MR. REGISTRAR *Sprey*

Re *J. Stiggins.*

*Here insert the name of the creditor.

Ex-parte* *F. Sharpe.*

ON the petition (dated the *10th* day of *September,* 1932, and numbered *1436* of 193.) of

a creditor, filed the *tenth* day of *September,* 193., and on reading *the affidavit of the said F. Sharpe dated 10th September, 193., and that of the said J. Stiggins in reply thereto*

†Set out the nature and date or dates of the act or acts of bankruptcy on which the order is made.

and it appearing to the Court that the following act of bankruptcy has been committed, viz.†: *the said F. Sharpe having obtained final judgment against the said J. Stiggins for £50 and having served on him a bankruptcy notice, he has not within seven days complied with the notice or satisfied the Court that he has a counter-claim which equals or exceeds the amount of the judgment debt.*

‡Insert name, addresses, and description of debtor as set out in petition.

a receiving order is hereby made against‡ *the said John Stiggins of 3 Dunham Avenue, Stoneyhurst, Tailor*

and *Robert Grinder* one of the Official Receivers of this Court is hereby constituted receiver of the estate of the said debtor.

Dated this *10th* day of *October,* 193..

By the Court,

B. Sprey, Registrar.

NOTE. The above-named debtor is required, immediately after the service of this order upon him, to attend the Official Receiver of the Court at his offices, Bankruptcy Buildings, Carey Street, Lincoln's Inn.

The Official Receiver's offices are open (except on Holidays) every week-day from 10 a.m. to 4 p.m., except Saturdays, when they close at 1 p.m.

*Insert name and address.

The name and address of the solicitor to the petitioning creditor are*

FIRST MEETING OF CREDITORS

This meeting is summoned within fourteen days after the receiving order. The meeting is called by the O.R. by notice in the *London Gazette* and in a local paper. He also sends notice of the meeting to each creditor mentioned in the debtor's statement of affairs. With the notice he encloses a summary of the statement of affairs including the cause of failure and his observations thereon. The O.R. acts as chairman at the meeting and only those creditors who have proved are entitled to vote. Secured creditors can only vote in respect of the balance due after deducting the value of the security. The secured creditor may estimate the value of his security in his proof, and then the O.R. may require him to give up the security on payment of the value so estimated plus 20 per cent.

The chairman at the meeting can admit or reject a proof for purpose of voting. Creditors may vote either in person or by proxy. A general proxy may be given to a manager or clerk, while a special proxy may be given to any person; but the latter entitles the proxy to vote only at a specified meeting or adjournment thereof upon the following matters—

1. Upon a specific proposal for a scheme of arrangement.

2. As to the appointment of a specified person as trustee or member of the committee of inspection.

3. On other matters arising at the specified meeting or adjournment.

Proxies must be deposited with the O.R. before the meeting. Solicitation on behalf of a trustee is not allowed. The meeting cannot act (except for the election of a chairman, the proving of debts, and the adjournment of the meeting) unless three creditors at least are present. Otherwise the meeting must be adjourned for at least seven days. The minutes of the meeting must be kept and signed by the chairman, or by the chairman of the next meeting.

The rules for the meeting are set out at length in the first schedule to the Act.

At the first meeting the creditors consider any composition or scheme put forward by the debtor, and if they do not approve it they may resolve that the debtor be adjudged bankrupt.

COMPOSITION OR SCHEME

When a composition or scheme is proposed by the debtor he must lodge his proposal in writing with the O.R., setting out any sureties or securities proposed. This he should do within four days after submitting his statement of affairs. The O.R. sends a copy to each creditor with a report thereon. If the meeting of creditors resolves by a majority in number and three-fourths in value of creditors who have proved, the scheme is deemed to be accepted by the creditors. A creditor may express his assent or dissent by letter to the O.R. not later than a day before the meeting. If the scheme is accepted, the debtor or the O.R. will apply to the Court to approve it. The application is not heard until after the public examination of the debtor. Before expressing its approval the Court hears the report of the O.R. as to its terms, as to the conduct of the debtor, and any objections by creditors. If the terms of the proposal are unreasonable or contrary to the interests of the general body of creditors the court must refuse its approval. If upon the facts the Court would be required to refuse, suspend, or attach conditions to the debtor's discharge, were he adjudged bankrupt, it must refuse its approval unless the scheme provides security for payment of at least five shillings in the pound on the unsecured debts. Approval is expressed by attaching the seal of the Court or by embodying the terms in an order of Court. The scheme so accepted and approved will bind all creditors as regards debts provable in the bankruptcy but in respect of other debts the debtor is not released. If default is made in payments of instalments, or if some fraud is shown, the court may annul the scheme and declare the debtor bankrupt.

ADJUDICATION

If the creditors do not approve the proposal for a composition or if it is rejected by the Court, the debtor is adjudged bankrupt. The same result follows if the creditors pass a resolution for his adjudication, or if they pass no resolution at all. The order for adjudication is made by the Court, and the bankrupt's property then becomes divisible among his creditors and vests in a trustee. Notice of the order giving the bankrupt's name, etc., the date of adjudication, and the Court which makes the order, is gazetted and advertised.

The Court may also make the order on the application of the debtor himself, and this may be done on making the receiving order. In all cases the date of the order is the date of the adjudication for the purposes of the Act.

Even after adjudication the creditors by a majority in number and three-fourths in value may accept a scheme or composition, and the proceedings are the same as in a scheme before adjudica-tion. If the Court approves the scheme it may order the adjudica-tion to be annulled and vest the property in the bankrupt upon terms. The adjudication may also be annulled if, in the opinion of the Court, the debtor ought not to have been adjudged bank-rupt, or if it is proved that his debts have been paid in full. This power is discretionary, and such an application by the debtor for annulment may be refused if the debtor has committed offences against the Bankruptcy Laws.

APPOINTMENT OF TRUSTEE

When the debtor is adjudged bankrupt or the creditors have so resolved they may appoint a trustee of the property of the bankrupt. Or they may resolve to leave his appointment to the Committee of Inspection. In many cases they leave it to the O.R. to act as trustee. The trustee is appointed by ordinary resolution of creditors, and his first duty is to give security to the satisfaction of the Board of Trade, which then certifies that his appointment is duly made. Appointment of a trustee takes effect as from the date of the certificate. If a trustee is not appointed within four weeks from the adjudication the O.R. reports the matter to the Board of Trade and that Board then appoints the trustee. If the creditors or Committee of Inspection subsequently appoints a trustee that person takes the place of the trustee appointed by the Board of Trade. Notice of his appointment is gazetted by the Board of Trade, but the trustee himself notifies his appointment in a local paper.

The remuneration of the trustee is voted by creditors or the Committee of Inspection and consists partly of a percentage on the amount realised and partly of a percentage on the amount distributed in dividend.

COMMITTEE OF INSPECTION

The creditors may appoint a committee of inspection to super-intend the administration of the property by the trustee. This committee will consist of not more than five or less than three persons with the following qualifications—

1. Being a creditor or the holder of a general proxy from a creditor.

2. Being a person to whom the creditor intends to give a general proxy.

The Committee meets at least once a month, and the trustee or any member of the committee may call a meeting when he thinks fit. The committee may act by a majority of the members present but can only act if a majority of the committee are present. A member may resign office by written notice signed and delivered to the trustee. If a member becomes bankrupt or compounds with his creditors, or is absent from five consecutive meetings his office becomes vacant. A member may also be removed by resolution passed at a meeting of creditors of which seven days notice has been given. Vacancies on the committee are filled by appointments made at a meeting of creditors. If no committee is appointed the authority given to the committee by the Act is exercised by the Board of Trade on the application of the trustee. No member of the committee may derive any profit from transactions arising out of the bankruptcy except where payment is authorised by the Court, and no payment is allowed for services rendered as a member of the committee.

COMMENCEMENT OF BANKRUPTCY

On being adjudged bankrupt the debtor's property vests in the trustee. The trustee's title to this property commences, not at the date of his appointment, but relates back to the first act of bankruptcy committed by the bankrupt within the three months preceding the date when the petition was presented (Section 37).

The trustee is thus entitled to claim property which the bankrupt may have disposed of some time before the petition. But this rule is subject to three exceptions, as follows—

1. Where a creditor has levied execution on the debtor's goods, and the execution is completed before the receiving order, and without notice of the bankruptcy petition or of an available act of bankruptcy, his title prevails against that of the trustee. An execution is said to be "completed" when the goods are seized and sold.

If the sheriff receives notice of a receiving order before sale he must hand over to the O.R. the debtor's goods which he has seized, but the costs of the execution are a first charge on the goods in question. If the execution is in respect of a judgment for more than £20 the sheriff, after deducting his costs, retains the balance for fourteen days. If within that time notice is served on him of a petition against the debtor and a receiving order is made thereon he pays the balance to the O.R. or trustee who retains it as against the execution creditor.

2. Payments by or to the bankrupt are protected if they take place before the receiving order and without notice of an available act of bankruptcy (Section 45).

3. By Section 46 a payment of money or delivery of goods to a person afterwards adjudged bankrupt, or to his assignee, is a good discharge if made (a) before the receiving order; (b) without notice of the bankruptcy petition, and in the ordinary course of business or otherwise *bona fide*.

The only case in which a payment made after the receiving order is protected as against the trustee arises under the Bankruptcy Amendment Act, 1926, Section 4. By that Act persons who have paid money or transferred property to the bankrupt after the receiving order, but before notice of the order has been gazetted, are protected if they acted without being aware of the order. The trustee is then not allowed to recover against them (i.e. to make them pay twice over) except where the Court is satisfied that it is not practicable for the trustee to recover from the person to whom the money was paid or the property transferred.

DIVISIBLE PROPERTY

The property divisible among creditors includes all property vested in the bankrupt at the commencement of the bankruptcy as above defined, or acquired by him before his discharge. It also includes all powers exercisable by the bankrupt between the same dates; and, lastly, all goods at the commencement of the bankruptcy in the possession, order, or disposition of the bankrupt in his trade or business by the consent of the true owner: provided that things in action other than debts due or growing due to the bankrupt in his trade or business are not deemed goods within the meaning of the section (Section 38). This latter clause is sometimes called the "reputed ownership" clause, and, as will be seen, affects only traders.

A typical instance of the working of this clause will be found in *Sharman* v. *Mason* (1899), 2 Q.B. 679, in which the trustee in bankruptcy claimed some dress stands which the maker had allowed to remain in the shop of a mantle dealer for use in her business. The stands were in the possession of the bankrupt in her trade with the consent of the true owner, and it was held that the trustee could claim them on behalf of the creditors. Where, however, it is the custom in a trade for goods to remain in the possession of a trader of which he is not the owner the effect of the section is excluded. Instances of this are found in a watchmaker's business where watches are left for repair, or in a hotel-keeper's business, where hired furniture is often used. In neither of these cases would the claim of the trustee succeed against that of the true owner. The true owner can, of course, prove in the bankruptcy for the value of the goods as a creditor if the trustee is successful against him.

PROPERTY WHICH IS NOT DIVISIBLE

By Section 38 the following property of the bankrupt is not divisible amongst creditors.

1. Property held by the bankrupt on trust for another person.

2. The tools of his trade and the necessary wearing apparel of himself, his wife, and children to a value not exceeding £20 in all.

Although the trustee's rights over the bankrupt's property are strictly exercised, the bankrupt is always allowed to retain out of his personal earnings enough for the support of himself and his family. Beyond this his earnings go to the trustee. In *re Roberts* (1900), 1 Q.B. 122, Roberts was a professional billiards player earning £2,000 a year. In addition to his salary he had a contract with the Bonzoline Company that if he would use their balls they would supply him with 2,000 billiard balls annually free of cost. The trustee in his bankruptcy claimed the balls as not necessary for the support of the bankrupt and his family— and in this he succeeded. By Sections 50 and 51 of the Act, where the bankrupt is a clergyman, or an officer in the Army or Navy, or is otherwise in receipt of salary or income, or is entitled to a pension granted by the treasury, the trustee can apply to the court and obtain an order for the payment of part of the bankrupt's salary to the trustee.

PREFERRED DEBTS

Debts proved in the bankruptcy are paid *pari passu* with certain exceptions. These are to be found in Section 33 of the Bankruptcy Act and are as follows—

1. Rates payable within twelve months before the receiving order and taxes assessed on the bankrupt up to 5th April before the receiving order and not exceeding one year's assessment.

2. Wages or salary of a clerk or servant for services rendered to the bankrupt during four months before the receiving order up to £50. This applies whether the wages were or were not earned by way of commission (see Bankruptcy Amendment Act, 1926, Section 2).

3. Wages of a workman not exceeding £25 whether for time or piece work for two months before the receiving order.

4. Compensation under the Workmen's Compensation Act, 1925. There is now no limit to the amount of this priority.

5. Contributions payable by the bankrupt under the National Health Insurance Act, the Pensions Act, and the Unemployment Insurance Acts in respect of his employees during twelve months before receiving order.

The above debts rank equally among themselves but before all other unsecured debts, and are paid in full if the assets permit; if not, they abate in equal proportions.

LANDLORD'S RIGHTS

Rent due to the landlord from the bankrupt is not entitled to priority among the above debts. Indeed, if the landlord distrain for his rent within three months before the receiving order the above debts are a first charge on the goods distrained on. But the landlord in that case will stand in the shoes of the preferred creditor and enjoy the same rights of priority to the extent of such payment.

Further, by Section 35 the landlord may distrain on the bankrupt's goods even after the bankruptcy has commenced. But if he does so the distress is only available for six months rent accrued due prior to the order of adjudication and is not available for rent payable in respect of a period after the date when the distress was levied. Apart from this the landlord must prove in the bankruptcy for the surplus due.

DEFERRED DEBTS

Two classes of debts rank for payment only after all other creditors for valuable consideration are satisfied. These are (1) persons who have lent money to the bankrupt in consideration of a share in the profits of his business, and (2) loans by a wife to her husband or a husband to the wife for the purpose of a trade or business.

INTEREST

A creditor is entitled to prove for interest on his debt at 4 per cent per annum (1) if the debt is payable by virtue of a written instrument at a certain time; or (2) if payable otherwise then from the time when written notice has been given to the debtor that interest will be claimed until payment. Apart from this,

Section 33 (8) provides that if there is a surplus after payment of debts it is to be applied in paying interest from the date of the receiving order at 4 per cent on all debts proved.

PARTNERSHIP DEBTS

In the case of partners, the partnership assets (called the joint estate) are applied in the first instance in payment of the firm's creditors, while the separate estate (i.e. the estate of each partner) is applied in the first instance to pay his separate debts. If there is a surplus of the separate estates it is dealt with as part of the joint estate. If there is a surplus of the joint estate it is dealt with as part of the separate estate of each partner in proportion to his interest in the joint estate.

OFFENCES IN BANKRUPTCY

Fraudulent conduct by the bankrupt in the course of the bankruptcy or leading up to it is a ground for prosecution, and the various offences are set out in Sections 154 to 156 of the Act. Perhaps the most important are (1) if the bankrupt, before his discharge, obtains credit for ten pounds or upwards without informing the other person that he is an undischarged bankrupt; (2) if he engage in a trade or business under a different name without disclosing to manufacturers, customers, etc., the name under which he was adjudged bankrupt; and (3) if he does not keep proper books of account within the two years before the bankruptcy. This last only applies to traders and only applies on a *first* bankruptcy where the unsecured liabilities exceed £500. If the liabilities are under £100 no offence is committed. If they are between £100 and £500 the trader can only be prosecuted if he has *previously* been made bankrupt. In any case it is a good defence if the trader can show that the failure to keep accounts was in the circumstances honest and excusable. The books of account which are deemed necessary by the Act as amended by the Act of 1926, Section 7, are (a) a day book showing in detail all cash received and paid; (b) statements of annual stocktaking (where the trade involves dealing in goods); and (c) except in a retail business, accounts of all goods sold and purchased showing the buyers and sellers in detail, so as to enable them to be identified.

SECOND OR SUBSEQUENT BANKRUPTCY

In the event of a second bankruptcy, any property acquired by the bankrupt since his adjudication which was not distributed at the date of the subsequent petition will vest in the trustee in the second bankruptcy; but the trustee in the first bankruptcy may prove for any unsatisfied balance of debts. The same applies if there are other bankruptcies after the second—and such cases do occur! The duty of a trustee on receipt of a subsequent petition is to hold any after-acquired property until the subsequent petition has been disposed of, and if an order of adjudication is made on the subsequent petition, to transfer the property to the trustee in the subsequent bankruptcy.

PROPERTY ACQUIRED AFTER ADJUDICATION

Property acquired by the bankrupt after adjudication and before discharge does not vest in the trustee until he (the trustee) intervenes (Section 47). The result is that if the bankrupt disposes of the property before the trustee's intervention the transaction is good as against the trustee provided that it is a transfer *bona fide* and for value. Mere knowledge of the bankruptcy does not invalidate the sale. When a banker finds that a customer is an undischarged bankrupt he should inform the trustee of the existence of the account: after that he should not make any payments out of the account except under order of Court or on instructions from the trustee unless on the expiration of a month after giving notice he is without instructions from the trustee.

Upon a man's second or subsequent bankruptcy the trustee of the previous bankruptcy is a creditor for the unsatisfied balance of provable debts. After-acquired property now vests in the trustee in the subsequent bankruptcy. This does not affect dealings by the trustee in the first bankruptcy made without knowledge of a subsequent petition, but on receiving notice of a fresh petition the trustee should hold after-acquired property until the fresh petition is disposed of, and, if necessary, transfer it to the new trustee.

VOLUNTARY SETTLEMENTS

The Act of 1914 contains provisions to prevent a debtor who wishes to avoid the consequences of bankruptcy from settling property belonging to him upon trust, so as to put the capital and income out of reach of his creditors. Any settlement made within two years before bankruptcy is void against the trustee in bankruptcy if it is not either a marriage settlement or one made in favour of a purchaser in good faith and for value. If the settlor becomes bankrupt within ten years it remains valid if the parties claiming under it can prove that the settlor, when he made the settlement, was able to pay his debts without the aid of the property comprised in it, and that the interest of the settlor really passed to the trustee of the settlement on its execution.

Thus, J. Trotter settles £5,000 Consols by deed upon trust to pay the interest to his wife for life with remainders over. If he goes bankrupt within two years the deed is void and the stock belongs to the trustee in bankruptcy. If he goes bankrupt within ten years his wife must show that he was solvent at the date of the deed, without the aid of the £5,000 stock, and that the stock was duly transferred to the trustee of the settlement.

It should be added that if the debtor has acquired property since his marriage in right of his wife and settles it upon his wife or children, the settlement is protected against the trustee in bankruptcy.

The same section (Section 42) avoids covenants made in a marriage settlement for the future payment of money for the benefit of the settlor's wife or children when he has not, at the date of his marriage, any actual interest in the money. It became a practice for insolvent persons who had "expectations" to enter into covenants of this kind upon marriage, and the Bankruptcy Act, 1914, puts a stop to this by providing that the person entitled under the covenant shall only be able to claim as a creditor in the settlor's bankruptcy, and that only after other creditors for value are paid out. Apart from this, unless the covenant is actually carried out at the commencement of the bankruptcy, it is void against the trustee. Payments made under the covenant are, however, valid if the payee can show either that the payment was made more than two years before the commencement of the bankruptcy, or that the settlor was able to pay his debts without the aid of the money so paid, at the date when the transfer took place. An exception is made in the Act where the payment consisted of money expected to come to the settlor on the death of a particular person named in the covenant, provided that payment took place within three months after the money came into the settlor's possession.

FRAUDULENT PREFERENCE

Fraudulent preference of one creditor over another can be set aside by the trustee quite apart from being itself an act of bankruptcy. In order to set aside a payment by the debtor on this ground the trustee must show (1) that the debtor was insolvent, i.e. unable to pay his debts as they became due; (2) that he acted with a view to giving one creditor a preference over the rest; and (3) that the debtor was adjudged bankrupt upon a petition presented within three months after the payment. If the payment was made under pressure from the creditor it is not a fraudulent preference, and each case must be decided on its own facts.

BOOK DEBTS

In order to obtain further credit a trader sometimes assigns his book debts to a particular creditor. If this is done the assignment should be registered as a bill of sale under the Bills of Sale Act, 1878. Otherwise book debts not paid at the commencement of the bankruptcy will belong to the trustee. This provision does not affect the assignment of book debts from specified debtors, or of debts under specified contracts, or of book debts included in a *bona fide* transfer of a business, but it does affect an assignment for the benefit of creditors generally.

DUTIES OF TRUSTEE

The trustee takes possession of the deeds, books, and documents of the bankrupt, and of his movable property. He has all the powers of a receiver appointed by the Court and, as regards stocks and shares in the bankrupt's name, he can transfer them to the same extent as the bankrupt. All rights of action are deemed to be assigned to the trustee, and a banker or agent of the bankrupt must hand over to the trustee monies and securities in his possession belonging to the bankrupt. Reference has already been made to his rights to other property and to the commencement of his title.

DISCLAIMING ONEROUS PROPERTY

It may be that some parts of the property are of no use to creditors, and as to these the Act gives him the power of disclaimer. The Act (Section 54) provides that where land belonging to the bankrupt is burdened with onerous covenants, or where stocks and shares are subject to calls, or there is a liability on contracts which are unprofitable the trustee may, by writing signed by him, disclaim the property at any time within twelve months of his appointment. Where the property has not come to his knowledge within one month after his appointment he may disclaim it within twelve months after he became aware of its existence. The disclaimer operates to determine as from its date the rights and liabilities of the bankrupt in the property disclaimed, but it does not affect the rights or liabilities of other persons. In the case of a lease the trustee cannot disclaim without leave of the court, and before giving leave the court may require notice to be given to persons interested and may impose conditions as to fixtures, tenants improvements, etc.

Any person interested may apply in writing to the trustee to decide whether he will disclaim or not, and the trustee has then twenty-eight days in which to make his decision, after which he loses his right. Persons interested may apply to the Court in the case of *contract* for an order rescinding the contract on such terms as to damages as the court may think fit. As regards property disclaimed any person interested may apply for an order vesting the property in him, but a person claiming as sublessee from the bankrupt or as mortgagee by demise is only entitled to an order subject to the same liabilities as the bankrupt at the date of the petition, and, if the Court thinks fit, subject to the same liabilities as if the lease were assigned to him at that date. Any person injured by the operation of the disclaimer becomes a creditor and may prove for the debt to the extent of the damages suffered.

GENERAL POWER OF TRUSTEE

The trustee may do any of the following things—

1. Sell any of the bankrupt's property, including the goodwill of his business and book debts due, or growing due, to him.

2. Give receipts for money so as to discharge the person making payment.

3. Prove and draw dividends for any debt due to the bankrupt.

4. Exercise any powers vested in the trustee under the Act, and exercise any deeds to effect the same.

5. Deal with property to which the bankrupt is entitled as tenant in tail.

The trustee can also do the following things *with the permission of the Committee of Inspection.* If there is no committee the O.R. gives permission, subject to the directions of the Board of Trade—

1. Carry on the business of the bankrupt so far as may be necessary for the beneficial winding up.

(For this purpose he may appoint the bankrupt as manager

and make him an allowance, but he cannot continue the business without the consent of the creditors.)

2. Bring or defend actions as to the bankrupt's property.

(For this purpose he is described as "the trustee of A.B. a bankrupt.")

3. Employ a solicitor or other agent.

4. Accept as consideration for the sale of property a sum of money payable at a future time, subject to such stipulations as to security as the committee thinks fit.

(NOTE. The trustee can sell for cash *without* leave.)

5. Mortgage or pledge part of the property to raise money for the payments of debts.

6. Refer disputes to arbitration, compromise any debts due to the bankrupt on such terms as may be agreed.

7. Compromise with creditors as to debts provable in the bankruptcy.

8. Make any compromise as to claims arising out of the bankrupt's property.

9. Divide in its existing form amongst the creditors any property which cannot be sold readily or to advantage.

TRUSTEES' ACCOUNTS

The trustee is required to keep proper accounts, and one-sixth of the creditors can require the trustee, at any time, to furnish a statement of accounts up to date: but the applicant must deposit with the trustee a sum sufficient to pay the costs, which sum is repayable out of the estate if the creditors and the Court so direct. The three books which the trustee must keep are the record book, the cash book, and the trading account. In the record book he enters all minutes, proceedings, and resolutions passed at meetings of creditors or of the committee of inspection.

In the cash book are entered from day to day receipts and payments made by him.

If he carries on the business of the debtor he also keeps a trading account and incorporates the total weekly receipts and payments in the cash book.

The trustee must submit the record book and cash book, with other requisite books and vouchers to the Committee of Inspection when required and not less than once every three months. The Committee of Inspection then audit the cash book and certify the date of audit. Every month the trading account must be submitted to the Committee of Inspection to be certified.

At the expiration of six months after the receiving order and every six months until his release the trustee must send the cash book accounts in duplicate for the six months to the Board of Trade, together with the necessary vouchers and copies of the certificates of audit by the committee. With his first accounts he forwards a summary of the debtor's statement of affairs showing in red ink the amounts realised and explaining the cause of non-realisation where necessary. When the account has been audited the Board of Trade certify that it has been duly passed, and the duplicate copy duly certified is transmitted to the Registrar who files the copy. If there are no receipts or payments for the period the trustee forwards to the Board an affidavit to that effect.

Once every year during the continuance of the bankruptcy the trustee sends a statement to the Board of Trade showing the proceedings in the bankruptcy up to date. Upon this statement the trustee is liable to be examined, and, if necessary, to make good any loss which the estate has sustained by his negligence (Section 87). The bankrupt himself or any creditor may inspect the books kept by the trustee, when filed.

In the case of partnerships distinct accounts must be kept of the joint and separate estate of the debtors, and no transfer from one to the other must be made without notice being gazetted.

BANKING ACCOUNT

The trustee should not pay money received by him as trustee into his private banking account but into the bankruptcy estates account at the Bank of England.

If, however, it appears to the Committee of Inspection that it is for the advantage of creditors to have an account at a local bank, the Board of Trade will authorise the trustee to do so on the application of the committee. If there is no committee then the application will be made by the O.R. or by the trustee. The account is opened in the name of the debtor's estate and payments in and out are made in the prescribed manner. Cheques are marked with the name of the estate and signed by the trustee: they are countersigned by a member of the committee and by some other person appointed by the creditors or the Board of Trade. If the trustee retains a sum exceeding £50 for more than ten days the Board of Trade may require him to pay interest on the excess at 20 per cent per annum, to forfeit his remuneration, and may remove him from his office.

PROOF OF DEBTS

All debts to which the debtor is subject at the date of the receiving order, or which may become due before his discharge, are provable in bankruptcy. The obligation, however, must have been incurred before the receiving order.

The following are not provable in bankruptcy—

1. Demands in the nature of unliquidated damages arising otherwise than by reason of a contract, promise, or breach of trust.

2. Debts incurred after notice of an act of bankruptcy.

3. Debts which are, in the opinion of the Court, incapable of being fairly estimated.

Unliquidated debts are those which have yet to be ascertained as regards the amount. Otherwise, future or contingent debts can be proved, the amount being estimated by the trustee. Gambling debts or debts barred by the Statute of Limitations cannot be proved in bankruptcy.

Where there are mutual dealings between debtor and creditor the balance only can be proved.

METHOD OF PROOF

Every creditor must prove his debts as soon as possible after the receiving order. This he does by sending an affidavit to the O.R. or trustee giving particulars of the debt.

He can then vote at creditors meetings. In proving his debt he must deduct trade discounts but he need not deduct discounts for cash which do not exceed 5 per cent on the net amount of his claim.

Secured creditors may either (1) realise their security and prove for the balance after deducting the net amount realised; or (2) surrender the security to the trustee and prove for the whole debt; or (3) assess the value of the security and claim a dividend in respect of the balance after deducting the value so assessed. In (3) the trustee may redeem the security on payment to the creditor of the assessed value or he may require that the security be offered for sale. The creditor may give notice in writing to the trustee requiring him to elect within six months which he will do.

The creditor should be careful to state in his affidavit that he is a secured creditor; otherwise the Court may order him to surrender his security, unless he can satisfy the court that his omission was inadvertent (Bankruptcy Amendment Act, 1926, Section 11).

ADMISSION OR REJECTION OF PROOFS

The trustee must now examine the proofs and decide which he will admit or reject. This he must do within twenty-eight days, but the O.R. is only allowed fourteen days if he is acting as trustee. If the creditor is dissatisfied with the trustee's decision he may within twenty-one days thereof appeal to the Court.

On the first of each month the trustee must send to the Registrar a certified list of proofs showing which he admits, which he rejects, and which stands over. The time has now come for the declaration of dividends.

DIVIDENDS

The first dividend must be declared and distributed within four months after the conclusion of the first meeting of creditors unless the Committee of Inspection agree to postpone it.

Subsequent dividends are declared and distributed at intervals of not more than six months. Not more than two months before declaring a dividend the trustee sends a notice to each creditor who has proved, showing its amount and when and how it is payable together with particulars of the estate. This notice is also sent to the Board of Trade in order that it may be gazetted. Any creditor who has not proved before the declaration of a dividend is entitled to be paid out of any money in the trustee's hand before future dividends are paid; but he is not entitled to disturb the distribution of any previous dividends in which he has not participated.

TRUSTEE'S RELEASE

When the trustee has realised all the bankrupt's property, or so much as he can realise without needlessly protracting his office, he declares a final dividend. But he must first give notice to all creditors, who have sent in their claims but have not established them, that they must establish them within a certain time to his satisfaction and that if not the final dividend will be paid without regard to them. After the expiration of the time stated in the notice the bankrupt's property is divided up without regard to the claims of creditors who have not proved. If there is any surplus it belongs to the bankrupt after creditors are paid in full and after the cost of the proceedings are paid. If the trustee has any unclaimed dividends in his hands after making a final dividend he should pay this to the Bankruptcy Estates Account at the Bank of England. He is obliged to pay in such dividends if they have not been claimed after six months. The Board of Trade then gives him a certificate of receipt which is an effectual discharge. No action for a dividend lies against the trustee, but the Court may order him to pay it with interest.

By Rule 338, before applying to the Board for his release, the trustee should give notice of his intention to all creditors who have proved and to the debtor, and should send them a summary of his receipts and payments. He should also hand over to the O.R. all material books, papers, and accounts. The Board will then grant his release and notice of the order will be gazetted. The Board acts upon a report as to his accounts, and if these are unsatisfactory or a creditor raises some valid objection the release may be withheld. In a bad case the Court may charge the trustee with the consequences of any breach of duty. But once the release is granted and the order gazetted the trustee is free from liability in connection with the bankruptcy.

BANKRUPT'S DISCHARGE

The application for discharge is made by the bankrupt himself and at his own cost. It is made to the Registrar who gives notice to the O.R., and fixes a day for the hearing. Before this, the O.R. makes a report on the matter and this is filed and taken into consideration. The hearing is in open court and any creditor may oppose. The Court may either grant or refuse the application; or suspend it for a specified time; or grant it, subject to conditions as to the bankrupt's subsequent earnings.

Cases in which the Court will refuse or suspend the discharge are—

1. That his assets are not ten shillings in the pound (unless he shows that he is not to blame for this).

2. That he has not kept proper books of account in his business within three years preceding his bankruptcy.

3. That he has continued to trade knowing himself to be insolvent.

4. That he has contracted debts without any expectations of being able to pay.

5. That he has failed to account for loss of assets.

6. That he has brought on his bankruptcy by rash speculation or gambling.

7. That he has within three months before the receiving order given an undue preference to a creditor.

8. That he has previously been adjudged bankrupt.

There are four more grounds which rarely occur, but which will be found in Section 26 of the Act.

In such cases the application may be refused or suspended for two years. The discharge frees the bankrupt from all debts payable in the bankruptcy but not from debts due to the Crown, debts incurred by fraud, or judgments against the bankrupt as co-respondent in a divorce suit.

DEEDS OF ARRANGEMENT

These deeds which are usually agreements for composition with creditors, but include other instruments, are now governed by the Deeds of Arrangement Act, 1914. By Section 2 such a deed is void unless registered with the Registrar of Bills of Sale within seven days after its execution. Upon the filed copy of the deed the person presenting it writes the date of the deed and of the filing, the amount of duty,* and a certificate is made by the debtor's solicitor or the person presenting it that it is a correct copy: he must also file an affidavit giving the debtor's residence, occupation, and place of business. The debtor will file an affidavit estimating his assets and liabilities included in the deed, and the amount of the composition, with the names and addresses of creditors.

The deed will be void (Section 3) unless within twenty-one days after registration it has received the assent of a majority in number and value of creditors. A creditor's assent is established by his attesting the deed or sending his assent in writing, attested by a witness, to the trustee. If the requisite majority have assented, the trustee files a statutory declaration to that effect within twenty-eight days.

In calculating a majority of creditors for the purposes of the deed a secured creditor is only reckoned as a creditor in respect of the balance after deducting the value of the security. Creditors whose debts do not exceed £10 are reckoned in the majority in value but not in number.

DUTIES OF TRUSTEE

Within seven days from the filing of the declaration as to creditors assent the trustee under the deed must give security to the Registrar unless the creditors dispense with this.

---

* NOTE. Stamp duty at 1s. for every £100 of the sworn value of the property passing, or (if no property passes) the amount of composition payable under the deed.

The deed itself is an assignment for the benefit of creditors and is, therefore, assailable as an act of bankruptcy. Therefore, the Act of 1914, Section 24, enables the trustee to serve a notice on creditors of the execution of the deed and of the declaration of assent. This notice informs the creditor that he has one month in which he may present a bankruptcy petition founded on the execution of the deed as an act of bankruptcy. After that period no creditor can present a petition on this ground unless the deed becomes void; and the trustee can then carry out its provisions and distribute the assets.

For this purpose the trustee should open an account at a bank in the name of the debtor's estate into which monies received may be paid. At the end of six months and of every subsequent six months the trustee will send to creditors a copy of his accounts (Section 14). He will also (Section 13) send an affidavit verifying these accounts to the Board of Trade. The Board may cause the accounts to be audited if a majority in number and value of the assenting creditors call for an official audit (Section 14). It is for the Board to decide who will pay the costs of the audit, to which the provisions of the Bankruptcy Act, 1914, apply. If the administration is not completed in two years the Court may order, on application of the trustee or of a creditor, that unclaimed dividends and funds shall be paid into Court (Section 16).

VOID DEEDS

Where a deed is void by reason that a requisite majority has not assented, or in case of a deed for the benefit of three or more creditors where the debtor was insolvent and the deed was not registered but is not void for any other reason, and a receiving order is made against the debtor upon a petition dated three months after the deed was executed, the trustee is not liable to account to the trustee in bankruptcy for his dealings with the property if he did not know that the deed was void (Section 19). It is the duty of the trustee, when the deed is void for any other reason than that it has not been registered within the proper time, to give notice to each creditor whose name and address he knows, that the deed is void. This he should do as soon as he discovers the fact. If he acts after knowing that it is void, or if he fails to give security within the proper time, he is liable to a fine. Where the deed is voided by the debtor's bankruptcy the trustee is entitled to recover any expenses incurred in the performance of his duty from the trustee in bankruptcy as a first charge on the estate. But this does not give him any remedy for expenses incurred apart from the Act of 1914, although he is entitled to reasonable expenses for services rendered where benefit has resulted to the estate (*Re Geen* (1927), 1 K.B. 183).

The Act of 1914 provides a convenient method of winding up a debtor's estate without the expense and formality of bankruptcy proceedings. Stress must be laid on the fact that deeds of arrangement must comply with the provisions of the Act, with which a trustee under such a deed should be familiar. Any other method constitutes an evasion of bankruptcy law. The above notes, while they are not exhaustive, indicate sufficiently how the deed should be registered and carried out and what are the trustee's duties under the Act.

PROPERTY RIGHTS AND DUTIES

TREASURE TROVE IS CROWN PROPERTY

OWNERLESS things are rare in developed communities. Wild animals and fish in the sea or navigable rivers are the chief instance; these become the object of property only when they are killed or caught. They are then "reduced into possession." Even as regards treasure trove, the Crown takes ownership. And treasure trove includes the following things, possession of which has been lost or abandoned by the owner: *Money or coin, gold, silver, plate, bullion,* hidden away; *waifs,* stolen goods "waived" or thrown away by the thief; *estrays,* valuable animals found wandering; *jetsam,* goods cast into the sea which sink and remain under water; *flotsam,* goods cast into the sea which float; *ligan,* goods sunk in the sea but attached to a cork or buoy.

REAL PROPERTY AND PERSONAL PROPERTY

In a developed community, nearly all desirable things are either public property (like most of our roads) or private property (like most of our railways). And property is divided into two big divisions, *Real Property* and *Personal Property.* In the event of a dispute arising about ownership, the claim to the property is now almost invariably decided upon by a Judge in a Court of Law; the old right of self-assertion of a claim has been gradually whittled down till it is no longer of much importance.

Where the law recognises a property right, there is imposed upon all persons an obligation to respect that right. Because the right is in a *thing (rem)* and is independent of promises by persons to respect the right, a property right is called a *jus in rem.* It exists against the world at large. The right I have against a person—the right, for instance, to payment of a debt, the right to go about my business without being attacked by him—is called a *jus in personam.*

ESTATES

We do not usually regard ourselves as owners of "estates" unless we are landed proprietors. After our death, however, the State assumes that we have estates that are to be distributed among new owners. It subjects what we have left, when it is sufficiently large, to "Estate Duty." And a new owner, other than the State itself, may have to pay a "Legacy Duty" also. The chief regulations relating to such estate duty are found on pages 308 and 309.

"POSSESSION" MAY NOT BE "PROPERTY"

When we say that "possession is nine points of the law," we mean only that he who has control of a thing need not surrender that control until another establishes a superior claim to it. The burden of proof, that is, rests upon the claimant; and normally he must assert his claim by due process of law. In order that peace shall be preserved—that there shall be no violence "against the peace of our Sovereign Lord, the King"—the ancient right of recovering one's own goods by one's own efforts has been narrowly limited. That is why the law protects possession against the spoiler. In *Armory* v. *Delamirie* (*Nisi Prius,* 1722), the plaintiff, a chimney-sweep's boy, found a locket set with diamonds. He took it to the shop of the defendant, a goldsmith, to learn its value; the goldsmith's apprentice, on pretence of weighing it, took out the stones, and called to the defendant that it was worth three-halfpence. The defendant offered the boy that amount; he refused it; and the apprentice gave him the locket without the stones. The chimney-sweep sued, and the Chief Justice said (1) that the finder, though he does not acquire an absolute ownership, yet has such a property as will enable him to keep it against all but the rightful owner; and he directed the jury (2) that unless the defendant did produce the jewel, and show it not to be of the finest water, they should presume the strongest against him, and make the value of the best jewels the measure of their damages— which they accordingly did.

PROTECTING ONE'S PROPERTY

A person is entitled to defend his property while it is in his possession, and by whatever degree of force is reasonably necessary. He is entitled also to recapture it from a thief when the theft is fresh, and he is in "hot pursuit" of the thief; and, provided he can do so without giving rise to a breach of the peace, he can take his own property when he finds it. But these rights of self-help are slight in regard to those of former times. Where land or houses are concerned the rightful owner can regain possession where he can do so by peaceful means. So long ago, however, as the reign of Richard II, a statute was passed punishing "forcible entry" as a crime. Where disputes arise they are to be settled by orderly argument and impartial decision in Court, not by the primitive method whereby might becomes right.

Real property consists in rights over "immovables," over land and buildings. Such property, therefore, is peculiar in this : that many may in succession become owners of it, or not being owners may have rights over it. Smaller rights (limited by years or by lives) can be carved out of the continuing existence.

Personal property consists in rights over "movables," over goods and chattels. Recent legislation, culminating in a series of Law of Property Acts (1922–25), and coming into operation on the 1st of January, 1926, has been devised mainly to facilitate dealings in real property. And it has been remarkably successful; real estate is now almost entirely free from the shackles in which the incidents of the feudal system had bound it.

HEREDITAMENTS, CORPOREAL AND INCORPOREAL

A *right* over land is known as a *hereditament* (something that could be inherited). It is a *corporeal hereditament* when the rights consist in actual ownership of land or building. It is an *incorporeal hereditament* when the right consists in a mere limited use of the land—a right to use a way across it, for instance. (See "Easements," page 480.)

LEGAL TENURE OF LAND

There is now only one tenure of land, a tenure indicated by saying that all land is held in "free and common socage." The only legal estates that can now be existent, and that can be bought, are—

1. An estate in fee simple absolute in possession (shortly known as a "freehold"). This is the greatest possible estate in land; all other estates are carved out of it.

2. A term of years absolute (shortly known as either a "leasehold" or a "mortgage"). Under the new law of property a lease can be created for as long as 999 years.

Other legal rights over land are, however, recognised—

1. Easements.
2. Rent-charges.
3. Charge by way of legal mortgage.
4. Land-tax or tithe-charges.
5. Rights of entry. (These are explained later.)

EQUITABLE RIGHTS OVER LAND

Any other rights over land are equitable rights only, enforceable only by equitable remedies. The distinction between *legal rights* and *equitable rights* may be put thus—

(*a*) A legal right exists whether or not the acquirer of land knows of it.

(*b*) An equitable right exists only so long as the acquirer of land knows of it, or ought to have known of it.

Thus, a legal mortgage, by which the estate in the land is conveyed to the lender of the money, is effective against even a *bona fide* buyer of land though he is quite unaware that the mortgage exists. If he should buy the land knowing of the mortgage, he gets no greater right to the land than the seller had; that is, he must, to obtain the fee simple of the land, pay off the mortgage.

A second mortgage, however, is effective only against such land buyers as have notice, or should have had notice, of its existence. When such a mortgage is, as it almost invariably will be, registered under the Land Clauses Act, 1925, anyone who buys the land is supposed to have had notice of it, whether he had or not.

The first mortgage is a legal right; the second mortgage is an equitable right.

TITLE TO LAND

By this is intended the manner of acquiring rights over land or buildings. I may, though very rarely in these days, obtain ownership simply by occupying land or buildings; if, without the sanction of the owner and without force or fraud, I retain the land or the building for twelve years without being challenged, I have an indisputable title to it. Though I have been a trespasser for twelve years, I become owner after the expiry of the period.

In ordinary events I acquire a title from the owner. The owner may divest himself of his rights (*voluntary alienation*), or he may, by process of law, be deprived of his rights (*involuntary alienation*).

Examples of the first are—

1. Conveyance by *sale*, or *settlement*, or *mortgage*.
2. *Gift by will.*

Examples of the second are—

1. *Bankruptcy*, which operates as a transfer of all the bankrupt's

16

property, with only slight exceptions, to the trustee in bankruptcy for the benefit of creditors.

2. *Distress* (distraint) for non-payment of rent.

3. *Execution of judgment.*

4. *By the State for public purposes* (always nowadays with compensation to the owner).

"VESTED" AND "CONTINGENT" OWNERSHIP

Since land endures and owners are transitory, the law allows future rights over land. We may speak of *vested* rights, those already in enjoyment, and *contingent* rights, those in expectation of an event.

A "vested" ownership exists when a definite person has a right over property, even though the actual enjoyment of the property is in the future. Thus, if property is granted to X for a lease of three years, with remainder to Y, then Y has a "vested ownership." He already has a right over the property though he must wait to obtain possession; and he can leave something of value in his will.

A "contingent" ownership exists when the right to enjoy property is dependent upon a condition that may not happen; if property is granted to A, then to B in the event of his surviving A, then B has only a contingent ownership. Unless he does survive A, he will get nothing.

The "vested ownership" will be of great value if the interval before actual enjoyment is short; it will be of little value if the interval is long. The "contingent ownership" will, in like manner, have much or little value in accordance with the degree of likelihood that the condition on which actual enjoyment is to depend will happen. One may, indeed, imagine a contingent ownership almost equal to actual enjoyment: a man given property "if and when the next Derby is run" might count with confidence on his getting the property. For the contingency is almost certain to be fulfilled.

The "vested ownership" depends upon something that is bound to happen; the "contingent ownership" depends upon something that may or may not happen. It is like the distinction between the "heir apparent" to the throne and the "heir presumptive." Nothing can happen to alter the first; subsequent births may alter the second. An eldest son is heir apparent. An eldest daughter may be "heiress presumptive"; but the birth of a son would destroy the presumption.

DUAL OWNERSHIP

There may be a double ownership, a *legal owner* and an *equitable owner*. The legal owner may, however, exist without an equitable owner; the equitable owner exists always along with a legal owner. Equity prevents the legal owner from using his Common Law rights as owner to the detriment of the equitable owner.

The recent Acts, passed in order to simplify property law and facilitate the transfer of landed property, utilised very effectively this idea of double ownership. Apart from a few legal estates all other interests in land are made into equitable interests, are placed behind a veil. He who buys a legal estate, in accordance with the forms laid down in regard to searches and so on, obtains a clear title. The equitable interests operate upon the purchase money only.

EMERGENCE OF PROPERTY RIGHTS

The recent advances in aviation afford illustrations of how property rights arise.

Men learn that rights over a thing, material or immaterial, are valuable. At once they seek to make the rights their own; and things become property that were before at anyone's disposal. The broad Atlantic itself may at some future date be charted as the territory of this or the other nation. Already—in the recognition of "territorial waters," of property in oyster fisheries and sealing grounds and the like—we see the process beginning. The air, happily, cannot be appropriated so as to deprive us of the breath upon which our being depends. But what about the air-space? Aviation, particularly in its application to advertising—sky-writing and sky-shouting—has made the question of more than merely academic interest. Who owns these air-spaces, or, more to the point, has anyone a right to prevent the use of the sky for purposes he dislikes? If the owner of the land surface resents the intrusion of an aeroplane above his property, can his resentment take legal effect?

THE LANDOWNER'S RIGHTS

The Common Law disliked the idea of ownerless things. It sought an owner for everything worth owning; and, having found that owner, it was not afraid to allot to him whatever benefits were derivable from his property. Thus it held that the man who was the owner of the surface of the land was also the owner of the column of air above it and of whatever rested below it. The maxim invoked was, *Cujus est solum, ejus est usque ad coelum et ad inferos*: Whose the soil is, to him also belongs up to the heavens above and down to the depths beneath. He can build a tower of Babel, can remove the branches of his neighbour's tree if they cross his boundary, can prevent the suspension of wires, however high above the soil. A landowner, true, had no property in a passing cloud any more than in a wild rabbit on his land. But if he could confine either—"reduce it into possession" is the phrase—he would have such property. He could catch the rabbit, and in one sense he can reduce the passing cloud itself into possession. He can "sky-write," whether by means of an aeroplane or a projector, and while he is "sky-writing" no one else can effectively do so. Anyone trying to do so would be interfering with the proprietary rights of the landowner, and would, therefore, be a trespasser.

THE AIR HIGHWAY

The Air Navigation Act of 1920—itself called for through the application of the new power that man had acquired over nature —prevents actions for trespass when an aeroplane is doing nothing but fly through the air. In effect that Act places the whole air space in the same position as a land highway. The air space is dedicated to the public for "passing and re-passing," and no action for trespass can be maintained "by reason only of the flight of aircraft" over property. A man may be, however, a trespasser on the land highway; a racing tout, walking up and down a stretch of road adjoining Newmarket Heath, was held to be a trespasser against the adjoining landowner. For property in the highway is vested either in the county authority or in the owner of the land adjoining the way. The public has the right of passage. But only this: a man dancing and shouting in order to scare game from the adjacent fields is trespassing. So in the air. An action for trespass might lie against a sky-writing aeroplane which hovered for a substantial time while writing. (See "Carriage by Air," page 812.)

TRESPASS IN THE AIR

Whether trespass could be maintained for sky-writing by means of projectors—searchlights—is a more difficult question. You have a blank wall to your house. Clearly, it is a trespass if, without your licence, one plays fives against it or throws stones against it. But what if he throws moving pictures, extolling the merits of So-and-so whisky, against it?

The more abstruse theories of physics tell us that even a beam of light is material enough to be affected by gravitation. No Court would hold, though, that the beams of light were material enough to be a physical interference with the property against which they impinged. Your only remedy would be to show that your comfort had been greatly diminished by the coming into your land of the obnoxious beams. In other words, you would seek damages for a private nuisance: the enterprising advertiser had caused to enter upon your land something that detracted from your enjoyment of it. If the sound-waves from a persistent pianoforte player, or the smell from an ill-kept stable, or the heat from a cooking stove could be judged to be nuisances, the beams of light could also be judged to be a nuisance. The problem would be to show that a real, not a fanciful, diminution of the owner's comfort had been caused by the unauthorised act. Pictures projected on the dining-room window would assuredly be deemed a nuisance. For such would detract to a perceptible degree from the occupier's enjoyment of the room. The question would be less easy to answer where a blank wall is the display surface.

" PUBLIC NUISANCE "

There is also, quite apart from the rights of ownership, the question of public nuisance. There is a public nuisance when the comfort or convenience of a community is disturbed by an act which is not authorised by law. To obstruct the highway, or to make it dangerous for traffic, is a public nuisance; it is a crime that the Attorney-General may be asked to prosecute. "Sky-shouting," or "sky-writing" over crowded industrial areas could be prevented, if at all, only by such a prosecution.

" SERVITUDES "

These are rights to use, for certain purposes, land in another's possession. Such are *rights of way (wayleaves), of light, of support, of shooting or fishing, of extracting minerals*. The right sometimes goes with the possession of adjoining land; this adjoining land (the "dominant tenement," as it is called) obtains a benefit from the "servient tenement." The servitude is then an *appurtenant* one: it appertains to the dominant tenement at the expense of the servient tenement.

When the right is unconnected with a dominant tenement it is called a "servitude in gross."

Servitudes are classed as follows—

1. *Public,* a right enjoyed by the public generally or by a defined part of the public. Such are a right of passage along public highways, and navigation and fishing in a navigable river.

2. *Private,* vested in specified individuals. Such private servitudes may be either—

(*a*) *Legal,* where they are protected not only against the first grantor of them, but also against all successive owners of the servient land;

(*b*) *Equitable,* when they are protected only against the first grantor and the successive owners who know of their existence.

Servitudes are again divided into—

1. *Easements,* rights of way, of light, of support, of water supply, "privileges that one neighbour hath of another, by writing or prescription (without profit) as a way or sink through his land, or the like."

2. *Profits,* rights to take away something—fuel, fish, pasture—from the servient tenement.

LICENCE

A right over land or building may also be given by licence. This is a permission (for entry into a theatre or a football ground) changing what would otherwise have been a trespass into a lawful act. A licence may be given in consideration of payment or other return; the owner of the land or building is then under obligation to make the land or building reasonably safe for the licensee. A licence may also be granted as an act of grace, the owner obtaining no benefit from its grant; the only obligation imposed upon the owner then is that he shall give the licensee due warning of dangers that could not be foreseen.

The old rule was that a licence could be revoked unless it was granted by a deed (a sealed writing). The modern rule is that, when it would be against equity to end the licence, the licence cannot be revoked. *Hurst* obtained damages of £150 against *Picture Theatres, Ltd.* (K.B. 1915), in the following circumstances. He had paid 6d. for admission; the attendant alleged he had not paid, ordered him out, and the porter took hold of him to remove him. He then walked out. The jury found that he had paid and awarded damages; and the verdict was upheld on appeal: "If there be a licence with an agreement not to revoke the licence, that, if given for value, is an enforceable right. Here the licence was a licence to enter the building and see the spectacle from beginning to end. There was included in the contract a contract not to revoke the licence until the play had ended. It was a breach of contract to revoke the licence." We should note, however, that the damages were not given for a breach of contract. They were for the force used against the plaintiff, force that would have been justified against a trespasser, but was unjustified against a licensee.

We are to note, also, that the occupier of building or land can himself determine the persons to whom he will grant licences. A theatre proprietor is not obliged to admit everyone who presents himself with the amount charged for admission: he is not like a railway company, which, in its capacity of "common carrier," is under obligation not to discriminate. The management ordered that a critic, biassed it would seem against the particular theatre, should not obtain a ticket of admission. He obtained one through a third person, was prevented from taking his seat, brought an action, but failed (*Said* v. *Butt*, K.B.).

LICENCE BY LAW

The law itself in some events confers a licence to enter upon property: "the law gives authority to enter into a common inn or tavern; so to the owner of the ground to distrain damage-feasant (i.e. to take another man's cattle if they should be trespassing on his land); to him in reversion to see if waste be done; to the commoner to enter upon the land to see his cattle; and such like." If, however, the man to whom the law grants a licence uses that licence for a purpose not contemplated, the man is a trespasser from the beginning of his entry: "If he who enters into the inn or tavern doth a trespass, as if he carries away anything; or if the owner, for damage-feasant, works or kills the distress (the animal taken while trespassing); or if he who enters to see waste break the house, or stays there all night; or if the commoner cuts down a tree: in these and the like cases, the law adjudges that he entered for that purpose; and because the act that demonstrates it is a trespass, he shall be a trespasser from the beginning."

The omission to do something that one ought to do is not, however, a trespass; and such omission cannot make a lawful entry into an unlawful one. "Six carpenters entered a common tavern, and bought and drank a quart of wine, and paid for it;

the taverner, at the request of the defendants, did then deliver them another quart of wine and a pennyworth of bread, amounting to 8d., and they did drink the wine and eat the bread, and did refuse to pay for the same." The taverner sued them for trespass; but the Court told him that his only remedy was to bring an action for debt against them. The carpenters' default was a breach of contract, not an actionable wrong.

RIGHT OF SUPPORT

This is either (1) *natural* (a piece of land—in its natural state, unweighted by buildings—has a right to be supported by adjoining or underlying land), or (2) *acquired by grant, express or implied*, or (3) *acquired by prescription, by twenty years' open enjoyment* (a house attached to another acquires this right in course of twenty years' time).

When there is withdrawal of the right of support the possessor of the land or building can bring an action *only when actual damage is apparent*. The wrong consists not in withdrawing the support, but in doing the damage, so that if substituted support is effectively supplied no wrong results.

NOTES ON RIGHT OF SUPPORT

1. It seems that, when an owner sells part of his land for building, there is an implied undertaking that he will not excavate on the land he retains so as to withdraw support from the buildings erected. That is, there is a right of support even apart from the right acquired by twenty years' enjoyment (*Rigby* v. *Bennett*, Ch. 1882).

2. The right by prescription is acquired (*a*) by twenty years' peaceful enjoyment without deception or concealment, (*b*) in conditions where it is obvious that the support is being enjoyed.

3. The withdrawal of support is only actionable when damage is caused to the land or building entitled to support. If, therefore, timber supports supply the requisite amount of upholding to prevent subsidence, no right of action accrues even though the minerals underneath the surface are abstracted or the adjoining house taken away. The unsightly baulks against certain old houses are tangible evidence that the buildings propped up have acquired a prescriptive right of support.

4. A curious case (*Solomon* v. *Vintner's Co.*, 1860, H. & N.) establishes the rule that it is the *adjoining* owner only who has the duty of support. Three houses leaned out of the upright for thirty years, A resting on B, B on C. The owner of C took down

his house ; the others fell ; the owner of A sought damages against
C. The owner of B would certainly have succeeded. The owner
of A, however, failed : A was not supported by C, and the owner
of B had done nothing to withdraw support.

RIGHT TO LIGHT—" ANCIENT LIGHTS "

This is acquired by grant or by uninterrupted enjoyment over
twenty years. Acquired by prescription in this way it constitutes
an " ancient " light. The right applies to the windows of a building only, not to land.

Nor is it every impediment to light that constitutes an actionable wrong : there must be a substantial deprivation of light,
enough to make a dwelling-house uncomfortable, or business
premises much less adapted for their purpose. " It might," said
Chief Justice Best, " be difficult to draw the line : but the jury
must distinguish between a *partial inconvenience* and a *real injury*
to the plaintiff in the enjoyment of his premises." There is a
rough practical " rule of forty-five degrees " (see page 502). An
obstruction is not actionable when the building complained of is
so low that the line drawn from the *centre* of the window to the
top of the obstruction is inclined at less than forty-five degrees to
the horizontal.

Where the inconvenience is slight from the obstruction, the
Court will not grant the extraordinary remedy of an injunction.
In the well-known case *Colls* v. *Home & Colonial Stores* (A.C.
1904), the principle was thus laid down : " In some cases an injunction is necessary ; for instance, if the injury cannot fairly be
compensated by money ; or if the defendant has acted in a high-
handed manner ; or if he has endeavoured to steal a march upon the
plaintiff or to evade the jurisdiction of the Court. In these cases
an injunction is necessary in order to do justice to the plaintiff
and as a warning to others.

" But if there is really a question as to whether the obstruction
is legal or not, and if the defendant has acted fairly and not in an
unneighbourly spirit, the Court ought to incline to damages
rather than to an injunction. The Court ought to be very careful
not to allow an action for the protection of ancient lights to be
used as a means of extorting money."

THREATENED OBSTRUCTION

It was in this spirit that the House of Lords decided (*Slack* v.
Leeds Co-operative Society, 1924) that, instead of a prohibitive

injunction of a building, damages might be a reasonable remedy. The Court of Appeal had held that a defendant could not, in effect, buy the power of doing a wrong against his neighbour, that it had no jurisdiction to award damages in lieu of a prohibitive injunction, where unlawful interference with light is threatened, but has not as yet been actually caused. The House of Lords, however, adjudged itself to have such jurisdiction; for the damage to the plaintiff would have been trifling and an injunction would have been a great detriment to the defendants.

RIGHTS TO WATER

This easement gives rise to difficult questions. An owner of land on the banks of a stream may have a claim for damages against a defendant who—

1. Takes water from the stream so as substantially to reduce the level flowing past the plaintiff's land.

2. Pollutes the water.

3. Obstructs the flow so as to injure the plaintiff's land.

Apparently, even the owner on whose land a natural stream originates cannot deprive owners lower down the stream of water. Where a dispute arises the task of the Court is difficult. For the principle is put thus: "This right to the benefit and advantage of the water flowing past his land is not an absolute and exclusive right to the flow of all the water in its natural state. It is a right only to the flow of the water and the enjoyment of it subject to the similar rights of all the proprietors of the banks on each side to that reasonable enjoyment of the same gift of Providence. It is only, therefore, for an unreasonable and unauthorised use of this common benefit that an action will lie."

Thus, in *Baily* v. *Morland* (Ch. 1902), the plaintiff, a mill-owner, asked for an injunction against the defendant, who extracted water for purposes of manufacture. The Court of Appeal held that he could not succeed; for he could not prove substantial damage; "The defendant's right to use the water is limited by this: that they must not so use it as to cause sensible injury to the plaintiff. The plaintiff, coming here to complain of the defendant's use, must prove sensible injury."

UNDERGROUND WATER

An owner can, however, use as he chooses underground water, not flowing in a stream, even though it would ultimately feed a stream. The town of Croydon got part of its water supply by sinking wells in its own land; the effect was to diminish sensibly the supply to a neighbouring stream; a mill-owner along the stream brought action, but failed.

The right to use one's property as he pleases is usually qualified by the maxim "so as not to harm another" (*sic utere tuo ut alienum non laedas*); the right to disturb the soil of your own land and all *underground* water that percolates without a known channel is, however, unqualified. "As the great interests of society require that the cultivation of every man's land should be encouraged, and its natural advantages made fully available, the owner must be permitted to dig in his own soil, and, in so doing, he can very rarely avoid interfering with the subterraneous waters flowing or percolating in his neighbour's land " (*Chasemore* v. *Richards*, H.L. 1859).

RIGHT SUBSISTS, THOUGH MOTIVE BE ILL

And, apparently, this unqualified right is not affected even though it should appear that it is being used with a wish to injure another, rather than to benefit oneself. The Corporation of Bradford sought an injunction to restrain an owner of land adjoining its water supply area from sinking wells that would substantially diminish the supply. The Corporation declared, and brought evidence to show, that the owner's intention was not to work his minerals, but to force the Corporation to buy his land. The Supreme Court held, however, that no injunction could be issued: "No use of property, which would be legal if due to a proper motive, can become illegal because it is prompted by a motive which is improper or even malicious. Motives and intentions in such a question as is now before your Lordships seem to me to be absolutely irrelevant " (*Mayor of Bradford, etc.* v. *Pickles*, A.C. 1895).

WATER RIGHTS INVOLVE DIFFICULTIES

The exceedingly great difficulty that often emerges when disputes regarding water supply arise is well illustrated in *Bartlett* v. *Tottenham*, decided in the Chancery Court in 1932. Plaintiff and defendant were adjoining landowners, conveyance of plaintiff's land having been made in 1919, of defendant's land in 1929, and by the same owners. These owners, more than forty years before, had built on the land, now the defendant's, a collecting tank, near the edge of what was now the plaintiff's land. This tank, used as a drinking trough for cattle and horses, had no outlet. But it was tipped, so that the outflow came on to plaintiff's land, and was carried by a stone drain to an open water-course. There were two watering points along this water-course, one used by the cottagers living on the plaintiff's land, the other used for watering cattle.

Improvements made by the defendant upon his land diminished the flow of the water. He substituted for the open tank a covered brick tank. This was connected by an underground pipe to a ram that pumped water into the defendant's house. The overflow still went in the old channel. But it was sensibly decreased. Moreover, in laying the pipe, springs were tapped and damage done to the plaintiff's land by the escape of water. The petitioner claimed a right by prescription to the full flow of water; he claimed also compensation for the damage by the springs.

On all points judgment went against the plaintiff. The tank had been built only for supplying water to cattle and horses. There could be no expectation that the outflow would be other than temporary. Nor did the right to the continuance of the overflow pass to the plaintiff by virtue of Section 62 of the Law of Property Act, 1925. The plaintiff had a right to the water naturally flowing in a stream through his land; but he could not obtain a right by prescription to have that natural flow augmented by an artificial water-course, built for a temporary purpose only.

Nor could the plaintiff obtain relief in regard to the water discharged on his land through the tapping of springs. For this tapping was caused by a natural and proper use of the defendant's own land.

RIGHTS OF WAY (PUBLIC)

These are rights enjoyed by the public at large of passing along highways or navigable rivers. As a rule the public does not own the highway: "the property is in the owner of the soil, subject to an easement for the benefit of the public." The owner or owners of the land adjoining own the highway or the river bed; and it is these owners that have the right to extract minerals from below the surface. Such extraction must not, however, interfere with the safety or the public enjoyment of the way. For there has been an actual or a presumed dedication by the owners to the use of the public; and a man cannot derogate from his own grant. Having made a grant he must do nothing that would tend to render that grant of no utility.

RIGHTS OF WAY ACT, 1932

The Rights of Way Act, enacted in 1932, makes clear the law in relation to public rights of way. The Common Law rules have been modified and made statutory.

All public highways which have not been created under statutory authority are deemed to have arisen from dedication. By this is implied a grant by the landowner to the public of a right of passage. It is, of course, seldom that an owner is willing, deliberately and voluntarily, to burden his estate with a perpetual public right of way. What usually happens is that for a long period of time the local population have used a track openly, freely, and without asking or obtaining permission or licence (*Nec vi, nec clam, nec precario*). In such circumstances, a Court, in the absence of evidence to the contrary, will presume that at some time some owner must have dedicated it, even though no evidence exists that he has ever definitely expressed his intention to do so. This presumption is the more readily drawn when the path is crossed by stiles or wicket gates, or other conveniences for the use of pedestrians, or when it has been repaired at public expense.

The only person who can burden his estate with a highway is the absolute owner of the freehold. Tenants for life of entailed properties, and trustees who have not complete power of disposition, do not enjoy absolute ownership. They are, therefore, incapable of dedicating. In order to get over the technical difficulty most judges, if satisfied that no beginning of the public use can be shown during the settlement, have been prepared to assume that the way in dispute was dedicated before the estate became entailed. The Prescription Act of 1832 provided that claims to private paths across freehold land might be established by proof of twenty years' enjoyment. Where land is subject to family settlement the period required is forty years.

The Rights of Way Act applies this to the proof of public rights of way. It provides that where a way has been used by the public as of right and without interruption for twenty years, in the case of land owned by an absolute freeholder, or for forty years where land has been entailed or subject to a limited interest, it "shall be deemed to have been dedicated as a highway unless there is sufficient evidence of circumstances existing during that period which negative the intention to dedicate such way."

For the security of landowners, who are entitled to protection from the possible effect of permitting the use of a short cut for the benefit of their tenants or of the public, without an intention of dedicating it as a highway in the strict sense, the Act contains the following provisions. By erecting a notice making it clear that a public right of way is not admitted, or, alternatively, by subsequently giving notice in writing to the county and district council concerned, an owner may fully safeguard himself against the risk of dedication being presumed from a neighbourly action. He may also deposit with the local authorities a map and a statement indicating the ways he admits to be public, and he can keep the record up to date by similar action every six years. The Court or Tribunal called upon to decide as to rights of way may take into consideration any maps, documents, plans, or historic records, which may throw light upon the dispute. Most of these, till the Act, have been inadmissible as evidence. The Act comes into operation on 1st January, 1934.

Clearly the Act improves upon the earlier position: "If the owner of the soil throws open a passage, and neither marks by any visible distinction that he means to preserve all his rights over it, nor excludes persons from passing through it by positive prohibition, he shall be presumed to have dedicated it to the public. Although the passage in question was originally intended only for private convenience, the public are not now excluded from it, after being allowed to use it so long without any interruptions."

OBLIGATION TO REPAIR

The Common Law rule was that when a road was dedicated to the public it was repairable by the public. The Highways Act, 1835, modified the rule to this extent: before the highway authorities "adopt" a road, they can require it to be made in a substantial manner. The cost of making the road to the satisfaction of the authorities is borne by the occupiers of the adjoining land in proportion to their frontages.

TRESPASS ON THE HIGHWAY

The road is dedicated so that persons may "pass and repass" along it. One who enters upon a highway for other purposes than passage may, accordingly, be a trespasser against the owners of adjoining land: "if a person uses the soil of the highway for any purpose other than that in respect of which the dedication was made and the easement acquired, he is a trespasser." So one who, remaining on the highway, sent his dog into the adjoining fields in order to flush pheasants, was held to be "trespassing in pursuit of game."

NUISANCE TO A HIGHWAY

This consists in obstructing the highway or in rendering it dangerous. It is a *public* nuisance. It is accordingly not a civil wrong, for which an individual may sue for damages. It is a crime, for which the person responsible may be prosecuted. Moreover, the Attorney-General may sue for an injunction to restrain the nuisance. To leave unguarded or unlighted a hole or a heap on the highway, to allow buildings adjoining the highway to become a source of danger, to have cellar gratings loose—all are public nuisances.

WRONGS TO PROPERTY RIGHTS

A person is protected in the enjoyment of what he has gained by bargain or obtained by gift. An interference with the enjoyment is a wrong for which he can claim damages. Such an interference may be the wrong of *Conversion*; the defendant has converted to his own use, or wrongfully deprived the plaintiff of the use and possession of the plaintiff's goods. He has, without legal justification—

1. Taken the property.
2. Detained it against the plaintiff's will.
3. Disposed of it without the plaintiff's authority.

A conversion is an actual interference with property; and it may be a conversion even though without wrongful intent. Thus, an auctioneer is liable for conversion when he sells property for one who has no title to it, and delivers it to the buyer. This is so whether or not he pays the proceeds to his customer (*Consolidated Co.* v. *Curtis*, Q.B. 1892). A railway company is liable for conversion if, after the transit is finished, it re-delivers goods to the sender. In *Taylor* v. *G. E. Railway* (K.B. 1901), the unpaid seller sought to exercise his right of stoppage *in transitu* upon learning of the insolvency of the buyer. The company let him have the goods back. But the goods were already lying at a railway station at the buyer's disposal; and that buyer had tried to resell them. The transit was therefore over; and the trustee in bankruptcy could successfully claim against the railway company.

On the other hand, a carrier, to whom reasonably prompt notice had been given to stop goods consigned to an insolvent buyer, is liable in conversion to the unpaid seller unless he acts promptly upon the instruction to stop delivery.

When the hirer of goods sells or pledges them he is guilty of a conversion; so is the buyer if he refuses to deliver the goods to the true owner. In an action against an auctioneer the judge said: "If goods be let on hire, although the person who hires them has the possession of them for the special purpose for which they are lent, yet, if he sent them to an auctioneer to be sold, he is guilty of a conversion, and, if the auctioneer afterwards refuses to deliver them to the owner, unless he will pay a sum of money, he is also guilty of a conversion."

The defendant, a warehouseman, was held liable for conversion in *Lilley* v. *Doubleday* (Q.B. 1881). The plaintiff had delivered the goods for deposit in a named warehouse, and had insured them as being there. In breach of his promise to store them in the warehouse named, Doubleday placed the goods in another of his warehouses. The things were burnt in the substituted warehouse; the insurance company was under no obligation to pay; and the warehouseman was held liable for the loss.

NO INVOLUNTARY BAILMENT

It may be noted, however, that to lose goods sent to you unasked for is not a conversion. A man cannot be made a bailee —a keeper of another's goods—against his will. If a tradesman sends good to a possible customer, the customer is under no obligation in regard to the goods; he need take no care of them; he need not, indeed, take them into his premises, but may leave them in the street. He is not intentionally to destroy or use the goods. For that would be an acceptance of the tradesman's offer. Otherwise he is under no duty in regard to the goods.

An author, being asked for the plot of a play he had written, sent not only the plot but the manuscript of the play to the manager of Drury Lane Theatre. The manuscript was lost, and the writer brought an action for conversion. He failed, however: "There is no case to go to the jury. The plaintiff was asked to send one thing. He sent another. His so doing cast no duty upon the defendant with regard to what was sent" (*Howard* v. *Harris, Nisi Prius,* 1884).

THE FINDER OF GOODS

The man to whom goods are sent without his asking is not like the *finder of goods*. The finder has, by his own action, taken another's property into his charge. He is, we say therefore, a "voluntary bailee." As a "voluntary bailee" he has the duty (1) of taking reasonable care of the goods for the rightful owner, (2) of taking reasonable steps to find the owner. He is entitled to retain the goods against everyone except the rightful owner; but if he sells them, or pledges them, or prevents himself in any other way from restoring them to the rightful owner, he may be made liable in conversion.

REMEDIES FOR CONVERSION

There are alternative remedies in an action for conversion—

1. The plaintiff may be awarded as damages the full value of the goods.

2. The Court may order restitution of the property. Such an order is enforced either by the sheriff's putting the plaintiff into possession, or by an attachment for contempt of Court if the defendant refuses to obey.

The second remedy is at the discretion of the Court. For, clearly, it would be sometimes injustice to the defendant to force restitution. If he has taken the plaintiff's corn and ground it into flour, the plaintiff may be allowed to have the flour. But if there has been a greater change—if the plaintiff's marble has been made into a statue—it is possible that the plaintiff would need to content himself with the cost of the marble.

Finally, it should be noted, the payment of damages in an action for conversion is equivalent to a buying of the goods. They are henceforth the defendant's property.

(See also pages 240 and 241, where the criminal aspects of conversion are considered.)

INTANGIBLE PROPERTY

Property nowadays consists of much more than the things we can see and handle. The development of trade has made many intangible rights into valuable property. Such intangible rights are "goodwill," "patents," "copyright."

PROTECTION OF GOODWILL

The reputation enjoyed by a trader and his goods in the market is property, sometimes valuable property. And English law adequately protects it. If a man sells his goodwill the law prevents him from canvassing his old customers; he will not be allowed to nullify the property he has sold.

There is also available an action for *injurious falsehood*, i.e. false statements made about a person whereby he suffers loss through the behaviour of those to whom the statements are made. Thus in *Ratcliffe* v. *Evans* (Q.B. 1892), the defendant was penalised

because he had published of the plaintiff the untrue statement
that he had ceased business. Trade thereby fell off. There is no
libel; for a libel is what tends to bring a man into hatred and
contempt. But it is established law that spoken or written false-
hoods, knowingly made and causing damage to another in the
way of his trade or profession, give a cause of action. They tend
to undermine the goodwill he has acquired.

" SLANDER OF TITLE "

One form of injurious falsehood is "slander of title"; the
plaintiff's trade has been lessened by a false statement that the
goods he offers are not his, or are the infringement of a patent
or of a copyright. "Slander" here is used in the old sense of
"scandal," "calumny." Thus, in *Royal Baking Powder Co.* v.
Wright, Crossly & Co. (Patent Cases Report, 1901), Lord Davey
said, "This is an action for slander of title—i.e. an action for
maliciously damaging the plaintiffs in their trade by denying
their title to the use of a certain label, and threatening to sue their
customers. To support such an action it is necessary for the
plaintiff to prove (1) that the statements complained of were
untrue, (2) that they were made without just cause or excuse,
(3) that the plaintiffs had suffered special damage thereby."
"Special damage" here means a money loss that can be traced
to the untrue statement.

Similarly, falsely to allege specific defects in a rival's goods is
an actionable wrong. But to allege, even falsely, that one's goods
are better than a rival's is not actionable. If it were to be made
actionable, traders would be under a constant temptation to use
the Courts as effective means of advertising.

" PASSING OFF "

There is also available an action for "passing off." A trader,
by one misleading device or another, takes to himself the benefit
of a rival's reputation. He sells goods under such a name as leads
the public to suppose the goods to be his rival's goods. Or he
uses the trade mark of his rival, or a mark closely resembling
it, or he imitates the "get-up" of the plaintiff's goods.

The essence of the wrong is the causing trade, by misleading
the public, to be diverted from the rival to himself; and the wrong
is independent of intention to deceive.

It is noteworthy that even a descriptive word may by long
usage become appropriated to a particular trade. A good instance

is afforded by the Appeal Court decision in *Reddaway* v. *Barton* (1932). Messrs. Reddaway sought an injunction to restrain another firm from selling "camel-hair belting," this name having by long usage become identified in the public mind with the belting manufactured by Messrs. Reddaway. The plaintiffs had, in 1896, obtained such an injunction (*Reddaway* v. *Banham*), on the intelligible ground that "it is not necessarily a defence that the name used by the defendant is descriptive of the goods, if it is calculated to deceive." In the later case the High Court judge refused an injunction, holding that the addition of the name of the competing firm distinguished the goods, and obviated the possibility of confusion. The Appeal Court unanimously reversed this decision. Any one, of course, can make belting from camel-hair; any one can put it on the market. But he must find a name other than "camel-hair" belting for it. This name is Messrs. Reddaway's.

FRAUD ON THE PUBLIC ESSENTIAL IN A PASSING-OFF ACTION

Passing-off consists in the fraud of imposing upon a customer other goods than the customer asks for and those he thinks he is about to receive. The customer is misled through the use of a name similar to the name he had in mind, or by appearances calculated to deceive him. The essence of passing-off is the likelihood that the public will be deceived. Whether or not the conscious attempt to deceive is present does not matter; if deception is likely to occur, that is enough.

So the owner of the copyright in a dramatic sketch succeeded in a passing-off action against the producer of a cinema picture (*Samuelson* v. *Producers' Distributing Co.*, C.A. 1932). There existed no film version of the sketch, but the picture might well be supposed to be such a version.

"REMEDIES" IN A PASSING-OFF ACTION

When a trader finds that his goodwill is being injured through the selling of another's goods where his own are asked for, he has an action for an injunction to restrain the misleading sales. He has, besides, a right to seek damages—damages that will be measured by the loss he can show, or by the profits the other seller has made by infringing the right of goodwill. The remedy is a Common Law remedy, dependent upon the rule that one may not attract the business of another, whether by misleading description, or make, or mark.

Thus in *Edge & Sons* v. *Nicholls & Sons* (H.L. 1911), the Supreme Court held that a manufacturer was entitled to an injunction against a rival, even though a patent the plaintiff had taken out had been revoked. The patent had been taken out in regard to the "get-up."

So, too, the name "Bolivar " had long been associated with a brand of cigar. The defendants put on the market a cigar which they called "La Molivar." The use of this name was forbidden by injunction (*Middlemas & Wood* v. *Molivar & Co.* (Ch. 1921). The public, never able to discriminate very keenly, might well confuse the names.

' DESCRIPTIVE " WORDS

There is no right to the exclusive use of any descriptive words. But where a name or anything else has come to summon into mind a specified commodity, a person will be restrained from using a similar association for a similar article. A maker may use "Swan " as a name for a match, even though the name should be already well known in connection with a pen. But he would not be allowed to use the name for a pen.

We may note in this connection that an ordinary English word is seldom protected as being distinctive of a particular trader's goods. Unless the conscious wish to deceive is proved, a trader cannot claim the exclusive right to a name. And, if an injunction should be granted, it is not the name that is protected but the goodwill that would be injured by its continued use.

" PASSING-OFF " IS AN ELASTIC TERM

It may be noticed that "passing-off" may take on a quite extensive meaning. Thus, *Vokes, Ltd.* v. *Evans, etc.* (Ch. 1932) was a case where an injunction was granted against quite innocent sellers of articles identical with plaintiff's articles, but obtained as a result of a third party's breach of contract. For some years the plaintiff had sold motor-car wind-screen wipers made by a manufacturer who had entered into an agreement that the plaintiff alone should have the right of selling these wipers. In breach of the agreement the manufacturer sold a number of such wipers, marked like the rest of the output with the plaintiff's name, to the defendants, who resold to the public. The plaintiff claimed an injunction to restrain the defendants from passing off their goods as the plaintiff's goods.

It was held that, since the wipers complained of had been manufactured and sold to the defendants wrongfully and in breach of duty to the plaintiff, an injunction could be granted. Such wipers not having been selected or marketed by the plaintiff were in fact spurious. Since, however, the defendants had bought innocently, no inquiry as to damage must be made.

"It is admitted, and there is no doubt about it, that it is exactly the same screen-wiper as the plaintiff has manufactured for him and sells. But the only authority to make these particular screen-wipers was an order given by the plaintiff company. Any screen-wiper, therefore, made to some other order, though precisely similar, would not in fact be the plaintiff's articles at all. Again it might well be said that a person in the position of the plaintiff company, having goods manufactured for him by a particular manufacturer, upon which his name and address were to appear, would take great care that the articles, when delivered to him, were in the best possible condition before he accepted them, and took delivery of them. For he would not desire a possibly defective article bearing his name to be offered to the public."

TRADE MARKS, PATENTS, AND COPYRIGHT

To infringe any of these is similar to the wrong of passing-off. But trade marks are also protected by the Trade Marks Act, 1905; patents are also protected by the Patents Act, 1907; copyright also by the Copyright Act, 1911.

The Merchandise Marks Act, 1877, makes it an offence to sell goods to which a false trade description has been applied. The master is liable under this section even if his servant disobeys his orders in regard to the sales. Otherwise, the Act would to a large extent be nugatory.

TRADE MARKS

The law relating to these is chiefly contained in the Trade Marks Act of 1905, and the Trade Marks Act of 1919. The earlier Act defines the trade mark as "A mark used or purposed to be used upon, or in connection with, goods for the purpose of indicat ng that they are the goods of the proprietor of such trade mark, by virtue of manufacture, selection, certification, dealing with or offering for sale." The 1919 Act enacts that, when a dealer in goods has used a mark for two years in the United Kingdom to denote that the goods are his, he may register this mark. Such a trade mark is an implied warranty that the goods to which it is applied are genuine (Merchandise Marks Act, 1877).

REGISTERING TRADE MARKS

Trade marks must be registered; the exclusive use of the trade mark is obtained only by such registration. To state untruly that the design of an article sold has been registered is a crime. The register is kept at the Patent Office.

Application for registration must be accompanied by the fee, by representations of the mark to be registered, and by details of the goods the mark is to be attached to. In order to obtain registration the trade mark must consist of either—

1. The name of a company, individual, or firm, represented in a special or particular manner.

2. The signature of the applicant or some predecessor of his.

3. An invented word or words.

4. A word or words having no direct reference to the character or quality of the goods and not being a geographical name or surname.

5. Any other distinctive mark; under this section a new design that cannot be patented may be protected.

6. An "old" mark; i.e. a mark existing and continuously in use before 13th August, 1875.

Some forms of wording cannot be registered as a trade mark. Such are *Patent*, *Registered Design*, and *Emblems of the Royal Family*, and, unless the trade mark incorporating them were used before 1875, *British National Flags* and the word *Royal* or the *Royal Arms*. Traders may, however, be appointed and may then use in their trade the Royal Arms. Anyone using them without authority in such a way as to imply that he supplies members of the Royal Family is liable to a fine of £20. He can also be restrained by injunction upon the application by anyone interested. An association of those having authority to use the Royal Arms is, in fact, mainly occupied in protecting their legal privilege. (See page 500.)

The main points that may cause controversy in regard to trade marks are illustrated in the *Bass* v. *Nicholson* case described below.

TO OBTAIN REGISTRATION

Upon application to the Registrar, he advertises the application. Letters relating to trade marks should be sent to Patent Office,

Trade Marks Branch, 25 Southampton Buildings, Chancery Lane, London, W.C.2. From this office full information as to the necessary procedure is obtainable. For cotton marks, however, the office is that of the Comptroller, Manchester Trade Marks Branch, 48 Royal Exchange, Manchester; and for steel goods, Law Clerk, Cutlers' Company, Cutlers' Hall, Sheffield. Any person may give notice of opposition on the ground of—

1. Incapability of registration.
2. Prior use belonging to some other person.
3. Previous registration.
4. Resemblance to an existing trade mark.
5. Lack of distinctive character.

The Registrar must not register anything likely to mislead the public; and when a word trade mark is registered which is the name of an article or substance manufactured under a patent, then the rights to the exclusive use of the trade mark cease upon the expiration of the patent.

Registration is for sixteen years. After this period, the trade mark may be re-registered so as to be permanently the exclusive possession of its owner. The trade mark may be assigned, but only in connection with the goodwill of the business to which it relates. An infringement consists in the unauthorised use of the actual mark, or in the use of a mark calculated, from its similarity to the registered mark, to deceive.

The Merchandise Marks Act, 1877, enacted that it shall be a criminal offence to forge a trade mark or to apply to goods falsely any mark which so nearly resembles a trade mark as to be calculated to deceive. In addition, the goods may be forfeited and destroyed. The Merchandise Marks Act, 1926, prevents the sale of imported goods to which are applied the name or trade mark of a dealer or trader in the United Kingdom, unless there is an accompanying indication of the origin of the goods. The trade mark is personal property.

FRAUD IS THE ESSENCE OF OFFENCES UNDER THE TRADE MARKS ACTS

The essence of an offence under the Trade Marks Acts is the deceiving of the public. This is well brought out in *Sykes* v. *Sykes* (K.B. 1824), decided, of course, on Common Law principles, made statutory by the Acts. There the plaintiff, who sold powder-flasks and similar goods marked with the words *Sykes Patent*, obtained damages against the defendant, even though the patent was invalid owing to a defect in the specification, and even though the defendant's real name was Sykes. It was urged that the dealers who bought the goods knew their origin well enough. But this was not enough. There was no actually false statement, yet the plaintiff obtained what he sought: the rival maker was prohibited from making goods that might well be confused with those already possessed of the market. The retail dealers knew the origin of the goods bought from the defendants; but the public to whom they resold did not. "No man," ran a later judgment upon much the same matter, "is entitled to represent his goods as being made by another; and no man is permitted to use any mark, sign, symbol, device, or other means whereby (even without making a direct false representation himself to a purchaser) he enables such purchaser to make a false representation to the ultimate customer."

A DISPUTE OVER TRADE MARKS

The principles under which the registration of trade marks is governed are well illustrated in *Bass, Ratcliffe & Gretton, Ltd.* v. *Nicholson & Sons, Ltd., and Registrar of Trade Marks* (H.L. 1931).

The respondent brewers had for a long time stencilled an outline triangle with "N" on their "best pale ale" casks, and had also branded "Nicholson" on them. In 1927, they applied to register the combination as a trade mark. Messrs. Bass opposed the application on the grounds of similarity with the Bass solid triangle mark registered in 1876. The Assistant Comptroller allowed registration, limiting the colours to be used by Nicholson to black and white. About the same time, Messrs. Nicholson applied for the removal of the word "Triangle" registered by Messrs. Bass in 1926, and the removal was ordered.

The Court of Appeal held (and the House of Lords affirmed with some modifications the judgment) that—

1. The respondents' mark, having been used as a mark of quality and of origin before 1875, was registrable as an "old mark." Whether or not the public recognised such a mark as distinctive did not matter; the test is simply, "Was the mark regularly used by the claimants before 1875?"

2. Though the mark might lead to confusion with that of Messrs. Bass, the Registrar was authorised (by Section 19 of the Trade Marks Act, 1905) to place upon the register an old mark so nearly resembling a mark of another already on the register as to be calculated to deceive.

3. That in view of the extensive use of the appellants' mark in connection with bottled beer and the absence of evidence that the respondents had used their mark for bottled beer, this should be excluded from the goods upon which Messrs. Nicholson's mark appeared.

4. That registering the respondents' mark involved the removal of the appellants' mark consisting of the word "Triangle."

"Unless it can be said that the casks of beer dealt with in the manner described cannot obtain a trade mark because the fact that the casks are constantly in the cellars of publicans and private customers prevents the public at large from seeing the mark, this mark seems to have satisfied all the necessary conditions.

"It was not merely a quality mark, but was exclusively used by Nicholson to denote a special quality, not of beer generally, but of beer brewed by them. The section contains no condition of general recognition of the mark.

"But the prohibition is a general one, and Section 19 states a definite exception. However, the Trade Marks Act of 1919 gives power to insert limitations in the mode or place of user. Under this power it is right to limit the respondents' mark to the use of goods other than bottled beer."

TRADE NAME

May an individual begin business under some such style as "Postal Supply Company"? Provided that the adoption of this name does not cause him to appropriate the trade of a competitor, he may; the "Co." may very well be his wife or son or daughter. The law of England is singularly liberal in this matter; a man is free to call himself by whatever name he chooses; he may, indeed, use different names for different purposes. Only, he must not use this liberty so as to interfere with the rights of his fellows. A trader must respect the trade names as well as the trade marks of other dealers. He must not trade under a name so closely resembling that of the plaintiff as to be mistaken for it by the public. Thus, the *Universal Life Assurance Society* obtained an injunction preventing a later incorporation from carrying on business under the name of the *Universal Life Assurance Association*. As for the assumption of the title "Company," it used to be said that it was an offence against the Crown (which alone could grant the privilege of incorporation) for a private person to "assume to act as a corporation." No machinery exists, it would seem, however, for punishing such an assumption; and the mere use of the word "Company," applicable as it is to both incorporated and unincorporated associations, does not constitute an offence. As one result of the panic legislation during the years of the Great War, certain formalities are now necessary when a man does choose to trade under a name other than his own. The Registration of Business Names Act, 1916, required registration under the Act.

" BY APPOINTMENT "

We may note in this connection the right cherished by many dealers of being able to describe themselves as suppliers to the Royal Household. A Royal Warrant Holders' Association exists in order to prevent unauthorised use of any device that would suggest such a relation to the public. The Association, in proper cases, petitions the Chancery Court for an injunction. A case in 1932 was the *Royal Warrant Holders' Association* v. *British Marketing Frames*. The defendants had been using on their stationery the device of the Prince of Wales' feathers with the words below, "By Appointment." They had no authority to do so, and the Court granted the injunction sought.

LAW RELATING TO ADVERTISEMENTS

Advertising is the necessary result of sale by description. It represents part of the work done in simpler times by middlemen who exhibited as well as sold their goods. As in all sales by description, the articles sold must answer to the description. Thus no wine may be sold as "Port," unless it is made within easy reach of Oporto and is so certified by the Portuguese Government.

" PUFFING " ONE'S WARES IS LAWFUL

"Puffing" one's own goods has never been held wrong. *Simplex commendatio non obligat* is the old Roman rule, "praising his wares binds no one." A line is drawn, however; though we must admit it is not always easy to say where. Land was advertised for sale as "very fertile and improvable," whereas it was in fact partly abandoned as useless. When the buyer made a complaint this advertisement was held to be "a mere flourishing description" by an auctioneer (*Dimmock* v. *Hallell*, Ch. 1866).

On the other hand, where, in the sale of an hotel, the occupier was stated to be a "most desirable tenant," whereas his rent was much in arrear and he shortly became bankrupt, such a statement was enough to justify the buyer in rescinding the contract. (*Smith* v. *Land and House Property Co.*, Ch., 1884.)

Perhaps we may say that the advertiser and those who act on the advertisement are expected to be reasonable men, and leave it at that. We should note, however, that the case where the buyer obtained no redress was an early one. The attitude of the old judges might be summed up in the question of one of them. "Shall we indict a man for making a fool of another?" Modern judges are less tolerant of sharp practice.

One thing is clear: if we make a definite promise in our advertisement, we are bound to fulfil our promise. During the prevailing influenza epidemic the Carbolic Smoke Ball Co., advertised widely that a person buying their remedy, lighting the smoke balls and inhaling the smoke four times a day, would be exempt from the devastating sickness. Probably no obligation was incurred by such a vague promise. But the Company went further; it promised £100 to anyone who, having carried out their instructions, did contract the disease. Mrs. Carlill bought the remedy, duly sniffed the smoke four times a day, and in spite of all she had influenza—and she sued for the hundred pounds. It was held that she was entitled to the promised £100 (Q.B. 1893). See also *Wood* v. *Letrik* (K.B. 1932), where, under very similar circumstances, the plaintiff obtained £500 because the electric comb he bought, relying on the defendants' promise that it would restore the youthful colour of his hair, failed to achieve the desired purpose.

RIGHT OF LIGHT

In erecting hoardings for advertisements we are constrained to obtain licences. Something else must be considered, too. There are rights of adjoining property to be regarded. One of these rights is that of receiving light. When during twenty years light has been received by the windows of a building—when these windows are, therefore, what are called "ancient lights"—no man is allowed to build so close to them or so high as to deprive these windows of a substantial part of the light. Mark that we say "substantial"; for clearly a building far away and quite low will obstruct *some* rays of light. "*Substantial*," like "reasonable," is a hard word to define. What is a "reasonable price" leads to many disputes. There is no absolute right to *all* the light that comes to a given window; there is, however, a right not to have windows so darkened that the obstructing building is a nuisance. It is perhaps difficult to know where to draw the line; a fair working rule—the "rule of forty-five degrees"—treats as innocent any building so low that the angle of obstruction does not exceed forty-five degrees. Thus, normally, a window *A* will not be legally obstructed by a building below the line *XY*.

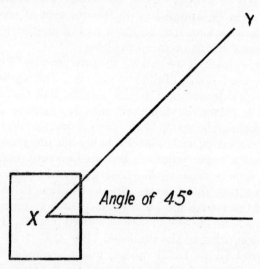

A WINDOW ENJOYING "ANCIENT LIGHTS"

Any building rising above the line *XY* would probably be regarded as infringing the legal right to light.

But varying circumstances will have weight. What would be regarded as an infringement in the country, where one spot is not necessarily the only spot for the building, would perhaps be without offence in the town.

In a much litigated case, the *Home and Colonial Stores* tried without success to prevent the erection of a building which when erected would not be as high as its own building. It was not disputed that the diminution of light received by one long room in the Stores would entail the burning of more electric light. But this was held by the House of Lords not to entitle the complaining Company either to an order forbidding the erection, or to damages. (See pages 483 and 484, where this question of the interference of "ancient lights" is discussed.)

INFRINGEMENT OF " GOODWILL "

The question of *goodwill*—for which the definition is suggested "the likelihood of getting whatever business is being done"—is more difficult than that of right to light. It includes the right to a registered trade mark, upon which we may say a word or two. The Trade Marks Registration Act of 1875 governs this part of the question; as time goes on, all parts of our Common Law will come under the general survey of Parliament and be codified in statutes. No registration is allowed that would monopolise part of the general vocabulary of trade, or would unduly restrict the use of words that a trader might be likely to use in describing his goods. The words must be "invented" ones, must apparently not be a mere modification of existing words : thus *Mazawattee* (tea), *Bovril* (meat extract), *Kodak* (photographic camera), and *Savoneol* (soap rich in oil), were considered invented words and duly registered. But *Panoram* and *Bioscope* (for camera), and *Orlwool* (for a particular cloth) were refused registration. A name when registered is protected against infringements ; and we may obtain some idea of what are regarded as infringements by noting that the following have been held to be such : *Securine* of the name *Seccotine* and *Condi-Sanitas* of the name *Sanitas*.

RIGHT TO TRADE NAME

"Goodwill" includes also the right to a trade name ; when, by intelligent advertising—backed up as this must be by real service to the community—a firm has won a reputation that draws business, it is unfair that another should step in and appropriate the business. A person may not trade even under his own name, if this would harm an established trader. Thus the well-known firm of Day & Martin had built up a large business by judicious publicity and by real polish. Both Day and Martin had long been dead when a real "Day" and a real "Martin" began to trade under the firm-name of "Day & Martin," as *makers of blacking*. An action was brought against the new firm and an injunction was granted restraining the defendants from using their real names when selling blacking, the reason given being that the defendants had the fraudulent purpose of representing and holding out to the public that they were the old and well-known firm. (*Croft* v. *Day*, Ch. 1843.)

Compare the case of *Harrods* v. *Harrod* (1923). A new firm had advertised, calling itself *R. Harrod, Limited* and describing itself as "the house of credit," the plaintiffs calling themselves "the house of quality." The Court held that the adopting of such a name was calculated to make people believe that the new firm was connected with the old one: "It should never be forgotten," is the judgment in *Levy* v. *Walker*, "in these cases that the right to restrain anybody from using the name that he likes in the course of any business that he chooses to carry on is a right in the nature of a trade mark. That is to say, a man has a right to say, 'You must not use the description whether true or not, which is intended to represent, or is calculated to represent to the world that your business is my business, and so by a fraudulent mis-statement deprive me of the profits of the business that would otherwise come to me.' That is the principle on which this Court interferes. The Court interferes solely for the purpose of protecting the owner of a trade or business from a wrongful invasion of that business by somebody else." We should note, perhaps, that the possibility of misleading the public is in the advertisements only; since 1917 there has been a statutory requirement that the true names of all partners are to appear on catalogues, and correspondence of the firm.

The case of *Sykes* v. *Sykes* illustrates the length to which our law goes in protecting traders who have earned a reputation for reliable goods (see page 497).

LIBEL LAW EXERCISES RESTRAINT

The advertiser should never be so ill-advised as to offend against the law of libel. Every man has a right to the reputation he and his goods have deservedly obtained, and the law protects this right. Praise your own goods as highly as you please—you need not fear lest the public, the much-confiding public, will be cloyed by the praise. But do not vilify another's goods; even though no actual damage be proved by words that affect a man in his calling (and a trader is very sensitive in this matter) the speaker or the writer of those words is liable to pay.

The law goes further in relation to written defamations: if a written statement exposes the libelled person to hatred and contempt, damages are awarded. The one defence available is that the statement is true, and, moreover, that it is to the interests of the people that it should be publicly known. For, of course, the advertiser cannot make use of the defence that he is privileged —as a Member of Parliament is—to make whatever statement he pleases, however damaging to another it may be.

ADVERTISEMENTS MAY ENJOY COPYRIGHT

In so far as we can describe an advertisement as a "production of genius"—a product embodying inventive skill and artistic production—it would seem subject to the law of copyright. No one is allowed servilely to copy it.

"Literary and artistic property" is acquired by producing and making public a work of literature or art; and copyright is allowed not only in books, paintings, and sculpture, but also for casts, engravings, photographs, and designs for articles, whether of ornament or use.

COPYRIGHT

There is no property which is more entirely the property of an individual than work which has been the direct results of the labour and the talent or genius of the author or composer who has given it to the world. The copyright which is given to him is not in derogation of the right of any other person. It is merely the right to prevent other people from copying and appropriating that which is the true property and the true invention of the original author or composer.

MEANING OF COPYRIGHT

Copyright means the exclusive right of multiplying copies of an original work or composition. By analogy it includes the exclusive right of performing a work in public.. This right involves the right of preventing other people from doing so, a right that can be made effective by means of an injunction. The statutory definition is contained in Section 1 of The Copyright Act, 1911: "Copyright means the sole right of reproducing or producing in any material form whatsoever, of performing, or, in the case of a lecture, of delivering, the work or any substantial part thereof in public; if the work is unpublished, it means the exclusive right to publish the work or any substantial part of it." What constitutes "performance in public" was discussed by the Court of Appeal in *Harms, Ltd. and Chappell & Co.* v. *Martans Club* (Ch. 1926). There it was decided that an infringement had occurred when, at a private dining and dance club to which guests had been invited, a performance had taken place.

The plaintiffs sued the club for performing in public the musical play called "Tip Toes." In this the plaintiffs had copyright. They had produced it in America but not yet in England. The

Court, affirming the judgment of the lower Court, held that the proprietary rights of the plaintiffs had been infringed. For the life of popular songs is usually very short, and premature performance of musical pieces may cause great loss to the copyright owners.

The contention of the defendants was that performance in a club could not be construed as performance in public. For the essential element of clubs is privacy; and the buildings they occupy are private premises. This contention the Court could not adopt: "There was an entertainment of members, and there were fifty guests, not members of the club. Is it possible to deny that they were properly called members of the public? The persons present would be able to pay for entrance to any public theatre where the play might be performed. I cannot deny that the author was injured. If it were possible to get round the Copyright Act by such a performance, it appears to me that a very serious inroad would have been made upon the property in copyright."

In a copyright test action (*Performing Rights Society, Ltd.* v. *Hammond's Bradford Brewery Co., Ltd.*, 1933) it was decided on similar grounds that the use of loud-speakers in public place? constituted a public performance that might be a breach of copyright.

The defendants admitted that on 1st October, 1932, the musical works referred to were broadcast by the British Broadcasting Corporation, and that they were audible to certain of the defendants' customers through a radio receiving set which was installed by the defendants at their premises and under the control of their servants.

The defendants denied that the audition constituted a further performance entitling the plaintiffs to royalties additional to the fees paid to them by the British Broadcasting Corporation.

"The plaintiffs claim that what has been done is an infringement; that it involves a performance in public of copyright work, and that such performance has not been authorised by them, or by any person empowered to give such authority. The original performance was relayed from a transmitting station under the control of the B.B.C.

The defendants say that the act of making audible to guests in the hotel of the musical works being broadcast is not a performance at all, or, at any rate, it is not furnished by the defendants. They take the further point that, assuming that they are wrong on the first point, the plaintiffs, licensing the broadcasting of the three musical works in question, put it out of their power to prevent people with receiving sets and using loud-speakers from using them for the purpose of making audible sounds to anybody they please.

I think that it is important to note in the first place that the Copyright Act, 1911, was passed with a single object—namely, for the benefit of authors of all kinds, whether the works are literary or dramatic or musical; and secondly, that the subject matter with which the Act was dealing is of a very practical kind. I think that one ought to bear these two circumstances in mind when one begins to construe the meaning of the word ' performance.'

The first question is whether the act of the defendants, or their servants, in tuning-in their receiving set and rendering audible the Hertzian waves which are being transmitted through the so-called ether is a performance. In answering this question I do not think that it is necessary to go into great detail. The loud-speaker is the translating device in that it converts the electrical current into sound vibrations.

That process is, in my opinion, essentially a reproduction and is not similar to the step of making distant sound audible by some magnifying device. The sounds are produced by an instrument under the direct control of the hotel proprietor, and to my mind they are as much under his control as if his employee were turning a barrel-organ—one of those distressing musical affairs that we sometimes hear. The fact that there is no power of selection is, I think, irrelevant to the question whether the sounds amount to a 'performance.'

The reproduction is, in my opinion, as much a 'performance' as is the reproduction of a musical piece by a gramophone apparatus.

As regards the second point, as to the effect of the licence given to the B.B.C. by the owners of the performing rights in question, Section 2 of the Act of 1911 provided that copyright in a work should be deemed to be infringed by any person who, without the consent of the owner of the copyright, does anything the right to do which is conferred by the Act on the owner of the copyright. Translating that into the subject matter of the present discussion, the copyright of the musical works has been infringed by the defendants, who, without the consent of the plaintiffs, have performed the works in public. The defendants cannot

17

justify their action by saying that the B.B.C. broadcast the musical works. Accordingly, the action, having regard to the view which I have expressed on 'performance' is an infringement of copyright.''

FOUNDATION OF COPYRIGHT

The copyright is a species of property founded on labour and invention. That is, it is property acquired by occupancy, the oldest and most widely recognised mode of acquiring property. If I take and make valuable what no one else wants or has thought about, it seems only fair that I should enjoy rights over what without me would not have existed as property. In this respect there may be copyright even in an original advertisement or trade "slogan." The test is always: Does this order of words indicate a substantial effort and material result of imaginative power? Has the work called for skill in composition? The protection afforded goes far, however. Thus a compilation even of unoriginal matter—a selection of poems, a broadcasting programme, a directory—is entitled to copyright when it means original effort. It has even been decided that an engraving or a photograph of a picture is protected.

NO COPYRIGHT IN IDEAS

There is no copyright in ideas; the protection of an idea falls within the patent law and is available only when the idea is embodied in manufacture.

To take an idea from a book or even to adopt its "plot," is no infringement if the idea is clothed in original literary or artistic form. True, if there is a close resemblance in the "situations" and incidents, the copying can hardly be negatived. But resemblance is by no means conclusive as to infringements. "A copy," it has been judicially defined, "is that which comes so near the original as to suggest the original to the mind of every person seeing the copy and knowing the original."

When the ideas have been embodied in words they can be regarded as property. The claim is to the order of words, the order having a marked identity and a permanent endurance.

COPYRIGHT IN PHOTOGRAPHS

When a person sits for his portrait, there will usually be implied a contract on the part of the taker that he will not sell or exhibit copies without the sitter's consent. Occasionally this consent may be implied, as when a sitter accepts an invitation for a free sitting. So with a photograph; the assumption is that the copyright belongs not to the photographer but to the photographed. If persons visit a photographer and arrange a sitting, paying for the resulting photograph, they own the copyright; and they have control over the use to which the photographs may be put. If persons accept an invitation for a free sitting, even if they subsequently buy copies of the photograph made, the copyright belongs to the photographer, who may use the photographs as he pleases.

COPYRIGHT IN LETTERS

It seems that a letter is an original literary work and is therefore entitled to copyright (*British Oxygen Coal Co.* v. *Liquid Gas Co.*, Ch, 1925). It seems, too, that the reporter of a speech has copyright not in the speech but in the report of it. Thus, in *Walter* v. *Lane* (A.C. 1900), *The Times* succeeded in an action against a person who took from *The Times* reports of certain speeches delivered by Lord Rosebery. *The Times* reporters were employed on the undertaking that the copyright in all articles and reports composed belonged to *The Times*. *The Times* sought to restrain the defendant from copying the reports, and ultimately obtained the injunction sought. It was urged that a verbatim reporter, however learned, artistic, and accomplished, acts simply as the echo, the mocking bird, the slave of the speaker. But the Lord Chancellor said—

"I should very much regret it, if I were compelled to come to the conclusion that the law permitted one man to make profit by appropriating to himself the labour, skill, and capital of another. Those who preserve the memory of spoken words that are assumed to be of value to the public are entitled to protection. The proof of piracy may be difficult, but that has no bearing upon the existence of piracy. Here there is no difficulty; the defendant's report of these speeches is not the result of independent labour, but is simply taken from *The Times*."

AUTHOR'S RIGHTS

The author of an original work is entitled to the exclusive rights
1. Of producing or performing any translation of the work.

2. Of converting a dramatic work into a novel or a non-dramatic novel.

3. Of converting a novel or other non-dramatic work into a dramatic work.

4. In the case of a literary, dramatic, or musical work to make any record, perforated roll, cinematograph film, or other contrivance by means of which the work may be mechanically performed or delivered.

5. To authorise any of such acts by other persons.

THE "FIRST AUTHOR"

Usually, there can be no doubt about the identity of the first author. In exceptional circumstances the Court may be called upon to decide. Thus, in *Cummins* v. *Bond* (Ch. 1926), the plaintiff sought a declaration that she was the owner of the copyright of the "Chronicle of Cleophas," written by her as a medium under the influence, as she declared, of an external psychic agent. The defendant, who had transcribed and annotated the writing, claimed to be joint author. He based his claim also on the assertion that his presence was necessary before the psychic being would manifest himself.

Mr. Justice Eve gave the plaintiff what she sought: "So far as this world is concerned there can be no doubt who is the author here, for the plaintiff has written every word of this script. But the plaintiff and the defendant are of opinion that the true originator is some being no longer inhabiting this world, and who has been out of it long enough to hope that he has no reasons for wishing to return to it. It would seem as though the individual who has been dead and buried for some 1900 years and the plaintiff ought to be regarded as the joint authors and owners of the copyright. But, inasmuch as I do not feel myself competent to make any declaration in his favour, and recognising as I do that I have no jurisdiction extending to the sphere in which he moves, I think I ought to confine myself, when inquiring who is the author, to individuals who were alive when the work first came into existence, and to conditions which the legislature of 1911 may reasonably be presumed to have contemplated. The defendant invites me to declare that the authorship and copyright rest with someone already domiciled on the other side of the inevitable river. But I can only look upon the matter as a terrestrial one, of the earth earthy, and I deal with it on that footing. The plaintiff has made out her case, and the copyright rests with her."

ALLOWABLE DEALINGS WITH COPYRIGHT WORKS

Copyright is not infringed by the following dealings with an original work—

1. Any fair dealing with the work for the purposes of private study, research, criticism, review, or newspaper summary.

2. The use by an artist who is not the owner of the copyright in his work of his sketches or models, provided that he does not repeat or imitate the main design.

3. Publishing sketches, engravings, or photographs of sculpture if permanently situate in a public place, or the publishing of sketches, engravings, or photographs (not in the nature of architectural drawings or plans) of any architectural work of art.

4. The publication, under certain restrictions, of short passages in collections intended for the use of schools.

5. The publication in a newspaper of a public lecture, unless prohibited by written notice exhibited in the building in which the lecture is delivered; but this does not prevent the publication of a newspaper summary.

6. The reading or recitation in public by one person of any reasonable extract from any public work.

7. The publication in a newspaper of a report of a political address, whether in the form of a lecture or otherwise.

WHEN "FIRST AUTHOR" IS NOT THE OWNER OF THE COPYRIGHT

The first author of a work has no copyright in the following events—

1. When a person has commissioned him to make an engraving or photograph or portrait. This becomes the copyright of the person who has given the money consideration. In ordinary cases the painter of a picture will be the owner of the copyright; and he may, in the absence of an agreement to the contrary, prevent the reproduction of the picture by the buyer.

2. When the author is in the employment of another person under a contract of service or apprenticeship and the work is done in the course of the employment, the employer is the owner of the copyright, in the absence of an agreement to the contrary. Where, however, the contributions are to newspapers or other

periodicals, the first author may be entitled to restrain publication otherwise than as part of the newspaper.

TO OBTAIN COPYRIGHT

1. The first publication must take place in such parts of the British Empire as are covered by the Copyright Act. Where the work has not been published the author, at the time of the making of the work, must have been a British subject or have been domiciled within the Empire.

2. The name or *nom-de-plume* of the author must appear on the title page. If no author's name appears, the publisher whose name appears will be presumed to be the owner of the copyright.

LENGTH OF COPYRIGHT

The right of copyright exists for the life of the author and for fifty years after his death. Where two writers have collaborated the term is fifty years after the death of the author who dies first or during the life of the longer liver, whichever period is longer. Where the work is not in publication during the author's lifetime, copyright exists until the publication or the performance in public, and of fifty years after such publication. For photographs, records, perforated rolls, and the like, the term of copyright is fifty years from the making of the negative or the plate.

After twenty-five years from the author's death any person may reproduce a work on payment to the owner of the copyright of a ten per cent royalty on the published price. Moreover, the Privy Council has power to grant a licence to reproduce a work after the author's death, if it should be proved that the work is withheld from the public by the owner of the copyright. The clause of the Act enacting this is as follows—

"Provided that at any time after the expiration of twenty-five years from the death of the author of a published work, copyright in the work shall not be deemed to be infringed by the reproduction of the work for sale if the person reproducing the work proves that he has given a prescribed notice in writing of his intention to reproduce the work, and that he has paid in the prescribed manner, to, or for the benefit of, the owner of the copyright, and that royalties in respect of all copies of the work sold by him were calculated at the rate of ten per cent on the price at which he published the work." The Board of Trade makes regulations prescribing the modes in which notices are to be given and payments made.

ASSIGNMENT OF COPYRIGHT

The owner of copyright may by personal contract assign his rights to another; such an assignment must be in writing and signed by the owner or his agent. A curious case of reversion of property exists in regard to copyright. The owner can assign copyright only until twenty-five years after the date of the author's death. After that period the copyright reverts to his legal representative. Such legal representative will normally enjoy the copyright for a further twenty-five years.

LIMITATION OF ACTION

The period of limitation applicable to copyright is three years. One complaining of an infringement must bring his action before three years have elapsed from the cause of the action. The owner of the copyright may apply for an injunction to restrain further infringement, and he may apply for damages and for the delivery of any copies of the infringement. Action must be brought, however, within three years from the date of the infringement. A summary remedy is also available, penalties for infringement ranging from 40s. to £50. Imprisonment, too, is possible.

WHAT CONSTITUTES INFRINGEMENT

Copyright is infringed—

1. If a persons sells or offers for sale copies of the work in question in such manner as to affect prejudicially the owner of the copyright.

2. Exhibits such copies in public.

3. Imports for sale or hire a copy that infringes the copyright.

4. Allows, for his personal profit, a theatre to be used for the performance of a copyright work, unless such allowance was given in ignorance of the existence of the copyright.

EXTENSION OF COPYRIGHT

The rights protected by the Copyright Act may be extended by Order in Council to works first published in a foreign country or produced by other than a British subject, if the foreign country gives similar protection to works first published in this country and produced by a British subject. Under this arrangement conventions have been made between the United Kingdom, Belgium, Denmark, France, Germany, Hayti, Holland, Italy, Portugal, Spain, Switzerland, Norway, Sweden, Finland, Tunis, Liberia,

Luxembourg, Monaco, Austria, Hungary, and Japan, and of most of the British Colonies and Dependencies.

COPYRIGHT IN RECORDS

Under the Dramatic and Musical Performance Protection Act, 1925, it is an offence to make, sell, or use in public unauthorised records.

COPYRIGHT IN A TITLE

Can there be copyright in a title? It depends upon the kind of title. Is the title calculated to produce an impression that the book is the work of someone other than the author? Probably, for instance, Mr. Priestley could restrain any one, if he thought it worth the trouble to do so, from publishing a novel under the title of *The Good Companions*. Does the title contain some element of fancy? Can we really say that it constitutes the literary composition of the author, or is it what any one would quite naturally hit upon to indicate the nature of the book? A man would be foolish who sought to prevent another from calling his book *English Grammar and Composition* or *A Textbook of Arithmetic*.

We might have a whole page of title; the subject-matter would then be substantial enough to enjoy copyright. Perhaps, however, a distinctive title would be better protected by means of a "passing-off" action.

Similarly, a name, even of a descriptive nature, may by long and exclusive use become property so that others may be debarred from its use. But a heavy burden is placed upon the man who wishes to assert such property. He must show in a convincing manner that the name has acquired a secondary meaning—that ordinary people look upon it as the name of goods supplied by him and no one else.

PATENT

This is a valuable kind of intangible property. It is a right granted by the Crown to the authors of new inventions, giving them the exclusive right to use, exercise, and sell their inventions and to secure the profits arising from them for a limited period. The grant from the Crown is contained in a "letter patent" (an open letter): "Patents are not sealed up, but exposed to open view with the great seal pendant at the bottom, and are usually directed or addressed by the King to all his subjects at large."

The granting of patents was taken into consideration by Parliament in the Statute of Monopolies of 1624. This Act, which prevented the Crown from granting trading monopolies in general, made an exception in favour of a grant of the privilege, for *fourteen years or under* (now sixteen years) "of the sole working or making of any manner of new manufactures within this realm, to the true and first inventor of such manufactures." The proviso was added that the grant should not be contrary to law, nor mischievous to the public welfare by the raising of prices of commodities at home, or the hurt of trade, or the general inconvenience.

A kind of bargain is made between the inventor and the public. In the interest of progress he should make known his invention. The patentee is, indeed, bound to work his patent as to give the public the benefit of it. If he does not, any person interested may apply to the Board of Trade for a licence to work the patent, or for the revocation of the patent. The Board of Trade, if a case is made out and if no arrangement can be reached by the parties, refers the application to the Court. The Court will make what order it thinks good so that the reasonable requirements of the public with reference to the patented invention shall be satisfied. It will order the patentee to grant licences, or it will revoke the patent and thereby allow the world at large to use it. Order for revocation cannot, however, be issued before three years have passed from the grant. The inventor must use his patent. But if he were left to the Common Law, the inventor would get no benefit from his invention. On the other hand, if he held a monopoly of it for ever, the public interest would suffer through the high prices imposed by him whenever his invention was valuable.

THE SUBJECT-MATTER OF A PATENT

The Patents and Designs Act of 1907 (amended by various Acts, the Patents and Designs Act of 1932 being the latest) now determine the law.

This must be a manufacture, some article of value produced by the art and skill of men. The invention must be embodied in something tangible. There can, for instance, be no patent in an idea; the idea must be combined with the material in which it is moulded. Moreover, the manufacture must be a new invention within the realm. "The consideration for a patent is the communication to the public of a process that is new."

SPECIFICATION OF PATENT

Publication is effected when a clear and concise description of the invention—a *specification*—is deposited for registration at the Patent Office. The specification may be *provisional*, describing the nature of the invention, or *complete*, particularly describing the nature of the invention and the manner of its working. A provisional specification must be followed by a complete specification within twelve months. On the acceptance of a specification the Comptroller of the Patent Office notifies the applicant and advertises the fact in the *Illustrated Official Journal*. Grant of a patent may be opposed on the following grounds—

1. That the opposer is the real owner of the patent.
2. That the invention has been "anticipated." It is covered by a specification made within the past fifty years.
3. That the nature of the invention is not sufficiently or fairly described in the specification.

If there is no opposition, or if the opposition is over-ruled, the grant of the patent ensues.

" INVENTION " AND DISCOVERY

Once made public an invention cannot be patented. And we should note that an invention is different from a "discovery." The discovery cannot be patented unless, besides adding knowledge, it enables the production of a new and useful thing. The invention must possess *utility* measured by worth in money : "A very small amount of utility is enough to support a patent. Utility, in patent law, does not mean abstract or comparative, or competitive or commercial utility ; but as applied to an invention. It means that the invention is better than the preceding knowledge of the trade as to a particular fabric ; better that is, in some respect, though not necessarily in every respect. For instance, an invention is useful by which an article good, though not as good as one previously known, can be produced more cheaply by a different process. And an invention is useful when the public are thereby enabled to do something which they could not do before, or to do in a more advantageous manner something which they could do before . . . or, in other words, an invention is patentable which offers the public a useful choice." (*Welsbach Incandescent Gas Light Co.* v. *New Incandescent* (*Sunlight Patent*) *Gas Lighting Co.* (Ch. 1900).)

WHO APPLIES FOR A PATENT?

The proper applicant for a patent is "the true and first inventor," British subject or not. The executor or administrator of a deceased inventor may apply at any time within six months after the death. Who is the true and first inventor may sometimes be difficult to decide. The Master of the Rolls discussed the matter (*Plimpton* v. *Malcomson*, 1876)—

"Shortly after the passing of the statute, the question arose whether a man could be called a first and true inventor who in the popular sense had never invented anything, but who, having learned abroad (that is, out of the realm, in a foreign country, because it has been decided that Scotland is within the realm for this purpose) that somebody else had invented something, quietly copied the invention, and brought it over to this country, and then took out a patent. As I said before, in the popular sense he had invented nothing. But it was decided that the legal sense and meaning of the statute is this, that if the invention, being in other respects novel and useful, was not previously known in this country—known being used in that particular sense, as being part of what had been called the common or public knowledge of the country—this was "invention." That was the first thing. Then there was a second thing. Suppose there were two people, actual inventors, in this country who invented the same thing simultaneously : could either be said to be first and true inventor? It was decided that the man who first took out the patent was the first and true inventor. Then there was another point. If the man who took out the patent was not, in popular language, the first and true inventor, because somebody had invented it before, but had not taken out a patent for it, would he still, in law, be the first and true inventor? It was decided that he would, provided the invention of the first inventor had been kept secret, or, without being actually kept secret, had not been made known in such a way as to become a part of the common knowledge, or of the public stock of information. Therefore, in that sense also, there was a person who was legally the first and true inventor, although, in common language, he was not, because one or more persons had invented it before him, but had not sufficiently disclosed it."

In order to obtain a patent for a thing, that thing must be—

1. Something which is tangible—a manufacture.
2. It must be new within the United Kingdom.
3. It must be of some utility, however small.

The patent may be granted to any person, natural or artificial, whether British or foreign. It is obtainable by filling up a form of application to be obtained from the Patent Office. This form, completed by the applicant and bearing the appropriate fee stamp, is lodged at the Patent Office. Along with it is given a specification, describing the nature of the invention.

OPPOSING A GRANT

The application may be opposed upon the following grounds—

1. That the applicant obtained the invention from the opposer.

2. That the invention has already been granted in a complete specification.

3. That the nature of the invention is not fully described in the specification.

4. That the specification is not in accordance with the provisional specification.

The Comptroller of the Patent Office hears the opposing claims. In the event of an appeal, the appeal lies either to the Attorney-General or to the Solicitor-General.

If there is no opposition or successful opposition, the patent is sealed within eighteen months from the date of application. It is granted or the period of sixteen years, and the High Court may extend this for an additional five or ten years if it should appear that the patentee has not been sufficiently remunerated for his invention.

REVOKING A GRANT

The Act of 1932 sets forth the grounds upon which a grant of letters patent may be revoked—

1. The invention is subject to a valid, prior grant;

2. The true and first inventor was not the applicant or one of the applicants for the patent;

3. The patent was obtained in fraud of rights of the person applying for the order of revocation, or of the person for whom the applicant claims;

4. The article is not a "manner of new manufacture" within the Statute of Monopolies;

5. The article is not new or not useful;

6. The article does not represent a step forward in invention;

7. The article is not fairly described or is intended for illegal purposes.

A Register of Patents is kept at the Patent Office. Any

assignment or licence under the patent must be entered upon this Register.

CROWN RIGHTS

When it seems likely that an invention may prove of value to the Crown, the inventor is required to agree to special terms upon application. Moreover, the War Office and the Admiralty have the right to acquire and keep secret an invention likely to prove useful in war, on paying to the inventor a sum sanctioned by the Treasury.

On the death of the owner of a patent, the patent vests in the personal representative of the deceased. Patent rights are property, and the rules as to the transmission of property on the death of the owner apply to it.

LETTERS PATENT

Here is given a form of Letters Patent (i.e. "Open Letters")—

GEORGE THE FIFTH, by the Grace of God, of the United Kingdom of Great Britain and Ireland, and of the British Dominions beyond the Seas, King, Defender of the Faith: To all to whom these presents shall come, Greeting:

WHEREAS John James, of 236 Short Street, Longtown, in the County of Whiteshire, Engineer, hath by his solemn declaration represented unto us that he is in possession of an invention for "Improvements in spring buffers," that he is the true and first inventor thereof, and that the same is not in use by any other person to the best of his knowledge and belief:

And whereas the said inventor hath humbly prayed that we would be graciously pleased to grant unto him (hereinafter together with his executors, administrators, and assigns, or any of them, referred to as the said patentee), our royal letters patent for the sole use and advantage of his said invention:

And whereas the said inventor hath by and in his complete specification particularly described the nature of his invention:

And whereas we being willing to encourage all inventions which may be for the public good, are graciously pleased to condescend to his request.

Know ye, therefore, that we, of our especial grace, certain knowledge, and mere motion, do by these presents, for us, our heirs and successors, give and grant unto the said patentee our especial licence, full power, sole privilege, and authority, that the said patentee by himself, his agents, or licensees, and no others, may at all times hereafter during the term of years herein mentioned, make, use, exercise and vend the said invention within our United Kingdom of Great Britain and Ireland, and Isle of Man, in such manner as to him or them may seem meet, and that the said patentee shall have and enjoy the whole profit and advantage from time to time accruing by reason of the said invention, during the term of sixteen years from the date hereunder written of these presents: and to the end that the said patentee may have and enjoy the sole use and exercise and the full benefit of the said invention, we do by these presents for us, our heirs and successors, strictly command all our subjects whatsoever within our United Kingdom of Great Britain and Ireland, and the Isle of Man, that they do not at any time during the continuance of the said term of sixteen years either directly or indirectly make use of or put in practice the said invention, or any part of the same, nor in anywise imitate the same nor make or cause to be made any addition thereto or subtraction therefrom, whereby to pretend themselves the inventors thereof, without the consent, licence or agreement of the said patentee in writing under his hand and seal, on pain of incurring such penalties as may be justly inflicted on such offenders for their contempt of this our Royal command, and of being answerable to the patentee according to law for his damages thereby occasioned: Provided that these our letters patent are on this condition, that, if at any time during the said term it be made to appear to us, our heirs, or successors, or any six or more of our Privy Council, that this our grant is contrary to law, or prejudicial or inconvenient to our subjects in general, or that the said invention is not a new invention as to the public use and exercise thereof within our United Kingdom of Great Britain and Ireland, and Isle of Man, or that the said patentee is not the first and true inventor thereof within this realm as aforesaid, these our letters patent shall forthwith determine, and be void to all intents and purposes, notwithstanding anything hereinbefore contained: Provided also, that if the said patentee shall not pay all fees by law required to be paid in respect of the grant of these letters patent, or in respect of any matter relating thereto at the time or times, and in manner for the time being by law provided: and also if the said patentee shall not supply or cause to be supplied, for our service all such articles of the said invention as may be required by the officers or commissioners administering any department of our service, in such manner, at such times, and at and upon such reasonable prices and terms as shall be settled in manner for the time being by law provided, then, and in any of the said cases, these our letters patent, and all privileges and advantages whatever hereby granted, shall determine and become void, notwithstanding anything hereinbefore contained: Provided also, that nothing herein contained shall prevent the granting of licenses in such manner and for such considerations as they may by law be granted: And lastly, we do by these presents for us, our heirs and successors, grant unto the said patentee that these our letters shall be construed in the most beneficial sense for the advantage of the said patentee. In witness whereof we have caused these our letters to be made patent this　　　　day of　　　　　　, one thousand nine hundred and　　　　, and to be sealed as of the day of　　　　　　, one thousand nine hundred and　　　　.

　　　　　　　　　　　　　L.S.　　　(*Seal of Patent Office*)

WORKER AND PATENT

Adamson v. *Kenworthy* (K.B. 1932) establishes the broad rule that, where a worker is instructed by his employer to prepare a design to get over a particular difficulty, he must do his best.

If he solves the problem, then normally the design and the invention are the employer's property. The plaintiffs were makers of machinery and, having had trouble through the jarring of brake mechanism, adopted the suggestion of the defendant, a draughtsman in their service, to embody springs in the brakes. The invention was patented by Kenworthy, the employers bearing all expense. The employers claimed that Kenworthy held the patent as trustee for them; and their claim was admitted. "A draughtsman," said Mr. Justice Farwell, "does not perform his duty unless he exercises skill and invention to the best of his power."

ALIENATION OF PERSONAL PROPERTY

A man transfers personal property by—

(a) *Gift* while alive (*inter vivos*), the gift being effective when delivery has been made to the donee. Unless a gift is so completed it is, except in one event, void at law and gives no title to the donee. The one event is where the gift has been made by a deed; then, though the giver may retain possession, the ownership passes. A grant of personal chattels by deed is irrevocable, even though the giver gets no valuable consideration; and the execution of the deed at once transfers ownership.

(b) *Creation of Trust* in favour of another. Thus, though I may retain possession, I may declare that I hold goods in trust for another. Then equity will enforce the trust.

(c) *Sale.* In what are called "hire-purchase" agreements there may be a sale though payments are deferred. The trader may, and usually does, however, so frame the agreement that he retains the property until his charges are fully met. Thus the trader (the bailor of the goods hired) may agree that the hirer may at any time return the goods on payment of rent due. In this event property is retained and a sale or pledge of the goods gives no right to the buyer from the hirer or to the pawnbroker who has lent to the hirer on the security of the goods. So, too, property is retained in such an agreement as this: the hirer is given an option of buying at a price exceeding (even very slightly) the total amount of rent payments.

(d) *Legal Assignment of Rights.* Certain rights—"choses in action" they used to be called, benefits that could if need arose be recovered by the aid of the Court—can now be legally assigned. The assignment is regulated by the Law of Property Act, 1925 (Section 136 (i)): "Any absolute assignment by writing under the hand of the assignor (not purporting to be by way of charge only) of any debt or other legal thing in action, of which express notice has been given to the debtor, trustee, or other person from whom the assignor would have been entitled to claim such debt or thing in action, is effectual in law (subject to equities having priority over the right of the assignee) to pass and transfer from the date of such notice—

(a) the legal right to such debt or thing in action;

(b) all legal and other remedies for the same; and

(c) the power to give a good discharge for the same without the concurrence of the assignor.

"Provided that, if the debtor, trustee, or other person liable in respect of such debt or thing in action has notice—

(a) that the assignment is disputed by the assignor or any person claiming under him; or

(b) of any other opposing or conflicting claims to such debt or thing in action;

he may, if he thinks fit, either call upon the persons making claim thereto to interplead concerning the same, or pay the debt or other thing in action into Court under the provisions of the Trustee Act, 1925."

There is some restriction upon the right to keep what has been given—

1. When a gift has been given by one who gives only because he thinks himself about to die, the giver can, in the event of his recovery, annul the gift.

2. When a gift has been induced by undue influence, it may be recovered. (See below.)

REPUDIATING A GIFT OBTAINED BY UNDUE INFLUENCE

No one standing in a fiduciary relation or one of authority to another can retain a gift made to him by that other, if the latter impeaches the gift within a reasonable time, unless the donee can prove that the donor had independent advice, or that the fiduciary relation had ceased for so long that the donor was under no control or influence whatever. It is necessary for the donee to prove that the gift was the result of the free exercise of independent will. The most obvious way to prove this is by establishing that the gift was made after the nature and effect of the transaction had been explained to the donor, by some independent and qualified person, so completely as to satisfy the Court that the donor was acting independently of any influence from the donee, and with full appreciation of what he was doing. Revocation of a gift, in order to be effective, must, however, be without great delay.

Allcard v. *Skinner* (Ch. 1887) illustrates the matter admirably.

This was an action to recover money and railway stock alleged to have been transferred by the plaintiff to the defendant, Miss Skinner, whilst subject to undue influence. Miss Skinner was the superior of a sisterhood of ladies who devoted themselves to works of charity. The plaintiff joined the sisterhood and conformed eagerly to its rules. She made a will in favour of Miss Skinner, and also made her gifts of money exceeding £7,000. After about eleven years the plaintiff left the sisterhood. She revoked the will made in Miss Skinner's favour, but made no claim for the return of the money until over six years later. The Court held that her continued acquiescence, after she had left the sisterhood, was such a ratification of the gifts as to make them then not recoverable.

"If her delay has been so long as reasonably to induce the recipient to think, and to act upon the belief, that the gift is to lie where it has laid, then, by estoppel, the donor of the gift would be prevented from revoking it. But I do not base my decision here upon the ground of estoppel. During five years she has had the opportunity of reflecting upon what she has done. She was surrounded by persons perfectly competent to give her proper advice. I draw unhesitatingly the inference that she did consider the matter and determine not to interfere with her previous disposition."

BILLS OF SALE

A *Bill of Sale* is an instrument in writing whereby the owner of goods transfers to another the property he has in goods or chattels, whilst retaining the possession of them. The holder or grantee of the bill is given power (in a special event), either with or without notice, and either immediately or at a future time, to take possession of the specified personal chattels. The power to seize will usually depend upon some condition, in general a condition relating to payment.

The Bills of Sale Acts (1878–1882) now regulate bills of sale. The object of the earlier, the principal, Act, was to enable people to get credit on the security of personal property, yet to give some amount of protection to lenders by preventing the obtaining of false credit. The object of the Act was mainly to protect the lender. The Amending Act of 1882 was devised mainly to protect the borrower; it was enacted largely to prevent needy people from being trapped into signing documents they did not really understand, and then finding themselves subject to harsh provisions. The Act prescribes a particular form if the bill of sale is to be a valid one. This form plainly indicates the contract and the consideration given for the bill.

POSSESSION DIVORCED FROM PROPERTY

The need for the 1878 Act arose mainly from the fact that, in general, retention of possession of goods was looked upon as evidence of fraud. By the Act of 1571 (the famous 13 Elizabeth), aiming at prevention of fraud upon creditors, it was enacted that all gifts and conveyances, whether of lands or chattels, made for the purpose of delaying or defrauding creditors, shall be null and void, as against such creditors. But this does not affect "conveyances made upon valuable consideration and to persons having no notice of the fraud." When the question comes before the Court, whether or not to set aside the conveyance, the intention of the transferor is sought. Did he in fact make the conveyance with the object of defeating and delaying his creditors?

That the result of a conveyance does in fact defeat creditors is not enough; if a man has enough means, even outside the settled property, to pay his present debts, the statute does not apply (*In re Lane* v. *Fox* (Q.B. 1900)). The Act alters the presumption of fraud in regard to conveyances that are *bona fide* either absolute sales or for security.

" ABSOLUTE " BILLS AND " SECURITY " BILLS

Bills of sale are either *Absolute Bills* (the intention being to transfer out and out the property in the goods) or *Security Bills* (the intention being to redeem the goods by repayment). The absolute bill not registered may be set aside as being in fraud of creditors. But it is not void, as a security bill is if not registered.

RULES RELATING TO BILLS OF SALE

1. A bill of sale is void (except as against a grantor) when made by one who is not a true owner. Only the true owner can give a valid bill of sale. Thus, where a husband by deed of gift conveyed his furniture to his wife, she became the true owner and could grant a bill of sale whereby a lender had a good title against the execution creditor of the husband (*Harrods, Ltd.* v. *Stanton*, I.B. 1923). A hirer of goods, with an option to purchase, but no

obligation to do so, has not sufficient interest to constitute him the true owner. Nor can a bill of sale be given in respect of future chattels.

2. Where registration of a bill of sale has become void for want of renewal, the guarantor again becomes the "true owner" for the purposes of the Act and can give another bill of sale.

3. A bill of sale is void if given for any sum under £30. This sum may not necessarily be handed to the borrower. Thus a bill of sale correctly stating that £2 2s. is deducted by the guarantee (with the consent of the guarantor) towards the expenses of the transaction, is a valid one (*London & Provinces Discount Co.* v. *Jones*, K.B. 1914). In this case the borrower had mortgaged his furniture to the Standard Development for £30, less £2 2s. costs to the solicitors. The London & Provinces Discount Co., recovered judgment against Jones and took the furniture in execution. The mortgagee claimed the furniture under the bill of sale and was successful. The argument of the plaintiff was that since less than £30 was given to the borrower, the bill of sale was void under Section 12 of the 1882 Act. The County Court judge over-ruled the contention, and the judgment was upheld in the King's Bench.

4. The statement of the consideration must show the whole transaction on the face of the bill of sale. The transaction must not be subject to any collateral agreement.

5. The registration of bills of sale is effected in the Bills of Sale Department of the Central Office at the Royal Courts of Justice, London, or at a District Registry. It must be done within seven clear days from the making of the bill. If the last of these days should be a Sunday, the registration may take place the following day. The registration must be renewed at least once every five years if the Bill of Sale is to be kept on foot.

6. A declaration of trust of chattels may be made by word of mouth. But a declaration of trust without transfer, if contained in a document, may be a bill of sale.

7. Since the bill of sale by way of security for payment is required to be in a special form, the 1882 Act prescribes the form. This is as follows—

BILL OF SALE TO SECURE MONEY AND INTEREST

THIS INDENTURE made the   day of
One thousand nine hundred and
BETWEEN   of
of the one part and   of
of the other part.

WITNESSETH that in consideration of the sum of £   now paid
to   by   (the receipt
of which the said   doth hereby acknowledge) he
the said   doth hereby assign unto
       his Executors Administrators and Assigns All and singular
the several chattels and things specifically described in the Schedule
hereto annexed by way of security for the payment of the sum of £
and Interest thereon at the rate of   per centum per annum. And
the said   doth further agree and declare that
he will duly pay to the said   the Principal Sum
aforesaid together with the   Interest then due on the   day of
       next and if the said Principal Sum shall not be paid on
the said day then will pay Interest thereon or on so much thereof as shall
for the time being remain unpaid at the rate aforesaid half-yearly on the
       day of   and the   day of   .
     And the said   doth agree also with the said
       that he the said   his
Executors Administrators or Assigns will not during the continuance of
this security remove the said chattels and things or any of them from the
premises where they may at any time be without the consent in writing
of the said   and further that the said
       his Executors Administrators or Assigns will at all times
during the continuance of this security keep the said chattels and things
insured against loss or damage by fire in the sum of £   at the least
in the   Insurance Office or in some other Insurance Office
to be approved by the said   his Executors
Administrators or Assigns And will punctually pay the rent rates taxes
and outgoings to become due and payable in respect of the premises on
which the said chattels and things or any of them are or may be and also
will on demand in writing produce to the said
his Executors Administrators or Assigns the last receipt for such rent rates
taxes and outgoings and also the policy of such insurance as aforesaid and
the receipt for the last premium payable thereunder unless he shall have
reasonable excuse for not so doing.

AND IT IS HEREBY AGREED AND DECLARED that if default shall at any
time be made by the said   his Executors or
Administrators in insuring or keeping insured the said chattels and things
or in paying the said rent rates taxes and outgoings it shall be lawful for
the said   his Executors Administrators or
Assigns to insure or keep insured the said chattels and things or to pay
the said rent rates taxes and outgoings (as the case may require) and that
all moneys expended by him for any of the purposes aforesaid together
with Interest thereon after the rate of £   per centum per annum
from the time of the same having been expended shall on demand be repaid
to him by the said   his Executors or Adminis-
trators and until repayment thereof shall be a charge on all the said
chattels and things.

PROVIDED always that the chattels hereby assigned shall not be liable
to seizure or to be taken possession of by the said
for any cause other than those specified in Section 7 of the Bills of Sale
Act (1878) Amendment Act, 1882.

IN WITNESS whereof the said parties to these presents have hereunto set their hands and seals the day and year first above written.

SIGNED and SEALED by the said ⎱

in the presence of me ⎰

This Bill of Sale is assumed to be well within the understanding of anyone raising money upon it.

A bill of sale may be created under the power of attorney, even though such a power has been given to the proposed guarantor; and the Court will not restrain the attorney from executing the bill of sale in proper form. If power has been given to him he may use the power for his own purposes.

8. Ordinary powers of distraint are not within the Acts, but the power to seize chattels contained in a lease (by way of distraint for recovery of debt) may be (as a licence to seize) a bill of sale. Thus a brewer's lease, containing in it the power to seize stock-in-trade and effects of the lease in default of payment, is a bill of sale, and therefore void unless duly registered (*Stevens* v. *Marston*, Q.B. 1890).

9. The Bills of Sale Acts do not apply to hire-purchase agreements, where, till the stipulated payments are made, the chattels are not the property of the hirer. The licence contained in the agreement to seize, is simply the power to retake possession of one's own property.

10. Bills of sale do not include the following—

(*a*) Assignments for the benefit of creditors of the person making or giving the assignment. Such an assignment must, however, be available for creditors generally. If the deed of assignment is for the benefit of certain creditors only, it is a bill of sale.

(*b*) Marriage settlements. A post-nuptial settlement may, however, be a bill of sale. When two persons are together in the enjoyment of chattels, the law refers possession to the one who is the legal title-holder.

(*c*) Transfers of ships.

(*d*) Transfers of goods in the ordinary course of business. Thus bills of lading, warrants, warehouse receipts, and the like do not need registration. Nor do letters given to bankers for advances on goods in the hands of third parties with their receipts attached, stating that the borrowers hold goods in the third parties' hands. For these letters are used in the ordinary course of business as proof of the possession or control of goods. They protect, without registration, goods returned to the borrower by third parties, as well as goods still in the third parties' hands.

(e) Debentures and mortgages giving charges upon a company's property. But, apparently, debentures issued by a society registered under the Industrial and Provident Societies Act are not exempted from the necessity for registration.

The personal chattels to which bills of sale refer comprise—

1. Articles capable of complete transfer by delivery.
2. Growing crops assigned separately from the land.
3. Fixtures when assigned from the land.
4. Trade machinery.

A schedule is essential to the validity of the absolute bill of sale. But the 1882 Act requires a schedule when a bill of sale is given by way of security. An inventory of personal chattels is valid only in respect of chattels that can be identified from it. Thus "household furniture and effects" and a "number of oil paintings with gold frames" have been ruled insufficient as a specification. On the other hand, " farming stock, comprising four horses and five cows," has been held sufficient.

ATTESTATION OF ABSOLUTE BILLS OF SALE

An absolute bill must be duly attested by a solicitor who must also state that before execution the effect of the bill was explained by him to the guarantor.

The circumstances under which seizure of the goods denoted in the bill of sale can be made are restricted to the following—

1. If the guarantor makes a default in payment of debt, or in performing anything in the maintaining of the security.
2. If the guarantor becomes bankrupt, or suffers distraint for rents, rates, or taxes.
3. If the guarantor fraudulently removes the chattels covered by the bill.
4. If the guarantor does not show, upon reasonable request, the last receipt for rent, rates, or taxes.
5. If the guarantor suffers execution under judgment.

When the goods are seized they must not be removed before a lapse of five clear days, so that if necessary the right to seize may be tested.

INTERFERENCE WITH PROPERTY RIGHTS—PRIVATE NUISANCE

There are two kinds of interference, other than trespass, with property rights. One kind is a disturbance of a person's rights over another's land. Such is the impeding of a right of a path across another's land, or the obstructing of a right to the light received across another's land, or the taking away of a right of support by another's land. Another kind of interference is the causing or the allowing of the escape of harmful things—smoke, smell, noise, vibration, and so on—into another's land. The person injured by such interference may sustain an action against the injurer; for the wrong of *private nuisance* has been committed. Thus— "If A dig a trench across the highway this is a public nuisance, the subject of an indictment. But if B fall into it, the particular damage sustained by him will support an action."

ACTION FOR PRIVATE NUISANCE

Some points should be carefully weighed before deciding to bring, or defend, an action for private nuisance.

1. Though the term "private nuisance" is a wide and very elastic one, it does not include every act whereby a man's rights lose in value. The land I occupy, the house I own, the shop by which I gain my livelihood may fall—or indeed rise in value—through my neighbour's action or omissions, and quite independently of what I do or omit doing. The law gives a remedy for some only of the causes of loss. My neighbour turns his parkland into a building site upon which, to his great profit but to my loss and vexation, he erects small houses closely packed together. I should fail if I brought an action against him for nuisance. My neighbour lets his shop to one who opens a business that diverts much custom from my shop; such competition is one of the risks that society, signifying its wishes in rules of law, calls on me to bear myself.

2. When a question arises, whether or not a particular injury is or is not a private nuisance,—whether it interferes with health, comfort, or convenience in the use of my property,—the standard of the ordinary man is the measure. Though a highly sensitive man is greatly perturbed when his neighbour plays jazz tunes on a high-power radiogram with the window open, he is probably ill-advised to bring an action to restrain the playing. He would be obliged, to succeed in his action, to show some particularly annoying features—a playing far into the night, for instance, or the concourse of rowdy dancers, and possibly, too, a malicious desire to annoy.

The character of the neighbourhood is also a relevant consideration: "In matters of this kind," said the Lord Chancellor (*St. Helen's Smelting Co.* v. *Tipping*, 1865), "it is a very desirable thing to mark the difference between an action brought for a nuisance upon the ground that the alleged nuisance produces material damage to property, and an action brought for a nuisance on the ground that the alleged nuisance is productive of sensible *personal* discomfort. With regard to the latter, namely, personal inconvenience and interference with one's enjoyment, one's quiet, one's personal freedom, anything that discomposes or injuriously affects the senses or the nerves, whether that may or may not be denominated a nuisance, must undoubtedly depend greatly on the circumstances of the place where the thing complained of actually occurs.

" If a man lives in a town it is necessary that he should subject himself to the consequences of those operations of trade which may be carried on in his immediate locality, which are actually necessary for trade and commerce and also for the enjoyment of property and for the benefit of the inhabitants of the town and of the public at large. If a man lives in a street where there are numerous shops, and a shop is opened next door to him which is carried on in a fair and reasonable way, he has no ground for complaint because to himself individually there may arise much discomfort from the trade carried on in that shop.

"But when an occupation is carried on by one person in the neighbourhood of another and the result of that occupation is a material injury to *property*, then there unquestionably arises a very different consideration. The submission which is required from persons living in society to that amount of discomfort, which may be necessary for the legitimate and free exercise of the trade of their neighbours, would not apply to circumstances the immediate result of which is sensible injury to the property."

3. An action for nuisance can be brought only by an occupier, of land or of building, or by an owner when his property is being depreciated by the nuisance. A stranger, even though the stranger may lose through the persistence of the nuisance, may not maintain an action. In *Cattle* v. *Stockton Waterworks* the facts were these. The defendants, under the powers conferred by their Act, laid a waterpipe under a turnpike road. Plaintiff contracted to make a tunnel under the road for one of the adjoining landowners. His work was delayed and made more costly through a leak in the defendants' waterpipe. He sued for negligence; but it was held that the damage was too remote. Courts of Justice, declared Lord Blackburn in his humility, should not "allow themselves, in the pursuit of perfectly complete remedies

for all wrongful acts, to transgress the bounds which our law, in a wise consciousness of its limited powers, has imposed on itself, of redressing only the proximate and direct consequences of wrongful acts." (*Cattle* v. *Stockton Waterworks*, Q.B., 1875.)

4. The law provides two remedies for the person injured by a nuisance. It awards a money compensation for loss caused, *Damages*, that is. It also, in suitable cases, takes steps to make the wrongdoer remove the nuisance; the Court issues an *Injunction*. But an injunction is a serious interference with the freedom of a man; and the Court is reluctant to issue one. It will not do so unless justice clearly demands it. Where damages are an adequate remedy an injunction will be refused.

Plaintiffs, makers of matting, filed a petition in Chancery asking for an order to restrain the defendants, makers of sulphate of ammonia, from allowing the escape of fumes that, when the wind was in a certain quarter, discoloured the fibres.

The defendants answered that they took elaborate precautions both for the sake of economy and in order to obviate injury, to prevent the escape of ammonia and sulphuretted hydrogen. In fact, the petitioners were able to show only slight damage on isolated occasions.

The Court therefore dismissed the bill: "This is an instance of a person carrying on a manufacture which, if his neighbour had not happened to have another manufacture of great delicacy, probably would not have caused any damage to the neighbour. Still, he has no right to injure his neighbour's manufacture at all. And, if it had been proved to me that a grave injury occurred every time an escape took place, or that there had been a constant repetition of the injury, the proper course would have been to grant an injunction. But I do not find that there were more than three occasions, at most, during the period of four and a half years since the defendant's manufacture commenced, that injury of any kind was done. The result is that I must dismiss the bill. This is not a case for an injunction. And the bill being filed so late, and the plaintiffs failing after many opportunities to make out his case, I am bound to dismiss it with costs, without prejudice to any action he may be advised to bring if he thinks he can get damages" (*Cooke* v. *Forbes*, Ch. 1867).

CREATING A PRIVATE NUISANCE

In an action by a farmer against the Manchester Corporation for an injunction and damages on the ground of nuisance the defendants pleaded that the acts complained of were done in pursuance of the powers conferred on them by the Manchester Corporation Act, 1914. This Act authorised the Corporation to erect and work an electrical generating station. The nuisance complained of was the emission of poisonous fumes from the chimneys. The House of Lords, by a majority decision, held the Corporation liable, in that it had not used all reasonable diligence to prevent their operations being a nuisance to their neighbours.

MEANING OF " REASONABLE DILIGENCE "

The undertakers of an enterprise for which Parliamentary sanction has been obtained are not called upon to be inventors. They are not bound to devise something that will prevent the enterprise from being a nuisance. "But they must have regard to expert advice; they must try to obtain the best devices, with a view to minimising any inconvenience that may be caused. The absence of reasonable precautions and the meagre extent of inquiries are not wrongs in themselves. If the Corporation had been able to prove that, however keen the search, safeguards could not have been found, they could escape liability. Their doing a work authorised by legislation would, in that event, justify their creating a nuisance."

JUSTIFYING A NUISANCE

But the task of justification is a difficult one. How difficult is shown in the *Metropolitan Asylum District* v. *Hill*.

The presumption is, when we are interpreting an Act of Parliament, that it never intended to give power to interfere with private rights—particularly if the interference amounts to a nuisance. Parliament does, indeed, often interfere with the rights of private persons; but, normally, it gives compensation to those injured. If no compensation is given, the assumption is that the thing authorised to be done must be done without injury to others.

The managers of the asylum district had erected a smallpox hospital at Hampstead, and the inhabitants objected. The objection was sustained: "I do not think," ran one judgment in the House of Lords, "that the legislature can be held to have sanctioned that which is a nuisance at Common Law, except where it has imperatively directed that a building be provided for a specific purpose, it being obvious that the nuisance must be the result. The onus of proving that the creation of a nuisance will be the result of carrying out the direction of the legislature lies upon the persons seeking to justify the nuisance. They must make good these two propositions : that such are the imperative orders of the legislature ; and that they cannot be carried out without the infringement of private rights."

The Corporation had not justified the measure, and were liable. "It must be remembered," said Viscount Sumner, "that, in making reasonableness the measure of what must be done, before the production of a nuisance can be excused, the law, as it always does, means reasonable according to all the circumstances, and reasonable not only in the interest of the undertakers but also in that of the sufferers. The legislature, in authorising a very great concern, must not be taken to be chary of requiring great care to be taken. Great powers often involve great responsibilities."

PROVING A NUISANCE

Still, the law in this country is not unkind to those who commit nuisances in the way of their trade. The complainant must prove a substantial injury, and this as an effect of the defendant's act or omission ; and it is no light matter when so many are doing the same thing—sending out smoke, or fumes, or noise, or even vibration—that his particular injury is the defendant's doing. First, the inconvenience shown must be more than fanciful, more than one of mere delicacy or fastidiousness. It must be an inconvenience that materially interferes with physical comfort, not merely according to elegant or dainty habits of being, but according to plain, sober, simple notions of reasonable people. Second, the damage must be effectively brought home to the defendant.

Yet it is not necessary to show that the particular defendant is wholly responsible. Two rival proprietors of merry-go-rounds brayed with powerful organs against each other on Ashstead Common. A neighbouring resident obtained an injunction restraining both defendants from making the noise. The suggestion of the defence was that the act of each would be quite innocent, possibly quite agreeable, but for the other's act; and that two rights cannot make a wrong. The Court, however, explained the position thus : "It was said that if one man makes a noise not of a kind, duration, or degree sufficient to constitute a nuisance, and another man, not acting in concert with the first, makes a similar noise at the same time, each is responsible only for the noise made by himself, and not also for that made by the other. In my opinion each is separately liable. Suppose one person leaves a wheelbarrow standing on a way. That may cause no appreciable inconvenience. But, if a hundred do so, that may cause a serious inconvenience, which a person entitled to the use of the way has a right to prevent; and it is no defence to one person among the hundred to say that what he does causes of itself no damage to the complainant. If the acts of two persons amount in the aggregate to what is an actionable wrong, each is answerable to the remedy against the aggregate cause of complaint" (*Lambton* v. *Mellish*, Ch. 1894).

MEANING OF " SUBSTANTIAL DAMAGE "

In a case where a petitioner failed to obtain relief for what he described as a nuisance, a Lord Justice in the Chancery Court of Appeal explained in picturesque manner the burden upon the petitioner to show *substantial* damage.

The petitioner (*Salvin* v. *North Brancepeth Coal Company* (Ch. 1874)) complained that the amenities of his pleasure grounds were being destroyed by the activities of the company. But, in effect, the Court advised him to enjoy with pleasure his mineral rights, though some slight annoyances resulted from the working of the minerals.

"It amounts to this, that although when you once establish the fact of actual substantial damage it is quite right to have recourse to scientific evidence upon the question of the causes to which that damage is to be referred, yet if you are obliged to start with scientific evidence (such as the microscope of the naturalist or the tests of the chemist) for the purpose of establishing the damage itself, that evidence will not suffice. There must be actual damage capable of being shown by a plain witness to a plain common juryman. The Court does not presume to measure with a microscopic eye.

" The damage must be substantial; and it must be, in my view, actual; that is to say, the Court has no right whatever, in dealing with questions of this kind, to have regard to contingent, prospective, or remote damage. I would illustrate this by analogy. The law does not take notice of the imperceptible accretions to a river bank, or to the sea shore, although after the lapse of years they become perfectly measurable and ascertainable; for if in the course of nature the thing itself is so imperceptible, so slow, so gradual, as that it requires a great lapse of time before the results are made palpable to the ordinary senses of mankind, the law disregards that kind of imperceptible operation.

AN INJUNCTION GRANTED ONLY UPON WEIGHTY REASON

"So, if it were made out that every minute a millionth of a grain of poison were absorbed by a tree, that would not do, although after the lapse of a million minutes the grain of poison would be easily detected. It would never have done, as it seems to me, for this Court, in the reign of Henry VI, to have interfered with the further uses of sea coal in London because it had been ascertained to their satisfaction, or predicted to their satisfaction, that by the reign of Queen Victoria, roses, both white and red, would have ceased to blow in the Temple. If some picturesque haven opens its arms to invite the commerce of the world, it is not for this Court to forbid the embrace, although the fruit of it should be the sights and sounds and smells of a common seaport and shipbuilding town, which would drive the Dryads and their masters from their loved solitude.

AN INJUNCTION REFUSED

"With respect to this particular property before us, I observe that the defendants have established themselves on a peninsula which comes forth into the very heart of the ornamental and picturesque grounds of the plaintiff. If, instead of erecting coke ovens at that spot, they had been minded, as apparently some persons in the neighbourhood on the other side had been, to import ironstone and erect smelting furnaces, forges, and mills, and had filled the whole of the peninsula with a mining and manufacturing village, with beer-shops and pig-styes and dog-kennels, with pigs, dogs, and children, which would have utterly destroyed the beauty and amenity of the plaintiff's grounds, this Court could not in my judgment have interfered. A man to whom Providence has given an estate under which there are seams of coal worth perhaps hundreds of thousands of pounds per acre, must take the gift with the consequence and concomitants of the mineral wealth in which he is a participant."

THE LAW AND TRIFLES

It is sometimes said that the law does not concern itself about trifles. There is, in fact, an often quoted legal maxim, *de minimis non curat lex*, and this is usually translated, "the law does not trouble itself about trifles." The meaning is that our judges, being sensible men, decline to undertake the measurement of what cannot be measured with any precision, and that they decline to push a legal rule to an absurd extent. If I dipped my pen into another's ink-well I am taking some of his property; but no Court would convict me of theft. The maxim certainly does not mean that I may do wrong with impunity so long as the damage does not exceed a substantial sum.

"The least touching of another in anger is a battery," said Chief Justice Holt, "and will sustain an action." And a later Chief Justice said, "By the laws of England every invasion of private property, be it ever so minute, is a trespass. No man can set his foot upon my ground without my licence, but be liable to an action though the damage be nothing."

To ask the Court for an injunction is, however, asking for much. The injunction is heavy artillery; and the Court will bring it into action only when weighty reasons call for it.

ABATING A NUISANCE

When a man suffers from a nuisance, can he himself remove the cause of it—abate it, we say? To some extent this right of self-help is recognised. And must he give notice to the wrongdoer before he takes action? It is perhaps socially desirable to give such notice; but usually there is no legal obligation to do so.

The question was, indeed, raised though not answered in the House of Lords, whether the right to lop without notice applied to trees so young that the owner might remove them intact if he chose to lift them, or to shrubs capable of being transplanted. Perhaps a prosecution under the Malicious Damages Act, 1861, might succeed in such an unneighbourly case.

The whole question was considered in *Lemmon* v. *Webb* (C.A. 1894). Plaintiff and defendant were adjoining landowners. Some trees on the plaintiff's land—trees so old that the defendant thought them about to fall—had branches projecting over the defendant's land. Without going off his own land, but also without giving previous notice to the plaintiff, the defendant cut off as much of the branches as projected over his own land.

ACQUIRING RIGHTS BY PRESCRIPTION

Was he justified in so doing? The Court of Appeal said "Yes." On behalf of the plaintiff it was urged that he had acquired a right to the exclusive ownership of so much of the space above the defendant's soil as the branches actually filled. Certainly, if I encroach upon a common or my neighbour's land, perhaps extending my shed over it, or moving my fence beyond the boundary, and he does not trouble to object to my trespass, after a period his right to object is gone. If, without force, without concealment, and without a grant from the owner, I occupy land for twelve years I become undisputed owner.

Up to twelve years I am a trespasser, and can be ejected; and the owner upon whose rights I have made trespass could sustain an action against me. After twelve years I am lawful owner; the former owner it is who would now be a trespasser if he intruded. For the Real Property Limitation Act, 1874, enacts: "No person shall make an entry or distress, or bring an action or suit to recover any land or rent, but within twelve years next after the time when the right accrued to make an entry or bring an action."

The Court refused to extend this to the acquisition of space by growing plants: "The owner of a tree which gradually grows over his neighbour's land is not regarded as insensibly and by slow degrees acquiring a title to the space into which its branches gradually grow. The analogy between an artificial projection or building hanging over a man's head is not close enough to serve any useful purpose."

RIGHT TO ABATE IS NO RIGHT TO APPROPRIATE

The right of an owner of land, or the occupier on the owner's behalf, to cut away the boughs of trees which overhang it, although those trees are not his, is too clear to be disputed. True, the branches still belong to the trespasser; if an owner of land lops off branches of fruit trees belonging to his neighbour, he must not sell or eat the fruit on them.

The law does not permit the abatement to result in a windfall for the abator. This was explained in *Mills* v. *Brooker* (K.B. 1919), discussed below. The position as regards the mere removal of a nuisance is clearly stated in the earlier case. "The owner of a tree has no right to prevent a person, lawfully in possession of land into or over which its roots or branches have grown, from cutting away so much of them as projects into or over his land; and the owner of the tree is not entitled to notice unless his land is entered in order to effect such cutting. However old the roots or branches may be, they may be cut without notice, subject to the same condition. The right of an owner or occupier of land to free it from such obstructions is not restricted by the necessity of giving notice, as long as he confines himself and his operations to his own land, including the space vertically above and below its surface."

ABATOR MAY NOT APPROPRIATE

Mills v. *Brooker* was an appeal from the Maidstone County Court to the King's Bench. The defendant had picked apples from the overhanging branches of the plaintiff's trees, to the amount it was said of several bushels, and had sold them. He claimed the right to do this in that the greater includes the less; if he had a right to lop the particular branches on which the apples grew, he certainly had the right to take part of the branches.

But the County Court judge held that, though a man may remove a nuisance, he cannot convert the material of the nuisance to his own use, and he gave the plaintiff judgment for ten pounds. The King's Bench confirmed the judgment. "He is given the right to lop for the purpose of abatement of nuisance, and for that alone. The right of lopping does not carry with it a right to appropriate the severed branches or the fruit growing on them."

CAN I JUSTIFY A TRESPASS?

It would indeed seem that the owner of the fruit can justify the trespass of going upon his neighbour's land; he can plead that otherwise he could not recover his property, that it fell into his neighbour's property without his act and against his will, and that the law will not willingly let the apples rot—because the owner of the soil cannot use another's apples, and because the owner of the apples cannot trespass to recover them. Necessity will excuse a trespass: "If a man, who is assaulted and in danger of his life, run through the field of another without keeping in a footpath, an action for trespass will not lie. Because the doing of this—it being necessary to the preservation of his life—is lawful" (Bacon's *Abridgement*). So it was laid down in the *Year Books*: "That, if a tree grow in a hedge, and the fruit fall into another's land, the owner may go upon the land and fetch it."

Clearly, however, the necessity must be obvious and great to justify the trespass. It would be intolerable if, whenever an apple drops into my garden, a neighbour could maintain a right to enter for its recovery. Here, as elsewhere, the law expects neighbours to act with reasonable regard towards one another.

It should be remembered, too, that I cannot justify a trespass, even to take my own goods, when I myself have intruded them into my neighbour's close. I shake the tree to dislodge the apples. Some fall into my neighbour's garden; I must depend upon his courtesy, not upon my legal right, to get them. A bad stroke sends the tennis ball or the badminton shuttlecock off my property; again I may not legally intrude.

So explains the famous *Case of Thorns* in the Court of Common Pleas, 1466. One brought an action of trespass "for breaking into his close, with force and arms (*vi et armis*) and destroying the herbage by tramping it under foot." The other sought to justify the trespass by stating that he only entered to take up his property, the thorns he had cut down. Counsel for the defendant says, "The cutting of the thorns was lawful, and the falling of them on your land was against my will; and therefore the entry to retake them was good and permissible. And, sir, I put this case, that if I am cutting my trees, and the boughs fall upon a man and kill him, in that case I shall not be attainted as guilty of felony; for my cutting of the boughs was permissible and their falling upon the man was against my will. And just so here."

ILL INTENT NOT NECESSARY FOR A CIVIL WRONG

"I hold the contrary," said plaintiff's counsel. "And I say that there is a difference between a man's doing a thing so as to become liable for felony, and doing it so as to become liable for the mere trespass. For felony is of malice aforethought, and what is done against the man's will is not done with felonious intent. But, if someone cuts trees and the boughs fall on a man and hurt him, that man would have an action for trespass. So, sir, if an archer shoots at a mark, and his bow swerves in his hand, and against his will he kills a man, this is no felony. But if he hurts a man with his archery, this man will have a good action of trespass against him, although archery is lawful, and the wrong which the archer did was against his will. And so here."

This argument was adopted by the Court, Littleton, J., adding, "And, sir, if it were law that he could enter and take the thorns, then, on the same principle, if he cut down a great tree he might come with carts and horses to carry the tree away. But that would not be reasonable at all; for peradventure there might be wheat or other crop growing upon the land. So no more will his entry be reasonable in the present case; since the law is all one for great things and for little." The modern way of putting the distinction between crime and wrong is this: in wrongs, for which the individual can sue, the intention of the wrongdoer is for the most part ignored; in crimes no external conduct, serious or even fatal as the consequences may have been, is punished unless a guilty intention (*mens rea*) is proved.

18

PRIVATE RIGHTS AND PUBLIC NEED

When a *public* necessity comes into contact with a *private* right, the justification of a trespass is not difficult. One who travels on the highway is exercising a public right. If an extraordinary occurrence, a heavy drift of snow, a fallen tree, shuts him out of the highway, he can justify a trespass to right or left. The private owner is obliged to submit to an interference with his property that arose from public necessity.

The justification is more difficult when a private right is in question. One who had a private right of way across another's land found his way so cut up by cart wheels that he was gravely inconvenienced in his use of the way. He, therefore, filled up the ruts and cut a trench to drain off the water. The Court held his action to be an unjustifiable trespass; and, when his counsel asked what other remedy he had, the Court answered, "If he went that way before in his shoes, let him now pluck on his boots." Even if the unlawful act should improve the land, the trespasser is not justified: "if a drain is cut in the soil by a man who has only a right of common in the land, though the drain improves the land, yet he will be liable to an action for cutting it."

Public necessity has been held to excuse all manner of interference with private rights. The safety of the State overrides any private right—*salus populi suprema est lex* ("the most important law of all is the safety of the State"). Military needs justify the requisitioning of property, the destruction of property, the curtailing of freedom of movement, the restriction of activities pursued without question in peace time. But I cannot justify harming my neighbour by a plea that the harm was necessary for the preservation of my property, my *private* rights.

AVERTING AND EXPELLING

To avert a source of danger is not the same as expelling it. If the harm to my neighbour's property happens as a result of my protecting my own against a threatened danger, I am not liable. By smoke clouds I drive off a swarm of locusts coming towards my fields, by embanking I ward off a flood from my lands. In so acting, in defence of myself or of my property, I cannot be held answerable when the danger, diverted from myself, has done mischief to another. It is a different matter, though, if I should turn off what is already on my property into my neighbour's property. This I may not do.

EXPELLING WHAT CAUSED DAMAGE

So the Court of Appeal decided in *Whalley* v. *Lancashire & Yorkshire Railway Company* (C.A. 1884). The defendants' railway was on a low embankment. The surrounding land sloped to the north-west, so that land on this side of the embankment was lower than the land on the other side. The plaintiff farmed land north-west of the line. In the August of 1881 there was an unprecedented rainfall, the ditches cut to drain the embankment overflowed, and a mass of water became dammed against the south-east side of the embankment. To preserve the embankment the Company cut trenches in the embankment, and the flood water went over the plaintiff's fields damaging his crops.

The jury answered questions to this effect—

1. The cutting of the trenches caused the flood over the plaintiff's land and inflicted damage of £130.

2. The cutting was reasonably necessary for the protection of the defendants' property, and it had not been done negligently. On these findings the judge gave judgment for the plaintiff; and the Court of Appeal confirmed his finding. The contention for the defendants was that what they did was implied in the powers given by Parliament. For a Railway Act had authorised the erection and maintenance of the embankment. It would seem, indeed, that if the harmful cutting had been necessary to preserve a public highway, or if the railway had been a State undertaking, the injured farmer would have had no remedy.

This was, however, a case of defending private property; and the Master of the Rolls explained the position in this way: "There is something existing which is injurious to your property, and the question is whether, by any active act of yours in order to get rid of that mischief, you are entitled to do something which would cause a misfortune to your neighbour. Now, it has been held that if a person brings something on to his own land, which if he does not take precautions may produce danger to his neighbour, he is liable though he does not do any second act whatever; because he did the act which brought about the danger, and he failed to guard against it. One of these cases is where a man brings water on the land which is his own, and dams it up, so that if it breaks away it must be a danger to his neighbour, and must do him injury; there such man is liable though he does nothing to let the water out, but it bursts away without any act of his.

"But then it is suggested that if a person has not brought the danger on his land it makes a difference. So it does. If he has not brought the danger there, and without any act of his it breaks through his land to his neighbour's land, I take it he is not liable. In that case both have suffered from a common extraordinary danger, but one has suffered before the other. That is all. But now comes this question : the danger has not been brought by a person on his own land, but it has come there—an extraordinary danger, which, if left standing there, will injure his property, but not that of his neighbour. Can he then, in order to get rid of and to cure the misfortune which has happened to himself, do something which will transfer that misfortune to his neighbour ? That seems contrary to the maxim that you must not, when you have the choice, elect to use your property so as to cause injury to your neighbour. The defendants did something for the preservation of their own property which transferred the misfortune from their land to that of the plaintiff, and therefore it seems to me that they are liable."

AN OWNER'S RIGHT ON ANOTHER'S LAND

Where a man is suffering from a nuisance on another's land his right to abate the nuisance is modified to this extent. If that other has himself created the nuisance—if, for instance, he has kindled a fire that threatens to spread to his neighbour's land—or if it is a matter of emergency, then the injured man can enter upon the land without notice to abate the nuisance. In all other events, a request to the wrongdoer to abate the nuisance and a non-compliance with such request are necessary to justify an entry by the person aggrieved.

NUISANCE ON A COMMON

Where the nuisance has been created on a common—where one has built upon it or has placed obstructions upon it—so that the enjoyment of the common is greatly lessened, any commoner on giving notice may remove the obstruction. He may do no unnecessary damage ; but his right is undoubted.

LIABILITY FOR DAMAGE THROUGH NUISANCE

The person responsible for the nuisance is answerable for any damage done by it. Whether such responsible person is the owner or the occupier may sometimes be a doubtful point. The Court of Common Pleas had such a point to settle (*Todd* v. *Flight*, 1860). The owner of a chapel sued the defendant for the destruction of the chapel roof, through the fall of the chimneys of his building.

The defendant had let the building to a tenant, though he knew the chimneys to be in a dilapidated and dangerous state, and he had done nothing to remedy the matter. The chimneys fell and damaged the chapel.

The owner, not the occupier, was held liable. If a man leases lands or buildings on which a nuisance exists, or if a nuisance arises and he is under a duty to remove it, he is answerable for any damage: "In this case the chimneys were known by him to be ruinous; he was guilty of the non-repair that led to the damage."

In general, however, it is the *occupier*, not the landlord, who is answerable for injury to a third person owing to disrepair of a building. "There are only two ways in which landlords or owners can be made liable in the case of an injury to a stranger by the defective repair of premises let to a tenant, the occupier, and the occupier alone, being *prima facie* liable; first, when there is a contract by the landlord to do the repairs, where the tenant can sue him for not repairing; second, where there is an actual wrong-doing by the landlord, as, for instance, where he *lets* premises in a ruinous condition." An owner, on the other hand, cannot be made liable for an accident due to a defect in his property of which he had no knowledge.

In *Noble* v. *Harrison* (K.B. 1926), the plaintiff claimed for damage done to his coach by the falling of a branch from a tree growing in the defendant's garden, and overhanging the road. The County Court judge awarded damages. But on appeal the decision was that the defendant was not liable. For a tree is not in itself a dangerous thing, and to grow trees is a natural use of the soil. The principle of *Rylands* v. *Fletcher*, that a man is responsible when he himself brings upon his land things which on escaping may do damage to his neighbours does not apply. Nor does the mere fact that the branch overhung the highway make it into a nuisance. It did not prevent the passage along the road. Nor had the defendant created a danger; nor, it appeared, had he any knowledge, actual or imputed, of its existence.

LIABILITY OF LANDLORD

In *Fairman* v. *Perpetual Investment Building Society* (H.L. 1923), the respondents owned a block of flats in the New Kent Road. The flats were let to various tenants, the common staircase remaining under the control of the Society. The appellant, who lodged with her sister in a fourth floor flat, caught her foot in a hollow of the cement of the staircase; she fell, and was severely injured. At the trial the judge, upon the evidence, came to the following conclusions: (1) There was no negligence on the part of the respondents; no complaint had ever been made, to them or to the caretakers at the flats, that either the staircase as a whole or that particular step on which the appellant fell was dangerous; (2) the depression could not be looked upon as a trap or concealed danger. And he gave judgment for the Society.

The House of Lords, by a majority, agreed with this judgment: "The liability of the owner of premises to those who use them varies; it is lowest to the trespasser, next to a licensee, and greatest to the person whose position, owing to the defects of the English language, is called an 'invitee'—persons invited to the premises by the owner or occupier for purposes of business or of material interest. Now, the lady was undoubtedly, when using the stairs, using them as the invitee of the tenant, not of the landlord. So far as regards the landlord she was, at best, merely his licensee. Towards her he owes the duty not to lay a trap for her."

MEANING OF " INVITEE "

It will be noted that the owner has some advantage which can be measured in money from an "invitee's" using his property. "Invitee," therefore, does not include a social guest, however warm the invitation that had preceded his coming. Such a non-paying guest is a "licensee" only; though he contracts cold through being put into a damp bedroom he has no legal remedy against his host—except, no doubt, in the very unlikely event of the host's being well aware of the danger and neglecting to warn his guest.

The owner who lets out flats, retaining the common staircase under his control, may be liable to his tenants if he neglects to repair or to light the staircase. That depends upon the contract between landlord and tenant. But to those who are merely given permission to use the staircase—to licensees, that is—he is liable only for a concealed danger of whose existence he was aware or ought to have been aware.

MEANING OF " TRAP "

I obtain permission to use another's house or land. In general I am, while availing myself of the permission, obliged to take care of myself. The owner has the duty of letting me know of dangers that I might not have expected. A farmer giving me permission to cross his fields must warn me if one field contains a vicious horse. For the horse is a legal "trap"; there is an appearance of safety and a reality of danger. The trespasser is not entitled to a warning. Nor, indeed, is it easy to see how a warning could be effectively given. The licensee is entitled to be, at all events, guarded against concealment and surprise: "A permission to use a way is of the character of a gift. The principle of law as to gifts is that the giver is not responsible for damage resulting from the insecurity of the thing, unless he knew its evil character at the time and omitted to caution the donee. There must be something like *fraud* on the part of the giver, before he can be made answerable."

Corby v. *Hill* decided in the Court of Common Pleas (1858) on appeal, turned on the question whether or not the defendant's action constituted a trap. The Court said it did. The plaintiffs' horse was severely injured by being driven against a stack of slates left on the road by the defendant. The road was a private one leading to Hanwell Asylum, and the defendant was employed upon building work at the Asylum. The jury found that the owners had allowed the slates to be stacked, but upon the usual terms of providing for the safety of such as had a right to use the road (of which people the plaintiff was one), that the defendant had shown negligence in leaving the stack without a warning light, and that the plaintiff was entitled to damages.

The Appeal Court confirmed this verdict: "The defendant had no right to set a trap for the plaintiff. One who comes upon another's land with the owner's permission has a right to expect that the owner will not dig a pit thereon, or permit another to dig a pit, so that persons lawfully coming there may receive injury."

WARNING AGAINST DANGERS

The warning must be sufficient; a licensee cannot complain of injury received from a danger of which he had adequate notice. But what may be an effective warning to an adult may be no warning at all to an infant. In one case (*Sarch* v. *Blackburn*, 4 C.P.) the Court decided that a notice "Beware of the Dog" was no answer to the claim of a visitor, who, not being able to read, had been bitten. The question was discussed at length in *Cooke* v. *Midland G.W.R. of Ireland* (H.L. 1909). On land belonging to the railway lay a disused turn-table. Though a notice-board forbade trespass, children did—with the knowledge of the Company's servants—habitually play on the turn-table. The plaintiff, four years old, playing there had his leg crushed. The jury said that he had been allured to the turn-table by the Company's negligence, that this negligence was the effective cause of the accident, and that £550 damages were payable.

It was urged on behalf of the Company: "It would be a novel doctrine that a trespasser is converted into a licensee by the mere fact that the owner had not turned him off when he was committing similar previous acts of trespass. The trespasser must take the consequences of his trespass." But the House of Lords agreed with the jury's verdict: "To the blind the most obvious danger may be a trap. To the idiotic the most perilous act may appear safe. The duty the owner of premises owes, to the persons to whom he gives permission to enter them, must be measured by his knowledge (actual or imputed) of the habits, capacities, and propensities of those persons. If the owner of premises, on which dangerous and alluring machines are placed, gives to boys of a mischievous and intermeddling age, or to children of such tender years as to be quite unable to take care of themselves, leave to enter, he will be responsible for injury."

That is, so far as regards children, both "licence" and "trap" receive a wide meaning. The attraction of a plaything may be an invitation to a child. The adult would be supposed not to feel, or be required to resist, the temptation to enter upon the land. The danger, too, may be plain to the adult, who cannot, therefore, call it a trap; it may be unrealised by the child, to whom it is, therefore, a trap.

TRESPASSERS INJURED DURING TRESPASS

The intruder on a man's property can, if injured during his trespass, rarely obtain compensation. He can when the occupier or owner has actually created a peril so serious that it is calculated to do grievous bodily harm, or when the injury is caused by something—spring-guns, for instance—that the law has forbidden. But for a trap for which a licensee can hold the owner liable, the trespasser has no remedy.

Indeed, an owner or occupier, in his wish to restrain trespass, is not prevented from creating perils that are obvious and that are unlikely to do serious harm. He can protect his walls by spikes or glass; but not in such a manner that the passenger on the highway, having no wish to trespass, may be hurt by the device. To place glass on a low wall would be to create a public nuisance. The rule was thus put in a case where the occupier was held liable for the death of an inadvertent trespasser, killed by falling into an area beside an unfinished house. The defendant was erecting a row of houses in the Uxbridge Road. There was no fence to guard the area, only a low coping into which iron railings were to be placed. The night was dark; the deceased was passing along an immemorial public way near the place; she unluckily diverged a little and was fatally injured. "The jury expressly found the way to have existed immemorially; they must be taken to have found that the state of the area made the way dangerous for those passing along it, and that the deceased was using ordinary caution in the exercise of the right of way at the time the accident happened. The result is—considering that the newly-made excavation adjoining the public way rendered the way unsafe to those using it with ordinary care—that the defendant was guilty of a public nuisance, even though the danger consisted in the risk of accidentally diverging from the road. For the danger thus created may reasonably deter prudent persons from using the way, and thus the full enjoyment of it by the public is as much impeded as in the case of an ordinary nuisance to a highway" (*Barnes* v. *Wood*, Court of Common Pleas, 1850).

PROTECTING ONE'S PROPERTY

The owner has ample means of guarding his property against intruders. The Court held that, during the night, an owner may let loose within a walled yard or garden a dog known to be fierce. And a case in the Bournemouth County Court (*Giles* v. *Garnett*, 1932), illustrates the extent of an owner's rights against marauding cats and dogs. The plaintiff claimed for the loss of a terrier, killed by contact with live electric wires placed in the defendant's garden to protect it from stray cats. The dog, when being taken out, had run into the garden. The plaintiff failed to recover damages.

"In *Jordan* v. *Crump*," said his Honour, the County Court judge, "the question was whether the plaintiff was entitled to compensation for injury done to his dog by certain spears set by the defendant in his wood. The Court said that the setting of the dog spears was a lawful act; that the accident occasioned by them was the act of the dog, not of the defendant; and that the plaintiff was bound to keep his dog on the path. The facts of this case are even more in favour of the defendant, with the exception that in the earlier case notice of the presence of the dog spears was exhibited; but the Court held that even without such notice the defendant was not liable. I have come to the conclusion that Ginger, not being controlled by the person in charge of him, became a trespasser and thereby met his death; and that the defendant is not responsible in law by reason of the electric wire fixed in her garden." But he added, "The fixing of electric wires in a garden so near the public road for the purpose of scaring stray cats, but which in this case proved fatal to a dog, is—though it may be legal—an undesirable practice."

UNLAWFUL MEANS OF PROTECTION

The question of how much force may be used against trespassers has, indeed, usually been raised in regard to trespassing animals. The owner has the right to protect his property, it is true, but the right is limited by the provision, "using no more force than is reasonably necessary." And very different opinions may be held, on the one hand, by an owner irritated or annoyed by repeated or impudent trespass, on the other hand by a judge and jury coolly examining all the circumstances in a quiet court where passion seems an undesirable stranger.

In one particular case, an owner on whose game-land boys were constantly trespassing placed notices threatening to shoot at intruders. He did so fire small shot, intending to frighten, or at all events to do only slight harm to the legs of some boys who defied his threat. Unluckily for him, a shot had effect, the wound took an ill turn, the wounded boy died, and though the penitent owner had himself paid for the best medical attention he was, deservedly, hanged. His use of weapons was no legitimate extension of his clear right, *molliter manus ponere*, "to lay hands gently on the intruder." (See the case *R.* v. *Cory Bros.*, discussed on page 391.)

Doubtless, the law will be less scrupulous where animals are concerned. Even so, the Court is reluctant to admit extreme measures.

"The question is," was the retort to an attempted justification, "whether the plaintiff's dog incurred the penalty of death for running after a hare in another's ground. And if there be any precedent of that sort, which outrages all reason and sense, it is no authority to govern other cases." In another case, where the plaintiff sought and obtained damages for the shooting of his dog, it was proved that the dog had worried sheep belonging to the defendant. The dog had, however, left the field where the sheep were when the shooting occurred, and the judgment was,

"Whatever the provocation the verdict must be for the plaintiff. For it was clear that the dog was not shot in protection of the defendant's property; he was shot after he had left the sheep. But, though there could not be a verdict for the defendant, the habits of the dog might be considered in mitigation of damages" (*Well* v. *Head*, 1831, 4 Carrington).

In short, the occupier, suffering from or threatened by an unwarranted intrusion or an unlawful injury, is under an obligation to make sure of two things before he uses force: (1) Is the damage I propose to inflict indispensable to guard against the loss I fear? Are not less severe measures available? (2) Is the harm to my property likely to be so great that I can justify my action in doing harm to guard it? A great teacher, Prof. Kenny, gives a good illustration: "If other people's hens are scratching up your seeds you must consider not only whether you can chase them out instead of shooting them, but also whether the damage done to the seed beds may not be less than the damage that would be done by shooting them. It is one thing to kill a mongrel cur which is worrying your prize poultry, and another to kill a well-bred retriever which is chasing your barn-door fowls."

OWNER'S RESPONSIBILITY TO INVITEES

To those whom the owner invites upon his premises for his own purposes—to buy in his shop, to stay in his hotel, to effect repairs upon his building—he owes a higher duty than to the licensee. He must take all reasonable precautions to make his premises safe. The clearest exposition of the duty is in *Indemaur* v. *Dames* (C.C.P. 1886).

Plaintiff was a journeyman gas-fitter, employed by a patentee, who had fitted a gas-regulator in the defendant's business premises. Defendant was a sugar-refiner, and, apparently, his business required an open shaft in the floor. Whilst the plaintiff was testing and examining the gas appliances on the floor where the shaft was, he fell down the shaft, which was unfenced. He was badly hurt and the jury awarded £400 damages. On appeal the Court confirmed the jury's finding: "It was argued that the plaintiff was at best in the condition of a bare licensee or guest, who, it was urged, is only entitled to use the place as he finds it (and whose complaint may be said to wear the colour of ingratitude, so long as there is no design to injure him). This argument fails: the capacity in which the plaintiff was there was that of a person on lawful business, in the course of fulfilling a contract in which both the plaintiff and the defendant had an interest. He was not there upon bare permission.

"What is the duty of the occupier of a building towards persons resorting thereto in the course of business, upon his invitation, express or implied? The common case is that of a customer in a shop. Whether the customer actually buys or not, he is entitled to the exercise of reasonable care by the occupier to prevent damage from unusual danger, of which the occupier knows or ought to know—and such is a trap-door left open, unfenced and unlighted. The protection depends upon the fact that the customer has come into the shop in pursuance of a tacit invitation given by the shopkeeper.

"The class to which the customer belongs includes persons who go—not as licensees or guests or servants—upon business which concerns the occupier, and upon his invitation. Such a visitor is entitled to expect that the occupier shall use reasonable care to prevent damage from unusual danger.

"We think there was evidence for the jury that the plaintiff was in the place by the tacit invitation of the defendant; that there was, by reason of the shaft, unusual danger known to the defendant, and that the plaintiff sustained damage by reason of that danger and of the neglect of the defendant and his servants to use reasonably sufficient means to avert it or warn him of it."

PRIVATE NUISANCE AND PUBLIC NUISANCE

It will be noticed that a "public nuisance" is a *crime*. When such a crime is prosecuted it is usually by the Attorney-General, who gathers up the complaints of a whole district and lays them before the Court. An individual may bring an indictment for a public nuisance, as he can prosecute any other crime; but the Court does not encourage an indictment when a civil action for a private nuisance would be the appropriate course.

In *Rex* v. *Lloyd* (*Nisi Prius*, 1803), the Society of Clifford's Inn preferred an indictment against Lloyd, who was a tinman. The prosecutors, who were attorneys, asserted that the noise the tinman made so disturbed them in their arduous and delicate duties—the examination of title deeds and so on—that their business was substantially injured. But Lord Ellenborough said the indictment could not be sustained. "If anything, it is a *private* nuisance. It is confined to only three members of Clifford's Inn; it does not extend to even the rest of the Society. And it can be avoided by shutting the windows. It is therefore not of sufficient *general* extent to support an indictment; and I think this kind of indictment has been already carried on far enough."

The damage to the public that will justify an indictment was, in a later case, explained by the same judge. The defendant, a timber merchant, had been indicted for depositing, hewing, and sawing logs in the street. His counsel claimed that he had a right to do this; it was necessary for his business, and it could not occasion more inconvenience to the public than draymen taking hogsheads of beer from their drays and rolling them down into the cellar of a publican. "If," answered the judge, "an unreasonable time is occupied in the delivery of beer, this is certainly a nuisance. A cart or wagon may be unloaded at a gateway, but this must be done with promptness. So as to the repairing of a house, the public must submit to the inconvenience occasioned necessarily to the repairing of the house; but, if this inconvenience is prolonged for an unreasonable time, the public have a right to complain and the party may be indicted for a nuisance. The rule of law upon the subject is much neglected, and great advantages would arise from a strict and steady application of it. I cannot bring myself to doubt of the guilt of the present defendant. He is not to eke out the inconvenience of his own premises by taking in the public highway into his timber-yard; and if the street be narrow he must remove to a more commodious situation for carrying on his business."

CAUSING A PUBLIC NUISANCE

Causing a crowd to collect may be a public nuisance. In *Rex* v. *Carlile* (1834), at the Central Criminal Court the defendant was indicted for a public nuisance in that he "near a public highway called Fleet Street, did exhibit two scandalous and libellous effigies representing a bishop with his arm tucked under that of the devil, and did unlawfully cause divers persons to assemble, by means of which the highway was greatly obstructed." The defendant had been distrained on for church rate, and had retaliated in this manner. The defendant, who conducted his own case in able fashion, asked, "Why do we pay for situations and disburse large sums of money annually in high rents in Fleet Street, if it is not to have the opportunity of putting things in our windows to attract the attention of customers?" And he suggested that Mr. Verry, a confectioner in Regent Street, might equally have been indicted for having his daughter in his shop—a daughter so beautiful that crowds used to gather daily to watch her and police officers were constantly moving the crowds until Mr. Verry, being inconvenienced himself as well as his neighbours, was obliged to dispense with her services. The jury found the accused guilty in spite of his suggesting that the annual procession of the judges to St. Paul's, the Lord Mayor's Show, and Bartholomew Fair, were all likewise public nuisances. (See "Sky-writing, etc.," on page 478.)

ACTION FOR NUISANCE

A public nuisance, of course, harms some of the public more than others. If one particular person suffers special damage from it, he can bring a civil action and claim damages for a private nuisance. But the plaintiff, to sustain an action, must show that he has sustained special injury other and different from what was common to the rest of the public. "There are three things the plaintiff must substantiate—beyond the existence of the public nuisance—before he can be entitled to recover. *First*, he must show a particular injury to himself beyond that which is suffered by the rest of the public. It is not enough for him to show that he suffers the same inconvenience as others do: in *Winterbottom* v. *Lord Derby* (Ex. 1862), the plaintiff proved no damage peculiar to himself beyond being delayed on several occasions, and he was held not entitled to maintain the action. *Second*, the injury must be direct, and not a mere consequential injury. Thus a vessel damaged a dock and the dock had to be closed for repair. Another vessel was delayed as a result; and its owners sought damages from the owners of the vessel causing the damage. The damage was held to be too remote from the loss (*Anglo-Algerian S. Co.* v. *Houlder Line*, K.B. 1908). *Third*, the injury must be shown to be of a substantial character. The damage, in short, must be *particular*, *direct*, *substantial* (*Benjamin* v. *Storr*, C.C.P. 1874). In this particular case the plaintiff, a coffee-house keeper near Covent Garden, was successful against auctioneers whose horse-vans blocked the approaches to his shop, obstructed his light, and caused offensive smells.

OBSTRUCTION OF LIGHT MAY BE A NUISANCE

The test of the right—to maintain an action for diminution of light—is whether the obstruction complained of is a nuisance. The value of the test is that it makes the amount of light acquired depend upon the surroundings. A dweller in towns cannot expect to have as pure air (as free from smoke, smell, and noise) as if he lived in the country; and yet an excess of smoke or smell or noise may give a cause for action. But it is all a question of degree. So with light.

" After an enjoyment of light for twenty years would the owner of the tenement be entitled to *all* the light, without any diminution whatsoever at the end of such a period? If that were the law it would be very far-reaching in its consequences. The strict application of it would render it almost impossible for towns to grow, and would formidably restrict the rights of people to utilise their own land. If that broad proposition is true, it is not a question of forty-five degrees; but *any* appreciable diminution of light which has existed uninterruptedly for twenty years constitutes a right of action, and gives to the proprietor of a tenement that has had the enjoyment a right to prevent his neighbour's building on his own land. My Lords, I do not think this is the law. The argument rests upon a false analogy, as though the access to and enjoyment of light constituted a sort of proprietary right in the light itself. In short, he who would obtain an order to prevent such building as would diminish his light must show that, if persisted in, it would amount to a nuisance. Light, like air, is the common property of all, or, to speak more accurately, it is the common right of all to enjoy it, but it is the exclusive property of none."

There has been a substantial privation of light so that the house is rendered much more uncomfortable to live in, or the shop is much less suited to the carrying on of business. A *partial inconvenience* one must be prepared to endure; a real injury one may have remedied. Nor does the fact that the complainant is using his property in a manner that requires more than the ordinary amount of light in any way affect the question.

Clearly, it must be a hazardous business to test the question at law; and reasonable give-and-take would meet most cases. For mostly the injury can be compensated by a money payment; and, where this is so, the Court is reluctant to allow the extraordinary remedy of an injunction. "It is quite true," said one of the Law Lords in the *Colls* case, "that a man ought not to be compelled to part with his property against his will, or to have the value of his property diminished without an Act of Parliament. On the other hand, the Court ought to be very careful not to allow an action for the protection of ancient lights to be used as a means of extorting money."

In one case (*Kelk* v. *Pearson*, Ch. App. 1871), where the Court of Appeal in Chancery confirmed an injunction, the facts were these: The plaintiff owned and occupied a house, "Ness Cottage," at Notting Hill. The principal windows were to the north, where there was a garden, bounded on the east by a wall six feet high. Beyond the wall was open garden ground. The twenty years' period requisite for the acquisition of the right of ancient lights had long passed when the defendants began to build on the open ground a row of houses one of which would almost touch the plaintiff's garden wall and, when finished, would have a dead wall over forty feet high. The plaintiff protested; but the defendants proceeded with the building.

In the end the plaintiff filed his suit in Chancery. He obtained the injunction he sought, the Appeal Court saying: "The plaintiff's bedroom, which may be taken as a test room, was formerly a light and cheerful room; the light had been taken from it to such an extent that it is gloomy and uncomfortable. It may be that we should interfere more readily in a case of this kind than if it had been a street in London, where a person was employing his house for city purposes. But, in this case, to the defendants it is the mere loss of a piece of building land, the site of one house, which they will have to convert into a garden or keep as a piece of pasture-land; whereas to the plaintiff it is a very serious deprivation of the comfort of his house, and a very serious diminution of the lettable value of his house as a residence.

"I have no hesitation in saying that the legal right ought to be enforced by the equitable remedy, that the Court ought to interfere and grant an injunction. There must now be a mandatory order to restore that which now exists as a brick wall to the height at which it stood before the building was commenced."

EXTENT OF RIGHT TO PROTECTION

When Messrs. MacAlpine were driving in piles to form a good foundation for Thames House, the vibration shook an old inn of Messrs. Hoare to such an extent that it became, to the eyes of the London County Council surveyor, a "dangerous structure." The builders were held liable for the damage done; for much of the inn had to be reconstructed. The suggestion for the defendants was that the inn had already reached an age of decrepitude, that because it was peculiarly liable to damage it was unfair to limit the reasonable activities of those working in its neighbourhood. But the Court said that a building—and the same rule is applicable to a person—does not lose its right to be undamaged, however old it is (*Hoare* v. *MacAlpine*, Ch. 1923).

SALE OF GOODS

THE rules which are considered later when dealing with "Contracts" apply to contracts for the sale of goods as they do to all other forms of contract. There must be an offer made by one person and an acceptance by another person. If A tells B he can have his car, or his watch, or anything else for that matter, for thirty shillings, A has made an offer. If B replies that he will give A the thirty shillings he requires in return for the thing offered, then and only then is there a binding contract of sale, breach of which by one party will entitle the other party to sue for damages.

SPECIAL FEATURES OF A CONTRACT OF SALE

These requirements, agreement, common intention, and intention to be bound by law which are essential to any contract are dealt with later (see page 682). Contracts of sale have special characteristics which are not common to all contracts, and it is with these that we are at present concerned.

The law as to the sale of goods is consolidated in the Sale of Goods Act, 1893, which deals with such matters as conditions implied in the contract, when ownership of a thing passes to the purchaser, the rights of a person who is not paid for the goods he has sold. All these matters are peculiar to the sale of goods and are therefore dealt with specially by statute and not left to the ordinary common law, though the statute of 1893 did little more than re-state the common law. Further, when any matter arising out of a contract of sale is not dealt with in the statute the common law applies.

THE SALE

It is important that the distinction between an agreement to sell and a sale should be clearly understood. The term contract of sale is frequently used to include both. The agreement to sell is purely and simply a *contract*, whereas the sale itself includes a conveyance. As a rule the contract to sell and the sale take place practically at the same time. Thus, if A goes into a shop and sees a book he likes, he picks it up and offers the price to the salesman. There is an offer to buy, the salesman takes the money, and the contract to sell is complete. But more has happened, the ownership in the book has been transferred to A, there has been a sale. In this example, A might have asked the salesman to get the book for him and promised to call later. This would be a contract for sale. When A called, paid, and took the book, the ownership of the book would be transferred to him and the sale complete. The importance of this distinction is clear when it is considered that the thing sold or to be sold may be broken or destroyed, and the loss falls upon the owner who, if the sale is complete, is the purchaser.

SALE OF GOODS, OR CONTRACT FOR SERVICES?

Whether a contract is or is not one for the sale of goods may sometimes be debatable.

The point is important. For a contract to do work may be made without the need for writing, even if it is a contract to execute a piece of sculpture or to paint a picture. But, if the law is to aid in enforcing the bargain, a contract for the sale of goods needs writing where the amount involved is £10 or over. The distinction has been put thus: "If the contract be such that, when carried out, it would result in the sale of a chattel, the party cannot sue for work and labour; if the result of the contract is that the party has done work and labour which ends in nothing that can become the subject of a sale, the party cannot sue for goods sold and delivered."

SALE OR GIFT?

It may be desirable, too, to discriminate between sale and gift. A gift of goods may be effected by sealed writing: a "deed of gift" transfers the property in the goods even though possession remains with the giver. Apart from a deed, however, a gift is incomplete until the thing given is put into the possession of the donee. A statement of intention is not enough. We should note, too, that a gift may be a conditional one, the condition being either expressed or implied. Thus gifts between an engaged couple may not be absolute gifts. The engagement ring, it seems for instance, must be returned unless the projected marriage becomes a fact. In a contract of sale, however, property in the goods passes at the time it is intended to pass; the goods may remain in the possession of the seller when they have already become the property of the buyer.

NECESSARIES

An infant—one who has not yet reached the last day of his twentieth year—is under an incapacity to bind himself by contract. When, however, "necessaries" are delivered to him, he is under obligation to pay a reasonable price for them. And "necessaries" are defined as having two characteristics—

(a) They must be suitable to the infant's condition of life.

(b) They must not be in excess of his actual requirements at the time.

Moreover, if the question should arise whether or not things supplied are necessaries it is for the judge to explain to the jury the legal meaning of the term. It is then for the jury to say whether in the particular case the goods supplied are necessaries.

LIABILITY FOR SUPPLY

As regards liability for the supply of necessaries to others, the following are the rules—

(a) A *Husband* is bound to supply his wife with necessaries for herself and the household. If he neither does this nor makes a suitable allowance for their provision, the wife is entitled to pledge his credit for them.

(b) Neither *Father* nor *Mother* is liable for goods supplied without authority to an infant child, even though the goods are necessaries.

(c) The *Shipmaster* has an implied authority to bind the owner for the price of necessaries supplied to the ship.

WHERE WRITING IS WANTED

Most contracts, whether of sale or otherwise, can be made without formality of any kind. One exception exists in regard to sales: a contract cannot be sued upon when the goods in question are £10 or more in value, unless there is written evidence of the contract. Such evidence must clearly identify the goods, the price, and the persons entering into the contract; and it must have the signature of the person whom it is desired to sue upon the contract. If the goods have been delivered and accepted, or if an earnest to bind the contract has been given, then the written evidence is not needed.

It should be noted that the evidence required may be given after the contract has been made. A man has, indeed, been held liable on a contract, the necessary written evidence being supplied

by him in a letter in which he declared himself unwilling to carry
out the contract.

It should be noted, too, that, since signature is needed to bind
a party, the contract may be enforceable against one party and
not against the other, who has not signed. And it appears that
any mark, written name, initials, stamp, added by a party for
the purpose of adopting the document, is enough. At an auction sale the auctioneer, though he is the agent of the seller, is
looked upon as the agent of the buyer also for the purpose of
signing so as to provide the written evidence.

When, in carrying out a contract, skilled labour has been
expended on something sold, the transaction is still a sale of
goods. And if the thing is valued at £10 or more there must be
a note or memorandum (signed by the defendant) to make the
contract enforceable.

Artificial teeth costing £21 were supplied. There was no note
sufficient to satisfy the Statute of Frauds. The dentist failed to
recover the price. If the contract had been one for the hire of
services, there would have been no impediment to recovery.

"I do not think that the test to apply in these cases is whether
the value of the work exceeds that of the materials used in its
execution. For, if a sculptor was employed to execute a work of
art, greatly as his skill and labour, supposing it to be of the
highest description, might exceed the value of the marble on
which he worked, the contract would be, nevertheless, for the
sale of a chattel." (*Lee* v. *Griffin*, 1861, B. & S.)

DEPOSIT

When money has been paid as a deposit, this is usually a
security to the seller that the buyer will complete the sale. In
that case if the sale goes off through the buyer's fault he forfeits
the deposit. "The deposit serves two purposes. If the purchase
is carried out, it goes against the purchase-money. But its primary
purpose is this; it is a guarantee that the purchaser means
business."

REPRESENTATIONS UPON SALE

The seller may—

(*a*) *Express an opinion* about his wares and commend them.
The buyer must not rely upon the opinion but, unless he decides
to trust to his own judgment, must seek a warranty.

(*b*) *Give a description.* The buyer can then rely upon the
description and, if it is misleading, he can sue for breach of con-

tract; and he can regard himself as discharged from obligation under the contract. Such a representation is a *condition*, a vital term going to the root of the contract.

IMPLIED UNDERTAKINGS (ABOUT RIGHTS TO THE GOODS SOLD)

Whether or not anything is actually said or written, the seller is understood to assure the buyer that—

(*a*) He has a right to sell the goods.

(*b*) The buyer will not be subjected to claims, undisclosed by the seller, in respect of the goods.

(*c*) The buyer will not be obliged to make further payments in respect of the goods.

Thus in *Niblett* v. *Confectioners Materials Co.* (K.B. 1921), the buyer of preserved milk found that he could not sell the tins without infringing a third party's trade-mark. The implied promise under (*b*) had been broken; and the buyer was held entitled to damages.

IMPLIED CONDITIONS (ABOUT NATURE OF GOODS)

(*a*) When goods are sold by *description* the goods must correspond with the description. This is a statutory condition (Section 13 of the Sale of Goods Act); and a seller cannot avoid it by any device. Pratt sells seed to Wallis as "English sanfoin," the seller declaring "seller gives no warranty express or implied as to growth, description or any such matters." The seed was not in accordance with the description and, despite the disclaimer, the seller was obliged to pay damages.

Even if a sample has been shown and the goods are in accordance with the sample, this is not enough if the description is not answered.

(*b*) When a buyer tells the seller for what purpose the goods are wanted, relying upon the seller's skill and judgment to supply the requisite goods, then—provided that the seller deals in goods of this description—the goods must be reasonably fit for the purpose.

This, too, is a statutory condition (Section 14 of Sale of Goods Act), and applies in all cases except when patented goods are sold under the trade name.

(*c*) Goods sold by description must be of "merchantable quality." What this term implies was laid down by the Court of

Appeal in *Sumner Permain & Co.* v. *Webb & Co.* (1921). The sellers knew that the mineral waters supplied by them were for resale in the Argentine; the mineral waters contained some salicylic acid; there is a prohibition in the Argentine of sale for human consumption of articles containing salicylic acid. Upon these facts the buyers claimed that the waters were not "of merchantable quality." But the Court held that the term did not imply a compliance with foreign law. The foreign law exists outside the goods, and the term applies to the quality of the goods themselves.

Yet, when goods are contracted for of a specific description, the fact that they can be sold at a good price—that they are in the commercial sense "merchantable"—does not exempt the seller from the obligation of supplying the particular goods. The appellants (*Arcos, Ltd.* v. *Ronaasen*, H.L. 1933) contracted to supply the respondents with a quantity of staves, the dimensions being specified, c.i.f. the River Thames. The timber, shipped at Archangel, was found when delivered to deviate from the specified measures.

The umpire, under the arbitration clause, found that although the goods tendered were not strictly within the specification they were so near as to be commercially within it, and that—since the goods were of the same value as those specified—the buyers were not entitled to reject. But the three Courts in succession determined that the buyers had the right to reject: the difference was not of such a trivial nature as would entitle the Court to disregard it; the goods themselves, not their commercial equivalent, were what the buyers were entitled to: "The fact that the goods are merchantable is no proper test in determining whether the goods satisfy the contract description. If the article delivered is not the article purchased, the buyers are entitled to reject it."

Lord Justice Scrutton's remarks in the Court of Appeal are illuminating: "The commercial mind and the legal mind are at variance as to the obligation of seller and buyer. The Sale of Goods Act provides that, if a person undertakes to deliver goods of a certain measure and number, he must deliver the goods accordingly. Otherwise, the buyer may reject. The commercial mind, naturally, does not like rejection. It is inclined to take the view that it is sufficient if delivery is made somewhere near the description, and that, if the buyer is not satisfied, he may make a claim.

"Here the arbitrator had thought that a 5 per cent margin might be allowed, although it was not specified in the contract. That was a misunderstanding on a point of law—one which was continually made by arbitrators. It was not a microscopic difference to which the Court could shut its eyes."

"CAVEAT EMPTOR"

One making a bargain is expected to look after his own interests; he cannot expect the other party to watch over them. "*Caveat emptor* does not mean in law or Latin that the buyer must 'take chance'; it means that he must 'take care.' It applies to the purchase of specific things, e.g. to a horse or a picture, upon which the buyer can, and usually does, exercise his own judgment. It applies also whenever the buyer voluntarily chooses what he buys. But it has no application to any case in which the seller has undertaken, and the buyer has left it to the seller, to supply goods to be used for a purpose known to both parties at the time of the sale."

The buyer can always guard himself by requiring express undertakings from the seller. If he chooses to rely upon his own skill and judgment, he must not complain when he deceives himself.

A WARRANTY OF GOODS

If he takes a warranty he is partly protected; for a warranty is usually limited to specific points. Obviously the seller of goods is reluctant to assume unrestricted obligations. The buyer may, in truth, suppose that he is guarded against every eventuality in reference to the thing he has bought; and one is at times forced to the conclusion that the wording of the warranty (or "guarantee," as it is often but erroneously called) is purposely misleading. Even a close scrutiny may fail to reveal the catch.

You buy a car, for instance, and get with it "a perpetual guarantee" to the effect that "Should this car develop any defect it will be put in order free of charge, irrespective of the age of the car." Now, it is hardly too much to say that such a warranty adds nothing to the rights of the buyer. For whether such an express warranty is given or not, there is an implied condition that no disabling defect exists.

So enacts Section 14 (1) of the Sale of Goods Act: "Where the buyer, expressly or by implication, makes known to the seller the particular purpose for which the goods are required, so as to show that the buyer relies on the seller's skill or judgment, and the goods are of a description which it is in the course of the seller's business to supply, there is an implied condition that the goods shall be reasonably fit for such purpose." Where a hot-water bottle burst, and the contents scalded the buyer's wife, the buyer successfully sued for breach of implied warranty.

But it would be unwise to sue, though on an express warranty, for damage through accident or ordinary "wear and tear," a term as illusive as one could find. A flaw or fault in manufacture becoming evident in use must be repaired by the maker quite apart from his express warranty. The replacement of worn-out parts is, however, a quite different matter. As the case discussed below illustrates, however, the old rule of *caveat emptor* no longer subsists in its old severity upon the buyer. As a part of his duty to the community at large, the maker of goods is obliged to be careful, even though the ultimate buyer of the goods makes no contract with him.

DUTY TOWARDS NEIGHBOUR

I have a duty towards my neighbour. On the high moral plane the duty is wide-sweeping. I must hurt no one by word or deed; I must be true and just in all my dealing. The legal duty is less exacting. Law refuses to follow out the remote consequences of a failure in duty. It gives a narrow answer to the question: Who is my neighbour? For acts or omissions that any moral code would censure cannot, in practice, be treated so as to give a right to every person injured by them to demand relief. *We must not injure our neighbours by our negligence.*

NEGLIGENCE

But the legal meaning of "negligence" is a narrow one. There can be negligence only when the defendant owes a duty to the plaintiff; and our law has not gone far in its recognition of duties towards people in general. A duty is owed—

1. Where a person has entered into a contract to perform a service. Thus a carrier is under a duty to carry his passenger safely; a doctor is under a duty to use reasonable care and skill towards his patient.

2. Occupiers of land or houses are under varying degrees of duty towards those who enter upon the land or into the house. (See "Landlord and Tenant.")

3. Those who hand to others (whether by way of sale or for carriage) things that may be dangerous are under a duty to give reasonable warning. The consignor of goods likely to leak or explode if carried in the ordinary way must give warning, so that

the carrier may make suitable provision against the danger. Otherwise the consignor is answerable for any damage done.

4. Those who handle things, guns and the like, that are apt to injure others must observe reasonable care in the handling.

And the lawyer's notion of "neighbour" is the man or woman who will be closely and directly affected by one's act. When I bring an action claiming damages for negligence, I am called upon to show that I have been injured by the defendant's breach of his duty to exercise care towards me. His duty was, as a user of the road, to exercise care towards other users; his duty as seller was to take care that the goods sold did not harm the buyer; his duty as occupier was to make his premises reasonably safe for those who resorted to them upon his express or implied invitation. Failure in this duty gives an injured neighbour a cause of action.

But it must often be a question of surpassing difficulty to determine whether the one injured is the neighbour contemplated by law. The seller of an apparently innocuous drink is undoubtedly liable to the buyer when that drink, being contaminated, causes a serious illness. For the seller has, expressly or by implication, warranted the drink to be what it pretends to be.

DONOGHUE (PAUPER) v. STEVENSON (H.L. 1932)

Suppose though, the negligence is the manufacturer's, and the injured complainant is the remote consumer. Is such a consumer a neighbour near enough to be entitled to care? He cannot sue for a breach of contract. For no contract was made with him. But can he not sue for a wrong committed against him? This interesting case, decided in the House of Lords, says Yes. The appellant was a shop assistant; yet, by means of our facilities for helping poor litigants, her name will go down to posterity in a leading case. The respondent was an aerated water manufacturer from whom she claimed, and after many vicissitudes obtained, £500 as damages for negligence. Her friend had bought her a bottle of ginger-beer in a Paisley shop. She drank part of the contents before discovering that there was a dead snail in the bottle; and the shock of discovery, together with the contaminated drink, caused her serious illness.

Lord Atkin, who delivered the majority judgment, pointed out the injustice that would follow if no legal remedy existed: "A manufacturer put up an article of food in a container, which he knew would be opened by the ultimate consumer. There could be no inspection by any purchaser and no reasonable preliminary inspection by the consumer. Negligently, in the course of preparation, he allowed the contents to be mixed with poison. It would be a grave defect in the law if the poisoned consumer had no remedy against the negligent manufacturer. I confine myself to articles of household use—soap, ointment, cleaning powder. Every one, including the manufacturer, knew that the articles would be used by other persons than the actual purchaser—by members of his family, or his servants, or his guests. I do not think so ill of our law as to suppose it to deny a legal remedy where there is so obviously a social wrong."

"CAVEAT EMPTOR" WHITTLED AWAY

The decision certainly extends legal liability, and adds another restriction to the rule of *caveat emptor*. Nor can any reason be adduced against the extension. In a simple state of society, where the ultimate consumer was in reasonably close contact with the maker, the rule, that the buyer must rely upon his own skill and judgment for his protection, probably did little harm. It is different now. The great bulk of things sold in the chemist's or grocer's shop consists of proprietary articles. The buyer from the retailer has no contractual relation with the original maker, and unless there is a liability for negligence he could have no remedy for injury. The remedy does not arise from contract. It arises from the social duty to conduct our business without wronging our neighbour; it is analogous to the duty of the occupier of a house abutting on the highway to keep that house in such a state of repair as will prevent its being a source of danger to passers-by. If I know that a thing is dangerous, or if, but for my negligence, I ought to have known it to be dangerous, then it is my duty to warn possible recipients. A manufacturer labels "extract of belladonna" (which is a poison) as "extract of dandelion" (which is a harmless drug). He is liable to any sufferer deceived by that label, even though the sufferer is not the original buyer: "If a person dealing with an article of a dangerous nature hands it over to somebody else, who is ignorant of its true nature, without warning him, he commits a breach of duty not only to the person who contracts with him, but to all the persons who, to his knowledge, may use it." So, in *George* v. *Skivington* (Ex. 1869), frequently referred to in the *Donoghue Case*, the defendant was a chemist. He made a hair-wash, which his negligence made harmful to any user, and sold it to the plaintiff's husband. The

Court of Exchequer held that the plaintiff could recover for personal injuries through using the hair-wash.

CONDITIONS AS TO PRICE

The practice of fixing the prices of goods has of late extended greatly: it applies to books, drugs, photographic goods, gramophones and records, motors, tobacco, confectionery, groceries. And it is usual to enforce the conditions upon retailers by a threat of boycott, or of actual boycott, if prices are cut. (See "Trade Associations," page 93.) Evidently, business men, both merchants and makers, are satisfied that the system is sound, and, in spite of some powerful and ominous monopolies, we may presume that the ultimate consumer is not unduly prejudiced by the system.

PRICE MAINTENANCE

In some ways it may be that the consumer is benefited. The price-maintenance system tends to promote harmony between the retailer and the customer, and to make selling easy and expeditious; there is nothing of the "higgling of the market," no feeling that others may get better terms or that elsewhere lower prices are charged. The maker, who has branded his goods, spent much on advertising them at definite prices, fixed those prices with careful reference to costs, must look on price cutting with something like dismay. Customers are bound to lose confidence in the quality of the goods, in the reasonableness of the prices ordinarily charged, in the good faith of the maker, when they see that the prices fixed for branded goods are not enforced. Selling of branded goods at low prices in order to induce customers to buy other goods disorganises the maker's selling organisation. Shopkeepers near the price-cutters cease to stock the goods affected, and the maker's sales diminish. Ultimately, the price-cutters, finding the goods no longer an effective decoy, may cease to stock them.

The difficulty is how to enforce fixed prices. The goods may come to a retailer who has had no contract with the maker, and who is, therefore, under no contractual obligation towards the maker. Or the retailer may disregard the conditions under which he had been supplied. Is there any legal remedy? Apart from an action for breach of contract, where this is available, there is none.

CONDITIONS ATTACHED TO GOODS

A condition of sale cannot attach itself to goods as it can to land. I may sell a piece of land's upon condition that no public-house shall ever be erected upon it; and every subsequent buyer who has notice of the condition is under the restriction imposed. If necessary, I, or any one interested, can obtain from the Court an injunction that will prevent the land's being used contrary to the stipulation. So, too, I may sell goods upon condition that they shall not be resold below a fixed price. Yet that condition is not binding upon subsequent buyers; they may have had notice of the condition, but they can ignore it. See the well-known case, *Dunlop Pneumatic Tyre Co.* v. *Selfridge & Co.* (1915, H.L.). The only course for the maker, as the law stands, if he wants to maintain his prices, is to take effective steps for preventing supplies from reaching the price-cutters.

Conditions cannot be imposed by law so as to follow goods. The plaintiffs (*Ajello* v. *Worsley*, 1896, Ch.) sought to prevent the defendant from advertising their pianos at cost price. For other traders, who retailed at twenty-four guineas the pianos they bought for fifteen guineas, could not sell and thereupon ceased ordering. Though it seemed that the defendant in fact had no pianos to sell, the plaintiffs failed to get the injunction they sought.

In some events the law of copyright gives a remedy. Thus, a gramophone company makes records of music of which it owns the copyright. It sells the records on the condition that the records must not be played in public, in cinemas and dance-halls, for instance. For the bloom upon popular melodies soon goes, and with the freshness sales also go. Can the company enforce the condition? The company cannot sue for breach of contract when the records have passed out of the immediate buyer's hands. But it can sue for an infringement of copyright.

RIGHT TO STOP IN TRANSIT

A seller who has actually transferred the property in goods, and has handed them to a carrier for transmission to the buyer, can resume property in the circumstances below. He learns that the buyer is insolvent; he stops the goods during the transit by giving timely notice to the carrier; he directs the carrier to redeliver the goods. He then has a right of resale.

If the consignor stops goods in transit and the carriers deliver them to the consignee, the consignor has choice of two courses: he can sue the carrier for conversion, obtaining as damages the value of the goods; or he can adopt the transaction and rely on his contractual rights against the consignee. But the consignor must elect the course of conduct, and he is bound by his election.

The plaintiffs had delivered goods to the defendants for carriage to Hull and thence to Manchester. At Hull the plaintiffs instructed the defendants not to deliver; but, through some confusion, the goods were, in fact, delivered to the customer. The plaintiffs then invoiced the goods to the customer, sued him, and recovered judgment. The judgment being unsatisfied, the plaintiffs sued the defendants for negligence and breach of duty.

The Court of Appeal held that, as the plaintiffs had treated the delivery as authorised, they could not now treat it as a misdelivery.

"The owners of the goods might have sued for conversion. They sued in contract and thereby waived the tort. A party cannot accept a transaction for one purpose and reject it for another." (*Verschure's Creameries* v. *Hull & Netherlands S.S. Co.* (C.A. 1921).)

TRANSFER OF PROPERTY FROM SELLER TO BUYER

In regard to this we are to keep in mind these rules—

1. In general only the owner can divest himself of property.

2. He may, however, give another the necessary authority.

3. He may, without intending to, lead buyers to think he had given authority.

We need to remember, too, that often legal possession is with one person, property is with another. The owner of the property is the bailor; he has transferred a limited right to a bailee—a carrier or a pawnbroker or a repairer or a warehouseman—for a particular purpose to be effected.

Where goods ready for delivery are identified and agreed upon by buyer and seller they are "specific goods"; the property in these passes, unless there is an express agreement to the contrary, from seller to buyer *as soon as the contract is made*. Contract operates as conveyance. With the property the risk passes to the buyer. I buy a stack of hay; it remains in the farmer's field; it is accidentally burnt. I must pay the price. For it is my property that has been destroyed.

Baxter agreed in writing with Tarling to sell a stack of hay, then standing in a field at Islington, for £145. Payment was to be made in a month's time; but the stack could remain till May Day. The seller stipulated that it was not to be cut till paid for. Before it was removed an accidental fire destroyed it. The loss was held to fall on the buyer. He must pay the contract price, since, at the time of agreement, the property had passed to him.

"The rule of law is that where there is an immediate sale, nothing remaining to be done by the vendor, the property in the thing sold vests in the vendee. Then all the consequences resulting from the vesti ig of the property follow, one of which is that, if it be destroyed, the loss falls on the vendee." (*Tarling* v. *Baxter*, K.B. 1827.)

Where the goods that are the subject-matter of the sale are not yet ready for delivery, or are not yet separated from a greater bulk, the property does not pass until they have been *selected and appropriated to the contract* by the seller and *approved of and assented to* by the buyer. Such goods may be "generic goods," defined by description only like "a dozen copies of Slater's *Mercantile Law.*" Or the goods may be an undivided part of a whole.

Thus in *Hayman* v. *M'Lintock* (1907), the seller sold to the buyer fifty sacks of flour out of his 200 sacks warehoused. He gave the buyer a delivery order which the buyer presented to the warehouse-keeper, obtaining a storage warrant in exchange. The fifty sacks were not separated so that no property in them passed to the buyer, and when, as did happen, the seller became bankrupt, his trustee could claim all the flour.

To deliver goods to a carrier for transmission to the buyer is to appropriate them to the contract: "the moment the goods which have been selected in pursuance of the contract are delivered to the carrier, the carrier becomes the agent of the buyer, and such a delivery amounts to a delivery to the buyer."

Where there is a contract for the sale of specific goods, and the goods, without the knowledge of the seller, have perished at the time when the contract was made, the contract is void.

A cargo of corn, supposed by both of the parties to be on the way from Salonica to England, was no longer in existence when the parties made their agreement for a sale. Before the date of the sale the shipmaster, finding the corn heated and in danger of taking fire, had unloaded it at Tunis and sold it for what it would fetch. The buyer was not liable for the price.

"It plainly imports that there was something to be sold, and something to be purchased, whereas the object of the sale had ceased to exist." (*Couturier* v. *Hastie*, H.L. 1856.)

PROPERTY IN GOODS

The owner can transfer ownership; he can give or sell or bequeath. But, in general, no one else can. Where goods are sold by one who is neither the owner, nor is possessed of the owner's authority to sell, then the buyer gets no better title than the seller had. A second-hand bookseller buys books borrowed from a library. The library marks have been eliminated, and the bookseller has no reason to question the right of the seller to sell. Nevertheless, he must give up the books to the library, and his only hope of recovering the money he paid for them is to trace the seller. Nor does "finding" goods enable one to transfer the property to them; he who finds goods and who turns them to his own use, though he has reason to believe at the time of finding that the owner can be found, is guilty of theft.

Business considerations have, however, brought about great modifications of this general rule. If a person is put in possession of goods or of documents of title then, as regards innocent third parties, he is, as a rule, to be regarded as owner of the goods. The merchant has in this matter gained a victory over the English Common Law. Common Law said *Nemo dat quod non habet* (nobody gives what he hasn't got); mercantile custom would have it that, if an owner allowed the world at large to suppose another to have authority to give (or sell) his goods, then the owner must not be allowed to say that that other had no authority. A diamond merchant let a broker have a parcel of diamonds, the broker saying he had a customer for them. The broker pledged the diamonds. Apparently, it is not customary in the diamond trade for a broker to have authority to pledge. The pawnbroker, however, who had had previous dealings with the broker, believed him to be principal. The pawnbroker was held to have a lien over the diamonds for his loan and charges. (*Oppenheimer* v. *Attenborough*, K.B. 1908.) For Section 2 of the Factors Act, 1889, enacts that where a mercantile agent is, with the consent of the owner, in possession of goods or of the documents of title to goods, any sale, pledge, or other disposition of the goods, made by him when acting in the ordinary course of business of a mercantile agent shall be as valid as if he were expressly authorised by the owner of the goods; provided that the person taking acts in good faith.

DELIVERING GOODS TO CARRIER

Apart from special arrangements, the delivery of goods to a carrier is equivalent to delivery to the buyer. If the goods are damaged in the transit, it is the buyer who must take the matter up with the carrier, and, again apart from special arrangement, it is the buyer who pays the carriage. Moreover, the buyer takes the risk of ordinary deterioration of the goods during transit.

When the seller does deliver the goods to the carrier he must make, on behalf of the buyer, such a contract for carriage as is reasonable. And, if the transit involves a sea journey, the seller must give adequate notice to the buyer so that, if the buyer chooses, the goods may be insured.

RESERVING RIGHTS OVER GOODS

The parties may introduce into their contracts terms that show an intention of the seller to reserve rights over the goods. Where there is this reservation, the property in the goods passes to the buyer only when the condition specified is fulfilled. Thus, the ordinary contract where documents are to be handed over upon payment (a D/P contract) implies that the seller retains a right of disposal. And when goods are shipped and, by the bill of lading, are made deliverable to the order of the seller or his agent, the seller may be taken to have reserved a right of disposal.

Moreover, if the seller draws upon the buyer for the price and sends the bill of exchange and the bill of lading to the buyer, then the buyer must either honour the bill of exchange (accept it or pay it) or return the bill of lading. If he does retain the bill of lading without accepting or paying the bill of exchange, property in the goods does not pass to him. We must note this, however; if he retains the bill of lading and sells it to a *bona fide* buyer, he does give property to that buyer. The seller cannot then exercise a right of stoppage in transit against the goods.

GOODS " ON SALE OR RETURN "

The rule as to these is that the property passes to the buyer—

(*a*) When he signifies his approval or acceptance to the seller, or does any other act adopting the transaction.

(*b*) If he retains the goods without giving notice of rejection, then, if a time has been fixed for the return of the goods, on the expiration of this time. If no time has been fixed then on the expiration of a reasonable time.

To "adopt" the transaction is to treat the goods as an owner only is entitled to. A lady wears, at a banquet, a dress sent on approval; she has adopted the transaction and may not, legally, now return the dress. The seller delivers goods "on sale or return"; the receiver pledges them. The act of pledging adopted the sale and the seller could not recover the goods from the pawnbroker. (*Kirkham* v. *Attenborough*, Q.B. 1897.)

The seller, however, can effectively protect himself. For he may make it clear that he does not intend the property to pass until he is assured of payment. The approbation note in one case had the words: "Goods had on approbation remain the property of Samuel Weiner until such goods are paid for or charged." The receiver under this agreement was unable to give a title to the pawnbroker with whom he pledged the goods, and Weiner could recover them. (*Weiner* v. *Gill*, C.A. 1906.)

What constitutes a "reasonable time" of retention is a question of fact, dependent mainly on the usage of the market.

The precise moment when an article ceases to be the property of the seller and becomes the property of the buyer often matters a great deal. I ask the waiter to bring me a glass of beer. When does the beer become mine? When it is drawn, or when it is handed to the waiter, or when he places it within my reach? If, unluckily, a clumsy guest jogs the waiter's elbow making him spill some of the longed-for liquor, whose is the loss? Must I pay as for a full glass, or may I require it to be replenished? The question was in 1932 considered by a Divisional Court, presided over by the Lord Chief Justice, and sitting as a Court of Appeal from a decision of the Licensing justices. The justices had convicted a hotel proprietor of selling intoxicants in an unlicensed building. No! he said, the drink was certainly consumed in an unlicensed building; but it was sold in a licensed building. And the Divisional Court accepted his contention, and quashed his conviction. (*Nelson* v. *Mighall*, K.B. 1932.)

WHEN DOES PROPERTY PASS?

There had been a meeting of the Royal Antediluvian Order of Buffaloes. For the meeting the licensee of the Bromborough Hotel had assigned a room to be used exclusively by the Lodge. The room was not in the hotel proper, but in a separate building called the "Café," and, though the Café was in the hotel grounds, it had never been licensed. On the night in question two members of the Cheshire Constabulary entered the room. They saw Mr. Jones come in carrying a tray bearing a dozen half-pints. He distributed the glasses among the members and received payment. Here apparently was a clear case, and an information was preferred by the Superintendent of Police against Jones and against the

19

licensee—against Jones for selling the beer, against the licensee for allowing the sale. But appearances are at times deceptive. They were here. For Jones was not a servant of the licensee; he was a member of the Lodge, and on that evening was taking his turn as "city waiter." The members of the Lodge adopt the peculiar machinery of appointing their own waiter. That he paid the licensee's servant before he collected payment from the members did not affect the essence of the transaction. "There was," said Mr. Justice Avory in his agreeing judgment, "no buying in order to resell to the members. The justices had founded their decision on the view that, when Mr. Jones returned carrying the beer, it was then his own property. There was no evidence that it was the property of the waiter, any more than if a man sent out his servant to buy a newspaper, for which the servant paid with his own money." The property had passed to the member within the hotel. Jones was only the conduit pipe and, if he had stumbled and spilt the beer, the unlucky Buffaloes would have been obliged to go thirsty and yet pay their money.

HIRE-PURCHASE AGREEMENTS

Now that these agreements have entered into all manner of trading, the time at which property passes affects the dealer very materially. How can he let the goods go out of his possession and yet retain the property in them until the hirer makes full payment? There is his problem. For, in great measure, the goods are his security; his power to retake them in default of payment gives some assurance that the debt will be paid. His difficulty is that mercantile law tends, whenever a trading transaction has taken place, to protect the party who has acted in good faith. If a man buys goods having no reason to doubt the right of the seller to sell them, or if he advances money not doubting the right to pledge them, the view of the business community is that he should be protected. In regard to his transaction possession should be construed as property.

Our law does not go so far as that; yet it has gone far. The Sale of Goods Act, 1893, gives indeed a statutory protection in many cases. Section 25 (2) enacts: "Where a person, having bought or agreed to buy goods, obtains with the consent of the seller possession of the goods . . . the delivery of the goods, under any sale or pledge, to any person receiving the same in good faith and without notice of any lien of the original seller in respect of the goods, shall have the same effect as if the person making the delivery were a mercantile agent in possession." That is, how-ever fraudulent the buyer may have been in obtaining possession, however great his violation of the agreement not to part with the property till payment is made, he can give a good title to a purchaser. So he can when goods are delivered "for sale or return." His dealing with the goods as though he were the owner is construed as his expression of approval.

RETAINING THE PROPERTY

If, however, the hirer has merely an option to buy at a price (however small as compared with the rent he pays), that agree-ment does not pass the property. A well-drawn clause to that effect is: "If and when the full amount firstly above named and all further moneys payable by the Hirer to the Owner under this Agreement shall have been duly paid, and provided that the Hirer shall not have committed any antecedent breach of the Agreement, then the Hirer shall have the option (but shall not be bound) to purchase the said Vehicle and Accessories, for the sum of one shilling." Under such a clause the trader can recover the goods or part of their price, even from a buyer in good faith. The Belsize Motor Supply Co. delivered a cab under an agreement giving an option. The hirer pledged the cab while in arrears with the instalment. The pledgee gets no better right to the cab than the hirer's right. But, apparently, he gets that right; if he pays the arrears and the amount named in the option clause the cab becomes his. (*Belsize Motor Supply Co.* v. *Cox*, K.B. 1914.) That is to say, so long as there is no express agreement to the contrary, a man may assign his rights under a hire-purchase agreement. The Court of Appeal came to this conclusion in *Whiteley* v. *Hilt* (C.A. 1918). For his own protection, therefore, a dealer will usually introduce a stipulation forbidding assignment; he is entitled to know from whom he is to expect payment.

So, too, it was held in *Helby* v. *Matthews* (H.L. 1895) that the property in the goods hired had not passed.

The hirer of a piano paid 10s. 6d. per month as "a rent or hire instalment." The agreement provided that the hirer might ter-minate the agreement at any time by returning the piano. But if the hirer should punctually pay all the monthly instalments the piano should become his absolute property; until full pay-ment the piano should continue the sole property of the owner. The hirer pledged the piano after he had paid a few instalments.

The House of Lords decided that the pawnbroker must give

the piano up. For the hirer had not agreed to buy. From a legal point of view the owner was in exactly the same position as if he had made an offer to sell on certain terms, and had undertaken to keep the offer open for a definite period. Until acceptance by the person to whom the offer is made there can be no contract to buy.

RESCUE OF GOODS

A risk run by a dealer selling on hire-purchase terms consists in this ancient right of the landlord to distrain for rent due. Self-help is almost wholly eliminated from our system of law. One remnant is the right of "distress" (or *distraint*). The landlord can enter upon the land or the building he has leased and, in order to receive his rent by sale of them, can seize the personal chattels there. That the goods seized are the property of another than the tenant in debt does not matter (with exceptions); and articles on hire-purchase are not within the exceptions. In *Worksop Public Utility Co.* v. *Sugden* (1931) the plaintiffs claimed damages for the wrongful taking of possession of a wireless set held under hire-purchase agreement. The set had been distrained upon and the defendant removed it. The value was £3. But under the Distress for Rent Act (1690) a "rescue of goods" is penalised by treble the value, and the County Court judge awarded the plaintiffs £9.

At Common Law, besides being a civil wrong of trespass, the forcible rescue of goods distrained, or of cattle from the pound in which they have been placed, is an indictable crime. For it is likely to lead to a breach of the peace.

MARKET OVERT

Sales in open market (market overt) give a good title to the buyer, whether or not the seller has a good title. Special market days in various towns have been appointed by Act or Charter, or in some cases by old custom. Within the City of London every day except Sunday is market day, and every shop, except a pawnbroker's, is market overt for its own trade.

But the market overt rule applies only when the goods are sold in the ordinary way to a customer. The case of *Ardath Tobacco Co.* v. *Ocker* (1931), through the discussion it aroused, probably settled one doubtful point about the extent of the privilege afforded to sales in market overt. All shops within the City of London are within the privilege; but how far does the privilege extend?

BUYING FROM TRADER

One who buys from a shopkeeper is protected in his ownership of the goods bought, even though it should afterwards prove that the shopkeeper had no right to sell them. The custom of market overt has ousted the Common Law rule that a man can give only such rights over goods as he himself has. But is a sale *to* a shopkeeper in his shop protected? if the shopkeeper bought from a thief would he be able to resist a claim by the rightful owner? It seems not. Certainly, in the *Ardath Case*, the whole of the transaction had not taken place in the shop; and this is essential, if the rule of market overt is to be invoked. Yet, even if the deal had been wholly transacted in the shop, Lord Finlay would not have held it to constitute a sale in market overt. The custom, in his view, applies only to the goods displayed and sold by the tradesman, not to goods sold to the tradesman. This seems clear from *Hargreave* v. *Spink and Another* (Q.B. 1891).

There is no sale "in market overt" when goods are sold in the City of London in a showroom over the shop, to which customers are admitted only by special invitation. Nor does it seem, in spite of the custom of market overt in the City of London, that "market overt" applies where the shopkeeper is the buyer, not the seller, of goods.

"The plaintiff owned jewellery which was stolen from her. The defendants are silversmiths and jewellers. They bought the jewellery *bona fide* from a person who brought it to their business premises for sale, and under circumstances which would entitle them to keep the stolen property if the sale to them was made in market overt.

" The defendants' place of business is within the City of London. It consists of a shop in the ordinary acceptation of the term. Behind the counter is a staircase leading to a showroom on the first floor. The person who brought the jewellery for sale explained her business, and was thereupon taken into the upper room where the purchase was effected.

" By the custom of London every shop in which goods are exposed publicly to sale is market overt for such things only as the owner professes to trade in. But by no reasonable stretch of language can the showroom be called a shop. Publicity is required in the transaction to bring it within the principle of a sale in market overt.

"Moreover, sales effected in a shop *to* a shopkeeper stand upon a footing differing in substantial respects from sales by the shopkeeper."

THE WRONG OF CONVERSION

In the *Ardath Case*, the defendant, a retail tobacconist in the City, bought in his shop cigarettes that had been stolen from the plaintiff. His good faith was not questioned. Still, being sued for *conversion*—for using another's goods without that other's authority—he was obliged to pay the value to the plaintiff.

The Common Law rule remains, therefore, unimpaired; only the owner, or one invested with authority by the owner, can transfer property. It is, perhaps, hard that the man who has bought suspecting no irregularity may find himself deprived of his money, and nothing to show for it. On the other hand, a relaxing in the watch over property rights might make the way of the transgressor too easy.

PASSING OF PROPERTY: COMMON LAW RULE

The judgment in the well-known case, *Cundy* v. *Lindsay*, gives this Common Law rule lucidly and concisely. In that case a fraud practised upon a linen manufacturer had caused him to part with the possession of a quantity of goods. He supposed he was selling to a man of substance; he was, in fact, selling to a man of straw. Must the buyer from the trickster be constrained to pay for the goods twice? Yes, said the Court; innocent though he has been in the transaction, he has acquired no property in the goods. For the trickster had no property to give.

The Lord Chancellor said: "My Lords, you have in this case to discharge a duty which is always a disagreeable one for any court, namely, to determine upon which of two parties, both of whom are perfectly innocent, the consequences of a fraud practised upon both of them must fall. In discharging that duty your Lordships can do no more than apply, rigorously, the settled and well-known rules of law. Now, the purchaser of a chattel takes the chattel as a general rule subject to what may turn out to be certain infirmities in the title.

"If he purchases the chattel in market overt, he obtains a title which is good against all the world. But if he does not purchase the chattel in market overt, and if it turns out that the chattel has been found by the person who professed to sell it, the purchaser will not obtain a title good as against the true owner. If it turns out that the chattel has been stolen by the person who has professed to sell it, the purchaser will not obtain a title."

RESTITUTION OF PROPERTY

The rightful owner of *stolen* goods may, in one event, regain his goods even though there has been a sale in market overt. He, or another, prosecutes the thief; and the thief is convicted. Then it is that the former owner can ask the Court for an order of restitution; and in all but the rarest cases the Court will grant it.

The language of the Sale of Goods Act, Section 24, is that where goods have been stolen and the offender is prosecuted to conviction, the property in the goods so stolen reverts to the person who was the owner of the goods, notwithstanding any intermediate dealing with them, whether by sale in market overt or otherwise.

Thus, if the Court had decided for the defendant on the market overt point in the *Ardath Case*, the plaintiff would have had yet another recourse. He could have seen to it that the thief was convicted. Indeed, the statutory revesting of stolen goods was designed in order to foster the prosecution of thieves. The conviction would not alter the fact that property had passed by the sale in market overt. Temporarily, the buyer had property and could give property; the tobacconist could not have been sued for conversion, but, having sold the cigarettes, could retain what he got for them. The buyers of the cigarettes—if they could be found and *if* the cigarettes remained unsmoked—could be forced to give them up. The very remote possibility of getting restitution in these circumstances is, however, obvious. For the revesting of property does not take place until ten days after conviction. For a convicted person is allowed an interval of ten days within which to appeal.

PROPERTY OBTAINED BY FRAUD

Property may pass by means of a contract that is voidable; the seller has been misled by the buyer and can, when he discovers that he has been defrauded, cancel the contract. Till, however, he does choose to rescind the contract, the property belongs to the buyer. And—this is the important point about the matter—the fraudulent buyer can give a good title.

The seller, therefore, if he is to recover his property, must act promptly. For, after the property has passed to a *bona fide* buyer, the original owner is left with nothing except a right to sue his defrauder for damages. And this right is usually not worth pursuing. "The fact that the contract was induced by fraud did not render the contract void, or prevent the property from passing, but merely gave the party defrauded a right, on discovering the fraud, to elect whether he would continue to treat the contract as binding, or would disaffirm the contract and resume his property. He can choose either course, but if, in the interval whilst he is deliberating, an innocent third party has acquired an interest in the property, it will preclude him from exercising his right to rescind." So ran the judgment in a leading case, *Clough* v. *L.N.W. Ry. Co.* (Ex.C. 1871).

Thus, an impostor bought goods from Phillips, paying for them by a worthless cheque. Before the fraud was discovered the impostor sold the goods to Brooks, who bought in good faith. Brooks obtained property in the goods. For the first transaction was not void. It was only voidable, and the property had temporarily passed to the fraudulent buyer. (*Phillips* v. *Brooks*, K.B. 1919.)

" ACCEPTANCE OF GOODS "

It is worth noting that "acceptance" is used to signify two slightly different senses—

1. The need for written evidence to make contracts valid for the sale of goods £10 or over in value, does not exist when the buyer has accepted part of the goods. Acceptance here means an act in relation to the goods which recognises a pre-existing contract of sale. Thus, where a buyer takes samples of hay and then rejects the bulk as not according to the contract, there is a sufficient acceptance for the purpose of evidencing the contract.

2. There is an acceptance of goods in fulfilment of a contract when—

(*a*) The buyer tells the seller that he accepts them.

(*b*) The buyer takes delivery and does any act in relation to the goods inconsistent with the seller's ownership.

(*c*) The buyer retains the goods beyond a reasonable time without telling the seller he has rejected them.

REJECTED GOODS

Apart from agreement a buyer is not obliged to return rejected goods to the seller. It is enough that the buyer tells the seller of the rejection. Where there is no right to rejection, the seller has his remedy in an action for the price.

RIGHT TO REJECT GOODS

A contract has been made for the supply of goods, and goods are delivered in fulfilment of the contract. The other party affirms that the goods delivered are not in accordance with the goods stipulated for, and he refuses to take delivery. Is any definite limit set upon his right to reject? If barley is delivered when oats are bargained for, the right is incontestable. But how if the oats delivered are a little more, or a less less, than the quantity ordered; how if they are, in a minute though ascertainable degree, inferior in quality? Cannot the slight discrepancy be met by a modification of payment?

The business world thinks it can and looks upon it as a matter of course that slight variations in quantity or quality may be offset by an adjustment of price. The anxiety of the law to ensure certainty in contracts brings about, unluckily, a divergence from the business attitude. What might seem to be quite negligible deviations from the strict letter of the contract have been considered to justify rejection of goods. In one case (*Moore* v. *Landauer*, K.B. 1921) a variation in packing was held to be justification for refusing the goods tendered; the contract had stipulated for cases each containing thirty tins, and a considerable part came in cases of twenty-four tins.

RIGID COMMON LAW RULES

It would almost seem that some of the rigidity of the old Common Law is again appearing to irritate the ordinary man, and make him exclaim against the unreason of law. In two important points, the bond and the mortgage, insistence upon the strict letter was tempered by the work of the Chancellor. An insurance company enters into a bond with a bank to pay the bank £500, with a condition that if a named employee of the bank faithfully performs his duties the bond is to be void. Any, even the slightest, breach of the condition would at Common Law entitle the bank to claim the entire £500. Equity long ago, and now Statute Law, limits the payment due to the actual damage suffered.

So with a mortgage. Common Law looked upon it as a transfer of ownership to the lender, unless the borrower repaid promptly; Equity insisted that the land was merely a security for the loan and preserved for the borrower, his "equity of redemption." Certain of our judges deplore that they cannot, by a similar ingredient of elasticity, give effect to the business way of regarding contracts; but, confronted with the definite words of an Act of Parliament, they are impotent in the matter.

CONDITION OR WARRANTY

It comes to this. The quantity stipulated for is, according to law, a *condition* of the contract; if that condition is unfulfilled the buyer can regard the contract as broken in its entirety. He is not obliged to be content with partial fulfilment, even though a right to claim damages is added. When the seller sends more, or less, than the contract stipulated for, the sending is interpreted as an attempt to make a fresh contract in lieu of the former one; the seller makes an offer that the buyer is entitled at his option to accept or reject. The relevant Section of the Sale of Goods Act is 30: (1) "Where the seller delivers to the buyer a quantity of goods less than he contracted to sell, the buyer may reject them; but if the buyer accepts the goods so delivered he must pay for them at the contract rate, (2) where the seller delivers to the buyer a quantity of goods larger than he contracted to sell, the buyer may accept the goods included in the contract and reject the rest, or he may reject the whole. If the buyer accepts the whole of the goods so delivered he must pay for them at the contract rate."

According to commercial usage, on the other hand, a variation not substantial in the quantity delivered is looked upon as giving rise merely to an adjustment of price. There has been a breach of a *warranty*, not of a condition, and a breach of warranty can be compensated for without supposing the whole contract broken. It is this second attitude of mind that is the more in keeping with commercial convenience.

The seller, uncertain about the exact quantity or the exact quality of the goods he will be able to deliver, can always protect himself. He can introduce terms like "more or less," "about," and so on, and he can agree to submit to an umpire's decision when an adjustment of price is called for. The buyer, having assented to the saving clause, must then be prepared to allow a reasonable margin.

It should be noted, too, that the buyer's right to reject has been lost when he has acted as owner of the goods delivered. Hardy buys wheat from Hillerns to be shipped from Rosario on a c.i.f. contract. On arrival of the wheat he makes no proper examination, yet he sells quantities to various buyers. He makes a thorough examination, when complaints reach him, and finds that the wheat is inferior to the quality bargained for. He is now restricted to an action for damages; for he has foregone his right of rejection. (*Hardy & Co.* v. *Hillerns and Fowler*, K.B. 1923.)

MORTGAGES

"Neither a borrower nor a lender be" was a sound enough maxim in the days of Shakespeare, when economic arrangements were comparatively uncomplicated. But under modern conditions, whether for the purpose of enabling the ordinary citizen to buy his house and live in it before he can find the full purchase price, or of permitting capital to find secure investment, or of enabling business people to tide over times of depression, borrowing on security is one of the commonest of legal transactions.

The safest form of security is land. A lender who knows that the money which he has lent can in any case be recovered by selling or taking the rents from a plot of land or the buildings on that land, has a security which cannot be bettered. The lender on such a security is known to the law as the mortgagee, while the borrower is called the mortgagor. The deed by which the contract of loan is made is called the mortgage deed.

Before the Law of Property Act, 1925, came into operation on 1st January, 1926, the law with regard to mortgages was, in many respects, different from what it is to-day. The mortgage deed was actually a conveyance from the borrower to the lender of the whole legal estate in the land in consideration of the advance. The legal estate was the full right of ownership recognised by the law, and it differed from an equitable estate, which might, for example, be the right of a beneficiary under a trust or the right of a borrower to redeem his security, which were recognised by the old courts of equity but not by the courts of law. This conveyance or transfer of the legal estate was known as a legal mortgage, and it contained a covenant by the borrower to repay the loan within a stipulated period (usually six months), and a covenant by the lender to re-transfer the property on such repayment being made. This did not mean that the lender either at once or on failure of repayment within the stipulated period became entitled to sell the land or lease it or build upon it unfettered by conditions. He was not the owner in that full sense, for the borrower retained what was called an "equity of redemption," which meant that he had a right to redeem the land at any time and become full owner again, provided that he had in the meantime kept up his payments under the mortgage deed, and provided that he paid the residue of principal and interest.

When a mortgagee desires to mortgage his own rights under a mortgage deed, he may enter into an agreement called a sub-mortgage. Under the old pre-1926 law he did this simply by conveying the land and transferring the mortgage debt to the new lender. The original borrower would still retain his equity of redemption, and the original lender (and new borrower) would also have an equity of redemption, which he could exercise by repaying what he had borrowed from the new lender, or sub-mortgagee.

Similarly, when a borrower desired to raise more money on the land, all he could do was to pledge his equity of redemption. When he did this, he was said to have entered into a second mortgage, and he could enter into a third mortgage and a fourth mortgage, and so on, so long as he could find persons willing to advance him money on the security of his new equity of redemption.

As land would frequently be made the subject of several mortgages in this way, there grew up certain rules with regard to the right of priority of payment as between different lenders. Sometimes a lender to whom the legal estate in the land had been conveyed had to compete in priority of payment with "equitable mortgagees" or "equitable chargees." An equitable mortgage was created by a deposit of title deeds with the lender, and was frequently accompanied by a document known as a memorandum of deposit. If a legal mortgagee had not been negligent in not asking for production of the deeds, he would have priority over an equitable mortgagee. As between several equitable mortgagees or chargees, the person who obtained his charge first was entitled to the first right of payment, and the others were entitled to payment in the order of the dates of their charges. A charge on the land was usually made by deed. It might, however, be made by writing or by conduct, without any conveyance of the land to the lender.

Where a legal mortgage co-existed with equitable mortgages the lender with the legal estate had priority, provided that he had no notice of previous mortgages when he lent his money. It followed that if a lender with the legal estate made any subsequent advances he would also have a prior right of payment with regard to those advances, provided that at the time of making them he did not know of the existence of previous mortgages. This process was described as "tacking" subsequent advances to previous advances, and it could be utilised by any lender who obtained the legal estate, whether he was a first mortgagee or not, provided that at the date when he lent his money he had no notice of the existence of other mortgages. .

MEANS OF EFFECTING A MORTGAGE

The alterations in the law of mortgages effected by the Law of Property Act, 1925, were designed with a view to making the law on this subject more simple and convenient than it had hitherto been. The principal alteration is that set out in Section 85. Under the old law, it will be remembered, a mortgage of the fee simple (i.e. of the full ownership) was effected by means of a conveyance of the legal estate. There was another method which had long been obsolete, and that was effected by granting to the lender a long lease. Section 85 revived this method. It provides that after 1st January, 1926, the only methods of effecting a mortgage of the fee simple estate (i.e. of the full ownership) shall be either by means of a lease for years, subject to a proviso for cesser on redemption (a condition that the lease shall automatically come to an end as soon as the mortgaged property is redeemed), or by a charge by deed expressed to be by way of legal mortgage. The lender's security in the case of a lease is the lease itself, but it is provided that in either case the first mortgagee shall have the same rights to the possession of documents of title as if the fee simple estate had actually been conveyed to him. The section goes on to enact that whenever the estate in fee simple is conveyed as a security after 1st January, 1926, the conveyance by which it is made shall operate as a lease of the land to the lender, subject to a proviso that the lease shall terminate on redemption of the mortgage. A first mortgagee is then deemed to take a term of three thousand years from the date of the mortgage, and any second or subsequent lender is deemed to take a term one day longer than the first or other lender whose security ranks immediately before that of such second or subsequent lender. It is clear from this that a sub-mortgage (i.e. a mortgage of his estate by a lender) is now effected by means of a lender granting a term less by one day than his own term to the person from whom he desires to borrow.

In the case of a charge by deed expressed to be by way of legal mortgage the lender has exactly the same protection, powers, and remedies as in the case of a mortgage by lease or sub-lease. This includes the right to take proceedings to obtain possession from the occupiers and the persons in receipt of the rent and profits. Any mortgage which was created before 1st January, 1926, and has become automatically converted into a lease or sub-lease on that date may be converted into a charge by way of legal mortgage by means of a declaration in writing signed by the lender, and the lender has in such a case the same protection, powers, and remedies, including the right to take proceedings to obtain possession from the occupiers and the persons in receipt of rents and profits, as if the mortgage term or sub-term were still subsisting.

There is a special form of the charge by way of legal mortgage which is known as the statutory mortgage. Four forms in use for this type of mortgage are set out in the Fourth Schedule to the Law of Property Act, 1925, but variations or additions may be made as the circumstances require. Covenants for payment of the mortgage money and interest by the borrower and for d'scharge of the mortgage by the lender on full payment by the borrower are deemed to be implied in such mortgages. Three forms of transfer of the statutory mortgage are contained in the Fourth Schedule, but they may be varied or added to as the circumstances require. In whatever form the deed of transfer is made, the transferee becomes entitled to recover and sue for the unpaid part of the mortgage money and interest if any then due, and to give receipts for it, and generally to exercise all the rights of the original lender. The Fourth Schedule also contains a form of receipt, which may be varied or added to in order to suit the circumstances, and on which a statutory mortgage may be surrendered or discharged.

MORTGAGES OF LEASEHOLDS

The new law also prescribes and restricts the form of mortgages of leaseholds. Formerly it was possible to effect a mortgage of leaseholds either by a sub-lease or by an assignment of the lease. Since 1st January, 1926, it has no longer been possible to create a mortgage of leasehold property by means of an assignment of the term of the lease, for the Law of Property Act, 1925, provides that the only methods of creating such a mortgage are by means of a sub-lease for a term of years absolute less by one day at least than the term vested in the borrower, or by means of a charge by deed expressed to be by way of legal mortgage. Any such sub-lease must be subject to a "provision for cesser on redemption," and, where the owner of a lease must obtain from his landlord a licence to sub-demise by way of mortgage, the landlord must not unreasonably refuse such licence. Whenever, after 1st January, 1926, a mortgage of leaseholds purports to have been effected by way of an assignment, such a mortgage is to operate as a sub-lease, subject to a provision for cesser on redemption. A first mortgagee is then deemed to take a term less by ten days than the term expressed to have been assigned. Any second or subsequent lender takes a term one day longer than the first or other lender whose security ranks immediately before that of the second or subsequent lender, and in any case for a term less by one day at least than the term expressed to be assigned. To what sort of a sub-lease an eleventh mortgage by way of assignment is deemed equivalent is not dealt with by the Act, but as it is hardly likely that a mortgage of leaseholds by way of assignment will be attempted so many times in succession, the point is of little practical importance.

TRANSITIONAL PROVISIONS

In order to bring about the transition from the state of the law as it existed before 1926 to the law as enacted in the Law of Property Act, 1925, it is also provided that all mortgages created before the operation of that Act by means of the vesting of the fee simple estate in the first or only lender, shall be construed to vest a term of three thousand years in the first or only mortgagee. The term of three thousand years begins from 1st January, 1926, and is subject to a provision for cesser on redemption. A second or subsequent lender, whose mortgage was created before the Act, is deemed to obtain a term one day longer than that of the first or other lender, whose security ranks immediately before that of such second or subsequent lender. A sub-mortgage by conveyance of the fee simple which is subsisting immediately before 1st January, 1926, is deemed to be a term less by one day than the term created by the principal mortgage.

Similar provisions exist with regard to mortgages of leaseholds created by assignment before 1926. Such mortgages are to be construed as vesting, from and after 1st January, 1926, in the first or only lender for a term equal to the term assigned by the mortgage, less the last ten days thereof, subject to a provision for cesser on redemption. Each subsequent lender on the security of the leasehold property is then deemed to take a term longer by one day than the term vested in the lender whose security ranks immediately before such subsequent lender, subject to the usual provision for cesser on redemption. A sub-mortgage by assignment becomes a lease for a term less by one day than the term vested in the principal lender, subject to a provision for cesser on redemption.

THE RIGHT TO REDEEM

It will be seen therefore that although the borrower's interest in the land is still called an "equity of redemption," his right is in reality a legal estate in the fee simple, subject to the mortgage term or the interest of the chargee by way of legal mortgage. The effect of this is to enable the land to be conveyed to a purchaser free from equities of which he had no notice at the time of the purchase. The borrower who desires to exercise his equity of redemption must give the lender either six months' notice of his intention, or six months' interest in lieu of such notice. He then exercises his right to redeem by repaying the principal money, interest, and costs due under the mortgage, and performing any other legal obligation which remains to be performed under the mortgage deed.

No limitation or "clog" on the borrower's right of redemption is recognised by the law as valid. This means that once it is established that a mere security for a loan was intended, no term in the mortgage deed which prevents the lender from obtaining the return of the property transferred to the full extent of the transfer will be construed as valid. For example, in *Bradley* v. *Carritt* (1903), A.C. 253, a mortgage of shares in a tea company contained a clause enabling the lender to take over the shares as absolute owner in case repayment of the mortgage money was not made on the date fixed for repayment. This was held to be void, as a clog on the equity of redemption. This rule is often expressed by the legal maxim "Once a mortgage always a mortgage." Transactions between the borrower and the lender, with regard to the right to redeem subsequent to the creation of the mortgage, are not affected. The borrower may, for example, desire to sell his right of redemption to the lender. There is no rule of law which prevents him from doing so. He may even agree in the mortgage deed to give some commercial or other benefit to the lender, which shall be binding not only during the continuance of the mortgage, but also after he has exercised his right to redeem. So long as such a condition does not prevent him from getting back the full extent of the interest which he transferred to the lender, it will not operate as a clog on the right to redeem, and will be quite valid. The best illustration of such a condition is to be found in the leading case of *Kreglinger* v. *New Patagonia Meat Co.* (1914), A.C. 25, in which the defendant company had in 1910 borrowed £10,000 from the plaintiffs on the security of a floating charge over the whole of the company's undertaking. Repayment of the loan was not to be called for until 1915, but the company was empowered to give one month's notice at any time to determine the loan. It was provided that the defendant company should not, for a period of five years from the date of the loan, sell sheepskins to any person other than the lenders, so long as the latter were ready to pay the best price offered by any other purchaser, and that in the case of sales by the company to any other person, the lender should obtain a commission on the purchase price. It was held by the House of Lords that although the loan was paid off in January, 1913, the agreement as to the sale of sheepskins was not a "clog" on the right of redemption, and could be enforced for the full period of five years. Viscount Haldane said: "If it was the intention of the parties, as I think it was, to enter into this contract as a condition of the respondents getting their advance, I know no reason either in morals or in equity which ought to prevent this intention from being left to have its effect. What was to be capable of redemption was an undertaking which was deliberately left to be freely charged in its details by ordinary business transactions with which the mortgage was not to interfere."

THE BORROWER'S RIGHTS

The normal state of affairs after the creation of the mortgage is for the borrower to remain in possession of the land as he was before the mortgage. The result of this is that he has full rights to take and keep all the rents and profits of the land, and there is no obligation upon him to render accounts of his receipts to the lender. It follows that he can sue in his own name for any rents or profits from or injury to the mortgaged land, and also sue for possession of the land in his own name. He may not do so, however, if the lender has given notice of his intention to take possession or to enter into the receipt of the rents and profits of the land. Nor may he do so where the cause of action arises upon a lease or other contract made by him jointly with any other person. Moreover, the borrower has power while he is in possession to make certain leases of the mortgaged land or any part thereof. These leases are the same as those which may be made by a lender in possession, and are as follows: (1) agricultural or occupation leases for any term not exceeding twenty-one years, or in the case of a mortgage made after 1st January, 1926, fifty years; and (2) building leases for any term not exceeding ninety-nine years, or in the case of a mortgage made after 1st January, 1926, nine hundred and ninety-nine years. Every such lease must be made to take effect in possession not later than twelve months after its date, and must reserve the best rent that can reasonably be obtained. It also must contain a covenant by the lessee for payment of the rent, and a condition of re-entry on the rent not being paid within a time specified in the lease and not exceeding thirty days. Every building lease so made must be made in consideration of the lessee, or some person by whose direction the lease is granted, having erected, or agreeing to erect within not more than five years from the date of the lease, buildings, new or additional, or having improved or repaired buildings, or agreeing to improve or repair buildings within that time, upon the land leased, an improvement for or in connection with building purposes. Where such a building lease is made, a peppercorn rent or a merely nominal rent may be reserved for the first five years or any less part of the term. Within one month after the making of the lease, the borrower must deliver to the lender first in priority a counterpart of the lease, duly executed by the lessee. The borrower and lender may of course modify their rights of leasing either by conditions inserted in the mortgage deed or by a contract in writing, and they may also extend their leasing powers.

The result of this is that while the borrower may make what leases he likes outside the limits set out above, if he does so the lender may treat any lease so made as void, unless he has given his consent to its being so granted. The lease will, however, be perfectly binding between the parties who have made it, and as against everybody but the lender, who may eject the lessee at any time during the continuance of the lease. The consent of the lender may refer to a specific lease, or may be gathered from the general terms of the mortgage.

A borrower on the security of land while in possession also has power to accept from time to time a surrender of any lease of the mortgaged land or any part of the land comprised in the lease, with or without an exception of or in respect of all or any of the mines and minerals, and on such a surrender of a part of the land or mines and minerals, the rent may be apportioned. If, however, a surrender to the borrower is made for consideration other than

an agreement to accept an authorised lease, the consent of the
lender must be obtained. Similarly, a surrender to a second or
subsequent lender cannot be made without the consent of every
prior lender. Moreover, no surrender is valid unless an authorised
lease is granted of the whole of the land or mines and minerals
comprised in the surrender, to take effect in possession immediately or within one month after the date of the surrender. The
interest granted by the new lease must not be less in duration
than the unexpired term or interest which would have been subsisting under the original lease if that lease had not been surrendered. Where there is a total surrender of the whole of the
land mines and minerals originally leased, the rent reserved by
the new lease must not be less than the rent which would have
been payable under the original lease if it had not been surrendered. Where only part of the land or of the mines and minerals
has been surrendered, the aggregate rents remaining payable or
reserved under the original lease and new lease must not be less
than the rent which would have been payable under the original
lease if no partial surrender had been accepted. The borrower
and lender may modify or extend these powers of surrender,
either in the mortgage deed or in a separate written agreement.
These powers of accepting surrenders are also possessed by a
lender in possession, as against all prior or other lenders, and as
against the borrower.

Technically the position of the borrower in relation to the
lender is that of a tenant on sufferance, as he can be turned out
of possession of his land by the lender at any time after the
creation of the mortgage and no notice need be given to him by
the lender before turning him out or bringing proceedings to claim
possession. There may be a provision in the mortgage deed that
the borrower "attorn tenant" to the lender. A useful form of
attornment clause in the case of a building society mortgage
occurs in *Dudley and District Benefit Building Society* v. *Gordon*
(1929 K.B.). The mortgage in that case was by way of
legal charge, and the attornment clause provided that "the
mortgagor hereby attorns and becomes tenant from year to year
to the society of the said property or of such part thereof as is
in the occupation of the mortgagor at the yearly rent of ——.
. . . If the society shall at any time by virtue of these presents
. . . become entitled to enter into possession or receipt of the
rents of the said property, then the society may at any time
thereafter on giving to the mortgagor seven days' notice in writing

in that behalf determine the tenancy hereby created." The object of inserting such a clause is to enable the lender to obtain summary judgment for possession of the mortgaged land under Order 3, rule 6, of the Rules of the Supreme Court, and so expedite his entry into possession, and not, as at one time was the case, to enable the lender to distrain for the interest, as such a power is void unless the mortgage is registered as a bill of sale.

Apart from these limitations, the legal position of the borrower in relation to the mortgaged land is one of complete ownership. He may sell the mortgaged land either subject to or freed from the mortgage. If he sells it subject to the mortgage, the lender's consent must be obtained to the substitution of the liability of the person to whom the land is sold for that of the borrower. If, however, he sells it freed from the mortgage term, he must pay off the mortgage debt, interest, and costs by giving the proper six months' notice of his intention to redeem or six months' interest in lieu of such notice. The fact of full ownership by the borrower has the further consequence that on his death his right of ownership passes to his executors or administrators for distribution among the persons entitled under his will or under the law of intestacy, which applies where there is no will. Where mortgaged property changes hands in this way owing to the death of the borrower, the property charged remains primarily liable for the payment of the mortgage money, and every part of the property is liable to pay a proportionate part of the mortgage money, according to its value. The deceased may, of course, expressly direct that the mortgage should be redeemed by payments made out of other parts of his estate, and if that direction is capable of being performed, the mortgaged property does not remain primarily liable for the mortgage debt.

THE LENDER'S RIGHTS AND REMEDIES

The lender also has certain rights which arise directly from the fact that he is full legal owner of a lease for years. On his death the mortgage or lease passes to his executors or administrators for distribution under the will or under the laws applying where there is no will, as the case may be. Where the money is advanced by a number of persons, jointly or on a joint account, owing to a curious rule known as the rule of survivorship the mortgage term passes to the survivors on the death of one of the lenders. This is because the money so advanced is deemed to be money or money's worth belonging to the lenders on a joint account. As far as the borrower is concerned in such a case, the receipt in writing of the survivors or last survivor, or of the executors or administrators of the last survivor, is a complete discharge for all money or moneys' worth for the time being due. This rule takes effect subject to the terms of the mortgage, and may be excluded by a contrary intention expressed in that document.

One of the most important of the methods by which a lender of money on mortgage may enforce his security is by going into possession of the mortgaged land. He may do this at any time after the end of the period which the mortgage deed fixes for repayment of the mortgage money. If he enters into possession he must take the greatest possible care to receive all the rents and profits which are properly due, as he is liable to account on the footing of wilful default, i.e. not only for all rents and profits which he has actually received, but also for all those which, but for his own wilful default, he might have received. If the lender was not justified in entering into possession by reason of danger to the security and the fact of interest being in arrear, any excess of rents and profits over the amount of interest must be applied every year in reducing the principal debt. The lender is not entitled to remuneration for any services which he may render while in occupation, but he is entitled to the cost of any necessary repairs.

The lender in possession of the mortgaged land has power to make the same leases as those which the borrower in possession can make. While in possession he, furthermore, has power to accept the surrender of any lease, subject to the same conditions as those on which a borrower in possession may accept the surrender of a lease.

If the mortgage is by deed, the lender further has power to sell the mortgaged property when the mortgage money has become due, i.e. when the period fixed for payment has expired. But he cannot exercise this power unless and until one of three events has occurred. The first is that notice requiring payment of the mortgage money has been served on the mortgagor or one of two or more mortgagors, and default has been made in payment of the mortgage money or part thereof for three months after the service of such notice. The second event on which the lender can exercise his power of sale occurs when some interest under the mortgage is in arrear and unpaid for two months after becoming due. The third occurs where the borrower has broken a provision of the mortgage deed, or any other of his legal obligations, other than payment of the mortgage money or interest thereon. The lender exercising the right of sale has power to convey by deed the property sold free from all rights to which the mortgage has priority, but not from those which have priority to the mortgage. The purchaser is not concerned with the question, nor is he bound to inquire whether a case has arisen to authorise the sale or whether due notice has been given, or whether leave of the Court, if this is required, has been obtained, or whether the power has in any other respect been irregularly exercised, and the purchaser's right to the property cannot be attacked on any of these grounds. Any person who actually suffers loss through an improper or irregular exercise of the right of sale can obtain damages against the person exercising the power. Executors and administrators of the lender's estate, and persons to whom the mortgage has been assigned, may also exercise the power of sale. The person entitled to exercise the power of sale has a right to recover the deeds and documents of title to the property from anybody except a person having a right in priority to the mortgage. He can only do this, however, after the right to sell has become exerciseable.

The money which the lender receives as the proceeds of sale must be held in trust to be applied by him, first in payment of all costs, charges, and expenses properly incurred by him as incident to the sale, and secondly in discharge of the mortgage money, interest, and costs, and other money, if any, due under the mortgage. The rest of the proceeds must be paid to the person entitled to the mortgaged property, or authorised to give receipts for the proceeds of sale of the property. Any prior charges to which the sale is not made subject must, of course, be paid off first.

Where the mortgage is by deed, the lender also has implied power to insure and keep insured against loss or damage by fire any building or effects or property which form part of the mortgaged property and which can be insured. The premiums paid for any such insurance become a charge on the mortgaged property, with the same right of priority and at the same rate of interest as the original mortgage money. The amount of insurance effected by a lender acting under this power must not exceed the amount specified in the mortgage deed, or, if no amount is specified, two-thirds of the amount that would be required to restore the insured property in the case of its total destruction.

In three cases, however, the lender is not permitted to effect an insurance of the mortgaged property. One of these occurs where there is a declaration in the mortgage deed that no insurance is required. The second occurs where an insurance is kept up by or on behalf of the borrower in accordance with the mortgage deed. The third is where the mortgage deed contains no stipulation respecting insurance and an insurance is kept up by or on behalf of the borrower with the consent of the lender to the amount to which the lender is authorised to insure by the law as stated above.

If the lender requires it, all money received on an insurance of mortgaged property against loss or damage by fire, or any insurance which the borrower is liable to maintain under the mortgage deed, must be applied by the borrower in making good the loss or damage in respect of which the money is received. The lender may, on the other hand, require that all moneys so received be applied in or towards the discharge of the mortgage money. The mortgage deed may vary, or altogether exclude these provisions, which only apply in the absence of agreement to the contrary.

In addition to these powers a lender who is in possession has power to cut and sell timber and other trees ripe for cutting and not planted or left standing for shelter or ornament, or to contract for any such cutting and sale, to be completed within any time not exceeding twelve months from the making of the contract.

A fourth method by which the lender may enforce his rights where the mortgage is by deed is by the appointment of a receiver of the income of the whole or part of the mortgaged property. He may not do so, however, unless and until he has become entitled to exercise his power of sale. The appointment of the receiver must be in writing signed by the lender, who may choose any person whom he thinks fit to fill the office. He may also remove the receiver and appoint a new receiver at any time by means of a signed writing. A receiver so appointed is deemed to be the agent of the borrower, who is solely responsible for the receiver's acts and defaults, except where the mortgage deed otherwise provides. If he is directed in writing by the lender the receiver must insure to the extent if any to which the lender might have insured. He must also, if so directed, keep insured out of the money received by him, any property comprised in the mortgage, against loss or damage by fire. The receiver has power to demand and recover all the income of which he is appointed receiver, by action at law, distress, or otherwise, in the name of either the borrower or the lender, and to give effectual receipts.

A person who pays money to the receiver is not concerned to inquire whether any case has arisen authorising the receiver to act.

The remuneration, costs, and expenses of the receiver are met by means of the receiver retaining a commission at the rate specified in his appointment. Such rate must not exceed 5 per cent on the gross amount of all money received. Sometimes no rate of commission is specified in the appointment, and in such case the rate allowed is 5 per cent on the gross amount of all money received, or such other rate as the Court, on application by the receiver, thinks fit to allow. All moneys taken by the receiver must be applied (1) in discharge of all rents, taxes, rates, and outgoings whatever affecting the mortgaged property; and (2) in keeping down all annual sums or other payments, and the interest on all principal sums, having priority to the mortgage in right whereof he is receiver; and (3) in payment of the receiver's commission and of the premiums of any insurances properly payable, and the cost of executing any necessary or proper repairs directed in writing by the lender; and (4) in payment of the interest accruing due in respect of any principal money due under the mortgage; and (5) in or towards the discharge of the principal money if so directed in writing by the lender. The remainder, if any, of the money received must be paid to the person who, but for the possession of the receiver, would have been entitled to receive the income of which he is appointed receiver, or who is otherwise entitled to the mortgaged property.

If the lender desires to put an end to the borrower's right to redeem and so become complete owner of the mortgaged property he must do so by means of an application to the Court for an order of foreclosure. He cannot do this until the end of the period fixed in the mortgage for repayment. At the end of this period he may bring proceedings asking that the borrower be foreclosed (i.e. prevented from exercising his right to redeem) unless he pays what is owing under the mortgage deed. If the lender succeeds in his action he does not become absolute owner at once. The Court makes an order for foreclosure nisi, and fixes a date by which the money must be paid. This date is usually six months later, and, if the mortgage money is not paid by then, the Court, on the application of the lender, makes an order for foreclosure absolute. The result of this order is that the lender becomes absolutely entitled to the property, and his mortgage term is automatically brought to an end, as are all subsequent mortgage terms. In order to protect the rights of subsequent lenders it is usual to direct in the order for foreclosure nisi that any subsequent lender may repay the amount due to the first lender on the date fixed for foreclosure absolute. Where any subsequent lender obtains foreclosure, the rights of a previous lender remain unaffected, unless his mortgage is redeemed by the subsequent lender. Where a lender on the security of a mortgage created by means of a lease for a term of years or a charge by deed expressed to be by way of legal mortgage obtains an order for foreclosure absolute, he becomes the owner of the fee simple estate, subject to any legal mortgage which has priority to that of the lender. The lender's mortgage thereupon becomes merged in the fee simple estate, and any subsequent mortgage term or charge by way of legal mortgage bound by the order thereupon becomes extinguished.

Another right which the lender possesses after the expiration of the time fixed for repayment is to sue the borrower on his personal covenant to repay the mortgage money with interest. Where the mortgaged property depreciates in value this right becomes of practical importance, and a lender may exercise it after exercising his right to foreclose. If, however, he does so, the borrower becomes again entitled to his equity of redemption.

An equitable mortgagee who is entitled under his memorandum of deposit to call for a legal mortgage may apply for foreclosure, but if he has no right to call for a legal mortgage his proper method of enforcing his security is to apply to the Court for a sale. In any action, whether for foreclosure, redemption or sale, or for the raising or payment in any manner of the mortgage money, the Court may direct a sale of the mortgaged property on the request of the lender or any person interested in the mortgage money or in the right of redemption. It does not matter in such a case that any other person dissents, or the mortgagee or any person so interested does not appear in the action. The sale may be directed without allowing any time for redemption or for payment of mortgage money, and the Court may order such terms as it thinks fit, including the deposit in court of a reasonable sum fixed by the Court to meet the expenses of sale and secure performance of the terms.

TRANSFER OF MORTGAGE

A lender may desire to transfer his mortgage. He must do this by deed, and unless a contrary intention is expressed, the deed operates to transfer (a) the right to demand, sue for, recover, and give receipts for the mortgage money or the unpaid part thereof and the interest then due, if any, and thenceforth to become due thereon and (b) the benefit of all securities for the mortgage money and the right to sue on all covenants with the lender and the right to exercise all powers of the lender and (c) all the estate in the land vested in the lender, subject to the right of redemption and the provision for cesser. This also applies when a mortgage is transferred to personal representatives by the death of a lender.

RECEIPT FOR MORTGAGE MONEY

Since 1st January, 1926, a receipt endorsed on or written at the foot of or annexed to a mortgage, for all money thereby secured, which states the name of the person who pays the money and is executed by the lender or the person legally entitled to give a receipt for the mortgage money operates as a surrender of the term of the lease, if the mortgage is by means of a lease, or as a reconveyance of the property to the person who was entitled to redeem. The receipt operates as a discharge of the mortgaged property from all principal money and interest secured thereby, and from all claims under the mortgage. A statutory form of receipt is set out in the Third Schedule to the Law of Property Act, 1925, but this form may be varied or added to in such manner as is deemed expedient.

If the receipt shows that the money has been paid off by a person who is not entitled to the immediate right to redeem, the receipt operates as if a deed had been drawn up and signed, transferring the benefit of the mortgage to the person who paid the money. This, however, does not apply if the contrary is expressly provided. Nor does it apply where a trustee, or a personal representative of a deceased person's estate pays off the mortgage out of capital money or other money which may properly be applied to the discharge of the mortgage. In the last case the receipt will operate as a transfer only if express provision is made to that effect. Where a mortgage consists of a mortgage and a further charge, or where it consists of more than one deed, the receipt is sufficient if it refers either to all the deeds in which the mortgage money is secured or to the aggregate amount of the mortgage money secured and for the time being owing.

PRIORITY OF MORTGAGES

In view of the fact that property may be incumbered with a number of mortgages to different lenders, it is of the highest importance to have a clear notion of the rules by which the order of payment to different lenders is determined. Since 1st January, 1926, these rules have been vitally altered by the new law of registration of mortgages and charges set out in the Land Charges Act, 1925. Under Section 10 of that Act, certain mortgages and charges may be registered in the register of land charges. A number of these are specified in the section, but for present purposes it will be sufficient to refer to the following: (1) Any legal mortgage which is not protected by a deposit of title deeds and which is not registered in any local deeds register (sometimes called a "puisne mortgage"); (2) any equitable charge acquired by a tenant for life or statutory owner under the Finance Act, 1894, or any other statute, by reason of the discharge by him of any death duties or other liabilities, and to which special priority is given by the statute (sometimes called a "limited owner's charge"); (3) any other equitable charge, which is not secured by a deposit of documents relating to the legal estate affected, and does not arise or affect an interest arising under a trust for sale or a settlement, and is not included in any other class of land charge. This is technically known as a "general equitable charge."

All of these charges rank for payment in the order of their date of registration in the register of land charges. This makes it of vital importance for lenders who are not protected by a deposit of documents to register their mortgages as early as possible. The lender whose mortgage is protected by a deposit of the title deeds has the full priority that he had before 1926, that is to say, he has priority to all subsequent lenders on the security of the property. With regard to prior lenders, whether legal or equitable, the lender with the title deeds has priority over such persons only if they were not negligent in not demanding production of the title deeds.

TACKING

One of the most curious rules in the law of mortgages is that which is concerned with the doctrine of "tacking." The old pre-1926 law was that any lender who obtained the legal estate, whether he was first mortgagee or not, could tack subsequent advances to his previous advance, so as to have a right of payment with regard to such subsequent advances which could take precedence over the rights of any intermediate lenders of whose mortgages the lender who tacked had no notice at the time of his subsequent advances. The Law of Property Act, 1925, has now abolished the right of tacking except in any of the following circumstances. A prior lender since 1st January, 1926, has a right to make further advances to rank in priority to subsequent mortgages (a) if an arrangement has been made to that effect with the subsequent lenders; or (b) if he had no notice (i.e. knowledge) of the subsequent mortgages at the time when the first advance was made by him; or (c) whether or not he had such notice, where the mortgage imposes an obligation on him to make such further advances. This applies whether or not the prior mortgage was made expressly for securing further advances. The mere fact that a subsequent mortgage was registered as a land charge or at a local deeds registry does not mean that the lender has notice (i.e. knowledge) of its existence unless it was registered at the date when the original mortgage was created, or at the date when the last search, if any, by or on behalf of the lender, was made, whichever last happened. For instance, if A mortgages his house, "Fernlea," to B for £250 and deposits the title deeds with B, and then mortgages "Fernlea" to C for £300, then to B for a further £100, and then to D for £400, and finally to C for £100, B can tack his second advance of £100 to his first advance of £250, provided that either of the three contingencies mentioned above are fulfilled. The aggregate loan by B of £350 will rank in priority to the loans of C and D. Suppose, further, that C registered his charge for £300 before D registered his charge for £400, then, again, if any one of the three conditions mentioned above are fulfilled, C's aggregate loan of £400, which is formed by tacking his subsequent advance of £100 to his advance of £300, will rank in priority to D's loan of £400. But under no circumstances could D make his loan of £400 prior to C's loan of £300, as he might have done under the law as it stood before 1st January, 1926, by purchasing B's interest. One of the most frequent cases where tacking occurs in practice is where an overdraft on a current account at the bank is secured by a mortgage of the customer's real estate. In such a case, the mortgage binds the bank to make further advances when called upon to do so, and those further advances can be tacked to the previous advances, even though the bank has notice of intermediate mortgages.

CONSOLIDATION

Consolidation is another doctrine which is peculiar to the law of mortgages. It is applied where different pieces of land belonging to the same borrower are mortgaged to the same lender, and the right is expressly given in one or more of the mortgage deeds. The rule is that where this doctrine applies, the lender is entitled to refuse the redemption of one of the pieces of land unless at the same time all the other properties mortgaged to him are redeemed. It does not matter that the original lenders on the different securities were not one and the same person, provided that there is only one mortgagee at the time when the right of consolidation is sought. If, for example, A mortgages "Fernlea" to B, "Thornholme" to C, and "The Acacias" to D, and E subsequently has transferred to him the mortgages of B, C, and D, E is entitled to say to A, "You cannot redeem 'Fernlea' unless at the same time you redeem 'Thornholme' and 'The Acacias'."

A more difficult case occurs where the rights to redeem different properties pass to different persons. The rule in such a case is that if the rights to redeem have become the property of different persons after all the mortgages have become vested in one person and after all the rights to redeem have become vested in one person, consolidation is permitted, but not otherwise. For instance, in the example given above, if after E has purchased all the mortgages, A sells the rights to redeem the various properties to F, G, and H respectively, F will find that if he wants to redeem "Fernlea" he may be called upon to redeem "Thornholme" and "The Acacias" as well, and G and H may find themselves in a similar position. If, however, after the sale of the rights to redeem the various properties to F, G, and H respectively, A mortgages his property "Avondale" to E, neither F nor G nor H can be compelled by E to redeem "Avondale" as a condition of exercising their respective rights of redeeming "Fernlea," "Thornholme," and "The Acacias." Moreover, though F, G, and H are penalised to some extent by the doctrine of consolidation, they nevertheless have compensating rights; if, for example, G finds himself compelled to redeem "Fernlea" and "The Acacias," he stands in the same position as E with regard to those properties, and F and H will have to pay him the mortgage money which they would otherwise have had to pay to E.

LIMITATIONS

The Real Property Limitation Act, 1874, provides that if a lender on mortgage of land remains in possession of the land for twelve years without acknowledging the title of the borrower to the land, the lender becomes absolute owner of the land, and the borrower's right of redemption comes to an end. On the other hand, if for a period of twelve years the borrower pays neither principal nor interest the lender's security comes to an end, the borrower becomes full owner of the land free from the mortgage. If no part of the principal or interest is paid, the lender cannot even sue for the debt after twelve years.

BUILDING SOCIETY MORTGAGES

The building society mortgage furnishes the means by which an increasingly large number of householders buy their houses "out of income," paying in many cases a very small proportion of the purchase price on deposit, and the remainder by instalments spread over periods of varying length. We are not concerned here with the technical distinction between "terminating" and "permanent" building societies, except to note that the former class is now decreasing in number, no more being formed owing to their actuarial unsoundness. Societies may also be either incorporated under the Building Societies Act, 1874, or unincorporated and governed by the Building Societies Act, 1836. The property of the unincorporated society is vested in the trustees or in the treasurer. There are very few unincorporated societies left, as all societies formed since 2nd November, 1874, must be incorporated, and any societies formed before that date may obtain a certificate of incorporation from the Registrar of Friendly Societies. The rules of an incorporated society must specify, among other matters (1) the purposes to which the funds of the society are to be applied, and the manner in which they are to be invested; (2) the manner of altering and rescinding the rules and of making additional rules; (3) whether disputes between the society and any of its members or any person claiming by or through any member or under the rules shall be settled by reference to the Court, or to the registrar, or to arbitration; (4) provision for the custody of the mortgage deeds and other securities belonging to the society; (5) the fines and forfeitures to be imposed on members of the society; (6) the manner of calling general and special meetings of the members. Moreover, a society established, or substituting a new set of rules after 25th August, 1874, must, under Section 1 of the Building Societies Act, 1894, provide in its rules for (1) the manner in which the stock or funds of the society is or are to be raised; (2) the terms upon which unadvanced subscription shares are to be issued; the manner in which the contributions are to be paid to the society, and withdrawn by the members, with tables, where applicable in the opinion of the registrar, showing the amount due by the society for principal and interest separately; (3) the terms upon which paid-up shares, if any, are to be issued and withdrawn, with tables, where applicable in the opinion of the registrar, showing the amount due by the society for principal and interest separately; (4) whether preferential shares are to be issued and, if so, within what limits; (5) the manner in which advances are to be made and repaid; the deductions, if any, for premiums, and the conditions upon which a borrower can redeem the amount due from him before the expiration of the period for which the advance was made, with tables, where applicable in the opinion of the registrar, showing the amount due from the borrower after each stipulated payment; (6) the manner in which losses are to be ascertained and provided for; (7) the manner in which membership is to cease; and (8) whether the society intends to borrow money, and, if so, within what limits.

Alterations of the rules must affect members only, but they may be retrospective; they may reduce the sums standing to the credit of investing members or increase the amounts payable by borrowing members on redemption, and they may vary the rights of members among themselves. Advances to members must be by mortgage on the security of real or leasehold estate, and in England must not be on second mortgage unless the first mortgage is in favour of the society making the advance. The legal position of the borrowing member is to be gathered partly from the rules of the society and partly from his contract of mortgage, and no alteration in the rules can alter a member's rights under the mortgage. The mortgage deed overrides the rules, where a covenant in the former is inconsistent with the latter. Usually he must pay his subscriptions when due, on pain of fines and forfeitures set out in the rules. When a borrowing member redeems his mortgage before the prescribed period has come to an end, he must pay the difference between the amount which he has subscribed and the amount of the advance. A borrowing member is not liable to share any losses made by his society unless the rules so provide, and the mere fact that he is given the right to share profits does not mean that he also shares losses. A receipt endorsed on or annexed to the mortgage deed in the form provided in the schedule to the Building Societies Act, 1874, under the seal of the society and countersigned by the secretary or manager, vacates the mortgage and vests the mortgaged property in the

person for the time being entitled to redeem, and there is no need
to reconvey the property. The receipt may also be given under
the Law of Property Act, 1925 (see above, page 585), but in such
a case it must be made in the manner provided by the Building
Societies Act, 1874. The receipt is in all cases exempt from stamp
duty.

STAMP DUTIES

A legal mortgage, which is the only or principal or primary
security for the payment of money, must bear an *ad valorem* stamp
which is calculated as follows—

					s.	*d.*
When the money secured does not exceed £10	.	.			–	3
Exceeds	£10	and does not exceed	£25	.	.	–	8
,,	£25	,,	,,	£50	.	.	1	3
,,	£50	,,	,,	£100	.	.	2	6
,,	£100	,,	,,	£150	.	.	3	9
,,	£150	,,	,,	£200	.	.	5	–
,,	£200	,,	,,	£250	.	.	6	3
,,	£250	,,	,,	£300	.	.	7	6

For every additional £100 and for every fractional part of £100
of the money secured, 2s. 6d. stamp duty must be imposed.
Where a collateral or additional or substituted security (not being
an equitable mortgage) is given by way of further assurance
where the principal or primary security is duly stamped, a stamp
duty of 6d. is payable for every £100 and for every fractional part
of £100 of the amount secured, but the whole amount of the duty
payable must not in this case exceed 10s. In the case of an equitable mortgage a stamp duty of 1s. is payable for every £100
secured, and for every fractional part of £100 of the amount
secured. In the case of a transfer or assignment or disposition
of any mortgage, a duty of 6d. is payable for every £100 and also
for every fractional part of £100 of the amount transferred or
assigned. Finally, in the case of a reconveyance, which includes
a receipt endorsed on or written at the foot of or annexed to the
mortgage, a stamp duty of 6d. is payable for every £100, and also
for every fractional part of £100 of the total amount or value of
the money at any time secured.

SALE OF LAND

CONVEYANCING is the branch of law which regulates the transfer of land from one person to another. As land is the ultimate source of wealth, so, prior to the growth of a commercial civilisation, the possession of land was regarded as its main essential. Therefore the sale of "real property" as the term is, in distinction to "personal property," has become hedged about with a great number of rules and safeguards. Even to-day, though the importance of "real" in relation to "personal" property has considerably diminished, it is clear that a completely different order of considerations prevails in the purchase of a house and in the purchase of a piano. Moreover, there enters into the subject not only the safeguarding of the purchaser, but also the regulation of the rights and duties of the old owner and the new owner respectively in relation to the land in question.

CONTRACT OF SALE OF LAND

The first main division of the subject to be considered is the contract of sale, which constitutes the first step towards the transfer of land. Turning, then, to this, those aspects which fall within the province of the general law of contract need not be touched on here, but it is enough to make the starting point Section 40 of the Law of Property Act of 1925, which provides that: "No action may be brought upon any contract for the sale or other disposition of land or any interest in land, unless the agreement upon which such action is brought or some memorandum or note thereof is in writing and signed by the party to be charged or by some other person thereunto by him lawfully authorised." This re-enacts the corresponding section of the Statute of Frauds of 1677. Although it might not appear so at first sight from the words of the section, it lays down a rule of evidence only, and, therefore, should the person against whom a contract is sought to be enforced neglect to put forward the defence that this Act has not been complied with, the action may lawfully go forward.

FORM OF CONTRACT

As to the form of the memorandum, the law specifies nothing. The contract may be contained in one document only or in several

20

documents relating to one another. In *Dewar* v. *Mintoft*, [1912] 2 K.B. 373, even a written repudiation of liability was in the circumstances of the case held to be sufficient, when a purchaser who wished to avoid completion wrote a letter setting out what had occurred at an auction, where he was alleged to have bid for the property in question, and contending that the facts set out did not bind him. Mr. Justice Horridge put the matter very clearly in his judgment. He said: "In the present case it is true that the defendant does not merely acknowledge the contract and refuse to carry it out, but first sets out the bid and the knocking down of the property which would make a verbal contract, and then writes, 'The point is that I have paid no deposit and signed no contract'; but, in my view, he repudiates on the ground that the facts he has set out do not render him liable and his so doing does not prevent the documents from containing a signed note of the verbal contract on which this liability arises if there is a sufficient note within the Statute of Frauds."

An even more striking warning for the unwary is found in the case of *Grindell* v. *Bass* (1920 Ch.). There, a Mrs. Bass, finding herself sued for specific performance of a contract to sell a house, put in the defence that she had already contracted to sell the house to a Mr. Earle. This gentleman having been joined with her as a defendant proceeded to counterclaim for a declaration that he was entitled to the house. Against this it was contended that there was no proper contract because there was not sufficient written memorandum to satisfy the Statute of Frauds. However, the Court took the view that the defence signed by the counsel for Mrs. Bass, and setting out all the terms of the contract with Mr. Earle, satisfied all requirements. In the same way, no formalities are prescribed in regard to the requisite signature, the use of initials, for example, being permissible, and, under the section, the signature of an authorised agent is sufficient. In this connection, it may be noted that an auctioneer has the authority of both the vendor and the purchaser to bind them by his signature. The auctioneer's clerk, however, cannot sign on behalf of the parties unless they have specially authorised him to do so. Moreover, the authority of the auctioneer himself only endures during the time of the actual transaction of sale.

CONTENTS OF CONTRACT

Now, what should this written contract of sale contain? In the first place, the names of the parties must be specified; secondly the price, though this need not be actually named in figures, so long as a mode of ascertaining it be specified as, for example, by arbitration or valuation, and thirdly, a description of the property which is to change hands. If this is all that is set down, it is called an "open contract." In addition, however, the contract may contain any special terms which the parties have agreed upon. Those who are familiar with the general law of contract will know the circumstances which clinch negotiations and form a binding agreement, and, before passing on, it is only necessary to add that if there is any reservation, as there frequently is, whereby the agreement reached is made "subject to a formal contract," then the contract of sale is not complete, unless it is clear that there has been an unconditional offer or acceptance, and the words meant only that it was to be drawn up in legal form.

WHEN WRITTEN CONTRACT NOT REQUIRED

It is now necessary to consider the exceptions to the rule that the contract of sale must be in writing. In the first place, the Statute of Frauds was not designed to promote fraud, and the absence of writing will not be regarded if it can be shown that one of the parties fraudulently prevented the reduction of the contract to writing. Again, when a sale is made by order of the Court, there need be no written contract of sale. The main exception, however, depends on the "doctrine of part performance," as it is called, in pursuance of which the Court of Chancery established that it would decree specific performance of a contract for the sale of land, even in the absence of writing, if the party seeking to enforce the agreement had already carried out his obligations or some of them on the faith that the other party would do so likewise. In order to establish a good case for enforcement on this ground, certain essential factors must always be present. In the first place, the act or acts relied on must have been done by the plaintiff himself. Next, it must have been done exclusively in pursuance of the contract and must not be connected with any other motive. Thirdly, though it seems hardly necessary to draw attention to it, the act must actually be one of part performance. One that is merely introductory or preparatory to performance is not sufficient. Finally, the circumstances must be such that it would be a fraud on the plaintiff to allow the defendant to take advantage of the statute.

REGISTRATION OF CONTRACT

Once a completed contract has been reached, the first problem which will occur to the purchaser is whether to register it as a land charge under the Land Charges Act of 1925 (Section 10). If an immediate purchase is in contemplation, the step is unusual; otherwise, however, it is advisable, for so long as the contract remains unregistered it is void against anyone who purchases the land and gives value for it.

" OPEN CONTRACT "

Contracts of sale fall under two main heads. There is the "open contract," by which the parties reach an agreement to sell, but fix no terms or conditions between them and therefore leave them to be implied by the general law. In contrast to this, there is the "formal contract" whereby the parties set down their own terms in so far as the law allows. Generally speaking, it may be said that an open contract puts the purchaser in a favourable position, while a formal contract usually tends to reduce the rights otherwise implied for his benefit by law.

Turning first to open contracts, the most important provisions governing them are to be found in Sections 44 and 45 of the Law of Property Act, 1925. Both of these sections, of course, apply only in so far as no contrary intention has been expressed in the contract. Section 44 treats of the title to the land which it is incumbent upon the vendor to show in his "abstract of title," —the name given to the chronological statement of the documents under which the property is held. In the case of freeholds, he must prove a good title, going back at least thirty years, this being now fixed as the period of commencement of title which a purchaser of land may require. It should be noted that under the same section a proposed lessee has no right to call for any title at all to establish the lessor's right to the freehold, unless he has stipulated to the contrary. Running briefly through Section 45, the first subsection debars the purchaser from requiring the production of any document "made before the time prescribed by law or stipulated for the commencement of the title." Three exceptions are, however, allowed, and the purchaser may call for any power of attorney under which any document included in the abstract of title is executed. When any part of the property is disposed of by a document in the abstract of title subject to an interest, power, or obligation which is not shown to have ceased, the document creating or disposing of the interest, power, or obligation may be required. Lastly, the purchaser may require " any document creating any limitation or trust by reference to which any part of the property is disposed of by an abstracted document." Under subsection 2, the purchaser of a lease must assume, unless the contrary appears, that the lease was duly granted and on production of the receipt for the last payment of rent due must similarly assume that all covenants have been observed. Subsection 3 makes similar provisions in regard to the sale of under-leases. Subsection 4 lays on the purchaser the burden of paying for the expenses incurred in the production if he requires it, of wills, probates, letters of administration, and other documents not in the possession of the vendor, his mortgagee, or his trustee. The vendor, of course, is assumed to have borne the expense of compiling the abstract of title. So, too, the purchaser must pay for procuring, making, verifying, and producing all certificates, declarations, evidences, and information not in the possession of the vendor or his mortgagee or trustee. Subsection 5 makes only one abstract of title necessary where several lots of property held under the same title are sold. Under subsection 6, statements and descriptions of facts in documents twenty years old at the date of the contract are to be taken as true, unless proved inaccurate. Subsection 7 provides that "the inability of a vendor to furnish a purchaser with an acknowledgment of his right to production and delivery of documents of title . . . shall not be an objection to title, in case the purchaser will, on the completion of the contract, have an equitable right to the production of such documents." Such acknowledgments, as also covenants for the safe custody of documents, must under subsection 8 be at the purchaser's expense if he requires them. Under subsection 9, the vendor is entitled to retain documents of title where he retains any part of the land to which they relate, or where the document is a trust instrument creating a trust which is still subsisting.

" CONTRACTS BY CORRESPONDENCE "

Any of these provisions, as already pointed out, can be varied if the parties enter into a formal contract, but before passing on to these, note must be made of an important subdivision of open contracts created by Section 46, which provides that the Lord Chancellor may from time to time prescribe and publish forms of contracts and conditions of sale of land, and the forms so prescribed shall, subject to any modification or any stipulation or intention to the contrary expressed in the correspondence, apply to *contracts by correspondence*. The "Statutory Form of Conditions of Sale, 1925," published in pursuance of the power thus bestowed, may be briefly reviewed. Under these conditions, completion must take place seven weeks from the making of the contract at the office of the vendor's solicitors. On payment of the purchase money, the purchaser is entitled to possession and to receipt of the rents and profits of the land as from the date fixed for completion. He is also liable for all outgoings in connection with the land. If the purchase money is not paid on the date fixed for completion, it bears interest at 5 per cent, but, if the delay is not the fault of the purchaser, he may deposit the money at the Bank of England, giving the vendor notice of the fact, after which the vendor must accept the bank interest. If the fault lies with the vendor, no interest is, of course, payable to him. The abstract of title must be delivered within fourteen days and within another fourteen days after such delivery, any requisitions or objections arising out of it. Otherwise, he will be taken to have waived his rights in this respect. When the answers to the requisitions have been sent, they are taken to be satisfactory unless the purchaser objects to them in seven days. If the purchaser makes any objection or requisition which the vendor is unable to remove or comply with and the purchaser shall not withdraw such objection or requisition within ten days after being required in writing so to do, the vendor may by notice in writing delivered to the purchaser or his solicitor and notwithstanding any intermediate negotiations rescind the contract. This does not give the vendor an arbitrary power to rescind the contract without doing his best to make out a good title in answer to the requisitions. He must satisfy the Court that there is reasonable ground for his not doing so, as, for example, if he entered into the contract in ignorance of some material fact or document. If this occurs, the vendor must return any deposit and the purchaser any papers relating to the land within a week. The draft conveyance or instrument of transfer must be prepared at the purchaser's expense and delivered at the office of the vendor's solicitor ten days before the date fixed for completion. When it has been returned approved, the actual document which the parties will execute—the engrossment as it is called—must be delivered within four days. If the purchaser neglects to perform his part of the contract, the vendor can give him twenty-one days' notice to make good the default and, on non-compliance, the deposit money is forfeited, unless the Court otherwise directs, and the property may be resold.

" FORMAL CONTRACTS "

Having now dealt with the terms of "open" contracts, we turn next to the other great class of "formal" contracts, which includes both sales by auction and sales by private treaty. This aspect of the subject also divides itself into two branches—the "particulars of sale" and the "conditions of sale."

"The proper office of the particulars is to describe the subject matter of the contract, that of the conditions to state the terms on which it is sold." This is the definition of Vice-Chancellor Malins in the case of *Torrance* v. *Bolton*.

PARTICULARS OF SALE

Dealing first with the particulars of sale, they must not misrepresent the facts concerning the property either by asserting an untruth or suppressing the truth. Any misrepresentation of a material fact whereby a purchaser has been misled will form a ground for rescinding the contract, whether the vendor made the misstatement honestly or fraudulently. Concealment of a fact which it was his duty to reveal is, of course, the same thing as misrepresentation. The contract, however, will not be rescinded unless the matter is so serious as not to be amenable to the remedy of mere compensation. Lastly, the purchaser must claim rescission within a reasonable time and before any third parties have acquired rights under the contract. As to the vendor's duty of disclosure, he must reveal all material defects in his title to the property (any easement over it, for example), and all latent defects in its physical nature. Latent defects are specified because where a defect is visible to the eye, there can be no duty to indicate it explicitly, since it is assumed that the purchaser will not buy property without examining it or procuring its examination. Concealed defects of which neither of the parties is aware will be ground for recission of the contract if, by reason of it, the land cannot be used for the purpose for which it was sold to the purchaser, as in the case of *Re Puckett & Smith's Contract* (1902 Ch.). There, a contract to sell land which the vendors knew was required for building purposes was rescinded by the Court on the discovery that there was a hidden watercourse beneath the property of which neither party had been till then aware.

CONDITIONS OF SALE

Turning now to the subject of conditions of sale, it is first necessary to see those which are forbidden by the Law of Property
Act, 1925. Section 42, subsection 1, provides that "a stipulation
that a purchaser of a legal estate in land shall accept a title made
with the concurrence of any person entitled to an equitable
interest shall be void if a title can be made discharged from the
equitable interest without such concurrence (a) under a trust for
sale, or (b) under this Act or the Settled Land Act, 1925, or any
other statute." Briefly, this makes it impossible to deprive the
purchaser of land subject to a trust of his right to insist on a
conveyance from the person who actually holds the "legal estate"
in the property. Subsection 2 makes void "a stipulation that a
purchaser of a legal estate in land shall pay or contribute towards
the costs of or incidental to (a) obtaining a vesting order or the
appointment of trustees of a settlement or the appointment of
trustees of a conveyance on trust for sale or (b) the preparation,
stamping, or execution of a conveyance on trust for sale or of a
vesting instrument for bringing into force the provisions of the
Settled Land Act, 1925." Subsection 3 makes void a stipulation
in any contract of sale or exchange of land made after the Act
"to the effect that an outstanding legal estate is to be traced or
got in by or at the expense of a purchaser, or that no objection
is to be taken on account of an outstanding legal estate." These
three subsections, it has been seen, deal with circumstances
arising from trusts and settlements of land and with these it is
beyond the scope of the present work to deal. Section 48, subsection 1, deals with a less technical point, making void stipulations preventing a purchaser from employing his own solicitor,
although a vendor may still reserve to himself the right "to furnish
a form of conveyance to a purchaser from which the draft can be
prepared, or to charge a reasonable fee therefor." Finally, Section
117 of the Stamp Act of 1891 makes void every condition of sale
framed with the view of precluding objection or requisition upon
the ground of absence or insufficiency of stamp upon any instrument.

STATUTORY FORM OF CONDITIONS OF SALE, 1925

The formal contract, as has been already remarked, expressly
sets forth the terms and conditions by which the parties are bound.
It is, therefore, obviously impracticable to deal with all its possible
variations. Sometimes the parties may adopt *en bloc* or in part
the "Statutory Form of Conditions of Sale, 1925," which has been
treated of above. It will be enough to indicate briefly the matters

to which regard must be had. The property must be described and, if the sale is by private treaty, the price stated. If the conditions are being prepared for a sale by auction, the bidding must be duly regulated. They may make the deposit payable either to the auctioneer or to the vendor's solicitor. If it be to the former, he may insist on payment in cash or he may accept a cheque, but not an IOU. If there is a reserve price, it must be stated. The signing by the purchaser of a memorandum must also be stipulated in the case of auctions. In all formal contracts, the title to be made out by the vendor and the purchaser's requisitions thereon should be dealt with, fixing such time limits as are reasonable. If the vendor wishes to be relieved of the responsibility of answering any requisitions or to rescind the contract in the event of his being unable to do so, the necessary stipulations should be made. In restricting length of title, however, the vendor must not seek to cover up earlier defects of title. These he must disclose and, if the purchaser discovers such a defect, he can refuse to complete the purchase. If the sale is subject to any restrictive, covenants, tenancies, easements, or the like, these should similarly be disclosed. The condition as to "identity" which is one of the usual conditions has the object of disentitling the purchaser to call for any evidence that the property described in the particulars is the property described in the documents of title. Such a condition, however, amounts to a contract that these documents do actually show identity. Another condition usually anticipates errors in the particulars of sale, stipulating that misdescription shall not annul the sale and dealing with the question of giving compensation to the purchaser in such an event. The effect of this condition is not, however, to force the completion of the purchase unless the purchaser is receiving substantially what he undertook to buy. The date of completion and the payment of the purchase money, as also the place, should be fixed. Moreover, the failure of the purchaser to carry out his contract should be anticipated as a possibility, and provision made for forfeiting the deposit and enabling the vendor to resell in such an event. As to taking possession of the property, this usually coincides with completion. The purchaser should not, however, take possession if he has knowledge of any defects in the title to the property, since this would be taken to amount to a waiver. The usual condition which gives the vendor the right to rescind the contract, if the purchaser makes any requisition with which he is unable to comply, has been already dealt with in the discussion of the "Statutory Form of Conditions of Sale, 1925." The conditions of sale which have been touched on are naturally not exhaustive. In almost every case, special circumstances will arise calling for special conditions, such as can only be framed in relation to the particular problem in hand.

EFFECT OF CONTRACT OF SALE

Once the contract has been entered into, what is the relation existing between the vendor and the purchaser until the time of the conveyance? The classical definition of the position was given by Lord Cairns in the case of *Shaw* v. *Foster* (H.L.). He said: "There cannot be the slightest doubt of the relation subsisting in the eye of a Court of Equity between the vendor and the purchaser. The vendor was a trustee of the property for the purchaser; the purchaser was the real beneficial owner in the eye of a Court of Equity of the property, subject only to this observation that the vendor, whom I have called the trustee, was not a mere dormant trustee; he was a trustee having a personal and substantial interest in the property, a right to protect that interest, and an active right to assert that interest, if anything should be done in derogation of it. The relation, therefore, of trustee and *cestui que trust* subsisted subject to the paramount right of the vendor and trustee to protect his own interest as vendor of the property." One or two observations must be added to fill in the implications of this definition. Thus, the vendor is entitled to remain in possession till payment of the purchase money. Furthermore, he is entitled to the rents and profits until the date fixed for completion of the purchase. The rents and profits falling due after that date belong to the purchaser, and he then becomes correspondingly liable for all outgoings. While the vendor remains in possession, he is answerable to the purchaser for any deterioration in the property which may be due to his negligence. He is not, however, liable for accidental damage of which the tenant must bear the risk. Once a binding contract has been entered into, the purchaser can sell or otherwise dispose of the property. The vendor, on the other hand, possesses what is called an "equitable lien" on the property to secure the payment of the purchase money—a right not dependent on the continued possession of the property. It entitled him to apply to the Court to have the property sold for the purpose of satisfying his claim. So, too, a purchaser has a lien on the land for the whole or any part of the purchase money paid by him before conveyance.

His lien extends to the costs of any proceeding to enforce specific performance and the costs of investigating the vendor's title when the contract fails through some defect of title. The lien either of the vendor or the purchaser may be enforced against the land either in the hands of the other party or in the hands of persons who have succeeded to the property on his death. It cannot, however, be enforced against anyone who has acquired the property for value without notice of the lien.

REMEDIES FOR BREACH OF CONTRACT

Various legal remedies are open to the parties in the event of the breach by one or the other of a contract of sale. The most obvious of these is an action for damages. The amount recovered will vary according to circumstances. If the vendor, without being personally at fault, has been unable to make out a good title and so cannot complete the conveyance, the purchaser is only entitled to recover his deposit and the expenses incidental to the agreement. If, on the other hand, the vendor is at fault, the damages will be substantial. So, too, if the purchaser has failed to carry out his contract, the vendor may recover the difference between the value of the land as it remains in his possession and the price agreed to under the contract. Side by side with this remedy, there exists, also, the remedy of specific performance, an action to enforce the completion of the contract according to its terms. This is open to either party, but the granting of specific performance lies in the discretion of the Court, in the sense that if the defendant can show that circumstances independent of the contract itself render the making of such a decree unfair or inequitable, the Court will withhold this remedy. Sometimes the Court will decree specific performance on condition that the party seeking to enforce it pays compensation for some fault on his own part, if, for example, he failed to complete the conveyance on the date fixed in the contract.

In contrast to the action for specific performance is the action for rescission which is open to an innocent party if some term of the contract which is a condition precedent to his liability has been broken. It entails a right to recover any deposit paid and, conversely, if it is the vendor who is seeking to rescind, he must pay back any deposit in his hands if this was received by way of part payment, even though the purchaser is at fault. If, however, the money was paid as a guarantee of performance, then it need not be returned on recission at the suit of the vendor.

VENDOR AND PURCHASER SUMMONS

A useful remedy in connection with a contract of sale is known as a "Vendor and Purchaser Summons," initiated by the Vendor and Purchaser Act of 1874, and continued by the Law of Property Act of 1925. It provides machinery whereby summary application may be made to a judge in chambers in respect of disagreements preventing the completion of a contract of sale, for example, the construction of the contract or the sufficiency of an answer made to a requisition on title. The value of this procedure lies in offering a speedy solution to isolated points in dispute. It cannot, however, be invoked to adjudicate on the validity of the contract itself, and it is not available to decide difficult points of construction.

BANKRUPTCY OR DEATH

It may here be noted that on the bankruptcy of a vendor or a purchaser, the trustee in bankruptcy of either can enforce the contract. The contract can also be enforced against a trustee in bankruptcy unless he chooses to disclaim not only the contract but the land as well. So, too, the personal representatives of a vendor or purchaser who dies before completion of the contract, can sue or be sued for its enforcement.

ABSTRACT OF TITLE

Once a valid contract of sale exists, the next step towards the conveyance is the abstract of title—the connected summary of documents and events by which the vendor shows that he is able to convey the property to the purchaser or to compel the conveyance of the property to him, as, for example, if he is himself a purchaser of the property under a contract of sale which has not yet been completed. The abstract of title must be prepared at his expense.

The starting point of the abstract must be what is known as a good "root of title," that is to say, a document which deals with the entire legal and equitable estates in the property. The best possible root of title is therefore a conveyance on sale, as it contains a full description of the property and imports an investigation of the earlier title. A voluntary conveyance (or one made otherwise than for valuable consideration) is also a good root of title, though obviously not so satisfactory as a conveyance on sale. Again a specific devise (or disposition by will) of the property in question is also a good root of title. From this starting point, the history of the property in the land should be traced chronologically showing conveyances, wills, legal mortgages, births, marriages, and deaths, and, in short, every link in the chain leading to the vendor. On the vendor also lies the additional duty of producing for the purchaser to examine all the deeds set out in his abstract of title, together with proper proof of the facts mentioned in it, though, as has been already pointed out in dealing with Section 45, subsection 4, of the Law of Property Act of 1925, the purchaser must ordinarily bear the cost incurred in producing evidence not in the possession of the vendor, his mortgagee, or his trustee.

OBJECTIONS AND REQUISITIONS

When the abstract of title has thus been delivered and its contents duly verified, the purchaser, if he is not satisfied in any particular, may make further inquiry by putting objections or requisitions on title to which the vendor must give satisfactory answers. In the words of Lord Justice James in the case of *In re Ford and Hill*, 10 Ch. D. 365: "A vendor is bound to furnish an abstract of title and upon the requisition of the purchaser to verify it or complete it on any point on which it appears defective." In regard to the preparation of the abstract, Section 183 of the Law of Property Act of 1925 renders guilty of a misdemeanour, punishable by fine and imprisonment, any person selling property, or the solicitor or agent of such person, who "(a) conceals from the purchaser any instrument or incumbrance material to the title, or (b) falsifies any pedigree upon which the title may depend in order to induce the purchaser to accept the title offered or produced." They are also liable to an action for damages.

Among the points to which a purchaser should have regard in considering the adequacy of an abstract of title, he should consider whether the root of title is a good one, observe whether there are any mortgages or charges of any kind affecting the property, and whether all the documents are properly stamped. It may here be noted that by contracting to accept a shorter title than that to which he is legally entitled, a purchaser cannot escape the legal presumption that he has notice of all equitable rights which he would have discovered had he thoroughly investigated the vendor's title. Legal rights, generally speaking, bind a purchaser whether or not he has notice of them. As to matters discoverable only on an investigation of the title earlier than the period fixed by law, a purchaser is not affected by them unless he actually makes investigation and discovers them.

If a purchaser has notice of a death affecting the devolution of the property, he should satisfy himself as to the due payment of the death duties which may be a charge on the land. His liability is, however, limited in that he is absolved from liability if the death occurred more than twelve years prior to the purchase. In the case of a death occurring since 1925, death duties, in order to constitute a charge upon the land, must be registered as a land charge by the Inland Revenue. The same considerations also apply in the case of succession duty and estate duty.

Finally, a general inquiry should be made as to whether there are any legal easements affecting the land, for example, whether there are any rights of way over it.

The right to put objections and make requisitions may, of course, be waived by the purchaser, either expressly or impliedly, by his acts. For example, an attempt to resell the property in question would be evidence of waiver, though in itself not conclusive in establishing it.

SEARCHES OF REGISTERS

The final step to be taken before completion is the search by the purchaser's solicitor for registered incumbrances. The usual searches are for the most part made in the Land Registry, in Lincoln's Inn Fields, in London. There five registers are kept: (1) a register of pending actions, (2) a register of annuities, (3) a register of writs and orders affecting the land, (4) a register of deeds of arrangement, and (5) a register of land charges. These may be briefly reviewed, following the provisions of the Land Charges Act of 1925, which defines their respective functions.

As to pending actions, these, if duly registered, remain effectively on the register for a period of five years, after which they must be re-registered. This proceeding has the result of rendering any decree made in the action in question binding on any purchaser of the property, since he is taken to have notice of that which is registered. These matters are dealt with in Sections 2 and 3. Annuities for the purposes of the register of annuities, which is treated of in Sections 4 and 5, are defined by subsection 5 of the former section as comprising "a rent charge or an annuity for one or more life or lives or for any term of years or greater estate determinable on one or more life or lives created after the twenty-fifth day of April, eighteen hundred and fifty-five, and before the commencement of this Act and not being a rent charge or an annuity created by a marriage settlement or will." Unless such an annuity is registered, it is void against a purchaser of the land charged with it. Sections 6 and 7 deal with the register of writs and orders affecting land. These include (*a*) any writ or order affecting land, issued or made by any Court for the purpose of enforcing a judgment statute or recognisance, (*b*) any order appointing a receiver or sequestrator of land, (*c*) any receiving order in bankruptcy made after the commencement of the Act. In order not to be void against a purchaser of land, the writ or order must be registered, but a receiving order in bankruptcy, even if it is unregistered, is only void against a *bona fide* purchaser for money or money's worth. Unless the writs or orders are re-registered every five years, they become void against purchasers of the land. In the same way, deeds of arrangement which are dealt with by Sections 8 and 9, must be re-registered every five years. Most important of the five registers is the register of land charges. These are divided by the Act into five classes. Class A comprises "a rent or annuity or principal money payable by instalments or otherwise, with or without interest, being a charge (otherwise than by deed) upon land created pursuant to the application of some person either before or after the commencement of this Act, (i) under the provisions of any Act of Parliament for securing to any person either the money spent by him or the costs, charges, and expenses incurred by another person under the authority of an Act of Parliament, (ii) under s. 9 of the Land Drainage Act, 1930, (iii) under s. 20 or s. 41 of the Agricultural Holdings Act, 1923, or any previous similar enactment, or (iv) under s. 4 or s. 6 of the Tithe Act, 1918, or (v) under s. 5 of the Tithe Annuities Apportionment Act, 1921, or (vi) under paragraph 6 of the Twelfth Schedule of the Law of Property Act, 1922, but not including a rate or scot." Class B comprises the charges described above, if created otherwise than pursuant to the application of any person. Class C includes puisne mortgages (or legal mortgages not protected by a deposit of documents relating to the land affected), limited owner's charges (or equitable charges acquired by a tenant for life under the Finance Act, 1894, or any other statute by reason of the discharge by him of any death duties or other liabilities and to which special priority is given by the statute), general equitable charges (or charges not secured by a deposit of documents relating to the legal estate affected), and, finally, estate contracts (or contracts made by an estate owner or a person entitled to a conveyance of the legal estate). Class D comprises charges acquired by the Commissioners of Inland Revenue in respect of death duties payable on a death occurring

after 1925, covenants entered into after 1925 restricting the user
of the land, and equitable easements over land, created after 1925.
Class E includes annuities created before 1926, but not entered
before the commencement of the Act in the register of annuities.

The requisite searches may be made either by the purchaser of
land himself or by his solicitor, but this trouble can be saved by
having an official search made and obtaining a certificate of
search showing the result. Provided the purchase is completed
within two days of the date thereof, the purchaser will not be
affected by charges registered in the interval.

Other searches which it is in some cases expedient to make may
be briefly mentioned—the Middlesex and Yorkshire Registries,
the registers kept by local authorities (for local land charges and
town planning schemes), and in the Bankruptcy Court, to find
whether the vendor was made bankrupt before 1926.

FORM OF CONVEYANCE

It is next necessary to examine the subject of the actual
purchase deed—its form and its contents. To start with the
opening words, these need no longer be as formerly, "This Indenture." The document may be described simply as "This Conveyance." The date should be stated, although omission does not
invalidate the deed. The parties to the conveyance must next be
specified. These are, of course, the vendor and purchaser. In
addition, the expression includes all the persons whose concurrence
may be requisite for the validity of the conveyance and any persons who enter into covenants by the deed. Next come what are
termed "the recitals," or what might be called in non-legal
language, the explanations. These fall into two categories:
narrative recitals and introductory recitals. The former set out
the facts which go to show the title to the property and its past
history. The latter show the purpose of the deed as, for example,
the agreement in pursuance of which the conveyance is made.
The purposes fulfilled by recitals are various. Sometimes it may
be necessary to explain the interests of the various parties joined
in the deed or to show that the conveyance duly complies with the
terms of an earlier deed. In short, their purpose is to render the
document intelligible. A more remote purpose may be to provide
evidence for the future of the facts stated in the recitals, since
by Section 45, subsection 6, of the Law of Property Act of 1925,
recitals of facts contained in deeds twenty years old shall, except
so far as they are proved to be inaccurate, be taken to be sufficient

evidence of the truth of such facts. It may be mentioned that the modern tendency to cut down excessive verbiage tends to reduce the recitals to what is strictly necessary.

The matters hitherto dealt with have formed the introduction to the conveyance proper. The operative part of the deed is prefaced with the words: "Now this conveyance witnesseth . . ." followed by a statement of the consideration and an acknowledgment of its receipt and, finally, by the words to which everything has been leading up—the declaration that the vendor "hereby conveys" the property which is being dealt with. In passing, it may be noted that although the conveyance is not invalidated by an omission to state the consideration, there are several other reasons for such inclusion—to make clear the liability to stamp duty, to show that the conveyance is not "voluntary" (or made without receiving an advantage in return), and to show that the purchase price has been duly paid. A voluntary conveyance, it may be noted, suffers various disadvantages. For example, the law does not imply in its case the usual covenants for title discussed hereafter. The details of the property conveyed by the vendor (or, as they are called, the "parcels") must, of course, be described with the utmost accuracy, if necessary setting them out in a schedule to the conveyance. In regard to the meaning of the words used, "messuage" or "house" include as well the curtilage and garden attached to it; "land" includes, besides the surface, whatever may lie above or below it, and also, in the case of land adjoining a non-tidal river or a highway, the soil over which these run up to the centre of the river bed or the road. The conveyance carries besides the land all the profits à prendre, easements and the like, legally appurtenant to it. Formerly, in order to achieve this result, it was necessary to include in the deed certain "general words," as they were technically called. However, since the Conveyancing Act of 1881, this has become obsolete, inasmuch as by the section of that statute re-enacted by Section 62 of the Law of Property Act of 1925, "a conveyance of land shall by virtue of this Act operate to convey with the land all buildings, erections, fixtures, commons, hedges, ditches, fences, ways, waters, watercourses, liberties, privileges, easements, rights, and advantages whatsoever appertaining or reputed to appertain to the land or any part thereof." When, therefore, it is desired that any of these shall not pass, such an intention must be clearly stated. So, too, exceptions and reservations made by the vendor must be clearly and expressly set out. It should be noted that these two terms are not synonymous. An exception operates to take away a part of the whole property in question, as when a conveyance contains an exception of mines and minerals. In contrast, a reservation creates something entirely new in favour of the vendor, as when he reserves a right of way for himself over the land conveyed, since, of course, previous to the conveyance he could not be said to have a right of way over his own land.

Next in the deed comes that part known as the habendum, the purpose of which is to define the extent of the interest conveyed to the purchaser. Recent legislation has reduced the technical importance of this also, and since 1925 it has not been necessary in conveying an estate in fee simple to include that expression in the deed. However, to avoid ambiguity it is still highly desirable to do so. The creation of an entailed interest, however, still requires a conveyance containing explicit words.

COVENANTS ON CONVEYANCE

The covenants entered into by the parties constitute the next point for consideration. By Section 76, subsection 1, of the Law of Property Act of 1925, re-enacting a section of the Conveyancing Act of 1881, four covenants on the part of a vendor who is beneficial owner of land are implied. These are first, that he has full power to convey the property expressed to be conveyed; second, that the purchaser shall have quiet enjoyment of the property; thirdly, that the property is free from all incumbrances other than those subject to which the conveyance is expressly made, and, finally, that the vendor shall execute and do all such lawful assurances and things for further or more perfectly assuring the subject-matter of the conveyance to the person to whom the conveyance is made. These covenants bind the vendor as regards his own acts and omissions, and also those of any persons through whom his title was derived otherwise than for value. He is also liable for the acts or omissions of persons claiming under him or in trust for him. These covenants, as the term goes, "run with the land"; that is to say, any person in whom the purchaser's estate becomes subsequently vested can enforce them. It should be noted that these covenants can, of course, be varied by express provisions in the deed. Otherwise, they will always be construed literally.

The purchaser also may enter into various covenants in relation to the property conveyed. If these be of a positive nature, they are effective only as between the vendor and the purchaser, and do not bind subsequent purchasers. Restrictive covenants may, however, be enforced by the equitable jurisdiction of the Court against subsequent purchasers also. In the case of covenants entered into before 1926, this will depend on whether the person against whom enforcement is sought had notice either actual or constructive of the restriction in question. Thus, for example, the decision in the case of *Tulk* v. *Moxhay*, 2 Ph. 774, in 1848, saved Leicester Square from being built over and prevented the defendant from violating a covenant entered into by a predecessor in title when the land was conveyed to him in 1808. In the case of covenants entered into since the legislation of 1925, a restrictive covenant, in order to be enforceable at all against a subsequent purchaser, must be registered as a land charge. However, a covenant since that date runs with the land, even though the purchaser has not expressly referred to his successors in title. It should be noted that a restrictive covenant, in order to bind a subsequent purchaser, must operate for the benefit of other land, so that in the case of a vendor who conveys all his land to one purchaser, any covenants entered into restricting the user of the land are purely personal and do not remain effective if the property is sold again. Section 84 of the Law of Property Act of 1925, provides a method by which restrictive covenants affecting land may be discharged or modified. Any person interested in freehold land affected by a restrictive covenant may apply to a body of arbitrators defined by the section, who have power to discharge or modify the restriction on the ground either of the changed character of the neighbourhood, or that the person entitled to the benefit of the covenant has by act or omission, expressly or impliedly, agreed to such discharge or modification or, finally, that such discharge or modification will not injure the person entitled to the benefit of the restriction. It may also be that the vendor will enter into covenants relating to the land retained by him. These the purchaser has a right to have endorsed on the common title deed.

The conveyance closes with what is called the "testimonium." This sets forth that the parties to the deed have affixed thereto their hands and seals. This is attested by at least one witness.

COMPLETION OF CONVEYANCE

This being the form of the conveyance, the next point which arises is its completion. In the case of an open contract by correspondence, the date will ordinarily be seven weeks after the making of the contract. In the case of an ordinary open contract, the criterion will be what is reasonable in the circumstances. A formal contract will specify the time. It may also expressly stipulate that time shall be of the essence of the contract, in which case, if completion does not take place within due time, the contract may be rescinded. Otherwise, however, this is not usually the case, except when the nature of the subject-matter of the sale is such as to lead to the conclusion that time is of the essence. This has been held to be so in the case of a furnished house and of a public house. Even under an ordinary open contract, if one of the parties is guilty of undue delay, the other may specify in writing a date for completion reasonably remote which will then be of the essence of the contract.

It is the duty of the purchaser or his solicitor to prepare a draft of the conveyance for the vendor's approval. After this, it is ready to be engrossed or written out in its final form for execution, which generally takes place at the office of the solicitors acting for the vendor. The conveyance is handed over to the purchaser when he pays the price agreed, and with it all the necessary title deeds previously held by the vendor. The purchaser cannot insist on paying by cheque, but owing to the obvious drawbacks of payment in notes an arrangement is usually arrived at and a banker's draft accepted. If the vendor does not attend in person at the completion, the purchaser may safely pay the purchase money to the solicitor of the vendor if he produces an executed deed containing a receipt clause or having a signed receipt for the consideration money endorsed on it. In regard to the payment of the purchase money, apportionments of rent must frequently be made. If, for example, completion does not take place on the day fixed, the purchaser is entitled to the rent accruing since that date and, if it has been received by the vendor, to deduct such amount from the purchase money, together with the interest thereon.

On completion, a further duty of the vendor is to deliver up to the purchaser either possession of the property or receipt of the rents and profits according to the circumstances.

LAND REGISTRATION

The last point which must be regarded in connection with conveyancing is the system of registration of title now governed by the Land Registration Act of 1925. This must not be confounded with the registration of land charges and the like, already discussed, which protect the rights of third parties in land vested in another. Registration of title, on the contrary, deals with the actual ownership of the land. The Land Registry is conducted by the Chief Registrar, and is situated in Lincoln's Inn Fields. Registration is at present voluntary, except in the county of London and also in Eastbourne and Hastings. That is to say, within this area every conveyance or sale of freehold land, every granting of a lease of not less than forty years, and every assignment or sale of a lease with not less than forty years to run imposes on the grantee an obligation to be registered as proprietor of the land. The main advantage is, of course, that it greatly facilitates the transfer of land by the simplification of the investigation of title.

The Register is divided into three parts: First, the Property Register, which contains a description of the property in question; second, the Proprietorship Register, which contains the name, address, and description of the registered proprietor, and sets out the interest held by him, whether absolute, leasehold, qualified, or possessory; third, the Charges Register, containing (a) incumbrances subsisting at the date of first registration, (b) subsequent charges and other incumbrances, (c) such notes as have to be entered relating to covenants, conditions, and other rights adversely affecting the land, (d) all such dealings with registered charges and incumbrances as are capable of registration.

The only interests in land which may be registered are legal estates, that is to say, the fee simple absolute and the term of years absolute. The persons entitled to apply for registration are the estate owner or any person who has a right to require the legal estate to be vested in him. A person who under the Limitation Acts has acquired a title to registered land by adverse possession, may apply for registration if he can satisfy the Registrar.

Other interests besides the above are classed either as minor interests or as overriding interests. Minor interests, of which a typical example is found in the equitable interests arising under a settlement of land creating a trust for sale, cannot be registered, since on sale of the land the interests thereupon attach to the proceeds of sale. It should be noted, however, that in the case of a "voluntary" transfer of land (that is, one which is not made for value) the transferee takes subject to any minor interests. Overriding interests, on the other hand, bind purchasers of the registered land, whether they appear on this register or not. An easement created by an instrument and affecting the land at the time of registration must be noted, but otherwise there is no obligation to enter it. These interests are defined as including "all the incumbrances, interests, rights, and powers not entered on the Register, but subject to which registered dispositions are by this Act to take effect." These are fully set out in Section 70 of the Act, and include rights of common, rights of way, and other easements (not including equitable easements), land tax, tithe rent charge, fishing, sporting, and manorial rights generally.

In regard to freehold titles, there are three classes of registration: the absolute title, the qualified title, and a possessory title. The first registration of freehold land with an absolute title has the effect of vesting in the registered proprietor the fee simple in possession. Subject, of course, to registered incumbrances, over-riding interests, and, in the case of a first registered proprietor who does not hold the land for his own benefit, but, for example, as a trustee for sale, subject also to minor interests of which he has notice. Such a title is guaranteed by the State, which undertakes to indemnify any persons injured by errors or omissions in the Register, or through the registered title turning out to be defective. If it happens when an absolute title is applied for that the title can be established subject only to certain reservations or for a limited time, it may be registered subject to such appropriate exceptions as the circumstances call for—that is to say, with a "qualified title" as it is called. It has the effect of an absolute title, save in respect of the possible adverse interests excepted by the qualification. Again, land may be registered in respect of a possessory title only. Such registration, however, carries with it no State guarantee, and does not prejudice any interest adverse to the title of the registered proprietor, whether subsisting or capable of arising at the time of registration. Land may further be registered with a good leasehold title in the case of leases of which more than twenty-one years are unexpired. The applicant cannot be registered as proprietor unless and until the title to the leasehold has been approved by the Registrar. Such registration does not, however, prejudice the enforcement of any estate, right or interest affecting the title of the lessor to grant the lease. If an absolute title is required, the Registrar must be satisfied both in regard to the title to the leasehold and the title to the freehold, and the effect of such registration is to vest in the first registered proprietor the absolute title of the leasehold interest described, subject, of course, to implied and express covenants and obligations similar to those mentioned in discussing the registration of the absolute freehold title. Leaseholds can also be registered with a possessory title or a qualified title.

APPLICATION FOR REGISTRATION

Application for registration is governed by the Land Registration Rules, 1925. In the first place, it must be made in the prescribed form and accompanied by all such original deeds and documents relating to the title as the applicant has in his possession or under his control. These include opinions of counsel, abstracts of title, contracts for sale, conditions of sale, requisitions, and the like. There must also be a copy or sufficient abstract of the latest document of title not being a document of record. The Registrar may also require an affidavit from the applicant or his solicitor that to the best of his knowledge and belief all deeds, wills, instruments of title, and the like, and all facts material to such title have been disclosed. Sufficient particulars must also be furnished to enable the land to be fully identified. Along with these must go a list in triplicate of all documents delivered. In the case of leaseholds, a copy of the lease, or with the approval of the Registrar, an abstract or other sufficient evidence of its contents, must accompany the application. The lease must always be produced when it is in the possession or control of the applicant. The title shown by these documents must be examined by or under the superintendence of the Registrar, who may make such searches and inquiries as he may deem expedient. Before any registration is completed with absolute or good leasehold title, an advertisement must be inserted in the *Gazette* and in local or other newspapers if the Registrar so requires. These must describe the land and its situation, and require objections to be made within a stated period of not less than fourteen days. Any person may by notice in writing object to such registration, and the title cannot be registered until the objection has been withdrawn or otherwise disposed of after it has been heard by the Registrar. Incumbrances and other burdens to which the land is subject must be entered on the register. Notice of an easement, right, or privilege created by an instrument and operating at law which appears to the Registrar to affect adversely the land, shall if the Registrar thinks fit be entered in the register. The Registrar may also require the applicant to produce to him such documents of title as will, when stamped or otherwise marked, give notice to any purchaser of the fact of registration. When all requirements have been fulfilled, the registration may be completed. When this is done, the applicant receives a land certificate setting out full particulars of his registration, or if he wishes, it may be deposited for him at the registry. In order that the fullest advantages may be derived from the system of registration, other registered titles may in some circumstances be converted into absolute or good leasehold titles. For example, when freehold land has been registered for fifteen years or leasehold land for ten, the Registrar, if satisfied that the proprietor is in possession, must enter the title of the proprietor of the freehold land as absolute and of the leasehold land as good leasehold.

TRANSFER OF REGISTERED LAND

The registration of land considerably simplifies its transfer, and the Land Registration Rules, 1925, provide a form of transfer which, executed as a deed, completes the operation. In its turn it must be registered, the name of the transferee being entered on the register. The land certificate, unless deposited in the registry, must be produced. Though registered land may be dealt with apart from registered transfer, such a conveyance only goes so far as to create a "minor interest," which may be over-reached by a registered transfer for value, unless it is protected by notice on the register.

The vendor of registered land is not obliged to furnish the purchaser with any evidence of title, except that notwithstanding any stipulation to the contrary he must at his own expense furnish him with an authority to inspect the register, and if required, with a copy of the subsisting entries in the register and of any filed plans and copies or abstracts of any documents noted on the register so far as they affect the land to be dealt with. If, however, the purchase price does not exceed £1,000, the purchaser must, in the absence of special stipulation, bear the costs of these copies or abstracts. Subject to stipulation to the contrary, the vendor must at his own expense furnish the purchaser with such copies, abstracts, and evidence in respect of any subsisting rights and interests appurtenant to the registered land, and of any matters excepted from the effect of registration as the purchaser would have been entitled to if the land had not been registered. These requirements apply to the sale of land registered with an absolute title, and also with reservations when the title is possessory or qualified. In the former case, the purchaser must investigate the title prior to registration, and in the latter case, he is entitled to such evidence in regard to the estate or interest excluded from the effect of registration as he could have called for in the case of unregistered land.

SETTLEMENTS

OBJECTS AND DEFINITION

The law recognises the common wish of men to control or limit the enjoyment of their property by others, even after it has actually passed out of their hands. One of the principal devices through which it permits this control to be effected is the "settlement." This may be broadly defined as "an instrument or instruments under which property is limited to several persons in succession, so that the person for the time being in possession has no power to deprive the others of their future right of enjoyment."

Generally speaking, therefore, it is employed to preserve property for the purpose of providing for a given person or class of persons during life or for some limited period. Any property which is susceptible of private ownership, whether it be "real property"—that is, land—or personal property is also susceptible of being settled. Thus, for example, stocks and shares, money secured by mortgage, policies of insurance and even debts may be the subjects of settlements. In the past, land used to be more commonly settled than other forms of property, but now the position is reversed.

WHO CAN MAKE SETTLEMENTS

As to persons capable of making a settlement, one may say in general that whoever can hold and dispose of property can also settle it. An adjudicated bankrupt cannot make a settlement, nor can a convict. Settlements by lunatics are liable to be set aside if the persons benefiting thereby knew of the settlor's mental condition. An infant cannot ordinarily be bound by a settlement or an agreement for a settlement entered into by him. But if it be held to be for his benefit, it may be confirmed by him on coming of age. The exceptions created by the Infant Settlements Act of 1855 will be dealt with at a later stage. Now, it is enough to say that an infant's settlements are usually voidable, not void. It is desirable, though not essential, that they should be confirmed after the infant attains twenty-one but they will stand if not repudiated by him within a reasonable space afterwards.

TIME LIMIT

It should be noted at the outset that settled property cannot be indefinitely bound. Because the main use to which settlements have been put in the past has been to make provision for the parties to a marriage and their children, the property settled cannot be tied up for a longer period than the lifetime of any specified person actually living at the date the settlement is made and a further period of twenty-one years after his death (or, if more than one person was specified, after the last survivor of them). The settlor cannot ensure the further postponement of the final and absolute vesting of the property. The principle of law by which this limitation is laid down is known as the Rule against Perpetuities and the reason which underlies it is that it was found harmful to permit property to be tied up indefinitely so as to prevent its free alienation. This fact was early reflected in the policy of the law. It is as well to state here that dispositions which are legally held to be charitable do not come within the rule.

MODES OF CREATION

Settlements can be created by a number of different methods. The most impressive, but, for the purposes of the ordinary man, by far the least important way is settlement by means of an Act of Parliament. It cannot, however, be passed over without some explanation. When they occur, such settlements are frequently made for the purpose of rewarding eminent public services of which the State desires to perpetuate the memory. The Marlborough Estates present a notable instance of a settlement of this class and one which is in the nature of a national memorial. Apart, however, from such rare events as these, it has on occasion been found advisable in the past to consolidate or confirm the settlement of the estates of a particular family by means of the passing of an Estate Bill through Parliament, as, for example, in the case of the settlement of the lands of the Earls of Shrewsbury in 1719, when special measures were regarded as necessary for the purpose of safeguarding the interests of the then Bishop of Salisbury, a distant kinsman of the family, and also for other purposes.

However, the methods of settling property in common use on ordinary occasions are either by deed or else by will.

SETTLEMENTS—"VOLUNTARY" AND FOR VALUE

It is now necessary to draw attention to the very important distinction which the law makes between (1) settlements made for "valuable consideration" on the one hand; and (2) "voluntary settlements" on the other hand, that is to say, between settlements for which the settlor obtains in return some advantage recognised by the law, and settlements for which he receives no such advantage and which are, therefore, in the nature of a gift.

This is a distinction which common-sense would be compelled to draw from human observation and which could certainly not have escaped the vigilant wisdom of our ancestors. It is unfortunately a fact that in most of the relations of life men are not in the habit of bestowing benefits from spontaneous benevolence, and generally give only in so far as they receive an advantage in return. When, therefore, the law sees a settlor making a settlement without receiving any "valuable consideration," it treats the action with a certain suspicion, lest in reality he may be secretly receiving some dishonest advantage.

DISADVANTAGES OF VOLUNTARY SETTLEMENTS

Formerly, the law carried this suspicion so far that, under a statute of Queen Elizabeth's reign, a voluntary settlement of land might be defeated by any subsequent conveyance for value; but this is not any longer the law. If, however, the Court discovers that a voluntary settlement has been made with the object of defrauding or prejudicing the settlor's creditors, any person who has suffered damage through the subterfuge may have the transaction set aside.

In some circumstances, the subsequent bankruptcy of the settlor may operate so as to defeat an earlier voluntary settlement. If, for example, a settlor goes bankrupt within two years of making a settlement, his trustee in bankruptcy has the right to apply to the Court to have it set aside. A further complication may, however, arise if a beneficiary under a voluntary settlement has sold his interest to an innocent purchaser who knew nothing of the bankruptcy. If these circumstances occur, the settlement cannot be set aside. Even after so long a lapse of time as ten years, bankruptcy may upset a settlement if the beneficiaries are not in a position to show that the bankrupt was solvent at the time the settlement was made, and that he was then able to pay all his debts without having recourse to the property settled.

When settled property is thus taken for the benefit of creditors, it should be borne in mind that, after such claims have been satisfied, the beneficiaries under the settlement still retain their rights over whatever may remain.

" VALUABLE CONSIDERATION "

What then is this "valuable consideration" which takes a settlement out of the "voluntary" category? It was defined in a very comprehensive manner by Mr. Justice Lush in the leading case of *Currie* v. *Misa* (1875), L.R. 10 Ex. 153, where the learned judge said: "A valuable consideration in the sense of the law may consist either in some right, interest, profit, or benefit accruing to the one party or some forbearance, detriment, loss, or responsibility given, suffered or adopted by the other." Concrete examples will help to clarify this definition. Thus in the case of *In re Johnson*: *Golden* v. *Gillam*, 20 Ch. D. 389, an old and bed-ridden woman settled her farm and its stock, together with her household goods, on her daughters, while they, in return, were to provide a home for her and keep her in good clothing and medicines. This was held to constitute valuable consideration. Again, in the case of *Townsend* v. *Token*, L.R. 1 Ch. 446, an aunt settled property on her nephew who in return moved into a larger house so as to permit her to live with him. Subsequently, she left his roof and agreed to sell the property to a purchaser for value, but the settlement was upheld as having been made for valuable consideration.

MARRIAGE AND " POST NUPTIAL " SETTLEMENTS

So wide a definition could hardly fail to include marriage within its ambit and, in fact, the law recognises marriage in itself, apart altogether from any pecuniary advantage which, in different instances, may or may not follow in its train as being valuable consideration for the making of a settlement. That is to say, a prospective marriage is valuable consideration, but once it has been celebrated, it ceases to be so and all settlements made in favour of a wife during the married life—they are known as "post-nuptial" settlements—are regarded by the law as "voluntary" unless it can be proved that they were, in fact, made in pursuance of an agreement entered into prior to the marriage and in contemplation of it.

At one time, some doubt existed in regard to the proper classification of settlements made after marriage in pursuance of a pre-nuptial agreement which had not been reduced to writing. The difficulty arose out of the provisions of the Statute of Frauds which required, as a matter of evidence, that an agreement made in consideration of marriage should be in writing and signed by the party to be charged. This point was settled by the Court of Appeal in the case of *In re Holland*: *Gregg* v. *Holland* [1902], 2 Ch. 360. In that instance, the settlement contained a recital in the following words: "And whereas the said parties hereto of the first part intermarried on the 27th day of August, 1872, and, previously to such marriage, the said Isidore M. Bourke agreed to make such settlement of the future of his said wife as is hereinafter contained . . ." The difficulty arose on the subsequent bankruptcy of the husband, but the Court of Appeal decided that the inclusion of the above words in the settlement constituted a sufficient memorandum in writing of the pre-nuptial agreement to satisfy the requirements of the Statute of Frauds. Accordingly, it was upheld.

"GOOD CONSIDERATION"

Just as post-nuptial settlements are regarded by the law as "voluntary," so, too, settlements created for motives of natural affection, blood relationship, moral duty, or benevolence, of course, fall for most purposes into the same category. It should be added, however, that, in one respect, the Law of Property Act, 1925 (Section 172), puts settlements such as the last-mentioned— made, as the term goes, for "good consideration"—on the same footing as settlements made for valuable consideration, in that, even if the settlor's intention was to defraud his creditors, the settlement will not be upset, provided the person benefiting was not aware of this and took in good faith.

EXTENT OF MARRIAGE CONSIDERATION

A further difficulty may also arise from the fact that the same settlement may on occasion conceivably be "voluntary" from one point of view and made for valuable consideration from another. In the case of a marriage settlement, for example, the marriage consideration extends only to the husband, the wife, and the children of the marriage. So that if any person but these derives benefit under a settlement, it is, so far as he is concerned, a "voluntary settlement." This may be made more clear by taking as an illustration the case of *de Mestre* v. *West*, [1891] A.C. 264. There the Judicial Committee of the Privy

Council held that a limitation in a marriage settlement in favour of the settlor's illegitimate child and his issue was not within the marriage consideration and was therefore "voluntary."

REVOCATION

In emphasising the distinctions existing between "voluntary" settlements and settlements made for valuable consideration, the points in which they resemble each other must not be lost sight of. Thus, it is very important to remember that the distinction is drawn first and foremost for the protection of innocent third parties and not for the protection of the settlor himself. Therefore, once the property has been duly settled, the settlor cannot revoke the settlement merely on the ground that it was voluntary. A settlement may, however, be revoked if the settlor has been sufficiently far-sighted to insert a power of revocation into the deed. That he was induced to make the settlement by undue influence or fraud constitutes, of course, good ground for revocation.

FRAUD AND CONSPIRACY

Again for precisely the same reason—namely, the protection of third parties—even settlements for valuable consideration may be upset if the beneficiary was aware that the settlor made it with the intention of defrauding his creditors. The most obvious instance of this is a marriage settlement made in circumstances which amount to a conspiracy between the man and the woman. A rather curious example of this type of fraud caused the point to be decided in the case of *Columbine* v. *Penhall* (1853), 1 Sm. & Giff. 228. An unsuccessful London solicitor, finding himself insolvent and in pecuniary difficulties, hit upon what seemed to him an extremely ingenious way of saying good-bye to his embarrassments and starting life anew. He decided to marry the woman with whom he had been living for the past eight years or so. Accordingly, on the 12th January, 1847, he executed a marriage settlement in her favour, and two days later married her by special licence in the parish church of St. Nicholas, Brighton. Within two months of the ceremony, a fiat of bankruptcy had issued against the bridegroom under whose control the property settled had, of course, remained. At this point, the bride took steps to get the settlement recognised by the Court of Chancery, but she did not succeed because " where a marriage and a settlement are made under such circumstances, the consideration of marriage, if allowed to prevail, would only afford a secure means of defrauding creditors."

In connection with matrimonial frauds of this description, there is a further point which should not be overlooked. Clearly, the unbegotten children of such a union cannot be parties to the fraudulent intention behind it, and therefore even a settlement made under such circumstances as these would stand in so far as it conferred any benefit on the issue of the marriage.

DUTY OF LAWYERS

In regard to voluntary settlements more than any others, a special point remains to be considered, though it may not be strictly within the scope of the law of this subject—namely, the duty of barristers and solicitors towards clients who consult them in connection with the settling of property. It is mentioned because it is very desirable that the layman should appreciate the light in which he is considered by his legal advisers and the services which they regard themselves as owing to him. The lawyer's primary obligation is, of course, to make absolutely certain, by means of personal contact with the proposed settlor that he is capable of appreciating and does in fact appreciate the nature and consequences of the step which he is about to take in limiting or abrogating his control over his property. It must be ascertained that such are in fact his wishes and his instructions and that whatever influence may have helped to bring him to this decision was not in any way in the nature of undue influence. Beyond this, he must consider whether, from all points of view, the proposed settlement is a suitable one, and give clear advice accordingly. His position becomes very difficult indeed if the client perversely insists on following a course which he considers open to serious objection. In deciding the case of *Powell* v. *Powell*, [1900] 1 Ch. 243, Mr. Justice Farwell took a very extreme view of the duties of a legal adviser. Setting aside a voluntary settlement made by a young lady very shortly after she had attained the age of twenty-one, he declared that the solicitor must "satisfy himself that the gift is one that it is right and proper for the donor to make under all the circumstances; and if he is not so satisfied, his duty is to advise his client not to go on with the transaction and to refuse to act further for him if he persists. He certainly ought not to go on if he disapproves, simply because, as was suggested in this case, he thinks that someone else will do the work if he does not. The plea that offences must needs come does not exonerate the man by whom the offence cometh. The more foolish and wilful the conduct of the youthful donor appears to the solicitor, the less should he lend the sanction of his countenance to the gift."

The learned judge's own words make as clear as possible the most extreme view of a lawyer's duty in this connection. It can, however, be in the most exceptional cases only that he is justified in refusing to act.

UNDUE INFLUENCE

This case constitutes a convenient bridge for passing over to the subject of undue influence, against which, in the making of a settlement, it is the lawyer's special duty to guard, and which constitutes a ground for setting the transaction aside. *Powell* v. *Powell* provides as clear an example of undue influence as could be found. The young lady who made the settlement in dispute was an orphan whose father had married a second time. For three years prior to her twenty-first birthday, she had remained at school abroad, though her father had died during that period leaving her under the guardianship of her step-mother. This lady seems to have shared the instincts tradition-ally associated with step-mothers, for on the very day the child came of age, she confronted her with a document signed by the father in which he expressed an earnest wish that the personal property which came to her should be divided with his two other children. On this pretext, she was persuaded to make a settlement which, amongst other things, gave her step-mother two-thirds of the income from the property for life. Further than this, there was no power of revocation inserted in the deed. In setting the settlement aside, the learned judge remarked in regard to the use made of the document signed by the father that "such a memorandum is an improper attempt to exercise post-humous pressure and is most obnoxious to the rule of the Court. It is an appeal of a nature most difficult for a young person just twenty-one to resist, especially if the child is told at the same time (as in the present case) that she is bound in honour to obey and will be regarded as a social pariah if she does not."

When any question of this sort arises, the responsibility lies on the person who takes advantage under a voluntary settlement to show that the settlor at the time of the transaction was adequately and competently advised in the matter.

SETTLEMENTS BY WILL AND BY DEED

Regarding undue influence, a practical distinction is drawn between settlements created by will and settlements created by deed. The former represent, in effect, a posthumous control which the testator, having himself passed beyond the enjoyment of all descriptions of property, yet continues to exercise over what was once his own. The latter take away from him in his lifetime the full enjoyment of that which otherwise would have remained under his absolute dominion until death. It is not difficult to see that the latter class of settlement, operating as it does to the detriment of the settlor, gives rise more readily to a suspicion of undue influence. Generally speaking, therefore, it may be said that in such cases when a settlement in his favour is brought about by the influence of a parent or guardian, religious, medical, or legal adviser, it is liable to be set aside, unless the party deriving the benefit can show that the settlor was absolutely free in his judgment. In the case, however, of settlements by will, the mere fact that some degree of influence has been exercised will not in itself raise presumptions adverse to the beneficiary, so long, of course, as the testator acted freely.

INFANTS' SETTLEMENTS ON MARRIAGE

The general principles governing the law of settlements have hitherto been treated of. It is now time to turn to special kinds of settlements, and of these the principal is the marriage settlement. The object which it sets out to achieve is to assure to the respective parties the enjoyment of an income, and often, in addition, of other privileges, as, for example, the use of furniture or of a dwelling-house and to preserve the property settled for the benefit of the children of the marriage.

In the past the law has attached such importance to arrangements of this description that the case of marriages of minors was specially provided for by the Infant Settlements Act of 1855. By its provisions, male infants of twenty and female infants of seventeen may make valid and binding settlements of their property in contemplation of marriage. This power is exercisable under the superintendence of the Chancery Division of the High Court of Justice and must receive its sanction. It is well to note in the case of infants who are not already wards of court that the mere application for such a sanction does not

21

serve to put them in that category. Even in the case of wards, however, the Court has no power to compel the making of a marriage settlement, as was decided in the case of *In re Leigh : Leigh* v. *Leigh*, 40 Ch. D. 290. There, a young man of twenty, a ward of court, married without the consent of the Court. The hideous nature of the "contempt" of which he had been guilty was duly explained to him by the managing clerk of the family solicitors. An application was made by his mother to Mr. Justice Kay, and a settlement was ordered to be drawn up and executed by him under the provisions of the Infant Settlements Act. Cowed by the instinctive belief of the uninitiated in the law's universal power of compulsion, the young man did as he was told, though much against his will. After he came of age, however, he questioned the right of the Court to exercise such compulsion, and the Court of Appeal eventually upheld his contention and set the settlement aside.

MARRIAGE SETTLEMENTS

To return to marriage settlements generally, the marriage must be one which the parties can legally contract. Otherwise, if the trusts are expressed to take effect "from and after the solemnisation of the marriage," they must wholly fail. For example in *Phillips* v. *Probyn*, [1899] 1 Ch. 811, such an effect was produced. In 1873 a widower executed a settlement in contemplation of a proposed marriage with his deceased wife's sister —a union which at that time was illegal and invalid. In 1877, he went through a ceremony of marriage with her and they lived together as man and wife till his death in 1891. The Court held that though "on the face of it, the settlement appears to be a valid one, and it would have been valid if Clara Probyn had not been the sister of the settlor's deceased wife," the trust must in these circumstances fail.

In the forming of marriage settlements, so many eventualities unlikely to occur to the non-professional mind must be considered and provided for that it is practically impossible to carry them through without professional assistance. For example, it is prudent to make provision for subsequent marriages, since, if the property in question is made subject to trusts in favour of the issue of that marriage only and one of the parties having died, the other marries again, an injustice may result in regard to the children of the second union.

SETTLEMENTS ON CHILDREN

Again, apart from marriage settlements, property is often settled for the special purpose of providing for the education and maintenance of sons and daughters. Of late years, the practice has become much more common as a means of reducing the sum payable by the parent in respect of income tax and surtax. Such settlements perform the double function of reducing the taxable income and at the same time fulfilling a duty which the parent would in any case have been obliged to discharge. Section 20 of the Finance Act of 1922 was designed to put a check on the scope of settlements made with this object, but it has by no means done away with their general utility. The dispositions which it has made ineffective for this purpose are (a) in the first place, settlements subject to a power of revocation which the settlor could operate for his own benefit; (b) in the second place, voluntary settlements under which he has made the income "payable to or applicable for the benefit of any other person for a period which cannot exceed six years"; and (c) finally, settlements under which the income is payable to or applicable for the benefit of a child of the settlor (including a step-child or illegitimate child) "for some period less than the life of the child." In all these cases, the income remains, for the purposes of income tax, the settlor's income, except that in settlements falling within the last-mentioned class, it only remains so while the child is still unmarried or a minor. Of course, even after a child has married or come of age, a settlement on him may still be caught in either of the two preceding classes, which, though not confined to the case of children, may apply to them. The general effect of this enactment is that a settlor cannot obtain exemption from taxation if, while purporting to make provision for his child, he actually retains an indirect hold on the property settled.

Settlements of this character have been discouraged by the authorities by the imposition of a very heavy stamp duty often amounting to a year's income tax, but settlors have not been thereby discouraged from purchasing subsequent immunity by this means. It may be noted that as the stamp duty is payable on the first periodical payment, monthly rather than yearly payments are sometimes arranged for.

SETTLEMENTS OF LAND

Having dealt generally with the subject of settlements, an important practical distinction must now be drawn between

settlement of "realty" (or land) and settlements of other forms
of property which go under the name of "personalty." The law
relating to real settlements has been fundamentally revised by
the Settled Land Act of 1925, and it is proposed to deal with
these first.

Section 1, subsection (1), defines the range of circumstances
which constitutes a settlement for the purposes of the Act and
it is impossible to explain them as fully as might be desirable
without going so far into the law of real property as to depart
unduly from the present subject. In the actual language of the
Act, a settlement is created when any land stands for the time
being—

"1. Limited in trust for any persons by way of succession.

"2. Limited in trust for any person in possession.

"(a) For an entailed interest, whether or not capable of
being barred or defeated.

"(b) For an estate in fee simple or for a term of years absolute, subject to an executory limitation gift or disposition
over on failure of his issue or in any other event.

"(c) For a base or determinable fee or any corresponding
interest in leasehold land.

"(d) Being an infant for an estate in fee simple or for a term
of years absolute; or

"3. Limited in trust for any person for an estate in fee simple
or for a term of years absolute on the happening of any event; or

"4. Limited to or in trust for a married woman of full age in
possession for an estate in fee simple or a term of years absolute
or any other interest with a restraint on anticipation.

"5. Charged whether voluntarily or in consideration of marriage or by way of family arrangement and whether immediately
or after an interval with the payment of any rent charge for
the life of any person or any less period or of any capital annual
or periodical sums for the portions, advancement, maintenance,
or otherwise for the benefit of any persons with or without any
term of years for securing or raising the same."

It has been thought proper to set down these provisions in full,
but, summarising them for the benefit of the non-professional
reader, it may be said that the circumstances here defined leave
the person or persons in possession of the land in question with
something less than an absolute interest and complete dominion
whether because other people's interests await the determination
of his own or because the duration of his interest is dependent

upon the happening or not happening of some event in the future or because the beneficial owner is an infant and is therefore in law incapable of dealing with the land—to select a few instances for exemplification.

TRUSTEES OF SETTLED LAND

For the purposes of the Act there must also be trustees of the settlement. The persons who, for the purposes of the Act, come within this class are specifically defined by Section 30, but at the present stage, it is not necessary to analyse its provisions. As to their functions, they are briefly stated by Mr. Justice North in the case of *In re Hotchkin's Settled Estates,* 35 Ch. D. 41, when he said: "Trustees are appointed in order that they may act as a check upon the tenant for life in the interest of the other persons who are entitled under the settlement." In the discharge of this duty, their consent is sometimes required for the exercise of the powers under the settlement. Speaking generally, however, their function is passive rather than active, for they are not held strictly accountable for all the acts of the tenant for life in connection with the land, and Sections 97 and 98 enumerate the instances in which they are not liable, in respect of various dealings with the settled property, as, for example, "for adopting a contract made by the tenant for life" on a purchase, exchange or lease or for the acts of any agent of the tenant for life "on the investment of capital money in any authorised security."

THE TENANT FOR LIFE

It is therefore the tenant for life who holds the key position in relation to the settlement and the subject can be most conveniently investigated from his point of view. He is defined by Section 19 as "the person of full age who is for the time being beneficially entitled under a settlement to possession of settled land for his life." If more persons than one are beneficially entitled as joint tenants, they constitute together the tenant for life for the purpose of exercisng the powers under the Act. If of these one is an infant, the legal estate in the property vests in the person or persons of full age until the infant reaches his majority. In the case of an infant who would be tenant for life alone if he was of full age, the powers under the Act vest meanwhile in the trustees of the settlement. Under Section 28: "Where a tenant for life is a lunatic or a defective, his committee or receiver may in his name and on his behalf, under an order in lunacy, exercise the powers of a tenant for life under this Act."

In a way "tenant for life" is a misleading term, and must be taken to include a large number of persons who, though not in the literal sense "life tenants," can yet exercise the powers conferred upon that class. These are enumerated in Section 19 and are—

1. A tenant in tail.

2. A person entitled to an estate in fee simple subject to an executory limitation, gift or disposition over or failure of his issue or in any other event.

3. A person entitled to a base or determinable fee or to any corresponding interest in leasehold land.

4. A tenant for years determinable on life not holding merely under a lease at a rent.

5. A tenant for the life of another, not holding merely under a lease at a rent.

6. A tenant for his own or any other life or for years determinable on life whose estate is liable to cease in any event during that life, whether by expiration of the estate or by conditional limitation or otherwise or to be defeated by an executory limitation, gift, or disposition over or is subject to a trust for accumulation of income for any purpose.

7. A tenant by the curtesy.

8. A person entitled to the income of land under a trust or direction for payment thereof to him during his own life or any other life or until sale of the land or until forfeiture, cesser, or determination by any means of his interest therein, unless the land is subject to an immediate binding trust for sale.

9. A person beneficially entitled to land for an estate in fee simple subject to any estates, interests, charges, or powers of charging subsisting or capable of being exercised under a settlement.

10. A married woman entitled to land for an estate in fee simple or for a term of years absolute subject to a restraint on anticipation.

MODES OF SETTLING LAND

Land may be settled in one of two ways. On the one hand, the legal estate may be conveyed to trustees on trust for sale, a proceeding which transforms it into a settlement of the proceeds of the sale and therefore into a settlement of personalty. On the other hand—and this is the method relevant to the present discussion—the legal estate may be conveyed to the tenant for life upon the trusts declared in another deed. Section 4 of the Act provides that "every settlement of a legal estate in land *inter vivos* shall, save as in this Act otherwise provided, be effected by two deeds, namely a vesting deed and a trust instrument."

The function of the trust instrument as set out in the same section is to declare the trusts affecting the settled land, appoint trustees of the settlement, and contain a power, if this is intended, to appoint new ones. Finally, it must set out whatever powers are intended to be conferred by the settlement in addition to those conferred by the Act. It must, of course, be duly stamped.

Section 5 deals with the vesting deed which must contain a description of the settled land, a statement that it is vested in the persons to whom it is conveyed upon the trusts affecting the settlement, the names of the trustees and of the person entitled to appoint new trustees and any additional powers conferred by the settlement, beside those conferred by the Act.

At first sight, there may seem to be a certain anomaly in transferring the legal fee simple to the tenant for life who, in fact, is only entitled to a limited interest. The advantage of the transaction is, however, to enable him to offer a satisfactory title to the land should it in the future be thought advisable, in the interests of all the beneficiaries under the settlement, to sell the land and realise the proceeds of the sale for their benefit.

POWERS ON TENANT FOR LIFE

The tenant for life being now in the saddle, the next question to be examined is the extent of his powers in relation to the settled land and his duties touching their exercise. In most cases it is sufficient for him simply to give notice to the trustees, but Section 58 provides two cases in which he must obtain their actual consent in writing. The first instance is when he desires to "compromise, compound, abandon, submit to arbitration or otherwise settle any claim dispute or question whatsoever relating to the settled land." The second instance is when he desires "to release, waive, or modify any covenant, agreement, or restriction imposed on any other land for the benefit of the settled land."

In other cases, the tenant for life has the alternative of obtaining either such written consent as has been mentioned or an order of the Court. Under Section 65, this is necessary before "the powers of disposing of settled land conferred by this Act on the tenant for life may be exercised, as respects the principal mansion house, if any, on any settled land and the pleasure grounds parks and lands, if any, usually occupied therewith," in the case of settlements made or coming into operation before the 1st January, 1926, and not expressly dispensing with the necessity for such consent, and, in the case of settlements coming into operation after that date, only if they expressly provide for the necessity of such consent. A house usually occupied as a farm or one which with its park and lands does not occupy more than twenty-five acres is not regarded as a "mansion house." Under Section 66, the same consents are necessary for the cutting and selling of timber ripe for cutting, in the case of a tenant for life who is "impeachable for waste," as the phrase goes, or, in other words, accountable for acts done by him which are a lasting detriment to the land.

Finally, for the exercise of certain other powers, an order of the Court is always requisite. This is so in regard to the sale of personal chattels "settled to devolve with the settled land," or, as they are more popularly described, heirlooms, the relevant provision being contained in Section 67. The same applies to the case of building on mining leases which the tenant for life wishes to grant "for a longer term, or, on other conditions than the term or conditions specified in that behalf in this Act," to use the words of Section 46. Finally, under Section 57, an order of the Court is required to permit a tenant for life to lease more than two acres of land in an urban district or ten acres in a rural district for the provision of working-class dwellings or for the purposes of the Small Holdings and Allotments Acts, 1908 to 1919.

Having now summarised the various circumstances under which the tenant for life in the exercise of his powers must do more than give the trustees due notice, one can approach the general subject of the exercise of these powers, bearing in mind the reservations implied by the provisions which have just been discussed.

RIGHTS AND LIABILITIES OF TENANT FOR LIFE

However, before turning to the rights of the tenant for life under the Settled Land Act, 1925, his rights and liabilities under the Common Law must be considered. He is entitled to the general profits of the land and to the harvest of the crops he has sown which may, therefore, be claimed by his personal representatives on his death. As to fixtures, he may remove such as have been created for the furtherance of trade and such as come within the class generally described as "ornamental." Tapestries fixed to the walls often fall within this category, but so much depends on the particular circumstances of the individual case, especially the solidity of the mode of fixing, that it is impossible to discuss the subject fully within the bounds of relevance. It is enough here to mention two contrasting cases: *Leigh* v. *Taylor* (1902, H.L.), and *In re Whaley* (1908, Ch.). In the former, certain tapestries were held to be removable, and in the latter not removable.

LIABILITY FOR "WASTE"

Again the tenant for life is checked, quite apart from the Act of Parliament, in the commission of certain acts of destruction which change the character of the land and which are known under the general term of "waste." If, under the settlement, he is "impeachable for waste," he cannot fell timber, alter or pull down houses, open mines, or change the character of arable land, pasture or woodland. If, however, as is usually the case with modern settlements, he is "unimpeachable for waste," he can do all these things, though he must, of course, stop short of acts of wanton destruction. The classical instance of this sort of malicious folly is the case of *Vane* v. *Lord Barnard* (1717), 2 Vern. 738, and related to Raby Castle. In the words of the report: "The defendant, the Lord Barnard, having taken some displeasure against his son, got two hundred workmen together, and of a sudden, in a few days, stript the castle of the lead, glass-doors, and boards, etc., to the value of £3,000." When the matter came before the Court of Chancery, the fact that he was tenant for life "without impeachment for waste" availed him nothing and he was ordered by injunction to stop committing waste and to repair the castle. The wanton destruction of ornamental timber is also restrained on the same principle.

POWERS UNDER SETTLED LAND ACT, 1925

Next the statutory powers conferred on the tenant for life by the Settled Land Act of 1925 must be examined. He "may sell the settled land or any part thereof or any easement, right, or privilege of any kind over or in relation to the land," or he "may make an exchange of the settled land or any part thereof or any easement, right, or privilege of any kind" for other land easements, rights, and the like. This right is conferred by Section 38. All sales must be made for the best consideration in money that can reasonably be obtained, but certain provisions are made allowing sales to be carried through "in consideration wholly or partially of a perpetual rent. In case of sale or exchange, the tenant for life may, under Section 50, reserve all or any of the mines and minerals in the land together with all "easements, rights, and privileges for or incident to or connected with mining purposes."

The leasing powers of a tenant for life are regulated by Sections 41 to 48 of the Act. Building and forestry leases may be for nine hundred and ninety-nine years, mining leases for a hundred years, and other leases fifty years. All leases must, of course, be for the best rent obtainable. The decision in the recent case of *In re Grosvenor Settled Estates ; Duke of Westminster* v. *McKenna* (1933, Ch.), laid down that in the case of a building lease granted by a tenant for life, no time limit for the rebuilding need be specified. As to the proceeds of mining leases where the tenant for life is impeachable for waste in respect of minerals, three-quarters of the rent must be set aside as capital money arising under the Act. Otherwise, the proportion is one-quarter. Notice must, of course, be given to the trustees of the settlement before the tenant for life grants any lease, but an exception is made in the case of a term not exceeding twenty-one years, when the best rent has been obtained and "the lessee is not exempted from punishment for waste." Besides granting leases, a tenant for life may, under Section 53, "accept a lease of any land or of any mines and minerals or of any easement, right, or privilege convenient to be held or worked with or annexed in enjoyment to the settled land or any part thereof." In the case of *In re Savile Settled Estates ; Savile* v. *Savile* (1931, Ch.), it was held that a tenant for life has power to vary by deed the terms of leases already granted by him so long as they do not, after variation, contravene the provisions of the Settled Land Act of 1925.

Finally, a tenant for life may mortgage the settled land for any of the purposes set out in Section 71. The most noteworthy of these are discharging an incumbrance on the settled land, paying for an improvement authorised by the Act or by the settlement, and paying the costs of any transaction authorised by this section and of the two preceding sections which relate to incumbrances.

IMPROVEMENTS TO SETTLED LAND

The mention of improvements leads naturally to Sections 83 to 89 of the Act which deal with this subject. The improvements authorised by the Act are enumerated in the Third Schedule and are much too numerous to set out in full, and fall into three categories. The first are improvements of which the costs paid out of capital money are not liable to be replaced by instalments. They comprise such works as drainage, bridges, irrigation, embanking rivers or lakes, sea walls, roads, clearing, trenching, planting, cottages for labourers, tramways, railways, canals, and docks. In the case of improvements of the second class, the trustees of the settlement or the Court may require the costs to be replaced by instalments. Instances of the works specified include residential houses for land or mineral agents, managers, clerks, bailiffs, woodmen, gamekeepers, and other persons employed on the settled land, restoration of buildings damaged by dry rot, boring for water, and similar enterprises. The third class of improvements are those the costs of which the trustees of the settlement and the Court must require to be replaced by instalments. Amongst these are heating, hydraulic or electric power apparatus, engine houses, engines, gasometers, dynamos, steam rollers, traction engines, and the like.

" CAPITAL MONEY "

Before abandoning the discussion of the Settled Land Act, the meaning and nature of "capital money" must be treated of, for when the tenant for life exercises his powers to dispose of the settled land, the proceeds realised become capital money which he cannot pocket for himself, but which must be paid over to the trustees of the settlement though he still retains certain powers of control over it. Thus, a purchaser of settled land must pay the purchase money to the trustees and receive a receipt from them. The tenant for life can only dispose for his own benefit of the annual produce of the settled property. When he disposes of more, that is, when he touches the body of the property itself, he has to resign it for the common good of all the beneficiaries under the settlement. In the case of a sale, as noted above, this is self-evident, but the same principles apply to mining leases in the case of which a certain proportion of the rent paid must be dealt with as capital money since it is paid in respect of an actual diminution of the land itself. Though such capital money is in the hands of the trustees, its investment is controlled by the tenant for life, and, so long as his interest subsists, cannot be changed without his consent.

THE " FAMILY SETTLEMENT "

The main provisions of the enactment which at present governs settlements of land having been thus reviewed, one can now glance at the disposition known as the "family settlement." It is a device designed primarily to keep land in the settlor's family as long as the Rule against Perpetuities, which has already been touched upon, will permit. Such a settlement, in the first place, makes due provision for the settlor's family and in particular for his wife should she survive him and his children, other than his eldest son. For himself, he retains a life interest. The descent of the property to the eldest son is insured by the creation of an estate in tail male, as it is called. So far so good. But supposing the son on coming into the estate, should not feel inclined to allow it to descend to his eldest son in turn, should, in technical phrase, "bar the entail" : is he entitled to do so ? The eventuality is forestalled by the device of the resettlement, an ingenious invention attributed to Sir Orlando Bridgeman, an eminent lawyer of Stuart times, who was shrewd enough to see how youth could be played off against age. The son attains the age of twenty-one. He has no idea how long his father's life will keep him out of the enjoyment of the estate, but a regular income in the immediate present would be most desirable. This his father offers him on terms. He must execute a disentailing deed to "bar the entail" and convey the fee simple to his father upon such trusts as the two shall jointly declare. A deed of resettlement is then executed. The father gets a life interest ; the son gets a life interest, and meanwhile a yearly rent charge to be paid to him while his father lives. An entailed interest is created for the son's sons. These are the main provisions which constitute the framework of the scheme. It is easy to see that by the time the son's eldest son is twenty-one, he himself will have acquired the paternal point of view and will offer that son the same terms as he himself accepted. This device for many generations preserved the integrity of the great estates, but the power of sale, given to the tenant for life under the Settled Land Act of 1925, has considerably undermined its efficacy. Another characteristic development of modern times is the turning of the great estates into limited companies of which the shares are held by members of the family. For this reason many settlements which have hitherto been "real" settlements will tend to become settlements of "personalty."

THE "TRUST FOR SALE"

At this point one may pass on to the other method by which "real" property is settled, namely, the "trust for sale" and here it is not the property so disposed of but the proceeds of sale which must be primarily regarded. In every such trust, a power to postpone the sale indefinitely is implied unless the trust instrument expressly directs the contrary, but in the interval the law in pursuance of the "doctrine of conversion" regards the land as having been immediately converted into money and treats it accordingly. However, a settlor may declare the same trusts in creating a settlement of this description as in the case of a "strict" settlement of land, but in this case, the main power over the property is swayed, not by the tenant for life, but by the trustees, though they may delegate to him their powers of leasing and management. While the sale is postponed, the trustees wield the powers conferred on a tenant for life by the Settled Land Act of 1925, for the property is vested in them and not in him. As to the postponement of sale, a problem may arise when there are several beneficiaries under a trust and the interest of one of them vests in possession. Does this put an end to the discretion to postpone the sale and must the estate be realised forthwith so as to give this beneficiary his share? The situation arose in the case of *In re Kipping; Kipping* v. *Kipping* (1914 Ch.), where one of seven children, beneficiaries under a trust for sale, put forward this contention on attaining the age of twenty-one, but the Court decided against him for reasons very concisely stated by Lord Justice Buckley: "The will gives him not a distributive share of a sum of money, but a distributive share of the income of the property so long as it remains unsold, and a distributive share of the proceeds of sale when the property is sold. There is no gift of the proceeds of sale until the property is sold and he is not entitled to interfere with the *bona fide* exercise by the trustees of their discretion and to call upon them to sell." Shortly afterwards, however, it was held in the case of *In re Marshall; Marshall* v. *Marshall* (1914 Ch.), that in similar circumstances when the settled property consisted of company shares, and could therefore easily be divided up without prejudice to the interests of the other beneficiaries, the transfer could be required.

MARRIAGE SETTLEMENTS

The other broad class of settlements contrasted with settlements of "real property" comprises settlements of "personal property." It may be said that they are made most frequently on the occasion of a marriage, and the trusts ordinarily declared have, in the course of long development, attained a considerable degree of uniformity. The settled property may be provided either by the husband or by the wife, and is known as the "Husband's Trust Fund" or the "Wife's Trust Fund," according as it belonged to the one or the other. The first obvious object of the settlement is to provide for the respective spouses, so, to begin with, the settlor is given a life interest in the property. Perhaps the settlor will be the first to die, so the next provision usually entitles the survivor to receive the income for life. Both are now adequately provided for and the next problem is to consider the possible children of the marriage. In this it is considered wise to preserve to the parents a free hand, so the next trust is usually for such of the children of the marriage as they shall jointly appoint or if they do not exercise this power in the lifetime of both of them, then the power of appointment vests in the survivor. There is, of course, a possibility that the appointment may never be made either by the husband or by the wife, and so the next trusts declared provide for this eventuality, in which case they operate in favour of all the male children of the marriage who reach the age of twenty-one, and of all the female children of the marriage who either attain that age or marry. So far then the property has been completely and satisfactorily disposed of, but the possibility remains either that there may be no issue at all or else that none of the children will live to attain a vested interest under the terms already set out. With this in view, it is usual to declare further trusts designed to give back to the settlor dominion over the settled property so far as is compatible with the benefits secured by the previous trusts. Ordinarily, it is directed that the fund shall in such circumstances be held in trust for the settlor absolutely. In the case of a wife's fund, trusts are further declared in favour of such persons as she shall appoint by will, and, finally, if she dies before her husband and leaves no will, in favour of the persons who would have been entitled in law to succeed to her personal property had she died intestate and unmarried. This last provision fulfils the very reasonable function of bringing back the wife's property to her own family after her death instead of allowing it to devolve upon the relatives of her husband. Of course, if she survives her husband, the precaution is unnecessary, while if she does not, she has always possessed the power to benefit him by her will. If the marriage on which this settlement is made be a second marriage and the wife has children by her first union whom she wishes to benefit under this last trust, it should, of course, be made to operate not as if she had died a spinster, but as if she had died a widow. Finally it may be noted that when the husband alone is settling property it is often desirable to give the first life interest to the wife.

" HOTCHPOT " CLAUSE

Such is the usual structure of marriage settlements of personalty, subject, of course, to convenient variations in each particular case. Complications most often arise in connection with the trusts in favour of issue of the marriage. In particular the "hotchpot" clause, as it is called, requires a brief explanation. Its object is to secure equality of benefit among the children of the marriage and its operation, and, in particular, to avoid any injustices which might in some circumstances result from the exercise of the power of appointment. Its operation is to oblige a child, to whom a part of the fund has been appointed, to treat what he has thereby received as going to satisfy the share he would be entitled to on equal division of the settled property between all the children under the trust, which operates in default of appointment.

POWER OF ADVANCEMENT

Appointment in this connection must not be confused with "advancement." The latter is a power designed to provide for a very common eventuality, the necessity of raising an unusually large sum of money for the purpose of establishing the career of a son or daughter. The importance of realising the distinction will be seen in relation to the "hotchpot" clause already discussed, for if a lump sum of money paid for the "advancement" of a child were the same as an "appointment" to the child, it would come within that principle. The question arose in the case of *In re Fox; Wodehouse* v. *Fox*, [1904] 1 Ch. 430, in connection with a sum of £705 advanced to one of several children, and it was held by Mr. Justice Byrne that the "hotchpot" clause was not applicable to this sum. It should be noted that in the case of trusts coming into force since the Trustee Act of 1925, a power to apply capital money for the advancement of a child is implied to the extent of half "the presumptive or vested share or interest" of the individual benefited. When this occurs, the money so applied must be brought into account. These provisions, however, are subject to any express variation in the instrument creating the trust. The sum paid out must always be in respect of some definite and legitimate purpose such as the Court will recognise and approve. This, of course, results in the drawing of some very fine distinctions. Thus, for example, in the case of *In re Kershaw's Trusts*, L.R. 6 Eq. 322, Vice-Chancellor Malins approved the payment of £5,000 for the purpose of setting up in business the husband of one of the settlor's daughters, since, if he could not get the capital, he would have been obliged to go abroad and leave his wife and children. On the other hand, in *Molyneux* v. *Fletcher* (1898, Q.B.), the trustees of a settlement were held not to be justified in parting with a sum of money to pay a debt of the husband of a beneficiary.

In the case of *In re Stimpson; Stimpson* v. *Stimpson* (1931, Ch.), it has been held that trustees holding land upon trust for sale may exercise the power of advancement out of capital bestowed by Section 32 of the Trustee Act of 1925, in favour of a remainderman.

COVENANT TO SETTLE AFTER-ACQUIRED PROPERTY

A settlement, whether made by a husband or a wife, may deal, not only with property actually in the possession of the settlor, but may also contain a covenant to settle property which may be subsequently acquired. Both divorce and judicial separation put an end to the operation of such a covenant, though, curiously enough, it continues to be effective between the granting of the decree nisi and of the decree absolute. Till then, generally speaking, the covenant can be enforced by the trustees of the settlement with whom it is made, although, as in the case of *In re Pryce; Nevill* v. *Pryce* (1917, Ch.), the Court may direct them to refrain from taking such a step when the only persons to benefit thereby would be the next of kin, there being no issue of the marriage. A husband's bankruptcy also renders such a covenant unenforceable as against his trustee in bankruptcy.

" PROTECTIVE TRUSTS "

The treatment of this subject calls for some mention of the important provisions of Section 33 of the Trustee Act of 1925. Under that section, a direction that income shall be held on "protective trusts" operates to create a trust for the beneficiary during the trust period specified, or else until he does, or attempts to do, or suffers any act or thing or until any event happens whereby, if the income were payable to him absolutely, he would be deprived of the right to receive it—until, for example, he goes bankrupt. In such a case, the income is to be held at the absolute discretion of the trustees upon trust for "the application thereof for the maintenance or support or otherwise for the benefit" of all or any of a defined class of persons, including the beneficiary as well as his or her husband or wife and children. Thus he may in effect continue to enjoy his income under circumstances which would normally have deprived him of it.

DIVORCE COURT VARYING SETTLEMENTS

It is now necessary to turn to another aspect of this subject, the power of the Divorce Court to vary settlements. This now depends on Section 192 of the Supreme Court of Judicature (Consolidation) Act of 1925 under which "the Court may, after pronouncing a decree for divorce or for nullity of marriage, inquire into the existence of ante-nuptial or post-nuptial settlements made on the parties whose marriage is the subject of the decree, and may make such orders with reference to the application of the whole or any part of the property settled, either for the benefit of the children of the marriage or of the parties to the marriage, as the Court thinks fit." Either the husband, the wife or, in cases where the petitioner is dead, the guardian of the children of the marriage may apply for such variation and the ordinary time for doing so is within a month of the decree being made absolute.

Moreover, under the preceding section of the Act (Section 191) "in any case in which the Court pronounces a decree for divorce or for judicial separation by reason of the adultery of the wife" and she is entitled to any property in possession or reversion, the Court may order a settlement of such property or part of it to be made for the benefit of her husband or of the children of the marriage. Such an order may also be made on an application by a husband for restitution of conjugal rights.

The object of these enactments is to make proper provision for an injured spouse and for the children of the marriage. The Court does not use them for the purpose of punishing the guilty party, though, of course, certain aspects of personal conduct may be very material to the consideration of the questions which arise. For example, in the case of *Chetwynd* v. *Chetwynd*, L.R. 1 P. & D. 39, a wife having obtained a divorce from her husband and petitioned for variation of the marriage settlement in her favour, the extravagance of which she had been guilty during the marriage was taken into consideration by the Court as a factor in the husband's favour in settling the future destination of the income. Again, the benefits to be conferred by the exercise of this power are purely personal, being confined to the parties, to the marriage, and the children. Thus, as was held in the case of *Thompson* v. *Thompson and Rodschinka*, [1896] P. 263, that when a husband dies after obtaining a dissolution of his marriage and after presenting a petition for variation of the marriage settlement, the proceedings cannot be continued by his personal representatives for the benefit of his estate and the petition abates unless there are children of the marriage whose interests must be provided for.

The power of variation extends to every part of the marriage settlement. It can, however, only be exercised once and a change of circumstances occurring subsequently to the date of the order can constitute no basis for a further variation of the settlement. Thus in *Benyon* v. *Benyon* (1890) 15 P.D. 54, after a divorce had been granted to a husband, the marriage settlements were varied and the wife ordered to pay him £300 a year. Some years later, she applied to have this amount reduced on the ground that her own income had shrunk as a result of the depreciation of securities. The application was dismissed.

Examples of the Court's exercise of its discretion in particular instances might be more misleading than helpful and it is best to say no more than that it looks primarily at the welfare of the children of the marriage and secondly to securing a competency to the innocent party.

*   *   *

This subject may be concluded with a specimen form of marriage settlement designed to demonstrate its elementary outline, eliminating, however, for the sake of simplicity even some very ordinary provisions.

SPECIMEN MARRIAGE SETTLEMENT

This Settlement made the 1st day of April, 19—, between John Truelove hereinafter called the husband of the first part, Jane Darling hereinafter called the wife of the second part and John Doe trustee and Richard Roe trustee of the third part.

Whereas a marriage is intended shortly to be solemnised between the husband and the wife.

Now this deed witnesseth that in consideration of the said intended marriage it is hereby agreed and declared as follows—

1. That until the said intended marriage the trustees shall hold the settled fund upon trust for the husband.

2. That from and after the said intended marriage the said trustees shall pay the interest of the settled fund to the husband during his life and after his death to the wife during her life if she shall survive him.

3. That from and after the death of the survivor the trustees shall hold the settled fund upon the trusts following—

4. Upon trust for all or such of the children of the marriage as the husband and wife jointly shall by deed appoint, and in default of such appointment as the survivor shall by deed, will, or codicil appoint.

5. In default of such appointment in trust for all the children of the marriage who shall attain the age of twenty-one years in equal shares.

6. No child shall be entitled to participate in the unappointed part of the settled fund without bringing into hotchpot the part appointed to him or her under the power hereinbefore contained.

7. Upon failure or determination of the said trusts the trustees shall hold the settled fund in trust for the husband or his personal representatives absolutely.

WILLS

A *Will* (or *Testament*) is a statement of what the maker (the *testator*) wishes to be done on or after his death. The will may give directions about the distribution of his property; for English law recognises in the fullest measure the right of bequest. True, the State, by way of Estate Duties, makes itself to some extent the heir of every one. But, apart from the State's share, the testator is at complete liberty.

One who dies without leaving a will is "intestate"; one who does not deal fully with his property is partially intestate. The property left by such persons is dealt with in accordance with the Administration of Estates Act, 1925. This Act in effect makes a will for him, such a will as the ordinary reasonable person, anxious to satisfy "legitimate expectations," might be expected to make.

Apart from declarations made by soldiers on active service or mariners at sea—declarations called *nuncupative wills*—a will, in order to be effective, must be in writing, and its preparation must be attended with the formalities (or "solemnities") noted below.

The will may appoint persons to see to the carrying out of the testator's intentions; the persons appointed by the will are *executors* (*executrix* is the word sometimes used when a female is appointed). When no executor is appointed in the will the Probate Court itself appoints a person or persons (*administrators*) to carry out the directions of the will. The Court also appoints administrators when there is no will, when there is an intestacy.

The making of a new will in itself revokes a former will. For the will has no legal effect during the testator's lifetime. Till the testator's death it is *ambulatory* (movable): it can be revoked. The addition to an existing will of a supplementary disposition—a *codicil*—also modifies the will. The codicil, to be effective, must be executed in the same manner as the will. There need not be the *same* witnesses as to the will itself. But there must be the two witnesses and the testator's signature.

Intentional destruction of the will by the testator also revokes it; and he can revive it only by means of the same formalities as attended the destroyed will. Accidental destruction or loss does not revoke the will. But proof of the testator's intentions is peculiarly difficult, and the Probate Court may be obliged to consider him an intestate.

Regulations about wills are contained in the Wills Act, 1837.

PROPERTY TRANSFERRED BY THE WILL

A testator has, of course, no power over property disposed of before death: if his will gives "my piano" to X, X has no claim against the estate when the testator has sold the piano. Moreover, the property available for distribution may be lessened by payment of funeral expenses, death duties, and debts. On the other hand, and operating to increase the estate of the deceased, we are to remember that gifts (other than gifts of small amount, of customary donations to charity, of allowances to children and the like) made more than three years before the death are made inoperative.

Apart from these limitations, English law gives the fullest freedom of bequest. A man is master of his estate so long as he is of sound mind. Where other systems of law secure to a widow or children a share of a deceased's property, in England a man can do what he chooses with his property even to the extent of ignoring entirely his widow and children. He can settle his property so as to defeat all manner of legitimate expectations; and it needs very weighty reasons to induce the Probate Court to disregard his wishes. The old idea, that property really belongs to a family group, and that the right of an individual is no more than to manage his share during his lifetime, has quite gone from our system of law.

MANNER OF MAKING A WILL

An effective disposition of property can be made only by a person who has *legal capacity to make a will*, and who *makes it in the prescribed manner.*

To make a will a person must be—

(a) *Twenty-one years old.* (An exception to this rule exists: a soldier, being on active service, and a mariner, being at sea, can make a will at the age of 16. Nor need they observe the formalities necessary in other cases.)

(b) *Of sound mind.* He must have sufficient capacity to understand the disposition of property he is making, and he must show clearly that he intends to make the dispositions. Subsequent insanity or senile decay does not revoke the will already made.

The burden of proof that the testator was of sound mind at the date of executing the will is upon the person who sets up the will. The Probate Court will not, however, except for very strong reasons, conclude against a properly signed and witnessed will.

CAPACITY TO MAKE WILL (CONVICTS)

When a person has been convicted of felony, his property is vested in administrators appointed by the Crown. The convict cannot, during the service of his sentence, divest himself of this property. But he may make a will, and, even if he dies before regaining his freedom, his intentions are carried out.

CLEARNESS IS IMPERATIVE

The testator expresses his intentions in his last will and testament; he is not available for explanations of his meaning. It is, therefore, most desirable that both ambiguity and obscurity should be absent from a will. Some rules worth observing by the testator making his own will are these—

(i) Make your intentions clear to yourself, and then express them in *few and simple words*. The Court is anxious to give effect to the intentions, but it must be in no doubt about what the intentions are.

Perhaps the statement of Lord Chief Justice Hale is no longer entirely applicable: "Judges ought to be curious and subtle to invent reasons and means to make acts effectual according to the just intention of the parties." For nowadays the Courts do not assume that they can enter into the testator's mind and grasp his intention, in spite of the ambiguity or want of meaning of his words. What the Courts take upon themselves power to do is this: "Omitted words may be supplied; words may be transposed; parenthesis may be inserted; false grammar and incorrect spelling may be disregarded if the intention of the parties sufficiently appears from the context." The rule that the Probate Court acts upon was thus expressed by one of its Presidents:

"I have been long impressed with the wisdom of the rule, now, I believe, universally adopted, at least in Courts of law, that, in construing all written instruments, the grammatical and ordinary sense of the words is to be adhered to, unless that would lead to some absurdity, or some repugnance, or inconsistency with the rest of the instrument, in which case the grammatical and ordinary sense of the words may be modified, so as to avoid that absurdity and inconsistency, but no further."

(ii) Do not use technical legal terms like "real property" or "hereditaments." Thus, a husband willing his property to his wife need say nothing more than: "This is the last will and testament of me, John Jones. I leave to my wife, Ellen, all the property I have, and I appoint her the sole executrix."

(iii) If you wish a person to deal with part of your property in a particular way, say so definitely: "I wish my wife to give to Henry Smith ten of my law books at his choice." Avoid phrases like "knowing that my wife will give suitable memorials of me to my friends." Let both the property you have in mind and the person to whom you allot it be clearly identified.

(iv) If a number of specific legacies have been left, make it quite clear who is to have what is left (the *residue*) of the estate after debts have been met and legacies handed over.

A *specific* legacy is property specially intended for a named person. It is the last thing that will be sold in order to pay the deceased debts. But, if it is no longer the property of the testator at the death, the specific legatee gets nothing.*

A *general* legacy is paid out of the whole estate.

" ADEMPTION " OF LEGACY

A man may leave part of his property—"my house in Waterloo Park Road," "my gold hunter watch"—to a specific person.

---

* Where an obvious ambiguity exists, the Court will admit outside evidence in order to reach a decision upon what the words of the will mean. Thus (*in re Jackson*, Ch. 1932), a testratrix left the residue of her estate in equal shares to two brothers, two sisters, "and my nephew, Arthur Murphy." The difficulty arose from the fact that three nephews (two legitimate and one illegitimate) bore that name, and the difficulty was thus resolved by Mr. Justice Farwell—

"She had two legitimate nephews bearing that name. That being so, evidence is clearly admissible to show, not indeed her intention, but the meaning of the words which she used. So far as concerned the legitimate nephews, it is impossible for me to determine which she meant, and, had the matter ended there, there would have been intestacy. But it did not end there; for one of the sisters of the testatrix had a son born out of wedlock, and he also is named Arthur Murphy.

"It is clear on authority that *prima facie* an illegitimate relative cannot claim against a legitimate relative; that is to say, if one finds a legitimate relative properly answering the description in the will, that person must take, and evidence cannot be received that someone else who does not answer the description is the person intended. Therefore, if there were only one legitimate Arthur Murphy and one illegitimate, the former would clearly take.

"But, as there are two legitimate nephews, both named Arthur Murphy, an ambiguity exists and I have come to the conclusion that evidence can be received to show who is the person really intended, even if it leads to the result that a third person who does not accurately answer to the description in the will is the person to benefit.

"I have accordingly admitted the evidence, and, having considered it, have come to the conclusion that the word 'nephew' is not used in the strict legal sense, but refers to the person who is the son of her sister and with whom she was on terms of considerable friendship, and I declare that Arthur Murphy, the son of Margaret Murphy, is the person entitled to one-fifth of the residuary estate."

He may afterwards sell or give away the particular property. To that extent he has revoked the will. The particular property has been "adeemed"; and the legatee has no claim against the estate in respect of it.

ADEMPTION OF LEGACIES BY " PORTIONS "

So with the making of advances to children. Equity, in its anxiety to promote fairness, leans against what are called "double portions." If, therefore, a father leaves a legacy to a child and *afterwards* gives that child a "portion," a marriage portion perhaps, or an advance to begin business, the presumption is that he intended the portion as a substitute in part or in whole of the legacy. The "legacy is adeemed by the portion": the testator has omitted to alter his will; but the Court will do it for him and fulfil his intention. If the child should wish to take the benefit given by the will, he must give back his portion to the estate— "bring the portion into hotchpot" is the phrase used.

Of course, the presumption is not acted upon where the testator makes quite clear that he intends the child to have both portion and legacy. And, as reason would suggest, the fact that small gifts from time to time have been made has no effect upon the dispositions made in the will.

" LAPSE " OF LEGACY

When a person entitled to a benefit under a will dies before the testator, the legacy destined for him "lapses." Unless the testator makes another disposition of the property covered by the legacy, it passes according to the rules laid down to govern an intestacy. Or it may be that the testator has indicated a person who will take all that is left of the property after legacies are paid. This person is called the "residual legatee": he will, in general, take any legacy or devise that has lapsed.

There are two cases, however, where the death of the named legatee before the death of the testator does not mean a total failure of the testator's gift—

(i) The testator has intended property for a *descendant* (a son or daughter, grandson or granddaughter); the descendant has died in the testator's lifetime, but has left a descendant of his or her own. Then a legal fiction comes into operation. It is assumed that the original legatee dies immediately after, not before, the testator. The intended legacy, therefore, is looked upon as the descendant's property. If he has disposed of it in his will, it goes according to his intentions; if not, it goes to the descendant's next-of-kin.

(ii) The testator has created by his will an *entailed interest* in favour of a person, whether relative or not, who pre-deceases the testator. The entailed interest—a right that can descend on the owner's death *only* to his descendant—goes to the heirs of the legatee. For again it is assumed that this legatee dies after, not before, the testator.

DONATIO MORTIS CAUSA

(Gift made in contemplation of death.) A person, believing himself about to die, may deliver property or a document evidencing the title to property to another. This is a gift that becomes effective only upon death; if the giver recovers, he may resume the property. Such a gift, moreover, is of no effect where the deceased's estate is inadequate to meet his debts.

PERPETUITIES

The policy of the State is to make property circulate. For each change of ownership nowadays means revenue. The law, therefore, places obstacles in the way of him who would lock up property for great lengths of time. The most recent obstacle is the attack, by the Finance Act, 1930, on the making of the family into a limited liability company—which may endure indefinitely and so escape death duties. (See "Estate Duties," page 302.) So with the appointment of property by deed or by will. The deed or the will can tie up property during the lifetime of people living at the time ("lives in being") and for 21 years after the death of the last survivor (with possibly an added period for an unborn child actually conceived). This is the longest period allowed.

The settlement may be made by will. Then the measurement of the allowable period begins from the death of the testator.

A future gift evading the rule is void from the outset, even though it is unlikely that a very long period will elapse before the property is "vested" (that is, before the property comes to one who may deal with it as he chooses, all other rights being merged in his). Thus, the Court held void a bequest of "an annuity of £100 to the Central London Rangers on the appointment of the next lieutenant-colonel." For, though unlikely even with a dilatory Department, over 21 years *might* pass before the War Office appointed a successor.

The rule against perpetuities sets no limit to the enjoyment of an estate. It is enough that it has come into the hands of a legal person—a corporation, such as a limited liability company, for instance—that can sell the estate. Yet, where there is a condition attached to the gifts, the condition may invoke the rule. I bequeath land to Dr. Johnson and his heirs to the use of Guy's Hospital. That is a quite effective gift. If, however, I add, "In the event of the establishment of hospitals financed by the State the land shall go to the use of the London University," that makes the gift bad. Neither Guy's Hospital nor London University can claim the gift. For the condition may not occur within the period fixed by the rule.

VALIDATION OF CERTAIN GIFTS VOID FOR REMOTENESS

The Law of Property Act, 1925, by a statutory fiction, protects a testator in one event from the effect of his own reluctance to give uncontrolled power to a very young person. The testator's intention is not made void; it is modified. Section 163 of the Act enacts: "Where, in a will, settlement or other instrument the absolute vesting either of capital or income of property, or the ascertainment of a beneficiary or class of beneficiaries, or members of the class of an age exceeding 21 years, and thereby the gift is (or, but for this section, would be) rendered void for remoteness, the will shall take effect as though 21 years were substituted for the age stated."

"DOUBLE POSSIBILITY RULE"

This was a curious limitation on a testator's power, whereby he could not settle property under a condition depending on a condition: he could not give land for life to a son *if* a son is born and then, after the life interest, to a grandson *if* a grandson is born. This rule is abolished by the Law of Property Act, 1925 (Section 161):

"ABOLITION OF THE DOUBLE POSSIBILITY RULE.

The rule of law prohibiting the limitation, after a life interest to an unborn person, of an interest in land to the unborn issue of an unborn person is hereby abolished, but without prejudice to any other rule relating to perpetuities." That is, the general rule against perpetuities remains untouched.

ACCUMULATION OF INCOME

The Law of Property Act, 1925, also makes statutory the prohibition against the accumulating of incomes for longer than specified periods. Section 164 enacts:

GENERAL RESTRICTIONS ON ACCUMULATION OF INCOME

1. No person may settle or dispose of any property in such manner that the income thereof shall, save as hereinafter mentioned, be wholly or partially accumulated for any longer period than one of the following—

(a) The life of the grantor or settler; or

(b) A term of 21 years from the death of the grantor, settler, or testator; or

(c) The duration of the minority or respective minorities of any person or persons living or *en ventre sa mere* at the death of the grantor, settler, or testator; or

(d) The duration of the minority or respective minorities only of any person or persons who under the limitations of the instrument directing the accumulations would, for the time being, if of full age, be entitled to the income directed to be accumulated.

In every case where any accumulation is directed otherwise than as aforesaid, the direction shall (save as hereinafter mentioned) be void, and the income shall go to and be received by the person or persons who would have been entitled thereto if such accumulation had not been directed.

2. This section does not extend to any provision—

(i) For payment of the debts of any grantor, settler, testator, or other person;

(ii) For raising portions for—

(a) Any child, children, or remoter issue of any grantor, settler, or testator; or

(b) Any child, children, or remoter issue of a person taking any interest under any settlement or other disposition directing the accumulation or to whom any interest is thereby limited;

(iii) Respecting the accumulation of the produce of timber or wood;

and accordingly such provisions may be made as if no statutory restrictions on accumulation of income had been imposed.

DISPOSING OF ENTAILED PROPERTY

The Act makes possible the disposing of entailed property as though it were owned without limitation. Section 176 enacts—

1. A tenant in tail of full age shall have power to dispose by will, by means of a devise or bequest referring specifically either to the property or to the instrument under which it was acquired or to entailed property generally—

(a) Of all property of which he is tenant in tail in possession at his death; and

(b) Of money subject to be invested in the purchase of property, of which if it had been so invested he would have been tenant in tail in possession at his death;

in like manner as if, after barring the entail, he had been tenant in fee-simple, or absolute owner thereof for an equitable interest at his death, but, subject to and in default of any such disposition by will, such property shall devolve in the same manner as if this section had not been passed.

PRESUMPTION OF SURVIVORSHIP

The Law of Property Act, 1925, made yet another innovation. At Common Law there was no presumption regarding survivorship; apart from evidence the Court was not entitled to say that the strong survived the weak, nor the young the old. Section 184 of the Act now establishes the presumption: "where two persons have died in circumstances rendering it uncertain which of them survived the other, such deaths shall (subject to any order of the Court), for all purposes affecting the title to property, be presumed to have occurred in order of seniority, and accordingly the younger person shall be deemed to have survived the elder."

DECEASED'S DIRECTIONS ABOUT DISPOSAL OF BODY

A deceased's directions in his will as to the disposal of his body after death are without legal force. His executors (or administrators) may disregard his wishes.

WILLS SECRET TILL "PROVED"

A will can be published only after it has been proved in the Court, and the Court will, on suitable occasion and where no alteration in the disposal of the goods is caused, permit words to be omitted. The Court will do this (as was shown "in the Goods of *Bowker*, Probate Division, 1932), though they make no personal allusion to any individual. In the particular case, the executor supported his motion, which was granted, by swearing "that the words were offensive and objectionable and repugnant to the members of the deceased's family and, unless omitted, would be broadcast in the Press and particularly in the locality where the deceased was well known and where the deponent and other members of the family lived."

The publication of the details of a will deposited at Somerset House, before the will has been proved, is heavily penalised under the Official Secrets Act; and, of course, though wills proved are open to public inspection at Somerset House, wills unproved are kept rigorously private.

INTENTIONS OF TESTATOR ARE SOUGHT

The rules for finding out the intentions of the testator are less exacting than the rules for constructing a deed. The Courts try to obey the instructions of the testator, no matter how loosely he conveys his instructions.* Still, there must be some canons of interpretation, and, where the testator's words are ambiguous, his intentions may be defeated.

PUBLIC POLICY AGAINST BENEFIT FROM CRIME

That the person who commits murder, or any person claiming under him or her, should be allowed to benefit by his or her criminal act, would be contrary to public policy. Thus, *In re Crippen* (1911) the wife died intestate. The husband had murdered her, and his executrix and universal legatee was not allowed to take out administration, the President of the Probate Court saying: "No person can obtain or enforce any rights resulting to him from his own crime; neither can his representative, claiming under him, obtain or enforce any such rights. The human mind revolts at the very idea that any other doctrine could be possible in our system of jurisdiction."

DOMICILE MAY DETERMINE VALIDITY

Whether a will is valid or not may depend upon the domicile of the testator. Thus, one domiciled in Scotland may write out

---

* Thus, *in re Price* (Ch. 1932), the testatrix had given direction about "5% War Loan," though her securities were Treasury bonds. The Court held that she must have meant the latter: "The conclusion seems irresistible that the testatrix regarded any investment she made in securities created for the purpose of helping the country during the War as 'War Loan'; and I should be shutting my eyes to what everybody must regard as obvious if I were to hold that the misdescription is fatal to the gift."

his will in his own handwriting (*holograph will*), and it is valid even though no witnesses attest it. One domiciled in England must observe the formalities of the Wills Act in order to make a valid will. And domicile does not mean residence. Even a long stay in another country may not entail a change of domicile. For besides residence, the *intention* to change residence must be present. *Ramsay* v. *Liverpool Royal Infirmary* (H.L. 1930) is a good illustration. The testator whose will was in dispute was a Scotsman who had for many years lived in Liverpool. He had made a holograph will under which the Infirmary was a beneficiary. If, however, he had changed his domicile so that English law governed, the Infirmary would get nothing; all would pass as on an intestacy. The House of Lords decided that the testator was still domiciled in Scotland when he made his will. A change of domicile must be made *animo et facto* (by the intention and by the fact). The fact is the bare fact of residence within the new domicile. No amount of assertion of change will be effectual if unaccompanied by actual residence. But the bare fact is not enough. There must also be some evidence of intention.

LEAVING POWERS TO ANOTHER

The Court is anxious that the intentions of the deceased, as expressed in his written and witnessed instructions, shall be carried out. But it will not recognise the giving of power to another to make a will: if no clear instructions are to be found duly attested we have the Administration of Estates Act, which, in effect, makes a will for the intestate. And to leave unrestricted power to another to dispose of property is, says the law, to die intestate.

Thus, in regard to the estate of *Park* (*Public Trustee* v. *Armstrong*, Chancery, 1931), an unsuccessful attempt was made to show that the will did actually leave the disposition of the property involved to a third party, and that the Court ought to declare an intestacy. The testator had appointed the public trustee to be his sole executor and trustee. He directed that certain bequests should be paid and that the rest of the estate should be turned into money for investment. The trustee was to pay over the income from the investments to such persons (other than herself) or to such institutions as his sister should direct in writing. At her death both capital and income were to come to the Imperial Merchant Service Guild.

The judgment of *Clauson, J.*, puts the matter clearly and

brings out effectively what manner of trust it is that the Court will recognise and enforce. It illustrates also the distinction between a *general power*, unfettered in every way, so that if he chose the owner of the power could direct payment to himself, and a *particular* or *special power*, limited by precise directions of the testator. The person endowed with the power "appoints" the property; if he or she does not, then the property goes, "in default of appointment," as if no power had been given. Thus, in the case noted, whatever income the sister did not allot—"appoint"—would, on her death, go to the Merchant Service Guild.

"On the true construction of this clause it seems to me to be an absolute gift to the 'stress fund' of the Imperial Merchant Service Guild, with the proviso that during her life Jane Armstrong may by writing, to such an extent as she thinks proper, direct any part of the income to any object other than to her own personal use.

"Now, Jane Armstrong is not a trustee. If she refused to act in the matter the Court could not appoint another person to act in her place.

"It is clearly settled that, if a testator creates a trust, he must mark out the metes and bounds which are to fetter the trustee, or, as has been said, the trust must not be too vague for the Court to enforce, and that is why a gift to trustees for such purposes as they may in their discretion think fit is an invalid trust. There are no metes and bounds within which the trust can be defined, and, unless the trust can be defined, the Court cannot enforce it.

"The trust here created seems to me to be perfectly definite and marked out by definite metes and bounds. If Jane Armstrong designates a definite object in writing, that will be the object to which the trustees or the Court will apply the income. In so far as there is no such direction, the charitable gift to the stress fund of the Imperial Merchant Service Guild will operate.

"A testator must define for himself the trusts which he created; he must not leave it to his trustees to define them; he cannot leave it to his trustees to make a will for him."

Here the testator has marked out the trust quite definitely, and left nothing indefinite about the trustee's duties.

"A testator may by will confer on any person a power to appoint to whomsoever such person pleases, i.e. a general power, and also may confer on any person a power to appoint with a restriction, namely, that the appointees are to be among certain objects designated in the will, i.e. a particular power. The Court recognises the validity of a power created by will for the donee to appoint to anyone except certain persons named as indicated. I know of no authority to justify me in holding that a power to A B to appoint to any object except himself is invalid, while a power to A B to appoint to any object except to X Y is valid. I hold that the trust is an effectual and valid trust, and that the power conferred thereby on Jane Armstrong is a valid power exercisable by her."

FAILURE OF GIFT THROUGH RULE AGAINST PERPETUITIES

The case *In re* Davies (*Lloyds Bank* v. *Mostyn*, C.A., 1932) illustrates the failure of an attempted gift. Since it created a perpetuity it could succeed only if it were a "public charity"; and the Court was obliged to conclude that it was a "private charity," not "a public charity." Lloyds Bank, executor and trustee under the will, took out (as the bank was obliged to, in order to protect itself against claims by the next-of-kin) a summons in order to determine the meaning of the will. The residue of the estate, about £15,000, was left "upon trust to pay the income thereof to the Archbishop for the time being of the Archdiocese of Cardiff for work connected with the Roman Catholic Church in the said Archdiocese."

Mr. Justice Clauson thought that "work connected with the Roman Catholic Church" must cover many objects which were not, in their strict legal sense, charitable. It was not, he thought, a purely charitable gift and therefore it failed. He seems to have been most influenced by *Morice* v. *Bishop of Durham* (9 Ves.), where a gift for "such objects of benevolence and liberality as the trustee in his discretion should approve" was held not "charitable," and was therefore a gift over to the next-of-kin. The Archbishop appealed.

The Master of the Rolls, giving judgment, said that Mr. Justice Clauson had put to himself the right test when he said that he could not escape from the conclusion that the words used would cover much work which was not in the strict sense charitable. It was not every bequest which could be called charitable because the testator intended his money to be used for purposes which commended themselves to him as right and proper ones. There were many purposes importing piety, philanthropy, or benevolence which, however meritorious in themselves, were not in the strict sense charitable.

It was contended for the appellant that the words of the will meant to indicate simply the work of the Roman Catholic Church; but the words "connected with" had been used by the testatrix, and the Court must construe them. To do so could only mean that something must be added on to the scope of the ordinary work of the Roman Catholic Church, making the words used and the choice of work open to the appellant even wider than they would otherwise have been.

CONDITIONS IN A WILL

A testator may make the taking of property under the will dependent upon the fulfilment of a condition, upon the adoption perhaps of the testator's name. Where the condition is clearly against the interest of the State, the Probate Court will allow the legatee to ignore it. Where, however, the condition is not against public policy or against morality, the Court will enforce it. Whether it is a reasonable condition or not is a matter for the testator. We cannot compel a person to accept a gift; and he is entitled to decline it if he refuses to be bound by the condition attached to the gift.

"PROVING" A WILL

The property left by a testator does not, immediately on the death, become the property of the executor so that he can at once deal with it. He must first obtain permission from the Probate Court. If he meddles with the estate before obtaining this permission—before "obtaining probate" or "proving the will"—he may find himself liable to those having claims against the estate. He may become an "executor *de son tort*," a manager to his cost.

The Court obtains his promise upon oath to carry out the deceased's wishes subject, of course, to the legal claims against the estate. The Court may, indeed, also require security. It is only then that the executor (or administrator) becomes the owner of the property.

AN INTESTATE'S ESTATE

The Administration of Estates Act, 1925, enacts the following mode of disposing of the property of an intestate. Whether *real*

22

(land or what is attached to the land) or *personal* (movable property and intangible rights) the division is as follows—

1. The surviving husband or wife takes absolutely all "personal chattels," together with £1,000; and

(*a*) If there are no children and no statutory next-of-kin, then the rest of the estate absolutely. (The statutory next-of-kin are shown below.)

(*b*) If there are no children, but statutory next-of-kin, then a life-interest in the remainder.

(*c*) If there are children, then a life interest in half the remainder.

Subject to these rights of the surviving spouse, the whole of the estate passes to the following groups of persons, each to the exclusion of the following groups.

1. To *children* if any. These, no distinction being made of age or sex, share equally the income of half the estate during the lifetime of the surviving spouse, and receive the whole of the estate afterwards. If no children, then

2. To *parents* of the deceased in equal shares. If no children or surviving parents, then to the other relatives in equal shares and in the following order—

3. (*a*) To *whole-blood brothers and sisters.*
   (*b*) To *half-blood brothers and sisters.*
   (*c*) To *grandparents.*
   (*d*) To *whole-blood uncles and aunts.*
   (*e*) To *half-blood uncles and aunts.*

It will be noticed that these groups take only in the event of there being none of a preceding group alive.

4. In the event of there being no children, or parents, or statutory next-of-kin, the estate passes to the *Crown.*

BONA VACANTIA

Where there is no recognised claimant for property left by an intestate, or after the winding-up of a company, the property reverts to the Crown. As regards intestates, the Administration of Estates Act, 1925, abolished escheat; but it enacted that the estate of an intestate, without relatives in the prescribed degrees, gives to the Crown. As regards undistributed assets, coming in after the winding up, the rule is laid down in Section 296 of the 1929 Companies Act: "Where a company is dissolved, all property and rights vested in the company, immediately before its dissolution (including leasehold property but not including property held in trust for any other person) shall be *bona vacantia*, and shall accordingly belong to the Crown."

TO MAKE A WILL

The intentions of a testator as to the disposal of his property after his death need not be expressed in any particular form of words. It is enough that the property dealt with is clearly identified, and the manner of disposal stated so as to avoid possibility of mistake.

The formalities upon completion of the statement of intention are, however, important.

The *first signature* to the will must be that of the *testator*, who must write his name opposite the attestation clause in the presence of at least two witnesses, who should sign the attestation clause in the presence of the testator and in the presence of each other. The attestation clause may be in some such form as this: "Signed by the above-named.............as and for his last will in the presence of us both being present at the same time who, at his request and in the presence of each other, have hereunto subscribed our names as witnesses."

The Wills Act, 1837, which governs the formalities of execution, provides: "No will shall be valid unless it shall be in writing, and executed in manner hereinafter mentioned. It shall be signed at the foot or end thereof by the testator, and such signature shall be made or acknowledged by the testator in the presence of two or more witnesses present at the same time, and such witnesses shall attest and shall subscribe the will in the presence of the testator."

It is sufficient if a testator has already signed his will and acknowledges it as his signature to the two witnesses, all being present at the same time; it suffices, even if the witnesses had an opportunity of seeing the signature so acknowledged, though they cannot state that they did see it. But the Court must, of course, be satisfied that the signature was on the will at the time. Nor is there any set form of acknowledgment, which may be by word or act or gesture.

WHO MAY BE WITNESSES?

Any person who understands that he is providing evidence that the testator is acknowledging his signature is a competent witness. He may be a witness even if the will gives him some benefit.

But he cannot take the benefit. So far as this part of the testator's property is concerned, there is a distribution as upon an intestacy. Nor can the wife (or the husband) of a witness take any benefit under the will witnessed. It is not necessary, but it is desirable, to describe the witnesses fully. For, if question arises later about the execution of the will, these witnesses may be wanted. This rule, that a witness can take no benefit under the will he or she witnesses, has no application to the executor or executrix appointed in the will. The testator will, indeed, normally direct that the executor receives some compensation out of the estate for his work in collecting and distributing the deceased's property; and, where there is a sole legatee competent to transact business, there is no reason why he (or she) shall not also be sole executor (or executrix). The executor, or executrix, must not in such event, however, be a witness also.

CAN A WILL BE ALTERED?

Not after it has been executed. If the testator changes his intentions, he must make a new will with the same formalities as attended the first. If he wishes to add something he can do so; but this addition—this *codicil*—must be signed by the testator and witnessed as though it were a new will.

CAN A PERSON, TOO ILL TO SIGN HIS NAME EVEN BY A MARK, MAKE A VALID WILL?

Yes. It is enough that another person, in the presence of the testator and by his direction, signs the testator's name. The witness must be able to attest to the giving of the authority to sign, and must be prepared to affirm that the testator knew the contents of the will. The attestation clause should then run in some such form as this—

Signed by Henry Jones, by the direction and in the presence of the testator, Thomas Parnell, in the presence of us, who thereupon signed our names in the testator's presence and in the presence of each other, the will being first read over to the testator who appeared to understand it fully.

In a similar manner, a blind person may make a valid will.

CAN I MAKE CERTAIN OF THE SAFE-KEEPING OF MY WILL?

The Wills Department of Somerset House (Strand, London, W.C.2), takes care of wills deposited in London or at any district registry. A fee of 15s. is charged for deposit in London, 5s. in addition when deposited in a district registry. A will, once in the depository will not be given up until the testator's death, and then for probate. If the depositor wishes to destroy the will, he can do so in the presence of the Registrar. The deposit of a will in no way affects the right of the testator to revise his directions. A later will, properly executed, even if not deposited at Somerset House, will render the earlier one inoperative.

WILL MADE "IN CONTEMPLATION OF MARRIAGE"

The law, though perhaps with much creaking and groaning, is changed to meet changing needs. Formerly, the marriage of either man or woman meant an automatic revocation of a will made before the marriage. For the change of status meant so much that the intention to make a different disposition of property must be presumed. Moreover, till 1888, when a woman married, she, by the very act of marriage, assigned her proprety to her husband; any previous directions with regard to it were inoperative, and the views of the husband were not yet expressed. This general law relating to wills made before marriage remains: subsequent marriage still revokes a will made before the marriage. But the Law of Property Act, 1925, introduces this sensible modification that, when the will is made in actual contemplation of marriage, and the contemplated marriage takes place, the will is not annulled.

Pilot v. *Gainfort* (Probate Court, 1931), where a will was pronounced valid in the circumstances noted below, illustrates Section 177 of the 1925 Property Act: "a will expressed to be made in contemplation of a marriage . . . shall not be revoked by the solemnisation of the marriage contemplated." The testator had married; his wife had left him; he met the plaintiff, lived with her and bequeathed to her, "my wife, Diana Pilot, all my worldly goods." Seven years after his first wife left him he married the plaintiff. The President said: "At a time when this marriage was obviously within the contemplation of the testator, if he could validly contract it, he wrote out this holograph document, the material part of which is a bequest to the plaintiff, whom he described as his wife, of all that he had. According to the former law, the document would have been ineffective. But the testator must be taken to have had knowledge of the Act of 1925. Under the circumstances I do not think that it can be doubted that the will was in contemplation of the subsequent marriage and is good."

WITNESSES (TIME OF ATTESTING)

Note that the witnesses must sign *after* they have seen the signature of the testator appended. In a case of 1932, the probate judge, much against his will, was obliged to pronounce against a will where this was not done. The intentions of the testator were clear; he was of mental capacity for making a will; there was no suggestion of trickery. Yet, because he had asked the witnesses to sign before he did, his will was void. Where the statute lays down a strict injunction, the judge cannot exercise a discretion.

TAMPERING WITH WILLS

An attempt to defeat a testator's disposition of his property by destroying or altering his will is a serious offence, is regarded as a felony, and is punishable by penal servitude: "Whoever shall, either during the life of the testator, or after his death, steal or for any fraudulent purpose destroy, cancel, obliterate, or conceal, the whole or any part of any will, codicil, or other testamentary instrument, will be guilty of felony." Provision is made, however, that a person cannot be convicted under the Act if he has himself disclosed his fault in consequence of proceedings in a court of law.

" SECRET " TESTAMENTARY INTENTIONS

To what extent is it possible to give effect to testamentary intentions that are not contained in a written document duly executed as a will? To some extent. In *Blackwell* v. *Blackwell* (H.L. 1929) the Appeal Court held a trust "for the purposes indicated by me to them," purposes declared orally by the testator to one of the trustees, to be valid. Where there is a secret trust, or where there is a right created by a personal confidence reposed by a testator in any individual, the breach of which confidence would amount to a fraud, the title of the party claiming under the secret trust, or claiming by virtue of that personal confidence, is a title outside the will. What is enforced is not a trust imposed by the will, but one arising from the acceptance by the legatee of a trust, communicated to him by the testator, on the faith of which acceptance the will was made.

A " PUBLIC CHARITY "

Property given, either by settlement or will, to trustees for the benefit of charity must be for the accomplishment of purposes of benefit to the public at large, or to an undefined part of the public. Thus (*In re Smith, Public Trustee* v. *Smith*, Ch. 1931) the question at issue was whether a gift "to my country England" is a public charity. The contention of the claimant against the Public Trustee was that the bequest was so vague as to be void for uncertainty; it could not be held to be a charitable bequest so as to take it out of the rule against perpetuities. The Court, however, held the gift to be a valid public charity. England is an entity, and the residuary estate must be transferred to such persons as His Majesty should direct under his sign mannual: these persons would determine the purposes.

The Court, that is, leans in favour of making the testamentary dispositions of a testator effective.

Unlike a trust for definite persons, the public trust can endure as long as its purposes remain possible of accomplishment.

It is not subject to the rule against perpetuities. Moreover, even if it becomes, owing to changed conditions, undesirable to carry out the original purposes of the settler, it may be possible, with the assent of the Chancery Court, to devote the charity to other purposes "closely akin"—*cy pres* is the phrase used—to those original ones. The Court will try to decide what the settler, if he had been alive, would have arranged in the altered conditions. But, unless such a decision is fairly obvious, the failure of the original trust will mean that the property reverts to the settler or his next of kin, or failing them to the Crown as *bona vacantia*.

Public charities do not include every benevolent purpose: they are restricted to relief of poverty, advancement of education, the promotion of religion, and objects that may reasonably be supposed to benefit the public or a large portion of it. The varied judgments suggest that the question "Is this a public charity?" may well have different answers at different times and by different judges.

The public character of the trust and the fact that there are no defined beneficiaries to guard against its mismanagement, render it necessary for the Attorney-General to take charge of trusts. He may bring an action to compel the trustees to conform to the terms of the trust.

PERSONAL REPRESENTATIVE (EXECUTOR OR ADMINISTRATOR)

Till Letters of Administration are granted by the Probate Court, all the property of a deceased person vests in the Judge of the

Probate Court; when letters are granted, the property becomes that of the executor or administrator, whose duty it is to deal with the property. The executor or administrator is the "personal representative"; and, in order that he may fulfil his duty, he has all the powers of a trustee for sale, including the powers of a tenant for life under the Settled Land Acts.

The *executor* is named in (or inferred from) the will of the deceased; the *administrator* is a court agent, appointed for the purpose of settling the estate. The Grant of Probate to an executor supplies evidence of an existing title; the Grant of Letters of Administration confers a title to deal with the estate left. An executor, therefore, can begin his duties in regard to the estate at once; the administrator is obliged to await his grant. Any acts he may do pending the grant are, strictly, *ultra vires* and therefore void. But, once the grant is made, the powers conferred are "related back"; and his past acts are valid and are binding upon all parties concerned.

APPOINTMENT OF EXECUTOR OR ADMINISTRATOR

There may be—

1. An *express appointment*, as when the executor is named in the will, or when a person is named who will nominate the executor.

2. An *implied appointment*, as when a person is asked in the will to do an act coming within an executor's duties.

If no executor is named or if the person named will not or cannot act, an interested party (usually a creditor or a legatee of the deceased) applies for Letters of Administration.

QUALIFICATION

Any person of full age, not obviously disqualified for the transacting of business, may act if properly appointed by the will. Thus—

1. *Idiots* and *persons of unsound mind* cannot, in any event, obtain probate of a will.

2. An *undischarged bankrupt* will be restrained from acting by the Court of Chancery and a receiver will be appointed to perform the executor's duties. This is not refusing probate, but simply transferring it to a more competent party.

3. *Infants* cannot act until they attain majority: when infants are named in the will as executors, the guardians obtain the grant of administration "during period of pupillage" (*durante minore*

aetate); upon his attainment of majority the infant applies for grant of probate.

TRUST CORPORATIONS

Any bodies (including the Public Trustee, under the Public Trustee Act, 1906) may be executors. But the Judicature Act, 1925 (Section 161) has prohibited the Grant of Letters of Administration to the nominee of a Trust Corporation.

If the person named as executor dies, the will can be treated as though no executor had been named or as if the executor had refused to act. If an executor dies before finishing his task, it is finished by—

1. The surviving executors, where there were more than one appointed, *or by*

2. The executor named in the will of the deceased executor, *or*

3. Through the grant of letters *de bonis non administratis* (concerning goods not settled) to an interested person.

EXECUTOR DE SON TORT

One who interferes with a deceased's estate without authority may incur liabilities. He becomes "executor *de son tort*" (executor who takes upon himself personal responsibility for wrong). The duly appointed executor or administrator, on the other hand, is responsible only so far as funds from the deceased's estate come or should come into his hands. The liabilities incurred by meddlers are—

1. Penalties under the Probate Rules, 1862.

2. Possible actions for conversion by the true representative.

3. Possible actions by creditors and legatees as if he were the personal representative.

In these actions, however, he has available whatever defences would have been available to the true representative such as (*a*) the insolvency of the estate, (*b*) the stature-barring of the debt.

OTHER RULES RELATING TO EXECUTORS

1. A testator may limit the powers of an executor to dealing with part only of the estate : then a limited Grant of Probate is made ("save and except") the counterpart being a *grant caeterarum*.

2. Special executors who are trustees at death may apply for a grant limited to the settled land (Section 22, A.E.A., 1925).

3. No executor may be compelled to obtain probate, and he

may renounce the whole appointment. But he cannot, except in one instance, renounce a part only. The exception is that the executor may renounce a part of the will that concerns settled land, but may carry on with the rest (Section 23, A.E.A., 1925). An executor loses his right to apply for probate if—

(a) He dies before obtaining probate.

(b) He does not appear when cited.

(c) He renounces probate.

QUALIFICATION OF ADMINISTRATOR

Where the deceased died wholly intestate the administration shall be—

1. Unless by reason of the insolvency of the estate or any other special reason, by Letters of Administration granted to some persons interested in the estate of the deceased upon application to the Court.

2. The trustees of settled land may act if they are willing (Judicature Act, 1925, Section 162). Where the deceased leaves a number of persons interested, the Court shall decide which shall receive a Grant of Letters of Administration. Such a grant may not be given to more than four persons.

Where an infant is the beneficiary under a will or an intestacy, the administration will be given to—

1. A trust corporation; or

2. To not less than two persons.

APPOINTMENT

In general, the administrator obtains his grant of letters after a hearing in Court. By Section 167 of the Judicature Act, 1925, an administrator renders to the probate judge a bond with one or more securities. If this bond is broken, the administrator is liable for double the estate value, unless such amount is remitted by the Court.

The bond usually contains the following obligations—

1. That the administrator will make a true inventory or list of the properties of the estate.

2. That he will duly administer the estate.

3. That he will render a true account of his office.

4. That he will follow, in distributing the proceeds of the estate or the residue of the proceeds, either the will or (if there is no will) the rules of intestacy.

The Court may, however (Section 2, A.E.A., 1925) dispense with the securities to the administrator's bond when dealing with trust corporations in the capacity of administrators, but may not dispense with the bond itself.

Where the executor dies without obtaining probate, or when he cannot or will not take out probate, the Court grants Letters of Administration *cum Testamento Annexo* (with the will attached) to the principal legatee or devisee. The Court wishes that the estate shall be settled according to the desires of the testator, and to the best benefit of those interested in the estate. The Court gives its grant for a specific purpose; so the executor may himself only obtain a Limited Grant of Probate. Thus, there are limitations—

1. *Durante Minore Aetate.* During the age of minority: where an infant receives a benefit, or is appointed as the executor, the guardian receives Letters of Administration, until the infant reaches majority.

2. *Durante Dementia.* During temporary unsoundness of mind.

3. *Durante Absentia.* If after twelve months from the date of death the true personal representative is out of bounds of the jurisdiction of the High Court of Justice, any interested person may apply for Letters of Administration *durante absentia* (during the absence). In that event, the Court may order that the money and securities in the estate shall be transferred to the Court, and may hold the personal representative liable for any charges incurred when he eventually returns.

4. *De Bonis non Administratis.* (In relation to the goods not settled.)

This grant is given where—

(*a*) The sole executor dies after obtaining probate but before completion of his office.

(*b*) Where an administrator dies under the same circumstances.

5. *Pendente Lite* (pending a lawsuit).

If there is any dispute on the will or estate, the Court may appoint a fully empowered administrator, so that the estate may be represented and not be prejudiced. The Court may award him reasonable remuneration out of the estate.

6. *Ad Litem* (for the conducting of a case).

If, for any reason, the executor or administrator refuses to take part in an action, the Court may appoint an administrator of the action only. His powers cease after the action, but he may have reasonable remuneration.

PROBATE

Wills may be proved in common or in solemn form. For the latter it is necessary to undergo a Court hearing.

In both cases the executor files at the District or Principal Probate Court—

1. The Estate Duty Account.

This must be on the official form, obtainable from Somerset House, Estate Duties Department. The form itself contains full and fairly clear instructions.

2. The will and the certified epitome of it.

3. Payment of the estate duty on the estate.

This gives the executor probate in Common Form. It may, however, be revoked within 30 years, and the executor may be then called upon to prove in Solemn Form. This necessitates, in addition, that—

1. All parties interested should be cited in the Court.

2. Examination of witnesses on oath in the Court.

This solemn form of proof of probate is irrevocable.

Anyone objecting to the probate of or grant of Letters of Administration must lodge a caveat at the Probate Court. The chief grounds for opposition are concerned with lack of the mind to bequeath (*animus testandi*) or testamentary capacity on the part of a testator; or upon grounds of wrongful appointment or incapacity to act on the part of the personal representative.

Probate cannot be obtained within three days from the date of death. Letters of Administration cannot be obtained within seven days from the date of death.

DUTIES OF PERSONAL REPRESENTATIVES

These are—

1. The burial of the deceased in a manner suited to his station in life.

2. The preparation of an account of the assets and liabilities of the estate, and the rendering of it to the Inland Revenue Office.

3. The obtaining of probate of the will.

4. The getting in of all the property of the deceased and realising where necessary.

5. The advertising for, and paying of all debts and claims against the estate of the deceased.

6. The paying of legacies, legacy and other duties, and executorship expenses.

7. Dealing with the residue as instructed by the will or distributing among the next of kin in accordance with the rules of intestate succession.

8. The rendering of an account of his dealings to the persons entitled to the residue, and the obtaining of his discharge.

THE APPLICATION OF THE TOTAL ASSETS

1. *Where the Estate is Solvent.*

(*a*) Costs of realisation, (*b*) funeral and administration expenses, (*c*) debts, (*d*) pecuniary legacies, (*e*) residue.

2. *Where the Estate is Insolvent—*

(*a*) Items of 1 (*a*) and (*b*) above; (*b*) in accordance with the Bankruptcy Rules as to: Secured creditors, unsecured creditors, debts and liabilities provable, valuation of annuities, priorities of debts and liabilities.

DUTIES PAYABLE ON THE ESTATE

1. *Estate Duty* on the whole of the estate varying in amount according to the value of the estate.

2. *Succession Duty* on all land, including leaseholds.

3. *Legacy Duty* on all legacies of personal property other than leaseholds. (This duty is payable by the personal representative, but it is recoverable from the legatee.)

RIGHT OF REMUNERATION

1. For all reasonable expenses incurred. Thus where an accountant does any professional work, if he is the personal representative himself he cannot charge, but if he is employed by a personal representative the estate bears the charge.

2. Where the will authorises payment.

3. Where a judicial or public trustee is appointed.

MARSHALLING THE ASSETS

The application of assets in payment of the debts is prescribed in the Administration of Estates Act, 1925. The order is as follows—

1. Property disposed of by will, SUBJECT TO RETENTION OF FUND TO MEET THE PECUNIARY LEGACIES.

2. Residuary property, SUBJECT TO A RETENTION FOR THE PECUNIARY LEGACIES NOT SATISFIED UNDER No. 1.

3. Property left specifically for the payment of debts and liabilities.

4. Property which has been charged for the purpose of the payment of the debts.

5. The fund retained in Nos. 1 and 2 for the payment of the pecuniary legacies.

6. The specific legacies and devises, rateably according to value.

7. Property appointed by will under a general power of appointment.

EXECUTOR'S POWER TO GIVE PROPERTY

Attenborough v. *Solomon* (H.L. 1913), illustrates the difference between the legal position of an executor and that of a trustee. A testator appointed two persons as executors and trustees, giving the residue of his estate to them upon trust for distribution. Fourteen years after the death, one of the executor-trustees pledged part of the estate and appropriated the money. His fellow executor-trustee was unaware of the pledging, and the lender supposed he was dealing with the true owner. If the property was vested in executors, the pledge was valid; *for a single executor* can *deal with property*. If the property was vested in trustees, the pledge was invalid; *for the trustees must agree.* It was held that, since so long a time had passed, the executors must be taken to have assented to the trust. They were trustees, not executors.

Trustees are not one personality; there is no implied authority to bind one another, as there is in a partnership.

EXECUTORS CALLING FOR CLAIMS

When an executor advertises, calling for claims upon a deceased person's estate, he is taking advantage of the Trustee Act, 1925, passed so as to relieve him of a too long period of administration. There is no legal obligation to advertise; and, when it is quite certain that all legal claims against the deceased are known, it is needless expense to do so. But it is the executor's duty to liquidate outstanding debts before he pays over legacies, and he may find himself liable to a creditor unless he avails himself of the statutory protection. The Act requires him to advertise in the *London Gazette* and other selected newspapers, one being a local paper, calling upon creditors to make good their claim before a fixed date. The executor is thereby completely exonerated from a claim not made before the date.

The Law of Property (Amendment) Act, 1926, introduces a modification of the statutory protection. There need now be advertisement only in the *Gazette* and in one paper of the district where the property is.

The advertisement should be in this form—

MRS. CHARLOTTE BROWN, DECEASED: Pursuant to the Trustee Act, 1925. All persons having any CLAIM against the ESTATE of Mrs. Charlotte Brown, late of 25 High Street, Croydon (who died on the 20th April, 19—, and whose Will was proved by the Public Trustee and Herbert James Hunt, the Executors therein named, on the 16th day of May, 19—, in the Principal Probate Registry) are required to send particulars thereof in writing to the undersigned on or before the 31st day of July, 19—, after which date the Executors will proceed to distribute the assets having regard only to the claims of which they shall then have had notice.

Dated this 20th May, 19—.

TAMPLIN AND BERNEY, 27 Cheam Walk, Croydon,
Solicitors for the Executors.

CONTRACTS

BEGINNING OF CONTRACTUAL OBLIGATION

We have no need to incur contractual obligations; we take them upon our shoulders because it is to our interest or our pleasure to do so. Though the obligations are made binding by law, they are voluntary burdens; and the question may sometimes be a material one: at what moment did I assume those obligations? When was the law entitled to say to me: "You are bound now, it's too late to retreat?" Not that, in the overwhelming number of instances, I wish to retreat. Still, there may be occasions when I have regretted my precipitancy and should withdraw if I could. The question when the binding contract comes into being is important. It is difficult, too.

The following case, for instance, is put: "If A writes to B offering to grant a lease of an office subject to 'proper lease to be drawn up with all proper clauses and to be approved by my solicitor,' and B accepts without qualification, is there a binding contract?" It may be remarked in passing that for B to accept "without qualification" is indicative of boundless confidence in his ability to perform whatever conditions are imposed, or of boundless confidence in the fairness of the other party. In either event, he would be foolish; and the Court, not lightly imputing to a business man so complete a disregard of his own interests, would probably construe B's acceptance as conditional upon some such proviso as: "If, when I see the conditions in the lease as drawn by your solicitor, I think the conditions fair." An almost identical question was, indeed, before the Court when Mr. Winn claimed that Mr. Bull should carry out the arrangement made between them (*Winn* v. *Bull*, Ch. 1879).

AGREEMENT " SUBJECT TO CONDITIONS "

The plaintiff agreed to let the defendant have a certain dwelling-house on lease, allowing him the first year's rent "to be laid out by him in substantial repairs to the property," the signed agreement ending: "This agreement is made subject to the preparation and approval of a formal contract."

When the formal lease came, the defendant objected that it contained onerous conditions not contemplated by him; he refused to take a lease in that form; and the plaintiff brought his

682

action for specific performance of the agreement. The plaintiff failed, the Master of the Rolls saying: "I am of opinion there is no contract. The principle is clear. If in a proposed sale or lease of an estate two persons agree to all the terms and say: 'We will have the terms put into form,' then there is a contract. If two persons agree in writing that up to a certain point the terms shall be the terms of the contract, but that the minor terms shall be submitted to a solicitor, then there is no contract because all the terms have not been settled. It comes to this: where you have a proposal made in writing expressed to be subject to a formal contract being prepared, it means what it says; it is subject to and is dependent upon a formal contract being prepared."

It would have been different if the conditions of the lease had been already embodied in writing and were known to both parties. Then the offer and acceptance, though couched in general terms, would have created a binding contract.

LATITUDE FOR NEGOTIATION

English law recognises no contract except where a definite offer has been definitely accepted. There may be all sorts of preliminary inquiries, of expressions of willingness to treat, of modifications of offers made; but till the point comes when both parties are at one, without doubt or difference, there is no contract. English law gives far greater latitude than most people think to dalliance with a proposal. Even when one makes a definite offer he may withdraw it at any moment before acceptance; I bid for an article offered at auction, or rather not offered but exhibited in the hope of securing offers; I can still repent and withdraw my offer unless the auctioneer promptly clinches the matter by dropping his hammer in token of acceptance. A would-be buyer sends a telegram: "Will you sell us Bumper Hall Pen? Telegraph lowest cash price." The recipient answers: "Lowest price for Bumper Hall Pen, £900"; and to this comes the reply: "We agree to buy Bumper Hall Pen for £900 asked by you." Did this correspondence constitute a valid contract? The Court said "No." Giving of information relative to the lowest price acceptable is not an offer to sell at that price; a man usually hopes, and expects, to sell for much more than he would be prepared to accept if pushed to extremes. So, in the curious case *Canning* v. *Farquhar* (Q.B. 1885), Canning had filled in a proposal form for insurance. He was accepted subject to the condition that "no assurance can take place until the first premium is paid." He suffered a serious injury before the premium was paid; the insurance company declined to accept his premium and issue a policy; and the Court held that the company was entitled to take that course.

It is true, too, that we may—and the law countenances the action—enter into all manner of agreements without intending them to have *legal* consequences. Even in business matters, the House of Lords decided in *Rose & Frank Co.* v. *Crompton* (H.L. 1925), such agreements may be made: "The over-riding clause in the document is that which provides that it is to be a contract of honour only and unenforceable at law."

ENTERING UPON OBLIGATIONS

A moral compulsion may, indeed, exist where there is no legal compulsion; a man may think he has treated so long, has given the other party so much trouble, that it would be shabby not to conclude the bargain. Sometimes, too, the preliminary negotiations lead one almost imperceptibly to a finished contract. The timid bather deliberates long, he has many mental promptings to jump from the diving-board, he has in fact tentative bodily motions towards the water—yet he draws back in time. A moment of resolution comes and a reasonably elegant dive follows; or, maybe, he goes a little too far in his anxious bendings to look at the water below, and, not quite knowing whether he wanted to or not, he topples in. So, too, with the formation of a contract. I may negotiate long; I may never dive. But, normally, there comes a point where, whether I would or not, I cannot withdraw.

CONCLUDING OF AGREEMENTS (CONTRACTS)

In most cases it is not necessary to have an agreement in writing. It may be made quite well by word of mouth. But it is usually desirable to have the writing. For the writing acts as a record and a reminder. *Vox perit, litera scripta manet* (the spoken word ever grows fainter in our minds, the written word stands as a permanent memento) is the maxim. And in some cases writing and even a deed are necessary if the contract is to be enforceable. Parliament, for one reason or another, has prescribed the evidence that must be forthcoming. The Statute of Frauds, 1677, requiring for certain contracts written evidence to render them enforceable at law, is probably the best known of these Parliamentary requirements. It was meant to prevent litigation. It has in fact given rise to an enormous mass of litigation.

AGREEMENT UNDER SEAL

An agreement under seal, that is by means of a deed, differs from an ordinary agreement in these respects—

1. An agreement by means of a deed is binding upon the promisor even though he gets nothing (no legal consideration) from making his promise.

On the other hand, an agreement by word of mouth or in simple writing is not enforceable unless some consideration is obtained for the promise.

2. An agreement under seal may be enforced during a period of twenty years; but a simple contract is not enforceable after a period of six years.

The signatures of the parties should be appended to the agreement. There is, as a rule, no need for a witness. But it is well to have the signature attested against the possible arising of dispute.

RECOGNISANCES

These are undertakings entered into (usually by or on behalf of one who is released upon "bail," or by one against whom a person threatened has "sworn the peace,") with the Crown. They are agreements entered into with the Crown in its judicial capacity. He who enters upon a recognisance acknowledges himself to be "bound" to pay the King a specified sum. The bond is, however, expressed as being void *if* so-and-so surrenders himself for trial at the appointed place and time, or *if* so-and-so keeps the peace towards all of the King's subjects but especially towards X.Y. (the person dreading violence). Such a bond is a "promise defeasible upon condition subsequent"; the condition being the object meant to be achieved by the making of the bond.

ACCEPTANCE OF OFFER MAKES CONTRACT

An offer being accepted, a contract is made and both parties are placed under obligation towards one another. Both become bound when one is bound. But an offer, though once available for acceptance, may have ceased to be so. It may have been withdrawn by the person making it, or the person to whom it has been made has delayed long before he decided to accept. In the first case the offer has been revoked. In the second case it is said to lapse. As a well-known illustration puts it: "Acceptance is to offer what a lighted match is to a train of gunpowder. It produces something which cannot be recalled or undone. But the powder may have lain till it has become damp, or the man who laid the train may remove it before the match is applied. So an offer may lapse for want of acceptance, or be revoked before acceptance." Moreover, an offer is to be understood as rejected when the person to whom it was made makes a counter offer. "I will sell you my horse for £50," is an offer; "I will give £45 for it," is also an offer; but it is also an implied rejection of the first offer.

DEATH OF OFFEROR

The question, "Is this offer still open for acceptance?", is ordinarily easy enough to answer. Its withdrawal before acceptance, its lapsing after a reasonable time has passed, its refusal by the one to whom the offer has been made—either his direct refusal or the implied refusal through the making of a counter offer—all these admit of no doubt. The death of either the offeror or the offeree is another cause that makes an offer no longer open for acceptance. This rule may at times lead to difficulties. For, in modern business, intermediaries often come between the parties ultimately concerned; and the intermediary may go on bargaining though his principal is dead. The question may arise, therefore, whether an offer has been accepted before death, whether or not, therefore, a contract exists.

An agent may be employed to accept an offer for his principal. But, then, the power of an agent to make a valid acceptance depends upon the authority given him by his principal. And with the death of the principal the authority ceases. The question considered in *Kennedy, etc.* v. *Thomassen* (Ch. 1929) affords a good illustration of the rule that acceptance after the death of the offeree (or of the offeror) is not effective.

The plaintiffs, trustees under a will, sought in this case to recover money paid to the defendant's solicitors in accordance with an offer made by the plaintiffs. They succeeded, the judge deciding that acceptance of the offer had been communicated after the death of the person to whom the offer was made; and it was then too late.

X, living in Holland, was an annuitant under the will of which the plaintiffs were the trustees. The trustees negotiated with her for the redemption of the annuity by payment of a lump sum. The negotiations were conducted through X's solicitors. After a while these wrote to the plaintiffs that if the plaintiffs would make X an offer for £6,000 they would advise X to accept. This offer was made; and a deed of release was sent for X's signature. She executed the deed and returned it to her solicitors. A few days after her signing the deed of release, and before her solicitors had communicated her acceptance to the plaintiffs, X died.

This was unknown at the time both to the plaintiffs who paid the £6,000 and to the solicitors who received it. The matter in controversy was whether the trustees could recover the money from X's executors. The judge decided that there was no concluded contract, and that accordingly the money was recoverable. X had, it is true, sent her acceptance to her solicitors; but this sending did not complete the contract. For these were her agents, not agents of the trustees. And, since her death ended the authority given to her solicitors to act for her, their so-called acceptance was inoperative. This was so in spite of the fact that no lack of good faith was suggested.

An attempt was made to show that acceptance had been completed when X had executed the deed of release. This, it was asserted, the plaintiffs had asked to be done. It was done, and a binding contract was thereby concluded. The contention was based upon the well-known case *Carlill* v. *Carbolic Smoke Ball Co.* There it was held that the company's offer had been accepted when Mrs. Carlill had fulfilled the conditions detailed in the advertisement. Performance was acceptance. It is, indeed, beyond dispute that the offeror may indicate a mode in which acceptance of his offer should be communicated. He will then be bound by such a communication, whether it reaches him or not. Moreover, the offeror may—as when a reward is offered to the finder of lost property—invite performance without communication of acceptance. The acting on his proposal will then complete this contract.

The judgment of the Smoke Ball case stated the law thus: "Notification of acceptance is required for the benefit of the person who makes the offer. But that person may dispense with notice to himself if he thinks it desirable to do so. If the person making the offer expressly or impliedly intimates in his offer that it will be sufficient to act on the proposal without communicating acceptance of it to himself, then the performance is a sufficient acceptance without notification."

The Court very wisely refused to see in the present case a similarity. For here it was obviously understood that the mode of acceptance should be by letter posted to the offeror. And the agent's authority had ended by the death of his principal before posting.

AGENT'S ACCEPTANCE IS USUALLY EFFECTIVE

An agent is a representative employed by a principal to make contracts for him and given authority, to a greater or less extent, to act at discretion. In modern English law there is the fullest recognition of such agency, both as giving the principal a right and as imposing on him a duty: *Qui facit per alium est perinde ac si faciat per se* (one who acts through another is in the same position as if he had acted by himself). The authority ceasing, however, the principal can neither incur obligations nor obtain rights through the one who has ceased to be agent.

Clearly the authority given is terminated by the death of the principal. It is terminated also by the bankruptcy of the principal, bankruptcy being in fact a kind of temporary death, an inability for the time to enter upon any business arrangement of consequence. More doubtfully, it may be taken to cease when the principal has become mentally incapable of making contracts for himself. Nor does the fact that the agent is ignorant of the cessation of the authority affect the matter. Thus, in *Yonge* v. *Toynbee* (K.B. 1910), a firm of solicitors was instructed to defend a libel action. The defendant became insane; but this fact was not communicated to the firm, which continued to act. Yet they were held liable to all costs incurred on both sides from the date of the insanity of the defendant. For it was their continuing the case, though their authority to do so had ceased, that gave rise to those costs.

STATEMENT OF INTENTION

A mere statement of intention cannot be treated as an offer capable of being turned into a binding contract by being accepted. In *Spencer* v. *Harding* (Q. B. 1870) an attempt failed to make the defendants act upon a circular: "We are instructed to offer to the wholesale trade for sale by tender the stock in trade." There is a distinction between definite *offers* (that may be turned into binding contracts by being accepted) and *undertakings to consider offers* (that impose no liability upon the party giving the under-taking). The circular did not compel the advertiser to accept the highest (or any tender): it was "a mere proclamation that the defendants are ready to chaffer for the sale of the goods and to receive offers for the purchase of them." Though the advertise-ment was awkwardly couched—"We are instructed to offer to the wholesale trade for sale by tender"—it could not be regarded as an offer. It was an invitation to make offers.

AN ACCEPTANCE

To be effective an acceptance must—

1. Be made before the offer has been revoked, or has lapsed.
2. Be communicated to the offeror.
3. Not introduce any variation of the terms proposed.

With regard to 1 it should be noted that a revocation is effective only from the time when it is brought to the notice of the offeree. On the other hand, an acceptance is complete as soon as the offeree's agreement to the terms proposed has been signi-fied in the manner indicated or suggested by the offeror. A revocation is then too late, even though the acceptance has not been actually received by the offerer.

What constitutes a reasonable time for acceptance varies with the nature of the offer. The time may be fixed in the offer; after that fixed time the offer automatically lapses, though it can be revoked before that time if unaccepted. An offer also lapses after a reasonable time has passed. Then an attempted acceptance is merely an offer which the original offeror can accept or reject as he chooses. An acceptance with modification of the terms of the offer is a new offer, and is construed as a rejection of the offer made.

BUYING AN OPTION

It should be noticed that the party who wishes to have an offer kept open may, by paying an agreed sum, buy an option. He obtains time during which an acceptance makes a binding con-tract: the offeror cannot withdraw the offer until the expiration of the stipulated period. The buying of an option is a contract quite distinct from the main contract; the main contract, indeed, may never be entered into. What the offeree buys is an exten-sion of time within which to make up his mind. What the offeror sells is his freedom to revoke the offer before the stipulated time.

STATEMENTS NOT ALWAYS OFFERS

It remains to note that statements may be made and be acted upon by the other party that do not contemplate legal obligations. Domestic and social arrangements are illustrations. In *Balfour* v. *Balfour* (K.B. 1919), Lord Justice Atkin became quite lyrical over agreements between husband and wife: "The Common Law does not regulate the form of agreements between spouses. Their promises are not sealed with seals and sealing wax. The consideration that really obtains for them is that natural love and affection which counts for so little in these cold Courts."

CREATION OF A CONTRACT

A contract is formed when a definite offer has been definitely accepted. The offer may be accepted by writing or by word of mouth. The offer may even be accepted and a binding contract be concluded by a person's doing what the offer suggests: "When an offer has been made to another party, and in that offer there is a request, express or implied, that he must signify his acceptance by doing some particular thing, then as soon as he does that thing, the offeror is bound. If a man sent an offer abroad to take goods at a price, adding: 'If you agree, ship the first cargo as soon as you get this letter,' there is no doubt that as soon as the cargo was shipped the contract would be complete; and if the cargo went to the bottom of the sea it would be to the loss of the orderer" (*Brogden* v. *Metropolitan Ry. Co.*, A.C. 1877).

SALE WITHOUT RESERVE

The putting up of property at an auction advertised as "without reserve" is an undertaking to accept the highest offer; and when the highest bid is made, there is a binding contract between the auctioneer and the bidder. "The sale," ran one judgment, "was announced 'without reserve'. This means that neither the vendor nor any person on his behalf shall bid at the auction, and that the property shall be sold to the highest bidder, whether the sums bid be equivalent to the real value or not. We cannot distinguish the case from that of the loser of property offering a reward, or that of a railway company publishing a time-table. It has been decided that the person giving the information advertised for, or a passenger taking a ticket, may sue as on a contract with him."

ADVERTISEMENT AS OFFER

So, since the *Carbolic Smoke Ball Case* (Q.B. 1892), it has been repeatedly held that one who fulfils the conditions of an advertisement is entitled to hold the advertiser to his offer. In *Wood* v. *Letrik Limited* (K.B. 1932), the plaintiff obtained judgment for £500 because an electric comb failed to do what was promised: it would not restore his hair, going grey, to its original colour. "It was," said Mr. Justice Rowlatt, "rather a windfall for the plaintiff. But I do not see why Mr. Wood should not say: 'Here is a man who says that my hair will be turned to the colour of my boyhood and if it is not, I shall get £500. I will try it.' A man is entitled to remain an elderly optimist. We must assume that Mr. Wood bought and tried the comb in good faith, hair restoration not reward being his primary purpose."

CONTRACT UNDER SEAL (" SPECIALTY CONTRACT ")

This is a written promise accompanied by a number of formalities. The person giving the promise—

1. *Signs the paper.*
2. *Seals it,* that is, *he places upon it a piece of wax or lead or other material with a device on it to guarantee the authenticity of the document.*

(In days when the power to write was narrowly confined, this sealing was the only "signature" that most people could make.)

This sealing is almost invariably witnessed. An Act of Parliament in some instances makes a witness (or witnesses) necessary to the validity of a deed. In an ordinary agreement under seal, however, the "witnessing" of a signature proceeds from what is sometimes called the excess of caution on the lawyer's part. The "attesting" makes provision against the possibility of a disputed signature. The witness is, however, not necessary to the validity of a deed. The deed becomes operative when its maker—

3. *Delivers it—*

He places his finger on the seal and says: "I deliver this as my act and deed."

It is then, we say, *executed*—made conclusive as between the parties.

A deed which sets out in formal fashion a bargain between two or more parties is often called an "Indenture." Such is the partnership agreement given on page 374.

A deed which sets out in formal fashion and which is available as evidence of a single person's undertaking, is often called a "Deed Poll." The terms are reminiscent of ancient custom: the formal contract was once written on a single piece of paper or of parchment, which was then cut into two, and the edges being designedly irregular (indented). The counterparts would be handed to each of the two consenting parties, the possibility of fitting the parts together again, if necessary, serving to identify the agreement. The deed poll was made with smooth (polled) edges. Such is the deed of gift below.

In modern times the seal is a formality only. Formerly, the seal betokened the individuality of the man. He was in no danger from forged grants of his land, so long as he kept his seal carefully. A man may say that this formality—of sealing, signing, and delivering a deed—is a quite foolish survival of what, in simpler times, may have had a real purpose. Perhaps he would be right. Yet if, in certain business transactions, he ignores the formality, he suffers from his resolution to take no part in the foolishness. For the law ignores his transaction. The doing of what we might think applicable to the dark ages only is needed in what we consider our enlightened times.

CHARACTERISTICS OF PROMISES UNDER SEAL

A promise made with these ancient formalities has some differences from a simple contract (one entered into by word of mouth or by ordinary writing)—

1. *A man is not allowed to disprove what he asserts as facts in his deed* (see Rule of Estoppel, p. 893).

2. *Right of action, in order to enforce the contract, is not barred until the lapse of twenty years ; right of action under a simple contract is barred after six years.*

3. *A gratuitous promise (one for which the promisor gets nothing in return) is binding under seal ; it is of no legal effect if made by word of mouth or in writing not under seal.*

Thus, if a man wishes to make a gift to his wife of the house in which he lives, or the furniture in their joint possession, he can only do so by executing a "deed of gift." Making the gift by word of mouth, even before a multiplicity of witnesses, is not effective: in the event of the man's bankruptcy the things he tried to give may yet be taken to pay his debts. Such a deed of gift is the following—

THIS DEED OF GIFT made the

day of   19

BETWEEN

of

(hereinafter called the Grantor) of the one part

and

wife of the said

(hereinafter called the Donee) of the other part.

Witnesseth that in consideration of the natural love and affection of the Grantor for the Donee the Grantor as Beneficial Owner hereby assigns unto the Donee ALL THAT the household furniture chattels and effects now in or upon the dwelling-house occupied by the Grantor and the Donee at

aforesaid except money and securities for money all of which said furniture chattels and effects are particularly set forth in the schedule hereto TO HOLD the same unto the Donee absolutely as and for her separate property free from all rights and control of the Grantor.

IN WITNESS whereof the said parties to these presents have hereunto set their hands and seals the day and year first above written.

THE SCHEDULE above referred to—

(Here follows a list of goods included in the gift)

SIGNED SEALED AND DELIVERED by

the said

in the presence of—

{ Here is the signature and the description of a witness }

SIGNED SEALED AND DELIVERED by

the said

in the presence of—

{ Here is the signature and the description of a witness }

It should be noted that the possession of the goods noted must be given up by the grantor of the deed of gift. If he should retain possession, his deed would need registration as a Bill of Sale (see Bills of Sale, page 524).

FIDELITY BOND

So, too, to be operative, a fidelity bond must be under seal; for it is a gratuitous promise, made by an insurer to an employer.

that an employee will be honest. The bond is expressed as being void if the employee faithfully fulfils his duties.

Note that, though the insurer binds himself to pay a lump sum, the employer can recover only the actual loss he sustains through the dishonesty of his employee.

CONTRACT UNDER SEAL NEEDED

A deed is essential for the validity of—

1. *A transfer of a British ship, or a share in it (a form of transfer is given in the Merchant Shipping Act*, 1894).

2. *A lease of land or building for more than three years.*

3. *A gratuitous promise*, i.e. one where there is not material consideration for the promise made on one side and accepted on the other. I can make a gift—

    (*a*) *By handing over the thing with the intention of giving it ; or*

    (*b*) *By executing a deed of gift* (see above).

4. *Assignment of a lease or of sculpture.*

5. *Contracts with corporations (including limited liability companies).*

The exceptions to the last, however, have almost eaten up the rule : "A company can only carry on business by agents, managers, and others ; and if the contracts made by these persons relate to the objects and purposes of the company, and are not inconsistent with the rules and regulations which govern their acts, they are valid and binding on the company, though not under seal." The rule remains, though, where an Act of Parliament prescribes a deed. The Public Health Act, 1875, enacts that contracts of an urban authority, involving over £50, must be under seal. In *Nixon* v. *Erith U.D.C.* (K.B. 1924) the urban council obtained the full benefit of a contract, but had a complete defence to a claim for payment in the absence of a scaled writing : "There being no contract under seal the plaintiff cannot recover."

A deed may be prepared, the seal affixed, and the signature of the party promising may be appended. Till it is "delivered," however, till the person executing it goes through the ancient formalities, it remains what is called an *escrow* (or "scroll") : the delivery puts it into effect. If a condition should be attached, the document remains an escrow till the condition is fulfilled.

CONTRACTS NEEDING WRITTEN EVIDENCE

Certain statutes prescribe written evidence. Where such evidence is not available the contracts noted below cannot be enforced; they may be quite valid in law, but for want of the requisite evidence they cannot be sued upon.

1. The Companies Act, 1929, prescribes a written form of transfer and acceptance of shares in a company.

2. The Copyright Act, 1911, enacts that an assignment of copyright must be in writing.

3. The Railways Act, 1921, requires special contracts for carriage of goods to be in writing.

4. The Sale of Goods Act, 1893, requires (in the absence of certain conditions) writing for contracts for the sale of goods worth £10 or over.

5. The Statute of Frauds, 1677 (in part repealed and re-enacted by the Law of Property Act, 1925), enacts that no action shall be brought, in the case of certain specified contracts, unless some note of the agreement shall be in writing, signed by the defendant or his agent. These contracts are: i. *Promises by an executor or administrator to answer damages out of his own estate*; ii. *Guarantees* (special promises to answer for the debt, default, or miscarriage of another); iii. *Agreements made in consideration of marriage*; iv. *Transfers of an interest in land or buildings*; v. *Agreements that are not intended to be fully performed within a year from the making*.

STATUTE OF FRAUDS

The statute was passed with a view to limiting litigation; it was thought that, by reason of the written evidence available, there would be fewer disputes. In fact, the statute has given rise to more litigation than any other. The statute was meant to be a shield against fraud. It became a means of evading liabilities. From the beginning men tried to get out of their obligations by pleading the statute; from the beginning the judges have whittled away its effect. Thus, very soon, it was settled that promises to marry could be sued upon without there being writing: "An agreement in consideration of marriage" applied, it was held, only to collateral agreements.

And, if what one party undertakes to do is intended to be done within a year, the statute does not apply: the statute applies only when it appears "by the whole tenor of the agreement that it is to be performed after the year." Peter was apparently a confirmed bachelor; Compton one day jokingly said: "Give me a guinea now, and I will give you a thousand guineas on your wedding day." "Done," said Peter, and paid the guinea. Two years later Peter married, and then claimed the promised guineas. Compton demurred and, when Peter brought his action, sought to support his refusal by the Statute of Frauds. His defence failed, however, the judges holding that the clause applied only to such agreements as are *incapable of performance within the year*; and Peter might have married the very day after the agreement (*Peter* v. *Compton*, 1694).

The strangest departure from what Parliament probably intended when it passed the Act is the admitting, as the requisite evidence, of writing made before or after the actual agreement. So long as the parties to the contract and the subject matter of their agreement are clear from the writing, and so long as it is signed by the party who is to be made defendant, that is taken to satisfy the statute. Actually a letter in which a defendant repudiated a contract was accepted as the written evidence to make him liable (*Buxton* v. *Rust*, Ex. 1872).

Possibly, too, "agreements made in consideration of marriage" were intended to have a wider scope than their modern limited one. They are now restricted to promises to pay money or settle property in consideration of a marriage actually taking place; they do not include promises to marry though at first thought to do so.

THE WRITING REQUIRED

The statute prescribes "some memorandum or note in writing" as the requisite evidence to make the contract enforceable. The Courts have explained that this does not mean "a document in writing." For many documents, capable of being connected with one another by outside evidence, have been admitted as "some memorandum." One party to the contract signs a rough draft of its terms; when the draft has been corrected, he acknowledges his signature. That supplies the evidence. It is even held that evidence by word of mouth may be admitted to connect two documents, where each obviously refers to another, and where the two thus connected give the complete contract without further explanation.

So, too, we have what is called the "equitable doctrine of part performance": when one party, acting in accordance with the contract, does the whole or part of what he has promised to do, and the other party has accepted what has been done, this is evidence enough to supply the lack of written evidence. The defendant agreed, by word of mouth not by writing, with the plaintiff to buy a plot of land on which the plaintiff would build a dwelling-house according to the defendant's special plan. This agreement is contemplated by the statute : it is one for the buying of an interest in land. Consequently, written evidence should be available. But during the building of the house the defendant often came, asked for alterations and additions, and had her wishes granted. Being sued on her refusal to carry out her bargain, she pleaded the Statute of Frauds. But the Court declared the alterations to be available to prevent the defence (*Dickinson* v. *Barrow*, Ch. 1904).

The Moneylenders Act, 1927 (Section 6) makes necessary a written memorandum signed by the borrower of any contract to repay money lent on interest. Within seven days a copy must be delivered to the borrower. Without such evidence the money-lender cannot enforce the contract, nor can he avail himself of a security given. It should be noted that the memorandum must be signed before the money is lent. It is not possible, as it is with contracts covered by the Statute of Frauds, to have the written evidence supplied subsequently to the making of the contracts.

GRATUITOUS PROMISE

Under English law a promise, in return for which the promisor gets nothing, has no legal effect unless made in a writing under seal : "If a person undertakes to perform a voluntary act, he is liable if he performs it improperly, but not if he neglects to perform it." Thus, a promise to release the residue of a debt upon payment of a smaller sum does not prevent the creditor from suing for the residue : he gets nothing for his promise, since the debtor did no more than he was legally bound to do.

" CONSIDERATION " IN CONTRACT

It should be noted, however, that the Courts will consider that a man has had something in return for his promise—"considera-tion for the promise" is the phrase—even when he has been benefited only very slightly. The comprehensive definition is : "A valuable consideration in the sense of the law may consist either in some right, interest, profit, or benefit accruing to one party, or some forbearance, detriment, loss, or responsibility given, suffered, or undertaken by the other." In one strange case Bainbridge owned two boilers. Firmstone asked to weigh them, undertaking to return them in as good a condition as when lent ; he took them to pieces for convenience of weighing, returned them in pieces, and was held liable in damages. "The consideration," said the Court, "is that the plaintiff, at the defendant's request, allowed the defendant to weigh the boilers. I suppose the defendant thought he had some benefit: at any rate there is a detriment to the plaintiff from his parting with the possession for ever so short a time." (*Bainbridge* v. *Firmstone*, 1838, A. & E.)

RULES RELATING TO CONSIDERATION

The rules evolved in English law in regard to consideration are these—

1. *For every promise (other than one under seal) consideration is necessary if the Court is to enforce it.* The rather cynical view is that a man makes no promise unless he gets something for making it: "It is undoubtedly true," said a famous chief baron, "that every man is by the law of nature bound to fulfil his engagements." It is equally true that the law of this country supplies no means nor affords any remedy to compel the performance of an agreement made without sufficient consideration. Such an agreement is *nudum pactum ex quo non oritur actio* (a bare promise which affords no basis for an action).

2. *The Courts are not concerned with the adequacy of the consideration : that is a matter for the parties themselves.* So long as a man gets what he bargained for, the other party can enforce the contract. In *De la Bere* v. *Pearson* (K.B. 1908) the plaintiff suffered loss through following advice given by the defendant. He sued for damages; the defendant pleaded "no consideration, no contract "; the Court, however, held that there was sufficient legal consideration for the promise. "The defendants advertised, offering to give advice with regard to investments. The plaintiff, accepting that offer, asked for advice, and asked the name of a good stockbroker. The questions and answers were, if the defendants chose, to be inserted in their paper as published; such publication must obviously have a tendency to increase the sale of the defendant's paper. I think that this offer, when accepted, resulted in a contract for good consideration." The consideration may, indeed, be so trifling as to need a good deal of thought to find it.

3. *A past consideration is no consideration on which to found an action.* For, though the promisor had obtained something and might be expected to show gratitude, he need not have given the promise. Yet, if the consideration was rendered at the request of the defendant, and if it is reasonable to suppose that at the time

there was an understanding that a reward would be given, the consideration is good. In the old case, *Lampleigh* v. *Braithwaite*, decided in 1615, the plaintiff sued on a promise to pay £100 for services rendered at the defendant's request. The defendant had feloniously killed a man and anxiously asked the plaintiff "to labour and do his endeavour to obtain pardon from the King." This the plaintiff did making many journeys, though apparently the pardon did not result from the plaintiff's efforts. The defendant afterwards promised the money. At the trial it was decided "that a mere voluntary courtesy [a gratuitous act] will not have a consideration to uphold an Assumpsit [a promise]. But if that courtesy were moved by a suit or request of the party that gives the Assumpsit, it will bind. For the promise, though it follows, yet it is not naked, but couples itself with the suit before." The request (or suit), that is, may imply a promise to pay; the subsequent promise of a definite sum may be treated as a bargain which fixes the amount of the reasonable remuneration on the faith of which the service was rendered.

We may perhaps say that, when a promise has been given, the Courts will try to find a consideration in order to make it enforceable. Thus, the payment by the debtor of a smaller sum is no good discharge of a debt of a larger sum, even if the creditor promises to accept the smaller sum in full satisfaction. Yet, if the payment is in any way different from what the creditor could have insisted upon, the debtor is fully discharged. Thus, the creditor can insist upon full payment of the amount due in legal tender; if he offers to accept a cheque for a smaller amount, the debtor is discharged. For a creditor cannot demand to be paid by cheque. Drake owed Wilby £18 3s. 11d.; for Wilby was holder of a bill, drawn by Drake, that had not been accepted. Wilby agreed that if Drake's father paid £9, he would take it in full satisfaction. The father did so pay; Wilby sued for the balance, but failed: "If the father did pay the smaller sum in satisfaction of the debt, it is a bar to the plaintiff's now recovering against the son; because by suing the son he commits a fraud on the father, whom he induced to advance his money on the faith of such advance being a discharge of his son from further liability" (*Wilby* v. *Drake*, 1825, C. & P.).

ABSENCE OF EVIDENCE

It is important from the practical point of view to note the result of the absence of the prescribed evidence.

23

When an Act of Parliament calls for specific evidence of a transaction, the Court cannot recognise the transaction in the absence of the evidence. Business men do; for business men fulfil their obligations not because the law constrains them to do so. They fulfil them because they are honourable business men; and a surprisingly large number of bargains are faithfully carried out when there is no legal compulsion to do so. It is enough that an undertaking has been given. Still, it is desirable to recognise the distinction between a moral claim and a legal claim.

Thus, the trustee in bankruptcy may find himself obliged to ignore the moral claim of one creditor in order not to deny the legal claim of another creditor. The legal results of initialing a marine insurance policy affords as good an illustration as can be wished of the distinction. (See page 876, where a case in point is discussed).

MISTAKE AND CONTRACT

Can one be relieved of liability under a contract because he was mistaken when he entered into it? Only rarely.

1. He is sometimes protected by statute as when he buys seeds "tested in accordance with the Seeds Act, 1920."

2. There are also certain contracts, like insurance, where the utmost good faith on both sides is required: if a man enters into such a contract and the other party has concealed a material fact, he can avoid the contract.

3. And if the mistake has been actively induced by the other party he has his remedies—

   (a) He may rescind the contract.

   (b) He may sue for damages for the fraud.

Ordinarily, however, he must abide by his bargain. He must not assume that every one with whom he deals will act with scrupulous good faith. He must exercise care (caveat emptor); if the terms of the bargain are unfavourable to him, he has only himself to blame. For he has reached maturity of judgment, and he may propose what terms he pleases.

CAVEAT EMPTOR

The other party is under no legal obligation to disclose what might make the bargain more unfavourable to himself. A seller is under no obligation to disclose the existence even of hidden defects in his wares; he is only liable if, by act or implication, he represents such defects to be absent. "Ordinarily, the failure to disclose a material fact which may influence the mind of a prudent contractor does not give the right to avoid the contract." So declared Lord Atkin in his judgment allowing the appeal of their former servants against Lever Brothers. These servants had obtained large sums of money for giving up their contracts of employment; and facts had afterwards emerged which showed that these sums need not have been paid (*Lever* v. *Bell*, 1932).

"The servant," explained Lord Atkin, "owes a duty not to steal. But having stolen is there super-added a duty to confess that he has stolen? I am satisfied that to imply such a duty would be a departure from the well-established usage of mankind, and would be to create obligations entirely outside the normal contemplation of the parties concerned. If a man agrees to raise his butler's wages, must the butler disclose that two years ago he received a secret commission from the wine merchant. And, if the master discovers it after the servant has left, can he avoid the agreement and get back the extra wages paid? I think not."

The Court cannot imply terms into a contract. We must have certainty in contract; and, if it were possible to modify, we should have doubt and confusion where certainty is essential.

The law, it is true, will not allow a man to have the benefit of a bargain when he knows that the other party understands the bargain in a different sense from that in which he himself understands it. Apart from this a bargainer must look after himself. "If, whatever a man's real intention may be, he so conducts himself that a reasonable man would believe that he was assenting to the terms proposed by the other party and that other party upon that belief enters into the contract with him, the man thus conducting himself would be equally bound as if he had intended to agree to the other party's terms."

A much discussed case (*Smith* v. *Hughes*, Q.B. 1871), illustrates the latitude given by our English law to bargainers. A man may not make or accept a promise, when he knows that the other party understands it in a different sense from that in which he understands it himself. But a man is under no legal obligation to undeceive a self-deceiver. Hughes, a horse-trainer, obtained a sample of oats from Smith. Hughes wanted old oats and thought, from the sample, that the oats offered were old. He bought them; but, on learning that they were new oats, he refused to accept them. The judge in the lower court considered Hughes to be justified in refusing. But on appeal the Court of Queen's Bench sent the case for a new trial : Smith could recover if he had known that Hughes thought he was buying old oats ; Smith could not recover if he had known that Hughes thought he was being promised old oats. The burden was upon the defendant to show that Smith did know this.

"In this case I agree that on the sale of a specific article, unless there be a warranty making it part of the bargain that it possesses some particular quality, the purchaser must take the article he has bought though it does not possess that quality.

" And I agree that even if the vendor was aware that the purchaser thought that the article possessed that quality, and would not have entered into the contract unless he had so thought, still the purchaser is bound, unless the vendor was guilty of some fraud or deceit upon him, and that a mere abstinence from disabusing the purchaser of that impression is not fraud or deceit; for whatever may be the case in a court of morals, *there is no legal obligation* on the vendor to inform the purchaser that he is under a mistake, not induced by the act of the vendor." The defendant believed the oats to be old. The plaintiff was conscious of the existence of such belief. But he did nothing, directly or indirectly, to bring about the belief. He offered his oats and exhibited his sample, remaining passive as to what was happening in the mind of the other party. Did the passive acquiescence of the seller in the self-deception of the buyer entitle the buyer to avoid the contract? The Court agreed that it did not.

BUYING OF SHARES

Full disclosure is called for in a prospectus. The omission, however, if it is to give a right of rescinding, must actually be misleading. The position was stated in *New Brunswick Railway Co.* v. *Muggeridge* (1860) ; and the Companies Act, 1929, makes the obligation upon share sellers a statutory one :

"Those who issue a prospectus holding out to the public the great advantage which will accrue to persons who will take shares in a proposed undertaking, and inviting them to take shares on the faith of the representations therein contained, are bound to state everything with strict and scrupulous accuracy, and not only to abstain from stating as fact that which is not so, but to omit no one fact within their knowledge the existence of which might in any degree affect the nature, or extent, or quality of the privileges and advantages which the prospectus holds out as inducements to take shares."

CONTRACT OF GUARANTEE

In this contract, too, the surety must be kept informed by the creditor (whose debt he guarantees) of any agreement altering the relations of creditor and debtor, or of any other matter giving him a right to cancel his contract.

The guarantee (or surety) is given to the creditor (not to the debtor); and the guarantor is liable only on the failure of the debtor (who is primarily responsible) to fulfil his obligation. Like all other written agreements not under seal it requires a six-penny stamp.

The written evidence called for to make a guarantee enforceable need not, since the Mercantile Law Amendment Act, 1856, contain a note of the consideration for the promise: "No special promise made by any person after the passing of this Act to answer for the debt, default, or miscarriage of another person, being in writing and signed by the party to be charged or some other person authorised by him, shall be deemed invalid to support an action by reason only that the consideration for such promise does not appear in writing."

INDEMNITY, DISTINCT FROM GUARANTEE

An indemnity, which in some respects is like a guarantee, differs from it in this: an indemnity (a promise to see that a person suffers no loss) makes the promisor liable to remedy a loss, however the loss occurs; a guarantee makes the promiser liable only in the event of the default of the primary debtor. An indemnity needs no formal evidence; it is valid and enforceable though made by word of mouth. A man may, therefore, be concerned to show that a promise he made is a guarantee (for in the absence of writing he is not liable) and not an indemnity (for which he is liable). In *Harburg India Rubber Comb Company* v. *Martin* (K.B. 1902) the defendant orally promised the plaintiffs that he would endorse bills drawn on a company in which he was interested.

The plaintiff company had obtained judgment against the debtor company, and had delivered a writ of *fi. fa.* for the execution of the judgment. The defendant made his oral promise and thereby obtained the release of the goods. It was held that the promise was one of indemnity, not of guarantee: there was no expectation of payment by a primary debtor.

INDEMNITY

To indemnify a person is to make good a loss he has sustained; a contract of indemnity is an undertaking to make good a loss in a specified event. Thus, if by accident I lose or destroy a cheque sent to me in payment, I can require my debtor to pay another. But he is entitled to ask for an indemnity: if the first cheque he has paid should get into circulation and he be obliged to pay it, I must recoup him. Here is a letter of indemnity in relation to a lost share certificate.

I, Tom Smith, do hereby desire the A.B. Company Ltd., to issue a Certificate to me for Ordinary Shares in lieu of Certificate No.
dated　　　　　　　which has been lost by me, and in consideration of the Company so doing I hereby agree to indemnify the said Company against all claims, demands, and charges which may be brought against the said Company by reason of the issuing to me of the said Certificate.

　　　　　Dated this　　　　　　day of

Signed by the said Tom Smith

in the presence of

Name and description　　　————————————————　　6d.

of Witness who attests　　　————————————————　　Stamp.

An old case, *Birkmyr* v. *Darnell* (1704, 1 Salkeld), gives a good illustration of the difference between a guarantee and an indemnity.

"If two come to a shop and one buys, and the other, to gain him credit, promises the seller '*If he does not pay you, I will*,' this is a collateral undertaking and void without writing by the Statute of Frauds (i.e. it is a guarantee, which is enforceable only if evidenced by writing). But if he says: '*Let him have the goods, I will be your paymaster*,' or '*I will see you paid*,' this is an undertaking as for himself, and he shall be intimated to be the very buyer and the other to act as but his servant" (i.e. there is an indemnity, a promise to preserve from loss). Perhaps "unenforceable without writing" would be a more accurate phrase than "void without writing": the contract of guarantee is perfectly valid, it is only the absence of writing that makes it unenforceable. See page 358 for a difference between an indemnity and a *del credere* agency agreement.

AN ENDORSEMENT IS A GUARANTEE

It is worth remembering that, whenever a man places his name upon the back of a cheque he becomes a guarantor. He promises the person who takes the cheque from him that, in the event of its not being met, he himself will meet it.

GUARANTOR'S RIGHTS

When a guarantor has discharged a debt under the guarantee he has given—

1. He can claim against the primary debtor for the amount paid.

2. He has a right to take the creditor's place towards the primary debtor (a right of subrogation); thus securities deposited in regard to the debt must be transferred to him.

3. He can obtain contribution from a co-surety, if any.

RELEASE OF A GUARANTOR

1. When there is an alteration (without the guarantor's knowledge) of the contract between creditor and the debtor, the guarantor is discharged: "If there is any agreement between the principals with reference to the contract guaranteed, the surety ought to be consulted." In *Ellesmere Brewery Co.* v. *Cooper* (Q.B. 1896), four persons executed a joint and several bond of suretyship, the liability of two being limited to £25 each, of the other two to £50 each. One of the latter, executing the bond after the other three, added "£25 only" to his signature; and the creditor accepted the bond without objection. This material alteration released the first three sureties.

2. If the creditor gives time to the principal debtor, the surety is discharged. For the creditor has deprived the surety of his remedies against the debtor—for a time only, it is true; but then the remedies may be lost through lapse of time. In *Midland Motor Showrooms* v. *Newman* (K.B. 1929), a surety was held discharged from liability where, under a hire-purchase agreement, the creditor had given time for payment of instalments in arrears.

A case that came before the Court of Appeal in 1932 illustrates the point (*Eshelby* v. *Federated European Bank, Ltd.*). A surety is discharged unless the creditor informs him promptly of any default on the part of the primary debtor; and the contract of surety may indicate the degree of promptitude. Two Italians in Soho were converting an old pickle factory into a night club. Eshelby contracted to design and execute work on the building. Payment was to be by instalments as the work proceeded. The parties to the agreement with the contractor were a company called Olympas, Ltd. (controlled by Taglioni, one of the Italians), Taglioni himself, and the bank (of which the other Italian was managing director). The principal debtor was Olympas, Ltd. Taglioni undertook that upon any default for three days or more ("written notice of which shall be given by the contractor to the guarantor within six days of such default") he would make the payment. The bank became surety for Taglioni on similar conditions.

Olympas, Ltd., failed to make the stipulated payment. The appellant, possibly because he knew that Taglioni was well aware of the default, gave no written notice within the time stated. Such omission barred his claim upon the guarantors, in spite of the fact that these guarantors were virtually the debtors : " This is an unsatisfactory case because the respondents have no merits. The event on which Taglioni has agreed to make the payment is not the default by itself but upon notice of default. The notice is just as much a condition on which Taglioni becomes liable as the default itself is. Inasmuch as the notice was never given there was no default on the part of Taglioni ; and therefore the liability of the respondents never came into existence."

3. Where, in the case of a "fidelity guarantee," the employee's duties have been changed, the surety, unless assenting to the change, is discharged from liability.

NOTICES, WHEN EFFECTIVE

A man may be under obligation though he is unaware of it. But no one can place him under an obligation by notices ineffectively displayed.

The law relating to these was stated in *Lewis* v. *Dart* (K.B. 1932), a case where a motor-car owner recovered against a garage proprietor. An employee of the defendant had stolen the car; and, on the ground of negligence and breach of contract, the defendant was adjudged to pay. He pleaded that the car was garaged on the terms that no responsibility for theft or damage was taken. There was, in fact, a notice to this effect; but the owner could, and did, assert that he had not seen it. "When a person in the position of the defendant seeks to protect himself from a liability which the law would otherwise cast on him, he must do it clearly and unambiguously, and must show that the terms of the contract were accepted by the other party. The best way of doing that is to get the terms set out and the owner of the car to sign the form. Or there should be a receipt on which the terms are pointed out. A third method is to exhibit a notice in such a way that the owner must be taken to be familiar with it." The notice in this case, written on foolscap paper and pinned on a baize board with other notices, could not protect the proprietor.

CONDITIONS UNASCERTAINED MAY YET BE BINDING

When a man accepts a document containing the terms of an offer he is bound by those terms. For they have been communicated to him, even if he does not trouble to read them and understand them.

This "constructive notice" has been recently much developed. For if a man could get out of a bargain by pleading ignorance, or misunderstanding, or inadvertency, modern business would be impracticable. A man might well choose to remain in ignorance when he knew that knowledge might place legal-obligations upon him. So it is that men making a contract may be bound by conditions that they could have ascertained, perhaps ought to have ascertained, but did not. Thus, in *Thompson* v. *L.M.S. Railway Co.* (1930, K.B.), the King's Bench gave judgment for the defendants, and the Court of Appeal affirmed the judgment. The plaintiff had sued the defendants for negligence, causing personal injuries. The defendants claimed that the terms of the contract excluded their liability. The excursion ticket bought by the plaintiff bore clearly on its face the words: "Excursion ticket. For conditions see back." On the back of the ticket were the words: "Issued subject to conditions in the Company's Time Tables." To find the conditions involved, therefore, some trouble. The time tables included a condition negativing liability for injury in regard to excursions; and the point at issue was whether the plaintiff must be supposed to have assented to the condition.

The plaintiff was unable to read; but, nevertheless, she was held to be subject to the condition. For reasonable efforts had been made to bring the condition to her notice; and the question always is in such circumstances: Was the notice such as is reasonably sufficient for an ordinary person—not for the rather peculiar person unable to read? Perhaps it was hard on the plaintiff. But the obvious inconvenience that would be caused by admitting exceptions is clear.

The well-known case of *Parker* v. *South-Eastern Railway Co.* (C.A. 1876) established the rule; and the opinion of one of the Lords Justice in the case is relevant to the present attitude towards the communicating of the terms of a contract: "The question is, whether the plaintiff was bound by the conditions contained in the ticket. Now, if in the course of making a contract, one party delivers to another a paper containing writing, and the party receiving the paper knows that the paper contains conditions which the party delivering it intends to constitute the contract, I have no doubt that the party receiving it, does, by receiving and keeping it, assent to the conditions contained in it, although he does not read them, and does not know what they are. The railway company, as it seems to me, must be entitled to make some assumptions. I think they are entitled to assume that persons can read, that they understand the English language, and that they pay such attention to what they are about as may reasonably be expected. I think that a particular plaintiff ought not to be entitled to a better position than other persons on account of his exceptional ignorance or stupidity or carelessness."

Where a party to a contract has done what may be reasonably required to draw the attention of the other party to the conditions of the contract, that other party is bound by the conditions. Applying this general rule to the Thompson case, we may say that where a contract is made by the delivery and acceptance of a document in common form, which indicates clearly that there are conditions and where they may be found, the acceptor—if he does not then and there object—is bound by the terms of the contract. This is so even if he does not read the document or acquaint himself with the conditions.

REVOKING AN OFFER

An offer subjects me to no legal liability till it has been accepted. But I may sell an *option*, undertaking thereby not to revoke the offer before a stipulated time. Apart from this I am at liberty to withdraw an offer at any time before acceptance. After acceptance my attempted revocation is too late.

And an acceptance may be on its way without my knowing; if I made an offer by post the posting of a letter accepting the offer concludes the contract. This is so even though I have sent off a revocation. For—different in this from the acceptance—a revocation is effective only when it comes to the notice of the man to whom the offer was made.

Van Tienhoven of Cardiff sent on the 1st of October to Byrne of New York an offer of tinplates. The offer reached New York on the 11th and was at once accepted by telegram. A confirming letter followed. There had been after the 1st a startling rise of prices, and Van Tienhoven on the 8th wrote a letter withdrawing the offer made on the 1st. The withdrawal preceded Byrne's acceptance of the 11th; but, since on the 11th the withdrawal was still making its way across the Atlantic, it did not reach New York till the 20th. The offer had then been accepted; the tinplates had been resold. Revocation was, therefore, inoperative. "Where an offer is made and accepted by letter sent through the post, the contract is complete the moment the letter accepting the offer is posted; even though it never reaches its destination. The principle upon which the rule is based is that the writer of the offer has made the post office his agent to receive the acceptance. The letter of the 8th cannot be treated as communicated to the plaintiffs before the 20th, when the letter reaches them. But before that letter had reached the plaintiffs they had accepted the offer; and a complete contract binding upon both parties was entered into. Any other conclusion would produce extreme injustice and inconvenience. If the defendant's contention were to prevail, no person who had received an offer by post and had accepted it would know his position, until he had waited such a time as to be quite sure that a letter withdrawing the offer had not been posted before his acceptance of it. Both legal principles and practical convenience require that a person who has accepted an offer not known by him to have been revoked, shall be in a position to act upon the footing that the offer and acceptance constitute a contract binding on both parties." (*Byrne* v. *Van Tienhoven*, C.P. 1880.)

CONDITIONS IN A CONTRACT

Risk is inherent in all business; a man entering upon an engagement may well find that he has made a losing bargain. When what is called an "entire contract" is made, for instance, the party undertaking the service may give much and yet receive nothing, because he has, for one reason or another, left his service incomplete. The cook who agrees to serve for £8 a month and who leaves in disdain at the end of a fortnight has no legal right to any wage. Captain Powell taking on board a mate gave to him a note: "I promise to pay to Mr. T. Cutter, the sum of thirty guineas provided he does his duty as second mate to the port of Liverpool."

Mr. Cutter died at sea, and although two-thirds of the voyage had been accomplished, his representatives could obtain nothing. Appleby, likewise, was unlucky, or imprudent. He agreed with Myers to install new machinery for a fixed sum. The installation being well advanced, a fire in the factory destroyed the machinery, and Appleby could recover neither the stipulated sum nor an amount proportionate to the work done (a *quantum meruit*, the term is): "The plaintiffs, having contracted to do an entire work for a specific sum, can recover nothing unless the work be done, or it can be shown that it was the defendant's fault that the work was incomplete. Where, as in the present case, the premises are destroyed without fault on either side, it is a misfortune equally affecting both parties; excusing both from further performance of the contract, but giving a cause of action to neither" (*Appleby* v. *Myers*, C.P., 1867).

ADVISABILITY OF INSURANCE

The contingency that a prospective payment may fail to come, although much has been done to earn it, impels to one of two alternatives. A condition is introduced whereby, in the event of the contract becoming impossible of performance, the party unable to earn the full amount is yet paid *quantum meruit*, what he has already earned. Or the risk is devolved upon an insurer. It is the second alternative that is adopted by the ship-owner. He is entitled to freight only when the cargo is safely delivered. Wishing in no event to lose the entire earnings of his vessel, he hands a part of those earnings over to an underwriter shouldering the risk.

Controversy may arise over the extent of the risk transferred. The insurance case, *Gulf and Southern Steamship Co.* v. *British Trade's Insurance Co.* (K.B. 1929), supplies a good commentary. The case arose out of a claim to be indemnified for loss of freight. Collision occasioned the total loss of ship and cargo. The goods were being carried with all charges "collect." That is, they were payable by the consignee at the ultimate destination. In such a case, in the event of loss, no charges are payable. Some of the goods were being carried on through bills of lading. The Steamship Company was only one of a succession of carriers.

In such case, freight or other charges of the carrier are considered earned on the safe termination of the part of the whole transit that that carrier may be responsible for. They are paid by the carrier next in the series. This next carrier adds them to his own charges, and collects them either from the person to whom he hands the goods for the ensuing carriage, or from the actual consignee. The charges paid to previous carriers are known as "back charges." They are at the risk of any carrier who has paid them. If goods are lost while in the charge of the carrier, he cannot recover charges either from the previous carriers or from the consignor or consignee. In this particular case there was no dispute about the liability of the insurance company regarding these "back charges." The dispute arose regarding the freight that was being earned when accident ended the life of the ship. The shipowner had lost the right to recover this freight. For it only became payable on the right and true delivery of the goods by the plaintiff. Was he entitled to be indemnified for his loss by the insurance company? That, of course, depended upon the form of the insurance contract.

The claim for freight was based upon the undertaking by the insurers "to indemnify the assured against all advances made by and payments of back charges made by or due from the assured and all charges of the assured upon cargo." Did "all charges upon the cargo" include freight in process of being earned? The Court said yes; and the claim of the shipowner succeeded. True, it is customary when you insure freight to use the word "freight." But then "any apt wording undertaking the risk will extend the protection policy to freight." Here the words were "charges upon the cargo." And in using these words in the policy the parties must have intended to cover the freight in process of being earned by the ship. The very definition of freight is "the charge made by the shipowner for the carriage of goods on board his ship." And the only reason why freight was not specifically mentioned was because that is the first and most natural thing which the parties would think of as being a charge upon the cargo.

CONSTRUING A CONTRACT

When a dispute arises regarding the interpretation of a contract, the effort of the Court is directed to the question: What would reasonable men in the circumstances conclude as to the intention of the parties? The Court will, indeed, sometimes give effect to an unexpressed condition, but only if it is obvious, if it is one that the parties must, almost of necessity, have had in mind at the time of making the contract.

IMPLIED TERMS

An implied term, or, as it is called, a "covenant in law," as distinguished from an express agreement, really is in all cases founded upon the presumed intention of the parties and upon reason. Taylor sued Caldwell because, having hired from him a music hall in which, during four successive nights, he hoped to entertain the public, and, incidentally, to make a profit for himself, the music hall was not available on those nights. For an accidental fire had destroyed the building. Although Taylor had spent much in making his project widely known he could recover no damages. The parties must be taken to have contracted on the basis of the continued existence of the building.

"There is a class of contracts in which a person binds himself to do something which requires to be performed by him in person; and such promises, e.g. promises to marry, or promises to serve for a certain time, are never in practice qualified by an express exception of the death of the party; and therefore in such cases the contract is in terms broken if the promisor dies before fulfilment. Yet it was very early determined that, if the performance is personal, the executors are not liable : 'if an author undertakes to compose a work, and dies before completing it, his executors are discharged from this contract ; for the undertaking is merely personal in its nature, and, by the intervention of the contractor's death, has become impossible to be performed.' In contracts in which the performance depends on the continued existence of a given person or thing, a condition is implied that the impossibility of performance arising from the perishing of the person or thing shall excuse the performance " (*Taylor* v. *Caldwell*, 1863).

Yet the law is not foolish in applying the "Rule of *Cutter* v. *Powell.*" It will not deny a claimant merely because he has failed in some slight respect. *De minimis non curat lex* (about things negligible the law does not trouble): otherwise we might be charged with theft for filling our fountain pens at the bank. If the claimant has substantially performed his contract, he is entitled to the payment stipulated for, less an allowance in regard to the points wherein he has come short of his promise. Dakin & Co. agreed to repair Mrs. Lee's house according to a specification. They completed the repairs, but where four feet of concrete had been specified two feet only were given, where five-inch iron rods were specified, four-inch rods were supplied. Still, Dakin & Co. recovered the agreed sum less a deduction in regard to the shortcomings. Their failure to do what they had undertaken was the breaking of warranty, not the breaking of a condition (*Dakin & Co.* v. *Lee*, K.B. 1916). It would seem that a builder who contracts for a lump sum is entitled to a *quantum meruit*—a reasonable payment for what he has actually done, even though he has not fulfilled the entire contract—so long as the work benefits the owner of the property, and is work of the kind contemplated in the contract.

Yet even a slight departure from the terms of the contract may be held to enable the other party to treat the contract as broken.

To the business man, accustomed in his transactions to a reasonable amount of give-and-take, it not seldom appears that the law is even too scrupulous about trifles. What he regards as a minor matter, capable of being adjusted by a small payment one way or the other, the law may regard as a serious matter upsetting the whole transaction. Thus, in *Moore & Co.* v. *Landauer & Co.*, decided in the Commercial Court in 1921, the buyer was held entitled to reject goods tendered in fulfilment of a contract, though the ordinary man can see only a negligible departure from what was bargained for. The contract was for the buying of 3,000 tons of Australian fruit, packed in cases each containing thirty tins. The goods tendered in London were, for a large part, in cases containing twenty-four tins; and, since the Sale of Goods Act enacts "Where there is a contract for the sale of goods by description, there is an implied condition that the goods shall correspond with the description," the right of rejection was upheld. If the description of the article tendered is different in any respect, it is not the article bargained for, and the other party is not bound to take it. So, too, with delivery of a wrong quantity; in strict law the buyer may reject what is tendered if it is appreciably more or less than he contracted to buy, in actual practice an adjustment of price occurs. But, of course, this does not mean that a few pounds difference in a cargo of many tons will nullify the contract. It is difficult sometimes to draw the line.

Here is a question that must find many sympathetic readers in these days when houses, in many a growing suburb, are being thrown up with little thought of permanence. The good builder builds a house to live in; the jerry-builder builds a house to sell. Spacious and showy he makes it; but the lasting comfort of its occupants is little concern of his. "I bought," writes a suffering correspondent, "a new house just over six years ago. During that period three ceilings have fallen down. The builders made the necessary repairs without charge; but now another ceiling has come down, and they refuse to meet the expense. Is there any legal claim against them?" Probably not; even if we would assume at the time of sale an implied promise to remedy any latent defects, we could not sue on such a promise after the lapse of six years. As the builders apparently recognise by their undertaking of previous repairs, there is a moral obligation. Statute Law does give a buyer some protection in regard to commodities; the Sale of Goods Act, 1893, modifies in great measure the rule that in making a bargain a man must either rely upon his own judgment or else bind the other party by definite agreements. This rule, of *caveat emptor* it is sometimes called, is modified by the Act in that where goods are bought by description or in reliance on the judgment of the seller who knows the purpose intended by the buyer, there is implied a condition that the goods shall be reasonably fit for the intended purpose. Common Law itself will not permit a man to make a bargain when he *knows* the other is mistaken in the offer he accepts. A man takes rooms at the seaside for his one brief holiday. Clearly, he contracts for something inhabitable at once; if he doesn't get it, he can not only leave without notice but also claim for what loss he sustains.

CONTENTION OVER TERMS

An inevitable risk of business arises from the use of language. One party to the agreement chooses unlucky words, or the other interprets the words clumsily. For, at its best, language is not perfect for the conveyance of thought from man to man; and, for one reason or another, parties may attach different meanings to the same words. Both parties hold strenuously, and in all good faith to the meaning they suggest; and where the difference is material and the parties uncompromising, litigation results.

The very nature of language, the fact that it is living and therefore developing, now and again brings about divergence of interpretation. The meaning of a word or phrase has changed, and for one party it has changed more speedily than for another.

Unilever Ltd. agreed to buy "the entire production of whale oil for the season 1930 to 1931" of two named vessels belonging to Norwegian whaling companies. "Entire production" in these days of scientific planning is a very elastic term. "Increasing returns" seem to be incident not to manufactures only, but to the produce of field and forest and sea; and the amount of whale oil tendered to Unilever's far exceeded what the company anticipated, and what the company desired. It exceeded, indeed, the carrying capacity of the vessels concerned. There was plausibility therefore in the buyers' contention that they had a right to reject, since the amount tendered was in excess of what the contract stipulated for. The Sale of Goods Act, by Section 30, gives this right. When the seller sends more than the contract amount, the sending is construed as an attempt to make a fresh contract in lieu of the former one. The seller makes an offer that the buyer may at his option either accept or reject. On the ground that more than the entire production had been sent, Unilever did exercise their option to reject; and the Norwegian companies claimed damages for non-acceptance. For, they asserted, they had tendered no more than the entire production.

A development had in fact taken place in the particular season. The whaling trade was first conducted on a system of land factories, to which the whalers brought their catch. At a later stage ships were fitted as factories and conducted their producing operations in sheltered harbours. Later still the ships producing the oil were kept in the open sea, and still later the whalers by using the carcass of a whale as a fender, succeeded in transferring oil from the factory ship to the tanker. Till that was possible the production of a floating factory had to be carried home in the whaler's own tanks.

The House of Lords, reversing in so doing, the opinion of the lower Courts, decided that the sellers' contention was the correct one (*Unilever Ltd.* v. *S.S. Polaris, etc.*, H.L., 1933).

CARE STILL NEEDED

Because the law introduces terms into a contract, the parties are not thereby exonerated from the duty of taking care of their own interests. The law cannot undertake to make bargains for people of mature intellect. The well-known case *Ward* v. *Hobbs* (A.C., 1878) illustrates this effectively. The pigs that Hobbs sent to market were, he suspected, suffering from typhoid fever; and he expressly declined to warrant their condition, selling them "with all faults." Ward, buying them, made an unlucky speculation; most of them died, and other pigs in Ward's possession were infected. Ward could not sue on any express warranty; but he sought to establish an implied representation by Hobbs that the pigs were not suffering from any contagious disease. To exhibit such for sale is to break an Act of Parliament; and, his counsel said, we are entitled to assume that a man is not consciously breaking the law. Ward's ingenious attempt failed, however; though he had temerity (or obstinacy) enough to take the case to the House of Lords. The Lord Chancellor said: "Upon the question of implied representation I have never felt any doubt. Such an implication should never be made without facts to warrant it, and here I find none except that in sending for sale these animals a penal statute was violated. To say that every man is always to be taken to represent in his dealings with other men that he is not, to his knowledge, violating any statute is a refinement which would not appear reasonable to any man."

WARRANTY, A PART OF BARGAIN

It must be remembered that, for a warranty to be of any value, it must be made as part of the bargain, not after the bargain has been struck and the price settled or paid. A warranty, given then, after the contract has been concluded, is in the category of gratuitous promises involving no legal constraint. The seller need not have made it; and English law assumes that no man will place himself under a legal obligation unless he gets something for doing so. Roscorla bought a horse from Thomas, who, *after* the sale was over, warranted the horse sound and free from vice. The horse was in fact vicious; but Roscorla failed in his action. The promise was independent of the sale. It was based upon a consideration past and executed; and a past consideration supports no promise. It is worth noting, too, that expressions of opinion, lauding the merits of the thing offered for sale, are not warranties.

CONDITIONS ATTACHED TO COMMODITIES

The buyer of goods may, indeed, find that he has obtained no title to them: he may have bought them from a thief, or from one who has found them. In either event he may be called upon to give them up without compensation. He is, however, free from the many anxieties that may beset a buyer of land. For several tenants may have interests in the land, settlements may prevent its alienation, various covenants may limit its use, it may be charged with mortgages.

The Law of Property Acts, certainly, now relieve the buyer of land of most of his anxieties. For they require all legal charges to be registered where the information is available for him; and, unless he has notice of them, he can ignore any equitable charges.

Conditions, however, cannot follow goods as they follow land. In *McGruther* v. *Pitcher* (Ch. 1904), where an unsuccessful attempt was made to prevent revolving heel pads from being sold below specified prices, the judgment was: "Can the plaintiffs succeed by saying that they sold goods and attached a condition to the resale, and that the defendant was told of this condition when he purchased the goods? Clearly, they cannot. A vendor cannot in that way enforce a condition, and by printing the so-called condition upon some part of the goods say that every subsequent purchaser of the goods is bound to comply with the condition, so that if he does not comply he can be sued by the original vendor. That is clearly wrong."

The buyer has property in the goods he has bought and may do with them what he pleases. In this matter movable goods differ from land. For the land may be sold with conditions attached; and a subsequent buyer, provided that he has notice of the condition, is bound by it. Even though the buyer of commodities knows of the conditions he may, as owner, ignore them. If I buy a razor marked "No stropping," I can ignore the prohibition.

In an Appeal Court case (*National Phonograph Co.* v. *Menck*, 1911), the position was thus put: "The owner may use and dispose of ordinary goods as he thinks fit. He may have made a certain contract with the person from whom he bought; and to such a contract he must answer. Simply in his capacity as owner, he is not bound by any restrictions in the use of sale of the goods; and it is out of the question to suggest that restrictive conditions run with the goods." Yet the buyer is bound by a personal contract. If he breaks this contract he may very well be liable for damages. So G is, in the circumstances detailed below: "G, the retailer, makes a contract with H, a soap manufacturer, whereby for a special discount of 25 per cent he agreed not to sell any other maker's soap for ten years and not to sell below cost prices. During the ten years G does both. What are H's rights?" Here G made a promise; he obtained consideration for it; he broke it. True, the undertaking is in some sense, a restraint of trade; it prevents G from carrying on his business according to his unfettered discretion. But then, all contracts in greater or less measure, limit the parties from freedom of action; and the Courts are nowadays much less reluctant than formerly to enforce such contracts. He will show that he has suffered damage, that his sales' organisation has been upset, that his sales are less than they would have been if the contract had been carried out. Having shown this he will recover damages.

This rule—that conditions do not follow goods—does not apply to a patented article. A purchaser who buys such an article with knowledge of the conditions under which his vendor is authorised to use the patented invention, is bound by the conditions. But this using of a patent is not a contract of sale: it is rather a licence to use, and the grantor of the licence is entitled to impose what conditions he pleases to his grant. If the conditions are not observed, there is no grant. To some extent conditions may follow land.

COVENANTS AFFECTING LEASES

If a lessee assigns his lease the man to whom he assigns it is, as regards the property, under the same liabilities and has the same rights as the assignor. But the assignee has no personal claim against the landlord though his assignor might have had. Thus a landlord leased a public-house to X, agreeing with X that he would not build another public-house within half-a-mile. X assigned his lease; the landlord built another public-house within half-a-mile; and the new lessee had no remedy. For the agreement was a personal one (*Thomas* v. *Hayward*, Ex. 1869).

COVENANTS AFFECTING FREEHOLDS

An agreement by the owner of land restricting his use of it does not bind his assignee unless—

1. He has created an *easement* or *profit* recognised by law;
2. The assignee has obtained the land with notice of the restrictions placed upon it.

CONDITIONS IMPORTED INTO CONTRACT

Unrestricted competition for a restricted market may induce one of the competitors, in order to lower prices, to cut his costs by methods harmful to the community. He may sell his goods under one name. They ought to be called by another name. He may sell as butter what should be called margarine, may exhibit stockings made from a tree as being the product of an insect. The community tries to protect itself against this possibility by legislation; adulteration and fraud are restrained in the first place by being penalised, in the second place by being made vitiating factors in contracts. The man who sells adulterated goods cannot insist on the benefit for which he has bargained. Formerly, a buyer was left almost wholly to his own devices for assurance that he was buying what he was trying to buy; and when buyer and seller were in close contact with one another, the evil of adulteration could hardly have been great. Now, when a buyer obtains his provisions from the ends of the earth, added protection is called for; and this added protection is sometimes given by positive injunctions of law. It does in regard to fertilisers and cattle foods. The case considered below brings out a most important point. Even an express stipulation to be held exempt from a liability imposed by Act of Parliament is of no avail (*Dobell* v. *Barber*, Com. Court, 1930, and see also page 8).

Both parties were wholesale dealers in cattle foods, with which the Fertilizers and Feeding Stuffs Act, 1926, deals. This Act enacts among other things that, on the sale of feeding stuff: "There shall be implied, notwithstanding any notice or contract to the contrary, a warranty by the seller that the article is suitable to be used as such." This implied warranty applies, therefore, to linseed cake. Apparently, this is very liable, when it comes from India, to contain irritating and injurious castor-seed. These facts, dictating the greatest caution in dealing with Indian cake, were familiar to the parties.

The controversy concerned a parcel of India cake sold by Dobell in terms clearly intimating that he himself gave no sort of warranty of its freedom from the injurious mixture: "The cake is sold *tel quel* in all respects, but So-and-so's analysis, for which sellers accept no responsibility is 8·93 per cent oil, 29·22 albumenoids, castor free." The analysis was misleading; for when, after cattle had contracted illness through eating the cake, other analyses were made, castor was found. The amount though small, was still enough to make the cake unfit for food. There is no doubt that the declining by the sellers to give a warranty, the selling the cake *tel quel* (with all faults, that is) would, apart from the Act, have absolved the seller from liability.

But there is the Act to be reckoned with; and the attempt to disclaim liability failed. The Act imported into the contract a warranty that the article was suitable food for cattle; it was not suitable, and the defendants were liable for breach of warranty.

IMPLIED CONDITION IN A CONTRACT

It may be, indeed, that one party to a contract has not fulfilled a promise never mentioned in the bargaining. The promise was so obviously called for that neither party imagined it to be necessary to speak of it. Yet the promise may be of the very essence of the contract, and its non-fulfilment entitle the aggrieved party to damages. The Banco de Portugal contracted with Messrs. Waterlow for the printing and supply of Portuguese bank-notes. That Messrs. Waterlow should take precautions to prevent forgery of notes, and that they should not print from the plates except on the express authority of the bank, were obvious implications. Messrs. Waterlow, deceived by a plausible rogue, printed unauthorised notes and handed them to him. The notes got into circulation; the bank was obliged to withdraw all notes, genuine and counterfeit, and honour them; the bank claimed damages for negligence and breach of duty.

The Court held that there was an absolute duty on the defendants not to print notes without authority, and that breach of this duty entitled the bank to damages—damages assessed by the House of Lords at over half a million pounds: "Such unauthorised printing was a breach of contract, and Waterlows' dealing with the notes so printed was a conversion of the notes both at Common Law and under the provisions of the Copyright Act, 1911, the notes being copies of an engraving in which the bank had the copyright."

RESTRICTIONS ON CONTRACTS

Freedom of contract is not absolute. In the interests of the community the chosen representatives of the community restrict the area of bargaining. The State will, obviously, try to prevent agreements to do what the State forbids—to commit a crime. It will also try to restrict bargains that, though to the advantage of at least one of the parties making them, are against the general good. Such restriction is an embodiment of the recognition that private interest may not, as the classical economists used to assert peremptorily, be coincident with public welfare. When this restriction does exist, some involuntary obligation is introduced into the bargain. The introduction into the bargain may conflict with the specific bargain; and then it is that the actual agreement becomes inoperative. The statute governs. A good example is supplied by the Carriage of Goods by Sea Act of 1924. The contract between the shipowner and the shipper is contained in bills of lading. Some of these bills, despite much simplification, are still astonishing documents. But, as a result of the Act, many of the clauses that formerly exempted the shipowner from liability or loss, and which still persist in many bills, are of no effect.

The State—

1. Prohibits the making of some contracts (a contract to commit a crime would be punishable as a criminal conspiracy).

2. Subjects others to scrutiny and possible revision (see the Moneylenders Act, page 38).

3. Modifies others by introducing statutory stipulations (see pages 9–15).

4. Allows others to be made, but ignores them (this is its usual attitude in regard to wagers).

UNDESIRABLE CONTRACTS

Judges, like other men, reflect their period; and in their interpretation of law they make evident the spirit of the age. When the bias was towards non-interference, bargains were tolerated and enforced that very likely would nowadays be declared void as being against public policy. "Shall we indict a man for making a fool of another?" would have been answered "No!" in former days. Now, the Courts are not content to see undesirable bargains made; and they may treat those bargains as though they had never been made. The contract between *Foster* and *Driscoll* (A.C., 1929) was thus treated. The parties had agreed about the loading of a ship with whisky to be carried to some point in Canada, whence it could be smuggled into the United States. The Court of Appeal held that, since the performance of the contract was bound to impair our friendly relations with the United States, the agreement was contrary to public policy, and, therefore, void. In 1875, on the other hand, a famous judge had declared with emphasis: "If there is one thing which more than another public policy requires, it is that men of full age and competent understanding shall have the utmost liberty of contracting."

If a contract is illegal, no Court of law will help either party to enforce the contract.

Scott and McNab made a bargain for the buying of shares in a company, the object of the bargain being the wish to create in the public mind the idea that a market existed for the shares. McNab, though employed as a broker to buy shares at a premium, transferred his own shares to the plaintiff. Scott sought rescission of the contract. Neither party alleged that the contract was one incidental to "market-rigging," incidental that is to an attempt to mislead the public. But upon its becoming clear that such was the purpose of the bargain, the Court declined to interfere (*Scott* v *Brown, Doering, McNab & Co.*, Q.B., 1892).

RESTRAINT OF TRADE

Some obvious difficulties arise, though. There should be freedom to make what bargains one thinks good. If the person who has made a bargain, leading thereby the other party to expect performance, can get out of it when he finds it more irksome than he anticipated, an added risk is introduced into business life. The law is uncertain enough as it is. To make it more uncertain by entrusting to judges a discretion to declare contracts void upon some vague notion of what "public policy" requires, would be a backward step. "Judges," says one of their number, "are more to be trusted as interpreters of the law than as expounders of what is called public policy." A rule of law is established: and people act in accordance with it. Such a rule should remain till Parliament thinks fit to modify it. For Parliament alone has the right and the power to determine what public policy requires. It is not for a judge, from some notion of policy or expedience, to prevent a party from getting a benefit for which he bargains.

There should be freedom of contract. But, then, suppose the making of one contract restricts the freedom to make other contracts? I judged it wise to make the restricting bargain; ought I to be allowed to ignore it? The answer seems to be: "Only when the bargain is manifestly oppressive." The Court, asked to maintain freedom of contract, may be asked to enforce a contract to restrict freedom.

ENFORCEABLE OR VOID

Where one species of freedom conflicts with another species, which is to be preferred? The old cases show the judges eager to uphold the doctrine that a man cannot sell his freedom. To be sure, even to-day he cannot sell his freedom in its entirety; a contract whereby he bargained to become a slave would be regarded as non-existent. Much less encroachments upon liberty were formerly frowned upon. Thus, an apprentice entered into a bond not to compete with his master within a limited area for four years; and the judges vigorously condemned it. For such an undertaking prevented the apprentice from making the most profitable use of his acquired skill and business capacity, prevented him, therefore, from adding as much as he might to the well-being of the community. "And all the justices agreed that the condition was against law, and then all is void. For it is against the liberty of a free man, and against the statute of Magna Charta. And one said that he might as well bind himself that he would not go to church. And judgment was given against the plaintiff."

It would have startled the old judges if they could have heard the Appeal Court approving of combination to avoid "cut-throat competition": "Unquestionably the combination in question was one the purpose of which was to regulate supply and keep up prices. But an ill-regulated supply and unremunerative prices may in point of fact be disadvantageous to the public. Such a state of things may, if it is not controlled, drive manufacturers out of business or lower wages, and so cause unemployment or labour disturbance. It must always be a question of circumstances whether a combination of manufacturers in a particular trade is an evil from a public point of view." (*North-West Salt Co.* v. *Electrolytic Alkali Co.* 1914, A.C.) The same case is noteworthy because of Lord Haldane's statement of the present attitude of the Courts: "Where the controversy is as to the validity of an agreement, say, for service, by which someone who has little opportunity of choice has precluded himself from earning his living by the exercise of his calling after the period of service is over, the law looks jealously at the bargain. But when the question is one of the validity of a commercial agreement for regulating their trade relations, entered into between two firms or companies, the law adopts a somewhat different attitude. It still looks carefully to the interests of the public, but it regards the parties as the best judges of what is reasonable between themselves."

CONTRACTS IN RESTRAINT OF TRADE

So with contracts "in restraint of trade." The modern tendency is to enforce them when they are not obviously unfair to one of the parties, and not against public interest. Shown to be unfair or harmful to the public, however, the Courts still declare them to be void.

Thus in *Vincents of Reading* v. *Fogden* (K.B. 1932) the Court decided that a restrictive undertaking need not be observed by the defendant. He had been a salesman for the plaintiffs, and one clause in his engagement contract stipulated that "for three years from the termination of this agreement" he would not compete, or help to compete, with the plaintiffs "within fifteen miles of Station Square, Reading." The Court's decision was based upon the principles : (1) one who seeks to enforce a restriction must show that it goes no further than is reasonably necessary for the protection of his business ; (2) an employer must not take from the employee a covenant protecting the employer, after the cessation of the employment, from the competition of his former servant. "Here the defendant has not acquired any information of a confidential character. The restrictive clause is, therefore, unenforceable and void."

EMPLOYEE'S AGREEMENT NOT TO COMPETE

An employee is now and again required to sign, as one condition of his employment, an undertaking not to compete with his employer when the contract of employment is ended. Where the restriction imposed is reasonable the Courts will enforce it. For they have long given up their traditional antagonism against any agreement that seeks to prevent a man from earning his living as he thinks best; and an employer would frequently be betraying his own interests if he neglected to obtain such an undertaking. The employer must, however, so frame the restriction that it is obviously no more than fair to both parties. A restrictive agreement imposing excessive restraint upon the employee can be safely ignored by that employee. The Courts, if invoked, would treat it as void.

Many such agreements, indeed, are only meant to be means of intimidating the employee. Their propounders would shrink from any attempt to enforce them. The fact that the agreement concludes with some such phrase as this : "The employee hereby acknowledges that this undertaking is fair and honourable," does not affect the matter. A palpably unfair stipulation does not become fair simply by asserting that it is so.

In *Morris* v. *Saxelby* (A.C., 1916), where an unsuccessful effort was made to enforce a restriction, it was clearly pointed out that restrictions quite fair when applied to the seller of the goodwill of a business may be quite unfair when applied to a servant or apprentice. "The goodwill of a business is immune from the danger of the owner's exercising his personal knowledge or skill to its detriment; and if the purchaser is to take over such good-will with all its advantages it must, in his hands, remain similarly immune. A covenant against competition is, therefore, reason-able. It is quite different in the case of an employer taking such a covenant from his employee or apprentice. I cannot find any case in which a covenant against competition by an employee or a servant has, as such, ever been upheld by the Court. Wherever such covenants have been upheld it has been on the ground that he might obtain such personal knowledge of and influence over the customers of his employer, or such an acquaintance with his employer's trade secrets as would enable him, if competition were allowed, to take advantage of his employer's trade con-nection or utilise information confidentially obtained."

What is *personal* to the employee—his acquired knowledge or his skill, derived though it may be from his experience with his employer—is his own; it would be wrong to prevent his using it to earn his living. What is *property* to the employer—secret processes, lists of customers, and the like—is the employer's; the employee would do wrong to appropriate it.

ENGLISH LAW AND COMBINATION

English law does not, as that of the United States does, make combinations in restraint of trade illegal. It does not penalise those who enter into them. English law ignores them in the sense that it will not lend its aid to enforce agreements to com-bine in restraint of trade. The strength of the combinations usually, depends, therefore, upon the continuing willingness of the members; any one may withdraw without incurring legal penalties.

Nor do the actions of the combinations to further their supposed interest come under the ban of the Courts. The actions may injure an outsider, may be intended to injure an outsider. Yet he cannot obtain an injunction to restrain them. Thus, the com-bination may deliberately undersell a rival though at a temporary loss; it may "sow one year a crop of apparently unfruitful process in order by driving away competition to reap a fuller harvest of profit in the future" (*Mogul Steamship Co.* v. *McGregor*). The ruined rival has no remedy.

The new attitude towards combinations for keeping up prices by restricting output was well illustrated in *English Hop Growers* v. *Dering* (C.A., 1928). Dering, a member of the combine, agreed to limit his crop to a quota approved by the combine, and to sell through the combine alone. He broke his agreement, affirming that he was not obliged to keep it since it was in restraint of trade and therefore illegal. The Court of Appeal was unanimous against him: "In view of the fluctuating yearly supply of hops, I see nothing unreasonable in hop-growers combining to secure a steady and profitable price, by eliminating competition amongst themselves and putting the marketing in the hands of one agent with full power to fix prices and hold up supplies."

LAW RELATING TO WAGERS

English law does not forbid a man to bet. The Street Betting Act of 1906 does forbid him to loiter in streets or public places for the purpose of bookmaking; but that is another matter. Still, though it does not penalise, the law does discourage betting. For it treats a bet as void. So far as the law is concerned the bet was never made. If a man makes a bet he cannot look to the Courts for the enforcement of any rights he acquires through it. The "welsher" may be prosecuted for obtaining money by false pretences; he cannot be sued for not paying his losses.

WHAT IS A WAGER

The essence of a wager, as distinct from an insurance contract, is that the interests of the parties to the agreement are divergent. When A insures his life, he wants to pay as many premiums as possible. The insurance company wants him to do so, too. When A, about to begin batting, agrees to pay B £1 on condition that B pays him a shilling for every run he makes, A wants to make a big score. B doesn't want him to do so. The first agreement is enforceable at law, the second is not; the first is an insurance contract that the law recognises and enforces, the second is a bet. Applying this rule for discriminating, it is apparent that a stock exchange bargain on "differences" is a wager. It has been held, too, that even where there is an option expressed in the contract to demand delivery or acceptance of the actual stocks the transaction is still one of gaming or wagering. The trustee in bankruptcy of Gieve (*In re Gieve*, C.A., 1899) succeeded in his appeal against a creditor, Moss, who claimed against the bankrupt in respect of stock exchange dealings on the "cover" system for payment of differences.

THE RELEVANT STATUTES

Section 1 of the Gaming Act, 1835, enacted that a security given for money lost in playing at games or in betting should be looked upon as given for an illegal consideration. The immediate recipient, therefore, could not enforce it. But a "holder in due course"—one who, without knowledge of its illegal inception, gave value for it—could enforce it. Section 2 of the Act was, however, designed to preserve the loser's right to recover his loss from the winner: it enacted that, if the loser had paid a holder in due course, he could claim the amount paid from the winner. In 1922, over eighty years later, it was decided (in *Sutters* v. *Briggs*, A.C.) that this section enabled every one who had paid losses by cheque to recover them if he, or his executor, or his trustees in bankruptcy, thought fit. Indeed, the trustee in bankruptcy had no option. Whether he liked the job or not, he was under legal obligation to recover the money paid in bets. For the winner would have, doubtless, endorsed the cheque to his banker. Whether or not Parliament wished to protect bookmakers from a spate of claims, the Gaming Act of 1922 was hurriedly passed. This repealed Section 2 of the 1835 Act, so that now the winner who gets payment through a cheque remains undisturbed.

GAMING ACT, 1845

The Gaming Act, 1845, made wagers of all kinds void: "All contracts or agreements, whether by parole or in writing, by way of gaming or wagering, shall be null and void." He who asserts that he has won a bet cannot, by process of law, get his winnings. The other party merely has to "plead the Gaming Acts." For the Act enacts that "no suit shall be brought or maintained in any court for recovering any sum of money or valuable thing alleged to be won on any wager, or which shall have been deposited in the hands of any person to abide the event on which any wager shall have been made."

GAMING ACT, 1892

The Gaming Act, 1892, went further still. Before that Act, if a man borrowed money in order to bet, he could be made to pay it back; if a man engaged another to make bets for him, he could be made to pay for the services rendered. The Act changed matters in both respects: "Any promise to pay any person any sum of money paid by him for betting debts, or by way of commission, shall be null and void."

RACECOURSE BETTING ACT, 1928

The wheel is being reversed in these days. The Racecourse Betting Act, 1928, made the use of totalisators legal, and established a Racecourse Betting Control Board—a body corporate with perpetual succession, its chairman certified as being of the utmost respectability. For he is appointed by the Home Secretary. The legalisation is hedged around by restrictions : (1) there must be no deduction from the pool for the benefit of the racecourses or of their owners; (2) a percentage of the takings is diverted to public purposes; (3) betting on the course is controlled by a statutory body. The Betting Act, 1853, which declared places used for betting as public nuisances, is abolished so far as applicable to approved racecourses. It would seem that, in view of the multiplicity of statutes bearing on betting, a codifying Act is long overdue.

Probably this is the view of the Government which, in 1932, set up a Royal Commission on Lotteries and Betting. The extraordinary interest in Irish sweepstakes and the almost continuous facilities for gambling on greyhound racing had made the question of the proper policy to be pursued an urgent one. Owners of greyhound courses had readily persuaded themselves that legalization of the tote on horse tracks entailed its legalisation on dog tracks, and that its use on these was freed from restrictions. *Shuttleworth* v. *Leeds Greyhound Association, Ltd.* (K.B. 1932) showed this view to be erroneous. This was an appeal from a decision of the Leeds stipendiary magistrate; the magistrate had decided in favour of the association, but the Divisional Court reversed the decision. The association had been summoned under the Betting Act, Section 1, 1853. This section is a little involved, since its draughtsman was anxious to guard against evasions of it. But the Lord Chief Justice helps to understanding by his careful dissection of it. The section is—

"No place shall be kept (1) for the purpose of the occupier thereof betting with persons resorting thereto, or (2) for the purpose of any money or valuable thing being received by or on behalf of such occupier as aforesaid : (*a*) as or for the consideration for any assurance, undertaking, promise, or agreement, express or implied, to pay or give thereafter any money or valuable thing on any event or contingency of or relating to any race; or (*b*) as or for the consideration for securing the paying or giving by some other person of any money or valuable thing on any such event or contingency as aforesaid."

A PIECE OF JUDICIAL ANALYSIS

"The first question," said the Lord Chief Justice, "of construction which is raised is as to the effect of the words, 'such occupier as aforesaid.' The magistrate adopted the contention put forward on behalf of the respondents that these words 'qualified the class of persons amenable to the provisions of the second part of Section I as being persons within the ambit of the first part of the section, such persons not being persons opening, keeping, or using a place *simpliciter*, but doing so for the purpose of betting with persons resorting thereto to conducting some kind of betting business.'

We do not agree with this view. In our opinion, the words are used to avoid repeating at length the words in the first part of the section, 'owner, occupier, or keeper, or any person using the same, or any person procured or employed by or acting for or on behalf of such owner, occupier, or keeper, or person using the same, or any person having the care or management or in any manner conducting the business thereof.' The first part of the section specifies (*a*) the place; (*b*) the persons who, in a variety of capacities, may be using it; and (*c*) a purpose for which it may not be used. The second part—introduced by the alternative 'or'—specifies the same variety of capacities in which a person may be using the place, but different purposes for which the place may not be used. The section concludes by declaring that a place kept for the aforesaid purposes or any of them shall be a public nuisance.

This is the view expressed by Lord Halsbury in *Powell* v. *Kempton Park Racecourse Company, Limited* (A.C. 1899), when he is dealing with the second part of the section. The passage to which we refer is the following—

'The second part of the section is in strict accordance with what I have suggested as the meaning of the statute. It assumes a place or establishment for receiving money or some valuable thing being received by or on behalf of an owner, occupier, keeper, or person; here the statute uses the words "as aforesaid" that is, "person using the same"—for the consideration for any assurance, undertaking, promise, or agreement, expressed or implied, to pay or give thereafter any money or valuable thing on any event or contingency or of relating to any horse-race or other race, fight, game, sport, or exercise.'

Such being, in our opinion, the true construction of the section, we proceed to consider, first, whether the facts found in the present case bring the respondents within its ambit; and, secondly, whether that is any authority for holding that the construction we have adopted is incorrect.

It is not, and could not be, contended that the respondents had committed any offence against that part of the section which is marked '1' in our dissection of it. This result follows from the decision of the House of Lords in *Attorney-General* v. *Luncheon and Sports Club, Limited* (A.C. 1929), where it was held that the operators of a totalisator do not make bets or wagers with the persons who stake their money through the totalisator.

"The operators of a totalisator, however, do receive money, and, if they receive it as the consideration for any promise, express or implied, to pay any money thereafter to any one on any event or contingency of or relating to a race, the place which they keep for the purpose of so receiving the money is, in our opinion, within the ordinary meaning of the language used in that part of the section which is distinguished above as '2 (a)'. The money paid to the operators of a totalisator is not a gift. They are entitled, in the ordinary course of the events contemplated alike by themselves and by those who pay their money to them, to put into their own pockets a percentage of each payment they receive. The consideration for the receipt by them of the money paid is their undertaking or promise that they will thereafter pay money to such person or persons as the event of the race shall entitle to receive it. Unless, therefore, any limitation is to be placed on the plain language of the section the facts establish an offence against that part of it which we have distinguished as '2 (a)'.

"The respondents contend that certain authoritative decisions of the Courts have established that the language of the section must be read in a limited sense, and that no part of it applies to any place kept or used by a person who does not himself enter into transactions which are either bets in the ordinary sense of that word, or of the nature of bets. The first case cited in support of this contention is *Powell* v. *Kempton Park Racecourse, Limited*; and reliance is placed in particular on certain passages in the opinion of the late Lord Halsbury. It is essential in approaching the consideration of this case to bear in mind what exactly was the point which arose for decision. The action was brought expressly to test the decision in *Hawke* v. *Dunn* (Q.B. 1897), in which five judges had held in similar circumstances that there

had been an infringement of the first part of Section 1 of the
Betting Act, 1853, without any reference to the second part.
The question was whether the enclosure on the racecourse which
was frequented by bookmakers could properly be said to be 'used
by' them for the purpose of betting with persons resorting thereto.
The decision was concerned, therefore, solely with that part of
the section distinguished above as '1,' and nothing turned upon
the construction of those parts distinguished as '2 (a)' and
'2 (b)'.

It is to be observed that in his dissection of Section 1 the
noble and learned lord stopped short at the end of that part of
it which we have called '1'.

It seems to me clear that the thing against which the enactment is levelled is any place used in the sense I have explained.
There must be a business conducted, and there must be an owner,
occupier, manager, keeper, or some person who, if these designa-
tions do not apply to him, must nevertheless be some other person
who is analagous to and is of the same genus as the owner, keeper,
or occupier, who bets or is willing to bet with the persons who
resort to his house, room, or other place. In this view it is not an
offence under this Act of Parliament to allow persons to assemble
for the purpose of betting with each other; there is, upon this
hypothesis, no business being conducted at all. The different
betting people, or each individual bettor, is conducting his own
business, and doing it in a house used indeed, but only used,
just as he might do it on the racecourse or on the high road.
There is no betting establishment at all, and there is no keeper
of one.'

If it were certain that, in the paragraph just quoted, Lord
Halsbury was referring to the section as a whole, this Court
would, as in duty bound, bow to his authority. But an examination of the language of the paragraph has convinced us that he
was not. He speaks of the necessity of the occupier being one
who is ready and willing to make a bet with persons resorting to
the place, a necessity which would clearly exist in cases to be
brought within '1' and which might possibly exist in cases
to be brought within '2 (a)'. But such a necessity cannot exist
in the cases contemplated in '2 (b)'; for a bet with a person
resorting to the place cannot result in a payment becoming due
from some other person. It follows that, in the paragraph in
question, Lord Halsbury has left the consideration of the latter
part of Section 1 and has gone back to that part which alone

24

was material to his decision. None of the other noble and learned Lords who delivered opinions in *Powell* v. *Kempton Park Racecourse Company, Limited* dealt with this point at all, and we are, therefore, of opinion that that case is no authority for placing any limitation on the plain words of the second part of the section.

The next case relied on by the respondents is that of *Reg.* v. *Hobbs* (Q.B. 1898). This was a decision of the Court for Crown Cases Reserved. From the case it appeared that Hobbs, a publican, had, for the amusement of his customers, organised a sweepstake on terms which resulted, and were intended to result, in his receiving nothing but his expenses in connection therewith and under which he entered into no contractual relationship with those participating in the sweepstake. On these facts it was held that Hobbs had not used his house for the purpose of receiving any money as or for the consideration of any promise to pay, on the event of a race, first because it did not appear that he had received the money as or for the consideration of any promise to pay at all, and, secondly, because the event was not the result of the race but the drawing of the sweepstake.

In our view *Reg.* v. *Hobbs* was decided on the particular facts of the case which differ from those of the present case in two most material respects. In the present case the respondents did receive money as or for the consideration of a promise to pay, and to pay on the event of a race.

The case must go back to the magistrate with the direction that the respondents were guilty of the charge made against them in the first summons.

In the result the appeal is allowed with costs. In our view, the proper course is that the magistrate do adjudicate on the first summons and do adjourn the second summons *sine die*.

EFFECT OF THE ACTS

The Gaming Act, 1892, relating to agreements arising out of bets or in contemplation of them, has been most discussed. Plimmer, needing £500 to deposit with a stakeholder, borrowed it off Carney. He was to repay the money in the event of his winning, not otherwise. He did win but refused to pay; and Carney failed to recover, since the money was paid in respect of a bet (*Carney* v. *Plimmer*, Q.B., 1897). Even before this Act it was held that money deposited with a stakeholder can be recovered if request is made before it has been paid away to the winner of the bet; for the money has not been "paid" in the sense of the Act. Hampden made a bet that the earth is flat, Walsh being the stakeholder. He was held to have lost; but, before Walsh paid the winner, Hampden reclaimed his stake. Walsh paid the winner, and was obliged to repay the amount to Hampden.

Stuart-King declined to pay losses; and, if he had been sued for payment, he would have had a defence in the Gaming Act, 1845. Hyams, however, threatened to declare him a defaulter; and Stuart-King promised to pay in a few days if the threat was not carried out. This was a new promise upon a new consideration. For the defendant it was urged that the bets were *illegal*, and that the new consideration was tainted with illegality. The Court, however, held the defendant liable on the new promise. The bets were not *illegal* but only *void*: "There is certainly nothing illegal in paying or receiving payment of a lost bet: it is one thing for the law to refuse to assist either party in their folly, if they will bet; it is quite another to forbid the loser to keep his word" (*Hyams* v. *Stuart-King*, K.B. 1908). The decision was in accordance with the early case where a promissory note, given in payment of a bet on the hop duty, got into the hands of an endorsee. It was held that he could recover payment upon it, though the first recipient could not have done so: "Is this note brought within the category of notes tainted with illegality in their inception by showing that it was given in payment of a wager on the hop duty. I am of opinion that it is not so tainted. A party without violating the Common Law may make such a wager and may pay the money if he lose it; and if instead of paying the bet he gives a note promising to pay at a future date, he still violates no statute."

MONEYLENDERS ACT, 1927

This Act allows a judge to reopen a transaction if he should deem its terms "harsh and unconscionable." Perhaps the Act has not afforded as effective a protection as was expected. Enacted primarily to safeguard the debtor compelled in some grave emergency to have recourse to more exacting creditors than bankers; it states that a rate over 48 per cent per annum will not be allowed unless the lender satisfies the Court that quite exceptional circumstances justify it. Such an exceptional circumstance would be the very slight security upon which the lender relies for repayment. The rate would assuredly not be allowed where security is good, where, for instance, a bill of sale is taken of the borrower's property. Yet many moneylenders, acting on the assumption that what the law does not expressly forbid the law sanctions, exact their 48 per cent; and, in their dire need for temporary accommodation, few debtors demur to the exorbitant rate. Or, perhaps, the borrowers can be induced to believe that, when the Act mentions 48 per cent, it authorises that rate.

In *South* v. *Carrington* (K.B. 1906), an instructive judgment explains the operation and effect of the Act. It is not intended to upset bargains entered into with due care: "The conclusion at which I arrive is that the judge is entitled to consider the fact that the borrower thoroughly understood the transaction, and without any misrepresentation, or any pressure, other than the mere request to pay so much interest, voluntarily agreed to pay it. When the judge finds these to be the facts, he ought to find that the interest which the man agrees to pay is reasonable. This view of the Act in no way interferes with its operation in all the cases to which it was really meant to apply. When the borrower is ignorant, when advantage is taken of him, when his necessities are such that he practically has no free will, his agreement is no test of what is reasonable. Judges will have no hesitation in applying the Act. But here the borrower was in a position to bargain on terms of equality with the moneylender."

Section 12 of the Act modifies the Statutes of Limitations to this extent: an action to recover loans must be begun within a year. The ordinary term of six years is not available for the moneylender; but, doubtless, this restriction will mean little.

PAWNING

This is a species of bailment whereby the owner of goods parts with the possession of them to one who lends upon the security of the goods. There is no need for writing or any other formality for a pledge, except for small loans made by a pawnbroker. For, when possession of the goods is given, the pledging is outside the scope of a bill of sale.

PAWNBROKERS

Pawnbrokers must obtain a certificate—in the metropolis, from a Metropolitan police magistrate; elsewhere, from the borough or district council. The annual licence is issued only on production of the certificate. Any person is a pawnbroker who keeps a shop where he lends out sums *not exceeding* £10 upon the security of goods placed in his possession—the understanding being that the borrower may afterwards redeem the goods (Pawnbrokers Act, 1872). The Act is inapplicable to those lending sums over £10. Every pawnbroker must take out from the Inland Revenue Commissioners an annual licence (duty £7 10s.) for each shop kept by him. The licence expires on 31st July.

CHARGES ALLOWED

The charges on small loans are fixed: ½d. per month on every 2s. or fraction of 2s. when the loan does not exceed 40s.; ½d. per month upon every 2s. 6d. when the loan exceeds 40s. The ticket costs ½d. for loans not over 10s.; it costs 1d. for loans above 10s. The Pawnbrokers Act, 1922, sanctions an additional ½d. for each 5s. or part of 5s. lent.

TIME ALLOWED FOR REDEMPTION

When goods are given into the pawnbroker's possession as security for a loan of 10s. or less, they must be redeemed within twelve months and a period of grace of seven days. Otherwise they become the pawnbroker's absolute property. When the loan is over 10s. the pawnbroker may sell by public auction the security for satisfaction of his debt and charges, handing over any surplus upon demand within three years to the pawner. Apparently, in the event of the sales realising less than the amount due, the pawnbroker may sue for the balance.

Till an actual sale, the security for a loan of over 10s. may be redeemed, though the year and seven days have passed. As noted above, if a sale realises less than the amount of debt and charges, the pawnbroker has strictly a personal claim for the balance against the debtor.

PAWN TICKET

The pawnbroker who delivers goods to the person presenting the pawn ticket relating to them is protected against any claim by the pawner. He is, however, still under a possible liability to the rightful owner if it should appear that the goods pledged had been stolen.

PAWNBROKER'S LIABILITY

If goods pledged are destroyed by fire the pawnbroker must pay to the pawner the value, less his debt and charges, the value being reckoned at 25 per cent of the loan more than this. A justice is empowered to order compensation when there has been damage by neglect.

UNLAWFUL PAWNING

This is a statutory offence created by the 1872 Act. It is committed when a person, not being employed or authorised by the owner, pawns another's property, intending and having reasonable hope of being able to redeem it. Where this intention and reasonable hope do not exist, the offence is larceny. When such a pawning takes place, the pawnbroker has no right to retain the goods. But he may prosecute and, on conviction of the offender, the pawnbroker is entitled to the sum lent from the forfeiture imposed (not exceeding £5 and the full value of the article). Any surplus is applied to defraying the costs of prosecution, and anything left is handed to the local authorities for the use of the poor.

DAMAGES

When a contract has been broken, the Court awards a monetary compensation to the aggrieved party. He has sustained a loss that can be calculated in money; and, obtaining the amount from the defendant, he is placed in the same position as he would have been if the contract had been duly performed. The rule was thus put in the well-known case *Hadley* v. *Baxendale* (K.B. 1854): "Where two parties have made a contract which one of them has broken, the damages which the other party ought to receive should be such as may fairly and reasonably be considered as either arising naturally (in the ordinary course of business, that is) from such breach of contract, or (where there are special circumstances) such as may reasonably be supposed to have been in the contemplation of both parties, at the time they made the contract, as the probable result of the breach."

COMPENSATION NOT PENALTY

The sum awarded is not a penalty imposed upon the contract breaker. However harsh and overbearing his conduct, however greatly he has distressed the plaintiff, he pays nothing beyond the actual monetary loss. It is true that, when a jury awards damages for breach of a promise to marry, a sum may be awarded for "injured feelings." In general, however, the monetary loss only is covered by the award. In an action for tort—for the wrong of libel or assault, for instance—the jury is entitled to take into account all manner of circumstances either to aggravate or to mitigate damages. Both the motive of the defendant who did the wrong and the conduct of the plaintiff who seeks redress may be taken into account. Damages are not limited to the actual loss sustained: "I remember a case," said one of the judges of the Court of Common Pleas, "where a jury gave £500 damages for merely knocking a man's hat off; and the Court refused a new trial." This was said in *Merest* v. *Harvey* (1814), where also a jury's verdict was allowed to stand.

DAMAGES IN CONTRACT

In contract, however, pecuniary loss is the one criterion; the defendant cannot be penalised as a wrongdoer. Merchants, in their curious retention of old forms, do retain in charter-parties the clause: "Penalty for non-performance of this agreement, estimated amount of freight." Yet in spite of the phrase only the actual damage suffered is recoverable. On the other hand, however good the intentions of the contract-breaker, however greatly to be commiserated upon his failure to perform what he had undertaken, he must make good the loss. Even if his undertaking is implied only, not expressed, he must compensate. If, as in the case given as illustration, his failure was due to a fraud unique in its audacity and scope, that makes no difference in his liability towards the other party. The possibility of being misled by fraud is a risk incident to business; and a man cannot evade his contractual liabilities by pleading that a third party has tricked him. The damages awarded are a money compensation to the plaintiff for the loss he has sustained through the breach of contract—no more, but also no less.

It will be readily seen that the measure of damages is often very difficult to determine. The point was thus put by a great judge: "There is no other universal principle as to the amount of damages than that it is the aim of the law to ensure that a person whose contract has been broken shall be placed as near as possible in the same position as if it had not. The assessment is sometimes a matter of great difficulty. It is impossible, in many cases, to regard the damage that has followed the breach as that for which the plaintiff is to be compensated; for the injury to the plaintiff may depend on matters which have nothing to do with the defendant. For example, an innkeeper furnishes a chaise to a son to drive to see his dying father; the chaise breaks down; the son arrives too late to see his father, who has cut him out of his will in his disappointment at his not coming to see him; in such a case it is obvious that the actual damage to the plaintiff has nothing to do with the contract to supply the chaise. Therefore, at an early stage the limitation was imposed that damages for breach of a contract must be such as might naturally be supposed to be in the contemplation of the parties at the time the contract was entered into; damages, in order to be recoverable, must be such as arise out of the contract and are not extraneous to it." Often, when parties enter upon a formal contract, they try to estimate the amount of damage that would arise through a complete or partial breach of contract. The amount stated in the contract is then recoverable; it is "liquidated damages" even though it should be called a "penalty." The proper form of words, where the parties do intend to provide for possible failure, is shown in paragraph 4 of the building contract form (page 752 below).

THE BANK-NOTES CASE

The Waterlow case, which aroused so great interest at the close of 1930, raised, among others, the question of measure of damages. The plaintiffs, asserting that they had suffered loss by the breach of an implied term in their contract with Messrs. Waterlow, claimed over half a million pounds as damages. The case arose in these circumstances. In addition to their ordinary business Messrs. Waterlow held themselves out as printers of banknotes, as being, therefore, worthy of trust in a highly responsible task. For the printer of banknotes is dealing with matter that may be as dangerous as dynamite; the credit upon which a country's currency is founded may be shattered by the knowledge that false notes have intruded among the true notes. The printer, accordingly, is bound to exercise the utmost vigilance in order to ensure that not a note is issued beyond those authorised by his clients, that none of those authorised gets into unauthorised hands. See page 720, where the case is discussed in relation to an implied term.

The plaintiffs pleaded that this implied undertaking had been broken; and it was not seriously contended to the contrary. The firm, having made plates for the notes authorised by the bank, had been deluded into using those plates for notes unauthorised. "There was," the decision went, "no express term in the contract that Messrs. Waterlow should not print or deliver notes without the authority of the bank. But that was accounted for by the fact that no one ever imagined that such a thing would occur. I hold that such a term must be implied in the contract; it is necessary to give effect to such business efficacy as the parties contemplated."

MEASURING THE DAMAGE

The unauthorised notes issued represented over a million pounds sterling. Was this the right measure of damage? That was the question upon which, ultimately, the House of Lords was asked to deliberate. The defendants contended that, even if there had been a breach of contract, the loss resulting was negligible. Since the bank was under no obligation to pay gold for notes, the bank had lost only the actual cost of printing the genuine notes issued in exchange for the spurious notes. This contention was easily countered. Whether convertible into gold or not, the notes constituted the currency of the country; the spurious ones jostled the genuine ones and competed with them. Each kind exerted command over the market. The unauthorised notes were "gate-crashers"; they elbowed away the invited guests, and took up much space upon the dancing floor and at the supper table.

The bank, however, had already recovered from the perpetrators of the fraud about half the total lost. The bank's claim was accordingly diminished by this recovered amount; for a man is not expected to profit by a broken contract. Then, too, the judge considered that the bank might have taken more energetic measures for minimising losses; after the gigantic fraud had become evident the bank could have done much to separate the genuine from the spurious notes. For Waterlows had furnished a key, enabling discrimination between the issues. If a plaintiff fails to do what a reasonable man would do to lessen losses, he cannot with justice ask the defendant to compensate him for what is due to his own remissness. The judge, therefore, allowed a comparatively small amount for the bank's failure to take the reasonable steps indicated. The higher Courts differed from him in regard to the action the bank might reasonably have been expected to take. But the principle is clear. As is noted below, a man is expected to act reasonably even when annoyed by a breach of contract. In the event Messrs. Waterlow were adjudged to pay over £600,000 as damages, together with the exceedingly high costs incurred on both sides.

COMMON MONEY BOND

Here, as another illustration, is a "Common Money Bond."

KNOW ALL MEN by these presents that I John Jones of 395 Eldon Road Southtoun in the County of Blankshire General Merchant am held and firmly bound to Samuel Smith of Sherston House Northbridge in the County of Whiteshire in the sum of ONE THOUSAND POUNDS to be paid to the said Samuel Smith or to his executors administrators or assigns for which payment to be well and truly made I bind myself my heirs executors and administrators firmly by these presents.

SEALED with my seal and dated this 2nd day of December 19...

Signed sealed and delivered ⎫
by the said John Jones in ⎬ JOHN JONES L.S.
the presence of ⎭

WILLIAM ROBINSON,

895 Round Street,

Southtoun,

Clerk.

NOW THE CONDITION of the above-written bond or obligation is such that if the above-bounden John Jones his heirs executors administrators shall pay unto the said Samuel Smith his executors administrators or assigns the sum of Five hundred pounds by the instalments following (that is to say) the sum of One hundred pounds on the 1st day of March next ensuing the sum of One hundred pounds other part thereof on the 1st day of June next ensuing and the sum of Three hundred pounds the residue thereof on the 2nd day of December 19 – – and if the said John Jones his heirs executors or administrators shall at the several times hereinbefore appointed for payment of the said several instalments of the said sum of Five hundred pounds pay unto the said Samuel Smith his executors administrators or assigns interest for the said sum of Five hundred pounds or such part thereof as for the time being shall remain unpaid after the rate of Five pounds for every One hundred pounds by the year (such interest to commence and be computed from the day of the date of the above-written bond or obligation) THEN the above-written bond or obligation shall be void otherwise the same shall remain in full force and virtue.

Stripped of its excess of words it comes to this : the borrower of £500 at 5 per cent interest undertakes in solemn form to pay to his creditor £1,000 in the event of failure to observe any of the conditions relating to repayment. If, however, as is contemplated by both parties, the conditions are duly fulfilled, the promise embodied in the bond becomes void, of no effect.

Common Law, interpreting the bond literally, would enforce the full payment. But equity intervened: it would be "against conscience" if the creditor stood upon his bond, when the failure put him to slight expense only. Yet, as Professor Holdsworth tells us in his monumental *History of English Law*, the Common Law judges themselves were reluctant to enforce a claim contrary to righteous dealing. He comments on a case in the Year Books of Edward II (*Umfraville* v. *Lonstede*): "A man has bound himself to pay a certain sum if he does not hand over a certain document on a certain day. Being sued upon his bond, he is unable to deny that he did not tender the document on the day fixed for the transfer; but he tenders it now, excuses himself by saying that he was beyond the sea, having left the document with his wife for delivery, and urges that the plaintiff has suffered no damage. The plaintiff relies upon the words of the bond, and we must confess to having thought that in and about the year 1309 judgment for the plaintiff would have followed as a matter of course. But to our surprise Bereford, C.J., after remarking that what is sought to be recovered is not properly speaking a debt (*purement dette*) but a penalty (*une peine*), exclaims: 'What equity would it be to award you the debt when the document is tendered and you cannot show that you have been damaged by the detention?' In the end the plaintiff is told that he will have to wait seven years for his judgment. Here certainly we seem to see 'relief against penalties' and relief that is granted in the name of 'equity,' though it takes the clumsy form of an indefinite postponement of that judgment which is dictated by the rigour of the law."

The equity rule now governs; there is no need for a subterfuge in order to enforce what is just. The creditor recovers no more than the actual loss that he proves from the debtor's failure.

PRICE-MAINTENANCE CONTRACTS

A price-maintenance case illustrates the points that may arise. The defendants had assented to the clause: "We agree to pay to the Dunlop Pneumatic Tyre Company the sum of £5 for each tyre sold in breach of this agreement, as and by way of liquidated damages and not as a penalty." The contention of the defendants was that, in spite of this statement, the sum stated must in fact be regarded as a penalty. The contention ultimately failed, and the Court awarded the sum stated; but the possibility of so contending illustrates the difficulty of discriminating between liquidated damages and penalty. Parties to a contract may be supposed to mean what they say; yet the expression is not conclusive. Contrary evidence may show that the parties in truth meant "penalty" when they spoke of "liquidated damages," or "liquidated damages" when they spoke of "penalty."

DIFFICULTY OF ASCERTAINING LOSS

The fact that the damages are indirect and difficult of ascertainment does not of itself prevent the sum specified from being the liquidated damages that can be recovered. Only by a rough computation can a manufacturer determine how much he loses when he finds his sales organisation upset, prices cut, good customers irritated, hostile traders supplied, and the like. In such a case, it is quite reasonable for the parties to estimate the damage at a figure; and if that figure is not extravagant, we must hold it as a bargain to assess damages, not a penalty to be held *in terrorem* over a possible delinquent.

If the sum is made payable by way of compensation on the occurrence of one or more or all of several events, some of which may occasion serious and others but trifling damage, the assumption then is that it is a penalty.

DAMAGES UNDER AN INDEMNITY PROMISE

An insurance company has, by an agreement under seal, promised to pay a bank the sum of £1,000. This agreement—this fidelity bond, as it is called—is not, however, to stand if an employee of the bank performs his duties faithfully and honestly during the year. To use the technical term, the bond is a promise defeasible upon condition subsequent. Now, strictly speaking, the promise ought to be fulfilled, however slightly the employee diverges from the straight path of industry and integrity. If he filches some of the bank's time by smoking a cigarette during office hours, if he is a penny out in hs accounts, then the condition upon which the promise depends has been satisfied.

Common Law did, in fact, so interpret such promises. It construed them to the letter; here are the plain words, we must take it that they mean what they say. Equity, however, stepped in to modify the harshness of adherence to a strict interpretation. Equity sought for the real intention of the parties when they framed their agreement. It was "sharp practice," "against conscience," "inequitable," "unconscionable"—these are the current terms of the Chancery Court—when one party tried to take advantage of the words, though he knew those words to bear a meaning other than the plain one. So here equity decided that what the parties meant was an indemnity against possible loss. The insurance company undertook to make good the loss; the exaction of a payment of £1,000 when a loss of £50 has occurred is unreasonable, and, therefore, unjust; the mention of £1,000 must be taken to be a fixing of the upper limit beyond which the company declined responsibility. Acts of Parliament have adopted the equity rule: the actual loss sustained by breach of the condition is all that is now recoverable.

"PENALTY" OR "LIQUIDATED" DAMAGES

This equitable rule governs throughout our law of contract. The man suffering from the breach of an agreement, the fulfilment of which he had a right to expect, gets a money compensation. The promise breaker is not to be penalised by being adjudged to pay more than the actual loss sustained. Yet agreements are made every day in which the parties stipulate for payment of a penalty in the event of the agreement's being broken. The law will enforce the "penalty" stated if, and only if, it appears to have been a genuine pre-estimate of the loss that would arise through the breach of contract. In such a case, no doubt, the term "penalty" is not the correct one; the proper term is "liquidated damages." Still, we can easily understand how business men are apt to use the shorter term. One of them has tried to calculate what he will lose if the agreement is broken; the other has assented to the calculation. Then it is that the Court will not interfere with the amount, though it is termed a "penalty."

To discriminate between a careful pre-estimation of loss and a sum intended to act as a powerful deterrent—between "liquidated damages" and "penalty," that is—calls at times for some close thinking. "The criterion," said Lord Dunedin, "of whether a sum—be it called 'penalty' or 'damages'—is truly liquidated damages (and, as such, not to be interfered with by the Court), or is truly a penalty (which covers the damage, but does not assess it) is to be found in this. Can the sum stipulated for be regarded as a genuine pre-estimate of the creditor's interest in the due performance of the obligation? Enormous disparity of the sum to any conceivable loss will point one way; the fact of the payment being in terms proportionate to the loss will point the other. But the circumstances must be taken as a whole, and must be viewed as at the time the bargain was made."

CODIFYING THE LAW OF CONTRACTS OF SALE

One might suppose that the codifying of a section of our law would diminish disputes. Parliament, with much strenuous debating, with scrupulous anxiety to provide for every conceivable happening, passes an Act; and henceforth we know where to find the law relevant to a particular matter. Perhaps, in fact, codifying does diminish disputes, though some loosely-drawn statutes have given abundant work to lawyers. And even the best drafted statute does not eliminate difficulties. A reading of the Act does not invariably provide plain answers to the questions that arise in practice; and disputes, deplorable and costly, still occur.

SPECIFIC PERFORMANCE IN CONTRACT

The Sale of Goods Act of 1893, for instance, is quite rightly looked on as an excellent exposition. Yet the proper application of its provisions is constantly a matter of controversy in the Courts. Section 4 of the Act seems particularly to afford scope for litigation: "A contract for the sale of any goods of the value of £10 or upwards shall not be enforceable by action unless the buyer shall accept part of the goods so sold, and actually receive the same, or give something in earnest to bind the contract, or in part payment, or unless some note or memorandum in writing of the contract be made and signed by the party to be charged or his agent in that behalf."

Does it apply to a ship? What constitutes the part payment spoken of? What note or memorandum satisfies it? These were the questions discussed in *Behnke* v. *Bede Shipping Co., Ltd.* (K.B. 1927).

Does this have any bearing upon the sale of a ship? Yes; a ship falls within the definition of "goods" as being "All chattels personal other than things in action and money." A ship is a personal chattel. The defendants contended that, even assuming that a valid contract for the sale of the vessel existed, the contract was unenforceable by reason of the section: the vessel had not been delivered, there was no part payment, there was no sufficient note.

The plaintiff had sent a deposit to the ship brokers. Was that part payment? Well, to constitute part payment, not only must the money be sent by the buyer, but also either accepted or in some way acknowledged by the sellers, so as to constitute a recognition by the sellers that there is a contract. Here the brokers held the deposit "pending completion of the contract." They received it, that is, not as agents for the defendants, but as stakeholders; there was, therefore, no part payment within the section.

But was there not "a note or memorandum of the contract . . . . . . signed by the party to be charged" (the defendant, that is)? Yes, said Mr. Justice Wright. The defendants had sent as their final offer a form of contract, headed with their name as sellers. "I think it must be held that the contract so headed constitutes an offer in writing which, if accepted either orally or in writing, would constitute a written note or memorandum. The contract is enforceable against the defendants."

The plaintiffs asked, however, for a decree of specific performance. Was that the proper remedy; would not an award of damages afford adequate compensation? For a Court will not decree specific performance unless damages are an altogether ineffective remedy. True, by Section 52 the Act does give the Court a discretion (in the event of a failure to deliver specific goods) to direct the contract to be performed, without allowing the seller an option to keep the goods and pay damages. And, even before the Act, equity would decree the specific performance of agreements to sell chattels having a special beauty, or rarity, or interest. Still, was a ship within the rule?

In the particular case it was, said Mr. Justice Wright. Ordinarily, no doubt, the loss suffered by the plaintiff could be readily computed; and an award of damages would satisfy the demands of justice. Here, however, evidence showed that the vessel, the subject-matter of the dispute, was of peculiar and practically unique value to the plaintiff. It was a cheap vessel, built in 1892; but her engines and boilers, being practically new, were such as to satisfy the German regulations. The plaintiff could, therefore, as a German shipowner, have her at once put on the German register. "The plaintiff wants the ship for immediate use; and I do not think damages would be an adequate compensation. I think he is entitled to his decree of specific performance in order that justice may be done."

WHEN SPECIFIC PERFORMANCE IS DECREED

The plaintiff who seeks specific performance must show that the ordinary remedy of a money award does not give him adequate compensation for the breach of contract. He must show that particular circumstances justify the Court in exercising its discretion, and in giving him the exceptional remedy. For specific performance is an equitable remedy, a device of the Chancellor in his efforts to supply the deficiencies of the Common Law Courts. It became available to the ordinary courts only in 1875; and it is still administered under rules evolved by the Lord Chancellor as keeper of the King's conscience. Men seeking an equitable remedy came as suppliants asking for a special intervention of the King's grace. In the Common Law Courts they were claimants of rights; in the Chancellor's Court they were suitors petitioning grace. Whether or not the suitor obtained the decree he sought depended largely upon his own conduct in the transaction. Was he one who deserved the King's grace? As was said in one judgment: "The remedy by specific performance was invented, and has been cautiously applied, in order to meet cases where the ordinary remedy by an action for damages is not an adequate compensation for breach of contract. The jurisdiction to compel specific performance has always been treated as discretionary and confined within well-known rules."

One of these rules illustrates the nature of the remedy. The Court will not grant its decree unless it can itself supervise the carrying out of the contract. It would not, for instance, try to enforce a contract of employment; for the attempt would involve "a series of orders and a general superintendence that could not conveniently be undertaken by any court of justice." The difficulty did not, of course, exist in the case.

There was, however, one other. When the Court grants a decree of specific performance, it directs the defaulter to do the thing he contracted to do. It explains to him what, as a conscientious man, he should do; and, if he disobeys, the Court commits him to prison for contempt. The defaulter here was a limited liability company; and a Court cannot imprison a company. But the Court can direct the officials of the company to perform an act, and, in the event of refusal, can commit the officials. Behnke, therefore, got his decree, and, thereby, the ship.

FURTHER RULES RELATING TO CONTRACTS

1. *Suing for Another's Benefit.* If A, not being an agent, makes a contract for the benefit of B, B himself cannot sue upon the contract. For there is no privity of contract between him and the

other contracting party. This is so, even if B, being an agent, conducts the bargaining on behalf of A. But A can sue upon it and recover for B's benefit. The House of Lords acknowledged the rule in *Les Affréteurs Réunis Société Anonyme* v. *Walford* (H.L. 1919). Walford as broker negotiated a charter-party, one clause of which stipulated that the owners would pay Walford a commission. Walford sued the owners, joining as plaintiffs the charterers. "The charterers," said Lord Birkenhead, "can sue as trustees on behalf of the broker. A charter-party is a contract between owners and charterers and, so far as brokers are concerned, it is *res inter alios acta* (a matter that gives outside parties no rights and imposes on them no liabilities). But, in the present case, the parties by a sensible arrangement have agreed that the matter shall be dealt with as if the charterers were co-plaintiffs."

2. *Interference with Contract.* The making of a contract cannot place liability upon a stranger to the contract. Still, there is a duty upon every one not to interfere with contractual rights. A man who induces one of two parties to a contract to break it, intending thereby to injure the other or to obtain a benefit to himself, does the other a wrong. Unless, as is possible, he shows that he had sound reason for persuading the breach, or unless he is protected by the Trade Disputes Act, 1906, he must pay damages.

3. *Duty of Mitigating Loss.* A plaintiff, though required to do what a reasonable man would do to lessen a loss caused by another's breach of contract, is not required to incur indirect losses in the effort. In *Finlay* v. *Kwik Hoo Tong* (C.A. 1929), the plaintiffs, dealers in sugar, could have avoided loss by making their sub-buyers take delivery under a bill of lading that was to be "conclusive evidence of the date of shipment." The B/L was in fact incorrect and the plaintiffs declined to insist on their right. Their attitude was upheld by the Court of Appeal: "I have little doubt that it would not have suited the respondents' business, nor would it be reasonable as a matter of business to require them, to do what is suggested in order to diminish the damages."

COMPETENCY TO TRANSACT BUSINESS

Before certain kinds of business can be transacted a legal qualification is needed—

1. A *solicitor* must be qualified; he must also take out an annual practising certificate. An unqualified person acting as a

solicitor is subject to penalties prescribed in the Attorneys and Solicitors Act, 1874. Moreover, one successful in his action cannot recover costs if the solicitor employed is uncertificated.

2. *Auctioneers* and *valuers* must have an annual licence.

3. A *County Court bailiff* and a *bailiff* to levy a distress must be certified by a County Court judge.

PERSONS OF UNSOUND MIND

There is a presumption that everything done by a person, while he is under the status of being a lunatic, is bad—i.e. is an act which the law cannot recognise. If a man becomes so far insane as to have no mind, perhaps he ought to be deemed dead for the purpose of contracting, even when the contract is in the form of a Contract of Record. So, too, an attempted gift of property would be void; a charge of crime would be countered by the defence "unfit to plead," whereupon the accused would be confined "during His Majesty's pleasure"; a contract made by him would be unenforceable, unless the other party could prove contractual capacity. A person of unsound mind sues, or defends an action brought against him, by his committee—by the individual to whose keeping the lunatic's person or estate is committed.

In the *Imperial Loan Company, Ltd.* v. *Stone* (C.A. 1892), the defendant had signed a promissory note as surety. After the signing he was found by inquisition to be a lunatic. At the trial the jury found that the defendant was insane when he signed the note; but they could not agree upon the question whether the plaintiff's agent knew of the insanity. On appeal it was held that there must be a new trial: "When a person enters into a contract and afterwards alleges that he was so insane at the time that he did not know what he was doing, and proves the allegation, the contract is as binding on him in every respect, whether it is executory (to be performed in the future) or executed, as if he had been sane when he made it, unless he can prove further that the person with whom he contracted knew him to be so insane as not to be capable of understanding what he was about. The burden of proof in such a case must lie on the defendant. The jury have disagreed on a material question, and the case must go back for a new trial." The old rule was that " Every deed, feoffment (a conveyance of freehold estate), or grant, which any man makes *non compos mentis* is avoidable; and yet shall not be avoided by himself, because it is a maxim of law that no man of full age shall be, in any plea to be pleaded by him; received by the law to stultify himself." That is, the man himself could not plead disability. One who claimed under him could, however. The old law is now altered in this respect, that the man himself by his committee can plead disability. The presumption is still, however, that the person making a contract is sane enough to know what he is doing. If he wishes to evade its obligations he, or his committee, must show (1) that he was insane at the time of making the contract, (2) that the other party knew this *at the time of making the contract*. And, even though he did know of insanity, one who supplies a lunatic with "necessaries" is entitled to a reasonable price.

The question was raised in *Rex* v. *Green-Emmott* (Court of Criminal Appeal, 1931) whether the recognisance of a certified lunatic is valid, a recognisance being a contract entered into with the Crown in its judicial capacity. The Court held that it was not. The accused had entered into a recognisance, into a contract of record entered upon the Court's rolls. He broke his undertaking and was convicted. The Court quashed the conviction in spite of the Crown's plea that the accused man was estopped from setting up his disability against a contract of record; "To render a contract binding upon him, it must be shown affirmatively that he understood what he was doing. No evidence has established that the appellant had a lucid interval so as to be capable of entering into a recognisance."

DRUNKENNESS AS AN EXCUSE

One who makes a contract while intoxicated may cancel it when he becomes sober. But he must act promptly. For the contract is not void but only voidable; if a third party acquires rights by it, an attempted rescission is too late.

FRAUD IN CONTRACT

This consists in an active intention to deceive: "Making a false statement through want of care falls far short of, and is a very different thing from, fraud; and the same may be said of a false representation honestly believed, though on insufficient grounds." This was in the judgment of *Derry* v. *Peek*, which settled definitely that an action for negligent misrepresentation, as distinct from fraudulent misrepresentation, could not be maintained. To constitute *fraud* the misrepresentation is known by the party making it to be untrue, or is made recklessly, its truth or falsehood, not troubling the maker. And to sustain an action for fraud the person suing must also show: (1) that he acted upon the misrepresentation; (2) that he suffered damage through doing so.

DURESS

This consists—

1. In actual or threatened violence.
2. Towards the person making the agreement, or to his wife, child, or parent.
3. By the other party.

He who enters into an undertaking under duress need not fulfil it.

UNDUE INFLUENCE

This arises when an unfair and unconscientious use of power over another brings about a transaction. If a gift or promise is made by child to parent, by client to solicitor, by ward to guardian, a presumption of undue influence arises: the burden of showing the fairness of the transaction is thrown upon the person who seeks to obtain the benefit of it. The presumption arises, too, where one of the parties is uneducated and inexperienced and the other educated and experienced; and where one is in urgent need of the other's help.

AGREEMENT NOT TO MAKE OFFERS

Q, a piano dealer, pays R, another dealer, £20 in consideration of his absenting himself from an auction. R does not attend the auction and Q buys there a piano for £40, which he resells to S for £120. Has the original owner of the piano any right of action against Q or S? Ever since the famous *Mogul Steamship Co.* v. *McGregor* case, trade competition has been almost exempt from restrictions. There it was decided that an individual trader could not recover damages against his rivals even though their business methods were designed with a view to harm him. In quite recent times the principle has been applied to an agreement to abstain from competing, an agreement that obviously must lessen the prices obtained by the seller. So the Court of Appeal decided in *Rawlings* v. *General Trading Co.*, 1921, a case arising out of a sale of Government stores where, through a "knock-out agreement" among intending bidders, goods were sold at absurdly low prices. At Common Law there is nothing illegal in persuading a man not to enter into contracts, nor does the fact of giving an inducement affect the matter. A third party may be injured by the success of the persuasion; but this is an injury incident to business life. It gives no cause of action.

The Auctions Bidding Agreements Act, 1927 attempts to provide a remedy in circumstances like the above. It is now an offence to give or to seek reward for not bidding at auctions; penalty of £100 or six months' imprisonment, or both is prescribed; and the seller may, against one who is a party to the agreement, treat the sale as one induced by fraud. He can rescind the bargain. So here both Q and R are liable under the Act. But the sale to S cannot be impugned; for S was no party to the agreement. The Act provides that, if a copy of the agreement is deposited with the auctioneer, traders can buy on a joint account.

A GENTLEMAN'S AGREEMENT

Is it possible to make a business arrangement without subjecting oneself to legal obligations under its stipulation? Nowadays it is. Formerly it was not; the Courts jealous of their standing as the final arbiters between parties in dispute, resented an agreement that sought to oust the jurisdiction of the Courts. Public policy demanded that the authority of the law should be upheld; and such an agreement was, therefore, against public policy. A more enlightened age recognises that the promotion of freedom is a higher public policy. Persons who have reached maturity of judgment may well be allowed to make what agreement seems good to them, even an agreement whereby either or both of the parties stipulate to be exempt from legal obligation.

In a well-known case, *Rosin and Turpentine Import Co.* v. *Jacobs* (1910), the House of Lords decided, though after much difference of judicial opinion, that a party might limit his obligations as he chose. The question at issue was whether a barge owner, guilty of negligence, was protected by the clause: "The rates charged by B. Jacobs & Sons, Ltd., are for conveyance only, and every reasonable precaution is taken for the safety of goods whilst in craft; they will not be liable for any loss or damage, including negligence, which can be covered by insurance." The clause did protect the defendants. The phrase: "Every reasonable precaution will be taken," merely advertised excellence as lightermen; it was not intended to be contractual.

In a more recent case (*Rose and Frank Company* v. *Crompton Bros.*, 1925), the Supreme Court went further. It held an agreement, settling the terms of a business arrangement, to be one upon which there could be no proceedings in the Law Courts.

It was a "gentlemen's agreement," the carrying out of which depends upon a sense of honour rather than upon legal constraint. For it had the clause: "This arrangement is not entered into as a formal or legal agreement, and it shall not be subject to legal jurisdiction, but it is only a definite expression and record of the purpose and intention of the parties concerned, to which they each honourably pledge themselves."

Stamp.
6d.

[FORM OF BUILDING CONTRACT.]

AN AGREEMENT made the 10th day of December 19— BETWEEN Joseph Jones of 385 Portland Square in the County of London Gentleman (hereinafter called "the Owner") of the one part and Samuel Smith of 794 Surrey Street Strand in the County of London Builder and Contractor (hereinafter called "the Contractor") of the other part WHEREBY it is agreed as follows—

1. The Contractor shall forthwith commence and before the expiration of two Calendar months from this date in all respects complete with the best materials in the best workmanlike manner and to the satisfaction of the Owner all the works and things mentioned or referred to in the particulars or specification hereunto annexed in and upon the house and premises therein mentioned.

2. The Contractor shall within one week from the completion of the said works and things remove all his scaffolding plant and materials from the premises.

3. The Owner shall pay to the Contractor the sum of £500 for the said works and things upon the completion thereof.

4. If from any cause whatsoever the said works and things shall not be completely finished and the said scaffolding plant and materials removed within the time and in the manner aforesaid then the Owner may deduct from any moneys then or thereafter due or payable to the Contractor the sum of £5 per day for every day after the expiration of two calendar months and one week from this date until such completion and removal shall be effected as and for liquidated damages and not by way of penalty.

5. In case there shall not be sufficient money due and payable to the Contractor to make such deduction then the excess shall be paid by the Contractor to the Owner.

6. In the event of such default the Owner may employ and pay other workmen to finish the said works and may use any scaffolding plant and materials on the premises belonging to the Contractor for such purpose and should the Owner pay or be liable to pay a larger sum for finishing such works than the amount he would be indebted for to the Contractor then the excess shall be paid to him by the Contractor.

7. The Owner may if he thinks fit require the omission of any of the works and in that case a proportionate sum shall be deducted.

8. All work rendered necessary in consequence of the doing of the work hereby agreed upon shall be deemed to be included in and to form part of this contract although not mentioned in the specification and no additional payment shall be made to the Contractor for the same.

9. No extra or additional work shall be done by the Contractor except upon the previous order in writing of the Owner agreeing to pay for the same and should the same be done without such order the Contractor shall not be entitled to any additional payment for the same.

10. The Contractor shall as well after as before he shall have been paid for the said works and things and without any further payment for a period of one year after completion make good any defects whatever in such works and things and especially in the roofs or drainage of the premises and the Owner may retain a sum not exceeding 15 per cent of the total contract price hereinbefore agreed upon until the expiration of such period as a security for the performance by the Contractor of this stipulation.

11. In case any dispute or difference shall arise between the Owner and the Contractor either during the progress or after the determination of the works and things or after breach of this contract as to the construction thereof or as to any matter or thing arising thereunder then such dispute or difference shall be referred to the arbitration and final decision of two impartial persons one chosen by each party and the award of such arbitrators shall be final and binding on both parties. The submission shall be deemed to be a submission to arbitration within the meaning of the Arbitration Act 1889.

IN WITNESS whereof the said parties have hereunto set their respective hand the day and year first above written.

Signed by the above named }
Joseph Jones and Samuel } JOSEPH JONES
Smith in the presence of me } SAMUEL SMITH
  THOMAS FIELD,
   185 Essex Street,
    Strand,
     W.C.2
      Solicitor.
(Here set out premises, specification, and plans.)

(N.B. The above form is one of the simplest character. In all works of any magnitude or importance an architect will be appointed, and also, perhaps, a surveyor or foreman of works. The payment will generally be made by instalments, dependent upon the granting of a certificate by the architect, as the work progresses. Provision will be made as to the ownership of the materials brought upon the property. Insurance will also be arranged for. And, lastly, there will frequently be a strike clause inserted, indemnifying the Contractor from loss or damage under certain circumstances. These matters, however, are noticed in the text.)

CARRIAGE BY LAND

THE CARRIER AS BAILEE

Goods are constantly in process of transit; they are in one person's possession, for the purpose of transit, though they are another person's property. The bailment thus created gives rise to many questions of law: in particular who is answerable for loss or damage of the goods? Persons, too, travel much more than in former days; and, in order to travel, they trust for their safety to carriers of various kinds. Through the advent and the almost startling development of mechanical means of transport on the roads, there has come a corresponding development of the carrying of one's own goods and person, by the ordinary individual in his own conveyance. The modern law of transport is, as a result, not only of great volume but also—by way of orders issued by the Minister of Transport—of almost daily addition or modification. Here is a branch of the law where ignorance may well be pleaded, though for obvious reasons it could not be admitted as an excuse for breaking the law. Details even in the most recently compiled account may, accordingly, be inaccurate at the time of reading. Information on such details, particularly in regard to the multitudinous orders issued under the Road Traffic Act, 1930, is available upon application to *His Majesty's Stationery Office, Adastral House, Kingsway, London, W.C.2.*

The main features of the law of carriage are, however, well established, and are here explained.

CARRIAGE OF GOODS

We must discriminate between a "common carrier," whose liabilities both at Common Law and by statute are onerous, and a "private carrier," whose liabilities are usually limited by the particular contract upon which he enters.

WHO IS A "COMMON CARRIER"?

A common carrier is one who makes a public profession to carry for all who will employ him: he is, therefore, to be distinguished from a carrier who takes what jobs suit him. The common carrier cannot limit those for whom he will convey. But he can limit the class of goods he conveys. Thus a railway company is not a common carrier of dangerous goods: the

Railways Act of 1921 (Section 50) declares: "Nothing contained in this Act shall impose any obligation on any railway company to accept dangerous goods for conveyance." So, too, any other common carrier may restrict himself to a particular description of goods. Or he may limit his profession to the carrying between specified places. He cannot then be compelled to carry between intermediate places.

The common carrier—

1. Is bound to accept consignments upon the fixed charges if he has accommodation; is bound to carry by the ordinary route (not necessarily the shortest) though he may be entitled to charge a mileage rate; is bound to deliver the goods without unreasonable delay.

2. Is, apart from very exceptional circumstances, the insurer of the goods placed in his charge for carriage. That is, he bears the risk of loss or damage, except under conditions that the Common Law was obliged to admit as excuses. Though negligence is absent he is liable for loss or damage, unless he can show that this loss or damage was caused by—

(a) Act of God.

(b) Act of the King's Enemies.

(c) Inherent Vice.

(d) Default of the Consignor.

Nugent v. *Smith* (C.P.D., 1875) illustrates the point well. A common carrier warrants the safe delivery of goods entrusted to him : apart from special contract he can escape liability for loss or damage only by proving that the loss or damage occurred through *Act of God,* or *act of the King's enemies,* or *defects in the thing carried (inherent vice).*

The defendant, a common carrier by sea, received the plaintiff's mare for carriage from London to Aberdeen. Rough weather was met, the frightened mare struggled, injured itself and died. Negligence was not proved against the defendant. It was, however, argued that the rough weather was not so unusual as to constitute an *Act of God,* nor the struggling of the mare enough to show that the loss occurred through *inherent vice.* But the Court of Appeal held the defendant free from liability.

"A carrier does not insure against acts of nature and does not insure against defects in the thing carried itself. But in order to make out a defence he must be able to prove that either cause taken separately or both taken together, formed the sole and direct and irresistible cause of the loss."

DISTINCTION FROM A PRIVATE CARRIER

A carrier other than a common carrier is exempt from this liability as an insurer. He is answerable for damage only when his negligence is established. Whether a carrier is a common carrier or not may, therefore, be a matter of moment when it is sought to fix liability for loss. The *Belfast Ropework Co.* sued *Bushell* (K.B. 1918) in the following circumstances. Bushell carried sugar from Liverpool to Manchester; he was continuously employed by one firm for this purpose. On the return journey he used to take whatever goods offered, rejecting them when the nature of the goods, or the destination, did not suit him, and varying his charges with the state of his business. That is, he made a special contract with the consignor.

It was held on these facts that he was not a common carrier and that, therefore, the plaintiffs could not recover for loss by accidental fire. That is, a man may carry on the business of a carrier; he may wish to extend his business and get new customers. But, if it is established that he reserves the right to decline offers—"being guided in his decision by the attractiveness or otherwise of the particular offer, and not by his ability or inability to carry having regard to his other engagements"—he is not a common carrier.

TERMINATION OF CARRIER'S LIABILITY

But the liability of a common carrier as an insurer of goods does not last longer than the time taken in transit and a "reasonable" time after. If, for instance, the consignee does not take prompt delivery the carrier's liability becomes lessened into the liability of a bailee: he is, in other words, liable only when the owner of the goods can establish negligence. The transit being ended he would not be answerable for an accidental fire that destroyed the goods in the warehouse; he would have been answerable for an accidental fire that destroyed the conveyance and the goods.

LIABILITY OF THE COMMON CARRIER

A consideration of common law exceptions from liability of the common carrier will make us understand why Parliament afforded him certain statutory defences. The Common Law exceptions are—

1. *Act of God.* An outbreak of natural forces such as could not by reasonable care have been foreseen or provided against.

2. *Act of the King's Enemies.* Constraint imposed by the armed forces of a State at war with this country.

3. *Inherent Vice.* The nature of the things carried (thus the carrier is exempt from the liability when loss is caused by the evaporation of liquids or the decay in organic matter). So too, a carrier must be told when special care is needed for the carriage of goods. Otherwise he cannot be fixed with liability.

4. *Default of the Consignor.*

Various Acts—from the Carriers Act, 1830 to the Carriers Act, 1924—enable the different types of carriers to limit their liability. And an *unambiguous special* contract may also limit liability. It should also be noted that the handing to a consignor of a notice specifying the terms makes the consignor subject to the conditions in the notice.

STATUTORY LIMITATIONS OF LIABILITY

The Railways Act, 1921, expands these common law exemptions from liability. Thus, for ordinary merchandise *Group A* carried at company's risk the condition is—

The company shall be liable for any loss or misdelivery of, or damage to merchandise during transit, unless the company shall prove that such has arisen from—

1. Act of God.

2. Act of War or the King's Enemies.

3. Arrest or restraint of princes, or rulers, or seizure under legal process.

4. Orders or restrictions imposed by the Government.

5. Act or omission of the trader, his servant, or agent.

6. Inherent liability to wastage in bulk or weight, latent defect or inherent defect.

7. Casualty (including fire or explosion).

Provided that—

(*a*) Where the company have failed to prove that they used all reasonable foresight and care in the carriage of the merchandise, the company shall not be relieved from liability.

(*b*) The company shall not incur liability of any kind in respect of merchandise when there has been fraud on the part of the trader.

" RESTRAINT OF PRINCES "

It is to be noted that this term does not of necessity imply force. Obedience to a command that it seems very inadvisable to disobey may very well be regarded as restraint. In *Sanday & Co.* v. *British and Foreign Marine Insurance Co.* (K.B. 1915), the insurance company disputed payment in these circumstances. Plaintiffs had shipped linseed on two British ships from the Plate River to Hamburg. The perils covered by the policy included "arrests, restraints, and detainments of Princes." While the voyage was proceeding, war ensued between Great Britain and Germany; the shipowners cabled to one ship to proceed to a British port; the other, being signalled to do so by a French cruiser, also put into a British port. The shipowners claimed for a total loss due to "Restraint of Princes."

The insurers contended that the declaration of war had made the adventure legally impossible. For not only does the Common Law forbid the carrying out of contracts with alien enemies, but various Trading with the Enemy Acts made commercial dealings of all kinds, direct and indirect, with the King's enemies, a criminal offence. It was the shipowners, by their voluntary submission to the law, that had frustrated the adventure, not the restraint of princes. This contention was negatived : "'Restraint of princes' does not necessarily involve the use of force; any authoritative prohibition on the part of a governing body, or the operation of municipal law, is sufficient." If one obeys an order, knowing that disobedience would result in the application of force, that is restraint.

CARRIERS' ACT, 1830

This Act limits the Common Law liability of carriers. Its effect has, with some modifications, been adopted in the Railways Act, 1921. If the carrier is to remain liable for certain specified and valuable articles, the nature and value of these must be declared to the carrier, and, if required, an additional amount as insurance must be paid.

The Railways Act places £25 as the limit of value. The limit of £10 is still applicable for a common carrier other than the railway. The additional charge must be notified conspicuously and a receipt for the goods must be given "acknowledging the same to have been insured." The goods in question include—

1. Gold or silver (whether as specie or bullion).
2. Precious stones, jewellery, watches.
3. Securities (notes, etc.).
4. Stamps, maps, writings, or pictures.

5. Plate, glass, china, furs, lace (not including machine-made lace).

Silk, which still applies where other carriers are concerned, disappears from the railway list.

PASSENGERS' LUGGAGE

The Carriers' Act is applicable even to passengers' luggage carried free; a declaration is necessary when the luggage includes the specified goods above the value of £25. In *Caswell* v. *Cheshire Lines Committee* (K.B. 1907), the plaintiff failed to recover for luggage lost. Plaintiff and his wife took with them on their railway journey a box containing articles of the specified kind. They made no declaration. Their argument was that, since the company could not charge for this luggage, a declaration would have been useless. But the Court held that the undertaking to carry luggage free referred only to the carriage; it did not refer to insurance. And, since the charges made under the Carriers Act were charges for insurance against the greater risk, a declaration was called for. In its absence the company was exempt from liability.

No special form of declaration is stipulated for; all that is necessary is enough information to enable the carrier to make his insurance charges. The maximum that can be claimed, if loss ensues, is the value declared. But a refund of the insurance charge is also due when damages are recovered.

MEANING OF " OWNER'S RISK "

Goods are carried " at owner's risk " rate only when the consignor has requested the company in writing so to carry them. The Railways Act prescribes a note to be signed by the consignor. His signing the note, whereby he undertakes—in consideration of his goods being carried at a lower than " company's rate "—to exempt the company from liability for negligence, is taken to be sufficient notice to him that he himself bears the risk arising from any negligence.

The company is not exempted entirely, even under owner's risk, from liability. Two liabilities are assumed—

1. For wilful misconduct: "The company shall not be liable for loss, damage, deviation, misdelivery, delay, or detention of a consignment, except on proof that the same arose from the wilful misconduct of the company or their servants." (That is, the claimant against the company has the heavy burden of proving intentional wrongdoing before he can recover damages.)

2. For the following causes of loss the company accepts responsibility unless it can disprove negligence; the presumption is that the company is l able; but the presumption may be rebutted by the company's proving the exercise of reasonable care.

(*a*) Misdelivery of a consignment.

(*b*) Pilferage.

(*c*) *For perishables by passenger train*: liability is accepted for half the loss caused by negligent delay over 36 hours, through which delay a loss of three-quarters of the value occurs.

(*d*) *For milk by passenger train*: liability is accepted for half the loss through negligent delay over 24 hours, whereby three-quarters of the value of the milk goes.

(*e*) Where other goods go by passenger train, liability is accepted for delay up to 75 per cent of the net invoice value of the goods.

MISDELIVERY OF GOODS BY CARRIER

This is a breach of his contract by the carrier; and where the goods are lost it may also give ground for an action for conversion. The carrier is a bailee of a person's goods and must obey his instructions. The consignor gives instructions in the first place. But, unless the consignor has indicated his wish to keep control over the goods, the consignee is entitled to issue fresh instructions. For in most events the property in the goods will have passed to the consignee by a contract of sale. And, where the consignor consigns to himself, he likewise may issue fresh instructions. In *Scothorn* v. *South Staffordshire Railway* (Ex. 1853), the plaintiff sailing to Australia consigned goods to a steamer. He then found that a berth was not available, and he instructed the L.N.W.R. clerk at Euston to send the goods to another address. The goods were, however, put on board the steamer, were lost in Australia, and the plaintiff recovered.

The wrong of conversion is independent of negligence. If a person obtained delivery through a fraud impossible of detection—by forged instructions for example, from the consignee—the carrier still is liable to the true owner.

UNREASONABLE DEVIATION

At Common Law, when an unreasonable deviation from the customary route took place, the carrier was unable to avail himself of any special clauses relieving him from liability. He was relegated to his status and became again the absolute insurer of goods placed in his charge. He cannot even plead the common exemptions from liability. For in fact the deviation is the cause of the loss.

This rule still operates at sea. In *James Morrison & Co., Ltd.* v. *Shaw, Savill and Albion Co., Ltd.* (K.B. 1916), the ship-owner was held liable for the cargo lost by the torpedoing of his vessel. His course was from New Zealand to London; and the bill of lading gave liberty to call at intermediate ports. But the master, in order to land other cargo, left the usual track to London in order to call at Le Havre. This was held to be a deviation. And, since the shipowner could not prove that in any event the cargo must have been lost by King's enemies, he had to pay damages. The Railways Act modifies the rule in land carriage by rail. The company is liable for loss caused by un-reasonable deviation, *unless they disprove negligence.* That is, the company is not remitted to its very narrow Common Law defences as a common carrier. For at Common Law even to disprove negligence does not exempt from liability.

ENDING OF TRANSIT

To determine this may be a matter of importance. The carrier's rights and obligations have ceased and have been re-placed by the warehouseman's rights and obligations. Or the consignee has obtained actual, or constructive, possession of the goods. In either event the seller-consignor can no longer stop the goods in transit.

Transit is over as regards railway transport—

1. When the consignor has effectively exercised his right of stoppage in transit; or when the consignee has taken delivery before the intended destination is reached.

2. When goods have been carted and offered for delivery at the usual delivery hours.

3. For goods "to await order" one clear day after notice is given to the address of the consignee (or to the consignor if this is unknown).

4. Where goods are to be transferred to an independent carrier (but not to another railway company in Great Britain), when the transfer has been made.

LIABILITY FOR LUGGAGE

A railway company is liable as a common carrier for loss of or damage to the luggage of a passenger lawfully travelling by the railway. This is so not only when the luggage is placed in the luggage van, but also when it is retained by the passenger as hand luggage. To evade the liability the company must prove that the passenger assumed the immediate care of the luggage, and that he had failed in his care.

The points were illustrated in *Vosper* v. *G.W.R. Co.* (K.B. 1927), where, on appeal from the county court, the plaintiff obtained damages. The plaintiff, holding a third-class ticket from Exeter to London, instructed a porter to place his suit-case in the London train. This the porter did; but, on arrival at Paddington, the suit-case could not be found. The company contested the claim because, apparently, the passenger had travelled in a third-class compartment though the luggage was in a first-class compartment. In his entertaining judgment, Lord Justice Atkin said: "It has been well established that railway companies are common carriers of passengers' luggage, whether it be luggage which is labelled and put in the luggage van or hand luggage taken by the passenger. But in respect of the latter, there is this modification of their ordinary liability, that they are not liable if they can show that the loss occurred through the negligence of the passenger. The difficulty arises in this case in that the goods were put into a first-class carriage whereas the passenger had a third-class ticket. But one knows that third-class passengers do from time to time, for different reasons, travel in first-class carriages. Sometimes they do so in open violation of their rights. Sometimes they do so because there is no room in the third-class carriages, and they think that that absolves them from paying the extra fare. Sometimes they do so because they think it convenient to take a third-class ticket and intend to pay the first-class fare. Sometimes there is a reservation, no doubt, that they will not pay the higher fare if no one comes and asks for it. Apart from that last case, however, those are lawful forms of uses of a railway. A third-class passenger is not an outlaw when he travels in a first-class carriage. The railway company are still under a duty to him personally and in respect of his luggage." I am injured by a railway collision: the fact that I am in a first-class compartment though I have a third-class ticket does not make me a trespasser, unable therefore to obtain damages against the company.

WHAT IS "PASSENGERS' LUGGAGE"?

This question is sometimes difficult to determine. Much guidance is afforded by the case *Buckland* v. *The King* (K.B. 1932), where the appellant's Petition of Right failed. He claimed that goods retained by the Custom's officials were not ordinary merchandise but passenger's baggage; that therefore they were wrongly detained; and he asked for damages. The goods in question were imported cinematograph films: the appellant had tried to anticipate the import duty upon such articles.

The Customs officials contended that the goods should have been entered as merchandise in accordance with Section 66 of the Customs Consolidation Act, 1876: "If any goods be taken or delivered out of any ship or out of any warehouse, not having been duly entered, the same shall be forfeited; provided always that no entry shall be required in respect of the baggage of passengers, which may be examined, landed, and delivered under such regulations as the Commissioners of Customs may direct."

"In Stroud's *Judicial Dictionary*," ran the judgment, "it was said that 'baggage' means such articles of necessity or personal convenience as are usually carried by passengers for their personal use. It is synonymous with *personal luggage*, and not merchandise or other valuables (although carried in the trunks of passengers) which were not designed for any such use but for other purposes, such as sale and the like. If those six parcels were to be deemed 'baggage of passengers,' why not also a dozen cases of cutlery, a dozen Turkey carpets, or a score of garden seats?"

Thus an army officer's valise, containing his equipment and revolver, is personal luggage (*Jenkyns* v. *Southampton Steam Packet Co.*, K.B. 1919). But a comedian's theatrical costume and properties is not personal luggage (*Gilbey* v. *G.N. Ry.*, K.B. 1920). The distinction seems to be very fine; for it may be urged that the articles in both cases were needed for the adequate performance of the respective services. It is consistent with the last case that a typewriter, a violoncello, an artist's sketches, the trust deeds taken by a solicitor for his client—all being carried in the way of business—have been excluded from the class of "personal luggage." As regards dogs accompanying passengers, (i) the company has power to make by-laws; (ii) when the company has undertaken to carry the dog, the undertaking being signified by the giving of a dog ticket, a guard or railway policeman may still (for good reason) prevent the dog's travelling; (iii) other passengers in the compartment have a right to object to the dog's presence.

25

COMMERCIAL TRAVELLERS' SAMPLES

A railway company may enter into a special contract (under Section 7 of the Railway and Canal Traffic Act, 1854) for the carriage by passenger train of samples as baggage.

If the consignor signs the contract, the company can rely upon a condition contained in it that it is exempt from all liability. If, however, no special contract is signed, the ordinary liability attaches to the goods.

RAILWAY COMPANY AS WAREHOUSEMAN

A warehouseman is liable for negligence. Whether, therefore, a company's liability is increased or diminished by the end of transit depends upon whether the goods are carried at company's risk or at owner's risk. In the first the liability is diminished, in the second it is increased. It seems, however, that the company's liability as a common carrier continues in respect of articles deposited in its cloak-rooms : "Having regard to modern decisions and the rising standard of convenience to which railway companies are obliged to conform, the cloak-room is now to be regarded simply as one of the necessary and reasonable facilities incident to the carriage of passengers and their baggage (*Singer Co.* v. *L.S.W.Ry.*, Q.B., 1894).

RAILWAY COMPANY'S LIEN ON GOODS CARRIED

The Common Law gave the carrier a right to retain the particular goods carried until his charges on those goods had been met. This *lien* was thus a particular, not a general, lien; he could not retain goods for money on outstanding accounts.

Such general lien could, however, result from a special contract : a trader might be permitted to settle his accounts at the end of specified periods. In exchange for this privilege the company would take a general lien authorising the retention of any consignment for charges due. A right of sale to cover charges—a right which is not included in an ordinary lien—would also be taken. It is this extended lien that is adopted in the *Standard Terms and Conditions*—

"Merchandise delivered to the company will be received and held by them subject—

(*a*) To a lien for moneys due to them for the carriage of and other proper charges or expenses upon or in connection with such merchandise ; and (*b*) To a general lien for any moneys or charges due to them from the owners of such merchandise for any other services rendered or accommodation provided in relation to the carriage or custody of merchandise;

and in case any lien is not satisfied within a reasonable time from the date upon which the company first gave notice of the exercise of their lien to the owners of the merchandise, the merchandise may be sold and the proceeds applied in or towards the satisfaction of every such lien and all proper charges and expenses in relation thereto, and the company shall account to the owners of the merchandise for any surplus.

"The general lien conferred by this condition shall not prejudice an unpaid vendor's right of stoppage in transit."

The lien referred to in paragraph (*a*) is the particular lien applicable to the occasional parcel sent by a non-trader; the lien referred to in paragraph (*b*) is the general lien applicable to a running account.

The concluding paragraph preserves the right of the consignor who is an unpaid vendor of recovering the goods sold by exercising his right of stoppage in transit. So long as the goods have not, actually or constructively, come into the possession of the consignee-buyer, the consignor can retake them on payment of the particular charges. That is, the general lien is only operative against the consignee who is demanding delivery and who owes on a current account: "if a person from whom no money is due is in a position to assert his right of the goods, the general lien is inoperative."

RAILWAY COMPANY'S RIGHT OF SALE

The conditions under which a railway company may exercise its right of sale of goods in its possession are—

1. That the company do what is reasonable to obtain the value of the merchandise.

2. That in all cases, save one, notice be given to the proper person if telegraph or telephone be available, and if it is reasonably practicable: failure to give the company immediate instructions in the manner indicated in the condition will enable the sale to proceed without them. The proper person to be notified is the consignee, or, if he is not available, the consignor. The case where no notice need be given at all is that of civil or industrial commotion.

This second paragraph bears upon the reluctance of English

law to admit the plea of "agent by necessity." The master of a ship may, in case of necessity, sell ship or cargo; and "the law as to power of sale and the duty to take care of the goods which is laid down in the case of a carrier by sea applies to a carrier by land where the necessary conditions exist." But "a real necessity must exist for the sale, and it must be practically impossible to get the owner's instructions in time as to what shall be done."

This was laid down in *Springer* v. *G.W. Ry.* (K.B. 1921), when the company was held liable to the owner of tomatoes, sent from Jersey and held up at Weymouth through a railway strike. The company sold the tomatoes lest they should become unsaleable, but without advising the owner and seeking his instructions, and was held liable for the full value.

RAILWAY RATES

These are under the control of the Rates Tribunal, the composition of which is determined by the Railways Act. The aim has been to make the Tribunal representative of all the interests concerned—the companies, the traders, the manufacturers, the public at large. Publicity is assured both as to the proceedings of the Tribunal and the publishing of the rates affecting the trader. Section 54 of the Act enacts—

1. That printed copies of the general classification of merchandise and a schedule of standard charges shall be kept for sale by every railway company to which the same apply;

2. That there shall be open for public inspection a copy of the general classification of merchandise carried on the railway; and

3. A book or books shall be kept stating—

(a) The chargeable distance from the station or place where the merchandise is received of every place to which the company book;

(b) The scales of standard charges applicable to each class of merchandise.

(c) All exceptional rates in operation from the station or place in question.

(d) Collection and delivery charges.

RAILWAY RATES TRIBUNAL

The Railways Act, 1921, set up this tribunal as a permanent part of the re-organization of the railways. Its offices are at 2, *Clement's Inn, London, W.C.2.* The three "permanent members" are the President, an "experienced lawyer," and two persons "of experience in commercial affairs and railway business." The term of office is seven years, but renewal is possible and usual. The Lord Chancellor, the President of the Board of Trade, and the Minister of Transport concur in the appointment. Two panels supplement the tribunal: a "general panel" of thirty-six representing the interests of trade, labour, passengers, agriculture, and horticulture; a "railway panel" of twelve representing the railways. Members from these panels are co-opted to help the permanent tribunal.

The Tribunal (1) classifies merchandise for carriage by rail; (2) settles standard terms and conditions; (3) fixes and, from time to time, modifies standard conveyance rates and terminal charges, and settles disputes regarding them; (4) sanctions exceptional rates; (5) fixes through rates and fares between the companies; (6) settles questions as to dangerous goods; (7) fixes a "standard revenue" for the companies.

PROCEDURE

The rules and forms to be observed in making application to the Tribunal are given in *Statutory Rules and Orders*, 1922, No. 906: this is obtainable from *H.M. Stationery Office, Kingsway, London, W.C.2*. Individuals, firms, or associations may apply; legal advisers may appear; attendance of witnesses may be enforced by *subpoena*; an appeal lies on point of law, not of fact.

The Tribunal, like the Railway and Canal Commission—much of the work of which has been taken over,—is therefore a judicial body. It is a Court of Record from which appeal lies to the Court of Appeal. The extension of Government activity into all manner of new fields has made inevitable the entrusting of the power of deciding administrative issues to executive bodies. One may indulge in adverse comments upon the growth of bureaucracy. But it is probably inevitable.

WAY-LEAVE

An interesting illustration of the kind of questions dealt with by the Railway and Canal Commission was afforded by the successful application of the *Hamsterley Ganister Company* (*Times* Law Report, 22nd April, 1931). Whenever a carrier cannot reach an agreement with a landowner, whose land or a right over whose land is desirable for the effective working of his enterprise, the Commission is authorised—by the Mines (Working Facilities and Support) Act, 1923—to make an order.

The applicants, the owners of a quarry at Hamsterley, conveyed their ganister, a material used in the making of fire bricks, to a siding of the L.N.E.R., a distance of about $3\frac{1}{2}$ miles, by means of an aerial ropeway which crossed the land of several owners, including that of Mr. William Frederick Brown, who opposed the application.

The right to carry the ropeway over Mr. Brown's land was the subject of a way-leave for 14 years at a rent of £200 a year. The way-leave expired in October, 1930. The land was crossed by the ropeway for a distance of 1,600 yards.

On the expiration of the way-leave Mr. Brown offered to grant a new way-leave at the former rent of £200 a year. The applicants contended that that was too much, and considered that a proper rent would be 2d. a yard plus 7s. 6d. a trestle a year, which worked out at slightly under £18 a year in all.

Mr. Justice MacKinnon, in delivering judgment, pointed out that an ancillary right such as that claimed by the applicants could only be granted if it could not be obtained by private arrangement. If the grantor asked for unreasonable terms, that was in effect the same thing as if he refused altogether. Further, the Court had to be satisfied that the making of an order was in the national interest.

The Court were of opinion that the rent asked was grossly excessive. Further, the Court considered it to be in the national interest that the applicants should obtain the use of the ropeway on reasonable terms, because, if they were unable to continue working at a profit, the quarries would be closed and many men thrown out of employment. What was a reasonable rent in the circumstances? Adopting the standard of allowing 7s. 6d. a trestle and 2d. a yard, a fair rent in the present case would be £18 a year. The Court accordingly directed that an order should be drawn up in similar terms to the way-leave which expired in October, 1930, except that £18 should be substituted for £200 in the clause fixing the rent.

THE CARRIER'S LIABILITY : HOW FAR LIMITED

Rules of law applicable to days when men had leisure enough to discuss their contracts need modification in these quick-moving times. Recent decisions have, for instance, increased the railway company's power to bind the passenger by conditions of which the passenger was unaware at the time of making the contract. That time is when the passenger proffers his fare in payment for a ticket. The ticket is evidence that the contract has been made. Now, suppose the ticket contains an instruction, "For conditions see time-tables." Is the passenger subject to those conditions, which he has not seen and which possibly would be difficult for him in the circumstances to see? Apparently he is. In *Thompson* v. *L.M. & S. Railway* (K.B. 1930), the plaintiff argued that she should not be subject to a condition never brought to her notice. For in fact she could not read.

She failed, however, in her contention. The law cannot cater for exceptional persons; and what is adequate notice to the average person is notice also to the exceptional one. She was therefore subject to the condition whereby the railway company limited its liability. The case of *Penton* v. *Southern Railway* (K.B. 1931), seems even harder on the passenger. Penton intended to buy an ordinary ticket. The booking clerk gave him a cheap ticket under which the passenger travels at his own risk. Injury ensued, and a claim followed. The evidence was that Penton, though surprised at the change handed out, was too hurried to note the nature of the ticket. Yet he failed in his claim. By something very like a legal fiction, notice had been given of the limitation of railway company's liability.

We have travelled some way from *Parker* v. *S.E. Railway* (1887). In that case the Court of Appeal decided that, where ignorance of conditions is urged, the Court (judge or jury) must ask itself the questions: Did the claimant know that the writing on the ticket expressed conditions of the contract? Did the carrier do what was reasonably sufficient to give the claimant notice of the conditions. If either question can be answered, Yes, then the conditions form part of the contract. The railway company is entitled to assume that those entering into contracts with it can read and understand English, that they are intelligent enough to realise that a contract of carriage will contain many conditions besides the undertaking on the one hand to carry, and the undertaking on the other hand to pay the fare. Presumably, answers to the same questions would still be the basis of a decision, but "sufficient notice" is now construed in an elastic point of view, and a point of view much more favourable to the railway company than when Parker sued for his lost luggage.

LIABILITY FOR LOST LUGGAGE

In another matter, the question of liability for loss of the passenger's luggage, things are moving in a direction less satisfactory from the railway company's point of view. It used to be accepted that the fact of taking one's luggage into one's compartment, instead of handing it over to the guard for conveyance in the luggage van, absolved the company from the duty of taking care of it. For the passenger had constituted himself its one guardian. If it were stolen in transit, he could recover its value only in the very unlikely event of his being able to prove wilful negligence on the part of the company's servants. The provision of racks for light luggage was not to be interpreted as an invitation to passengers to place luggage upon them. They were merely conveniences, out of the company's bounteous goodwill; and the passenger used them at his risk.

Two cases in 1931, both in favour of the passenger, call for a modification of this statement. In one case the passenger, after seeing her case placed on the rack by a porter, walked along the platform in order to buy literature at the bookstall. When she returned, the case had vanished; and, though she had left the compartment on her own initiative and for her own purpose, not at all upon the invitation of the railway company, she recovered the value of the lost case.

In the other case, the passenger had left the compartment in order to have luncheon in the special car; and a package was abstracted during his temporary absence. The company had invited the passenger to leave. It was not to be expected that he would carry his luggage about with him. Again the company was held liable.

PASSENGER WHO HAS LOST TICKET

The legal position when the passenger has lost his ticket still remains as it was stated by the Court of Appeal in *Butler* v. *Manchester S. & L. Railway* (1888). The contract of carriage is made when the passenger tenders his fare: the railway company is then under obligation to carry. The ticket affords evidence— mainly for the purpose of being shown to the company's servants —that the contract has been made. But the ticket is not the only possible evidence. If the passenger can show by any other evidence that he bought a ticket, the company must carry him. They cannot forcibly expel him from the train, as they can one who has not bought a ticket. For the latter is a trespasser; and one may remove a trespasser by force—using, however, no more force than is necessary. "One knows," said Lord Justice Lindley, "that railway companies may be placed in great difficulty by the unscrupulous attempts of fraudulent persons to cheat them. But there is nothing that authorises the company to remove from their carriage a passenger who fails to produce his ticket. The company cannot justify laying hands on the plaintiff. The plaintiff had taken his ticket and the effect was that there was a contract by the company to carry him to Manchester and back." The company, for its own protection, is entitled to make conditions, however. Thus, if a person leaves his season ticket at home a condition constraining him to pay the full fare—to be refunded upon application—is enforceable. So, too, is a condition obliging the passenger to pay a small fee upon the issue of a duplicate of the ticket that has been lost.

CARRIER'S OBLIGATION IN REGARD TO LUGGAGE

Furniture removers are not common carriers when, as almost invariably happens, they make a special contract with each customer. On the other hand a railway company and motor coach service are common carriers of such passenger's luggage as is carried without special agreement, including what is carried free.

As to this "free luggage" the service of the railway or the motor coach proprietors is not gratuitous, part of the fare paid by the passenger being the consideration for carrying the luggage. And a man travelling together with his wife can claim free carriage of double the weight allowed to a single passenger.

The liability of the carrier—railway or steamship or motor coach—begins from the moment the luggage is placed in the conveyance or is handed to a servant of the carrier. This last statement is, however, limited in that the luggage must not be handed to the servant an unreasonably long time before the journey is to begin. In *Bunch* v. *Great Western Railway* (H.L. 1888), the House of Lords decided that even forty minutes before the train left was not too long to prevent the passenger from succeeding in a claim. Mrs. Bunch reached Paddington, gave a Gladstone bag to a porter who undertook to put it into her compartment, went away for ten minutes to get her ticket and to find her husband in the station, and missed the bag when she returned. The company was held liable. Indeed, though the luggage is under the immediate care of the passenger and in his compartment, the company is still liable for it as a common carrier.

When a company seeks to escape from its liability to insure passenger's luggage by showing that the passenger took the control of it into his own hands, the burden is upon the company to prove (1) that the passenger actually assumed control; (2) that his own negligence caused the loss.

DUTIES OF PASSENGERS

1. A passenger is bound, on request by a servant of the company, to produce and—if required—to deliver up a ticket showing that his fare is paid; or else to pay the fare from the place whence he started; or else to give the servant of the company his name and address. Refusal to do any of these three renders him liable, on summary conviction, to a fine of forty shilling (Regulation of Railways Act, 1889). For subsequent offences the penalty is increased to one of £20 or a month's imprisonment. Failure to do one of the three things also entitles a servant of the company to detain him till he can be brought before a magistrate. If the passenger does give a name and address the company's servants have no right to detain him—even though they suspect the address to be incorrect. (See *Knights* v. *London, Etc., R. Co.,* Q.B. 1893.)

2. A passenger must not travel beyond the point to which he has paid his fare, nor, unless with the express or implied authority of the company's servants, in a carriage of a superior class to that authorised by the ticket. Travelling *with intent to avoid payment* is punishable by a fine on summary conviction of £2 (subsequent offences £20 or month's imprisonment). The "intent to avoid payment" is usually established by showing that the passenger passed the barrier at his destination without offering to pay the extra amount due from him. In the absence of fraud (which must be proved by the company) none of these things is an offence: travelling without a ticket, travelling in a class superior to that for which the ticket is available, using a ticket on a day for which it is not available, refusing to produce a ticket. The presumption is always in favour of innocence. The onus, therefore, is upon the company to establish the intent to avoid payment due.

RIGHT TO REMOVE PASSENGER

Since 1926 English railway companies have issued fresh sets of by-laws. The need for the new sets arose from the fact that some of the former by-laws were *ultra vires*. When a railway company obtains from Parliament its special enabling Act, it is given powers—within strictly defined limits—to make laws. To the extent that these laws are consistent with the powers given, they become part of English law. But the company must have regard to the limits imposed, just as a joint-stock company must frame its Articles of Association so as to fall within the powers taken in its Memorandum of Association. If beyond those powers, both the by-laws and the company's articles are of no legal effect. Thus, a railway had a by-law that a person travelling without a ticket was liable to a fine, even in the absence of fraud. A passenger, fined under the by-laws, appealed against his conviction, and the fine was remitted.

The Regulations of Railways Act, 1889, provided what Parliament considered adequate protection for the railways. A by-law authorising fine or detention, when Parliament had not thought fit to authorise it, was *ultra vires*. One of the new by-laws illustrates the fact that the passenger is a licensee of the company when it has agreed to carry him; till then if he enters a carriage he is a trespasser and may be removed even though willing to pay the fare. The by-law is "No person shall enter any carriage or vehicle using the railway, for the purpose of travelling, unless and until he or some one on his behalf shall have obtained a ticket entitling him to travel therein. Any person infringing or not observing this by-law and regulation, and failing to leave the carriage or vehicle immediately on request by any duly authorised servant or agent of the company, may be removed therefrom by or under the direction of such servant or agent."

COMMUNICATION CORDS

When a train is intended to run more than twenty miles before stopping the company is bound to provide and to keep in good order means of communication between the passengers and the company's servants in charge of the train (Regulation of Railways Act, 1868).

RAILWAY TIME-TABLES

These are continuous offers to the general public. Any one who proffers the stipulated fare at the booking office accepts the offer. The company is then under contractual obligation to carry out the undertaking. Through a mistake in the time-table Denton lost his connection and failed to keep an appointment: the railway company was held liable to compensate him. "It is all one as if a person, duly authorised by the company had, knowing it was not true, said to the plaintiff: 'There is a train from Milford Junction to Hull at that hour.' The plaintiff believes this, acts upon it, and sustains loss. Where a person makes an untrue statement, knowing it to be untrue, to another, who is induced to act upon it, an action lies" (*Denton* v. *G.N.R.*, Q.B. 1856).

It seems, however, that lateness of arrival will give a passenger a valid claim for damages only when he can show that the lateness is due to negligence. For the company usually restricts its liability by some such condition as: "Though every effort is made to ensure punctuality, the company does not warrant the departure or arrival of trains at the times specified." This condition does not, of course, wholly exempt the company from liability. It does, however, throw upon the complaining passenger the burden of proving that "every effort" was not in fact made.

CONSIGNOR'S DECLARATION OF VALUE

When the consignor declares the goods to be of a certain value, or when he acts in such a way as to represent them to be of a certain value—in order, for instance, to secure a lower rate of carriage—he cannot afterwards be heard to say in an action that the goods were of a higher value. This is another example of the rule of estoppel.

CONDITIONS, REASONABLE AND UNREASONABLE

Examples of the conditions imposed by a railway company upon its customers that have been held to be unreasonable are—

1. The company will not be liable for loss or deterioration of goods improperly packed.

2. The company will not be liable for imperfections or defects in its own stations or premises, or for insufficiency of its vehicles.

3. The company will not be responsible for passengers' luggage unless it is fully addressed with the name and destination of the passenger (*Cutler* v. *North London R. Co.*, Q.B. 1881).

4. The company will not be liable for an injury unless the alleged injury was pointed out at the time of unloading (on the other hand a condition that notice of a claim must be made within fourteen days has been held reasonable).

LUGGAGE LEFT IN TRAIN

Railway servants have orders to take forgotten packages to a particular place. To this place the passenger, seeking to recover his property, resorts. The railway employee, therefore, who "finds" and takes to his own use a package left in a train is guilty of larceny of the thing appropriated. Whenever in like manner a finder has directions which he should obey regarding the disposal of the thing found, he is a thief when he disregards the directions and converts the thing to his own use.

This, of course, does not apply to articles of trivial and perhaps transitory value like newspapers. These being "abandoned" by their owner become the property of the first occupant, of the first person who chooses to take them up.

LIABILITY TO " INVITEES "

A railway company is liable for negligence to persons who come to a station merely to see friends off, and whether or not those persons have bought a platform ticket. For such persons are in the position of invitees upon the railway premises.

CARRIAGE OF ANIMALS

Railway and canal companies must afford facilities for the carriage of animals. Any special conditions in the contract that seek to limit their liability for negligence are void unless—

1. They are contained in a writing signed by the consignor or his agent.

2. They are just and reasonable.

LIMITATION OF LIABILITY

The Railways Act, 1921 (amending the Railway and Canal Traffic Act, 1854) limits liability for loss or injury to a horse to £100, to a head of cattle to £50, to any other animal to £5. But if the consignor at the time of delivery to the company declares them to be of higher value, the declaration being made with a view to paying a higher rate posted up in the company's office, the company incurs the higher liability. The higher rate charged includes, that is, an insurance premium against the risk of loss.

CARRIER'S LIABILITY FOR " MISCONDUCT "

Though a carrier's contract may relieve him from liability for "fault or negligence," he is still liable for misconduct; and misconduct implies that a person clearly appreciates that he is acting wrongly. The party alleging it must prove the misconduct; it will not be presumed from a misdelivery or delay or unexplained injury.

SPECIAL RAILWAY ACT

A railway will need to acquire land. It, therefore, promotes and obtains a Private Act giving it powers of compulsory purchase. Parliament usually takes the opportunity of imposing terms upon the company. The Act will specify the gauge, usually the standard gauge of 4 ft. 8½ in. Where the railway crosses a public road, a bridge must be built, except in places where a level crossing is authorised. If such a level crossing is authorised, the company must provide suitable gates and a gate-keeper to control them. The Minister of Transport has powers to make regulations about such crossings, and about the speed at which trains may pass over them.

SAFETY ON RAILWAYS

Railway companies are obliged to report to the Minister all accidents causing personal injury, and all derailments and collisions in which passenger trains are involved. Inquiries may be made into such accidents, and the inquiries are made public.

SEATS IN RAILWAY TRAINS

It seems that a railway company is under no obligation to find a seat for a particular passenger on a particular train : it is a matter of chance whether the passenger travels sitting or standing. This is a contrast to the practice of the road competitors : to buy a ticket for a motor-coach journey is to obtain a certainty of obtaining a seat.

LETTER CARRYING

The Post Office Act, 1908, gives the Postmaster-General a monopoly of the business of letter-carrying, although there are certain exceptions. It also grants him the exclusive privilege (with exceptions) of "performing all incidental services of receiving, collecting, sending, dispatching, and delivering letters."

Among the exceptions are : a letter sent by a private friend who is travelling and who is delivering it to the person to whom it is directed ; letters sent by messengers concerning the private affairs of the sender or receiver.

House-to-house delivery of trade announcements or advertisements is permitted ; but the documents become liable to the provisions of the Act if they are placed within envelopes or wrappers and addressed. Even if unaddressed, they come under the

Postmaster's monopoly if they are delivered according to a list of addresses.

"This means that you are not entitled to select certain houses for delivery," an official of the G.P.O. stated. "It is also unlawful to make a business of keeping messengers and letting them out on hire to carry letters.

"A servant or messenger may carry a letter for his employer, but must not collect letters from several persons. In other words, your servant may take a note for you, but if he calls at several of your friends' houses and collects notes from them for delivery elsewhere you are breaking the law. Carriers, too, are prohibited from carrying letters except those relating to the goods carried."

STOPPAGE IN TRANSIT

Stoppage in transit is the right of the unpaid seller, *if the buyer has become insolvent,* to require a carrier to deliver goods back to him. And if the carrier, ignoring or forgetting the unpaid seller's request, does deliver to the insolvent buyer, then the carrier is liable for a conversion; and the unpaid seller may recover the value of the goods from him. Nevertheless, the buyer, once the goods are in his possession, can deal with them as he pleases. They are his property. For the exercise of the right of stoppage in transit does not of itself annul the sale. The buyer, though he has not paid for the goods, may, therefore, sell them to a third party; and the third party cannot be disturbed in his ownership.

Thus, M sells a piano on credit to O and delivers it to a carrier. Hearing that O is insolvent, he instructs the carrier to redeliver the piano. The carrier, through a mistake of his servant, delivers the piano to O, who forthwith sells it to P. O is, in fact, insolvent. What are M's rights against O, P, and the carrier?

Against P, none at all; against O a claim for the amount due, a claim to be proved in the bankruptcy proceedings; against the carrier, a claim for the loss sustained through the carrier's failure to follow instructions. And he must elect between the claims: he cannot enforce both.

When the seller does resume possession of the goods it amounts to this: the contract of sale still stands and he can, if he chooses, sue for payment; but he can now exercise his lien for the price.

RULES REGARDING STOPPAGE IN TRANSIT

The rules regarding stoppage in transit are clearly set out in Sections 44–46 of the Sale of Goods Act, 1893. These rules make it clear that in one event only can the goods be stopped, that event being when the buyer has become unable to pay his debts. Whether or not his being unable to pay past accounts is a proof of insolvency, depends upon circumstances. Apparently the furthest guide given by the Courts is in *National Bank* v. *Morris* (A.C. 1892), that a creditor could assume insolvency if he knew of circumstances from which ordinary men of business would judge the debtor unable to meet his liabilities. No Court would compel a seller to deliver goods for which the price would not be paid. On the other hand, the seller who does stop the goods in transit makes himself liable to heavy damages if he should stop them and yet the buyer be solvent.

DURATION OF TRANSIT

Difficulty may arise about the ending of the transit. Perhaps the clearest statement is: "When the goods have not been delivered to the purchaser or to any agent of his to hold for him, *otherwise than as a carrier*, but are still in the hands of the carrier as such, and for the purposes of the transit, then, although such carrier was the purchaser's agent to accept delivery so as to pass the property, nevertheless the goods are *in transitu* and may be stopped."

When the goods are sent on a liner bill of lading they are certainly in transit. In that event stoppage may be effected. The procedure is to give notice to the shipowner or his representative; and the shipowner or his representative is under duty to forward the notice as speedily as possible to the shipmaster. If the goods should be delivered to the buyer after the notice has been given and a reasonable time for its effective communication to the master has elapsed, the shipowner is liable to the seller in damages.

Where the goods are shipped on a steamer chartered by the buyer, the freight being credited on the invoice, the matter becomes doubtful. If the ship chartered is for the time being at the absolute disposal of the buyer, so that the master and crew are his servants and not the servants of the shipowner, the transit is at an end as soon as the goods are delivered to the ship.

If, however, the chartering of the ship is not absolute, the ship remains under the control of the shipowner. The goods are then in transit. It may be taken as almost invariably the case that the latter is the correct position, so that goods may, even where the ship has been chartered by the buyer, be stopped.

The right to stop goods in transit is gone when an innocent party has bought (or taken in pledge) the bill of lading or other document of title for the goods. Mercantile custom, seeking to promote confidence in dealings with documents of title, has brought about the rule of law: an assignment to a *bona fide* purchaser of a bill of lading defeats the right of stoppage in transit. It should be noted that a sub-sale, otherwise than by the transfer of such a document, does not defeat the right. When the document has been taken as a pledge the unpaid seller can recover the goods by paying off the banker or other party who has advanced money on the goods.

The lien of the carrier for his charges on the actual goods carried remains, in spite of there quest to stop; and the carrier may require from the unpaid seller payment of these charges. But the goods cannot be retained to satisfy the carrier's claim on general balance against the buyer.

IMPLIED WARRANTY OF FITNESS FOR CARRIAGE

The consignor who delivers goods without special description to a common carrier warrants by implication that the goods are fit to be carried in the ordinary way. When the goods are dangerous, the consignor is bound to inform the carrier. *Bamfield* v. *Goole and Sheffield Transport Co.* (K.B. 1910), is a good illustration. The plaintiff's husband, owner of a barge, carried for the defendants some casks of chemical. The chemical gave off fumes that poisoned the husband and made the plaintiff ill. The consignors were held liable, in spite of the fact that they did not know the dangerous nature of what they had sent as "general cargo."

"There is a common law obligation of the carrier to carry according to his profession; there is the correlative obligation of the consignor to tender for carriage such goods only as can safely be carried. Every consignor who tenders goods to a common carrier, to be carried by him in performance of his common law obligation to carry, thereby impliedly warrants to the carrier that the goods so tendered are fit to be carried in the ordinary way and are not dangerous."

ROAD TRAFFIC

This is now regulated by the Road Traffic Act, 1930, and the orders issued by the Minister of Transport under that Act. The

Act prescribes the construction, weight, and equipment of the vehicles that may use the roads; it regulates the granting of licences for driving them; and it makes provision that third party risks arising out of the use of motor vehicles shall be insured.

HIGHWAY CODE

Under the Act, too, the Minister has issued a code of good manners which should be in the hands of every motorist. Most do not need the injunctions—the injunction to be careful of the rights of pedestrians, for instance, or the injunction not to use the horn unnecessarily, and never as a means of showing irritation. Some motorists do, however, need them; and it is well that they are issued. The code marks an innovation in English law. For no penalty is prescribed for breach of the code. But it is stated that, in the event of an accident, whether or not the motorist has acted in accordance with the code will be evidence in his favour or against him. The Highway Code is obtainable at 1d.

LICENCES TO DRIVE

The applicant for a licence must apply to the council of the county or county borough where he lives. He makes a declaration of fitness on a prescribed form. Unless from the declaration it appears that the applicant is suffering from a disease or disability likely to cause a motor vehicle driven by him to be a source of danger to the public, the licensing authority grants the licence.

An appeal is possible by an applicant who has been refused because of disease or disability to a court of summary jurisdiction.

A curious case in regard to this driving licence came before the courts in 1931. Under Section 5 of the Road Traffic Act, 1930, an application for a driving licence must be made on a prescribed form, the applicant stating that he is free from specified physical disabilities. One question asks whether the applicant is able to see twenty-five yards away in good daylight (with glasses if worn) a motor-car number-plate of six letters and figures. When there is physical disability "the licensing authority shall refuse to grant the licence." Appeal by one aggrieved through refusal to issue a licence lies to a Court of summary jurisdiction, which can make an order binding on the licensing authority.

The authority refused an applicant's request for a licence. For, though he had driven extensively for eight years without accident, he could not truthfully answer the question in the affirmative. Nor were his successive appeals of any avail. The last was to the Court of Appeal which, very reluctantly as it appeared, decided that it could not issue a *mandamus*, commanding the Justices to make an order. It would seem that the man who refuses to palter with his conscience is under a handicap when faced by official forms. The Master of the Rolls said: "It is matter of regret to the Court, as I dare say it was to the Justices, that the licence had to be refused. The applicant had written a letter, obviously frank and truthful, which showed him to be a competent driver but which said: 'I cannot conscientiously say that I can read the figures and letters on a number plate at a distance of twenty-five yards, as they seem blurred to me.' One cannot avoid regretting that this question should be put in the form in which it is put; because a driver of great experience, of great care and consideration for others, is unable to answer a test which may be framed ill for the purposes of securing competence. But still, there it is. The duty of the licensing authority stands unqualified, and they are required to refuse to grant the licence. It may, however, well be a matter for consideration whether this question could not be somewhat differently framed" (*R.* v. *Justices of Cumberland, Ex parte Hepworth*, C.A. 1931).

DUTY TO PRODUCE LICENCE

A driver of a motor vehicle must, on requirement by a constable, produce his licence for examination so as to enable the constable to ascertain the name and address of the holder, and the date of issue and the issuing authority. £5 penalty is attached to the refusal. But if within five days the licensee takes his licence in person to a police office (named by him at the time when he could not produce the licence) he is excused.

DISQUALIFICATIONS FOR HOLDING LICENCE

1. A person under sixteen may not drive a motor vehicle in a road.

2. A person under seventeen may not drive a motor vehicle other than a motor cycle or an invalid carriage.

3. A person under twenty-one may not drive a heavy locomotive, light locomotive, motor tractor, or heavy motor car.

4. A person may be disqualified by the Courts.

DISQUALIFICATION FOR CONVICTIONS

The Court convicting of an offence under the Act may order the offender's licence to be *endorsed* and must do so when the conviction results in disqualification for holding, either temporarily or permanently.

OFFENCES UNDER THE ROAD TRAFFIC ACT

The chief offences are—

1. *Driving at a speed greater than the maximum applicable to the particular vehicle.* As to this note that (a) a person cannot be convicted solely on the evidence of one witness who expresses his opinion of the speed ; (b) a first or second conviction does not render the offender liable to disqualification.

2. *Driving on a road recklessly, or at a speed or in a manner which is dangerous to the public, having regard to all the circumstances.* As to this, note that (a) these circumstances include the nature, condition, and use of the road, and also the amount of traffic on it at the time or which might reasonably be expected to be on it; (b) the penalty prescribed is on *summary conviction* (the defendant having been told that he can, if he chooses, be tried by jury) £50 or imprisonment for four months, on *conviction on indictment* imprisonment for six months or fine, or both ; (c) the Court must order particulars of conviction for this offence to be endorsed on licence ; (d) on a second or subsequent conviction, unless a special reason exists, the Court must exercise its power of disqualification : one special reason would be the lapse of time since the former conviction.

3. *Driving or being in charge of a motor vehicle on a road or other public place when under the influence of drink or drug to such an extent as to be incapable of having proper control of the vehicle.* As to these, note (a) the penalty prescribed is that for 2 ; (b) unless for a special reason, the Court must disqualify the person convicted for at least twelve months.

MOTOR CYCLE PASSENGER

A penalty of £5 (second offence £10) is imposed upon a driver of a motor cycle who carries more than one person (in addition to the driver). The person carried must sit astride and on a proper seat securely fixed behind the driver's seat.

MOTOR DRIVER'S DUTY TO STOP

1. A person driving a motor vehicle on a road must stop at the request of a constable in uniform.

2. If an accident, whether to person or animal occurs through the motor vehicle, the driver must stop. To any person who may reasonably seem to have a right to require it he must give his name and address and the identification marks of the vehicle. Failing this, he must report the accident to the police within twenty-four hours ("Animal" is interpreted to mean horse, cattle, ass, mule, sheep, pig, goat, or dog—not cat nor poultry).

UNPERMITTED "JOY RIDES"

An essential element of theft is the intention at the time of the taking to despoil the owner permanently of his property. When a person was charged with stealing a motor car it was difficult to contradict the assertion that he intended to return it, that therefore he had no intention to steal (*animus furandi*). This difficulty prompted the creation of the new statutory crime; *taking and driving away a motor vehicle without the consent either of the owner or of other lawful authority*. As to this, note that (1) the prescribed penalty is, on summary conviction, £50 fine or three months imprisonment, on indictment, £10 fine or twelve months imprisonment or both; (2) it is a valid defence if the alleged offender had reasonable belief that, in the circumstances, the owner would have given his consent or that he had lawful authority; (3) the jury may, on the trial of an indictment for stealing a motor vehicle, find the offender guilty of this offence instead of stealing.

INSURANCE AGAINST THIRD PARTY RISKS

The Act makes it an offence (penalty £50, or three months, or both) to use, or cause another to use, a motor vehicle in the road unless there is in force such a policy of insurance as will effectively protect third parties against risks.

If a person is convicted for this offence the Court *must*, in the absence of some special reason, disqualify the person from holding a driving licence for at least twelve months.

TRAFFIC SIGNS, ETC.

Where a constable is directing traffic, or where a traffic sign in accordance with the Act indicates a route, it is an offence when a person driving or propelling *any* vehicle (1) neglects or refuses to follow the directions of the constable (2) or fails to conform to the indication given by the sign.

LIGHTING OF VEHICLES

The Road Transport Lighting Act, 1927, enacts that every vehicle on any public highway or any other road to which the public has access shall carry (1) two lamps, each showing to the front a white light visible from a reasonable distance; (2) one lamp showing to the rear a red light visible from a reasonable distance.

(A bicycle not having a sidecar, propelled by mechanised power or not, need have only a single white light to the front. This applies also to a tricycle not propelled by mechanical power. For these vehicles, too, an unobscured and efficient red reflector can be used for the red light.)

LIGHTING UP TIME

Hours of darkness mean (1) during summer time the hours between one hour after sunset and one hour before sunrise; (2) during the rest of the year, the hours between half an hour after sunset and half an hour before sunrise.

" SUMMER TIME "

This is defined in the Summer Time Act, 1925. It begins at 2 a.m. (Greenwich time) of the Sunday after the third Saturday in April, or, if that is Easter Sunday, after the second Saturday in April. It ends at 2 a.m. (Greenwich time) of the Sunday after the first Saturday in October.

HOTEL KEEPER'S LIABILITY AND LIEN

The hotel keeper is under a Common Law obligation to provide accommodation and refreshment for whatever traveller seeks it, is prepared to pay for it, and against whom no reasonable objection can be urged. When he declines to receive he is (unless he can show that the traveller was not in a fit condition to be received) : (1) guilty of an indictable offence ; (2) liable to an action for damages at the suit of the aggrieved traveller. That is, he can be prosecuted for a crime or sued for a civil wrong. Nor does the time, whether of day or night, at which the traveller presents himself make any difference.

As some balance to his inability to select his guests, the Common Law gives the hotel keeper—though not the boarding-house keeper, who can select his guests—a lien on the guest's luggage for sums due from him. This lien includes goods sent by his firm to a traveller. It would not apply, however, to something hired from outside for a temporary purpose—to a piano, for instance.

It is because of this obligation to receive that Common Law gives the innkeeper a lien over whatever luggage his guest brings into the inn. This is so even if the goods are not the guest's own, but those of his employer: in *Robins* v. *Gray* (Q.B. 1895), the plaintiffs had sent goods to their commercial traveller staying in the defendant's inn, and the defendant retained these goods on account of the traveller's failure to pay his hotel bill. The defendant was held to be entitled to do so. The innkeeper cannot, of course, place any constraint upon the guest himself. Nor may he take from the guest anything he is carrying, or any of his wearing apparel. The Innkeeper's Act, 1878, gives the innkeeper the right to sell the goods retained if his bill is not paid within six weeks. Notice to the guest must be given. The person buying the goods gets a valid title to them.

A boarding-house keeper, able to determine whether or not he will provide accommodation, has no corresponding lien; he cannot retain the luggage even of a defaulting guest. His only remedy for failure to pay is to bring an action for breach of contract.

INNKEEPER'S LIABILITY

The innkeeper's liability in regard to the safe keeping of his guest's property is also greater than that of the boarding-house keeper. Common Law made the innkeeper responsible unless he could show that the losses occurred through—

1. The Act of God or the King's Enemies; or
2. Through the guest's own fault.

The Innkeeper's Act, 1863, lightened the Common Law liability to this extent. If the innkeeper exhibits, in plain type and in a conspicuous part of the entrance hall, a copy of Section 1 of the Act—the section limiting liability—a guest, unless in specified events, can recover no more than £30, however great his loss

The specified events, when the innkeeper is again relegated to his Common Law liability as being practically the insurer of the goods, are—

1. Where the loss is in regard to a horse or other live animal, or any gear appertaining thereto, or any carriage.

2. Where the loss has occurred through the wilful act, default, or neglect of the innkeeper, or of one of his servants.

3. Where the property has been deposited for safe custody with the innkeeper.

Caldecutt v. *Piesse* (K.B. 1932), illustrates the points that may arise. The plaintiff, a lady staying with the defendant, lost a diamond ring, stolen, it seemed, by a "charming and affable man who had left without notice and without luggage." The plaintiff asserted that her complaint to the manageress about a defective lock on her room door had been ignored, and that the loss had occurred through this and not through her own negligence. The Court accepted the contention "Either the defendant was an innkeeper, in which case she insured the safety of her guest's property; or she received them into her house for reward and was bound to take reasonable care of their property. I do not consider the defendant an innkeeper. She could pick and choose; she did not take guests for less than a week. She is the keeper of a guest house. But, as such, she is bound to use at least ordinary care for the protection of the guest's goods. She was not fulfilling her duty if she provided a room that could not be locked from the outside by the guest."

CARRIAGE BY SEA

AT Common Law there attached to the shipowner the same very heavy liability as fell to the lot of the carrier on land. But it was the custom of business men who had need of a ship to transport their wares overseas to allow the shipowner to relieve himself of some of his great responsibility. This he did by stipulations contained in charter-parties and bills of lading.

And, as the Common Law liability of the land carrier became limited by statutes, so in like manner the liability of the carrier by sea became limited. Various measures were passed which lessened the liability of the sea carrier; and a codification of the law was contained in the Merchant Shipping Act, 1894.

The relieving provisions of this Act were—

1. Where loss or damage by fire has occurred without the fault or privity of the shipowner, he is exempted from all liability. At Common Law accidental fire was no excuse.

2. No claim will be sustained for loss or damage caused by robbery, theft, or embezzlement of gold, silver, jewellery, or precious stones, unless the nature and value of such articles have been declared in writing to the shipowner or master at the time of shipment.

3. The amount of damages recoverable, where such loss or damage has occurred without the fault or privity of the owner, is now limited, in respect of goods, to £8 per ton of the ship's tonnage, and in respect of loss of life or personal injury, either alone or together with damage or loss to goods, to £15 per ton of the ship's tonnage.

CARRIAGE BY SEA

This is now mainly regulated by the Carriage of Goods by Sea Act, 1924.

A *contract of affreightment* places an obligation upon the shipowner to carry goods, upon the shipper to pay *freight*. The shipowner's obligation to carry the goods is limited by conditions, some implicit in this contract, some expressed in the *charter-party* or the *bill of lading*.

The charter-party (c/p) is an agreement to hire out the ship, the *charterer* undertaking to provide a full cargo for it.

The *bill of lading* (b/l), besides serving to show the conditions on which part of the cargo space is hired, is also a receipt for goods. Moreover, the custom of merchants has made it a *document of title*, delivery of which enables the goods covered by it to be dealt in though out of possession of the owner. Statute (the Bills of Lading Act, 1855) gives to the indorsee of a bill of lading the same rights and liabilities as if the contract of affreightment had been made with him.

A charter may temporarily transfer the ownership of a vessel. In such a case the master and crew are for the stipulated time the servants of the charterer; and he is answerable for their acts performed in the scope of their employment. Almost invariably, however, the charter merely gives the charterer a right to have his goods carried by the particular vessel. The master and crew remain the servants of the shipowner.

THE BILL OF LADING

The shipper of goods will usually be bound by the conditions in the bill of lading, even though he may be unaware of them. Most shipping lines have their own prepared bills, so that shippers by those lines have no excuse for being ignorant of conditions limiting liability.

Occasionally a usage of the port may add something to the contents of the bill of lading, the assumption being that "parties did not mean to express in writing the whole of the contract by which they intended to be bound, but to contract with reference to those known usages." Whether a usage is binding or not has been expressed thus: "In order that the shippers should be taken to have implicitly given leave to stow the goods on deck, the shipowners must prove a practice so general and universal in this trade, and in the particular port from which the goods were taken, that every one shipping goods there must be taken to know that other people's goods, if not his goods, might probably be stowed on deck."

Where the bills are printed with blanks to be filled in by writing, it may happen that the writing is inconsistent with the written clauses. The writing, expressing as it does the immediate intention of the contractors, governs.

A through bill of lading is a contract for the carriage of goods by several shipowners or railway companies. The carrier delivering the bill is liable for loss on any part of the journey unless he has expressly limited his liability. Usually, the carrier does limit his liability to "damage or loss that may occur while the goods are in his possession, and for which he is legally liable."

SEAWORTHINESS

Whether he expressly says so or not, the shipowner, when he enters into a contract to carry goods, gives the shipper assurance : (1) that before and at the beginning of the voyage he will exercise due diligence to make the ship seaworthy; that he will properly man, equip, and supply the ship; that he will make the holds, the refrigerating and cool chambers, fit and safe for the reception and preservation of the goods; (2) that his ship will begin and carry out the voyage with reasonable diligence; (3) that his ship will not deviate without necessity.

The test of "seaworthiness" suggested is : Would a prudent owner, if he had known of the defect, make it good before he sent out the ship to sea? If he would, the ship was not seaworthy. The ship should be in a condition to encounter whatever perils a *ship of that kind, laden in that way*, might be expected to encounter on *such a voyage* at *such a time of year*.

GENERAL AVERAGE CONTRIBUTION

This is a contribution by all parties in a sea adventure, to make good the loss sustained by one of their co-adventurers for sacrifices made, or expenses incurred, for the preservation of the whole. He who seeks a general average contribution must show that : (*a*) There was a common danger; (*b*) there was a necessity for sacrifice; (*c*) the sacrifice was voluntary and real; (*d*) there was a saving of the imperilled property through the sacrifice; (*e*) the common danger did not arise through his default.

MARITIME LIEN

This is a peculiar claim, made effective by the Admiralty action *in rem* (against this thing), against ship or cargo. The lien arises and the ship can be arrested or its cargo attached in the circumstances following :

1. Damage done by the ship through collision.
2. Salvage services rendered to the ship.
3. Bottomry bonds securing the payment of money upon the ship or cargo or freight.
4. Respondentia bonds securing the payment of money upon cargo.
5. Liability for the payment of seamen's wages.

FORM OF CHARTER-PARTY

It is not necessary that a charter-party should be drawn up in any particular form, and different trades have drawn up their own special forms of charter-parties. The general stipulations of a charter-party, however, will be found to be expressed similarly to the following example—

London, 1st June, 19..

It is this day mutually agreed between A. B., owner of the good ship or vessel, called.., of the measurement of........tons or thereabouts, now in the port of..(or now at sea having sailed............................), and C. D. on behalf of E. F., merchants: that the said ship being tight, staunch, and strong, and in every way fitted for the voyage shall with all convenient speed sail and proceed in the usual and customary manner with usual dispatch according to the custom of the port (or in regular turn) (or shall sail from............................on or before the............................), except in the case of accidents beyond the charterer's control to............................, or so near thereunto as she may safely get, and shall load from the factor of the said........................a full and complete cargo, say about............tons, not exceeding what she can reasonably stow away and carry, over and above her tackle, apparel, provisions, and furniture (the charterer's stevedore to be employed by the ship), and being so loaded shall therewith proceed to........................, or so near thereunto as she may safely get and deliver the same in the usual and customary manner on being paid freight as follows........................(or agreeably to the bills of lading), the Act of God, the King's enemies, fire, and all and every other dangers and accidents of the seas, rivers, and navigation, of whatever nature and kind soever during the said voyage, always excepted. Freight to be paid on unloading and right delivery of the cargo. The said C. D. to be allowed................days for the loading and unloading of the said ship and................days on demurrage over and above the said lay days and time herein stated at £................ sterling per day. Penalty for non-performance of this agreement ....

The signatures of the various parties to the contract must be attested by one or more witnesses.

"Lay days" are the time allowed for loading and unloading the ship, and "Demurrage" signifies the sum which is payable when the stipulated number of lay days have been exceeded.

The term "perils of the sea" signifies damage caused by storms, typhoons, collisions, or any occurrence which could not have been foreseen. The term does not cover every loss or damage of which the immediate cause is the sea, and does not include ordinary wear and tear occasioned by wind or sea waves.

WARRANTIES AND CONDITIONS

Various trades have their own stipulations and conditions to be included in charter-parties, but there are certain warranties which are common to all contracts of carriage of goods by sea. They are—

1. Seaworthiness.
2. Dispatch.
3. Non-deviation.

By seaworthiness it is meant that the vessel is properly equipped and manned, and in a thoroughly competent condition to commence a voyage.

A ship with an incompetent crew is not considered seaworthy (*Watson* v. *Clarke*, 1813). The term does not signify that the vessel shall be seaworthy for the duration of the voyage; it merely signifies that the ship is fit to put to sea. But, should any mishap or accident occur some time after the vessel has been under way, the cause of which may be suspected to be due to some defect in the condition of the vessel, the onus is upon the shipowner or the assured to show that the cause arose subsequent to the vessel commencing her voyage.

By dispatch it is meant that the vessel shall commence and complete the voyage within a reasonable time, and that there shall be no delay upon the course of the voyage without very good cause.

DEVIATION PERMISSIBLE

Non-deviation is a warranty that the ship will not turn aside or in any way deviate from her proper and usual course of navigation. But there arose many cases in which deviation took place, and in which it appeared to be justified by the circumstances. These numerous instances resulted in the law upon the subject being codified, and it is now enacted in the Marine Insurance Act, 1906, that deviation is permissible in the following circumstances—

1. Where deviation is authorised by any special term in the policy of insurance.

2. Where deviation is necessary in order to comply with an express or implied warranty.

3. Where the deviation is caused by circumstances beyond the control of the master and shipowner.

4. Where the deviation is reasonably necessary in order to ensure the safety of the vessel or the subject-matter insured.

5. Where the deviation is necessary in order to obtain medical or surgical aid for some person on board.

6. Where the deviation is for the purpose of saving life at sea, or for assisting a vessel in distress where human life may be in danger.

7. Where the deviation has been caused by the barratrous conduct of the master or crew, if barratry be one of the perils insured against.

When deviation has taken place and there has been an intentional departure from the proper course, not occasioned by any of the above causes, the shipowner can no longer rely upon any exemptions he has incorporated into the bill of lading or charterparty. His position is that of a general carrier. He is liable for any loss caused, unless he can show that the loss would have happened in any case, whether he had deviated or not.

A cargo was shipped from New Zealand to London, and the bill of lading gave permission to call at any intermediate port. The vessel put in at Havre to land some other cargo, and while approaching that port she was torpedoed by a German submarine. It was held that Havre was not an ordinary port of call on the ordinary course of the voyage and that in calling there, the vessel had deviated, and the shipowner had to pay damages. For he could not prove that the loss would have occurred in any event. (*Morrison* v. *Shaw Savill Line*, 1916.)

A vessel may be guilty of deviation even without departing from her proper course. If, for example, she tows a disabled vessel, this will be a deviation, because the voyage will thereby be prolonged and the risk increased.

BILL OF LADING AS DOCUMENT OF TITLE

A bill of lading (b/l) is a document which contains the conditions of the carriage of goods, and acts as an acknowledgment that the goods are on board. It is usually signed by the ship's master.

The bill of lading acts as a document of title, and the holder of it can demand delivery of the goods. It is not, however, a negotiable instrument: any person to whom it is transferred gets no better title to it than the person had from whom he obtained it.

The rights of the transferee of a bill of lading were made statutory by the Bills of Lading Act, 1855. Delivery of the B/L confers on the transferee all the rights of the original shipper of the goods. It imposes upon the transferee all the liabilities also. That is where a B/L differs from a negotiable instrument like a cheque. The man who takes a cheque in good faith for value takes it "free from equities," free from claims that would have been good against former holders. The man taking a B/L is not so freed. If the transferor has no valid title to the B/L, then he can give the transferee no valid title. In one point only may the transferee obtain a better title than his transferor had. This point is that a right of stoppage in transit, that would have been available against an insolvent transferor, cannot be exercised against a transferee who has bought the B/L in good faith. See, for instance, the case of *Cahn & Mayer* v. *Pockett's Bristol Channel Steam Packet Co.* (Q.B. 1899).

A cargo of copper was shipped. The sellers sent to the buyer a bill of exchange to be accepted and a bill of lading endorsed in blank. The intention was that property should not pass till the bill had been accepted. The buyer was insolvent; he did not accept the bill; contrary to the understanding, he endorsed the bill of lading to the defendants. Such a transfer prevented the unpaid vendors from exercising their right of stoppage in transit.

[NOTE. The original plaintiffs were Cahn & Mayer, against whom the right of stoppage had been exercised, and against whom the decision had gone in the lower court. The defendants were the carriers who stopped delivery of the copper upon obtaining an indemnity from the sellers.] The gist of the judgment is: "By sending the bill of lading and the bill of exchange direct to Pintacher [the bankrupt], Steinmann & Co [the sellers] constituted him bailee of both of them. It seems impossible to say that there was any wrongful taking. There was no trick which would have negatived a bailment. If he became criminally responsible for his subsequent dealing with the bill of lading, it must have been as bailee, which presupposes a taking by consent. It would defeat the purpose of the Act, and work a public mischief, if a vendor who had himself placed the bill of lading in the hands of his purchaser were entitled as against a *bona fide* sub-purchaser from the latter to enter into nice questions as to the intention with which the original purchaser took the document of title into his possession. The legislature has deliberately chosen to alter the Common Law, which made a transfer of a bill of ladng ineffectual if the person transferring were not himself the owner of the goods. It has, step by step, enlarged the class of persons who, having possession, may give a better title than they have themselves got, and has relaxed the conditions under which they may do so."

BILLS OF LADING ACT

The preamble of the Act explains the purpose of Parliament in passing the Act: "Whereas by the custom of merchants a bill of lading of goods being transferable by endorsement, the property in the goods may thereby pass to the endorsee, but nevertheless all rights in respect of the contract contained in the bill of lading continue in the original shipper or owner, and it is expedient that such rights should pass with the property; and whereas it frequently happens that the goods in respect of which bills of lading purport to be signed have not been laden on board, and it is proper that such bills of lading in the hands of a *bona fide* holder for value should not be questioned by the master or other person signing the same on the ground of the goods not having been laden as aforesaid; be it enacted, etc.:"

As in the case of charter-parties, forms of bills of lading vary considerably. The fact that no particular form was necessary for a bill of lading encouraged shipowners to lessen their heavy responsibility in many ways, and the result of this was that cargo owners were apt to suffer hardship. Before the 1924 Act, some of these bills of lading were amazing documents, containing exemptions from liability printed in type almost illegible. Of one the judge remarked: "There seems to be no other obligation on the shipowner than to receive the freight." In order to prevent this, the Carriage of Goods by Sea Act, 1924, contained many provisions relating to bills of lading. It does not, however, apply to charter-parties; but bills of lading issued under charter-parties must comply with the Act. The Act clearly lays out the duties of carriers of goods by sea, which may be briefly stated as follows—

DUTIES OF SEA CARRIERS

At the beginning of the voyage the carrier must exercise due care to see that the ship is—

1. Seaworthy.
2. Properly manned and equipped.
3. In a fit and proper condition to be used for the safe carrying and preservation of goods.

When the goods have been shipped, the carrier must issue a

bill of lading if the shipper demands one, and the bill of lading must show—

1. The identification marks of the goods.
2. The condition of the goods.
3. The number of the packages or the total weight or quantity of the goods, which information shall be supplied by the shipper.

If a bill of lading has been issued acknowledging receipt of goods in good condition, the shipper cannot afterwards assert to a holder of the bill that they were damaged before shipment. He must abide by the terms of the bill.

In order to claim any compensation for goods damaged in transit, a consignee must give notice to the shipper or carrier, and if he does not give such notice within a year the shipper or carrier is discharged from all liability.

There are seventeen clauses in the Act which exempt a carrier from all responsibility for loss or damage. These cannot all be cited here, but they include—

1. The Act of God.
2. Act of war.
3. Riots and civil commotions.
4. Strikes or lock-outs.
5. Quarantine restrictions.

FREIGHT

Freight is what we pay the shipowner in consideration of his lending his vessel for the carrying of our goods. It is payable on delivery; if the ship is lost and the goods not delivered, there is no freight. It has been held that where a ship is abandoned, the contract to pay freight is dissolved. It is obvious that there is a big risk to shipowners of losing their freight, and it is not unusual, therefore, for them to stipulate that payments of freight should be made in advance. When this advance freight has been paid it cannot be recovered. A condition that freight should be paid at the port of loading is insufficient to constitute "advance freight."

Sometimes payment is made by what is called "lump freight." When this is the case, it is not necessary that the shipowner should deliver the whole of the cargo before he is entitled to the freight, so long as the rest of it has been lost without his fault. The amount of freight which is to be paid is usually clearly set out in the charter-party or bill of lading; but where this is not so, and it is yet clear from the terms of the contract that

26

freight is to be paid, the amount is calculated according to the freight rates ruling at the time of shipment. Where freight is due and has not been paid, the shipowner has a lien upon the goods until the freight has been paid. He has, however, no lien for "advance freight," unless there is a special contract for such.

In the case of *Gardner* v. *Trechmann* (1884, Q.B.), a charter provided for the payment of freight at the rate of 33s. 6d. a ton; and the shipowner was to have an absolute lien on the cargo for the freight. The captain could sign bills of lading at any rate of freight, but should the total amount of freight as per the bills of lading be lower than the amount estimated to be earned by the charter, the captain could demand payment of the difference in advance. The captain signed bills of lading under the chartered rate, but did not demand payment of the difference. It was held that there was no lien for this difference.

CHARTERER'S DUTY

Unless express stipulations provide otherwise, it is the charterer's duty to furnish a cargo according to the terms of the charter. And, unless there are express provisions covering the case, the charterer will not be relieved of his liability merely by reason of strikes, or the bankruptcy of the merchants who have agreed to supply the cargo.

Any terms in the charter-party regarding the method of loading or unloading the vessel, must be construed with reference to the customs of the port of loading or discharge. The mere fact that one or a few merchants go about their business in a certain way will not constitute a custom. But, if such method is universally followed at the port in question, it will be binding even upon persons who did not know of its existence.

It is the shipowner's duty to provide ballast for the ship, and he cannot require the charterer to load such a cargo as will do away with the need for ballast.

MATE'S RECEIPT

On delivery of the goods to the shipowner or to his agent, the shipper will receive a mate's receipt, unless there is a contrary custom ruling at the port. (For instance, in the Port of London only waterborne goods receive a mate's receipt. Goods sent by land receive a "wharfage note" from the Port Authority.) Usually, a person producing a mate's receipt is entitled to the bills of lading in exchange, and the ship's master will be justified in giving them to such a person. A mate's receipt is a "clean" receipt unless it contains any reference to damage or bad condition of goods. Then it is a "foul" receipt.

MARINE INSURANCE

The insuring of goods carried by sea is the oldest form of insurance, and with the increase of commerce and transport it has grown greatly, and it is necessarily, with modern conditions, much more complex.

Marine insurance is a contract whereby one party, for a specified sum, undertakes to indemnify another for loss arising through the carriage of goods by sea. The insured usually employs an insurance broker to negotiate the policy of insurance. The broker acts as middleman between the insurer and the insured. His position is not merely that of an agent, because he is answerable to the insurers for the premium due. The broker prepares a brief memorandum setting out the terms of the intended insurance, and the underwriters (as the insurers are usually called) initial this document (known as the "slip") for the amount for which each will be personally liable. The policy of marine insurance is drawn up from this slip.

The insured must have an "insurable interest," just as in other forms of insurance. This is provided for by the Marine Insurance Act, 1906, which further sets out that "the assured must be interested in the subject-matter insured at the time of the loss, though he need not be interested when the insurance is effected."

An insurance may sometimes be taken out when a ship is still upon a voyage, and neither party may know if she has not gone down. In such a case, the insertion of the words "lost or not lost" into the policy of insurance will make the policy valid, even although it subsequently turns out that the ship was indeed lost at the time the insurance was effected. Of course, in such a case, if the insured knew that the vessel was actually lost at the time of effecting the insurance, he could not recover. And if the underwriter knew that the voyage had safely terminated, he would have to return the premium.

The policy of marine insurance is a complex document and it may be well to define some of the clauses which have given rise to litigation.

Goods are sometimes insured against loss occasioned by the acts of pirates, thieves, or robbers. The New English Dictionary

definition of the term "piracy" is: "Robbery and depredation
on the sea or navigable rivers, etc., or by descent from the sea
upon the coast, by persons not holding a commission from an
established civilized state." "Thieves and robbers" are thieves
and robbers external to the ship. Two cases illustrate the
meaning of these words.

Goods were shipped from P. to London, under the exceptions,
"robbers, the dangers of the seas, roads, and rivers." The goods
were stolen on the railway journey between Southampton and
London. It was held that the shipowner was liable. (*De Roths-
child* v. *Royal Mail Co.*, 1852, Q.B.)

Goods were shipped under the exceptions, "pirates, robbers,
or thieves of whatever kind, whether on board or not, by land
or sea." After shipment, some goods were stolen by one of the
stevedores employed by the ship. It was held that the exceptions
did not apply to men employed by the ship, and the shipowner
was liable. (*Steinman* v. *Angier Line*, 1891, Q.B.)

Some of the large steamship lines have now widened their
exceptions to meet this.

In the policy, a ship is sometimes given permission to touch
and stay "at any port or place whatsoever" ("touch and stay
clause"); but this does not permit the ship to deviate from her
proper course of navigation.

"Barratry" constitutes any wrongful act committed by the
captain or crew of the ship; but this appears to be an exception
that will be null and void under the Carriage of Goods by Sea
Act, 1924.

CONTINUATION CLAUSE

This is a term often met with. In time policies, where an
insurance is taken out for a specified time, provision is sometimes made by means of a continuation clause for that time to
be extended. It had been previously held that a policy for longer
than twelve months was illegal; but provision was made for this
clause by the Finance Act of 1901.

"RUNNING DOWN" OR "COLLISION" CLAUSE

The riverways of our busy ports are often so crowded with
various craft that collisions may be difficult to avoid. A "running
down" or "collision" clause is usually, therefore, inserted in the
policy, under which the underwriters agree, in the event of a
collision, to pay three-fourths of the claim against the owners.

LOSSES

Losses under a policy of marine insurance may be either actual or constructive. An actual loss occurs when the subject-matter is so lost or destroyed as to be beyond recovery; a constructive total loss occurs when the subject-matter is in such a position that the best course would be to abandon it as a total loss rather than to go to the expense of recovering it, such expense probably exceeding the total sound value.

GENERAL AVERAGE

From very early days, various kinds of losses have occurred for which certain parties to the contract could not be held liable, and it would have been unfair to lay the blame upon one party alone. So there arose what is known as general average, and under this type of loss various parties have to contribute their part to indemnify the chief sufferer. A general average loss must be a voluntary act, done for the benefit of the cargo or ship as a whole, under which all parties must have benefited. It can be resorted to only in times of real danger, and a real sacrifice must be incurred.

An example of a general average loss would be the throwing overboard (i.e. the jettison) of some part of the cargo in a time of storm, for the purpose of lightening the vessel and enabling it to reach a place of safety, and so avoid a probable loss of property and life.

In such a case, the owner of the cargo thrown overboard would be indemnified by the other cargo owners, who had benefited by the sacrifice.

A GENERAL AVERAGE CLAIM

One of the most interesting and instructive cases decided by the House of Lords in 1931 was *Louis Dreyfus and Co.* v. *Tempus Shipping Co., Ltd.*

In essence, the question before the successive Courts was the constantly recurring one: Where loss has occurred in a joint adventure, neither party being to blame, who must bear the loss? Are there any rules of law to rebut the presumption that the loss lies where it falls—that if the ship sinks, it is the ship-owner's loss, if the cargo is destroyed, it is the cargo owner's loss? The case entailed a survey of *General Average Contribution* and the principles governing its allocation; it placed in clear light the limitation of the shipowner's liability by statute, and it occasioned a restatement of the rules by which the law lords conceive themselves bound when hearing appeals. The respondents in the House of Lords were the owners of the S.S. *Campus*; the appellants were the owners of a cargo of grain from the River Plate to the United Kingdom. Shortly after starting on the voyage, fire broke out in the ship's bunkers; the fire destroyed part of the grain and threatened the safety of the ship. The captain put into Monte Video and there incurred general average expenditure in discharging and reloading the grain and in obtaining fresh bunker coal. The ship claimed against the cargo owners for a contribution to the general expenses. The cargo owners denied liability, contending that the fire was due to the bad bunker coal, and they counter-claimed for damage to their cargo. On both points the cargo owners lost.

LOSS THROUGH FIRE

Apart from statute law or from special arrangement, the carrier's liability is heavy; few excuses are available for failure to transport safely the goods entrusted to him. Even accidental fire was a risk incident to his profession. The Merchant Shipping Act, 1894, relieves the sea-going carrier from many of his Common Law burdens, Section 502 relating to fire among other risks:

"The owner of a British sea-going ship shall not be liable to make good any loss happening without his actual fault or privity where merchandise on board his ship is damaged by reason of fire on board the ship." But, contended the cargo owners, a ship with bunker coal that takes fire spontaneously is an unseaworthy ship, and in every contract of carriage by sea a warranty of seaworthiness is implied. Whether the shipowner knows of the fact constituting unseaworthiness does not matter.

That is so, agreed the Court, but we have the clear words of the Merchant Shipping Act. In spite of the fact, therefore, that the trouble arose from the unsuitable coal—that is, from the unseaworthiness of the ship—no part of the loss can be recovered from the shipowners. Damage done to the ship, on the other hand, must be borne by the shipowner. That disposed of the counterclaim by the cargo owners. The question of average contribution was more intricate. The appellants had lost some part of their cargo; were they, despite their loss, obliged to pay contribution before they could get the part saved? The House of Lords said, yes.

GENERAL AVERAGE

The rules of maritime law when merchandise is sacrificed for the general good, for the safety of the ship and the rest of the cargo carried, have long been settled—

1. Each owner of jettisoned goods becomes the creditor of ship and cargo saved.

2. He has a direct claim against each of the owners of ship and cargo for a *pro rata* contribution towards his indemnity.

3. This contribution he can recover in one of two ways—

(*a*) By enforcing through the shipmaster, who is his agent for that purpose, a lien on each parcel of goods sold to answer its proportionate liability.

(*b*) By direct action.

4. When a person who would otherwise have been entitled to claim contribution has, by his own fault, occasioned the peril which gave rise to the claim, it would be manifestly unjust to permit him to recover from those whose goods are saved.

In a sense, they have certainly benefited by the sacrifice of the property. But, in relation to them, he is a wrongdoer, and, as such, under obligation to ward off or repair by every means within his power the natural consequences of his wrongful act. He cannot be allowed to claim either recompense for services rendered, or indemnity from losses sustained by him in his effort to save property imperilled by his act.

Very well, said the cargo owner, these being the rules, does not No. 4 bar the shipowner's claim? His fault, the neglect that there must have been in selecting coal, was the immediate cause of the loss. That would be so, said the Court, if the shipowner had committed an actionable wrong against the shipper. Here, however, the Act declares that, if accidental fire is the cause of the trouble, that is no "fault" of the shipowner. There is no "fault,"—"legal fault," if you like—because of the statutory protection given to the shipowner.

The decision followed that given in the case of the *Carron Park* (1890). There, a cargo of sugar was loaded, the charter-party containing the exception clause, "neglect or default of the pilot, master, crew, or other servants of the shipowner always excepted." One of the engineers negligently left a valve open, and water damaged the cargo. The shipowner pleaded the exception and counterclaimed for general average contribution, and he succeeded in both contentions: "The claim for contribution as general average cannot be maintained when it arises out of any negligence

for which the shipowner is responsible, but negligence for which
he is not responsible is as foreign to him as to the person who has
suffered the loss." So said the President of the Admiralty Court.

AUTHORITY OF DECIDED CASES

The decision of the Admiralty Court need not have been
followed by the Court of Appeal; there was still less compulsion
upon the House of Lords. The Court of Appeal feels no compunc-
tion in upsetting a decision of a lower court when it thinks that
decision clearly wrong. It is, however, bound by its own decisions, and, when a recorded judgment has been accepted law for
a number of years, it is reluctant to judge counter to the judgment
even of a lower court. So with the House of Lords. It considers
itself bound by its own decisions; it disturbs the decisions of
lower courts only when irrefutable arguments show those decisions to have been erroneous, and when they have stood long its
reluctance to overrule them is increased.

The *Carron Park* decision was, in fact, followed by the Court
of Appeal decision in *Melburn* v. *The Jamaica Fruit Company*
(1900); of which case Lord Atkin said: "My Lords, since that
date the decision has stood undisturbed. It has been followed
in Scotland. Countless contracts of carriage by sea must have
been made on the footing that it was correct, and general average
claims adjusted accordingly. Even if the balance of argument
had been on the side of the cargo owners, I apprehend that
at the present date your lordships would have felt the greatest
difficulty in overruling a decision not unreasonable in itself upon
which so many people have regulated their material obligations
in an important branch of commerce."

DELAY NOT COVERED BY GENERAL AVERAGE

The limits within which general average can be claimed is
illustrated in *Wetherall* v. *London Assurance* (1931, Commercial
Court).

The plaintiff's vessel, swerving to avoid a collision, grounded,
thereby incurring *particular damage*. Payment for the services
of tugs and other measures for preserving ship and cargo was
general damage. Could such a loss be allowed in general average?
The Court thought not. Loss consequential on the actual damage,
but outside the cost of repair, cannot be recovered. In the
Leitrim case, 1902, it was said: "It does not follow that the

mere loss of the profitable employment of the vessel as distinguished from actual expenses should be allowed. A loss of this character has never been claimed in general average. It is not introduced in the York-Antwerp Rules, nor can I find any trace of its being allowed by the laws of any foreign country, though many of them contain provisions as to the allowance in general average of the wages and maintenance of the crew. It may be said: Why on principle should not the loss of time be compensated for, where that loss is due to the necessity for repairing damage, itself the subject of general average? I think the answer is that the loss of time is common to all the parties interested and all suffer damage by the delay, so that the damages by loss of time may be considered proportionate to the interests, and may be left out of consideration."

PRIVILEGES OF BRITISH SHIP

In order that a vessel shall be a British ship, it must be owned entirely by British subjects, natural born or naturalised, or by a company which has been established under and is subject to the laws of some part of the British dominions, and which has its principal place of business somewhere therein.

The ship must be registered as a British ship, which may be done at any port in the British dominions, and such port is subsequently known as the port of registry. But before an application for registration can be made, there are certain things which must be done. The name of the ship must be clearly marked on the bows, and the name and intended port of registry on the stern. The official number and tonnage must be cut on the main beam, and her draught must be shown either in letters or figures on the stern post.

A "Certificate of Survey" giving various particulars, and, on first registration, a "Builder's Certificate" are also required. The shipowner is required to sign a declaration to the effect that he knows of no reason why the ship should not be registered as a British ship, and he must also state the name of the master.

OWNERSHIP OF A BRITISH SHIP

1. The property in a ship must be divided into sixty-four shares.

2. Not more than sixty-four individuals can be registered as owners at the same time.

3. No person may be registered as owner of a fractional part

of a share, but any number of persons, not exceeding five, may be registered as joint owners of a ship or of any share or shares in a ship.

The registered owner of a ship or share in a ship may deal with his interest or dispose of it in any manner he wishes as provided by the Act.

MANAGEMENT

In cases where a ship is owned by several persons, they usually appoint an individual as manager, called the "managing owner." He was formerly called the "ship's husband," but this latter term is now usually applied to the employee of the shipowner who looks after the equipment of the vessel. The managing owner has full power over the use and employment of the ship. If a managing owner is not appointed, the will of the majority of the owners governs the use and employment of the vessel. But a voyage cannot be undertaken to which the minority of the owners object, unless the majority agree to indemnify the minority against any loss which may arise. But, in this event, if the voyage concludes safely and turns out to be profitable, the minority are not entitled to share in any of the profits.

MORTGAGES AND TRANSFERS

The owners of a ship or of a share in a ship may dispose of the same by way of either a sale or a mortgage. Special rules govern these transactions.

A sale can be effected only by a document called a bill of sale. This is a misleading term, for the Bills of Sale Acts do not apply to it. The form of this particular bill of sale is laid down in the Merchant Shipping Act, 1894, and must be strictly followed. It must be under seal, and it must contain a description of the ship sufficient to identify it. The bill of sale and the declaration are handed to the registrar who records the transaction and endorses the bill. The transferee of the bill must sign a declaration to the effect that he is qualified to own a British ship. Until he has done this, he cannot be registered as owner.

TRANSFER BY OPERATION OF LAW

The transfer of the ship or shares in a ship may take place through operation of law, that is to say, by the death or bankruptcy of the owner. In this event no executor, administrator, or trustee can be registered as a transferee unless he is properly qualified to own a British ship. If he be not qualified, he may apply to the Court, and the Court will order that the ship be sold within four weeks of the transmission of the interest of the former owner.

MASTER OF THE SHIP

The master of the ship must be a properly qualified person according to the rules laid down in the Merchant Shipping Acts. He must provide a competent crew for the vessel, must arrange for adequate equipment and proper navigation of the ship. He must do all he can to protect the interests of the owners. He has power to control all on board.

Owing to the "perils of the sea," the master of the ship has always enjoyed peculiar authority, and he is enabled to exercise some remarkable powers in regard to the ship and the cargo. He must not use these powers in any arbitrary manner; he must have due regard for the interests of all concerned.

He must pay great attention to the safety of the cargo, and if through some special reason this seems to be in danger, he may tranship it, sending the cargo to its destination by another vessel. Technically, such an act involves a breach of the contract of carriage; but the shipowner will still be entitled to receive the full freight provided the cargo does safely reach its destination.

If the ship is damaged, and the master cannot raise money to effect repairs, he may sell the cargo for this purpose; but the shipowner must indemnify the owners of the cargo.

BOTTOMRY AND RESPONDENTIA BONDS

These bonds are documents which charge the ship, freight, or cargo for the payment of money which the master has borrowed to enable the ship successfully to carry out her voyage.

These bonds are usually made by deed and are signed by the master. They are repayable on condition that the ship safely reaches her destination. It was decided in the case of *The Haabet* (1899) that, where there was an agreement to repay the money in any case, the bond was not a good one.

This power of hypothecation, as it is called, is a very formidable one, and it may not be used until every other possible means of raising money has been tried, and communication with the shipowner is either impossible or rendered impracticable by a delay which would imperil the safety of the vessel.

In these days of means of rapid communication, such as the

cable and the wireless, bottomry or respondentia bonds are rarely called for and are not used nearly so much as was the case in the days of sail.

CONFLICT OF LAWS

Since a ship passes into many jurisdictions, it may sometimes be a question: what law is to govern a contract (evidenced by a charter-party or a bill of lading)? A shipowner may be liable to make payment under one law, exempt under another. The parties to a contract may themselves make clear what law is to be applied: English Courts will then apply that law. When the intention is unexpressed, the Court will ascertain the intention. The assumption is that the law of the place where the contract was made (*Lex Loci Contractus*) governs the contract. So far as charter-parties and bills of lading are concerned, however, this rule is modified; the law applicable is, apart from evidence to the contrary, the law of the ship's flag.

From the British shipowner's point of view, one of the most serious of these conflicts of law results from the United States Act of Congress (the "Harter Act") of 1893.

Even before this Act a clause in a bill of lading that exempted a shipowner from liability for negligence was held in the United States Courts to be void as being against public policy. In the case of "The Guildhall" there was a claim for loss of goods from negligence, the shipment being on a British ship from Rotterdam to New York. The negligence clause, though valid and effective by both English and Dutch law, was held not to protect the shipowner and the claim was allowed. In another case (*Botany Worsted Mills* v. *Knott*), the bill of lading expressly stated that the contract should be construed according to English law; yet the clause was held void.

THE " CLAUSE PARAMOUNT "

A British or other shipowner issuing a bill of lading in the United States is now obliged to incorporate in the bill of lading the provisions of the Harter Act. This he does by adding a governing clause—a "clause paramount"—that "It is also mutually agreed that this shipment is subject to all the terms and provisions of, and all the exceptions from liability contained in the Act of Congress of the United States, approved 13th February, 1893." This clause makes the Act, therefore, a part of the contract; and when, as is possible, other clauses in the bill of lading are in conflict with those of the Harter Act, the latter clauses govern.

IMPLIED CONDITIONS

Perhaps the best example of conditions not necessary to be expressed are in contracts of carriage of goods by sea. The shipowner may expressly stipulate not to be bound by the conditions; but, apart from such express bargains, he undertakes—

1. Before and at the beginning of the voyage to exercise due diligence to make the ship seaworthy. (This enactment of the Carriage of Goods by Sea Act, 1924, replaces the Common Law undertaking "That his ship is seaworthy.")

2. That his ship shall begin and carry out the voyage contracted for with reasonable diligence.

3. That his ship shall carry out the voyage contracted for without unnecessary deviation.

Seaworthy implies that the ship is in a condition to encounter whatever perils a ship of that kind, laden in that way, might fairly be expected to meet upon the contemplated voyage. For example, the ship must be properly ballasted; if it is chartered to carry gunpowder it must have the magazine prescribed by the Board of Trade regulations; its master and crew must be efficient (thus, in *Standard Oil Co.* v. *Clan Line*, A.C. 1924, the condition of seaworthiness was held to have been broken because the owners had failed to give the master special information furnished by the builders, about the proper method of stowage in a vessel of that type. This failure occasioned a "disabling want of knowledge.")

Delay may be such as to render the voyage useless for the particular enterprise contemplated by the charterer. This delay, going as it does to the essence of the contract, is the breach of a CONDITION; it enables the charterer both to repudiate the contract and to claim damages. Where the delay does not so "frustrate the adventure," the charterer can only claim damages.

NEGLIGENCE OF CARRIER OR HIS SERVANTS

The carrier who would disclaim liability for the negligence or default of himself or his servants must say so in clear terms. Thus, in *Steinman* v. *Angier Line* (C.A. 1891) an excepted risk clause protecting the shipowners from liability for losses due to "pirates, robbers, or thieves of whatever kind, whether on board or not, or by land or sea," did not cover thefts by the stevedore's men. For they were in the service of the shipowner, and "this question of construction must be decided on the broad principle which has been so long and so constantly invoked in the interpretation of contracts with carriers, by sea as well as land, viz. that words of general exemption from liability are only intended (unless the words are clear) to relieve the carrier from liability where there has been no misconduct or default on his part or that of his servants." An ambiguous document is not a protection; for the rule is that the words of a contract are taken most strongly against the party who uses the words and relies upon them as his excuse (*verba chartarum fortius accipiuntur contra proferentem*).

SALVAGE

This is a reward paid by the shipowner or the owner of goods to the person who performs extraordinary services at sea as a result of which the ship or goods are saved from wreck or other kind of loss. We also use the term to describe the property so saved.

In order to claim salvage, a person must show that he performed the act voluntarily, and that without it the goods or other property would have suffered loss. As a rule, there is no claim for salvage for saving human life; and the passengers or crew of the vessel saved, whatever their exertions may have been, are also not usually entitled to salvage.

SHIP'S PAPERS

A British ship must carry the following papers—

1. Certificate of Registration, recording the name and particulars of the ship.

2. The Articles, which state particulars of the voyage, description of the crew, scale of wages, etc.

3. The Manifest, which contains particulars regarding the cargo.

4. The charter-party and bill of lading.

5. Bill of Health, stating that the vessel is free from all infectious disease.

6. Official Log-book, in which the master records any noteworthy incidents of the voyage.

CARRIAGE BY AIR

CHANGES come; and the law must develop and adapt itself to the changes. The great ruling principles of the common law remain unimpaired. A statute continues to be good law until Parliament sees fit to repeal or to modify it. The Courts are, however, constantly exercised in applying the old rules to new facts and new problems certainly never contemplated when the rules were first enunciated. It may be that a word used in an Act of Parliament enlarges its connotation: it is applied to products of men's inventive genius that were in the distant future when the Act was passed. The Bread Act, 1836, for example, prescribes that any person carrying bread for delivery in a "cart or carriage" shall be provided with scales and weights with which, on demand by any purchaser, the bread may be weighed. Is a bicycle such a "cart or carriage"? The Court of Appeal (*Pollard* v. *Turner*, 1912) decided that it is, and affirmed the conviction of the appellant.

The Common Law, too, has enough vitality to cope with new situations. So with the new means of transport. The old rules, formulated in the days when alliance between carrier and highwayman was a likelihood, still are the basis of the law relating to the common carrier. How far are they applicable to the air-carrier? The questions will be gradually answered at the expense of litigants; the persons going to law upon novel points may derive what satisfaction they can from the thought that, at all events, they have helped to fix a part of English law. The general principles of air transport are to be found in the Air Navigation Act, 1920, while the Carriage by Air Act, 1932, has been passed regulating such matters as tickets, luggage, and liability for safety of passengers and goods. This latter Act may be applied to international and inland carriage by order in council.

CARRIER BY AIR MAY BE A COMMON CARRIER

This was decided in *Aslan* v. *Imperial Airways, Limited* (K.B., 1933), a case that affords an admirable setting for a modern detective story. Effraim Heskel Aslan claimed damages. His local agents at Baghdad had handed to the defendants a box of bullion for carriage to London. During the transit the box mysteriously vanished. The defendants were, said the plaintiff, liable for the loss. He founded his claim both on contract and in tort. Either they had broken their contract to carry safely, or, as an alternative claim, they had been guilty of the wrong of negligence.

The first question was this: "Are the defendants common carriers?" If they are, they are—apart from the common law defences noted above—the absolute insurers of the goods carried. They hold themselves out as carriers of goods and passengers; and this would imply a warranty that their aeroplanes are suitable for the purpose. Besides, they charged a special high rate for the conveyance of bullion; and this would seem to warrant that the aeroplanes had a thief-resisting room.

As regards an implied warranty by a shipowner the obligation is a heavy one. There had been an extension of the implied warranty for seaworthiness to an implied warranty of cargo-worthiness, even to the provision of suitable receptacles for particular goods. Still, there is the very nature of an aeroplane to be considered. That a ship should have an efficient bullion room is reasonable enough. But to instal a burglar-proof room in an aeroplane would destroy its stability, and would probably prevent its owners from obtaining a certificate of airworthiness under the Air Navigation Air, 1920.

It is true that a common carrier could not bring forward to excuse the loss even the contention that such a room would be inconsistent with the nature of a flying machine. Were the defendants such, though? On the back of the consignment note —which had been signed by the plaintiff and which, therefore, bound him to its conditions—the defendants declare that they are not common carriers and do not accept the liability of common carriers. Was this notice effective? For, of course, one cannot yet get out of one's responsibilities simply by declaring oneself exempt from them. It was effective, said the Court. "I see no reason why a carrier by air should not be a common carrier, and subject to the liabilities of a common carrier. But see what terms have been agreed upon as basis of the contract of carriage. The sender has signed the consignment note, which says he agrees that the goods are accepted subject to the conditions on the back. The carriers, on the back, reserve the right to refuse any goods offered for carriage, and state that they are not common carriers. In face of these terms it is impossible to hold that the defendants are common carriers; and I hold that they are only bailees and so only liable for negligence."

NEGLIGENCE OF A BAILEE

Another point arose, therefore, upon the contract of carriage. One who has charge of another's property is a bailee. If he gets nothing for his service, he is a gratuitous bailee; he is obliged to take such care of the goods entrusted to him as an ordinary prudent man would take of his own goods of the same kind. If, as in the case, he does get something, he is a bailee for reward; he is bound to adopt all precautions and means of assuring safety. The contract of carriage contained, however, a condition that "Goods are accepted for carriage only at the risk of the owner. Imperial Airways undertake no responsibility for loss, damage, or delay caused directly or indirectly during the conveyance by aeroplane." Did this comprehensive clause protect the defendants even assuming the loss occurred through negligence?

It will be noticed that the clause is in general words and that it does not specially mention negligence; and, so far as ships are concerned, there is a stream of authorities to the effect that the general words do not exclude liability for negligence. Other authorities, dealing mainly with railways, hold that liability for negligence is also excluded. Here there is no doubt about the exclusion. The one thing for which the carriers were liable was negligence as a bailee. Unless that liability was covered by the condition, the clause would be meaningless: "The nature of the contract here is such that the defendants would have been liable only for negligence in the carrying of the goods, and in failing to exercise reasonable care and skill to make the aeroplane fit for the carriage. For the defendants are not common carriers and, therefore, give no absolute warranty of fitness. As the defendant's only liability is for negligence, the clause—though in general words and not mentioning negligence specifically—is sufficient to protect the defendants."

The conclusion follows. The air-carriers, like the railways, are common carriers unless they enter into special agreements. But, by means of the special agreements, they can limit their liabilities to any extent that the consignor agrees with.

PAYMENT OF DEBTS

At Common Law I could not give to another my legal right so that he could sue upon it in his own name. "A 'chose in action' (a thing to which I can enforce my right by appeal to the Courts) is not assignable." For, though some think and many assert otherwise, the law discourages litigation. Legal rights have something of sanctity; they must not become the base material of commerce. Besides, if one could buy a right of action as a speculative venture, the Courts would be overwhelmed.

This doctrine of non-assignment, like so many of those old rules, "whereof the memory of man runneth not to the contrary," is wellnigh eaten away by its exceptions. True, from the very nature of the contracts, it remains intact where the bargains concern personal relations; if Joan Smith promised to marry Tom Jones, Tom Jones may not—whether he gets a consideration or not—assign to William Sykes his right to the marriage. For, clearly, Joan will claim to have some voice in the matter. In such a case as this the old rule remains, that a contract can affect only the parties to it. Where, however, the right is to receive a sum of money or a specific piece of property, the doctrine has gone by the board. Such a right is freely transferable.

The bill of lading, for instance, is the symbol of a right to cargo; and with the transference of the symbol the right to the cargo passes from owner to owner. Modern commerce would be hampered, would, in fact, be impossible, if the Common Law doctrine still ruled.

CHEQUES AND BANK-NOTES

This is particularly so in regard to payments. There the custom of merchants has gained a complete victory over the Common Law; and, in respect of negotiable instruments, the victory has its statutory recognition in the Bills of Exchange Act. The promise to pay, being embodied in a piece of paper, becomes the merchant's currency. He still uses the money that the State prescribes as legal tender. But he uses this for the trivial transactions of life, to pay for his cup of coffee or his bus fare. For settlement of the vast bulk of his bargains he uses cheques and bills and notes. All these promises to pay are accepted in lieu of payment of money; and, promises only as they are, they effect the same purpose as money itself. The promise of a new suit at Easter won't keep me warm to-day; but the promise of £5 will pay just as effectively as £5 will.

Nor is this a matter for astonishment. For, after all, the hand-to-hand currency is itself only a symbol of debt. Money was once something one could wear or eat. It was wanted for its own sake as well as for the power it gave its owner. Now, it is only the second that counts; we want money because we want claims. He who has a shilling may be presumed to have rendered a shilling's worth of good service to the community. The community is ready to acknowledge and to cancel its debt. It does, when he spends the shilling in the market. Essentially, the money is a promise by the community that it will satisfy the holder's wants up to the amount of the money; and the promise can, without the least formality, be assigned to others.

PAPER PROMISES TO PAY

But there can be other promises to pay besides the silver shillings and the paper pound; and, like these, the other promises have become freely assignable either by delivery or by endorsement. There is no need to tell the debtor that his creditor has been changed; there is no need to trouble about the past history of the documents that represent debts. He who takes the documents in good faith may look for the fulfilment of the promises. For no counterclaim is possible upon them. Nor can his ownership of them be challenged. These documents—these *negotiable instruments*—are like money in this respect: the man taking them in good faith, for value, gets a good title to them, however defective the title of the former possessor was.

The custom of merchants made it imperative that every business man should honour the bill he had accepted, no matter into whose hands it had come. If the holder had taken it in the ordinary course of business, taken it in good faith, he could exact payment. The thing that *was done* by honourable merchants became the thing that *must be done* by all merchants whether honourable or not, and now—by the Bills of Exchange Act, 1888—has become what all must do, merchants or not.

A NEGOTIABLE INSTRUMENT

For the bill could become an acceptable means of payment only when people had confidence in it. And one way of promoting confidence was to assure the taker of the bill that his right to it would be no more contested than his right to the shillings he had taken in payment. The man who gives the bill, or the shilling, may not be the rightful owner: he may have found it or stolen it. That does not affect the taker's right. So long as his own conduct in the transaction is straightforward, so long as he has no suspicion of anything wrong, he is entitled to payment on the bill just as he is entitled to spend the shilling. The shilling is not earmarked. The rightful owner cannot follow it and recover it—as he can every other kind of movable property *except negotiable instruments.*

CHEQUE NOT LEGAL TENDER

The cheque differs from coin, however, in this: it is not endowed with the privilege of legal tender. Parliament has not enacted— as it has done in regard to coins and to Bank of England notes— that a debtor may, whether his creditor likes it or not, cancel a debt with it. A creditor need not take a cheque in payment; he can demand legal tender. Nor is a creditor entitled to demand one. That is the reason for the strange rule of English law: a cheque for a smaller amount, taken by a creditor "in full settlement," frees the debtor from his debt; a money payment of a smaller amount than the debt, though accepted by the creditor "in full settlement," does not discharge the debtor. The creditor may, if he chooses, sue for the balance. True, he has given his promise to remit the remainder. But then he has gained nothing in return. The promise is gratuitous, and it will be no bar to his recovering the balance by legal process.

MEANING OF " NEGOTIABLE "

The bill—or the cheque, itself a bill drawn on a banker—is a *negotiable instrument.* This means something more than a document for transferring rights. A bill of lading is a transferable document; but it is not, strictly speaking, a negotiable instrument. A man may buy it believing that he is, by doing so, becoming owner of the cargo covered by the bill. In the vast majority of instances, his belief is justified. On rare occasions, however, it is not. The seller of the bill of lading may have no right to it; and the rightful owner will be able to claim the goods. Or the buyer of the bill of lading may find that the shipowner has a lien on the cargo until certain charges are met.

True it is, that the assignee of the bill of lading may in some events get a better claim than that of his assignor. If the seller learns that the buyer is insolvent, he can ask the carrier not to deliver the goods. He can, we say, exercise the right of stoppage in transit. The seller cannot exercise this right against an honest buyer of the bill of lading. We say that the transference to a *bona fide* buyer, to one who has no reason for suspecting anything wrong, defeats the unpaid vendor's right of stoppage in transit. Or fraud of the buyer may taint the bargain. The seller, finding the fraud, may cancel the bargain. Once, however, an innocent third party has obtained rights to the goods the defrauded seller's option to rescind is lost.

"NEGOTIABLE" MEANS MORE THAN "TRANSFERABLE"

Yet the buyer of the bill of lading runs the risk that the seller pretends to more right than he really has. The risk, seeing that most business men are eager to keep faith with one another, is only slight. But it exists. No such risk attaches to a negotiable instrument. The taker of a cheque, if he takes it in good faith, cannot, when he seeks payment, be met with defences that would have been valid against the giver of the cheque. He takes it, we say, "free from equities," free from any claims that might in fairness have been advanced against the original holder of the cheque. It is this immunity from risk that distinguishes a negotiable instrument from one merely transferable.

RAPHAEL v. BANK OF ENGLAND

We can best illustrate this by referring to the well-known case, *Raphael* v. *Bank of England*. It concerned a promissory note, a Bank of England note of large denomination that had been stolen. But the principle applies to all negotiable instruments, to cheques and bills and bearer bonds no less than to promissory notes. The principle is that the taker in good faith gets a good title and that negligence itself does not affect his right. He may have acted in a blundering, stupid way; yet, if he acted in an honest way, his right cannot be assailed.

The theft of a number of notes caused the Bank, acting for the despoiled owner, to give particulars of the stolen notes in quarters where the notes might be presented. The Bank notified, among others, Raphael's principal, a Parisian money-changer. The money-changer had, for his guidance, particulars of the stolen notes at hand; yet, through forgetfulness or carelessness, he failed to consult the particulars when a customer presented one of the notes. The fact of weight was that he turned pounds into francs at the current rate; and this fact sufficed to establish his good faith in the matter. Negligent he may have been. Of his good faith there was no doubt. He was, therefore, able to recover from the Bank the amount of the note. That is, the Bank's customer lost the amount.

"GOOD FAITH"

"Good faith" is, indeed, one of the terms glibly and frequently used, but often with no very clear notion of the quite definite meaning attached in law to the term. I tell a man hurrying for his train that it has already gone. My statement subjects him to a great deal of irritation and some pecuniary loss. For, as it appeared, the train had not left and he could have caught it; my solicitude, lest he should harm himself by his precipitation, caused him damage. Has he any legal right against me? Apparently not. If I honestly believed what I said, however unfounded my belief, however careless I was in the matter, I am exempt from liability. For I have acted *bona fide*, in good faith. Business men would, perhaps, like to have it recognised that gross negligence, failure, for instance, to make inquiries that a prudent business man would think incumbent upon him, should be looked upon as being quite inconsistent with good faith. Formerly, indeed, a tendency to do this was observable in the Courts. It is now, however, established—it is, indeed, defined by statute—that "good faith" may be consistent with both foolishness and carelessness: "a thing is deemed to be done 'in good faith' when it is in fact done honestly, whether it be done negligently or not." To bring "bad faith" home it is not enough to show that there was carelessness or negligence or foolishness. The man taking a bill of exchange from another, and showing all of these, may yet be a "*bona fide* taker for value." The question is not whether he ought to have suspected some irregularity about the bill, that perhaps the profferer had stolen it or had obtained it by trickery. The question is—a question of fact to be determined by the jury—did he actually suspect anything wrong? To suspect wrongdoing, though one refrains from questioning, negatives the assertion of "good faith."

STOPPING A CHEQUE

The stoppage of a note, or a cheque, has thus a quite restricted effect. It may prevent a thief from obtaining payment. But, once the note or the cheque has got into circulation, once a man has taken it in good faith and given value for it, the drawer is responsible for its payment.

INSTANCES OF NEGOTIABLE INSTRUMENTS

The negotiable instruments that enter most frequently into business practice are bills of exchange (including cheques) and promissory notes. What made these into a kind of money was the custom of merchants; and the custom of merchants still makes law. We are not to regard the list of negotiable instruments as closed. When the convenience of trade leads business men to accept the holder of a paper claim to money as the one entitled to payment, then this paper claim is on its way to becoming a negotiable instrument. If question is raised about his right to payment, he may be called upon to show that he gave value for the claim, and that he had no reason for doubting the right of the previous holder to pass the claim on. Once he satisfies reasonable people upon these matters his claim is acknowledged, even though the previous holder could have established no claim at all. Merchants get into the habit of acknowledging the claim; the Courts in time recognise the habit. When they do so recognise it, when the custom of merchants has been proved to the satisfaction of the judge, the document in question has become a negotiable instrument.

CHEQUE CONTRASTED WITH POSTAL ORDER

The difference between documents that are negotiable and those that are not may be realised by contrasting a postal order with a cheque. The words "Not Negotiable" upon the former indicate that he who takes the order in payment may find his rights to it limited. He will find them limited if some previous owner was not fully entitled to it. If, in the course of its passage from one post office to another, it has been stolen, the true owner can make good his claim even against one who takes it in good faith for value. In the case of postal orders the general rule of law is applicable: that I can give no better right than I have myself.

With a cheque, however, it is different. Though I have stolen the cheque or obtained it by trickery, I can still give a good title to it. He who takes it from me is not concerned with the manner in which I have obtained it. If his own conduct cannot be impeached in the matter he is entitled to claim on the instrument.

It is true that the cheque may be restricted as regards negotiability. I may place upon it an endorsement like "Pay John Smith only," or I may cross it with the words "Not Negotiable." In either of these events a person taking the cheque has not, and cannot give, a better title than the person from whom he took it. One may be willing to take such a cheque, as one may be willing to take a postal order payment. But he takes it at his risk.

The holder of a negotiable instrument has power to give a good title to any person honestly acquiring it. "It is of the very essence of a negotiable instrument that you may treat a person in possession of it as having authority to deal with it unless you know to the contrary, and you are not compelled, in order to secure a good title for yourself, to inquire into the nature of his title or the extent of his authority."

BILLS OF EXCHANGE

Some points about the bill of exchange, of which the cheque is a species, are these—

1. The written order must be an unconditional one. Thus, a request to pay "if the horse I now sell you wins the Derby" would not be a true bill of exchange.

2. The subject-matter must be a sum of money definite at the time or calculable at the time. Thus "Pay to my order £500 with interest at 5 per cent" is good. But a request to "Deliver a thousand tons of iron to bearer" is not. Nor would the request "Pay to me a reasonable price for the cottages I have built" be a good bill; for reasonable "is a word of many interpretations."

3. The kind of payment must be either fixed in the bill or be ascertainable of a certainty. "Pay a month after the Liberals come into power" is not a good bill. For there is no certainty of time. "Pay a month after the death of George V" is good. For the event will happen, and the date when the bill becomes due will ultimately be fixed.

4. Once a negotiable instrument gets into circulation a "holder in due course" (as one is called who takes it in good faith, for value, and before it is overdue) is protected. If we should stop a cheque, our stopping is effective against the payee. But it is not effective against one to whom the payee has passed a cheque for value and who has no notice of any irregularity about it.

5. No title can be obtained through a forged endorsement.

THE CHEQUE

The cheque is in form an order addressed to the banker. The presumption is that the banker has promised to pay the drawer a sum of money. The drawer has either paid money into the bank or, more usually, the banker has lent him money. In either event a deposit is placed to his account. He who signs a cheque says in effect to its recipient: "The banker has promised to pay this amount in accordance with my instructions. You can take the cheque in full confidence; for I, too, promise to pay in the event of the banker's failure to do so." That is to say, the drawer of the cheque is in the legal position of guarantor. So, too, is every endorser of a cheque: he also adds his guarantee that the payment will be forthcoming. Indeed, when deciding whether or not to take a cheque in payment, it is the guarantor's credit rather than the banker's that we consider. For, if the cheque is not paid upon its presentation to the banker we have no right of action against that banker. The drawer of the cheque may have such a right. The receiver has not: no privity of contract exists between him and the banker.

ACCEPTANCE OF BILL OF EXCHANGE

There may be a *"general acceptance"*: the drawee of the bill assents, without any qualification, to the order of the drawer. This he does by writing his name across the bill, adding, if he thinks fit, where the bill is payable.

There may be a "qualified acceptance": the drawee assents to the order of the drawer but modifies it: *he adds a condition*; he expresses his willingness to pay *if* something happens.

HOLDER IN DUE COURSE BEFORE ACCEPTANCE

May a person be a holder in due course of a bill of exchange before it has been accepted? Certainly. The very purpose of a foreign bill is usually negotiation before presentation for acceptance; and a cheque—which is a bill drawn on a banker—though never accepted, may pass through the hands of many holders in due course. Any of these would be able to sue either the drawer or a prior acceptor. It should be noted, indeed, that the Bills of Exchange Act, when defining a bill, makes no mention of an acceptor. There must be a drawer; he must address his order to a particular person; he must give definite directions about the payment of a determinable sum of money. If he does this, the bill is "complete and regular on the face of it." That the bill of exchange is dishonoured by non-acceptance prevents the "holder in due course" from claiming against the drawee. For no one can be sued on a bill whose name does not appear on it. Against all other parties his claim remains, provided that—

1. He becomes the holder of it before it was overdue, and without notice that it had been previously dishonoured, if such was the fact.

2. That he took the bill in good faith and for value, and that at the time the bill was negotiated to him he had no notice of any defect in the title of the person who negotiated it.

This very question was answered in the affirmative in the case of *National Park Bank* v. *Berggren & Co.* (K.B. 1914).

" FICTITIOUS PAYEE "

By the Bills of Exchange Act (Section 7) a cheque made payable to a fictitious or non-existent person is to be treated as one payable to bearer. This rule is founded upon the well-known principle of the Courts that a thing, on the face of it impossible, should be so interpreted as to make it possible; *ut res magis valeat quam pereat* (in order that the matter should rather stand than fall). But when is a payee fictitious? Certainly when he is the offspring of imagination; a cheque made payable "to the Man in the Moon or Order" is regarded as a bearer cheque. Yes; but even a real name may be regarded as fictitious. It is when the name is inserted simply by way of pretence, when there is no intention that payment shall be made in conformity with the order. So it was held in the important case, *Vagliano* v. *Bank of England*, where the House of Lords gave judgment in favour of the Bank. A confidential clerk of the plaintiff had forged a drawer's name, had made bills payable to a real person who had no knowledge of them, had obtained the acceptance of Vagliano, and then, by a forged endorsement, had obtained payment from the Bank. The Bank was justified in debiting Vagliano with the amount paid. A useful appendix to one of the judgments is this : "In the case of a real drawer, that the payee is a fictitious person (unless it is obvious on the face of the bill) must be proved by the holder. But in the case of an unreal drawer, the unreality, and, therefore, fictitiousness of the person named as payee, follows necessarily."

RISKS INCIDENT TO CHEQUES

The economising expedient of the cheque has, along with its enormous advantages as an easy way of setting off debts against credits, its risks also. The business community, in view of the convenience it derives from the cheque, willingly faces the risks. The case decided in July, 1931 (*Slingsby and Others* v. *The District Bank*), illustrates certain of these risks. One is that of forgery. A banker undertakes to pay out his customer's money only in accordance with his customer's mandate; by implication he undertakes not to part with it otherwise. If the banker pays when the customer has given no mandate at all, or if an unauthorised alteration has defeated the customer's intention, then the banker can only very rarely debit his customer with the amount paid. He can do so only by showing that the customer's fault had invited the fraud.

For one thing, the banker must see to it that the endorsement of an order cheque corresponds with the designation of the payee: if the payee is described as agent for a principal, he must endorse as agent. The cheque in question, on being presented to the bank, appeared to be drawn in the form "Pay A B, per X, or Order." Such a direction is not common. It is used, however, when a banker is to collect dividends for his customer, or when, as in the case, an agent is to receive money for a principal. Payment is to be made to A B, but through the instrumentality of X. He alone can give a valid discharge for the payment. But he gives the discharge in a representative capacity—as agent or trustee for the principal for whom the money is destined. Apparently, banking practice has accepted "X" as a sufficient endorsement. This practice, we may assume, will now cease. The endorsement will correspond with the designation of the payee. Indeed, the *Journal of the Institute of Bankers* in "Answers on Banking Practice" gives, as the proper form of endorsement, "A B, per X." "The Bank," ran the judgment, "had no right to pay except under an endorsement corresponding to the mandate expressed on the cheque. Otherwise, the bank could not claim to have discharged the cheque in accordance with the mandate."

ALTERATION IN A CHEQUE

The case cited above raised another interesting point in banking law: when has a cheque been "materially altered"? To what extent is a banker protected when he pays such a cheque? The alteration in the cheque had succeeded in effecting an ingenious fraud. Executors, deciding to invest £5,000 in War Loan, signed an order cheque to the stockbroker, and handed it to their solicitor for transmission. The solicitor when writing out the cheque had left a space between the name of the intended payee and the printed words "or Order." Into that space and after signature he inserted his own name as agent for the stockbroker, "per X." He was thereby enabled to divert the money from the direction intended by the executors and to his own purposes. Was this a material alteration? Certainly, said Mr. Justice Wright; it clearly came within the scope of the judicial definition, "Any alteration is material which would alter the business effect of the instrument." The alteration had changed the nature of the mandate in an essential particular, namely, the description of the payee. The alteration avoided the cheque. The defendant bank could not charge the plaintiffs with a payment made, however innocently, on a void instrument. But, then, was not the bank entitled to say that the plaintiff's lack of care had invited the fraud? They ought to have noticed the space; ought to have foreseen that the space might be filled in such a manner as would defeat their intention; ought, therefore, to have filled the inviting space. It is true that the customer owes the duty of care towards his banker, a duty defined by the House of Lords "to be careful not to facilitate any fraud, which when it has been perpetrated, is seen to have in fact followed in natural and uninterrupted sequence from the negligent act." The banker is bound to pay on the customer's mandate; but he is entitled to have that mandate expressed in clear terms, and in a form not lending itself to alteration by a forger. Yes; but even the most prudent, the most suspicious signer of the cheque could not be expected to have in mind the possibility of the addition actually made. "Reasonable precautions" are essential; and "reasonable precautions" do not imply the anticipation of an occurrence quite unprecedented. There was no breach of duty by the plaintiffs towards the defendant bank (*Slingsby* v. *The District Bank*, K.B. July, 1931).

MATERIAL ALTERATION IN A CHEQUE

When a cheque is altered in a material point, when the name of the payee or the amount to be paid is changed, the cheque is made void. For the drawer has given one direction to his banker about his money; the cheque form now bears a different direction, unauthorised by the banker's customer. Yet this general rule must be interpreted, if possible, in such a sense as to make the cheque valid for what it seems to be. Certainly, if the drawer, filling in his cheque, leaves the amount blank, he cannot complain when an amount other than he intended is inserted by the payee. The drawer must be taken to have authorised the amount; the ostensible authority must be taken to be the real authority. Actual alteration of an amount already inserted is another matter. To insert 20 in front of 7, is obviously alteration in a point that matters. It voids the cheque. Even here, though, the banker has some protection; he can charge his customer with the increased amount, when it is that customer's carelessness that has, in a manner, invited the alteration. "There is a special duty imposed on the banker's customer to exercise care in framing what is a mandate—a duty not to facilitate any fraud, which, when it has been perpetrated, is seen to have in fact flowed in natural and uninterrupted sequence from the negligent act." So declared the Lord Chancellor in the well-known case, *London Joint-Stock Bank* v. *Macmillan* (H.L. 1918).

The answer to this question is thus clear: "E who owed G £3, drew a cheque payable to G or order, but omitted to fill in the amount. G inserted £7, and endorsed the cheque for value to H. H inserted 20 in front of the 7 and cashed the cheque at E's bank, receiving £27. What are the rights and liabilities of E, G, H, and the bank?"

The cheque was good for £7, except as regards G. Any one who took the cheque from G in good faith could enforce payment of the amount. E, however, had a separate right against G for the added £4. The bank paying out £27 when £7 only was authorised could debit E with £7 only, unless—as appears to have been the case—E's negligence had invited the fraud. In that event, E's only prospect of recovering the £20 was by action against H.

What constitutes a material alteration in a bill of exchange was discussed in *Kock* v. *Dicks* (K.B. 1932); (*Action under Order XIV*).

The plaintiff claimed as indorsee of bills of exchange accepted by the defendant and drawn by Radio Actien Gesellschaft. The bills had purported to be drawn in London and were accepted in London. The plaintiff to whom the bills had been endorsed sought to discount them at Deisslinger. The bank would not discount unless, by altering "London" on the face of the bill to "Deisslinger," the bills were made foreign bills. Plaintiff consented; but no communication was made to defendant. Was the alteration a material one? Yes; for the alteration would alter the business effect. In the case of an inland bill it was not necessary to note or protest the bill upon dishonour. But in the case of a foreign bill, notice and protest were essential, and charges were recoverable (Section 57).

A further point was that the amount payable may vary considerably owing to rate of exchange.

REQUIREMENT OF ENDORSEMENT ON CHEQUES

The question has been raised whether the now common requirement of endorsement before payment makes the cheque no longer a negotiable instrument, makes it no longer "an *unconditional* order on the banker." It depends upon whether the requirement is imposed upon the banker or the payee. If, at the foot of the draft, are the words: "The receipt on the back hereof must be signed, which signature will be taken as an endorsement of the cheque," the draft is still a cheque. For no condition is imposed upon the banker. If, however, the draft reads: "Pay to John Smith, fifty pounds, provided the receipt form at foot hereof is duly signed, stamped, and dated," then there is a condition. The draft is no longer a cheque within the meaning of the Act.

ENDORSEMENTS OF CHEQUES

A cheque drawn to order is not transferable by mere delivery; before transfer, the payee must give his order; and this he does upon the back of the cheque. He endorses it. By writing his name he gives an order that the cheque is to be paid to the holder in due course; he has made an "endorsement in blank," and thereby has turned the order cheque into a bearer cheque. He may, however, prefix his signature by a direction; he may make a "restrictive endorsement." In that event, his direction must be respected. If he writes "Pay P for the account of Q," then he has ended the negotiability of the cheque; it can no longer be mercantile money. Yet, clearly, he cannot be allowed entire freedom in his endorsements. The person liable to pay must not be put into a quandary as to whether he should or should not pay. If the direction is "Pay P on his passing the Intermediate Examination" the payer is not obliged to make himself certain that the condition of payment has been fulfilled; his payment of the bill discharges his obligation even though the condition has not been fulfilled. Nor can the payee require payment in separate sums; he must transfer his whole right or none. An endorsement on a bill for £100, "Pay P £50, the balance of £50 having been received by me" is invalid. We may have an acceptance for a smaller amount than that of the bill; we cannot have a partial endorsement. But it would seem that as between an indorser and his indorsee, the latter, if he took the instrument under a conditional endorsement, holds it, or the proceeds thereof, subject to the rights of the person endorsing conditionally.

CUSTOMER'S DUTY TOWARDS BANKER

The reciprocal duties of banker and customer were discussed at length in *London Joint-Stock Bank* v. *Macmillan* (H.L. 1918), where as in the Greenwood case the rule of estoppel was invoked with success against the customer. The banker undertakes to deal with his customer's money in accordance with the customer's mandate; and the customer's mandate is usually given by way of cheque. The banker, however, has a right to insist that the mandate he gets, if he is to act upon it without delay and without loss, should be carefully drawn. The customer owes to the banker a duty to be careful not to facilitate any fraud which, when it has been perpetrated, is seen to have, in fact, flowed in natural and uninterrupted sequence from the negligent act. The Macmillan case concerned a cheque signed for £2 that was fraudulently raised and cashed for £120. By his negligent conduct the customer was estopped from asserting that he had drawn the cheque for £2 only. "For all practical purposes," ran the judgment, "the cheque was in blank. The figure '2' in its isolated position afforded no security whatever against a fraudulent increase. The clerk had the authority of the customer to fill in the words denoting the amount in the body of the cheque; and to put other figures before and after the '2' was quite easy. Examination of the cheque when filled up shows how impossible it was to detect the fraud. The customer is under a legal obligation to see that any cheque which he signs, to be subsequently filled in and presented, is in order when presented. The existence of this obligation precludes him from setting up that the clerk had not authority in fact." The customer has, in effect, led the banker to believe one thing; he is, quite reasonably and fairly, estopped from giving evidence of a different thing. The Greenwood case develops the idea. It makes clear the customer's duty even when fulfilment of that duty is a confession of his wife's liability—and as a consequence of his own liability—for fraud. He knows that the bank is being defrauded. He must give timely warning so that the bank may guard itself. Otherwise, he may find his remedy against the bank gone. (See page 888.)

PRACTICAL ASPECTS

Perhaps what has been said about negotiable instruments may be illustrated by considering two practical questions—

The first is: X buys a motor cycle from Y and gives him in payment thereof a promissory note for £30. Y endorses it for value to Z. Z demands payment, and X refuses payment on the ground that he (X) is an infant. What are the rights of Y and Z?

The second is: R finds in the road a crossed cheque, drawn by S in favour of T. He forges T's endorsement and cashes the cheque with W. W pays it into his bank, and the bank collects from S's bank and credits W. On whom does the loss fall?

Both the note and the cheque are negotiable instruments, evolved by traders as safe, convenient, and elastic means of settling debts. Both are like coin of the realm or bank notes in this important respect, that he who takes them in the ordinary course of business need not be troubled about whether or not he can enforce the promises embodied in them. He himself has a perfect right to them, however defective or non-existent the right of the previous holder. Certainly, if they are not what they purport to be—if the note or the cheque bears a forged signature —the holder has a claim no more enforceable than that given by a spurious bank note or a counterfeit coin. When, however, the instruments are what they profess to be, when his own action in taking them is honest, he is entitled to the full amount of the bill or cheque or note.

One other point, however, must be noted. The negotiable instrument is the written embodiment of a contract, it is essentially the written evidence of a promise to pay. Now, an infant cannot—without exceptions not applicable here—make a binding contract. His signature upon a negotiable instrument places him under no obligation whatever in regard to that instrument. Statute law has indeed gone to a quite extraordinary length in the protection it affords to the infant. If, after coming of age and prompted by feelings of what honour would constrain him to do, he gives a negotiable instrument in respect of a loan made to him when an infant, this instrument is, so far as regards him, void. This protection is given by the Betting and Loans (Infants) Act, 1892. Any one else who places his name upon the bill (or cheque) can be held liable : the infant cannot.

Bearing this in mind, consider the first case. Z has a promissory note upon which two signatures appear, that of X, the infant, and that of Y, the dealer. Against X, despite the making of the note by him, Z is powerless ; X in refusing to pay is within his legal rights, though morally he may be reprehensible. But Y, too, has signed the negotiable instrument and thereby made himself liable in the event—which has happened—of X's unwillingness or inability to pay. Z therefore recovers from Y. Whether or not Y can obtain payment from X will depend, not upon the promissory note, but upon whether he can convince a jury, or a judge sitting without a jury, that the motor cycle is a "necessary." Conceivably, he may be able to do so ; though it must be admitted that his chances are slight. For the Courts tend to narrow rather than to widen the interpretation of the term. It is still much wider than what is absolutely essential for the maintenance of life ; it extends to "goods suitable to the station in life." Even so, Y's task is difficult.

In the second case, we have the position, frequently realised in practice, where one of two innocent people are to suffer through the fraud or dishonesty of a third. This third is, presumably, one whom we cannot attach and constrain to undo his delinquency, or, more likely, is not worth attaching. The cheque is to be paid to T, who may assign his right by endorsing. Since it is a crossed cheque he will invariably do so when his own banker is, as here, other than the drawer's banker ; for the cheque, being crossed, is paid by one banker to another banker. Now R, finding the cheque, acquires no right to payment ; nor can any one else acquire a right through the forged endorsement placed upon it. True, the banker who pays the cheque, without negligence be it noted, in conformity with a forged endorsement, is given a statutory protection. Section 60 of the Bills of Exchange Act, 1882, runs thus : "It is not incumbent on the banker to show that the endorsement of the payee was made by or under the authority of the person whose endorsement it purports to be." And Section 82 of the Act extends the

27

protection to the collecting banker: "Where a banker in good faith and without negligence receives payment for a customer of a cheque crossed generally or specially to himself, and the customer has no title or a defective title thereto, the banker shall not incur any liability to the true owner of the cheque by reason only of having received such payment." The two banks concerned in the transaction being exempt from liability, it remains to consider the position of W. It is quite true that W has given value for the cheque, and we may assume that he took it believing that no irregularity existed in regard to it. Nevertheless, he has no other right to it than R had; and just as R could not substantiate a claim to the amount of the cheque, neither can W. The cheque, in the form taken by him, was not a completely negotiable instrument; it lacked the necessary authority of T for its transfer. What money W has received upon the cheque he must refund to S, to whose account the cheque has been debited. W certainly has an indisputable claim against R, if only R could be found and made to pay. We may probably take it that the claim is of negligible value, so that the whole loss falls upon W.

A case in point is *Goldman* v. *Cox* (C.A. 1923).

BANKERS AND CHEQUES

1. On the service of a garnishee order *nisi*, made on a judgment against the customer, the whole credit balance on current account is impounded, irrespective of the relative amounts of such balance and the judgment debt. The banker must not reduce this balance even by paying out cheques drawn before the garnishee order was served.

2. Unless precluded by agreement (as he was in *Greenhalgh* v. *Union Bank of Manchester*, K.B. 1924), a banker is entitled to combine different accounts kept by the customer in his own right, even though at different branches of the same bank. The agreement may be express, or it may be implied by the course of business. The customer, however, has no converse right: he cannot use a credit balance at one branch in order to draw cheques on another branch.

3. There is no protection for the banker collecting uncrossed cheques. If the customer has no title, or only a defective title, the banker is liable to the true owner for conversion, or for money had and received (*Reckitt* v. *Midland Bank*, C.A. 1930). Yet he may escape liability if he can establish an independent

title as owner in that: (1) he has given cash for the cheque; (2) that cheque has been paid in to reduce an overdraft ; (3) where he has given sanction to the customer to draw against it before it is cleared; (4) where there is a lien on the cheque.

4. A banker may not pay an unstamped cheque: he may, however, affix an adhesive twopenny stamp, and cancel it, charging the twopence to the *drawee* of the cheque. He may not pay a cheque with an uncancelled adhesive stamp unless he is prepared to prove that the drawer affixed the stamp. (By the Stamp Act, 1891, where the drawer does use an adhesive stamp, he must cancel it before letting it out of his hands, subject to a penalty of £10.) The Midland Bank's attempt to create unstamped "chequelets" for amounts below £2 failed (*Midland Bank* v. *Inland Revenue*, 1927).

MONEY AND PAYMENTS

The recent changes in the legal tender of the country illustrate in striking form the supremacy of Parliament, its power of adding to or of modifying the laws we must obey. "Money" in the narrowest sense means whatever Parliament prescribes as a means of cancelling debts. That means may be bits of metal (coins, the contents of which Parliament settles) or bits of paper. Parliament enacts. It issues its decree, its fiat, "This shall be money"; and immediately it is money. True, our money of account, the unit by means of which we compare the value of things and by reference to which we calculate, has retained the name "pound" from the days of the earliest transactions among us. But though the name has persisted, the thing denoted by the name has passed through many vicissitudes; a pound, to the first traders who bargained on the little hill where St. Paul's Cathedral was later to rise above the roar of traffic, meant something very different from a pound to those who now transact their business in and about Lombard Street. The name remains. What the name denotes is transitory. The change in the answer to the question of "What is a pound?" used to be so gradual as to be imperceptible to ordinary people. In these days the passing of an Act of Parliament both brings about the change and makes obvious that a change has been effected.

"WHAT IS A POUND?"

In 1816 we led the way to the once almost universal gold standard, now almost universally abandoned. Parliament enacted that the pound, which, until then, ought to have been an actual pound weight of silver, should be the value of a fixed weight of gold. The value of this fixed weight should be a "pound," the pull over the market of everything else should be measured by reference to this value. This is, in fact, what we understand by a "gold standard"; the purchasing power of the specified weight of gold is what we compare all other purchasing powers with. And a new coin, the sovereign, was to be issued containing exactly this specified weight of gold. The sovereign was no mere token of value. It contained in itself the value it represented; and hammering it into a shapeless piece of yellow metal would not have diminished its power over the market. It still had its value of a pound; the transforming of it into a coin neither augmented nor diminished its value. Moreover, there was freedom to use the sovereign as its owner pleased, to export it or to use it as material for manufacture at his will. It was a commodity put upon the market in such a form as made quantity and quality determinable without difficulty. The weight and the degree of purity were guaranteed by the State. Indeed, any one could, if he cared to do so, take his gold to the Mint and have it made into coins without charge.

WAR CHANGES IN THE POUND

The year 1914 brought the first of recent changes in the meaning of "pound sterling." The Defence of the Realm Act, among other measures apparently called for by the appalling menace to the country, decreed the withdrawal of gold from circulation and prohibited the melting or exporting of sovereigns. The gold coins were replaced by Treasury notes. We still, nominally, remained on the gold standard. The Bank of England was still under a statutory obligation to give gold for notes. But, in practice we had, temporarily it was expected, abandoned it. The year 1925 restored the effective gold standard, but in a modified form. The piece of paper that circulated as a pound, was again made at one point equivalent to a specified weight of gold. Provided that the holders of the notes were prepared to buy 400 oz. of gold at once, the Bank of England was put under obligation to provide it. And again, as before 1914, no restrictions were placed upon the use of the gold. In 1928 came the Bank Notes and Currency Act, transferring to the Bank of England the issue of the paper notes representing gold. The war-time treasury notes became replaced by Bank of England pound and ten-shilling notes. Shortly afterwards, the Macmillan Committee of Finance was appointed; and its members determined that the gold standard was the only possible one for this country. Its report was hardly out when, in spite of strenuous efforts of the Government and the Bank of England, we were forced off the gold standard. Here is yet another instance of admirable, well-reasoned conclusions meeting shipwreck upon the hard rocks of intractable facts.

THE 1931 ACT

The meaning of the 1931 emergency Act is simply this. The Bank of England is relieved of the statutory duty, placed upon it by the Act of 1925, of selling bar gold to all comers at a fixed price. With the removal of this obligation the former parity between paper and gold no longer obtains. The amount of *gold* now obtainable for a pound has become less; how much less depends upon market conditions. Therefore it is that the pound, in relation to the franc, in relation to any monetary unit that still retains its former power over gold, has depreciated. The pound buys less than 113·0016 grains of fine gold. The franc still buys ·9097625 grains. The pound, therefore, buys fewer francs. But it is no necessary result that the pound buys fewer yards of calico or fewer pounds of bacon. The result of the 1931 Act is to make the "pound" into an abstraction. The pound has now no tangible representative except the green embellished pieces of paper issued by the Bank of England. And the total amount of these that the Bank can issue is in accordance with what Parliament has decreed. He who has a pound, whether the pound is attested by his possessions of this note, or whether the pound is placed to his credit at his banker's, commands the market still—to the extent of his pound. But he commands it in competition with all other possessors of pounds.

BANKERS CREATE MONEY

They create other money than that prescribed by the State.

Our bankers long ago realised that promise, in matter of money, is as good as performance. That is why they are able to create money. They promise to pay; and since their promise is widely credited it becomes money. When the old private bankers issued their promissory notes, they hoped that each one would go through a long drawn-out series of adventures before it returned to him to test whether his promise would be kept.

The modern banker lends John Smith £10,000 by putting that amount to John Smith's credit. But he trusts that John Smith will not ask for legal money, that he will draw cheques, will even cross them so that they are not intended to be paid in money, will, in short, cancel his own debts by writing them off against another's debts to him. He can do this if he transfers his credits to the banker. For, of course, John Smith also has promised to pay the banker £10,000; but John Smith's promise is not widely enough credited to serve as money. The promise to the banker is redeemed when John Smith passes to the banker the claims he has upon others. "You cannot ride on a claim to a horse, but you can pay with a claim to money."

The bill of exchange is like the cheque in this, that it asks an identifiable person to pay a sum of money. The drawer issues his request. The debtor accepts the bill. By writing his name across it, that is, he both acknowledges his indebtedness and he promises to pay. The acceptor is the primary debtor. He it is who is responsible in the first place to any one who gets the bill of exchange in the ordinary course of trading. But, here, as in the cheque, the drawer is a guarantor that the bill will be duly met.

DUTY OF DEBTOR

The legal rules relating to payment are not always obvious. Some are, indeed, not easily reconcilable with reason. Yet, once we place ourselves upon the standpoint of the Common Law, we can understand them. They may at times conflict with our sense of reason, with our sense of justice, in fact. Still, we can appreciate them as logical conclusions from the assumptions that law makes—from fictions, the practical man, in his impatience, declares. These assumptions are founded on the legal view of what a reasonable man, anxious to fulfil his obligations to his fellows, unwilling, however, to stretch those obligations farther than is needed, would do.

One of the assumptions is that a debtor, the moment payment is due, will seek out his creditor and pay him. Eager to discharge his obligations, he will not await a demand note, much less delay until a "final notice" reaches him. Income tax being due on New Year's Day, he writes a cheque to the collector on New Year's Eve. The payment, too, must be proffered in "legal tender" if the creditor insists. An offer up to 10s. in copper is good tender; up to 40s. in silver; and to an unlimited extent in Bank of England notes. Refusal of the proffered amount does not discharge the debtor from his debt. But he has fulfilled his duty; and, provided he remains ready to hand over the requisite legal tender, he need do no more. He has an answer to a possible action for debt. The creditor, however, is not obliged to give change, so that it is not good tender unless he can take from the paper or coins offered the exact sum due to him.

On the other hand, the creditor, since he has a legal right to the money, is not entitled to charge interest on the sum due. In theory, the legal right to money is equivalent to the money itself. Apart from definite agreement, therefore, no interest can be charged on overdue accounts; if the creditor has not promptly issued his writ, the loss is partly due to his own remissness, but by virtue of the Law Reform (Miscellaneous Provisions) Act, 1934, the Court may, if it thinks fit, order interest to be paid on a debt or damages in respect of which judgment is given for the creditor.

AGREEMENT TO PAY INTEREST

But, then, what does constitute agreement about interest payment? Does the statement upon an account rendered that "Interest will be charged at 5 per cent on overdue accounts" constitute such an agreement? It does if the creditor intends to act in accordance with the statement, and if the debtor knows, or should know, of the intention at the time of making the contract. A man who takes a document containing the terms of the contract he makes is bound by those terms, if his attention has been directed to them in a reasonably effective manner. That is the rule reached in the well-known case of *Parker* v. *The South-Eastern Railway*. A man may be bound by a condition of which he was unaware. Very little, however, suffices to show that the creditor has not intended to enforce his claim. If he has in the past accepted payment without exacting interest, it will be taken that he has waived his right to interest. On the other hand, where a creditor did actually charge interest on overdue accounts in accordance with the notice of his invoice, it was held that he was entitled to prove for the interest payment in a bankruptcy. This is the often quoted case of the Marquis of Anglesey.

APPROPRIATION OF PAYMENTS

Another rule, less susceptible to ridicule than the interest rule, exists in regard to the appropriation of payments. The man having money has a general power over the market; he can exert that power in whatever direction he pleases. If he chooses to pay the bet he lost rather than the grocer's bill, he cannot be restrained from exercising that choice; the grocer has his legal remedy, and in the eyes of the law that is enough. If he chooses to pay a debt he incurred yesterday rather than one incurred six years ago, none can prevent him. When the creditor of long standing laments his hard lot, laments that lapse of time has now barred his recovery by legal process, the answer of the law is again that he has himself been remiss. He has slept when he should have been awake, and *vigilantibus non dormientibus jura subveniunt* (laws come to the help of those awake to their own interests, not to those asleep over them). So we have the rule that a creditor is bound by the debtor's appropriation; the creditor cannot divert to another debt, perhaps to one about which dispute exists, the money paid to cancel a different debt. Apart from an appropriation by the debtor, an appropriation that he may make by implication as well as by express terms, the creditor can appropriate; and, when he is an astute business man, he will appropriate to the debt difficult to recover by legal process. A quite interesting illustration is *Seymour* v. *Pickett* (K.B. 1905). Seymour was not registered under the Dentists' Act. He could not, therefore, recover any fee for an operation. But he could sue for materials supplied. He operated on Pickett and charged him £45. Pickett paid him £20 without making any specific appropriation. Seymour brought an action for £25 unpaid, and at the trial the judge found that the cost of the materials supplied was £21, the balance of £24 being the fee for the operation. In the witness box Seymour claimed to appropriate the £20 to payment of fees. He was held entitled to do so, since the debtor had made no appropriation. Seymour, therefore, recovered the £21 as cost of materials.

PART PAYMENT NO GOOD DISCHARGE

At another rule of English law relating to payments, the judges themselves now and then laugh. This is the rule that the payment of a smaller sum cannot operate as a discharge of a larger sum. Even if the creditor promises to accept the smaller sum in full settlement he is not, except in so far as he has regard to the sanctity of a promise, prevented from suing for the balance. Prompt payment is his due; his promise to release the debtor from the unpaid balance is, therefore, a gratuitous promise. And, unless made by a sealed writing, a gratuitous promise is not enforceable. Yet, if the creditor promised to accept a cheque for a smaller amount as complete discharge, he would be bound by his promise. For the debtor has given something, a negotiable instrument, that the creditor could not demand; the creditor can demand legal tender only. A cheque for £10 accomplishes in this case more than £10 in good pound notes can. The absurdity of the rule has caused the judges to exert their ingenuity in finding points where what is done is different from what is legally exigible. The difference found is then a consideration for the promise made, and the promise is enforceable. Thus, the payment of part only of a debt has been held to be a good discharge of the whole when a person other than the debtor advanced the sum.

LEGAL MONEY

1. The amount of cheque circulation is left uncontrolled. The Bank of England note circulation is carefully regulated. For, since 1833, Bank of England notes have been endowed with the privilege of "Legal Tender." By enacting this Act, Parliament in effect guaranteed the goodness of the notes; and, as a result, felt itself obliged to determine the conditions of issue.

2. Before the autumn of 1931 the regulations about notes were directed to the one point of assuring their immediate convertibility into gold. It was thought that, as long as parity between gold and the token paper was maintained, the increase or decrease of the currency would depend solely upon the efflux or influx of gold. The devices adopted for securing convertibility were—

(a) A fixed fiduciary issue was appointed: an issue well within the limits of the note circulation.

(b) The Bank of England was empowered to issue further notes against gold.

(c) The Bank of England was placed under a statutory duty to buy or sell gold to all comers at a fixed rate.

(d) The Bank of England was, until 1914, obliged to pay all claims upon it in gold, not notes.

(e) The Bank of England was obliged to show in a Weekly Return that Parliament's directions were duly observed.

3. Since 1931, though the Bank is relieved of its obligation to sell gold at a fixed price, the issue of notes is still controlled. There is the fixed fiduciary issue of £260,000,000 (an issue that the Bank, with the consent of the Treasury may expand): there is the gold backing for the rest of issue.

4. That the State's fiat may enhance or diminish the purchasing power of the monetary unit, introduces a risk into business relations; and many cases since the unsettling of the currencies as a result of war conditions, show that the risks have often been realised. The effect of the various decisions seems to be that payments made in what constitutes the "Legal Tender" of the place of payment are good, even though the money should have greatly depreciated since the making of the contract. Dorman, Long & Co., for instance, contractors for the Harbour Bridge at Sydney, lost about a quarter million on the contract made in 1924. The company could not foresee that on the completion of the bridge in 1932 the Australian pound would be worth only 16s. in London.

Depreciation has proceeded further in other currencies. One curious case will serve to illustrate this, and also the difference between lending money and depositing it for safe custody.

An owner may let another have property on the understanding that the actual property be returned to him later.

This is a species of bailment that is sometimes called *Commodatum*. I lend a textbook, from my point of view enhanced, from another's point of view depreciated in value, by copious annotations. I expect the same book back, not merely a similar one, though fresh from the printer. In many incidents of business life, however, the intention is that the property handed over may be used as he pleases by the possessor, his agreement being to restore similar property. Such is the relation with the banker. The customer lends him money. The banker is under no obligation to keep intact the actual notes or coins deposited. It is enough that he maintains power to pay out other money according to his undertaking. Such a transfer of property, where there is neither express nor implied undertaking to restore the identical property, is sometimes called *mutuum*. Illustration of the distinction between *Commodatum* and *Mutuum* was afforded in *Kricorian* v. *Ottoman Bank* (K.B., 1932). The plaintiff in 1913 deposited with the Smyrna Branch of the Ottoman Bank 12,500 gold piastres. In 1930 he demanded repayment of his account in gold, the original deposit at compound interest apparently amounting to something like £8,000. The bank offered payment in the paper piastres then current in Smyrna, equivalent to about £12. Now, it seems that a good Mohammedan, like the good Christian in days of old, refuses to accept interest. If he deposits money he expects back the same money, neither more nor less. It is *Commodatum*. Here, however, there was the agreement for interest payment; the bank had the implied authority to make the deposit fructify by the financing of trade and industry. It was *Mutuum*; and the bank's contention prevailed. The plaintiff was obliged to be content with what the Turkish Government had made "Legal Tender." The extraordinary depreciation of the currency had so lightened the burden of the bank's debt as to enable it to release itself from its obligations by handing back only a small fraction of what had been deposited.

CUSTOMS DUTY AND CONTRACT OF SALE

When a duty has been imposed upon goods that are the subject-matter of a contract of sale, who bears the added cost? The rule in relation to this is laid down in the Finance Act of 1901. Section 10, Paragraph I, enacts: *Addition or deduction of new or altered duty in the case of Contract*: "Where any new customs import duty or new excise duty is imposed, or where any customs import duty or excise duty is increased, and any goods in respect of which the duty is payable are delivered after the day on which the new or increased duty takes effect in pursuance of a contract made before that day, the seller of the goods may, in the absence of agreement to the contrary, recover, as an addition to the contract price, a sum equal to any amount paid by him in respect of the goods on account of the new duty or the increase of duty." And Paragraph 3 of the same section indicates how the added price shall be calculated. "Where any addition to the contract price may be made under this section, such sum as may be agreed upon or in default of agreement determined by the Commissioners of Customs in the case of a customs duty, and by the Commissioners of Inland Revenue in the case of an excise duty, as representing in the case of a new duty any new expenses incurred, may be included in the contract price." That is to say, the buyer, apart from a stipulation to the contrary, bears the added cost. This is in accordance with the underlying idea of "indirect" taxes: the ultimate consumer is intended to bear the tax; the actual payer of the tax is expected to shift its burden along.

STAMPS ON RECEIPTS

It appears that some doubt exists in regard to the stamping for revenue purposes of receipts when goods are sold for cash. Quite often, it is true, the seller gives no receipt, nor is he asked for one. The transfer of the goods and the transfer of the money being concurrent, neither party anticipates further question about the transaction. Nevertheless, the buyer who pays £2 or upwards may require a receipt properly stamped. The payer may, frequently does, waive his right; and then no penalty attaches to the receiver's omission to give an acknowledgment. Where the payer does ask for a receipt, and where it is refused, the receiver of the money is liable to a £10 penalty. The relevant section of the Stamp Act, 1891, is 103: "If any person—

1. Gives a receipt liable to duty and not duly stamped; or

2. In any case where the receipt would be liable to duty refuses to give a receipt duly stamped; or

3. Upon a payment to the amount of £2 or upwards give a receipt for a sum not amounting to £2, or separates or divides the amount paid with intent to evade the duty; he shall incur a fine of £10."

DOCUMENTS OF TITLE

The bill of exchange, as we have seen, developed into a means of assigning credits in order to cancel debits. In its origin it was a written agreement by the acceptor to pay the drawee. It has become mercantile money. Several other business documents have similarly developed as means of facilitating trade. They have become something more than clear records of agreement or clear statements concerning the disposal of goods. They have become *Documents of Title*. That is, these documents—bills of lading, warehouse warrants, dock warrants, and others—afford evidence of ownership of the goods noted in them. The holder of the document is presumed to have power to dispose of the goods. Though the goods may be another's, his having the document of title proclaims to the world that the owner has given him authority to deal with the goods. By handing over the document of title he can sell the goods or can pledge them. The goods remain in the warehouse or the ship. Yet transfer of the document transfers ownership, or, when the document has been given as security, transfers the right to retain the goods till charges are met. To effect the transfer of ownership, or part ownership, the holder of the document may need to endorse it. But simple delivery may suffice.

WAREHOUSE WARRANT

The business community deals freely in documents of title, because confidence exists that the goods noted are really available, that the rights pretended to be assigned are really assigned. Consider an iron warrant, for instance, issued by a warehouse-keeper in respect of iron put into his custody. The ironmaster cannot lightly suspend production; he must, at times, continue making though he is selling little. He can make for stock, he can hold out for better terms, when, by means of his warehouse warrant, he can get money for his iron though he has not yet sold it. True, he might get an advance from his banker upon the security of stock at the works. He gets the advance more readily when, by his signature on a warrant, the warehouse-keeper gives assurance to the world that the iron is in the warehouse ready for delivery.

Dealing in goods by means of these documents of title is greatly promoted by the growing practice of grading according to widely recognised standards. When a trusted party grades corn or cotton or rubber the buyer need not trouble about examining samples; the grader, interested only in giving the right classification so as to be fair to both buyer and seller, gives certainty about quality. The Canada Grain Act of 1912, for instance, enacts that all wheat grown in Canada and dispatched from elevators must be inspected and graded by Government officials. Prospective buyers, knowing the grading, can buy the farmer's warehouse receipt and be certain of getting the wheat they want. The buyer does not get the actual wheat delivered by the farmer to the elevator. That wheat has long lost its identity. He does get wheat of the same grade. For the warehouse receipt is a *general warrant*; it is a document of title, not to a particular parcel of wheat, but to a given quantity of a defined quality of wheat.

A " GENERAL " WARRANT

By a "General Warrant" we do not mean a receipt for a specific lot of iron or wheat or cotton. We mean a transferable *order* for an equal quantity of the same grade of the commodity. In an important case decided in 1877, the legal view of such general warrants was put very clearly.

"This form of iron warrant was invented about 1844 and the practice grew general about 1866, and from that time till now we must consider it on the evidence as an established custom, that any man who gives this warrant intends that it shall pass from hand to hand for value by endorsement, and that the indorsee is to have the goods free from any claim for purchase money. He is not to be asked whether he has a claim or not; if he chooses to issue it in this shape he tells the trade that they may safely deal on the faith of that warrant, and whether or not it becomes a negotiable instrument in Common Law as distinct from equity is, to my mind, purely immaterial. That is the custom. And, as a man who issues such a warrant knows that custom, it appears to me that the Phoenix Bessimer Co. have issued this exactly as if they had stated they were to be deliverable according to the custom of the iron trade, that is, to be deliverable free from any vendor's lien to Messrs. Smith & Co., or their assigns by endorsement. For had these words been inserted, as I think it will be desirable in future they should be inserted, can anybody doubt that the company, by assigning the warrant in that form, would be precluded in effect from afterwards alleging that they were unpaid vendors?"

BILL OF LADING

The bill of lading, again, has been called "the key to a warehouse afloat." He who has obtained the bill in the normal course of business can require the shipmaster to give him the cargo covered by the bill. The merchant buying the bill buys the goods; and, if he chooses, he can resell them before they reach port. The banker, taking the bill into his possession, gets good collateral security for the advance he makes.

The New Orleans exporter has bought cotton from growers in the Mississippi Valley. He sends samples by post to Liverpool firms likely to want cotton, and offers to sell *c.i.f. on type.* He warrants, by this offer, that the cotton delivered will be in quality equal to the sample; and he undertakes to pay the freight and the cost of the marine insurance. The Liverpool buyer, that is, learns the amount of all expenses up to landing the cotton on the quay, or wagon, or canal boat at Liverpool; he learns also when he must begin to defray expenses.

Can the exporter make certain of his being paid; and can he have payment without awaiting the expiry of the credit term? The banking system enables him to do both. The Liverpool man arranges with his banker for a "documentary credit." The banker will accept a bill of exchange drawn by the New Orleans man, but only when the banker knows that cotton has been shipped to Liverpool. The New Orleans exporter ships the cotton, obtaining from the shipmaster a bill of lading; he insures the cotton; he prepares his c.i.f. invoice. He then draws a bill of exchange upon the Liverpool bank. And he sells the bill of exchange, to which are attached the shipping documents, to his own bank. The New Orleans bank, having the bill of lading, is now the temporary owner of the cotton.

BANK'S FINANCING OF TRADE

The bank has no wish to deal in cotton, though. It looks forward to the transfer of the bill of lading and the repayment of its advance. It sends, therefore, the documents to its Liverpool agent. The agent presents the draft to the Liverpool bank for acceptance, handing over at the same time the shipping documents. These being in order, the Liverpool bank accepts the bill of exchange. Now it is the Liverpool bank that is the temporary owner of the cotton. The American bank has not, in fact, received cash for its bill of lading. It has, however, received a banker's acceptance; and this, at the end of the sixty or ninety days specified, will certainly become cash. The Liverpool bank, in accordance with the arrangement made with its customer, sends to him the shipping documents enabling him to claim the cotton and attend to it. A formal letter accompanies the documents instructing the customer to warehouse the cotton in the name of the bank, or to retain it in trust for the bank till sale has been effected.

The importer has the bill of lading. This he presents to the shipmaster, probably through the agency of a master porter or of a warehouse-keeper, and the shipmaster will give him possession of the cotton. The cotton will then be dealt with by means of warehouse warrant or of delivery order.

BILL OF SALE, EFFECT OF

The Bill of Sale as security for a loan effects a transfer of the property in the goods enumerated. But it leaves the possession of the goods with the borrower. The buyer of the goods from the borrower gets no title to them; yet, if they are sold by a mercantile agent, the buyer gets a perfectly good title. The lender's remedy is to sue the agent for conversion. Thus, X borrowed and assigned, by a bill of sale, the furniture of her house as security. X asked Curtis, an auctioneer, to sell the furniture for her. He did so, she obtained the proceeds, and the lender sued the auctioneer for conversion. Curtis did not know of the bill of sale, though he could have known by consulting the County Court Register, and he was obliged to satisfy the lender's claim (*Consolidated Co.* v. *Curtis*, K.B. 1930).

LEGAL REMEDIES

POSSIBLE REMEDIES

ONE whose legal rights have been invaded may ask the Court for (1) *damages*, a money compensation for the wrong or breach of contract; (2) *specific performance of a contract*, an order from the Court to the defendant that he carry out the contract according to its terms; (3) *injunction*, an order from the Court to the defendant that he refrains from action constituting a wrong or a breach of contract.

RIGHTS AND REMEDIES

We have a legal maxim which says: "No right without a remedy"; if the law does not prescribe a remedy, it does not recognise a right. For every legal wrong there is a legal remedy. Perhaps it would be well if the law did recognise a right in some particular matter; and, in the development of our law, new rights are from time to time being recognised and new remedies being created. Nor is this enlargement of legal rights confined to what Parliament does in its conscious and deliberate examination of the law relating to a special topic. The enlargement comes also from an adaptation of Common Law principles to the changing conditions of life. An Act of Parliament, for example, provides a remedy for the unlucky pedestrian who, injured by the carelessness of a motorist, finds that his injurer is a man of straw so that an action for damages would be a foolish waste of money. The Road Traffic Act of 1930 enjoins that every driver shall be in possession of an insurance policy covering the risks of such a pedestrian. Statute law has thereby given a right against an insurance company, in this manner providing a remedy for an obvious evil. In like manner the Common Law may take cognisance of altered conditions. Before the snail in the ginger-beer bottle case (*Donoghue* v. *Stevenson*), decided in the House of Lords in the autumn of 1932, it was not clear that (apart from contract) a consumer, made ill by contaminated food or hurt by a defective implement, had any remedy against the manufacturer of the food or the maker of the implement. The decision in that case makes abundantly clear the citizen's duty not to turn dangerous or noxious things loose on the world; those damaged as a result of failure in that duty are provided with a remedy in an action for damages.

RIGHTS AND REMEDIES ARE CORRELATIVES

The rule remains, however, *ubi jus, ibi remedium*; if the law
has provided a remedy there, and only there, it has recognised
a right. The law provides no remedy for one whose photograph
has been taken and published much against his will, nor for one
whose customers have been lamentably lessened by the opening
of a rival enterprise, nor for one who, acting upon the faith of
a telegram wrongly transmitted, has suffered loss by his action.
The converse is that the law recognises no right of privacy, no
right to freedom from competition, no right to protection against
misleading statements—unless, indeed, these statements are wilfully made. In *Le Lievre* v. *Gould* (Q.B. 1893) the defendant, a
surveyor, had given certificates relating to work done. The
certificates were not accurate; the surveyor had been tricked by
the builder to whom he gave them. Relying on these certificates,
the plaintiffs made advances on mortgage to the builder. They
lost money; and they sued the surveyor, since it was upon his
misleading statement that they had lent. The Court considered,
however, that, in the absence of a duty owed by the surveyor
towards the mortgagees, they had no remedy against him. "No
doubt," said the Appeal judge, "the defendant did give untrue
certificates. It was negligent on his part to do so. But can the
plaintiffs rely upon negligence in the absence of fraud? The
question of liability for negligence cannot arise at all until it
is established that the man who has been negligent owes some
duty to the man who seeks to make him liable. What duty is
there when there is no relation between the parties by contract?
A man is entitled to be as negligent as he pleases towards the
whole world if he owes no duty to them."

THE APPROPRIATE REMEDY

A knowledge of the remedies available is, therefore, wellnigh
as necessary as a knowledge of the legal rights we enjoy, if we
are not to be baulked of those rights. The facts may be the
same in two cases. Yet in one case the suitor succeeds because
he has asked for the fitting remedy; in the other case he fails
because he has asked for a remedy that is not applicable. He has
suffered loss because another has failed to fulfil his contractual
obligations. He can get damages, a monetary compensation
for the non-performance of the contract; and he can get this
because the law owes it to him as a right. But it is no necessary
consequence that he can, if he chooses, ask and obtain from the

Court an order, addressed to the defaulter, that he shall carry out the contract in accordance with its terms. He will get this order—this decree of specific performance—only in a limited number of events: if one broke a promise to marry, for instance, it would hardly be possible (it would certainly be very undesirable) for the Court to compel performance of the promise. The jilted party must be contented with damages, however ineffective a money payment is towards the healing of a broken heart. Besides, he who seeks the Common Law remedy of damages will get it, provided he establishes his claim, though his conduct in the matter has been harsh and overbearing, though he may have been guilty of sharp-practice. He who seeks the equitable remedy of specific performance must, however, show that his conduct throughout has been straightforward, that he has come into the Court with clean hands, and is a worthy recipient of its grace.

BREACH OF CONTRACT AND TORT

Moreover, the same wrongful action may be both a breach of contract and a tort. The person wronged may state his claim in either of two ways; he may seek damages either for a breach of contract or for a failure in a duty owed to him.

In what way he shall frame it is, indeed, sometimes a question of moment. A servant has been dismissed unjustifiably—without the requisite notice and under circumstances that must damage his reputation in the world. He will get as damages for breach of contract, at the most, payment for the period of notice that should have been given. He may get heavy damages if he sues in tort. For in the case of a wrong the damages are entirely with the jury; and they may take into account other elements than the actual monetary loss shown.

TECHNICAL DEFENCE MAY DEFEAT CLAIM

One contemplating going to law in order to vindicate his rights must consider this point, too. His claim may be one that all fair-minded people would admit. Yet it may fail in law because of some point he had overlooked, perhaps because his opponent could take advantage of a technical point. For the reiteration is well worth while that a statute may afford a perfectly good defence against a claim—good from the legal point of view that is, though not palatable to the honourable business man. Common Law would admit the claim; Statute Law bars it. The Court may be reluctant to admit such a defence; but the Court has no option. Parliament has spoken; and the duty of the Court is to interpret the law as laid down by Parliament. The defence is possible that the statute governing the matter requires a specific piece of evidence in order to make the contract enforceable; and the specified evidence is not forthcoming. Or possibly the Stamp Act calls for the payment of revenue before the Court can admit documents; and the revenue has not been paid. Then it may be that an obligation, which honour requires to be fulfilled, is no legal obligation. The marine insurance case (*Motor Union Insurance Company* v. *Mannheimer Versicherungsgesellschaft*, Com. Cases, 1932) appears to illustrate the point.

ARBITRATOR AND " SPECIAL CASE "

The arbitrator had decided against the German company; but he submitted a special question to the decision of the Court. The question was whether the relation between the parties had been that of principal and agent, or that of insurer and re-insurer. If the first, then the arbitrator's finding was good against the appellants. If the second, then the claim failed owing to the absence of the statutory requirements.

In 1925, the appellants, a German insurance company, carrying on business at Mannheim, wished to undertake marine insurance business in the English market. At that time German policies were not looked upon with any confidence in this country. The appellants, therefore, entered into an agreement with the respondents, the Motor Union Insurance Company. The policies, however, were to be issued in the name of the Motor Union; and ostensibly the business should be Motor Union business. One term of the agreement stipulated that, when issuing a policy, the Motor Union should itself be liable for half the total sum insured. This stipulation was intended to secure the appellants against the risk of the Motor Union taking up undesirable insurances. Policies were issued by the Motor Union in accordance with the agreement, and in course of time heavy losses were incurred. The Motor Union paid the losses and sought to recover over £40,000 from the appellants. The appellants refused to pay; and the claim was referred to arbitration.

MARINE INSURANCE MUST BE EVIDENCED BY POLICY

At the appeal against the arbitrator's award, the German company contended that the agreement was in fact one relating to reinsurance. The agency agreement masked the reality. That being so, the claim of the Motor Union must depend upon the existence of a reinsurance policy. No such policy had ever existed, and, therefore, the claim could not succeed owing to the requirements of the Marine Insurance Act. This Act declares that "a contract of marine insurance is inadmissible in evidence unless it is embodied in a marine policy." Further, the agreement between the parties was a reinsurance contemplated by the Stamp Act, 1891, and since no policy existed, the claim of the Motor Union was barred by the Stamp Act, too. For the Stamp Act declares that "a contract for sea insurance (including reinsurance) shall not be valid unless the same is expressed in a policy of sea insurance."

The contention of the appellants prevailed. The judgment brings out very clearly the law relating to the undisclosed principal, as well as the effect of a statute upon the possibility of enforcing a contract. "It is a commonplace of the law of agency that an undisclosed principal may sue or be sued upon a contract made on his behalf; but in the case of sea insurance the marine insurance is inadmissible in evidence unless embodied in a marine policy in accordance with the Act, and by Section 23 the policy must specify, among other things, the name or names of the underwriters. Clearly, therefore, as the name of the Mannheim Company did not appear in the policies issued in pursuance of the agreement, they could not have intervened as principals so as to sue the assured for a premium, nor could they have been sued for a loss. In either case the absence of a policy subscribed in their name would have been fatal. The statutes prevent any privity of contract being established between the Mannheim Company and the assured by the action or agency of the Motor Union Company; and the latter, and they only, in my judgment, are the insurers. Any premiums received were received by them, and any losses paid were paid by them as principals in respect of a liability which was their's and only their's. If that be so, it seems to me that any claim they may have against the Mannheim Company is not for indemnity against loss sustained as agents, but is in the nature of reinsurance.

"I must hold that the claim here is in effect a claim for reinsurance, and so must fail for want of a policy."

TWO SYSTEMS OF LAW

Statements like these meet us; "Common Law has differed from equity in its treatment of bonds much as it did in its

treatment of mortages. Common Law took the contract in its
literal form and enforced the fulfilment of the entire promise upon
breach of the condition. Equity looked to the object which the
bond was intended to secure and would restrain the promisee
from obtaining more than the amount of damages which accrued
to him by its breach." We read also that the Common Law
Courts gave one remedy for legal wrongs; the Court of the Chancellor, which applies equity, gave a different remedy. If injured
by a breach of contract, a man could claim damages at Common
Law; and he could claim damages as his right. He could go to
equity only for remedies like specific performance or injunction
that would be given at the discretion of the Court. He was a
petitioner asking for grace. For the equity remedies were special
interventions of the King's Grace, where it appeared that the
Common Law Courts were unable to do complete justice. If his
petition were to be granted, the suitor was obliged to show that
he could not otherwise obtain a remedy appropriate to his case.
He had also to show that he was a worthy recipient of the favours
that he sought: his own conduct had been that of an upright
and conscientious man. He came into the Chancellor's Court of
conscience "with clean hands."

EQUITY AND COMMON LAW NOW MERGED

A man may fairly ask in exasperation, even in dismay, whether
he has two systems of law to deal with, whether he must choose
between two sets of principles for the ordering of his life. Nowadays, he has not. For, one of the great legal reforms of the
nineteenth century was the happy marriage of equity and the
Common Law. Up to a quite recent date in our legal history, a
man would have been obliged to cope with two systems, administered in two different courts, by different judges, upon different
principles. If he sought a particular remedy for a grievance in
one court he might be disappointed, whereas, in the other court
he would obtain the remedy. Equity was not, it is true, a rival
to the Common Law. Equity was, in fact, meaningless, apart
from the structure of the Common Law. It was really in the
nature of a supplement to correct the defects of justice inherent
in any rigid system. Still, the possibility of a clash between the
two systems was a grave defect in our law.

RIVAL TRIBUNALS

A suitor in equity would bring a bill to the Chancellor as
keeper of the King's Conscience, begging "of his grace" that he

would bring about equity between the suitor and his adversary. That adversary had, by means that no upright and conscientious person would adopt, obtained an unfair advantage. The Common Law Courts could afford no remedy. For the Common Law remedies were rigidly confined to a limited number of causes; and here the adversary had devised a new species of trickery. Though the adversary was a rogue, he had the law on his side. Or, perhaps, the adversary was so powerful as to overawe the ordinary Courts. The one chance for the suitor was to invoke directly the King, or the King's Deputy. The Chancellor reads the bill; he summons the unrighteous dealer before him; he makes it a matter of conscience that right shall be done. If the wrongdoer should prove to be impervious to the Chancellor's admonition, to go and sin no more and to annul the effects of his former offence, then the Chancellor would take effective steps to prevent the inequity.

Thus, in a dispute about ownership of land before the Common Law Court, one of the parties had kept his opponent's witnesses drinking in an ale-house during the period of trial; and the decision of the Court, in the absence of these witnesses necessary to his case, was against the right claimant. An appeal is made to the Chancellor. He hears the appeal; he learns what trick has been practised; he feels he must intervene. He cannot disturb the decision of the Common Law Court; that is in accordance with the law; and, once a dispute is decided by judgment entered upon the rolls of the Court, it cannot be reopened. It is *res judicata*, a matter upon which judgment has been finally entered; and the judgment must stand. But the Chancellor can tell the successful litigant that it would be wrong to take advantage of the judgment gained by so unworthy a means; that if he persists in trying to enforce the judgment, the Chancellor will, in order to save him from this burden upon his soul, this deadly sin, restrain him. Neglect of the advice would mean attachment for "contempt of court."* The successful litigant would, if he

---

* The "advice" in modern times is an order. A person disobeying the order is still attached. Thus, on the opening of the Michaelmas Law Sittings in 1932, application was made in the Chancery Court on behalf of one who had disobeyed an injunction. He had been told not to sell oil and call it Castrol when it was not Castrol; but he had reverted to his evil way. Counsel read an affidavit in which the defendant apologised for his contempt and gave an undertaking never again to do what had been forbidden. He had been seven weeks in prison, and had, counsel submitted, "purged his contempt." Mr. Justice Eve said: "I shall now order release. I think it was a case of gross contempt of Court; and I do not feel sure that seven weeks are enough. But it was a satisfactory time for reflection and, I hope, for repentance."

defied the Chancellor, enjoy the right that the Common Law gave him to the land. But he would enjoy it in gaol till he had purged his contempt by submitting to the Chancellor's direction. In short, the Chancellor could make a decision of the Common Law judges to be of no effect.

REFORMS IN LAW

This correcting of injustice, sometimes wrought by rigid adherence to Common Law principles, did not exhaust the Chancellor's incursions into litigation. Certain matters of which the Common Law took no notice, were dealt with by him. Notably, the enforcing of trusts was his province. A testator would leave property to a friend upon the friend's assurance that he would use the property for no other purpose than the benefit of one whom the testator wished to benefit. Common Law disregarded the trust, and would allow the trustee to deal with the property as his own. It was, in fact, his own. But, if he should use it otherwise than for the benefit of the person intended by the testator, the Chancellor intervened. He would not deal with the property involved; he would instead issue a *decree* against the fraudulent trustee: "It is decreed that the defendant refrain from such and such conduct." The Chancellor's action was, we say, *in personam*, it was directed against a person. Failure to obey his decrees might result in "attachment" an imprisonment until the implied contempt had been purged.

Clearly, the Common Law judges would be inclined to resent an interference by the Chancellor with their decisions; and we need not be surprised to find that clashes occurred between the jurisdictions. That there should exist two systems of law side by side, dealing with the same matters in varying ways, added to the law's uncertainty. It also added to the law's expense; and the merging of the two systems into one by the Judicature Act of 1873 was a long overdue reform. The Common Law Courts and the Chancellor's Court were replaced by the Supreme Court of Justice; the judges presiding in the various divisions of the Court are to give the appropriate remedy, whether a Common Law remedy or an equitable remedy; and, if there should be a divergence between the Common Law and equity on the particular question before the Court, the rules of equity are to prevail. And procedure once peculiar to the Chancery Court is now available in all courts. In the Chancery the defendant would be required to give a sworn answer to the charges made against him in the bill. The Chancellor could thereby "scrape the conscience" of the defendant, and obtain discovery of facts that would help him to a decision. One can now "obtain discovery" in proper cases, whatever the court of trial.

COURT OF TRIAL

Since 1875, therefore, we have had in this country not a multiplicity of legal systems but one. Many reminders there are still, though, of the former multiplicity. The High Court has three divisions called by different names; yet the judges who preside, whether in the *King's Bench* or the *Chancery* or the *Probate, Divorce, and Admiralty Court,* administer the same law and afford the same remedies; and the judges may be called upon for a case in any Court. A judge, too, may one day be presiding over a criminal trial, the next day over a civil trial. As one branch of the High Court the *Commercial Court* was set up as the place where important questions of mercantile law might be discussed under the presidency of a judge eminently qualified to decide the questions.

The assizes, held in the various county towns, are also presided over by the High Court judges. These travel under the King's Commission; and at the assizes there is not only a "gaol delivery" of prisoners, but also a number of such civil cases as can be tried locally. As auxiliaries of the High Court judges some of the ablest barristers of old standing also travel on the King's Commission to the assizes. They become temporary judges.

NO CONTRIBUTION AMONG WRONGDOERS

Where two or more agree together for the commission of a wrong, there is the implied understanding among them that—if the wronged should recover damages—all should contribute to pay them. Such an implied contract is one that the law declines to countenance, and consequently to help. This is sometimes called the rule of *Merryweather* v. *Nixon* (K.B. 1799): "No contribution among joint tort-feasors." A person had recovered damages against the two parties for a joint wrong; he had levied judgment upon the plaintiff; and the plantiff sought—unsuccessfully—to make the defendant pay his share. But, as was pointed out in a later case: "From reason, justice, and sound policy, the rule that wrongdoers cannot have redress or contribution against each other is confined to cases where the person seeking redress must be presumed to have known that he was doing an unlawful act." The rule itself has been criticised; the law imposes a burden on two men; why should it not interfere to prevent its being borne wholly by one? There are, in fact, statutory exceptions to the rule—all the directors, for instance, are jointly liable for misrepresentations in prospectuses, and a right of contribution is given. And the tendency is to restrict the application of the rule.

INTERPLEADER

A person may be in possession of property, or may owe money, claimed by more than one. Under certain conditions he is relieved of liability to both by requiring them to bring their claims before a legal tribunal for determination. When the tribunal makes the order, the question is settled once for all.

Thus, a sheriff may, in order to execute a judgment, take property claimed by a person other than the one against whom the judgment has been given; or a stakeholder may be sued by two claimants. The sheriff then takes out an *interpleader summons*; he serves it on the judgment creditor and the claimant who has intervened; and the three parties appear before a Master of the Supreme Court. The Master may dispose of the case: he will, if it involves no difficult point of law. Or he may direct an issue to be tried in open court.

The applicant for relief by way of interpleader must be able and willing to dispose of the property, or pay the money, as the Court directs.

" MANDATORY INJUNCTION "

The strict legal remedy may be inadequate. It is, for instance, where a house is made uninhabitable by the creation of a nuisance. The legal right might be measured in money, and its infringement be met by an assessment of damages. But, for all sorts of quite sound reasons, people may object to giving up their property or suffering it to be diminished in value, even upon a monetary compensation. Then it is that equity, supplementing the Common Law and making it fairer between man and man, steps in. Equity issues an order to the wrongdoer to desist from his wrongdoing. Formerly, this order—this injunction—was confined to orders *not* to do something, *not* to allow a certain state of things to persist. Any positive acts necessary by the defendant were implied. Now the Court grants a "mandatory injunction" when equity demands that something should be done by the defendant.

AN " INTERIM INJUNCTION "

The Court has power not only to award damages, but also to issue orders. It may command a person to do what he had undertaken to do : it may, that is, issue a *decree of specific performance*. It may command a person not to do something that infringes another's legal rights : it may, that is, issue an *injunction*. The Court may even—though rarely, and only where the matter is unusually urgent—issue an *interim injunction*, pending the trial of an action.

The rules governing the last are well explained by the Lord Chief Justice in the *Mogul* case (Q.B. 1885): "If the plaintiffs establish their case by the verdict of the jury or the decision of the judge, they will get as damages all they are entitled to. The injury is not irreparable. If a fine old ornamental tree in a nobleman's park be cut down, the injury is practically irreparable, and cannot be compensated in damages. It is in cases of that nature that an interim injunction issues. The injury complained of is not irreparable ; there is no infringement of any right which affects the enjoyment of life ; no restraint of freedom of personal action ; none of those considerations which have induced the Courts to interfere by injunction before the trial of the action."

" CONCEALED FRAUD " AND STATUTE OF LIMITATIONS

Where a hidden fraud prevents discovery of a right of action, time does not run against a plaintiff until he discovers the fraud. This is well illustrated in *Lynn* v. *Bamber* (K.B. 1930). Plaintiff had in 1921 bought from the defendant young plum trees sold and warranted as "Purple Pershore." After some years the plaintiff found that the trees were "Coe's Late Red," apparently an inferior plum. The question was : " Did the Statute of Limitations apply ?" The Court held that it did not. The plaintiff's action was not barred. For "where the existence of the cause of action is concealed by the fraud of the person who creates it, such person shall not take advantage of the wrong which he himself has done. A fresh cause of action accrues from the moment that the fraud is discovered."

LIMITATION UPON POWER TO BRING CIVIL ACTIONS

In general any one can bring a civil action, however groundless his cause of complaint. The possible great hardship upon a defendant is met in part by the power of the Court to award him his costs. It is also met in part by: (1) the power of the Court, on the application of the defendant, to stay proceedings until the plaintiff shall have given security for costs; (where a person with no property within the jurisdiction of the Court brings an action, such a stay will usually be granted; or he will be required to find security for the possible costs that may be awarded against him.) (2) making another person than the actual plaintiff liable for costs, when the plaintiff cannot himself be made liable. Thus, a lunatic sues in the name of his committee ("committee" here meaning the individual to whom charge of the lunatic's affairs has been committed, and in this connection being pronounced committēē); and an infant sues by his "next friend." The "committee" or the "next friend" will be called upon to pay the defendant's costs, if the plaintiff is ordered to pay them.

MEASURE OF DAMAGES

The salutary rule: "to agree with thine adversary quickly," is well illustrated in actions for damages. The person injured by breach of contract or by neglect of duty can demand monetary compensation. To open the mouth wide at the outset may do no harm; but to persist in a claim, against reasonable arguments for abating it, is foolish. No doubt, it evidences resolution, a sturdy will to accept no compromise, on the part of the plaintiff. It is, nevertheless, foolish; for the Court will award only such damages as would, on the supposition least favourable to the plaintiff, cover his loss.

In breach of contract or in breach of trust damages are not intended to punish the defendant. There is nothing similar to the punitive or vindictive damages that are occasionally given by a jury in actions of wrong. Consider an example or two. In *Kaye Navigation Co.* v. *Barnett, Ltd.*, reported in *The Times* of 10th May, 1932, the defendants were charterers of a ship owned by the plaintiffs. The defendants had undertaken to provide a cargo in the River Plate; but various untoward events prevented their fulfilling the undertaking. Their liability for loss of the anticipated earnings of the ship was not disputed. Two contentions of the defendants, whereby they sought to reduce the amount claimed, were disputed; and in both contentions the Court agreed with the defendants. In the first place, the charter-party gave liberty to hold the ship at the wharf for twenty-three days. The failure to find a cargo had obviated the expenses that the plaintiffs would have incurred during that period. Should not this saving be set against the loss of freight? The Court said: Yes. Further, the charterers had liberty to name any one among a number of home ports for delivery. Landing charges at these ports are not uniform; and the charterers claimed to name the most expensive port, and to set off the charges that would have been incurred there against the damages. This set-off, too, was allowed. In support of his judgment, Mr. Justice Branson cited the Chancery case (*Robinson* v. *Robinson*) where a trustee had two courses open to him. He took neither; and the Court estimated the damages by calculating what the result would have been if the trustee had taken the course the less favourable to the beneficiary.

DUTY TO MITIGATE LOSS

The practical deduction emerges: when we see that we shall be unable to carry out the contract we have made, we should give prompt notice to the other party. He can then take reasonable steps to lessen his loss. He is not entitled to remain passive, counting upon full satisfaction of his claim. For "in assessing the damages for breach of performance, a jury will take into account what the plaintiff, as a prudent man, ought in reason to have done, whereby his loss has been or would have been diminished." By taking timely measures he might have averted, or materially lessened, the harm that would have flowed from the non-fulfilment of the contract. In so far as the plaintiff's loss can be reasonably ascribed to his failure to take such measures, he himself is the immediate cause of the loss, not the defendant. Resentment the plaintiff may feel. That is to be expected; for a man is entitled to fulfilment of promises made to him. But he must not, by his own conduct, aggravate his loss.

The principle was applied by Mr. Justice McCardie in the interesting case *Payzu Ltd.* v. *Saunders* (K.B. 1919), and his judgment was approved in the Court of Appeal. The defendant, a dealer in silk, bargained to supply the plaintiffs at a specified price with 400 pieces of silk "delivery as required January to September, 1918: conditions, $2\frac{1}{2}$ per cent 1 month." That is, payment for goods delivered up to the twentieth day of any month should be made on the twentieth day of the following month, subject to $2\frac{1}{2}$ per cent discount. One consignment of silk was delivered: there was some delay in payment; and the defendant, fearing that the plaintiff's financial position did not warrant the giving of credit, asked for cash with each order. This the plaintiffs refused and claimed damages for breach of contract. Now, the ordinary measure of damages, when goods contracted for are not delivered, is the difference between the contract price and the market price at the time when delivery should have been given. But here, if the defendant's offer to sell for cash had been accepted, the plaintiff would have lost only the discount stipulated for in the contract. Was not this smaller amount the measure of damages? Yes said the Court: "The fundamental basis is compensation for pecuniary loss naturally flowing from the breach. But this first principle is qualified by a second, which imposes on a plaintiff the duty of taking all reasonable steps to mitigate the loss consequent on the breach, and debars him from claiming any part of the damage, which is due to his neglect to take such steps. The law does not ask the plaintiff to do anything outside the ordinary course of business; it does ask him to act as a reasonable man would."

"PENALTY" OR "LIQUIDATED DAMAGES"

Some such phrase as "Penalty for breach of this agreement is fixed at £100" is not unknown, and seems to conflict with the statement above that the idea of penalty is absent from contract. But this is not so. Even though the word "penalty" is used, the Court will award nothing except what will cover the actual loss sustained. That this assessment of damages is difficult affords no reason why damages should not be given. A contract has been broken; the injured party seeks redress, and the Court awards it. But how translate the loss entailed, the annoyance and distress caused, into the right number of monetary units? An actor was engaged to play "a leading comedy part" at the London Hippodrome. He was offered a part that none could regard as a leading one. Was he entitled to compensation for loss of advancement of his reputation or for loss of publicity? The Court of Appeal decided that he was. An actor's real income includes much more than the actual money he gets; and, apparently, an actor considers that a substantial part of that income consists in being prominent in the bill, in being elaborately advertised. Indirect losses are usually too remote to allow of just assessment; and the Court declines the attempt to do so. And "injured feelings" are compensated by a money award only in quite exceptional circumstances: "As a general rule, the measure of damage for breach of contract is unaffected by the motives or manner of its breach. What are known as vindictive or exemplary damages in tort find no place in contract; nor can injury to feelings or vanity be regarded." The actor's profession, though—peculiar in many respects—justifies a departure from the general rule (*Clayton*, *etc.* v. *Oliver*, H.L. 1930). The arduous task of fixing the adequate sum is for the jury of reasonable men and women; that an actor's "loss of publicity" constitutes a claim cannot now be disputed.

REMOTE DAMAGES SOMETIMES RECOVERABLE

Damages recoverable are such as may reasonably be supposed to have been in the contemplation of both parties at the time they made the contract, as the probable result of the breach. The *immediate* loss is usually all that could be in contemplation; but circumstances may arise that would make a more remote loss payable by the defendant.

Defendant was a coal merchant. Plaintiffs were shipping agents at Dover. The defendant knew that the plaintiff supplied "steam coal," and he sold coal warranted fit for use in steam-ships. The plaintiffs resold it with the same warranty. A claim was made against the plaintiffs by their sub-vendors in respect of the bad quality of the coal. Before the trial the defendant reiterated that the coal was of the description specified in the contract.

The jury awarded damages against H., the plaintiff, in the action. B., the defendant, was willing to pay these damages; and he did pay the amount into Court. Plaintiffs claimed also the cost of defending the action brought against them. It was this amount that was in dispute. Bussey was held liable: "He knew for what purpose the plaintiffs were purchasing the coal, viz. to resell it to the owners of steamers, and he must have known as a business man what damages might naturally result if it was not reasonably fit for the purpose. He must have known, too, that if claims were made against the plaintiffs they would be in a difficult position: on the one side would be those who had tried the coal insisting that it was bad; on the other would be the defendant who might object to a recognition of the claim. If the defendant had acknowledged the coal to be bad the action would not have been brought" (*Hammond & Co.* v. *Bussey*, A.C. 1887).

COSTS MAY EXCEED DAMAGES

The "FALLS CITY" (*Joseph Rank Ltd.* v. *Dimitrios N. Rallias*, Admiralty Division Court, 1932) illustrates very effectively how costs may be accumulated when litigants are obstinate. The case was tried on appeal from the Liverpool County Court. The original action was brought by millers against shipowners in respect of damage by sea water to a cargo of wheat. The defendants pleaded that they were covered by exceptions contained in the bill of lading. The sea water had penetrated through leaks in the shell of the vessel; but the defendants claimed that, if there were any defects, they were latent and not due to want of due diligence on their part.

The president in giving judgment made some scathing remarks about the pursuit of such actions: "The defendants' ship *Falls City* loaded in Seattle in the autumn of 1927 a full cargo of wheat in five holds. It consisted altogether of 7,200 tons. The ship was directed to deliver 3,000 tons at Birkenhead and then proceed to Hull to deliver the rest. At Birkenhead and Hull it was found that water had entered at three points on deck and side. The damage to the wheat delivered at Birkenhead was something over £100 and at Hull over £70—under £200 in a cargo of 7,200 tons. The damage was there, the cause leakage: and thereupon, I suppose because there were underwriters in some form or other concerned, Messrs. Joseph Rank, Ltd., the cargo owners, and the shipowners, instead of putting their heads together and saying: 'There has been this little damage, relatively very small. What about it?' embarked upon this litigation which began in 1928. Five years after the events in question the case comes here—I will not say microscopic but trifling in its original character—comes here wrapped up in these massive documents, eight inches high, most of them printed, and we have had the opportunity for three days of listening to very capable arguments of counsel on both sides, and they dealt with the matter as thoroughly as though £100,000 was involved. Really in these times there is something exemplary in the occurrence of litigation of this kind."

In the event, the shipowner was held responsible for the loss. For it arose from the unfitness of the vessel; and the latent defect must be considered as the result of want of due care in survey. But, of course, the point of importance to the litigants was "Who is to bear the costs?"

DAMAGES IN COLLISION ACTIONS

In *Admiralty* v. *S.S. Chekiang* (H.L. 1926) a law lord considered at length the rules applicable to the measure of damages in collision actions: "To say, as judges have come as near to saying as decorum permits, that juries must find a figure as best they can and escape criticism by being anonymous and dumb, and accordingly proof against everything but 'perversity,' is a poor position. In this class of cases, there is an opposite system of practice, and, in lieu of a jury, a highly important and experienced official of the Court acts judicially in the first instance. He has to arrive at a conclusion without any previous directions upon the law from the learned judge, and then to state that conclusion in writing, and—unless he wishes such a criticism, erroneous as I venture to think, as was passed on him in this case by the Court of Appeal, namely, that he had proceeded on a rule of thumb, as if it was binding law in all cases— he must give the legal reasons, which support his conclusions. The measure of damages ought never to be governed by mere rules of practice, nor can such rules over-ride the principles of the law on this subject.

"The data for estimating the amount of substantial damage are not precise. In cases like the present that difficulty is sometimes inevitable and is of common occurrence; but it is a difficulty which can be easily and is often satisfactorily overcome by a jury under proper directions. Personally, I have a dislike, which I believe is shared by other judges, to the task of assessing damages."

PAYMENT INTO COURT (LIBEL ACTIONS)

One curious rule exists in regard to libel actions. In the hope of saving costs a defendant may pay money into Court, admitting liability. In other actions, a defendant may pay money into Court and also deny liability: he cannot do this in a libel action. If the plaintiff should decide to go on with the action on the ground that the money is insufficient, or on the ground that he wishes to vindicate his character in open Court, he can yet take the money out of Court; and it becomes his property. When the jury awards a less sum than the amount paid in, the plaintiff may indeed be obliged to pay the defendant's costs following the time of payment into Court. But if, in his prudence, he has taken the money out of Court, he cannot be asked to repay it.

In one case (*Morriss* v. *Baines & Co.*, K.B. 1933), when £525 was paid in by the defendants, when the jury awarded a farthing damages, and when the astute plaintiff declined to return any of the money he had taken out, Mr. Justice McCardie severely criticised the rule: "The question" said his lordship, "is one of practical importance in view of the many actions for defamation which are brought before the Courts, and in view also of the fact that certain persons at the present time carry on a considerable and profitable trade in actions for defamation brought against newspaper proprietors and others.

"It seems to be the moral duty of the plaintiff to return to the defendants the difference between the farthing and the £525. Counsel for the plaintiff does not dispute that duty, but relies on the existing state of the law as precluding the Court from making any order for the return of the £524 19s. 11¾d. Counsel for the plaintiff is, of course, bound to act on the direct and personal instructions received by him.

"I regret that my powers are not wider in such a case as the present. A plaintiff, where the defendant has paid in with an admission of liability, may take out the money at any time, not only on the morning of the day of trial but even when the trial is actually taking place, and he sees that the case is going against him.

"I venture to express the view that the present rule does more harm than good. Too often it prevents exposure in cases where exposure should be made in the public interest. No real hardship could result to honest plaintiffs from an alteration of the present rule, provided (a) that the judge at the trial has a full and complete discretion as to costs; and (b) that a plaintiff who desires to take money out of Court and end the action should have liberty to apply to a judge in chambers for an order that for special reasons the case be mentioned in open Court. The judge can ensure that the true nature of the action is disclosed.

"I recognise the power of the Press to injure reputations, and I agree that the law must be strong to enable a good character to be vindicated and to penalise baseless imputations. But I know quite well how large a number of fraudulent or undesirable persons remain undisclosed through the severity of the rules of law with respect to defendants in cases of defamation. The public, too, often loses the protection which it so greatly needs. I know also of the large trade that exists in seeking to extort damages from newspaper proprietors and others in circumstances which are little better than disguised blackmail."

28

CONTRACT DEBTS OF MARRIED WOMEN

The position, since the Married Women's Property Act, 1882, of a married woman in regard to debts incurred by her is well illustrated in *Scott* v. *Morley* (K.B. 1887). When a judgment is obtained against the married woman, it is not executed in the ordinary way. Execution issues upon it against the only portion of her property which can be got at, her separate estate not specially protected. For the restraint on anticipation operates as long as her husband is alive.

The particular case was an appeal against an order committing a married woman, Julia Morley, to prison for six weeks for non-payment of a judgment debt. The Appeal Court decided that such an order could not be issued.

"The Act provides that a 'married woman shall be capable of entering into and rendering herself liable on any contract.' That must mean that a woman shall after she is and whilst she is married, be capable of entering into and rendering herself liable upon any contract. She could enter into a contract before the Act, and therefore the Act must mean that she shall be capable of entering into a contract so as to render herself liable upon it. A liability is thus imposed on her which did not exist either at law or in equity before the Act. If Sub-section 2 had stopped there, I should have thought that the same consequences would follow as in the case of a contract entered into by a *feme sole*. If no remedy were given by the Act for a breach of the contract, the remedy must be that Common Law remedy which is applicable to the case. But, if a remedy is given by the statute which imposes the new liability, that must be the only remedy. Sub-section 2 goes on to provide that the woman shall be capable of rendering herself liable 'in respect of and to the extent of her separate property' and 'of suing and being sued, either in contract or in tort, or otherwise in all respects as if she were a *feme sole*, and her husband need not be joined with her as plaintiff or defendant, or be made a party to any action or other legal proceeding brought by or taken against her' (that again alters the law) and any damages or costs recovered against her in any such action or proceeding shall be payable out of her separate property, and not otherwise.

"If this be so, does Section 5 of the Debtors Act, 1869, apply to a judgment of this nature? Section 5 says that the Court may commit to prison any person who makes default in payment of 'any debt due from him' in pursuance of any order or judgment of the Court. What is the real meaning of those words 'due from him.' It appears to me that they point to a debt which the defendant is personally liable to pay. If you treat the Debtors Act as an Act which authorises the Court to commit people to prison, then you must construe it strictly. It is a highly penal Act, affecting the liberty of the subject and you must not say that a sum which is payable only out of a person's property is a sum 'due from' that person.

If, on the other hand, you treat the Act as a remedial Act, then it only enables the Court to modify the imprisonment which should have been inflicted at Common Law, so as to prevent it from being so large as it was at law before the Act; and, treating the Act in that way Section 5 cannot apply to such a case, because there was nothing to modify, there being no power to arrest a married woman before the Act. If it is treated as a penal Act it must not be stretched. In either view of the Act, it appears to me that Section 5 of the Debtors Act does not apply to the judgment which can be recovered against a married woman only by virtue of the Married Women's Property Act, 1882."

EXECUTING A JUDGMENT

A litigant has obtained a judgment in his favour; his opponent must pay him damages assessed at so many pounds sterling. Yes; but how is he to get the money from the judgment debtor? For clearly this debtor, who very likely feels himself hardly dealt with, will be reluctant to pay and will avoid payment if he can. Well, of course, if he has no money and no property in this country, the judgment debt is worth nothing. If, however, he has money or property, the law is not so futile as to leave its judgment without effect. The judgment being given, the law provides a machinery for carrying it into effect. The successful litigant has several devices available. His money is not forthcoming. Very well, he knows what bank the debtor uses, and he obtains from the Court a *garnishee* addressed to the banker. This is an order to pay the amount of the judgment debt, not to his customer but to the litigant who has obtained judgment against that customer. To obtain a "garnishee order nisi" the judgment creditor must swear an affidavit showing—

1. That judgment has been recovered and is still unsatisfied.

2. That a certain person named, within the jurisdiction of the Court, owes money to the judgment debtor.

Application is made to a Master in Chambers.

Money not being attachable, property may be. The judgment creditor obtains a writ of *fieri facias* (*fi. fa.*, is the recognised abbreviation), a writ addressed to the sheriff directing him "to make good" (*fieri facias*) out of the debtor's property the amount of the debt. The writ commands the sheriff to seize and sell as much of the debtor's personal property as will produce an amount equal to—

1. The judgment debt.
2. Interest from the date of judgment at 4 per cent.
3. Costs of the execution.

When the debtor has land the creditor may take out a writ of *elegit*. Under this writ the creditor obtains the legal estate in the land.

There is now no imprisonment for debt, even for a judgment debt. But when the Court has ordered a defendant to pay and he neglects to do so, he may be committed to prison for six weeks (Debtors Act, 1869), the imprisonment not operating as a cancelling of the debt. The Court, it should be noted, gives only such orders as it knows the debtor can obey; and the debtor is imprisoned not for his debt but for his disobedience of the Court— for contempt of Court, that is.

Again there may be no tangible property, but there may be the intangible property so important in these days—stocks and shares. The creditor in that event applies to the Court for a *charging order*. If the application is granted, then any Government stock or stock in any English public company stands charged with payment of the amount of the judgment debt. The creditor gives notice of his order to the Bank of England or to the secretary of the company: his claim is thereby established.

ARBITRATION A CONDITION PRECEDENT

The parties to a contract may make what bargain they choose; and, unless an imperative reason exists to the contrary, the Courts will enforce the bargain. Where arbitration is stipulated for they can, therefore, consent to submit the dispute to any one, lawyer or not. And they can make submission to arbitration a condition necessary before an action can be brought. Thus, in *Ayscough* v. *Sheed Thomson & Co.* (K.B. 1925), the buyers of goods agreed that, if goods of inferior qualtiy were delivered, they would refer the claim for damages to an arbitrator within three days. Failure to do so barred their action.

This simply followed the leading case *Scott* v. *Avery* (H.L. 1855), where the plaintiff brought action against the defendant, both being members of the Newcastle Insurance Association, one of the rules of which was that no member was to sue upon a policy until arbitrators had determined the amount to be paid. Plaintiff claimed that this stipulation, ousting as it did the jurisdiction of the Courts was void; but the judgment held that such a clause "did not oust the jurisdiction, but only created a condition precedent to an action."

The Arbitration Act emphasises this position. Except by leave of the Court, a submission to arbitration is irrevocable. If after such arbitration a party begins an action, the other party can apply to the Court for a stay of proceedings. And the stay will be granted unless good reason is shown why arbitration should not proceed. One such good reason is where the party desiring a stay has charged the other party with fraud, and the latter seeks a public inquiry. Thus, in *Jureidini* v. *National, Etc., Insurance Co.*, the Appeal Court in 1915 held that since the assurance company charged the plaintiff with arson and fraud, it could not bar his action by invoking the Arbitration Clause.

PARTNER'S SUBMISSION TO ARBITRATION

In partnerships, an arbitration agreement is something outside the ordinary business of a firm. A partner, therefore, has no implied authority—merely from the fact of partnership—to bind his colleagues by an arbitration.

ARBITRATORS AND THE COURT

The Courts were formerly punctilious in asserting their claims against possible rivals. In particular, they were alert to frustrate any attempt to usurp their functions: "to oust the jurisdiction of the Court" deserved drastic penalty. The legality, and indeed the wisdom of submitting most business disputes to arbitration other than that of the judges are nowadays freely recognised. Yet a term in an agreement stipulating that no recourse to the Courts should be made would still be regarded as void.

Thus, in *Czarnikow and Co., Ltd.* v. *Ruth Schmidt and Co.* (C.A. 1922) the parties agreed to submit disputes to the Refined Sugar Association, one of whose rules ran thus: "Neither buyer, seller, trustee in bankruptcy, nor any other person shall require, nor shall they apply to the Court to require, any arbitrators to state in the form of a special case for the opinion of the Court any question of law arising in the course of the reference, but such a question of law shall be determined by arbitration." A dispute having arisen, one of the parties asked the arbitrators to state a case. The arbitrators refused; but, on appeal to the Court, they were obliged to do so. The judgment explains the position very clearly: "The agreement ousts the jurisdiction of the courts of law, and is consequently against public policy and void. Commercial arbitrations are undoubtedly and deservedly popular. I entertain no doubt that they will continue so, so long as the law retains sufficient hold over them to prevent and redress any injustice on the part of the arbitrator, and to secure that the law administered by the arbitrator is the law of the land and not some home-made law of the particular arbitrator or the particular association."

" SPECIAL CASE " IN ARBITRATION

That the King's Courts should guide arbitration tribunals in matters of law was, in fact, contemplated in the codifying act relating to arbitration. This is the Arbitration Act, 1889. It would be a palpable injustice if, through an arbitrator's mistake of law, a party who had striven to conform to law should be penalised. The Master of the Rolls put the matter thus: "The Arbitration Act confers on the parties to an arbitration the right to apply to the Court for an order directing the arbitrator to state in the form of a special case for the opinion of the Court any question of law arising in the course of the reference. This right must be respected by the arbitrator. But if an application for a special case is frivolous and unreasonable, the arbitrator may refuse it, and his refusal would in such case be upheld by the Court."

The kind of question that may be raised in the form of a special case is well illustrated in *Burnett Steamship Co.* v. *Joint Danube and Black Sea Shipping Agencies* (K.B. 1933), the real meaning of a clause in the charter-party being the point at issue.

By a charter-party dated 9th April, 1931, the steamer *Burnhope* belonging to the appellant shipowners was chartered by the respondents to go to certain ports on the Danube and there to load a grain cargo. The cargo was to be loaded at a certain specified rate per day, and Clause 4 of the charter-party provided as follows—

Should any time be lost while the steamer is in a landing

berth owing to work being impossible through rain, snow, or storm, this time to be added to the loading time.

The *Burnhope* loaded her cargo in due course, and if she had loaded continuously at the specified rate the time allowed for loading would have been 15 days 13 hours. Rain, however, occurred at intervals during the period, and while it was falling loading would have been impossible. The total time during which rain was falling amounted to two days. The charterers therefore contended that their time for loading had been extended by two days and they had 17 days 13 hours before demurrage began to run. But in fact the charterers had no cargo alongside ready for loading at the time when the rain occurred, and the shipowners therefore contended that loading had not been prevented by rain within the meaning of Clause 4. The arbitrator found as a fact that, even if the charterers had had cargo alongside, the rain would have prevented its being loaded, and he allowed the charterers the extra two days. On appeal to the High Court, however, the decision was reversed: "The award in favour of the charterers is wrong. The clause does not say: 'should rain occur to an extent which would render loading impossible'; it said: 'should time be lost.' It is impossible to say that any time has been lost owing to rain. The charterers neither had the cargo alongside nor had they made arrangements under which it would have come forward without delay. Loading was not interrupted by rain."

EVIDENCE

GENERAL RULE

ENGLISH Courts are careful that no man shall be penalised, either in person or in pocket, without his having ample opportunity of putting his own case. Evidence against him comes under the scrutiny of a judge whose whole training, backed by age-long tradition, enables him to brush away whatever is irrelevant. Material witnesses against him undergo rigorous cross-examination. He learns, well before the trial, what case he has to answer.

On rare occasions, indeed, a judge makes an order or an *ex parte* application: he grants a request though he hears only one of the parties. But this is only where speed is essential lest irreparable damage be done; the order is strictly limited in time; and, if it should appear at the trial of the case that the request should not have been made, the other party obtains adequate compensation. Normally, both parties are present and have a right to be heard.

BURDEN OF PROOF

Besides, the prosecutor in a criminal case, the plaintiff in a civil case, must prove his contention. Till prosecutor or plaintiff brings forward material evidence, neither prisoner nor defendant need answer. "It would be a monstrous thing if the mere fact of not answering a letter which charges a man with some misconduct was held to be evidence of an admission by him that he had been found guilty of it." So it was judged in a breach of promise case, where the fact had been relied upon as the corroborative evidence needed in such a suit. Silence is not evidence of an admission, unless there are circumstances which render it more reasonably probable that a man would answer a charge made against him than that he would not (*Wiedemann* v. *Walpole*, C. A. 1891).

We must not presume that because a man is accused he is guilty of a crime, or that because he is sued he is liable to pay damages. And, where crime is charged, the weight of evidence needed to convince is greater than the weight requisite to establish liability in civil cases.

Mr. Justice Humphreys, in trying Mrs. Barney at the Central Criminal Court in 1932, put the matter thus to the jury: "You must be satisfied that she pulled the trigger intentionally, not accidentally. The prosecution must prove that to your satisfaction; and by proof in a criminal case is meant something more than probability, something more than suspicion. Probability and suspicion will not do. You must be satisfied that the prosecution has proved, not that it is quite likely that the accused may have murdered the deceased or that it is quite open on the evidence that it may be so. You must be satisfied that she did it." In short, if there is reasonable doubt, the verdict must be "Not Guilty." In a case that came before the Criminal Appeal Court, the L.C.J. said, in allowing the appeal: "There is certainly grave suspicion. But we are not concerned with suspicion, however grave, or with theories, however ingenious. And Section 4 of the Criminal Appeal Act of 1907 enjoins that we shall allow the appeal where the evidence is consistent with innocence or guilt."

DUTY OF PROSECUTOR

Moreover, in a criminal trial it is the duty of the prosecution to place all the evidence before the Court, whether it tend to prove or disprove guilt. Rejection of evidence legally admissible served to quash the conviction for obtaining by false pretences of *W. L. Thomas* (C.C.A. 1931). Appellant had been convicted at Quarter Sessions, but certain letters had not been put in by the prosecution, and when counsel for the defence sought to put questions on the letters he was stopped. "The whole story as it is known to the police must be placed before the jury," said the Court.

DRAWING INFERENCES

"Circumstantial" (*or indirect*) *evidence* may serve to establish a case; and often this is the only evidence available. Witnesses of the actual commission of a crime are seldom forthcoming; and they are not always available in civil cases. It may, indeed, be that, in the absence of explanation, the Court is obliged to draw inferences. Consider, for instance—
Fisher (Pauper) v. *L.M.S. Rly.* (H.L. 1931).
A railway guard met his death through an unexplained accident. The House of Lords decided, in spite of the lack of evidence, that his widow could recover under the Workmen's Compensation Act, 1925. The accident had happened "in the course of his employment," and there was nothing to negative the contention that the risk of the employment had become reality and

caused the death. Lord Tomlin said : "Where the evidence establishes that in the course of his employment the workman was properly in a place to which some risk particular thereto attaches, and an accident occurs capable of explanation solely by reference to that risk, it is legitimate to attribute the accident to that risk, and to hold that the accident arose out of the employment. But the inference as to the origin of the accident may be displaced by evidence tending to show that the accident was due to some action of the workman outside the scope of his employment."

That is, unless a presumption is rebutted by evidence to the contrary, it establishes the case.

REASONABLE INFERENCES ARE DRAWN

In a similar case (*Jones* v. *G.W.Rly.*, 1930), the House of Lords was urged to follow *Wakelin* v. *London S.W.Rly.* In the Wakelin case the plaintiff failed. Neither the allegation of the plaintiff nor the denial of the defendant was supported by evidence, and the Court could not let conjecture take the place of evidence. In the later case, however, there were pieces of evidence pointing to negligence on the part of the railway company's servants. "The accident," said Lord Hailsham, "took place in the course of shunting operations, and the known facts fairly admit of the inference that it is explained by the neglect of the respondents to give to the deceased due warning of impending danger. Familiar with the crossing the deceased certainly was. But the movement of wagons during a shunting operation are mysterious except to the man in control. Not only is it a reasonable inference that due warning from him would have effectually kept the deceased in a place of safety, but the absence of such a warning was well calculated to put the deceased off his guard. We are in the domain of reasonable inference and have passed beyond the region of pure conjecture."

WHO MAY BE WITNESSES

In civil cases, all persons competent to give evidence may be compelled to give it. A refractory witness would be liable to fine in the County Court, or to attachment for contempt of court in the High Court. It seems that even confessions made to a spiritual adviser are not, technically, exempt from disclosure. Nor are the statements made to a medical attendant. In all probability, however, no Court would, in the exercise of its discretion, try to compel an unwilling breach of the seal of confession. The only causes of incompetency recognised by the law are obvious immaturity of intellect (though quite young children have recently been admitted as witnesses) and deficiency of intellect.

EVIDENCE OF A CHILD

" Where a child of tender years who is tendered as a witness does not in the opinion of the Court understand the nature of an oath, the evidence of that child may be received, though not given upon oath, if, in the opinion of the Court, the child is possessed of sufficient intelligence to justify the reception of the evidence, and understands the duty of speaking the truth . . . provided that a person shall not be liable to be convicted unless the testimony admitted by virtue of this section is corroborated by some other material evidence." (Children Act, 1908, Section 30.)

WITNESSES IN COUNTY COURT

The County Courts Act, 1888, Section 86, enacts that a person—

(1) Being summoned as a witness; and

(2) Being paid or offered his expenses, who refuses to be sworn or to give evidence shall be liable to a fine up to £10.

The fine levied goes towards the compensation of the party injured by the refusal.

When either party wishes to call as a witness a person in custody for crime, he makes a sworn statement (an affidavit) to the judge that " E. F., now a prisoner confined in ——— will be a material witness for me," and asks for an order. The judge then issues a warrant to bring him up. Where the prisoner is in custody on civil process, he can only be brought up by a writ of *habeas corpus ad testificandum* (thou mayst have his body for the purpose of his giving evidence), for which application is made to a High Court judge.

PRISONER CHARGED WITH CRIME

English law is insistent that no man need answer questions tending to incriminate him. If he chooses, he can remain silent. If he calls no witnesses, he can make an unsworn statement without rendering himself liable to cross-examination. But now (since the Criminal Evidence Act, 1898) both a prisoner and the wife or husband of the prisoner are *competent* to give sworn evidence, subject to a limited cross-examination. Neither spouse, however (except where the Common Law already sanctioned the calling), is a *compellable* witness against the other spouse.

The points below are to be noted—

(*a*) *A person charged by the police with a crime* need make no statement but may reserve his defence to the trial. Before he is questioned, the police are obliged to inform him of this, and to warn him that "You are not obliged to say anything; but if you do say anything it will be taken down and may be used as evidence at the trial." It will be noted that to include "against you" in the warning is wrong.

(*b*) Failure of the accused to avail himself of the privilege of giving sworn testimony on his own behalf must not be commented upon by the prosecution. (The judge, however, has discretion in the matter, and probably a jury will not fail to note the absence of the accused from the witness box, and will draw unfavourable conclusions from it.)

(*c*) The wife or husband of an accused can be called as a witness without the accused's consent in charges relating to—

(i) Desertion of wife or family.

(ii) Offences against the person (e.g. assault of wife by husband).

(iii) Various sexual offences.

(*d*) The prosecution must, in the cross-examination, ask no questions directed to show—

(i) That the prisoner has committed an offence other than the one on which he is charged.

(ii) That he has a bad character in general (unless he has given evidence of his own good character, or has sought to show bad character of the prosecution's witnesses).

WIFE SOMETIMES A COMPELLABLE WITNESS

When is a wife a compellable witness against her husband? This question is answered in *R.* v. *Lapworth* (Court of Criminal Appeal, 1930). *Where one spouse is at Common Law a competent witness against the other spouse, as on a charge involving personal violence committed by the one against the other, the first-mentioned spouse is not merely a competent but also a compellable witness.*

The appeal was against a conviction of a husband for causing grievous bodily harm to his wife, with intent. At the trial, the wife was unwilling to give evidence against her husband. But, Rowlatt, J., ruled that she could be compelled to give evidence.

The Court at the appeal said: "A wife was always a competent witness on a charge against her husband of having assaulted her. If it is once established that she was competent, it follows that she was compellable at Common Law, and remains so under Section 4, subsection (2) of the Criminal Evidence Act, 1898, which provides that: *Nothing in this Act shall affect a case where wife, or husband, of a person charged with an offence may at Common Law be called as a witness without the consent of that person.* The Court of Criminal Appeal said:

" It has been suggested that in the case of *Leach* v. *Regem* (A.C. 1912), a charge of incest, there are expressions inconsistent with this view, one such expression being: 'The principle that a wife is not to be compelled to give evidence against her husband is deep seated in the Common Law of this country, and I think if it is to be overturned it must be overturned by a clear, definite, and positive enactment.' But it must be borne in mind that the House of Lords in that case was dealing with the effect of a statute—the Criminal Evidence Act, 1898—which had expressly authorised a wife or husband to give evidence in certain cases.

The learned judge was right in telling this witness that she was bound to give evidence, and there was no misdirection by him in law."

WITNESSES' EXPENSES

In civil proceedings a witness may claim his expenses before giving evidence. His claim is against the party who has had him served with the subpœna (i.e. the notice to attend as a witness under a penalty for default). In criminal affairs, his attendance as a witness is a part of his duty to preserve the King's peace: he is not entitled to payment *as of right*; but the Court has power to award reasonable compensation, whether he appears for prosecution or defence.

DISCLOSURE BY JURORS, ETC.

Jurors are not to disclose what took place upon their retirement before they reached their verdict. And it is settled practice not to receive a verdict till all the jurors are in Court and within hearing: when received, the Court officer rehearses it to them as recorded by him and asks if it is the verdict of them all. So, too, the grand jurors—like the petty jurors—are under an oath of secrecy and must not say what induced them to "find a true bill" against a person charged.

WITNESSES OUT OF COURT

The judge may, on either party's application, order all witnesses (except the parties, their legal advisers, and the witness being examined) to be out of Court.

WITNESS ENJOYS "ABSOLUTE PRIVILEGE"

Whatever a witness says in evidence is privileged; no action for defamation can be entertained in respect of it. "In certain relations of life," said Lord Justice Scrutton, "it is so important that the persons engaged in them should be able to speak freely that the law takes the risk of their abusing the privilege." But if a witness commits perjury, he is liable to seven years' penal servitude. And the ingredients of perjury are, (i) giving of evidence which is false, (ii) which is material to the question at issue, (iii) in a judicial proceeding after being sworn (or making solemn affirmation), (iv) not believing it to be true.

WITNESSES NEEDED

A single witness, provided that the jury, or the judge in the absence of a jury, is prepared to accept his evidence, suffices in all except the cases below to establish a fact—

(i) By the Treason Act, 1359, no person may be tried for *treason* or for *misprision of treason* (i.e. knowing of treason and not disclosing one's knowledge) unless upon the testimony of two lawful witnesses.

(ii) By the Perjury Act, 1911, some strengthening of the evidence tendered by a single witness is necessary before conviction of an accused. Otherwise, it is simply oath against oath.

(iii) By the Wills Act, 1837, two witnesses are needed for the attestation of a will.

(iv) By the Bastardy Laws Amendment Act, 1872, before an order of affiliation is made against the putative father of an illegitimate child, the mother's evidence must be corroborated on a material point.

(v) By the Evidence (Further Amendment) Act, 1869—the Act which made parties to an action for breach of promise of marriage competent to give evidence—the plaintiff's evidence must be corroborated, by other material evidence, before a verdict can be given against the defendant.

The question, what constitutes evidence in corroboration, is one of law—a question, therefore, for the judge. It was startling, for instance, to find the Court of Criminal Appeal unanimously deciding that passionate love letters—which did not, however, mention marriage—were not such evidence.

The question of the adequacy of the corroborative evidence is one of fact—a question, therefore, for the jury.

(vi) In practice, the evidence of an accomplice is rarely enough to convict an accused.

WITNESSES GIVE EVIDENCE ONLY

Witnesses are spoken of as being for the prosecution or for the defence. This is convenient. But they are, or should be, witnesses of what they saw or heard, indifferent as to the result of their evidence. That result is for the Court. It may be, indeed, that the " evidence in chief," itself tendered to support the contention of one party, supports rather the contention of the other party. And, of course, the evidence brought out in "cross-examination" may give more effective support.

PRESUMPTIVE AND CONCLUSIVE EVIDENCE

Most kinds of evidence raise a *presumption* only. Such evidence may be rebutted by stronger evidence. Some evidence is, however, *conclusive*; being tendered and being believed, there is no more to be said. I produce a birth certificate showing that a defendant, who has not paid for goods other than necessaries, is an infant. That establishes at once his freedom from liability.

RECEIPT AS EVIDENCE

On the other hand, a receipt is only presumptive evidence of payment. It is only one of many kinds of evidence: a cheque may be equally good evidence. Moreover, the fact that a creditor has given a receipt does not preclude him from asserting that his debt remains unpaid. He may rebut the evidence of the receipt by showing that it was given under a misunderstanding— given in exchange, perhaps, for a cheque that proved worthless. The receipt, we say, is not *conclusive* evidence of payment.

BILL OF LADING MAY BE CONCLUSIVE EVIDENCE

In order to promote confidence in dealing with Bills of Lading, Parliament has enacted (Bills of Lading Act, 1855, Section 3) that when the Bill of Lading has come into the hands of a consignee or indorsee for value, it is *conclusive* evidence that the goods shipped were actually shipped, unless—

(1) The holder took the bill with actual notice that the goods were not on board; or

(2) The signer of the bill shows that the mistake arose through the fraud of the shipper, or the holder, or some person under whom the owner claims.

CONFESSIONS AND ADMISSIONS "WITHOUT PREJUDICE"

We speak of "confessions" in criminal and divorce causes, of "admissions" in civil causes. A confession is admissible evidence against a person accused provided that it has not been extorted from him by threats, or cajoled from him by offers of favour. But, in English law confessions are not freely admitted. Cave, J., explained the matter thus in *Reg.* v. *Thompson* (1893):

"Many reasons may be urged in favour of the admissibility of all confessions, subject to the cross-examination of those who heard and testify of them. But this is not the law of England. By that law, to be admissible, a confession must be free and voluntary. If it proceeds from remorse and a desire to make reparation for the crime, it is admissible. If it flows from hope or fear, incited by a person in authority, it is inadmissible."

Therefore it is that, before the police question a person whom they have made up their minds to charge, a caution must be given in this form—

"Do you wish to say anything in answer to the charge? You are not obliged to say anything unless you desire to do so, but whatever you say will be taken down in writing, and may be given in evidence at the trial."

It is not corroboration of incriminating evidence that the accused did not deny the charge or was silent about it. To be silent must not be construed as an admission of guilt.

An "admission" can be received as evidence. But communications between parties, perhaps in the attempt to effect a compromise, that are marked or are indicated as "Without Prejudice" (see the solicitor's letter on page 940), are not admissible as evidence. An admission or confession usually needs corroborative evidence before it is acted upon. Thus, in *Simpson* v. *Simpson* (Divorce Court, 1932), the husband petitioned for a dissolution of marriage, the cause alleged being the adultery of his wife. The only evidence tendered was the wife's oral confession to the petitioner, together with statements in her letters as to her association with men—including a letter after petition in which she admitted her unfaithfulness. The President pronounced a decree *nisi*, holding it to be strong corroboration that the wife made the confession and stood by it though she had everything to lose thereby.

FIRST-HAND KNOWLEDGE NEEDED

A witness deposes about what he himself has heard or seen relevant to the question at issue. "Hearsay evidence" is admissible only rarely, and usually when the witness who might have given it is not available. Second-hand evidence is admitted, that is, when first-hand evidence is impossible (or at all events very difficult) to obtain.

But "*hearsay*" is admissible in the following forms—

1. "Dying declarations" (statements made by a person thinking himself about to die as to the cause of his death).

2. Declarations against their own interest or in the course of their duties, whether written or spoken, made by persons since dead.

3. As reputation in proving matters of *public* interest, like the boundaries of parishes or common rights.

4. Current opinion in pedigree cases.

5. The depositions of witnesses at a preliminary inquiry may be read at the actual trial of a criminal if the witnesses have died in the interval.

EVIDENCE NOT ADMISSIBLE

In order that the question at issue shall be decided without undue delay or bias the Court rejects evidence—

(*a*) Of facts having no *direct* bearing upon the question to be decided; thus, when a person is accused of a crime, evidence that previously he had committed the same kind of crime is not admitted. His "record" may be known to the police, and it may be weighed by the judge when he passes sentence. But it is not allowed to point to guilt on the present occasion.

(*b*) Of the general bad character of the accused.

(*c*) Of the prevalence in the accused's neighbourhood of the particular crime.

And *facts*, not *opinions*, are evidence. A witness called as an expert, a doctor or an engineer, may be asked for his opinion upon a question he has studied intensely. But the ordinary witness must confine himself to what he knows and must not say what he merely surmises.

PUBLICITY OF EVIDENCE

As a rule, cases must be tried and witnesses give evidence *in public*. The evils of secret trials in cases of divorce—trials *in camera*—were made so obvious to the legal authorities during a short experiment in 1929 that publicity again became the rule. A man accused must be allowed to clear himself in public. The exceptions to this rule are few—

(*a*) In the preparatory (or "interlocutory") proceedings of a *civil action*, sworn statements (or "affidavits") may take the place of the oral evidence that will be given in court.

(*b*) Witnesses too old or infirm to attend Court may be examined by a magistrate. In civil cases the Court may appoint persons "on commission" to examine witnesses that, living outside the jurisdiction, cannot be summoned.

EVIDENCE IN RELATION TO BUSINESS AFFAIRS

This, particularly as regards the manner in which the Court interprets business documents, merits more detailed notice. Not that business men fulfil their obligations because the law constrains them to do so. They fulfil them because they are honourable men, and they faithfully fulfil bargains though there is no legal compulsion to do so. It is enough that an undertaking has been given. Still, it is desirable to recognise the distinction between a moral claim and a legal claim. The trustee in bankruptcy may find himself obliged to ignore the moral claim of one creditor in order not to deny the legal claim of another creditor.

The legal results of initialing a marine insurance slip and of executing a marine insurance policy afford as good an illustration as can be wished of the distinction.

THE " SLIP " IN MARINE INSURANCE

The Marine Insurance Act requires the contract of insurance to be evidenced by a formal policy. In the absence of such a policy, the contract is unenforceable. Yet it is customary to consider risks as being covered from the moment that the slip has been initialed by the underwriter as a preliminary to the preparation of a formal contract. No company would dream of not standing by a contract so evidenced. Nevertheless, a liquidator must not pay upon such evidence ; if he does, he may be required to replace the amounts paid. Where legal claims would be prejudiced by a satisfying of claims that are not legal, the law requires justice before generosity. A case in point arose in 1929.

The Home & Colonial Insurance Co., Ltd., had in 1918 entered into an agreement with another insurance company, by which, in effect, it undertook to reinsure marine risks undertaken by the latter, the London Guarantee & Accident Co., Ltd. The agreement proved so disastrous that the Home & Colonial Co. had to wind up in 1922. A chartered accountant was appointed as liquidator. Apart from the claim of the London Guarantee & Accident Co., the Home & Colonial was solvent. The latter's claim amounted to £89,000, and the liquidator admitted this on the mere evidence of the slip. In doing so, he was simply following the practice of accountants and insurers. Yet he was making a mistake in law. The Court, therefore, on the application of a creditor of the Home & Colonial Insurance Co., held that the liquidator was liable to repay the money: "He had been guilty of a misfeasance or breach of trust in relation to the Company." (In *re Home & Colonial Insurance Co., Ltd.*, 1929, Ch.D.)

KIND OF FORMAL EVIDENCE NEEDED

Most business arrangements call for no special formalities. Certainly, if dispute should arise regarding them, the Court will want to know that the agreements were really made. In ordinary cases, the testimony of the parties, or of those having direct knowledge of what took place, is usually enough for this. Sometimes, however, the Court asks for special evidence upon the matter in dispute. A long-established rule of law may require a particular proof of the intention of the party who promises; or an Act of Parliament enacts that certain particular agreements must be made in particular ways.

GRATUITOUS PROMISE

We have, for instance, the rule about a gratuitous promise— a promise, that is, for which the promisor gets nothing in return. Such a promise, if made by word of mouth or in an ordinary writing, places the promisor under no legal constraint. It is not binding upon him. For our law takes the view that a gratuitous promise may be ignored. It must have been made on the foolish impulse of the moment, and its maker should be allowed to change his mind about it. Made, however, by a *deed*, *a sealed writing*, a gratuitous promise becomes binding. The deed being a writing attended with unusual solemnities—the affixing of a seal, the delivery as the promisor's "act and deed," very often the attesting of witnesses—expresses clearly the intention of the party to be under an obligation. It "imports consideration" we sometimes read; we may take it that in some way, perhaps not expressed, there has been a benefit received for the burden undertaken.

FIDELITY BOND

Take as an illustration a "fidelity bond." By the bond an insurance company, it may be, promises to pay a bank a large sum of money. But the promise is a conditional one; if a certain employee of the bank, on whose behalf the bond has been made and who pays the insurance company a premium for making it, performs his duties faithfully, the promise is to lapse. So far as the bank is concerned, the insurance company makes a gratuitous promise; for the bank has given nothing in return. The sealed writing is, therefore, needed to make the promise into one that the bank can, in the event of the condition unhappily not being performed, enforce against the company.

LEGAL REQUIREMENTS ABOUT WRITING

From their very nature, some business transactions must be embodied in writing. An acknowledgment of debt and undertaking to pay must be shown by a *bill of exchange* before they could serve as a means of payment; the promise of a merchant to pay had to be signified in an easily recognised document, in a *promissory note*, before it could be used as mercantile money. This practice of the merchants is now embodied in the Bills of Exchange Act, 1882, and this Act also requires the acceptance of a bill to be in writing. Convenience dictates the preparation of other documents.

Where transactions are incessantly repeated, the business men concerned devise a document for general use. The shipper, wishing to send a cargo to Calcutta, would never dream of making his bargain with the shipowner by word of mouth or even by letter. Nor would the shipowner care to state the multitudinous ways in which he limits his liability. A *bill of lading* is available. This shows the shipper what he is to expect from the shipowner; it protects the shipowner against risks he himself might have been unable to foresee.

The formal document being there, drawn up with deliberate care and scrutinised by the keen eyes of those whose interests are involved, neither party need trouble about the general nature of the transaction. He simply fills in the details of the bargain.

CONTRACTS NEEDING WRITTEN EVIDENCE

In order to ensure that satisfactory evidence shall be forthcoming, the law has, in all developed systems, prescribed writing for specified documents. Our law, for instance, not apt to attribute disinterested generosity to those involved in litigation, requires unmistakable evidence of a person's undertaking to be answerable for another's debt or default. I say to a tailor, "Make him the suit; if he doesn't pay, I will"; and, so doing, I am giving a guarantee. I am making a conditional promise. But the only constraint upon me to keep the promise is my respect for my plighted word. Since the promise is not expressed in writing, I may legally disregard it; it is not enforceable by action. Bankers and others in the habit of requiring guarantees know all this very well, and they usually have special forms for signature. Some of these forms are terrifying documents, binding the guarantor beyond possibility of doubt and on every conceivable happening.

Other contracts not enforceable at law unless evidenced by "some note or memorandum signed by the party to be charged or his agent" are—

1. Contracts relating to an interest in land.
2. Contracts made in consideration of marriage.
3. Contracts not to be completed within a year.
4. Contracts by an executor or administrator to pay a deceased's debt out of his own pocket.
5. Contracts of sale to the value of £10 or over.

Such contracts made by word of mouth are valid contracts. It is only because Parliament has thought fit to prescribe the particular evidence that they cannot be legally enforced. And, if a defendant provides the written evidence even after the formation of the contract, that is enough. The contract is enforceable at law.

See, for instance, *Buxton* v. *Rust* (Ex. 1871) where the defendant, in the very act of repudiating the contract, supplied the written evidence needed. The Appeal judge said: "The plaintiff and defendant met and made a bargain for the purchase by the plaintiff from the defendant of some wool, and as the purchase money was more than £10, it was necessary that the terms of the bargain should be evidenced by writing. Accordingly, a memorandum was drawn up and signed by the plaintiff, and handed by him to the defendant, which, we must take it, correctly represented what the contract really was, and according to which the wool was to be cleared in 'about twenty-one days.' More than this period having elapsed, the defendant wrote: 'It is now twenty-eight days since you and I had a deal for my wool, which was for you to have taken all away in twenty-one days. I do not consider it business to put it off like this, therefore I shall consider the deal off, as you have not completed your part of the contract.' This was a sufficient recognition of a contract to satisfy the statute of frauds."

" STATUTE-BARRED " DEBTS

The law assumes, too, taking a cynical view of human nature, that a man will not pay a debt he can avoid paying. Just as a tax that can be evaded will be evaded, so a debt that can be dodged will be dodged. Now, a debt that has been dormant for six years, the debtor not having acknowledged it within that period nor paid anything upon its account, can be dodged. It is "statute-barred." That is to say, the legal remedy available for recovery of the debt has been withdrawn. So enacts the Statute of 1624: "All actions of debt without specialty shall be sued within six years after the cause of such action."

For a debt with specialty—a debt in respect to an agreement under seal—the limiting period is extended to twenty years. The right to the money is not, however, extinguished, and the power of the creditor to bring an action may be revived. But it needs a written acknowledgment to bring about the revival, and the acknowledgment must either contain an express promise to pay, or such a promise must be clearly inferable. If I wrote, "I know I owe the money. But I was badly treated in the matter, and I refuse to pay," that would not revive the right of action. We could hardly imply a promise to pay where there is a definite refusal to do so.

EVIDENCE OF SEALED WRITING NEEDED

It was a rule of Common Law that to make a contract enforceable against a corporation the attachment of the corporate seal was needed. This rule has been largely relaxed. But it still exists where Parliament has enacted that a sealed writing is requisite. Thus, in *Nixon* v. *Erith Urban District Council*, the plaintiff failed to recover payment for work done, since his contract with the Council was not under seal. For, by the Public Health Act, 1875, contracts of a value over £50 made by an urban authority under the powers conferred by the Act must be under seal. Joyce, J. (in *Douglass* v. *Rhyl Urban Council*, Ch. 1913), put the matter thus: "It is now settled that, in the absence of an express statutory provision requiring a contract under seal, the requirements of the corporate seal at Common Law is subject to this exception: Wherever the purposes for which a corporation is created render it necessary that work shall be done or goods supplied to carry such purposes into effect, and orders are given at a corporate meeting regularly constituted, and having power to make contracts authorised and necessary for the purposes for which the corporation is created, and the work is done or goods supplied and accepted by the corporation and the whole consideration for the payment executed, there is a contract to pay implied from the acts of the corporation; the corporation cannot keep the goods or the benefit and refuse to pay on the ground of mere absence of a formality, as that the fixing of a seal was wanting."

HOW CONTRACTS ARE INTERPRETED

When a man has made a contract, using words that reasonable men will interpret in one way, he cannot be allowed to assert that he means them to be interpreted in a different way. If a dispute arises, the question to be determined is not what the man had in his mind when he agreed to the terms, but what others are justified in thinking he had in his mind. Where the terms of a contract are so obscure that it is impossible to attach a definite meaning to them, the Court will refuse to enforce the agreement. It is for the parties themselves to make their bargains, not for the Court when dispute arises. The buyer of a horse promised that if the horse was lucky he would "give £5 more or buy another horse." The Court held such a promise to be too loose and vague to be considered. The seller of a business undertook to retire wholly from the trade, "so far as the law allows." It was held that the agreement was worthless: the parties must assign their own limits, not ask the Court to assign them. But, if it is possible to read a definite meaning into the words used, the Court will enforce the agreement.

DIFFICULTIES OF INTERPRETATION

That difficulties shall arise is perhaps unavoidable. For language is not a perfect embodiment of thought. The parties may, in quite good faith, interpret the one word in two ways, and judicial decision may be necessary to determine the right interpretation. So with this marine insurance case (*Lindsay Blea Depôts* v. *Motor Union Insurance Co.*, 1930). The plaintiff asserted that the coal insured had not been "landed"; the defendant asserted that it had been "landed." The plaintiff—a firm of merchants at Oran—imported a cargo of bunker coal from the Tyne. The insurance policy covered the risk of transit until the coal was discharged "and safely landed including all risks of craft awaiting landing." The coal did, in fact, reach Oran. There it was discharged into a barge, and the barge sank the following night. The plaintiff claimed under the policy; for the coals had not been "safely landed." But, then, it appeared that the method of dealing with the imported coal did not entail the placing of the coal ashore. The bunker coal was discharged into barges and was left there until a vessel needed coal. Then the barge moved alongside the vessel and bunkered it. In these circumstances, the Court held that the safe landing contemplated had been accomplished. The company's risk ceased when the coal was where the plaintiff intended to keep it until resold.

AN UNDERSTANDING

The difficulty is greater where implications are in question. The parties to a contract often leave unexpressed what is perfectly well understood. For it is not always necessary to use words, whether spoken or written, to express one's intention. My intention may be readily and certainly inferred from my conduct. I insert two pennies into an automatic ticket machine; there is no doubt about my having thereby accepted the offer of the Railway Company to carry me to the Bank or a dozen other stations at my option. The understanding, though unexpressed, may, in fact, be the very essence of the bargain. It may, that is, be a *condition*. It is as though one party had said, "Of course, if such-and-such a thing happens, the bargain is off," or "You will, of course, undertake to do so-and-so when executing the contract," and the other party had replied, "Certainly, that is understood." The condition, which might have been expressed, is only implied. It is none the less a term of the contract; and its breach may give rise to an action for damages.

IMPLIED WARRANTY OF SEAWORTHINESS

This is one of the most familiar of such implied terms. The Common Law imposed upon every shipowner proposing an insurance the obligation to make the ship "sea-worthy." That he had striven diligently to make it seaworthy was not enough;

the ship must really be fit in all respects to carry her cargo safely to its destination, having regard to the ordinary perils to which such a ship would be exposed on such a voyage.

In contracts of affreightment to which the Carriage of Goods by Sea Act, 1924, applies this implied warranty will be replaced by one less onerous to the shipowner. It is replaced by the statutory undertaking that the shipowner will "before, and at the beginning of the voyage, exercise due diligence to make the ship seaworthy" (Art. III, Rule I).

AN IMPLIED TERM

The astonishing case in which Messrs. Waterlow were called upon to pay over half a million pounds as damages affords a capital illustration of an implied term. *Banco de Portugal* v. *Waterlow and Sons, Ltd.* (K.B. 1930).

The law does not presume to make bargains for the parties; nor does it claim a power to release a party from the legal obligations he has undertaken. Then, on what principle does a Court imply conditions in a contract? We might answer generally that the law has in every country supplemented the shortsightedness of individuals; it has done for them what they would have done for themselves if their imagination had anticipated the course of nature. We need, however, in regard to practical application, a less general answer, and this is supplied in the Waterlow case. The term implied must be such as is required to carry out the real intentions of the parties; or, as it was put, "to give effect to such business efficacy as the parties contemplated."

By a series of successful tricks, a gang of swindlers had induced Waterlow's to print a number of notes, not authorised by the Bank of Portugal. It was the printing of these unauthorised notes that constituted the breach of an implied condition. The relevant part of the judgment is: "On the construction of the contract of November, 1922, which provided for the printing by Messrs. Waterlow and Sons of the authorised notes for the bank, it seems that the plates are the property of Waterlow only to be available for the purposes of the bank. There is no express term in the contract that Messrs. Waterlow shall not print or deliver notes without the authority of the bank. But that is accounted for in that no one imagined such a thing would occur.

In my view, it is of the essence of a contract like the one in question that the printers of bank-notes are left in possession of the plates on condition that there was not to be any use of the plates for any purpose other than that of the bank which issued the notes. Such a term is necessary to give effect to such business efficacy as the parties contemplate. It is obvious that if the defendants print unauthorised notes from the plates, even in good faith and without negligence, they are doing something that can have the most disastrous effect upon the whole credit system of the country. If the printer does use the plates and print the notes, he must be in a position to justify his doing so if there is any challenge by the bank of issue. I, therefore, hold that such a term must be implied in the contract between Messrs. Waterlow and Sons and the Bank of Portugal, and that the duty on Messrs. Waterlow was absolute."

That is, it was a duty of so binding a nature that no excuse about its non-fulfilment could be entertained. The Court will not, has, indeed, no power, to imply in a contract a term or condition inconsistent with the express provisions of the contract. The intention of the parties is gathered from the express provisions, and only in obvious instances is an additional term applied. If the contract is for the hire of *a particular* horse for a particular day, it is easy to imply a condition that the horse shall be alive on that day. If the contract is simply for the hire of *a* horse, we could not imply such a condition.

RULES FOR CONSTRUING CONTRACTS

When dispute does arise as to the real meaning of a business document, the Court invoked to determine the dispute—

1. Will try to interpret the document so that the intention of the bargainers, at the time of making the contract, is fulfilled.

2. Will not, except to a very limited extent and for special purposes, admit anything that will add to or vary the written contract.

As to the first, we are entitled to suppose that a man means what he says, and that when he signs a document he assents to what the document contains. Business would be sadly impeded if people were allowed to say that though, in fact, they did sign the document, they were unaware of its terms or that they understood the terms in a meaning different from the ordinary one. To avoid possible recriminations in the future, a party proffering a document as containing the terms of the contract made may make some such statement as this: "There are no agreements or understandings other than those contained in this form." The statement really adds nothing to the legal view. It is useful, though, as a reminder to the party signing the form that he cannot be heard to say that he understood something else (other than, or in addition to, what is in the form) at the time. As the judge said in a case where one party sought to prove an understanding modifying the written agreement: "They put on paper what is to bind them, and so make the written document conclusive evidence between them." Or, as an old book puts it: "It would be inconvenient that matters in writing, made by advice and on consideration, and which finally import the certain truth of the agreement of the parties, should be controlled by averment of the parties, to be proved by the uncertain testimony of slippery memory."

AMBIGUOUS WORDS OR PHRASES

True it is that occasionally the words of the document admit of two meanings. In an interesting insurance case, the phrase in dispute was: "In consideration of the premium mentioned, we who have hereunto subscribed our names agree to insure her against all loss wheresoever which the assured may sustain by the loss of or damage to the property herein specified." This was the underwriters' undertaking to insure Mrs. Payne's jewellery. A pearl necklace valued at £600 was missed; a claim was made, and the underwriters satisfied the claim. Some months after, the missing necklace dropped from an evening cloak that Mrs. Payne's sister was trying on. The underwriters were told of the recovery, and the necklace was offered to them as salvage. They claimed, however, that the money paid out on account of its loss should be returned. There had been no "loss" within the meaning of the policy. Decision was given in the lady's favour. Was there a "loss"? *Holmes* v. *Payne* (K.B. 1930).

It was contended that a thing cannot be lost when it is in the owner's house. The contention is not supported by experience. The Marine Insurance Act has defined losses for the purpose of marine insurance: *unlikelihood of recovery* is the test. It is true that a thing may be mislaid, yet not lost; but if a thing has been mislaid, and a reasonable time has elapsed to allow of diligent search, and such diligent search has been made and has been fruitless, then the thing may properly be said to be lost.

ORAL EVIDENCE MODIFYING WRITTEN EVIDENCE

Henderson v. *Arthur* (K.B. 1907) affords a good example of the second rule, that in general outside evidence is not admissible to vary the terms of a written contract. Henderson leased a theatre to Arthur. The lease stipulated for payment of rent quarterly in advance. Arthur contended, however, that an agreement by word of mouth permitted him to pay by a three months' bill. Henderson refused such a bill, sued for immediate payment, and succeeded. The Court of Appeal declared that the written agreement contemplated payment in cash, so that the bill at three months did not satisfy it. The parol arrangement alleged by Arthur, contradicting as it did the written agreement, could not be admitted in evidence.

MODIFYING A WRITTEN AGREEMENT

The rule in regard to this was put thus by Chief Justice Lord Denman: "By the general rule of the Common Law, if there be a contract that has been reduced into writing, verbal evidence is not allowed to be given of what passed between the parties, either before the written instrument was made, or during the time that it was in a state of preparation, so as to add to or subtract from, or in any manner to vary or qualify the written contract. But, after the agreement has been reduced into writing, it is competent to the parties, at any time before breach of it, by a new contract not in writing, either altogether to waive, dissolve, or annul the former agreements, or in any manner to add to, or subtract from, or vary or qualify the terms of it, and thus to make a new contract. This is to be proved, partly by the written agreement, and partly by the subsequent verbal terms engrafted upon what will be thus left of the written agreement." The verbal terms are operative. None the less, it is obviously desirable, for the avoidance of possible disputes, to have these modifying terms put into writing.

USAGE MODIFYING A DOCUMENT

Yet it may be that some of the terms in the contract need explanation. Certain usages of a trade or of a locality may be so well known to the parties that they must be taken to contract with those usages in mind. In one case, for instance (*Smith* v. *Wilson*, 1802), evidence of a local custom, that the 1,000 in the agreement meant 1,200, was admitted. "There is a presumption that in such transactions the parties did not mean to express in writing the whole of the contract by which they intended to be bound, but to contract with reference to those usages." One ignorant of the usage would fail to understand the document; there is, we say, a *latent ambiguity*. Where such exists the Court admits evidence to show what the parties intended. This is not to modify or add to the contract in any way. It is simply to show what the contract really means.

Where the ambiguity is *patent*, however, where one part of the document is inconsistent with another part, outside evidence is not admissible to remove the ambiguity. Unless certain rules of construction enable the Court to see what the parties intended, the Court will refuse to enforce the agreement on the ground of uncertainty. Some rules there are.

By the Bills of Exchange Act, 1882, for example, the written words in the body of the bill override the figures, where these differ, in the margin. Or the Court will read the document in the sense the more unfavourable to the party whose document it is. And, where blanks in the document are filled in then, when the written words are inconsistent with the printed form, the Court may take the written words as the more immediate expression of intention.

USAGES AND CUSTOMS

To what extent are customs of trade incorporated into a bargain? Only so far as they are consistent with the expressed terms of the bargain. Thus, goods were shipped under a bill of lading with the words: "Freight payable in London." Evidence, that by the custom of the steam shipping trade this meant "Freight payable in advance in London," was rejected. Here there were no qualifying words, and "freight" must be taken to have its ordinary mercantile meaning, "the reward payable to the carrier when the goods arrive in merchantable condition, ready for delivery to the merchant." On the other hand, evidence of a custom in the trade was accepted, that brokers were liable as principals if they do not disclose the name of their principal when making the contract, in *Pike* v. *Ongley* (Q.B. 1887). The sold note given by the broker to the buyer was in the form, "Sold by B to C for and on account of owner."

Where the customs are well known to both parties they must be assumed to have contracted upon the tacit undertaking that these customs are to be observed. A custom is a reasonable and universal rule of action in a locality, and, when custom is pleaded, the legal position has been put thus: "In order that the shippers should be taken to have impliedly given leave to stow the goods on deck, the shipowners must prove a practice general and universal in the trade, and in the particular port, that every one shipping goods there must be taken to know that goods might probably be stowed on deck." Thus, a claim for demurrage was made against the charterer of a vessel, the cargo not having been discharged at a stipulated rate "per working day." The charterers showed that by the custom of the port a "surf day," when the surf prevented the lighters from discharging, was not a "working day." The Court held that evidence of the custom was admissible. (*British & Mexican Co.* v. *Lockett*, K.B. 1911.)

"EJUSDEM GENERIS" RULE OF CONSTRUCTION

Where specific words are followed and amplified by general words, these last are to be confined to things *of the same kind* as the preceding specific words. The rule received a striking illustration in a deviation case. The cargo owners recovered from the shipowners because there had been a deviation uncovered by the charter party (*Mango and Co.* v. *Stag Line*, C.A. 1931). A steamer had been chartered to carry coal from Swansea to Constantinople. On the voyage a new piece of apparatus was to be tested, and the company's engineer went on the ship from Swansea. The steamer put in to St. Ives to land him, shortly afterwards stranded, and both ship and cargo were lost. A clause in the charter party stated, "The vessel shall have liberty to call at any ports in any order for bunkering or other purposes." Could this call at St. Ives be regarded as covered by this clause. No! it was held; the "other purposes" must be of the *same kind* (*ejusdem generis*) as "bunkering." That is, the words must be restricted to ports having some relation to the joint adventure. "It could not be that the ship might call for ' any purpose,' as if the captain wanted to see his wife. The mere presence of the word 'bunkering' showed that; this word was not wanted if calling for any purpose was allowed." Now, since there had been an unauthorised deviation, the shipowner could not excuse his failure to carry unless from the act of God or the King's enemies or vice in the goods themselves. He was thrown back upon his Common Law rights and obligations, and, though "perils of the sea" had been among the "excepted risks" of the charter party, he could no longer take advantage of the clause. He had undertaken to carry the goods; he had failed; no excuse was available; and he must pay as damages the market price of the cargo.

THE RULE OF ESTOPPEL

One rule of evidence has been severely criticised—unjustly, though. This is the rule that prevents a man from asserting the truth, when he has led the other party to act on a lie. This rule of evidence had a very effective illustration in the case *Greenwood v. Martins Bank, Limited*, decided in 1932 by the House of Lords in favour of the bank. To state the matter bluntly, the rule prevents a litigant from telling the truth concerning the matter in dispute. He has evidence available which, being received, would determine the litigation in his favour; but he is not permitted to give the evidence. This seems at first glance a stupid rule, harsh to the litigant who is estopped from giving the evidence, and inconsistent with the normal duty of the Court— which is to bring forth truth and make it prevail. Yet we can easily imagine conditions that would make it a greater hardship upon the other litigant to allow the evidence to be given. Here is a statement to which I have, in solemn and formal manner, set my seal: I am estopped from denying the truth of the statement. A man leads me to believe what is not true; I act in accordance with the belief he has induced in me; to let him now reveal the true state of things would be unfair to me if it meant my loss. I ought to be able to put faith in the representations of my fellows. So it has been laid down, "Where one by his words or conduct wilfully causes another to believe the existence of a certain state of things, and induces him to act on that belief so as to alter his own previous position, the former must not aver against the latter the existence of a different state of things." The Greenwood case shows that omission to act, where a duty is cast upon a person to disclose the truth, has the same effect. An estoppel arises, that is, when there is—

1. A representation, or conduct amounting to a representation, tending to induce a course of conduct on the part of the person to whom the representation was made.

2. A resulting act or omission by the person to whom the representation was made.

3. Detriment to such person as a consequence of the act or omission.

GREENWOOD v. MARTINS BANK (H.L. 1932)

The facts of this unhappy case were these. Greenwood had his account with Martins Bank. His wife, in order to finance some litigation by her sister, depleted the account by means of forged cheques, and confessed the forgeries to her husband, begging him not to tell the bank. Greenwood refrained; but some time after, upon his refusal to supply more money for the sister's litigation, his wife shot herself. He afterwards told the bank about the forgeries, claiming that his account should not be debited with the amounts paid without his authority. Of course, however careful a banker may be, he cannot charge his customer with the amount paid out upon a forged cheque. Once the customer establishes that the signature is not his, the bank must restore to his account the amount paid.

But, ought Greenwood to be allowed to say that the signatures were not his? Timely notice might have enabled the bank to lessen its loss; was it justice to make the bank pay when this possibility had gone through the death of the wife? The members of the Court of Appeal and of the House of Lords were all of the opinion that the answer must be "No." By his delay, Greenwood had deprived the bank of its power to sue the wife for fraud. For the death of a person prevents an action from being pursued against that person.

The position was curious and, from Greenwood's point of view, most difficult. His wife had committed the crime of forgery, and might have been prosecuted for it; and his disclosure to the bank would have enabled the bank to sue his wife for fraud. For a prosecution for crime does not exclude an action for wrong. Now, in spite of the Married Women's Property Act, 1882, a husband is still liable for his wife's wrongs, including the frauds she perpetrates. The one exception is when the fraud is directly connected with a contract, and is the means of effecting the contract. Here there was no contract between Mrs. Greenwood and the bank. The husband was, therefore, impaled upon one of the horns of a dilemma. If he disclosed his knowledge during his wife's lifetime, he could certainly have his account rectified; but the bank could recover the necessary amount from him. If he did not he was estopped from his claim. It would seem that, for practical purposes in regard to the signing of cheques, a man and his wife are one.

EVIDENCE TENDING TO ILLEGITIMATISE A CHILD

Akin to this rule of estoppel is the rule, reiterated by the House of Lords in the Russell divorce case, 1924, that neither husband nor wife may give evidence tending to show that a child born in wedlock is not the child of the husband. This rule is grounded upon the policy of the law, that what takes place between spouses shall not be matter for legal consideration.

PROCEDURE

PROCEDURE is the mode by which a legal right is enforced. Procedure is the machinery; the enjoyment of the right is the product. If a man wishes, by invoking the aid of the Courts, to vindicate his rights, he must proceed according to the rules laid down. For the rules are themselves laws. They have been formulated by the Judges in accordance with the powers conferred on them by Parliament; and the object of the rules is to ensure reasonable speed and economy, so far as can be consistent with perfect fairness of trials. Perhaps the effort "to abridge process" has been less successful than the effort to ensure complete and impartial investigation. But, at any rate, efforts are made to shorten trials.

Part of procedure, therefore, consists of the rules adopted in order to narrow the questions at issue—

1. The *Pleadings* on both sides must be clear and without irrelevancies; the plaintiff must state briefly what his claim is; the defendant must state briefly what his defence is. The facts upon which both sides agree are ascertained. The facts in dispute thereby emerge of themselves. The answers of the Jury settle the disputed facts; the Judge can then give clear decisions on points of law without being distracted by having to make up his mind upon disputed facts.

2. The *Evidence* available at the time of the trial is hedged round by restrictions; only such evidence may be presented as has a direct bearing upon the case, and only such evidence as can be thoroughly tested. Hearsay gossip is rigorously excluded. Witnesses confine themselves to answering questions propounded by counsel, who are aware of what is evidence, aware also that the Court will resent attempts to obscure truth by adducing what is not evidence. The statements of witnesses are, indeed, absolutely privileged. But the statements are subject to cross-examination; and the penalty when perjury is proved is heavy.

We are not to suppose that the Courts have a method of their own for bringing out the truth of matters. But witnesses can be kept to the point; cross-examination, in the hands of a competent counsel, is a potent instrument; and in general the truth emerges soon or late.

29

THE MACHINERY OF LITIGATION

It is little to the purpose to have legal rights, unless one knows the method of enforcing those rights. It is little to the purpose to know that claims are unjust unless one knows the method of resisting them. We may—and we are probably wise in doing so —leave the working of the machinery that has been evolved in our legal system, to the experts, to the solicitors and barristers, who have suitably equipped themselves for working it. None the less, a knowledge of the machinery is desirable. Men and women of all classes are nowadays called upon as justices of the peace, as members of a jury, as witnesses, even as prosecutors for crime, to help in the working. And many a litigant conducts quite successfully his own case, vindicates his own legal rights, or repels unjustified attacks by another; and English judges seem to be peculiarly tolerant of those litigants who choose to appear in person. There is no very strong reason why a litigant should not so appear, for the procedure to be followed is carefully indicated. There is less need to conduct one's own case, now, however. The poorest can, in suitable cases, pursue their cause to the House of Lords. To the Poor Prisoners' Defence Act (1930) on the criminal side there is on the civil side the machinery whereby a person can sue *in forma pauperis*. (See page 136 where such a person succeeded in the Supreme Court.)

PROCEEDINGS BY POOR PERSONS

A person unable to finance a lawsuit, whether as plaintiff or defendant, can obtain a certificate from the Law Society (or a provincial branch of that society) that will enable him without payment to have all the help he needs. Such a certificate is granted after inquiry by a committee of the Society, the inquiry being directed to the following points—

1. Has the person applying £50 (in special circumstances £100)?

2. Does his weekly income exceed £2 (in special circumstances £4)?

3. Has he a reasonable cause of action or reasonable defence?

Application should be made to *Secretary, Law Society's Hall, Chancery Lane, London, W.C.*2. He will give applicants outside London the name of the Secretary of the appropriate local committee.

The certificate being obtained and filed in the Supreme Court, the litigant is not liable for Court fees, nor (except when in very rare cases the Court orders otherwise) is he liable to pay costs (except reasonable out-of-pocket expenses to the solicitor assigned to him) or to receive from the other party any profit, costs, or charges. Of course, he receives for himself any damages he may recover.

Our helping of poor litigants is a late imitation of Scottish practice. In Scotland the legal profession have for 500 years been obliged to conduct the causes of the poor under authority of a statute of the Scottish Parliament in 1424, which may be translated—

"If there be any poor creature that for lack of wisdom or means cannot follow his cause, the King for the love of God shall ordain that the judge before whom the cause shall come shall provide and supply a good and wise advocate to follow such poor creature's cause. And if such cause be successful, the wrongdoer shall pay both the party injured and the advocate's costs and efforts."

In the Supreme Court the Faculty of Advocates—the Scottish Bar—appoint each year six of its members to be counsel for the poor, and solicitors appoint certain of their number to act as solicitors for the poor, and both bodies appoint certain others to be reporters on the "*probabilis causa*" of those who applied to be admitted as poor litigants. For not only must the poverty of the intending litigant be proved, but he must be found to have a probable cause, a reasonably good claim or defence.

NOTES ON PROCEDURE

A few preliminary notes are necessary—

1. *Ubi jus, ibi remedium* (where there is a legal right, there is a legal remedy). The law does not provide a remedy for all the ills of life. Most of them we must bear as best we can without help from the Courts. It may be that the law is defective in that it has not made provision for our special grievance. It may be that, as in regard to trade competition, public policy calls for our own exertions against the grievance. At any rate unless a legal remedy exists, there is no legal right (*ubi jus, ibi remedium*): "It is a vain thing to imagine a right without a remedy, for want of right and want of remedy are reciprocal." If my rival supplants me in my lady's affections I suffer a loss, but the law provides no compensation: it is *damnum sine injuria* (a loss without being a legal wrong).

2. *Infant Litigant.* An infant litigant is subject to special rules of procedure. He sues by his "next friend," who is personally liable for the costs of the action. If he sues in his own

name the writ may be set aside with costs against the solicitor issuing it. An infant is sued in the ordinary way. But he enters appearance and defends by a "guardian *ad litem*," such guardian not being personally liable for costs.

3. *Publicity is Desirable.* Except in very rare cases—where official secrets are concerned, for instance, or where secret processes are in dispute, or where, having regard to the nature of the evidence that will be tendered, the judge decides on holding the trial *in camera*—all trials, civil and criminal, are open to the public. A man is accused; he clears himself in public, if he can; and his reputation suffers no damage from the accusation. Moreover, the publicity of trials for crimes acts both as a deterrent to the criminal and as an effective way of instructing people about the laws they must obey. Thus in 1908 an Act enacted punishment for incest. Proceedings under the Act were to be held *in camera*, that is, without the admission of the public and without the publication of what took place. The secrecy clause was repealed in 1922, the judges reporting that the suppressing of public trials had resulted in ignorance that the practices penalised were in fact criminal.

There is some restriction of publicity, too, in regard to the publication by newspapers of evidence of an indecent character or of more than the bare outlines of divorce and other matrimonial causes. The Judicial Proceedings (Regulations of Reports) Act, 1926, makes it a penal offence (punishable by fine of £500 or four months imprisonment) to publish in relation to any judicial proceedings—

(i) any indecent matter, or medical or surgical details;

(ii) where matrimonial causes are concerned, particulars other than (*a*) witnesses, (*b*) concise statement of charges and defence, (*c*) submissions on points of law, (*d*) judge's summing-up, verdict, and judgment.

But only people connected with newspapers can be convicted under the Act, and the sanction of the Attorney-General must be obtained before proceedings are begun. It is a tribute to the good sense and good taste of newspaper men that the Act has not yet been invoked.

Apart from these exceptions, publicity is the rule.

The great importance attached by English law to publicity in order to ensure a fair trial for a prisoner is illustrated in *Rex* v. *Dunne* (1929). The Court of Criminal Appeal quashed the conviction for incest of a man sentenced to three years' penal servitude. The material witness, a girl of seven, was questioned in private by the judge in order that he might form an opinion whether she could be sworn. We may assume, with a great deal of confidence, that not a question was asked about the case. The judge was acting in all kindness. Yet, as the C.C.A. decided: "Something was said to or by this witness which was not in the hearing or presence of the jury or of the accused. The Court is clearly of the opinion that, in these circumstances, the appeal must be allowed and the conviction quashed."

4. *Expense of Litigation.* It is often good business to bear, with such equanimity as we can bring to our aid, what one knows is injustice. It certainly is so when he who has infringed our legal rights is a man of straw, against whom a judgment would be of no value. Yet, even when our opponent is opulent enough, the wise man shrinks from litigation, and enters upon it with fear and trembling. For one can hardly ever be perfectly certain about the issue of a case; and one can be perfectly certain that the costs will be great. The criticism long ago urged by Mill is still pertinent: "The procedure of the tribunals is so replete with delay, vexation, and expense, that the price at which justice is at last obtained fully outweighs a very considerable amount of injustice."

In a High Court action, the costs to be borne by the unsuccessful litigant are often excessively high in relation to the amount in dispute. The judges themselves sometimes lament the fact. In *Addis* v. *Gramophone Co.* (H.L. 1909), the Lord Chancellor said: "My Lords, this is a most unfortunate litigation, in which the costs must far exceed any sum there may be at stake. A little common sense would have settled all these differences in a few minutes. . . . Litigation between exasperated litigants can breed barren controversies and increase costs in a matter of itself simple enough."

County Courts. The institution, in the middle of the nineteenth century, of the County Courts, did much to remedy the matter. In County Court actions, the possibility of excessive expense and of great delay has been in great measure lessened. For the power to appeal is narrowly restricted and can be exercised only by leave of the Court and the scale of fees and costs is much lower.

County Courts were set up primarily so that poor people, even in contention with the rich, might obtain justice, and might obtain it without great delay and expense and vexation of spirit. They have been wonderfully successful and rightly enjoy the confidence of all classes, so that questions involving property of great value are now brought for the decision of the County Court judge. These Courts are the poor man's Courts. They were, indeed, designed in 1846 to supply justice cheaply where no very great sum depended upon the litigation, and where no difficult point of law was to be decided. The ordinary limit is £100; and where the amount is not over £20, no appeal is allowed, except by leave of the judge. The judge usually decides both law and fact; but, except where the sum involved is very small, either party may claim a jury of eight persons. The County Courts have abundantly justified themselves.

High Courts. Litigation in the High Courts is, however, still a most expensive luxury, mainly because a disappointed litigant has power, provided that his purse is deep enough, to carry the case first to the Court of Appeal, then to the House of Lords, the Supreme Court. Why there should be a possibility of two appeals is not obvious. If the House of Lords is more fitted for revising the decision reached by the High Court Judge, there seems no real necessity for an intermediate Appeal Court. True, there must be in any legal system some arrangement for reaching finality; but, where there are two possible appeals, the reversal by the House of Lords of a decision might well make suitors rankle with a quite understandable sense of injustice. In one much-discussed case—the Russell divorce case of 1924—the judgment of the High Court Judge, that of the three judges in the Appeal Court, and that of two of the five judges in the House of Lords were in the petitioner's favour. These six judgments were, however, outweighed by the judgment of the three majority judges in the House of Lords; so that in the event the respondent won, six judges being against her and three for her. This would seem to be an absurdity; and it is explainable only by our traditional respect for vested rights. When, in 1873, the great reform of the Courts took place, the first intention was to set up a special Court of Appeal and to abolish appeal to the mixed gathering of lawyers that constituted the House of Lords in its aspect as a tribunal. Second thoughts restored the House of Lords to its ancient privilege; and thereby produced the anomaly of two Appeal Courts.

5. *Costs.* The Court has a considerable amount of discretion in regard to costs. Here, for instance, is the House of Lords judgment in *Tolley* v. *Fry* (1932).

"Judgment be entered for the appellant for damages to be

assessed, and that a new trial be had between the parties for the assessment of such damages. The respondents to pay the costs of the trial before Acton, J., and also the costs of the appeal to this House. Each party to bear and pay their own costs in the Court of Appeal. Cause remitted back to the King's Bench Division to do therein as shall be just and consistent with this judgment."

That is, the party unsuccessful in the final court was not obliged to bear his opponent's costs in the Appeal Court, where he had been successful, but had to bear them in the Court of first instance where he had been unsuccessful.

Some general rules relating to costs are these—

(1) In regard to criminal cases (where the contention is between the King and accused) the old rule was "the Crown neither receives nor pays costs"; a man, even if he clears himself triumphantly from an accusation, must bear the cost of his defence; a criminal, however wealthy, did not bear the cost of his prosecution.

This rule has been departed from in these matters—

(a) By the Criminal Law Amendment Act of 1867 the Court is given power, when a person has been acquitted of an indictable offence, and when it thinks the prosecution unreasonable, to order the prosecutor to pay all costs. The Costs in Criminal Cases Act, 1908, extends the rule to all criminal cases. The later Act gives power also to make a convicted person pay all the costs of the proceedings.

(2) In civil cases costs usually follow the event; the successful party gets his costs from the unsuccessful, since the costs were incurred by the latter making an unjust claim or resisting a just one. But the Court may for good reason vary the rule.* Only, in no case would a successful litigant be obliged to bear his opponent's costs.

---

* Here, for instance, is the concluding paragraph of the Lord Chancellor's judgment in *Maddison* v. *Alderson* (H.L. 1883), a case where failure of a testator to execute his will properly prevented the appellant from getting what had been intended for her: "I am sorry for the appellant's disappointment, through the ignorance of her late master as to the attestation requisite for a valid testamentary act. But the law cannot be strained for the purpose of relieving her from the consequences of that misfortune. It would be much strained if your Lordships were to reverse the order of the Court of Appeal. I should have been glad if that Court had dealt differently with the costs; for she has lost not only the estate intended for her, but also her wages. Costs were, however, within their discretion, and their decree cannot be altered in that respect, being otherwise correct. This House has also to exercise a discretion as to the costs of this appeal; and I humbly venture to recommend to your Lordships that it should be dismissed without costs."

6. *House of Lords as Supreme Court.* When the House of Lords has spoken we do know the law upon a matter. For the House considers itself bound by its own decisions : if the law is to be altered Parliament must act. The benefit and the drawback of this state of affairs was thus expressed by a Lord Chancellor : "I do not deny that cases of individual hardship may arise, and there may be a current of opinion in the profession that such and such a judgment was erroneous. But what is that occasional interference with what is perhaps abstract justice as compared with the inconvenience—the disastrous inconvenience—of having each question subject to being re-argued and the dealings of mankind rendered doubtful by reason of different decisions, so that in truth and in fact there would be no real final court of appeal." A decision of the House of Lords must be followed by all other Courts. A decision of the Court of Appeal must be followed by all the lower Courts.*

By the Appellate Jurisdiction Act, 1876, it is enacted that no appeal can be heard in the House of Lords unless at least three *Law Lords* are present. These Law Lords are either life members of the House specially appointed to hear appeals, or former holders of high judicial office who have been made peers. In practice (though in theory any member of the House, lawyer or not, may be present and vote) only the Law Lords and the former judges take part. Judgment depends upon a majority vote.

When, as may happen, the votes are equal, that is regarded as a dismissal of the appeal. This happened, for instance, in *Paquin* v. *Beauclerk* (H.L. 1906), where it was held that a married woman, who in fact has authority from her husband to deal with tradesmen as his agent, does not bind her separate estate, whether present or after-acquired. This is so even though the tradesmen may be unaware of her agency, or, indeed, of her marriage. Votes in the House of Lords being equal for the plaintiff who appealed and for the defendant who responded, the Lord Chancellor said : "My Lords, I find among the precedents the record : 'It being moved to reverse the judgments or decrees complained of, the same was objected to, and inasmuch as the votes were equal, two for reversing and two for affirming, thereupon, according to the ancient rule of law *semper præsumitur pro*

---

* Doubtless this is at times irksome. As one High Court Judge expressed it : "No more unpleasant duty has to be performed by a judge than the duty of deciding a case in accordance with a previous decision of the Court which is binding on him but which he thinks, as applied to the facts of the case before him, is both unreasonable and unjust. That is the task I have before me."

*negante,** the question for reversal was determined in the negative;
therefore the judgment or decree complained of was affirmed and
the appeal dismissed.' There is a note that costs are never given
in such a case. I propose to your Lordships that that rule be
adopted in this case."

7. *Barristers and Solicitors.* In the development of division of
labour in legal matters, there has come about a separation between the lawyers who come into contact with the general public
and those who concentrate upon the work of advocacy. A man
or woman can change from barrister to solicitor (attorney), or
from solicitor to barrister, but cannot be both. The solicitor
alone, like the Stock Exchange broker, comes into contact with
his lay clients; the barrister, like the Stock Exchange jobber, is
commissioned by the solicitor, and is not approached by the
person whose cause he pleads. The solicitor, indeed, does work
for his clients quite unconnected with action in Court. He is
their business factotum; he draws up their agreements, makes
their wills, settles their marriage portions.

The solicitor's branch of the legal profession is under the control of the Incorporated Law Society; and this Society has done
much in recent years to raise the standard of those placed upon
the roll of solicitors of the High Court. And the dread penalty
of being "struck off the rolls" is an effective curb upon the
predatory projects of a solicitor who might be tempted. The
would-be solicitor serves an apprenticeship—"takes out articles,"
that is, with a firm of solicitors; and he must pass a series of
quite searching examinations. The law relating to solicitors is
now carefully codified and made easily accessible in the Solicitors
Act, 1932. The Act sets out clearly the conditions of admission
and enrolment of solicitors; the conditions under which a
solicitor may be struck off the roll, or possibly restored to it; the
qualification for admission with a full account of the examinations
to be passed; and the privileges and monopolies to be reserved
to solicitors.

The Act is obtainable at 1s. from the Stationery Office.

The would-be barrister has a less arduous journey to traverse
before he is "called to the Bar" and allowed the privilege of
advocating causes before all English Courts, even the most
august. He eats six dinners a term for twelve terms (three years,
that is) and passes a few not exacting examinations. Now, as
formerly, whether or not the Masters of the Inn will admit him

* Till something convinces us to the contrary, we must say "No."

as a student and ultimately "call" him or her, is the important matter. The Benchers of each of the four Inns of Court are the autocratic controllers of the members. Even when "called," a barrister who fails to conform to the standard of professional etiquette may be "disbarred"; the Benchers of his Inn screen his name in hall together with a note of how he has fallen short of their requirements; and either permanently or, when his shortcoming has not been serious, for a limited time he is deprived of his privilege. When a barrister seeks to be enrolled as a solicitor, then he must ask to be disbarred—the disbarring being in such an event, of course, no mark of dishonour.

The old idea was that the barrister was in court ready and anxious to give help to embarrassed litigants. Fee was not the matter of weight with him; what concerned him was to make truth prevail. As still illustrative of this old idea, a barrister cannot sue for fees due to him for services rendered in the ordinary course of his professional duties. It seems, however, that he can prove in a bankruptcy for a debt due to him.

Judges, both High Court Judges and County Court Judges, are recruited solely from among the barristers.

NOTE ON THE COURTS

The Supreme Court of Judicature (Consolidation) Act, 1925, establishes as the High Court of Justice the three divisions of judges, the *Chancery Division* (of which the Lord Chancellor is President), the *King's Bench Division* (of which the Lord Chief Justice is President), and the *Probate, Divorce, and Admiralty Division* (of which the head is the President). The judges (puisne judges) are called Justices of the High Court; they are addressed in court as "Your Lordship."

The *Judicial Committee of the Privy Council* (which is in practice composed of the same members as the *House of Lords* as a Court) is the Supreme Court of Appeal for ecclesiastical causes.*

---

* A decision in 1932, approving of a scheme involving the demolition of St. Mary's in Charing Cross Road, is noteworthy for a vigorous attack upon an attempt to influence decisions. Lord Atkin said—

"Each of your Lordships has received a document, signed by the vicar and churchwardens of St. Mary's, of a most improper nature, because it refers to this scheme which is *sub judice*, and it concludes by saying: 'We look to you as an honourable member of the Final Court of Appeal to use your influence to quash this proposed demolition.' Nothing can be more improper than that. I cannot understand how any educated people can put their hands to a document which suggests to members of a Court of Justice, in advance, that they should use their influence to secure a particular result; and it is still more offensive if the suggestion is that honourable conduct requires that to be done."

THE EXISTING COURTS

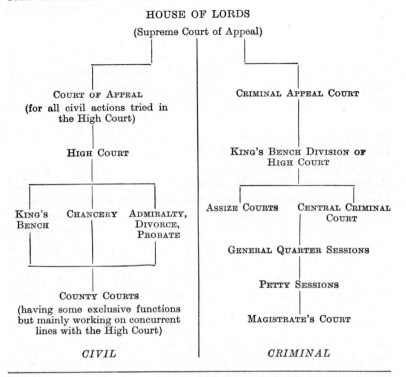

HOUSE OF LORDS
(Supreme Court of Appeal)

COURT OF APPEAL
(for all civil actions tried in
the High Court)

HIGH COURT

KING'S BENCH   CHANCERY   ADMIRALTY, DIVORCE, PROBATE

COUNTY COURTS
(having some exclusive functions
but mainly working on concurrent
lines with the High Court)

CIVIL

CRIMINAL APPEAL COURT

KING'S BENCH DIVISION OF HIGH COURT

ASSIZE COURTS   CENTRAL CRIMINAL COURT

GENERAL QUARTER SESSIONS

PETTY SESSIONS

MAGISTRATE'S COURT

CRIMINAL

NOTES. 1. (*a*) The *House of Lords* as the Supreme Court of Appeal is not the House of Lords as a House of Parliament. As the Supreme Court it consists solely of the Lord Chancellor, members of the House who have held high judicial office, together with specially appointed Appeal Judges (seven Lords of Appeal in Ordinary).

(*b*) The Court of Appeal contains six permanent members (the Master of the Rolls and five Lords Justices), together with the heads of the three divisions of the High Court and the Lords of Appeal in Ordinary.

2. The superior Courts exercise control, where necessary, over the inferior Courts by means of the writs—

(*a*) of *certiorari*, whereby proceedings are called for to be reviewed and if necessary quashed;

(*b*) of *mandamus*, whereby a court is commanded to do justice in specified matters;

(*c*) of *prohibition*, whereby a court is forbidden to do something not within its jurisdiction;

(*d*) of *error*, whereby an error in point of law, apparent on the record, is rectified.

The writs issue from the King's Bench Court and are prerogative writs, issued, that is, at the discretion of the Court.

3. The County Courts were established in 1846 with the design of making justice cheaper.

4. The Criminal Appeal Court was established in 1907. Very rarely, and only on the certificate of the Attorney-General that an important question of law is involved, an appeal lies to the House of Lords.

The Judicial Committee is also the Supreme Court of Appeal from the Empire. An appeal lies of right where certain conditions are fulfilled, a value of £500 in dispute usually being one. In other cases special leave, either from the Court below or from the Privy Council itself, must be obtained. The Judicial Committee will intervene in criminal cases only when there has been a serious error in the administration of justice, or a serious error in a judge's interpretation. Thus, it intervened (in *R.* v. *Knowles*, A.C. 1930) where the judge had overlooked the possibility that an alleged accident causing death might not have been murder but only manslaughter. In 1833 the Judicial Committee, till then a varying and indefinite one, of the Privy Council was given a statutory form. It was to consist of members who held, or had held, high judicial office. Four paid members, Law Lords having a life title, were appointed in 1871. These, with the Lord Chancellor, form in effect the panel from which the judges of the Supreme Court of Appeal for all the King's lands beyond the seas, and all Ecclesiastical Courts, are selected. The four are also "Lords of Appeal in Ordinary" who, again with the Lord Chancellor, constitute the House of Lords in its function as Supreme Court of Appeal from home courts.

The form of judgment in the Judicial Committee is a curious one. It is not a decision, but is humble advice to the King; and, though many judges may form the Court, one opinion only is given. In accordance with the advice, an Order in Council affirms or reverses the judgment against which appeal has been made.

RULES IN CRIMINAL PROCEDURE

1. Guilt must be established beyond reasonable doubt. The anxiety shown in English law that no man shall be punished for a crime, until the fact of his having committed it has been fully established, was admirably shown in the appeal case *Rex* v. *Hart* (Court of Criminal Appeal, 1932). The Court allowed the appeal and quashed the conviction of the prisoner on the grounds that the evidence he brought forward was not challenged, and was able to support an alibi. The Lord Chief Justice said, "In support of the alibi raised by the defence various witnesses were called. A remarkable feature of the case was that three of the witnesses for the defence were not cross-examined. If the jury accepted their evidence it appeared to be a physical impossibility that the appellant could have been at the spot at the time of the assault.

In the opinion of the Court if, on a crucial part of the case, the prosecution intended to ask the jury to disbelieve the evidence of a witness, it was right and proper that that witness should be challenged in the box, or that it should be made plain while the witness was in the box that the evidence of that witness was not accepted."

2. It is a rule of English law that no person can be placed in peril twice for the same offence; it is a good defence to a criminal charge that the person charged has formerly been acquitted or convicted on that same charge. Therefore it is probably, that the Criminal Appeal Act makes no provision for a new trial, a deficiency sometimes lamented as a defect. Thus in *R. v. Dyson* (C.C.A. 1908), a father was found by a jury guilty of the manslaughter of his infant child. The evidence showed that he had injured its skull more than a year before the death, and had inflicted later injuries. The trial judge directed the jury that, if they thought the earlier injuries had accelerated the death, they could find the prisoner guilty of manslaughter.

This was a misdirection. For, as the Chief Justice said when appeal was made: "Whatever one may think of the merits of such a rule of law, it is still undoubtedly the law of the land that no person can be convicted of manslaughter where the death does not occur within a year and a day after the injury was inflicted. For in that event the death must be attributed to some other cause." That is, in spite of the advance in "medical science," which can prolong life far beyond what was once possible after fatal injuries, the old definition of manslaughter still holds, and may prevent deserved punishment. It clearly happened in this particular case.

The Criminal Appeal Act certainly allows the Court to dismiss the appeal when, though the particular point raised might be decided in the appellant's favour, no substantial wrong has been done. But the C.J. referred to the decision of the Appeal Court in *Makin v. Attorney-General of New South Wales*, 1894—

"Their Lordships do not think it can properly be said that there has been no substantial wrong or miscarriage of justice, where on a point material to the guilt or innocence of the accused the jury have been invited by the judge to consider in arriving at their verdict matters which ought not to have been submitted to them." And he added: "It is to be regretted that the Legislature, when passing the Criminal Appeal Act, did not empower the Court to order a new trial. For the present is a case in which it is eminently desirable that such a power should exist. But they did not think fit to do so, and we have no choice but to allow the appeal."

3. *The Plea of "Not Guilty."* Why a judge usually advises a prisoner to withdraw his confession of guilt and to plead "not guilty" is the humane reason that a thorough and impartial investigation into what took place may put the prisoner's conduct in more favourable light. For the same act may, in varying circumstances, range through all degrees of crime, may even constitute no crime whatever; the killing of a man is at one time a murder, at another a more or less culpable manslaughter, at another a justifiable, even a meritorious, homicide. A man may believe himself guilty where the judge, weighing the matter, believes him innocent. In *R.* v. *Plummer* (K.B. 1902) one of three defendants, charged with conspiracy, pleaded "guilty." His co-defendants pleaded "not guilty," and were acquitted. Appeal against the conviction of the first defendant was made and was successful. No man can conspire alone. The acquittal of his fellows showed his belief in his and their guilt to be unfounded. So, too, it is the duty of an advocate to make out the possible case for his client. Even if, as the expression goes, he believes that client guilty, he must do his best for acquittal. For he might be mistaken in his belief

NEW TRIAL

In civil cases—not criminal cases—a Court of Appeal may direct a new trial.

The reasons for granting a new trial comprise—

(a) *Verdict against Evidence.* No reasonable body of persons, basing their conclusions upon the evidence given at the trial, could find such a verdict. In suitable cases, instead of ordering a new trial, the superior Court will itself give the remedy sought. This happened, for example, in *Croker* v. *Croker* (*South, co-respondent*, C.A. 1932). The case raised the question whether the Court of Appeal, after finding that the verdict was against the weight of evidence and that adultery between the respondent and corespondent had in fact been proved, could at once make a *decree nisi*, or whether the power of the Court was limited to ordering a new hearing of the petition. The judge in the Divorce Court, in dismissing the petition, said that, but for his loyalty to the jury's verdict, he should have granted the petition. "In the present case," said the Master of the Rolls, "the evidence practically compelled a verdict in one way; and, as it was laid down in the Court of Appeal in *Rugg-Gunn* v. *Rugg-Gunn and Archer* (C.A. 1931), that parties to a matrimonial suit had now no inherent right to insist on having trial by a jury, it seemed unnecessary to send the case back for a new hearing. The Court would be failing in its duty if it did not give the relief which ought to have been given below."

(*b*) *Improper Damages*. The damages awarded are so far in excess or so far below what are reasonable that it is clear the jury must have taken into account factors not relevant: "Judges have no right," said Lord Justice James in *Phillips* v. *L.S.W. Rly.*, "to overrule the verdict of a jury merely because they take a different view but, for the sake of justice, they must send the matter for consideration by another jury if it is evident that certain topics have not been taken into account" (Q.B. 1879).

(*c*) *Compromise by the Jury*. For example, it may be evident, from the smallness of the award, that the jury has avoided its duty of deciding the real questions, and has agreed to "split the difference."

(*d*) *Misconduct of the Jury*. For example, a member's conversing with one of the parties would probably invalidate a verdict against the other party.

(*e*) *Discharge of Jury by Judge*. For example, a rule of practice is that, in an accident case, the jury shall not be told that the defendant is insured. A judge has discretion to discharge the jury at the expense of the party whose advocate has transgressed the rule.

(*f*) *Misdirection by the Judge, Improper Rejection or Acceptance of Evidence by Him*. These are the points upon which reliance is most often placed.

LAPSE OF TIME

(*Vigilantibus Non Dormientibus*, For the watchers, not for the sleepers.)

We are to vindicate our rights speedily, lest time should set an obstacle against us. Laws exist to protect the rights of those who are awake to those rights, not for those asleep to them. Unless an aggrieved party invokes the law without excessive delay, his legal remedies are barred. For lapse of time means that possible witnesses of what actually happened are no longer available, that imagination cannot be discriminated from recollection, that all manner of transactions involving many parties have followed upon the transaction now challenged.

DEFENCE OF LIMITATIONS

Mill wrote: "It may seem hard that a claim, originally just, should be defeated by a mere lapse of time; but there is a time after which (even looking at the individual case, and without regard to the general effect on the security of possessors), the balance of hardship turns the other way. With the injustices of men, as with the convulsions and disasters of nature, the longer they remain unrepaired, the greater becomes the obstacles to repairing them, arising from the aftergrowths which have to be torn up or broken through."*

PERIODS OF LIMITATION

We have, therefore—we are almost bound to have—definitely limited periods within which action must be brought: it is for the well-being of the State that contention shall cease (*interest reipublicae ut sit finis litium*). The periods, as one would anticipate, differ with the nature of the right to be vindicated. An *action for slander*, for defamation by word of mouth, that is, must be brought *within two years*; what we really heard, even a week ago, may differ materially from what we think we heard; when two years have passed since the witnesses heard the words complained of, the deepest impression must have been nearly smoothed away. So, too, the Maritime Conventions Act of 1911 imposed a limiting period of two years in respect of claims for damages at sea; in view of the fact that possible witnesses might belong to widely separated parts of the world, such limitation was probably imperative. The difficulty, again, of determining who first put a new idea into abiding form has led Parliament, in the Copyright Act of 1911, to make the limiting period *three years*.

In contrast to these periods of less than the usual six years, there is the longer period, when the cause of action is evidenced

---

* Perhaps *Harnett* v. *Fisher* (H.L. 1927) affords an illustration of such hardship. The defendant, a doctor, had certified Harnett's insanity; Harnett was upon the certificate confined as a lunatic for nine years; he escaped and some months after brought an action for negligence against the doctor. The jury found that Harnett was not insane when so certified, and awarded damages. The judge decided, however—and his decision was upheld in the superior Courts—that the action was statute-barred. The period of limitation began when the certificate was granted, since Harnett was not then insane. He, therefore, had had a right (though obviously his confinement prevented his exercising the right) of action for longer than the statutory six years.

by a deed or a sealed writing, when there has been made a *Specialty Contract*, as it is called. Thus, the dividends of a company, when declared, are debts due to the shareholders. The holders of shares, the certificate of which is under the seal of the company, are not barred from bringing a claim until *twenty years* have elapsed. The general period remains as it was fixed by the Statute of James I (1624), one of *six years* : after that period has elapsed, the right to bring an action is "statute-barred."

It may seem an unfair method of defence to base it upon lapse of time, to penalise a plaintiff for his forbearance. No one, therefore, is obliged to take advantage of the Statutes any more than a person sued in relation to a bet is obliged to take advantage of the excuse given to him by the Gaming Acts. In either case the statute must be specially pleaded. That is, the defendant must definitely state at the outset that he relies upon his statutory defence. If not so pleaded, it will be understood that the defence is waived : trial will proceed as if the defence did not exist. For *The Statutes of Limitation*—with the one exception of those affecting rights to land—are rules of the Court only. They do not affect the rights but only the means of enforcing them. Thus, a right under contract may be "barred by statute." But subsequent conduct by a possible defendant may enable an action to be brought. The right remains. Thus, money paid by a debtor to his creditor, without the debtor's appropriation to a specified debt, may be appropriated by the creditor to a statute-barred debt. (See page 908.)

SIX YEARS' LIMITATION

The general period in actions of tort and contract (otherwise than by sealed writing) is six years from the time when the right to bring an action began (Limitation Act, 1623).

The following causes of actions are exceptions—

1. Assault and false imprisonment : *four years*.

2. Slander, when the words spoken are actionable in themselves : *two years*.

The limitation does not begin to run when the possible plaintiff, at the time when the right to bring action arose, is either *under age or of unsound mind*.

Nor does it begin if the defendant is beyond seas and, therefore, outside the jurisdiction of the Court. But it does begin where the defendant comes within the jurisdiction for ever so short a time, even though the plaintiff is unaware of the fact.

EXTENDING THE PERIOD

Part payment of a debt, or of interest upon it, revives the cause of action for debt; and the period of limitation begins from such payment. So also will an "acknowledgment" operate to extend the period. In *Spencer* v. *Hemmerde* (H.L. 1922) it was held that the words, "It is not that I don't want to pay but that I cannot do so," constituted an acknowledgment sufficient to prevent the Statute from debarring the claim. For the Lord Chancellor said: "It is settled law (1) that a written promise to pay a debt, given within six years before action, is sufficient to take the case out of the statute of James I; (2) that such a promise is implied in a simple acknowledgment of the debt; but (3) that where an acknowledgment is coupled with other expressions (such as a promise to pay at a future time, or on a condition, or an absolute refusal to pay, it is for the Court to say whether those other expressions are sufficient to qualify or negative the implied promise to pay." Note that (*a*) if one of several executors acknowledges a testator's debt, that is enough; for the executors form a unit; (*b*) the acknowledgment must be in writing; (*c*) a letter stated to be written "without prejudice" cannot be brought forward as evidence of an acknowledgment.

PERIOD FOR MORTGAGE DEBT

As a result of the extinguishing of rights to land, when twelve years have elapsed without challenge of a "squatter's right," the limitation to a debt upon mortgage of land is *twelve years* (Real Property Limitation Act, 1874).

LEGACY AND INTESTACY

Any proceeding to recover a legacy must be brought within *twelve years*; but to recover the personal estate of an intestate the period is *twenty years*.

PERIOD FOR LAND

The period of limitation for the recovery of land is twelve years from the time when the possessor first trespassed upon the land. When the period has elapsed, the right of the former owner of the land is extinguished (Real Property Limitation Act, 1874).

PUBLIC AUTHORITIES

The Public Authorities Protection Act, 1893, provides a special limitation of *six months* in regard to any act done in carrying out an Act of Parliament or of any public duty.

AFFILIATION ORDER

Application for an affiliation order cannot be made after *twelve months* from the birth of the child, unless the putative father has, meantime, paid for the child's maintenance.

LIMITATIONS IN CRIMINAL PROSECUTIONS

Lapse of time rarely affects a criminal prosecution. But limitations are prescribed in—

1. *Treason.* Within three years from commission, unless the treason was an actual plot to kill the King or was committed abroad.

2. *Riot.* (Under the Riot Act, 1715, whenever an unlawful assembly of *twelve* or more persons do not disperse within an hour after a J.P. has read a proclamation in terms of the Act, they become guilty of a felony, punishable with penal servitude for life). Within twelve months.

3. *Carnally knowing a girl between thirteen and sixteen.* Within twelve months.

4. *Offences punishable on summary conviction.* Within six months.

CLAIMS UNDER WORKMEN'S COMPENSATION ACT

The Workmen's Compensation Act, 1925, requires that a claim be made within six months from the occurrence of the accident, unless the failure to make it is caused by mistake or other reasonable cause. It was held in the Court of Appeal (*Templeton* v. *Coupe & Sons, Ltd.*, 1932) that if a workman honestly believed an accident not to be serious, but it proved serious, there was reasonable cause.

LAYMAN AND LAWYER

In the English legal system the co-operation of the ordinary individual and the expert in law began early. It is still a striking feature of our system. In the administration of criminal justice particularly, the tendency is growing for all but the most serious crimes to be adjudicated upon by Justices of the Peace, either in summary manner or upon indictment at the Quarter Sessions, rather than by the High Court Judges at the Assizes or at the Central Criminal Court. In civil cases the jury is still important, though now and again attacked as being a cumbrous survival of old custom.

Two cases of 1932, in both of which the jury awarded damages for injuries sustained, and in both of which the Court of Appeal set the jury's verdict aside, illustrate admirably one aspect of co-operation that exists in our law between judge and jury. The determination of fact is for the jury; the statement of law is for the judge. The jury, men and women whose sound sense and knowledge of the world will guide them aright, determine questions of fact. The judge, expert in law, determines questions of law.

The *verdict*, the statement of what the jury has found to be the truth, is the basis upon which the judge enunciates the relevant rules of law.

The verdict may be a *general verdict*, disposing of the whole question before the Court: in a criminal case, the jury declares that the accused is "guilty" or "not guilty." It may be a *special verdict*, the jury answering a number of specific questions put by the judge. The judge, though he almost invariably does, is not bound to accept the jury's verdict. Moreover, the judge may or, rather, ought to decline to submit the case to the jury when the evidence brought forward is too flimsy to support the case. It was put thus in *Ryder* v. *Wombwell*, the well-known case that settled the law concerning legal necessaries: "In so far as the question is one of fact, it must be determined by a jury, subject no doubt to the control of the Court. This may set aside the verdict and submit the question to the decision of another jury. But there is, in every case, a preliminary question, which is one of law, whether there is any evidence on which the jury can properly find a verdict for the party on whom rests the burden of proof. If there is not, the judge ought to withdraw the question from the jury." The opinion of the judge may, indeed, be wrong. And the Court of Appeal may order a new trial so that the question may be submitted to a jury. The Court of Appeal did this in the notorious "Helen of Troy" case (*Place* v. *Searle*, K.B. 1932). The possibility of error on the part of the judge is, however, much less serious than to leave to the jury the power that might be used in a most arbitrary manner. The Courts are, it must be emphasised, reluctant to disturb a jury's verdict. It is only rarely that it is set aside, and only when it is clear that it is against the weight of evidence or is given under a mistake of law. Justice to one litigant then compels action.

DRAWBACKS OF JURY SYSTEM

Some control of a jury's verdicts there must be. For we are bound to recognise that the jury system has some unavoidable drawbacks. Admirable it is in many ways. The sturdy independence of juries has long been the subject's defence against officialism. And the requirement of unanimity where a prisoner is charged with a grave crime, would seem to give assurance that no innocent man can be found guilty of a crime at all serious. Still, a jury is, from its nature, swayed by matters not relevant. Such matters are apt to affect people who are not skilful in discriminating. Thus, Soames in the *Forsyte Saga*, when wondering what the result of the libel action would be, carefully sized up the attractions of his daughter, Fleur, as one of the witnesses. How would she in the witness box appeal to a jury? Would she make a man of sentiment, perhaps even a woman of sentiment, feel incapable of recording a verdict against so charming a creature? In particular, a jury is apt to be unduly biased towards the individual and against the impalpable company or local authorities. It is, the members of the jury instinctively feel, another instance of David against Goliath, the weak individual against the powerful corporation. Indeed, it is hard to feel sympathetic towards an abstract idea; and when it is a company against an individual, the jury is likely to favour the individual. The balance is weighted in favour of the visible person.

Thus, in *Jones* v. *London County Council* (K.B. 1932), the plaintiff was awarded damages by a jury for injury through an accident at school. A game was being played under the supervision of the drill instructor; the plaintiff hurt his knee; and damages were awarded against the London County Council. The Court of Appeal agreed that the verdict should be set aside. The judgment ran: "The infant plaintiff has undoubtedly suffered serious injury, but it does not follow that he is entitled to compensation. To be so entitled he must show some breach of legal duty on the part of the defendant. Now, the London County Council has put physical exercises under the charge of an instructor of twenty years' experience. When a game has been played for twenty years without any serious accidents, it cannot be said to be negligence to allow the game to be played."

HALL v. BROOKLANDS (K.B. 1932)

The second case was one where the seriously injured plaintiff must have excited the sympathetic feelings of the jury. A spectator at Brooklands was badly hurt when a racing car leaped from the track into the spectators. Was the Brooklands Company liable? When they invited him to attend, when they took payment for him to attend, did they thereby undertake to make the attendance safe for him? The Court of Appeal thought not. Lord Justice Scrutton's judgment gives an illuminating account of the principles involved. This was a case where the spectator of his own accord encountered whatever risks were to be met. "Spectators at Lord's run risks of being hit by a cricket ball, spectators at football matches run similar risks, both from the ball and from collision with the players. Spectators who obtained admission to golf courses run risks of the players slicing balls, which might hit them with considerable velocity and damage. The spectators at Brooklands were absolutely safe in the greater part of the grounds where they could watch the racing. But, naturally, they liked to get as near the racing as they could, and they placed themselves along the railing. If there are any incidents in a play which are dangerous unless carefully performed, especially if they involve the use of firearms, then it is an implied term in the contract between the playgoers and the other party that such other party will use reasonable care and diligence to see that such incidents are performed without risks to a playgoer. He is not, however, liable for any accident which he could not have prevented by the exercise of reasonable care or supervision. The duty of the invitor towards the invitee is to use reasonable care to prevent damage about which he knows or ought to know. In view of the facts, there was no evidence to justify the verdict of the jury. In view of the pace of motors and of motor racing at the present day, I cannot think that there was a failure to use reasonable care or that it was negligence not to inform spectators that a car running at the rate of 100 miles per hour might leave the track." The verdict and judgment for the plaintiff was set aside, and judgment was entered for the defendant company.

OBJECTIONS TO THE JURY SYSTEM

The writer of a vigorous letter to the Editor of the *Times* puts the matter very effectively—

Sir,—You say in your leading article this morning—

It has always been recognized that proceedings for libel and slander, malicious prosecutions, and actions in which fraud is alleged, are unsuited to any form of abbreviated procedure which would withdraw them from a jury's cognizance.

The grounds of this opinion are not very clear to me. Why should the functions of a jury be specially valuable in proceedings of the three classes you describe? In libel actions the verdict of the jury is notoriously undependable. In cases where fraud is alleged, if the fraud is at all complicated, the average juror soon completely loses track of the argument. Having served as a juryman myself, I have long been convinced that the jury system is a bad one; and that the common opinion of its merits is a superstition. So far as I can see, there is only one thing to be said for it—namely, that if the law ever becomes too flagrantly out of harmony with public opinion, juries may refuse to convict. But this, of course, applies only to criminal cases.

The principal objections to the jury system as I see it, are these—

1. The average man (or woman) is totally unable to retain the arguments or the evidence in his head; and equally unable to select what is important from the mass of conflicting material suddenly thrown at him. The natural capacity to do so is extremely rare; and the juryman has no training whatever to equip him for so difficult a task. Nor is he assisted (so far as my experience goes) with any documents. I sat on the jury in a complicated and prolonged action a few years ago. We had nothing to help us—not even a copy of the pleadings. I was told subsequently that it was most undesirable for juries to have copies of the pleadings. Why? Because they might get even worse tied up with the pleadings than without them! As the case dragged on, the Judge and the counsel were supplied with verbatim reports of the evidence given on the preceding days. Not the jury. Again, why not? Not, I was told, because of the expense, but because we should be even more muddled if we had the evidence to refer to than we were already. I have no doubt that this was quite true. But it is surely a *reductio ad absurdum* of the whole system.

2. The formation of opinion by a jury, as expressed in its verdict, is the result of sentiment rather than of reason. Discussion in the jury-room can take the most farcical turn. There is always the amateur lawyer, concerned to confuse the issue of fact; the bored juryman; the inconceivably stupid juryman. The issue may easily turn on the presence of one man with a stronger personality than the rest.

3. These weaknesses of the jury have a most debasing effect upon the conduct of a case. Instead of presenting a rational argument for dispassionate consideration, counsel are tempted to employ every tawdry device of rhetoric and theatricalism to impress the jury. These devices often defeat themselves by their own crudity. But they are responsible for much popular mistrust of the Courts. Skilfully used by a clever advocate they may pervert the course of justice.

4. There is also an argument against the jury system from the juryman's own point of view. It is very difficult to secure exemption. I have tried to do so, without success, on the perfectly true ground that I could not afford the time away from my business. It is, in fact, an almost intolerable nuisance to be obliged to desert one's proper work in order to waste days sitting in Court waiting one's turn to settle (more likely than not) some petty squabble which no man of sense would have allowed to get as far as the High Court. For the whole of the week for which he is summoned he can make no business engagements; he must arrange in advance for his work to be done by others. If the purposes of justice were being really served by his inconvenience he would make light of it; but not if he has come to believe that the whole thing is a farce.

I am, Sir, &c.,

GEOFFREY FABER.

24 Russell Square, W.C.1.

COUNTY COURT PROCEDURE

COUNTY COURTS HAVE POWER

1. To decide on claims for damages up to £100.
2. To exercise chancery jurisdiction where the property involved is not over £500.
3. To determine claims under Workmen's Compensation Acts.
4. To exercise bankruptcy jurisdiction.

But, unless parties agree to submit to its jurisdiction, the County Court cannot entertain actions for *libel, slander, seduction,* or *breach of promise.* That is, though the County Courts administer exactly the same law as the High Court does, its jurisdiction is limited (*a*) in regard to the amount of money involved, (*b*) in regard to the presumed difficulty of the law involved.

COUNTY COURT PROCEEDINGS

The information below is given in essence in the "default summons" that follows. This summons is, indeed, an earnest and successful attempt to explain to the defendant what steps he must take if he wishes to contest the claim, what courses are open to him if he admits the claim whether wholly or in part.

1. Notice of intention to defend is requisite within eight days from the personal service of the summons; the defendant will then receive due notice of the day of trial.

2. No notice being given, the plaintiff is at liberty, at any time within two months from the service of the summons, to "enter judgment" and to "proceed to execution"; the entering of judgment implies that the Court has turned the ordinary debt into a "judgment debt," and the plaintiff now has the right of "Execution" by way of—

(*a*) *Obtaining a fieri facias (fi. fa.* is the usual abbreviation), a writ addressed to the sheriff ordering him to take and sell such goods of the debtor as will cover the debt. The sheriff may seize what goods he chooses either as being in effect money (as bank-notes, cheques, and so on), or as being most readily saleable. But he must not take the clothes or bedding of the debtor or his family, nor his tools up to £5. Certain claims have preference over *fi. fa.*—

(i) Before the goods are removed, debts due to the Crown by way of taxes (to the amount of one year's arrears) must be paid.

(ii) Rent due to the landlord (to the amount of one year's arrears) must be paid.

The effect of such a writ as regards the transfer of property in the goods is explained in Section 26 of The Sale of Goods Act: "A writ of *fieri facias* or other writ of execution against goods shall bind the property in the goods of the execution debtor as from the time when the writ is delivered to the sheriff to be executed; and it shall be the duty of the sheriff, without fee, to endorse upon the back of the writ the hour, day, month, and year when he received it; Provided that no such writ shall prejudice the title to such goods acquired by any person in good faith and for valuable consideration." That is, the judgment debtor if he acts promptly can sell his goods and the buyer gets a good title. But the knowledge of the buyer that an unexecuted writ is in the hands of the sheriff destroys his title; for he has not then bought in good faith.

In his execution of the writ of *fieri facias* the sheriff is under some restrictions—

(i) "An Englishman's house is his castle": the sheriff is not justified in breaking any outer door or window in order to effect an entrance. The matter is different when it is a case of arresting a felon, or one against whom a warrant has been issued. Then, when the sheriff (or other officer) has given notice of his business and has demanded admission "in the name of the law," he is justified in obtaining entry as best he can.

(ii) Apparently, if he has reason to suspect that the debtor has removed his goods to another's house, the sheriff can follow them there. But if the goods are not there he is liable for trespass.

Or the creditor who has obtained judgment for his debt may—

(b) *Charge the real estate of the debtor*, by registering, under the Land Charges Act, 1925, a writ of *Elegit*. By this writ of *Elegit* the creditor is given possession of the real property until such time as his debt has been satisfied from the profits of the land seized.

Or he may—

(c) *Obtain a garnishee order*, whereby he secures payment to himself of debts due to the judgment debtor (as, for instance, by his banker). The debts that can be attached by the garnishee order are in general such as the judgment debtor could have sued for. But the following cannot be attached—

(i) Money in the hands of the Government, such as deposits in the Post Office Savings Bank;

(ii) wages;

(iii) half-pay of Naval or Military or Air Force officers;

(iv) pensions.

Or he may—

(*d*) *Make the debtor a bankrupt* if the judgment debt is £50 or over and is not paid.

Or he may—

(*e*) *Obtain a charging order* upon stocks and shares owned by the debtor.

DEBTOR ACKNOWLEDGING CLAIM

The debtor who knows that he owes the money claimed is faced with several possibilities—

1. If he pays before the summons is issued he pays only the amount of the debt. The fact that he has had a solicitor's letter is immaterial; the solicitor cannot charge the debtor.

2. If he pays the debt and the costs indicated on the summons within eight days, he avoids further costs; and, even if he has given notice to defend, he may at any time before the action is called on for trial pay the debt and costs up to date, thereby incurring no further costs.

3. If he allows judgment to go against him by default he will be required to pay, in addition to the amount indicated in the summons, *half* the hearing fee. An order will be made that he should pay at once or by instalments. Though the Debtors Act, 1869, abolished imprisonment for debt in general, it retained power to commit where the County Court judge is satisfied that the debtor could pay in accordance with such an order, but has neglected to do so. Strictly speaking, this is imprisonment for contempt of court rather than for debt. The maximum period is six weeks, and the imprisonment does not extinguish the debt.

DEBTOR ACKNOWLEDGING PART OF CLAIM

The debtor admitting part only of the claim should pay to the Registrar's office the amount he admits with costs *proportionate* to the amount. Unless the plaintiff succeeds at the action in obtaining a further amount no other payment is due.

DEFENDANT DISPUTING PLAINTIFF'S CLAIM

The defendant intending to dispute the claim must—

1. Give the required notice of his intention.

2. Five clear days before the trial give to the Registrar of the Court particulars of his defence.

In the Lambeth County Court of Surrey

BETWEEN   JOSEPH SIMPSON   *Plaintiff,*

and

JAMES ALFRED THOMPSON   *Defendant.*

PARTICULARS OF PLAINTIFF'S CLAIM.

19..

		£	s.	d.
March 25.	To one Quarter's rent of the premises, No. 953 Faithful Road, West Norwood, Surrey, due from the Defendant to the Plaintiff under an Agreement dated the 29th day of September, 19.., made between the Plaintiff of the one part and the Defendant of the other part	10	10	0

Dated this 14th day of May, 19..

Yours, etc.,

JONES & ROBINSONS,

784 Essex Street,

Strand,

London, W.C.,

Plaintiff's Solicitors who will accept
service of all notices on his behalf.

To the *Registrar of the Court*
and to the Defendant.

Copies enough of these particulars to give to the plaintiff (or plaintiffs) and one for the Court are needed. Where the claim exceeds £5, the defendant may if he chooses have the action tried by a jury. If he does so choose he must give to the Registrar ten clear days' notice before the day fixed for trial, and pay eight shillings as the fees of the jury. The plaintiff also may obtain a jury on the same conditions.

POSSIBLE GROUNDS OF DISPUTE

1. The defendant may have a set-off, an actual sum of money owing to him by the plaintiff, against the plaintiff's claim; particulars of such set-off must be delivered to the Registrar.

2. The defendant was under 21 when the debt was contracted, and the goods supplied were not necessaries.

3. The defendant was at the time of contracting the debt, or is now, a married woman.

4. The debt claimed is more than six years old; no acknowledgment of it has been made during the six years; nor has there been any part payment or payment of interest. That is, the defendant pleads the Statute of Limitations.

5. The defendant has been adjudicated bankrupt, and has thereby been discharged of all his debts including the plaintiff's.

6. The defendant has tendered to the plaintiff what is due, and he brings the amount tendered into Court.

7. An Act of Parliament or a principle of equity furnishes a defence.

WITNESSES AND DOCUMENTS

Where the defendant requires witnesses to be summoned or documents to be disclosed he makes applications to the Registrar, and the Registrar, upon payment of the proper fee, issues the necessary summonses or orders.

PAYMENT INTO COURT

Where a defendant admits liability but disputes the amount claimed as damages, he is at liberty to pay into Court what amount he chooses. The plaintiff is told of the payment and may accept it as full settlement, the defendant in that event paying the costs incurred by the plaintiff. If the plaintiff prefers to continue and if the Court awards him no further sum than what has been paid into Court, any costs incurred by the defendant subsequent to the paying in are paid by the plaintiff.

A COUNTY COURT JUDGMENT

A typical County Court judgment will illustrate much of what has been said. It is that of Judge Barnard Lailey, K.C., adjudicating in *Etheridge* v. *Pink* at the Bishop's Waltham County Court, and is reported in *The Law Journal* of 30th July, 1932—

JUDGMENT

The plaintiff brings this action alleging a nuisance to him in the use and enjoyment of his dwelling-house by noise and vibration caused by an oil engine installed and worked by the defendant to generate electricity for the purposes of a cinema, and claiming damages and an injunction.

The plaintiff's premises consist of a small six-roomed house, with scullery, etc., fronting to a narrow street in Bishop's Waltham known as Brook Street, with a smithy in the rear, in which he works in his trade as a blacksmith, and another detached building in which his wife carries on a day school. The premises are about an acre in extent, and include a garden and tennis ground. The rateable value of the whole is £27.

The defendant occupies as a cinema a hall on the opposite side of Brook Street, opening on to that street and also to the parallel High Street, and in a building standing some 40 ft. from the plaintiff's house and on the same side of Brook Street, he, in January, 1932, installed the engine complained of, which previously to that time was placed in or under the cinema. The engine is in use every weekday from 6 or 7 p.m. until 9.30 or 10.30 p.m. on days other than Saturday, and on Saturday from 6 p.m. to 10.45 or 11 p.m. with, on one occasion, a *matinee*.

Having heard the evidence for the plaintiff, I, at the request of the parties, viewed the *locus in quo*, and in the course of my inspection the engine was started and run at varying speeds, up to the maximum load. The parties expressed themselves as satisfied that I had full opportunity of hearing what happens.

When the engine was running it could be heard in all the rooms of the plaintiff's house and there was vibration to a slight extent. The question for determination is whether, within the principles established by the authorities, a nuisance has been created. In *Broder* v. *Saillard* (2 C.D.), Jessel, M.R., said: "The law is this, that a man is entitled to the comfortable enjoyment of his dwelling-house. If his neighbour makes such a noise as to interfere with the ordinary use and enjoyment of his dwelling-house, so as to cause *serious annoyance and disturbance* (the italics are mine) the occupier of the dwelling-house is entitled to be protected from it." Very similar language was used by Warrington, J., in *Rushmer* v. *Polsue*, 1906 (1 Ch.): "The question I have to consider is whether the defendants, by working the machine in question, seriously interfere with the comfort, physically, of the plaintiff and his family in the occupation of his house, according to the ordinary notions prevalent among reasonable English men and women." See also *Hussey* v. *Bailey* (11 T.L.R.), where Chitty, J., said: "The question is whether the alleged nuisance was of such a character as to materially interfere with the ordinary comfort of the plaintiff." It is not every act which is distasteful—and not unreasonably so—to a neighbour which amounts to an actionable wrong. Some inconveniences are part of the price one pays for living as a member of a civilised community, instead of on a desert island. In *Colls* v. *Home and Colonial Stores* (A.C. 1904), Lord Halsbury, L.C. observed that a dweller in towns cannot expect to enjoy as much freedom from noise as if he lived in the country, and Lord Selborne, L.C., pointed out with emphasis in *Gaunt* v. *Fynney* (8 Ch. App.), that the question of nuisance by noise is in every case one of degree. Those are the principles which have to be applied, and in considering a given case one has to take the surrounding circumstances into account, e.g. the character of the neighbourhood, the class of house affected, and so on.

At the outset of the hearing the defendant's solicitor stated that, whilst not admitting any nuisance, his client intended to make certain alterations in connection with the engine with a view to removing or minimising any cause of complaint, and that steps in that direction were being taken. I had no doubt that improvements were practicable, and at the close of the plaintiff's case the parties agreed that it was desirable for the hearing to stand adjourned until to-day to enable the proposed alterations to be carried out, as they have been.

I have to-day paid a second visit to the premises in company with the experts, and I am satisfied that there is no ground for complaint.

The question remains whether a nuisance existed when the action was commenced and brought to trial. If it did, I agree with Mr. Hughes that the remedial steps taken since, though they might effect the form of remedy, would not ordinarily prejudice the plaintiff as regards costs. But, applying the established principles and giving full consideration to the evidence and all

relevant circumstances, in particular the limited periods of the
day during which the engine was in use, I have come to the conclusion that the matters complained of fell short of an actionable
nuisance. The case is, however, near the line, the complaint was
not frivolous, and the defendant not pressing for costs, I think
justice will be met by the action being dismissed and the parties
being left to bear their own costs; and that is the order.

In view of my finding, I do not propose to call for any undertaking from the defendant, but if his arrangements, as they now
stand, should hereafter be so altered as to cause a nuisance, this
judgment will, of course, not preclude the plaintiff from coming
to the Court and obtaining any relief to which he may then be
entitled.

DEFAULT SUMMONS AND ORDINARY SUMMONS

Note that a *default summons* (of which an example is given) is
used by the plaintiff when a definite sum of money is due to him
from the defendant; an *ordinary summons* is used when the
amount to be paid by the defendant will be decided by the Court.
The former is a liquidated demand; the latter an unliquidated
claim, the amount of which will depend upon the event of the
trial.

In deciding which form to issue, the following points need consideration: 1. For the *Default Summons* personal service is
needed, and the date of trial is not fixed as it is in an *Ordinary
Summons*. 2. The *Default Summons* gives a right to the claimant
to sign final judgment for payment and costs (without further
proof of the debt than the affidavit he swore), unless within eight
days the defendant gives notice of an intention to defend the
action. Notice of defence is easily given, and may be given when
there is no real intention to defend and merely in order to delay
satisfaction of the claim. Notice is given by the defendant's signing the form at the foot of the summons, and posting the form so
signed to the judge.

On the whole, perhaps, an ordinary summons obtains the
speedier settlement.

The cheap method of obtaining justice in the County Court is
guarded by not permitting appeals except upon point of law.
The County Court judge, who hears the evidence and observes
the witnesses, decides upon the facts of the case. When he has
decided, these facts are the basis upon which the relative law
depends. He may be mistaken in applying the law to the facts.

This Paper marked " A " is the Paper referred to in the annexed affidavit.

" BY LEAVE OF THE REGISTRAR."

No. of Plaint O O 796

23.—*Default Summons under Sect. 86 of The County Courts Act, 1888.*

In the Lambeth County Court of Surrey,

holden at the Camberwell New Road, Camberwell.

BETWEEN   JOSEPH SIMPSON,   *Plaintiff.*
of 392 Conduit Street,
London,
Solicitor.

AND   JAMES ALFRED THOMPSON,   *Defendant.*
of 485 Thames Street,
Lambeth,
Electrician.

TAKE NOTICE, That unless within **Eight Days after the personal service of this Summons on you, inclusive of the day of such service,** you return to the Registrar of this Court at the Camberwell New Road, Camberwell, the Notice given below, dated and signed by yourself or your Solicitor, you will not afterwards be allowed to make any defence to the claim which the Plaintiff makes on you, as per margin, the particulars of which are

hereunto annexed; but the Plaintiff may, without giving any further proof in support of such Claim than the affidavit filed in Court herein, proceed to judgment and execution. If you return such notice to the Registrar within the time specified, the Registrar will send you by post notice of the day upon which the action will be tried. (*See* below.)

Dated this 14th day of May, 19..

	£	s.	d.
Claim . . .	10	10	0
Fee for Plaint .		13	0
Solicitor's Costs .	1	3	2
Total Amount of } Debt and Costs }	12	6	2

W. B. PRITCHARD, *Registrar.*

To the Defendant.

N.B.—SEE BACK.

[N.B.—This Summons must be served personally on the Defendant within a period of twelve months from the date thereof, or within such extended period as may be allowed.]

Hours of attendance at the Office of the Registrar, Camberwell New Road, Camberwell, from Ten till Four o'clock, except on Saturdays, when the Office will be closed at One o'clock.

Notice of Intention to Defend.   No. of Plaint O O 796

In the Lambeth County Court of Surrey,

holden at the Camberwell New Road, Camberwell.

*   SIMPSON   *v.**   THOMPSON

I intend to defend this Action.

Dates this   day of   19..

....(1) *Defendant.*

Address to which Notice of Trial is to be sent......................................

....

(2207)

If you pay the Debt and Costs, as per margin on the other side, into the Registrar's Office, before **the expiration of EIGHT Days from the date of service of this Summons, inclusive of the day of such service,** and without returning the Notice of Intention to Defend, you will avoid further Costs.

If you do not return the Notice of Intention to Defend, but allow Judgment against you by Default, *you will save Half the Hearing Fee,* and the Order upon such Judgment will be to pay the Debt and Costs forthwith, [*or by instalments, (to be specified as in Plaintiff's written consent)*].

If you admit a part only of the Claim, you must return the Notice of Intention to Defend within the time specified on the Summons; and you may, by paying into the Registrar's Office at the same time the amount so admitted, together with Costs proportionate to such amount, avoid further Costs, unless the Plaintiff proves at the trial an amount exceeding your payment.

[If you return the notice of Intention to Defend, you may pay the Debt and Costs, or, if you admit a part only of the Claim, the amount so admitted, together with Costs proportionate to such amount, into the Registrar's office at any time before the action is called on for trial, and by so doing you may avoid further Costs, unless the Plaintiff proves at the trial an amount exceeding your payment, or the Judge orders you to pay any further Costs properly incurred by the Plaintiff before receiving notice of such payment.]

If you intend to dispute the Plaintiff's Claim on any of the following grounds—

    1. That the Plaintiff owes you a debt which you claim should be set off against it;
    2. That you were under Twenty-one when the debt claimed was contracted;
    3. That you were then, or are now, a married woman;
    4. That the debt claimed is more than six years old;
    5. That you have been discharged from the Plaintiff's claim under a Bankrupt or Insolvent Act;
    6. That you have already tendered to the Plaintiff what is due;
    7. That you have a Statutory or Equitable Defence;

You must give notice thereof to the Registrar FIVE CLEAR DAYS before the day fixed for the trial; and such notice must contain the particulars required by the County Court Rules; and you must deliver to the Registrar as many copies of such notice as there are Plaintiffs, and an additional Copy for the use of the Court. If your DEFENCE be a SET-OFF, you must, with the Notice thereof, also deliver to the Registrar a statement of the particulars thereof. If your DEFENCE be a TENDER, you must pay into Court the amount tendered.

[If the Debt or Claim exceeds five pounds you may have the Action tried by a Jury, on giving notice in writing at the Registrar's office TEN CLEAR DAYS before the day fixed for the trial, and on payment of eight shillings for the fees of such Jury.]

Summonses for witnesses and for the production of documents by them will be issued upon application at the office of the Registrar of this Court, upon payment of the proper fee.

Order II.
Rule 23.

No. of Plaint O O 796

The Summons of which this is a true copy [*add, if so, with copy of* affidavit annexed] was served by me, the undersigned, personally on the Defendant ,

at

on the

day of

19...

Bailiff
to sign
full
names,

Bailiff of the

County Court.

Then it is that an appeal is sanctioned, is indeed necessary, for ensuring justice. Thus in *Baker* v. *Longhurst* (Court of Appeal, 1932), we have Lord Justice Scrutton explaining the position. The County Court judge had awarded damages to an injured motor-cyclist, but, it seems, under a mistake of the law relating to contributory negligence. "The case," he said, "was an appeal from the decision of a County Court judge, from whose finding of fact there was no appeal. The appellants must, therefore, satisfy the Court that on the facts proved at the trial the finding of the County Court judge that there was no contributory negligence proved against the plaintiff could not stand.

"On the principle of *Sharpe* v. *Southern Railway* (K.B. 1925), the plaintiff, himself, on his own evidence, was negligent. His own evidence was that he could pull up his motor-cycle in ten yards. His lamp enabled him to see a vehicle thirty yards off. Either he was going so fast that he could not pull up within range of vision, or he was not looking to see what was in front of him. In either case he was negligent. It was no use saying that the vehicle was unlighted. If people who rode motor-cycles went at such a pace on dark nights that they could not pull up when they saw something they must take the consequences of their own negligence. There might have been a pedestrian there, who was not required by law to carry a light, or, as in the New Forest, there might have been cattle. People must go at such speed that they could pull up within range of vision. It was clear in this case that the County Court judge had no ground for finding that the plaintiff was free from negligence. The appeal would be allowed."

HIGH COURT PROCEDURE

A WRIT

To enforce one's rights in the High Court, the first step is the preparation of a writ. This is a formal command, issued over the signature of the Lord Chancellor, commanding the defendant to appear and answer the claim of the plaintiff.

The effective part of the writ is—

In the High Court of Justice,
King's Bench Division,
Between Richard Roe, Plaintiff
and
John Styles, Defendant.

George the Fifth, etc. . . . to John Styles of 69, High Street in the County Borough of Croydon. We command you, that within eight days after the service of this Writ on you, inclusive of the day of such service, you do cause an Appearance to be entered for you in an action at the suit of Richard Roe, draper. And take notice that in default of your so doing, the plaintiff may proceed therein and Judgment may be given in your absence.

Witness, John, Baron Sankey, Lord High Chancellor of Great Britain.

The defendant may appear hereto by entering an appearance either personally or by solicitor, at the Central Office, Royal Courts of Justice, London.

INDORSEMENT OF WRIT

On the back of the writ the plaintiff states what it is that he claims from the defendant. Thus, in an action for deceit the indorsement would be of this nature—

Fraud

The plaintiff's claim is for damages for fraudulent misstatement in a prospectus issued by the defendant as director of the Deeper Reef Gold Mines, Limited.

Usually the indorsement will be of a general nature, omitting details. But, in certain defined cases, where the action is of a simple nature, and when the plaintiff thinks that a speedy decision is possible, a special indorsement, giving details of claim, may be prepared. Such an indorsement would be—

Bill of Exchange

The plaintiff's claim is for £400 10s. 9d., for principal, interest, and notarial expenses, payable by the defendant to the plaintiff on a bill of

922

exchange for £385, dated 3rd January, 19—, drawn by X Y on the defendant, and accepted by him, payable three months after date to the plaintiff.

PARTICULARS

				£	s.	d.
Principal due	.	.	.	385	–	–
Interest	.	.	.	15	9	3
Noting	.	.	.		1	6

The plaintiff also claims interest on £385 at £5 per cent from the date hereof until payment.

(The "New Procedure Rules," designed with the object of still further saving of time and expense, are noted below.)

"ISSUE" AND "SERVICE" OF WRIT

To "issue a writ" means to have it made into an official document. This is done by the plaintiff or his solicitor going either to the Law Courts in the Strand or to a District Registry. The larger towns have Registries. There he signs one copy, pays the fee, and the official files it. The other copy is stamped by a "seal" and becomes "the writ in the action."

"Service of the writ" is made by delivering to the defendant a copy after showing him the original.

"ENTERING AN APPEARANCE"

If a defendant decides to contest the claim he "enters an appearance." That is, he attends at the Central Office or the District Registry, gives two copies of a memorandum in the form—

MEMORANDUM OF APPEARANCE

Enter an appearance for John Styles in this action.

Henry Stephens, of 68 Old Broad Street, E.C.2, whose address for service is the same, Solicitor for the defendant.

He pays the appropriate fee, the official seals one copy and hands it back, retaining the other.

"SUMMONS FOR DIRECTIONS"

The plaintiff takes out a "summons for directions." That is, he applies to a Master of the Supreme Court or to a District Registrar. These officials decide all the preliminaries to a trial.

Actions for breach of contract or for wrongs (torts) are begun by the issue of writs or summonses.

Divorce suits, bankruptcy proceedings, application to wind up a company are begun by petition.

Motions are applications to the Court for immediate action, as to attach a person for contempt of Court.

30

THE CHOICE OF COURT

This is a matter of importance to a plaintiff. In some respects he is restricted. In the *County Court*—

1. The jurisdiction is limited to defined areas; the plaintiff may sue in the Court having jurisdiction where the cause of action arose, or where the defendant resides.

2. The amount he can recover, whereby as damages for wrong or for breach of contract, is limited.

3. Certain actions that may involve difficult points are not to be tried in the County Court. For, where appeals are justifiable and perhaps desirable, the High Court is the proper place of trial.

These are actions—

1. For breach of promise of marriage.

2. For libel or slander.

3. For seduction.

4. In relation to an interest in land where the value of the interest in disputes exceeds £100 a year.

The jurisdiction of the High Court is unlimited (except as regards those enjoying diplomatic immunity and as regards a peer charged with felony) so far as regards people living under the permanent or temporary protection of the King. And, even when a defendant is outside the jurisdiction, but where the matter of dispute is land within jurisdiction, leave will be granted by the Court to serve a writ.

Any action may be brought in the High Court. There is this drawback, however, to the litigant. If he recovers less than £40 in an action upon a contract he can obtain none of his costs from the defendant. If he recovers less than £100 he can obtain costs only on the lower County Court scale.

If he recovers less than £10 in an action for wrong, he can obtain none of his costs from the defendant. If he recovers less than £50, he can obtain costs only on the County Court scale.

SPECIAL INDORSEMENT

When a claimant is, in the following six cases, seeking a definite sum of money ("liquidated damages" it is called) he can probably shorten proceedings by placing a "special indorsement" upon the writ. The six cases are—

1. Upon a contract (e.g. on a bill of exchange, or promissory note, or cheque).

2. On a bond for payment of a defined sum.

3. On a statute stipulating a fixed sum.

4. On a guarantee.

5. On a trust.

6. When a landlord seeks recovery of land from a tenant whose term has expired or has been ended by a notice to quit, with a claim for rent.

When a writ has been specially indorsed—

1. In default of the defendant's appearance the plaintiff can, if he files an affidavit that the writ was properly served, sign final judgment for the full amount claimed.

2. Where the defendant appears, the plaintiff takes out a summons under Order XIV (for which see below). The master will then give leave to the plaintiff to sign final judgment unless the defendant shows that he has a possible defence.

3. The indorsement is a statement of claim and the need for "pleadings" is avoided.

The precaution necessary for the plaintiff is thus put by Chief Justice Coleridge: "if a man employs the machinery of the specially indorsed writ, he must make his indorsement a full and complete statement of his cause of action." He must give dates and items so that the defendant, knowing exactly the claim against him, may be able to decide whether or not to contest the claim. *Order XIV* has been thus explained by a former Master of the Rolls. When the plaintiff shows, to the satisfaction of a master or a judge, that he has a cause of action which the defendant cannot answer, then the master or judge "will give leave to sign judgment at once without going through all the unnecessary and expensive preliminaries of a trial or the expense of the trial itself. It is a strong thing to give such a power to a judge, and the Courts have said, therefore, that they would watch strictly the exercise of that power. But this does not mean that they would give effect to every pettifogging objection which the ingenuity of a defendant could raise."

In other words, a plaintiff asks for, and usually obtains, summary judgment.

SUMMONS FOR DIRECTIONS

When the defendant has put in an appearance, the plaintiff must take out a "summons for directions." That is, he applies to the master to settle matters preliminary to and relating to the trial. The summons needs a 10s. stamp. A copy must be served upon all parties affected; they are entitled to attend and, if they think it desirable, to enter into the discussion upon the directions.

If the plaintiff does not take out a summons for directions within fourteen days of the defendant's appearance, the defendant may apply for an order to dismiss the action.

Some noteworthy matters are these—

1. *Security for Costs.* It is only fair to the defendant in some cases (as, for instance, where the plaintiff has no substantial property) to require the plaintiff to provide security against the awarding of costs to the defendant. The master will, in suitable cases, make such an order.

2. *Stay of Proceedings.* The master may stay proceedings. He will if it is proved to him that the action is frivolous, or is designedly oppressive to the defendant.

3. *Particulars.* Either party may apply for particulars in addition to those given in the statements of claim and defence, and, if the master thinks it fair that the particulars should be given he makes the order.

4. *Place, mode* (whether with or without a jury and the kind of jury), and *time* of *trial*: these are fixed by the master.

5. *Taking of Evidence on Commission.* Where it is shown to be necessary, or highly expedient, that witnesses should give their evidence out of Court and before the trial, the master makes the requisite order.

6. *Pleadings.* The matters to be decided at the trial should be clearly set out. To determine upon what points controversy arises, the parties may be required to make clear their cases; the plaintiff shows precisely in what his claim consists, the defendant shows precisely what his defence is.

As a result of such pleadings, it is often unnecessary to go into Court: a settlement satisfactory to both parties is reached out of Court.

The master makes the order for pleadings.

On all questions there is possible an appeal to the judge from the master's decision.

ORDER XIX, RULE 4

Order XIX, Rule 4, of the Supreme Court indicates the nature of the "Pleading" required in order to make plain where the controversy lies.

Every pleading shall contain, and contain only, a statement in a summary form of the material facts on which the party pleading

*relies for his claim or defence, as the case may be, but not the evidence
by which they are to be proved.*

The party pleading must state all the facts upon which he intends to found his case. Without leave he cannot give evidence
of such facts as are not pleaded. But he need not anticipate
what may be urged in answer. "It is," said Lord Justice James,
"no part of a Statement of Claim to anticipate the defence, and
to state what the plaintiff would have to say in answer to it.
That would be a return to the old inconvenient system of pleading in Chancery, when the plaintiff used to allege in his bill
imaginary defences of the defendant, and make charges in reply
to them."

The general rule was thus put: "What particulars are to be
stated must depend upon the facts of each case. But, in my
opinion it is absolutely essential that the pleading, not to be
embarrassing to the defendants, should state those facts which
will put the defendants on their guard, and tell them what they
will have to meet when the case comes on for trial."

PARTICULARS

Before the trial, parties are entitled to know what case they
are to meet. This saves expense and prevents parties from being
taken by surprise. The Supreme Court (Order XIX) enjoins,
therefore, "A further and better statement of the nature of the
claim or defence, or further and better particulars of any matter
stated in any pleading may in all cases be ordered, upon such
terms, as to costs and otherwise, as may be just." That is, a
litigant who considers that he has not received the information to
which he is entitled may make application to the master for
further particulars, and in suitable cases his application will be
granted. The old system of pleading was to conceal as much as
possible of what was going to be proved at the trial; the new system insists upon clear and definite information.

A litigant is not now liable to be deprived of his legal remedy
owing to some technical error of himself or his advisers. Modern
procedure is this, according to Lord Justice Scrutton (*Oakley* v.
Lyster, C.A. 1931): "The Courts find out the facts and endeavour
to give the right legal judgment on those facts. So in this case
I begin by ascertaining the facts in order to see whether the
form in which the plaintiff is claiming is substantially right, or,
if not substantially right, whether any injustice is done by giving
him the real remedy which the facts justify."

" NEW PROCEDURE " RULES

"Procedure" means the ordered and orderly method through which a plaintiff's claim is determined. It is often, too, a slow and tedious and astonishingly costly method; the remedy to enforce a right may cost more than the right is worth. Mainly to diminish the cost of litigation, but also to shorten the interval between the beginning and the ending of an action, the "New Procedure Rules" operate from 24th May, 1932. That these rules constitute a great and valuable reform in our law administration is certain. The Rules, given in Order XXXVIII (a) of the Supreme Court, apply to the more straightforward actions in the King's Bench Division. They do not apply to actions for libel, slander, malicious prosecution, false imprisonment, seduction, or breach of promise of marriage, and, where fraud is alleged by the plaintiff, even a simple action is removed from the "New Procedure List" and enters into the "Ordinary List." Two judges, continuously working in London, will give their time to trials of cases under the new rules.

MODE OF PROCEDURE

The responsibility of deciding whether a case is fit for the abridged new procedure rests, in the first place, upon the solicitor who is acting for the plaintiff. He will endorse the writ, the issue of which is the first step in every action, with the words "Fit for the New Procedure," and will add his signature. Unless the judge decides that the solicitor is wrong, several important innovations tend to shorten the action and lessen its costs. The writ is served upon the defendant; the defendant enters an appearance, showing that he means to contest the claim; within seven days the plaintiff makes out his claim with all particulars; within four days, the defendant delivers his defence, with all particulars. Then the plaintiff takes out a "summons for directions," and, within four days, the judge gives instructions to the parties about the procedure to be followed. In his discretion, he is enabled to do much to abridge an action. The judge has power to limit the number of expert witnesses; the rather ridiculous array of opposing experts, all armed with elaborate opinions clothed in the latest scientific jargon, will be absent from new procedure cases, and with them will be absent also their fees as expert witnesses. The presence of witnesses, other than experts, will be necessary only "where it appears to the judge that the other

party desires the production of a witness for cross-examination."
The evidence of witnesses can, in most cases, be given by a
statement on oath—by an affidavit, that is. In many cases of
dispute, there is agreement upon facts; the dissension is about the
legal consequence of the facts. It is to those cases where the testing of evidence by cross-examination is uncalled for that the new
procedure rules are applicable.

JURY ACTIONS

There is discretion about the summoning of a jury: "the judge
may order the action or any issue therein to be tried with a jury
or without a jury as, in his discretion, he may think fit." If he
should decide to dispense with the help of a jury, he will constitute himself a judge of fact as well as of law. This will have
several results, all tending to the shortening of trials with, we
may assume, at least as great a chance of the truth becoming
apparent. For the mind of the judge, trained to brush away
what is irrelevant and to distinguish between sincere belief and
bold assertion, is likely to be less easily misled than the minds
of twelve persons untrained in these directions. The speeches of
counsel will only deal with what really tells in favour of their
contentions: impassioned appeals, which make so great a show
and mean so little, but which may well sway a jury, weigh not at
all with the judge. Counsel may try to throw dust in the juryman's eye; they will hesitate to try this with the judge. There
will be no careful stage management, as when, in order to impress
a jury, an injured claimant is carried into Court to give evidence.

The discretion to try an action without a jury, was in operation
during the War, when the empanelling of a jury often presented
some difficulty; and the exercise of the discretion aroused little
resentment then. Perhaps in other less happy days, when judges
were the creatures of the monarch, the subject needed the protection of a jury. It is not so now, and those liable to be summoned to serve as jurymen may welcome this rule.

APPEALS LIMITED

The chief cause of expense in litigation is, however, the possibility of a double appeal, first to the Court of Appeal, then to the
House of Lords. One whose purse would not enable him to stay
the course might well submit to injustice rather than enter the
lists against an opponent more lavishly supplied with money.
The threat "to take the case to the House of Lords" is likely

to intimidate, and is intended to intimidate. Faced with that prospect, a diffident suitor may relinquish a valid claim. The new rules enable the parties concerned, if they choose, to get rid of this terrifying prospect. They may agree to accept the decision of the judge as final or to limit the right of appeal to one Court only. Or, they may agree to accept the judge's decision upon the facts as final, and limit their right of appeal to questions of law. The judge may "record the consent of the parties either wholly excluding their right of appeal, or limiting it to the Court of Appeal, or limiting it to questions of law only."

FIXING THE DATE

An attempt is made to remove another prolific source of expense. It is difficult to foretell, with any degree of accuracy, *when* an impending trial will take place. The law's delays in adjusting claims are a great nuisance; they would be less of a nuisance, much less of an expense, if something like certainty about the date of trial could be assured. The new rules try to give the certainty. The judge fixes a day for the trial of the action, about which he has given directions, and, so far as possible, he himself will take the case on that day. If the desired certainty can be achieved, even approximately, much waste of time and money would be avoided. At present, even when a case is on the "warned list" it may be held up for days; witnesses brought to London kick their heels in boredom and run up hotel bills; solicitors' and counsels' fees are swollen; all sorts of irritating items add to the burden of even the successful litigant.

CONDUCT OF A CASE

A sketch of the procedure in an actual case will help to make matters clear. An instructive one, having a number of most interesting features, is *Murray* v. *"Croxteth Hall"* (Admiralty Court, 1929). The amount in dispute was small, a tiny fraction of the costs involved in getting a final decision; the elucidation of the relation between an Act of Parliament and a judicial decision perhaps made the costs worth while incurring. Whether that is much comfort to the shipping company, which had to bear the costs, is doubtful.

Correspondence takes place between the men's union and the shipowners. The letters, in which the points in dispute become crystallised, follow. No agreement being reached, a claim for wages alleged to be due is made in the Magistrate's Court.

The case comes before the stipendiary magistrate; it is found to involve an important point of law; it is therefore a suitable case for remission to the High Court. Remission is made by the order—

Ellerman Lines. 19— —Letter M—No. 2355

Murray v. *"Croxteth Hall"*

Order of the Stipendiary Magistrate. 6th August, 19—.

Court of Summary Jurisdiction in Liverpool.

BETWEEN   John Murray   PLAINTIFF

and

The Ellerman Lines, Limited   DEFENDANTS

Upon Hearing Counsel for each of the above-named parties,

It is ordered that the claim for the sum of £31 4s. wages and subsistence allowance alleged to be due to the Plaintiff, under Section 1 (1) of the Merchant Shipping Act, 1925, and instituted in this Court of Summary Jurisdiction, and all questions arising therein be referred to the Probate, Divorce, and Admiralty Division of His Majesty's High Court of Justice.

The Writ of Summons, initiating the High Court proceedings, is issued by the plaintiff. The face of the writ contains the command to appear—

Writ of Summons, dated 9th August, 19—

19— —Letter M—No. 2355

In the High Court of Justice,
  Probate Divorce and Admiralty Division,
    Admiralty,
      Liverpool District Registry.

John Murray   PLAINTIFF

               and

The Ellerman Lines, Limited
the owners of the S.S. "Croxteth Hall"   DEFENDANTS

George the Fifth by the Grace of God, of Great Britain, Ireland, and the British Dominions beyond the Seas, King, Defender of the Faith.

To the Ellerman Lines Limited (Owners of the S.S. "Croxteth Hall") of 19–21, Moorgate, London, E.C.2.

We Command You, that within eight days after the service of this Writ on you, inclusive of the day of such service, you do cause an appearance to be entered for you in the Probate, Divorce, and Admiralty Division of our High Court of Justice in an Action at the Suit of John Murray.

And Take Notice that in default of your so doing the Plaintiff may proceed therein and Judgment may be given in your absence.

Witness, John, Baron Sankey, Lord High Chancellor of Great Britain.

The back of the Writ of Summons gives such a statement of the claim as will enable the defendant to realise what is being asked of him—

The Plaintiff's Claim is £31 4s., being wages and subsistence for two months from the 4th March, 1929, due to him under the provisions of the Merchant Shipping (International Labour Conventions) Act, 1925, he being engaged as a Quartermaster and Able-Bodied Seaman on board the S.S. "Croxteth Hall" of which vessel the defendants were the owners when she was wrecked off Flushing on the 27th February, 1929, and the plaintiff's service having terminated as a result of such wreck on 4th March, 1929, before the date contemplated in the Agreement and he having remained unemployed during each day during the period of two months from 4th March, 1929.

And the sum of £5 10s. (or such sum as may be allowed upon taxation) for costs.

If the amount claimed be paid to the plaintiff or his solicitors or agent within four days from the service hereof, further proceedings will be stayed.

The *Statement of Claim* expands the summary upon the back of the writ and includes paragraph

7. On 5th August, 1929, the Court of Summary Jurisdiction sitting at Liverpool, acting under the authority of the Merchant Shipping Act, 1894, and of the Merchant Shipping (International Labour Conventions) Act, 1925, referred the plaintiff's claim herein to the Probate, Divorce, and Admiralty Division of His Majesty's High Court of Justice.

The Statement of Claim is delivered to the solicitors of the defendants, who in a series of paragraphs numbered for purpose of reference, prepare a defence. The defence makes clear how far the defendants agree with the Statement of Claim; how far they deny the Statement. The points that will be put in issue at the trial then clearly stand out—

DEFENCE

1. The defendants admit—

(*a*) That they are the Owners of the S.S. "Croxteth Hall."

(*b*) That the plaintiff was thereon employed as quartermaster and able-bodied seaman under an agreement in writing to which they will refer for its full and/or true terms.

(*c*) That the said ship was wrecked and/or lost on 27th February, 1929.

(*d*) That the service of the plaintiff was terminated on 4th March, 1929.

(*e*) Paragraph 7 of the Statement of Claim.

2. Save as above the defendants deny each and every allegation of fact contained in the Statement of Claim as though the same were herein set out and specifically traversed.

3. They deny that the plaintiff would have been employed or paid and/or that it was contemplated that he would be employed or paid as in the Statement of Claim alleged.

4. They deny that the plaintiff was in fact unemployed during the period and/or as the result of the wreck or loss of the said ship.

5. Alternatively, the defendants will rely upon the release given by the plaintiff at Liverpool dated 4th March, 1929, and duly signed and attested as required by Section 136 of the Merchant Shipping Act, 1894.

6. In further alternative the plaintiff was, on and after the 8th day of March, 1929, able to obtain suitable employment.

7. Also in the alternative if the plaintiff was in fact unemployed on any day after 10th March, 1929, such unemployment was not due to the wreck or loss of the said ship.

PARTICULARS

On 10th March, 1929, the S.S. "Croxteth Hall" would have arrived at Middlesbrough and on that date the voyage, in respect of which the said agreement was made, would have ended and the crew including the plaintiff would have been discharged from the service aforesaid.

8. The defendants will further and in the alternative contend that any claim under the Merchant Shipping (International Labour Conventions) Act, 1925, is by that Act limited to an indemnity against unemployment resulting from loss of the S.S. "Croxteth Hall."

By reason of the premises such indemnity cannot exceed the amount of the wages which the plaintiff would have earned under the agreement aforesaid between the 27th February, 1929, and the 10th March, 1929. The plaintiff has been paid such wages up to 4th March, 1929, and the defendants before the commencement of any proceedings herein offered to pay to the plaintiff any balance of such indemnity and/or amount. They will refer to letters dated 5th and 9th April between the defendants and the plaintiff and/or his agents.

9. And the defendants while denying liability bring into Court herewith the sum of £5 and say that as above appears such sum is more than enough to satisfy the claim (if any) of the plaintiff herein.

Correspondence referred to and forming part of the documents in the case—

10 Water Street,

LIVERPOOL.

5th April, 19—.

Henry O'Pugh, Esq., J.P.,

    Area Secretary,

        Transport and General Workers' Union,

            41 Islington,

                LIVERPOOL.

Dear Sir,

HP/AW/LH "Croxteth Hall"

H. Roberts, J. Murray, and H. Collins

We refer to our letter of the 20th ultimo.

We are instructed that your three members were paid off at Liverpool up to and including 4th ultimo. We are further instructed that in any event the services of your members would have terminated at Middlesbrough before 12th ultimo.

In these circumstances it appears to us that any unemployment of your members after 12th ultimo was not due to the wreck or loss of the ship and the case falls within subsection 1 of the Merchant Shipping (International Labour Convention) Act, 1925. Our clients are, therefore, prepared to pay your members' wages for the period 5th March to 12th March inclusive and we shall be glad to hear from you whether our clients are to send the amount in question to you or to your members direct. In the latter event, you will no doubt furnish us with their addresses.

Should it be your members' intention to proceed further with the matter, our clients reserve the right to rely upon the statutory release signed by your members and it is without prejudice to that right that our clients offer to make the payment in question.

Yours truly,

Hill, Dickinson & Co.

The Transport and General Workers' Union,
Smith Square,
LONDON, S.W.1.
9th April, 19—.

Messrs. Hill, Dickinson & Co.,
    10 Water Street,
      LIVERPOOL.

Dear Sirs,

S.S. "Croxteth Hall"

The correspondence which has passed between yourselves and our Mr. Pugh of Liverpool relative to the above question, has been forwarded to me. I have looked into the matter and cannot agree that in any event the services of our members would have terminated at Middlesbrough before the 12th ultimo, and I fail to see that the shipowners have discharged the onus of proof which is imposed upon them in subsection 2 of Section 1 of the Merchant Shipping (International Labour Conventions) Act, 1925, and therefore the offer of your clients to pay wages for the period 5th March to 12th March inclusive is not satisfactory.

With reference to the last paragraph of your letter, I have to suggest that the statutory release signed by our members has no force in respect of a claim under the 1925 Act, which clearly imposes upon the employers an obligation which accrues from day to day after the wreck up to a period of two months. May I ask, therefore, that you give the matter further consideration with a view to meeting the men's claim up to the time they obtained employment.

I shall be glad to hear from you at your early convenience as the men expect shortly to obtain work, and they would like the matter cleared up before they leave for their next voyage.

Yours faithfully,
F. Stillwell.

At the trial, the counsel for the plaintiff "opens the case," states concisely what his claim is, and the circumstances that justify it. Then he calls and questions such witnesses as he thinks fit, in order to bear out the assertions made in the Statement of Claim. Counsel for the defence may, if he chooses, cross-question any witness; he will do so when he thinks it possible to shake the testimony telling against him, or to make it assume a different aspect.

At the end of the plaintiff's case the counsel for the defence sketches his defence; he calls his witnesses who, he hopes, will support the written defence he has tendered to the plaintiff; these witnesses, too, may be cross-questioned—this time on behalf of the plaintiff. At any point the judge may, some judges do frequently, intervene and question the witness. The judge, moreover, takes such notes as he considers desirable for his own guidance and as a help to the appeal judges, if an appeal from his decision should follow.

The witnesses being heard, the counsel for the plaintiff makes his concluding speech and emphasises how thoroughly his preliminary statement has been justified, how completely the defence has proved insubstantial. The counsel for the defendant follows with his attempt to explain how triumphantly the defence had emerged from its ordeal, how flimsy the claim appeared once it was tested.

Where a jury is present to answer questions, it is the duty of the judge to sum up the matter for their benefit. He cuts away irrelevancies, shows the varying weights to be attached to the evidence tendered, and carefully directs their attention to the questions they must answer. In accordance with their answers upon questions of fact, he bases his judgment of what the law demands.

In non-jury actions, the judge gives his decision, explaining in open Court the reasons prompting the decision.

Judgment goes against the shipowners (the defendants) in the Admiralty Court, and they give—

NOTICE OF APPEAL

19——Letter M—No. 2355

In the Court of Appeal.

Take Notice that this Honourable Court will be moved at the expiration of fourteen days from the date hereof or so soon thereafter as Counsel can be heard by Counsel on behalf of the above named Defendants for an Order that the Decree or Judgment of the Right Honourable the President whereby the learned Judge pronounced for the Plaintiff's claim together with costs, and condemned the said Defendants, be set aside and that the Plaintiff's claim be dismissed, and that the

Plaintiff be condemned on the costs of the proceedings in the Court below and of this Appeal.

Dated this 13th day of December, 19—.

Hill, Dickinson & Co.,
10 Water Street, Liverpool.
Defendants' (Appellants') Solicitors.

To the Plaintiff (Respondent)
and to Messrs. G. J. Lynskey & Sons,
30 Lord Street, Liverpool,
his Solicitors.

CRIMINAL TRIALS

RULES RELATING TO THE TRIAL OF CRIMES

These are for the most part rules of the Common Law, evolved so that a person accused of a crime might be sure of a fair and open trial before he can be convicted and punished. A person charged is bound to be to some extent flustered and bewildered in the court of trial. Besides, however much we may strive against it, we all have a tendency to suppose that a man would not be charged unless some evidence of his guilt existed. It is, perhaps, an adequate balance of this handicap upon an accused that the rules relating to criminal trials are weighted against the police and the prosecution.

1. The King as Preserver of Peace

The King's Peace is a synonym for the good order of the realm: "peace is the very end and foundation of civil society." By his office and dignity the King is the chief Conservator of Peace; and his officers include the High Court Judge, the Sheriff, the Coroner, and the Constable. But unofficial persons are appointed "On the Commission of the Peace"; these are the Magistrates. In all Courts, the King, as the fountain of justice, is supposed to be always present, being represented by his Judges.

Even when disturbance of the peace may only be threatened, one who fears such disturbance may swear to his fears before a Justice of the Peace. If the Justice should consider the fears to be reasonable, he has the power to summon the persons named before him and require them to enter into sureties (recognisances) that they will keep the peace, adding where necessary "particularly towards so-and-so." This is "swearing the peace."

2. Conduct of Criminal Proceedings

A special department under the Treasury—that of the "Director of Public Prosecutions"—conducts most criminal proceedings in England. The right—in many conditions the duty—of the private individual to prosecute for crime is, however, preserved intact. But the Crown can, by a *nolle prosequi* ("to be unwilling to prosecute") of the Attorney-General or the Solicitor-General, stop any criminal proceeding even when begun by a private citizen. Moreover, in many statutory offences, the mandate of the Attorney-General is needed before prosecution can begin.

3. Power of Pardon

The King, on the advice of the Home Secretary, can pardon an offender, either before or after conviction. But (under the Act of Settlement, 1701) no pardon can be pleaded against an impeachment. Nor can offenders against the Habeas Corpus Act, 1679, obtain pardon.

4. Crimes Tried in County of Commission

The men of each county were responsible for the preservation of "the King's Peace" in their county. And the rule that has come from the earlier times is that a crime is still usually tried,

1. In the county town.
2. Before a jury selected from the men and women of the county.
3. By a commissioner of the Crown, who thrice a year comes for a "gaol deliverance," and at the "Assizes" tries prisoners brought before him.

Moreover, the "warrant" (or *authorisation*) for the arrest of one accused is issued by a Justice of the Peace (a Magistrate) of the county. In order to authorise the arrest the accused *outside* the county, the warrant must be "backed" by a Magistrate of the county where the accused is to be found.

5. Grand Jury and Petty Jury

The "Grand Jury" were, in effect, accusers. They found that there was at all events a case (a *prima facie* case) against a prisoner; he might not be guilty, but the police had raised a presumption of his guilt. Whether or not he successfully rebutted this presumption at his trial was a question for the "Petty Jury." They determine the *facts*, upon which the presiding Judge declares *the law*. "Grand Juries" were abolished as from 1st September, 1933, on the recommendation of a committee on procedure.

6. Central Criminal Court (Old Bailey)

Parliament set up this Court, the noteworthy exception to the county idea, in 1834. The Central Criminal Court is a special, and statutory, court of *oyer and terminer* (to hear and to determine) and of gaol delivery. It was to exercise criminal jurisdiction over the London area. To administer justice in this crowded area, covering parts of four counties, was most inconvenient on the county system. The Court was empowered to try—

1. Crimes committed in London and (by Order in Council) in the Home Counties.

2. Crimes committed at sea or abroad.

3. Crimes of such a nature that the accused could not be fairly tried in the county of commitment.

4. Crimes under the Official Secrets Acts and the Corrupt Practices Acts.

The Recorder of the City of London, the Common Sergeant, and the Judge of the Mayor's Court of the City of London, are full-time judges, appointed by the Crown to preside over this Court, and they try the bulk of the cases. Judges, taken in rota, from the King's Bench Division of the High Court try the more serious charges.

7. The Magistrate's Courts

A large number of offences are dealt with in the magistrates' courts, and are not transferred to *Quarter Sessions* or to the Assizes. Because tried summarily, these offences, minor breaches of the law, are called "summary offences."

The magistrates' courts comprise—

1. *Courts of Quarter Sessions.* Each county and a number of populous boroughs have a Court of Quarter Sessions comprised for the counties, in theory, of all the magistrates commissioned, but, in practice, of a varying number of active members. The Chairman may have some legal training. But most of the magistrates (or Justices of the Peace) have not. In the boroughs the jurisdiction is exercised by a Recorder.

The Courts conduct trial in all but a very few serious offences. Whether or not an accused is tried at Quarter Sessions, or at the Assizes, depends normally upon the time of sitting of the Court.

2. *Petty Sessions Court.* Two magistrates at least comprise this Court, which can try only summary offences. It may, indeed, be regarded as a committee of Quarter Sessions, to which an appeal may ordinarily be made.

The preliminary examinations of even serious crimes is conducted by this Court, for the purpose of determining whether an accused should be "committed for trial," the police having shown that there is reason to believe him guilty.

In many of the more important boroughs a Stipendiary or Police Magistrate in himself constitutes a Petty Sessions Court.

He is a trained lawyer, and his office is a full-time and paid appointment.

8. Criminal Appeals

There is now a limited right of appeal in criminal cases. The Criminal Appeal Act, 1907, gave a right of appeal to a convicted prisoner in criminal cases on questions of law and, with the permission of the Court of trial or of the Appeal Court, on questions of fact or (again with permission of the Court) against the sentence. The prosecution cannot appeal even if convinced that acquittal was wrong; for none can be placed in jeopardy twice upon the same charge.

Where an unusually important point of law is involved, the Attorney-General may grant a certificate that will enable an appeal to be made to the House of Lords. The Home Secretary can himself, though the prisoner does not appeal, seek the views of the Court.

The Court of Criminal Appeal regards itself as being under obligation to ensure that a criminal trial should admit no suspicion of unfairness to the accused. *Rex* v. *Southern* (C.C.A. 1930) is an illustration. The appellant had been convicted by a jury apparently so satisfied of his guilt that they did not retire. The judge had not, however, called their attention to the statutory need for corroboration, and the conviction was quashed. The judgment ran: "The Court approaches the consideration of this case with a natural reluctance, in view of the fact that both the judge who tried the case and the jury concluded without any doubt that the appellant was guilty; and if, as is our conclusion, this conviction cannot stand, we feel it means that a guilty man escapes punishment. The rules of the criminal law should be maintained; and for the safety of the innocent they must be maintained impartially in all cases, although the result be that in some cases a guilty man escapes punishment."

9. Court of Criminal Appeal and Court of Appeal

There may, apparently, be divergence of opinion between these Courts. In a "stop list" case the Court of Criminal Appeal upheld the conviction of an agent of a Trade Association (*Rex* v. *Denyer*, 1926). In a civil case, where the same Association was sued, the Appeal Court refused to entertain the action of the threatened trader (*Hardie and Lane* v. *Chilton*, 1928); and Lord Justice Scrutton said: "In my opinion *Rex* v. *Denyer* was wrongly decided. There was no evidence upon which a jury could find want of reasonable and probable cause, no evidence of any menace constituting a crime. The judge should have withdrawn the case from the jury."

It seems, however, that a Criminal Court must still follow the earlier decision. For the Lord Chief Justice has said : "The Lord Justice is reported to have said that *Rex* v. *Denyer* was wrongly decided. It may be well, therefore, to make it clear for the purposes of the administration of the criminal law that unless and until the decision of *Rex* v. *Denyer* in this Court is reversed by the only competent tribunal—the House of Lords—it is binding upon and will be enforced by this Court against any person offending in this manner."

10. Indictment

This is a formal charge of crime in the name of the Crown. The person charged has done wrong not only to the actual sufferers but to the nation ; and the King, as representative of the nation, demands punishment. By Magna Carta an accused person has a right to be indicted, a right to be exempt from punishment until convicted by a verdict of his peers. Such an indictment is—

THE KING v. A. B.

COURT OF TRIAL: CENTRAL CRIMINAL COURT.

Presentation of the Grand Jury.

A. B. is charged with the following offences.

STATEMENT OF OFFENCE.

First Count.

Arson, contrary to Section 2 of the Malicious Damage Act, 1861.

PARTICULARS OF OFFENCE.

A. B., on the 3rd day of January, 19—, in the County of Middlesex, maliciously set fire to a dwelling-house, one F. G. being therein.

STATEMENT OF OFFENCE.

Arson, contrary to Section 3 of the Malicious Damage Act, 1861.

PARTICULARS OF OFFENCE.

A. B., on the 3rd day of January, 19—, in the County of Middlesex, maliciously set fire to a house with intent to injure or defraud.

The Criminal Justice Act, 1925, has, however, given to the Justices power to deal with minor offences, always subject to this right of an accused person of going before a jury. To a rapidly increasing extent persons accused are preferring to be tried without great delay—tried summarily—before the Justices. The Justices in Petty Sessions are much more narrowly confined than Quarter Sessions or the Assizes in regard to punishment. This may have something to do with the fact.

11. Arresting under Warrant

Any warrant lawfully issued by a Justice for apprehending a person charged with an offence may be executed by a constable at any time, though the warrant is not in his possession at the time. The warrant must, however, be shown to the person apprehended as soon as practicable after his arrest. (C.J. Act, 1925.) This does not, however, apply to warrants in respect of affiliation or maintenance arrears. The person apprehended is not charged with an offence; and a constable arresting without a warrant may be, as he was in *Horsfield* v. *Brown* (Manchester Assizes 1931), cast in heavy damages.

12. Release on Bail

A man arrested has a right to be released upon bail, unless a good reason exists for refusing release. Such good reason would be his failing to present himself for trial on a previous occasion. Where the crime is a *misdemeanour* the person charged has a right to release on bail; where it is a *felony* the magistrate has discretion: "A man steals 5s. and can be refused bail, because larceny is a felony. A man can obtain thousands of pounds and is entitled to bail if that fraud is a misdemeanour. . . . The mischief is the more serious as many of the heaviest commercial frauds are made misdemeanours by their creative statutes."

Release is usually conditional upon the finding of guarantors who will promise that the accused will present himself for trial. If their promise is not fulfilled they forfeit to the Crown a stipulated sum. (See "Recognisances," below.)

13. Recognisances (" Swearing the Peace ")

These are enforced undertakings to pay to the Crown a sum of money unless peace is kept or appearance is made for trial. One who has reason to fear violence appeals for protection to the Court; where sufficient cause is shown the judge summons the person complained of before him and constrains him to make a promise (subject to prescribed penalties if he breaks it) to be of good behaviour. Similarly, one may "enter into his own recognisances" to appear at the assizes.

Here is a recognisance—

Be it remembered, that on ....X Y of .... comes into the King's Bench Division of the High Court of Justice before me, one of His Majesty's Justices, and acknowledges to owe our Sovereign Lord the King the sum of £ .... upon condition that if the said X Y shall be of good behaviour for the space of .... and keep the peace towards all His Majesty's liege subjects, and especially towards A B .... then this recognisance to be void, or else to remain in full force.

If the undertaking is broken the recognisance is *estreated*; that is, the record is taken to the Court of Exchequer, which collects the sum named.

14. Protection of Liberty

Habeas Corpus is a writ that prevents any dweller in the United Kingdom from being confined against his or her own will, whether by the Crown or by private individuals, unless in accordance with an act of law. The procedure is this. The person who alleges that he is wrongfully imprisoned, or more usually one who has an interest in him, makes application to a Judge of the High Court. Even in vacation time such a Judge is always available. The applicant makes an affidavit; and, unless the affidavit in itself shows that the person is rightly confined, the Judge makes a *rule nisi*. That is, he issues an order to the custodian of the person, ordering that he shall produce the body of the person imprisoned "together with the day and cause of his taking and detaining, to undergo and receive all and singular such matters and things as Our Court shall then and there consider of concerning him in that behalf."

At the time appointed the Court either makes the *rule nisi* into a *rule absolute* by releasing the prisoner, or, being satisfied that he is properly in custody, remands him into the custodian's keeping.

A judge who denies the writ where a *prima facie* case is made out by the affidavit is liable to forfeit £500 to the party aggrieved by the refusal.

"Returns" that would justify detention are—

1. Internment as an alien enemy (*Rex* v. *Superintendent of Vine Street Police Station, Ex parte Leibman*, K.B. 1916).

2. Arrest or imprisonment on a criminal charge.

3. Commitment for contempt of court.

4. Commitment by either House of Parliament for a breach of its privileges.

5. Safeguarding of a lunatic, or of an infant.

Offenders against the Habeas Corpus Act (1679) cannot be pardoned by the Crown. But Parliament has (e.g. in the O'Brien case of 1923, where the Home Secretary had incurred heavy penalties for illegal arrest and the sending of prisoners beyond sea) sometimes passed an Act of Indemnity, made retrospective and thereby remitting penalties already incurred.

15. Defence of Poor Prisoners

The Poor Prisoners' Defence Act, 1930, makes provision for the granting of free legal aid to persons charged with either an indictable or a summary offence.

A "defence certificate" is granted on *committal for trial*, either by the committing Justices, or by the Judge or the Chairman of Quarter Sessions. It should appear to the certifying authority that the person's means are insufficient. Where it does so appear, a certificate *must* be granted where there is a charge of murder, and it *may* be granted in any other case where it is desirable in the interests of justice. In summary cases it is the Justices that grant the certificate.

An order under the Costs in Criminal Cases Act, 1908, then directs that payment out of local funds shall be made.

16. Fairness to the Accused is Ensured

by reason of these facts—

1. The publicity of trials.

2. The prosecutor must make out the charge beyond reasonable doubt.

3. Evidence only must be considered; not, for instance, the bad repute of the person charged.

4. The jury must be unanimous.

5. The judgment is given and reasons rendered in open Court.

6. An appeal is possible.

7. The preliminary proceedings are open.

8. The accused is not compelled to incriminate himself by answering questions that would be equivalent to an acknowledgment of guilt.

17. Publicity of Trials

The Courts of this country must administer justice in public; but the need for secrecy may be established and then a case is heard *in camera*.

Thus, the public may be excluded when—

1. There is no contention but only a desired settlement of questions affecting the person in guardianship, wards, and lunatics.

2. Secret processes are in dispute.

3. Presence of the public would make the administration of justice impracticable.

18. Dealing with Young Offenders

There are no separate prisons for young offenders. The only establishments set apart entirely are the five Borstal institutions. Among these, young offenders are distributed, after being classified in a boys' prison at Wormwood Scrubbs. Classification requires from one to three months. The more hardened criminals are sent to one institution, and at the other end is one for novices in crime. In that institution the normal period of detention is one year. A boy can be licensed any time after he has served six months, but a longer period is usually necessary.

If a young offender at a Borstal institution misconducts himself, he is sent to a special block set apart at Wandsworth Prison.

If a boy is sentenced to imprisonment, he goes to an ordinary prison; but, as far as possible, he is kept apart from the adult prisoners.

19. No Second Trial upon Same Charge

There is a valid defence in the plea of *autrefois convict* or *autrefois acquit* (i.e. "convicted before" or "acquitted before"). The plea prevailed in *Rex* v. *King* (Q.B. 1897). A defendant who has been convicted upon an indictment charging him with obtaining credit for goods by false pretences cannot be afterwards convicted upon a further indictment charging him with larceny of the same goods. It is against the very first principles of the criminal law that a man should be placed twice in jeopardy upon the same charge; the offences are practically the same, though not their legal operation.

It is important to note the limitations of the plea, however. The *facts* relied upon by the prosecution may be the same. The offences may be different. Thus under Section 31 of the Larceny Act (1916) it is a *misdemeanour*, punishable by two years' imprisonment, to theaten to print or publish matters concerning a prosecutor, with intent to extort money from him. Under Section 29 of the same Act, to utter a letter demanding money with menaces, and without reasonable or probable cause, is a *felony* punishable by penal servitude for life. That a jury has found the accused guilty on the former count, while disagreeing on the latter count, does not prevent a new trial on the more serious charge. In *Rex* v. *Kendrick and Smith* (Central Criminal Court, 1931) the Recorder instructed the jury that, since the offences were not the same, the trial should proceed; and on appeal to the Criminal Appeal Court the Recorder's attitude was approved: "It is not enough to say that the evidence tendered on the second charge was the same evidence as that offered to prove the first charge." It is the offence that is material; and as regards the more serious one, the Court said, in answer to Kendrick's appeal against sentence: "The crime of which he was convicted is a very terrible crime— one of the most serious crimes dealt with in courts of justices— that of preying on the weakness or folly of persons who, by their stupidity or wickedness, have put themselves into a position which renders them an easy prey to those who desire to extort money from them."

20. Plea of " Not Guilty "

When a prisoner pleads "Not Guilty," it is the jury that must answer whether his plea is true or false. Even though, during the course of the trial, the accused makes statements apparently tantamount to an admission of guilt, the jury's verdict is necessary to convict him. His statement is merely evidence on which the jury may act. The judge must not discharge the jury and sentence the prisoner. See *Rex* v. *Hancock* (Court of Criminal Appeal, 1931), where the question arose. The Lord Chief Justice said: "The appellant was charged at Derbyshire Assizes on an indict- ment which charged him with having carnal knowledge of a woman without her consent. At first he pleaded 'Not Guilty,' but afterwards he appears to have made a confession of some sort in the presence and hearing of the jury, and that confession was acted upon, although no verdict of the jury was taken. A verdict of the jury ought to be taken. The conviction of the appellant should be set aside and he be ordered to appear at the next Assizes there to take his trial." This, it will be noted, was not a second trial upon the same charge. For the first trial had not been completed.

21. Insanity as Excuse for Crime

To be excused on the ground of insanity, the defence must show that, at the time of doing the act, the prisoner did not know the nature and quality of the act he was doing, or, if he did know it, he did not know that he was doing what was wrong. Would he have done it if a policeman had been at his elbow ?—is suggested as a test question.

22. Statements made by Prisoners or Persons Suspected

In 1918 the Home Office issued for the guidance of the police a set of rules approved by the King's Bench judges—

1. A police officer may seek information from any person, suspected or not.

2. When he has made up his mind to charge a person with crime, he should first caution him before asking any question.

3. He must not question persons in custody before cautioning them.

4. He must not accept a volunteered statement without a caution.

5. The caution to the prisoner when *formally* charged should be : "Do you wish to say anything in answer to the charge? You are not obliged to say anything unless you wish to do so, but whatever you say will be taken down in writing and may be given in evidence."

6. A statement made by a prisoner before there is time to caution him is not inadmissible, but he should be cautioned as soon as possible.

7. A prisoner making a voluntary statement must not be cross-examined.

8. When two or more persons are charged with the same offence and separate statements are taken, the police should not read these statements to the other people charged, but each of such persons should be furnished by the police with a copy and nothing should be said or done by the police to invite a reply.

9. Any statement made in accordance with the above rules should, whenever possible, be taken down in writing and signed by the person making it, after it has been read to him, and he has been invited to make any corrections he may wish.

23. Benefit of the Doubt

Guilt must be brought home beyond reasonable doubt; we must assume innocence till guilt is proved. Where the evidence is equally consistent with innocence and guilt there ought not to be a conviction. Thus, an appellant to the Court of Criminal Appeal had been convicted as an accomplice of a "welsher"—

of one, to quote the language of the charge, who "had decamped from a race meeting with a sum of money which he had accepted by way of bets on a horse which won a race." He had helped to book the bets; but there was no evidence that he knew that the bookmaker intended to run away. He himself had run away, but this was because he wanted police protection from an angry crowd. The Court said that his explanation *might* be the true one, and quashed the conviction (*R*. v. *Bookbinder*, C.C.A. 1931).

24. A Penal Statute is Interpreted in Favour of an Accused

A rule of our criminal law similar to the last is that, when an Act of Parliament prescribes a penalty, it must be quite clear that the penalty attaches to the accused before he can be punished.

In *R*. v. *Chapman* (C.C.A. 1931) the appellant had been convicted of unlawful carnal knowledge of a girl under the age of sixteen. The Criminal Law Amendment Act of 1922 enacts that even reasonable cause to believe that a girl is sixteen shall not be a defence; but it makes a proviso "that, in case of a man of twenty-three years of age or under, the presence of reasonable cause to believe that the girl was over the age of sixteen years shall be a valid defence on the first occasion on which he is charged with the offence." The prisoner had passed his twenty-third birthday and so was in his twenty-fourth year. Did the proviso apply to him? Yes, said the Chief Justice: "Where an equivocal word or ambiguous sentence leaves a reasonable doubt of its meaning, the benefit of the doubt should be given to the subject and against the legislature which has failed to explain itself."

25. Ignorance of the Law is Usually No Excuse

In *R*. v. *Prince* (1875) a man was convicted, under Section 55 of the Offences Against the Person Act, 1861, of unlawfully taking an unmarried girl under the age of sixteen out of the possession and against the will of her father. It was no defence that he believed and had reasonable grounds for the belief that she was over sixteen. For her father has a right to her personal custody up to the age of twenty-one, and to appoint a guardian by deed or will, whose right to her personal custody would have extended to twenty-one. By taking her, even with her own consent, he must at least have been guilty of aiding and abetting her in doing an unlawful act—in escaping, against the will of her natural guardian, from his lawful care and charge.

26. Prosecution for Felony must Precede a Civil Suit for Damages

Where the wrongful act is at once a felony and a civil wrong, the wronged person must fulfil his duty to the community and prosecute for felony before he brings his suit for damages. Thus, in *Midland Insurance Co.* v. *Smith* (Q.B. 1881), the plaintiffs contested payment under a fire policy, alleging that the wife of the holder of the policy had purposely caused the fire. It was held that the suit could not proceed until the wife had been prosecuted for arson. There is a duty imposed upon the injured person not to resort to the prosecution of his private suit to the neglect and exclusion of the vindication of the public law. "A man is not permitted to abstain from prosecuting an offender by receiving back property or any equivalent or composition for a felony."

The rule does not apply where the criminal offence is a mere misdemeanour or one punishable only on summary conviction. Nor does it apply to actions under the Fatal Accidents Act, 1846: an action lies "although the death shall have been caused under such circumstances as amount in law to felony."

27. Presumption of Marital Coercion

As regards crime, the wife formerly incurred no liability if she committed one in her husband's presence. For she was presumed to act under his coercion. This presumption of coercion was abolished by statute in 1925. It can, however, of course still be pleaded as a fact to exculpate the wife. The operative section is: "Any presumption of law that an offence committed by a wife in the presence of her husband is committed under the coercion of the husband is hereby abolished. But on a charge against a wife, for any offence other than treason or murder, it shall be a good defence to prove that the offence was committed in the presence of, and under the coercion of, the husband." (Criminal Justice Act, 1925, Section 47.)

28. Accessories in Crime

In felonies—not in treasons or misdemeanours—a distinction is drawn between *principals* and *accessories*.

Those who comfort and assist a criminal after a felony or treason has been committed are "accessories after the fact." They commit no crime where a misdemeanour only has been committed.

29. Principal and Accessory in Crime

Note that "principal" in criminal law is used in a sense other than its sense in "principal and agent." The principal in criminal law is he who actually carries out the crime; he who would be called principal in the law of contract is the "accessory before the fact."

The case *Rex* v. *Betts and Ridley* (C.C.A. 1930) makes clear the position of an aider and abettor of a felony—a *principal in the second degree*, as he is called. In pursuance of a plan to rob a man known to be in the habit of taking money to the bank for his employers, Ridley had a motor-car in waiting while Betts knocked the man down and snatched his bag. The blow struck resulted in death. Betts was, therefore, clearly guilty of wilful murder. The death was caused by some act done by him *in the furtherance of a felony involving violence*. Betts was, in fact, convicted and sentenced to death; for it was no alleviation of his offence that he did not intend all the mischief that followed his larceny with violence. But what about Ridley, the principal in the second degree? He, too, said the Court, agreeing with the jury's verdict, was guilty of murder. He was at hand to render help or give warning, and was properly convicted of the same crime.

POLICE

HOME SECRETARY

The Secretary of State for Home Affairs is responsible for the quiet ordering of affairs at home. He it is, therefore, that must control police and prisons, reformatories, and all other institutions for dealing with the activities of the predatory class among us, or for preventing the growth of that predatory class.

The Home Secretary exercises control by reason of the fact that half the cost of upkeep of the police is borne by the Central Government, and that the grants to the "Watch Committees" are conditional upon a certificate of efficiency granted by the Home Office Inspector-General.

POLICE ARE SERVANTS OF THE CROWN

Though the Watch Committee of a borough or a county appoints the police, and though they are paid out of the rates, yet in law the police are the servants of the Crown. If, therefore, the police commit a wrong, the only remedy available to the wronged person is an action against the individual officers. He cannot sue the county or the borough council; for the relation of master and servant does not subsist. He cannot sue the Crown; for "the only cases in which the petition of right is open to the subject are for restitution of property that has found its way into the possession of the Crown; or, where the claim arises out of a contract, as for goods supplied to the Crown or to the public service."

ACTION FOR FALSE IMPRISONMENT

In *Fisher* v. *Mayor, etc., of Borough of Oldham* (K.B. 1930), the plaintiff, who was mistakenly arrested on a police warrant and kept for one night in a cell before his identity was established, brought an action against the corporation. The action was based upon the assumption that "the defendants, acting through their watch committee, are the police authority for the county borough of Oldham, and are the employers of the police." The decision showed that this assumption is unfounded.

MUNICIPAL CORPORATION ACT, 1882, AND POLICE

The Act enjoins a corporation to appoint a watch committee, which "shall from time to time appoint a sufficient number of fit men to be borough constables." The "borough constable shall be sworn in before a justice of the borough." And "the watch committee, or any two justices having jurisdiction in the borough, may at any time suspend, and the watch committee may at any time dismiss, any borough constable whom they think negligent in the discharge of his duty, or otherwise unfit."

SECRETARY OF STATE CONTROLS POLICE

Nevertheless, the police are servants of the Crown, not of the local authority. For—

1. The Police Act, 1890, provides for a scheme of pensions, allowances, and gratuities for police officers throughout the kingdom—indicating thereby the fullness of central control.

2. The Police Act, 1919, creates a *police federation* "that shall be entirely independent of and unassociated with any body or person outside the police service"; and under this Act, "it shall be lawful for the Secretary of State to make regulations as to the government, mutual aid, pay, allowances, pensions, clothing, expenses, and conditions of services of all police forces within England and Wales, and every police authority shall comply with the regulations so made."

3. The Police Appeals Act, 1927, provides that "A member of a police force who is dismissed, or required to resign as an alternative to dismissal, may appeal to a Secretary of State."

CONSTABLE'S OATH

The administration of the oath to constables by justices of the peace (themselves appointed by the central government to administer justice and keep order) converts what was once a local administrative officer into a ministerial officer of the Crown. The oath is, "I will well and truly serve and act as a constable for preserving the peace by day and by night and preventing robberies and other felonies and misdemeanours and apprehending offenders against the peace."

PROTECTION OF CONSTABLE AGAINST ACTION

The orders of a civil public authority are a good defence for a constable obeying them, as in effecting an arrest. So an eighteenth-century case (*Aill* v. *Bateman and Another*): "Bateman, being a J.P., had convicted the plaintiff for destroying game. And, though the plaintiff had effects which might have been distrained, yet the defendant sent him immediately to Bridewell without endeavouring to levy the penalty upon his goods. An action of trespass and false imprisonment being brought against Bateman for his commitment and heard at Westminster, the Chief Justice held that the action succeeded. The other defendant was the constable who had executed this warrant of commitment. And as to him, it was agreed that the warrant was a sufficient justification, it being in a matter within the jurisdiction of the justice of the peace." But if a justice of peace makes a warrant which is plainly out of his jurisdiction, such warrant is no justification to a constable. As it was put in the judgment of *Hogg* v. *Ward* (Ex. 1858): "It is absolutely essential for the prevention of crime that the police throughout the country should be supported in the execution of their duty; on the other hand, it is equally important that persons should not be arrested upon frivolous or untenable charges."

PROTECTION OF SHERIFF

So with a sheriff, who is bound to execute process issuing out of a court of competent jurisdiction: it would be wild work if an officer were entitled to scan the warrant delivered to him for the purpose of deciding whether it is regular or not. The interesting *Countess of Rutland's Case* (reported by Coke three centuries ago) well illustrates this. A judgment had been obtained against the countess in an action for debt. Then, unlike now, an order to arrest for debt (a *capias ad satisfaciendum—ca. sa.*) could be issued, and was issued by the Court of Common Pleas, forgetful of the fact that the debtor, as wife of a peer of the realm, was privileged from arrest. The sheriff executed the order and was sued in the Court of Star Chamber, which, however, held him exempt from liability: "The sheriff or his officer might execute it without offence. For they ought to execute the writs directed to them: to this they are sworn. And though it appears in the *capias* that she was a countess (against whom no *capias* lies), and *ignorantia juris non excusat* (especially in sheriffs and other ministers of law and justice), yet the sheriff and his officers ought not to examine the judicial act of the Court but execute the writ."

PAYING THE POLICE FOR PROTECTION

The circumstances under which the police can demand payment for affording special protection were discussed in *Glassbrook Bros.*,

31

Ltd. v. *Glamorganshire County Council* (H.L. 1925). During the national coal strike of 1921 the management sought and obtained protection, but only upon agreement to pay the cost involved. The Courts upheld the charge made. "If," said the Lord Chancellor, "in the judgment of the police authorities, formed reasonably and in good faith, the garrison was necessary for the protection of life and property, then they were not entitled to make a charge for it. For that would be to exact a payment for the performance of a duty which they clearly owed to the appellants and their servants. But if they thought the garrison a superfluity, then they were entitled to treat the garrison duty as special duty and to charge for it." The police are not to incur expenses because of the excessive timidity or the excessive imagination of citizens. Yet, in their primary duty of preserving the peace, they are bound to weigh warnings from whatever quarter the warnings come. The problem of discriminating must be difficult.

POLICE HELP TO EVICT

The limitations to which this is subject was illustrated in *R.* v. *Tobin*, heard in August, 1932, at Old Street Police Court. The charges were, under the Vagrancy Act, 1924, that of being found on enclosed premises for an unlawful purpose, and of obstructing a police officer in the execution of his duty. Both charges were dismissed. The premises concerned had been obtained by the landlord upon an order of the County Court; the bailiffs took possession, locked the doors, and screwed up the windows. The defendant, the secretary of a local tenants' protection association, obtained entry and refused to leave at the request of the landlord's agent, who came along with a police sergeant. The sergeant gained entry by breaking a window and evicted the intruder.

The defendant was undoubtedly a trespasser. But this is not a criminal offence; and "an unlawful purpose" under the Vagrancy Act must be a criminal one. The landlord or his agent have a right to expel a trespasser, using no more force than is reasonably necessary. But he cannot call in the police to vindicate a civil right unless there is an urgent necessity. The only occasions when a constable is entitled to break open a private dwelling house is to take a suspected felon, or to prevent a felony, or "where a constable hears an affray in a house he may break in to suppress it, and may, in pursuit of an affrayer, break in to arrest him."

POLICE AT MEETINGS

There is nothing to prevent the hiring of a constable *off duty*, or of a police reservist, to help in keeping order at a meeting. Police on duty may be called in to suppress an actual or to prevent a threatened breach of the peace. When police are called in, the chairman must first ask disorderly persons to leave. Only after a reasonable time can such persons be forcibly removed, and then *not* by the police. It is only when the person resists in such a way as to cause a breach of the peace that the police can intervene.

CHURCH LAW

THE ecclesiastical law with which we deal in this book is part of the general law and applies, therefore, to every one living under the King's peace, whether he is a member of the Church of England or not. The peculiar position exists that laws affecting the church, "as by law established," are made by men of all churches and creeds, by men of no creed at all. When we speak of the Church of England as being the "Established Church," we mean simply that the State gives to the Church of England a legal position involving disabilities as well as privileges. We do not, of course, mean to suggest that out of a number of competing faiths Parliament has determined that only one may be lawfully entertained. Religious freedom can quite well consist with an established church.

CHURCH AND STATE

The relationship includes the following: (*a*) The King is head of Church as of State. As such head he summons convocations and in fact appoints bishops on the nomination of the Prime Minister of the time, who often is not a member of the Church of England, who may indeed, like Disraeli, belong to the Jewish faith ;

(*b*) Parliament controls the forms of worship and, in some sense, the teachings of the Church. In this the Church of England, in common with other Protestant Churches, is fundamentally different from the Roman Catholic Church. This consistently maintains the principle that the duly ordained clergy alone have control over the church and its members. The layman has no part—whether to make laws or to administer laws or to give decisions upon laws. From the outset, however, the Protestant Churches have admitted laymen to share in the ordering of church affairs.

In this country, the last vestige of the power of a Consistory Court against laymen has been taken away by the Chancel Repairs Act, 1932 (which came into operation on the first day of 1933). Section 1 of the Act prohibits any proceedings in any ecclesiastical court to enforce liability to repair the chancel.

The old names remain. But they are applied to Courts and to persons shorn of secular power. In some cases the power of Church Courts has been taken away directly. Thus the

Ecclesiastical Courts Jurisdiction Act, 1860, abolished the former jurisdiction of such courts to try cases of "brawling in church." The Act provided, in lieu, that a churchwarden or constable may arrest any person making a disturbance in church or churchyard, during service or not, and take him before a court of summary jurisdiction. So, too, the setting up in 1857 of the Divorce and Matrimonial Causes Court and the Court of Probate transferred to the temporal Courts jurisdiction over divorces and over wills. In other cases the power of the Church Courts has been taken away by implication. Bigamy and incest were once punishable in the Ecclesiastical Courts. Both are now punishable in the criminal courts, bigamy under the Offences Against the Person Act, 1861, incest under the Punishment of Incest Act, 1908. In a case where an attempt was made to revive an ecclesiastical jurisdiction, which, "if it has not expired, has so long slumbered in peace," the presiding judge in the Probate Court declared, "It cannot, I think, be doubted that a recurrence to the punishment of the laity, for the good of their souls, by the Ecclesiastical Courts would not be in harmony with modern ideas, or with the position which ecclesiastical authority now occupies in the country" (*Phillimore* v. *Machon*, Probate Division, 1876).

The Reformation did not in this country, as in most countries it did, bring about a complete severance with the system of the medieval Church. The episcopacy, the division into parishes, convocation, and the presence of the spiritual peers in the House of Lords—all these come down from the earliest times. And in the services appointed are innumerable echoes of the Middle Ages. But the Reformation did make a fundamental change in that the supreme head of the State became the supreme head of the Church, and the church Courts became controlled by the law Courts;

(c) Every person, in permanent or temporary allegiance to the King, has a right to baptism, marriage, and burial according to the rites of the Church. This is so whether or not the person is a member of the Church;

(d) Every person has a right to attend divine service at the parish church. Indeed, until the Religious Disabilities Act, 1846, a fine was payable by any person failing to attend divine service at their parish church on every Sunday and Holy Day "having no lawful or reasonable excuse to be absent." Such an excuse was, however, attendance at another place of worship: "If," ruled Holt, C.J., "a man repaired to any other chapel, it would be a good excuse for his not coming to his parish church";

(e) The Church of England can, through the powers delegated to it by the Church of England Assembly (Powers) Act of 1919— the "Enabling Act," it is sometimes called—make laws that have the force of Acts of Parliament;

(f) The decrees of the Ecclesiastical Courts, such as do continue to function, acting in accordance with Act of Parliament, will be enforced by the State. For, different in this matter from the purely domestic tribunals of the other churches, they rank as Courts of the land. The High Court will punish any contempt of the Ecclesiastical Courts; a writ of prohibition may issue against an excess of jurisdiction; and a mandamus may proceed against a reluctant bishop (see, for instance, the order in Chancery for a bishop to admit to a perpetual curacy a duly nominated person: *Notley* v. *Bishop of Birmingham*, 1930).

"FREE CHURCH" AND "ESTABLISHED CHURCH"

We will understand the relation better, perhaps, by looking at the difference from the legal point of view between the laws of a "free church" and those of an "established church." Indeed, we are incorrect in calling the former "laws." For, lacking the sanction of the State, they are rules of much the same nature as those of any voluntary association. They concern the members; and the Courts take cognisance of them only when they conflict with the State's laws. That his particular church countenanced a plurality of wives, for instance, would be no answer to a charge of bigamy. When the church is "established," however, its laws are given to it by the State, and will be enforced by the State. The method by which Parliament now exercises authority over the Established Church is described later. The church may have its own Courts, and their actions are valid in so far as they come within the powers delegated to them by Parliament, but no further.

From the strictly legal point of view, the Church of England is dependent upon the State. It is not a unity like a joint-stock company. Even the representative government spoken of below is by a delegated authority. The Church Courts have laymen as their officials; and, though these laymen are nominally in subordination to the hierarchy, in reality they are answerable to the Crown. Parliament is supreme over Church as over State. And, on all questions of ecclesiastical law, the final Court of Appeal is the Judicial Committee of the Privy Council.

An old book puts the matter thus: "The ecclesiastical law of England is compounded of these four main ingredients: The civil law, the canon law, the common law, and the statute law. When these laws do interfere and cross each other, the order of preference is this: The civil law submitteth to the canon law; both of these to the common law, and all three to the statute law." Under statute law, we should note, are included the Thirty-nine Articles of Religion, agreed upon in Convocation in 1562, and the Rubrics (i.e. directions for the conduct of the services) of the Book of Common Prayer. For both Articles and Rubrics were adopted by Act of Parliament.

DEFINITIONS AND NOTES

The "civil law," spoken of as occupying the lowest seat of authority, is the old Roman Law. To this, in the absence of other guidance, all our Courts resort. It forms the foundation of Scots law and is a boundless source of legal rules. Chief Justice Tindall declared, indeed, (*Acton* v. *Blundell*, 1843): "The Roman Law forms no rule binding in itself on the subjects of these realms. But, in deciding a case upon principle, where no direct authority can be cited from our books, it affords no small evidence of the soundness of the conclusion at which we have arrived, if it prove to be supported by that law,—the fruit of the researches of the most learned men, the collective wisdom of ages, and the groundwork of the municipal law of most of the countries of Europe."

"Canon law" is the collection of rules binding upon the clergy, but binding upon the laity only when they have been enacted by Parliament and turned thereby into statute law. The Act for the Submission of the Clergy, 1533, enacted that canon law is valid only to the extent that it is not repugnant to the laws of the realm or derogatory from the King's prerogative. The canons are made in Convocation; and they bind the clergy when the Royal assent has been signified. The canons usually referred to are those settled by the Convocation of Canterbury in 1603. 141 canons were agreed upon, mostly dealing with the duties of the clergy and the church officers. Canon 71, for instance, enjoins the minister to give the Communion to a person dangerously ill, or through infirmity unable to go to church, and who wishes to receive it; Canon 90 enjoins that two or three or more discreet persons in every parish be chosen for sidesmen or assistants to the churchwardens.

For purposes of church administration England is divided into two provinces, Canterbury and York, each having at its head an Archbishop. The Archbishop of Canterbury has, curiously enough, the style of "Primate of All England," while the Archbishop of York has the style of "Primate of England." Each province is divided into dioceses (districts administered by Bishops): the Bishop is sometimes called the *diocesan*; and this term is also applied to a member of the diocese (as *parishioner* is the term for a member of the parish). In many of the more populous dioceses the administrative work of the Bishop has become so overwhelming that it has been necessary to consecrate an assistant, or Suffragan Bishop. The Bishop may also have as his deputy a Surrogate.

Each diocese is divided into archdeaconries, the Archdeacon having the duty of superintending the Rural Deans. The Archdeacon's Court once of importance has ceased to be so, the Archdeacon's power of imposing penalty being confined to spiritual censure.

The Rural Deans administer the sub-divisions of the Archdeaconry: their office in these days does little more than give them precedence over the other clergymen in the rural deanery. The Dean of a cathedral or collegiate church controls the services and sees to the maintenance and improvement of the fabric.

The Rector or Parson, the incumbent of the parish church, had once rights to all church dues. Often the dues were "impropriated" by the monasteries and later by "lay impropriators" like some of the ancient colleges. The impropriators were, however, bound to provide for the services of the church; and the person appointed for the purpose was their Vicar, their substitute, or a Perpetual Curate, one to whom the care of souls is entrusted. Properly, we should use Rector as the term for the parson of a parish church whose tithes are not impropriate.

The benefice (or living) consists of the emoluments attached to the church; the parson is said to be appointed to a benefice (or to be beneficed); and the formal introduction to his parish church —an introduction called his induction—entitles him to the amounts payable.

Patronage (*congé d'élire*) is the process by which certain clergymen are appointed to office. Bishops, deans, some canons and incumbents, are appointed by the Crown on the advice of the prime minister. In the ancient sees the middle-age proceeding still prevails though it is, in fact, only a formality: there goes from the Crown a *congé d'élire* (a permission to choose) addressed to the dean and chapter; an accompanying letter announces the name of the person whom they may elect; this person is elected, his election is confirmed by the archbishop, he is consecrated to his office, does homage to the King, and is ceremoniously enthroned in his cathedral. Where there is no cathedral chapter, appointment is by letters patent.

Canon (or Prebendary), used of a church dignitary, is a clergyman who owns a prebend in a cathedral or collegiate church—the prebend being that portion of the revenues forming his stipend. Where, as in most of the newer cathedrals, no stipend is attached to the office, the term "canon" is restricted to one who forms part of the "chapter," or governing body, of the church or cathedral. This is the distinction between *canonry* and *prebend*: a canonry is the right to be a member of the chapter; a prebend is the right to receive certain revenues appropriated to the place.

A canon at first had his *praebenda* (his share) of the general funds. He lived with others in a clergy-house (or *claustrum*); and he ordered his life in accordance with the canons (or rules) of the church. Later each canon had a particular estate attached to his office; and he sometimes took his title from that estate. Thus a clergyman may be "Canon of St. Paul's and Prebendary of Finsbury."

The title of "honorary canon" is often conferred by the bishop upon clergymen of special distinction. Clergymen who help in the services of the cathedral, but who are not members of the chapter, are sometimes called "minor canons" or "petty canons."

The duties of a canon include residence near the cathedral (an Act of 1840 fixing the minimum period at three months in the year), and preaching in it and in other churches of the diocese.

"Secular Canon": the canons who adopted the ancient rule of having property in common were "regular canons" as contrasted with "secular canons" who had their private property. Since the Reformation the canons of the Church of England have all been secular.

REPRESENTATIVE GOVERNMENT IN THE CHURCH

In each parish there is an "electoral roll" upon which all parishioners, and also all those attending the church from without the parish, have a right to appear. Those upon the roll are called together to the *Annual Parochial Church Meeting* to elect their representatives to the *Parochial Church Council*, and also to the councils of the larger units of church organisation, to the *Ruri-decanal Conference* and the *Diocesan Conference.*

It is the diocesan electors that, every five years, elect members of the *House of Laity.* The *National Assembly of the Church of England* consists of this *House of Laity* together with the *Upper and Lower Houses of Convocations.*

By the "Enabling Act," the Church Assembly passes measures relating to the Church, as, for instance, the adoption of the revised Prayer Book.[1] These measures are then reported upon to Parliament by its Ecclesiastical Committee. The Committee is technically the "Ecclesiastical Committee of the Privy Council," and its composition is laid down in s. 2 of the 1919 Act :

The Ecclesiastical Committee shall consist of fifteen members of the House of Lords nominated by the Lord Chancellor, and fifteen members of the House of Commons, nominated by the Speaker of the House of Commons, to serve for the duration of each Parliament. The Committee is expected to make a report upon the legal effect of the measure proposed and of its expediency, particularly in reference to the constitutional rights of all his Majesty's subjects.

When Parliament enacts that the measure shall receive the royal assent, it is presented to the King; and his signing it makes it a part of the general law.

PAROCHIAL CHURCH COUNCIL

This council governs the financial affairs of the parish, taking over in this matter the functions of vestry meeting and churchwardens. But s. 2 of the 1921 Act setting up the parochial councils suggests that this should not curtail church activities—

It shall be the primary duty of the Council in every parish to co-operate with the Incumbent in the initiation, conduct, and development of church work both within the parish and outside.

---

[1] A striking illustration was afforded in 1928. The Prayer Book of 1662 seemed to many capable of improvement and, after strenuous debate, the Church Assembly authorised the use of a Prayer Book—"the Deposited Book"—having additions to and modifications of the older one. In two successive years, though the House of Lords approved the measure, the House of Commons refused its sanction of the use. For the "Deposited Book" seemed to countenance doctrines not consistent with those of the Tudor Reformers. Strictly, therefore, the Prayer Book annexed to the Act of Uniformity (1662) is the only one that should be used; and the full, not the curtailed, forms of Morning and Evening Prayer in that book should be used every Sunday in the year. The revised services are, indeed, being used—in some instances with the bishop's sanction. The old question of the desirability of a continuing connection between Church and State is, thereby, again raised in a new form.

ELECTORAL ROLL

The Parochial Church Council is elected by those whose names appear on the Electoral Roll. The qualifications for enrolment are shown in the form of Application for Enrolment—

I, ...[*Full Christian Name and Surname*]......., of ....[*Full Postal Address*], declare that I have attained the age of eighteen years and reside in the parish of ...., and am a member of the Church of England and do not belong to any religious body which is not in communion with the Church of England.

I hereby apply to be entered on the Church electoral roll of the parish of .... in the diocese of ...., in which parish I am resident *or* in which parish for the period of six months last past I have habitually attended public worship.

I declare that my name is not on the church electoral roll of any other parish in the said diocese *except that of the parish of* ...., *from which roll I desire my name to be removed.*
[Date]   [Signature]

CHURCHWARDENS

The churchwardens are relieved of duties relating to the collection and spending of money on the church building and on its services. They are still, however, responsible to the "Ordinary" —the Bishop whose orders are valid through the diocese—for the order and discipline of church and parish. They are guardians of the parishioners' rights, and they are the legal owners of the goods of the church. The freehold of the church, on the other hand, is, in general, vested in the incumbent.

Any person, including a woman, qualified to be a member of the Parochial Church Council, may be elected as churchwarden, residence in the parish not now being necessary. The churchwarden must, that is, be an actual lay communicating member of the Church of England, and be at least twenty-one years of age.

The Vestry and the Parochial Church Meeting, forming one body for this special purpose, elect the churchwardens. The incumbent must consent to the choice and, in the event of failure to agree, the meeting elects one churchwarden and the other is nominated by the incumbent. Election takes place either in Easter week or the week after; but, till the bishop or the archdeacon admits (upon their undertaking to fulfil their duties faithfully) the newly-elected wardens, the old ones retain office. In practice the Parochial Church Council has absorbed the Vestry, a meeting of representatives of the congregation for the transaction of parish business.

RIGHTS AND DUTIES OF CHURCHWARDENS

As their name implies, the churchwardens are guardians of the interests of the church. It is their duty to inform the bishop of any neglect of duty or impropriety of conduct of the incumbent; they maintain order during the services, allocating seats and collecting alms; they are charged with the protection of church property, being able, if necessary, to invoke the Courts; and they ought, in strictness, to present for the bishop's censure all—including the clergy—who have transgressed ecclesiastical law.

Though the general finance of a parish is controlled by the Parochial Council, the churchwardens, with the consent of the incumbent, still dispose of the money collected at Holy Communion to "pious and charitable uses," these uses being determined by the bishop in the event of disagreement.

Where the Parochial Church Council does not appoint a treasurer, the churchwardens are joint treasurers of the money collected in church.

The Act of 1921 transferred to the Parochial Council the former liabilities of the churchwardens to maintain, preserve, and insure the fabric of the church. Yet the churchwardens must, from the essential nature of their office, take the initiative in any matter relating to repairs. They, too, are the owners of the goods, ornaments, and furniture of the church, for the use of parishioners. But their old obligation, to provide what are necessary for the right and reverend conduct of the services—including such things as "a bell and rope, to ring to church and to toll at funerals," "a communion table and a fair linen cloth to cover it," and "a surplice with sleeves for the minister"—is now, it would seem, transferred, along with the funds available, to the Parochial Council.

CHURCHWARDENS AND SITTINGS

It is the duty, and the right, of the churchwardens to arrange the sittings in the church. All the parishioners have a right to a seat in the parish church without payment; but the churchwardens may allot seats to such parishioners as require them, and then they must not allow any other person to sit in these seats until after the service begins. When a person has been accustomed to occupy a seat at an ordinary service, it appears that the churchwardens must not deprive him or her of it without such notice as will allow of a protest.

The practice of receiving a payment from those to whom the churchwardens allot seats is not illegal. But, in all churches built under the Church Building Act of 1818, at least one-fifth of the seats must be set apart for the use of the poor without payment.

The right of the churchwardens to control sittings is limited to this extent: (a) The chief seat in the chancel may by custom be appropriated to the use of the rector (or vicar) and his family; (b) A private person may own an aisle or a chapel, and in this the churchwardens cannot allot sittings; (c) A parishioner may have a right vested in him, possibly through his occupation of a certain house in the parish, to occupy a special seat. That, indeed, is the real meaning of "pew": it was a raised, sometimes enclosed, seat for a particular person or family. Now, of course, the name is applied indiscriminately to all the seats of the congregation.

The churchwardens' duty of maintaining order and decorum in church and churchyard has already been noted.

SIDESMEN

These are chosen to help the churchwardens in the maintenance of order and in other duties, including the collection of voluntary offerings connected with the church and its services. They are "two or three or more discreet persons in every parish chosen for sidesmen or assistants."

PARISH CLERK AND SEXTON

These church officers are from old time. The parish clerk is noted in Canon 91, which declares that "he shall be of twenty years of age at the least, known to the Parson to be of honest conversation, and sufficient for his reading, writing, and also for his competent skill in singing, if it may be."

The sexton, whose office may be held by a woman, has as chief duty the care of church and churchyard, possibly including the digging of graves.

APPOINTMENT OF INCUMBENT

The Benefices (Exercise of Rights of Presentation) Act of 1931 made a great change in the method of appointment of the incumbent of a parish. Till that Act neither the churchwardens nor the parishioners generally had any voice in the matter; the patron and the bishop of the diocese were uncontrolled.

The present law is this: the parishioners now have much

control. (*a*) When a vacancy occurs, or is about to occur, the bishop must notify the patron and the Parochial Church Council. The Council then has power to "make representations in writing to the patron as to the conditions, needs, and traditions of the parish, but without mentioning the name of any particular clerk," sending also a copy to the bishop. (*b*) The Council may then resolve that the rights given by the Act shall be claimed. Then—

(i) The patron must confer with the churchwardens, acting as the representatives of the Parochial Church Council, and obtain their consent to the presentation. Having this consent he may immediately present.

(ii) If *sixty days have passed* since the vacancy was notified, and (*a*) *the conference between patron and churchwardens has taken place and the churchwardens have not given assent to the presentation*, or (*b*) *the conference, for some reason other than the neglect or refusal of the patron, has not taken place*, then the patron must obtain the bishop's approval of the clerk presented as being suitable. In each diocese a body of advisers has been established; and the bishop may (if patron or council require, he must) consult this body before giving or withholding approval. An appeal lies by the patron to the archbishop.

CLERGYMAN (Ordination, Holy Orders, Thirty-nine Articles, etc.)

The incumbent is a clergyman, an ordained minister of the Established Church. This "ordination" consists in his receiving, from the hands of his bishop (who himself has the power as being in the direct line of "apostolic succession") and after suitable tests as to character and capacity, authority to act as a deacon. Under this authority he is endowed with the power to officiate in the Church services, to administer the sacraments, and to pronounce absolution to such as "do earnestly and truly repent"; he becomes, in virtue of his office, endowed with the power to bind and to unbind; he may celebrate marriages and conduct burials in accordance with the rites of the Church. At his ordination he accepts certain fundamental doctrines, prescribed by the Clerical Subscription Act, 1865, and based on the Thirty-nine Articles of Religion drawn up by the Convocation of 1562, and he undertakes to obey his "Ordinary" (the Bishop or other superior officer entitled to give him orders).

Being ordained he is in one of the "holy orders"—grades or degrees in the Church ministry—the orders recognised in the Anglican Church being *bishop*, *priest*, and *deacon*, the orders recognised in the Roman Catholic Church being *bishop, priest, deacon,* and *sub-deacon* (in the Roman Catholic Church are also the minor orders of *acolyte, exorcist, reader,* and *doorkeeper*). As a "clerk in holy orders" a clergyman is under some disabilities. He is, for instance, ineligible for election to the House of Commons; though, in the event of his becoming a senior bishop, he automatically becomes a member of the House of Lords. Nowadays, however, he may renounce holy orders, and he is then remitted to the ordinary civil status.

The privileged position once held by a clergyman as distinct from a layman has disappeared. In particular, the "benefit of clergy"—exemption in the earliest period from trial by the secular Courts, and, later, exemption from sentence for the first conviction—has long gone. Like his parishioners the clergyman is now subject to the ordinary Courts and is required to conform to the ordinary law. (See page 951 where the subject of "marital coercion" is discussed.)

An age limit is prescribed: "And none shall be admitted a Deacon, except he be Twenty-three years of age, unless he have a Faculty. And every man which is to be admitted a Priest shall be full Four-and-twenty years old. And every man which is to be ordained or consecrated Bishop shall be full Thirty years of age."

Since a most important part of his duties is to minister the sacraments (religious ceremonies, like baptism and communion, that are regarded as outward and visible signs of inward and spiritual grace) he is sometimes called a Minister. But this term is not commonly applied to a clergyman of the Church of England.

DUTIES OF AN INCUMBENT

From the fact that the Church of England is "established" it follows that the incumbent's duties to his parishioners are in many matters prescribed by law. The penalties attached to breaches of the earlier Acts, are, indeed, seldom invoked; and many of Parliament's directions are habitually flouted. Still, the laws remain.

Obedience to Law

(*a*) Thus, the Act of Uniformity of 1662, directs the incumbent to perform the morning and evening services contained in the Book of Common Prayer on every Sunday, and on every Holy day and its eve. By the Revised Tables of Lessons Act, 1922, he may vary the lessons prescribed, and the Act of Uniformity

Amendment Act, 1872, allows a shortened form of service for days other than Sunday, Christmas Day, Ash Wednesday, Good Friday, and Ascension Day. Deviations apart from these—the common practice of abbreviating the Invocation and the substitution of modern prayers for the collects provided in the book, for instance— are illegalities.

Visiting the Sick

(b) On being told that a person is dangerously ill in the parish, the incumbent is bound to go and give that person instruction and comfort. The Prayer Book prescribes a service for Visitation of the Sick. The incumbent must also administer the Communion if the sick person wishes to receive it.

Communion

(c) The incumbent must administer the Communion often enough to enable all parishioners to communicate at least three times a year, of which Easter is to be one.

Baptism

(d) The incumbent must baptise the child of any parishioner brought to him on a Sunday or Holy day, and he must go to baptise any child in the parish that is dangerously ill. He must enter particulars in a baptismal register; and, in accordance with the Baptismal Fees Abolition Act, 1872, no one shall take a fee for the service.

Marriage

(e) By the Marriage Act, 1823, he must publish banns on three Sundays at morning service. (See page 53.)

Burial in Churchyard

(f) The incumbent owns the freehold of the churchyard and may give consent for the burial of a non-parishioner, dying outside the parish, to be buried there. For this, however, he must obtain the consent of the churchwardens as representing the parishioners. But a parishioner, wherever he may die, has a right to be buried in the churchyard or other burial place of his own parish. A non-parishioner, too, dying in the parish has also a right to be buried there. Except for the cases noted below the incumbent must perform the service provided in the Prayer Book for the Burial of the Dead. The Births and Deaths Registration Act, 1926, forbids him to allow burial till a certificate of registration of death, or a coroner's order, has been issued, and within ninety-six hours he must deliver to the Registrar notification on a prescribed form of the burial.

The Burial Service must not be used for such as are not baptised members of the Church of England, nor for such as, having been excommunicated for a grievous and notorious crime, have not repented. He must, however, allow burial in the consecrated ground. For any one who has "laid violent hands upon himself" —one against whom the coroner has recorded a verdict of *felo de se*—the Burial Laws Amendment Act, 1880, prescribes alternative burial services.

Conduct of Services

(*g*) The incumbent determines the manner in which the services are to be performed. He determines, therefore, whether or not there shall be music, whether also there shall be a choir or an organist. Apparently it follows that, though the Parochial Church Council provides as a general rule the salary payable, the organist is appointed by the incumbent—normally no doubt with the Council's approval.

Alteration of Structure

(*h*) Though the incumbent has, in general, the freehold of the church, he has it in trust and must maintain the property as it is. For, a judgment declared, "the church belongs not to any one generation, nor are its interests and conditions the exclusive care of those who inhabit the parish at any one period of time. It is in entire conformity with this aspect of the parish church that the law has forbidden any structural alteration to be made in it, save those which are approved by a disinterested authority in the person of the Ordinary." Apart, therefore, from trivial matters, the incumbent must obtain approval before a structural alteration is effected in the church, and before any modification of existing ornaments alters the character of the church. He obtains what is called a "faculty." (See page 972.)

Tombstones

(*i*) The incumbent has the duty, and the right, to determine whether tombstones and monuments of ordinary kind shall be placed in church or churchyard. He may permit these at his discretion without a faculty; but, where a monument out of the ordinary is in question, a faculty is needed. As the protector of the churchyard, it is his duty to prevent unsightly erections or improper inscriptions. The tombstones and monuments remain the property of those who erected them; and they can protect their property by an action for trespass. Accordingly, the Parochial Council is under no obligation to maintain tombstones in repair.

Commission of Inquiry

(*j*) The Benefices (Ecclesiastical Duties) Act of 1926 supplies a good summary of the duties. The Act enables a bishop to appoint a commission of inquiry whenever he has reason to suppose that the duties are inadequately performed; and these include a duty "to manifest, in his acts, conduct, and course of life, due respect for his sacred office, and a due solicitude for the moral and spiritual welfare of his parishioners."

FACULTY: CONSISTORY COURT: COURT OF THE ARCHES

An addition or alteration that sensibly changes the character of a church is illegal unless the previous approval of the bishop has been obtained. Yet the former state cannot be restored without a faculty, and the application for a faculty for removal usually elicits an application for a "confirmatory faculty." Like an Act of Indemnity the confirmatory faculty legalises an illegality.

Application for a faculty is made in each diocese to the Consistory Court (called in the diocese of Canterbury the Commissary Court). This Court, presided over by the bishop's chancellor, is the general court for church affairs, and is the one ecclesiastical court left of any importance. Appeal lies to the Archbishops' Provincial Courts over which one judge, appointed by the archbishops jointly, presides. This judge has the title "Dean of the Arches" when president of the Provincial Court of Canterbury, a Court to which the name "Court of the Arches" is given.

CONSISTORY COURT AND CLERGY DISCIPLINE

It is this court, too, before which a clergyman is prosecuted under the Clergy Discipline Act of 1892. For an alleged offence against morality either a parishioner or the Bishop prosecutes the clergyman.

TITHE RENT-CHARGE AND QUEEN ANNE'S BOUNTY

Payments to many incumbents come from "Queen Anne's Bounty"; and the source is to a great extent "tithe rent charge."

In 1704, by letters patent, Queen Anne created a corporation to which she assigned all her revenue of first-fruits and tenths. The full name of the Corporation explains its object : "The Governors of the Bounty of Queen Anne for the Augmentation of the Maintenance of the Poor Clergy." It is to this corporation that landowners, holding their land subject to the payment, pay the amount due, and the corporation distributes to the incumbents entitled. The Tithe Act, 1925, makes provision for its extinction. Meantime, it is, by the Law of Property Act, 1925, a legal interest in land. It by no means goes all to the beneficed clergy : a High Court case in 1933 arose from the fact that Merton College, Oxford, levied an illegal distress upon one who had defaulted in respect of tithe rent-charge payment. Doubtless, the prejudice against the payment is due now to its name (with the associations that name has) rather than to its nature. For it is to-day on the same footing as ground-rent.

Under the Tithe Act, 1891, in order to collect tithe rentcharge from landowners in default, Queen Anne's Bounty applies to the County Court of the district in which the land concerned is situated. The County Court Judge then makes an order under which a distress is levied. The County Court Judge may, upon his refusal to make the order, be obliged to do so by a *mandamus* from the High Court. A striking illustration occurred in Kent during a period of acute agricultural depression (*Rex* v. *Judge Clements*, on the application of *Queen Anne's Bounty*, July, 1933). Attempts to levy distresses had led to violence and disorder, and the County Court Judge was reluctant to issue an order that apparently could not be executed: "I am," he said, "not going to make these orders until you give me the name of a person who can carry them out." Queen Anne's Bounty obtained a rule *nisi* and the Divisional Court made the rule absolute. The Lord Chief Justice, in the course of his judgment said : "It is a very unfortunate case. I sympathise very much with the County Court Judge. But, in view of the Tithe Act, 1891, the Court has no alternative but to make the order asked for. I hope most sincerely that wise counsels will prevail in the present and in similar cases." The Tithe Act, 1925, s. 10, does in fact give Queen Anne's Bounty a discretion not to take proceedings in cases of hardship.

INCOME TAX

GENERAL CONSIDERATIONS

THIS is a "direct tax," being levied upon the person who is expected to bear the burden of it, and there being as a rule no method of moving the burden on to another. It is no longer a single tax, but a great code of taxation; and it seeks to bring about fairness by a complexity of devices. There are allowances and remissions; there is a discrimination between "earned" and "unearned" incomes; there is a lower limit income exempt from the tax, and a higher limit income about which an additional—or *surtax*—is enacted.

The resulting difficulty of determining what amount of tax is payable increases the cost of collection. It increases, too, the troubles of the income-tax payer anxious to fill up his assessment form correctly; and he is often left under the, probably erroneous, impression that he is paying more than the income tax law obliges him to.

It may be noted, too, that the attempt to bring about fairness has brought some inconsistencies into income tax law. Thus, the exemption of insurance premiums lessens the burden upon those whose responsibilities and whose precarious incomes oblige them to insure. Such exemption is, however, a discrimination against other desirable forms of saving. Something like one-tenth of the tax arises, for instance, not from individual incomes, but from the profits placed to the reserves of joint-stock companies. This part of the tax diminishes, therefore, the flow of savings nourishing the capital equipment of the country. Such social savings might well, perhaps, be relieved.

WHO SHOULD PAY INCOME TAX ?

The persons liable to the tax are (1) all persons resident in Great Britain and Northern Ireland, whether British subjects or not; (2) all persons not resident (whether British subjects or not) to the extent that they derive income from property, trade, employment, or vocation in Great Britain and Northern Ireland. (Where "United Kingdom" occurs in the Income Tax Acts, the term must be understood to refer to Great Britain and Northern Ireland only.)

"Persons" include the artificial persons created by law, in particular, joint-stock trading companies.

SCHEDULES

Taxable incomes are classed under five schedules—

Schedule A. From property in land and buildings. The tax is levied upon the occupier of the property, who, if he is not also the owner, may deduct the amount paid from the rent. The tax is payable in one instalment, on or before the 1st January. Where the annual value does not exceed £40, relief is granted to the extent of one-fourth of the value; where the annual value is between £40 and £50, relief is granted to the extent of £10; where the annual value is between £50 and £100 relief, is granted to the extent of one-fifth; where the annual value is above £100, relief to the extent of one-fifth on the first £100, to the extent of one-sixth on the remainder is granted.

Schedule B. From the occupation of lands, the basis of the assessment being the full annual value. But farmers may, if they choose and if they give notice before the 6th July, be assessed under Schedule D.

Schedule C. From interest and dividends arising out of the public funds.

Schedule D. By way of profits from professions, trades, or other callings. The trader making his annual return must show his profits for the year *preceding* the year of assessment. But, if the trade has begun during the assessment year, the actual profits of the year are the basis of the tax.

Schedule E. By way of annuities, salaries, or pensions arising from employment under the Crown, public bodies, societies, companies, and traders generally. The assessment is on the actual income from employment during the preceding year.

The fiscal year runs from the 6th April to the 5th April following; assessments are made in the autumn; and the tax is payable in two equal instalments on the 1st January and the 1st July.

NOTES RELATING TO THE ASSESSMENT FORM

In filling up the assessment form the following should be noted—

1. *Offices, Employments, or Pensions.* The amounts of the emoluments to be entered are the amounts for the year ended 5th April.

Where income tax in respect of any emoluments is borne by

the company or employer, the amount so borne is required to be treated as additional remuneration.

Wounds, disablement, and disability pensions granted on account of military, etc., service, and allowances in respect of children granted by the Ministry of Pensions to widows of members of the naval, military or air forces, are exempt and should be omitted.

2. *Offices and Employments : Expenses that may be entered as deductions*—

(*a*) Expenses which the taxpayer is necessarily obliged to incur and defray out of the emoluments either in travelling in the performance of the duties, or otherwise wholly, exclusively, and necessarily in such performance. (The cost of travelling between the place of residence and the place of employment is, for example, not allowable.)

(*b*) Annual contributions paid to a Superannuation Fund approved by the Commissioners of Inland Revenue under the provisions of the Income Tax Acts.

(*c*) Contributions made under the requirements of any public general Act of Parliament towards the expenses of providing a superannuation allowance or gratuity on retirement or death, e.g. contributions required under the Teachers' (Superannuation) Acts, 1918 to 1925, the Police Pensions Act, 1921, etc. The name of the Fund or Act should be quoted.

(*d*) So much of any amount expended in replacing obsolete machinery or plant as is equal to the cost of the machinery or plant replaced, after deducting from such cost (*a*) the total amount of any allowances made at any time in respect of such machinery or plant for wear and tear and the additional deduction of one-tenth (see Note 3) and (*b*) any sum realised by its sale.

(*e*) In the case of a clergyman or minister who uses any part of his dwelling-house mainly and substantially for the purposes of his duty, a corresponding part of the rent or annual value of the house, not exceeding one-eighth.

The expenses to be entered as above are the expenses of the year ended 5th April.

3. *Allowance in respect of Machinery and Plant* (*Wear and Tear and Additional Deduction*). A deduction may be claimed in respect of wear and tear of machinery or plant (e.g. a motor car) necessarily used for the purposes of the office or employment. An additional deduction will be allowed equal to one-tenth of the wear and tear deduction appropriate to the year.

4. *Profits of Trade, Profession, or Vocation.* The amount of profits entered in the return should be calculated from the accounts of the business for the year ended on the date, not later than 5th April, to which the accounts are usually made up.

Exception. Where the trade, etc., was set up on the assessment year, the profits to 5th April, should be computed to the best of the taxpayer's knowledge and belief, and the basis of the computation should be stated.

Information as to the deductions allowable in arriving at the amount to be returned may be obtained from the Inspector of Taxes.

5. *Allowance in respect of Losses in a Trade, Profession, or Vocation.* An adjustment of tax may in certain circumstances be cla'med—

(*a*) Where a loss is sustained in a trade, etc., during the year to which the tax relates—provided that the claim is made within twelve months after the end of the year.

(*b*) Where a loss has been sustained in a trade, etc., during an earlier year and relief has not already been wholly given in respect of such loss.

Further information may be obtained from the Inspector of Taxes. Any claim in respect of a loss should be made, not on the return form, but by letter addressed to the Inspector.

6. *Interest, Dividends, Annuities, and other Annual Payments and Dominion and Foreign Securities and Possessions, not taxed at the source.* Care should be taken to include any income received or credited in respect of interest on bank accounts or deposits, interest from Co-operative Societies on loans, deposits or share capital (but not dividends on purchases), and dividends or interest on Government and Corporation securities from which tax is not deducted at the time of payment.

Among the dividends or interest on Government and Corporation securities from which tax is not deducted are the following—

(*a*) Dividends or interest, of any amount on 5 per cent War Loan Stock, registered or inscribed at the Bank of England or the Bank of Ireland—except where application has been made to the Bank to deduct tax—or held on the books of the Post Office. (Tax is deducted where the securities are held in the form of "bearer bonds.")

(*b*) Dividends or interest, of any amount, derived from the Post Office issues (except of "bearer bonds") of Funding Loan Stock, registered Victory Bonds, 5 per cent and $4\frac{1}{2}$ per cent

Treasury Bonds, 3 per cent, 3½ per cent, 4½ per cent, and 5 per cent Conversion Loan, 4 per cent Consolidated Loan, and 4 per cent National Savings Bonds.

(*c*) Dividends not exceeding £5 per annum from Government or Corporation securities inscribed at the Bank of England or the Bank or Ireland; interest on registered Housing Bonds, where the aggregate holding does not exceed £100.

(*d*) All dividends from stocks purchased and held through any Savings Bank; dividends on 4½ per cent War Loan Stock registered at the Post Office, where the holding does not exceed £200.

The accumulated interest on National Savings Certificates is exempt from Income Tax, and should be omitted from Sections B and C.

As regards income from Dominion and Foreign Securities and Possessions, the amount to be entered is the full amount arising in the year ended 5th April (whether or not received in the United Kingdom), except that in the case of Possessions other than Stocks, Shares, or Rents, the amount to be entered is the amount received in the United Kingdom in that year.

7. *Other Profits or Income not taxed at the source.* Having entered in Section B his income from the sources described above, the taxpayer should consider carefully whether he had any other income of any description not taxed at the source, and, if so, should enter it in the space provided in Section B. Examples of such other income are the profits from letting a furnished house and underwriting (or sub-writing) commissions.

8. *Wife's Income.* The income of a married woman living with her husband is deemed to be his income for the purposes of the Income Tax Acts. Her income must be included in his return (in Section B in so far as it is not taxed at the source, and in Section C in so far as it is taxed) unless an application for separate assessment has been made. The amount of tax payable by husband and wife together will not be diminished by separate assessment.

9. *Income from Ownership of Land, Houses, etc., in the United Kingdom*—

(*a*) Enter description and precise address of each property owned and the net annual value as assessed to Income Tax, Schedule A, or the amount of the rent if less than the net annual value assessed. If the annual value assessed is not known, state so and give the best estimate you can, and the figure entered will be corrected when the return is examined.

(*b*) A person occupying property either rent free, or at a rent below the net annual value of the property, as assessed under Schedule A, should enter in space (*a*) of Section C the net annual value of the property; if the property is occupied rent free, he should add the words "rent free"; if a rent is paid, he should enter such rent in Section D. Property occupied rent free by an employee, as such, will not usually fall to be entered in his return, but a full statement of the facts should be annexed to the return form, unless this has already been done in a previous year. If further information is desired, apply to the Inspector of Taxes.

(Where a clergyman or minister occupies a dwelling-house rent free by virtue of his office in such circumstances that the annual value of the house does not fall to be regarded as part of his income, he is neverthless entitled, on giving notice for any year to the Inspector of Taxes, to require that the annual value of such house, after deducting therefrom the amount of any annual sum payable in respect of the house, shall be treated as part of his earned income for that year. Any such notice must be given either by 30th September in the year of assesssment, or within three months after the commencement of occupation by the clergyman or minister, and may be given by entering the situation and annual value of the house in the space provided in Section C, and adding the words : "occupied rent free—claimed as earned income." Any rent, ground rent, interest on mortgage or loan, or other annual sum paid in respect of the house, either by the clergyman or minister or by the trustees, etc., should be entered in Section D.)

10. *Income from Occupation of Land in the United Kingdom.* State situation and enter the amount of the assessment to Income Tax, Schedule B. If this is not known, state so and enter (*a*) the amount of the annual value (inclusive of any tithe) where the lands are occupied wholly or mainly for husbandry; or (*b*) one-third of such annual value, where the lands are not so occupied.

11. *Dividends, Interest, Annuities, etc., Taxed before Receipt.* (*a*) Enter the gross amounts receivable in the year ended 5th April, and include any dividends declared "free of tax." Where the gross amount is not shown on the counterfoil of the dividend warrant or on a similar document, it may usually be calculated by adding one-third (5s. for every 15s.) to the net amount received. If you are unable to ascertain the correct amount to be added, you may enter the net amount, provided you add the word

"Net," and the proper addition will be made when the return is examined.

If in any case United Kingdom Income Tax has been deducted at a rate reduced in consequence of the allowance of relief in respect of Dominion Income Tax, enter the actual rate of tax deducted opposite the item of income concerned.

Include any Building Society interest received or credited.

(b) Dividend counterfoils or other certificates of deduction of tax need not be forwarded with the return unless a request for such certificates accompanies the return form.

12. *Statement of Charges (Section D of the Return Form).* Enter the gross amounts payable in the year ended 5th April. Any interest paid to a Bank in respect of which you have obtained re-payment (or set-off) of Income Tax for that year should be included.

Voluntary payments are not admissible as deductions and should not be entered.

13. *General Explanation.* From the tax chargeable at the standard rate on the net income remaining after deducting any annual charges such as ground rent and interest on mortgages or loans, the undermentioned reliefs at the standard rate (except where otherwise specified) may be claimed by individuals provided the conditions indicated below are satisfied.

Before the reliefs can be granted the Acts require a declaration of the statutory income of the year from all sources.

14. *Earned Income Allowance.* A deduction of the tax on one-fifth of the net amount of any earned income will be allowed subject to a maximum of the tax on £300.

15. A similar *allowance in respect of other income* may be claimed where either the taxpayer, or, in the case of a married man, his wife living with him, was on 6th April 65 years of age or more and the total statutory income does not exceed £500.

Where the total income exceeds £500, the tax payable on the total income will be reduced, where necessary, so as not to exceed a sum equal to the total of (1) the amount of tax which would have been payable if the total income had been just £500, and (2) one-half of the amount by which the total income exceeds £500.

16. A *Personal Allowance* will be made of tax on £100, or, in the case of a married man whose wife is living with him, a personal allowance of tax on £150 may be claimed.

Where the total income includes any earned income of the wife, an additional deduction will be allowed of tax on $\frac{4}{5}$ of the amount of such earned income (subject to a maximum additional deduction of tax on £45).

17. A deduction of tax on £50 may be claimed by (*a*) a *Widower* who has a female relative of his or of his deceased wife resident with him for the purpose of having the charge and care of any child or adopted child of his in respect of whom the deduction for children is given, or in the capacity of a housekeeper; or (*b*) a *Widow* who has a female relative of hers or of her deceased husband resident with her for the purpose.

If the widower or widow proves that he or she has no such female relative who is able and willing to take such charge or act in such capacity, the same deduction may be claimed in respect of some other female person employed for the purpose.

18. A deduction of tax on £50 may be claimed by an *Unmarried Person* who has living with him and maintains at his own expense either his mother (being a widow or living apart from her husband) or some other female relative for the purpose of having the charge and care of any brother or sister of his in respect of whom the deduction for children or adopted children is given. (A female taxpayer may claim in respect of either her mother or a female relative in the circumstances set out.)

19. A deduction may be claimed in respect of any *child*, step-child, or adopted child who is living and under the age of 16 years at any time within the year ending 5th April, or who, if over that age on 6th April, is receiving full-time instruction at any university college, school, or other educational establishment. ("Adopted child" means, for this purpose, a child of whom the individual has the custody and whom he or she maintains.) The deduction allowable is tax on £50 in respect of *one* child, and tax on £40 in respect of each subsequent child.

No deduction can, however, be allowed in respect of any child or adopted child who is entitled in his or her own right to an income which, after excluding any income from a scholarship, bursary, or other similar educational endowment, exceeds £50 a year.

20. A deduction of tax on £25 may be claimed in respect of any person whom the individual maintains at his own expense, and who is (1) a *relative* of his, or of his wife, and *incapacitated by old age or infirmity* from maintaining himself or herself; or (2) his or his wife's *widowed mother*, whether incapacitated or not; or (3) his *daughter* who is resident with him and *upon whose*

services he is compelled to depend by reason of old age or infirmity. (A female taxpayer may claim in respect of (1) a relative of hers or of her husband; or (2) her or her husband's widowed mother; or (3) her daughter, in the circumstances set out.)

No deduction can, however, be allowed under (1) or (2) if the income of the dependent relative, exclusive of voluntary allowances, exceeds £50 a year.

Where two or more persons jointly mantain a dependent relative as above, the deduction is to be apportioned between them in proportion to the amount or value of their respective contributions.

21. An allowance will be made of *half the tax remaining chargeable at the standard rate* after the allowances specified in Notes 16 to 22 have been made—but *subject to a maximum of half the tax on* £175. The effect of this allowance is to reduce the tax on an amount of income not exceeding £175 to half the standard rate.

Where the £175 of income in question includes income from dividends, mortgage interest, etc., taxed before receipt, an allowance of tax representing the difference between tax at the full standard rate and at half the standard rate on the amount of such income will be made as far as possible as a set-off against the tax chargeable on other income.

Where the £175 of income in question includes income from property, the allowance due in respect of such income will normally be made in the assessment on the property. An owner may, if he desires, make application for the tax on any property to be recovered from him instead of from his tenant (without prejudice, however, to the right of recovery, if necessary, upon the property). Any such application should be made before 31st July in the first year for which it is intended to take effect, upon a form to be obtained for the purpose from the Inspector of Taxes.

22. From the tax remaining chargeable after the allowances specified have been made, an allowance may be claimed in respect of premiums paid for *Life Assurance* or for contracts for deferred annuities. The allowance is authorised in respect of (a) premiums (whether annual or not) paid by the claimant on his own life or on that of his wife; (b) premiums (whether annual or not) paid by the claimant's wife out of her separate income on her own life or on that of her husband; and (c) any sum which the claimant, under any Act of Parliament or under the conditions of his employment, is liable to pay, or to have deducted from his salary, to secure a deferred annuity to his widow or provision for his children after his death.

The amount of premiums on which the allowance is to be calculated is subject to the following limitations—

(*a*) In the case of any policy securing a capital sum on death (whether in conjunction with any other benefit or not) the amount on which the allowance is calculated is not to exceed 7 per cent of that capital sum, exclusive of any additional benefit by way of bonus or otherwise.

(*b*) In the case of policies or contracts which do not secure a capital sum on death, the total amount on which the allowance is calculated is not to exceed £100, and the policies must have been taken out not later than 22nd June, 1916. In the case of such policies or contracts effected after that date, no allowance is to be made, except where they were effected in connection with certain superannuation or pension schemes.

(*c*) In the case of a deferred assurance made after 22nd June, 1916, no allowance is to be made in respect of premiums payable during the period of deferment, except where the assurance was effected in connection with certain superannuation or pension schemes.

(*d*) The total amount on which the allowance is calculated is not to exceed one-sixth of the claimant's total statutory income from all sources for the year.

The allowances due will be calculated at the following rates—

(i) Where the policy was effected after 22nd June, 1916: at half the standard rate in all cases.

(ii) Where the policy was effected on or before 22nd June, 1916: (*a*) at half the standard rate if the total statutory income does not exceed £1,000; (*b*) at three-fourths of the standard rate if the total statutory income exceeds £1,000 but does not exceed £2,000; (*c*) at the full standard rate if the total statutory income exceeds £1,000, but does not exceed £2,000; (*c*) at the full standard rate if the total statutory income exceeds £2,000.

The receipts for the premiums, or the policies, should be produced to the Inspector of Taxes if required.

An allowance of tax may be claimed in respect of compulsory contributions under the Widows', Orphan's, and Old Age Contributory Pensions Act, 1925.

Penalties. The penalty for neglecting to make a return, or for making an untrue or incorrect return, is a sum not exceeding £20 and treble the tax chargeable. A penalty not exceeding £5 may be imposed for neglecting to make a return, even though the person proceeded agai̇nts may prove that he was not charge-able to Income Tax.

The penalty for fraudulently concealing or untruly declaring any particulars in making any claim for any allowance or deduc-tion is £20 and treble the tax chargeable in respect of all the sources of income.

If any person, for the purpose of obtaining any allowance, reduction, rebate, or repayment in respect of Income Tax, either for himself or for any other person, or in any return made with reference to Income Tax, knowingly makes any false statement or false representation, he is liable, on summary conviction, to imprisonment for a term not exceeding six months with hard labour.

SURTAX

This is an added income tax payable by persons whose incomes exceed a specified limit, at present £2,000. The rates chargeable vary with the exigencies of the Chancellor of the Exchequer: to raise the rate is a much easier way of meeting a financial difficulty than to devise a new way of obtaining revenue. The rates noted below should, therefore, be checked by reference to current rates. Those in force at the moment are those fixed in the Finance Act, 1930, together with a uniform *addition of* 10 *per cent*, authorised by Parliament in 1932. They are—

	In the £ s. d.
On first £2,000	nil
,, ,, £500 in excess of £2,000	1 0 + 10 per cent
,, ,, £500 ,, £2,500	1 3 ,, ,,
On £1,000 in excess of £3,000	2 0 ,, ,,
,, ,, ,, £4,000	3 0 ,, ,,
,, ,, ,, £5,000	3 6 ,, ,,
,, £2,000 ,, £6,000	4 0 ,, ,,
,, ,, ,, £8,000	5 0 ,, ,,
,, £5,000 ,, £10,000	5 6 ,, ,,
,, ,, ,, £15,000	6 0 ,, ,,
,, £10,000 ,, £20,000	6 6 ,, ,,
,, £20,000 ,, £30,000	7 0 ,, ,,
For every £9 remainder	7 6 ,, ,,

No deduction is allowable in regard to "earned" income or to family. The allowances in regard to fixed loan interest, ground rent, annuities, and other compulsory payments out of income, however, remain.

Those liable to surtax are required to give notice to the

Special Commissioners of Income Tax, Kingsway, London, W.C.2. The wife's income must be included in the husband's statement of aggregate income. Either husband or wife may ask for a separate assessment. The tax due is still calculated on the total joint income; but it will be payable by husband and wife in proportion to their shares.

CO-OPERATIVE SOCIETIES

The Income Tax Act, 1918, Section 39, exempted from tax under Schedules C and D a society registered under the Industrial and Provident Societies Act, 1893, "unless it sells to persons not members thereof, and the number of its shares is limited by its rules or practice." Most co-operative societies were exempt under the section. The idea was that just as an individual cannot make a profit out of himself, so the "artificial person" that we call an incorporated society cannot make a profit out of itself. (*Styles* v. *New York Life Insurance Co.*, H.L., 1889.)

The Finance Act of 1933 repeals the section. The position now is, therefore, that co-operative societies are on the same footing as other companies and societies and will be assessed on profits under all the Schedules. Certain points, however, are to be noted—

A. DIVIDENDS

The "divi" is still allowable as an expense if it is (as it will usually be) a discount or bonus on transactions, not a dividend on shares. The Act provides that discounts, rebates, dividends, or bonuses granted to members or non-members on transactions which have been taken into account in computing the taxable profits, may be treated as expenses if these are paid in reference "to the magnitude of the said transactions and not by reference to the amount of any share or interest in the capital of the company or society." Nor will the individual recipient of the "divi" need to include it in his income tax return.

B. CLUBS AND MUTUAL SOCIETIES

A company carrying on a social club in the usual way—on the mutual principle, that is—is not carrying on a trade. Any surplus it makes is, therefore, still exempt.

C. MUTUAL INSURANCE COMPANIES

Even before the 1933 Act a Mutual Life Assurance Company was taxable on its investment income. The Act places other mutual insurance companies under the same obligation.

D. PROFESSIONAL AND TRADE PROTECTION SOCIETIES

Since these rarely engage in trade the Act is not applicable to them.

E. CHARITABLE EXPENSES

These are allowable deductions in so far as designed for the welfare of the *employees of the society*, not in so far as designed for the welfare of *members of the society* who are not also employees.

F. EDUCATIONAL ALLOCATIONS

These are allowable deductions if for the welfare of *employees* or if for advertising.

The net result of the 1933 Act, as regards co-operative societies is this : amounts carried forward as reserves will be taxed as in the ordinary joint-stock company.

RATING

THE levying of rates is now governed almost wholly by the Rating and Valuation Act, 1925. This codifies the law relating to rates. Some later modifications are the following—

(i) The Landlord and Tenant Act, 1927, gives a landlord the right to obtain an increase of rates from his tenant when that increase is due to the tenant's own improvement of the occupied premises;

(ii) The Rating and Valuation Act, 1928, relieves certain holdings of a part or the whole burden of rates.

(iii) The Local Government Act, 1929, exempts wholly from rates agricultural land and buildings, and gives part relief to industrial and freight-transport holdings.

RATING AUTHORITIES AND THE LEVY

The councils (county borough, urban district, and rural district) are the rating authorities for their areas. They levy a consolidated rate called the "General Rate." This is a uniform rate per pound on the rateable value of the holding. The authority has power, however, to reduce or to remit payment when it is satisfied of the poverty of the person liable.

GENERAL RATE

The rate is made for the financial year beginning 1st April. It is due from the person in occupation. Where occupation has been for part only of the period the amount payable is made in proportion.

PRECEPTS

These are the demands, served directly on the various rating authorities, by the County Councils to levy a specified amount in the pound. And, in order that the County Councils may know what precept to make, each rating authority must before 1st February inform the County Councils the amount that will be produced by each penny in the pound.

ASSESSMENT OF RATES

In each area an assessment committee is appointed. It consists of persons, some appointed by the rating authority, some by the

County Council, in the proportion sanctioned by the Minister of Health. In every county, too, a *"Valuation Committee"*—with the duty of helping rating authorities and bringing about uniformity in valuation—is appointed.

VALUATION

1. The rateable value is the net return an owner may expect from the property. That is, from the annual rent, a tenant would, on the average pay, the landlord may deduct whatever outgoings he has. Thus, if the landlord pays rates, taxes, and tithe rent-charge, if he also bears the average cost of repairs and insurance sufficient to maintain the property, these outgoings are deducted from the gross rent to find the rateable value.

2. Where machinery or plant is included in the valuation the assessment committee must, on the request in writing of the occupier, furnish particulars of the things that have been treated as part of the holding. The general idea is that machinery is taken into account when it is of the nature of a building; "process machinery" and loose tools or plant are excluded.

3. The rating authority prepares a *"draft valuation list."* Anyone—including the county valuation committee—may object to a valuation, and the assessment committee holds meetings to consider the objections tendered. From its decision an appeal lies to Quarter Sessions. The list is revised every five years, and is therefore called the "quinquennial list."

RATEPAYERS' RIGHT TO INSPECT DOCUMENTS

Section 60 of the 1925 Act gives ratepayers the right to inspect and take extracts from rate books, valuation lists, notices of objection and appeal, and the like. No payment for such inspection is to be exacted, and anyone having the custody of the documents is liable to a fine of £5 if he obstructs ratepayers in regard to this right. (It seems that a fee of 2s. 6d. may be charged for inspection of documents more than ten years old.)

EXEMPTION FROM RATES

The following are exempt from payment of rates—

(*a*) Churches and other buildings used exclusively for religious services;

(*b*) Premises belonging to scientific and literary societies and used exclusively for their purposes;

(c) "Non-provided" public elementary schools, such that is as are not built by the education authority;

(d) Houses occupied by ambassadors, their staffs, and servants;

(e) Public parks;

(f) Agricultural holdings, industrial undertakings, freight-transport undertakings (De-rating Act, 1928).

NOTES ON " OCCUPATION " AND " RATEABLE VALUE "

(a) *Allotments.* The council providing land for allotments may require the rating authority to regard the council as occupier for the purposes of rating;

(b) *Advertising Station.* These are rateable according to the value for advertisement, and the occupier is he who permits the exhibition;

(c) Beneficial use of premises constitutes *occupation* for purposes of rating. Thus, it was explained in *R. v. St. Pancras*, 1877, Q.B.—

So long as an owner leaves a house vacant, he is not rateable. If, however, he furnishes it, and keeps it ready for habitation whenever he pleases to go to it, he is an occupier, though he may not reside in it one day in a year. On the other hand, a person who, without having any title, takes actual possession of a house or piece of land, whether by leave of the owner or against his will, is the occupier of it. Another element, however, besides actual possession of the land, is necessary to constitute the kind of occupation which the Act contemplates, and that is permanence. An itinerant showman who erects a temporary structure for his performance may be in exclusive actual possession, and may, with strict grammatical propriety, be said to occupy the ground on which his structure is placed, but it is clear that he is not such an occupier as the statute intends.

Moreover, the occupation must be exclusive in the sense that the occupier may bring an action for trespass against anyone who enters without his licence.

(c) *Caretaker in Occupation.* Where a caretaker is put in to preserve and guard the house till it is sold or let, neither the caretaker nor the owner is rateable.

(d) *Ascertaining Rateable Value.* The rental that a tenant undertaking his own repairs might be expected to pay is the ordinary test. Where this test is inapplicable—provided schools, for instance—a reasonable rate of interest on the cost of construction serves as a basis for valuation. Profits is the basis for such holdings as hotels, race-courses, theatres.

(e) *Notice to Ratepayers.* In the following events immediate notice must be served by the rating authority on the person liable, so that he may, if he thinks fit, lodge an objection—

(i) A holding not previously assessed is inserted in the quinquennial list;

(ii) The rateable value is raised.

ENFORCING PAYMENT OF RATES

A distress warrant, whereby the occupier's goods are taken and sold to the amount of the rate, may be issued upon the default of the person liable to pay rates. Where goods sufficient are not available a warrant may be issued by the justices of commitment to prison for a period not exceeding three months. But the Rating and Valuation Act, 1925, expressly enacts that "the justices shall not issue a warrant of commitment, in default of distress for non-payment of the general rate, against any person who proves to their satisfaction that his failure to pay is due to circumstances beyond his control." The justices also have authority to remit the payment, thereby preventing the rating authority from renewing its demand. Moreover, under the 1925 Act, the rating authority itself has power to reduce or remit the payment of any general rate on account of the poverty of any person liable to the payment thereof.

" DE-RATING " ACT OF 1928

With a view to affording some relief to industry from its burdens, this Act remitted rates on certain enterprises. The enterprises relieved are—

(a) *Agricultural holdings*, land or buildings. (By the Local Government Act of 1929 these are totally exempt from rates);

(b) *Industrial holdings*, including mines, mineral railways, factory, workshops; but not including retail shops, wholesale distributive warehouses, store-houses, public supply undertaking (i.e. for the supply of gas, water, and so on);

(c) *Freight-transport holdings*, including railways and light railways, canal buildings, dock buildings, but not including buildings primarily occupied for office purposes.

APPORTIONMENT OF RATES

On industrial holdings and freight-transport holdings the amount of rates to be paid is calculated in this way. The "annual value" is found in the ordinary manner. But where the building or land is used *solely* for industrial or freight-transport purposes the rate due is 25 per cent only and not the full annual value. Where apportionment is necessary, the 25 per cent is applicable to so much of the land as is devoted to industrial or freight-transport purposes; the remainder pays at the ordinary rate.

INDEX

NEW BRUNSWICK RAILWAY CO. *v.* MUG-
GERIDGE, 702
NEW
houses, warranty of fitness, 113
trial, 904
NEWBOULD *v.* ATTORNEY-GENERAL, 33
NEWMAN *v.* SLADE, 107
NEWS, CRYING OF FALSE, 248
NEWSHOLME BROS. *v.* ROAD TRANSPORT
AND GENERAL INSURANCE CO., 416
NEWSPAPER,
advice, loss through, 168
editor, termination of employment, 72
libels in, 239
picture publication without sanction,
317
reports, 176, 239
reproduction of photographs, 22
NEXT FRIEND, SUING BY, 853
NIBLETT *v.* CONFECTIONERS MATERIALS
CO., 559
NIECE, MARRIAGE WITH, 49
NIGHT OFFENCES, 245
NIXON *v.* ERITH URBAN DISTRICT COUNCIL,
696, 880
NOBLE *v.* HARRISON, 543
NON-ACCESS OF HUSBAND, 33
NORTH WESTERN SALT CO. *v.* ELECTRO-
LYTIC ALKALI CO., 103, 723
NOT
guilty, plea of, 904, 948
negotiable, meaning of, 814
NOTICE,
appeal, of, 937
board and trespass, 545
dismissal without, 72
domestic servant, 71
quit, to, 107, 119
ratepayers, 989
terminating employment, 71, 72
NOTLEY *v.* BISHOP OF BIRMINGHAM, 960
NOVATION, 369, 372
NUGENT *v.* SMITH, 755
NUISANCE, PRIVATE, 528
abatement of, 145, 536
action for, 529
creating a, 531
injunction for, 535
justification of, 532
proof, 533
public nuisance, contrasted with, 550
NUISANCE, PUBLIC, 117, 189
action for, 552
definition of, 146, 253, 479
causing a, 551
liability for damage, 542
on common, 542
on highway, 253, 489
private nuisance, contrasted with, 550
NUNCUPATIVE WILLS, 655
NURSING FOR REWARD, 266

O

OAKLEY *v.* LYSTER, 927
OATH OF ALLEGIANCE, 283
O'BRIEN, *ex parte*, 158
OBSCENE PUBLICATIONS, 240
OBSTRUCTION,
common, on, 542
strikes, in, 98
threatened, 483
view, of, 20
OCCASIONAL EXCISE LICENCES, 274
OCCUPIER'S RESPONSIBILITY, 118, 989
OCEANIC STEAM NAVIGATION CO. *v.*
COMERFORD, 10
OFFENCES,
bankruptcy, 459
liquor laws, against, 279–80
persons, against, 155, 217
OFFER,
acceptance of, 689
revoking an, 708

OFFER—(*contd.*)
statement not always, 690
(*See also* CONTRACT)
OFFICIAL
receiver, 446
Secrets Act, 218
OFFICIALS AND EMPLOYEES OF LOCAL
AUTHORITIES, APPOINTMENT OF
344
OFF-LICENCE, 274
OGDEN *v.* OGDEN, 45, 56
O'HARA, *In re*, 32
OLD AGE PENSIONS, 434, 436, 441
OLD BAILEY, 206, 211, 940
OLD METAL PURCHASE, 266
OLIVER *v.* BIRMINGHAM & MIDLAND
OMNIBUS CO., 138
OMNIBUS PASSENGER, INJURY TO, 138
ONE-MAN COMPANY, 388
ONEROUS PROPERTY, DISCLAIMING OF,
462
ON-LICENCE, 274
ON SALE OR RETURN, 570
OPEN
contract, 605, 606
letters, 519
market, 574
OPENING HOURS OF LICENSED PREMISES,
276
OPERATION BY UNQUALIFIED PERSON
233
OPINIONS NOT EVIDENCE, 875
OPPENHEIMER *v.* ATTENBOROUGH, 569
OPTION,
buying an, 689
clause in contract, 25
ORAL EVIDENCE MODIFYING WRITTEN
EVIDENCE, 886
ORDER,
maintenance, 47
XIV, summons under, 925
XIX, rule 4, 926
ORDERS IN COUNCIL, 10, 282
ORDINATION, 968
ORPEN *v.* HAYMARKET CO., 3
OVERCROWDING,
factories and workshops, in, 79
railway carriage, in, 135
OVERDUE
accounts, interest on, 833
rent, landlord's remedies, 110
OVERHANGING BRANCHES, 145, 536, 543
OVERLOOKED BY NEIGHBOURS, 23
OWNER,
responsibility to invitees, 549
who is the, 243
OWNER'S RISK, MEANING OF, 759
OWNERSHIP,
contingent, 476
dual, 477
vested, 476
OYER AND TERMINER, COURT OF, 940

P

PAQUIN *v.* BEAUCLERK, 41, 898
PARDON,
power of, 940
Sovereign, by, 230
PARENTS,
consent to marriage, 46, 51
educate children, duty to, 31
maintain children, duty to, 29
PARISH, THE, 324
Clerk, 967
Council, 325–7
meetings, 325
PARISHIONER, 962
PARKER *v.* MCKENNA, 359
v. SOUTH-EASTERN RAILWAY CO., 708,
769, 833
PARLIAMENT,
Acts of, 3, 4, 5
authority of, 3